T   V

Vol   E

V

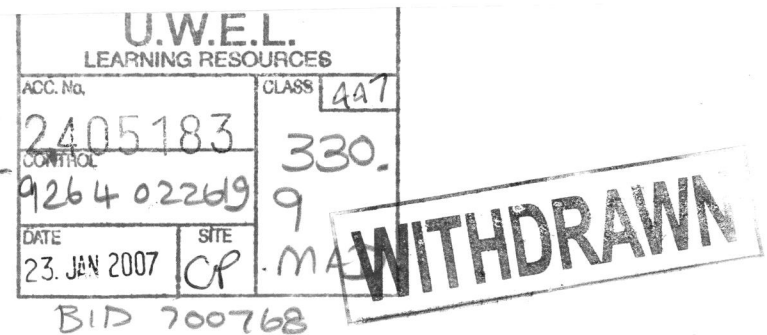

D1395037

OECD

DEVELOPMENT CENTRE OF THE ORGANISATION
FOR ECONOMIC CO-OPERATION AND DEVELOPMENT

ORGANISATION FOR ECONOMIC CO-OPERATION AND DEVELOPMENT

Pursuant to Article 1 of the Convention signed in Paris on 14th December 1960, and which came into force on 30th September 1961, the Organisation for Economic Co-operation and Development (OECD) shall promote policies designed:

- to achieve the highest sustainable economic growth and employment and a rising standard of living in member countries, while maintaining financial stability, and thus to contribute to the development of the world economy;
- to contribute to sound economic expansion in member as well as non-member countries in the process of economic development; and
- to contribute to the expansion of world trade on a multilateral, non-discriminatory basis in accordance with international obligations.

The original member countries of the OECD are Austria, Belgium, Canada, Denmark, France, Germany, Greece, Iceland, Ireland, Italy, Luxembourg, the Netherlands, Norway, Portugal, Spain, Sweden, Switzerland, Turkey, the United Kingdom and the United States. The following countries became members subsequently through accession at the dates indicated hereafter: Japan (28th April 1964), Finland (28th January 1969), Australia (7th June 1971), New Zealand (29th May 1973), Mexico (18th May 1994), the Czech Republic (21st December 1995), Hungary (7th May 1996), Poland (22nd November 1996), Korea (12th December 1996) and the Slovak Republic (14th December 2000). The Commission of the European Communities takes part in the work of the OECD (Article 13 of the OECD Convention).

The Development Centre of the Organisation for Economic Co-operation and Development was established by decision of the OECD Council on 23rd October 1962 and comprises twenty member countries of the OECD: Austria, Belgium, the Czech Republic, Finland, France, Germany, Greece, Iceland, Ireland, Italy, Korea, Luxembourg, Mexico, the Netherlands, Norway, Portugal, Slovak Republic, Spain, Sweden, Switzerland, as well as Chile since November 1998 and India since February 2001. The Commission of the European Communities also takes part in the Centre's Governing Board.

The purpose of the Centre is to bring together the knowledge and experience available in member countries of both economic development and the formulation and execution of general economic policies; to adapt such knowledge and experience to the actual needs of countries or regions in the process of development and to put the results at the disposal of the countries by appropriate means.

The Centre is part of the "Development Cluster" at the OECD and enjoys scientific independence in the execution of its task. As part of the Cluster, together with the Centre for Co-operation with Non-Members, the Development Co-operation Directorate, and the Sahel and West Africa Club, the Development Centre can draw upon the experience and knowledge available in the OECD in the development field.

 THE OPINIONS EXPRESSED AND ARGUMENTS EMPLOYED IN THIS PUBLICATION ARE THE SOLE RESPONSIBILITY OF THE AUTHOR AND DO NOT NECESSARILY REFLECT THOSE OF THE OECD OR THE GOVERNMENTS OF THEIR MEMBER COUNTRIES.

Reprinted 2006

Foreword

This publication brings together two reference works by Angus Maddison: *The World Economy: A Millennial Perspective*, published in 2001 and *The World Economy: Historical Statistics*, which was released in 2003.

The first volume provides a comprehensive view of the growth and levels of world population since the year 1000, when rich countries of today were poorer than Asia and Africa. It is a pioneering effort to quantify the economic performance of nations over the very long term, identifying forces which explain the success of the rich countries, and exploring the obstacles that hindered advance in less developed regions.

In the second volume, Angus Maddison offers a rare insight into the history and political influence of national accounts and national accounting. Based on revised and updated population estimates for 1950-2003 and GDP and per capita GDP estimates for 1820 to 2001, he demonstrates that such statistical data can shed light on the analysis of economic phenomena like growth, market formation and income distribution. This approach is particularly interesting for developing countries often lacking the expertise or data to produce good national accounts. It also serves as a reminder for OECD countries that effective policy making depends on verifiable economic data.

The World Economy is a monumental work of reference and a "must" for all scholars and students of economics and economic history, as well as a mine of fascinating facts for everyone else. An attractive feature of this new edition is the inclusion of Statlinks, which provide access to the underlying data in Excel® format.

Further analysis and data compiled by Angus Maddison can be found at: www.ggdc.net/Maddison

THE WORLD ECONOMY

Volume 1: A Millennial Perspective

Foreword

Shortly after my arrival at the OECD in 1996, I came upon the study by Angus Maddison "Monitoring the World Economy 1820–1992". It is a fascinating and stimulating work providing a complete coverage of the world economy during the period in question. It brought together data of some 56 countries accounting for 93 per cent of the world output and 87 per cent of the world population and world exports. It never left my desk. Probably I was not alone in my appreciation of this quite extraordinary work, as I kept coming on references to it in the work of other authors.

As we were nearing the end of the twentieth century, it seemed to me that this study could undergo some slight revisions to make it more attractive to general readership, and brought up to the close of the century and of the second millennium. I discussed the project with Professor Maddison and, to my delight, he agreed.

From his enormous energy and intellectual capacity emerges a far greater work in depth and scope than anything I had imagined possible. This book covers the development of the entire world economy over the past two thousand years. The author takes a (quite literally) global view of world growth over that period, examining both changes over time and between different regions. The book has a wider ambit than any previous OECD publication or, indeed, than almost any other publication in the market worldwide. First, the scope of the analysis is breath–taking. Second, there must be few (if any) economic history books so wide in their reach, in terms of both geography and history. Third, although his approach is economic, it is not narrowly so and draws on many other subjects — history, geography, demography and more — on the path to its conclusions; this multidisciplinary sweep gives the book great value.

Because of its value and its global reach, I am sure it will find a global readership, as an authoritative reference for academics, students, professionals and general readership.

I predict it will find its place in homes, offices and libraries in every corner of the world, and for many years to come. It will undoubtedly be the foundation for further works of this kind during the millennium we have just entered.

We should all be extremely grateful to Angus Maddison for having taken on this challenge with results which far exceed my original expectations.

John Maynard Keynes wrote that the master economist should "examine the present in light of the past, for the purposes of the future". Never before have we had such a rich resource at our disposal to pursue that objective.

Donald Johnston
OECD Secretary–General

Table of Contents

Text Tables

Appendix Tables

Acknowledgements

I am grateful to Saskia van Bergen, Catherine Girodet, Ly Na Tang Dollon, and Erik Monnikhof for considerable help in processing statistical material and preparing graphs, and to Sheila Lionet for putting the manuscript in a form suitable for publication.

I am particularly indebted to my friend and mentor Moses Abramovitz (1912–2000), for his encouragement, wisdom and generosity in commenting on this manuscript and many others over the past 40 years.

I benefited from discussions that followed the 1998 Kuznets Memorial Lectures which I gave at Yale University, and from comments on presentations on this theme at the Academy of Social Sciences in Australia, the Brazil Forum in Porto Alegre, seminars at the Academia Sinica, Hitotsubashi University, Keio University at Fujisawa, Osaka University and Osaka Gakuin University. I remembered a lot that I learned from a three month stay at the Universita Ca' Foscari in Venice in 1990.

I received useful comments on different drafts from Bart van Ark, Ian Castles, François Crouzet, Charles Feinstein, Colm Foy, David Henderson, Paolo Malanima, Jim Oeppen, Osamu Saito, Graeme Snooks, Victor Urquidi and Sir Tony Wrigley.

I had advice or answers to queries from Michèle Alkilic, Heinz Arndt, Jean–Pascal Bassino, Joel Bergsman, Luis Bertola, Derek Blades, Yves Blayo, Lidia Bratanova, Henk–Jan Brinkman, J.W. Drukker, Nick Eberstadt, Pierre van der Eng, Jean–Yves Garnier, Roland Granier, Maria Alice Gusmâo Veloso, Akira Hayami, André Hofman, Yuri Ivanov, Masaaki Kawagoe, Peter Lindert, Cormac O Grada, Debin Ma, Elizabeth Maddison, Paul McCarthy, Nanno Mulder, Peter Hein van Mulligen, Konosuke Odaka, Dirk Pilat, Richard Ruggles, Serguei Sergueev, Miyohei Shinohara, Siva Sivasubramonian, Marcelo Soto, T.N. Srinivasan, Kaoru Sugihara, Jean–Claude Toutain, Richard Wall, Michael Ward, and Harry X. Wu.

My biggest debts are to my wife, Penelope Maddison, for continuous encouragement, sustained moral and material support.

Preface

Angus Maddison visited Nova University at Lisbon in 1986 and that is where we first met. I already knew of his work, since my late father, himself an economic historian, had mentioned its importance to me many years previously. It was therefore with some nostalgia that, as newly appointed President of the Development Centre, I found myself involved with Angus on a regular basis.

The Development Centre's association with Angus Maddison is a very long one. He was present at the birth of the Development Centre, influenced its evolution and the character of its research. In many ways, the Centre is indissociable from him. This is one reason why the writing of this extraordinary history of the world economy should have been entrusted to him. In addition, Angus is possibly the greatest living *chiffrephile*, as demonstrated by his earlier work for the Centre, most notably: *The World Economy 1820–1992* and *Chinese Economic Performance in the Long Run*, both of which have become works of reference in quantitative economic history the world over.

The Development Centre is preoccupied with the place of governance in the new world order. Our research effort is directed towards helping countries to find ways of reforming governance systems at every level of society. This is also a constant theme in this book. Throughout the thousand years under consideration, governance can be seen as a factor which either advantaged or disadvantaged growth. We therefore remain convinced that this is a vital issue confronting developing societies today. We are also persuaded that OECD countries have themselves a responsibility to implement good governance and to encourage it elsewhere.

Jorge Braga de Macedo
President
OECD Development Centre

April 2001

ISBN 92-64-02261-9 – © OECD 2006

Introduction and Summary

The Contours of World Development

Over the past millennium, world population rose 22–fold. Per capita income increased 13–fold, world GDP nearly 300–fold. This contrasts sharply with the preceding millennium, when world population grew by only a sixth, and there was no advance in per capita income.

From the year 1000 to 1820 the advance in per capita income was a slow crawl — the world average rose about 50 per cent. Most of the growth went to accommodate a fourfold increase in population.

Since 1820, world development has been much more dynamic. Per capita income rose more than eightfold, population more than fivefold.

Per capita income growth is not the only indicator of welfare. Over the long run, there has been a dramatic increase in life expectation. In the year 1000, the average infant could expect to live about 24 years. A third would die in the first year of life, hunger and epidemic disease would ravage the survivors. There was an almost imperceptible rise up to 1820, mainly in Western Europe. Most of the improvement has occurred since then. Now the average infant can expect to survive 66 years.

The growth process was uneven in space as well as time. The rise in life expectation and income has been most rapid in Western Europe, North America, Australasia and Japan. By 1820, this group had forged ahead to an income level twice that in the rest of the world. By 1998, the gap was 7:1. Between the United States (the present world leader) and Africa (the poorest region) the gap is now 20:1. This gap is still widening. Divergence is dominant but not inexorable. In the past half century, resurgent Asian countries have demonstrated that an important degree of catch–up is feasible. Nevertheless world economic growth has slowed substantially since 1973, and the Asian advance has been offset by stagnation or retrogression elsewhere.

The Purpose of this Study

The purpose of this book is to quantify these long term changes in world income and population in a comprehensive way; identify the forces which explain the success of the rich countries; explore the obstacles which hindered advance in regions which lagged behind; scrutinise the interaction between the rich countries and the rest to assess the degree to which their backwardness may have been due to Western policy.

There is nothing new about long–term surveys of economic performance. Adam Smith had a very broad perspective in his pioneering work in 1776. Others have had an equally ambitious vision. There has been spectacular progress in recent years in historical demography[1]. What is new in this study is systematic quantification of comparative economic performance.

In the past, quantitative research in economic history has been heavily concentrated on the nineteenth and twentieth centuries when growth was fastest. To go back earlier involves use of weaker evidence, greater reliance on clues and conjecture. Nevertheless it is a meaningful, useful and necessary exercise because differences in the pace and pattern of change in major parts of the world economy have deep roots in the past.

Quantification clarifies issues which qualitative analysis leaves fuzzy. It is more readily contestable and likely to be contested. It sharpens scholarly discussion, sparks off rival hypotheses, and contributes to the dynamics of the research process. It can only do this if the quantitative evidence and the nature of proxy procedures is described transparently so that the dissenting reader can augment or reject parts of the evidence or introduce alternative hypotheses. The analysis of Chapters 1, 2 and 3 is underpinned by six appendices which are intended to supply the necessary degree of transparency.

Explaining Economic Performance

Advances in population and income over the past millennium have been sustained by three interactive processes:

a)   Conquest or settlement of relatively empty areas which had fertile land, new biological resources, or a potential to accommodate transfers of population, crops and livestock;

b)   international trade and capital movements;

c)   technological and institutional innovation.

a) Conquest and Settlement

One important instance of this process was Chinese settlement of the relatively empty and swampy lands south of the Yangtse, and introduction of new quick–ripening strains of rice from Vietnam suitable for multicropping. This process occurred between the eighth and thirteenth centuries, during which population growth accelerated, per capita income rose by a third, and the distribution of population and economic activity were transformed. In the eighth century only a quarter of the Chinese population lived south of the Yangtse; in the thirteenth, more than threequarters. The new technology involved higher labour inputs, so productivity rose less than per capita income[2].

An even more dramatic case was the European encounter with the Americas. The existence of this continent was unknown to Europeans before the 1492 voyage of Columbus[3]. The discovery opened up an enormous area, for the most part thinly populated. Mexico and Peru were the most advanced and densely settled, but they were easily conquered and three quarters of their population was wiped out by diseases which the Europeans inadvertently introduced. The new continent offered crops unknown elsewhere — maize, potatoes, sweet potatoes, manioc, chilis, tomatoes, groundnuts, pineapples, cocoa and tobacco. These were introduced in Europe, Africa and Asia, and enhanced their production potential and capacity to sustain population growth. There was a reciprocal transfer to the Americas, which greatly augmented its potential. The new crops were wheat, rice, sugar cane, vines, salad greens, olives, bananas and coffee. The new animals for food were cattle, pigs, chickens, sheep and goats, as well as horses, oxen, asses and donkeys for transport.

The major initial attractions of the Americas were the rich silver resources of Mexico and Peru, and development of plantation agriculture with imports of slave labour from Africa. The neo–European economies of North America and the southern cone of Latin America developed later. The population of the Americas did not recover its 1500 level until the first half of the eighteenth century. The full potential of the Americas began to be realised in the nineteenth century with massive European immigration and the western movement of the production frontier made possible by railways.

The present variation in economic performance within the Americas — between the United States, Latin America and the Caribbean — is partly due to variations in resource endowment, but there are institutional and societal echoes from the past. In North America and Brazil the relatively small indigenous population was marginalised or exterminated, in former Spanish colonies the indigenous population remained as an underclass, and in all the areas where slavery was important their descendants have also remained an underprivileged group. Quite apart from this, there were important differences in the colonial period between Iberian institutions and those of North America. These continued to have an impact on subsequent growth performance[4].

b) *International Trade and Capital Movements*

International trade was important in the economic ascension of Western Europe, and much less significant in the history of Asia or Africa.

Venice played a key role from 1000 to 1500 in opening up trade within Europe (to Flanders, France, Germany and the Balkans) and in the Mediterranean. It opened trade in Chinese products via the caravan routes to ports in the Black Sea. It traded in Indian and other Asian products via Syria and Alexandria. Trade was important in bringing high value spices and silks to Europe, but it also helped the transfer of technology from Asia, Egypt and Byzantium (silk and cotton textile production, glassblowing, cultivation of rice in Italy, cane sugar production and processing in the Venetian colonies of Crete and Cyprus). To a significant degree the maritime expansion of Venice depended on improved techniques of shipbuilding in its Arsenal, use of the compass and other improvements in navigation. Institutional innovations — the development of banking, accountancy, foreign exchange and credit markets, creation of a solvent system of public finance, creation of a competent diplomatic service were all instrumental in establishing Venice as the lead economy of that epoch. Venice played an important part in fostering the intellectual development of Western Europe. It created manuscript libraries and pioneered in book publishing. Its glass industry was the first to make spectacles on a large scale. It played a leading role in the Renaissance by making Greek works known in the West. The University of Padua was a major centre of European learning, with Galileo as one of its distinguished professors.

Venetian contacts with Asia were eventually blocked by the fall of Byzantium, the rise of the Ottoman Empire, the collapse of the crusader states in the Levant and the Mameluke regime in Egypt. In the second half of the fifteenth century, a much more ambitious interaction between Europe and the rest of the world had started in Portugal.

Portugal played the main role in opening up European trade, navigation and settlement in the Atlantic islands, in developing trade routes around Africa, into the Indian Ocean, to China and Japan. It became the major shipper of spices to Europe for the whole of the sixteenth century, usurping this role from Venice. Its navigators discovered Brazil. Its diplomacy was astute enough to persuade Spain to endorse its territorial claim there, and to let it have a monopoly of trade with the Moluccan spice islands and Indonesia. Although Spain had a bigger empire, its only significant base outside the Americas was the Philippines. Its two most famous navigators were Columbus who was a Genoese with Portuguese training, and Magellan who was Portuguese.

Portugal had major advantages in developing its overseas commerce and empire. There was a clear strategic benefit in being located on the South Atlantic coast of Europe near to the exit of the Mediterranean. Deep–sea fishermen provided an important part of the Portuguese food supply and developed an unrivalled knowledge of Atlantic winds, weather and tides. The value of these skills was greatly enhanced by crown sponsorship of Atlantic exploration, research on navigation, training of pilots, and documentation of maritime experience in the form of route maps with compass bearings (rutters) and cartography. Portuguese shipbuilders in Lisbon and Oporto adapted the design of their ships in the light of increasing knowledge of Atlantic sailing conditions. The biggest changes were in rigging. At first they concentrated on lateen sails, then added a mix of square sails and lateen for deeper penetration into the South Atlantic, with further changes for the much longer route round the Cape. Another element in Portuguese success was the ability to absorb "new Christians" — Jewish merchants and scholars who had played a significant role in Iberia during Muslim rule. They were driven out of Spain, but many took refuge and increased the size of the community in Portugal. They were required to undergo proforma conversion and were subject to a degree of persecution, but they provided important skills in developing Portuguese business interests in Africa, Brazil and Asia, in scientific development, as intermediaries in trade with the Muslim world and in attracting Genoese and Catalan capital to Portuguese business ventures.

Portugal was responsible for transferring cane sugar production and processing technology into the Atlantic islands of Madeira and São Tomé, and later to Brazil. It inaugurated the slave trade to provide a labour force for the industry in the New World. It carried about half of the slaves who were shipped to the Americas from Africa between 1500 and 1870. In the fifteenth century, sugar was a very rare and expensive commodity in Europe; by the end of the eighteenth century it was an item of popular consumption, having grown much more in volume than trade in any other tropical product.

At the time Portugal was pioneering these worldwide linkages, trade relations between different parts of northern Europe were intensified by the phenomenal development of Dutch maritime activity. In 1570, the carrying capacity of Dutch merchant shipping was about the same as the combined fleets of England, France and Germany. Per head of population it was 25 times as big as in these three northern countries.

Development of shipping and shipbuilding, the transformation of Dutch agriculture into horticulture, the creation of a large canal network, use of power derived from windmills and peat made the Netherlands the most dynamic European economy from 1400 to the middle of the seventeenth century. It pushed international specialisation much further than any other country. Shipping and commercial services provided a large part of its income. It imported cereals and live cattle, exported herring and dairy products. In 1700 only 40 per cent of the labour force were in agriculture.

Until 1580 the Netherlands was part of a bigger political entity. It included Flanders and Brabant — the most prosperous industrial area in Europe and a centre for banking, finance and international commerce which was a northern counterpart to Venice. The whole area was under Burgundian control until the late fifteenth century, then fell into the hands of the Habsburgs who were also rulers of Spain. The Dutch revolted against their predatory empire because of its excessive fiscal demands, political and religious repression. They created a modern nation state, which protected property rights of merchants and entrepreneurs, promoted secular education and practised religious tolerance.

Most of the financial and entrepreneurial elite and many of the most skilled artisans of Flanders and Brabant emigrated to the new republic. The Dutch blockaded the river Scheldt and the port of Antwerp for more than 200 years, and destroyed the Iberian monopoly of trade with Africa, Asia and the Americas.

Dutch experience from 1580 to the end of the Napoleonic wars provides a dramatic demonstration of the way in which Western Europe interacted with the world economy in that epoch.

The initial economic success of the Dutch Republic, and its maritime and commercial supremacy, depended to a substantial extent on success in war and beggar–your–neighbour commercial policy in competition with Portugal and Spain. By the eighteenth century it had lost this supremacy, because two new rivals, England and France, had greatly increased their maritime strength, and used the same techniques to push the Dutch out of the markets they sought to dominate. The volume of Dutch foreign trade dropped 20 per cent from 1720 to 1820. During this period, UK exports rose more than sevenfold in volume, and French by two and threequarters. From 1700 to 1820, Dutch per capita income fell by a sixth, British rose by half and French by a quarter.

Britain had faster growth in per capita income from the 1680s to 1820 than any other European country. This was due to improvement of its banking, financial and fiscal institutions and agriculture on lines which the Dutch had pioneered, and to a surge in industrial productivity at the end of the period. It also derived great benefits from its rise to commercial hegemony by adroit use of a beggar–your–neighbour strategy.

Sixty years of armed conflict and the restrictive Navigation Acts pushed competitors out of the markets it sought to monopolise. It took over the leading role in shipping slaves from Africa to the Caribbean and created an overseas empire with a population of about 100 million by 1820.

Other European powers were losers in the British struggle for supremacy. By the end of the Napoleonic wars, the Dutch had lost all their Asian territories except Indonesia. The French were reduced to a token colonial presence in Asia, and lost their major asset in the Caribbean. Shortly after the war, Brazil established its independence from Portugal. Spain lost its huge colonial empire in Latin America, retaining only Cuba, Puerto Rico and the Philippines. Britain took over what the French and Dutch had lost in Asia and Africa, extended its control over India, and established a privileged commercial presence in Latin America.

Other losers included the former rulers of India, whose power and income were usurped in substantial part by the servants of the British East India Company. Under their rule, from 1757 to 1857, Indian per capita income fell, but British gains were substantial.

Between 1820 and 1913, British per capita income grew faster than at any time in the past — three times as fast as in 1700–1820. The basic reason for improved performance was the acceleration of technical progress, accompanied by rapid growth of the physical capital stock and improvement in the education and skills of the labour force, but changes in commercial policy also made a substantial contribution. In 1846 protective duties on agricultural imports were removed and in 1849 the Navigation Acts were terminated. By 1860, all trade and tariff restrictions had been removed unilaterally. In 1860 there were reciprocal treaties for freer trade with France and other European countries. These had most–favoured nation clauses which meant that bilateral liberalisation applied equally to all countries.

Free trade was imposed in India and other British colonies, and the same was true in Britain's informal empire. China, Persia, Thailand and the Ottoman Empire were not colonies, but were obliged to maintain low tariffs by treaties which reduced their sovereignty in commercial matters, and granted extraterritorial rights to foreigners. This regime of free trade imperialism favoured British exports, but was less damaging to the interests of the colonies than in the eighteenth century, when Jamaica could only trade with Britain and its colonies, Guadeloupe only with France.

The British policy of free trade and its willingness to import a large part of its food had positive effects on the world economy. They reinforced and diffused the impact of technical progress. The favourable impact was biggest in North America, the southern cone of Latin America and Australasia which had rich natural resources and received a substantial inflow of capital, but there was also some positive effect in India which was the biggest and poorest part of the Empire.

Innovations in communications played a major part in linking national capital markets and facilitating international capital movements. The United Kingdom already had an important role in international finance, thanks to the soundness of its public credit and monetary system, the size of its capital market and public debt, and the maintenance of a gold standard. The existence of the empire created a system of property rights which appeared to be as securely protected as those available to investors in British securities. It was a wealthy country operating close to the frontiers of technology, so its rentiers were attracted to foreign investment even when the extra margin of profit was small.

From the 1870s onward, there was a massive outflow of British capital for overseas investment. The United Kingdom directed half its savings abroad. French, German and Dutch investment was also substantial.

The old liberal order was shattered by two world wars and the collapse of capital flows, migration and trade in the beggar–your–neighbour years of the 1930s. Between 1913 and 1950, the world economy grew much more slowly than in 1870–1913, world trade grew much less than world income, and the degree of inequality between regions increased substantially, the setback being biggest in Asia.

By 1950 colonialism was in an advanced state of disintegration. With one or two exceptions, the exit from empire was more or less complete by the 1960s. The British imperial order was finished, as were those of Belgium, France, the Netherlands and Japan. In the West, the United States had emerged as the hegemonial power competing with the Soviet bloc for leverage in the newly independent countries of Asia and Africa.

The world economy grew very much faster from 1950 to 1973 than it had ever done before. It was a golden age of unparalleled prosperity. World per capita GDP rose nearly 3 per cent a year (a rate which implies a doubling every 25 years). World GDP rose by nearly 5 per cent a year and world trade by nearly 8 per cent a year. This dynamism affected all regions. The acceleration was greatest in Europe and Asia. There was also a degree of convergence between regions, though a good part of this was a narrowing of the gap between the United States and the other advanced capitalist countries (Western Europe and Japan).

There were several reasons for unusually favourable performance in the golden age. In the first place, the advanced capitalist countries created a new kind of liberal international order with explicit and rational codes of behaviour, and institutions for co–operation (OEEC, OECD, IMF, World Bank and the GATT) which had not existed before. There was a very serious East–West split from 1948 onwards, but the split reinforced the harmony of interest between capitalist economies, so the beggar–your–neighbour behaviour of pre–war years did not recur. The United States provided a substantial flow of aid for Europe when it was most needed, fostering procedures for articulate co–operation and liberal trading policies. Until the 1970s it also provided the world with a strong anchor for international monetary stability. North–South relations were transformed from the colonial tutelage of pre–war years to a situation where more emphasis was placed on action to stimulate development. The huge expansion of trade in the advanced capitalist economies transmitted a dynamic influence throughout the world economy.

The second new element of strength was the character of domestic policies which were self–consciously devoted to promotion of high levels of demand and employment in the advanced countries. Growth was not only faster than ever before, but the business cycle virtually disappeared. Investment rose to unprecedented levels and expectations became euphoric. Until the 1970s, there was also much milder inflationary pressure than could have been expected in conditions of secular boom.

The third element in this virtuous circle situation was the potential for growth on the supply side. Throughout Europe and Asia there was still substantial scope for "normal" elements of "recovery" from the years of depression and war. Additionally and more importantly, was the continued acceleration of technical progress in the lead country. Furthermore, the United States played a diffusionist role in the golden age in sharp contrast to its role in the interwar years.

Since the golden age, the world picture has changed a great deal. Per capita growth has been less than half as fast. There has been much greater divergence in the performance of different regions. In Western Europe and Japan, per capita growth fell well below that in the golden age, but was appreciably better than in 1870–1913. In the countries of "resurgent Asia", which have half the world's population, the success was quite extraordinary. Their per capita growth was faster after 1973 than in the golden age, and more than ten times as fast as in the old liberal order.

If the world consisted only of these two groups, the pattern of world development could be interpreted as a clear demonstration of the possibilities for convergence. By success in mobilising and allocating resources efficiently and improving their human and physical capital to assimilate and adapt appropriate technology, the countries of resurgent Asia achieved significant catch–up on the advanced capitalist group.

However, there is another group (168 countries, with about a third of the world's population) where the deterioration in performance since the golden age has been alarming. In Africa there has been no advance in per capita income in the past quarter century. In Eastern Europe and the former USSR, average per capita income in 1998 was about threequarters of that in 1973. In Latin America and in many Asian countries, income gains have been a fraction of what they were in the golden age. The economies of this heterogeneous group of "faltering economies" have been falling behind instead of catching up. Most of them have not been able to adapt successfully to an international economic order which has changed considerably from that in the golden age.

The way in which postwar order now operates is analysed in detail in Chapter 3. The structure of the analysis is based on Table 3–5 which summarises the comparative performance of the major regions.

c) Technological and Institutional Innovation

From the year 1000 to 1820, advances in technology were much slower than they have been since, but they were nevertheless a significant component of the growth process. Without improvements in agriculture, the increase in world population could not have been sustained. Without improvements in maritime technology and commercial institutions the opening up of the world economy could not have been achieved. Technical advance in important areas was dependent on fundamental improvements in scientific method, experimental testing, systematic accumulation and publication of new knowledge. The long centuries of effort provided intellectual and institutional foundations for the much more rapid advances achieved in the nineteenth and twentieth centuries.

This process of cumulative advance is clearly demonstrated in the history of maritime technology and navigation. In the year 1000, European ships and navigation were no better than in the Roman Empire. The advance started when Venice created its public shipyard, the Arsenal, in 1104 to build its oared galleys and improve ship design. The introduction of the compass and the sandglass for measuring time at sea helped to double the productivity of ships. They could navigate in bad weather and make two return journeys a year from Venice to Alexandria instead of one. The Portuguese preparations for the passage to India were a major research project involving years of experimentation in shipping technology, improvement of navigational instruments and charts, applied astronomy, developing knowledge of winds, currents and alternative routes. The Dutch created a new type of factory ship for processing the herring catch at sea. They developed mass production of a cheap general purpose cargo vessel (the fluyt). The British government financed and encouraged research into astronomy, terrestrial magnetism, production of the first reliable maritime chronometer and nautical almanacs. They also demonstrated the efficacy of sauerkraut and citrus juice in preventing scurvy.

By the end of the eighteenth century ships could carry ten times the cargo of a fourteenth century Venetian galley, with a much smaller crew. The safety of long distance sea travel was also greatly improved. In their first voyages to Asia, da Gama and Cabral lost half their crew and more than half of their ships. Magellan lost more than 90 per cent of his crew on the first circumnavigation of the globe. Cook's successful circumnavigation 240 years later approximated modern standards of maritime safety.

Until the fifteenth century, European progress in many fields was dependent on transfers of technology from Asia or the Arab world. In 1405–33, Chinese superiority in shipping technology was evident in seven major expeditions to the "Western Oceans" (see Table 2–11). Chinese ships were much bigger than those of the Portuguese, more seaworthy and more comfortable, with watertight compartments, many more cabins, and a capacity to navigate over large distances to Africa. Thereafter, China turned its back on the world economy, and its maritime technology decayed.

By the end of the seventeenth century, the technological leadership of Europe in shipping and armaments was apparent. There had also been important institutional advances. Banking, credit, foreign exchange markets, financial and fiscal management, accountancy, insurance and corporate governance (by the Dutch and British East India Companies) were more sophisticated than those in Asia, and were essential components of European success in opening up the world economy.

Within Western Europe the diffusion of technology was fairly rapid, and the technological distance between nations was not particularly wide in spite of the frequency of wars. Links were fostered by the growth of humanist scholarship, the creation of universities and the invention of printing.

In the sixteenth and seventeenth centuries, there was a revolutionary change in the quality of western science with close interaction of savants and scientists such as Copernicus, Erasmus, Bacon, Galileo, Hobbes, Descartes, Petty, Leibnitz, Huyghens, Halley and Newton. Many of them were in close contact with colleagues in other countries, or spent years abroad. This type of co–operation was institutionalised by the creation of scientific academies which encouraged discussion and research, and published their proceedings. Much of this work had practical relevance, and many of the leading figures were concerned with matters of public policy.

Diffusion of these advances outside Europe was relatively limited. There were Jesuit scholars in Peking for nearly two centuries, some of them like Ricci, Schall and Verbiest had intimate contact with ruling circles, but there was little curiosity amongst the Chinese elite about intellectual and scientific development in the West. Japanese exposure to western knowledge was more limited than Chinese, but its impact went deeper. The Portuguese and the Jesuits were in Japan for nearly a century, and there was considerable interest in European ships, maps, navigation and guns. After the Portuguese were expelled the only contact Japan had with western learning was with those Dutch East India Company officials who were scientists (Kaempfer, Thunberg and von Siebold). Although these contacts were limited, they helped destroy Japanese respect for "things Chinese" and accentuate their curiosity about "things Western" (see Appendix B).

The East India Company officers who controlled India from 1757 to 1857 had a strong streak of Benthamite radicalism, and a strong urge to modify Indian legal and property institutions. After the Indian Mutiny of 1857 and establishment of direct imperial control, these radical westernising ambitions were dropped. In Indonesia, there were somewhat similar ambitions in the period of British administration during the Napoleonic wars, but Westernisation was abandoned after the Diponogoro revolt in the 1830s.

The only effective overseas transmission of European technology and science by the end of the eighteenth century was to the 13 British colonies in North America. In 1776 they had nine universities for 2.5 million people and an intellectual elite (e.g. Benjamin Franklin and Thomas Jefferson) fully familiar with the activities of their European contemporaries. In the Spanish colonies, Brazil and the Caribbean there were more than 17 million people, but only two universities (in Mexico City and Guadalajara) which concentrated on theology and law.

The reasons for the accelerated growth of technical progress since 1820 are analysed in considerable detail in my earlier study, *Monitoring the World Economy* (1995), particularly in Chapter 2 and pp. 71–3, and are not treated at any length in this volume. However, it is clear that technical progress has slowed down. It was a good deal faster from 1913 to 1973 than it has been since. The slowdown in the past quarter century is one of the reasons for the deceleration of world economic growth. "New economy" pundits find the notion of decelerating technical progress unacceptable and cite anecdotal or microeconomic evidence to argue otherwise. However, the impact of their technological revolution has not been apparent in the macroeconomic statistics until very recently, and I do not share their euphoric expectations[5].

Notes

1. Wrigley and Schofield (1981) and Wrigley and Associates (1997) used techniques of family reconstitution and inverse projection to exploit church records of births, deaths and marriages. As a result, we now have annual estimates of English population and demographic characteristics since 1541. Bagnall and Frier (1994) used remnants of Roman censuses to reconstruct the demography and economy of third century Egypt. Thanks to the work of de Vries (1984) for Europe and Rozman (1973) for Asia one can measure the proportionate importance of urbanisation for long periods in the past. The Chinese bureaucracy kept population registers which go back more than 2 000 years. These bureaucratic records were designed to assess taxable capacity, and include information on cultivated area and crop production, which was used by Perkins (1969) to assess long run movements in Chinese GDP per capita. The work of Perkins encouraged me to write *Chinese Economic Performance in the Long Run* (OECD Development Centre, 1998) which has the same temporal perspective as the present study.

2. See Maddison (1998a), pp. 24–33 for an analysis of the historical development of Chinese agriculture; see Boserup (1965) for a brilliant refutation of the simplistic Malthusian view that population pressure on a fixed stock of natural resources will inevitably produce diminishing returns. She shows how "traditional" Asian agriculture accommodated population pressure by a whole series of changes of technical practice. Intensity of land use progressed from hunter–gatherer activities, to forest fallow, settled farming with improved tools, from dry farming and fallowing to irrigation and multi–cropping. In this process there was probably a significant drop in labour productivity before modern fertilisers and machinery came on the scene.

3. See Morison (1971) on the Norwegian movement from Iceland to Greenland and Leif Ericsson's trip in 1001 via Baffin island, Belle Isle and the Labrador sea to the northern tip of Newfoundland where there was a very brief and long forgotten settlement at l'Anse aux Meadows.

4. Adam Smith *The Wealth of Nations,* 1776, book IV, Chapter VII, Part II contains a prescient assessment of these institutional differences and their implications for subsequent development. Engrossment of land which hindered its development and transfer, the heavy burden taxes to support the pomp of civil and ecclesiastical government, and official control of markets were the shortcomings in the Spanish colonies which he emphasised. See Chapter 2 of this study for my assessment of the Portuguese influence on Brazil, and the difference between the colonial heritage in Mexico and the United States.

5. See the discussion of US economic performance in Chapter 3, and Box 3–1.

Chapter 1

The Contours of World Development

World economic performance was very much better in the second millennium of our era than in the first. Between 1000 and 1998 population rose 22–fold and per capita income 13–fold. In the previous millennium, population rose by a sixth and per capita GDP fell slightly.

The second millennium comprised two distinct epochs. From 1000 to 1820 the upward movement in per capita income was a slow crawl — for the world as a whole the rise was about 50 per cent. Growth was largely "extensive" in character. Most of it went to accommodate a fourfold increase in population. Since 1820, world development has been much more dynamic, and more "intensive". Per capita income rose faster than population; by 1998 it was 8.5 times as high as in 1820; population rose 5.6–fold.

There was a wide disparity in the performance of different regions in both epochs. The most dynamic was Group A: Western Europe, Western Offshoots (the United States, Canada, Australia and New Zealand) and Japan. In 1000–1820, their average per capita income grew nearly four times as fast as the average for the rest of the world. The differential continued between 1820 and 1998 when per capita income of the first group rose 19–fold and 5.4–fold for the second.

There are much wider income gaps today than at any other time in the past. Two thousand years ago the average level for Groups A and B was similar. In the year 1000 the average for Group A was lower as a result of the economic collapse after the fall of the Roman Empire. By 1820, Group A had forged ahead to a level about twice that in the rest of the world. In 1998 the gap was almost 7:1. Between the Western Offshoots and Africa (the richest and poorest regions) it is 19 to one.

Economic performance since 1820 within Group B has not been as closely clustered as in Group A. Per capita income has grown faster in Latin America than Eastern Europe and Asia, and nearly twice as fast as in Africa. Nevertheless, from a Western standpoint, performance in all these regions has been disappointing.

There have been big changes in the weight of different regions. In the year 1000, Asia (except Japan) produced more than two thirds of world GDP, Western Europe less than 9 per cent. In 1820 the proportions were 56 and 24 per cent respectively. In 1998, the Asian share was about 30 per cent compared with 46 per cent for Western Europe and Western Offshoots combined.

The World Economy: A Millennial Perspective

Table 1–1. Level and Rate of Growth of Population: World and Major Regions, 0–1998 A.D.

	0	1000	1820 (million)	1998	0–1000	1000–1820 (annual average compound growth rate)	1820–1998
Western Europe	24.7	25.4	132.9	388	0.00	0.20	0.60
Western Offshoots	1.2	2.0	11.2	323	0.05	0.21	1.91
Japan	3.0	7.5	31.0	126	0.09	0.17	0.79
Total Group A	28.9	34.9	175.1	838	0.02	0.20	0.88
Latin America	5.6	11.4	21.2	508	0.07	0.08	1.80
Eastern Europe & former USSR	8.7	13.6	91.2	412	0.05	0.23	0.85
Asia (excluding Japan)	171.2	175.4	679.4	3 390	0.00	0.17	0.91
Africa	16.5	33.0	74.2	760	0.07	0.10	1.32
Total Group B	202.0	233.4	866.0	5 069	0.01	0.16	1.00
World	230.8	268.3	1 041.1	5 908	0.02	0.17	0.98

Source: Appendix B.

Table 1–2. Level and Rate of Growth of GDP Per Capita: World and Major Regions, 0–1998 A.D.

	0	1000	1820 (1990 international dollars)	1998	0–1000	1000–1820 (annual average compound growth rate)	1820–1998
Western Europe	450	400	1 232	17 921	−0.01	0.14	1.51
Western Offshoots	400	400	1 201	26 146	0.00	0.13	1.75
Japan	400	425	669	20 413	0.01	0.06	1.93
Average Group A	443	405	1 130	21 470	−0.01	0.13	1.67
Latin America	400	400	665	5 795	0.00	0.06	1.22
Eastern Europe & former USSR	400	400	667	4 354	0.00	0.06	1.06
Asia (excluding Japan)	450	450	575	2 936	0.00	0.03	0.92
Africa	425	416	418	1 368	−0.00	0.00	0.67
Average Group B	444	440	573	3 102	−0.00	0.03	0.95
World	444	435	667	5 709	−0.00	0.05	1.21

Source: Appendix B.

Table 1–3. Level and Rate of Growth of GDP: World and Major Regions, 0–1998 A.D.

	0	1000	1820 (billion 1990 international dollars)	1998	0–1000	1000–1820 (annual average compound growth rate)	1820–1998
Western Europe	11.1	10.2	163.7	6 961	−0.01	0.34	2.13
Western Offshoots	0.5	0.8	13.5	8 456	0.05	0.35	3.68
Japan	1.2	3.2	20.7	2 582	0.10	0.23	2.75
Total Group A	12.8	14.1	198.0	17 998	0.01	0.32	2.57
Latin America	2.2	4.6	14.1	2 942	0.07	0.14	3.05
Eastern Europe & former USSR	3.5	5.4	60.9	1 793	0.05	0.29	1.92
Asia (excluding Japan)	77.0	78.9	390.5	9 953	0.00	0.20	1.84
Africa	7.0	13.7	31.0	1 039	0.07	0.10	1.99
Total Group B	89.7	102.7	496.5	15 727	0.01	0.19	1.96
World	102.5	116.8	694.4	33 726	0.01	0.22	2.21

Source: Appendix B.

http://dx.doi.org/10.1787/301542223888

ISBN 92-64-02261-9 – © OECD 2006   30

I
The Nature and Welfare Implications of Population Change

The acceleration of population growth over the past millennium could have come from increased fertility or reduced mortality. The evidence (Table 1–4) suggests that a slow and irregular decline in mortality was the predominant cause before 1820. Since 1820 the decline in mortality has been much sharper, and has clearly been the predominant influence. In fact fertility has declined substantially since 1820 (see Table 1–5a). Increases in life expectation are an important manifestation of improvement in human welfare. They are not captured by our measure of GDP, but there has been significant congruence, over time and between regions, in the patterns of improvement in per capita income and life expectation.

Table 1–4. **Life Expectation and Infant Mortality, Both Sexes Combined, 33–1875 A.D.**

Country and period	Years of life expectation at birth	Death rate per 1000 population in lst year of life	Source & authors
Roman Egypt, 33–258	24.0	329	Fragments of Roman Censuses Bagnall and Frier
England, 1301–1425	24.3	218	Very crude estimates derived from fiscal records: Russell
England, 1541–56	33.7	n.a.	Family reconstitution and
England, 1620–26	37.7	171	inverse projection from
England, 1726–51	34.6	195	birth and death records:
England, 1801–26	40.8	144	Wrigley, et al.
France, 1740–49	24.8	296	Family reconstitution:
France, 1820–29	38.8	181	Blayo
Sweden, 1751–55	37.8	203[a]	Parish records & census returns: Gille
Japan, 1776–1875	32.2	277	Temple records: Jannetta
Japan, 1800–50	33.7	295	Temple records: Yasuba
Japan, 1751–1869	37.4	216	Population registers: Saito

a) 1751–1800.

Source: Egypt from Bagnall and Frier (1994), pp. 70 and 100. England 1301–1425 from Russell (1948), pp. 186 and 218. England 1541–1826 (excluding Monmouth) from Wrigley et al. (1997), p. 614 for life expectation and p. 219 for infant mortality. France from Blayo (1975), p. 141 for life expectation, pp. 138–9 for infant mortality. Sweden from Gille (1949). Japan from Jannetta and Preston (1991), p. 428 and 433–5, Yasuba (1987), p. 291, deducting a year to adjust to Western reckoning. Saito (1997), p. 143 average for both sexes of his high infant mortality estimate. The first two estimates are derived from temple registers (kakocho), the third from population registers (shumon aratame cho). There is a much greater scarcity of information on infant mortality in Japanese sources than in the European records. Children were not covered in the registers. Temple records provide material on deaths by age but not population. There is a further problem that the Japanese system of counting age was different from that in the West and the degree of ambiguity was large for infants. Japanese children were presumed to be 1 year old at birth and two years old on the following New Year's day. A Japanese child could therefore be anywhere between 2 days and 1 year old when it became 2 years old in the Japanese system (see Saito, 1997). Estimates of infant mortality are therefore hypothetical or inferential. Saito used one of the probability models which Coale and Demeny (1983) constructed to fill gaps in information on deaths by age. Saito (1997), p. 136 shows other estimates with much higher life expectation than the three I show. In my view these are not plausible and either show or infer improbably low infant mortality. Kalland and Pederson (1984) pp. 54 and 61 show life expectation averaging 44 years for 1700–1824 in Kanezaki and an infant mortality rate of less than 100. Smith (1977) pp. 57 and 162 shows a life expectation of 43.2 for 1717–1830 in Nakahara, and a range of alternative infant mortality options which Saito averages at 145. Hanley and Yamamura (1977), p. 222 show a life expectation of 45 for Nishikata 1782–96 and 43 for Fujito 1800–35, without showing infant mortality.

http://dx.doi.org/10.1787/301542223888

In the year 1000, average life expectation at the world level was probably about 24 years — no better than at the beginning of our era. By 1820, it rose to about 26 years (see Table 1–5b). The rise was biggest — from 24 to 36 years — in Group A, and since then has risen to 78 years. The increase was ten times as fast from 1820 as in the previous eight centuries. In Group B countries, our very crude estimate suggests that there was no improvement between 1000 and 1820. By 1998 it had grown dramatically to an average of 64 years.

Table 1–5a. **Birth Rates and Life Expectation, 1820–1998/9**

	Births per 100 population				Years of life expectation at birth (Average for both sexes)			
	1820	*1900*	*1950*	*1998*	*1820*	*1900*	*1950*	*1999*
France	3.19	2.19	2.05	1.26	37	47	65	78
Germany	3.99	3.60	1.65	0.96	41	47	67	77
Italy	3.90	3.30	1.94	0.93	30	43	66	78
Netherlands	3.50	3.16	2.27	1.27	32	52	72	78
Spain	4.00	3.39	2.00	0.92	28	35	62	78
Sweden	3.40	2.69	1.64	1.01	39	56	70	79
United Kingdom	4.02[a]	2.93	1.62	1.30	40[a]	50	69	77
West European Average	3.74	3.08	1.83	1.00	36	46	67	78
United States	5.52	3.23	2.40	1.44	39	47	68	77
Japan	2.62[b]	3.24	2.81	0.95	34	44	61	81
Russia	4.13	4.80	2.65	0.88	28[c]	32	65	67
Brazil	5.43[d]	4.60	4.44	2.10	27[e]	36	45	67
Mexico	n.a.	4.69	4.56	2.70	n.a.	33	50	72
Latin America Average	n.a.	n.a.	4.19	2.51	(27)	(35)	51	69
China	n.a.	4.12[f]	3.70	1.60	n.a.	24[f]	41	71
India	n.a.	4.58[g]	4.50[h]	2.80	21[i]	24[g]	32[h]	60
Asian Average[j]	n.a.	n.a.	4.28	2.30	(23)	(24)	40	66
African Average	n.a.	n.a.	4.92	3.90	(23)	(24)	38	52
World	n.a.	n.a.	3.74	2.30	26	31	49	66

a) 1821; b) 1811–29; c) 1880; d) 1818; e) 1872; f) 1929–31; g) 1891–1911; h) 1941–51; i) 1833; j) excluding Japan.

Source: Birth rates 1820 and 1900: European countries mostly from Maddison (1991a) p. 241; 1821 for England from Wrigley *et al.* (1997), p. 614; Brazil 1818, from Marcilio (1984), otherwise Brazil and Mexico from Maddison and Associates (1992); United States 1820 and 1900 from *Historical Statistics of the United States*, (1975), vol.1, p. 49; China 1929–31 from Barclay *et al.* (1976); India entries for 1900 and 1950 from Mari Bhat (1989), p. 96; Japan 1816–20 (in Yokoucho) from Hayami (1973), p. 160, 1900 and 1950 from Japan Statistical Association (1987). 1950 generally from OECD (1979) and national sources. 1998 from OECD, *Labour Force Statistics, Population et Sociétés,* INED, Paris July–August 1999, and UN Population Division (1997).

Life expectancy 1820: France from Blayo (1975); Germany from Knodel (1988), p. 59 (average of his alternative estimates); Italy derived from Caselli (1991), p. 73; Spain derived from Livi Bacci and Reher (1993), p. 68; Sweden from Gille (1949), p. 43; the United Kingdom from Wrigley *et al.* (1997), p. 614; Russia (1874–84) from Ohlin (1955), p. 411; the United States from *Historical Statistics of the United States* (1975), vol. 1, p. 56 (refers to Massachusetts in 1850); Japan 1820 — average of three estimates in Table 1–4; Brazil 1872 and 1900 from Merrick and Graham (1979), pp. 41, 42 and 57; China , 1929–31 from Barclay, Coale, Stoto and Trussell (1976, p. 621); India, 1833 for Delhi from Visaria and Visaria (1983), p. 473, 1891–1911 and 1941–51 from Mari Bhat (1989), pp. 92, using an average of the three alternative measures shown. 1900 from Maddison (1995a), p. 27, except for the United Kingdom, from Wrigley *et al.* 1950 for most OECD countries from OECD (1979), Mexico from Maddison and Associates (1992), China from Lee and Wang (forthcoming). India from Mari Bhat (1989). Japan from Japan Statistical Association (1987). Other countries and regions 1950 from UN Population Division (1997). 1999 from *Population et Sociétés*. Regions 1820–1900 derived by weighting country estimates. World averages derived by weighting regional averages by regional population.

http://dx.doi.org/10.1787/301542223888

Life expectation in 1999 in the Group A countries was fairly closely clustered. In Group B, there was not much difference between Russia, Latin America and Asia, with an average of 67 years. But in Africa, life expectation was significantly lower at 52 years.

Although the pattern of improvement in life expectation and per capita income has been similar, the present interregional dispersions are much bigger for income. In 1999 the gap in life expectation between the lead country, Japan, with 81 years and Africa with 52 years was distressingly wide. But it was much smaller than the 15:1 spread in per capita income level between Japan and Africa.

Table 1–5b. **Average Life Expectation for Groups A and B, 1000–1999**
(years at birth; average for both sexes)

	1000	1820	1900	1950	1999
Group A	24	36	46	66	78
Group B	24	24	26	44	64
World	24	26	31	49	66

Source: 1820–1999 from weighted average of regions shown in Table 1–5a. Figure for 1000 is a rough inference from first two entries in Table 1–4 and other fragmentary clues.

Table 1–5c. **Rate of Growth of Life Expectation in Groups A and B, 1000–1999**
(annual average compound growth rate)

	1000–1820	1820–1900	1900–50	1950–99
Group A	0.05	0.31	0.72	0.34
Group B	0.00	0.10	1.06	0.77
World	0.01	0.22	0.92	0.61

http://dx.doi.org/10.1787/301542223888

West European Experience

Table 1–6 presents the evidence on long run growth of West European population. The pace of change has been very uneven. There were major disasters in the sixth and fourteenth centuries and a substantial setback in several countries in the seventeenth century. Until the nineteenth century population growth was repeatedly interrupted by crises of varying frequency and severity. These were of three main types: hunger crises due to harvest failure, waves of infectious disease, or war. These different types of causality were of course interactive in varying degree.

As European countries operated much nearer to subsistence levels in the past than is now the case, with poor transport and storage facilities, harvest failures could create big spikes in mortality. They also affected birth rates, because dietary deficiencies caused amenorrhea or led young couples to postpone marriage. A major instance of this type of crisis was the potato famine which doubled the normal death rate in Ireland over the six years 1846–51. "Excess" deaths were nearly one million or about 12 per cent of the 1845 population (see Ó Gráda, 1988).

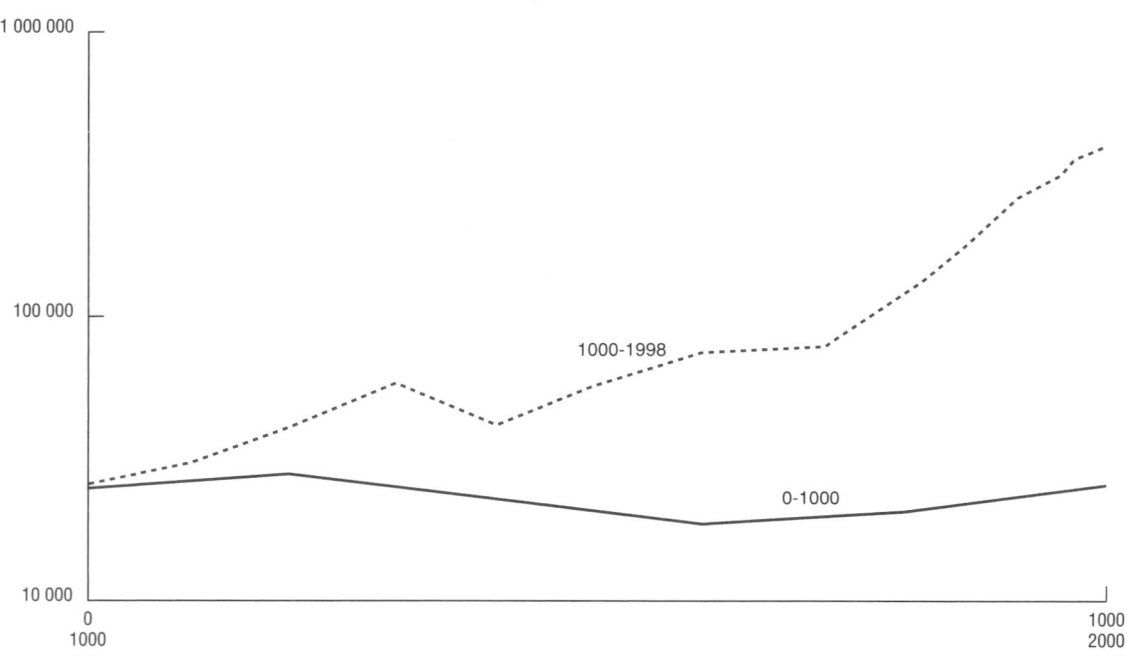

Figure 1-1. **Population of Western Europe: Confrontation of Two Millennia**
(000)

Source: See Table 1-6*a*. Vertical scale is logarithmic.

Table 1–6a. **West European Population Levels, 0–1998 A.D.**
(000)

0	200	400	600	800	1000	1200
24 700	27 600	22 900	18 600	20 400	25 413	40 885

1300	1400	1500	1600	1700	1820	1998
58 353	41 500	57 268	73 776	81 460	132 888	388 399

Source: McEvedy and Jones (1978) and Appendix B. The share of five Mediterranean countries (France, Greece, Italy, Portugal, Spain) dropped from 77 per cent in the year 0 to 67 per cent in 1000, 60 per cent in 1500, 52 per cent in 1820, and 45 per cent in 1998.

Table 1–6b. **West European Population Growth Rates, 0–1998 A.D.**
(annual average compound growth rates)

0–200	200–600	600–1000	1000–1300	1300–1400
0.06	−0.10	0.08	0.28	−0.34

1400–1500	1500–1600	1600–1700	1700–1820	1820–1998
0.32	0.24	0.08	0.41	0.60

Source: As for 1–6a.

http://dx.doi.org/10.1787/301542223888

ISBN 92-64-02261-9 – © OECD 2006

Figure 1-2. **Annual Movement in Swedish Birth and Death Rates, 1736-1987**
(per 1 000 population)

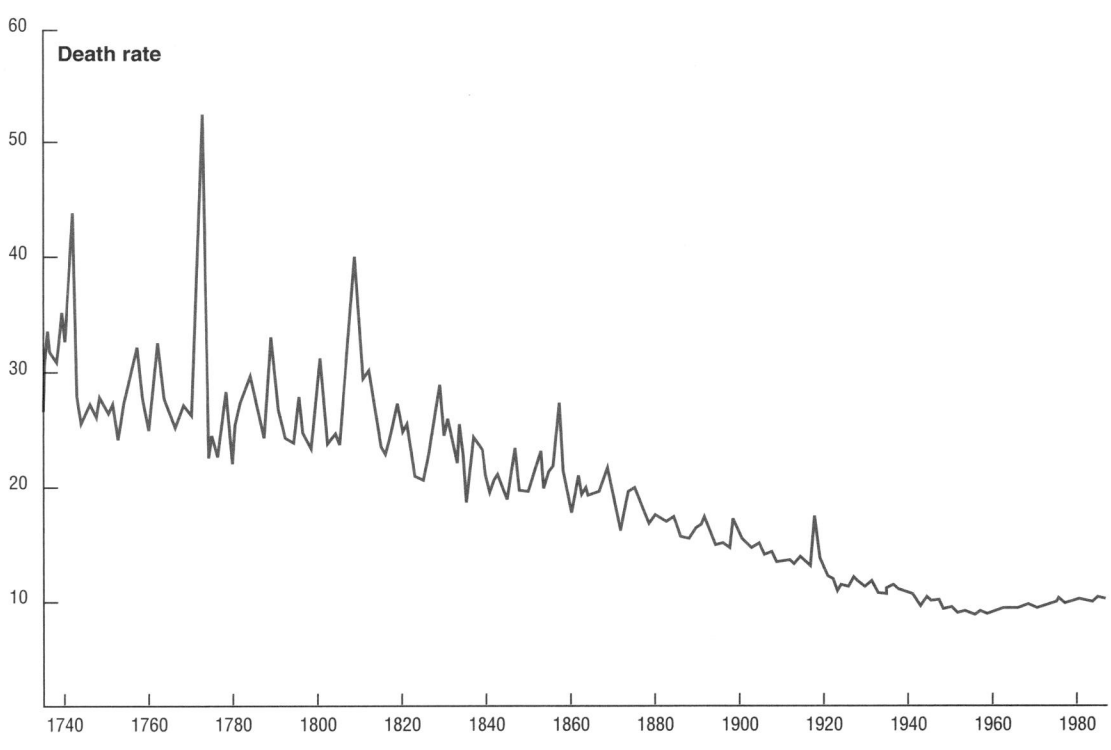

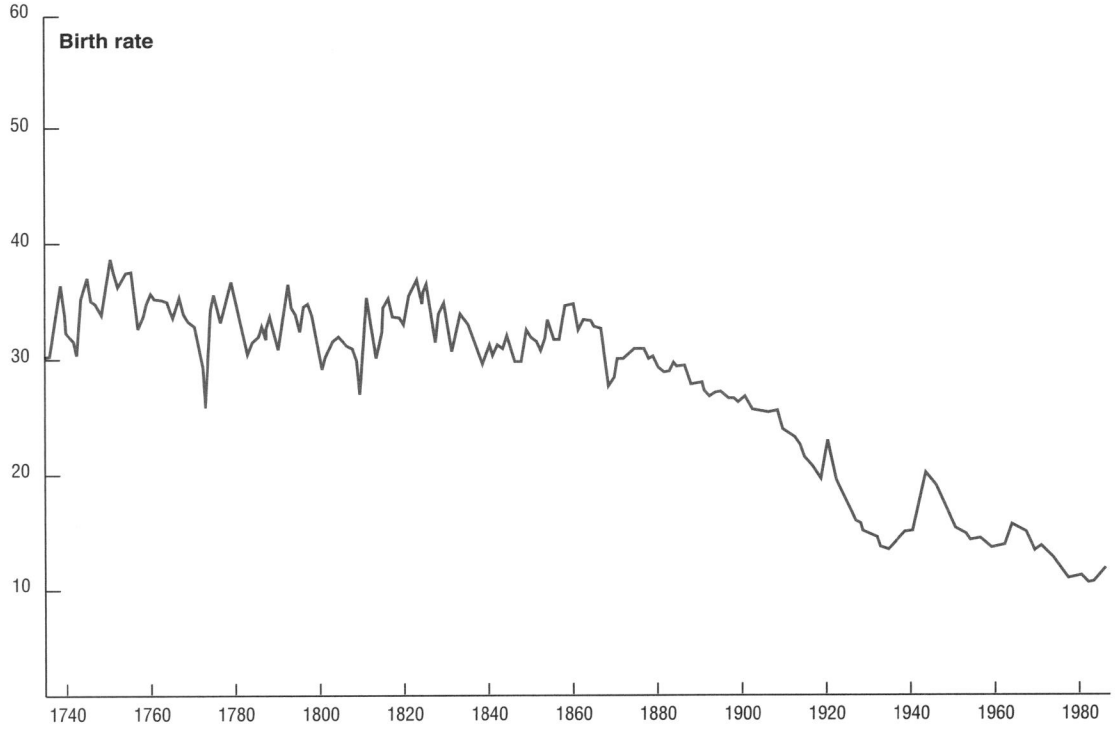

Source: H. Gille "The Demographic History of the Northern Countries in the Eighteenth Century", *Population Studies,* June 1949; *Historical Statistics for Sweden,* vol. i, CBS, Stockholm, 1955; and *OECD Labour Force Statistics,* Paris, various issues.

http://dx.doi.org/10.1787/301542223888

Recurrent episodes of infectious disease caused major surges in mortality. The worst was bubonic plague which wiped out a third of the European population in the sixth century and again in the fourteenth. The second plague lingered for centuries, finally dying out in England in 1665 and in France in 1720–21. John Graunt, the first scientific demographer, chronicled its impact in London for the years 1592, 1603, 1625, 1630, 1636, and 1665, the worst year, when a total of 97 000 burials were recorded (about 16 per cent of the population). Biraben (1972) estimated a total of 94 000 plague deaths in Provence in 1720–1 (about 32 per cent of the population) due to the arrival of a ship in Marseilles which brought the disease from Syria. The impact of this plague was limited by strict control of movement in and out of the region. The plague disappeared, but many other lethal diseases remained — cholera, diphtheria, dysentery, influenza, measles, smallpox, tuberculosis, typhus and typhoid. Their incidence receded temporarily after epidemics had wiped out the least resistant. In some cases, like the plague, repeated exposure seems to have generated resistance or immunity in the long term. In other cases, the bacterial and viral organisms responsible for infection may have changed. The pattern and duration of acquired immunities varied for reasons not fully understood, but the impact of epidemic disease declined sharply in Western Europe in the late nineteenth and in the twentieth century. However deaths surged again in the global influenza epidemic of 1918–19. The new threat from Aids seems to have been contained in Group A countries.

Until the twentieth century, a major countervailing force in the process of mortality reduction was increased urbanisation. Although city dwellers had higher incomes and better organised food markets than rural areas, their mortality rates were distinctly higher. John Graunt discovered this for London in the seventeenth century where burials were substantially higher than christenings. Mortality rates were a good deal higher in London than in small towns like Romsey, Tiverton and Cranbrook whose experience he also investigated. London's expansion was due to high net immigration, but the big city was a reservoir of infection, with poor sanitation, most lethal in its impact on infants and recent immigrants. Wrigley et al. (1997), p. 218, note that in the early eighteenth century London's infant mortality rate was about twice as high as for the country as a whole. Hayami (1986a) notes the same phenomenon in Japan, citing evidence for the capital city Edo for 1840–68. In the course of the twentieth century this differential has disappeared (see Preston and van der Walle, 1978, for the decline in the differential in nineteenth century France).

Over the long run, in the centuries before 1820, there was a slow increase in agricultural productivity and improvements in food availability. Hunger crises became less frequent or severe. Increased resistance to disease was also helped by rising living standards, substitution of wine, beer and tea for contaminated water, improvements in clothing and bedding. In the nineteenth and twentieth centuries, better sanitation and public health facilities, improvements in medical knowledge and facilities greatly reduced the incidence of premature death by infectious disease (see Fogel, 1986, for a causal analysis of mortality decline). The most striking feature has been the reduction in infant mortality. Around 1820, it was probably between 150–200 per 1 000 population in Western Europe and about 200 in Japan. In the 1990s, it was about seven in Western Europe and four per 1 000 in Japan. The increase in life expectation for the elderly in Western Europe, the Western Offshoots and Japan since 1950 involved a big rise in health expenditure. Earlier decreases in mortality in the nineteenth and twentieth centuries were much cheaper to obtain.

Figure 1–2 provides a fairly representative picture of European mortality and fertility experience since 1736 when such records first became available in Sweden. Vallin (1991) presents similar charts for English, French, Finnish and Norwegian mortality back to 1720. Until the latter half of the nineteenth century, the pattern in all these countries was more irregular than it has been since because crisis mortality has been greatly mitigated. Figure I–2 also shows the demographic transition which started in the mid–nineteenth century throughout most of Western Europe.

Birth rates have fallen more than death rates. In 1998, they were about a third of their 1820 level. As a consequence population growth is much slower and demographic structure has changed dramatically. In England, which is fairly typical of West European experience, nearly 39 per cent of 1821 population were below 15 years of age and less than 5 per cent were 65 or over. In 1998, 19 per cent were below 15 and nearly 16 per cent 65 or over. The proportion aged 15–64 rose from 60 to 65 per cent.

Table 1–7a. Population Growth: Western and Iberian Offshoots in Comparative Perspective, 1500–1998
(annual average compound growth rates)

	1500–1700	1700–1820	1820–1950	1950–73	1973–98
United States	−0.35	1.94	2.12	1.45	0.98
Canada	−0.11	1.18	2.20	2.18	1.19
Australia & New Zealand	0.00	− 0.20	2.45	2.16	1.27
Brazil	0.11	1.07	1.92	2.91	2.00
Other Latin America & Caribbean	−0.21	0.36	1.63	2.65	2.02
Western Europe	0.18	0.41	0.64	0.70	0.32
Japan	0.28	0.12	0.77	1.15	0.61
Rest of World	0.17	0.47	0.58	2.09	1.85

Source: Appendices A and B.

Table 1–7b. Comparative Population Growth in the Americas and Former European Metropoles, 1500–1998

	Population level (million)		Coefficient of multiplication 1500–1998		Population level (million)		Coefficient of multiplication 1500–1998
	1500	1998	1500–1998		1500	1998	1500–1998
Brazil	1	170	170	United States	2.00	271	136
Portugal	1	10	10	United Kingdom	3.94	59	15
Other Latin America	16.5	338	20	Canada	0.25	30	120
Spain	6.8	39	6	France	15.00	59	4

Source: Appendices A and B.

Table 1–7c. Shipment of African Slaves to the Americas, 1500–1870
(000)

	1500–1600	1601–1700	1701–1810	1811–70	1500–1870
Brazil	50	560	1 891	1 145	3 647
Caribbean[a]	–	464	3 234	96	3 793
Spanish America	75	293	579	606	1 552
United States	–	–	348	51	399

a) British, French, Dutch and Danish colonies.
Source: Curtin (1969), p. 268. See also Table 2–5 below.

Table 1–7d. Net Migration to Brazil, Australia and United States and from the United Kingdom, 1500–1998

	1500–1600	1600–1700	1700–1820	1820–69	1870–1913	1913–50	1950–98
Brazil	+40	+60	+400	+400	+2 200	+1 294	n.a.
Australia	–	–	+33	+1 069	+885	+673	+4 184
United States	–	+131	+587	+6 131	+15 820	+6 221	+24 978
United Kingdom	n.a.	−714	−672	−5 548	−6 415	−1 405	+132

Source: Brazil from Marcilio (1984), Merrick and Graham (1979) and IBGE (1960); Australia 1788–1973 from Vamplew (1987), pp. 4–7; thereafter from OECD, *Labour Force Statistics;* United States 1630–1780 from Galenson (1996), p. 178, and Potter (1965) for 1790–1820. I assumed that 1780–90 immigration was the same as Potter's estimate for 1790–1800; United Kingdom 1600–1820 from Henry and Blanchet (1983) who show net migration from England (their figures exclude deaths at sea and in wars abroad; 1820–69 from Mitchell (1975), pp. 137–40, gross emigration 1820–54 was reduced by one sixth, using the same emigrant/immigrant ratio available for 1855–69. United Kingdom and United States for 1870 onwards from Maddison (1991a), p. 240 and from OECD *Labour Force Statistics.*

http://dx.doi.org/10.1787/301542223888

Figure 1-3. **Comparative Population Levels in the Three Biggest Countries of the Americas and their Former European Metropoles, 1500-1998**

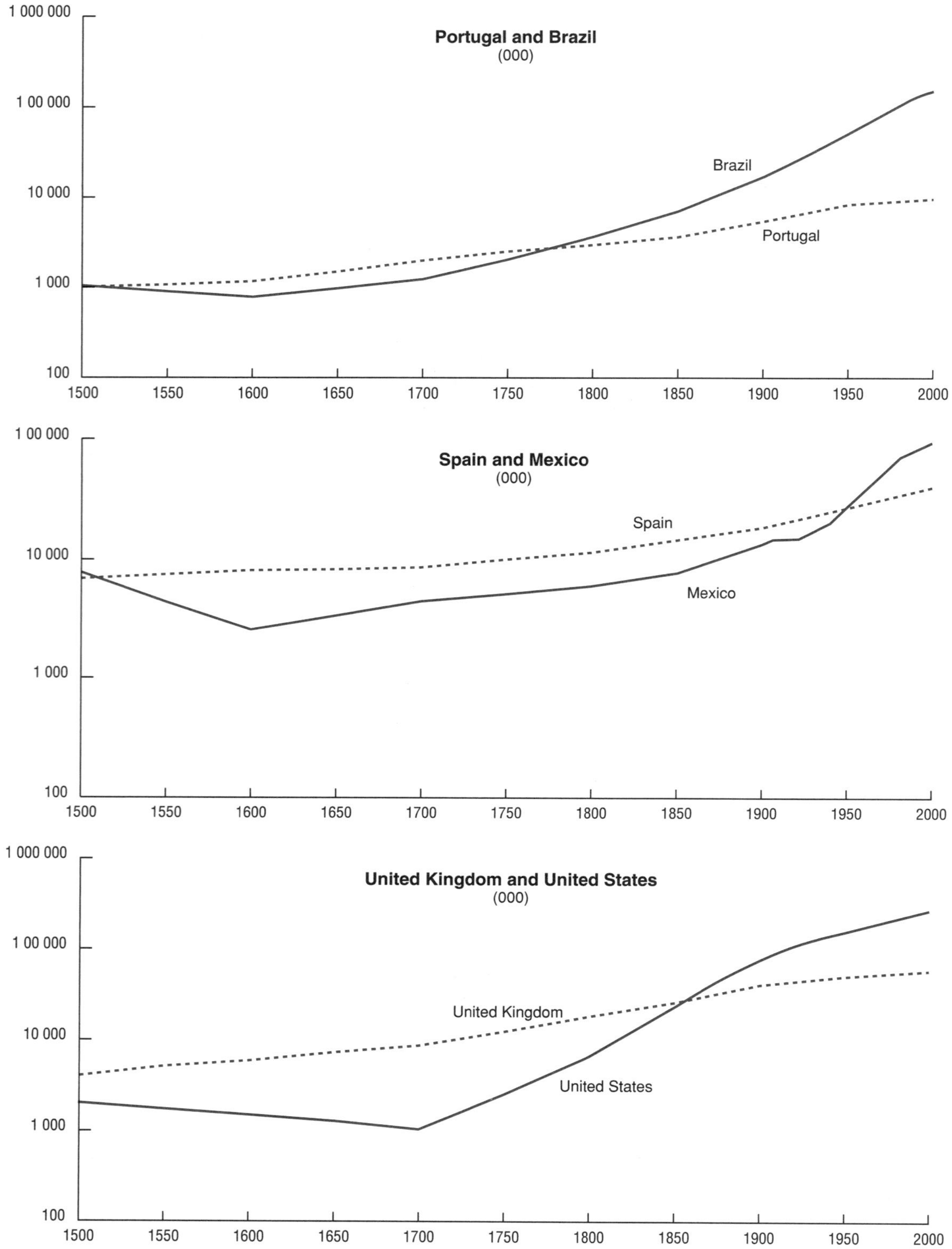

Source: See Appendices A, B, C. Vertical scale is logarithmic.

http://dx.doi.org/10.1787/301542223888

ISBN 92-64-02261-9 – © OECD 2006

The Americas and Australasia

The pattern of mortality, migration and population growth in the Americas and Australia was changed drastically by the encounter with Western Europe. The relatively densely populated agrarian civilisations of Mexico and Peru were quickly destroyed by the sixteenth century Spanish conquest mainly because of the inadvertent introduction of European diseases (smallpox, measles, influenza and typhus). Shortly thereafter the traffic in slaves introduced yellow fever and malaria. The consequences were devastating for the indigenous population. At least threequarters of them perished (see Appendix B). In Latin America as a whole, mortality was about twice as big proportionately as Europe's loss from the Black Death.

In parts of the Americas where the population was mainly hunter–gatherers and less densely settled (e.g. Brazil, and the areas that subsequently became Canada and the United States), the impact of disease mortality was somewhat smaller.

Western contact with Australia and other Pacific islands occurred towards the end of the eighteenth century. The impact of disease on mortality was similar to that in the Americas, and there was a more deliberate policy of exterminating the native population than in Spanish America (see Butlin, 1983 and 1993).

Although the initial impact of conquest and colonisation was massively destructive for the indigenous population, the long term economic potential of the Americas was greatly enhanced. Capacity to support a bigger population was augmented by the introduction of new crops and animals (see Crosby, 1972). The new crops were wheat, rice, sugar cane, vines, salad greens, olives, bananas and coffee. The new animals for food were cattle, pigs, chickens, sheep and goats. The introduction of transport and traction animals — horses, oxen, asses and donkeys — along with wheeled vehicles and ploughs (which replaced digging sticks) were another major addition to productive capacity. There was also a reciprocal transfer of New World crops to Europe, Asia and Africa — maize, potatoes, sweet potatoes, manioc, chilis, tomatoes, groundnuts, pineapples, cocoa and tobacco — which enhanced the world's production potential and capacity to sustain population growth.

New economic horizons and acquisition of vast territories led to a large scale transfer of population from Europe and Africa. Between 1500 and 1870 almost nine and a half million African slaves were shipped to work in plantation agriculture (sugar, tobacco, coffee and cotton) in Brazil, the Caribbean and the southern United States.

The migration of Spanish and Portuguese settlers to Latin America in the colonial period (before 1820) was smaller than the movement of slaves. Portuguese emigration was probably about half a million (Marcilio, 1984), and Spanish less than a million (Sanchez–Albornoz, 1984). Galenson (1996) estimates British migration to the Caribbean to have been about a quarter of a million from 1630 to 1780. If we include French and Dutch migration, the net white migration to Latin America probably totalled two million before 1820, compared with imports of 7.5 million slaves. However the life expectation of slaves was a good deal lower. Merrick and Graham (1979, pp. 56–7) estimate 18 years for male slaves in Brazil in 1872, compared with 27 years for the total population. Fertility of slaves was also lower because of the precarious nature of their opportunities for family life. The proportion of females in the white immigrant population was low. Threequarters or more consisted of adult males. Their fertility was quite high because of informal unions with the indigenous and black population. As a result there was a much greater ethnic mix in Latin America than in North America.

Since 1820, Latin American population has grown faster than that of Western Europe. The main reason has been higher birth rates, as the decline in mortality came later and has been smaller. Migration from Europe to Latin America accounted for a substantial part of the differential before 1913, but has been less important since then.

In the area of the United States and Canada, European settlement started in the seventeenth century, and expanded rapidly in the eighteenth, when there was also a large import of slaves. The indigenous population was killed off or pushed out of the areas of European settlement. In 1700, threequarters of the population had been indigenous, by 1820 they were only 3 per cent (see Table B–15). In the South, there was a heavy concentration on plantation agriculture, with slaves as the main component of the labour force. In the North, white settlers predominated and were mainly occupied on family farms.

White life expectation in North America was similar to that in Western Europe. It was lower for slaves, but the differential was smaller than in Brazil. Merrick and Graham (1979, p. 57) show 35.5 years for slaves in the 1850s and 40.4 for the US population as a whole. Fertility was high. In the United States, the birth rate was 5.5 per 100 population in 1820, in Canada (Quebec) 5.7. This was much higher than the United Kingdom (4.0) or France (3.2).

Since 1820 the US population has grown a good deal faster than that of Western Europe. The death rate has been similar. The birth rate has remained higher but has declined proportionately as much as in Western Europe. Immigration to the United States has continued at a high level. Most of the immigrants came from Europe before the 1960s, so migration explains a good deal of the US/ European growth differential.

Japan

From the seventh to the mid–nineteenth century, Japan tried to model its economy, society and institutions on those of China, but its demographic experience was very different:

a)   over the long run, the major check to Japanese population expansion came from famines and hunger crises. Disease and war were much less important than in China (and Europe);

b)   by the second half of the eighteenth century, and perhaps earlier, Japanese life expectation was similar to that in Western Europe, and much higher than in China.

Comparative Incidence of Hunger, Disease and War

Macfarlane (1997) provides a comparative survey of the long run forces affecting mortality in England and Japan; Jannetta (1986) a detailed study of Japanese experience with epidemic disease, and Saito (1996) an assessment of the comparative incidence of famine and disease in Japan over the long term.

The major point which emerges from their work is that Japan was not affected by bubonic plague. The main reason was Japan's isolation. Two hundred kilometres of stormy seas separated it from Korea. The nearest point in China was 750 kilometres away. This sea barrier, and official policy, imposed an effective *cordon sanitaire*. Travel into and out of Japan was very restricted. Foreigners trading with Japan were more or less permanently quarantined in a small area near Nagasaki. There was no import of grain or other products likely to introduce pests. The two Mongol attempts to invade Japan in 1274 and 1281 were unsuccessful. If they had succeeded Japan's demographic history (and much else) would have been very different.

Freedom from the plague was the main reason why Japanese population growth was faster than that of Europe and China in the first millennium and a half of our era.

Smallpox was the most significant cause of Japanese epidemics. Mortality from other diseases — cholera, dysentery, malaria, measles, tuberculosis and typhoid fever was milder than in Europe, and epidemic typhus was absent. This situation was mainly due to hygienic habits, and very limited contact with animals. Japanese had an abundant supply of mountain streams and hot springs, and the Shinto emphasis on physical purity led to daily bathing at home or in bathhouses. Japanese houses were austere but kept spotlessly clean and well ventilated. Shoes were left at the entry, there was virtually no furniture or hangings except mosquito nets. Most water consumption was in the form of tea made with boiling water. The Japanese diet consisted of rice, fish, soyabeans, a considerable variety of vegetables, bamboo shoots and giant radishes. Buddhist tradition meant that Japanese ate virtually no meat. They had no cows, pigs, sheep, goats or animal dung. Although human wastes were used for manure, the few foreigners who visited Japan were greatly impressed by the immaculate privies, and the sanitary treatment of sewage. In 1853, foreigners were able to force an entry into Japan and greatly increased the range of foreign contacts. This resulted very quickly in a major cholera epidemic in 1858–60, and much greater exposure to influenza, tuberculosis, typhoid, typhus and diphtheria (see Saito, 1996 and Honda, 1997). As a consequence the Japanese death rate rose significantly until the 1890s (see Ishii, 1937, pp. 124–5).

Saito (1996) has collated the historical records of famine and crop failure from the eighth to the twentieth century for Japan. Although it is not possible to measure the intensity of these hunger crises one can get an idea of changes in their frequency. From the eighth to the tenth centuries, there was one every three years, in the eleventh to fifteenth centuries one every five years, in the sixteenth to eighteenth one every four years, in the nineteenth every nine years, and none in the twentieth century.

It is not possible to compare the importance of Japanese hunger crises with those in China or Europe. However, the nature of the Japanese and European diets was very different. Europeans had substantial consumption of meat, milk and other animal products which were absent in Japan. They had sufficient cereal production to make large quantities of ale and beer which the Japanese did not have. Land scarcity was much greater in Japan, and Japanese had to work much more intensively than Europeans. The combination of greater austerity and greater physical strain may well have made Japanese more vulnerable to hunger crises than Europeans, but the susceptibility was probably similar to that of Chinese.

A third major check to population comes from war. Here Japanese experience was very mild compared with China, and probably milder than in Western Europe.

China suffered major losses from the Mongol invasion of North China in 1234. The Mongols razed many cities, inflicted great damage on agriculture, enserfed or enslaved part of the rural population and displaced them by pastoralising cropland to make way for horses. Their later assault on South China in 1279 was much less destructive, but Mongol horsemen brought bubonic plague in 1353. Total population loss from the encounter with the Mongols was around 30 million.

The transition from the Mongol to the Ming dynasty did not involve substantial mortality. The next big disaster was the replacement of the Ming by the Manchus. The Manchu takeover was rapid in North China in 1644, but the struggle with Ming loyalists in the South lasted till 1683. The savagery of war, combined with smallpox and famine, reduced population by more than 20 million. There was also significant migration from mainland China. In the struggle with Koxinga who operated from Taiwan, the Manchus carried out a scorched earth policy on the opposite coasts of Kwangtung, Fukien and Chekiang provinces, burning crops and villages to a depth of about eight to 30 miles. There was significant move of population from this area to Taiwan, and a wave of "overseas" Chinese migrants to Southeast Asia (see Purcell, 1965).

There were other major population losses in the Taiping and other anti–Manchu rebellions in the 1850s and 1860s. As a result of these and associated famine and disease, Chinese population dropped by more than 50 million from 1850 to 1870.

China also suffered significant losses from 1840 to 1945 from aggression by West European countries, Japan and Russia and from its own civil war from 1937 to 1949.

Japan never suffered from foreign invasions, and the two main episodes of civil war in the latter half of the twelfth century when the first (Kamakura) shogunate was established, and from 1467 to 1568, were much smaller in their impact than the wars China experienced.

Table 1–8a. **Comparative Population Growth: Japan, China and Western Europe, 0–1998 A.D.**
(000)

	Japan	China	Western Europe
0	3 000	59 600	24 700
1000	7 500	59 000	25 413
1300	10 500	100 000	58 353
1400	12 700	72 000	41 500
1500	15 400	103 000	57 268
1600	18 500	160 000	73 778
1700	27 500	138 000	81 460
1820	31 000	381 000	132 888
1850	32 000	412 000	164 428
1870	34 437	358 000	187 532
1998	126 469	1 242 700	388 399

Source: China from Appendix B and Maddison (1998a): Western Europe from Table 1–6a: Japan from Farris (1985), Honjo (1935), Taeuber (1958), with some interpolation.

Table 1–8b. **Population Growth Rates: Japan, China and Western Europe, 0–1998 A.D.**
(annual average compound growth rate)

	0–1500	1500–1700	1700–1850	1850–1998
Japan	0.11	0.28	0.10	0.93
China	0.04	0.15	0.73	0.75
Western Europe	0.06	0.18	0.47	0.58

Source: Derived from Table 1–8a.

Table 1–8c. **Urbanisation Ratios: Japan, China and Western Europe, 1000–1890**
(per cent of population in towns of 10 000 inhabitants and more)

	Japan	China	Western Europe
1000	n.a.	3.0	0.0
1500	2.9	3.8	6.1
1820	12.3	3.8	12.3
1890	16.0	4.4	31.0

Source: Appendix Table B–14, de Vries (1984), Perkins (1969) and Ishii (1937).

http://dx.doi.org/10.1787/301542223888

A Precocious Demographic Transition in Tokugawa Japan

After a century of rapid expansion, Japanese population growth slowed markedly from the early eighteenth to the mid–nineteenth century.

The slowdown reflected a precocious transition to lowered levels of mortality and fertility, and to life expectation higher than the Asian norm. The transition was analogous in some respects to that experienced in West European countries from the mid–nineteenth to the twentieth century.

Japanese demographic records for the eighteenth century have certain deficiencies, but they are much better than those for earlier centuries. In the past 40 years they have been subjected to meticulous scrutiny by a new generation of historical demographers inspired by the pioneering and prolific work of Akira Hayami. As a result the interpretation of this period has changed completely. The eighteenth century slowdown was once attributed to Malthusian immiseration but is now characterised as a period of rising welfare.

There is little doubt that population was stagnant from 1721 to 1846 when the best Tokugawa statistics were available, and there is reasonable evidence that it was expanding much faster in the seventeenth century. There are grounds for believing that birth rates were relatively low and life expectation relatively high, but there is controversy about life expectation. The most credible estimates range from 32 to 37 years. The spread reflects uncertainty which arises from the absence of direct evidence on infant mortality and the need for inferential procedures as explained in the notes to Table 1–4.

The traditional method of family limitation in Japan (as in China) was abortion and infanticide. In the eighteenth century, family size was further reduced by late marriage, and lower levels of marital fertility. The change was induced by new institutional arrangements, rising per capita income and increased per capita labour inputs.

Early in the seventeenth century, the Tokugawa regime compelled its military elite (*daimyo*) to move their vassals (*samurai*) from the countryside to castle towns. The peasantry were no longer closely controlled, and were much freer to capture gains in productivity for themselves. There were large rice levies to provide stipends for the *samurai*, but these were more or less fixed and the tax burden declined over time.

In the seventeenth century, there were large land reclamation and irrigation projects, improved seeds, increased use of fertiliser. The proportion of land devoted to double cropped rice increased significantly, there was a rapid expansion of new commercial crops (cotton, sericulture, oil seeds, sugar and tobacco) and industrial by–employments. These changes brought increased real income, but required more intensive labour, with a particularly heavy additional load for women (Saito, 1996).

In these circumstances, large families came to be regarded as a burden. By reducing dependency, per capita income could be raised or more easily sustained. Family restriction was also socially acceptable. Villages had a collective responsibility to provide the compulsory rice levy, so the welfare of the whole village community was safeguarded by lower dependency rates. The danger that the family line would die out was covered by the widespread practice of adopting adults (e.g. sons–in–law) who would take over the family name and ultimately the family assets. The Japanese inheritance system was more or less equivalent to primogeniture with reversion to a single heir, rather than the system of partible inheritance which prevailed in China.

Japanese death and birth rates increased somewhat in the last quarter of the nineteenth century. Some of the rise may have been more apparent than real because of a change in official attitudes and practice. These changed from Tokugawa tolerance of abortion and infanticide to repression, and these practices were easier to detect because the new Meiji population registration system had much more effective coverage. However, Japanese family size and population growth continued to be fairly modest by subsequent standards elsewhere in Asia.

Figure 1-4. **Comparative Levels of GDP Per Capita: China and West Europe, 400-1998 A.D.**

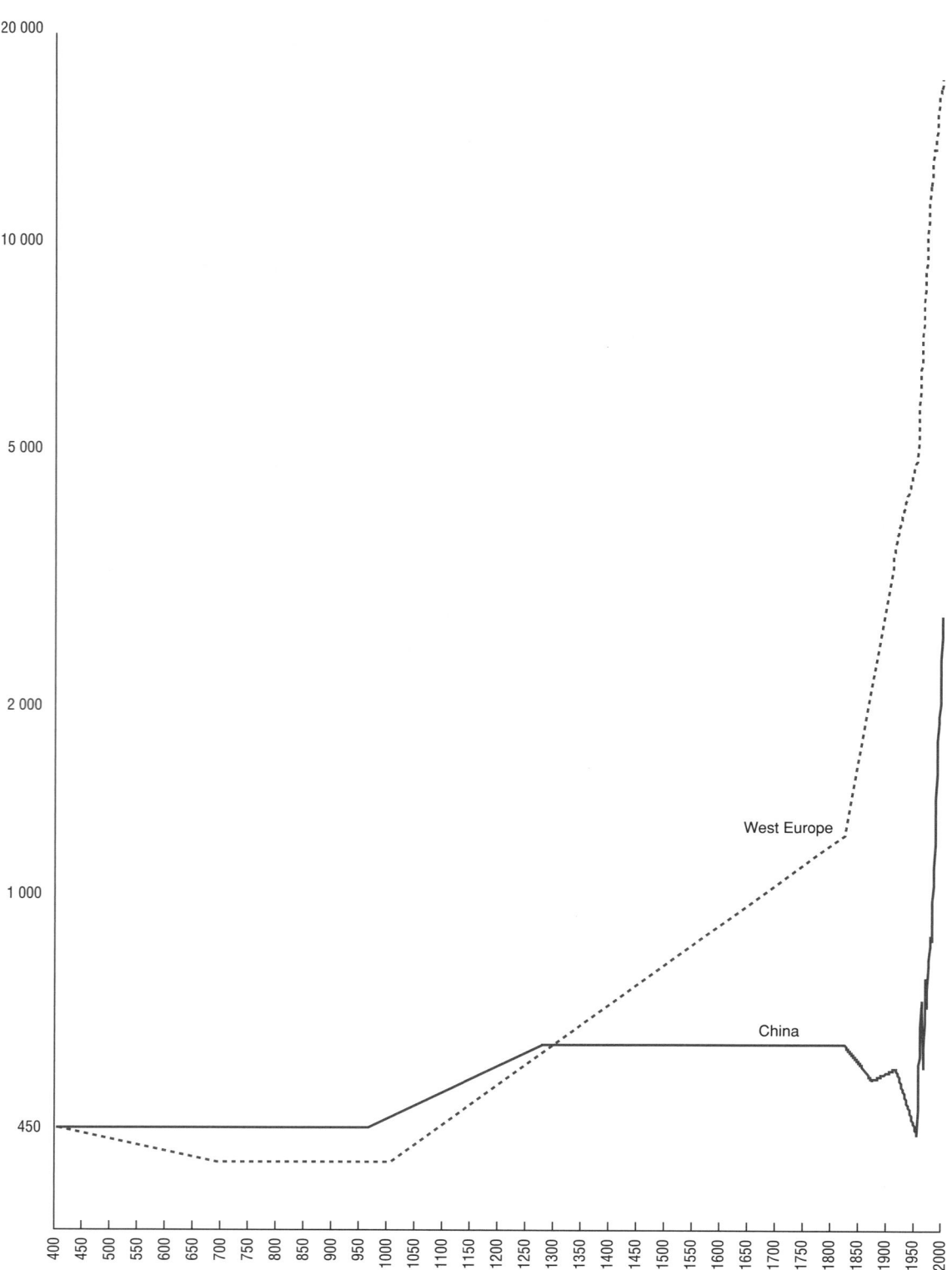

Source: Appendices A, B and C. Vertical scale is logarithmic.

http://dx.doi.org/10.1787/301542223888

ISBN 92-64-02261-9 – © OECD 2006

Figure 1-5. **Comparative Levels of GDP Per Capita, China and the United Kingdom, 1700-1998**

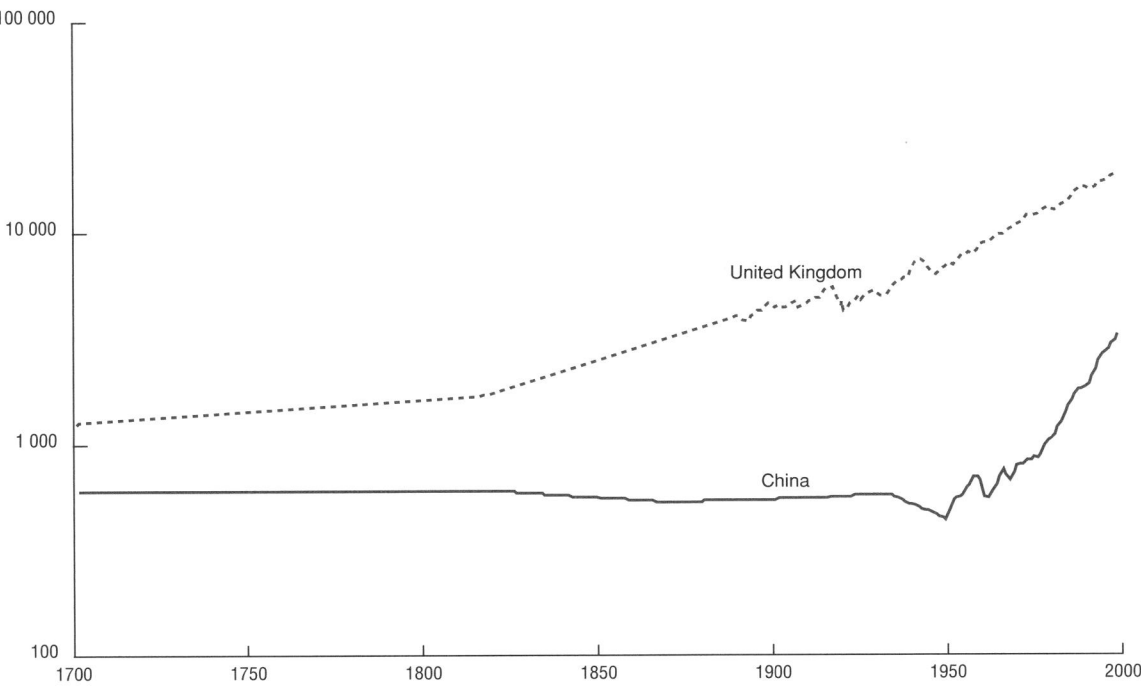

Figure 1.6. **Comparative Levels of GDP Per Capita, China and the United States, 1700-1998**

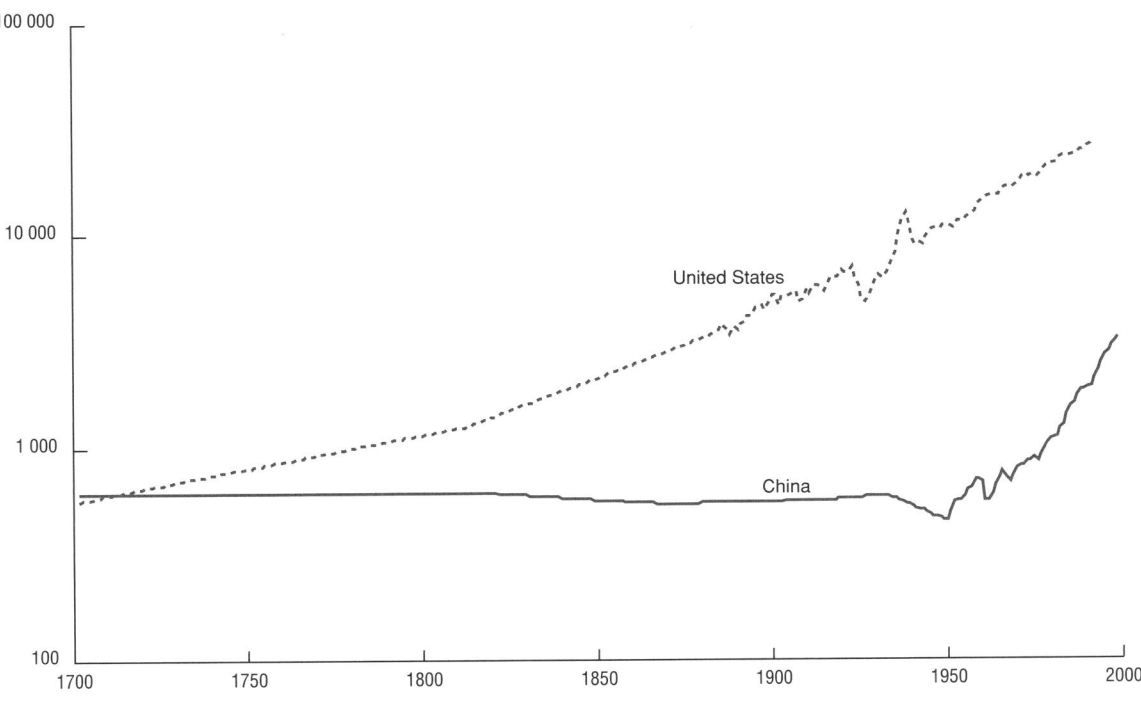

Source: Appendices A, B, C. Vertical scale is logarithmic.

http://dx.doi.org/10.1787/301542223888

II
GDP Per Capita

Long–term estimates of world GDP are very recent. Research on real income growth by quantitative economic historians has been heavily concentrated on Europe, and generally confined to the past two centuries. Until recently what was known about earlier centuries was in large degree conjectural.

Maddison (1995a) contained detailed estimates for different parts of the world economy for 1820 onwards, with a very crude provisional assessment for 1500 to 1820. Here I have made a much more careful scrutiny of the evidence for centuries before 1820 and incorporated the results of Maddison (1998a) on Chinese economic performance over two millennia. There is still a substantial degree of conjecture, but Appendices A and B present my evidence and assumptions as transparently as possible, so that critical readers can easily modify, adjust or augment my results where they find them open to question.

The level and movement of per capita GDP is the primary general purpose indicator of changes in well–being and production potential, but one should keep in mind that per capita consumption has increased less over the long run because of the increased share of product allocated to investment and government. Labour productivity does not always move parallel to per capita income. The advances achieved in Sung China (960–1279) and in Japan in the seventeenth and eighteenth centuries required substantial increases in per capita labour effort. In the twentieth century we find the opposite phenomenon. Labour input per person fell substantially in Western Europe and Western Offshoots (see Appendix E).

Table 1–3 summarises my findings for the past millennium. It shows clearly the exceptionalism of Western Europe's very lengthy ascension, and origins of the great divergence between the West (Group A) and the rest of the world (Group B).

The major conclusions I draw from the long term quantitative evidence are as follows:

a)   West European income was at a nadir around the year 1000. Its level was significantly lower than it had been in the first century. It was below that in China, India and other parts of East and West Asia;

b)   There was a turning point in the eleventh century when the economic ascension of Western Europe began. It proceeded at a slow pace, but by 1820 real income had tripled. The locus and characteristics of economic leadership changed. The North Italian city states and, in particular, Venice initiated the growth process and reopened Mediterranean trade. Portugal and Spain opened trade routes to the Americas and Asia, but were less dynamic than the Netherlands which became the economic leader around 1600, followed by the United Kingdom in the nineteenth century;

c)   Western Europe overtook China (the leading Asian economy) in per capita performance in the fourteen century (see Figure 1–4). Thereafter China and most of the rest of Asia were more or less stagnant in per capita terms until the second half of the twentieth century. The stagnation was initially due to indigenous institutions and policy, reinforced by colonial exploitation which derived from Western hegemony and was most marked from the eighteenth century onwards;

d)   West European appropriation of the natural resources of North America, introduction of European settlers, technology and organisation added a substantial new dimension to Western economic ascension from the eighteenth century onwards. Towards the end of the nineteenth century, the United States became the world economic leader;

e)   Japan was an exception to the Asian norm. In the course of the seventeenth, eighteenth and the first half of the nineteenth century, it caught up with and overtook China in per capita income. The Meiji takeover in 1868 involved massive institutional change aimed at catching up with the West. This was achieved in income terms in the 1980s, but not yet in productivity;

f) The colonial takeover in Latin America had some analogy to that in North America, but Iberian institutions were less propitious to capitalist development than those in North America. Latin America included a much larger indigenous population which was treated as an underclass without access to land or education. The social order was not greatly changed after independence. Over the long run the rise in per capita income was much smaller than in North America, but faster than in Asia or Africa;

g) African per capita income was lower in 1820 than in the first century. Since then there has been slower advance than in all other regions. The income level in 1998 was little better than that of Western Europe in 1820. Population growth is now faster than in any other region — eight times as fast as in Western Europe;

h) The most dynamic growth performance has been concentrated on the past two centuries. Since 1820 per capita income has risen 19–fold in Group A, and more than 5–fold in the rest of the world — dwarfing any earlier advance and compressing it into a very short time span.

One may ask what is new in these findings. In the first place there is the quantification which clarifies issues that qualitative analysis leaves fuzzy. It helps to separate stylised facts from the stylised fantasies which are sometimes perceived to be reality. It is more readily contestable and likely to be contested. It sharpens scholarly discussion, and contributes to the dynamics of the research process. It is also useful to have a world picture because it helps to identify what is normal and what is exceptional.

My findings differ in some respects from earlier interpretations of the length and pace of Western Europe's economic ascension. There has been a general tendency to date it from 1500 when Europeans encountered America and first made a direct entry into the trading world of Asia. Max Weber attributed Europe's advance to the rise of protestantism, and this thesis attracted attention because it was congruent with the conventional wisdom about the beginning of the European ascension. I no longer believe that there was a sharp break in the pace of advance of per capita income around 1500.

Kuznets (1966, Chapter 1) suggested that "modern economic growth" is a distinctive economic epoch preceded by merchant capitalism in Western Europe "from the end of the fifteenth to the second half of the eighteenth century," and an "antecedent epoch of feudal organisation." In Kuznets (1973, pp. 139–41), he advanced what seemed to be a reasonable view about the rate of per capita GDP growth in Western Europe in the merchant capitalist period. In Maddison (1995a), I accepted Kuznets' hypothesis for his merchant capitalist period, but I now believe that growth was slower then than Kuznets suggested, and that the pace of advance between the eleventh and the fifteenth centuries was not much different. For this reason, it does not seem valid to distinguish between epochs of "feudal organisation" and "merchant capitalism". Instead I would characterise the whole period 1000–1820 as "protocapitalist".

I also differ from Kuznets on the timing of the transition to what he called "modern economic growth" (which I call "capitalist development"). The evidence now available suggests that the transition took place around 1820 rather than in 1760. The revisionist work of Crafts (1983 and 1992) and others has helped to break the old notion of a sudden take–off in the second half of the eighteenth century in England. Recent research on the Netherlands shows income to have been higher there than in the United Kingdom at the end of the eighteenth century. Work in the past twenty years on the quantitative history of other West European countries provides further reason for postdating the transition and modifying the old emphasis on British exceptionalism.

My analysis of US economic performance shows a rapid advance in the eighteenth century in contrast to the findings of Gallman (1972) and Mancall and Weiss (1999). The essential reason for the difference is that I include rough estimates of the indigenous population and its GDP as well as the activity of European settlers (I also did this for Australia, Canada and New Zealand).

My assessment of Japanese development differs from the conventional wisdom. I have quantified its economic performance in the Tokugawa period and compared it with China. Most analysts concentrate on comparisons between Japan and Western Europe in the Meiji period, and ignore the Asian context.

Table 1–9a. **Growth of Per Capita GDP by Major Region, 1000–1998**
(annual average compound growth rate)

	1000–1500	1500–1600	1600–1700	1700–1820	1820–1998
Western Europe	0.13	0.14	0.15	0.15	1.51
Western Offshoots	0.00	0.00	0.17	0.78	1.75
Japan	0.03	0.03	0.09	0.13	1.93
Average Group A	0.11	0.13	0.12	0.18	1.67
Latin America	0.01	0.09	0.19	0.19	1.22
Eastern Europe & former USSR	0.04	0.10	0.10	0.10	1.06
Asia (excluding Japan)	0.05	0.01	−0.01	0.01	0.92
Africa	−0.01	0.00	0.00	0.04	0.67
Average Group B	0.04	0.02	0.00	0.03	0.95

Table 1–9b. **Level of Per Capita GDP, Groups A and B, 1000–1998**
(1990 international dollars)

	1000	1500	1600	1700	1820	1998
Average Group A	405	704	805	907	1 130	21 470
Average Group B	440	535	548	551	573	3 102

Table 1–9c. **Population of Groups A and B, 1000–1998**
(million)

	1000	1500	1600	1700	1820	1998
Total Group A	35	76	95	110	175	838
Total Group B	233	362	461	493	866	5 069

Table 1–9d. **GDP of Groups A and B, 1000–1998**
(billion 1990 international dollars)

	1000	1500	1600	1700	1820	1998
Total Group A	14.1	53.2	76.1	100.0	198.0	17 998
Total Group B	102.7	194.0	252.9	271.8	496.5	15 727

Source for Tables 1–9a to 1–9d: Appendix B.

http://dx.doi.org/10.1787/301542223888

Gerschenkron (1965) and Rostow (1960 and 1963) both emphasised the idea that "take–offs" were staggered throughout the nineteenth century in West European countries. Kuznets (1979, p. 131) endorsed this view. In fact growth acceleration was more synchronous in Western Europe than they believed.

There are two schools of thought about the relative performance of Europe and Asia. The mainstream view was clearly expressed by Adam Smith in 1776. He was not a practitioner of political arithmetic but on the basis of the "price of labour" and other evidence, his ordinal ranking from the top downwards was as follows for the 1770s:

Netherlands

England

France

British North American colonies

Scotland

Spain

Spanish colonies in America

China

Bengal (depressed by the East India Company's plundering)

This mainstream view is reflected in Landes (1969, p. 13–14) whose overall assessment, like that of Smith, was similar to mine. "Western Europe was already rich before the Industrial Revolution — rich by comparison with other parts of the world of that day. This wealth was the product of centuries of slow accumulation, based in turn on investment, the appropriation of extra–European resources and labour, and substantial technological progress, not only in the production of material goods, but in the organisation and financing of their exchange and distribution ... it seems clear that over the near–millennium from the year 1000 to the eighteenth century, income per head rose appreciably — perhaps tripled."

In Maddison (1983), I contrasted the Landes view with Bairoch's (1981) assessment of relative income per head. He suggested that China was well ahead of Western Europe in 1800, Japan and the rest of Asia only 5 per cent lower than Europe, Latin America well ahead of North America, and Africa about two thirds of the West European level. This highly improbable scenario was never documented in the case of Asia, Latin America or Africa. His figures for these areas were essentially guesstimates. Bairoch consistently took the position that the third world had been impoverished by the rich countries (see Bairoch, 1967), and he was, in fact, fabricating ammunition for this hypothesis (see the critique of Chesnais, 1987).

In spite of its shaky foundations, Bairoch's assessment has been influential. Braudel (1985, vol. 3 pp. 533–4) acknowledged "the great service Paul Bairoch has rendered to historians" and believed "it is virtually beyond question that Europe was less rich than the worlds it was exploiting, even after the fall of Napoleon". Andre Gunder Frank (1998, pp. 171 and 284) cites Bairoch and suggests that "around 1800 Europe and the United States, after long lagging behind, suddenly caught up and then overtook Asia economically and politically". Pomeranz (2000) cites Bairoch more cautiously (p. 16) but his sinophilia drives him to the same conclusion. He suggests (p. 111), there is "little reason to think that West Europeans were more productive than their contemporaries in various other densely populated regions of the Old World prior to 1750 or even 1800."

Maddison (1983) contrasted the assessments of Landes and Bairoch and commented: "These remarkably different quantitative conclusions have very different analytical implications. If Bairoch is right, then much of the backwardness of the third world presumably has to be explained by colonial exploitation, and much less of Europe's advantage can be due to scientific precocity, centuries of slow accumulation, and organisational and financial prosperity."

In view of the laborious efforts I have since made to accumulate quantitative evidence on this topic, I now conclude that Bairoch and his epigoni are quite wrong. To reject them is not to deny the role of colonial exploitation, but this can be better understood by taking a more realistic view of Western strength and Asian weakness around 1800.

The major problem in growth analysis is to explain why such a large divergence developed between the advanced capitalist group and the rest of the world. There are, of course, some examples of past convergence, e.g. Europe's rise from its nadir to overtake China , the Japanese catch–up with China in Tokugawa times, and subsequently with the advanced capitalist group. Western Europe achieved a very substantial degree of catch–up on the United States in the golden age after the second world war; resurgent Asia (China, India, the so–called tigers and others) have narrowed their degree of backwardness substantially over the past quarter century.

In attempting to understand the causes of divergence and the possibilities for catch–up in different parts of the world economy, there is no universal schema which covers the whole millennium. The operative forces have varied between place and period. Chapter 2 attempts to illuminate the changes in the character of economic leadership and backwardness which have occurred over the past millennium.

Chapter 2

The Impact of Western Development on the Rest of the World, 1000–1950

A major feature of world development which emerges from our macro–statistical evidence is the exceptionalism of Western Europe's long–run economic performance. By the year 1000, its income levels had fallen below those in Asia and North Africa. In its lengthy resurrection, it caught up with China (the world leader) in the fourteenth century. By 1820, its levels of income and productivity were more than twice as high as in the rest of the world. By 1913 , the income level in Western Europe and its Western Offshoots was more than six times that in the rest of the world.

In order to understand the forces which made for the Western ascension, and the reasons for its greater dynamism than the rest of the world, it is useful to scrutinise the interaction of the West with the Rest over the long run. It is not feasible to embark on a comprehensive survey of all parts of the world economy. This chapter therefore presents four case histories. A great advantage of this detailed scrutiny is that it demonstrates how misleading it is to treat Western experience as homogeneous or monolithic.

The first deals with the Venetian Republic — the richest and most successful West European economy from the eleventh to the sixteenth century.

Portugal is the second case. It was never as rich as Venice, but developed ship design and navigational techniques which made it possible to open up new routes and commercial contact with Africa and Asia. Portugal pioneered European expansion into the Atlantic, discovered Brazil in 1500 and began three centuries of colonial development in the Americas.

The Netherlands is the third case. It was the European leader in terms of per capita income between 1600 and 1820, with a high degree of international openness and specialisation, and a very large trading empire in Asia.

The United Kingdom is our fourth case. It followed the Dutch model of international specialisation and commercial development, built a much bigger colonial empire, and was a pioneer in industrial and transport technology.

Concentration on Western exceptionalism may be considered Eurocentric, but Western countries were the most successful and their experience is the best basis for understanding the roots of economic growth. Analysis of their interaction with the rest of the world throws light on the origins of economic backwardness, and the extent to which Western advance may have contributed to this.

The process of Western ascension involved violence against other parts of the world. European colonisation of the Americas involved the extermination, marginalisation or conquest of its indigenous populations. European contact with Africa was for three centuries concentrated on the slave trade. There were European wars with Asian countries from the mid–eighteenth to the mid–twentieth century designed to establish or maintain colonies and trading privileges. However, Western economic advance also involved devastating wars and beggar–your–neighbour policies. Venetian advance provoked conflicts with Genoa,

Portugal clashed with the Dutch. The Netherlands was involved in an 80 year struggle for independence from Spain, four wars with Britain and more with France. The United Kingdom was involved in over 60 years of war with other West European countries from 1688 to 1815, and another ten years from 1914 to 1945.

Before starting on the detailed case studies, it is useful to present a brief overview of West European performance from the first to the tenth centuries, and from 1000 to 1500.

I
EUROPE'S DECLINE FROM THE FIRST TO TENTH CENTURIES

In the first and second centuries, the Roman Empire was at its peak, a political entity that stretched from the Scottish border to Egypt, with a population of 20 million in Europe, another 20 million in Western Asia and 8 million in North Africa[1]. Within this area there was a common legal framework, and the security of the *pax romana*. There were about 40 000 miles of paved road[2]; 5 per cent of the population was urban with an active secular culture[3]. The major cities were supplied with aqueducts, public baths and fountains, amphitheatres, libraries, temples and other public monuments. The Mediterranean was a Roman lake with tribute shipments of grain from Alexandria and Carthage to the Roman ports of Puteoli (near Naples) and Portus Novus (near Rome). Silk and spices from Asia came overland via Antioch, and up the Red Sea to Egypt. By the first century, Roman citizens (Greeks, Syrians and Jews) had discovered how to use the monsoon winds to trade directly with Western India[4].

Roman imperialism was based on plunder, enslavement and ability to exercise control through military force. The strains in running such a large system were already obvious when Diocletian created separate Western and Eastern Empires in 285. Eventually the Western Empire's capacity to levy taxes and tribute eroded. It relied increasingly on barbarians to man its armed forces. When they revolted, the system collapsed.

By the fifth century the West Roman Empire had disintegrated. Gaul, Spain, Carthage and most of Italy were taken over by illiterate barbarian invaders and Britain was abandoned. There was a brief reprise in the sixth century when the East Roman Emperor recovered Italy, Spain and North Africa. The final blow came with the Arab takeover of Egypt, North Africa, Spain, Sicily, Syria and Palestine between 640 and 800. The only remnant of Roman civilisation was the rump of the Byzantine Empire.

The main changes between the first and tenth centuries were a) the collapse of a large scale cohesive political unit which was never resurrected, and its replacement by a fragmented, fragile and unstable polity; b) disappearance of urban civilisation and predominance of self–sufficient, relatively isolated and ignorant rural communities where a feudal elite extracted an income in kind from a servile peasantry; c) the virtual disappearance of trading links between Western Europe, North Africa and Asia[5].

The Belgian historian Pirenne (1939) provided a succinct description of the situation in the ninth century: "If we consider that in the Carolingian epoch, the minting of gold had ceased, the lending of money at interest was prohibited, there was no longer a class of professional merchants, that Oriental products (papyrus, spices and silk) were no longer imported, that the circulation of money was reduced to a minimum, that laymen could neither read or write, that taxes were no longer organised, and that the towns were merely fortresses, we can say without hesitation that we are confronted by a civilisation that had retrogressed to the purely agricultural stage; which no longer needed commerce, credit and regular exchange for the maintenance of the social fabric."[6]

II
WESTERN EUROPE RECOVERS AND FORGES AHEAD, 1000–1500

Between the years 1000 and 1500, Western Europe's population grew faster than any other part of the world. Northern countries grew significantly faster than those bordering the Mediterranean. The urban proportion (in terms of towns with more than 10 000 population) rose from zero to 6 per cent, a clear indicator of expansion in manufacturing and commercial activity. Factors making it possible to feed the increased population were an increase in the area of rural settlement, particularly in the Netherlands, Northern Germany and the Baltic coast and the gradual incorporation of technological changes which raised land productivity. The classic analysis of these rural changes is by Lynn White (1962): "...the heavy plough, open fields, the new integration of agriculture and herding, three field rotation, modern horse harness, nailed horseshoes and whipple tree had combined into a total system of agrarian exploitation by the year 1100 to provide a zone of peasant prosperity stretching across Northern Europe from the Atlantic to the Dnieper." White probably exaggerated the precocity of their impact and the degree of prosperity, but these technical improvements were clearly of fundamental importance. The switch from a two–field to a three–field system also increased food security and reduced the incidence of famine. A growing proportion of agricultural output went as inputs into clothing production (wool), wine and beer (cereals and vines) and fodder crops for an increased horse population. There was a degree of regional specialisation in food production with growing international trade in cereals, live cattle, cheese, fish and wine. Increased trade in salt and the reintroduction of spice imports helped improve the palatability and conservation of meat and fish.

Increased use of water and windmills augmented the power available for industrial processes, particularly in new industries such as sugar production and paper making. There was international specialisation in the woollen industry. English wool was exported to Flanders for production of cloth which was traded throughout Europe. The silk industry was introduced in the twelfth century and had grown impressively in Southern Europe by 1500. There were big improvements in the quality of textiles and the varieties of colour and design available. Genoa introduced regular shipments of alum from Chios to Bruges in the thirteenth century. There were improvements in mining and metallurgy which helped transform and expand European weapons production (see Nef, 1987 and Cipolla, 1970). Improvements in shipping and navigation techniques from the eleventh to the fifteenth century underpinned the increase in trade in the Mediterranean, the Baltic, the Atlantic islands and the Northwest coast of Africa.

There were big advances in banking, accountancy, marine insurance, improvements in the quality of intellectual life with the development and spread of universities, the growth of humanist scholarship and, at the end of the fifteenth century, the introduction of printing.

There were important changes in the political order. Scandinavian raiders who had made attacks on England, the low countries, Normandy and deep into Russia had become traders and established effective systems of governance in Scandinavia itself, in England, Normandy and Sicily. The beginnings of a nation state system had emerged, with a reduction in the fragmentation of political power that had characterised the Middle Ages. The hundred years war (1337–1453) was not the last of the conflicts between England and France, but the national identity of the two countries was much more clearly defined after it was over. At the end of the fifteenth century, the *reconquista* had established Spanish identity in its modern form. In the Eastern Mediterranean, the situation was the reverse. The Ottoman Empire had taken Constantinople in 1453, and quickly extended its hegemony to the Balkans, Syria, Palestine, Egypt and North Africa.

Estimates of what happened to GDP in Europe and the rest of the world over this period are obviously subject to a wide margin of error. Chapter 1 and Appendix B explain the basis for my estimates as transparently as possible. I concluded that there was almost a doubling of West European per capita income from 1000 to 1500 compared with an improvement of about a third in China, less elsewhere in Asia, and some regression in Africa. It seems clear that West European levels of income and productivity were higher than in Asia and Africa at the end of the period whereas they had been lower in the year 1000. As far as West Asia and Egypt are concerned, this view seems to be shared by specialists in Muslim history, e.g. Abulafiah (1987) and Abu–Lughod (1989); for China/West European performance the evidence for this conclusion is examined in detail in Maddison (1998a).

Within Europe, the areas which made the most economic progress in this period were i) Flanders, which was the centre for wool production, international banking and commerce in Northern Europe; and ii) Italian city states — Florence, Genoa, Pisa, Milan and Venice. Of these the most successful and the richest was Venice. The dynamic forces of Venetian capitalist development are therefore scrutinised in some detail in the following section.

III
THE VENETIAN REPUBLIC

Venice played a major role in reopening the Mediterranean economy to West European commerce and developing links with Northern Europe. It created an institutional basis for commercial capitalism, made major progress in shipping technology, and helped transfer Asian and Egyptian technology in cane sugar production and processing, silk textiles, glassblowing and jewellery to the West.

Venice was the most successful of the North Italian city states in creating and maintaining a republic dominated by a merchant capitalist elite. Thanks to its geographic position and willingness to defend itself, it was able to guarantee its autonomy and freedom from exactions by feudal landlords and monarchs.

It created political and legal institutions which guaranteed property rights and the enforceability of contracts. It was a pioneer in developing foreign exchange and credit markets, banking and accountancy[7]. It created what was effectively a government bond market, starting with compulsory loans on which interest was paid regularly. Its fiscal system was efficient and favourable to merchant profits and the accumulation of capital. The revenues came from excise levies and property taxes based on cadastral surveys.

It was a tolerant and fairly secular state where foreign merchants (Armenians, Greeks and Jews) could operate as freely as locals. Although it was theoretically part of the catholic world, it enjoyed privileged relations with the Byzantine empire. It buttressed its ecclesiastical independence by acquiring the relics of St. Mark from Alexandria in 828. It was effectively independent of both Pope and Patriarch.

Venetian diplomacy was highly professional, pragmatic, opportunistic and dedicated to the pursuit of its commercial interests. It adjusted amazingly well to political changes. In the ninth and tenth centuries its main commerce was to provision Constantinople with grain and wine from Italy, wood and slaves from Dalmatia and salt from its lagoons, taking silk and spices in return. Towards the end of the eleventh century, Byzantium was under pressure from the Seljuk Turks who seized Anatolia, and Frankish incursions into its Southern Italian territories. Venice secured commercial privileges (exemption from excise taxes) from Byzantium in 1082 in return for help in bolstering its naval defences. In 1204, by contrast, it played a major role in persuading the leaders of the fourth crusade to target Constantinople instead of Islam. As a result Venice acquired bases in Dalmatia and an empire in the Aegean. It took the southern half of the Peloponnese, Corfu and Crete. It occupied nearly half of Constantinople and gained access to trade in the Black Sea and Sea of Azov. In 1261, the Byzantine Emperor recaptured Constantinople and gave trade preferences and a territorial base to Venice's rival, Genoa. However, Venice retained its Greek colonies and Venetian shipping was soon able to re–enter the Black Sea where trade was booming due to the Mongol reopening of the silk route through Central Asia.

West European crusaders successfully attacked the Syrian and Palestinian coast and established small christian states in Antioch, Acre and Jerusalem between 1099 and 1291. They gave commercial privileges to Pisan and Genoan traders who had helped finance their conquest. The Venetians had not helped, but nevertheless managed to establish a trading base in Tyre.

The Turkish Mameluke regime recaptured Syria and Palestine in 1291 and ruled Egypt until 1517. Here too, Venice managed to establish a privileged trading relationship, buying a large part of the Asian spices which the Karimi merchants of Alexandria brought to Egypt from Asia via the Red Sea. In return the Venetians sold metals, armour, woollens and slaves. The slaves came from the Balkans and Russia: males were destined for service in the Mameluke army, females for their harems.

When the Ottoman Turks captured Constantinople in 1453, Venice quickly negotiated the maintenance of its trading rights, but in 1479, the Ottomans closed their access to the Black Sea. In 1517, they took over Egypt and terminated most of the Venetian trade in spices.

Venice had important connections with Northern Europe. Trade with Flanders was carried out mainly at the Champagne fairs where Italian merchants bought woollen goods and sold silk, spices, alum, sugar and lacquer[8]. When the sea route was opened between the Western Mediterranean and the Atlantic, trade with Flanders was carried out directly by ship.

A second route linked Venice with Augsburg, Nuremberg, Prague and Vienna via the Brenner Pass. German merchants brought metals and metal products (including silver). Venetians traded these metals up the Po Valley and in the Mediterranean. In 1318 the Fondaco dei Tedeschi was created in Venice to provide for the trading needs and lodging of German merchants.

In building up its trade, Venice created a political empire. In 1171, the city had about 66 000 inhabitants, and was one of the three biggest in Western Europe until the sixteenth century when its population peaked around 170 000. Venice experienced three demographic catastrophes. In 1347–48, nearly 40 per cent of the population died when a galley brought the plague from the Black Sea port of Caffa. Two other attacks occurred in 1575–77 and 1630; each killing about a third of the population of the city[9].

The Empire overseas (*dominio da mar*) included about half a million people. Between 1388 and 1499, Venice acquired territory on the Italian mainland (*terraferma*) which included Udine, Friuli, Vicenza, Padua, Verona, Bergamo, Rovigo and Cremona. In 1557 the population of these territories was about 1.5 million (see Table 2–1).

The Venetian state played a leading role in commercial activity, being the major shipbuilder, leasing state–owned galleys to private enterprise, arranging the organisation and timing of convoys. It developed types of ship suitable for Venetian commerce and the conditions of trade in the Mediterranean. This state activity reduced costs for private traders by making commerce more secure from enemy attack. It also permitted smaller traders, with limited capital, to participate in international trade.

Table 2–1. **Population of the Venetian Empire in 1557**
(000)

City of Venice	158	Ionia	52
Islands of the Lagoon	50	Crete	194
Istria	52	Terraferma	1 542
Dalmatia	93	Total	2 141

Source: Beloch (1961), pp. 164 and 352. The population of Cyprus (under Venetian control 1489–1573) in the mid–1550s was probably about 160 000, see McEvedy and Jones (1978), p. 119.

---

http://dx.doi.org/10.1787/723137538677

Table 2–2. **Size and Carrying Capacity of Venetian Merchant Galleys, 1318–1559**

	Length	*Breadth (metres)*	*Depth*	*Cargo capacity (metric tons)*
1318 for voyages to Cyprus	40.4	5.3	2.4	110
1320 for voyages to Flanders	40.4	5.7	2.4	115
1420 for voyages to Flanders	41.2	6.0	2.7	170
1549–59 merchant galleys	47.8	8.0	3.1	280

Source: Lane (1966), p. 369.

Table 2–3. **Population of 31 Biggest West European Cities, 1500–1800**
(000)

	1500	*1600*	*1700*	*1800*
Italy				
Naples	150	281	216	427
Venice	100	139	138	138
Milan	100	120	124	135
Florence	70	70	72	81
Genoa	60	71	80	91
Rome	55	105	138	163
Bologna	55	63	63	71
Palermo	55	105	100	139
France				
Paris	100	220	510	581
Lyon	50	40	97	100
Rouen	40	60	64	81
Bordeaux	20	40	50	88
Low Countries				
Antwerp	40	47	70	60
Ghent	40	31	51	51
Brussels	35	50	80	74
Bruges	30	27	38	32
Amsterdam	14	65	200	217
Germany and Austria				
Nuremburg	36	40	40	27
Cologne	30	40	42	42
Lubeck	24	23	n.a.	23
Danzig	20	50	50	40
Augsburg	20	48	21	28
Vienna	20	50	114	231
Iberia				
Granada	70	69	n.a.	55
Valencia	40	65	50	80
Lisbon	30	100	165	180
Barcelona	29	43	43	115
Cordoba	27	45	28	40
Seville	25	90	96	96
Madrid	0	49	110	167
Britain				
London	40	200	575	865

Source: de Vries (1984), pp. 270–77.

http://dx.doi.org/10.1787/723137538677

The biggest enterprise in Venice was the Arsenal, a public shipyard created in 1104. It was operative for centuries, and employed thousands of workers.

There were major changes in ship construction and navigation techniques between the tenth and fourteenth centuries. Roman ships had been constructed hull first, held together by careful watertight cabinetwork of mortice and tenon; the second stage was the insertion of ribs and braces. In the eleventh century there was a switch which made a major reduction in costs. The keel and ribs were made first and a hull of nailed planks was added, using fibre and pitch to make the ships watertight. A later development was the stern–post rudder which replaced trailing oars as a more effective means for steering ships. The power of the rudders was strengthened by use of cranks and pulleys[10]. There were improvements in sails, notably the introduction of a triangular lateen rig set at an angle to the mast instead of a rectangular sail square to the mast. There was a long run increase in the size of ships (see Table 2–2).

Soon after 1270, the compass came into use in the Mediterranean. This, together with improved charts, made it possible to sail all year round. Previously ships trading with Egypt had not ventured out between October and April. With the compass the same ship could make two return trips a year from Venice to Alexandria instead of one.

There were two main kinds of Venetian ship. General purpose cargo ships ("cogs") were built in private shipyards. Their length was about three times their breadth, and they relied entirely on sails. Galleys for passengers, high value cargo and naval duties were built in the Arsenal. These were longer, had a wide beam and a crew of 200 most of whom were oarsmen. Galleys were speedier, more manoeuvrable for entering and leaving harbour, and for occasions when there was no wind. The general Venetian practice was to have 25 benches on each side of the galley, each bench having three oarsmen. The benches were set at an angle and the oars were of different lengths so that the rowers would not interfere with each other. On such a ship there would be 150 oarsmen and about 30 crossbowmen for defence and attack, who would also take turns at rowing. Galleys were owned by the state and rented out for each venture to the highest bidder in public auctions. Galleys also acted as public carriers, as those who leased the ships had to accept goods from other merchants if they had spare capacity.

In 1291, the Genoese defeated a Moroccan fleet controlling the straits of Gibraltar, and opened the way for European commerce from the Mediterranean to the Atlantic[11]. Thereafter Venetian galleys used this route to trade with London and Bruges.

Although international trade, banking, shipbuilding and associated trades in timber, carpentry, rope and sailmaking etc. were the biggest sectors of the Venetian economy, there were also sizeable manufacturing activities producing goods for local use and export. One of the earliest was the glass industry which had already started in the tenth century. Venice was a pioneer in glassblowing technology in Europe and made glasses, goblets, pitchers, dishes, bottles, vases, mirrors, jewellery, candelabra and decorative products of very high quality. From the thirteenth century Venetians produced delicate, carefully blown sand–glasses as a time–keeping device for mariners. From the fourteenth century onwards they started making spectacles — an Italian invention which greatly increased the productivity of artisans and scholars[12]. Angelo Barovier, the most famous glassblower of the fifteenth century, perfected the process for making crystal. By that time, polychrome, engraved, filigree, enamelled and gold–leafed glassware was available in a profuse variety of designs. In 1291 all glassblowing was shifted to the island of Murano by decree of the Maggior Consilio. This enabled Venice to keep tighter control of its trade and technological secrets.

Equally precocious were the skills and products of Venetian goldsmiths, mosaicists, woodcarvers and decorative artists who were in heavy demand in turning the inside of churches, civic monuments and private palaces into works of art. Venetian style was influenced by the work of previous generations of mosaicists and iconographers in Ravenna and the thirteenth century inflow of objects looted from Constantinople.

The trade with Asia in raw silk and silk products eventually led to import substitution in Europe. Silk production had already spread from China to India and Syria, and came to Italy in the twelfth century — initially to Lucca, then to Venice, Florence, Genoa, Milan and Bologna, and later to Lyon in France. Within the Arab world, silk production came to Spain from Syria. Venetian silk production is documented as early as the thirteenth century. The Venetian government regulated production to guarantee quality, keep out competitors and reduce the risk of industrial espionage. The silk, satin and velvet products of Venice were of the highest quality, and designs were a distinctive mix of indigenous creativity and oriental influence. Multicoloured velvet brocades, often executed with gold and silver thread, were produced as items of ceremonial clothing for Venice's governing elite, for furniture, wall hangings, table coverings, decorative items for gondolas etc. These products made a substantial contribution to Venetian exports.

Another important field was book production. In the ninth and tenth centuries, scribes and illuminators were mainly active on sacred books in the scriptoria of monasteries. Later there were civic records, histories, translations of Aristotle and other Greek texts destined for the libraries of San Marco, ducal, civic and private collectors. This gave employment to professional scribes, bookbinders, specialists in ornamented calligraphy and illustration. Less than 15 years after Gutenberg's invention of printing, a German immigrant brought the technique to Venice in 1469. It led to an enormous improvement in the productivity of the industry, with print runs up to 4 500 copies. A very much larger proportion of output was destined for export than had been the case for manuscript books. Venice quickly became the principal Italian typographical centre, and one of the biggest in Europe. By the middle of the sixteenth century, some 20 000 editions had been published. Venetian publishing helped invigorate the cultural and intellectual life of Europe by providing music scores, maps, books on medical matters and translations of the Greek classics. The Aldine Press (set up in 1494) edited and published original Greek texts, and Venice became the major publisher of books for the Greek–speaking world[13].

Sugar was another major product. Venice created plantation agriculture and processing facilities with slave labour in Crete and Cyprus, using techniques borrowed from Syria. Venetian practice was copied later by the Portuguese in Madeira and in Brazil.

The Venetian role in the spice trade was greatly reduced at the beginning of the sixteenth century because of restrictions on trade with Syria and Egypt imposed by the new Ottoman authorities, and competition from direct Portuguese shipments from Asia. Lane (1966, p. 13) suggests that Venetian spice imports fell from around 1 600 tons a year towards the end of the fifteenth century to less than 500 tons by the first decade of the sixteenth century. Lane thought that the absolute size of the pepper component of these shipments had recovered by the 1560s, but Venice's leading role in this trade had obviously evaporated.

Venetian shipping also faced increased competition on Western routes to England and Flanders, and its sugar industry in Crete and Cyprus declined because of competition from Portuguese production in Madeira and later in Brazil.

There were also changes in shipbuilding technology in the Atlantic economies which quickly rendered the oared Venetian galley obsolete. The two main changes were in the rigging of round ships and the development of firearms during the fifteenth century. Lane (1966, pp. 15–16) described these changes as follows: "The transformation of the one–masted cog into a full–rigged, three–masted ship possessed of spritsail, topsail and mizzen lateen occurred about the middle of the century — the sailing ships of 1485 differed less in appearance from the sailing ships of 1785 than they did from those of 1425 — equally important in robbing the merchant galley of the special security which had alone justified its existence was the increase in the use of guns in naval warfare."

As a result there was a sharp decline in the main product of the Arsenal and a rise in the share of cogs in the Venetian merchant fleet. There was increased purchase by Venetian merchants of ships from abroad, as problems of adapting to technological change were compounded by much poorer Venetian access to cheap timber than shipbuilders in the Atlantic economies.

From 1500 onwards, a significant proportion of Venetian capital was reoriented to agrarian reclamation and development and creation of Palladian villas and country estates in the *terraferma*.

Over the sixteenth, seventeenth and eighteenth centuries, Venice did not expand much in population or per capita income, but it remained one of the richest parts of Italy and Europe until overtaken by the Dutch in the seventeenth century.

IV
PORTUGAL

Portugal emerged from Arab rule between 1147 when Lisbon was captured and 1249 when full sovereignty was established in an area corresponding roughly to its present boundaries. Its political regime was very different from that of Venice. Its *reconquista* was due mainly to militant crusading orders of knighthood. The military aristocracy and the church became the major landowners. In Portugal, as in Spain, the interests of church and state were closely linked. The crown was able to nominate bishops and collect ecclesiastical taxes, under a patronage system known as the "padroado real". Although there were some clashes between Portugal and Spain, and for a time (1580–1640) Portugal had a Spanish king, there was a remarkably effective long–term territorial division of interests between the two countries. Under various treaties sanctioned by the Papacy, Portugal was able to develop its commercial and imperial interests in Africa, in the whole of Asia except the Philippines, and in Brazil without significant Spanish interference.

Portugal had three major advantages in developing its overseas commerce and empire. There was a clear strategic benefit in being located on the South Atlantic coast of Europe near to the exit of the Mediterranean. Deep–sea fishermen provided an important part of the Portuguese food supply and developed an unrivalled knowledge of Atlantic winds, weather and tides. The value of these skills was greatly enhanced by crown sponsorship of Atlantic exploration, research on navigation technology, training of pilots, and documentation of maritime experience in the form of route maps with compass bearings (rutters) and cartography. Portuguese shipbuilding in Lisbon and Oporto adapted the design of its ships (caravels) and rigging in the light of increasing knowledge of Atlantic sailing conditions. The biggest changes were in rigging. At first they concentrated on lateen sails, then added a mix of square sails and lateen for deeper penetration into the South Atlantic, with further changes for the much longer route round the Cape. Knowledge of these techniques was protected by forbidding sales of ships to other countries. A third commercial advantage was Portugal's ability to absorb "new Christians" — Jewish merchants and scholars had played a significant role during Muslim rule. They were driven out of Spain, but many took refuge and increased the size of the community in Portugal. They were required to undergo proforma conversion and were subject to a degree of persecution, but they provided important skills in developing Portuguese business interests in Africa, Brazil and Asia, in scientific development, as intermediaries in trade with the Muslim world and in attracting Genoese and Catalan capital to Portuguese business ventures.

A fourth important influence on the pattern of Portuguese business interests was the heritage of slavery. In most parts of Western Europe, slavery had more or less disappeared in the middle ages, though it was a peripheral part of Venetian trade with Byzantium and the Muslim world. Portugal had lived in closer contact with the Muslim world than any other part of Western Europe. Portuguese themselves had had experience of being slaves and about ten per cent of the population in Lisbon were berber or black slaves. They were also used as a labour force in the sugar plantations and sugar mills which Portugal developed in Madeira and São Tomé.

Significant Portuguese activity in slave trading in Africa began around 1445 shortly after Portuguese navigators discovered and settled the Cape Verde islands (opposite Senegal). They were able to buy slaves from African merchants in this region in return for cloth, horses, trinkets and salt. Between 1450 and 1600

Table 2–4. **Sugar Production by Area of Origin, 1456–1894**
(metric tons)

	Cyprus	Madeira	São Tomé	Brazil	British Caribbean	French Caribbean	Other Caribbean	Rest of World
1456	800	80						
1500	375	2 500						
1580		500	2 200ᵃ	2 300				
1700				20 000	22 000	10 000	5 000	
1760				28 000	71 000	81 000	20 000	
1787				19 000	106 000	125 000	36 000	
1815				75 000	168 000	36 600	66 200	18 500
1894				275 000	260 200	79 400	1 119 000	6 523 600

a) 1550s.

Source: 1486–1787 from Blackburn (1997), pp. 109, 172, 403 and Schwartz (1985), p. 13; 1815–94 from Williams (1970), pp. 366, 377–80. The figure for rest of world includes 10 000 tons of beet sugar in 1815 and 4 725 000 tons in 1894. Sugar beet production started in Europe during the Napoleonic wars.

Table 2–5. **Atlantic Slave Shipments by Portugal and Its Competitors, 1701–1800**
(000)

England	2 532	North America	194
Portugal	1 796	Denmark	74
France	1 180	Other	5
Netherlands	351	Total	6 132

Source: Lovejoy (1982), p. 483.

http://dx.doi.org/10.1787/723137538677

about 175 000 slaves were shipped to Portugal and its Atlantic islands. Later, as the trade developed, Portugal became more directly involved in capturing slaves further south in Angola. The crown organised the Casa de Escravos in Lisbon in the 1480s. The trade was highly profitable and expanded enormously at the end of the sixteenth and in the seventeenth century when Portugal shipped slaves to Brazil and handled most of the slave shipments to Spanish America (under slave trading permits (*asiento*) sold by the Spanish government). The slave trade received Papal legitimacy in 1455 with the bull *Romanus Pontifex*, which construed it as a form of missionary activity. Between 1500 and 1870, 9.4 million slaves were shipped to the Americas. About 4.5 million of these were supplied by Portugal.

The Portuguese crown took the initiative in exploring and developing the Atlantic islands and their sugar industry, and in creating a maritime bypass of the old caravan route which carried gold from Timbuktu in Mali to the Moroccan coast. This route had supplied two thirds of the gold entering Europe.

The leading role in these two developments was played by Prince Henrique (third son of the Portuguese king, John I, and nephew of the English king, Henry IV). For four decades (1420–1460) he applied his considerable financial resources to these ventures and prepared the ground for the later Portuguese breakthrough into Asian trade by developing navigational expertise[14].

In 1420, the crown took over the administration of the wealthy military orders. Henrique became administrator of the Order of Christ (successor to the Templars in Portugal), and his brother acquired a similar position in the Order of Santiago. Henrique used the assets of his Order to finance ventures in the Atlantic and Africa, and persuaded successive rulers (his brothers) to invest him personally with significant property rights in both areas.

Madeira (about 560 km into the Atlantic from the Moroccan coast) was discovered in 1420. It was uninhabited and extremely fertile. A sugar industry was developed with use of slave labour on similar lines to Venetian practice in Cyprus and Crete. The two sectors of the industry were cane plantations and sugar mills, with the bigger enterprises covering both activities. The industry was developed by leases to Genoese and "new Christian" entrepreneurs. Capital requirements were fairly substantial and the newest techniques were adopted in the mills. Instead of the large circular stone that was rolled over cut cane in the Venetian controlled mills, a new type of press with two cylindrical rollers was able to get more juice from the cane which no longer needed to be cut. The presses were operated with animal or water power rather than manually[15]. Production expanded faster after Henrique's death, when the industry was less tightly controlled. By 1500 Madeiran production was more than six times as big as that of Cyprus where output had plummeted. Portuguese sugar replaced it on the markets of Antwerp and Bristol. In addition to sugar, Madeira was a major source of timber. Wheat and wine production was also significant. The wine was of the malmsey type which the Venetians had brought to Crete from Syria.

The uninhabited Azores were discovered in mid–Atlantic (about 1 300–1 500 km from Portugal) in 1427 and settlement started in 1439. They were not very suitable for sugar production, but were a useful staging post for subsequent Atlantic trade, and augmented Portuguese knowledge of navigation in the Atlantic.

In developing navigation on the African coast, Portugal established settlements in two other significant island outposts. The Cape Verde islands were settled in 1460 and acted as a staging post for the slave trade. In this area, the Portuguese found malaguette (a coarse pepper substitute) and later a better quality pepper in Benin. Further east, São Tomé and Principe (in the Bight of Guinea) were settled after 1480. Sugar production was introduced and by the 1550s had supplemented Madeira as the major centre of Atlantic production.

In 1482, Elmina fort was built on the coast of what is now Ghana. This was centre of the gold trade. Gold became the biggest source of income for the Portuguese crown. At Elmina the main source was Ashanti gold, at trading points on the Guinea coast it was gold diverted to Portuguese traders from the caravan route from Timbuktu to Morocco. Total gold exports of West Africa between 1471 and 1500 amounted to 17 tons. This helped the Portuguese crown to finance its most expensive venture — the opening of a Cape route to Asian trade[16].

Circumnavigation of Africa in order to get direct access to the spices of Asia was not a new idea. The Vivaldi brothers had set out from Genoa in 1291 and disappeared in the attempt. By the end of the fifteenth century, it was clear that such a venture would be very expensive and highly risky, but political developments in the Eastern Mediterranean suggested that the old Venetian route through Egyptian and Syrian middlemen was under threat, and that the potential profits from a new route would be very rewarding.

The Portuguese had an unrivalled knowledge of sailing conditions in the Atlantic and halfway down the African coast. There had been developments in ship design, rigging and seamanship which made it possible to contemplate long–distance trips in stormier seas than the Venetians encountered in the Mediterranean.

The preparations for this venture were carefully planned and spread over a couple of decades. They involved research on techniques of navigation, astronomy and cartography and collection of information on trading conditions in Asia and East Africa. The second component was a series of trial voyages to explore possible routes and wind patterns down the whole length of the African coast. The third component was a voyage to India to explore trading conditions and possibilities for establishing the sort of bases already established on the African coast.

In the Mediterranean, navigators from the thirteenth century had relied on the compass to determine direction, a sandglass to measure time and a traverse board to measure deviations from course. As the main routes had been known since antiquity, they had reasonable charts, a fair idea of the distances they had to travel and rough methods for judging speed.

The Portuguese were now exploring unknown waters, and had to rely much more on celestial navigation. In the Northern hemisphere Portuguese navigators knew that the pole star provided a roughly constant bearing and altitude, maintaining roughly the same height on a particular parallel of latitude. On a north–south passage a navigator could observe the pole star each day at dawn and dusk (when he could see both the star and the horizon). By noting changes in altitude he could get some idea of changes in his position. In sailing east–west, he could keep a steady course by maintaining a constant polar altitude. All this had to be done very crudely using finger spreads or other rough means to estimate changes in altitude. Measurement was greatly refined by the invention of the quadrant, first recorded in 1460 by Gomes, a professional navigator in the employ of Prince Henry. Parry (1974, p. 174) describes the quadrant as follows: "The seaman's quadrant was a very simple device; a quarter of a circle, with a scale marked on the curved edge, and with two pinhole sights along one of the straight edges. A plumb line hung from the apex. The sights were aligned on the star and the reading taken from the point where the plumb line cut the scale. Polar altitude in degrees gave the observer's latitude." This way a navigator could measure his distance from Lisbon, or some other place whose polar altitude he already knew.

In the Southern hemisphere, the pole star was not visible, and there was no other star with the same properties. Instead the altitude of the sun had to be used but one could not study its position with the naked eye. In 1484, John II created a commission of mathematical experts and astronomers to observe and measure solar altitude. The instrument for measuring distance from the equator was the mariner's astrolabe, derived from astrolabes used by medieval astronomers. It was a graduated brass disc, with a bar which was rotated until the point of light shining through the upper sight fell on to the lower one. It was used at midday when the sun was at its zenith. As there were no accurate clocks a series of readings had to be taken around what appeared to be midday, to derive the maximum altitude. As the distance between the equator and the sun changes from day to day and year to year, mariners needed accurate tables of the sun's declination. John II's commission produced a simplified version of the *Almanach* of the Jewish astronomer Zacuto, and successfully tested the possibilities of finding latitude on a trip to the African coast in 1485. Estimates of the sun's declination were incorporated in a navigational manual *Regimento do Astrolabio e do Quadrante* which was available to da Gama when he sailed to India in 1497. Da Gama had direct contact with Zacuto who had come to Lisbon as a refugee from Spain. The *Regimento* also contained a translation of a work by a thirteenth century English mathematician, Holywood (known as Sacrobosco), who was a pioneer of spherical astronomy, pointed out the errors in the Julian calendar and suggested a correction more or less the same as that incorporated in the Gregorian calendar 350 years later. All this Portuguese research and development was done 50 years before Copernicus published his work on celestial orbits in 1543, but the committee would surely have had an immediate understanding of its significance.

There were preparatory voyages to gauge the feasibility of a passage to India by Diogo Cão in 1482–4 and another by Bartolomeu Dias in 1487–8. Cão found the mouth of the Congo river and went past the future sites of Luanda and Benguela in Angola. The voyage of Dias was more rewarding. He had two caravels and a store ship, found a better route to Angola, and at Lüderitz Bay on the coast of Namibia, in the face of adverse winds, discovered it was useful to veer well out west into the Atlantic to catch winds which took him round the Cape. He sailed 1 000 kilometres east of the Cape before turning back. The trip took 18 months. He had sailed nearly 13 000 kilometres from Lisbon. The return passage was somewhat shorter because he found favourable winds from the Cape to the Azores. He had demonstrated that the Atlantic and Indian oceans were connected.

There was also an exploratory trip by land. Pero da Covilhã had been a spy in Spain and Morocco, spoke fluent Arabic and could pass for a Muslim. Armed with letters of credit he went to Cairo via Barcelona, Naples, Rhodes and Alexandria, down the Red Sea coast by caravan, took a ship at Aden for Calicut (in Kerala) which was known to be the major Indian emporium for the spice trade with a hinterland in a rich spice–growing region. He made an extensive reconnaissance of the west coast of India as far north as Goa and the East African coast down to the port of Sofala. He sent a report on his findings in 1490 via a Portuguese emissary in Cairo, and acting on a second set of instructions he visited Hormuz, the centre of the spice trade in the Persian Gulf.

Thus the Portuguese committee was well briefed on trading conditions in India and East Africa and possibilities of navigation in the Atlantic before entrusting Vasco da Gama with a passage to India in 1497–9.

In 1484, John II received a proposition for a westward passage from Christopher Columbus, a Genoese navigator who had spent eight years in Portuguese ships sailing to the Atlantic islands and the Guinea coast. He asked the king "to give him some vessels to go and discover the Ile Cypango by this Western Ocean" (Morison, 1974, p. 31). The committee rejected the proposal because they thought Cypango (Japan) was a fiction of Marco Polo and that Columbus greatly underestimated the distance to Asia. Eventually the Columbus venture was financed by Queen Isabella of Spain. In 1492, he sailed to the Canary Islands, and from there reached the Bahamas in 33 days. He spent more than three months in the Caribbean where he found Cuba and Haiti without realising that the islands were in the middle of a huge unknown continent. Because of stormy weather on his return voyage, he was forced to land in Lisbon in 1493 for refitting, and had to brief John II. The Portuguese did not believe that Columbus had reached Asia, and knew he had not found spices. However, in anticipation of a flurry of Spanish maritime exploration, and to protect Portuguese interests, the Treaty of Tordesillas was negotiated with Spain in 1494. This stipulated that Portugal would not compete in the West Atlantic. On Portuguese insistence, the dividing line was fixed 370 leagues west of the Azores (about 48 degrees west of the Greenwich meridian). Portugal not only got a free hand for its Asian project and African interests, but established a legal claim to Brazil (which was found six years later).

The last step in the preparation for da Gama's voyage was to provide two specially built ships, constructed with advice from Dias. Jones (1978), p. 30, compares them with the caravels used by earlier navigators as follows: "a stouter, roomier craft, standing higher in the water and able successfully to navigate in coastal waters, better able to stand long periods in the ocean, safer in the tempests of the tropics, and with better quarters for the crew. He designed the vessels to have a foremast, and mainmast, square rigged with mainsail and topsail, a square spritsail at the bow and a small lateen–rigged mizzen stepped right aft on the castle. These probably provided a sail area, without bonnets, of about 4 000 sq. feet. Main and fore each had a crow's nest — Length of hull was probably slightly under seventy–five feet, with a beam a third of that." The ships "were about 200 tons register in present day terms", they each had 20 guns firing stone balls weighing a few ounces. In addition, da Gama had a 50 ton caravel and a small supply ship. His crew of about 160 included gunners, musicians and three Arabic interpreters. He carried trade goods of a type used in West Africa (coarse cloth, bells and beads) which were virtually useless in Asia.

Da Gama sailed from Lisbon in July 1497 to Cape Verde. Shortly thereafter (about 150 kilometres off Sierra Leone) instead of heading southeast which was the normal route down the African coast, he veered southwest far into the Atlantic and eventually caught winds which blew him southeast around the Cape. By Christmas he had rounded Africa, and moved up the East coast, visiting Mozambique, Mombasa and Malindi. Economic life there was much more sophisticated than in West Africa. The coastal towns had merchants — Arabs, Indians from Gujarat and Malabar and Persians — who imported silk and cotton textiles, spices and Chinese porcelain and exported cotton, timber and gold. They had professional pilots familiar with monsoon conditions in the Indian ocean. Their ships were sturdy, but the Portuguese noted that they were constructed without nails. Instead the timbers were stitched and bound together with ropes made of coconut fibre (coir) which was widely available in Southern India and Ceylon. The local population were an Afro–Arab mix, speaking Arabic and Swahili, wearing cotton clothing and using coined money. He was able to get a competent Gujarati pilot from the ruler of Malindi (in Kenya), who got him to Calicut (in Kerala) in less than a month.

The Portuguese remained in Calicut for three months, discovered a good deal about prices and conditions in the spice market, but failed to establish amicable relations with the local ruler or to sell their trade goods. The return trip to Malindi took three months. They found it difficult to man the ships as many of the crew had died of scurvy, so they burned the São Gabriel (one of the specially built ships). They had already dismantled the supply ship on the outward journey.

The caravel returned to Lisbon in July 1499, and da Gama got back in August (having stopped to bury his brother in the Azores). In the two year voyage, he had lost half the crew and two of the ships, and had very little in the way of cargo. However, he had proved the feasibility of the route, found a new source of gold in East Africa, had established that there were no maritime fleets in the Indian Ocean which could impede Portuguese access to the spice trade. He also let it be known that there were Christians in Kerala[17].

This news was received enthusiastically in Lisbon, and there was a quick follow–up. In March 1500, Pedro Cabral was given command of 12 ships and more than 1 000 men to improve on the route, bring back a significant cargo and establish a base on the Kerala coast. There was fairly extensive private participation in the cost and benefits of the trip.

Cabral went farther west in the Atlantic than da Gama and had the good luck, after a month at sea, to be the first navigator to encounter Brazil. He stayed a few days at a point he called Porto Seguro (about 350 km south of Bahia), and immediately sent a ship back to Lisbon to announce his finding territory which lay well within the area allotted to Portugal in the Treaty of Tordesillas[18].

On the East African coast he stopped off at Sofala and Kilwa which da Gama had missed, got a pilot in Malindi and was in Calicut within six months of leaving Lisbon. He stayed in Calicut for two months and was given a large house as a trading base (known as a factory). However, he had to leave in a hurry. The Portuguese seized a local vessel on its way to Gujarat and another leaving for Jedda on the Red Sea. In retaliation, local muslim traders attacked the Portuguese factory, killed over 50 Portuguese and took the trade goods. In return Cabral captured ten more local vessels and bombarded the unfortified town (see Subramanyam, 1997, pp. 180–1). He sailed 150 kilometres further down the coast to Cochin, where he was able to load additional cargo and create the basis for a permanent factory. He left some of his people behind for this purpose and took three Cochin representatives back to Portugal. Before leaving for Malindi, he stopped in Cannanur (about 70 kilometres north of Calicut) to pick up a cargo of cinnamon.

Cabral arrived back in Lisbon around the beginning of July 1501 with five vessels. The cargo, mostly pepper, appears to have been around 700 tons[19], but the loss of seven ships (six on the way out, one on the way back) and the violence in Calicut were not encouraging.

Da Gama was sent on a second mission to India with a fleet of 20 ships, leaving Lisbon in February 1502. Fifteen of the ships were for the return journey, and another five (under the command of da Gama's uncle) were destined to stay behind to protect Portuguese bases in India and to blockade shipping leaving India for the Red Sea. By June, da Gama had traversed the Cape and stopped at Sofala to buy gold. At Kilwa, he forced the local ruler to agree to pay an annual tribute of pearls and gold, and left there for India. He waited offshore at Cannanur, for ships returning from the Red Sea. He captured one returning from Mecca with pilgrims and a valuable cargo. Part of the cargo was seized and the ship was burned with most of the passengers and crew (see Subrahmanyan, 1997, pp. 205–9). Then he put into Cannanur, and exchanged presents (he offered silver and got precious stones) with the local ruler, but did no business as he found the price of spices too high. He headed in the direction of Cochin, stopped his ships opposite Calicut and demanded that the ruler expel the whole Muslim merchant community (4 000 households) which used the port as a basis for trading with the Red Sea. The Samudri, the local Hindu ruler, refused, so da Gama bombarded the city as Cabral had done. He got to Cochin at the beginning of November, where he was able to buy spices against silver, copper and the textiles he had taken from the ship he sank. A permanent factory was set up in Cochin, and five ships were left to protect Portuguese interests.

Before leaving for home, da Gama's fleet was attacked by more than 30 ships financed by the Muslim traders of Calicut. They were routed after Portuguese bombardment, and part of the Muslim merchant community in Calicut decided to move their operations elsewhere. These naval engagements showed clearly the superiority of armed Portuguese ships over those of Asian countries.

Da Gama returned to Lisbon in October 1503, with 13 of his ships and nearly 1 700 tons of spices, i.e. about the same as annual Venetian imports from the Middle East at the end of the fifteenth century. However, the Portuguese margins on this trade were much bigger than the Venetian. Most of these spices were marketed in Europe via Antwerp, which was the chief port of the Spanish Netherlands.

The voyages of Dias, Cabral and da Gama had laid the foundations of the Portuguese trading empire in East Africa and Asia. Portugal held a monopoly of the traffic round the Cape until the last decade of the sixteenth century.

The Mameluke regime in Egypt sent a fleet in 1509 to try to stop interference with shipping to the Red Sea but they were defeated by the Portuguese at Diu off the coast of Gujarat. However, Portugal did not succeed in establishing a base in the Red Sea, Aden was taken by Turkey in 1538, and the old Asian trade to Egypt was reopened from about the middle of the sixteenth century. Portugal did acquire a fortified position at Hormuz which dominated the entry to the Persian Gulf for about a century. There was no blockade of trade with the newly established regime in Safavid Persia, but traders entering the Gulf and those using other Portuguese bases had to pay for safe–conduct passes (cartazes). In addition Portugal levied customs duties on goods travelling through its Asian bases.

Wake (1979), p. 377, provided a rough estimate of annual Portuguese spice imports. In the first half of the sixteenth century they averaged 1 475 metric tons a year, 1 160 in the second half. In 1600, total West European consumption was probably about twice the 1500 level, and per capita consumption had risen by half[20].

Table 2–6. **Number of Ships Sailing to Asia from Seven European Countries, 1500–1800**

	1500–99	*1600–1700*	*1701–1800*
Portugal	705	371	196
Netherlands	65[a]	1 770	2 950
England		811	1 865
France		155	1 300
Other		54	350
Total	770	3 161	6 661

a) 1590s.

Source: Portugal 1500–1800 from Magalhães Godinho in Bruijn and Gaastra (1993), pp. 7 and 17; otherwise from Bruijn and Gaastra (1993), pp. 178 and 183. "Other" refers to ships of the Danish, Swedish trading companies, and the Ostend Company.

http://dx.doi.org/10.1787/723137538677

Table 2–7. **Movement of Portuguese Ships to and from Asia, 1500–1800**

	Departures from Lisbon to Indian Ocean	Arrivals in the Orient	Departures from India and Malacca	Arrivals in Lisbon
	(totals for period)			
1500–49	451	403	262	243
1550–99	254	217	212	170
1600–35	207	152	95	74
1636–1700	164	n.a.	n.a.	n.a.
1701–1800	196	n.a.	n.a.	n.a.
	(annual average)			
1500–49	9.0	8.1	5.2	4.9
1550–99	5.1	4.3	4.2	3.4
1600–35	5.8	4.2	2.6	2.1
1636–1700	2.5			
1701–1800	1.9			

Source: Magalhaes in Bruijn and Gaastra (1993), pp. 7 and 17. The difference between departures from Lisbon and returns is due to losses, and in some cases returns to home port, but also to ships which remained in Asia to defend the bases or to participate in intra Asian trade. Once the trade was firmly established, the average duration of the outward trip Lisbon–Cochin was about 5.75 months, and 6.5 months for the return journey. The average size of vessels increased over time with a carrying capacity of 300 tons in the sixteenth century and up to 1 000 tons in the seventeenth.

Table 2–8. **Gold and Silver Shipments from the Americas to Europe, 1500–1800**
(metric tons)

	Gold	Silver
1500–1600	150	7 500
1600–1700	158	26 168
1700–1800	1 400	39 157
Total 1500–1800	1 708	72 825

Source: Morineau (1985), p. 570.

Table 2–9. **Chinese Imports of Silver by Country of Origin, 1550–1700**
(metric tons)

	Japan	Philippines	Portuguese shipments to Macao	Total
1550–1600	1 280	584	380	2 244
1601–40	1 968	719	148	2 835
1641–85	1 586	108	0	1 694
1686–1700	41	137	0	178
Total 1550–1700	4 875	1 548	428	6 951

Source: Von Glahn (1996), pp. 140 and 232.

http://dx.doi.org/10.1787/723137538677

Table 2–10. **Exports of Silver and Gold from Western Europe, 1601–1780**
(tonnes of "silver equivalent")

	To the Baltic	To Eastern Mediterranean	Dutch (VOC) to Asia	British (EIC) to Asia	Total
1601–50	2 475	2 500	425	250	5 650
1651–1700	2 800	2 500	775	1 050	7 125
1701–50	2 800	2 500	2 200	2 450	9 950
1751–80	1 980	1 500	1 445	1 450	6 375
Total 1601–1780	10 055	9 000	4 845	5 200	29 100

Source: Barrett, in Tracy (1990), p. 251 (he does not show his equivalence conversion ratio for gold).

http://dx.doi.org/10.1787/723137538677

V
THE TRADING WORLD OF THE INDIAN OCEAN

The population of Asia in 1500 was five times as big as that of Western Europe (284 million compared with 57 million), and the ratio was about the same in 1600. It was a very large market with a network of Asian traders operating between East Africa and India, and from Eastern India to Indonesia. East of the straits of Malacca, trade was dominated by China. Indian ships were not sturdy enough to withstand the typhoons of the China sea, and not adequately armed to deal with pirate activity off the China coast (see Chaudhuri, 1982, p. 410).

The Portuguese displaced Asian traders who had supplied spices to Red Sea and Persian Gulf ports for onward sale to Venetian, Genoese and Catalan traders. But this was only a fraction, perhaps a quarter, of Asian trade in one group of commodities. In addition there was trade within Asian waters in textiles, porcelain, precious metals, carpets, perfume, jewellery, horses, timber, salt, raw silk, gold, silver, medicinal herbs and many other commodities.

Hence, the spice trade was not the only trading opportunity for the Portuguese, or for the other later European traders (Dutch, British, French and others) who followed. Silk and porcelain played an increased role, and in the seventeenth and eighteenth centuries, cotton textiles and tea became very important. There were possibilities of participating in intra–Asian trade as well. In the 1550s to the 1630s this kind of trade between China and Japan was a particularly profitable source of income for Portugal.

Asian merchants were familiar with the seasonal wind patterns and problems of the Indian Ocean, there were experienced pilots, scientific works on astronomy and navigation, and navigational instruments not greatly inferior to those of the Portuguese[21].

From East Africa to Malacca (on the narrow straits between Sumatra and Malaya), Asian trade was conducted by merchant communities which operated without armed vessels or significant interference from governments. Although Southern India, where the Portuguese started their Asian trade, was ruled by the Empire of Vijayanagar, conditions in coastal trade were set by rulers of much smaller political units, who derived income by offering protection and marketing opportunities to traders. The income of the rulers of Vijayanagar and later the Moghul Empire was derived from land taxes, and they had no significant financial interest in foreign trade activities. In China and Japan the situation was different.

Asian merchants operated in mutually interactive community networks with ethnic, religious, family or linguistic ties and an opportunistic concentration on profit. In this respect their trading habits were not very different from those of Venetians or of Jewish traders in the Arab world of the Mediterranean[22]. In Western Asia and the Middle East merchants were generally Arabs and Muslims, but further east they included "Gujarati *vaniyas*, Tamil and Telugu Chettis, Syrian Christians from Southwestern India, Chinese from Fukien and neighbouring provinces"[23]. If they paid for protection and market access, they found that they were free to trade. If the protection became too expensive they usually had some leeway for moving elsewhere.

The Portuguese trading network was different in two respects. It consisted of a string of strongly fortified bases linked by a fleet of armed ships, so market forces were modified by coercion. Unlike the Asian trading communities or in the European trading companies which penetrated Asia at a later date, Portugal was involved in religious evangelism.

The headquarters of the Portuguese trading empire was established in 1510 at the captured Arab port of Goa, an island harbour halfway up the west Indian coast which was a Portuguese colony for nearly 460 years[24]. It was the residence of the Portuguese Viceroy, and from 1542 it was the headquarters of the Jesuit order for all its operations in Asia. Malacca, the port which controlled trade and shipping from India to Indonesia and China, was captured in 1511 and kept until 1641 when it was taken by the Dutch. A base was established at Jaffna in Sri Lanka for trade in cinnamon. Most Portuguese shipments of pepper and ginger originated from the Malabar coast of India, but for higher value spices they obtained a base at Ternate in the Moluccas (between Celebes and New Guinea) for trade in cloves, nutmeg and mace.

VI
THE TRADING WORLD OF CHINA, JAPAN AND THE PHILIPPINES

Trading conditions were very different in Asia east of the Malacca straits. Establishment of trading relations with China and Japan was a much more difficult proposition than with countries in the Indian Ocean. Requests for access to China in 1513 and 1521–22 were rejected. It was not until 1557 that Portugal acquired Macao though it participated earlier in clandestine trade off the Chinese coast. Contact was made with Japan in 1543 and trade started there in earnest in the 1550s from the base in Macao.

China

China had withdrawn from an active role in Asian trade in the fifteenth century, imposed tight controls on private trade, and an embargo on trade with Japan. In view of the historic importance of this withdrawal, it is worth retracing Chinese experience from the 1100s to 1433 when it was the most dynamic force in Asian trade.

China's exposure to world trade had been greatly enhanced when the Sung dynasty were driven out of North China and relocated their capital at Hangchow, south of the Yangtse. It was a prosperous and densely populated region of rice cultivation. It was not necessary to bring food supplies from distant areas. They relied more heavily on commercial taxes than most Chinese dynasties and fostered the development of ports and foreign trade. Their major port was Ch'üan–chou, about 600 kilometres north of Canton. They developed large scale production of ceramics for the export market, and the kilns of Ching–te–chen (in Kiangsi) prospered greatly.

In order to defend the Yangtse and coastal areas against Mongol attacks the first Chinese professional navy was created in 1232. Within a century it had grown to 20 squadrons with 52 000 men, with its main base near Shanghai. The ships included treadmill operated paddle–wheelers with protective armour plates, for service on the Yangtse. These were armed with powerful catapults to fling heavy stones or other missiles at enemy ships.

After the Sung were defeated, the Mongol (Yuan) dynasty continued with even larger scale shipbuilding activities for foreign trade, for grain transport to Peking (their new capital) in North China, for maritime commerce with Asia and for naval operations. In 1274 and 1281, two massive fleets were assembled in an unsuccessful attempt to invade Japan. The first fleet included 900 ships, the second was much larger and carried an invasion force of quarter of a million soldiers. They reopened overland commerce to Europe and the Middle East on the silk route.

As in the Sung, a large proportion of the trading community in the Yuan dynasty were from all parts of the Muslim world. This is clear from the observations of Marco Polo, the Venetian who came to China in the last quarter of the thirteenth century, and Ibn Battuta from Morocco more than 50 years later. Both left striking testimony to the vigour of the international trade of China at that time.

In the early years of the Ming, the Yung–lo emperor embarked on a series of naval expeditions outside the area of the "Eastern Oceans" which were the traditional Chinese sphere of interest. These expeditions were massive exercises whose basic motivation was political, though they did include an important element of state trading.

Yung–lo was a usurper, who had deposed his nephew in a successful military rebellion. The naval ventures were intended to display China's power and wealth and enhance his own legitimacy. They were also intended to extend Chinese suzerainty over a much wider area. Korea was a permanent member of this system of tributary relationships and Yung–lo persuaded Japan to accept a similar status in 1404 (which lasted with a brief interruption until 1549). In the tribute system, there was an initial exchange of "gifts" (consisting on the Chinese side of specialties such as silk, gold, lacquer and porcelain) and the other side would reciprocate. These exchanges were renewed at intervals of a few years, and in the past had been followed up by private trade relations. However, Yung–lo prohibited private trade.

Table 2–11. **Chinese Naval Diplomacy: Voyages to the "Western Oceans", 1405–33**

Time	Number of ships	Number of naval military & other personnel	Places visited in Western Oceans	Places visited in Eastern Oceans
1405–7	62 large vessels	27 000	Calicut	Champa, Java, Sumatra
1407–9	n.a.	n.a.	Calicut & Cochin	Siam, Sumatra, Java
1409–11	48	30 000	Malacca, Quilon	Sumatra
1413–15	63	29 000	Hormuz, Red Sea, Maldives, Bengal	Champa, Java,Sumatra
1417–19	n.a.	n.a.	Hormuz, Aden, Mogadishu, Malindi	Java, the Ryuku islands, Brunei
1421–2	41	n.a.	Aden, East Africa	Sumatra
1431–33	100	27 500	Ceylon, Calicut, Hormuz, Aden, Jedda, Malindi	Vietnam, Sumatra, Java, Malacca

Source: Needham (1971) and Levathes (1994). The detailed official records of these trips were destroyed later by the bureaucracy who were opposed to renewal of such expeditions. The evidence is based on the writings of participants and later imperial histories.

http://dx.doi.org/10.1787/723137538677

These tributary relations were conceived as a vehicle for assertion of China's moral and cultural superiority, to act as a civilising force on barbarians at the frontiers, and thereby enhance China's security. For this reason the government expected to play a leading role in developing and supervising the trade relationships. The underlying idea was not to create a colonial empire, but to assert Chinese hegemony. This traditional view of Chinese relations with the outside world was very different from that of the Mongol dynasty whose objective was world conquest, and Yung–lo probably felt the need to re–establish a more attractive image of Chinese civilisation.

Seven expeditions between 1405 and 1433 penetrated very deep into the "Western Oceans". They were commanded by Admiral Cheng–ho, a member of the emperor's household since he was 15 years old who had become a comrade in arms. Cheng–ho was a eunuch. There were thousands of them in the Ming imperial household. Emperors of this dynasty used them as a trusted and loyal counterweight to the power of the bureaucracy. Most of the latter regarded the expeditions as a waste of money, at a time when there were very large commitments in moving the Ming capital from Nanking to Peking and in rebuilding the Grand Canal. They involved very heavy fiscal burdens, and special levies on the coastal provinces. Yung–lo augmented his revenues by printing massive quantities of paper money. The resulting inflation (see Table 2–12) led to a disappearance of paper money transactions in the private economy. From the 1430s, silver became the predominant instrument of exchange and tax payments.

Table 2–12. **Exchange Rates between Ming Paper Currency and Silver, 1376–1426**

	Official	*Market*
1376	1.00	1.00
1397	0.07	
1413	0.05	
1426	0.0025	
1436	n.a.	0.0009

Source: Atwell in Twitchett and Mote (1998), p. 382.

---

http://dx.doi.org/10.1787/723137538677

Under the Yung–lo emperor, the Ming navy "consisted of some 3 800 ships in all, 1 350 patrol vessels and 1 350 combat ships attached to guard stations or island bases, a main fleet of 400 large warships stationed near Nanking and 400 grain transport freighters. In addition there were more than 250 long–distance Treasure–ships" (Needham, 1971, p. 484). The treasure ships were the most important vessels in the maritime expeditions to the Western Oceans. They were five times as big as any of the ships of da Gama, 120 metres long and nearly 50 metres broad.

Chinese ships differed substantially from those in the Indian Ocean or Portugal. The treasure ships had nine masts, and smaller ships also had multiple masts. Transverse laths of bamboo attached to the sail fabric permitted precise and stepwise reefing. When sails were furled, they fell immediately into pleats. If tears developed in the sail, the area affected was restricted by the lathing. Big ships had 15 or more watertight compartments, so a partially damaged ship would not sink and could be repaired at sea. They had up to 60 cabins so the crew quarters were more comfortable than on Portuguese ships.

Table 2–11 shows the characteristics of the six naval expeditions of the Yung–lo emperor, and the seventh which was sent after his death. The fleets were very large and the big ships were intended to overawe the rulers of the countries which were visited. The intentions were peaceful but the military force was big enough to deal effectively with attacks on the fleet, which occurred on only three occasions. The first had India and its spices as their destination. The rest explored the East Coast of Africa, the Red Sea and the Persian Gulf.

A major purpose of these voyages was to establish good relations by presentation of gifts and to escort ambassadors or rulers to or from China. There was no attempt to establish bases for trade or for military objectives. There was a search for new plants for medical purposes, and one of the missions was accompanied by 180 medical personnel. There was also an interest in types of African livestock which were unknown in China. The expeditions brought back ostriches, giraffes, zebras, elephant tusks and rhinoceros horns. However, these were exotica, and there was no significant replication of the international interchange of flora and fauna which the European encounter with the Americas inaugurated.

After the death of Cheng–ho, support for this distant diplomacy faded very quickly. The broadening of China's tributary relations with countries of the "Western Oceans" did not enhance China's security and the cost of the naval expeditions had exacerbated a situation of fiscal and monetary crisis. The meritocratic bureaucracy had always opposed a venture which promoted the leverage of the eunuch interest. They consolidated their gains by destroying the official records of the overseas expeditions. There was increasing concern to defend the new northern capital against potential invasions from Mongolia or Manchuria. The new capital's food supply was guaranteed by the Grand Canal which had been reopened in its full length in 1415 (2 300 kilometres — equivalent to the distance from Paris to Istanbul). It functioned better than ever before because of new locks which made it operational on a full–time basis[25]. Grain shipments by sea to the capital had already ceased and sea–going grain ships were replaced by canal barges.

As the oceanic diplomacy had been ended, there was no longer a need for Treasure ships, coastal defences had been reduced and there was strong pressure to reduce the hard core of the navy. By 1474 the fleet of large warships had been cut from 400 to 140. Most of the shipyards were closed, and naval manpower was reduced by retrenchment and desertions.

The tributary arrangements for countries within the Eastern Ocean continued, e.g. ships from Japan were able to come at intervals of several years, but the Yung–lo ban on private trade continued, and sea–going junks with more than two masts were prohibited.

This regime of interdiction and regulation eventually sparked large scale development of illicit private trade and piracy. The coastguards were open to bribery. By the time the Portuguese established their base in Macao in 1557, they were fully aware of the trading situation and had easy contacts with Chinese and Japanese pirates.

In 1567, the Chinese authorities ended the prohibition on private trade but banned trade with Japan. This gave the Portuguese an unbelievably favourable window of opportunity.

Japan

In 1539, the Chinese had confiscated the cargo of Japanese ships participating in the tribute trade. In 1544 they had turned away Japanese attempts to renew the tributary trade. This was enough to induce Japanese hostility, and enmity was further heightened by political changes in Japan. By the middle of the sixteenth century the Ashikaga shogunate which had accepted nominal Chinese suzerainty was on its last legs. It was succeeded by a series of three ruthless military dictators, Nobunaga, Hideyoshi, and Ieyasu, who created a powerful unified system of government. They completely repudiated the idea of Chinese suzerainty.

These political developments occurred at the same time as Japan became a major silver producer. Rich deposits were discovered in the 1530s. The export potential was very large. The Chinese market was hungry for silver, and the gold/silver price ratio was much more favourable to silver in China than in Japan. As the Chinese would not allow Japanese ships to enter their harbours, the main carriers of Japanese silver to China were Chinese pirates and the Portuguese.

Portuguese ships were able to bring Indonesian spices from Malacca to Macao, sell them in China, buy Chinese silks and gold, go from Macao to harbours in the south of Japan (first Hirado and then Nagasaki), sell these products, buy Japanese silver, sell it in Macao, and buy silk again for shipment to Japan or their depot in Goa.

Portuguese trade was also accompanied by Jesuit missions. Francis Xavier was in Japan in 1549–51, and Jesuits were very successful in getting converts in the south of Japan. Eventually, the number of Japanese Christians rose to about 300 000 (many more converts than the Jesuits made in Goa or in China). Japanese were interested in Portuguese ships, maps and navigation, and learned something of these two techniques. They were even more interested in guns. Portuguese technology of that epoch was reproduced in Japanese *namban* (southern barbarian) art which is displayed most clearly in very large multi–panelled lacquer screens. The first Portuguese to arrive in 1543 had firearms which were new to Japan. The potential of this new weaponry was quickly appreciated by the military who managed to copy the guns and manufacture them in Japan. They had an important effect in deciding the outcome of the Japanese civil wars. After 1615, the new shogunate began a successful policy to eliminate firearms and restrict the use of swords to the *samurai*.

In 1596, the Spanish authorities in Manila tried to replicate Portuguese successes in Japan, and sent a mission of Franciscan missionaries to proselytise. The Japanese got the impression that Spain might want to take over as they had the Philippines, and on Hideyoshi's order the Spanish missionaries and 19 of their converts were crucified at Nagasaki. From that point on, Japan became increasingly hostile to Portuguese missionary activities, and made contact with English and Dutch traders who had no religious ambitions. Eventually Christianity became illegal, and the Portuguese were expelled in 1639. Henceforth trade with the Japanese mainland was confined to Chinese and Dutch traders.

Manila

Fernao de Magalhaes had participated in the first Portuguese expedition to the Moluccan spice islands in 1511, and was disappointed with his pay and prospects when he returned to Portugal. In 1517, he defected to Spain, changed his name to Magellan, and persuaded the Spanish crown to finance a voyage by a Western route. The expedition he commanded (1519–22) was the first to circumnavigate the globe. It established a route around the south of Argentina. Magellan was killed in combat in the Philippines, but the voyage continued to the spice islands and eventually got back to Spain. Fifteen men returned, more than 200 failed to survive the voyage.

Spain surrendered its claim to the Moluccas to Portugal for a cash payment, but gained effective control of the Philippines in 1571. It was the only significant part of the Spanish empire outside the Americas. The route between Acapulco (on the west coast of Mexico) and Manila had a monopoly in trading Spanish silver against Chinese silks and porcelain. Spaniards took little direct part in China trade, which was mainly conducted by Chinese ships, using the large overseas Chinese population of Manila as intermediaries. At the end of the sixteenth century there were 2 000 Spanish living in Manila and 10 000 Chinese.

Relations with China were never very friendly. In 1603, a visit by rather pushy Chinese traders representing the provincial authorities of Fukien gave the misleading impression that China intended to invade the Philippines. The Spanish reaction was to attack and kill most of the Chinese community in Manila. The Chinese Wan–li emperor executed the trader who had provoked the Spanish, and the trade with China managed to survive this incident. However, possession of the Philippines was never a particularly profitable venture for Spain, and the flow of silver from Mexico via Manila to China was a good deal smaller than that from Japan (see Table 2–9).

VII
THE PORTUGUESE IN BRAZIL

When the Portuguese arrived in Brazil in 1500, their situation as colonialists was very different from that of Spain in Mexico and Peru. They did not find an advanced civilisation with hoards of precious metals for plunder, or a social discipline and organisation geared to provide steady tribute which they could appropriate. Brazilian Indians were mainly hunter–gatherers, though some were moving towards agriculture using slash–and–burn techniques to cultivate manioc. Their technology and resources meant that they were thin on the ground. They had no towns, no domestic animals. They were stone age men and women, hunting game and fish, naked, illiterate and innumerate.

In the first century of settlement, it became clear that it was difficult to use Indians as slave labour. They were not docile, had high mortality when exposed to Western diseases, could run away and hide rather easily. So Portugal turned to imported African slaves for manual labour. The ultimate fate of Brazilian Indians was rather like that of North American Indians. They were pushed beyond the fringe of colonial society. The main difference was greater miscegenation with the white invaders and with black slaves in Brazil.

A much bigger proportion of Portuguese gains from Brazil came from development of commodity exports and commercial profit than those of Spain from its colonies. In the sixteenth and seventeenth centuries official revenue from Brazil was small — about 3 per cent of Portuguese public revenue in 1588 and 5 per cent in 1619 (see Bethell, 1984, Vol. I, p. 286). In the sixteenth century, economic activity was concentrated on a small population of settlers engaged in a highly profitable export–oriented sugar industry in the Northeast. The techniques for this industry, including negro slavery, had been previously developed in Madeira and São Tomé. Cattle ranching in the dry backlands area (the *sertão*) provided food for those working in sugar production.

Brazilian sugar exports peaked in the 1650s. Earnings fell thereafter because of lower prices and competition from the rapidly growing output in the Caribbean (see Table 2–4).

The setback in sugar caused large parts of the Northeast to lapse into a subsistence economy. In the 1690s, the discovery of gold, and in the 1720s diamonds further south in Minas Gerais, opened new opportunities. During the eighteenth century, there was considerable immigration from Europe, and internal migration from the Northeast to Minas, to engage in gold and diamond development. The eighteenth century prosperity in Minas is obvious even today from the number of elaborate buildings and churches in Ouro Preto which was the centre of mining activity. As Minas Gerais is very barren, the food and transport needs of the mining area stimulated food production in neighbouring provinces to the South and in the Northeast, and mule–breeding in Rio Grande do Sul. The gold industry was at its peak around 1750, with production around 15 tons a year, but as the best deposits were exhausted, output and exports declined. In the first half of the eighteenth century profit remittances from gold averaged 5.23 million milreis (£1.4 million) a year, of which the identifiable royal revenues were around 18 per cent (Alden, 1973, p. 331). Total Brazilian gold shipments over the whole of the eighteenth century were between 800 and 850 tons (see Morineau, 1985).

In the second half of the eighteenth century, Portuguese finances were in desperate straits. Metropolitan revenues from Brazil were squeezed by the decline in gold production. Income from Asia had collapsed and Portugal had to bear the costs of reconstructing Lisbon after the 1755 earthquake. To meet this problem, the Portuguese prime minister, Pombal, expelled the Jesuits from Brazil (1759), confiscated their vast properties, and sold them to wealthy landowners and merchants for the benefit of the crown. Most of the property of other religious orders was taken over a few years later.

Table 2–13. **Commodity Composition of Brazilian Exports, 1821–1951**
(per cent of total)

	Cotton	Sugar	Coffee	Rubber	Cocoa
1821–3	25.8	23.1	18.7	0.0	n.a.
1871–3	16.6	12.3	50.2	0.0	n.a.
1901–3	2.6	2.4	55.7	22.5	2.5
1927–9	2.0	0.5	71.1	2.0	3.8
1949–51	10.0	0.3	60.5	0.2	4.8

Source: 1821–73 from Leff (1982), Vol.II, p. 9. 1901–51 from *O Brasil em Numeros.*

http://dx.doi.org/10.1787/723137538677

When gold production collapsed, Brazil turned back to agricultural exports. At independence in 1822, the three main exports were cotton, sugar and coffee. Coffee production started at the beginning of the nineteenth century after the slave revolt cut output in Haiti. Coffee was grown in the Southeast, whereas sugar and cotton were typical Northeast products.

At the end of the colonial period, half the population were slaves. They were worked to death after a few years of service, and fed on a crude diet of beans and jerked beef. A privileged fraction of the white population enjoyed high incomes but the rest of the population (free blacks, mulattos, Indians and large numbers of the whites) were poor. Landownership was concentrated on slave owners, thus a very unequal distribution of property buttressed a highly unequal distribution of income. There was substantial regional inequality. The poorest area was the Northeast. Minas Gerais had also passed its peak. The most prosperous area was around the new capital, Rio de Janeiro.

Independence came to Brazil very smoothly by Latin American standards. In 1808, the Portuguese Queen and the Regent fled to Rio to escape the French invasion of the motherland. They brought about 10 000 of the mainland establishment with them — the aristocracy, bureaucracy, and some of the military who set up government and court in Rio and Petropolis running Brazil and Portugal as a joint kingdom (both parts by then being about equal in terms of population). After the Napoleonic wars, the two countries split without too much enmity. Brazil became independent with an Emperor who was the son of the Portuguese monarch.

With independence, Brazil ceased remitting official tribute to Portugal, but the large imperial ruling establishment meant a higher internal tax burden. The British, the new protectors of Brazil, took out their growing commercial profits. However, independence meant that the country could create its own banking system, print paper money, indulge in mild inflation and borrow on the international capital market.

There was an intermittent inflow of foreign capital from the 1820s onwards, mostly in the form of direct loans to the government or the proceeds from sales of Brazilian government bonds abroad. There were 17 foreign loans in the Imperial period. There was no default on this debt, and Brazil remained in good standing with its British bankers who supplied all the funds.

There were changes in commercial policy which came with independence. Until 1808, Brazilian ports were open only to British or Portuguese ships[26], and mercantilist restrictions prevented production of manufactured items. These barriers were lifted in 1808, but the United Kingdom retained special extra–territorial rights and tariff preferences until 1827. The preferences were then abolished, but Brazil was obliged to limit tariffs to 15 per cent *ad valorem* until 1844. This was a serious fiscal constraint on a government with all the trappings of a monarchy to support, and without the political clout to impose land or income taxation. It encouraged the trend towards inflationary finance and a depreciating paper currency. In 1844, when Brazil regained its customs autonomy the general tariff level was raised to 30 per cent for manufactured goods, but duties on raw materials and machinery were lifted.

These measures stimulated the creation of the cotton spinning and weaving industry. In the Imperial period, tariff revenue provided two thirds of the government's tax receipts and their effect in protecting local industry was significant. Tariff receipts were a higher proportion of imports than those of any other country except Portugal[27].

In 1833, the United Kingdom abolished slavery in the West Indies and started to interfere actively with the slave trade. Between 1840 and 1851, the inflow of slaves to Brazil was 370 000, but thereafter the British Navy brought it to an end. Slavery continued for almost four more decades, but the economy was modified significantly by the ending of the trade. The immediate effect was to double the price of slaves and make it less profitable to work them to an early death. The sex and age structure of the black population began to change, making for lowered activity rates. In 1888, slavery was abolished without compensation, or any kind of resettlement help for slaves. By that time the slave population was only 7 per cent of the total compared with 13 per cent in the United States in 1860, on the eve of the US civil war.

The Emperor was deposed in 1889 by the military which established an oligarchic republic. Church and state were separated. The franchise was restricted to those with property. The Presidency generally alternated between politicians from São Paulo and Minas Gerais on a prearranged basis. The monarchy had exercised a centralised power, but now the provinces became states with a good deal of autonomy, including control over customs duties which could be levied on both foreign and interstate commerce. At the state level, power was concentrated in the hands of a small political class who favoured their cronies and relatives.

At local level, "coronelismo" (rule of the colonels) prevailed. This semi–bandit gentry built up their landholdings by means not always legal, and exercised seigneurial type power over the less prosperous citizenry.

In the initial years of the Republic, the strains involved in moving from slave to wage labour were obvious. Coffee was no longer profitable in the region around Rio, which switched to cattle raising. The competitive position of São Paulo was strengthened. Its climate and soils were better suited to coffee than the eroded valleys near Rio. It had been building a free labour force of white immigrants since the 1840s, when Senator Vergueiro introduced them to his plantation. The state government subsidised immigration (mainly of Italians) on a large scale from 1880 to 1928. In the 1920s, many of the immigrants to São Paulo were Japanese. This part of the country was further helped by the growth of rail transport and the development of the port of Santos. The average educational level of immigrants was considerably higher than that of native born Brazilians. They had twice the literacy rate and three times the level of secondary and higher education (Merrick and Graham (1979), p. 111). Their wage level made them more expensive than slaves, but their productivity was higher, and their number could be quickly expanded by immigration.

The Northeastern economy stagnated in the Republican period. There and elsewhere, the black and mulatto population generally got little of the benefits of growth in a country where they had no voting rights, access to land, education or any form of governmental help in adjusting to a wage economy.

Portuguese rule in Brazil had several lasting consequences:

a) Brazil is characterised by very wide disparities in income, wealth, education and economic opportunity. These are more extreme than in Asia, Europe or North America. The social structure still has strong echoes of the colonial period, when there was great inequality in access to landed property, and the bulk of the labour force were slaves. The continued neglect of popular education is very marked even by Latin American standards and has hampered the growth of labour productivity. Another aspect of inequality is regional. The per capita income disparity between the poorest state, Piauí, and the federal district is about 7:1. The only other countries with this degree of regional disparity are Mexico and China.

Table 2–14. Confrontation of Brazilian and US Economic Performance in the Five Major Phases of Brazilian Development, 1500–1998

	Population *(000)*	*Brazilian Growth Record* *GDP* *(million 1990 int. $)*	*GDP Per Capita* *(1990 int. $)*
1500	1 000	400	400
1820	4 507	2 912	646
1890	14 199	11 267	794
1929	32 894	37 415	1 137
1980	122 936	639 093	5 199
1998	169 807	926 919	5 459

Growth Rates in Each Phase (annual compound rate)

	Population	*GDP*	*GDP Per Capita*
1500–1820 Colony	0.47	0.62	0.15
1820–90 Empire	1.65	1.95	0.30
1890–1929 Oligarchic Republic	2.18	3.13	0.92
1929–80 Developmentalist Era	2.62	5.72	3.03
1980–98 Era of "Adjustment"	1.81	2.09	0.27
1500–1998	1.04	1.57	0.53

US Growth Record

	Population *(000)*	*GDP* *(million 1990 $)*	*GDP Per Capita* *(1990 $)*
1500	2 000	800	400
1820	9 981	12 548	1 257
1890	63 302	214 714	3 392
1929	122 245	843 335	6 899
1980	227 757	4 239 558	18 575
1998	270 561	7 394 598	27 331

US Growth Rates in Each Phase (annual compound rate)

	Population	*GDP*	*GDP Per Capita*
1500–1820	0.50	0.86	0.36
1820–90	2.67	4.14	1.43
1890–1929	1.70	3.57	1.83
1929–80	1.23	3.21	1.96
1980–98	0.96	3.15	2.17
1500–1998	0.99	1.85	0.85

Source: Appendices A, B and C, and Maddison (1995a).

http://dx.doi.org/10.1787/723137538677

b) Inequalities of income and opportunity in Brazil are closely associated with ethnicity, but the heritage of slavery has produced less social tension than in the United States. Gilberto Freyre (1959) argued that Brazilians are more or less colour blind, and that Brazil is a social continuum from rich to poor with no sharp social antagonisms. Brazil was different from the United States mainly because Portuguese society and mores at the time of colonisation were heavily influenced by close contact with the Muslim world. Florestan Fernandes (1969) took a much more critical view of a Brazilian society that practises *de facto* but generally discreet social discrimination.

ISBN 92-64-02261-9 – © OECD 2006

c) Brazil has been favoured by softer political transitions than other countries in Latin America. The Treaty of Tordesillas (1494) divided the Americas amicably between Portugal and Spain. Portugal got a slice extending 48 degrees West of the Greenwich meridian, but its present borders encompass nearly three times as much land — a situation peacefully endorsed by the Treaty of Madrid in 1750. Most of the territorial gains were made by frontiersmen. The only substantial invasion was the Dutch occupation of the Northeast (1630–54). Conflicts to preserve boundaries against French or Spanish incursions were insignificant, and the last territorial acquisition, the Acre territory, was by purchase from Bolivia. The biggest foreign war was with Paraguay (1865–70). This is in stark contrast with Mexico, which lost half its territory in wars with the United States, or to European and Asian experience of wars over boundaries.

d) Another striking feature has been the ease of Brazil's domestic political transitions. Independence was gained with no significant struggle, the Portuguese crown prince becoming Emperor of Brazil in 1822. Slavery was abolished without a civil war in 1888. The Empire became a republic without a struggle in 1889. The Vargas dictatorship of 1930–45 began and ended with relatively little violence, and this was also true of military rule from 1964–85.

e) The combination of smooth political transitions, freedom from foreign conflicts and relative ease of social relations between ethnic groups permitted Brazil to assimilate a cosmopolitan mix of the original Portuguese settlers, the descendants of African slaves, later immigrants from Italy, Japan, Germany and the Lebanon. It is a frontier country with a high degree of self–confidence, without a chip–on–the–shoulder feeling of exploitation by powerful neighbours. It is a looser federation than many big countries and has an intellectual life which is multipolar.

VIII
THE NETHERLANDS

From 1400 to 1700, Dutch per capita income growth was the fastest in Europe, and from 1600 to the 1820s its level was the highest. Before 1600 this performance was due to seizure of opportunities for trade in Northern Europe, and success in transforming agriculture by hydraulic engineering. Thereafter prosperity was augmented by its role in world trade.

The Dutch Republic became independent in 1579 by breaking away from a larger "Netherlands" ruled by Spain[28]. The struggle to achieve and maintain independence lasted for nearly 80 years. The Dutch defeated a Spanish empire which included Castile, Aragon, Portugal (from 1580 to 1640), Naples, Sicily, the Duchy of Milan, Franche Comté, Mexico, Peru, the Philippines, West Indies, Tunis, Flanders, Brabant, Luxembourg, Lille, Artois and Hainault.

It is useful to consider the economic and political context from which the Netherlands economy emerged. From the twelfth century onwards, Flanders and Brabant were the most prosperous part of Northern Europe. The leading cities of Flanders (Bruges, Ghent and Ypres) were the major centre of the European woollen textile industry, making very high quality draperies, tapestries and furnishing materials, which were sold all over Europe. The raw materials were to a substantial extent supplied by imports — wool from England and alum (a cleansing agent indispensable in the cloth industry) which Genoese traders brought from Chios. Woad and other dyestuffs, fuller's earth and other items were mainly local products. In the middle of the fourteenth century (see Postan, 1987, p. 180), English wool exports were running at nearly 7 000 tons a year, most going to Flanders via the English port of Calais. By the middle of the fifteenth, English wool exports had dropped by four fifths and the wool imports of Flanders came from Spain, being shipped from Bilbao and other Spanish Atlantic ports. England had become an exporter rather than an importer of woollen textiles, but a substantial part of its cloth exports were undyed and sent to Flanders for finishing. McNeill (1974) pp. 53–4 indicates the magnitude of the massive Genoese alum shipments to Flanders between the mid–fourteenth to mid–sixteenth century: "Having captured Chios in 1346, they used the island as an entrepôt, collecting the yield of all the mines of Asia Minor there. This assured a constant supply of adequate quantities of alum to fill the holds of vast specialised ships — some twenty such vessels, of a size greater than any wooden ship attained before or afterward, plied regularly between Chios and Bruges, winter and summer, stopping en route only at Cadiz to take on water and other supplies." Postan suggests that the annual production of Flemish woollen cloth in the fourteenth and fifteenth centuries was more than 150 000 pieces of 28 yards (25.8 metres) in length. In addition Flanders produced linens for export, using local supplies of flax.

Flanders was heavily urbanised and much of its food was imported. There were substantial imports of grain (wheat and barley from France and England, rye from the Baltic), fish from the Baltic and Holland, and wine from France. Postan suggests that wine exports from Bordeaux were running at 25 million gallons a year at the beginning of the fourteenth century. A large proportion of this went to England, some to the Baltic, and a substantial amount to Flanders and Brabant.

By the mid–fourteenth century, the cities of Brabant (Antwerp, Leuven and Brussels) gained an economic edge on Flanders, due to the silting up of water routes to Bruges, the greater enterprise of Antwerp and British competition with the Flemish woollen industry. In Flanders, output, marketing and production practices tended to be heavily regulated by guilds. Foreign trade was conducted through periodic fairs or "staple" arrangements which confined international transactions to particular towns and gave privileged access to the consortium of German merchants in the Hanseatic League. Antwerp had a magnificent harbour at the mouth of the Scheldt, and a more commercial, less regulatory approach. It was the major North European centre for international banking, and loans to foreign rulers, e.g. Henry VIII of England. The Antwerp bourse provided a model for the London Exchange.

Both Flanders and Brabant conducted a substantial amount of international business in their high value exports by land, but for heavy imported goods, sea transport was very much cheaper. A large part of these imports came by sea and river in ships and boats from Holland, Zeeland and the Northern Provinces.

The seven Northern Provinces which united to create the Dutch Republic (Holland, Zeeland, Utrecht, Gelderland, Overijssel, Friesland and Groningen successively in 1579–80) were very different from Flanders and Brabant[29]. They occupied a flat amphibious terrain where the relationship between land and water was very close. There were major natural waterways. The Rhine provided transport deep into Germany, to Cologne and Frankfurt–am–Main. Its delta was full of islands and natural harbours. The Ijssel led into the Zuider Zee, the Ems provided an excellent route to the North German coast. In such a setting, the leading industries were fisheries, sea and river transportation and shipbuilding. Agriculture was also deeply marked by the possibilities for hydraulic management and irrigation.

In the fourteenth century, the merchant marine of the Northern Provinces had established a major position in the North Sea and Baltic, carrying rye and timber from East Germany and Poland which was shipped via Danzig; furs, wax, honey, pitch, tar and timber from Russia via Narva and Riga; copper, iron ore, weapons and salt herring from Sweden; salted cod and timber from Bergen in Norway. In return they carried re–exports of English woollen textiles, salt (for preserving fish and meat) and re–exports of wine from France. Apart from these merchanting activities, they acted as carriers, e.g. between Danzig and Riga, when opportunities arose.

Shipping and trade in the Baltic had previously been monopolised by a consortium of German merchants (the Hanseatic League) with headquarters in Lübeck, and commercial bases in London, Bruges, etc. Hanseatic trade from the Baltic had relied to a large extent on the short land route from Lübeck to Hamburg. The Dutch pioneered the sea route through the Danish sound, which though longer, was cheaper. In 1437–41 the Hanseatic League engaged in hostilities to try to drive Dutch ships from the Baltic, but, with support from Danzig, the Dutch kept the right to trade. This trade was well

Table 2–15. **Carrying Capacity of Dutch and Other European Merchant Fleets, 1470–1824**
(metric tons)

	1470	1570	1670	1780	1824
Netherlands	60 000	232 000	568 000	450 000	140 000
Germany	60 000	110 000	104 000	155 000	
Britain	n.a.	51 000	260 000	1 000 000	
France	n.a.	80 000	80 000	700 000	
Italy, Portugal, Spain	n.a.	n.a.	250 000	546 000	
Denmark, Norway and Sweden				555 000 [a]	
North America				450 000	

a) 1786–87.

Source: 1470–1670 for Netherlands, Germany and France, and Britain 1570 from Vogel (1915), p. 331. 1670 and 1780 for Britain, 1780 and 1824 for the Netherlands, and 1780 for France from de Vries and van der Woude (1997), pp. 411, 484, 490 and 492. Denmark; Norway and Sweden; and Germany, Italy, Portugal and Spain 1786–87 from Unger (1992), p. 258. Italy, Portugal and Spain 1670 from Petty (1690), p. 251.

Table 2–16. **Dutch Merchant Ships by Area of Operation Around 1670**

	Ships	Carrying capacity (metric tons)	Average capacity per ship (metric tons)
Norway	200	40 000	200
Archangel	25	9 000	360
Greenland	150	40 000	267
Mediterranean	200	72 000	360
Baltic & Other Europe	735	207 000	282
Herring Fisheries	1 000	60 000	60
Coastal Traffic	1 000	40 000	40
West Africa & West Indies	100	40 000	400
Asia	100	60 000	600
Total	3 510	568 000	162

Source: Vogel (1915), p. 319.

Table 2–17. **Employment in Dutch Shipping by Area of Operation, 1610–1770**

	1610	1630–40	1680	1770
Baltic	4 000	4 000	2 000	n.a.
Norway	4 000	4 200	4 000	n.a.
Archangel	500	1 000	1 200	n.a.
North Sea	500	800	800	n.a.
England	1 000	1 000	500	n.a.
France	4 500	4 500	4 000	n.a.
Iberia & Mediterranean	5 000	6 000	6 000	n.a.
West Africa & Americas	2 000	4 000	2 000	n.a.
Total Merchant Marine	21 500	25 500	22 500	21 000
Asia[a]	2 000	4 000	8 500	11 500
Ocean Fisheries	6 500	7 000	6 500	4 000
Whaling	0	1 500	9 000	6 000
Admiralties[b]	3 000	8 000	11 000[c]	2 000
Total	33 000	46 000	57 500	44 500

a) monopoly of VOC (Dutch East India Company); b) naval defence forces; c),1670.

Source: De Vries and van der Woude (1997), p. 406, see pp. 98–100 for functioning of "admiralties"; figure for 1770 for admiralties is from Israel (1995), p. 263. In time of war, the naval defence forces could be augmented by drawing manpower from the merchant and fishing fleets — see Israel (1995), p. 768.

http://dx.doi.org/10.1787/723137538677

documented, because Denmark, whose territory then included Southern Sweden, controlled the entry to the Baltic and levied tolls. In 1500, 300–400 Dutch ships a year entered the Baltic, and by the 1560s, more than 1 300. Grain shipments amounted to about 100 000 tons a year in the latter period.

The Dutch ships involved in this trade operated from the coasts of Zeeland, Holland and Friesland. Dordrecht was the major port for traffic on the Rhine with Germany and with Liège via the Meuse. Middelburg (on the island of Walcheren), opposite the mouth of the Scheldt, imported English woollen cloth, French wine, grains and salt, and in the sixteenth century, spices and sugar from Portugal. The Dutch trading fleet was by far the biggest in Europe. By the 1560s, on the eve of independence, the province of Holland alone had 1 800 seagoing ships (Israel, 1995, p. 117). The carrying capacity of Dutch merchant shipping in 1570 was about the same as the combined fleets of France, Germany and England (see Table 2–15). Per head of population, Dutch shipping capacity was 25 times as big as in these three northern countries.

Herring fisheries were an important part of Dutch shipping activity. The herring were sold fresh or lightly salted near to the ports or were processed and barrelled for international trade. Before 1400, herring shoals best suited for salting were off the Swedish coast, but in the fifteenth century, they migrated into the North Sea, so the bulk of the catch was taken by Dutch ships. A technological breakthrough increased productivity substantially. Dutch shipyards developed a new type of factory ship (a herring "buss"), with nets, rigging and processing facilities which permitted crews of 18 to 30 men to gut, clean, salt and barrel the herring whilst at sea. Vessels of this type could make three trips a year of five to eight weeks during the open season from June to December. By the 1560s there were 400 Dutch vessels of this type operating from the province of Holland, with ownership concentrated on urban investors. At this time, the Dutch were exporting herring to the Baltic rather than importing (see de Vries and van der Woude, 1997, pp. 243–54). In the seventeenth century, Dutch ships embarked on whale fishing off Spitzbergen in the Arctic.

Water control played a major role in Dutch agricultural development. Marshes, bogs, low–lying land subject to frequent flooding were not attractive in their natural state. Agricultural settlers in the Middle Ages occupied mounds and turned them into polders by building dykes to keep off flood waters. In time, skills in hydraulic management improved, and large areas of new land were reclaimed. By the beginning of the sixteenth century, water management and engineering was entrusted to professionals responsible for development and maintenance. Farming communities raised taxes and provided funds for the waterboards. Windmills were used as a source of power for pumps which controlled water flow in canals. As de Vries (1974) p. 27 noted: "Much of fourteenth century Holland was, in effect, a new country. Only in east–Elbian Germany can one find reclamation being carried out in so systematic a manner and over such large tracts."

This conquest of nature had important social implications. Only a small part of the Dutch population was constrained by feudal restrictions. Peasants were freer than anywhere else in Europe. Some were landowners, many more paid money rents or worked for wages. The reliance on water control generated solidaristic attitudes which are still observable in Dutch society.

Dutch agriculture developed a high degree of specialisation. Much of the grain supply came from imports, and domestic production concentrated heavily on meat, milk, butter and cheese. Two features were more developed than elsewhere in Europe: a) stall feeding of cattle through the winter months, and b) large production of vegetables. Over time there was an increased emphasis on industrial crops — hops for the beer industry, flax, hemp and madder for textiles, and later, tobacco and tulip bulbs. There was a gradual transformation of agriculture into horticulture.

In large areas of the Northern Netherlands there were layers of peat several metres deep which were a potential source of cheap energy for many purposes. After 1600, about 275 000 hectares of these peat–bogs were stripped. Engineering skills in land reclamation, drainage, and pumping were easily transferable to peat extraction. In the Groningen area, urban investors set up companies to exploit this resource on a large scale on confiscated monastic lands.

Transport of peat, hay, wheat, cattle, timber, building materials and other heavy freight became a good deal cheaper in the middle of the seventeenth century, because of the creation of a network of canals equipped with tow–paths. Drawn by horses, canal barges carried freight, mail and passengers on regular schedules, at seven kilometres an hour, day and night, at frequent intervals between virtually all areas of the country. "In the 1660s, nearly 300 000 passengers travelled annually on the Amsterdam–Haarlem route, 140 000 glided between Haarlem and Leiden, and some 200 000 between Leiden and the joint destinations of the Hague and Delft" (de Vries and van der Woude, 1997, p. 187). No other country had such a cheap and dense transport network. Road freight carried by carts was slower and much more expensive. As Sir William Temple (1693), p. 152 put it: "one Horse shall draw in a Boat more than fifty can by Cart — And by this easie way of Travelling, an industrious Man loses no time from his Business, for he Writes, or eats, or Sleeps, while he goes."

The biggest industries in the Dutch provinces at the time of independence were shipbuilding, sailcloth, fishing nets, ropes, barrels and associated items, salt refining, breweries, brickworks and timber for buildings, and a substantial woollen and linen textile industry.

The circumstances under which the partition of the Netherlands occurred had an enormous positive impact on the economic potential of the new republic. They were also detrimental to the economic interests of Portugal, Spain and the Spanish Netherlands.

The struggle against the Spanish regime had involved repression and resistance in the Southern Netherlands as well as the North. The inquisition started in 1523 with the burning of two dissident clergy at the stake in Brussels. In the next 50 years more than 2 000 had met the same fate and a large proportion were from the South. The Count of Egmont, the governor of Flanders, a catholic who had been a distinguished general in the Spanish armies, was executed in 1567 because he had protested against Spanish fiscal demands and curtailment of previous political rights of the Southern nobility. Malines (Mechelen) was sacked by Spanish troops and part of its population massacred in 1572. Antwerp suffered deaths and serious property damage from the depredations of riotous Spanish soldiers in 1576. Its losses were even greater during the Spanish siege in 1583–85.

As a result, there was large scale migration from Flanders and Brabant to the new republic. Between 1583 and 1589 the population of Antwerp fell from 84 000 to 42 000. In Bruges and Ghent the exodus of refugees reached the same proportions. In Mechelen, the population fell by two thirds. In the Republic, the population of Middelburg trebled, in Leiden it doubled, 30 000 came to Amsterdam (see Israel, 1995, pp. 307–12). Altogether, the influx was about 150 000, more than 10 per cent of the population of the South, and a bigger proportionate addition to the North. As the North had huge imports of grain and fish which no longer went to the South, there was no problem feeding the new population. The northern confiscation of monastic properties helped in accommodating the influx.

The refugees included a large proportion of the merchant class and bankers of the Southern Netherlands (though some of the latter went to Germany). They brought capital, skills and international contacts. Virtually all of the Jewish population moved to the North. Migration of skilled workers strengthened the textile industry of Leiden. Immigrants also brought skills for other industries including printing, publishing and sugar refining. Before the partition, the only university had been in Leuven (founded 1425). This was one of the largest and most distinguished in Europe, but its freedom was curtailed by the inquisition. The university of Leiden was founded in the North in 1575 followed by Franeker (1585), Harderwijk (1600), Groningen (1614) and Utrecht (1634). Leiden was the biggest with a full range of faculties and offered a humanist education in the tradition of Erasmus. It soon began to attract a large international student body from Germany, Britain and Scandinavia, as well as the refugees from the South.

The political change opened possibilities for a worldwide expansion in Dutch shipping activity to the detriment of Portugal and Spain. In the 1590s, trade with Asia was inaugurated with trial voyages around the Cape into the Indian Ocean to the spice islands, and West via the Magellan Straits to Japan. Barents, 1596–7, made an unsuccessful attempt at a Northeastern passage via Archangel and Novaya

Zemlaya. Hudson discovered New York in 1609 whilst seeking a Northwest passage. Within 30 years the Dutch displaced the Portuguese as the dominant European traders with Asia. They seized Portuguese bases in West Africa, acquiring a substantial share of the trade in gold and slaves. They attacked the Spanish empire in the Americas, occupying Northeast Brazil and its profitable sugar industry from 1630 to 1654 (at that time Portugal was ruled by Spain), then moved their base to the Caribbean (Curaçao and Surinam). There was also significant pirate activity. The greatest coup was Piet Heijn's capture of the whole Spanish silver fleet off Cuba in 1628.

From 1585 to 1795, for reasons of military and naval security and commercial advantage, the Dutch successfully blockaded the mouth of the Scheldt, consolidated the ruin of Antwerp, and imposed a very serious constraint on the economic progress of the Spanish Netherlands. In the course of the seventeenth century, Spanish military potential weakened enormously, but the Dutch had no interest in conquering the Southern Netherlands, which was a useful buffer against French territorial ambitions.

Throughout the seventeenth and for most of the eighteenth century, British economists recognised the superiority of Dutch performance and policy. William Petty's pioneering work on *Political Arithmetick*, written in 1676 and published in 1690 was perhaps the most astute assessment. He demonstrated that a "small country and few people may be equivalent in wealth and strength to a far greater people and territory." He provided a foretaste of the type of reasoning used later by Adam Smith and Douglass North when he compared the performance of France and Holland. The population of France was more than ten times that of the United Provinces, but he estimated the Dutch merchant fleet to be nine times as big as the French, its foreign trade four times as big, its interest rate about half the French level, its foreign assets large, those of France negligible. The Dutch economy was highly specialised, importing a large part of its food, hiring mercenaries to fight its wars, and concentrating its labour force in high productivity sectors. Its flat terrain permitted substantial use of wind power. High density of urban settlement, good ports and internal waterways reduced transport and infastructure costs, cheapened government services and reduced the need for inventories. Dutch institutions favoured economic growth. Religious tolerance encouraged skilled immigration. Property rights were clear and transfers facilitated by maintenance of cadastral registers. An efficient legal system and sound banking favoured economic enterprise. Taxes were high but levied on expenditure rather than income. This encouraged savings, frugality and hard work. Thus the Dutch were a model of economic efficiency with obvious lessons for British policy.

In a similar vein, Gregory King (1696) made a comparative assessment of the resource mobilisation of England, France and the Netherlands in fighting the war of the League of Augsburg. For the nine year conflict, William III, the Dutch stadholder who had become King of England, organised a coalition of the United Kingdom, Netherlands, the German protestant states, Spain and Savoy against France, which had challenged the legitimacy of his succession to the English throne and annoyed its neighbours by trying to expand its frontiers. King estimated French and English per capita fiscal revenues in 1695 to be similar, but in the Netherlands the level was more than two and a half times as large.

The cost of maintaining Dutch independence was high, involving the creation of a chain of fortresses in the South and on the East (where the country was vulnerable from attack via catholic states in Germany — particularly the bishopric of Munster). Its army and naval expenditures were costly. It had to build up an armaments industry. It was involved in a series of wars in which England and France became the main enemies in the seventeenth and eighteenth centuries. Towards the end of the seventeenth century Dutch economic expansion faltered. The Netherlands became the victim rather than the beneficiary of the beggar–your–neighbour policies of the merchant capitalist era. British and French shipping, trade and industry grew much faster than those of the Netherlands. Both countries adopted protectionist policies which damaged Dutch interests. The most important were the British Navigation Acts and similar French provisions. From 1651 onwards Dutch shipping and Dutch ship exports had restricted access to the ports of the United Kingdom and were barred from trade with English and French colonies. When these countries waged war with the Netherlands they did so with the concentrated energy of modern nation states — very different from the way Spain had dissipated its energy.

Table 2–18a. **Dutch Involvement in European Military Conflicts, 1560s–1815**

Wars with Spain to establish and guarantee Independence	Wars of commercial interest with England	Wars over European balance of power, territory & religion
1560s–1609	1652–4	1618–48: 30 Years War
1621–48	1665–7	1688–97: War of League of Augsburg
	1672–4	1701–13: War of Spanish Succession
	1780–3	1756–63: Seven Years War
		1795–1815: Revolutionary & Napoleonic Wars

Source: Israel (1989 and 1995).

Table 2–18b. **Size of European Armies, 1470–1814**
(000)

	France	Spain	Netherlands	United Kingdom	Sweden	Russia
1470s	40	20	0	25	n.a	n.a.
1550s	50	150	0	20	n.a.	n.a.
1590s	80	200	20	30	15	n.a.
1630s	150	300	50	n.a.	45	35
1650s	100	100	29	70	70	n.a.
1670s	120	70	110	15	63	130
1700s	400	50	100	87	100	170
1812–14	600			250		500

Source: 1470s–1700s from Parker (1979), p. 96, except 1650 in the Netherlands which is from Israel (1995), p. 602, and the United Kingdom in 1670s from Brewer (1989), p. 8. 1812–14 from Kennedy (1987), p. 99.

Table 2–19. **Dutch Commodity Trade, 1650s to 1770s**
(million current guilders)

	1650s	1720s	1770s
Imports			
European Sources	125	84	105 [a]
Other	15	24	38
Total	140	108	143
Exports and Re–exports[b]			
European Destinations	115	83	92
Other	5	7	8
Total	120	90	100
Of which Re–exports	60	48	69

a) includes colonial products re–exported by Britain (5 million) and France (20 million); b) excludes exports of slaves and ships, earnings from shipping and insurance services, and earnings on foreign loans.

Source: De Vries and van der Woude (1997), p. 498.

http://dx.doi.org/10.1787/723137538677

The main reason for loss of dynamism in the eighteenth century was the destruction of monopolistic trading privileges in conflicts with France and the United Kingdom, which pushed the Dutch to the sidelines.

Population growth slackened as the economy ceased to attract migrants. There was stagnation in the industrialised western Netherlands and substantial growth in the agricultural province of Overijssel. Agricultural output increased, with a fall in imports and a growth in agricultural exports. There was a decline in production and exports of textiles (particularly the Leiden woollen industry), fisheries and shipbuilding. The volume of foreign trade dropped 20 per cent from 1720 to 1820. During this period UK exports rose more than sevenfold in volume, and French by two and threequarters.

Dutch service industries continued to play an important part in the economy, and there was a large increase in overseas investment. In 1790 total foreign investment probably amounted to 800 million guilders at a time when national income was around 440 million. If the rate of return on foreign investment was around 4 per cent, then foreign income would have been around 30 million guilders, giving a national income about 8 per cent higher than domestic product. The combination of rising rentier incomes, together with pauperism and unemployment in the old industrial areas, increased inequality.

Dutch Economic Activity Outside Europe

a) Africa

Dutch objectives in Africa were to get access to the gold of the Guinea coast, enter the slave trade to the Americas, and acquire a base for ventures in Asia.

They succeeded in capturing Elmina in 1637 and several other Portuguese bases in West Africa for trade in gold and slaves. For a time they captured a foothold in Angola (the main slave base for the Portuguese) but failed to keep it. They also failed to take Mozambique (in East Africa). They established a new base at the Cape in South Africa, introducing European settlers to provide a staging and supply post for their voyages to Asia.

The major economic gain came from participation in the slave trade. Slaves were shipped to Northeastern Brazil and to Surinam for Dutch sugar plantations, and to Curaçao for sale to British and French sugar planters. However, the Dutch role in the trade was a good deal smaller than that of Portugal, England and France (see Table 2–5).

b) Americas

In the Americas, the first major venture was the capture of the sugar producing region of Northeast Brazil (around Recife) from 1630 to 1654. Sugar was transported to the Netherlands where there were 40 refineries by 1650.

The venture in Brazil had substantial military and naval support but the sugar plantations were run by private enterprise. Most were owned by sephardic jews from Amsterdam, many of Portuguese origin. During the period when Portugal was governed by Spain, the Dutch were reasonably well received in Brazil, but after Portugal regained its independence, they were expelled. Many plantation owners then moved to the Caribbean where they introduced the same production techniques and marketing patterns. Their arrival transformed the economy of Barbados which the British had occupied in 1627 and grew tobacco with white settlers. Within a short time the island had 30 000 slaves and was totally devoted to sugar (see Eltis, 1995, for a proxy assessment of the GDP of Barbados in 1644–1701). Emigrant plantation owners from Brazil had a similar impact in Guadeloupe and Martinique which had been French since 1635 (see Verlinden, 1972, p. 642–4). By the 1660s and 1670s, the British and French had driven out the Dutch, who moved their sugar activities to Surinam.

In the early seventeenth century, sugar production in the Americas had been concentrated on Brazil. But from mid–century, Brazilian production stagnated and a hugely expanded market was dominated by France and Britain. Dutch production in Surinam was on a much smaller scale (see Table 2–4).

Another Dutch venture in the Americas was the inadvertent discovery of a magnificent harbour and huge river by Henry Hudson. He was on a Dutch East India Company mission to try to discover a Northwest passage to Asia in 1609 and hopelessly off course. In 1614 the New Netherlands Company was founded to settle a colony with its capital at New Amsterdam in 1623. In 1664 it was taken over by the British, and in 1674 formally ceded (as New York) in exchange for a free hand for Dutch sugar interests in Surinam (de Vries and van de Woude, 1997, pp. 397 and 467).

c) Asia

The most successful area of Dutch involvement outside Europe was in Asia.

The Dutch were extremely well informed about Asian trading prospects, for many had worked on Portuguese ships. One of them, Jan Huygen van Linschoten, produced two travel journals in 1595 and 1596 with detailed maps, information on markets, winds and potential routes. In 1602, under official pressure, all Dutch merchants in this trade were compelled to join the United East India Company (VOC) which was given monopoly trading rights and authority to establish military outposts and negotiate with foreign rulers. The Company owned and built all its own ships. The comparative volume of Dutch trading activity in Asia can be seen in Table 2–6. In the seventeenth century they sent out nearly five times as many ships as the Portuguese, and in the eighteenth, 15 times as many. The average size of their ships was smaller than the Portuguese who were then using huge carracks of 1 000 tons, against 600 tons for the average Dutch ship. The English East India Company (EIC) was a more important competitor than the Portuguese. They entered the Asian trade at the same time as the Dutch. Their main bases were at two towns they created in India (Madras 1639, and Calcutta in the 1690s) and Bombay which was a wedding gift from Portugal to Charles II in 1661. EIC operations in the seventeenth century were about half the size of those of the VOC, and about two thirds in the eighteenth. The French entered the Asian trade with the *Compagnie des Indes Orientales* which Colbert created in 1664. They established a base at Pondicherry (on the Coromandel coast) in 1673. By the eighteenth century, a new French company, created in 1719, had become a very significant presence. Later participants were Danish and Swedish companies, and from 1715–32, the Ostend company operating from the new port which the Austrian administration had created in the Southern Netherlands.

The total volume of European shipping in Asia in the eighteenth century was about nine times as big as it had been in the sixteenth, but the scope for traditional exports of pepper and spices was limited. This meant that the Dutch, who were more heavily involved in this trade than the English and French and other newcomers, had to be careful to control supply in order to maintain prices. The opportunities for new exports to Europe — a wide variety of cotton textiles, coffee and tea — were much more promising and their share of the trade rose rapidly, for all of the participants in the market (see Table 2–20).

Table 2–20. **Commodity Composition of European Exports from Asia to Europe, 1513–1780**

Portugal (Estado da India — state trading, headquarters Goa)
(per cent by weight)

	1513–19	*1608–10*
Pepper	80.0	69.0
Moluccan Spices	9.0	0.03
Other Spices	9.4	10.9
Textiles	0.2	7.8
Indigo	0.0	7.7
Other	1.4	4.6

Dutch East India Company (VOC corporate monopoly, headquarters Batavia)
(per cent by value)

	1619–21	*1778–80*
Pepper	56.4	11.0
Other Spices	17.6	24.4
Textiles & Raw Silk	16.1	32.7
Coffee & Tea	0.0	22.9
Other	9.9	9.0

English East India Company (EIC corporate monopoly operating
mainly from Bombay, Calcutta and Madras)
(per cent by value)

	1668–70	*1758–60*
Pepper	25.3	4.4
Textiles	56.6	53.5
Raw Silk	0.6	12.3
Tea	0.03	25.3
Other	17.5	4.5

Source: Prakash (1998), pp. 36, 115 and 120.

http://dx.doi.org/10.1787/723137538677

The initial thrust of the VOC was to bypass the Portuguese, using a new route via the Cape and sailing direct to Indonesia. This brought them directly to the Moluccan islands where the most valuable spices (cloves, nutmeg and mace) could be found. They were also able to get pepper in Indonesia, rather than India. The indigenous rulers in the Indonesian islands were much weaker than those in India, Persia, China and Japan, and more susceptible to Dutch pressure to enforce monopoly rights and low prices. The VOC established its headquarters in 1621 on the Javanese coast at Batavia (present–day Jakarta). They drove the Portuguese out of Ternate in 1603, and destroyed their base at Malacca in 1641. They also expelled the muslim merchants who had previously traded on the Javanese coast.

The population of the spice islands revolted in 1621. They were all killed or deported and replaced by Dutch planters working with slave labour.

In order to help finance its Indonesian operations, the VOC established a base at Masulipatnam on the East (Coromandel) coast of India. Here it obtained the agreement of the King of Golconda, who granted preferential trading conditions. The company's main interest was in cotton textiles, in particular painted chintz, which were in demand in Indonesia. Later the VOC moved further down the coast and shifted their base to Negapatam in 1690 where textiles were cheaper.

In 1617, the VOC obtained permission from the Moghul empire to establish a base in Surat in Gujarat in Northwest India, dislodging Portuguese operations in this area. Here they could exchange pepper and spices for coarse cotton textiles for use as a barter item in the African slave trade.

Later in the seventeenth century, the VOC tried to drive the Portuguese from their bases in Goa and Ceylon. It blockaded but did not capture Goa, but took Jaffna in Ceylon, replaced the Portuguese in the cinnamon trade and as rulers of the island. Portuguese trading on the Malabar coast was harassed, but that area did not have substantial commercial interest for the Dutch.

There was an early move to establish trading links with China and Japan which had been so lucrative for Portugal. Unlike the Portuguese, The Dutch felt no vocation for religious evangelism, and were the only Europeans allowed to trade in Japan between 1639 and 1853. From 1641 they were confined to a very small island (Deshima) in the harbour of Nagasaki. The profitability of this trade faded after a few decades because of a Japanese ban on export of precious metals and Japanese insistence on fixing the prices at which the Dutch could sell their goods. In this trade there was no question of Dutch exploitation. In fact they were used as a conduit by Japanese eager to know about Western technology (see Appendix B).

The VOC did not succeed in dislodging the Portuguese from Macao. In the 1620s they got a base in the Pescadores and from 1624 were allowed to shift to Taiwan. In 1662 they were forced to leave and never acquired another Chinese base. From the 1640s to 1660s the Ming dynasty was in a state of collapse. The great porcelain and pottery town of Ching-te-Chen was devastated and Chinese porcelain exports were interrupted until the 1680s. This encouraged the Dutch to develop their own pottery industry in Delft to produce cheap copies of Chinese blue-and-white ware. At the same time, the Japanese developed their own pottery and porcelain industry to substitute for Chinese imports, and the Dutch also copied Japanese copies of Chinese pottery. European production of porcelain in Sèvres and Meissen started later.

The VOC operated from the 1630s in Bengal because of its rich variety of high quality textiles (cotton and silk). Here they stepped in the shoes of the Portuguese who had been expelled from Hugli by the Moghul authorities in 1632.

At first the VOC concentrated on exporting Bengali raw silk and mixed cotton-silk textiles to Japan, and opium to Indonesia. In exchange they sold Japanese copper, silver and gold in Bengal. The Japanese market declined considerably after 1680, but European demand for Bengali textiles rose very rapidly. Between 1680 and 1740, textiles from Bengal were the largest component of VOC exports to the Netherlands (see Prakash, 1998, pp. 198 and 218). Fine cottons, muslins, silks and mixed piece goods appealed to new European tastes and rising incomes, though it was more difficult to know what the market might be for these fashion items than for raw silk or opium.

Bengali textiles were also of major interest to the British and French companies from the last quarter of the seventeenth century, and their textile exports were even bigger than those of the Dutch. However, both the French (1686) and the British (1700) forbade import of printed and painted cottons in order to protect their domestic textile producers. Both countries continued to import these goods for re-export (though a large part of these were smuggled back into England). The Dutch did not protect their own textile industry, and ended up marketing a large part of French and somewhat less of the British re-exports of Indian textiles within Europe (see Table 2–19). The British greatly increased imports of white bleached cloth from Bengal for processing in England (see Rothermund, 1999).

Towards the second half of the seventeenth century, European demand for coffee grew very fast. The first London café was opened in 1652. The beverage became popular in France in the 1660s and in the Netherlands in the 1670s. The VOC began buying coffee in Mokka in Yemen at the beginning of the eighteenth century, rising from 300 tons in 1711 to 875 tons in 1720. Shrubs were taken for planting in Java and by the late 1720s, Javanese production was about 2 000 tons a year. The VOC imposed cultivation quotas on petty Javanese rulers who compelled their subjects to raise coffee. From the 1730s there was competition from Surinam where output and exports rose much faster (see Bulbeck and Associates, 1998).

A few years later there was a great surge in European demand for tea, particularly in England and the Netherlands. The Chinese had opened Canton to foreign traders in 1685. British tea imports rose from about 100 kilos in 1669 to 28 000 tons in 1760 (see Chaudhuri, 1978, p. 539). The Dutch bought most of their tea from Chinese junks trading to Batavia, though there was a direct shipment from Canton to Amsterdam in 1729. The English company were able to finance their tea purchases in Canton by selling Bengali opium and raw cotton, but the Dutch were obliged to pay in bullion (see Glamann, 1981, pp. 212–43).

The new European taste for coffee and tea was complementary to the rise of sugar consumption. Growth of these items displaced a significant part of demand for beer and gin, both in England and the Netherlands.

In the second half of the eighteenth century, the VOC ceased to be a profitable organisation. It collapsed in bankruptcy in 1795, after several decades of distributing dividends bigger than its profits.

One of the causes was the disintegration of the Moghul Empire in India and the British takeover of the governance of Bengal in 1757. After that, discrimination against Dutch operations weakened the VOC considerably. Anglo–Dutch hostilities in 1781–84 (when the two countries took opposite sides in the American War of Independence) had serious repercussions in Asia. The outbreak of the Napoleonic wars led to a complete British takeover of Dutch interests in India, Malacca, Ceylon, South Africa and temporarily in Indonesia. It also ended any significant French connection with India.

Contributory factors to the profit decline were the very high overheads for the company in hiring military and naval personnel to run what had become a territorial empire in Java and Ceylon. The officers of the VOC were not well paid and conducted an increasingly large private trade in the company's ships. There was also a good deal of corruption in the administration of Java and Ceylon, which benefited the servants but not the shareholders of the company. Given the changing commodity structure of trade and the locus of operations, Batavia was no longer an ideal headquarters.

After 1815, Indonesia became a colony of the new Dutch kingdom. There was intensive development of tropical crop production for export. During the wartime period of British rule, there had been a policy of westernisation of the administration, property rights and land taxation. The Diponegoro revolt of 1825–30 ended this approach. Thereafter the Dutch stuck consistently to a policy of dual administration, retaining traditional rulers, law and custom as a major instrument of their rule. They also kept their trading monopoly, as most of the profits would have gone to powerful British and American traders under an open–trade regime.

In the 1830s the so–called "Cultivation System" was introduced. The Netherlands exercised its claims on indigenous income by increasing its demand for tribute — forced deliveries of crops or labour services in lieu of land taxation. From 1816 to 1914 movement and residence of the indigenous and Chinese populations were controlled by a system of pass–laws designed to maintain labour discipline and enforce ethnic *apartheid*.

From the 1830s, the Dutch were remarkably successful in raising the income flow from Indonesia. In the 1830–70 period, half of it went directly to the Dutch government as fiscal tribute from the cultivation system. In addition there was monopoly income from transport of export crops by the NHM shipping company owned by the Dutch King, and income from sales of monopoly franchises to dealers in opium. The government dominated production of sugar and coffee, but most of the tobacco crop was in private hands. Favoured individuals were subsidised to create sugar processing factories. There were ample opportunities for corruption in the Dutch administration, amongst the 76 local Regents and heads of the 34 000 villages of Java. In 1844 Indonesia was allocated a fictitious debt of 236 million guilders to cover the costs of liquidating the VOC's debts and those incurred in suppressing the 1825–30 revolt.

Table 2–21a. The Dutch "Drain" on Indonesia, 1698–1930

	Indonesian export surplus as per cent of Indonesian net domestic product	Indonesian export surplus as per cent of Dutch net domestic product
1698–1700	0.7	1.1
1778–80	0.9	1.7
1868–72	7.4	5.5
1911–15	7.6	8.7
1926–30	10.3	8.9

Source: Maddison (1989*b*), pp. 646–7. See van der Eng (1998) for a comment on these estimates.

Table 2–21b. The British "Drain" on India, 1868–1930

	Indian export surplus as per cent of Indian net domestic product	Indian export surplus as per cent of British net domestic product
1868–72	1.0	1.3
1911–15	1.3	1.2
1926–30	0.9	0.9

Source: Maddison (1989*b*), pp. 647–8 with revision of Indian/British income ratio. The "drain" (i.e. the colonial burden as measured by the trade surplus of the colony) figures prominently in the literature of Indian nationalism, beginning with Naoroji in the 1870s (see Naoroji (1901). I applied the same concept to Indonesia to compare the colonial burden in the two countries as a share of their own national income, and the colonialist's gain as a share of their respective national incomes. See also the discussion in Maddison (1971), pp. 63–6.

Table 2–21c. Growth of Indonesian Population and Real Income by Ethnic Group, 1700–1929
(population in 000, per capita income in 1928 guilders)

	Indonesians		Chinese & other foreign Asiatics		Europeans[a]	
	Population	Per capita income	Population	Per capita income	Population	Per capita income
1700	13 015	47	80	156	7.5	1 245
1820	17 829	49	90	193	8.3	2 339
1870	28 594	50	279	187	49.0	2 163
1913	49 066	64	739	240	129.0	3 389
1929	58 297	78	1 334	301	232.0	4 017

a) Includes Eurasians.

Source: Maddison (1989*b*), p. 665, with revised estimates of Indonesian population and income.

http://dx.doi.org/10.1787/723137538677

Export prices for sugar and coffee rose after the abolition of the African slave trade in the 1830s. This ruined competitors in the Caribbean and raised costs in Brazil.

From 1848, when the Netherlands acquired a more democratic political system, there was growing criticism of exploitative practices and bureaucratic cronyism in Indonesia. These pressures, plus the opening of the Suez Canal and the development of steam shipping, led the Dutch authorities to open the colony to private enterprise and investment. By the 1890s the government share of exports had dropped to zero.

Table 2–21a provides a crude measure of the burden of colonial rule and the colonialist gain for the Netherlands for the period 1700 to 1930. The volume of exports grew very much faster after the demise of the VOC, and became a much greater share of Indonesian GDP. The proportionate gains to the Netherlands also rose greatly. Table 2–21b provides similar estimates for India, where the colonial burden and gain were relatively much smaller.

Table 2–21c provides a crude estimate of population and income levels by ethnic group in Indonesia from 1700 to 1929.

IX
BRITAIN

In considering British economic performance, it is useful to distinguish between Ireland and the rest of the kingdom. Wales was incorporated politically in 1301. The incorporation of Scotland did not take place until 1707, but the ground was prepared by the advent of a Scottish king to the English throne in 1603. Ireland was subject to a brutal conquest in the 1650s. Petty's *Anatomy of Ireland* (1691) suggested that the population fell by a quarter because of war deaths, famine, plague and deportations. The war was followed by a massive confiscation of property and social restructuring. Two thirds of the land fit for agriculture was transferred from Irish to English landlords.

Ireland had a per capita income half of that in the rest of the United Kingdom from 1700 to the 1850s (see Table B–13) and a very different demographic history. As a result of the famine of 1846–51 and massive emigration thereafter, Ireland's population fell by half between 1840 and 1913. It therefore seems legitimate to treat Ireland as a British colony, as I have done in Table 2–22.

Between the Norman conquest of 1066 and 1950 there were several major phases of British economic and political development and overseas involvement.

The Norman–Angevin Regime, 1066–1485

Between the years 1000 and 1500, British population growth was somewhat slower than the West European average, and in all probability this was also true of per capita income. The income level in 1500 (see Tables B–21 and 2–22) was well below that in Italy, Flanders and Brabant which were the European leaders at that time.

From the eleventh to the mid–fifteenth century, British national identity was ambiguous. The monarchy and the ruling elite were Anglo–French warlords whose property rights and income derived initially from territorial conquests in England and France. The resources which the state could mobilise came from tribute received from feudal vassals and their servile peasantry. A fairly submissive church buttressed its political legitimacy and acted as an instrument of social control. William the Conqueror installed his friend Lanfranc as Archbishop of Canterbury, and Norman clergy to fill the other bishoprics. In 1170, when Henry II had problems with Archbishop Becket, he had him murdered. The main investments of the regime were fortified castles (such as those in Carnarvon and Harlech to consolidate the Welsh conquest) or imposing cathedrals and abbeys (such as the the Abbaye des Hommes — the tomb of the conqueror — and the Abbaye des Dames — the tomb of his wife — in Caen).

The acquisition of land and loot in France was pursued by war and matrimony. British possessions were biggest in the second half of the twelfth century after Henry II married Eleonor of Aquitaine, the divorced wife of the French King Louis VII. At that time, half of France was British. There were British victories at Crecy in 1346, Poitiers 1356, and Agincourt in 1415. With Burgundian help the British captured and killed Joan of Arc in 1430. Thereafter the Burgundians changed sides, and at the end of the Hundred Years war in 1453, all that was left was Calais, which the French recuperated in 1558.

There was some economic and political advance in this period. There was an extension of cultivated area by clearing of forests, and increases in land productivity because of changes in agricultural technology of the same kind as those elsewhere in Northern Europe (see White, 1962). There was a big expansion in wool production for export to Flanders, increasingly replaced from the second half of the fourteenth century by export of woollen cloth. However, a good deal of overseas trade was handled by foreign merchants and there was heavy dependence on Antwerp for banking and financial services. The level of urbanisation in 1500 was well below the West European average (see Table B–14). In England and Wales only 3 per cent of the population lived in towns of 10 000 and over compared with 21 per cent in Flanders and Brabant, 16 per cent in the Netherlands and 15 per cent in Italy.

The financial difficulties of the crown provoked a modicum of countervailing power in an emerging parliamentary process. There was some movement away from feudal property rights towards market forces in agriculture which was given a major push by the Black Death when plague reduced the population by a third, increased per capita land availability, and provoked claims for higher labour income.

An important step was taken in the fourteenth century to establish English as the dominant language. Until then French had been used in all legal proceedings, which had a distinctly discriminatory impact on property rights. The situation was changed by the 1362 Statute of Pleading, which stated that "the French tongue is much unknown in the realm, so that the people who do implead, or be impleaded, in the king's court, or in the courts of others, have no knowledge or understanding of that which is said for them or against them" (Baugh and Cable, 1993, p. 145).

Table 2–22a. **Levels of GDP Per Capita in European Colonial Powers and Former Colonies, 1500–1998**
(1990 international dollars)

	1500	*1700*	*1820*	*1913*	*1950*	*1998*
Britain[a]	762	1 405	2 121	5 150	6 907	18 714
France	727	986	1 230	3 485	5 270	19 558
Italy	1 100	1 100	1 117	2 564	3 502	17 759
Netherlands	754	2 110	1 821	4 049	5 996	20 224
Portugal	632	854	963	1 244	2 069	12 929
Spain	698	900	1 063	2 255	2 397	14 227
China	600	600	600	552	439	3 117
India	550	550	533	673	619	1 746
Indonesia	565	580	612	904	840	3 070
Brazil	400	460	646	811	1 672	5 459
Mexico	425	568	759	1 732	2 365	6 655
United States	400	527	1257	5 301	9 561	27 331
Ireland[b]	526	715	880	2 736	3 446	18 183

Table 2–22b. **Growth of Per Capita GDP in European Colonial Powers and Former Colonies, 1500–1998**
(annual average compound growth rates)

	1500–1700	*1700–1820*	*1820–1913*	*1913–50*	*1950–98*
Britain[a]	0.31	0.34	0.96	0.80	2.10
France	0.15	0.18	1.13	1.12	2.77
Italy	0.00	0.01	0.90	0.85	3.44
Netherlands	0.52	–0.12	0.86	1.07	2.56
Portugal	0.15	0.10	0.27	1.38	3.89
Spain	0.13	0.14	0.81	0.17	3.78
China	0.00	0.00	–0.08	–0.62	4.17
India	0.00	–0.03	0.25	–0.23	2.18
Indonesia	0.01	0.04	0.42	–0.20	2.74
Brazil	0.07	0.28	0.24	1.97	2.50
Mexico	0.15	0.24	0.89	0.85	2.18
United States	0.14	0.73	1.56	1.61	2.21
Ireland[b]	0.15	0.17	1.23	0.63	3.53

a) Refers to England, Scotland and Wales for 1500–1913. Northern Ireland is included for 1950 and 1998;
b) refers to all Ireland for 1500–1913, Irish Republic for 1950 and 1998.

Source: Appendices A and B.

http://dx.doi.org/10.1787/723137538677

Creation of a Modern Nation State and Institutions Favourable to Merchant Capitalism, 1485–1700

From the end of the fifteenth to the end of the seventeenth century, British population rose about fourfold, compared with a doubling in the Netherlands, a rise of less than half in France, and about a quarter in Germany and Italy. There was an increase in life expectation (see Table 1–4), to a level substantially higher than in France. The agricultural share of the labour force dropped considerably (in 1700 it was 56 per cent). Apart from the rise in farm productivity, the reliability of the food supply had been increased (see Wrigley, 1988). This, together with the efficacy of coastal shipping in mitigating local food shortages had more or less eliminated famine–related mortality in England and Wales, at a time when it was still significant in France[30]. The urbanisation ratio rose more than fourfold (Table B–14) and London's population 14–fold (it had become the biggest city in Europe, see Table 2–3).

Per capita income in Britain almost doubled from 1500 to 1700, compared with a rise of a third in France and Germany and stagnation in Italy (see Table B–21). The only country where income grew faster and achieved a higher level by 1700 was the Netherlands. Dutch income performance was better because of higher productivity in agriculture, shipping, banking and commercial services, and a bigger degree of international specialisation. Its shipping fleet was bigger than that of Britain though it had less than a quarter of the population. Only 40 per cent of its labour force was in agriculture.

British economists and diplomats of the seventeenth century (Petty, King, Davenant and Temple) regarded the Netherlands as the economic model to be emulated. To a large extent British economic institutions moved in a Dutch direction — a process which was consolidated in 1688 by the installation of a king who was also the Dutch Stadholder.

There were several stages in the creation of a modern nation state which favoured the interests of merchant capitalism. The old feudal fragmentation of power and resources was replaced by a much more centralised system. Henry VII, a Welshman who emerged as victor in the civil war in 1485, confiscated the estates of many of the feudal aristocracy in favour of the ascendant gentry. He eliminated the right of the nobility to keep armed retainers. Thereafter their country houses were no longer fortified. His son, Henry VIII, broke with the Papacy, created a national church which practised a lukewarm version of protestantism, abolished the monastic orders and seized their property (including about a quarter of English land). His daughter Elizabeth dilapidated the property of the bishops. The great bulk of these ecclesiastical assets fell into the hands of a secular elite of merchants and gentry, through royal sales and largesse.

In the seventeenth century, there were major changes in the British mode of governance (which involved the temporary establishment of a republic and abolition of the House of Lords). It ended with a monarchy dependent for its finance on a House of Commons controlled by a secular elite of landlords and merchants.

In the field of economic policy there was a modernisation of the administration at the end of the seventeenth century. Professional competence was increasingly relevant in public appointments, and improved statistics were becoming a significant guide to policy. Patronage was still important, but political cronyism was replacing nepotism.

The farmers of the hearth tax were obliged to show full accounts from 1679. Tax farming of customs duties was abolished in 1671 and an Inspector General of exports and imports was created in 1696. Tax farming of the excise was abolished in 1683, and the economist Davenant was appointed as the Commissioner. The Board of Trade was created in 1696, with John Locke, the philosopher, as one of the Commissioners. Samuel Pepys carried out a similar modernisation of the naval administration. In 1702, Gregory King, the economist, became Commissioner of Public Accounts. All of these new administrative posts were highly paid to ensure that the occupants were not corruptible. The Bank of England was created in 1694, and a major recoinage took place in 1696. Monetary policy was modernised and a properly managed market for public debt was emerging.

As a result, the British were able to develop a robust system of public finance in the eighteenth century in stark contrast to the weaknesses of the French regime. The government remained solvent with a large part of public debt in the form of perpetual annuities. There were no exemptions for privileged groups, no tax farmers, no sales of public office, no autonomous tax jurisdictions. The political legitimacy of taxes was guaranteed by parliamentary control and the number of public officials per head of population was a fraction of that in France[31].

Intellectual life was very vigorous and increasingly secular in the seventeenth century and there was close interaction with similar developments in Northern Europe. An organisational basis was created in Gresham College by the generous endowment in 1579 of Sir Thomas Gresham, an extremely wealthy banker and royal fiscal agent. The College provided open access to higher education in the form of daily lectures on different topics. It was particularly successful with applied mathematics and practical research into navigational instruments and shipbuilding. In the 1640s and 1650s it became a centre for intensive discussion of new results in experimental science, and was the precursor of the Royal Society which was founded in 1662 on its premises. The leading activists of the Society were Christopher Wren (professor of astronomy at Gresham and Oxford, and the architect who rebuilt London's churches after the great fire); John Wilkins, mathematician and Warden of Wadham College; Robert Boyle, the chemist and anatomist; and William Petty, a former professor of anatomy in Oxford, creator of political economy, director of the cadastral survey of Ireland, and inventor of a double–bottomed ship (like a catamaran), speedier forms of land carriage, schemes for improving the postal service, water pumps and sweetening sea water. In this century of enlightenment, many distinguished intellectuals, e.g. Bacon, Hobbes, Locke and Newton, were involved in practical matters of public policy (Newton was Warden and later Master of the Mint from 1695 to his death). In many cases, their work had an important impact on technology.

The restoration monarchy was interested in promoting research into practical and theoretical work on navigation, created the Royal Observatory and the post of Astronomer Royal. Edmund Halley, mathematician and astronomer, started his fruitful career at the age of 20, laying the foundations of stellar astronomy in the Southern hemisphere in two years of observation in St. Helena, and ended as Astronomer Royal. In 1693, he produced a fundamental paper on the mathematics of life expectation, using mortality data for Breslau supplied by Leibnitz. This laid the scientific foundation for life insurance.

These scientific investigations in England had their counterpart in the Netherlands and to a significant extent in France, but were in sharp contrast with the situation in Spain where religious bigotry and the Inquisition inhibited intellectual curiosity. In Italy too, the counter–reformation harassed Galileo and weakened the creativity of a country which had shown such brilliance in earlier centuries.

In terms of overseas commitments and foreign policy, there were major changes from the 1550s to 1700. The idea of European conquest was abandoned, and the strategic advantages of being an island were intelligently exploited. The British merchant fleet was greatly expanded. Naval forces were developed in the reign of Elizabeth which were adequate to beat off a Spanish attempt at invasion, and by 1700 had considerable offensive power. Gregory King estimated that in 1697 the merchant fleet comprised more than 2 000 vessels with a tonnage of 323 000 tons, and the navy had 189 vessels with a tonnage of 120 000[32]. This was bigger than any other power at that time (except the Netherlands, see Table 2–15).

There was a relatively small British commitment to land forces (see Table 2–18b). From 1688 to 1815 Britain was involved in many wars with continental countries, but most of the burden of land warfare was borne by Britain's allies. This division of effort was ensured by opportunistic diplomacy, subsidies, and the convenient persistence of enmities between major continental countries for dynastic, territorial or religious reasons.

From the sixteenth to the nineteenth century, commercial policy was dominated by mercantilist assumptions. In England and in continental Europe, it was taken for granted that international competition was a beggar–your–neighbour proposition. A major reason for this was that economic advance before the nineteenth century was based on what seems in retrospect to have been a quite slow pace of advance in technology, with rates of domestic investment which by present standards were low. In England in 1688, Gregory King's estimates suggest that the British investment rate was less than 7 per cent of GDP. The most promising opportunities for raising income were perceived to come from the increased specialisation and division of labour which the Dutch had achieved, or from exploiting new opportunities in the Americas, in the slave trade from Africa, and in imports of spices, textiles and porcelain from Asia. At the levels of income the Dutch and British had achieved there were funds available to finance these overseas ventures and corporate know–how to use them properly. Navigation and shipping technology permitted ventures which could be profitable even when the return voyage might last as much as two years in journeys to East Asia.

Table 2–23. **Structure of British Commodity Trade by Origin and Destination, 1710–1996**
(per cent of total current value)

	Europe	Asia	Africa	North America	British West Indies	Other America	Australia & New Zealand
				Imports			
1710[a]	63.6	6.9	0.4	7.3	21.7	0.1	0.0
1774	46.1	11.4	0.4	12.5	29.3	0.3	0.0
1820	26.8	24.6	0.5	14.6	26.0	7.5	0.0
1913	40.7[b]	15.7	3.0	22.6	0.8[c]	9.6	7.6
1950	27.8[b]	17.2	11.0	15.9	5.1[c]	8.6	14.4
1996	61.7	18.8	2.2	14.1	0.3[c]	1.7	1.2
				Exports and Re–exports			
1710[a]	87.6	2.1	1.2	5.1	3.4	0.6	0.0
1774	58.5	3.9	6.0	21.5	10.0	0.1	0.0
1820	61.8	7.1	1.1	11.7	9.0	9.3	0.0
1913	37.4[b]	22.7	6.4	13.5	1.0[c]	8.7	10.3
1950	28.8[b]	18.9	13.2	14.4	1.7[c]	7.2	15.8
1996	63.3	16.8	3.0	13.3	0.3[c]	1.5	1.8

a) England and Wales; b) includes North Africa; c) includes all Caribbean.

Source: Mitchell and Deane (1962), pp. 309–11 (for 1710–1820); pp. 317–23 (for 1913). Mitchell and Jones (1971) pp. 136–9 (for 1950). *UN Yearbook of International Trade Statistics* (1996), p. 1065 for 1996. From Mitchell and Deane (1962), pp. 2679–84, it appears that reexports were 58 per cent of domestic exports (i.e. 37 per cent of total exports) in the 1720s and 1770s. This compares with 53 per cent and 220 per cent in the Netherlands for these two periods (see Table 2–19 above). In 1913, British reexports were 20.8 per cent of domestic exports, and in 1950, 3.9 per cent. In 1710, woollen and worsted yarn and manufactures were 78 per cent of domestic exports; in 1774, 49 per cent; in 1820, 12 per cent; and in 1913, 6 per cent. Cotton yarn and manufactures were 2 per cent of domestic exports in 1774; 62 per cent in 1820; 24 per cent in 1913; and 11 per cent in 1938.

http://dx.doi.org/10.1787/723137538677

Another attraction of such commerce was that it involved new products. In the sixteenth century sugar was virtually unknown as an item of popular consumption. By 1700, consumption was 2.6 kilos per head of population in England and Wales. For tobacco it had risen from zero to about 1 kilo. Tea and coffee had begun to make an appearance[33]. Printed and painted cotton textiles from India had brought major changes in taste and fashion. Porcelain and pottery from China had a similar impact on domestic utensils. The elasticity of demand for these new consumer goods was high, and this category of goods was a very large proportion of personal consumption. Gregory King's estimates suggest that, in 1688, expenditure on food, drink and textiles in England and Wales was 58.5 per cent of gross domestic product (compared with about 16 per cent at the end of the 1990s).

There was an increasing frequency of wars to grab a bigger share of overseas opportunities. There were three Anglo–Dutch wars in the quarter century following 1652. They led to a significant constriction of Dutch trading opportunities in the Americas and Africa. There were also significant net additions to the British merchant fleet from capture of Dutch ships, particularly the Dutch "fluyts" which were designed for cheap mass production and reduced operating costs (through lower manning requirements) but were not armed[34].

Commercial policy reinforced the objective of these trade wars. There was a series of Navigation Acts, starting in 1651 and eventually repealed in 1849. These kept foreign ships from participation in trade with British colonies, and forced the colonies to route their exports through British ports. As a result, a pattern of trade developed which involved large imports of colonial goods for re–export. This pattern was also characteristic of Dutch and French trade (see Table 2–19 and the notes to Table 2–23). Table 2–23 shows clearly the switch in geographic orientation of British trade which had already started in the seventeenth century.

The British Advance to Hegemony, 1700–1820

Between 1700 and 1820, there was a marked acceleration in British population growth to a rate more than twice as fast as in the seventeenth century, when there were losses from civil war and plague. Growth was faster than in any other European country, and the urbanisation ratio rose substantially in all parts of the kingdom; again in sharp contrast to developments elsewhere in Europe (see Table B–14).

Per capita income growth was somewhat faster than in the seventeenth century, and more than twice as fast as the European average. By contrast, Dutch performance was disastrous. Its population growth decelerated sharply and per capita GDP fell. In 1700 British GDP (excluding Ireland) was twice as high as the Dutch. In 1820 it was seven times as big.

There were significant changes in British economic structure, with a substantial decline in the share of the labour force in agriculture, and a big rise in industry and services (see Table 2–24). In the Netherlands there was deindustrialisation, deurbanisation, and a rise in the share of the farm sector.

With the decline in domestic and overseas investment opportunities, Dutch savings were increasingly diverted to foreign investment, much of it in British public debt. Hence British growth was bolstered by Dutch finance (see Maddison, 1991a, pp. 34–5 and 45–6).

Between 1720 and 1820, the volume of British exports rose by 2 per cent a year, and Dutch fell at an annual rate of 0.2 per cent (see Maddison, 1982, p. 247). In 1700, the British share of world shipping capacity was little more than a fifth, the Dutch share more than a quarter. By 1820, the British share was over 40 per cent, and the Dutch little more than 2 per cent (see Tables 2–15 and 2–25a).

This was the period when the United Kingdom rose to world commercial hegemony by adroit use of a beggar–your–neighbour strategy. The Dutch decline was due in substantial part to British and French commercial policy and to the disastrous impact of war in 1795–1815.

From 1700–1820, Britain was involved in a series of major wars with different combinations of European powers (in 1700–13, 1739–48, 1756–63, 1793–1815) as well as the war of American independence (1776–83), which it fought alone against its colonies and their European allies (France, the Netherlands and Spain). British involvement in these conflicts was due in substantial degree to its pursuit of worldwide commercial supremacy. Britain made substantial gains in the peace treaties of 1713 and 1763. The latter eliminated the French from Canada and weakened the Spanish position in the Caribbean and Florida. The war of 1776–83 was a major defeat which involved the loss of the 13 British colonies in North America.

Table 2–24. **Structure of Employment in the Netherlands, the United Kingdom and the United States, 1700–1998**
(per cent of total employment)

		Netherlands	United Kingdom	United States
1700	Agriculture	40	56	n.a.
	Industry	33	22	n.a.
	Services	27	22	n.a.
1820	Agriculture	43[a]	37	70
	Industry	26[a]	33	15
	Services	31[a]	30	15
1890	Agriculture	36[b]	16	38
	Industry	32[b]	43	24
	Services	32[b]	41	38
1998	Agriculture	3	2	3
	Industry	22	26	23
	Services	75	72	74

a) 1807; b) 1889

Source: Maddison (1991a), p. 32 for 1700; Maddison (1995a), p. 253 for the United Kingdom and the United States 1820–90; Netherlands 1807 and 1889 from Smits, Horlings and van Zanden (2000), p. 19; 1998 from OECD, *Labour Force Statistics 1978–1998*. Agriculture includes forestry and fishing; industry includes mining, manufacturing, electricity, gas, water and construction; services is a residual including all other activity, private and governmental (including military).

Table 2–25a. **Carrying Capacity of British and World Shipping, 1470–1913**
(000 tons)

	Sail	Steam	Total carrying capacity in sail equivalent	Sail	Steam	Total carrying capacity in sail equivalent
	United Kingdom			World		
1470	n.a.	0	n.a.	320	0	320
1570	51	0	51	730	0	730
1670	260	0	260	1 450	0	1 450
1780	1 000	0	1 000	3 950	0	3 950
1820	2 436	3	2 448	5 800	20	5 880
1850	3 397	168	4 069	11 400	800	14 600
1900	2 096	7 208	30 928	6 500	22 400	96 100
1913	843	11 273	45 935	4 200	41 700	171 000

Source: UK 1470–1780 from Table 2–15, 1820–1913 from Mitchell and Deane (1962), pp. 217–9. World 1470–1780 from Table 2–15 with upward adjustments for the years 1470, 1570 and 1670 for incomplete coverage of European fleets. The adjustment coefficient for 1470 was 1.85, 1.34 for 1570, and 1.07 for 1670. I also added 100 000 tons as a rough estimate for the ships of Asian countries for 1470–1780. 1800–1913 from Maddison (1989a), p. 145. The equivalence coefficient, 1 steam — 4 sail, from Day (1921), p. 290, allows for the greater speed and regularity of steam ships.

Table 2–25b. **Comparative Rates of Growth of British and World Shipping Capacity and GDP, 1570–1913**
(annual average compound growth rate)

	UK shipping	British GDP	World shipping	World GDP
1570–1820	1.56	0.79	0.84	0.33
1820–1913	3.20	2.13	3.69	1.47

Source: Shipping capacity from Table 2–25a, GDP from Appendix B, Tables B–13 and B–18.

http://dx.doi.org/10.1787/723137538677

The revolutionary and Napoleonic wars were much less costly in real terms to Britain than to France, the Netherlands, Spain and other continental countries. The Napoleonic campaigns ranged from Moscow to Egypt, Northern Germany to Spain. On the French side more than half a million soldiers were killed, and at least as many in other countries. French troops were financed in substantial degree by levies or billeting soldiers at the cost of occupied territories. And there were swathes of devastation in Germany, Russia and Spain (see Kennedy, 1987, p. 115–39 on the costs of war). The war also involved commercial blockades which retarded industrial development on the continent (as analysed in Crouzet, 1964).

There were huge setbacks to the overseas commercial and colonial interests of the continental powers. The Dutch lost all their Asian territories except Indonesia, and their base in South Africa. The French were reduced to a token colonial presence in Asia, and lost Saint–Domingue, their major asset in the Caribbean. Shortly after the war, Brazil established its independence from Portugal. Spain lost its huge colonial empire in Latin America, retaining only Cuba, Puerto Rico and the Philippines.

Britain took over what the French and Dutch had lost in Asia and Africa, extended its control over India, and established a privileged commercial presence in Latin America.

In 1750, the British Empire included about one and half million people in the Americas (see Table 2–28), about 2.4 million in Ireland, and bases in Calcutta, Madras and Bombay. By 1820, although it had lost its 13 North American colonies, Britain had gained control of Indian territories with a population of about 100 million.

British growth was reinforced from 1700 to 1820 by successful pursuit of its beggar–your–neighbour commercial strategy, but its advance was buttressed by other factors. Unlike its continental counterparts, its domestic development was not disturbed by armed conflict (as it had been in the seventeenth century). The integration of domestic markets was greatly improved by creation of a network of turnpike roads and canals and development of coastal shipping. This permitted a more efficient specialisation and division of labour between different regions. Resource allocation was further strengthened by sound public finance and the growth of the banking sector.

From the 1760s, there was spectacular growth in the cotton textile industry. Demand for cotton clothing and household furnishings had been nurtured by a century and a half of imports from India. The prospects and profitability for domestic expansion were transformed by a wave of technological innovation. Cotton was much easier to manipulate mechanically than wool and mechanisation had a dramatic impact on labour productivity with modest levels of capital investment. Hargreaves' spinning jenny (1764–7) permitted a 16–fold productivity gain in spinning soft weft. Arkwright's spinning frame (1768) could produce a strong warp and used water power. Crompton's 1779 "mule" could produce both weft and warp. Cartwright's 1787 power loom extended the productivity gains to weaving; and, finally, the American Eli Whitney invented the cotton gin in 1793, which substantially reduced the cost of the raw cotton which was imported from America. Between 1774 and 1820, imports of raw cotton increased more than 20–fold. Employment in cotton textiles rose from a negligible level in the 1770s to more than 6 per cent of the labour force in 1820. Cotton yarn and manufactures rose from 2 per cent of British exports in 1774 to 62 per cent in 1820 (even though the price of these exports had fallen sharply). The share of woollen goods in exports fell from 49 per cent in 1774 to 12 per cent in the same period (see notes to Table 2–23).

There was also an expansion in cotton textile production and knowledge of the new techniques in Europe, but French per capita consumption of cotton textiles in 1820 was only about a quarter of that in the United Kingdom.

There were substantial improvements in navigational technology in the eighteenth century thanks to government support for the work of the royal astronomers, and the £20 000 prize offered for the development of a ship's chronometer robust and accurate enough to establish longitude at sea. The first of a series of Naval Almanacs (practical guides to navigators) was published in 1767, and the final instalment of the prize money was paid for John Harrison's chronometer in 1773. Armed with a replica of Harrison's chronometer, and an array of other instruments developed in the eighteenth century, Captain James Cook was able to explore and map the coasts of Australia and New Zealand with great success. He did it without loss of any of his crew to scurvy.

Acceleration of Technical Progress and Real Income Growth, 1820–1913

Between 1820 and 1913, per capita income grew faster than at any time in the past — three times as fast as in 1700–1820. It was a new era for Britain and the rest of Western Europe. The basic reason for improved performance was the acceleration of technical progress, accompanied by rapid growth of the physical capital stock and improvement in the education and skills of the labour force. The efficiency of resource allocation benefited from an improved international division of labour, with Britain's exports rising 3.9 per cent a year (almost twice as fast as the growth in GDP). Economic progress was facilitated by the absence of significant military conflicts. This contrasted sharply with experience from 1688 to 1815, when six major wars — 63 years of conflict — had put serious strains on economic development.

Britain added to its territorial empire from 1820 to 1913. There were major acquisitions from the 1870s in Africa, which included Egypt, Ghana, Kenya, Nigeria, Rhodesia, Sudan, Transvaal, the Orange Free State and Uganda. In Asia, Aden and the sheikdoms around Arabia, Burma, the Malay states, Hong Kong and some Pacific islands were added, and the British raj took control of the whole of India. The population in the African territories was about 52 million in 1913, in Asia about 330 million, in the Caribbean about 1.6 million, and in Australia, Canada, Ireland and New Zealand about 18 million. The total population of the Empire was 412 million — ten times as big as Britain itself. The hard core of the Empire was India, with threequarters of its population. Indian taxation financed a large army under British control, which could be deployed to serve British objectives elsewhere in Asia, the Middle East and eventually in Europe. The security of the Empire was guaranteed by British naval supremacy and a network of military/naval bases in Gibraltar, Malta, Cyprus, Egypt, the Suez Canal, Aden and Hong Kong.

In the course of the nineteenth century, there were major changes in British commercial policy. In 1846 protective duties on agricultural imports were removed and in 1849 the Navigation Acts were terminated. By 1860 all trade and tariff restrictions had been removed unilaterally. Dutch policy was similar to the British. In 1860 there were reciprocal arrangements for freer trade with France under the Cobden–Chevalier Treaty. The French made similar treaties with Belgium, Italy, Spain and Switzerland. These treaties had most–favoured nation clauses which meant that bilateral liberalisation applied equally to all countries. In the continental countries there was a reversal of this liberalisation later in the nineteenth century, but the United Kingdom stuck with free trade until 1931.

Free trade was adopted in India and other British colonies, and the same was true in Britain's informal empire. China, Persia, Thailand and Turkey were not colonies, but were obliged to maintain low tariffs by treaties which reduced their sovereignty in commercial matters, and granted extraterritorial rights to foreigners. In China, Britain took over the administration of its customs service, to ensure that China would service its debts.

Although the British empire was run on a free trade basis from the middle of the nineteenth century, colonialism favoured British exports. In Asian and African countries, British shipping, banking and insurance interests enjoyed a *de facto* monopoly. The colonies were no longer run by monopoly trading companies, but by an imperial bureaucracy which was efficient and free of corruption, but it was rule by white men, living in segregated cantonments, frequenting British clubs, so there was an automatic discrimination in favour of British goods, and some quite overt discrimination in government purchasing policies.

Britain's commercial policy and its willingness to import a large part of its food requirements had important positive effects on the world economy. They reinforced and diffused the impact of technical progress. The impact was biggest in the Western Offshoots which had rich natural resources to be exploited but there was also some positive effect in India which was the biggest and the poorest part of the Empire.

The accelerated technical progress which characterised the world economy from the early nineteenth century onwards is often designated as an "industrial revolution", but the word "industrial" suggests an inappropriately narrow sectoral impact of innovation. The acceleration of technical progress affected a very wide range of economic activity and there were improvements in organisation which also contributed to accelerated growth.

The innovations which were most important in diffusing growth worldwide were the advances in transport and communication. The first ship to use steam power appeared in the United Kingdom in 1812, and by the 1860s virtually all new ships used coal as the source of power. By 1913, less than 2 per cent of British shipping used sail. The power of ships' motors and their fuel efficiency increased steadily over the century. Iron and steel ships became much bigger, quicker and more reliable than wooden vessels. From the 1880s there were regular transatlantic shipping lines, which could get from Liverpool to New York in ten days. The opening of the Suez Canal in 1869 cut the distance from London to Bombay by 41 per cent, to Madras by 35 per cent, Calcutta 32 per cent and Hong Kong 26 per cent. This reduced the fuel costs of steam ships, and put sailing ships at a major disadvantage, because of the lack of wind in the canal.

As a result of cheap and reliable passenger services, there was a huge outflow of European migrants to the United States, Canada, Australia, New Zealand, Argentina and Brazil. The net outflow from the United Kingdom from 1820 to 1913 was about 12 million (half of it from Ireland). From the rest of Europe it was about 14 million. The net outflow from India was over 5 million — about 4.5 million to Burma, Malaya and Sri Lanka, a third of a million to Africa, and another third of a million to the Caribbean (see Davis, 1951, pp. 99–101). The outflow from China to other Asian countries was bigger than that from India (see Purcell, 1965).

Migration from Western Europe to North America, Latin America and Australia speeded the pace at which these areas could exploit their huge natural resources and raised the incomes of those who migrated. Emigrants' remittances helped the countries of emigration. Migration accelerated per capita income growth in Ireland and Italy by reducing excess labour in their impoverished rural areas (see O'Rourke and Williamson, 1999, p. 155). Migration from India and China to the "vent–for–surplus" economies of Southeast Asia (Burma, Malaya, Sri Lanka, Thailand and Vietnam), had a similar impact.

The acceleration in shipping and navigational technology was an extension of a process which had been under way since the thirteenth century[35]. American clipper ships were able to compete with steam in speed up to the 1860s. Long–term advances in land transport had been more modest, and the move from horse–drawn to railway freight was a more dramatic leap. Railway transport started in the North of England in 1826, and by 1913 there were nearly a million kilometres of railway track in service worldwide. Nearly half of these were in the United States and the other Western Offshoots. Another 30 per cent were in Europe, but both India and Argentina had a bigger rail network than the United Kingdom in 1913. This massive and costly railway investment opened up new lands for development, increased the effective size of markets, the scope for internal migration and urbanisation, changed the economics of industrial location, and greatly enhanced the possibilities for international specialisation (see O'Rourke and Williamson, 1999, pp. 41–54 for a detailed analysis of the fall in transport costs and their impact). In this railway development, as in shipbuilding, Britain played a leading part in diffusing and financing the new technology.

Table 2–26a. **Gross Nominal Value of Capital Invested Abroad in 1914**
($ million at current exchange rates)

	Europe	*Western Offshoots*	*Latin America*	*Asia*	*Africa*	*Total*
United Kingdom	1 129	8 254	3 682	2 873	2 373	18 311
France	5 250	386	1 158	830	1 023	8 647
Germany	2 979	1 000	905	238	476	5 598
Other	3 377	632	996	1 913	779	7 700
United States	709	900	1 649	246	13	3 514
Total	13 444	11 173	8 390	6 100	4 664	43 770

Source: Maddison (1995a), p. 63. "Other" includes Belgium, Netherlands, Portugal, Russia, Sweden, Switzerland and Japan.

Table 2–26b. **Gross Nominal Value of Capital Invested Abroad in 1938**
($ million at current exchange rates)

	Europe	*Western Offshoots*	*Latin America*	*Asia*	*Africa*	*Total*[a]
United Kingdom	1 139	6 562	3 888	3 169	1 848	17 335
France	1 035	582	292	906	1 044	3 859
Germany	274	130	132	140	–	676
Netherlands	1 643	1 016	145	1 998	16	4 818
Other[b]	1 803	1 143	820	101	646	4 579
United States	2 386	4 454	3 496	997	158	11 491
Japan	53	48	1	1 128	–	1 230
Total	8 331	13 935	8 774	8 439	3 712	43 988

a) includes investments not classified by region, of which 729 for the United Kingdom; b) includes 19 European countries.

Source: UK from Bank of England, *United Kingdom Overseas Investments 1938 to 1948*, London, 1950, p. 14; all other countries from C. Lewis, *The United States and Foreign Investment Problems*, Brookings, Washington, 1948, pp. 292 and 294.

Table 2–27. **Gross Nominal Value of Foreign Capital Invested in Nine Major Recipient Countries, 1913**

	Total ($ million at current exchange rates)	*Per capita* ($)
China	1 600	3.7
India	2 100	6.9
Indonesia	600	12.0
Argentina	3 136	409.8
Brazil	1 932	81.7
Mexico	1 700	113.6
Australia	1 800	373.4
Canada	3 850	490.3
South Africa	1 650	268.2

Source: Stock of foreign capital (portfolio and direct) from Maddison (1989a), p. 45. Population from Appendix A.

http://dx.doi.org/10.1787/723137538677

The invention of mechanical refrigeration created the possibility of long–distance transport of meat, dairy products and fruit by rail and by sea. In the 1870s refrigerator cars were introduced on US railroads. In 1879 the first shipments of frozen meat reached England from Australia, and in 1882 from New Zealand. In 1882, the first freezing plant was created in Buenos Aires for shipments of meat to England.

Britain created a modern postal service in 1840 which operated a system of standardised charges for letters and parcels throughout the United Kingdom, and exploited the new railway facilities to ensure more rapid deliveries than by stage coach. But introduction of the telegraph in the 1850s had a much more dramatic effect on the communications of business and government. By 1870 the United Kingdom had direct contact with India and North America. This innovation helped greatly to integrate international financial markets because access to information was more or less instantaneous. By 1913 the role of the telegraph had been reinforced by the advent of the telephone, and preliminary developments in radio communication.

Innovations in communications played a major part in linking national capital markets and facilitating international capital movements. The UK already had an important role in international finance, thanks to the soundness of its public credit and monetary system, the size of its capital market and public debt, and the maintenance of a gold standard since 1821 to stabilise its exchange rate. The existence of the empire had created a system of property rights which appeared to be as securely protected as those available to investors in British securities. It was a wealthy country operating close to the frontiers of technology, so its rentiers were attracted by foreign investment opportunities even when the extra margin of profit was small.

From the 1870s onward there was a massive outflow of British capital for overseas investment. The UK directed about half of its savings abroad. French, German and Dutch investment was also substantial. By 1913, British foreign assets were equivalent to one and a half times its GDP, income from them meant that national income was more than 9 per cent greater than its domestic product. Table 2–26a shows the origin and location of this foreign capital as it stood in 1914. Movement of capital made a significant contribution to growth in Australia, Canada, New Zealand, Argentina, Southern Brazil, Uruguay, Russia and South Africa, but its per capita impact was small in Asia (see Table 2–27). Most of it was in the form of bonds and a good deal was in railways.

From 1870 to 1913, world capita GDP rose 1.3 per cent a year compared with 0.5 per cent in 1820–70 and 0.07 per cent in 1700–1820. The acceleration was due to more rapid technological progress, and to the diffusionist forces unleashed by the liberal economic order of which the United Kingdom was the main architect. It was not a process of global equalisation (see Table 3–1b on the widened interregional spread of incomes), but there were significant income gains in all parts of the world. Australia and the United States reached higher levels than the United Kingdom by 1913. Growth was faster than in the United Kingdom in most of Western and Eastern Europe, in Ireland, in all the Western Offshoots, in Latin America and Japan. In India, other Asia (except China) and Africa, the advances were much more modest, but per capita income rose more than a quarter between 1870 to 1913.

Trade grew faster than income on a world basis and in virtually all countries from 1870 to 1913 (see Tables 3–2a and F–4).

In all of these dimensions, the situation was an enormous improvement on the eighteenth century, when shipments of slaves were bigger than the movement of migrants, when capital flows and transfer of technology were of limited significance, and when commercial policy was conducted on a beggar–your–neighbour basis.

Keynes (1919, pp. 9–10) provides an illuminating patrician perspective on the lifestyle and investment opportunities available to people like himself in Britain at the end of the liberal era:

"The inhabitant of London could order by telephone, sipping his morning tea in bed, the various products of the whole earth, in such quantity as he might see fit, and reasonably expect their early delivery on his doorstep; he could at the same moment and by the same means adventure his wealth in the natural resources and new enterprise of any quarter of the world. He could secure forthwith, if he wished it, cheap and comfortable means of transport to any country or climate without passport or other formality, could despatch his servant to the neighbouring office of a bank for such supply of the precious metals as might seem convenient, and then proceed abroad to foreign quarters, without knowledge of their religion, language, or customs, bearing coined wealth upon his person, and would consider himself greatly aggrieved and much surprised at the least interference — He regarded this state of affairs as normal, certain, and permanent."

Wars, Depression and Exit from Empire, 1913–50

This was a complex and dismal period, marked deeply by the shock of two world wars and an intervening depression[36]. The liberal economic order was shattered. World trade was much smaller in relation to world income in 1950 than it had been in 1913. International migration was a fraction of what it had been in the nineteenth century. Most of Western Europe's foreign assets were sold, seized or destroyed. Overseas empires disappeared or were in an advanced state of disintegration.

In spite of these disastrous shocks, and drastic reorientation of economic policy and policy instruments, their impact on world economic growth was smaller than might have been expected because the pace of technological advance was substantially faster in the twentieth century than in the nineteenth.

Development of road vehicles sustained the earlier transport revolution. The number of passenger cars in Western Europe rose from about 300 000 in 1913 to nearly 6 million in 1950, and from 1.1 to 40 million in the United States (see Maddison, 1995a, p. 72). There was a parallel transformation of road freight transport, and tractors had a significant impact in replacing horses in agriculture. Aviation had its main impact before 1950 on the technique of warfare, but its economic role in shrinking the significance of distance was already clear.

Development of electricity to produce heat, light and power also had massive ramifications: "electricity freed the machine and tool from the bondage of place; it made power ubiquitous and placed it within the reach of everyone" (Landes, 1966, p. 509). It made it possible to create new kinds of factories to assemble and mass produce automobiles and a huge range of new household products — sewing machines, refrigerators, washing machines, vacuum cleaners, radios and cameras. It contributed to a vastly popular new brand of popular cinematic entertainment.

There were important advances in chemistry, which made it possible to create synthetic materials, fertilisers, pharmaceuticals which had important implications for economic potential and medicine.

The leading role in developing these twentieth century technologies was played by the United States, which had become the world leader in terms of productivity and per capita income. The driving forces of innovation had changed from the nineteenth century, with a reduced role for the individual inventor, and greater emphasis on applied scientific research of a type which the United States pioneered. It institutionalised innovation in a way the United Kingdom had never done. In 1913, there were about 370 research units in US manufacturing employing 3 500 people. By 1946 there were 2 300 units employing 118 000. In 1946 there were four scientific workers in US manufacturing per 1 000 wage earners, five times the ratio in the United Kingdom. US government–sponsored research played a much more important role in agriculture and mining than in the United Kingdom, and the link between business firms and universities was closer (see Mowery and Rosenberg, 1989).

The United States developed new forms of professional business management, where large enterprises played a strategic role in standardising and enlarging markets. Multi–unit firms coordinated advertising, packaging, transport, sales and marketing. They allocated large amounts of capital, spread risks and increased productivity over a large range of new industries.

It is not easy to provide an aggregative estimate of the pace of technical change or its acceleration, but a rough proxy measure is the pace of advance in total factor productivity (the response of output to combined inputs of labour and capital) in the lead country with the highest productivity level. By 1913, it was the United States, not Britain, which operated closest to the technological frontier. Between 1913 and 1950, US total factor productivity grew by 1.6 per cent a year, more than four times as fast as it or the United Kingdom had achieved from 1870 to 1913. This was the first stage of a technological boom which lasted for 60 years. An acceleration of total factor productivity growth also occurred in the United Kingdom in 1913–50, though to a lesser degree than in the United States (see Maddison 1995a, pp. 40–50, and 252–5). There was also an associated acceleration of growth of labour productivity in most West European countries (see Appendix E, Table E–8).

The importance of this acceleration in growth potential was masked by the interwar behaviour of the United States, and the nature of its economic policy. In the 1930s, it had transmitted a strong deflationary impulse to the world economy by its deep depression which was reinforced by raising its tariffs and withdrawal from foreign investment. In Europe its potential was muted by two world wars which involved diversion of massive resources to mutual destruction.

In the first world war, threequarters of a million British troops were killed in combat, and 7.8 million tons of shipping were lost (mainly in submarine attacks). But these losses were proportionately much smaller than those of France, Germany and Russia. The nominal value of its foreign assets was more or less the same at the end of the war as in 1914, whereas German assets were confiscated as reparations, and two thirds of French were lost through inflation and Russian default. Britain added to its overseas empire by acquiring Germany's former colonies in Tanganyika and Namibia, and took over former Turkish possessions in the Middle East (Iraq, Jordan and Palestine), but a large part of Ireland became an independent republic.

In the 1920s British growth was hampered by highly deflationary policies to drive down wages and maintain an overvalued currency at its prewar parity. Their objective was to restore London's prewar role as an international financial centre and to serve the interests of rentiers who held bonds denominated in sterling. As a consequence, there were high levels of unemployment and loss of competitiveness in export markets. Britain had the worst performance in Western Europe in the 1920s, in terms of GDP growth and exports.

The depression of the 1930s led to devaluation of sterling, a large cut in interest rates, an abandonment of free trade, and creation of a network of imperial preferences. These policies cushioned the impact of the world depression on domestic economy. Housing investment had been depressed by high interest rates in the 1920s, and responded very favourably to their decline. There was no British counterpart to the collapse of the banking system which took place in the United States, Germany and Austria. Exports to the empire were bolstered by devaluation and imperial tariff preferences. As a result the impact of the world depression was milder in the United Kingdom than in all West European countries, except Denmark.

Britain came much closer to defeat in the second world war than in the first because Germany captured the whole of the West European continent in its rapid *blitzkrieg*. The eventual victory was due to very intensive domestic resource mobilisation, sale of foreign assets, financial, material and military support from the United States, Canada, India and Australasia, and Russian resistance to Germany on the Eastern front.

The war changed the economics of empire. The Japanese quickly conquered British colonies in East Asia which could not be adequately defended. The strength of the nationalist movement made it politically necessary to finance military expenditure in India by borrowing rather than local taxation. As a result India was able to liquidate $1.2 billion of prewar debt and acquired sterling balances worth more than $5 billion. The costs of maintaining the empire now greatly outweighed the benefits, and the acceleration of technical progress had reinforced the attractions of domestic investment.

The British withdrawal from India occurred in 1947, from Sri Lanka and Burma in 1948. The withdrawal from the African colonies followed a few years after the United States demanded the withdrawal of British forces from Egypt in 1956. The British imperial order was finished, as were those of Belgium, France, the Netherlands and Japan. In the West, the United States had emerged as the hegemonial power competing with the Soviet bloc for leverage in the newly independent countries of Africa and Asia. The foreign economic and commercial policy of the United States was very different from its prewar stance. It made major efforts to diffuse technology, to promote the outflow of capital and liberalisation of world trade. This new orientation was already manifest in 1948 in Marshall Plan aid for European reconstruction.

X
THE IMPACT OF BRITISH EXPANSION IN THE AMERICAS, AFRICA AND ASIA

As Europe's major offshore island, Britain always had substantial overseas involvements. Until the eleventh century, Britain was a target for conquest and barbarian invasion. Between the twelfth to the fifteenth centuries, under the Norman and Angevin dynasties, it was heavily engaged in attempts to acquire territory in France.

Thereafter Britain was involved in many wars in Europe, mainly with Spain, France and the Netherlands, but the objectives were commercial or diplomatic. By the middle of the sixteenth century, the idea of European conquest had been abandoned. Although trade was developed in the Baltic and Mediterranean overseas ambitions were concentrated on the Americas and Asia. Until the nineteenth century the only significant interest in Africa was the slave trade.

In the sixteenth century, the main activities outside Europe were piracy and reconnoitring voyages to explore the potential for developing a colonial empire. The boldest stroke was royal backing for the 1577–80 voyage of Drake, who took five ships and 116 men, rounded the Straits of Magellan, seized and plundered Spanish treasure ships off the coast of Chile and Peru, made useful contacts in the spice islands of the Moluccas, Java, the Cape of Good Hope and Guinea on his way back.

Piracy and Britain's support of the Dutch Republic provoked war with Spain from 1585 which lasted two decades. By this time, its maritime strength and skill were adequate to defeat the Spanish Armada. This was an invasion force of 130 ships from Cadiz which intended to rendezvous with a fleet of invasion barges in the Spanish Netherlands. The British victory at Gravelines prevented the rendezvous and forced the Spanish fleet to return home around the northwest of Scotland. Spain lost more than half of its fleet, and it was clear that Britain had acquired the naval power to support major ventures in the Americas and Asia.

As overseas ventures were varied in character and became bigger in scope than those of any other European power, our survey is necessarily selective and is presented below under four headings:

a)   development of sugar colonies in the Caribbean and associated participation in the slave trade from Africa from the 1620s onwards;

b)   settlement of 13 colonies in North America between 1607 and 1713 which became the United States in 1776;

c)   creation of an East Indian Trading Company in 1600 and its conquest of an Indian Empire after 1757;

d)   forcible opening of trade with China and establishment of the Treaty Port regime of free trade imperialism.

a) The Caribbean and the Slave Trade

The Caribbean islands were the first Spanish possessions in the Americas, but the native Arawaks in Hispaniola (Haiti and Dominican Republic) were quickly wiped out by disease and the Caribs in the Antilles were greatly depleted. Spanish interest switched to Peru and Mexico once large scale silver production started there in the middle of the sixteenth century. The British occupied the uninhabited island of Barbados in 1627 establishing tobacco plantations with a labour force of indentured white settlers. Dutch shippers in the Brazilian sugar trade promoted the idea of developing Caribbean sugar production with slave labour. Dutch entrepreneurs established sugar plantations in Barbados when they were expelled from Brazil. As the island was well watered, and the winds were favourable for a quick passage to Europe, it became Britain's biggest sugar colony until Jamaica was captured from Spain in 1655. With similar help from the Dutch, the French developed sugar production in Martinique and Guadeloupe and later took over a much bigger area in Saint Domingue (Haiti). The Dutch were pushed out of the British and French colonies and created a smaller sugar economy in Surinam. Britain took some French islands (St. Vincent, Grenada, Dominica and Tobago) in 1763, and Trinidad from Spain in 1727.

British entry to the slave trade was pioneered by Hawkins in 1562. Participation reached its peak in the seventeenth and eighteenth centuries when Britain became the main slave shipper, bringing a total of 2.5 million Africans to the Americas (see Table 2–5). The traffic was heaviest to the Caribbean. The British staked out Sierra Leone and the upper Guinea coast in the seventeenth century as their source of supply, the French took slaves mainly from the Senegal–Gambia region and the Dutch from the Gold Coast. The Portuguese operated the Africa–Brazil trade further south in Angola. The Royal Africa Company had a monopoly on British slave trading from 1672 to 1698, but in the eighteenth century "individual entrepreneurs who organised one or several voyages had become the norm in the trade" (see Klein, 1999, p. 80). Apart from European traders, there was financial backing from merchants in New England, Virginia, the West Indies and Brazil. Slavers generally financed their purchases with trade goods (East Indian textiles, alcohol, tobacco, bar iron, weapons, jewellery, or cowrie shells from the Maldives — for use in Africa as currency). "In the overwhelming majority of cases it was the Africans who controlled the slaves until their moment of sale to the captain — African slave traders came down to the coast or the riverbanks in a relatively steady and predictable stream to well–known trading places — European traders tended to spend months on the coast or travelling upriver gathering their slaves a few at a time" (Klein, 1999, pp. 90–1).

Within Africa, slaves were acquired as captives in local wars, as tribute from dependent tribes, or after condemnation as criminals, but there was also large scale slave raiding and kidnapping of individuals within Africa. Klein (1999, p. 129) estimated that of 18 million African slaves exported from 1500 to 1900, "11 million of them were shipped into the Atlantic economy. The other slaves were shipped into the Indian Ocean or across the Sahara to slave markets in the East."

The normal cargo per ship ranged between 400–500 slaves. Klein (1999, p. 139) estimates 12 per cent average mortality on the passage to America over the period 1590–1867 which he compares with 10 per cent in convict ships on the longer voyage to Australia in 1787–1800.

Table 2–28. **Population of British Colonies and Former Colonies in the Americas, 1750 and 1830**
(000)

	1750		*1830*	

A. 19 Caribbean Slave and Sugar Islands

	Total	*Per cent Slaves*	*Total*	*Per cent Slaves*
1625 St. Kitts	21.8	88.3	23.4	81.6
1627 Barbados	63.4	78.9	102.2	80.3
1632 Antigua	31.1	89.3	37.0	80.0
1655 Jamaica	127.9	90.1	378.1	84.4
1763 Grenada	12.0	87.3	28.4	84.1
1797 Trinidad	0.3	42.4	42.1	54.1
1803 British Guiana	8.0	91.0	100.6	88.1
12 Others	66.0	79.4	132.1	75.6
Total (19)	371.2	85.3	843.7	81.2

B. 13 North American Colonies and USA

	Total	*Per cent Black*	*Total*	*Per cent Black*
1679 New Hampshire	27.5	2.0	269	0.4
1620 Massachusetts	188.0	2.2	610	1.1
1635 Connecticut	111.3	2.7	298	2.7
1644 Rhode Island	33.2	10.1	97	4.1
1664 New York	76.7	14.4	1 919	2.3
1664 New Jersey	71.4	7.5	321	6.5
1681 Pennsylvania	119.7	2.4	1 348	2.8
1704 Delaware	28.7	5.2	77	24.7
1632 Maryland	141.1	30.8	447	34.9
1607 Virginia	231.0	43.9	1 221	42.6
1662 North Carolina	73.0	27.1	738	35.9
1662 South Carolina	64.0	60.4	581	55.6
1713 Georgia	5.2	19.2	517	42.6
Total (13)	1 170.8	20.2	8 443	19.2
Other States			4 458	15.7
Total			12 901	18.1

C. Canada

	1750	1830
		143
1713 Nova Scotia		612
1759 Lower & Upper Canada		83
Other		838
Total Canada		

Source: Panel A: Higman (1996), p. 302. Date of acquisition shown on left. Panel B: *Historical Statistics of the United States* (1975) Part I, pp. 14, 24–37 for 1830, Part 2, pp. 1168 for 1750. Date of acquisition shown on left, countries listed from north to south. The total black population in 1830 was 2.3 million of which 2 million were slaves (15.6 per cent of the total US population). Panel C: Pebrer (1833), p. 386, figures refer to 1829.

http://dx.doi.org/10.1787/723137538677

The average duration of a slave trading venture from Europe to Africa, the West Indies and back was about 20 months, including several months assembling the cargo in Africa, and two months for the voyage to the West Indies. Evidence for UK and French voyages suggests that the cost of trade goods was twice as big as the costs of shipping, insurance and wages of the crew. Klein (1999, p. 125) suggests that in the late eighteenth century, European trade goods represented less than 5 per cent of West African income. He (pp. 98) suggests that "slave trade profits were not extraordinary by European standards. The average 10 per cent rate obtained was considered a very good profit rate at the time, but not out of the range of other contemporary investments."

The impact of the Atlantic slave trade on African population growth was substantial. Between 1700 and 1800, African population increased from 61 to 70 million (see Table B–9a). In the same period, slavers delivered 6.1 million slaves to the Americas. With 12 per cent mortality on the voyage, this implies a shipment of about 6.9 million. After allowing for births foregone it seems possible that African population would have grown three times as fast in the eighteenth century without the Atlantic slave trade.

If there had been no export of slaves to the Americas, economic development in the Caribbean, in Virginia, Maryland and the Carolinas would have been much more meagre. Smaller profit remittances from the colonies and the absence of income from the slave trade would have slowed British growth and European consumption of sugar would have been much smaller. There would also have been an adverse impact on the New England colonies because their prosperity depended in part on commodity exports and shipping services to the West Indies.

The British abolished the slave trade in 1807, and slavery in 1833, with £20 million compensation to slaveowners and nothing for the slaves. France lost her major sugar colony in Haiti because of the success of the slave revolt which ended with independence in 1804. France abolished the slave trade in 1817 and slavery in 1848.

The British abolition was due in substantial part to the success of humanitarian reformers in convincing public opinion to end a repugnant form of exploitation. The success of independence movements in North America in 1783, and in Latin America in the 1820s, the successful slave revolt in Haiti and the unsuccessful revolt in Jamaica in 1831–2 persuaded the planting lobby that their days were numbered, and that it was in their interest to settle for compensation.

Brazil continued to import slaves until the 1850s when the trade was stopped by British naval intervention. Brazilian slavery was maintained until 1888. Spain restricted slave imports to its colonies until 1789, but thereafter opened them to all slave traders. It made a big push to increase sugar production in the nineteenth century in Cuba and Puerto Rico (the only colonies it retained in the Americas after the others became independent). Slavery was abolished in Puerto Rico in 1873 and in Cuba in 1880. In 1894, Cuban sugar production was 1.1 million tons, in the British Caribbean 260 000, French Caribbean 79 000, Puerto Rico 49 000 and Surinam 8 000 (see Williams, 1970, p. 378).

As a substitute for labour imports from Africa, indentured workers from India were first brought to British Guiana in 1838. From then until 1914, the inflow of Indians to the British Caribbean amounted to 450 000. Javanese were brought to Surinam in large numbers, and Cuba imported 150 000 Chinese on a similar basis from 1849–75. However, the ending of slavery raised costs in the Caribbean sugar industry and weakened its competitive position. In 1787 the Caribbean accounted for 90 per cent of world sugar production. In 1894 its share was only 22 per cent (see Table 2–4). There was a greater diversification of Caribbean production with a greater role for coffee and cotton, but the main impact was stagnant or falling per capita income. Eisner (1961, pp. 119 and 153) shows per capita real income in Jamaica in 1930 about threequarters of that in 1830. Table 2–23 shows the dramatic decline in the importance of British trade with the Caribbean after 1820.

b) The 13 North American Colonies

The situation in North America was very different from that in the Caribbean. In the five colonies which relied most heavily on slave labour (Maryland, Virginia, the Carolinas and Georgia) slaves were about 40 per cent of the population in 1750, compared with 85 per cent in the Caribbean colonies. Whites (indentured servants and others) were a significant part of the labour force. The main crops in plantation agriculture were tobacco, rice and indigo, where work intensity was less than in sugar, and the climate was healthier than in the Caribbean. Life expectation and possibilities for natural growth of the black population were greater than in the Caribbean. Growth of the labour force depended less on the slave trade.

In the Northern colonies, which had 56 per cent of the colonial population in 1750, slaves were less than 5 per cent. A large part of the labour force was employed in agriculture with very much greater land availability per capita than in the United Kingdom. The average family farm in New England, the mid–Atlantic States and Pennsylvania in 1807 had well over 100 acres (Lebergott, 1984, p. 17). Most of the northern colonies had been formed by protestants of various denominations who were keen on education. There were eight universities in the north (Harvard founded in 1636, Yale 1701, University of Pennsylvania 1740, Princeton 1746, Columbia 1754, Brown 1764, Rutgers 1766, Dartmouth 1769), only one (William and Mary, 1693) in the South (and none in the Caribbean). The level of education in the northern colonies was above that in the United Kingdom. Per capita income was about the same level as in the United Kingdom and more evenly distributed.

Although the British Navigation Acts made the colonies route their most important exports to Europe and their imports from Europe through the United Kingdom, they provided favoured access to markets within the empire which were particularly important for exports of shipping services and ships. On the eve of the war of independence, the merchant marine of the colonies was over 450 000 tons, all of which (coastal craft, West Indies schooners, fishing and whaling boats, and ships for trade with England) were built in New England shipyards which had easy access to cheap timber, pitch and tar (see Table 2–15).

In addition, American yards had built an increasing proportion of the British merchant fleet in the course of the eighteenth century. In 1774, 30 per cent of Britain's million–ton merchant fleet was American built (see Davis, 1962, pp. 66–8).

The North American colonies had a significant urban population in Boston, New York and Philadelphia. They had a politically sophisticated elite familiar with the ideas and ideals of the French enlightenment. Their incentive to break the colonial tie was reinforced in 1763, after the Seven Years war, in which the British ended French rule in Canada and French claims to territory west of the 13 colonies. Hitherto, the most likely alternative to British rule had been French rule. Thereafter it was independence.

A striking characteristic of US economic growth after independence was its much greater dynamism than that of its neighbour Mexico, which was a Spanish colony until 1825. It is therefore useful to compare the different institutional, societal and policy influences transmitted by Spain and the United Kingdom.

The main reasons for Mexican backwardness compared with the ex–British colonies in North America were probably as follows:

a)   The Spanish colony was subject to a bigger drain of resources to the metropole. In the first place a considerable part of domestic income went into the pockets of peninsular Spaniards who did not stay in the colony but took their savings back to Spain. Secondly there was official tribute of about 2.7 per cent of GDP (see Maddison, 1995b, pp. 316–7).

b)   The British colonial regime imposed mercantilist restrictions on foreign trade, but they were much lighter than in New Spain. Thomas (1965) has suggested that the net cost of British trade restrictions was about 42 cents per head in the American colonies in 1770 (about 0.6 per cent of GDP).

c)   The British colonies had a better educated population, greater intellectual freedom and social mobility. Education was secular with emphasis on pragmatic skills and yankee ingenuity of which Ben Franklin was the prototype. The 13 British colonies had nine universities in 1776 for 2.5 million people. New Spain, with 5 million, had only two universities in Mexico City and Guadalajara, which concentrated on theology and law. Throughout the colonial period the Inquisition kept a tight censorship and suppressed heterodox thinking.

d)   In New Spain, the best land was engrossed by hacienda owners. In North America the white population had much easier access to land, and in New England family farming enterprise was typical. Restricted access to land in Spanish colonies was recognised as a hindrance to economic growth both by Adam Smith and the Viceroy of New Spain. Rosenzweig (1963) quotes the latter (Revillagigedo) as follows (my translation): "Maldistribution of land is a major obstacle to the progress of agriculture and commerce, particularly with regard to entails with absentee or negligent owners. We have subjects of his majesty here who possess hundreds of square leagues — enough to form a small kingdom — but who produce little of value."

e)   At the top of New Spain there was a privileged upper class, with a sumptuary lifestyle. Differences in status — a hereditary aristocracy, privileged groups of clergy and military with tax exemptions and legal immunities — meant that there was much less entrepreneurial vigour than in the British colonies. The elite in New Spain were rent–seekers with a low propensity to productive investment.

f)   In the government of New Spain, power was highly concentrated on the centre, whereas in British North America there were 13 separate colonies, and political power was fragmented, so there was much greater freedom for individuals to pursue their own economic interests.

g)   Another source of advantage for North America was the vigour of its population growth because of the rapid inflow of migrants. Population in North America rose tenfold from 1700 to 1820, and by less than half in Mexico. Economic enterprise was much more dynamic when the market was expanding so rapidly.

c) India

The British connection with India started in 1600 with the creation of a monopoly trading company (the East India Company — EIC). For the first century and a half, it operated around the Indian coast from bases in Calcutta, Madras and Bombay. By the middle of the eighteenth century the main exports were textiles and raw silk from India, and tea from China. Purchases of Indian products were financed mainly by exports of bullion, and from China by export of opium and raw cotton from Bengal (see Table 2–20 and the above discussion of rivalry between the British, Dutch and French trading companies).

Until the eighteenth century the British generally maintained peaceable relations with the Moghul empire whose authority and military power were too great to be challenged. After the death of Aurangzeb in 1707, Moghul control disintegrated. The Moghul emperor became a token suzerain and provincial governors became *de facto* rulers as nawabs of successor states[37].

Given the size of India, with a bigger population than Europe, its racial, linguistic and religious complexity, it is not surprising that it fell apart. At the height of its power, under Akbar, the Moghul Empire practised religious toleration. This is one of the reasons why it was more successful in establishing an extensive domain than the earlier Muslim sultanates of Delhi. Aurangzeb abandoned the policy of religious tolerance, destroyed Hindu temples, reimposed the *jizya* (a capitation tax on non–Muslims) and confiscated some non–Muslim princely states when titles lapsed. After his death, there was a series of wars for the spoils of empire. In Western India, the Mahrattas established an independent

Hindu state with their capital at Poona. The *Nizam–ul–Mulk*, a high Moghul official who foresaw the collapse of the Empire, installed himself as the autonomous ruler of Hyderabad in 1724. In 1739, the Persian emperor Nadir Shah invaded India, massacred the population of Delhi and took away so much booty (including Shah Jehan's peacock throne and the Kohinoor diamond) that he was able to remit Persian taxes for three years. He also annexed Punjab and set up an independent kingdom in Lahore. The Punjab was later captured by the Sikhs. In other areas which nominally remained in the Empire, e.g. Bengal, Mysore and Oudh, the power of the Moghul emperor declined, as did his revenue. Continuous internal warfare greatly weakened the economy and trade of the country.

It was because of these internal political and religious conflicts that the EIC was able to gain control of India. It exploited the differences skilfully by making temporary alliances and picking off local potentates one at a time. Most of its troops were local recruits who were well disciplined and paid regularly. They conquered the Moghul province of Bengal in 1757, took over the provinces of Madras and Bombay in 1803, and seized the Punjab from the Sikhs in 1848. They also succeeded in driving their European commercial rivals — the French and Dutch — from India. The British government did not establish its own direct rule until after the Indian mutiny in 1857 when the East India Company was dissolved.

After its military victory at Plassey in 1757, the EIC operated a dual system in Bengal in which it had control and the nawab was a puppet. The main objectives of the Company were to enrich its officials and finance its exports from the tax revenues of the province instead of shipping bullion to India. The extension of the EIC's territorial conquests changed its role from trading to governance. The Company lost its trading monopoly in 1813 in India and in 1833 for China. Company policy was subjected to parliamentary surveillance in 1773, and the nawab was replaced by a Governor General (Warren Hastings) in direct charge of administration, but with Indian officials. Hastings was dismissed in 1782, and Cornwallis from 1785 created the basis on which colonial India was governed.

All high level posts were reserved for the British, and Indians were excluded. A civil administration was created which was much more effective and cheaper than that of the Moghuls. From 1806 the Company trained its young recruits at Haileybury College near London. From 1833 nominees were selected by competitive examination. After 1853, selection was entirely on merit. In 1829, the system was strengthened by establishing districts throughout British India small enough to be controlled by an individual British official who exercised autocratic power as revenue collector, judge and chief of police.

There was a strong streak of Benthamite radicalism in the EIC administration. James Mill, John Stuart Mill and Macaulay were influential Company officials, and Malthus was the professor of economics at Haileybury College. Bentham himself was consulted on the reform of Indian institutions and the Utilitarians used India to try experiments and ideas (e.g. competitive entry for the civil service) which they would have liked to apply in England. After the Indian Mutiny in 1857, when the British government took over direct control of India, these radical Westernising approaches were dropped, policy became more conservative, and there was no attempt at further extension of direct rule over provinces which were governed by Indian princes with British advisors[38].

The British raj was operated by remarkably few people. There were only 31 000 British in India in 1805 (of which 22 000 in the army, and 2 000 in civil government). In 1931, there were 168 000 (60 000 in the army and police, 4 000 in civil government and 60 000 employed in the private sector). They were never more than 0.05 per cent of the population — a much thinner layer than the Muslim rulers had been.

The changes which the British made in the system of governance had major socioeconomic consequences (see Boxes 2–1 and 2–2 which contrast the Indian social structure at the peak of the Moghul empire and at the end of British rule). The British took over a Moghul tax system which provided a land revenue equal to 15 per cent of national income, but by the end of the colonial period, land tax was only 1 per cent of national income and the total tax burden 6 per cent. The main gains from tax reduction and associated changes in property rights went to upper castes in the village economy, to zamindars who became landlords, and village moneylenders. The wasteful warlord aristocracy of the Moghuls was

Box 2–1. **Social Structure of the Moghul Empire**

Percentage of labour force		Per cent of national income after tax
18	*NON–VILLAGE ECONOMY*	52

1	Moghul Emperor and Court Mansabdars Jagirdars Native princes Appointed zamindars Hereditary zamindars	15
17	Merchants and bankers Traditional professions Petty traders & entrepreneurs Soldiers & petty bureaucracy Urban artisans & construction workers Servants Sweepers Scavengers	37

72	*VILLAGE ECONOMY*	45

Dominant castes
Cultivators and rural artisans
Landless labourers
Servants
Sweepers
Scavengers

10	*TRIBAL ECONOMY*	3

Source: Maddison (1971), p. 33.

Box 2–2. **Social Structure at the End of British Rule**

Percentage of labour force		Per cent of national income after tax
18	*NON–VILLAGE ECONOMY*	44
0.05	British officials and military / British capitalists, plantation owners, traders, bankers & managers	5
0.95	Native princes / Big zamindars and jagirdars	3
	Indian capitalists, merchants and managers	3
	The new Indian professional class	3
17	Petty traders, small entrepreneurs, traditional professions, clerical and manual workers in government, soldiers, railway workers, industrial workers, urban artisans, servants, sweepers & scavengers	30
75	*VILLAGE ECONOMY*	54
9	Village rentiers, rural moneylenders small zamindars, tenants–in–chief	20
20	Working proprietors, protected tenants	18
29	Tenants–at–will, sharecroppers, village artisans and servants	12
17	Landless labourers, scavengers	4
7	*TRIBAL ECONOMY*	2

Source: Maddison (1971), p. 69.

Table 2–29. **Population of British Territories in Asia, Africa, Australia and Europe in 1830**

	Population (000)	*Area* (Square Miles)
a) Asia		
Bengal Presidency	69 710	220 312
Fort St. George (Madras) Presidency	13 509	141 924
Bombay Presidency	6 252	59 438
Deccan districts	11 000[a]	91 200
Total EIC Territories	100 578	512 874
Areas under EIC "protection"	40 000[a]	614 610
Ceylon	933	
Mauritius	101	
Singapore, Malacca, Penang	107	
b) Africa		
Cape of Good Hope	129	
Sierra Leone	15	
Senegal, Goree and Fernando Po	10	
c) Australia (white population)	70[b]	
d) Europe		
Gibraltar	17	
Malta	120	

a) Pebrer's rough estimates; b) 1839.

Source: India from Pebrer (1833), pp. 454 and 465. EIC armed forces were 223,461 of which 36,606 Europeans. Ceylon and Mauritius from p. 410, Singapore etc. from p. 454. Ceylon was taken from the Dutch in 1795, Malacca in 1825; Mauritius from France 1795. The slave population of Mauritius was 79 000, in Ceylon 20 000. Africa from p. 418; the Cape was taken from the Dutch in 1806; in 1830 the slave population was 36 000. Australia 1839 from Vamplew (1987) p. 44. Gibraltar and Malta from Pebrer (1833), p. 374.

Table 2–30. **Comparative Macroeconomic Performance of India and Britain, 1600–1947**

	1600	*1700*	*1757*	*1857*	*1947*
Per capita GDP (1990 int. dollars)					
India	550	550	540	520	618
United Kingdom	974	1 250	1 424	2 717	6 361
Population (000)					
India	135 000	165 000	185 000	227 000	414 000
United Kingdom	6 170	8 565	13 180	28 187	49 519
GDP (million 1990 int. dollars)					
India	74 250	90 750	99 900	118 040	255 852
United Kingdom	6 007	10 709	18 768	76 584	314 969

Source: Appendix B and Maddison (1995a).

http://dx.doi.org/10.1787/723137538677

eliminated, and replaced by a small Westernised elite with a smaller share of national income. Until the 1920s, the new elite was almost entirely British, with British consumption patterns. This greatly reduced the demand for the luxury products of India's traditional handicrafts. The damage to India's main industry was greatly reinforced in the nineteenth century by duty–free imports of British cotton textiles.

In the first century of British rule, the changes in the social structure and replacement of old methods of governance led to continuance of the fall in per capita income which had started at the beginning of the eighteenth century as the Moghul state disintegrated. From 1857 to independence in 1947, there was a slow rise in per capita income, and faster population growth. Table 2–27 gives a rough comparative idea of changes in income and population in India and Britain from 1600 to the end of colonial rule in 1947.

Table 2–21 provides a rough idea of the dimension of the "drain" of resources from India to the United Kingdom as a consequence of having foreign governance. This drain was about 0.9 to 1.3 per cent of Indian national income from 1868 to the 1930s. This meant a transfer of about a fifth of India's net savings which might otherwise have been used to import capital goods. The drain was a major target of criticism by Indian nationalists from the end of the nineteenth century. Even more important from their point of view was the fact that 5 per cent of the national income represented consumption of British personnel in India. Most of this would have gone to an Indian elite if the British had left India 50 years earlier, and a modernising Indian elite might well have pursued policies more conducive to Indian development. However, if the British (or their French rivals) had not ruled India from the mid–eighteenth to late nineteenth century, it seems unlikely that a modernising elite or the legal and institutional framework for its operation would have emerged from the ruins of the Moghul Empire.

As my conclusions on the impact and consequences of British rule are contestable, it seems useful to set out the evidence for my viewpoint in more detail in the following sections on: the socioeconomic structure which the British inherited from Moghul India; the British impact on Indian agriculture; and its impact on industry.

The Socioeconomic Structure of Moghul India

Muslims were the ruling elite in India from the thirteenth century until the British takeover. The Moghuls had the military power to squeeze a large surplus from a passive village society. The ruling class had an extravagant lifestyle whose needs were supplied by urban artisans producing high quality cotton textiles, silks, jewellery, decorative swords and weapons.

The Moghul aristocracy were not landlords but were allotted the tax revenue from a specified area (i.e. they were given a *jagir*). Part of the revenue was for their own sustenance, the rest was paid to the central treasury in cash or in the form of troop support. The aristocracy was not, in principle, hereditary. Moghul practice derived from the traditions of the nomadic societies which had created Islam in Arabia and the Ottoman Empire. Nobles were regularly posted from one *jagir* to another and their estates were liable to royal forfeit on death. This system of warlord predators led to a wasteful use of resources. There was little motive to improve landed property. Moghul officials needed high incomes because they had many dependants to support. They maintained polygamous households with vast retinues of slaves and servants. Military spending was also large because soldiering and wars were the main duty of the Moghul elite. The *jagirdar* had an incentive to squeeze village society close to subsistence, to spend as much as possible on consumption and to die in debt to the state. There were also Hindu nobles (*zamindars*) who retained hereditary control over village revenues, and Hindu princes who continued to rule and collect revenues in autonomous states within the Moghul Empire, e.g. in Rajputana.

The reason why the Moghuls could raise so much revenue from taxation, without having a ruling class which directly supervised the production process, was that village society was very docile.

The chief characteristic of Indian society which differentiated it from others was the institution of caste. It segregated the population into mutually exclusive groups whose economic and social functions were clearly defined and hereditary. Old religious texts classify Hindus into four main groups: *brahmins,* a caste of priests at the top of the social scale whose ceremonial purity was not to be polluted by manual labour; next in priority came the *kshatriyas* or warriors, thirdly the *vaishyas* or traders, and finally the *sudras,* or farmers. Below this there were *melechas* or outcastes to perform menial and unclean tasks. Members of different castes did not intermarry or eat together, and kept apart in social life.

The theoretical model of the Rigveda is a very simplified version of the Indian situation. Brahmins and untouchables were distinguishable everywhere, but the hierarchy of intermediate castes was complex and often did not conform to the kshatriya, vaishya, sudra categorisation.

In relations with the state, the village usually acted as a unit. Land taxes were generally paid collectively and the internal allocation of the burden was left to the village headman or accountant. The top group were allies of the state, co–beneficiaries in the system of exploitation. In every village the bottom layer were untouchables squeezed tight against the margin of subsistence. Without the caste sanctions, village society would probably have been more egalitarian, and a more homogeneous peasantry might have been less willing to put up with such heavy fiscal levies.

From an economic point of view, the most interesting feature of caste was that it fixed occupation by heredity. For priests or barbers the prospect of doing the same job as a whole chain of ancestors was perhaps not too depressing, but for those whose hereditary function was to clean latrines, the system offered no joys in this world. One reason they accepted it was the Hindu belief in reincarnation which held out the hope of rebirth in a higher social status to those who acquired merit by loyal performance of their allotted task in this world.

Below the village society, about 10 per cent of the population lived in a large number of tribal communities. Aboriginal tribes led an independent pagan existence as hunters or forest dwellers, completely outside Hindu society and paying no taxes to the Moghuls.

The British Impact on Indian Agriculture

The colonial government modified traditional institutional arrangements in agriculture and created property rights whose character was somewhat closer to those under Western capitalism. Except in the autonomous princely states, the old warlord aristocracy was dispossessed. Their previous income from *jagirs* and that of the Moghul state was appropriated by the British. In the Bengal Presidency (i.e. modern Bengal, Bihar, Orissa and part of Madras) the second layer of Moghul property rights belonging to tax collectors (*zamindars*) was reinforced. They acquired hereditary status, so long as they paid their land taxes, and their tax liabilities were frozen at the 1793 level. In the Madras and Bombay Presidencies the British dispossessed most of the old Moghul and Mahratta nobility and big zamindars, and vested property rights and tax obligations in the traditionally dominant castes in villages. Lower–caste cultivators became their tenants.

Because of the emergence of clearer titles, it was now possible to mortgage land. The status of moneylenders was also improved by the change from Muslim to British law. There had been moneylenders in the Moghul period, but their importance grew substantially under British rule, and over time a considerable amount of land changed hands through foreclosures.

Over time, two forces raised the income of landowners. One of these was the increasing scarcity of land as population expanded. This raised land values and rents. The second was the decline in the incidence of land tax. As a result, there was an increased income and a widening of inequality within villages. The village squirearchy received higher incomes because of the reduced burden of land tax and the increase in rents; the income of tenants and agricultural labourers declined because their traditional rights were curtailed and their bargaining power was reduced by greater land scarcity. The class of landless agricultural labourers grew in size under British rule.

The colonial government increased the irrigated area about eightfold. Eventually more than a quarter of the land of British India was irrigated, compared with 5 per cent in Moghul India. Irrigation was extended both as a source of revenue and as a measure to mitigate famines. A good deal of the irrigation work was in the Punjab and Sind. The motive here was to provide land for retired Indian army personnel, many of whom came from the Punjab, and to build up population in an area which bordered on the disputed frontier with Afghanistan. These areas, which had formerly been desert, became the biggest irrigated area in the world and major producers of wheat and cotton, both for export and for sale in other parts of India.

Improvements in transport facilities (particularly railways, but also steamships and the Suez canal) helped agriculture by permitting some degree of specialisation on cash crops. This increased yields somewhat, but the bulk of the country stuck to subsistence farming. Plantations were developed for indigo, sugar, jute and tea. These items made a significant contribution to exports, but in the context of Indian agriculture as a whole, they were not very important. In 1946, the two primary export items, tea and jute, were less than 3.5 per cent of gross value of crop output. Thus the enlargement of markets through international trade was less of a stimulus in India than in other Asian countries such as Burma, Ceylon, Indonesia or Thailand.

Under British rule, the Indian population remained subject to recurrent famines and epidemic diseases. In 1876–8 and 1899–1900 famine killed millions of people. In the 1890s there was a widespread outbreak of bubonic plague and in 1919 a great influenza epidemic. In the 1920s and 1930s there were no famines, and the 1944 famine in Bengal was due to war conditions and transport difficulties rather than crop failure. However, the greater stability after 1920 may have been partly due to a lucky break in the weather cycle rather than to a new stability of agriculture.

The British Impact on Indian Industry

Moghul India had a bigger industry than any other country which became a European colony, and was unique in being an industrial exporter in pre–colonial times. A large part of this industry was destroyed as a consequence of British rule.

Between 1757 and 1857 the British wiped out the Moghul court, and eliminated three–quarters of the aristocracy (except those in princely states). They also eliminated more than half of the local chieftainry (zamindars) and in their place established a bureaucracy with European tastes. The new rulers wore European clothes and shoes, drank imported beer, wines and spirits, and used European weapons. Their tastes were mimicked by the male members of the new Indian "middle class" who acted as their clerks and intermediaries. As a result of these political and social changes, about threequarters of the domestic demand for luxury handicrafts was destroyed. This was a shattering blow to manufacturers of fine muslins, jewellery, luxury clothing and footwear, decorative swords and weapons. My own guess would be that the home market for these goods was about 5 per cent of Moghul national income and the export market for textiles probably another 1.5 per cent.

The second blow came from massive imports of cheap textiles from England after the Napoleonic wars. Home spinning, which was a part–time activity of village women, was greatly reduced. Demand for village hand–loom weaving changed with a substantial switch to using factory instead of home–spun yarn.

Modern cotton mills were started in Bombay in 1851, preceding Japan by 20 years and China by 40. Production was concentrated on coarse yarns which were sold domestically and to China and Japan. Exports were half of output. India began to suffer from Japanese competition in the 1890s. Exports to Japan were practically eliminated by 1898. Shortly after, Japanese factories in China began to reduce

India's market there. By the end of the 1930s, Indian exports of yarn to China and Japan had disappeared, piece goods exports had fallen off, and India imported both yarn and piece goods from China and Japan.

If the British had been willing to give tariff protection, India could have copied Lancashire's textile technology more quickly. Instead British imports entered India duty free. By the 1920s when Indian textile imports were coming mainly from Japan, British policy changed. By 1934 the tariff on cotton cloth had been raised to 50 per cent with a margin of preference for British products. As a result there was a considerable substitution of local textiles for imports. In 1896 Indian mills supplied only 8 per cent of Indian cloth consumption, in 1913 20 per cent and in 1945 76 per cent. By the latter date there were no imports of piece goods.

Modern jute manufacturing started in 1854 and the industry expanded rapidly in the vicinity of Calcutta. It was largely in the hands of foreigners (mainly Scots). Between 1879 and 1913 the number of jute spindles rose tenfold — much faster than growth in the cotton textile industry. Most of the jute output was for export.

Coal mining, mainly in Bengal, was another industry which achieved significance. Its output, which by 1914 had reached 15.7 million tons, largely met the demands of the Indian railways.

In 1911 the first Indian steel mill was built by the Tata Company at Jamshedpur in Bihar. The Indian industry started 15 years later than in China, where the first mill was built at Hangyang in 1896. The first Japanese mill was built in 1898. In both China and Japan the first steel mills (and the first textile mills) were government enterprises.

Indian firms in industry, insurance and banking were given a boost from 1905 onwards by the *swadeshi* movement, which was a nationalist boycott of British goods in favour of Indian enterprise. During the First World War, lack of British imports strengthened the hold of Indian firms on the home markets for textiles and steel. After the war, under nationalist pressure, the government started to favour Indian enterprise in its purchase of stores and it agreed to create a tariff commission in 1921 which started raising tariffs for protective reasons.

Many of the most lucrative commercial, financial, business and plantation jobs in the modern sector were occupied by foreigners. Long after the East India Company's legally enforced monopoly privileges were ended, the British continued to exercise effective dominance through their control of the banking sector[39] and the system of "managing agencies". These agencies, originally set up by former employees of the East India Company, were used both to manage industrial enterprise and to handle most of India's international trade. They were closely linked with British banks, insurance and shipping companies. Managing agencies had a quasi–monopoly in access to capital, and they had interlocking directorships which gave them control over supplies and markets. They dominated the foreign markets in Asia. They had better access to government officials than did Indians. The agencies were in many ways able to take decisions favourable to their own interests rather than those of shareholders. They were paid commissions based on gross profits or total sales and were often agents for the raw materials used by the companies they managed. Thus the Indian capitalists who did emerge were highly dependent on British commercial capital and many sectors of industry were dominated by British firms, e.g. shipping, banking, insurance, coal, plantation crops and jute.

Indian industrial efficiency was hampered by the British administration's neglect of technical education, and the reluctance of British firms and managing agencies to provide training or managerial experience to Indians. Even in the Bombay textile industry, where most of the capital was Indian, 28 per cent of the managerial and supervisory staff were British in 1925 (42 per cent in 1895) and the British component was even bigger in more complex industries. This naturally raised Indian production costs[40]. At lower levels in the plant there was widespread use of jobbers for hiring workers and maintaining discipline and workers themselves were a completely unskilled group who had to bribe the jobbers to get and retain their jobs. There were also problems of race, language and caste distinctions between management, supervisors and workers. The small size and very diversified output of the enterprises hindered efficiency. It is partly for these reasons (and the overvaluation of the currency) that Indian exports had difficulty in competing with Japan.

d) China

Until the nineteenth century China was a much bigger and more powerful state than any in Europe or Asia. Its technical precocity and meritocratic bureaucracy gave it higher levels of income than Europe from the fifth to the fourteenth century (see Figure 1–4). Thereafter Europe slowly forged ahead in terms of per capita income, but Chinese population grew faster. Chinese GDP in 1820 was nearly 30 per cent higher than that of Western Europe and its Western Offshoots combined[41].

In the first three centuries of European trade expansion, China had been much more difficult to penetrate than the Americas, Africa or the rest of Asia. Such trade as there was, was on conditions laid down by China.

Between the 1840s and 1940s, China's economy collapsed. Per capita GDP in 1950 was less than threequarters of the 1820 level. Population growth was interrupted by major military conflict. In 1950, China's GDP was less than a twelfth of that in Western Europe and the Western Offshoots.

The period of China's decline coincided with commercial penetration by foreign powers and the Japanese attempt at conquest. There are clear links between the two processes, but there were also internal forces which contributed to China's retrogression.

China turned its back on the world economy in the early fifteenth century, when its maritime technology was superior to that of Europe (see Table 2–11). Thereafter it was left without naval defences. China's highly educated elite showed no interest in the technological development and military potential of Western Europe. A British mission in 1793 tried to open diplomatic relations and demonstrate the attractions of western science and technology with 600 cases of presents (including chronometers, telescopes, a planetarium, chemical and metal products). The official rebuff stated "there is nothing we lack — we have never set much store on strange or ingenious objects, nor do we want any more of your country's manufactures." China did not start establishing legations abroad until 1877.

The Manchu dynasty was in a state of collapse from the mid–nineteenth century, and the Kuomintang regime which followed was equally incompetent. The dynastic collapse paralleled that of the Moghul regime in India, which led to British takeover there. However, Western colonialism in China was very different from that in India, and it was Japan, not the Western colonial powers, which attempted conquest.

Colonial penetration was inaugurated with the capture of Hong Kong by British gunboats in 1842. The immediate motive was to guarantee free access to Canton to exchange Indian opium for Chinese tea. A second Anglo–French attack in 1858–60 opened access to the interior of China via the Yangtse and the huge network of internal waterways which debouched at Shanghai.

This was the era of free trade imperialism. Western traders were individual firms, not monopoly companies. In sharp contrast to their hostile and mutually exclusive trade regimes in the eighteenth century, the British and French had made their Cobden–Chevalier Treaty to open European commerce on a most–favoured–nation basis. They applied the same principle in the treaties imposed on China. Hence 12 other European countries, Japan, the United States, and three Latin American countries acquired the same trading privileges before the first world war.

The treaties forced China to maintain low tariffs. They legalised the opium trade. They allowed foreigners to travel and trade in China, giving them extra–territorial rights and consular jurisdiction in 92 "treaty ports" which were opened between 1842 and 1917. To monitor the Chinese commitment to low tariffs, a Maritime Customs Inspectorate was created (with Sir Robert Hart as Inspector General from 1861 to 1908) to collect tariff revenue for the Chinese government. A large part of this was earmarked to pay "indemnities" which the colonialists demanded to defray the costs of their attacks on China.

The centre of this multilateral colonial regime was the international settlement in Shanghai. The British picked the first site in 1843 north of the "native city". The French, Germans, Italians, Japanese and Americans had neighbouring sites along the Whangpoo river opposite Pudong, with extensive grounds for company headquarters, the cricket club, country clubs, tennis clubs, swimming pools, the race course, the golf club, movie theatres, churches, schools, hotels, hospitals, cabarets, brothels, bars, consulates and police stations of the colonial powers. There were similar facilities, on a smaller scale, in Tientsin and Hankow. Most of the Chinese allowed into these segregated settlements were servants[42].

Apart from the British colony of Hong Kong, there were five "leased" territories ceded to Britain, France, Germany, Japan and Russia. These included Britain's 100 year lease on the New Territories adjacent to Hong Kong, granted in 1898.

Foreign residents and trading companies were the main beneficiaries of this brand of free trade imperialism and extra–territorial privilege. The settlements were glittering islands of modernity, but the character of other Chinese cities did not improve, and those which had been damaged by the massive Taiping rebellion of 1850–64 had deteriorated. Chinese agriculture was not significantly affected by the opening of the economy, and the share of exports in Chinese GDP was small (0.7 per cent of GDP in 1870, 1.2 per cent in 1913) — much smaller than in India. China regained its tariff autonomy in 1928 and there was some relaxation of other constraints on its sovereignty in the treaty ports. However, this was offset by intensified pressures from Japan.

The biggest intrusions into Chinese sovereignty and the biggest damage to its economy came from Japan. In the 1590s, Hideyoshi had made an earlier attempt to attack China by invading Korea, and the Meiji regime repeated this strategy with greater success in 1894–5.

There was a gradual build–up of pressure from the 1870s, when Japan sent a punitive force to Taiwan and asserted its suzerainty over the Ryuku islands (Okinawa). In 1876 a Japanese naval force entered Korea and opened the ports of Pusan, Inchon and Wonsan to Japanese consular jursidiction. In 1894, Japan declared war on Korea, and its forces crossed the Yalu river into China. In the Treaty of Shimonoseki, 1895, China was forced to recognise that its suzerainty over Korea had lapsed, Taiwan and the Pescadores were ceded to Japan. Japanese citizens (and hence other foreigners) were now permitted to open factories and manufacture in China. China was forced to pay an indemnity which amounted to a third of Japanese GDP, which China had to finance by foreign borrowing. This sparked off an avalanche of further foreign claims, and a Chinese declaration of war on the foreign powers in 1900. Within two months China was defeated by joint action of the foreign powers and Russia occupied Manchuria. Japan defeated Russia in the war of 1905, and took over Southern Manchuria. Korea became a Japanese protectorate, and in 1910 a Japanese colony.

Japan took Manchuria in 1931 and established a puppet state (Manchukuo) in 1933 which incorporated China's three Manchurian provinces, parts of Inner Mongolia, Hopei and Liaoning. China was obliged to turn the area around Peking and Tientsin into a demilitarised zone, which left North China defenceless. In July 1937, the Japanese attacked again. They presumably expected to take over the whole of North China after a short campaign, and thereafter to dominate a compliant government in the South as part of their new order in Asia. However, the Chinese government reacted strongly, and the war with Japan lasted for eight years. Its impact was compounded by the civil war between the Kuomintang and communist forces. Thus China endured 12 years of war from 1937 to 1949. The destructive impact was similar proportionately to that of the Taiping rebellion of 1850–64.

Notes

1. Beloch (1886, p. 507) estimated a total of 54 million (23 in Europe, 19.5 in West Asia, and 11.5 in Africa). My estimate is derived from Tables B–2, B–8 and B–9b of Appendix B.

2. See Needham, Vol.4 III (*Civil Engineering and Nautics*), 1971, p. 29 for his adjusted figures of paved roads in the 2 million square miles of the Roman Empire. His figure for the 1.5 million square miles of Han dynasty China was 22 000.

3. See Goldsmith (1984), pp. 271–2 for a discussion of the evidence on urbanisation. He suggests a ratio between 9 and 13 per cent, but my 5 per cent ratio refers only to places with 10 000 inhabitants or more.

4. See Warmington (1928) for Roman trade with Asia.

5. Hopkins (1980, p. 105–6) used information on 545 dated sea wrecks from the coasts of Italy, France and Spain to estimate changes in the volume of trade in the Western Mediterranean. He concluded that "in the period of Roman imperial expansion and in the High Empire (200 BC — 200 AD) there was more sea–borne trade in the Mediterranean than ever before and more than there was for the next thousand years." He shows that the level in 400–650 AD was about a fifth of that in the peak period. Ashtor (1976), p. 102 analyses Arab evidence on Mediterranean trade and concludes: "when the Arabs had established their rule over the eastern, southern and western coasts of the Mediterranean, it became the frontier between two civilisations, strange, unknown and hostile to each other. What had been a great lake on whose shores rulers, laws, religion and language were the same or similar became the scene of naval warfare and piracy. Trade disappeared almost entirely in the Mediterranean in the course of the eighth century. Spices, precious silk fabrics and other Oriental articles were hardly to be found in Western Europe."

6. See Pirenne, *Mohammed and Charlemagne* (1939), p. 242. Although Pirenne's description of the ninth century situation is succinct, striking and basically correct, his prior analysis of the timing and causes of Roman decline is difficult to swallow. He argued that the barbarian takeover in Gaul and Italy preserved a good deal of the advantages of Roman civilisation, and that its demolition was due to the Islamic invaders and Charlemagne. Hodges and Whitehouse (1998) summarise modern archaeological evidence and previous critical reactions to Pirenne's thesis. They conclude that Pirenne exaggerated the survival of Roman institutions: "By the end of the sixth century, conditions in the Western Mediterranean bore little resemblance to those in the second century. Before the Arabs arrived the transformation was virtually complete." (p. 53)

7. See Lane and Mueller (1985).

8. These fairs were held six times a year about 40 kilometres southeast of Paris and 110 kilometres from Bruges. Two fairs were held in Troyes, two in Provins, one in Lagny and the other at Bar–sur–Aube. They were the major centres of West European commercial activity from 1200 to 1350. They attracted merchants from all regions of France, northern and central Italy, Flanders, Hainault, Brabant, Spain, England, Germany and Savoy. The lords of the fair were the Counts of Champagne and later the French King. They derived income from taxes, tolls and safe–conduct charges on merchants. In return their agents kept law and order, helped to enforce contracts and kept notarial records. In cases of dispute, most Italian towns were represented by their consuls. The fairs petered out when the sea route from Italy to Flanders was opened (see Verlinden, 1963).

9. See Lane (1973), p. 19.

10. See Lane (1966), pp. 143–252 for an analysis of Venetian shipping techniques and navigation, and Unger (1980), pp. 161–94.

11. Possibilities for trade in the western Mediterranean had already been opened up by the recovery of Sicily (1090), Corsica (1091), Sardinia and Majorca (1232) from Arab control. This benefited the trade of Genoa, Barcelona and Provence.

12. See Landes (1998), pp. 46–7: "By the middle of the fifteenth century, Italy, particularly Florence and Venice, was making thousands of spectacles, fitted with concave as well as convex lenses, for myopes as well as presbyopes."

13. In the field of learning, it should be remembered that the University of Padua was part of the Venetian domain since its foundation in 1405. Its cosmopolitan faculty made major contributions to Renaissance scholarship and to scientific development. Its professors included Galileo, and the Flemish anatomist, Vesalius.

14. Henrique was influential in instigating a Portuguese attack on Morocco in 1415. The strategic port of Ceuta was captured and became a Portuguese stronghold (until 1580 when it was ceded to Spain). Ceuta was one of the terminals of the Sahara gold caravans. It was a useful port for Genoese, Venetian and Catalan merchants moving from the Mediterranean to the Atlantic, and seemed to be a first step in the conquest of Morocco. However, an attempt to take Tangier in 1437 was an ignominious failure. Henrique saved the remnant of his troops by promising to surrender Ceuta and leaving his younger brother as an Arab hostage. He kept Ceuta and left his brother to a nasty death (see Russell, 2000).

15. See Schwartz (1985), pp. 4, 7 and 504.

16. Barrett in Tracy (1990), p. 247, gives figures for West Africa gold exports for 1471 to 1800. From 1471 to 1700 they amounted to 145 tons of which most would have gone to Portugal.

17. The Portuguese were convinced that there were large Christian communities in Africa and Asia, and one of the missions of the explorers was to investigate the myth of the kingdom of Prester John. The Portuguese spy Covilhã went to Ethiopia in 1493 as part of this search. He stayed to work for the negus, the Ethiopian King and was found there in 1520. Elsewhere in Africa the only sizeable community was Copts in Egypt. There were small Christian communities in Southern India.

18. In order to check Cabral's discovery, the Portuguese engaged the Florentine navigator, Amerigo Vespucci to explore the Brazilian coast in 1501. He had carried out an exploratory trip two years earlier along the coast of Venezuela and Guiana for Spain. Needham (1971), Vol.IV:3, p. 513 refers to suggestions that the existence of Brazil was already known to the Portuguese before the Columbus voyage to the Caribbean.

19. Subrahmanyam (1997), p. 182 quotes a figure of "4 000 cantari". This measure has a wide range of possible meanings. Ashtor (1980) pp. 756–7, defines "kintars" (a measure used for Venetian spice exports from Alexandria) as 180 kg. I have assumed that this is the unit used in the source quoted by Subrahmanyam.

20. Needham (who was a biochemist) explains the European demand for spices as follows: "The usual idea is that pepper and spices were simply for table condiments or sauces designed to disguise the taste of tainted meat. But this could never have accounted for the vast imports of the Western Middle Ages –– we are bound to suppose that as in traditional China and the Islamic lands the pepper was actually mixed with the salt for — the meat to be preserved. The addition of spices in the correct amount permitted — inhibition of the autolytic enzymes as well as bacteriostatic action and an anti–oxidant effect on fats" (see Needham, Vol.IV:3, 1971, pp. 520–1). Landes (1998), pp. 132–3 makes the last point in different language: "people of that day could not know this, but the stronger spices worked to kill or weaken the bacteria and viruses that promoted and fed on decay."

21. See Tibbetts (1981) for a translation of the work of the leading Arab navigator Ibn Majid, and Jones (1978) for illustrations of Arab instruments to use stars and the sun for navigation.

22. See Goitein (1967) for the activity of Jewish communities throughout the Arab world of the Mediterranean.

23. See Subrahmanyam (1997), p. 96.

24. Albuquerque was Portuguese Viceroy in Asia in 1509–15. It was he who established the bases in Goa and Malacca. He selected Goa, after an attempt to take Calicut, where the Portuguese made a landing but were cut to pieces. The elimination of the Muslim position in Goa was welcome to the Hindu monarchs of Vijayanagar, with whom the Portuguese established friendly relations (see Panikkar, 1953, pp. 38–9).

25. The Grand Canal was about 10 times the length of the largest European venture — the Canal de Languedoc — built by Colbert and operational from 1681. Its length was 240 kilometres, and was confined to relatively small vessels (see Parry, 1967, p. 215).

26. In 1640 when Portugal regained independence from Spain, it allied itself closely with the United Kingdom. The British were allowed to have merchants in Brazil and Portugal, to engage in the carrying trade, were granted extra–territorial rights, and duties on British goods were bound at a fixed level. In 1703, the Methuen Treaty gave British goods free access to Brazil and the Portuguese market. In return, the United Kingdom propped up the Portuguese Empire with military guarantees.

27. Mulhall (1899), p. 172, shows Brazilian customs receipts equal to 21 per cent of trade turnover (about 37 per cent of imports after allowing for export taxes of about 5 per cent) in 1887 compared with a world average of 5.6 per cent. The ratio of customs receipts to trade turnover was highest in Portugal (41 per cent), next highest in the United States (15 per cent). In Holland it was 0.2 per cent; Belgium 1.1; India 2.2, and the United Kingdom 3.1. Mulhall also shows (p. 258) that in the decade 1871–1880 Brazil received 72 per cent of its revenues from customs duties (higher than any other country). In India it was only 4 per cent (the lowest).

28. From 1384 Flanders and Brabant, and from 1428 the province of Holland, were part of the Duchy of Burgundy whose headquarters were in Brussels. This was the main seat of the Duke and his court, with occasional sorties to Dijon and Bruges. The area of the future Belgium and the Netherlands had 17 provinces (staten) which sent representatives annually to a meeting of the States General where they were told what taxes they had to raise. The provinces were grouped under three governors (stadholders) selected from the nobility. The cities enjoyed considerable "liberties". These rights were exercised by a wealthy commercial elite which regulated industrial standards and arrangements for periodic fairs and staples for exports. There were three bishoprics within the area of the 17 provinces, and two others within the area of northern France under Burgundian control. It was a fragmented, and, by later standards, reasonably benign form of governance. The Duchy recognised French sovereignty, but was in fact autonomous. In 1477 the last Burgundian heir married Maximilian of Habsburg, and after her death in 1482, the territory became effectively a component of the Holy Roman Empire. Maximilian was Emperor from 1493 to 1519 and Charles V from 1519 to 1555. Habsburg rulers curtailed the privileges of the Burgundian nobility and the cities and imposed higher taxes. When the protestant reformation (Lutheran, Anabaptist and Calvinist) affected the provinces, there was a ruthless suppression of heresy. Charles V retired as emperor in 1555, and divided the Empire by giving the Austrian part to his brother, and the rest to his son, Philip II. In fact Philip was effectively in charge of the Netherlands for 50 years from his first visit to Brussels in 1548 until his death in 1598. The Netherlands was the richest region of his colossal empire and his intention was to squeeze it to finance his wider commitments and ambitions — which involved him in war with France, an attempted invasion of England and a massive naval conflict with the Ottoman empire. He used matrimony as well as war to further his ambitions, marrying successively Mary of Portugal (1543); Mary Queen of England (1554); Isabella of France (1559); Anne of Austria (1570). He squandered the silver tribute from Mexico and Peru, and fiscal irresponsibility led to a sequence of defaults on public debt in 1557, 1575, and 1597. The net impact of his activity was to weaken Spain.

Between 1609 and 1621 there was a truce in the war between Spain and the Dutch Republic. Hostilities were renewed in the 1620s when the two countries were on opposite sides in the 30 years struggle between protestant and catholic states in Germany. Spanish forces attacked the Netherlands from Germany, but after the 1630s were never again a serious threat to the Dutch. Spanish sovereignty in Belgium continued until 1714, when it was transferred to Austria, after the war of Spanish succession.

29. The seven provinces of the Netherlands emerged as an independent state with the formation of the Union of Utrecht in 1579, formally rejecting Spanish sovereignty in 1581. The new state was not quite a republic or a monarchy. It incorporated "generality" lands in northern Brabant including Breda, Bergen op Zoom and Maastricht. They were not treated as provinces, partly because the house of Orange enjoyed extensive seigneurial rights in Breda. William, Prince of Orange, Count of Nassau (1533–84) played a major part in the creation of the new state. He was the wealthiest of the Burgundian–Habsburg nobility, with extensive properties around Breda, in Germany and Provence. He was educated as a catholic in Brussels, served with distinction in the Spanish army against France, enjoyed high standing with the Emperor Charles V for whom he was governor (stadholder) of Holland and Zeeland. When he objected to the repressive policies of Philip II, his properties were seized, and a reward was offered for his assassination. He organised military and naval resistance to

the Spanish forces, converted to Calvinism and was recognised as stadholder of the provinces of Holland, Zeeland, Friesland and Utrecht in the new state. He was assassinated in 1584. Thereafter the House of Orange played a leading, but not continuous role as stadholders, and eventually in 1814 became hereditary monarchs of the Kingdom of the Netherlands. Their lands in Orange were seized by Louis XIV who incorporated them into France in 1685. The most prominent members of the house were Count Maurice (who had a leading role as a soldier defending the Republic from 1584 to 1625) and William, Prince of Orange, who was stadholder from 1672 and King of England from 1688 to his death in 1702. The British Ambassador to the Hague, Sir William Temple (1693, p. 133), described the situation in 1670s as follows: "the states general represented the Sovereignty, so did the Prince of Orange the Dignity, of this State, by Public Guards and Attendance of all Military Officers — by the Splendor of his Court, and the Magnificence of his Expence, supported not only by the Pensions and Rights of his several Charges and Commands, but by a mighty Patrimonial Revenue in Lands and Sovereign Principalities, and Lordships, as well in France, Germany, as in several parts of the Seventeen Provinces."

30. See Walter and Schofield (1989), p. 42: "Increased demand for non–cereal foodstuffs and non–agricultural products promoted mixed farming and a diversification of occupations in the countryside, leading to a better balance between cereal growing and animal husbandry, and, more generally to a strengthening of market networks. In addition, the increase in both the acreage and yields of oats and barley created a more advantageous mix to mitigate the impact of harvest failure by preventing the simultaneous failure of all crops." In the same volume (p. 199), Dupaquier makes another important point: "in France there was little movement of grain, and it was difficult to compensate for the effects of a poor regional harvest, whilst in England this could be done, thanks to the strategic role played by coastal shipping."

31. See Brewer (1989), pp. 14–20.

32. See Gregory King's manuscript notebook, p. 208, reproduced in Laslett (1973).

33. See Shammas, in Brewer and Porter (1993) pp. 182 and 184.

34. See Parry (1967) pp. 210–16 on the characteristics of the "fluyt", and Dutch shipbuilding techniques.

35. See North (1968) and Harley (1988) on the pace of decline in shipping costs, and Parry (1967) p. 216–17 on developments in land transport before the railways.

36. For a much more detailed analysis of this period, see Maddison (1976) and (1995a) pp. 65–73.

37. The present analysis of the British impact on India draws heavily on Maddison (1971). See also Habib (1995) and Lal (1988).

38. The "native states" ruled by princes with the guidance of British residents had about a fifth of India's population. There were several hundred of them. The really big ones were Hyderabad, Jammu and Kashmir and Mysore. Portugal retained Goa with 0.15 per cent of India's population, and the French had an even smaller toehold.

39. In 1913, foreign banks held over three–quarters of total deposits, Indian Joint Stock Banks less than one–fourth. In the eighteenth century there had been very powerful Indian banking houses (dominated by the Jagath Seths) which handled revenue remittances and advances for the Moghul Empire, the Nawab of Bengal, the East India Company, other foreign companies, and Indian traders, and which also carried out arbitrage between Indian currency of different areas and vintages. These indigenous banking houses were largely pushed out by the British.

40. See D.H. Buchanan, *The Development of Capitalist Enterprise in India*, Cass, London, 1966, pp. 211 and 321, who gives figures of the cost of European managerial personnel. In the Tata steelworks in 1921–2 the average salary of foreign supervisory staff was 13 527 rupees a year, whereas Indian workers got 240 rupees. These foreigners cost twice as much as in the United States and were usually less efficient. Use of foreign staff often led to inappropriate design, e.g. multi–storey mills in a hot climate or use of mule instead of ring spindles.

41. See Maddison (1998a), pp. 22–3 on the strength and shortcomings of the system of governance in traditional China; and pp. 39–54 on the economic decline and external humiliation of China between 1840 and 1949.

42. See Feuerwerker (1983) pp. 128–207 on the nature of the Treaty ports and settlements in China and on the lifestyle and privileges of the foreign community.

Chapter 3

The World Economy in the Second Half of the Twentieth Century

The world economy performed better in the last half century than at any time in the past. World GDP increased six–fold from 1950 to 1998 with an average growth of 3.9 per cent a year compared with 1.6 from 1820 to 1950, and 0.3 per cent from 1500 to 1820.

Part of the acceleration went to sustain faster population growth, but real per capita income rose by 2.1 per cent a year compared with 0.9 per cent from 1820 to 1950, and 0.05 per cent from 1500 to 1820. Thus per capita growth was 42 times as fast as in the protocapitalist epoch and more than twice as fast as in the first 13 decades of our capitalist epoch.

Interrelations between the different parts of the world economy have greatly intensified. The volume of commodity trade rose faster than GDP. The ratio of exports to world GDP rose from 5.5 per cent in 1950 to 17.2 in 1998 (see Table 3–2). There was a huge increase in international travel, communications and other service transactions. These improved the international division of labour, facilitated the diffusion of ideas and technology, and transmitted high levels of demand from the advanced capitalist group to other areas of the world.

The flow of foreign investment to poorer parts of the world (Africa, Asia excluding Japan, and Latin America) rose at an impressive pace in the past half century (see Table 3–3). As a result, the stock of foreign capital rose from 4 to 22 per cent of their GDP. However, the present ratio is only two thirds of its 1914 level. Most of the huge expansion in international investment in the past half century took place within the advanced capitalist group.

There was a resurgence in international migration. Table 3–4 shows that from 1950 to 1998, West European countries absorbed more than 20 million immigrants, Western Offshoots 34 million. There has been a distinct change in Western Europe. From 1870 to 1949 there was an exodus of people seeking better opportunities elsewhere. Since 1950 the situation has been completely reversed.

Within the capitalist epoch, one can distinguish five distinct phases of development (see Table 3.1a). The "golden age", 1950–73, was by far the best in terms of growth performance. Our age, from 1973 onwards (henceforth characterised as the "neoliberal order") has been second best. The old "liberal order" 1870–1913, was third best, with marginally slower growth than our age. In the fourth best phase (1913–50), growth was obviously below potential because of two world wars and the intervening collapse of world trade, capital markets and migration. The slowest growth was registered in the initial phase of capitalist development (1820–70) when significant growth momentum was largely confined to European countries and Western Offshoots.

Although our age is second best, and international economic relationships have been intensified through continuing liberalisation, the overall momentum of growth has decelerated abruptly, and the divergence in performance in different parts of the world has been sharply disequalising. In the golden age the gap in per capita income between the poorest and the richest regions fell from 15:1 to 13:1. Since then it has risen to 19:1 (see Table 3–1b).

Table 3–1a. **Growth of Per Capita GDP, Population and GDP: World and Major Regions, 1000–1998**
(annual average compound growth rates)

	1000–1500	1500–1820	1820–70	1870–1913	1913–50	1950–73	1973–98
				Per capita GDP			
Western Europe	0.13	0.15	0.95	1.32	0.76	4.08	1.78
Western Offshoots	0.00	0.34	1.42	1.81	1.55	2.44	1.94
Japan	0.03	0.09	0.19	1.48	0.89	8.05	2.34
Asia (excluding Japan)	0.05	0.00	−0.11	0.38	−0.02	2.92	3.54
Latin America	0.01	0.15	0.10	1.81	1.42	2.52	0.99
Eastern Europe & former USSR	0.04	0.10	0.64	1.15	1.50	3.49	−1.10
Africa	−0.01	0.01	0.12	0.64	1.02	2.07	0.01
World	0.05	0.05	0.53	1.30	0.91	2.93	1.33
				Population			
Western Europe	0.16	0.26	0.69	0.77	0.42	0.70	0.32
Western Offshoots	0.07	0.43	2.87	2.07	1.25	1.55	1.02
Japan	0.14	0.22	0.21	0.95	1.31	1.15	0.61
Asia (excluding Japan)	0.09	0.29	0.15	0.55	0.92	2.19	1.86
Latin America	0.09	0.06	1.27	1.64	1.97	2.73	2.01
Eastern Europe & former USSR	0.16	0.34	0.87	1.21	0.34	1.31	0.54
Africa	0.07	0.15	0.40	0.75	1.65	2.33	2.73
World	0.10	0.27	0.40	0.80	0.93	1.92	1.66
				GDP			
Western Europe	0.30	0.41	1.65	2.10	1.19	4.81	2.11
Western Offshoots	0.07	0.78	4.33	3.92	2.81	4.03	2.98
Japan	0.18	0.31	0.41	2.44	2.21	9.29	2.97
Asia (excluding Japan)	0.13	0.29	0.03	0.94	0.90	5.18	5.46
Latin America	0.09	0.21	1.37	3.48	3.43	5.33	3.02
Eastern Europe & former USSR	0.20	0.44	1.52	2.37	1.84	4.84	−0.56
Africa	0.06	0.16	0.52	1.40	2.69	4.45	2.74
World	0.15	0.32	0.93	2.11	1.85	4.91	3.01

Source: Appendices A and B.

Table 3–1b. **Levels of Per Capita GDP and Interregional Spreads, 1000–1998**
(1990 international dollars)

	1000	1500	1820	1870	1913	1950	1973	1998
Western Europe	400	774	1 232	1 974	3 473	4 594	11 534	17 921
Western Offshoots	400	400	1 201	2 431	5 257	9 288	16 172	26 146
Japan	425	500	669	737	1 387	1 926	11 439	20 413
Asia (excluding Japan)	450	572	575	543	640	635	1 231	2 936
Latin America	400	416	665	698	1 511	2 554	4 531	5 795
Eastern Europe & former USSR	400	483	667	917	1 501	2 601	5 729	4 354
Africa	416	400	418	444	585	852	1 365	1 368
World	435	565	667	867	1 510	2 114	4 104	5 709
Interregional Spreads	1.1:1	2:1	3:1	5:1	9:1	15:1	13:1	19:1

http://dx.doi.org/10.1787/170572737642

ISBN 92-64-02261-9 – © OECD 2006

Table 3–1c. **Shares of World GDP, 1000–1998**
(per cent)

	1000	1500	1820	1870	1913	1950	1973	1998
Western Europe	8.7	17.9	23.6	33.6	33.5	26.3	25.7	20.6
Western Offshoots	0.7	0.5	1.9	10.2	21.7	30.6	25.3	25.1
Japan	2.7	3.1	3.0	2.3	2.6	3.0	7.7	7.7
Asia (excluding Japan)	67.6	62.1	56.2	36.0	21.9	15.5	16.4	29.5
Latin America	3.9	2.9	2.0	2.5	4.5	7.9	8.7	8.7
Eastern Europe & former USSR	4.6	5.9	8.8	11.7	13.1	13.1	12.9	5.3
Africa	11.8	7.4	4.5	3.7	2.7	3.6	3.3	3.1
World	100.0	100.0	100.0	100.0	100.0	100.0	100.0	100.0

Source: Appendices A and B.

Table 3–2a. **Growth in Volume of Merchandise Exports, World and Major Regions, 1870–1998**
(annual average compound growth rates)

	1870–1913	1913–50	1950–73	1973–98
Western Europe	3.24	−0.14	8.38	4.79
Western Offshoots	4.71	2.27	6.26	5.92
Eastern Europe & former USSR	3.37	1.43	9.81	2.52
Latin America	3.29	2.29	4.28	6.03
Asia	2.79	1.64	9.97	5.95
Africa	4.37	1.90	5.34	1.87
World	3.40	0.90	7.88	5.07

Table 3–2b. **Merchandise Exports as Per Cent of GDP in 1990 Prices, World and Major Regions, 1870–1998**

	1870	1913	1950	1973	1998
Western Europe	8.8	14.1	8.7	18.7	35.8
Western Offshoots	3.3	4.7	3.8	6.3	12.7
Eastern Europe & former USSR	1.6	2.5	2.1	6.2	13.2
Latin America	9.7	9.0	6.0	4.7	9.7
Asia	1.7	3.4	4.2	9.6	12.6
Africa	5.8	20.0	15.1	18.4	14.8
World	4.6	7.9	5.5	10.5	17.2

Table 3–2c. **Regional Percentage Shares of World Exports, 1870–1998**

	1870	1913	1950	1973	1998
Western Europe	64.4	60.2	41.1	45.8	42.8
Western Offshoots	7.5	12.9	21.3	15.0	18.4
Eastern Europe & former USSR	4.2	4.1	5.0	7.5	4.1
Latin America	5.4	5.1	8.5	3.9	4.9
Asia	13.9	10.8	14.1	22.0	27.1
Africa	4.6	6.9	10.0	5.8	2.7
World	100.0	100.0	100.0	100.0	100.0

Source: Tables 3–2a and 3–2c are derived from Table F–3. In Table 3–2b, exports in 1990 US dollars from Table F–3 are divided by GDP in 1990 international dollars.

http://dx.doi.org/10.1787/170572737642

Table 3–3. Gross Value of Foreign Capital Stock in Developing Countries, 1870–1998
($ billion at year end and per cent)

	1870	1914	1950	1973	1998
Total in Current Prices	4.1	19.2	11.9	172.0	3 590.2
Total in 1990 Prices	40.1	235.4	63.2	495.2	3 030.7
Stock as per cent of developing country GDP	8.6	32.4	4.4	10.9	21.7

Source: The figures refer to the total for Africa, Asia (except Japan) and Latin America. 1870–1973 stock in current prices from sources cited in Maddison (1989a) p. 30. 1998 stock of foreign direct investment from UNCTAD, *World Investment Report,* Annex B; 1998 debt from World Bank, *Global Development Finance, Country Tables,* 1999; 1998 portfolio equity investment assumed to be $200 billion (derived by cumulating 1988–98 equity flows as shown in World Bank, *op. cit.*). Deflator is the US consumer price index, 1870–1980 from Maddison (1991a), Table E–2, updated from OECD, *Economic Outlook,* December 1999, p. 210. Denominator for third row is GDP in 1990 international dollars from Appendix A. The denominator for 1914 is 1913 GDP — 1914 not being available.

Table 3–4. Net Migration: Western Europe, Japan and Western Offshoots, 1870–1998
(000, negative sign means outflow)

	1870–1913	1914–49	1950–73	1974–98
France	890	−236	3 630	1 026
Germany	−2 598	−304[a]	7 070	5 911
Italy	−4 459	−1 771	−2 139	1 617
United Kingdom	−6 415	−1 405[b]	−605	737
Other[c]	−1 414	54	1 425	1 607
Total Western Europe	−13 996	−3 662	9 381	10 898
Japan	n.a.	197	−72	−179
Australia	885	673	2 033	2 151
New Zealand	290	138	247	87
Canada	861	207	2 126	2 680
United States	15 820	6 221	8 257	16 721
Total Western Offshoots	17 856	7 239	12 663	21 639

a) 1922–39; b) excludes 1939–45; c) Includes Belgium, Netherlands, Norway, Sweden and Switzerland.

Source: 1870–1973 generally from Maddison (1991a), p. 240; Australia 1870–73 from Vamplew (1987) pp. 4–7; New Zealand 1870–1973 from Hawke (1985) pp. 11–12; Canada 1870–1950 from Firestone (1958). 1974–98 from OECD, *Labour Force Statistics, 1978–1998.*

http://dx.doi.org/10.1787/170572737642

Table 3.5 compares the experience of different parts of the world economy in the three most successful phases of capitalist development. Performance in 1973–98 is compared with that of the golden age, and the "liberal order" (1870–1913).

Panel A shows the performance of 49 economies which produce more than threequarters of world GDP, and contain two thirds of world population. The advanced capitalist countries (Western Europe, Western Offshoots and Japan) together produce over half of world GDP. In this group, per capita growth in 1973–98 fell well below that in the golden age, but was appreciably better than in 1870–1913. The second part of Panel A shows the experience of "Resurgent Asia" — 15 countries which produce a quarter of world GDP and have half the world's population. The success of these countries has been extraordinary. Their per capita growth was faster after 1973 than in the golden age, and more than ten times as fast as in the old liberal order. They have achieved significant catch–up on the lead countries, and are replicating (in various degrees of intensity) the big leap forward achieved by Japan in the golden age.

Table 3–5. **Per Capita GDP Performance in the Three Most Successful Phases of the Capitalist Epoch**

	1950–73 (golden age)	1973–98 (neo–liberal order)	1870–1913 (liberal order)	1998 World GDP	1998 World Population
	Annual average compound growth rate of per capita GDP			Per cent share	
	Panel A				
Western Europe	4.08	1.78	1.32	20.6	6.6
Western Offshoots	2.44	1.94	1.81	25.1	5.5
Japan	8.05	2.34	1.48	7.7	2.1
Total Advanced Capitalist	3.72	1.98	1.56	53.4	14.2
Resurgent Asia	2.61	4.18	0.38	25.2	50.9
Advanced Capitalist & Resurgent Asia (49)	2.93	1.91	1.36	78.6	65.1
	Panel B				
40 Other Asia	4.09	0.59	0.48	4.3	6.5
44 Latin America	2.52	0.99	1.79	8.7	8.6
27 Eastern Europe & former USSR	3.49	−1.10	1.15	5.4	6.9
57 Africa	2.07	0.01	0.64	3.1	12.9
Faltering Economies (168)	2.94	−0.21	1.16	21.4	34.9
World	2.93	1.33	1.30	100.0	100.0

Source: Appendix A. The five phases of the capitalist epoch are the three indicated above, 1820–70, when world per capita growth was 0.53 per cent per annum and 1913–50 when it was 0.91.

http://dx.doi.org/10.1787/170572737642

If the world consisted only of the two groups of countries in Panel A, the pattern of world development could be interpreted as a clear demonstration of the possibilities for conditional convergence suggested by neo–classic growth theory. This supposes that countries with low incomes have "opportunities of backwardness", and should be able to attain faster growth than more prosperous economies operating much nearer to the technological frontier. This potential can only be realised if such countries are successful in mobilising and allocating resources efficiently, improving their human and physical capital to assimilate and adapt appropriate technology. Resurgent Asia has seized these opportunities. The countries of Panel B have not. Their relative position has deteriorated sharply since 1973.

Panel B shows the experience of "Faltering Economies". Collectively they produce about a fifth of world GDP and have about a third of world population. In all these regions, deterioration in performance since the golden age has been alarming. In the successor states of the former USSR, it has been catastrophic. The aggregate per capita income of Panel B countries actually declined by 0.21 per cent a year in the last quarter century. In the golden age, their aggregate per capita performance was identical with that of the countries in Panel A. In 1870–1913 their aggregate performance was not much below that of Panel A countries.

Before going into a detailed analysis of developments since 1973, one should note four major shocks which interrupted the momentum of growth and impacted unevenly in different parts of the world at different times. The first shock was a threefold challenge to the advanced capitalist group in the early 1970s (greatly accelerated inflation, the collapse of the Bretton Woods international monetary

Table 3–6. **Economic Characteristics of the 20 Biggest Countries, 1998**

	GDP in billion1990 PP dollars	Per capita GDP in 1990 PP dollars	Population million	Per cent of World GDP	Per cent of World Population
United States	7 394.6	27 331	270.6	21.9	4.6
China	3 873.4	3 117	1 242.7	11.5	21.0
Japan	2 581.6	20 410	126.5	7.7	2.1
India	1 702.7	1 746	975.0	5.0	16.5
Germany	1 460.1	17 799	82.0	4.3	1.4
France	1 150.1	19 558	58.8	3.4	1.0
United Kingdom	1 108.6	18 714	59.2	3.3	1.0
Italy	1 022.8	17 759	57.6	3.0	1.0
Brazil	926.9	5 459	169.8	2.7	2.9
Russia	664.5	4 523	146.9	2.0	2.5
Mexico	655.9	6 655	98.6	1.9	1.7
Indonesia	627.5	3 070	204.4	1.9	3.5
Canada	622.9	20 559	30.3	1.8	0.5
South Korea	564.2	12 152	46.4	1.7	0.8
Spain	560.1	14 227	39.4	1.7	0.7
Turkey	423.0	6 552	64.6	1.3	1.1
Australia	382.3	20 390	18.8	1.1	0.3
Thailand	372.5	6 205	60.0	1.1	1.0
Argentina	334.3	9 219	36.3	1.0	0.6
Taiwan	327.0	15 012	21.8	1.0	0.4
Total Top 20	26 755.0	7 023	3 809.7	79.3	64.5
World	33 725.6	5 709	5 907.7	100.0	100.0

Note: 1990 PP dollars are estimated by converting national currencies by purchasing power parities instead of exchange rates. The purchasing power parity estimates were derived mainly from the ICP (International Comparisons Programme) of OECD, Eurostat and the United Nations; see introduction to Appendix A for a detailed explanation.

http://dx.doi.org/10.1787/170572737642

order, and OPEC action to raise oil prices). The second was the debt crisis which hit Latin America in the early 1980s. A third was the collapse of Japanese asset prices around 1990 which had an extraordinarily deflationary effect on what was formerly the world's most dynamic economy. The fourth was the disintegration of the USSR in 1991. It involved collapse of Soviet control over the East European countries, dismantlement of COMECOM trade arrangements and the Warsaw Pact, and division of the USSR into 15 successor states.

Although these shocks had a profound influence, the liberal international order proved remarkably robust. There was no collapse of world trade or capital markets, and although there were a number of minor wars, the potentially lethal implications for global conflict inherent in the old cold–war standoff were substantially mitigated.

Developments within the fifth phase of capitalist development have been more complex in causality, have differed more between regions, and have been less synchronous than in the golden age. It is therefore necessary to examine the experience of each region separately.

I
ADVANCED CAPITALIST COUNTRIES

Western Europe

From 1973 to 1998, West European GDP grew at 2.1 per cent a year compared with 4.8 in the golden age. The deceleration had three components: *a)* a slowdown in population growth from 0.7 to 0.3 per cent a year, due to a significant and general fall in birth rates; *b)* very large rises in unemployment and other dimensions of labour slack; *c)* deceleration in labour productivity which grew at 2.3 per cent a year compared with 4.8 per cent in the golden age.

It was inevitable that West European productivity growth would decelerate. In 1950–73, once–for–all opportunities for catch–up on the United States were available and were seized, and the rate of technical progress in the lead country (the United States) was then much faster than it has been since 1973. In fact the catch–up process continued after 1973. The average productivity level in Western Europe rose from two thirds of the American level in 1973 to more than four fifths in 1998. However, per capita income in most Western European countries rose more slowly than in the United States because of slack in their labour markets (see Table 3–7).

The most disturbing aspect of West European performance since 1973 has been the staggering rise in unemployment. In 1994–8 the average level was nearly 11 per cent of the labour force (see Table 3–8). This is higher than in the depressed years of the 1930s, and four times the level in the golden age. Unemployment on this scale would have created a major depression if the unemployed had not received substantial income support from social security. The major reason for this rise was a change in macropolicy objectives. Initially, this was dictated by events but its continuance reflected a basic ideological shift.

The "establishment view" of economic policy objectives in the golden age was characterised by Erik Lundberg (1968, p. 37) as follows: "In the postwar period, the achievement of full employment and rapid economic growth have become a primary concern of national governments. Such policy targets did not ... guide government activities during most of the interwar period ... instead there were various policy aims that today would largely be considered as either intermediate, secondary, irrelevant or irrational targets, such as the restoration or preservation of a specific exchange rate, the annual balancing of the government budget, and the stability of the price level at a prevailing or previously reached niveau".

In the course of the 1970s, the objectives of full employment and rapid economic growth were jettisoned, and the major emphasis switched to achieving price stability. Initially, the change had considerable conjunctural validity. After the collapse of the Bretton Woods fixed exchange rate system, policymakers felt disoriented without a monetary anchor. This happened at a time of increased inflationary pressure, and expectations of accelerating inflation were greatly augmented by the first OPEC shock. It was felt that accommodation of inflation beyond a certain point would lead to hyperinflation, and that this would threaten the whole socio–political order. This was the razor's edge theorem. Income policies had been discredited so disinflation seemed the only option.

The change in the attitudes of policymakers was reinforced by changes in academic fashion. The Keynesians were pushed to the periphery, and lost their influence on policy. Politicians sought intellectual sustenance elsewhere. Friedman, Hayek and the neo–Austrians regarded unemployment as a useful corrective. The rational expectations school denied the usefulness of discretionary policy action. They argued that if simple rules were followed long enough, the economy would be self regulating. Responsibility for economic policy action should move from ministers of finance to central bankers. As far as possible, the latter should operate free from political pressure.

Table 3–7. **Western Europe and United States: Degree of Productivity and Per Capita GDP Convergence 1950–98**

	GDP per capita (annual average compound growth)		GDP per hour worked	
	1950–73	*1973–98*	*1950–73*	*1973–98*
France	4.1	1.6	5.0	2.5
Germany	5.0	1.6	5.9	2.4
Italy	5.0	2.1	5.8	2.3
United Kingdom	2.4	1.8	3.1	2.2
12 West Europe	3.9	1.8	4.8	2.3
Ireland	3.0	4.0	4.3	4.1
Spain	5.8	2.0	6.4	2.9
United States	2.5	2.0	2.8	1.5

	Level of GDP per capita US = 100			Level of GDP per hour worked		
	1950	*1973*	*1998*	*1950*	*1973*	*1998*
France	55	79	72	46	76	98
Germany	41	72	65	32	62	77
Italy	37	64	65	35	67	81
United Kingdom	72	73	68	63	67	79
12 West Europe	52	73	72	44	68	83
Ireland	36	41	67	29	41	78
Spain	25	52	52	21	46	64

	Employment as per cent of population			Hours worked per head of population		
	1950	*1973*	*1998*	*1950*	*1973*	*1998*
France	47.0	41.1	38.6	905	728	580
Germany	42.0	44.9	44.0	974	811	670
Italy	40.1	41.5	42.3	800	669	637
United Kingdom	44.5	44.6	45.8	871	753	682
12 West Europe	43.4	43.3	43.5	904	750	657
Ireland	41.1	34.7	40.6	925	698	672
Spain	41.8	37.4	34.0	921	805	648
United States	40.5	41.0	49.1	756	704	791

Source: Appendices A and E.

http://dx.doi.org/10.1787/170572737642

By 1983, deflationary policies had been quite successful, and the power of OPEC was greatly reduced. In 1973–83 inflation in Western Europe averaged 11.2 per cent a year, in 1983–93, it was 4.5 per cent. By 1993–8 it had fallen to 2.2 — about half the rate in the golden age (see Table 3–8).

The persistence of deflationary policies in the 1990s in the face of high unemployment and low inflation was due in large measure to a new objective of policy — monetary union.

Monetary union had been advocated within the EEC by the 1970 Werner Report, but this objective was abandoned in the monetary turmoil of the early 1970s and the collapse of the "snake" system (precursor of the EMS) in 1976. The EMS was created in 1979 to establish an area of exchange stability. From 1987 to 1992 it achieved reasonable success. As a result the objective of monetary union was disinterred and put forward in the Delors Report of 1989. This reiterated the importance of policy

Figure 3-1. **Binary Confrontation of United States/Japan, United States/European Per Capita GDP Levels, 1950-98**

(1990 Geary-Khamis dollars)

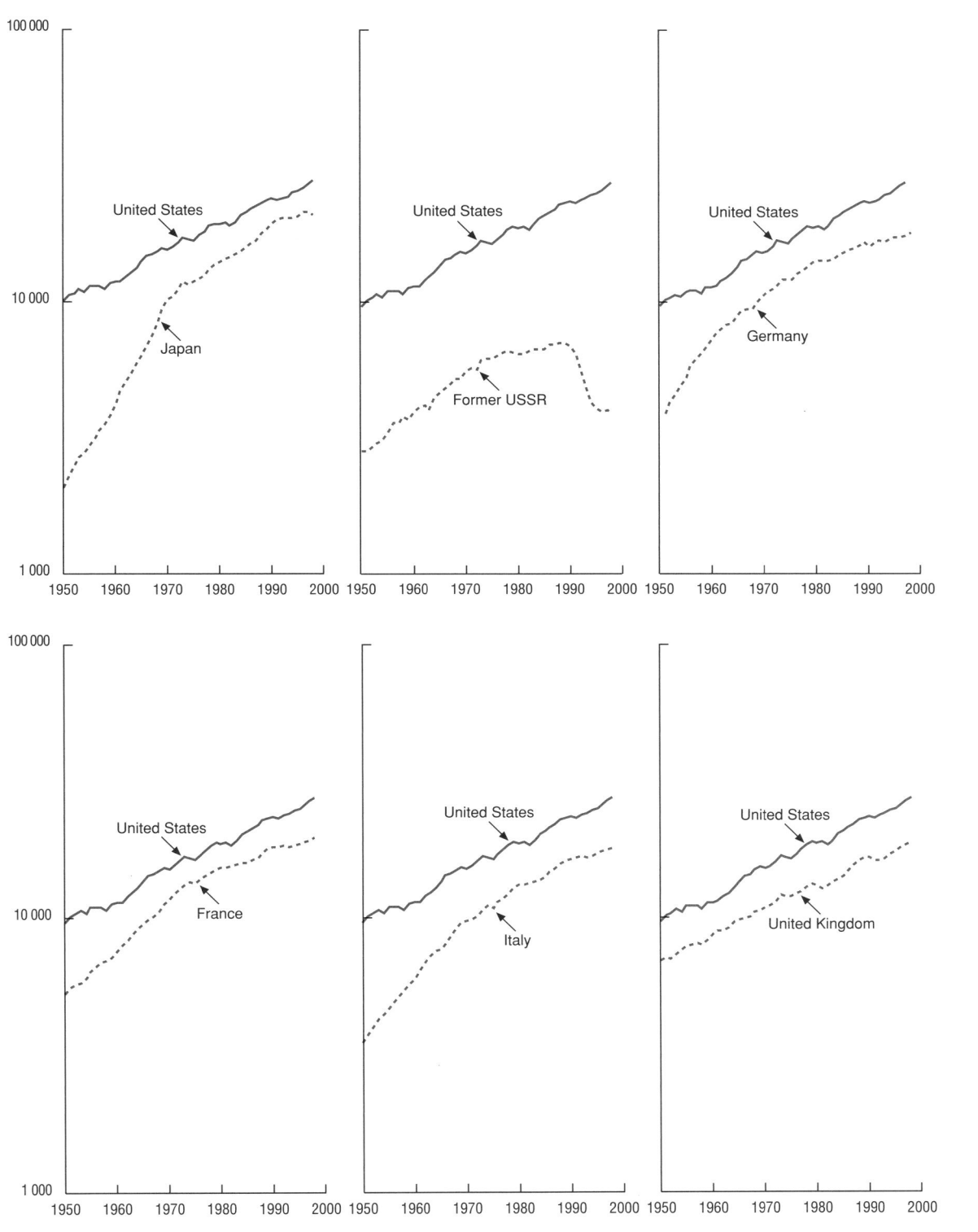

Source: Appendix C.

http://dx.doi.org/10.1787/170572737642

Table 3–8. **Experience of Unemployment and Inflation in Advanced Capitalist Countries, 1950–98**

	Level of Unemployment (per cent of labour force)				Changes in consumer price index (annual average compound growth rate)			
	1950–73	1974–83	1984–93	1994–98	1950–73	1973–83	1983–93	1994–98
Belgium	3.0	8.2	8.8	9.7	2.9	8.1	3.1	1.8
Finland	1.7	4.7	6.9	14.2	5.6	10.5	4.6	1.0
France	2.0	5.7	10.0	12.1	5.0	11.2	3.7	1.5
Germany	2.5	4.1	6.2	9.0	2.7	4.9	2.4	1.7
Italy	5.5	7.2	9.3	11.9	3.9	16.7	6.4	3.5
Netherlands	2.2	7.3	7.3	5.9	4.1	6.5	1.8	2.2
Norway	1.9	2.1	4.1	4.6	4.8	9.7	5.1	2.0
Sweden	1.8	2.3	3.4	9.2	4.7	10.2	6.4	1.5
United Kingdom	2.8	7.0	9.7	8.0	4.6	13.5	5.2	3.0
Ireland	n.a.	8.8	15.6	11.2	4.3	15.7	3.8	2.1
Spain	2.9	9.1	19.4	21.8	4.6	16.4	6.9	3.4
Western Europe Average	**2.6**	**6.0**	**9.2**	**10.7**	**4.3**	**11.2**	**4.5**	**2.2**
Australia	2.1	5.9	8.5	8.6	4.6	11.3	5.6	2.0
Canada	4.7	8.1	9.7	9.4	2.8	9.4	4.0	1.3
United States	4.6	7.4	6.7	5.3	2.7	8.2	3.8	2.4
Average	**3.8**	**7.1**	**8.3**	**7.8**	**3.4**	**9.6**	**4.5**	**1.9**
Japan	**1.6**	**2.1**	**2.3**	**3.4**	**5.2**	**7.6**	**1.7**	**0.6**

Source: Unemployment 1950–83 from Maddison (1995a), p. 84, updated from OECD, *Labour Force Statistics.* Consumer Price index 1950–83 from Maddison (1995a), updated from OECD, *Economic Outlook,* December 1999.

http://dx.doi.org/10.1787/170572737642

objectives which Lundberg had qualified as secondary or irrational in 1968. It made no mention of employment or growth objectives, nor did it give serious consideration to the institutional, social and economic costs of enforcing convergence and conformity in price, wage, monetary and fiscal behaviour. The major economic gain would be a reduction in transaction costs, improvement in economic stability, and economies of scale in a more integrated and more competitive European market. The proposal was adopted by the EC in 1991, and in the Maastricht Treaty of European Union which was ratified in 1993.

The path to monetary union was not smooth. In 1992 there was a major currency crisis. After a costly defence of their existing exchange rates, there were a number of devaluations. Italy and the United Kingdom left the EMS. In 1993 pressures on the French franc led the EMS authorities to widen the permitted fluctuation band from 2.25 to 15 per cent. Nevertheless, the determination to succeed was very strong, particularly in countries which had historically had the biggest problems of inflation and exchange rate instability and whose long term gains from monetary union seemed most promising. They were willing to prolong the period of high unemployment to fulfil the "convergence" obligations of membership — reducing inflation to what were to them very low levels, maintenance of exchange rate stability and reduction of budget deficits. These policies were successful in achieving a remarkable degree of convergence, and monetary union was inaugurated at the beginning of 1999 with all of the aspirants except Greece being accepted as members (Greece joined in 2001).

Although the intent of government policy in Western Europe was deflationary for a prolonged period, fiscal freedom was substantially constrained by welfare state commitments which are much larger than in the United States and Japan. When unemployment increased, transfer payments were triggered automatically. In many cases, particularly in France and the Netherlands, governments who considered unemployment to be caused by excess labour supply persuaded people to retire early or acquire "handicapped" status. There was also a steady build–up of pension benefits due to the ageing

Table 3–9. **Total Government Expenditure as Per Cent of GDP at Current Prices, Western Europe, the United States and Japan, 1913–1999**

	1913	*1938*	*1950*	*1973*	*1999*
France	8.9	23.2	27.6	38.8	52.4
Germany	17.7	42.4	30.4	42.0	47.6
Netherlands	8.2[a]	21.7	26.8	45.5	43.8
United Kingdom	13.3	28.8	34.2	41.5	39.7
Arithmetic Average	12.0	29.0	29.8	42.0	45.9
United States	8.0	19.8	21.4	31.1	30.1
Japan	14.2	30.3	19.8	22.9	38.1

a) 1910.

Source: 1913–73 from Maddison (1995a, p. 65); 1999 from OECD, *Economic Outlook,* December 1999, Table 28.

http://dx.doi.org/10.1787/170572737642

of the population. Budget deficits were much higher in 1974–96 than in the golden age. They fell in 1997–98 when the pressure to fulfil the convergence criteria for monetary union was at its height. The deflationary intent of government policy can be more clearly seen in the level of real interest rates. These were very much higher in the period of moderate price rises after 1982 than they were in the golden age and the years of high inflation 1974–81.

Since 1973, West European countries have given greater emphasis to use of market forces to improve efficiency of resource allocation. This was reflected in decisions to remove controls on international capital movements and privatisation of government enterprise. However, agriculture remains highly protected, regulation and tax policy are an impediment to efficient labour market functioning.

United States

American economic policy since 1973 has been much more successful than that of Western Europe and Japan in realising potential for income growth. The level of unemployment fell to less than half of that in Western Europe, whereas in 1950–73 it was usually double the European rate. Labour force participation increased, with employment expanding from 41 per cent of the population in 1973 to 49 per cent in 1998, compared with an average European rise from 42 to 44 per cent (see Table 3–7). Working hours per person rose whereas they fell in Western Europe. High levels of activity were achieved with a rate of inflation which was generally more modest than in Western Europe.

US policymakers have been less inhibited in operating at high levels of demand than their European counterparts. Having the world's major reserve currency, and long used to freedom of international capital movements, they generally treated exchange rate fluctuations with benign neglect. The Reagan administration made major tax cuts, and carried out significant measures of deregulation in the expectation that they would provoke a positive supply response that would outweigh potential inflationary consequences. The US operated with more flexible labour markets. Its capital market was better equipped to supply venture funds to innovators. Its economy was as big as Western Europe but much more closely integrated. Demand buoyancy was sustained by a stock market boom in the 1990s.

The United States was a major gainer from the globalisation of international capital markets. In the postwar period until 1988, US foreign assets always exceeded liabilities, but thereafter its net foreign asset position moved from around zero to minus $1.5 trillion (more than 20 per cent of GDP). Thus the rest of the world helped to sustain the long American boom and financed the large US payments deficit (see Table 3–10).

On the other hand there was a very large rise in US imports which helped to sustain world demand. From 1973 to 1998 import volume rose faster than in Western Europe and Japan. Imports grew at a rate not much less than in 1950–73, whereas in most of Western Europe and Japan there was a substantial deceleration (see Table 3–11). The rise in US imports reflected the strength of demand, and the impact of successive tariff reductions under GATT and WTO auspices, as well as regional arrangements such as the North American Free Trade Area (NAFTA).

In spite of American success in maintaining high levels of demand and activity, economic growth has been slower since 1973 than in 1950–73. The main reason was a sharp deceleration in productivity growth. In 1950–73 labour productivity rose by 2.8 per cent a year. From 1973 to 1998, this fell to 1.5 per cent, which is slower than for any sustained period since 1870. Between 1913 and 1973, US total factor productivity growth (the response of output to the combined inputs of labour and capital) averaged 1.6 to 1.7 per cent a year. From 1973 to 1998 it grew at about a third of this pace.

The productivity slowdown was masked by the improvement in use of potential, but has very serious implications for future growth if it continues, because it cannot continue to be offset by further improvements in the level of demand. The American slowdown probably contributed to slower productivity growth in other advanced capitalist countries which operate at levels of technology nearest to those in the United States. In the long run its impact would trickle down to poorer countries which operate at lower levels of technology.

Many participants in the "new economy" (information technology and associated activities) find the notion of decelerating technical progress unacceptable. It has accelerated dramatically in computer and communications technology and they assume that there have been big spillover effects in the rest of the economy. They justify their position by anecdotal or microeconomic evidence for their favourite sector, and point to the huge increase in share prices on the Nasdaq stock market (which specialises in the "new" economy). However the impact of this technological "revolution" has not been apparent in the macroeconomic statistics until very recently. Nasdaq gives high valuations for many enterprises which have low or no profits, and fell nearly 50 per cent from its peak in the second half of 2000.

New economy pundits argued that the national accounts statistics mismeasured growth. There was some truth in this because the traditional US growth estimates relied on fixed weights for a recent year to measure growth over a period of more than six decades. This did understate US growth compared with the weighting systems in vogue in Western Europe.

In 1993, the traditional approach to GDP measurement was modified by presentation of two new alternative measures: a) one where the weights changed every five years (a procedure then used in most EU countries), and b) a chain index with weights changing every year (a procedure then officially adopted only in the Netherlands). The 5 year segmented index showed the fastest growth (0.28 per cent a year more than the traditional measure and 0.04 per cent faster than the chained index). In Maddison (1995a) I used the 5 year segmented index as far as was then available (back to 1959).

Since then, US national accounts statistics have been further modified in ways which show faster growth and a higher level of GDP. With the new measures, one still finds a marked productivity slowdown from 1973 to 1995, but for 1995–8 there has been an acceleration to rates not far below the golden age. For 1973–95 labour productivity grew at 1.4 per cent, and in 1995–8 at 2.5 per cent. This recent acceleration is largely attributable to the increased weight of the "new" economy. Box 3–1 provides a detailed analysis of these changes in US statistical procedure and their impact. It also demonstrates that they do, in some degree, exaggerate US growth and levels of performance compared with the more conservative approach in measuring the impact of the new economy in European countries and Japan.

Recently, Jorgenson and Stiroh (2000) made an authoritative survey of US growth performance over the past four decades, using the revised GDP estimates. They found that accelerated technological change in computers and communications had its main impact in the production of these goods.

Table 3–10. Stock of Foreign Assets and Liabilities, the United States, Japan, Germany and the United Kingdom, 1989–98
($ billion at current exchange rates)

	Assets	Liabilities	Net assets	Assets	Liabilities	Net assets
	United States			Japan		
1989	2 348	2 397	−49	1 771	1 477	294
1990	2 291	2 459	−168	1 858	1 529	329
1991	2 468	2 731	−263	2 007	1 622	385
1992	2 464	2 919	−455	2 035	1 520	515
1993	3 055	3 237	−182	2 181	1 569	612
1994	3 276	3 450	−174	2 424	1 734	690
1995	3 869	4 292	−423	2 633	1 815	818
1996	4 545	5 092	−547	2 653	1 762	891
1997	5 289	6 355	−1 066	2 737	1 779	958
1998	5 948	7 485	−1 537	2 986	1 833	1 153
	Germany			United Kingdom		
1989	864	595	269	1 514	1 432	82
1990	1 100	751	349	1 728	1 744	−16
1991	1 146	818	328	1 756	1 750	6
1992	1 175	881	294	1 731	1 697	34
1993	1 285	1 080	205	2 001	1 948	53
1994	1 432	1 237	195	2 090	2 096	35
1995	1 656	1 537	119	2 386	2 394	−8
1996	1 691	1 612	79	2 775	2 778	−3
1997	1 759	1 695	64	3 212	3 348	−14
1998				3 521	3 695	−17

Source: IMF, *International Financial Statistics*.

Table 3–11. Growth in Volume of Merchandise Imports and Ratio of Imports to GDP, Western Europe, Japan and the United States, 1950–98

	Growth of import volume (annual compound rate)		Imports as ratio to GDP at 1990 prices		
	1950–73	1973–98	1950	1973	1998
France	9.3	4.6	6.1	15.2	27.7
Germany	12.6	4.7	4.1	17.6	36.1
Italy	11.3	4.0	4.9	16.3	24.9
United Kingdom	4.8	4.0	11.4	17.2	28.2
Japan	16.0	4.0	2.5	9.7	12.4
Arithmetic Average	10.8	4.3	5.8	15.2	25.9
United States	6.6	5.6	3.9	6.9	13.0

http://dx.doi.org/10.1787/170572737642

Box 3–1. Impact of Recent Revisions on Measurement of Level and Growth of US GDP, 1929–98
(million 1990 dollars)

	Maddison1995a updated	BEA (1998)	BEA (1999)	BEA (2000)
1929	844 324	740 311		711 309
1950	1 457 624	1 508 235	(1 455 916)	1 459 127
1959	1 981 830	2 068 828	1 997 061	2 006 235
1973	3 519 224	3 665 799	3 536 622	3 567 274
1990	5 464 795	5 743 800	5 803 200	5 803 200
1991	5 410 089	5 690 540	5 790 784	5 775 948
1992	5 562 302	5 844 986	5 983 457	5 952 089
1993	5 697 296	5 980 898	6 124 987	6 110 061
1994	5 907 953	6 187 856	6 371 321	6 356 710
1995	6 059 772	6 329 197	6 544 370	6 526 361
1996	6 276 136	6 547 387	6 784 105	6 759 427
1997	6 522 904	6 804 797	7 089 655	7 046 304
1998	6 777 297		7 394 598	7 349 878
1999				7 654 836

a) 1950–59 movement from BEA (1998).

Source: Col. 1 1913–90 from Maddison (1995a), updated 1990–7 from OECD *National Accounts 1960–97*, Paris 1999, 1997–8 from OECD, *Economic Outlook,* June 1999. Col. 2 1929–97 from *Survey of Current Business*, August 1998. Col. 3 from Seskin, *Survey of Current Business,* December 1999. Col. 4 from BEA internet web site June 2000. To facilitate comparison, I have converted BEA (1998) estimates from 1992 to 1990 dollars, BEA (1999 and 2000) from 1996 to 1990 dollars. Until the 1990s, the Bureau of Economic Analysis (BEA) published real GDP estimates back to 1929 with a single set of weights for the whole period. In 1993 it published three alternative estimates back to 1959: a) with old style fixed weights; b) a chain procedure where weights changed every year; c) a segmented index with weights changed every five years. In Maddison (1995a) I used the third procedure for reasons of international comparability (it was then standard practice for EU countries). In column 1, I used the 5 year segmented weights for 1959–90; it showed growth 0.28 per cent faster than the fixed weights and 0.04 per cent faster than the chain weights. BEA 1998 (col. 2) did not provide alternatives but switched completely to chain weights back to 1929. BEA (1999) made further changes for 1959–98 (including treatment of computer software as investment). BEA (2000) carried the new estimates back to 1929.

Impact of Recent Revisions on United States GDP Growth Rate
(annual average compound rate)

	Maddison1995a	BEA (1998)	BEA (1999)	BEA (2000)
1929–50	2.63	3.45	n.a.	3.48
1950–73	3.91	3.93	3.93[a]	3.96
1973–98	2.66	2.68[b]	2.99	2.93

a) 1950–59 movement from BEA (1998); b) 1997–98 from BEA (1999).

The impact of the revisions on growth rates is shown in the above table. For 1950–73, the new measures show little difference from those I used in Maddison (1995a). For 1973–98, BEA (1999), which I used in preparing the present study, shows growth about 0.3 percentage points higher than the old measure. However, the revisions for 1929–50 are much bigger. Their acceptance involves a major reinterpretation of American economic history. They imply a GDP level in 1929 16 per cent below the old index and would lower the level for earlier years correspondingly if used as a link. The 1913–50 growth of labour productivity would rise from 2.5 to 3 per cent a year and the 1913 level of labour productivity would be below that in the United Kingdom. The new BEA estimates also change the picture of the war and immediate postwar economy. It seems hazardous to use the new measures for 1929–50 without further investigation of the reasons why their impact is so big. One must also remember that no other country uses the chain index technique or hedonic price indices for such a long period in the past.

Many West European countries have also made recent changes in methods of measuring macroeconomic growth. In particular, most of them have adopted the new SNA recommendations which involve treatment of computer software as investment. However these changes have generally been less far–reaching and have had a smaller impact on growth rates than in the United States. Most other OECD countries have not adopted chain weights and of those which have, only Australia, France and Norway have carried them back very far (France and Netherlands to 1978, Australia to 1960). Most other countries do not use hedonic price deflators (which make a quality adjustment for changing product characteristics). Hedonic price indices are not used in Belgium, Finland, Germany, Greece, Italy, Japan, Spain or the United Kingdom. Wyckoff (1995) contrasted the 13 per cent a year decline in the US price index for computers and office machinery from 1976 to 1993 with the 2 per cent a year fall in Germany for the same period for this category of goods. Most of the difference appears to have been due to the technique of index number construction.

http://dx.doi.org/10.1787/170572737642

Productivity has continued to lag in the computer–using sectors. They state that "there is no evidence of spillovers from production of information technology to other industries — the empirical record provides little support for the 'new economy' picture of spillovers cascading from information technology producers on to users of this technology."

Oliner and Sichel (2000) reach more or less the same conclusion, as does Robert Gordon (2000), i.e. there has been a belated but positive payoff in macroeconomic productivity from a couple of decades of high investment in the "new economy".

The fact that there have been no very evident spillovers as yet in computer–using industries may well be due to the costs of absorbing new technologies which have involved a large input of highly trained people, rapid obsolescence of equipment and skills, and some serious blunders, such as those connected with the very costly Y2K scare. In the longer run, when the new technology has been fully assimilated, significant spillovers to other sectors of the economy may well occur.

It is too early to judge whether recent productivity improvements portend a return to the pace the US achieved from 1913 to 1973, but there are grounds for hoping that progress may be faster than in 1973–95.

Other Western Offshoots

Australia has been the most buoyant of the other Western Offshoots. It enjoyed favourable results from substantial reduction of trade barriers, increased competition, and its proximity to the fast growing Asian countries. The growth record was much less favourable in Canada and New Zealand.

Japan

During the golden age, the pace of Japanese growth was much faster than in Western Europe. Per capita income increased sixfold from 1950 to 1973, growing at 8 per cent a year compared with 4 per cent in Western Europe. Labour productivity grew by 7.7 per cent a year, compared with 4.8 in Western Europe, total factor productivity at 5.1 per cent a year compared with 2.9 per cent.

Japan did better than Western Europe for several reasons: a) its per capita income and productivity level in 1950 were little more than a third of the European level, so it had greater scope for exploiting opportunities of backwardness; b) the Japanese labour force already had an educational level not very different from the West European norm in 1950, and a huge reserve of technical skills acquired in military service which were fully available for peaceful pursuits; c) Japanese rates of investment were higher than in Western Europe; d) labour input per head of population was higher.

A major reason for Japan's capacity to mount such a large scale investment effort was the very high propensity to save in Japanese households. Horioka (1990) points to a number of complex reasons for this. They include traditional frugality which led to maintenance of modest lifestyles as income rose. Japanese had a high risk aversion and saved as a safeguard against illness and unforeseen risks. The smaller importance of social security than in Europe led to bigger private provision for old age. The significant role of remuneration in the form of twice–yearly lump–sum bonuses and relative scarcity of consumer credit were also contributory factors.

The Japanese catch–up effort was bolstered in unusual degree by government policy. Dedication to this goal was deeply rooted. In the seventeenth and eighteenth centuries, the Tokugawa regime sought successfully to catch up with and overtake Chinese levels of income. From 1868 onwards the objective was to catch up with the West.

In the postwar period, the developmentalist objective was pursued by a comprehensive interactive network of interest groups. There were close solidaristic links between Japan's highly educated bureaucratic elite, politicians of the Liberal Democratic party (in power with one brief interruption since 1955), big business and the banking system. Japan's large corporate groups (*keiretsu*) and banks had close interlocking financial ties. Large corporations often had long–standing symbiotic links with smaller firms. Japanese trade unions were organised on a company basis, workers had long–term job security, and identified their interests with those of their employers. The most successful members of the bureaucratic elite frequently moved into political office or careers of business leadership. MITI (the Ministry of Trade and Industry) provided "administrative guidance" to firms and banks which influenced the allocation of resources to what were considered key industries in terms of growth opportunities or export markets. The consensual character of all these relationships is reflected in the negligible importance of litigation or lawyers.

In the Tokugawa period, foreign trade was tightly controlled in a policy of seclusion (*sakoku*), designed to prevent foreign interference in Japan. In the postwar period trade was more open but the old autarkic emphasis remained. The government played a key role in promoting technological development, and assimilation of foreign technology, using techniques which preserved national independence. Foreign investment in Japan was very limited, and still is. Weak sectors, and some strong ones, were protected by a variety of restrictions on imports.

Although this version of capitalism was highly effective in producing rapid growth and high levels of per capita product it was more costly than it might have been with greater use of market forces, greater representation of consumer interests, and greater openness to foreign trade. By the early 1990s Japan had a capital stock per worker nearly a quarter higher than in Western Europe, but its productivity was substantially lower. Workers and "salarymen" worked very long hours and had little time for holidays. There was much greater unevenness of performance in different sectors than is normal for advanced capitalist countries — with very low productivity in agriculture and distribution, and a world leadership position in autos, steel, machine tools and consumer electronics.

In Japan, as in Western Europe, it was inevitable that the rate of growth would decline after 1973, and likely that the slowdown would be sharper, given the greater success in the golden age. The slowdown was indeed sharp, though per capita GDP and productivity grew faster in Japan than in Western Europe from 1973 to 1990. Thereafter things deteriorated badly. Per capita product rose only 1 per cent a year in 1990–98. Japan was clearly working below potential.

High Japanese investment rates continued in the 1970s and 1980s, and high expectations led to a boom in asset prices. But as the growth potential weakened there were diminishing returns and falling profits. This contributed to a collapse in share prices in 1989–92 from which Japan has not recovered. The Nikkei share price index in 1999 was at half its 1989 level compared with a fourfold rise in the United States, and a two–and–a–half–fold increase in Western Europe.

The stock price collapse was compounded by a fall in the price of residential land by a third from 1990 to 1998. This was proportionately more important than the stock market collapse. Household net worth of all kinds in Japan was 8.5 times as high as disposable income in 1990 and fell to 6.5 in 1998. In the same period the US ratio rose from 4.8 to 5.9, the German from 5.2 to 5.4, the French from 4.2 to 5.2.

The collapse in Japanese profits and asset values created a very deflationary situation. Consumers became extremely cautious in their spending. Many businesses became insolvent or bankrupt and banks found themselves with massive non–performing assets. This restricted their willingness and ability to extend new credits. The rate of price increase fell to 0.6 per cent a year in 1994–98.

Table 3–12. **Indices of Share Prices in National Currencies, Japan, the United States and Western Europe, 1950–99**
(1989 = 100)

	Japan	United States	France	Germany	Italy	United Kingdom
1950	4.4	5.2	2.4	3.6	3.5	3.1
1973	14.1	32.6	19.8	33.5	15.0	15.2
1989	100.0	100.0	100.0	100.0	100.0	100.0
1992	53.1	132.6	104.6	100.8	71.0	112.6
1998	45.9	344.4	209.7	238.7	211.8	217.4
1999	54.0	435.5	260.0	247.4	238.5	

Source: IMF, *International Financial Statistics*. The figures are averages for the years specified.

Table 3–13. **Exchange Rates: Units of National Currency per US Dollar, Japan and Western Europe, 1950–99**
(annual average)

	Japan	France	Germany	Italy	United Kingdom
1950	361	3.5	4.2	625	0.36
1973	272	4.5	2.7	583	0.41
1989	138	6.4	1.9	1 372	0.61
1992	127	5.3	1.6	1 232	0.57
1998	131	5.9	1.8	1 736	0.60
1999	114	6.2	1.8	1 817	0.62

Source: IMF, *International Financial Statistics*.

http://dx.doi.org/10.1787/170572737642

The government responded to this situation by a massive increase in extravagant public works rather than tax reduction. The Bank of Japan's discount rate fell nine steps from 6 per cent in 1991 to 0.5 per cent in 1995 and remained there for nearly five years. The interbank loan rate was virtually zero for two years from 1998. The government moved very slowly to clear up the mess in the financial system. It aggravated the long term problem by giving financial aid to institutions which should have been allowed to go bankrupt. Government measures prevented a major collapse in the economy, but they failed to revive demand.

The Japanese slowdown was transmitted to the rest of the world in two ways. Import growth was depressed but capital exports increased. Japan's high rate of saving continued but a larger share went to capital exports. Between 1990 and 1998 its net foreign assets rose from 10 to 30 per cent of GDP. Its impact on the world economy was a mirror image of that of the United States (see Table 3–10).

II
RESURGENT ASIA

In the half century since 1950, Asia has been the fastest growing part of the world economy, outperforming all other regions. This was in stark contrast with past experience. In the four and a half centuries from 1500 to 1950, Asia stagnated whilst all other regions progressed. In 1500 Asia accounted for 65 per cent of world GDP, and only 18.5 per cent in 1950. Since 1950, the Asian share has doubled.

In 1950–73, Japan had supergrowth, with per capita income rising over 8 per cent a year compared with the 2.6 per cent for resurgent Asia. In 1973–99 as a whole, per capita growth in resurgent Asia was twice as fast as in Japan. In the 1990s it was four times as fast.

Resurgent Asia consists of the 15 countries shown in Table 3–14. Seven of these (China, Hong Kong, Malaysia, Singapore, South Korea, Taiwan and Thailand) have been the most dynamic element in the world economy. Four now have a per capita income within the West European range. In 1999, the group had an aggregate income of 5.8 trillion international 1990 (PPP adjusted) dollars (not far below the aggregate for the 12 core countries of Western Europe, and more than double Japanese GDP of $2.6 trillion).

There are eight countries in a second group with an aggregate GDP of $3.1 trillion (more than twice as big as Germany). They have lower per capita income than the first group, and for 1950–99 as a whole their per capita growth rate was half as fast, at 2.2 per cent a year. Since 1973, their growth rate has been faster than in any part of the world outside Asia.

Table 3–15 indicates some proximate causes of Asia's growth. Within each category the countries are ranked in descending order of income level. The averages for each category are arithmetic, in contrast to the weighted averages in Table 3–14.

The supergrowth countries in the first group had high investment ratios. The combination of high investment rates and rapid GDP growth means that their physical capital stock was growing more rapidly than in other parts of the world. They also had a relatively high ratio of employment to population. This was partly due to a demographic transition with falling fertility and a rising share of population of working age, but also to the traditionally high labour mobilisation that characterises multicropping rice economies. In all cases which are documented they also had high rates of improvement in the quality of human capital (see Maddison 1995a for estimates of education levels). Equally striking was the rapid growth of exports and the high ratios of exports to GDP. This latter characteristic is in striking contrast to the Japanese model of development. Another contrast with Japan is the willingness of these countries to attract foreign direct investment as a vehicle for assimilation of foreign technology (see Table 3–16).

Countries in the second group have on average much lower income levels than the first, lower investment rates, lower ratios of labour mobilisation and less openness to international trade. To some extent, their slower growth suggests that "opportunities of backwardness" are not inversely related to income level. The ability to mount a successful process of catch–up seems to be greatest at somewhat higher levels of income.

It is difficult to draw sharp conclusions on the role of policy in the seven most successful countries, because their policy mix has been rather heterogeneous.

Three of the supergrowth countries are market oriented, open, highly competitive capitalist countries. *Hong Kong* comes closest to being completely driven by market forces, but its dynamism is also attributable to special circumstances. It was an unusually privileged entrepôt for trade and financial transactions between China and the rest of the world during the US embargo of 1952–73. It still benefits as an intermediary for trade between the Chinese mainland and Taiwan. Its low tax regime is partly attributable to the fact that the government has large revenues from monopoly ownership of

Table 3–14. **Variations in Per Capita GDP Growth Momentum: Resurgent Asia in Comparative Perspective, 1913–99**
(annual average compound growth rates)

	1913–50	1950–99	1950–73	1973–90	1990–99
Japan	0.9	4.9	8.1	3.0	0.9
China	−0.6	4.2	2.9	4.8	6.4
Hong Kong	n.a.	4.6	5.2	5.4	1.7
Malaysia	1.5	3.2	2.2	4.2	4.0
Singapore	1.5	4.9	4.4	5.3	5.7
South Korea	−0.4	6.0	5.8	6.8	4.8
Taiwan	0.6	5.9	6.7	5.3	5.3
Thailand	−0.1	4.3	3.7	5.5	3.6
7 Country Average	**−0.4**	**4.4**	**3.4**	**5.1**	**5.8**
Bangladesh	−0.2	0.9	−0.4	1.5	3.0
Burma	−1.5	2.0	2.0	1.1	3.8
India	−0.2	2.2	1.4	2.6	3.7
Indonesia	−0.2	2.7	2.6	3.1	2.1
Nepal	n.a.	1.4	1.0	1.5	1.9
Pakistan	−0.2	2.3	1.7	3.1	2.3
Philippines	0.0	1.6	2.7	0.7	0.5
Sri Lanka	0.3	2.6	1.9	3.0	3.9
8 Country Average	**−0.3**	**2.2**	**1.7**	**2.5**	**3.0**
15 Resurgent Asia	**−0.3**	**3.4**	**2.5**	**3.9**	**4.6**
Other Asia	1.8	2.3[a]	4.1	0.4	1.1[b]
Latin America	1.4	1.7	2.5	0.7	1.4
Africa	1.0	1.0[a]	2.1	0.1	−0.2[b]
Eastern Europe & former USSR	1.5	1.1[a]	3.5	0.7	−4.8[b]
Western Europe	0.8	2.9[a]	4.1	1.9	1.4[b]
United States	**1.6**	**2.2**	**2.5**	**2.0**	**2.1**

a) 1950–98; b) 1990–98.

Source: Appendix C, updated to 1999 from ADB, *Asian Development Outlook 2000*, Manila, 2000.

http://dx.doi.org/10.1787/170572737642

undeveloped land. It has access to an enormous pool of cheap labour on its doorstep. It has benefited from very large direct investment from abroad (see Table 3–16), and has made heavy investment in China's neighbouring enterprise zones where its stock of direct investment totalled $155 billion in 1998. In this situation, laisser faire worked wonders in achieving efficient resource allocation. In 1997, sovereignty reverted to China, but the nature of economic institutions and policy were not changed.

The reasons for *Singapore's* ascension resemble those operative in Hong Kong. It is a strategically placed city state with a vocation for entrepôt trade, but its growth got a bigger push from government. Its enlightened authoritarian regime pursued a policy of promoting high savings, improvement of education, encouraging exports and the acquisition of foreign technology. It benefited even more than Hong Kong from foreign direct investment (see Table 3–16). As its own manufacturing production grew more sophisticated, and labour costs rose, it became a major capital exporter, supporting partner enterprises in neighbouring countries. In 1998 its own stock of direct investment abroad was $48 billion.

The third country which is now a market oriented open capitalist economy is *Taiwan*. Its industry is characterised by highly competitive small scale firms with easy freedom of entry, and government willingness to let the failures go bankrupt. In the past two decades, as its manufacturing products became more sophisticated and labour costs rose, domestic investment ratios have fallen and there has been a substantial direct investment abroad, particularly in China. In 1998, its stock of foreign direct investment abroad was $38 billion. The government has maintained very large exchange reserves, as a hedge against its relative political isolation.

Figure 3-2a. **Binary Confrontation of Japan/East Asian Per Capita GDP Levels, 1950-99**
(1990 Geary-Khamis dollars)

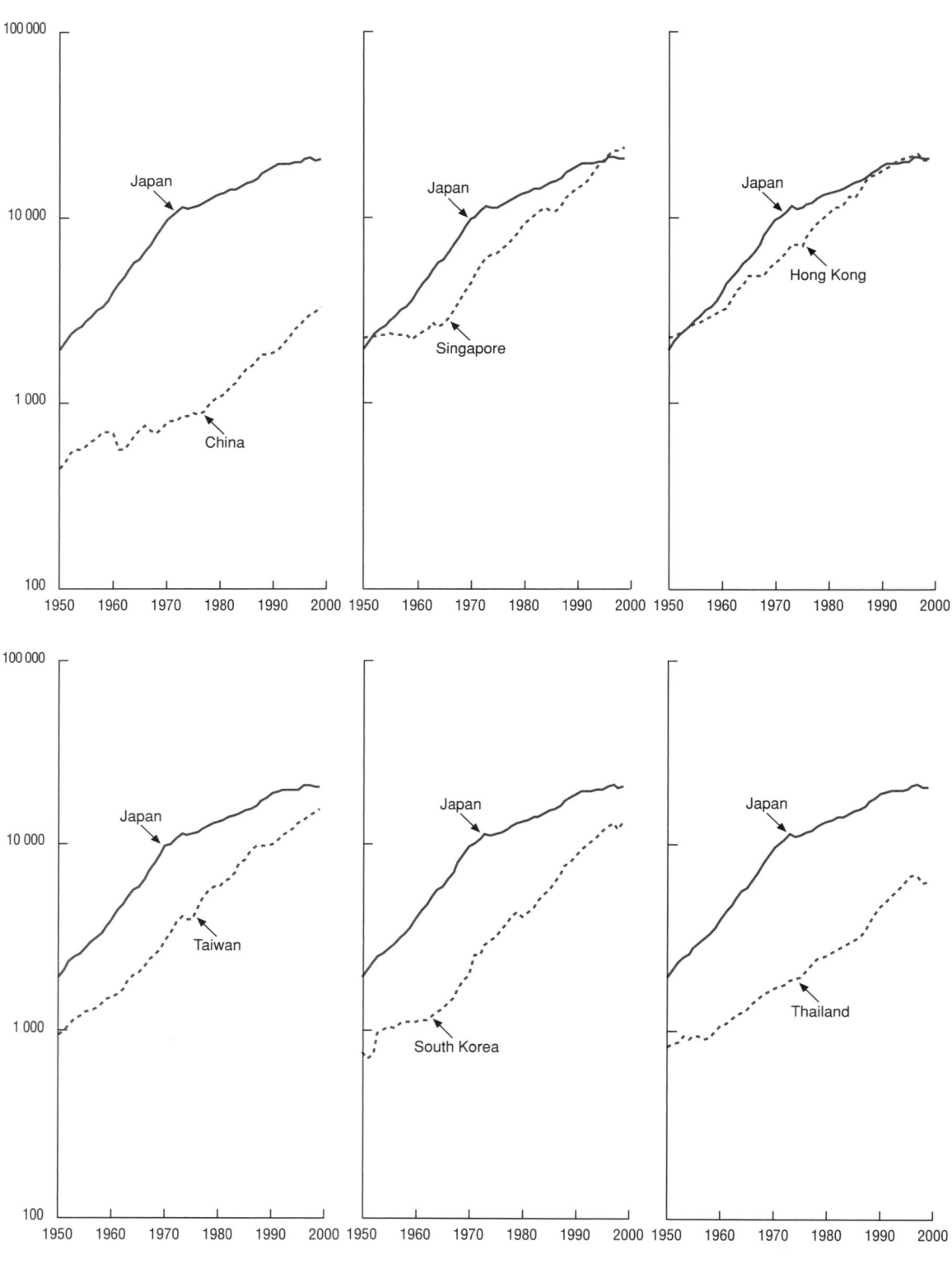

Source: Appendix C.

http://dx.doi.org/10.1787/170572737642

ISBN 92-64-02261-9 – © OECD 2006

Figure 3-2b. **Binary Confrontation of Japan/East Asian Per Capita GDP Levels, 1950-99**
(1990 Geary-Khamis dollars)

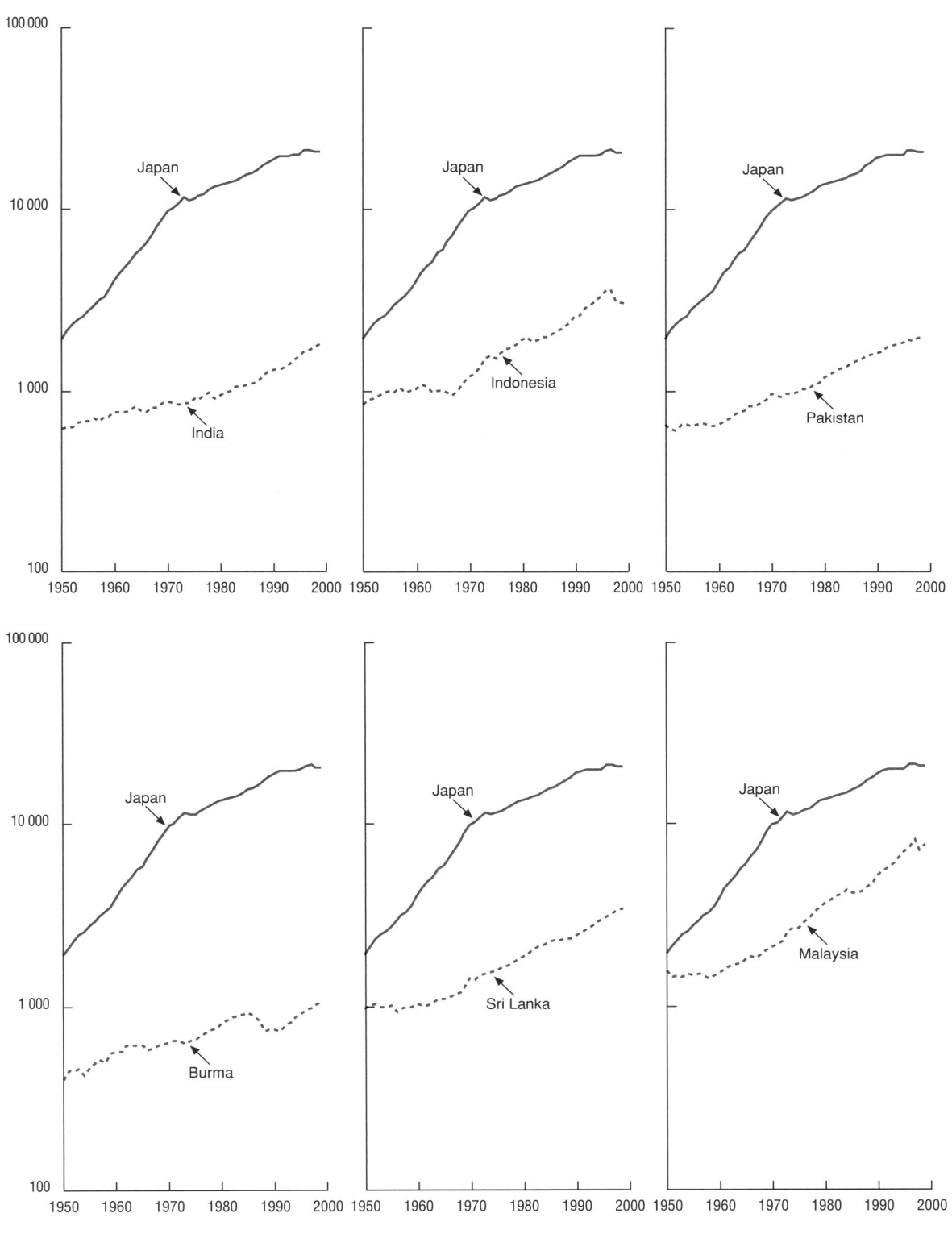

Source: Appendix C.

http://dx.doi.org/10.1787/170572737642

Table 3-15. **Characteristics of Growth Performance in Resurgent Asia, 1950–99**

	1999 per capita GDP Level	Per capita GDP growth rate	Fixed investment/ GDP Ratio	Annual export volume growth	Export/ GDP ratio	Employment/ population ratio
	1990 int. $	1973–99	1973–97	1973–98	1998	1997
Japan	20 431	2.3	.30	5.3	0.10	0.52
Singapore	23 582	5.4	.38	11.1	1.30	0.49
Hong Kong	20 352	4.1	.27	11.7	1.05	0.48
Taiwan	15 720	5.3	.24	12.1	0.42	0.44
South Korea	13 317	6.1	.31	13.9	0.41	0.46
Malaysia	7 328	4.1	.32	9.5	1.03	0.41
Thailand	6 398	4.8	.31	11.7	0.47	0.55
China	3 259	5.4	.30	11.8	0.19	0.52
Arithmetic Average	**12 851**	**5.0**	**.30**	**11.7**	**0.70**	**0.48**
Sri Lanka	3 451	3.3	.22	5.0	0.30	0.30
Indonesia	3 031	2.7	.24	7.3	0.25[a]	0.43
Philippines	2 291	0.6	.23	9.0	0.31[a]	0.38
Pakistan	1 952	2.8	.17	7.5	0.14	0.26
India	1 818	3.0	.20	5.9	0.08[a]	0.39[b]
Burma	1 050	2.0	.14	6.3	0.01[a]	0.40
Nepal	954	1.7	.17	4.8	0.09	0.39[c]
Bangladesh	835	2.0	.14	9.3	0.12	0.26[d]
Arithmetic Average	**1 923**	**2.3**	**.19**	**6.9**	**0.16**	**0.35**
United States	28 026	2.0	.18	6.0	0.08	0.52
Mexico	6 762	1.3	.19	10.9	0.16[a]	0.40
Brazil	5 421	1.3	.21	6.6	0.07	0.38[e]

a) 1997; b) 1995; c) assumed to be same as India; d) assumed to be same as Pakistan; e) 1994.

Source: Cols. 1 and 2 from Appendix A, updated to 1999 from *Asian Development Outlook 2000*, Manila, 2000. Col. 3 from ADB, *Key Indicators of Developing Asia and Pacific Countries*, Manila, 1999, except China (from *China Statistical Yearbook 1999*, p. 67–8 and Maddison 1998a, p. 164), Taiwan (from *National Income in Taiwan*, Executive Yuan, Taipei) and Japan (from OECD, *National Accounts 1960–97*, vol. 1, Paris 1999). Col. A from IMF, *International Financial Statistics*. Cols. 5 and 6 in most cases from ADB, *Key Statistics*.

http://dx.doi.org/10.1787/170572737642

China has totally different institutions and policy. Until 1978 virtually the whole economy was under state ownership and control. Economic performance was much better than in the past and the economic structure was transformed. The acceleration was due to a massive increase in inputs of physical and human capital, but there were self–inflicted wounds from the Great Leap Forward and the Cultural Revolution. For most of the Maoist period there was little contact with the outside world. From 1952 to 1973 the United States applied a comprehensive embargo on trade, travel and financial transactions, and from 1960 onwards the USSR did the same. Allocation of resources was extremely inefficient. China grew more slowly than other communist economies and somewhat less than the world average.

Since 1978, Chinese performance has been transformed by liberalisation of the economy. The relaxation of state control in agriculture was a massive success. There was a huge expansion in small–scale industry, particularly in rural areas.

The rigid monopoly of foreign trade and the policy of autarkic self–reliance were abandoned after 1978. Foreign trade decisions were decentralised. The yuan was devalued and China became highly competitive. Special enterprise zones were created as free trade areas. In response to the greater role for market forces, competition emerged, resource allocation improved, and consumer satisfaction increased. There was a massive increase in interaction with the world economy through trade, inflows of direct investment, a very large increase in opportunities for study and travel abroad, and for foreigners to visit China. At the same time, China was prudent in retaining control over the more volatile types of international capital movement. Although it has had to wait 15 years to be admitted to the World Trade Organisation, it is, together with Hong Kong, the world's fourth largest exporter.

Table 3–16. **Stock of Foreign Direct Investment, Total and Per Capita, Major Countries, Regions and World, 1998**

Country	Total ($ million)	Per capita ($)	Country	Total ($ million)	Per capita ($)
Japan	47 856	209			
			United States	875 026	3 234
China	261 117	183	Canada	141 772	4 679
Hong Kong	96 158	14 373	Australia	104 977	5 598
Malaysia	41 005	1 959	New Zealand	34 093	8 946
Singapore	85 855	24 600	Western Offshoots	1 155 868	3 574
South Korea	20 478	441			
Taiwan	20 070	921	Belgium[a]	164 093	15 448
Thailand	19 978	333	France	179 186	3 047
Total/Average	544 661	388	Germany	228 794	2 789
			Ireland	23 871	6 443
Bangladesh	652	5	Italy	105 397	1 830
Burma	1 139	24	Netherlands	164 522	10 798
India	13 231	14	Spain	118 926	3 021
Indonesia	61 116	299	United Kingdom	326 809	5 517
Nepal	81	3	Other Western Europe	264 441	4 311
Pakistan	8 221	61			
Philippines	10 133	130	Argentina	45 466	1 254
Sri Lanka	2 164	114	Brazil	156 758	923
Total/Average	96 737	60	Chile	30 481	2 061
			Mexico	60 783	617
Other Asia	75 492	198	Other Latin America	122 126	649
Total Asia	764 746	217	World	4 088 068	692
Africa	93 994	124			
Eastern Europe	66 397	549			
Former USSR	33 804	116			

a) includes Luxembourg.

Source: UNCTAD, *World Investment Report*, Geneva, 1999.

http://dx.doi.org/10.1787/170572737642

As a result China has had one of the fastest rates of growth of per capita GDP, and its growth path has been more stable since the 1970s than most of Asia. Its success is in striking contrast to the collapse of activity in the former USSR.

China still has some important problems to solve. It needs to shut down a large proportion of state industrial enterprises which are a hangover from the Maoist period. Most of them make substantial losses. They are kept in operation by government subsidy and default on loans which the state banks are constrained to give them. The relative importance of these enterprises is declining significantly. In 1996 43 million people were employed in the state industrial sector. By 1999 this had fallen to 24 million. Public employment in wholesale and retail trade and restaurants fell from 10.6 million to 6.0 million in the same period.

Another major (and related) problem is the large volume of non–performing loans in the banking sector which is largely controlled by the state. The importance of non–performing loans is smaller than in Japan, but the state does not make efficient allocation of the large funds which it captures from savers and the rapidly burgeoning private sector is starved of funds.

Korea's institutions and policy mix have been somewhat like those of Japan, with close interaction between government and large industrial conglomerates on strategic decisions. There has been a substantial liberalisation of the system in the past decade, with a reduced role for government. A major difference from Japan has been the high export orientation of the economy.

Table 3–17. **Annual Percentage Change in Real GDP Per Capita, Japan and Resurgent Asia, 1997–99**

	Japan	China	Hong Kong	Malaysia	Singapore	South Korea	Taiwan	Thailand
1997	1.2	5.4	2.1	5.4	6.2	3.8	5.8	−1.4
1998	−3.1	4.8	−7.8	−8.7	0.1	−6.7	3.9	−8.9
1999	0.1	4.6	.0.8	3.2	4.1	9.6	4.7	3.1

	Bangladesh	Burma	India	Indonesia	Nepal	Pakistan	Philippines	Sri Lanka
1997	3.7	2.8	3.3	2.8	1.4	−0.9	2.9	5.1
1998	3.7	4.5	4.1	−14.1	−0.6	3.1	−2.6	3.6
1999	2.7	2.5	4.1	−1.3	0.7	0.9	1.0	3.0

Source: Appendix C, updated to 1999 from ADB.

Table 3–18. **Exchange Rates: Units of National Currency Per US Dollar in Asian Countries, 1973–99**
(annual average)

	China	Hong Kong	Malaysia	Singapore	South Korea	Taiwan	Thailand
1973	1.99		2.44	2.46	398		20.62
1989	3.77	7.80	2.71	1.95	671	26.41	25.70
1997	8.29	7.74	2.81	1.48	951	28.70	31.36
1998	8.28	7.75	3.92	1.67	1 401	33.46	41.36
1999	8.28	7.76	3.80	1.70	1 189	32.27	37.84

	Bangladesh	Burma	India	Indonesia	Nepal	Pakistan	Philippines	Sri Lanka
1973	7.74	4.93	7.74	415	10.50	9.99	6.76	6.40
1989	32.27	6.70	16.23	1 770	27.19	20.54	21.74	36.05
1997	43.89	6.24	36.31	2 909	58.01	40.87	29.47	59.00
1998	46.91	6.34	41.26	10 014	65.98	44.92	40.89	64.59
1999	49.09	6.29	43.06	7 855	68.25	47.70	39.09	70.40

Source: IMF, *International Financial Statistics*, Hong Kong and Taiwan from national sources and Asian Development Bank.

http://dx.doi.org/10.1787/170572737642

Korea succeeded in achieving the fastest growth of per capita income in Asia and the world over the past half century. From 1950–73 it grew at 5.8 per cent a year, and from 1973–99 at 6.1 per cent. In the first of these periods it grew more slowly than Japan, in the second more than twice as fast. This was achieved despite very high military expenditure.

In 1998, there was a severe recession with a 6.7 per cent fall in per capita income. This was caused by flight of foreign short term capital in the Asian financial crises of that year. But Korea has a history of successful accommodation to external shocks, and in 1999 per capita income bounced up by 9.6 per cent. As in other Asian countries, the crisis was in large part a consequence of liberalisation of capital transactions in the early 1990s. There were large short term inflows from foreign investors seeking quick gains in a booming economy. The incentive to make such investments was particularly strong for Japanese investors whose own economy was stagnating, whose returns on equity investment were negative and on fixed rate securities virtually zero. In 1997–98, Korea was overexposed to changes in the expectations of foreign short term investors. They were panicked into sudden withdrawal of funds by the contagion effect of the crisis in Thailand.

The 1998 Korean crisis was overcome by substantial borrowing from the IMF, some degree of deflation in policy and the depressing effect of a temporary collapse in profits, stock prices and the exchange rate. There have been some beneficial effects of the crisis. The government is likely to be more cautious in encouraging the more volatile kind of capital inflow. It has moved to encourage bigger flows of foreign direct investment, pushed some of the large conglomerates (*chaebol*) to sell off distressed assets. The banking system has a significant portfolio of non–performing loans but these are proportionately smaller than in Japan.

Table 3–19. **Pre and Post–Crisis Savings as Per Cent of GDP in Five East Asian Countries, 1990–98**

| | 1990–96 | | 1998 | |
	National	Foreign	National	Foreign
Indonesia	29.3	2.6	15.5	−4.9
Korea	35.5	1.8	32.8	−12.8
Malaysia	34.2	6.0	41.8	−13.7
Philippines	19.3	3.9	16.3	−1.9
Thailand	34.8	7.1	32.2	−13.2

Source: Reisen and Soto (2000).

http://dx.doi.org/10.1787/170572737642

The 1997–98 recession had a serious impact in several Asian countries (see Table 3–17). The adverse effects were greatest in Indonesia where GDP per capita fell by one seventh in 1998. Bankruptcy and the social and political aftermath were much deeper than elsewhere, with negligible signs of recovery. The growth performance of Hong Kong, Malaysia and Thailand was also seriously interrupted. The basic cause was the reversal of massive short term capital inflows which had poured into the region in 1995–97 because of euphoria induced by rapid growth and liberalisation of capital movements (see Table 3–19). All of these countries have made some degree of recovery, but it is too early to assess the degree of damage to their long run growth momentum.

III
PROBLEM ECONOMIES OF EAST ASIA

There are six East Asian economies (Afghanistan, Cambodia, Laos, Mongolia, North Korea and Vietnam) where economic performance since 1950 has been considerably worse than in the rest of Asia, and where income levels are relatively low. Most of these were run for a lengthy period on communist lines, and economic advance was seriously interrupted by war. The worst cases are North Korea and Mongolia which were closely integrated in the Soviet orbit, and where aid and trade were disrupted after the collapse of the USSR in 1991. North Korea is an isolated outpost of Stalinism and has suffered the worst. Mongolia has privatised and marketised its economy and suffers from problems of transition which seem to be smaller than in some of the Asian successor states of the former USSR (see part VI below). Afghanistan has been shattered by foreign invasion and civil war and now has the lowest per capita income in Asia. Cambodia, Laos and Vietnam are making a more successful transition than the successor states of the USSR.

Table 3–20. **Per Capita GDP Performance in Six Problem Economies of East Asia, 1950–98**

| | 1950–73 | 1973–90 | 1990–98 | 1998 per capita GDP Level (1990 int. dollars) |
	(annual average compound growth rates)			
Afghanistan	0.3	−0.8	−1.9	514
Cambodia	2.0	0.9	1.4	1 058
Laos	1.0	1.1	2.1	1 104
Mongolia	3.0	2.6	−2.4	1 094
North Korea	5.8	0.0	−10.4	1 183
Vietnam	1.1	1.3	6.2	1 677

http://dx.doi.org/10.1787/170572737642

IV
WEST ASIA

West Asia consists of 15 economies. Ten of these are significant oil producers. The importance of oil helps to explain why they have relatively high per capita incomes, and why their growth momentum has differed from that in most of Asia. Per capita income of the oil producers in 1950 was much higher than in prewar years, and higher than in the rest of Asia. Oil production was 16 million metric tons in 1937, 86 million in 1950, and 1 054 million in 1973 — an increase of 11.5 per cent a year from 1950–1973. OPEC action in raising prices and restricting supply meant that aggregate oil production of West Asia was about the same in 1999 as in 1973 (see Table 3–21). Growth was significantly affected by war in Iraq, Iran, Israel, Kuwait, Lebanon, Palestine, Syria and Yemen. The aggregate GDP of this group was about 10 per cent of the Asian total in 1998.

It should be noted that our measure of real GDP per capita is in 1990 prices, and is not adjusted for changes in terms of trade. For most countries this is not important in assessing long term economic performance, but where exports are heavily concentrated on one commodity and prices are highly volatile, these movements are important. The average price of a barrel of crude oil quadrupled from 1972 to 1974. From 1978 to 1980 it rose nearly threefold. Between mid–1997 and mid–1998, it fell by half. At mid–year 2000 it was three times as high as in mid–1998.

Table 3–21. **World Production of Crude Oil and Natural Gas, 1950–99**
(million metric tons)

Country	1950	1973	1999	Country	1950	1973	1999
Bahrain	1.5	3.4	2.2	**Former USSR**	37.9	429.1	370.2
Iran	32.3	293.2	176.2				
Iraq	6.6	99.5	124.7	Romania		14.3	6.6
Kuwait	17.3	150.6	95.6	Other Eastern Europe		8.2	5.6
Oman		14.6	46.1				
Qatar	1.6	27.5	31.2	**Total Eastern Europe**		22.5	12.3
Saudi Arabia	26.6	380.2	426.3				
Syria	–	5.5	29.2	Argentina	3.4	21.9	43.0
United Arab Emirates	–	73.6	101.7	Brazil	–	8.3	57.4
Yemen	–	–	19.4	Colombia	4.7	9.8	41.8
				Ecuador	0.3	10.6	20.7
Total West Asia	**85.9**	**1 054.1**	**1 052.7**	Mexico	10.4	27.2	163.4
				Peru	2.1	3.6	5.3
China	n.a.	53.6	160.6	Venezuela	80.0	178.4	161.7
India	0.3	7.2	38.0	Other Latin America	n.a.	12.3	13.0
Indonesia	6.4	66.1	63.9				
Malaysia	n.a.	4.3	37.6	**Total Latin America**	**n.a.**	**272.1**	**506. 3**
Other East Asia	n.a.	13.6	37.6				
				Algeria	–	51.1	58.5
Total East Asia	**n.a.**	**91.3**	**177.0**	Angola		8.2	37.6
				Congo		2.1	12.9
Norway	–	1.6	149.3	Egypt	2.6	8.5	41.5
United Kingdom	0.2	0.5	139.2	Gabon		7.6	16.8
Other West Europe	n.a.	18.3	31.7	Libya		106.2	65.0
				Nigeria			99.5
Total Western Europe	**n.a.**	**20.4**	**320.2**	Other Africa	–	3.9	17.5
United States	266.7	513.3	359.6	**Total Africa**		**289.0**	**349.3**
Canada		94.1	114.1				
Australia		19.2	24.6	**World**	**523.0**	**2 858.9**	**3 449.5**
New Zealand		0.2	2.1				
Total Western Offshoots		**626.8**	**500.4**				

Source: 1950 from *UN Statistical Yearbook 1955*, New York, pp. 142–5. 1973 and 1999 supplied by International Energy Agency, Paris.

http://dx.doi.org/10.1787/170572737642

Another feature of the oil producing countries has been extremely rapid population growth as prosperity created a huge demand for foreign workers. Thus the population of Qatar increased 28–fold from 1950 to 1998, UAE 32–fold, Kuwait 13–fold, Saudi Arabia fivefold.

V
LATIN AMERICA

In Latin America, the Bretton Woods collapse and the acceleration of inflation in the early 1970s did not have the same effect on the policy–making establishment that it did in Europe. Most countries had never seriously tried to observe the fixed rate discipline of Bretton Woods. National currencies had been repeatedly devalued, IMF advocacy of fiscal and monetary rectitude had been frequently rebuffed, high rates of inflation had become endemic. The new disturbances were generally viewed as variations on a familiar theme. The acceleration of inflation was not regarded as a razor's edge situation, calling for drastic policy reorientation. The OPEC shock was important for Brazil as a large energy importer, but it brought windfall profits to oil exporting Mexico, Colombia and Venezuela, and was fairly neutral for self sufficient oil producers like Argentina, Chile and Peru.

Hence most countries reacted with insouciance to the worldwide explosion of prices, and governments felt that they could accommodate high rates of inflation. They were able to borrow on a large scale at negative real interest rates to cover external deficits incurred as a result of expansionary policies. As a result their GDP growth rate from 1973 to 1980 did not decelerate.

However, the basic parameters had changed by the early 1980s. By then, the OECD countries were pushing anti–inflationary policy very vigorously. The change to restrictive monetary policy initiated by the United States Federal Reserve pushed up interest rates suddenly and sharply. The dollar appreciated and world export prices began to fall. The average real interest cost of floating rate dollar debt rose to nearly 16 per cent in 1981–83 compared with minus 8.7 per cent in 1977–80. Between 1973 and 1982 external debt had increased sevenfold and the creditworthiness of Latin America as a whole was grievously damaged by Mexico's debt delinquency in 1982. The flow of voluntary private lending stopped abruptly, and created a massive need for retrenchment in economies teetering on the edge of hyperinflation and fiscal crisis. In most countries resource allocation was distorted by subsidies, controls, widespread commitments to government enterprise, and detailed interventionism. Most of them also had serious social tension, and several had unsavoury political regimes.

In the 1930s, most of the Latin American countries resorted to debt default. This path was pursued by some (Bolivia and Peru), but it was not a very attractive option in the 1980s. World trade had not collapsed, international private lending continued on a large scale. The IMF and World Bank had substantial facilities to mitigate the situation, and leverage to pressure Western banks to make involuntary loans and legitimate a substantial degree of delinquency.

In the course of the 1980s, attempts to resolve these problems brought major changes in economic policy. But in most countries, the changes were made reluctantly. After experiments with heterodox policy options in Argentina and Brazil, most countries eventually embraced the neoliberal policy mix pioneered by Chile. They moved towards more market oriented policy, greater openness to international markets, reduced government intervention, trade liberalisation, less distorted exchange rates, better fiscal equilibrium and establishment of more democratic political systems.

In economic terms, the cost of this transition was a decade of falling per capita income. After 1990, economic growth revived substantially but the process was interrupted by contagious episodes of capital flight. The first occurred in 1995 as a reaction to the Mexican debt crisis, the second in 1998 as a reaction to Russian debt default. Growth performance in the 1990s has been disappointing, considering the scope for recovery after the lost decade of the 1980s. For 1980–99 as a whole,

Figure 3-3. **Binary Confrontation of United States/Latin American Per Capita GDP Levels, 1950-98**
(1990 Geary-Khamis dollars)

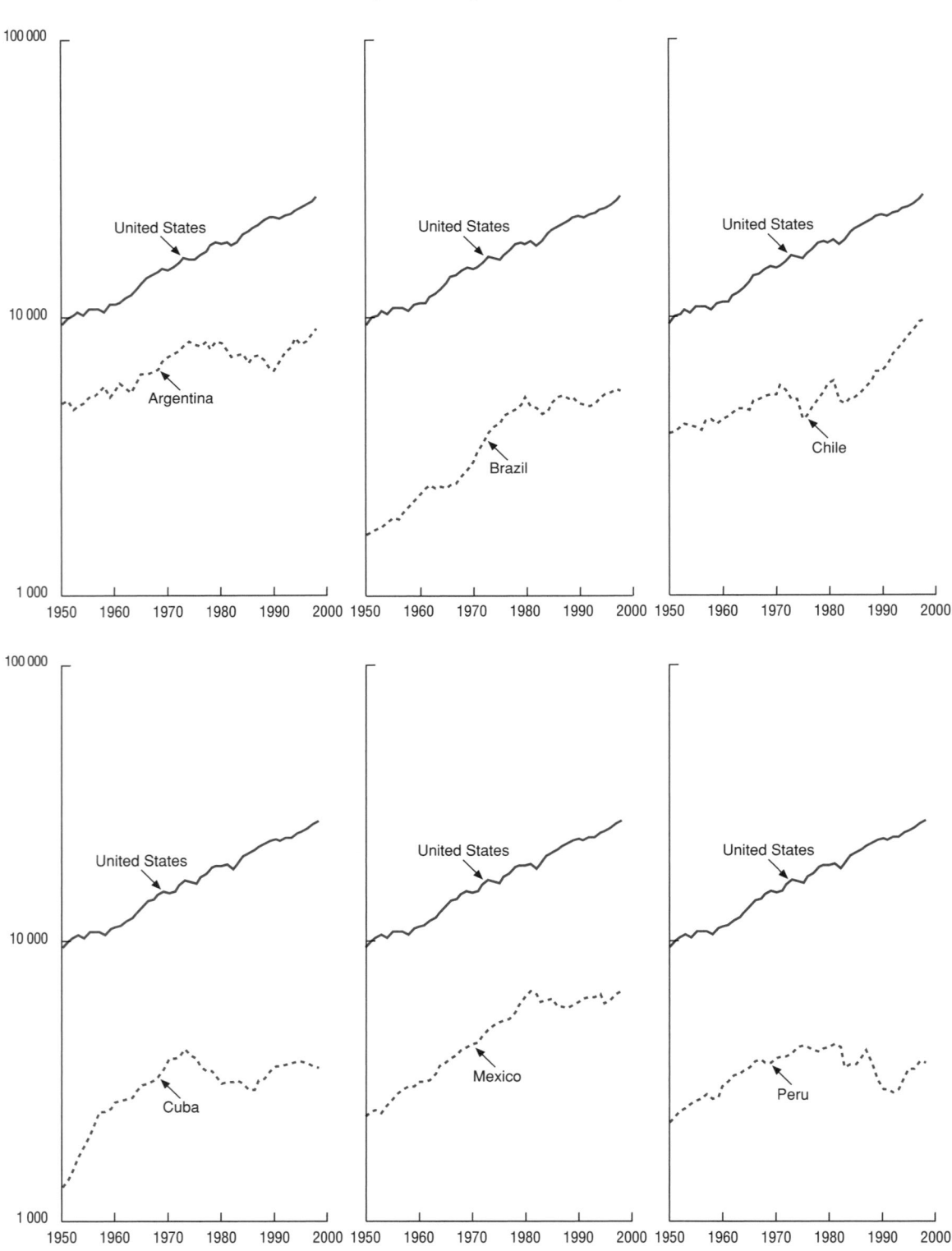

Source: Appendix C.

http://dx.doi.org/10.1787/170572737642

ISBN 92-64-02261-9 – © OECD 2006

Table 3–22. **Latin American Economic Performance, 1870–1999**

(a) Per capita GDP
(annual average compound growth)

	1950–73	*1973–80*	*1980–90*	*1990–99*	*1980–99*
Argentina	2.06	0.48	−2.33	3.38	0.33
Brazil	3.73	4.26	−0.54	1.07	0.47
Chile	1.26	1.72	1.10	4.47	2.68
Mexico	3.17	3.80	−0.31	1.16	0.38
40 Other Latin America	2.04	1.19	−0.67	1.28[a]	0.19[b]
Total Latin America	2.52	2.57	−0.68	1.36	0.28

a) 1990–98. b) 1980–98.

(b) Inflation
(annual average compound growth)

	1950–73	*1973–94*	*1994–98*	*1999*
Argentina	26.8	258.4	1.3[a]	−1.7[a]
Brazil	28.4	268.5	19.4[a]	8.0[a]
Chile	48.1[a]	71.8	6.7[a]	2.6[a]
Mexico	5.6	37.6	26.4[a]	13.9[a]
Arithmetic Average	27.2	159.1	13.5	5.7

a) consumer price index; otherwise GDP deflator.

(c) Volume of merchandise exports
(annual average compound growth)

	1870–1913	*1913–50*	*1950–73*	*1973–98*
Argentina	5.2[b]	1.6	3.1	6.7
Brazil	1.9	1.7	4.7	6.7
Chile	3.4[c]	1.4	2.4	9.1
Mexico	5.4[d]	−0.5	4.3	10.9
Total Latin America	3.4	2.3	4.3	6.0

b) 1877–1912; c) 1888–1913; d) 1877/78 to 1910/11.

(d) Ratio of Exports to GDP in 1990 prices
(per cent)

	1870	*1913*	*1950*	*1973*	*1998*
Argentina	9.4	6.8	2.4	2.0	7.0
Brazil	11.5	9.2	3.9	2.5	5.4
Chile	n.a.	7.5	5.0	4.0	12.6
Mexico	3.1	9.1	3.0	1.9	10.5
Total Latin America	9.2	8.9	6.0	4.7	9.7

http://dx.doi.org/10.1787/170572737642

per capita income in Latin America has risen by less than 0.3 per cent a year compared with over 2.5 per cent from 1950 to 1980. The earlier growth rate implied a doubling of per capita income every 28 years, the 1980–99 rate implies income doubling over 250 years.

Some idea of the difficulties and costs involved in switching policy regimes can be gained by detailed scrutiny of Chilean experience, where the transformation has been most complete.

The Chilean Paradigm

Chile is the economy with the longest history of substantial inflation. From 1880 to 1913, the annual price rise averaged 5.6 per cent, in 1913–50, 8.3 per cent, in 1950–73 48.1 per cent.

Chile was the heartland of the "structuralist" school which argued that economic rigidities made orthodox monetary remedies inapplicable to its inflationary problems. They argued that inflation could be mitigated by institutional reform, but basically one had to cohabit with it, tolerate or even use it as a positive instrument of policy. Economists of this school also had an instrumental bias towards detailed regulation and subsidies, exchange and trade controls, plus administered internal prices. These views led to early clashes with IMF orthodoxy in the 1950s.

The Allende administration which took over in 1970 was an ideological melange of structuralism, Marxism and a dash of Peronist–style populism. Its policy of nationalising foreign copper interests, increasing social expenditure, land reform and takeover of private business enterprises sapped investor confidence and lowered production at the same time as expansionary fiscal and monetary policies accelerated inflation.

The military who overthrew Allende in 1973 made a complete reversal of policy. They were substantially influenced and aided by Chicago University economists, who saw an opportunity for experiments with monetarism and *laisser faire* in a regime whose "credibility" was high because of its brutal hold on state power.

The new regime privatised the economy, restored land to previous owners, sold 472 of the 507 state enterprises cheaply, and gave gratuities to foreign copper interests deemed to have been inadequately compensated by Allende.

In order to break inflationary momentum shock treatment was applied — curbing public expenditure by a quarter, cutting the tariff level from 94 to 10 per cent, devaluing massively, abolishing exchange controls, suppressing trade union rights, tightening monetary policy, raising indirect taxes and lowering taxes on capital and profits. As a consequence per capita GDP fell by 24 per cent from 1971 to 1975. The rate of inflation was reduced to 375 per cent in 1975 but by 1982 it had fallen to 10 per cent.

After 1975, economic growth resumed, but there was another big recession from 1981 to 1983 when per capita GDP fell by 14 per cent. This setback was due to two major policy errors.

Around 1979, the emphasis in monetarist thinking moved away from controlling domestic monetary supply to fixed exchange rates which were expected to constrain domestic inflation to world rates. However, stable exchange rates and falling prices of copper exports in 1979–81 led to a very big current payments deficit (about 15 per cent of GDP), so the exchange rate was allowed to float sharply downwards.

The fall in the peso had major repercussions for the banks and financieras which had been sold back to private ownership subject to very lax supervision. These institutions made losses which they covered by heavy borrowing abroad. At the new exchange rate they could not service their debts. The government bailed them out and accepted responsibility for all their foreign debts. In this blundering way, there was a significant return to widespread public ownership and control of financial and productive assets (and liabilities).

After this episode the government managed to return to a more respectable growth path, swapped a quarter of the foreign debt for equity, subjected international capital movement to control, and after a short episode of higher tariffs, returned, in chastened mood, to a policy of budget balance, low inflation, floating exchange rates, and a judicious reprivatisation of government assets.

In 1990 the country returned to democratic government. The three successive civilian administrations of Aylwin, Frei, and Lagos have made no basic change to the neoliberal policy mix which they inherited, and in the 1990s it worked reasonably well for them.

VI
THE TRANSITION PROCESS IN THE FORMER USSR AND EASTERN EUROPE

a) Successor States of the Former Soviet Union

15 successor states emerged from the collapse of the former Soviet Union in 1991. In all of them, there had already been a very marked deceleration of economic growth in 1973–90. The reasons for the slowdown (or in some cases, decline) were very different from those in Western Europe. The USSR was relatively isolated from the world economy, and insulated from the inflationary shocks and speculative capital movements which induced caution in Western policy. There was no unemployment, and as the productivity level was less than half of that in Western Europe, the erosion of once–for–all catch–up factors should not have been operative in the USSR. What was most striking after 1973 was that total factor productivity became substantially negative, with labour productivity slowing down dramatically and capital productivity very negative indeed (see Maddison, 1989a, pp. 100–2).

There were three major reasons for the slowdown. One was the decrease in microeconomic efficiency, the second was the increased burden of military expenditure and associated spending. The third was depletion of natural resource advantages, or their destruction by ecological horrors.

The deficiencies in resource allocation were manifest. Average and incremental capital/output ratios were higher than in capitalist countries. Materials were used wastefully as they were supplied below cost. Shortages created a chronic tendency to hoard inventories. The steel consumption/GDP ratio was four times as high as in the United States, the ratio of industrial value added to gross output much lower than in Western countries. In the USSR, the average industrial firm had 814 workers in 1987 compared with an average of 30 in Germany and the United Kingdom. Transfer of technology from the West was hindered by trade restrictions, lack of foreign direct investment and very restricted access to foreign technicians and scholars. Work incentives were poor, malingering on the job was commonplace. The low wages which the system offered had a dulling effect on work incentives.

The quality of consumer goods was poor. Retail outlets and service industries were few. Prices bore little relation to cost. Bread, butter and housing were heavily subsidised. Consumers wasted time queueing, bartering or sometimes bribing their way to the goods and services they wanted. There was an active black market, and special shops for the *nomenklatura*. There was increasing cynicism, frustration, growing alcoholism and a decline in life expectation.

Soviet spending on its military and space effort was around 15 per cent of GDP in the 1970s and 1980s, nearly three times the US ratio and five times as high as in Western Europe. There were significant associated commitments to Afghanistan, Cuba, Mongolia, North Korea, Vietnam and Soviet client states in Africa.

Table 3–23. **Per Capita Growth Performance in Former USSR and Eastern Europe, 1950–98**

	1950–73	1973–90	1990–98	1998 per capita GDP (1990 int. $)	1998 GDP (million 1990 int. $)
	(annual average per capita growth rate)				
Former USSR	3.36	0.74	−6.86	3 893	1 132 434
Armenia		−0.04	−7.33	3 341	12 679
Azerbaijan		−0.29	−9.35	2 135	16 365
Belarus		1.85	−3.71	5 743	58 799
Estonia		1.27	−0.73	10 118	14 671
Georgia		1.48	−11.94	2 737	14 894
Kazakhstan		−0.23	−5.09	4 809	74 857
Kyrgyzstan		−0.18	−6.82	2 042	9 595
Latvia		1.39	−0.58	6 216	15 222
Lithuania		0.73	−4.55	5 918	21 914
Moldova		0.85	−10.77	2 497	9 112
Russian Federation		0.98	−6.53	4 523	664 495
Tajikistan		−1.84	−14.82	830	5 073
Turkmenistan		−1.67	−8.88	1 723	8 335
Ukraine		1.15	−10.24	2 528	127 151
Uzbekistan		−1.17	−3.32	3 296	79 272
Total Eastern Europe	3.79	0.51	0.06	5 461	660 861
Albania	3.59	0.57	−0.41	2 401	7 999
Bulgaria	5.19	0.29	−2.36	4 586	37 786
Czechoslovakia	3.08	1.12			
Czech Republic			−0.36	8 643	88 897
Slovak Republic			−0.01	7 754	41 818
Hungary	3.60	0.85	0.05	6 474	66 089
Poland	3.45	−0.35	3.41	6 688	258 220
Romania	4.80	0.08	−2.45	2 890	64 715
Former Yugoslavia	4.49	1.60	−3.45	4 229	95 337
Croatia			−1.93	5 963	27 858
Slovenia			1.09	11 980	23 625
Other former Yugoslavia			−6.37	2 758	43 854

Source: Appendices A and D.

http://dx.doi.org/10.1787/170572737642

There were increased real costs in exploiting natural resources. In the 1950s a good deal of agricultural expansion was in virgin soil areas, whose fertility was quickly exhausted. Most of the Aral Sea was transformed into a salty desert. Exploitation of mineral and energy resources in Siberia and Central Asia required bigger infrastructure costs than in European Russia. The Chernobyl nuclear accident had a disastrously polluting effect on a large area of the Ukraine.

In 1985–90 Gorbachev established a remarkable degree of political freedom, liberated Eastern Europe and disabled the command economy, but did little to change the economic system. Yeltsin (end 1991 to end 1999) created a market economy and broke up the Soviet Union.

Yeltsin's major initial concerns were to destroy the Soviet economic and political system. The USSR was dissolved at a clandestine meeting of Yeltsin as President of Russia, Kravchuk from the Ukraine and Shuskevich of Belarus early in December 1991. The Baltic states were left free to pursue the capitalist path. The old party bosses of the Asian republics had no prior warning, or ideas for change, but acquiesced, became presidents and entered into a loose federation (the Commonwealth of Independent States). The Soviet Communist Party was dissolved and its assets seized.

Table 3–24. Changes in Production and Consumption in Belarus, Russia and Ukraine, 1990–98
(1990 Volume = 100)

	Belarus	Russian Federation	Ukraine
GDP	80.1	57.7	41.1
Industrial Production	92.7	47.3	31.6
Agricultural Production	65.5	58.1	58.3
Financial Services	196.3	144.7	773.6[a]
Private Consumption	79.0	88.8	51.2
Government Consumption	79.4	70.8	76.9
Fixed Investment	62.9	17.5	15.5
Population	99.8	99.1	96.9

a) 1990–97.

Source: *The Main Macroeconomic Indicators of the Commonwealth of Independent States 1991–1998* (in Russian), Interstate Statistical Committee of the Commonwealth of Independent States, Moscow, 1999.

Table 3–25. Per Cent of Population in Poverty in Former USSR and Eastern Europe, 1987–88 and 1993–95

Country	1987–88	1993–95	Country	1987–88	1993–95
Estonia	1	37	Czech Republic	0	1
Latvia	1	22	Hungary	1	4
Lithuania	1	30	Poland	6	20
Average 3 Baltic States	1	29	Slovakia	0	1
			Slovenia	0	1
			5 Central Europe	1.4	12
Belarus	1	22			
Moldova	4	66	Bulgaria	2	15
Russian Federation	2	50	Romania	6	59
Ukraine	2	63	2 South East Europe	4	37
Average 4 Western CIS	2	52			
Kazakhstan	5	65			
Kyrgyzstan	12	88			
Turkmenistan	12	61			
Uzbekistan	24	63			
Average 4 Central Asian CIS	15	66			

Source: Branko Milanovic (1998), *Income, Inequality and Poverty during the Transition from Planned to Market Economy,* World Bank, Washington, D.C.

http://dx.doi.org/10.1787/170572737642

In the Russian republic a government of radical young economic reformers was installed in January 1992, who jettisoned the old command structure, freed most domestic prices, removed obstacles to foreign trade, cut the military budget to a fraction of its earlier level, abolished state trading, legalised all forms of private trading, and began a process of privatisation which eventually sold off most state enterprises at knockdown prices. Between 1990 and 1998, proceeds from Russian privatisation totalled $7.5 billion compared with Brazilian privatisation receipts of $66.7 billion in the same period. The average GDP of these two economies was similar over these years, but Brazilian sales were a very much smaller fraction of its capital stock (see World Bank, 2000, pp. 186-7).

The transition to a market economy was made rather quickly, but the economic outcome was a downward spiral of real income for the mass of the population which lasted almost a decade. In the Russian republic, GDP was 42 per cent lower in 1998 than in 1990. Fixed investment fell precipitously to 17.5 per cent of its 1990 level. There was a big drop in government military spending, so the fall in

Table 3–26. **Annual Average Rate of Change in Consumer Prices: Former USSR and Eastern Europe, 1990–98**

Country	1990–94	1994–98	Country	1990–94	1994–98
Estonia	333.7	15.2	Czech Republic	23.2	8.3
Latvia	320.3	11.5	Hungary	24.0	19.2
Lithuania	435.0	14.9	Poland	42.9	15.5
Average 3 Baltic States	363.0	13.9	Slovakia	26.1	6.2
			Slovenia	95.6	8.3
Belarus	1 402.0	132.1	Average 5 Central Europe	42.4	11.5
Moldova	825.5	17.1			
Russian Federation	927.8	61.5	Albania	96.9	18.6
Ukraine	3 361.8	62.7	Bulgaria	151.0	230.8
Average 4 Western CIS	1 629.3	68.4	Croatia	583.5	4.1
			Macedonia	615.4	2.0
Armenia	3 529.3	14.6	Romania	194.8	69.2
Azerbaijan	1 150.8	20.9	Average South East Europe	328.3	64.9
Georgia	3 817.6	22.4			
Average 3 Caucasus	2 932.6	19.3			
Kazakhstan	1 612.5	25.6			
Kyrgyzstan	721.9	25.0			
Tajikistan	2 228.2	585.0			
Turkmenistan	2 969.3	437.3			
Uzbekistan	811.3	64.3			
Average 5 Central Asia	1 268.6	227.4			

Source: EBRD, *Transition Report 1999*, London, p. 76.

http://dx.doi.org/10.1787/170572737642

real private consumption per capita was much milder (about 10 per cent) than in per capita GDP. In Belarus it fell by a fifth (see Table 3–24). The situation in the Ukraine was a good deal worse, with a 44 per cent fall in per capita consumption.

The transition to capitalism involved very big changes in income distribution. Under the old system, basic necessities (bread, housing, education, health, crèches and social services) had been highly subsidised by the government or provided free by state enterprises to their workers. These all became relatively more expensive, the real value of wages and pensions was reduced by hyperinflation, and the value of popular savings was destroyed. There were welfare gains from the ending of queueing, the improvement in quality and variety of consumer goods which came from freedom to import, but enjoyment of such gains was felt mainly by people able to succeed in the market economy.

Branko Milanovic recently estimated changes in the incidence of poverty (see Table 3–25). Between 1987–8 and 1993–5, the poverty ratio in four "Western" CIS countries (whose combined population was 212 million in 1998) had risen from 2 per cent to over half their total population. In four Central Asian states (with a combined population of 49 million), the ratio rose from 15 to 66 per cent, and in the three Baltic States from 1 to 29 per cent. This was much worse than the experience of Central and Southeast Europe, where the only country in a similar situation was Romania. Supplementary evidence of increased impoverishment is evident in reduced life expectation, reduced school attendance, and increased unemployment, though the latter was mitigated by the fact that many workers retained ties with enterprises which provided social benefits, even when their wages had stopped.

There are two major reasons why the transition was more painful in the former USSR than in Eastern Europe. One was the weakness of monetary and fiscal policy which led to hyperinflation. The other was what the EBRD calls the "capture" of the state by a new business oligarchy. Both of these were serious impediments to efficient resource allocation and helped to channel income to a privileged elite.

Macroeconomic Instability

Table 3–26 shows the average rate of inflation in 1990–94, and 1994–98. The first wave of hyperinflation has now been significantly tempered, but the momentum of price increase is still very much higher than the 2 per cent a year in Western capitalist economies (see Table 3–8). In the Baltics and Eastern Europe it is now similar to that in Latin America (13.5 per cent, see Table 3–22).

A bout of hyperinflation was an understandable consequence of the switch from the price structure of a command economy to one governed by market forces, but inflationary momentum was fed by fiscal weakness. This was inevitable in a state which previously derived its income from ownership of assets which had been sold for a song. It was also very difficult to devise and implement a new tax apparatus in an economy where enterprises had rapidly become adept at tax avoidance, tax evasion, concealment of profits at home and in foreign tax havens. In Russia the problem was exacerbated by devolution of spending power to 19 constituent republics and 61 other regional administrations.

Reckless monetary policy was the other major contributor to hyperinflation. In the first reformist phase, the Gaidar government took the advice of international agencies and maintained the rouble as a common currency for the CIS member states until 1993. Thus it had to cover their deficits which amounted to 10 per cent of Russian GDP. Between 1992 and 1994 hyperinflation was fuelled by an enormous increase in the volume of credits at negative real interest rates by the Central Bank to cover the federal budget deficit and to prop up enterprises that should have been forced into bankruptcy. At a later stage, deficits were financed by developing a Treasury Bill market and borrowing abroad. After the re–election of Yeltsin in July 1996, there was a large inflow of foreign investment in Russian equities and Treasury Bills. The stock market rose threefold from mid–1996 to the end of 1997 without much change in the exchange rate. Many foreign investors speculated heavily, hedging the exchange risk by buying forward dollar contracts from Russian banks. The dismissal of prime minister Chernomyrdin in 1998 and the Asian financial crisis caused large withdrawals of foreign funds. The Russian government propped up the exchange rate for a couple of weeks with nearly $5 billion from the IMF, but in mid–August 1998 devalued, defaulted on much of domestic debt and declared a moratorium on debt repayments to foreigners by Russian companies and banks.

The Rise of a New Financial Oligarchy

The other major problem with the Russian transition to capitalism was diagnosed by the EBRD (1999, pp. 110–11) as follows: "under the 'shares for loans' scheme implemented in 1995, many of the key resource–based companies fell into the hands of a small group of financiers, the so–called 'oligarchs'. This has led to very sharp increases in wealth and income inequality — by 1997 the Gini coefficient for income in Russia was around 0.5, a level comparable to those in Colombia or Malaysia. It has also helped to create an investment climate marked by corruption, non–transparent business practices — including barter — and cronyism." "Not only has income inequality increased substantially but spending on social benefits has actually become regressive over the course of the transition. This highlights the capture of the state by narrow interest groups."

There has been legislation to establish Western style property rights, but in practice accountancy is opaque and government interpretation of property rights is arbitrary. Many businesses are subject to criminal pressure. Property owners such as shareholders or investors are uncertain whether their rights will be honoured. Workers are not sure that their wages will be paid. These characteristics make resource allocation very inefficient.

Agriculture Untouched by Reform

A third major failure of transition policy was the treatment of agriculture. In Russia and the Ukraine, 1998 agricultural output was 42 per cent lower than in 1990. This is in startling contrast to China where agricultural output rose 56 per cent in the seven years following the 1978 reforms. Virtually nothing has been done to create dynamism in this backward sector, where effective action is difficult because of the heritage of the past. As Kornai (1992, p. 437) put it: "To this day the Soviet peasantry has not been able to get over the ghastly trauma of collectivisation. Even though the people who experienced it are no longer alive, their children and grandchildren feel there is no security for private property, and the land may be taken from them again. If they were to become prosperous farmers by farming individually, it could mean that they would be branded as *kulaks* again, which could bring persecution, deportation or death."

b) East European Countries

The economic system of the East European countries was similar to that of the former USSR until the end of the 1980s, and so was its macroeconomic performance. In the golden age, 1950–73, East European per capita GDP growth (like that of the USSR) more or less kept pace with that in Western Europe. From 1973 to 1990, it faltered badly as the economic and political system began to crumble, with aggregate per capita growth of about 0.5 per cent per annum compared with 1.9 in Western Europe.

Since 1990, East Europe has experienced major problems in the transition to capitalism, but the process has been much less traumatic than in the former USSR. Average per capita income in 1998 was similar to that in 1990, whereas it was more than 40 per cent lower in the former USSR.

There are in fact big differences in the success of the transition in different East European countries. Poland, by far the biggest economy and the worst performer in 1973–90, has had more rapid income growth since 1990 than any other European country except Ireland. The Czech and Slovak republics and Hungary have more or less recovered their 1990 levels of per capita income. The worst case is the former Yugoslavia which split into five separate states in the course of bloody conflicts. Bulgaria and Romania have also fared badly, in part because their economies were severely affected in various ways by wars in Bosnia and Kosovo, sanctions on Yugoslavia, and bombing of bridges on the Danube.

With the exception of Poland, economic performance has been disappointing. Given the fact that average per capita income in Eastern Europe is about 30 per cent of that in West Europe, there should have been scope for some degree of catch–up.

In fact the problems of transition are very profound. The easiest part was the freeing of prices and the opening of trade with the West. This ended shortages and queueing, improved the quality of goods available and increased consumer welfare in ways not properly captured in the GDP measures. However, much of the old capital stock became junk, the labour force needed to acquire new skills, the legal and administrative system and the tax/social benefit structure had to be transformed, and the distributive and banking system had to be rebuilt from scratch.

It is interesting to compare the situation in Eastern Europe with that in East Germany, which was incorporated into the Bundesrepublik in 1990. In other East European countries, the amount of Western aid has been relatively modest, and their access to Western markets is hampered by the EU's common agricultural policy and restraints on exports of sensitive industrial products. The Länder of East Germany, by contrast, have had completely free access to German and Western markets and have received transfers of various kinds of about a trillion dollars since reunification, but per capita product and labour productivity are still less than half the levels in the rest of Germany. The problem of transforming socialist firms into productive capitalist enterprises was more pronounced than elsewhere because East Germany was incorporated in a monetary union which greatly overvalued the old Ost Mark wages and assets. Most of the industrial capital stock has been scrapped. Employment is down by 30 per cent since 1990, as workers (as well as pensioners and other social categories) became eligible for much higher social security benefits.

The reasons why Eastern European countries have performed better than the states of the former USSR seem to be mainly as follows:

a)   the exposure to the command economy was shorter, about 40 years, as compared with more than 70 in most of the former USSR. This was also true of the Baltic countries, which have been more successful than the other economies of the former USSR;

b)   in several of the East European countries, there had been strong aspirations to break away from the command economy and Soviet hegemony — in Yugoslavia in the 1950s, in Hungary in 1956, in Czechoslovakia in 1968, and in Poland in the 1980s — and there was an active intellectual interest in problems of transition. Yugoslavia, Hungary and Poland were members of the IMF before the collapse of the Soviet system, and had acquired some knowledge of the macroeconomic policy mix and weaponry characteristic of capitalist economies. In the case of Czechoslovakia, Poland, Hungary and Slovenia, there was greater propinquity to and knowledge of Western capitalism than in the former USSR, Bulgaria or Romania;

c)   there was much greater concern to carry out transition policies within a framework of macroeconomic stability in Eastern Europe than in the former USSR. This is particularly true of Poland which started its radical reforms at the beginning of 1990 with an overhang of inflationary pressure engendered by wage indexation and other concessions to the militant trade unionism of the Solidarity movement (see Balcerowicz, 1995, pp. 324–6). Reform policy involved tight monetary and fiscal discipline;

d)   the reform process gave much greater emphasis to creating a transparent legal basis for contracts and property rights, and the privatisation process did not create a new oligarchy of predatory capitalists. Here again, the difference between policy in Poland and in the former Soviet Union is strongly emphasised by Balcerowicz, the main architect of the Polish reforms. As a result there was much less ambiguity about the direction and destination of the reform process.

VII
AFRICA

Africa has nearly 13 per cent of world population, but only 3 per cent of world GDP. It is the world's poorest region, with a 1998 per capita income only 5 per cent of that in the richest region, less than half of that in Asia (excluding Japan). It has the lowest life expectation (52 years compared with 78 in Western Europe). It has the most rapid demographic expansion — about nine times as fast as in Western Europe.

As a result of rapid population growth, age structure is very different from that in Western Europe. In Europe more than two thirds are of working age, in Africa little more than half. 43 per cent of Africans are below 15 years old and 3 per cent 65 or over. In Western Europe 18 per cent are under 15 and 15 per cent 65 or older. Almost half the adult population of Africa are illiterate. They have a high incidence of infectious and parasitic disease (malaria, sleeping sickness, hookworm, river blindness, yellow fever). Over two thirds of HIV infected people live in Africa. As a result the quantity and quality of labour input per head of population is much lower than in other parts of the world.

African economies are more volatile than most others, because their export earnings are concentrated on a few primary commodities, and extremes of weather (droughts and floods) are more severe and have a heavy impact.

Although African levels of performance are low in comparative terms, there has been economic growth in the capitalist epoch. Per capita income rose about 3.5–fold from 1820 to 1980 (see Tables 3–1b and C5–c), which is about the same as in Asia (excluding Japan). Since 1980 African per capita income has declined.

Figure 3-4. **Binary Confrontation of United States/African Per Capita GDP Levels, 1950-98**
(1990 Geary-Khamis dollars)

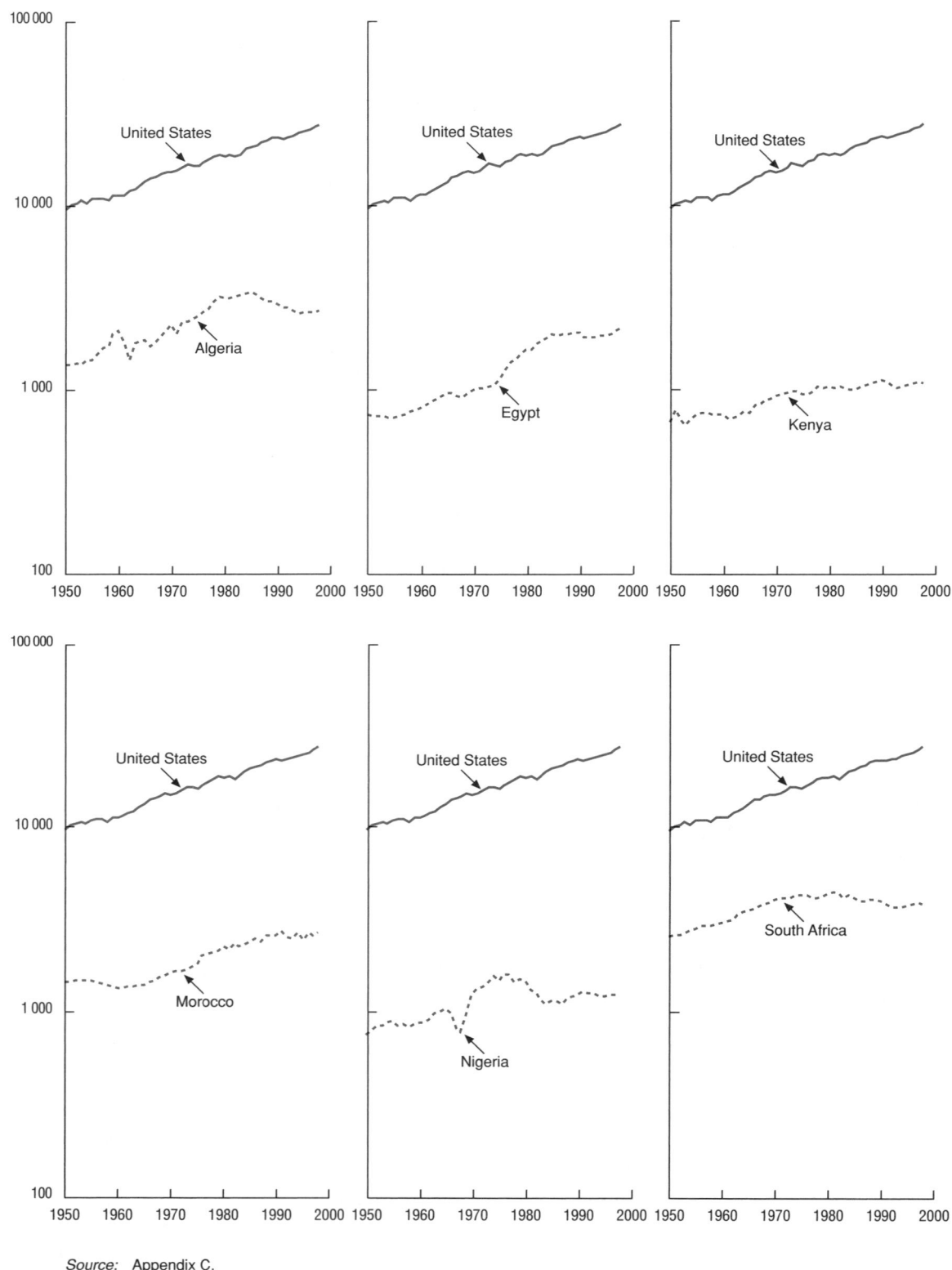

Source: Appendix C.

http://dx.doi.org/10.1787/170572737642

ISBN 92-64-02261-9 – © OECD 2006

162

Table 3–27. **Illiteracy Rates in Africa in 1997**
(percentage of adult population)

Algeria	40	Niger	86
Benin	66	Nigeria	40
Botswana	26	Rwanda	37
Burkina Faso	80	Senegal	65
Burundi	55	South Africa	16
Cameroon	28	Tanzania	28
Central African Rep.	57	Togo	47
Congo	23	Tunisia	33
Côte d'Ivoire	58	Uganda	36
Egypt	48	Zambia	25
Ethiopia	65	Zimbabwe	9
Ghana	33	Arithmetic Average	45
Kenya	21		
Malawi	42	Former USSR	4
Mali	65	Latin America	13
Mauritania	62	China	17
Morocco	54		
Mozambique	59		
Namibia	21		

Source: World Bank, *World Development Report 1999/2000*, Washington, D.C., 2000, pp. 232-3.

http://dx.doi.org/10.1787/170572737642

Poverty and economic stagnation or decline are predominant characteristics of Africa, but there are important variations in levels of income and growth performance. Table 3–28 distinguishes between the 14 countries where average income is above 2 000 international dollars a head and the 43 countries below this level. In the first group, 1998 per capita income averaged $2 816 and in the rest only $840. Countries in the first group now have an average income like that of Western Europe in 1900, in the rest it is below the Western European level in 1600.

The first relatively prosperous group consists of five countries on the Mediterranean littoral (Algeria, Egypt, Libya, Morocco and Tunisia). Of these Egypt, Morocco and Tunisia had reasonable growth performance in 1973–98, but 1998 per capita income in Algeria was 15 per cent below the 1985 peak, and in Libya about half of the 1973 level.

The second group, at the Southern tip of the continent, consists of Botswana, Namibia, South Africa and Swaziland. Botswana has been one of the world's fastest growing economies (5.4 per cent per capita from 1973 to 1998). Its growth performance was similar to that of Singapore, but was largely based on exploitation of its diamond resources. South Africa's per capita income in 1998 was 14 per cent below its 1981 peak, and Namibia's 9 per cent below 1981.

The third group of five small countries consists of special cases. Gabon and the Congo have relatively high and expanding levels of petroleum production and export. The three others are islands in the Indian Ocean with population growth rates well below the African average. Reunion is a French overseas department with a high degree of subsidy from the metropole. In the Seychelles and Mauritius the majority of the population are of Indian origin, bilingual in English and French. Seychelles has a high tourist income. Mauritius has been successful in developing exports of manufactures.

Threequarters of Africa's population belongs to a fourth group where per capita income peaked in 1980. By 1998 it had fallen by a quarter. This group of countries is the hard core of African poverty.

In explaining the reasons for African poverty, one must distinguish between longer term influences and the reasons for the reversal of economic advance over the past two decades.

Table 3–28. **Variations of Income Level Within Africa, 1998**

	GDP per capita (1990 int. $)	GDP (million 1990 int. $)	Population (000)
Algeria	2 688	81 948	30 481
Egypt	2 128	140 546	66 050
Libya	3 077	15 000	4 875
Morocco	2 693	78 397	29 114
Tunisia	4 190	39 306	9 380
5 Mediterranean Countries	2 539	355 197	139 900
Botswana	4 201	6 803	1 448
Namibia	3 797	6 158	1 622
South Africa	3 858	165 239	42 835
Swaziland	2 794	2 699	966
4 South African Countries	3 860	180 899	46 871
Gabon	4 885	5 901	1 208
Mauritius	9 853	11 508	1 168
Reunion	4 502	3 174	705
Seychelles	5 962	471	79
Congo	2 239	5 951	2 658
5 Special Cases	4 642	27 005	5 818
Total for 14 Countries with per capita GDP above $2000	2 816	563 101	192 589
Total for 43 Other Countries	840	476 307	567 365
Total Africa	1 368	1 039 408	759 954

Source: The estimates of GDP growth for African countries are of poorer quality than for other regions. National accounts were generally introduced by the colonial authorities in the late 1950s, and the quality and staffing of statistical offices since independence has been weak. There are also more serious problems in the estimates of comparative GDP levels than for other regions, see Table A4–g, and the accompanying commentary.

http://dx.doi.org/10.1787/170572737642

Until late in the nineteenth century, most of the continent was unknown and unexplored, occupied by hunter–gatherers, pastoralists or practitioners of subsistence agriculture. Levels of education and technology were primitive. Land was relatively abundant, was allocated by traditional chiefs, without Western–style property rights. The only territorial units which resembled those of today were Egypt, Ethiopia, Liberia, Morocco and South Africa. Slaves had been the main export.

The European powers became interested in grabbing Africa in the 1880s. France and Britain were the most successful. Twenty–two countries eventually emerged from French colonisation, 21 from British, five from Portuguese, three from Belgian, two from Spanish. Germany lost its colonies after the First World War, Italy after the Second.

The colonialists created boundaries to suit their own convenience, with little regard to local traditions or ethnicity. European law and property rights were introduced with little regard to traditional forms of land allocation. Hence the colonists got the best land and most of the benefits from exploitation of mineral rights and plantation agriculture. African incomes were kept low by forced labour or apartheid practices. Little was done to build a transport infrastructure or to cater for popular education.

European colonisers withdrew from the mid 1950s onwards. The British colonial bond with Egypt and the Sudan was broken in 1956. Ghana became independent in 1957, Nigeria in 1960, Tanzania in 1961, Kenya in 1963. White settler interests retarded the process in Zimbabwe and Namibia. In South Africa, the black population did not get political rights until 1994. French decolonisation

Table 3-29. **Degree and Duration of Per Capita Income Collapse in 13 Biggest African Countries South of the Sahara**

	1998 population (000)	*1998 per capita as per cent of peak*	*Peak year*	*Distance from peak (years)*
Angola	10 865	36.6	1970	28
Cameroon	15 029	60.0	1986	12
Côte d'Ivoire	15 446	64.7	1980	18
Ethiopia	62 232	95.0	1983	15
Kenya	28 337	97.5	1990	8
Madagascar	14 463	55.4	1971	27
Mali	10 109	92.3	1979	19
Mozambique	18 641	63.3	1973	25
Nigeria	110 532	77.1	1977	21
Sudan	33 551	75.5	1977	21
Tanzania	30 609	88.8	1979	19
Zaire	49 001	30.0	1974	24
Zimbabwe	11 004	100.0	1998	0
13 Country Total/Average	409 859	72.0	1980	18

Source: Appendix C.

http://dx.doi.org/10.1787/170572737642

started with Morocco and Tunisia in 1956. Guinea broke away in 1958, the rest of the sub-Saharan colonies became independent in 1960, and Algeria in 1962. Belgium abandoned Zaire in 1960, Burundi and Rwanda in 1962. Portugal and Spain made their exit in 1975.

In these years, the Cold War was at its height, and Africa became a focus of international rivalry. China, the USSR, Cuba and East European countries supplied economic and military aid to new countries viewed as proxies in a world wide conflict of interest. Western countries, Israel and Taiwan were more generous in supplying aid and less fastidious in its allocation than they might otherwise have been. As a result, Africa accumulated large external debts which had a meagre developmental pay-off.

Independence brought many serious challenges. The political leadership had to try to create elements of national solidarity and stability more or less from scratch. The new national entities were in most cases a creation of colonial rule. There was great ethnic diversity with no tradition or indigenous institutions of nationhood. The linguistic vehicle of administration and education was generally French, English or Portuguese rather than the languages most used by the mass of the population. Thirteen of the new francophone countries had belonged to two large federations whose administrative and transport network had been centred in Dakar and Brazzaville. These networks had to be revamped.

There was a great scarcity of people with education or administrative experience. Suddenly these countries had to create a political elite, staff a national bureaucracy, establish a judiciary, create a police force and armed forces, send out dozens of diplomats. The first big wave of job opportunities strengthened the role of patronage and rent-seeking, and reduced the attractions of entrepreneurship. The existing stock of graduates was too thin to meet the demands and there was heavy dependence on foreign personnel.

The process of state creation involved armed struggle in many cases. In Algeria, Angola, Mozambique, Sudan, Zaire and Zimbabwe, the struggle for independence involved war with the colonial power or the white settler population. A few years later, Nigeria, Uganda and Ethiopia suffered from civil wars and bloody dictators. More recently Burundi, Eritrea, Liberia, Rwanda, Sierra Leone and Somalia have all had the same problem. These wars were a major impediment to development.

Table 3–30. Total External Debt of Africa, Asia, Latin America, Eastern Europe and former USSR, 1980, 1990 and 1998
($ million)

	1980	1990	1998		1980	1990	1998
Algeria	19 365	27 877	30 665	Argentina	27 151	62 730	144 050
Angola	n.a.	8 594	12 173	Brazil	71 520	119 877	232 004
Cameroon	2 588	6 679	9 829	Chile	12 081	19 227	36 302
Côte d'Ivoire	7 462	17 251	14 852	Colombia	6 941	17 222	32 263
Egypt	19 131	32 947	31 964	Mexico	57 365	104 431	159 959
Ethiopia	824	8 634	10 351	Peru	9 386	20 967	32 397
Ghana	1 398	3 881	6 884	Venezuela	29 344	33 170	37 003
Kenya	3 387	7 058	7 010	Other Countries	43 471	99 143	112 041
Morocco	9 258	24 458	20 687	**Total Latin America**	**257 259**	**475 867**	**786 019**
Mozambique	n.a.	4 653	8 208				
Nigeria	8 921	33 440	30 315	Bulgaria	n.a.	10 890	9 907
Sudan	5 177	14 762	16 843	Czech Republic	–	6 383	25 301
South Africa	n.a.	n.a.	24 712	Slovakia	–	2 008	9 893
Tanzania	5 322	6 438	7 603	Hungary	9 764	21 277	28 580
Tunisia	3 527	7 691	11 078	Poland	n.a.	49 366	47 708
Zaire	4 770	10 270	12 929	Serbia	18 486	17 837	13 742
Zimbabwe	786	3 247	4 716	Russia[b]	n.a.	59 797	183 601
Other Countries	20 217	52 171	63 999	Other former USSR	–	–	34 888
Total Africa	**112 133**	**270 051**	**324 814**				
				Other Eastern Europe	n.a.	1 489	21 123
				Total Eastern Europe			
China	n.a.	n.a.	154 599	**& former USSR**	**56 263**	**171 004**	**383 842**
India	20 581	83 717	98 232				
Indonesia	20 938	69 872	150 875				
South Korea	29 480	34 986	139 097				
Pakistan	9 931	20 663	32 229				
Turkey	19 131	49 424	102 074				
Other Countries	83 688	284 759	375 775				
Total Asia[a]	**183 749**	**543 421**	**1 052 881**				

a) excludes Brunei, Japan, Hong Kong, Singapore and Taiwan; b) Russia assumed the debts of the former USSR.

Source: World Bank, *Global Development Finance 2000,* Washington, D.C., 2000. The figures are based on data for 137 reporting countries, and World Bank estimates for 12 other countries.

Table 3–31. Arrears on External Debt in Africa and Other Continents, 1980–98
($ million)

	1980	1990	1998	1998 Arrears as per cent of 1998 debt
Africa	3 907	32 704	55 335	17.0
Latin America	666	50 119	11 925	1.5
Asia	76	10 067	29 491	2.8
Eastern Europe & former USSR	576	19 509	22 923	6.0

Source: World Bank, *Global Development Finance 2000,* Washington, D.C., 2000. The figures reflect the combined effect of arrears on interest and principal.

http://dx.doi.org/10.1787/170572737642

Most of the recent attempts to explain Africa's weak economic performance (Bloom and Sachs, 1998; Collier and Gunning, 1999; and Ndulu and O'Connell, 1999) give major emphasis to the problem of "governance".

Ndulu and O'Connell found that in 1988 only five countries "had multi–party systems allowing meaningful political competition at the national level." They categorised 11 as military oligarchies, 16 as plebiscitary one–party states, 13 as competitive one–party, and two as settler oligarchies (Namibia and South Africa, where the situation has now changed). In most of the one–party states, the incumbent ruler sought to keep his position for life. In most states, rulers relied for support on a narrow group who shared the spoils of office. Corruption became widespread, property rights insecure, business decisions risky. Collier and Gunning (p. 93) suggest that nearly two fifths of African private wealth now consists of assets held abroad (compared with 10 per cent in Latin America and 6 per cent in East Asia). Such estimates are necessarily rough, but with Presidents like Mobutu in Zaire or Abacha in Nigeria, it is not difficult to believe that the proportion is high.

A major factor in the slowdown since 1980 has been external debt. As the Cold War faded from the mid 1980s, foreign aid levelled off, and net lending to Africa fell. Although the flow of foreign direct investment has risen it has not offset the fall in other financial flows. Table 3–30 shows clearly that lending to Africa has expanded less since 1990 than the flow to Asia, Latin America, Eastern Europe and the former USSR.

The aggregate external debt of African countries in 1998 was $427 per head of the population. In Asia it was $314, Latin America $1 548, and Eastern Europe and the successor states of the former USSR $932. Asian per capita income is more than twice as high as in Africa, Latin American more than four times as big and in the former communist group three times as big as in Africa. The African burden is clearly the heaviest, and African capacity to finance investment from domestic saving is lower than in other continents.

Although some African countries are scheduled to benefit from debt relief under the 1996 and 1999 HIPC (Heavily Indebted Poor Countries) Initiatives of the World Bank and IMF, and more have benefited from Paris Club debt relief, the scope of these debt restructuring operations has been much smaller in Africa than in Latin America (see Table 3–31). African access to IMF financing has also been much more restricted than that of countries in Asia and the former USSR in their recent debt crises.

Although the setback to African growth in the past two decades has been smaller in quantitative terms than that in the former USSR, the outlook for the future is more depressing. Levels of education and health are much worse, population growth is still explosive, problems of political stability and armed conflict are bigger, and problems of institutional adjustment and integration in a liberal capitalist world order seem just as great. Most of these problems require changes within Africa, but their course could obviously be influenced by outside help in reducing the debt burden.

Appendix A

Growth and Levels of World Population, GDP and GDP Per Capita, Benchmark Years, 1820–1998

This Appendix provides a quantitative picture of the world economy for the period 1820–1998. It presents estimates of population, GDP and GDP per capita for seven benchmark years and their rates of growth in five phases of development 1820–70, 1870–1913, 1913–1950, 1950–73, and 1973–98.

The first section covers Europe and Western Offshoots (the United States, Canada, Australia and New Zealand); the second, Latin America; the third, Asia; and the fourth, Africa. The source notes explain the derivation of the estimates.

Table A–a shows the coverage of our GDP sample. It represents 81 per cent of the world economy for 1820, 93 per cent in 1913, and over 99 per cent for 1950–98. As the objective is comprehensive coverage, proxy measures were needed to fill holes in the data set. The proxy procedures are explained in the text, and generally assume parallelism of per capita growth experience in the missing countries with that in other countries in the same region.

In order to add the individual country GDP estimates to obtain regional or world totals it is necessary to convert them into a common currency. Exchange rate conversion does not provide a satisfactory measure of real values. Purchasing power parity converters (PPPs) are preferable. These have been developed for use by international organisations over the past 50 years, and the best available are those from the International Comparison Programme (ICP) of the United Nations, Eurostat and OECD, though the coverage of these is not yet universal. Table A–b shows the nature of the converters used here. ICP measures were used for 70 countries representing 93.9 per cent of world GDP in the benchmark year 1990. Estimates from the Penn World Tables, version 5.6 (Summers and Heston, 1995) were used for 83 countries, representing 5.5 per cent of the world economy. Proxy measures were used for 45 (most very small) countries for which no ICP or PWT estimates were available. These represented 0.6 per cent of world GDP. 1990 benchmark levels were merged with the GDP time series in constant national prices, thus providing level comparisons for every year in terms of the benchmark *numeraire*. Table A–b also shows the nature of the converters used in Maddison (1995a).

Population figures do not pose the index number and aggregation problems which arise for GDP, and there are fewer holes in the data set. Figures for 1950 onwards were based on official sources, and where these seemed deficient, from the International Programs Center of the US Bureau of the Census. For years before 1950, estimates are based on census material and the work of historical demographers. Pre–1950 estimates are weakest for Africa, considerably better for Asia and Latin America, and best for Europe and Western Offshoots.

The present estimates are an update and revision of those in Maddison (1995a). That study concentrated on a sample of 56 countries, for which full source notes were given. Figures for other countries were given in summary form, with no detailed source notes (see Appendix F of Maddison, 1995a). Here the source notes cover many more countries, for which greater statistical detail is presented.

169

The revisions and expanded coverage are most significant for Asia; where source notes now cover 37 countries compared with 11 in Maddison (1995a). Estimates are also provided for the 22 new East European countries which emerged from the disintegration of the former USSR, Yugoslavia and Czechoslovakia in the 1990s (see also Appendix D). Estimates for Germany are revised to take account of the integration of new Länder in the East.

For Western Europe, Latin America and Africa, revisions in GDP indices are relatively modest, so for these regions it was not felt necessary to reproduce source notes from Maddison (1995a) *in extenso*, though a full description is given of the derivation of the benchmark levels of GDP in "international" Geary–Khamis dollars for 1990. There are significant revisions in population for Africa and Latin America. Table A–c provides a confrontation of the previous estimates of world and regional population and GDP, with those in the present study.

UPDATING THE ESTIMATES

GDP

The following international sources are useful for those who wish to update the GDP estimates.

For 21 European countries and the 4 Western Offshoots, OECD, *National Accounts of OECD Countries*, Vol. 1, presents the latest available national accounts in current and constant prices in standardised form, and has hitherto given retrospective coverage back to 1960. Because of the significant changes involved in the switchover to the new 1993 SNA system, the latest retrospective view goes back only to 1988 at best. OECD, *Economic Outlook* provides twice yearly provisional estimates of GDP volume change in the current and forthcoming year. These publications also cover Japan, Korea, Mexico and Turkey.

For 11 East European countries and the 15 successor states of the former Soviet Union estimates of GDP are available in constant prices for 1990 onwards (and for material product back to 1980) from the Statistics Division of ECE (Economic Commission for Europe of the United Nations). The Interstate Statistical Committee of CIS (Commonwealth of Independent States) has published detailed national accounts for 12 successor republics of the former USSR, *Osnovie Makroekonomikie Pokazateli Stran Sodruschestva Nezavisimich Gosudarstv 1991–1998*, Moscow, 1999.

For 32 Latin American countries, ECLAC (Economic Commission for Latin America and the Caribbean) publishes estimates of annual volume changes in GDP for the current year and the preceding nine years in its annual end December, *Preliminary Overview of the Economies of Latin America and the Caribbean*.

For 38 East Asian countries, ADB (Asian Development Bank) publishes *Key Indicators of Developing Asian and Pacific Countries* annually. This contains national accounts in some detail in current and constant prices, with an 18 year retrospective coverage.

For 11 West Asian countries and Egypt, ESCWA (Economic and Social Commission for West Asia) publishes *National Accounts Studies of the ESCWA Region* annually. It contains national accounts in current prices and summary annual estimates of GDP volume movement for the previous decade and provisional estimates for the current year.

For 51 African countries, the IMF (International Monetary Fund) twice yearly *World Economic Outlook* shows annual changes in GDP volume for the past decade. It provides similar indicators for the rest of the world. The IMF database is available back to 1970 on internet: http://www.imf.org/external/pubs/ft/weo/2000/01/data/index.htm.

There are two very useful sources of information which have now been discontinued but are still very useful for years before 1990. The OECD Development Centre set up the first international database. It published *National Accounts of Less Developed Countries, 1950–1966* in 1968 and issued 23 annual updates (*Latest Information on National Accounts of Developing Countries*) from 1969 to 1991. The World Bank's *World Tables* were first published in 1976 (with second and third editions in 1980 and 1983) and annually from 1987 to 1995.

Population

The International Programs Center of the US Bureau of the Census provides annual estimates from 1950 onwards, and annual projections to 2050 for all countries. The estimates are revised regularly, and retrospective estimates back to 1950 are included for the new countries which emerged in the 1990s. The estimates are available on internet: http://www.census.gov./ipc. I used their estimates for 1950 onwards for 178 countries (25 European, the United States, 44 Latin American, 51 Asian and 57 African).

Levels of GDP in International Dollars

In this study the benchmark GDP estimates are in 1990 international dollars. I explained the reasons for preferring PPP (purchasing power parity) converters rather than exchange rates, and the advantages of Geary–Khamis multilateral PPPs in Maddison (1995a) pp. 164–79. Such measures are available from the International Comparison Programme (ICP) of the United Nations, Eurostat and OECD.

The ICP exercise was initiated by Irving Kravis, Alan Heston and Robert Summers of the University of Pennsylvania, as a follow up and greatly expanded version of work undertaken in OEEC in the 1950s. Their *magnum opus* was Kravis, Heston and Summers, *World Product and Income: International Comparisons of Real Gross Product* (1982). Their approach was a highly sophisticated comparative pricing exercise in which national accounts expenditure in the participating countries in a given year was decomposed in great detail for representative items of consumption, investment and government services. The results were multilateralised using the Geary–Khamis technique which ensured transitivity, base country invariance and additivity. Their 1982 study covered 34 countries. The Pennsylvania team also created the Penn World Tables which updated and reconciled the material from all the preceding ICP rounds, and added short–cut estimates (using more limited price information) for many countries not covered by ICP. This important supplement to ICP was issued in several successively more ambitious versions from 1978 to 1995.

The ICP was taken over as a co–operative venture by UNSO (United Nations Statistical Office), Eurostat (Statistical Office of the European Union) and OECD in the 1980s. There was a division of labour in which the different agencies made estimates for their respective regions, and the results were adjusted for comparability and consolidated by the UN Statistical Office. UNSO produced such consolidated estimates for 60 countries for 1980 and 57 for 1985. Thereafter the arrangement for consolidating the results on a world–wide basis broke down but the regional exercises continued. For 1990 there were only two regional exercises; OECD estimates on a Geary–Khamis basis for the 22 countries shown in Table A1–g (as well as for Japan and Turkey) and an ECE study for five East European countries and the USSR (shown in Table A1–h).

At the time I wrote Maddison (1995a) there had been several ICP rounds for 87 countries for at least one year. I used the 1990 OECD and ECE estimates for 26 countries, and updated the available results of earlier ICP rounds to 1990 for 14 other countries (seven in Latin America, seven in Asia), and ICP equivalent estimates for East Germany, Bangladesh and Pakistan. Thus I used ICP or ICP equivalent estimates for 43 countries representing 79.7 per cent of world GDP. I used the Penn World Tables of

Robert Summers and Alan Heston (version 5.5 issued in 1993) for 106 countries, and their estimate for China. In total the Summers and Heston component represented 19.5 per cent of world GDP in 1990. For the remaining countries, representing 0.8 per cent of world GDP, I used proxy estimates (see Appendix F of Maddison, 1995a).

In the present study, I have continued to use 1990 as the benchmark year for several reasons: it is useful to retain the 1990 benchmark to ensure greater transparency in understanding the nature of the revisions and updating of Maddison (1995a); Maddison (1998a) made a very detailed reconstruction of Chinese GDP on the standardised SNA basis used in Western countries, with an estimate for 1990 in Geary–Khamis dollars; it would be a very complex exercise to switch from a 1990 to a 1993 benchmark on a consistent basis for different parts of the world, and the quality of the result would most likely be inferior to that for 1990.

For 1993 there are regional ICP estimates for 68 countries: OECD results for 24 countries, ESCAP for 14 East Asian countries, ESCWA for eight West Asian countries, and Eurostat for 22 African countries. All of these are available on a Geary–Khamis basis (as well as the EKS basis preferred for political reasons by Eurostat because it gives all countries the same weight). There are considerable problems in putting this material together on a comparable basis. The ESCAP estimates use the Hong Kong rather than the US dollar as a *numeraire*. ESCWA uses a short–cut, reduced information approach. The Eurostat results for Africa are intra–African relatives linked to the US dollar via a standardised exchange rate rather than a purchasing power parity with the United States as the *numeraire* country. To be useable for our purposes they need to be adjusted in the same way as the UN Statistical Office did for earlier Eurostat exercises for Africa (see note to Table A4–g).

OECD has recently published ICP8 estimates for 1996 for a total of 48 countries in two volumes: *Purchasing Power Parities and Real Expenditure*, 1999 covers the 28 OECD member countries and four others (Israel, Slovakia, Slovenia and the Russian Federation); and *A PPP Comparison for the NIS*, 2000. This covers the 15 successor states of the former USSR, Turkey and Mongolia. The ECE has made estimates which include five other East European countries for 1996 (Albania, Bulgaria, Croatia, Macedonia and Romania). The results of these three studies were multilateralised using the EKS procedure. Estimates on a Geary–Khamis basis have not yet been released. No 1996 estimates are available for other parts of the world. Appendix D assesses the results of these studies for Eastern Europe and the former USSR and describes the problems of reconciling them with those used in the present study.

In the present estimates for the 1990 benchmark, I have used the same ICP sources I used in Maddison (1995a), backcast ESCAP and ESCWA results in their 1993 exercise for eight Asian countries to 1990, the OECD 1993 exercise for Turkey and the OECD 1996 results for Mongolia. I dropped the Eurostat estimates for Africa in favour of Penn World Tables (version 5.6).

Table A–a. **Coverage of GDP Sample and the Proportionate Role of Proxy Measures, 1820–1998**
(GDP in billion 1990 international dollars and number of countries)

	1820	*1870*	*1913*	*1950*	*1998*
			Sample GDP		
Europe & Western Offshoots	180.3 (16)	579.5 (21)	1 785.9 (24)	3 729.7 (32)	17 197.1 (50)
Latin America	7.9 (2)	17.2 (5)	101.4 (8)	419.6 (23)	2 919.9 (23)
Asia	371.7 (4)	374.8 (6)	612.3 (12)	981.2 (37)	12 507.9 (37)
Africa	0.0 (0)	0.0 (0)	23.9 (4)	176.9 (42)	961.6 (42)
Total Sample	559.9 (22)	971.5 (32)	2 523.5 (48)	5 307.4 (134)	33 586.5 (152)
			Total GDP (including proxy component)		
Europe & Western Offshoots	238.	611.1	1 845.9	3 732.3 (42)	17 210.0 (60)
Latin America	14.1	27.9	121.7	423.6 (44)	2 941.9 (44)
Asia	411.2	422.2	664.2	985.7 (57)	12 534.6 (56)
Africa	31.0	40.2	72.9	194.6 (56)	1 039.4 (57)
World Total	694.4	1 101.8	2 704.7	5 336.1 (199)	33 725.9 (217)
			Coverage of Sample (Per cent of Regional and World Totals)		
Europe & Western Offshoots	75.8	94.8	96.7	99.9	99.9
Latin America	56.0	61.6	83.3	99.0	99.3
Asia	90.4	88.8	92.2	99.5	99.8
Africa	0.0	0.0	32.8	90.9	92.5
World	80.6	88.2	93.3	99.5	99.6

Source: "Sample" countries are those for which quantitative estimates of the volume movement of GDP are available. Proxy estimates are needed for missing countries in order to derive the regional and world totals (see the detailed explanation of the gap–filling procedure for 1820–1913 for Asian countries in section A–3 of the source notes). Generally proxies were derived by assuming that per capita GDP movement in the country and for period concerned moved parallel with that of other countries within the same region. The proxy GDP can then be derived by multiplying the per capita GDP by population (for which the coverage of the estimates is much more complete). Coverage is much higher for the period since 1950 as national accounts have been produced by official statisticians. For 1913 and earlier, the sample country estimates were mainly by quantitative economic historians. There were major political changes in the 1990s which increased the number of countries from 199 in Maddison (1995a) to 217. The former USSR has split into 15 countries, Yugoslavia into 5, Czechoslovakia into 2, and Eritrea has split from Ethiopia. The 2 Germanies have been reunited, and I have treated the West Bank and Gaza as if they were a consolidated unit. In most cases it is not possible to carry back the estimates for these new countries before 1990. However, the present estimates for new countries (e.g. the 15 successor countries of the former USSR) are (when consolidated) consistent with the historical estimates for the political entity to which they previously belonged.

http://dx.doi.org/10.1787/486663055853

Table A–b. Nature of the PPP Converters Used to Estimate Levels of GDP in international dollars in the Benchmark Year 1990
(billion 1990 Geary–Khamis dollars and number of countries)

	Europe & Western Offshoots	Latin America	Asia	Africa	World
ICP or Equivalent	15 273 (28)	2 131 (18)	8 017 (24)	0 (0)	25 421 (70)
Penn World Tables	59 (3)	71 (14)	524 (16)	846 (50)	1 500 (83)
Proxies	16 (10)	38 (12)	87 (16)	14 (7)	155 (45)
Total	15 349 (41)	2 239 (44)	8 628 (56)	860 (57)	27 076 (198)

Sources: Europe and Western Offshoots: 99.5 per cent of regional GDP from ICP, 28 countries shown in Tables A1–g and A1–h; Penn World Tables for 0.4 per cent of GDP (Bulgaria, Cyprus and Malta); proxy estimates for 0.1 per cent of GDP (Albania, Andorra, Channel Isles, Faeroe Isles, Gibraltar, Greenland, Isle of Man, Liechtenstein, Monaco and San Marino).

Latin America: 95.1 per cent of regional GDP from ICP (18 countries shown in Table A2–g); Penn World Tables for 3.2 per cent of GDP (Bahamas, Barbados, Belize, Dominica, Grenada, Guyana, Haiti, Nicaragua, Puerto Rico, St. Kitts Nevis, St. Lucia, St. Vincent, Suriname, Trinidad and Tobago); proxy estimates for 1.7 per cent of GDP (Antigua and Barbuda, Aruba, Bermuda, Cuba, Falkland Islands, French Guyana, Guadeloupe, Martinique, Neths. Antilles, St. Pierre and Miquelon, Turks and Caicos, and Virgin Islands).

Asia: 65.5 per cent of regional GDP from ICP, 27.4 per cent from ICP equivalent estimates (Bangladesh, China, Pakistan), see 23 countries listed in Tables A3–g, A3–h and A3–i, as well as Mongolia; Penn World Tables for 6.1 per cent of GDP (Bhutan, Burma, Fiji, Iraq, Jordan, Kuwait, Oman, Papua New Guinea, Saudi Arabia, Solomon Islands, Taiwan, Tonga, UAE, Vanuatu, Western Samoa, and Yemen); proxy estimates for 1 per cent of GDP (Afghanistan, American Samoa, Brunei, Cambodia, French Polynesia, Guam, Kiribati, Lebanon, Macao, Maldives, Marshall Islands, Micronesia, New Caledonia, North Korea, Pacific Islands, Wallis and Futuna, see Maddison, 1995a, pp. 214, 219–20).

Africa: Penn World Tables for 98.4 per cent of regional GDP (50 countries); proxy estimates for 1.6 per cent of GDP (Equatorial Guinea, Eritrea, Libya, Mayotte, St. Helena, São Tomé Principe and Western Sahara).

Table A–b cont'd. Nature of the PPP Converters Used to Estimate Levels of GDP in 1990 international dollars in Maddison (1995a)

	Europe & Western Offshoots	Latin America	Asia	Africa	World
ICP or Equivalent	14 847 (27)	1 835 (7)	5 111 (9)	0 (0)	21 793 (43)
Penn World Tables	72 (5)	232 (24)	4 211 (28)	813 (50)	5 328 (107)
Proxies	16 (10)	39 (13)	164 (20)	14 (6)	233 (49)
Total	14 941 (42)	2 106 (44)	9 486 (57)	827 (56)	27 359 (199)

Note: In Maddison (1995a), I used the different ICP rounds then available, with adjustment where necessary to 1990, for the 43 of the 56 sample countries. For the non–sample countries, and for the African sample countries (where I had doubts about the quality of the ICP estimates), I used Penn World Tables. In the present study, see Table AI–b above, I used the new estimates for China from Maddison (1998a) and made maximal use of the ICP results available from the 1975, 1980, 1985, and 1990 rounds, and partial use of the PPPs from the 1993 and 1996 rounds. In doing this I adjusted for revisions in nominal GDP in national prices. I did not use the ICP results for African countries (see Table A4–g). In Maddison (1995a) I used the Penn World Tables 5.5 version (1993), whereas the present study uses the PWT 5.6 version (1995) which is the latest available.

http://dx.doi.org/10.1787/486663055853

Table A–c. **Confrontation of Maddison (1995a) and Present Estimates of Regional and World Population and GDP, 1820–1990**

Population (million at mid–year)

	Europe & Western Offshoots		Latin America		Asia	
	Maddison (1995a)	*Present*	*Maddison (1995a)*	*Present*	*Maddison (1995a)*	*Present*
1820	228.7	235.3	20.3	21.2	745.8	710.4
1870	360.4	374.5	37.9	40.0	779.0	765.1
1913	595.0	608.2	80.2	80.5	987.0	977.6
1950	748.8	748.5	162.5	165.9	1 377.9	1 381.9
1990	1 087.6	1 086.7	444.8	443.0	3 106.2	3 102.8

	Africa		World	
1820	73.0	74.2	1 067.9	1 041.1
1870	82.8	90.5	1 260.1	1 270.0
1913	109.7	124.7	1 771.9	1 791.0
1950	223.0	228.3	2 512.2	2 524.5
1990	618.9	620.8	5 257.4	5 253.3

GDP (billion 1990 international dollars)

	Europe & Western Offshoots		Latin America		Asia	
1820	239.0	238.1	13.8	14.1	409.2	411.2
1870	607.7	611.5	28.8	27.9	451.7	422.2
1913	1 812.3	1 845.9	115.4	121.7	735.3	664.2
1950	3 718.7	3 732.3	404.0	423.6	1 064.6	985.7
1990	14 940.7	15 348.9	2 105.9	2 239.4	9 485.7	8 627.8

	Africa		World	
1820	32.9	31.0	694.8	694.4
1870	39.8	40.2	1 127.9	1 101.7
1913	63.1	72.9	2 726.1	2 704.8
1950	185.0	194.6	5 372.3	5 336.1
1990	826.7	859.8	27 359.0	27 076.0

Source: Maddison (1995a), and detailed tables and text below. Turkey is included in West Asia in this study; in Maddison (1995a) it was included in Europe. Here the earlier estimates are adjusted to conform with the regionalisation of the present study.

http://dx.doi.org/10.1787/486663055853

A–1

Population, GDP and GDP Per Capita in Western Europe, Western Offshoots, Eastern Europe and the Successor States of the Former USSR

12 West European Countries

The quantitative historical evidence for these countries is better than for most other parts of the world. It is set out in detail in Maddison (1995*a*).

GDP and population for Austria, Belgium, Denmark, Finland, France, Norway, Sweden and Switzerland for 1820–1960 and Italy 1820–1970 are from Maddison (1995*a*), updated (except as noted below for France and Norway) from OECD, *National Accounts 1960–1997*, Vol. 1, Paris 1999 to 1990 and for 1990 onwards from OECD, *National Accounts of OECD Countries, 1988–1998*, vol. 1, 2000. Figures are adjusted to exclude the impact of territorial change and refer to 1998 frontiers, except for Germany and the United Kingdom.

> **Germany:** Figures for 1950 onwards refer to 1991 frontiers, 1820–1913 to Germany within its 1913 boundaries (excluding Alsace–Lorraine). See Table A–d for details.

> **Netherlands:** 1820–1913 GDP movement derived from Smits, Horlings and van Zanden (2000). 1913–60 GDP movement and 1820–1960 population from Maddison (1995*a*) updated from OECD sources.

> **Switzerland:** It was assumed that the 1820–70 GDP per capita movement paralleled that in Germany.

> **United Kingdom:** 1820–1913 estimates include the whole of Ireland, see Maddison (1995*a*), p. 232, and Table B–13, those for 1950 onwards include Northern Ireland. 1960 onwards updated from OECD sources.

The latest OECD national accounts publication incorporates new estimates for 15 countries revised to conform with the SNA 1993 standardised system. This involves two significant modifications in statistical practice:

a)   treatment of computer software as investment rather than an intermediate product, which along with other changes has raised the 1990 benchmark GDP level as shown in Table A1–g;

b)   a recommendation that countries adopt chain–weighted indices to measure the movement in GDP volume. Such indices are now used by France, Greece, Luxembourg, Netherlands, Norway and Sweden. For most countries, the new estimates are available only for very recent years, which is one of the reasons why the new OECD yearbook no longer has the historical depth it has had for the past 30 years. GDP indices based on chain weights for France and Norway for 1978–98 were made available by OECD and used here, together with 1960–78 estimates for these countries from the 1999 OECD national accounts publication. The chain weights seem to make no difference to Norwegian growth, but made French growth slightly faster.

177

Table A–d. **The Impact of Border Changes in Germany**

	West Germany (1990 frontiers)	East Germany (1990 frontiers)	Germany within 1991 boundaries	Germany within 1936 boundaries	Germany within 1913 frontiers ex. Alsace–Lorraine,
GDP in million 1990 international dollars					
1820	16 390				26 349
1870	44 094				71 429
1913	145 045			225 008	237 332
1936	192 911	74 652	267 563	299 753	
1950	213 942	51 412	265 354		
1973	814 786	129 969	944 755		
1990	1 182 261	82 177	1 264 438		
1991	1 242 096	85 961	1 328 057		
(Population (000 at mid–year)					
1820	14 747				24 905
1870	23 055				39 231
1913	37 843			60 227	65 058
1936	42 208	15 614	57 822	67 336	
1950	49 983	18 388	68 371		
1973	61 976	16 890	78 866		
1990	63 254	16 111	79 365		
1991	63 889	15 910	79 799		

Source: West German GDP 1820–60 from Maddison (1995a) updated from OECD sources, with minor adjustment derived from change in 1990 GDP level as noted in Table A1–g. East German GDP index 1950–1991 from Maddison (1995a), p.132, benchmarked on official estimate for 1991 in 1990 DM (difference between West German and total German 1991 GDP as shown in OECD national accounts). The 1991 official benchmark level for East Germany is lower than I assumed in Maddison (1995a) which lowers the level of East German GDP 1950–91 shown there. 1936 level in East and West Germany, in the territories East of the Oder–Neisse, and for Germany in its 1936 frontiers from Maddison (1995a), p.131. 1820–1913 levels within 1913 frontiers from Maddison (1995a), p.231. Population in West Germany 1820–1991 and East Germany 1936–91 derived from Maddison (1995a), p.104–5, 132 and 231.

http://dx.doi.org/10.1787/486663055853

Greece, Ireland, Portugal and Spain

Greece: 1900–60 population and 1913–60 GDP from Maddison (1995a) updated from OECD, *National Accounts*. 1820–1913 per capita GDP assumed to move parallel to the aggregate for Eastern Europe. Population movement 1820–1900 derived from Mitchell (1975), p. 21, adjusted to offset changes in Greek territory. This involved a series of adjustments. Greece gained independence from Turkey in the 1820s, and gradually extended its territory to the Ionian Islands (1864), Thessaly (1881), Crete (1898), Epirus, Macedonia, Thrace and the Aegean Islands (1919) and the Dodecanese (1947).

Ireland: 1950–60 from Maddison (1995a), updated from OECD sources.

Portugal: 1820–1970 population and 1950–60 GDP from Maddison (1995a), updated from OECD sources. 1913–50 GDP from D. Batista, C. Martins, M. Pinheiro and J. Reis "New Estimates of Portugal's GDP 1910–1958", Bank of Portugal, October 1997. 1850–1913 derived from Pedro Lains (1989) as described in Maddison (1995a) p. 138. 1820–50 GDP movement assumed to be at same rate as shown by J. Braga de Macedo (1995) for 1834–50.

Spain: 1820–1990 population and 1820–73 GDP movement from Maddison (1995a) updated from OECD sources.

Table A–e. **Population and GDP: 13 Small West European Countries**

	1950	1973	1990	1998
	Population (000 at mid–year)			
Iceland	143	212	255	271
Luxembourg	296	350	382	425
Cyprus	494	634	681	749
Malta	312	322	354	380
9 Other	285	388	483	513
13 Country Total	1 529	1 906	2 155	2 337
	GDP (million 1990 international dollars)			
Iceland	762	2 435	4 596	5 536
Luxembourg	2 481	5 237	8 819	13 324
Cyprus	930	3 207	6 651	8 600
Malta	278	855	2 987	4 424
9 Other	1 429	4 718	8 152	9 615
13 Country Total	5 880	16 452	31 205	41 499
	GDP per capita (1990 international dollars)			
Iceland	5 336	11 472	18 024	20 205
Luxembourg	8 382	14 963	23 086	31 058
Cyprus	1 883	5 058	9 767	11 169
Malta	894	2 655	8 438	11 642
9 Other	5 013	12 159	16 877	18 742
13 Country Average	3 846	8 631	14 480	17 757

http://dx.doi.org/10.1787/486663055853

13 Small West European Countries

Iceland and Luxembourg 1950–1998 GDP from OECD sources; Cyprus and Malta 1950–90 GDP from Maddison (1995a) updated from IMF. Nine smaller countries (Andorra, Channel Islands, Faeroe Islands, Gibraltar, Greenland, Isle of Man, Liechtenstein, Monaco and San Marino), 1950–98 per capita GDP assumed to be the same as the average for the 12 bigger West European countries. 1950–98 population for the 13 countries from International Programs Center, US Bureau of the Census. 1820–1950, population movement and GDP per capita levels for the 13 country group assumed to move parallel to the average for the 12 bigger West European countries.

Western Offshoots: 4 Countries

United States: Population 1820–1949 from Maddison (1995a), 1820 and 1870 amended to include 325 000 and 180 000 indigenous population (see Maddison, 1995a, p. 97). 1950 onwards from US Bureau of the Census.

1820–1950 GDP movement from Maddison (1995a), amended for 1820–70 to include income of the indigenous population (taken to be $400 per capita in 1820 and 1870).

179

1950–59 GDP movement from "GDP and Other Major NIPA Series, 1929–97", Survey of Current Business, August 1998. This series is based on a chained index as described in J.S. Landefeld and R.P. Parker, "BEA's Chain Indexes, Time Series and Measures of Long Term Growth", Survey of Current Business, May 1997, p. 66, Table 5. 1959–98 GDP movement and 1990 benchmark level from the new estimates of BEA in Survey of Current Business, December 1999. The 1959–98 figures implement the recommendation of the new standardised System of National Accounts 1993 (published jointly by Eurostat, IMF, OECD, UN and World Bank) to include computer software as investment rather than intermediate input. The impact of the revisions, which raise the growth rate and the 1990 benchmark GDP level is described in E.P. Seskin, "Improved Estimates of the National Income and Product Accounts for 1959–98: Results of the Comprehensive Revision", Survey of Current Business, December 1999.

Australia, New Zealand and Canada: Population 1820–1973 from Maddison (1995a) updated from OECD sources. 1820 and 1870 amended to include indigenous population. Indigenous populations were as follows: Australia 300 000 in 1820, 150 000 in 1870; Canada 75 000 in 1820 and 45 000 in 1870, New Zealand 100 000 in 1820 and 50 000 in 1870 (see Maddison, 1995a, pp. 96–7).

1820–1960 GDP movement from Maddison (1995a) amended for 1820–70 to include income of the indigenous population (taken to be $400 per capita in 1820 and 1870). Canadian and New Zealand GDP movement 1960–98 from OECD sources. New Zealand estimates for 1969–87 refer to fiscal years. Australian GDP movement 1960–98 for calendar years based on the new official chain index (supplied by OECD) which shows slightly faster growth than the old index (annual compound growth of 3.95 per cent a year compared with 3.87 per cent for 1960–90). The Australian and Canadian GDP measures conform to the 1993 system of accounts, which New Zealand has not yet adopted.

Eastern Europe (7/12 Countries)

There have been major changes in the past decade in political and statistical systems which means that the estimates for these countries are of lower quality than for Western Europe.

Population of Albania 1820–1913, Bulgaria 1820, Poland, Romania and Yugoslavia 1820–70 from McEvedy and Jones (1978), otherwise 1820–1949 from Maddison (1995a), p. 110. 1950 onwards from International Programs Center, US Bureau of the Census.

East European GDP to 1990 from Maddison (1995a), Czech Republic, Hungary and Poland updated from OECD sources, other countries from the database of the Statistics Division of ECE (Economic Commission for Europe of the UN). 1820 estimates of GDP were available for only one country (Czechoslovakia); for 1870 for two countries (Czechoslovakia and Hungary); for 1913 for four countries (Bulgaria, Czechoslovakia, Hungary and Yugoslavia). In order to get a rough GDP estimate for the seven countries as a whole for 1820–1913, per capita GDP movement in the missing countries was assumed to move parallel to the average for the countries which were represented. In the 1990s, Czechoslovakia split into the Czech Republic and Slovakia, and Yugoslavia broke up into five republics; 1990–98 GDP volume movement in the five successor republics of Yugoslavia from ECE Statistics Division, 1990 breakdown of GDP by constituent republics derived from the Yugoslav Statistical Yearbook for 1990 (see Table A–f).

Table A–f. **GDP and Population in Successor Republics of Former Yugoslavia, 1990–98**

	1990	*1997*	*1998*
	Population (000 at mid–year)		
Bosnia	4 360	3 223	3 366
Croatia	4 754	4 665	4 672
Macedonia	2 031	1 996	2 009
Slovenia	1 968	1 973	1 972
Serbia–Montenegro	9 705	10 534	10 526
Former Yugoslavia	22 819	22 390	22 545
	GDP (million 1990 international dollars)		
Bosnia	16 530	9 028	9 261
Croatia	33 139	27 182	27 858
Macedonia	7 394	5 706	5 871
Slovenia	21 624	22 730	23 625
Serbia–Montenegro	51 266	28 000	28 722
Former Yugoslavia	129 953	92 646	95 337
	GDP per capita (1990 international dollars)		
Bosnia	3 791	2 801	2 851
Croatia	6 971	5 827	5 963
Macedonia	3 641	2 859	2 922
Slovenia	10 988	11 521	11 980
Serbia–Montenegro	5 282	2 658	2 729
Former Yugoslavia	5 695	4 138	4 229

Source: Population from US Bureau of the Census. 1990 GDP total for Yugoslavia from Table A1–h, broken down by constituent republic by applying the 1988 shares of gross material product shown in *Statisticki Godisnjak Jugoslavije 1990* (Statistical Yearbook of Yugoslavia), Statistical Office, Belgrade, 1990. GDP movement for successor republics 1990–98 from ECE Statistics Division, except for Bosnia, for which figures were not available. Bosnian GDP was assumed to move as in Serbia–Montenegro.

http://dx.doi.org/10.1787/486663055853

Former USSR

Population 1913–90 from Maddison (1995a), with revised estimates for 1820 and 1870 for the Asian population in the area of the former USSR (see Appendix B). 1950 population in each of the 15 successor republics from *Naselenie SSSR 1987*, Finansi i Statistika, Moscow, 1988, pp. 8–15 adjusted to mid–year; 1973 from *Narodnoe Khoziastvo SSSR*, 1972 and 1973 editions, p. 9, adjusted to mid–year; 1990 from *Mir v Tsifrakh 1992,* Goskomstat CIS, Moscow 1992; movement from 1990 onwards from ECE Statistics Division.

GDP 1870–1990 for the USSR within its 1990 boundaries from Maddison (1995a). Maddison (1998b) provides a detailed analysis of techniques for adjusting the national accounts of the Soviet era from an MPS to an SNA basis. 1820–70 per capita GDP assumed to move in the same proportion as the aggregate for Eastern Europe.

Breakdown of 1991 GDP level by successor republics derived from B.M. Bolotin "The Former Soviet Union as Reflected in National Accounts Statistics", in S. Hirsch, ed., *Memo 3: In Search of Answers in the Post–Soviet Era,* Bureau of National Affairs, Washington DC, 1992, cited in Maddison (1995a), p. 142, backcast to 1990 and adjusted to the USSR GDP total for that year. 1990–98 movement in GDP volume by republic from ECE Statistics Division.

A rough measure of the 1973–90 GDP volume movement in each of the 15 successor states was derived from official Soviet indices of real "national income" (MPS concept) which are available for 1958–90, see *Narodnoe Khoziastvo SSSR*, 1990 ed., p. 13; 1987 ed., p. 123; 1974 ed., p. 574; and 1965 ed., p. 590. Rates of growth of real "national income" 1973–90 were adjusted to a GDP basis, using the ratio which prevailed for the USSR as a whole for this period (.49075). See Maddison (1998*b*), p. 313 for a comparison of these two types of measure for 1913–90.

The official National Accounts of the Russian Federation (*Natsionalnie Schchota Rossii, 1999*) provide a breakdown of Russian GDP and GDP per capita for nine regions, and 90 administrative districts. The five Siberian regions and the Far East region together accounted for 29 per cent of product geographically allocable for 1997, and the Caucasus region 5.8 per cent. Thus, a little more than a third of GDP in the Russian Federation was generated in Asia, or about 232 billion international dollars of the Russian Federation's total GDP of $697 billion in 1997. Eight of the other successor republics of the USSR were in Asia (Armenia, Azerbaijan, Georgia, Kazakhstan, Kyrgyzstan, Tajikistan, Turkmenistan, Uzbekistan). Their total 1997 GDP was 216 billion international dollars. Thus the Asian part of the Russian republic, and the eight other successor republics in Asia together accounted for 448 billion international dollars or about 39 per cent of the total for the former USSR.

The per capita product of the different parts of the Russian Federation is also shown in the 1999 yearbook. In the city of Moscow, per capita income was 2.3 times the national average, in St. Petersburg about the same as the national average. Income levels in Siberia and the Far East were generally well above the national average. The lowest incomes were in the Caucasus region, less than a fifth of the national average in Ingushetia, 28 per cent in Dagestan, not available for Chechnya.

In the present exercise, the 1990 level of GDP in international dollars was derived from the ICP exercise for 1990 as shown in Table A–1h below. The breakdown by successor republic was based on the Bolotin estimates as indicated above. Recently the OECD, ECE, and the governments of most of the successor republics have collaborated on a new PPP exercise for 1996. This exercise was done using the EKS rather than the Geary–Khamis method. The results show significant differences from the ICP 6 estimates which I have used (see Appendix D).

Table A1–a. **Population (000 at mid–year): European Countries, the Former USSR and Western Offshoots**

	1820	1870	1913	1950	1973	1990	1998
Austria	3 369	4 520	6 767	6 935	7 586	7 729	8 078
Belgium	3 434	5 096	7 666	8 640	9 738	9 971	10 197
Denmark	1 155	1 888	2 983	4 269	5 022	5 138	5 303
Finland	1 169	1 754	3 027	4 009	4 666	4 986	5 153
France	31 246	38 440	41 463	41 836	52 118	56 735	58 805
Germany	24 905	39 231	65 058	68 371	78 956	79 364	82 029
Italy	20 176	27 888	37 248	47 105	54 751	56 719	57 592
Netherlands	2 355	3 615	6 164	10 114	13 438	14 947	15 700
Norway	970	1 735	2 447	3 265	3 961	4 241	4 432
Sweden	2 585	4 164	5 621	7 015	8 137	8 566	8 851
Switzerland	1 829	2 664	3 864	4 694	6 441	6 796	7 130
United Kingdom	21 226	31 393	45 649	50 363	56 223	57 561	59 237
12 West Europe	**114 419**	**162 388**	**227 957**	**256 616**	**301 037**	**312 753**	**322 507**
13 Small W.E. Countries	657	933	1 358	1 529	1 907	2 155	2 337
Greece	2 312	3 657	5 425	7 566	8 929	10 161	10 511
Ireland				2 969	3 073	3 506	3 705
Portugal	3 297	4 353	6 004	8 512	8 634	9 899	9 968
Spain	12 203	16 201	20 263	27 868	34 810	38 851	39 371
Total Western Europe	**132 888**	**187 532**	**261 007**	**305 060**	**358 390**	**377 325**	**388 399**
Australia	333	1 770	4 821	8 177	13 505	17 085	18 751
New Zealand	100	341	1 122	1 909	2 971	3 380	3 811
Canada	816	3 781	7 852	13 737	22 560	27 701	30 297
United States	9 981	40 241	97 606	152 271	211 909	249 984	270 561
4 Western Offshoots	**11 230**	**46 133**	**111 401**	**176 094**	**250 945**	**298 150**	**323 420**
Albania	437	603	898	1 227	2 318	3 273	3 331
Bulgaria	2 187	2 586	4 794	7 251	8 621	8 966	8 240
Czechoslovakia	7 190	9 876	13 245	12 389	14 550		
a) Czech Republic						10 310	10 286
b) Slovakia						5 263	5 393
Hungary	4 571	5 717	7 840	9 338	10 426	10 352	10 208
Poland	10 426	17 240	26 710	24 824	33 331	38 109	38 607
Romania	6 389	9 179	12 527	16 311	20 828	22 775	22 396
Former Yugoslavia	5 215	6 981	13 590	15 949	20 416	22 819	22 545
Total East Europe	**36 415**	**52 182**	**79 604**	**87 289**	**110 490**	**121 867**	**121 006**
Former USSR	**54 765**	**88 672**	**156 192**	**180 050**	**249 748**	**289 350**	**290 866**
Armenia				1 355	2 697	3 335	3 795
Azerbaijan				2 900	5 468	7 134	7 666
Belarus				7 755	9 235	10 260	10 239
Estonia				1 115	1 411	1 582	1 450
Georgia				3 261	4 857	5 460	5 442
Kazakhstan				6 711	13 812	16 742	15 567
Kyrgyzstan				1 742	3 182	4 395	4 699
Latvia				1 951	2 442	2 684	2 449
Lithuania				2 570	3 247	3 726	3 703
Moldova				2 344	3 743	4 365	3 649
Russian Federation				102 317	132 651	148 290	146 909
Tajikistan				1 534	3 235	5 303	6 115
Turkmenistan				1 222	2 395	3 668	4 838
Ukraine				36 951	48 280	51 891	50 295
Uzbekistan				6 322	13 093	20 515	24 050

http://dx.doi.org/10.1787/486663055853

Table A1–b. **GDP Levels (million 1990 international $): European Countries, the Former USSR and Western Offshoots**

	1820	1870	1913	1950	1973	1990	1998
Austria	4 104	8 419	23 451	25 702	85 227	130 476	152 712
Belgium	4 529	13 746	32 347	47 190	118 516	171 442	198 249
Denmark	1 471	3 782	11 670	29 654	70 032	94 863	117 319
Finland	913	1 999	6 389	17 051	51 724	84 103	94 421
France	38 434	72 100	144 489	220 492	683 965	1 026 491	1 150 080
Germany	26 349	71 429	237 332	265 354	944 755	1 264 438	1 460 069
Italy	22 535	41 814	95 487	164 957	582 713	925 654	1 022 776
Netherlands	4 288	9 952	24 955	60 642	175 791	258 094	317 517
Norway	1 071	2 485	6 119	17 838	44 544	78 333	104 860
Sweden	3 098	6 927	17 403	47 269	109 794	151 451	165 385
Switzerland	2 342	5 867	16 483	42 545	117 251	146 900	152 345
United Kingdom	36 232	100 179	224 618	347 850	675 941	944 610	1 108 568
12 West Europe	**145 366**	**338 699**	**840 743**	**1 286 544**	**3 660 253**	**5 276 855**	**6 044 301**
13 Small W.E. Countries	667	1 553	3 843	5 880	16 452	31 205	41 499
Greece	1 539	3 338	8 635	14 489	68 355	101 452	118 433
Ireland				10 231	21 103	41 459	67 368
Portugal	3 175	4 338	7 467	17 615	63 397	107 427	128 877
Spain	12 975	22 295	45 686	66 792	304 220	474 366	560 138
Total Western Europe	**163 722**	**370 223**	**906 374**	**1 401 551**	**4 133 780**	**6 032 764**	**6 960 616**
Australia	172	6 452	27 552	61 274	172 314	291 180	382 335
New Zealand	40	922	5 781	16 136	37 177	46 729	56 322
Canada	729	6 407	34 916	102 164	312 176	524 475	622 880
United States	12 548	98 374	517 383	1 455 916	3 536 622	5 803 200	7 394 598
4 Western Offshoots	**13 489**	**112 155**	**585 632**	**1 635 490**	**4 058 289**	**6 665 584**	**8 456 135**
Albania				1 228	5 219	8 125	7 999
Bulgaria			7 181	11 971	45 557	49 779	37 786
Czechoslovakia	6 106	11 491	27 755	43 368	102 445		
a) Czech Republic						91 706	88 897
b) Slovakia						40 854	41 818
Hungary		7 253	16 447	23 158	58 339	66 990	66 089
Poland				60 742	177 973	194 920	258 220
Romania				19 279	72 411	80 277	64 715
Former Yugoslavia			13 988	25 277	88 813	129 953	95 337
Total East Europe	**23 149**	**45 448**	**121 559**	**185 023**	**550 757**	**662 604**	**660 861**
Former USSR	**37 710**	**83 646**	**232 351**	**510 243**	**1 513 070**	**1 987 995**	**1 132 434**
Armenia					16 691	20 483	12 679
Azerbaijan					24 378	33 397	16 365
Belarus					48 333	73 389	58 799
Estonia					12 214	16 980	14 671
Georgia					28 627	41 325	14 894
Kazakhstan					104 875	122 295	74 857
Kyrgyzstan					11 781	15 787	9 595
Latvia					18 998	26 413	15 222
Lithuania					24 643	32 010	21 914
Moldova					20 134	27 112	9 112
Russian Federation					872 466	1 151 040	664 495
Tajikistan					13 279	15 884	5 073
Turkmenistan					11 483	13 300	8 335
Ukraine					238 156	311 112	127 151
Uzbekistan					67 012	87 468	79 272

http://dx.doi.org/10.1787/486663055853

ISBN 92-64-02261-9 – © OECD 2006

Table A1–c. **GDP Per Capita (1990 international $): European Countries, the Former USSR and Western Offshoots**

	1820	1870	1913	1950	1973	1990	1998
Austria	1 218	1 863	3 465	3 706	11 235	16 881	18 905
Belgium	1 319	2 697	4 220	5 462	12 170	17 194	19 442
Denmark	1 274	2 003	3 912	6 946	13 945	18 463	22 123
Finland	781	1 140	2 111	4 253	11 085	16 868	18 324
France	1 230	1 876	3 485	5 270	13 123	18 093	19 558
Germany	1 058	1 821	3 648	3 881	11 966	15 932	17 799
Italy	1 117	1 499	2 564	3 502	10 643	16 320	17 759
Netherlands	1 821	2 753	4 049	5 996	13 082	17 267	20 224
Norway	1 104	1 432	2 501	5 463	11 246	18 470	23 660
Sweden	1 198	1 664	3 096	6 738	13 493	17 680	18 685
Switzerland	1 280	2 202	4 266	9 064	18 204	21 616	21 367
United Kingdom	1 707	3 191	4 921	6 907	12 022	16 411	18 714
12 West Europe	**1 270**	**2 086**	**3 688**	**5 013**	**12 159**	**16 872**	**18 742**
13 Small W.E. Countries	1 015	1 665	2 830	3 846	8 627	14 480	17 757
Greece	666	913	1 592	1 915	7 655	9 984	11 268
Ireland				3 446	6 867	11 825	18 183
Portugal	963	997	1 244	2 069	7 343	10 852	12 929
Spain	1 063	1 376	2 255	2 397	8 739	12 210	14 227
Total Western Europe	**1 232**	**1 974**	**3 473**	**4 594**	**11 534**	**15 988**	**17 921**
Australia	517	3 645	5 715	7 493	12 759	17 043	20 390
New Zealand	400	2 704	5 152	8 453	12 513	13 825	14 779
Canada	893	1 695	4 447	7 437	13 838	18 933	20 559
United States	1 257	2 445	5 301	9 561	16 689	23 214	27 331
4 Western Offshoots	**1 201**	**2 431**	**5 257**	**9 288**	**16 172**	**22 356**	**26 146**
Albania				1 001	2 252	2 482	2 401
Bulgaria				1 651	5 284	5 552	4 586
Czechoslovakia	849	1 164	2 096	3 501	7 041		
a) Czech Republic						8 895	8 643
b) Slovakia						7 762	7 754
Hungary		1 269	2 098	2 480	5 596	6 471	6 474
Poland				2 447	5 340	5 115	6 688
Romania				1 182	3 477	3 525	2 890
Former Yugoslavia			1 029	1 585	4 350	5 695	4 229
Total East Europe	**636**	**871**	**1 527**	**2 120**	**4 985**	**5 437**	**5 461**
Former USSR	**689**	**943**	**1 488**	**2 834**	**6 058**	**6 871**	**3 893**
Armenia					6 189	6 142	3 341
Azerbaijan					4 458	4 681	2 135
Belarus					5 234	7 153	5 743
Estonia					8 656	10 733	10 118
Georgia					5 894	7 569	2 737
Kazakhstan					7 593	7 305	4 809
Kyrgyzstan					3 702	3 592	2 042
Latvia					7 780	9 841	6 216
Lithuania					7 589	8 591	5 918
Moldova					5 379	6 211	2 497
Russian Federation					6 577	7 762	4 523
Tajikistan					4 105	2 995	830
Turkmenistan					4 795	3 626	1 723
Ukraine					4 933	5 995	2 528
Uzbekistan					5 118	4 264	3 296

http://dx.doi.org/10.1787/486663055853

Table A1–d. GDP Per Capita Growth Rates: European Countries, the Former USSR and Western Offshoots

	1820–70	1870–1913	1913–50	1950–73	1973–98
Austria	0.85	1.45	0.18	4.94	2.10
Belgium	1.44	1.05	0.70	3.55	1.89
Denmark	0.91	1.57	1.56	3.08	1.86
Finland	0.76	1.44	1.91	4.25	2.03
France	0.85	1.45	1.12	4.05	1.61
Germany	1.09	1.63	0.17	5.02	1.60
Italy	0.59	1.26	0.85	4.95	2.07
Netherlands	0.83	0.90	1.07	3.45	1.76
Norway	0.52	1.30	2.13	3.19	3.02
Sweden	0.66	1.46	2.12	3.07	1.31
Switzerland	1.09	1.55	2.06	3.08	0.64
United Kingdom	1.26	1.01	0.92	2.44	1.79
12 West Europe	**1.00**	**1.33**	**0.83**	**3.93**	**1.75**
13 Small W.E. Countries	0.99	1.24	0.83	3.58	2.93
Greece	0.63	1.30	0.50	6.21	1.56
Ireland				3.04	3.97
Portugal	0.07	0.52	1.39	5.66	2.29
Spain	0.52	1.15	0.17	5.79	1.97
Total Western Europe	**0.95**	**1.32**	**0.76**	**4.08**	**1.78**
Australia	3.99	1.05	0.73	2.34	1.89
New Zealand	3.90	1.51	1.35	1.72	0.67
Canada	1.29	2.27	1.40	2.74	1.60
United States	1.34	1.82	1.61	2.45	1.99
4 Western Offshoots	**1.42**	**1.81**	**1.55**	**2.44**	**1.94**
Albania				3.59	0.26
Bulgaria				5.19	−0.57
Czechoslovakia	0.63	1.38	1.40	3.08	(0.67)
a) Czech Republic					
b) Slovakia					
Hungary		1.18	0.45	3.60	0.59
Poland				3.45	0.91
Romania				4.80	−0.74
Former Yugoslavia			1.17	4.49	−0.11
Total East Europe	**0.63**	**1.31**	**0.89**	**3.79**	**0.37**
Former USSR	**0.63**	**1.06**	**1.76**	**3.36**	**−1.75**
Armenia					−2.44
Azerbaijan					−2.90
Belarus					0.37
Estonia					0.63
Georgia					−3.02
Kazakhstan					−1.81
Kyrgyzstan					−2.35
Latvia					−0.89
Lithuania					−0.99
Moldova					−3.02
Russian Federation					−1.49
Tajikistan					−6.20
Turkmenistan					−4.01
Ukraine					−2.64
Uzbekistan					−1.74

http://dx.doi.org/10.1787/486663055853

ISBN 92-64-02261-9 – © OECD 2006

Table A1–e. **GDP Growth Rates: European Countries, the Former USSR and Western Offshoots**

	1820–70	*1870–1913*	*1913–50*	*1950–73*	*1973–98*
Austria	1.45	2.41	0.25	5.35	2.36
Belgium	2.25	2.01	1.03	4.08	2.08
Denmark	1.91	2.66	2.55	3.81	2.09
Finland	1.58	2.74	2.69	4.94	2.44
France	1.27	1.63	1.15	5.05	2.10
Germany	2.01	2.83	0.30	5.68	1.76
Italy	1.24	1.94	1.49	5.64	2.28
Netherlands	1.70	2.16	2.43	4.74	2.39
Norway	1.70	2.12	2.93	4.06	3.48
Sweden	1.62	2.17	2.74	3.73	1.65
Switzerland	1.85	2.43	2.60	4.51	1.05
United Kingdom	2.05	1.90	1.19	2.93	2.00
12 West Europe	**1.71**	**2.14**	**1.16**	**4.65**	**2.03**
13 Small W.E. Countries	1.70	2.13	1.16	4.58	3.77
Greece	1.56	2.23	1.41	6.98	2.22
Ireland				3.20	4.75
Portugal	0.63	1.27	2.35	5.73	2.88
Spain	1.09	1.68	1.03	6.81	2.47
Total Western Europe	**1.65**	**2.10**	**1.19**	**4.81**	**2.11**
Australia	7.52	3.43	2.18	4.60	3.24
New Zealand	6.48	4.36	2.81	3.70	1.68
Canada	4.44	4.02	2.94	4.98	2.80
United States	4.20	3.94	2.84	3.93	2.99
4 Western Offshoots	**4.33**	**3.92**	**2.81**	**4.03**	**2.98**
Albania				6.49	1.72
Bulgaria			1.39	5.98	−0.75
Czechoslovakia	1.27	2.07	1.21	3.81	(0.98)
a) Czech Republic					
b) Slovakia					
Hungary		1.92	0.93	4.10	0.50
Poland				4.78	1.50
Romania				5.92	−0.45
Former Yugoslavia			1.61	5.62	0.28
Total East Europe	**1.36**	**2.31**	**1.14**	**4.86**	**0.73**
Former USSR	**1.61**	**2.40**	**2.15**	**4.84**	**−1.15**
Armenia					−1.09
Azerbaijan					−1.58
Belarus					0.79
Estonia					0.74
Georgia					−2.58
Kazakhstan					−1.34
Kyrgyzstan					−0.82
Latvia					−0.88
Lithuania					−0.47
Moldova					−3.12
Russian Federation					−1.08
Tajikistan					−3.78
Turkmenistan					−1.27
Ukraine					−2.48
Uzbekistan					0.67

http://dx.doi.org/10.1787/486663055853

Table A1–f. **Population Growth Rates: European Countries, the Former USSR and Western Offshoots**

	1820–70	*1870–1913*	*1913–50*	*1950–73*	*1973–98*
Austria	0.59	0.94	0.07	0.39	0.25
Belgium	0.79	0.95	0.32	0.52	0.18
Denmark	0.99	1.07	0.97	0.71	0.22
Finland	0.81	1.28	0.76	0.66	0.40
France	0.42	0.18	0.02	0.96	0.48
Germany	0.91	1.18	0.13	0.63	0.15
Italy	0.65	0.68	0.64	0.66	0.20
Netherlands	0.86	1.25	1.35	1.24	0.62
Norway	1.17	0.80	0.78	0.84	0.45
Sweden	0.96	0.70	0.60	0.65	0.34
Switzerland	0.75	0.87	0.53	1.39	0.41
United Kingdom	0.79	0.87	0.27	0.48	0.21
12 West Europe	**0.70**	**0.79**	**0.32**	**0.70**	**0.28**
13 Small W.E. Countries	0.70	0.88	0.32	0.97	0.82
Greece	0.92	0.92	0.90	0.72	0.65
Ireland				0.15	0.75
Portugal	0.56	0.75	0.95	0.06	0.58
Spain	0.57	0.52	0.87	0.97	0.49
Total Western Europe	**0.69**	**0.77**	**0.42**	**0.70**	**0.32**
Australia	3.40	2.36	1.44	2.21	1.32
New Zealand	2.48	2.81	1.45	1.94	1.00
Canada	3.11	1.71	1.52	2.18	1.19
United States	2.83	2.08	1.21	1.45	0.98
4 Western Offshoots	**2.87**	**2.07**	**1.25**	**1.55**	**1.02**
Albania	0.65	0.93	0.85	2.80	1.46
Bulgaria	0.34	1.45	1.12	0.76	−0.18
Czechoslovakia	0.64	0.68	−0.18	0.70	(0.30)
a) Czech Republic					
b) Slovakia					
Hungary	0.45	0.74	0.47	0.48	−0.08
Poland	1.01	1.02	−0.20	1.29	0.59
Romania	0.73	0.73	0.72	1.07	0.29
Former Yugoslavia	0.59	1.56	0.43	1.08	0.40
Total East Europe	**0.72**	**0.99**	**0.25**	**1.03**	**0.36**
Former USSR	**0.97**	**1.33**	**0.38**	**1.43**	**0.61**
Armenia				3.04	1.38
Azerbaijan				2.80	1.36
Belarus				0.76	0.41
Estonia				1.03	0.11
Georgia				1.75	0.46
Kazakhstan				3.19	0.48
Kyrgyzstan				2.65	1.57
Latvia				0.98	0.01
Lithuania				1.02	0.53
Moldova				2.06	−0.10
Russian Federation				1.14	0.41
Tajikistan				3.30	2.58
Turkmenistan				2.97	2.85
Ukraine				1.17	0.16
Uzbekistan				3.22	2.46

http://dx.doi.org/10.1787/486663055853

Table A1–g. Derivation of 1990 Benchmark Levels of GDP in International Dollars, 22 OECD Countries

	GDP in national currency	Geary–Khamis PPP Converter	Exchange rate	GDP in million international dollars	GDP in $ million converted at exchange rate
Austria	1 813 482	13.899	11.370	130 476	159 497
Belgium	6 576 846	38.362	33.418	171 442	196 805
Denmark	825 310	8.700	6.189	94 863	133 351
Finland	523 034	6.219	3.824	84 103	136 777
France	6 620 867	6.450	5.445	1 026 491	1 215 954
West Germany[a]	2 426 000	2.052	1.616	1 182 261	1 501 238
Italy	1 281 207	1384.11	1198.1	925 654	1 069 366
Netherlands	537 867	2.084	1.821	258 094	295 369
Norway	722 705	9.218	6.26	78 333	115 448
Sweden	1 359 879	8.979	5.919	151 451	229 748
Switzerland	317 304	2.160	1.389	146 900	228 441
United Kingdom	554 486	0.587	0.563	944 610	984 877
Luxembourg	345 738	39.203	33.418	8 819	10 346
Iceland	364 402	79.291	58.284	4 596	6 252
Greece	13 143	129.55	158.51	101 452	82 916
Ireland	28 524	0.688	0.605	41 459	47 147
Portugal	9 855	91.737	142.56	107 427	69 129
Spain	501 452	105.71	101.93	474 366	491 957
Australia	393 675	1.352	1.281	291 180	307 319
New Zealand	72 776	1.5574	1.676	46 729	43 422
Canada	668 181	1.274	1.167	524 475	572 563
United States	5 803 200	1.000	1.000	5 803 200	5 803 200

a) East German GDP in international dollars was 82 177 million in 1990.

Source: GDP in national currency from OECD *National Accounts of OECD Countries, 1988–1998,* vol. 1, OECD, Paris, 2000, except for the Netherlands which is from OECD *Quarterly National Accounts* (1999:4), and the United States which is from *Survey of Current Business,* December 1999, p. 132. Official Italian GDP estimates reduced by 3 per cent as explained in Maddison (1995a), p. 133. Geary–Khamis purchasing power converters from the sixth round of the International Comparison Project (ICP) for 1990 — see Maddison (1995a) Table C–6, p. 172; exchange rates from the same source. PPPs and exchange rates are expressed in units of national currency by PPP per US dollar. GDP in million international dollars converted by PPP is derived by dividing column 1 by column 2. GDP in million US dollars converted at exchange rates is derived by dividing column 1 by column 3. When one makes binary comparisons of purchasing power, e.g. of France and the United States, there are three possible approaches. One can a) revalue French expenditure at US prices and get a "Laspeyres" comparison of GDP volume; b) revalue US expenditure at French prices and get a "Paasche" volume comparison; (c) make a compromise "Fisher" geometric average of the Laspeyres and Paasche measures. The results of such binary studies can be used to compare the situation in a number of countries, e.g. France/United States, Germany/United States and United Kingdom/United States comparisons can be linked using the United States as a "star" country. However, the derivative France–Germany, United Kingdom–Germany and France–United Kingdom results are inferential and will not necessarily be the same as one could derive from direct binary comparisons of each pair. Such comparisons are not "transitive", but transitivity and additivity can be achieved by use of a "multilateral" PPP. The Geary–Khamis measure is the multilateral measure I prefer as it gives weights to countries corresponding to the size of their GDP (see Maddison, 1995a, p. 163, for a detailed explanation). For most countries, the new GDP figures in national currencies are higher than those used in Maddison (1995a). They incorporate routine revisions and those resulting from adoption of the 1993 SNA (standardised system of national accounts). This was adopted by Norway in 1995, Denmark and Canada in 1997. Australia, Austria, Belgium, Finland, France, Germany, Greece, Ireland, Italy, Luxembourg, the Netherlands, Portugal, Spain, Sweden and the United Kingdom made the change later, and figures on the new basis were published for these 15 countries for the first time by OECD in the 1988–98 yearbook. The new system involves treatment of expenditure on mineral exploration and computer software as investment rather than intermediate input. In some countries, e.g. France and Italy "entertainment, literary and artistic originals" are also now treated as investment. Iceland, New Zealand and Switzerland still use the old 1968 SNA and have not made these methodological changes. As a result of these revisions the 1990 GDP levels have changed by the following ratios to the level shown in Maddison (1995a):

Austria	1.00676	United Kingdom	1.00928
Belgium	1.02342	Luxembourg	1.15206
Denmark	1.02779	Iceland	1.03700
Finland	1.01591	Greece	0.99539
France	1.01774	Ireland	1.06406
Germany	1.00033	Portugal	1.014765
Italy	1.00668	Spain	1.00051
Netherlands	1.04184	Australia	1.04055
Norway	1.09314	New Zealand	0.99290
Sweden	1.00000	Canada	1.00567
Switzerland	1.01041	United States	1.06192

http://dx.doi.org/10.1787/486663055853

Table A1–h. **Derivation of 1990 Benchmark Levels of GDP in International Dollars, Five East European Countries and USSR**

	GDP in national currency	Implicit PPP Converter	Exchange rate	GDP in million international dollars	GDP in $ million converted at exchange rate
Czechoslovakia	811 309	6.12	17.95	132 560	45 198
Hungary	1 935 459	28.89	63.206	66 990	30 621
Poland	608 347	3.12	9.5	194 920	64 037
Romania	857 180	10.678	22.43	80 277	38 216
USSR	1 033 222	0.520	1.059	1 987 995	975 658
Yugoslavia	1 113 095	8.565	11.318	129 953	98 347

Source: GDP in national currency from *International Comparison of Gross Domestic Product in Europe 1990*, United Nations Statistical Commission and ECE, Geneva and New York, 1994, p. 61. These comparisons were carried out in cooperation with the national statistical offices, with adjustments to make the coverage of the national accounts conform to the standardised national accounting system used in Western countries. Adjustments were also made to correct for lower quality of goods in the East European countries. The results were multilateralised using the EKS rather than the Geary–Khamis technique, and the PPP adjusted GDPs were expressed in Austrian schillings. The relative volume indices of GDP were converted to an approximate Geary–Khamis basis using Austrian GDP in international dollars in Table 2.4 as a bridge, see *op. cit.*, p. 5. This is how the column 4 results were estimated and the implicit PPP in column 3 was derived by dividing column 1 by column 4. Exchange rates were derived from IMF, *International Financial Statistics*, except for the USSR which is from World Bank, *World Tables 1995*. Since 1990, these six countries have become 25. Czechoslovakia has split into two countries, Yugoslavia into five, and the USSR into 15. In order to get rough provisional estimates for GDP in these 22 new successor states, I assumed that their proportional share in 1990 GDP was the same as it was in national currency. The OECD has released new estimates in international dollars for 20 of these new states (excluding Bosnia and Serbia), using the EKS technique of multilateralisation, see *A PPP Comparison for the NIS, 1994, 1995 and 1996*, OECD, February 2000. See Appendix D for a confrontation of these new estimates with those I use here.

http://dx.doi.org/10.1787/486663055853

A–2

Population, GDP and GDP Per Capita in 44 Latin American and Caribbean Countries

There are eight core countries for which GDP estimates are available before 1950. 1820–1990 GDP movement for Argentina, Chile, Colombia, Peru and Venezuela from Maddison (1995a), updated from ECLAC, *Economic Survey of Latin America and the Caribbean: Summary 1998–99*, 1999, p. 32. Brazilian GDP 1950–98 as above, 1820–1900 from Maddison (1995a); per capita GDP movement 1900–50 from Maddison and Associates (1992), p. 212. Mexican GDP movement 1870–1910 from Coatsworth (1989), 1910–60 from Maddison (1995a), 1960 onwards from OECD sources. I assumed a smaller drop in Mexican GDP per capita 1820–70 than Coatsworth. GDP 1820–1936 for Uruguay from Luis Bertola and Associates, *PBI de Uruguay 1870–1936*, Montevideo, 1998. 1936–90 GDP supplied by Luis Bertola, 1990 onwards from ECLAC (1999). Benchmark 1990 level of GDP in the eight countries in international dollars from Table A2–g.

Population 1820–1950 from Maddison (1995a) except Uruguay (supplied by Luis Bertola). 1950 onwards from US Bureau of the Census.

There are 15 other countries for which detailed estimates of population and GDP are shown. For 13 of them, 1870–1913 population was derived by interpolating the estimates of N. Sanchez Albornoz, "The Population of Latin America, 1850–1930", in L. Bethell, ed., *The Cambridge History of Latin America*, vol. 4, Cambridge University Press, 1986, p. 122. Jamaica 1870 and 1913 derived from G. Eisner, *Jamaica, 1830–1930: A Study in Economic Growth*, Manchester University Press, 1961, p. 134. 1870–1950 movement in Trinidad and Tobago was assumed to be proportionately the same as in Jamaica. 1820–70 population in the 15 countries assumed to move in the same proportion as the aggregate for the eight core countries. 1950–98 population movement from US Bureau of the Census.

1950–73 GDP movement for 11 of the 15 countries from ECLAC, *Series Historicas del Crecimiento de America Latina*, Santiago, 1978, 1973–90 from World Bank, *World Tables* (1995), and 1990 onwards from ECLAC (1999). Cuba 1950–90 from various ECLAC sources, 1990 onwards from ECLAC, *Preliminary Overview of the Economies of Latin America*, Santiago (1998 and 1999 editions). GDP of Puerto Rico 1950–98 from *PBI Historico*, Junta de Planificación, San José, 1998. Jamaica, Trinidad and Tobago 1950–73 from OECD Development Centre database, 1973–90 from World Bank, *World Tables*, 1990 onwards from ECLAC (1999). 1820–1950 movement in aggregate per capita GDP of the 15 countries assumed to move in the same proportion as the aggregate for the eight core countries.

Aggregate estimates for 21 small Caribbean countries are shown in Tables A–2a to A–2f; country detail for 1950–98 in Table A–g.

Table A2–g shows the derivation of 1990 benchmark GDP levels from ICP studies in 1990 international prices for the eight core countries and ten others. Penn World Tables were used for Bahamas, Barbados, Belize, Dominica, Grenada, Guyana, Haiti, Nicaragua, Puerto Rico, St. Kitts Nevis, St. Lucia, St. Vincent, Suriname, Trinidad and Tobago.

Table A–g. GDP and Population in 21 Small Caribbean Countries, 1950–98

	GDP in million 1990 international $				Population (000)			
	1950	*1973*	*1990*	*1998*	*1950*	*1973*	*1990*	*1998*
Bahamas	756	3 159	3 946	4 248	70	182	251	180
Barbados	448	1 595	2 138	2 366	211	243	255	259
Belize	110	341	735	929	66	130	190	230
Dominica	82	182	279	344	51	74	72	66
Grenada	71	180	310	388	76	97	94	96
Guyana	462	1 309	1 159	2 018	428	755	748	708
St. Lucia	61	199	449	508	79	109	140	152
St. Vincent	79	175	392	506	66	90	113	120
Suriname	315	1 046	1 094	1 209	208	384	396	428
Total Group A	2 384	8 186	10 502	12 516	1 255	2 064	2 249	2 339
Antigua & Barbuda	82	328	413	510	46	68	63	64
Bermuda	65	238	310		39	53	58	62
Guadeloupe	359	1 568	1 801		208	329	378	416
Guyana (Fr.)	138	238	516		26	53	116	163
Martinique	293	1 568	1 857		217	332	374	407
Neth. Antilles	393	1 097	980	1 100	159	225	253	274
St. Kitts Nevis	61	215	233	345	44	45	40	42
Total Group B	1 391	5 252	6 110	7 787	739	1 105	1 284	1 428
Other 5 Countries	181	667	1 094	1 446	68	139	183	233
21 Countries	3 956	14 105	17 706	21 749	2 062	3 308	3 726	3 990

Source: 1950–90 GDP movement from Maddison (1995a), p. 218, and the underlying database. For seven of the Group A countries, GDP movement for 1990 onwards from ECLAC, *Economic Survey of Latin America and the Caribbean 1998–1999*, Santiago, 1999, p. 32. 1990–98 per capita GDP movement for Antigua and Barbuda, Bahamas, Netherlands Antilles and St. Kitts Nevis from IMF. For other countries, aggregate GDP per capita movement assumed to be proportionately the same as the Group A average. Population 1950 onwards from the Division of Population Studies, US Bureau of the Census; 1820–50 aggregate population of the 21 countries assumed to move in the same proportion as the aggregate for the 15 countries specified in Table A2–a. The 5 countries in the third group are Aruba, Falkland Islands, St. Pierre and Miquelon, Turks and Caicos Islands and Virgin Islands.

http://dx.doi.org/10.1787/486663055853

For 11 small Caribbean countries and Cuba, neither ICP nor PWT estimates of PPP were available. It was assumed that the average per capita GDP level for these countries was the same as the average for the 32 countries for which indicators were available, and for Cuba that it was about 15 per cent below the Latin America average.

ICP estimates represented nearly 95.2 per cent of the aggregate GDP for Latin America in 1990, PWT nearly 3.2 per cent, and proxy valuations 1.7 per cent.

It was assumed that the aggregate proportionate GDP per capita movement for the three missing countries for 1870–1913 was the same as the average for the other five core countries. For 1820 it was assumed that the average level of per capita GDP for the missing core countries was the same as the average for Brazil and Mexico.

For the 36 other countries no estimates of GDP movement were available for 1820–1950. Their average per capita GDP movement was assumed to be proportionate to that in the eight sample countries (including the proxy element in the latter). Thus the total proxy component of Latin American aggregate GDP in 1820 was 44.0 per cent, for 1870 38.2 per cent, for 1913 16.7 per cent, and negligible for 1950 onwards.

Table A2–a. **Population (000 at mid–year): 44 Latin American Countries**

	1820	*1870*	*1913*	*1950*	*1973*	*1990*	*1998*
Argentina	534	1 796	7 653	17 150	25 174	32 634	36 265
Brazil	4 507	9 797	23 660	53 443	103 463	151 040	169 807
Chile	885	1 943	3 491	6 091	9 897	13 128	14 788
Colombia	1 206	2 392	5 195	11 592	23 069	32 985	38 581
Mexico	6 587	9 219	14 970	28 485	57 643	84 748	98 553
Peru	1 317	2 606	4 339	7 633	14 350	21 989	26 111
Uruguay	55	373	1 177	2 194	2 834	3 106	3 285
Venezuela	718	1 653	2 874	5 009	11 893	19 325	22 803
Total 8 Countries	**15 809**	**29 779**	**63 359**	**131 597**	**248 323**	**358 955**	**410 193**
Bolivia		1 495	1 881	2 766	4 680	6 620	7 826
Costa Rica		155	372	867	1 886	3 022	3 605
Cuba		1 331	2 469	5 785	9 001	10 545	11 051
Dominican Republic		242	750	2 312	4 781	6 997	7 999
Ecuador		1 013	1 689	3 310	6 629	10 308	12 337
El Salvador		492	1 008	1 940	3 853	5 041	5 752
Guatemala		1 007	1 486	2 969	5 801	9 631	12 008
Haiti		1 150	1 891	3 097	4 748	6 048	6 781
Honduras		404	660	1 431	2 964	4 740	5 862
Jamaica		499	837	1 385	2 036	2 466	2 635
Nicaragua		361	578	1 098	2 241	3 591	4 583
Panama		176	348	893	1 659	2 388	2 736
Paraguay		384	594	1 476	2 692	4 236	5 291
Puerto Rico		645	1 181	2 218	2 863	3 537	3 860
Trinidad & Tobago		210	352	632	985	1 198	1 117
Total 15 other Countries	**5 077**	**9 564**	**16 096**	**32 179**	**56 819**	**80 368**	**93 443**
Total 21 small non sample Countries	**334**	**630**	**1 060**	**2 062**	**3 308**	**3 726**	**3 990**
Total 44 Latin America Countries	**21 220**	**39 973**	**80 515**	**165 837**	**308 450**	**443 049**	**507 623**
Total 43 Latin America Countries (excluding Mexico)	**14 633**	**30 754**	**65 545**	**137 352**	**250 807**	**358 301**	**409 070**

http://dx.doi.org/10.1787/486663055853

Table A2–b. **GDP Levels (million 1990 international $): 44 Latin American Countries**

	1820	1870	1913	1950	1973	1990	1998
Argentina		2 354	29 060	85 524	200 720	212 518	334 314
Brazil	2 912	6 985	19 188	89 342	401 643	743 765	926 919
Chile			9 261	23 274	50 401	84 038	144 279
Colombia			6 420	24 955	80 728	159 042	205 132
Mexico	5 000	6 214	25 921	67 368	279 302	516 692	655 910
Peru			4 500	17 270	56 713	64 979	95 718
Uruguay		748	3 895	10 224	14 098	20 105	27 313
Venezuela		941	3 172	37 377	126 364	160 648	204 433
Total 8 Countries	**11 275**	**22 273**	**101 417**	**355 334**	**1 209 969**	**1 961 787**	**2 594 018**
Bolivia				5 309	11 030	14 446	19 241
Costa Rica				1 702	8 145	14 370	19 272
Cuba				19 613	29 165	31 087	23 909
Dominican Republic				2 416	9 617	17 503	25 304
Ecuador				6 278	21 337	40 267	51 378
El Salvador				2 888	9 084	10 805	15 627
Guatemala				6 190	18 593	29 050	40 522
Haiti				3 254	4 810	6 323	5 532
Honduras				1 880	4 866	8 898	11 929
Jamaica				1 837	8 411	8 890	9 308
Nicaragua				1 774	6 566	5 297	6 651
Panama				1 710	7 052	10 688	15 609
Paraguay				2 338	5 487	13 923	16 719
Puerto Rico				4 755	20 908	37 277	51 159
Trinidad & Tobago				2 322	8 553	11 110	13 683
Total 15 other Countries	**2 676**	**5 289**	**19 058**	**64 266**	**173 626**	**259 934**	**325 843**
Total 21 small non sample Countries	**169**	**335**	**1 206**	**3 956**	**14 105**	**17 706**	**21 749**
Total 44 Latin America Countries	**14 120**	**27 897**	**121 681**	**423 556**	**1 397 700**	**2 239 427**	**2 941 610**
Total 43 Latin America Countries (excluding Mexico)	**9 120**	**21 683**	**95 760**	**356 188**	**1 118 398**	**1 722 735**	**2 285 700**

http://dx.doi.org/10.1787/486663055853

Table A2–c. **GDP per Capita (1990 international $): 44 Latin American Countries**

	1820	1870	1913	1950	1973	1990	1998
Argentina		1 311	3 797	4 987	7 973	6 512	9 219
Brazil	646	713	811	1 672	3 882	4 924	5 459
Chile			2 653	3 821	5 093	6 401	9 756
Colombia			1 236	2 153	3 499	4 822	5 317
Mexico	759	674	1 732	2 365	4 845	6 097	6 655
Peru			1 037	2 263	3 952	2 955	3 666
Uruguay		2 005	3 309	4 660	4 975	6 473	8 314
Venezuela		569	1 104	7 462	10 625	8 313	8 965
Total 8 Countries	**713**	**748**	**1 601**	**2 700**	**4 873**	**5 465**	**6 324**
Bolivia				1 919	2 357	2 182	2 459
Costa Rica				1 963	4 319	4 755	5 346
Cuba				3 390	3 240	2 948	2 164
Dominican Republic				1 045	2 012	2 502	3 163
Ecuador				1 897	3 219	3 906	4 165
El Salvador				1 489	2 358	2 143	2 717
Guatemala				2 085	3 205	3 016	3 375
Haiti				1 051	1 013	1 045	816
Honduras				1 314	1 642	1 877	2 035
Jamaica				1 326	4 131	3 605	3 532
Nicaragua				1 616	2 930	1 475	1 451
Panama				1 915	4 251	4 476	5 705
Paraguay				1 584	2 038	3 287	3 160
Puerto Rico				2 144	7 303	10 539	13 254
Trinidad & Tobago				3 674	8 683	9 274	12 250
Total 15 other Countries	**527**	**553**	**1 184**	**1 997**	**3 056**	**3 234**	**3 487**
Total 21 small non sample Countries	**506**	**532**	**1 138**	**1 919**	**4 264**	**4 752**	**5 451**
Total 44 Latin America Countries	**665**	**698**	**1 511**	**2 554**	**4 531**	**5 055**	**5 795**
Total 43 Latin America Countries (excluding Mexico)	**623**	**705**	**1 461**	**2 593**	**4 459**	**4 808**	**5 588**

http://dx.doi.org/10.1787/486663055853

195

Table A2–d. **GDP Per Capita Growth Rate: 44 Latin American Countries**

	1820–1870	*1870–1913*	*1913–50*	*1950–73*	*1973–98*
Argentina		2.50	0.74	2.06	0.58
Brazil	0.20	0.30	1.97	3.73	1.37
Chile			0.99	1.26	2.63
Colombia			1.51	2.13	1.69
Mexico	−0.24	2.22	0.85	3.17	1.28
Peru			2.13	2.45	−0.30
Uruguay		1.17	0.93	0.28	2.08
Venezuela			5.30	1.55	−0.68
Total 8 Countries	**0.10**	**1.79**	**1.42**	**2.60**	**1.05**
Bolivia				0.90	0.17
Costa Rica				3.49	0.86
Cuba				−0.20	−1.60
Dominican Republic				2.89	1.83
Ecuador				2.33	1.04
El Salvador				2.02	0.57
Guatemala				1.89	0.21
Haiti				−0.16	−0.86
Honduras				0.97	0.86
Jamaica				5.06	−0.62
Nicaragua				2.62	−2.77
Panama				3.53	1.18
Paraguay				1.10	1.77
Puerto Rico				5.47	2.41
Trinidad & Tobago				3.81	1.39
Total 15 other Countries				**1.87**	**0.53**
Total 21 small non sample Countries				**3.53**	**0.99**
Total 44 Latin America Countries	**0.10**	**1.81**	**1.43**	**2.52**	**0.99**
Total 43 Latin America Countries (excluding Mexico)	**0.25**	**1.71**	**1.56**	**2.38**	**0.91**

http://dx.doi.org/10.1787/486663055853

Table A2–e. **GDP Growth Rate: 44 Latin American Countries**

	1820–1870	*1870–1913*	*1913–50*	*1950–73*	*1973–98*
Argentina		6.02	2.96	3.78	2.06
Brazil	1.77	2.38	4.24	6.75	3.40
Chile			2.52	3.42	4.30
Colombia			3.74	5.24	3.80
Mexico	0.44	3.38	2.62	6.38	3.47
Peru			3.70	5.31	2.12
Uruguay		3.91	2.64	1.41	2.68
Venezuela			6.89	5.44	1.94
Total 8 Countries	**1.37**	**3.59**	**3.45**	**5.47**	**3.10**
Bolivia				3.23	2.25
Costa Rica				7.04	3.51
Cuba				1.74	–0.79
Dominican Republic				6.19	3.95
Ecuador				5.46	3.58
El Salvador				5.11	2.19
Guatemala				4.90	3.17
Haiti				1.71	0.56
Honduras				4.22	3.65
Jamaica				6.84	0.41
Nicaragua				5.85	0.05
Panama				6.35	3.23
Paraguay				3.78	4.56
Puerto Rico				6.65	3.64
Trinidad & Tobago				5.83	1.90
Total 15 other Countries				**4.42**	**2.55**
Total 21 small non sample Countries				**5.68**	**1.75**
Total 44 Latin America Countries	**1.37**	**3.48**	**3.43**	**5.33**	**3.02**
Total 43 Latin America Countries (excluding Mexico)	**1.75**	**3.51**	**3.61**	**5.10**	**2.90**

http://dx.doi.org/10.1787/486663055853

Table A2–f. **Population Growth Rate: 44 Latin American Countries**

	1820–1870	*1870–1913*	*1913–50*	*1950–73*	*1973–98*
Argentina	2.46	3.43	2.20	1.68	1.47
Brazil	1.57	2.07	2.23	2.91	2.00
Chile	1.59	1.37	1.52	2.13	1.62
Colombia	1.38	1.82	2.19	3.04	2.08
Mexico	0.67	1.13	1.75	3.11	2.17
Peru	1.37	1.19	1.54	2.78	2.42
Uruguay	3.90	2.71	1.70	1.12	0.59
Venezuela	1.68	1.29	1.51	3.83	2.64
Total 8 Countries	**1.27**	**1.77**	**2.00**	**2.80**	**2.03**
Bolivia		0.54	1.05	2.31	2.08
Costa Rica		2.06	2.31	3.44	2.63
Cuba		1.45	2.33	1.94	0.82
Dominican Republic		2.67	3.09	3.21	2.08
Ecuador		1.20	1.84	3.07	2.52
El Salvador		1.68	1.79	3.03	1.62
Guatemala		0.91	1.89	2.96	2.95
Haiti		1.16	1.34	1.88	1.44
Honduras		1.15	2.11	3.22	2.77
Jamaica		1.21	1.37	1.69	1.04
Nicaragua		1.10	1.75	3.15	2.90
Panama		1.60	2.58	2.73	2.02
Paraguay		1.02	2.49	2.65	2.74
Puerto Rico		1.42	1.72	1.12	1.20
Trinidad & Tobago		1.21	1.59	1.95	0.50
Total 15 other Countries	**1.27**	**1.22**	**1.89**	**2.50**	**2.01**
Total 21 small non sample Countries	**1.28**	**1.22**	**1.81**	**2.08**	**0.75**
Total 44 Latin America Countries	**1.27**	**1.64**	**1.97**	**2.73**	**2.01**
Total 43 Latin America Countries (excluding Mexico)	**1.50**	**1.78**	**2.02**	**2.65**	**1.98**

http://dx.doi.org/10.1787/486663055853

ISBN 92-64-02261-9 – © OECD 2006

Table A2–g. **Derivation of Estimates of 1990 GDP in 1990 International Dollars, 18 Latin American Countries**

	GDP in million national currency units in reference year	PPP Converter for reference year (units of national currency per dollar)	GDP in reference year in million Geary–Khamis dollars	1990 GDP in Geary–Khamis dollars of reference year	1990 GDP in million 1990 Geary–Khamis dollars
	ICP 3 (Reference Year 1975)				
Jamaica	2 611	0.742	3 519	3 865	8 890
Mexico	1 007 036	7.4	136 086	224 649	516 692
	ICP 4 (Reference Year 1980)				
Argentina	3 840	0.02604	147 465	134 607	212 518
Bolivia	128 614	14.51	8 864	9 150	14 446
Brazil	13 164	0.03252	404 797	471 096	743 765
Chile	1 075 269	26.67	40 318	53 299	84 038
Colombia	1 579 130	21.99	71 811	100 736	159 042
Costa Rica	41 406	5.79	7 151	9 102	14 370
Dominican Republic	6 625	0.594	11 153	11 086	17 503
Ecuador	293 337	14.16	20 716	25 505	40 267
El Salvador	8 917	1.31	6 807	6 844	10 805
Guatemala	7 879	0.467	16 871	18 400	29 050
Honduras	4 976	1.12	4 443	5 636	8 898
Panama	3 559	0.564	6 310	6 770	10 688
Paraguay	560 459	83.87	6 682	8 819	13 923
Peru	5 970 000	129.6	46 065	41 157	64 979
Uruguay	92 204	7.58	12 164	12 734	20 105
Venezuela	297 800	3.14	94 841	101 753	160 648

Source: Column 1 shows GDP in the reference year in national currency units, in most cases as specified in the original ICP estimate. For Argentina, Peru and Venezuela, there were upward adjustments to the official estimates of nominal GDP in 1980, after the ICP exercise was conducted. These involved upward adjustments of 36 per cent, 6.5 per cent, and 17.2 per cent respectively to correct for previous underestimates for informal activity. In the case of Mexico my estimate is 12.2 per cent lower than the official 1975 figure shown in OECD, *National Accounts, 1960–97*; the adjustment was made to correct for official exaggeration of output levels in agriculture, manufacturing and some services. The rationale for this change is explained in Maddison (1995a), p. 166. The PPPs in column 2 are from ICP. Column 3 is derived from columns 1 and 2. Column 4 was derived by adjusting column 3 for the volume movement in GDP between the reference year and 1990. Column 5 is column 4 adjusted for the movement in the US GDP deflator from the reference year to 1990.

http://dx.doi.org/10.1787/486663055853

A–3

Population, GDP and GDP Per Capita in 56 Asian Countries, 1820–1998

The estimates for Asia are an update and substantial revision of those in Maddison (1995a). The biggest revisions to GDP growth are those for China which are described in Maddison (1998a), but there are improvements in those for India, Japan, the Philippines, Taiwan and a number of other countries. Source notes have been added for 26 countries, bringing the detailed coverage from 11 to 37 countries. There are also revisions to the population figures. The 1990 benchmark GDP estimates have been revised: for 24 countries representing 93 per cent of Asian GDP, they are based on ICP or ICP equivalent measures, for 16 countries (6 per cent of Asian GDP) they are derived from Penn World Tables version 5.6, and, for the remaining 1 per cent, GDP levels were measured by proxy estimates (16 countries).

There are three groups of countries. The most reliable estimates of GDP growth are for the first group of 16 East Asian countries for which there has been substantial research on historical national accounts. These countries represented 95 per cent of Asian GDP in 1820, 85 per cent in 1950 and 88.4 per cent in 1998. The proxy estimates used to fill holes in the GDP dataset are shown in Table A–m.

For the second group of 25 East Asian countries, the presently available GDP growth indicators have serious deficiencies and the quality of the 1990 benchmark estimates is poor. Detailed notes are given for Afghanistan, Cambodia, Laos, Mongolia, North Korea and Vietnam which all pose major problems. Conversion of their accounts from Soviet style material product to a GDP basis is one of these, and can only be done in rough fashion. The other countries in this group are Bhutan, Brunei, Macao, the Maldives and 15 Pacific islands. The 25 country group accounted for 3.7 per cent of Asian GDP in 1950 and 1.7 per cent in 1998.

The third group consists of 15 West Asian countries, many of which were provinces of the Ottoman Empire until the end of the first world war. For most of these there has been no quantitative research on their macroeconomic performance before 1950. In ten countries, the postwar economy was strongly affected by the oil industry. Per capita income of the oil producers in 1950 was much higher than in prewar years, and a good deal higher than in the rest of Asia. Oil production in the area was 16 million metric tons in 1937, 86 million in 1950, and 1 053 million in 1973 — an increase of 11.5 per cent a year from 1950 to 1973. OPEC action in raising prices and restricting supply meant that production in 1998 was about the same as in 1973 (see Table 3–21). Growth was also significantly affected by war in Iran, Iraq, Israel, Kuwait, Lebanon, Syria and Yemen. This group represented 11.2 per cent of Asian GDP in 1950, 14.4 per cent in 1973, and 9.9 per cent in 1998.

Our estimates for Asia exclude the eight Asian successor republics of the USSR (Armenia, Azerbaijan, Georgia, Kazakhstan, Kyrgyzstan, Tajikistan, Turkmenistan and Uzbekistan) and the Asian territory of the Russian Federation (see note on former USSR in Section A–1 of this Appendix, and Appendix D.).

16 East Asian Countries

Bangladesh: Maddison (1995a) provides separate GDP and population estimates back to 1820 for Bangladesh and Pakistan. In this study the figures for India 1820–1913 include Bangladesh and Pakistan.

1950–66, volume movement of Bangladesh GDP from A. Maddison, Class *Structure and Economic Growth,* Allen and Unwin, London 1971, p. 171. 1966–78 GDP movement from World Bank, *World Tables,* various issues, 1978 onwards from ADB. Figures for 1967 onwards are for fiscal years. Population 1950 onwards from the Center for International Research, US Bureau of the Census.

For India, Bangladesh, and Pakistan, it is necessary to have benchmark GDP levels which are compatible with the fact that the three countries were united until 1947. The ICP estimates for Bangladesh and Pakistan (see Table A–3g) are not compatible with those for India. I therefore assumed that Pakistan and Bangladesh combined had the same average per capita GDP (in 1990 international dollars) as India in 1950. In 1950 Bangladesh and Pakistan were two "wings" of the former Pakistan. Their relative levels of GDP in 1950 were taken from Planning Commission, Reports of the Advisory Panels for the *Fourth Five–Year Plan,* Government of Pakistan, Islamabad, July 1970, p. 136.

Burma (Myanmar): 1820–70 population movement assumed to be proportionately the same as in India, 1870–1941 population derived from Aye Hlaing (1964), 1950 onwards from US Bureau of the Census. 1901–38 net domestic product by industry of origin at 1901 prices from Aye Hlaing, "Trends of Economic Growth and Income Distribution in Burma 1870–1940", *Journal of the Burma Research Society,* 1964, p. 144 linked to 1938–59 estimates of GDP by industry of origin at 1947/8 prices in E.E. Hagen, *On the Theory of Social Change,* Dorsey, Homewood, Illinois, 1962, linked to OECD Development Centre estimates for 1950–78. GDP from 1978 onwards from ADB. Benchmark 1990 GDP level estimates in 1990 Geary–Khamis dollars derived from R. Summers and A. Heston, *Penn World Tables,* version 5.6.

China: 1820–1995 GDP levels and population from A. Maddison, *Chinese Economic Performance in the Long Run,* OECD Development Centre, 1998, pp. 158–9 and 169, 1950–52 GDP movement from Maddison (1995a). 1995–98 GDP movement derived from *China Statistical Yearbook 1999,* State Statistical Bureau, Beijing, 1999, p. 58. The Chinese authorities show GDP growth averaging 8.7 per cent a year for 1995–98. I reduced this to 6.6 per cent using a correction coefficient derived from Maddison (1998a), p. 160 for 1978–95. See Xu (1999) for a comment on the estimates in Maddison (1998a) by the acting head of national accounts in the Chinese statistical office (SSB). See Table A–3g for 1990 benchmark GDP level.

Hong Kong: 1820–1950 population from Maddison (1998a), p. 170, 1950–89 from US Bureau of the Census, 1990 onwards from ADB. 1950–61 GDP movement from K.R. Chou, *The Hong Kong Economy,* Academic Publications, Hong Kong, 1966, p. 81, and 1961–1998 from *Estimates of Gross Domestic Product 1961 to 1998,* Census and Statistics Dept., Hong Kong, March 1999, p. 14. Benchmark 1990 GDP level derived by updating ICP 5, see Table A3–g.

India: Population 1820–1900 from Maddison (1995a), thereafter from Sivasubramonian, figures refer to October 1st (middle of fiscal year). GDP at 1948/9 prices for fiscal years by industry of origin for undivided India 1900–46, and India 1946–98 from S. Sivasubramonian, "Twentieth Century Economic Performance of India", in A. Maddison, D.S. Prasada Rao and W. Shepherd, eds., *The Asian Economies in the Twentieth Century,* Elgar, Aldershot, London, 2001. 1870–1900 GDP movement derived by linking estimates of net product in nine sectors at constant prices in A. Heston, "National Income", in D. Kumar and M. Desai, *Cambridge Economic History of India,* Vol. 2, Cambridge, 1983, p. 397–8, to the Sivasubramonian estimates of the level of sectoral output in 1900 (see Table A–h). 1820 per capita product assumed to be the same as in 1870. Benchmark 1990 GDP derived from ICP 4, see Table A3–g.

Table A–h. **India: GDP, Population and Per Capita GDP, 1820–1998**[a]

	GDP (1990 million int. $)	Population (million)	Per Capita GDP (1990 int. $)		GDP (1990 million int. $)	Population (million)	Per Capita GDP (1990 int. $)
1820	111 417	209.0	533	1946	212 622	343	620
				1947	213 680	346	618
1870	134 882	253.0	533	1948	215 927	350	617
				1949	221 631	355	624
1900	170 466	284.5	599	1950	222 222	359	619
1901	173 957	286.2	608	1951	227 362	365	623
1902	188 504	288.0	655	1952	234 148	372	629
1903	191 141	289.7	660	1953	248 963	379	657
1904	192 060	291.5	659	1954	259 262	386	672
1905	188 587	293.3	643	1955	265 527	393	676
1906	193 979	295.1	657	1956	280 978	401	701
1907	182 234	296.9	614	1957	277 924	409	680
1908	184 844	298.7	619	1958	299 137	418	716
1909	210 241	300.5	700	1959	305 499	426	717
1910	210 439	302.1	697	1960	326 910	434	753
1911	209 354	303.1	691	1961	336 744	444	758
1912	208 946	303.4	689	1962	344 204	454	758
1913	204 242	303.7	673	1963	361 442	464	779
1914	215 400	304.0	709	1964	389 262	474	821
1915	210 110	304.2	691	1965	373 814	485	771
1916	216 245	304.5	710	1966	377 207	495	762
1917	212 341	304.8	697	1967	408 349	506	807
1918	185 202	305.1	607	1968	418 907	518	809
1919	210 730	305.3	690	1969	446 872	529	845
1920	194 051	305.6	635	1970	469 584	541	868
1921	208 785	307.3	679	1971	474 238	554	856
1922	217 594	310.4	701	1972	472 766	567	834
1923	210 511	313.6	671	1973	494 832	580	853
1924	220 763	316.7	697	1974	500 146	593	843
1925	223 375	319.9	698	1975	544 683	607	897
1926	230 410	323.2	713	1976	551 402	620	889
1927	230 426	326.4	706	1977	593 834	634	937
1928	232 745	329.7	706	1978	625 695	648	966
1929	242 409	333.1	728	1979	594 510	664	895
1930	244 097	336.4	726	1980	637 202	679	938
1931	242 489	341.0	711	1981	675 882	692	977
1932	245 209	345.2	710	1982	697 705	708	985
1933	245 433	345.8	710	1983	753 942	723	1 043
1934	247 712	350.7	706	1984	783 042	739	1 060
1935	245 361	355.6	690	1985	814 344	755	1 079
1936	254 896	360.6	707	1986	848 990	771	1 101
1937	250 768	365.7	686	1987	886 154	788	1 125
1938	251 375	370.9	678	1988	978 822	805	1 216
1939	256 924	376.1	683	1989	1 043 912	822	1 270
1940	265 455	381.4	696	1990	1 098 100	839	1 309
1941	270 531	386.8	699	1991	1 104 114	856	1 290
1942	269 278	391.7	687	1992	1 161 769	872	1 332
1943	279 898	396.3	706	1993	1 233 796	891	1 385
1944	276 954	400.3	692	1994	1 330 036	908	1 465
1945	272 503	405.6	672	1995	1 425 798	927	1 538
1946	258 164	410.4	629	1996	1 532 733	943	1 625
				1997	1 609 371	959	1 678
				1998	1 702 712	975	1 746

a) The figures for 1820–1946 refer to undivided India, 1946–1998 to modern India, 1946 is an overlap year where two figures are given which demonstrate the impact of partition.

http://dx.doi.org/10.1787/486663055853

Indonesia: 1820–70 real income for three ethnic groups (indigenous, foreign Asiatic, and "European", in A. Maddison, "Dutch Income in and from Indonesia", *Modern Asian Studies,* 23.4 (1989), pp. 663–5. 1870–1900 GDP movement by industry of origin at 1983 prices supplied by Pierre van der Eng. They are a revision of estimates in his article "The Real Domestic Product of Indonesia, 1880–1989", *Explorations in Economic History,* July 1992. 1900–98 from P. van der Eng, "Indonesia's Growth Performance in the Twentieth Century", in A. Maddison, D.S. Prasada Rao and W. Shepherd, eds., *The Asian Economies in the Twentieth Century,* Elgar, Aldershot, 2001. Population 1820–90 from same sources as GDP, 1990 onwards from ADB. Benchmark 1990 GDP level derived from ICP4 (see Table A–3g).

Japan: Population 1820–1960 from Maddison (1995a), updated from OECD sources. 1890–1940 GDP at 1934–36 market prices, by industry of origin, from K. Ohkawa and M. Shinohara, eds., *Patterns of Japanese Development: A Quantitative Appraisal,* Yale, 1979, pp. 278–80. This is a summary of the results of K. Ohkawa, M. Shinohara, and M. Umemura, eds., *Estimates of Long–Term Economic Statistics of Japan since 1868,* (LTES), which appeared in 14 volumes published between 1966 and 1988. Ohkawa and Shinohara (1979) reproduce the GDP by industry of origin estimates in LTES vol. 1 (1974) p. 227 with some tiny modifications. The LTES volumes were originally intended to cover the whole of the Meiji period back to 1868 but GDP aggregates were only published back to 1885, even though some of the volumes contained estimates for earlier years. The main reason for this reticence by Ohkawa and Shinohara was that the estimates in Vol. 9 *on Agriculture and Forestry,* published in 1966 had been criticised by James Nakamura, *Agricultural Production and the Economic Development of Japan, 1873–1922,* Princeton, 1966, for exaggerating the growth of rice production in the early years of the Meiji period. There were also some holes in the data base which reinforced their reluctance to estimate aggregate GDP for years before 1885. In 1979 new estimates of rice production became available for 1874–89 (see Saburo Yamada and Yujiro Hayami, "Agricultural Growth in Japan, 1880–1970", in Y. Hayami, V.W. Ruttan and H.M. Southworth, eds., *Agricultural Growth in Japan, Taiwan, Korea and the Philippines,* Asian Productivity Center, Honolulu, 1979, p. 233). This source was used to revise the LTES GDP estimate for the farm sector, with rough estimates to fill the holes in the data set, GDP for 1874–89 was estimated using the same 1934–36 price weights as in the LTES (see Table A–i). GDP growth 1820–74 from Appendix B.

The LTES (Vol. I, p. 214) GDP estimates for 1940–50 were revised by Toshiyuki Mizoguchi and Noriyuki Nojima, "Nominal and Real GDP in Japan: 1940–55", which was summarised in an English translation in T. Mizoguchi, *Reforms of Statistical System under Socio–Economic Changes,* Maruzen, Tokyo, 1995, p. 225. I used these estimates (at 1955 prices by industry of origin) for the years from 1940 to 1950. 1950–60 from Maddison (1995a), 1960–90 from OECD, *National Accounts 1960–1997,* vol. 1, 1999. 1990 onwards from *National Accounts of OECD Countries 1988–1998,* Vol. 1, 2000. Benchmark GDP level for 1990 derived from ICP6 (see Table A3–g)

Malaysia: Population of modern Malaysia (old federated and unfederated Malay states, Sabah and Sarawak) excluding Brunei and Singapore 1820–1913 from estimates supplied by Don Hoerr, 1913–50 movement kindly supplied by Pierre van der Eng. 1950 onwards from US Bureau of the Census.

GDP movement 1913–90 from provisional estimates by Pierre van der Eng. These are an extension of the estimates by industry of origin for West Malaysia in V.V. Bhanoji Rao, *National Accounts of West Malaysia 1947–1971,* Heinemann, Kuala Lumpur, 1976, adjusted to include Sabah and Sarawak. 1990 onwards from ADB. 1990 GDP benchmark level derived ICP 7, see Table A3–h.

Nepal: 1820–1913 population movement assumed to be proportionately the same as in India. 1913 from League of Nations, *International Statistical Yearbook, 1927,* Geneva, 1928, pp. 2–3; 1950 onwards from US Bureau of the Census. 1950–90 GDP movement from Maddison (1995a) database, 1990 onwards from ADB. 1990 benchmark GDP level derived from ICP 7, see Table A3–h.

Table A–i. **Reconstitution of Japanese GDP by Industry of Origin, 1874–90**
(million yen at 1934–36 prices)

	FFF (1)	MM (2)	Const. (3)	FI (4)	Subtotal (5)	OS (6)	DRR (7)	GDP (8)
1874	1 300	207	61	28	1 596	1 418	125	3 139
1875	1 444	225	50	30	1 749	1 506	126	3 381
1876	1 388	226	49	31	1 694	1 480	127	3 301
1877	1 437	240	48	33	1 758	1 520	128	3 406
1878	1 416	249	48	35	1 748	1 519	129	3 396
1879	1 514	266	57	38	1 875	1 593	130	3 598
1880	1 580	277	68	40	1 965	1 648	131	3 744
1881	1 497	274	73	42	1 886	1 608	132	3 626
1882	1 537	280	82	45	1 944	1 644	133	3 721
1883	1 529	281	85	48	1 943	1 648	134	3 725
1884	1 426	293	74	51	1 844	1 598	135	3 775
1885	1 637	266	88	54	2 045	1 713	136	3 894
1886	1 748	307	87	58	2 200	1 833	137	4 170
1887	1 808	328	116	60	2 312	1 908	137	4 357
1888	1 749	331	99	65	2 244	1 778	138	4 160
1889	1 578	374	115	67	2 134	2 085	142	4 361
1890	1 848	369	127	73	2 417	2 217	144	4 778

Source: The 1890 benchmark is from Ohkawa, Takamatsu and Yamamoto, *National Income* (1974) (Vol. 1 of LTES) p. 227. Col. 1 (FFF) refers to gross value added in farming, forestry and fishing. It adjusts the vol. 9, p. 152 estimate of gross farm output 1874–89 in line with the findings of Yamada and Hayami (1979) p. 233. Total farm inputs from vol. 9, p. 186, value added in forestry from p. 234. Value added in fishery from vol. 1, p. 228, linked to estimates for earlier years in Ohkawa (1957), p. 72. Col. 2 (MM) refers to gross value added in manufacturing and mining. 1885–90 from Vol. 1, p. 227; 1874–85 derived from Shinohara's estimates in vol. 10, p. 145 and 243 for gross output and assuming that the 1885 ratio of value added to gross output (30 per cent) was also valid for 1874–84. Col. 3 (Const.) refers to construction; 1885–90 from vol. 1, p. 227, 1874–85 assumed to move in line with investment in construction (vol. 4, p. 230). Col. 4 (FI) refers to transport, communications, electricity, gas and water, which Ohkawa called "facilitating industries". 1885–90 from vol. 1, p. 227, and it was assumed that this sector grew at the same rate in 1874–84. Col. 5 is the subtotal of cols. 1–4. Col. 6 (OS) refers to "other services", i.e. commerce, public administration and military, education, professional services and domestic servants; estimates for 1885–90 are from vol. 1, p. 227. For 1874–84 it was assumed that two thirds of the volume of these services moved parallel to the subtotal in col. 5, and one third in line with population. Col. 7 (DRR) refers to depreciation of residential buildings and "riparian" works. LTES made no imputation for house rent; 1885–90 from vol. 1, p. 227; for 1874–84 it was assumed that DDR rose with population. Col. 8 refers to GDP and is the sum of cols. 5, 6 and 7.

http://dx.doi.org/10.1787/486663055853

Pakistan: As for Bangladesh.

Philippines: Population 1820–1913 from Maddison (1995a), 1950 onwards from US Bureau of the Census. 1950–90 GDP movement from estimates of the National Statistical Coordination Board, Manila, 1990 onwards from Asian Development Bank (ADB), *Key Indicators of Developing Asian and Pacific Countries,* Manila updated from ADB. In Maddison (1995a), I used the estimates of Hooley (1968) for 1913–50, which showed 1950 per capita GDP well below the 1913 level. He has since made major revisions to his 1968 estimates showing substantially better performance for 1913–50. I have provisionally assumed that the 1950 per capita GDP level was about the same as in 1913. Benchmark GDP level derived from ICP4 (see Table A3–g).

Singapore: 1820–1998 population from same sources as for Malaysia. 1913–50 per capita GDP movement assumed to be proportionately the same as that for Malaysia. 1950–73 GDP movement from Maddison (1995a) database, 1973–90 from World Bank, *World Tables 1995,* 1990 onwards from ADB. 1990 benchmark GDP level derived from ICP 7, see Table A3–h.

South Korea: The estimates refer to the whole of Korea for 1820–1913, South Korea for 1950 onwards. 1820–1906 population movement from T.H. Kwon and Y–H. Shin, "On Population Estimates of the Yi Dynasty, 1392–1910", *Tong–a Munhwa,* 14, 1977, pp. 324–329. 1906–38 from Mizoguchi and Umemura (1988) p. 238. 1940 from Kim and Roemer (1979) p. 23. Population for 1950 onwards from Center for International Research, US Bureau of the Census.

Table A-j. **Japan: GDP, Population and Per Capita GDP, 1820-1998**

	GDP (million int. $)	Population (000)	Per Capita GDP (1990 int. $)		GDP (million int. $)	Population (000)	Per Capita GDP (1990 int. $)
1820	20 739	31 000	669	1934	142 876	68 090	2 098
				1935	146 817	69 238	2 120
1870	25 393	34 437	737	1936	157 493	70 171	2 244
1871		34 648		1937	165 017	71 278	2 315
1872		34 859		1938	176 050	71 879	2 449
1873		35 070		1939	203 780	72 364	2 816
1874	26 644	35 235	756	1940	209 728	72 967	2 874
1875	28 698	35 436	810	1941	214 392	74 005	2 897
1876	28 019	35 713	785	1942	214 853	75 029	2 864
1877	28 910	36 018	803	1943	211 431	76 005	2 782
1878	28 825	36 315	794	1944	206 747	77 178	2 679
1879	30 540	36 557	835	1945	156 805	76 224	2 057
1880	31 779	36 807	863	1946	120 017	77 199	1 555
1881	30 777	37 112	829	1947	125 433	78 119	1 606
1882	31 584	37 414	844	1948	135 352	80 155	1 689
1883	31 618	37 766	837	1949	138 867	81 971	1 694
1884	31 872	38 138	836	1950	160 966	83 563	1 926
1885	33 052	38 427	860	1951	181 025	84 974	2 130
1886	35 395	38 622	916	1952	202 005	86 293	2 341
1887	36 982	38 866	952	1953	216 889	87 463	2 480
1888	35 310	39 251	900	1954	229 151	88 752	2 582
1889	37 016	39 688	933	1955	248 855	89 790	2 772
1890	40 556	40 077	1 012	1956	267 567	90 727	2 949
1891	38 621	40 380	956	1957	287 130	91 513	3 138
1892	41 200	40 684	1 013	1958	303 857	92 349	3 290
1893	41 344	41 001	1 008	1959	331 570	93 237	3 556
1894	46 287	41 350	1 119	1960	375 090	94 053	3 988
1895	46 933	41 775	1 123	1961	420 246	94 890	4 429
1896	44 353	42 196	1 051	1962	457 742	95 797	4 778
1897	45 284	42 643	1 062	1963	496 514	96 765	5 131
1898	53 883	43 145	1 249	1964	554 449	97 793	5 670
1899	49 870	43 626	1 143	1965	586 744	98 883	5 934
1900	52 020	44 103	1 180	1966	649 189	99 790	6 506
1901	53 883	44 662	1 206	1967	721 132	100 850	7 151
1902	51 088	45 255	1 129	1968	813 984	102 050	7 976
1903	54 672	45 841	1 193	1969	915 556	103 231	8 869
1904	55 101	46 378	1 188	1970	1 013 602	104 334	9 715
1905	54 169	46 829	1 157	1971	1 061 230	105 677	10 042
1906	61 263	47 227	1 297	1972	1 150 516	107 179	10 735
1907	63 198	47 691	1 325	1973	1 242 932	108 660	11 439
1908	63 628	48 260	1 318	1974	1 227 706	110 160	11 145
1909	63 556	48 869	1 301	1975	1 265 661	111 520	11 349
1910	64 559	49 518	1 304	1976	1 315 966	112 770	11 669
1911	68 070	50 215	1 356	1977	1 373 741	113 880	12 063
1912	70 507	50 941	1 384	1978	1 446 165	114 920	12 584
1913	71 563	51 672	1 385	1979	1 525 477	115 880	13 164
1914	69 504	52 396	1 327	1980	1 568 457	116 800	13 429
1915	75 952	53 124	1 430	1981	1 618 185	117 650	13 754
1916	87 702	53 815	1 630	1982	1 667 653	118 450	14 079
1917	90 641	54 437	1 665	1983	1 706 380	119 260	14 308
1918	91 572	54 886	1 668	1984	1 773 223	120 020	14 774
1919	100 959	55 253	1 827	1985	1 851 315	120 750	15 332
1920	94 653	55 818	1 696	1986	1 904 918	121 490	15 680
1921	105 043	56 490	1 859	1987	1 984 142	122 090	16 251
1922	104 756	57 209	1 831	1988	2 107 060	122 610	17 185
1923	104 828	57 937	1 809	1989	2 208 858	123 120	17 941
1924	107 766	58 686	1 836	1990	2 321 153	123 540	18 789
1925	112 208	59 522	1 885	1991	2 409 305	123 920	19 442
1926	113 211	60 490	1 872	1992	2 433 924	124 320	19 578
1927	114 859	61 430	1 870	1993	2 441 512	124 670	19 584
1928	124 246	62 361	1 992	1994	2 457 252	124 960	19 664
1929	128 115	63 244	2 026	1995	2 493 399	125 570	19 857
1930	118 800	64 203	1 850	1996	2 591 213	125 864	20 587
1931	119 803	65 205	1 837	1997	2 613 154	126 166	20 712
1932	129 835	66 189	1 962	1998	2 539 986	126 469	20 084
1933	142 589	67 182	2 122				

http://dx.doi.org/10.1787/486663055853

ISBN 92-64-02261-9 – © OECD 2006

1911–38 Korean GDP derived from T. Mizoguchi and M. Umemura, *Basic Economic Statistics of Former Japanese Colonies, 1895–1938*, Toyo Keizai Shinposha, Tokyo, 1988, p. 238. They give annual estimates for two aggregate measures: gross domestic expenditure, and net domestic product at factor cost (both at 1934–6 prices). The latter showed a compound growth rate of 3.68 per cent per annum for 1913–38, the former 4.06 per cent. I used the expenditure estimate. Sang–Chul Suh, *Growth and Structural Changes in the Korean Economy, 1910–40*, Harvard University Press, Cambridge, Mass., 1978, p. 171 provides annual estimates of the net value of output for five commodity sectors (agriculture, forestry, fishery, mining, and manufacturing) for 1910–40 at 1936 prices. The aggregate measure shows slower growth for 1913–38 than Mizoguchi and Umemura (growth of 3.07 per cent per annum). I used the Suh commodity estimates together with a rough estimate for the service sector (assuming service output to move parallel to population) as a rough proxy for GDP movement for 1938–40. 1938–40 population movement from Suh, p. 41 adjusted from an end–year to mid–year basis.

In 1945, the Korean economy was split into two occupation zones and the peninsula has since become two very different economies. Suh (p. 136) provided a breakdown of commodity output for his five sectors between North and South Korea for 1934, 1935, 1939 and 1940. The commodity sectors can be aggregated using the current price market shares shown on pp. 160–6. The North Korean share rose from 1934 (37.2 per cent of total commodity output) to 1940 (45.2 per cent). In the same years the Northern share of population rose from 32.4 to 33.6 per cent, so it had higher per capita commodity output than the South in 1934 and the differential had increased very substantially by 1940, owing to the concentration of Japanese investment in Northern manufacturing and mining to complement its activity in Manchukuo. Augmenting Suh's commodity output estimates for North and South Korea by a rough adjustment for service activity, it would seem that in 1940, North Korean per capita GDP was about 49 per cent higher than that in South Korea. Kwang Suk Kim and M. Roemer, *Growth and Structural Transformation,* Harvard University Press, 1979, p. 35 estimate levels of commodity output by sector in South Korea in 1940 and 1953 in 1953 prices which I adjusted to a GDP basis by a rough allowance for service sector output. This link is not very satisfactory as it was made by revaluing Suh's estimate of 1940 South Korean commodity output (in 1940 prices) at 1953 prices, using a variety of price indices, and comparing this with an independently estimated figure of 1953 commodity output in 1953 prices. It would have been more satisfactory if Kim and Roemer had been able to find quantitative indicators of volume changes between the two years. However it is the best link available in the present state of research.

South Korean 1950–53 GDP movement from Maddison (1970) 300–1, 1953–70 from *National Income in Korea 1975*, Bank of Korea, pp. 142–3, 1970–90 from OECD, *National Accounts 1960–97,* vol. 1, Paris, 1999. 1990 onwards from *National Accounts of OECD Countries 1988–1998*, Vol. 1, 2000.

Sri Lanka: 1820–1913 population derived from N.K. Sarkar, *The Demography of Ceylon,* Ceylon Government Press, Colombo, 1957, p. 22, by interpolation of his benchmark estimates for 1814–1921; 1950 onwards from US Bureau of the Census.

GDP movement 1870–1950 derived from the substantial statistical Appendix of D.R. Snodgrass, *Ceylon: An Export Economy in Transition,* Irwin Illinois, 1966. Benchmark 1950 GDP at factor cost by industry of origin at 1950 prices, broken down into 14 sectors (p. 279). Annual volume movement in these sectors 1870–1950, derived as follows: export crops (tea and minor estate crops, rubber, coconut products) from pp. 357–60, food crops from cultivated area of paddy and other crops (p. 333); mining and manufacturing value added assumed to move with employment (p. 322); construction, wholesale and retail trade, banking and insurance assumed to move parallel to aggregate commodity output (in agriculture and industry); transport, communication, and utilities assumed to move parallel to movement of railway freight (p. 351). Other services (including dwellings, public administration and defence) assumed to move parallel with population. These crude estimates for 1870–1950 are provisional, and will be refined in a more careful analysis by Pierre van der Eng and myself. 1950–85 GDP movement from H.J. Bruton and Associates, *Political Economy of Poverty, Equity and Growth: Sri Lanka and Malaysia,* Oxford University Press, 1992, p. 375, 1985–90 from World Bank, *World Tables* (1995), updated from ADB. GDP level in benchmark year 1990 derived from ICP5 (see Table A3–g).

Taiwan: Population 1820–1990 from Maddison (1998a) updated from ADB. 1913–90 GDP from Toshiyuki Mizoguchi, *Long–Term Economic Statistics of Taiwan: 1905–1990,* Institute of Economic Research, Hitotsubashi University, 1999. There are two aggregate estimates (at 1960 prices), one for gross domestic expenditure, the other for GDP by industry of origin. There is not much difference in the volume movement for 1913–51, but there is a big discrepancy thereafter. I used the volume movement shown by his expenditure measure for 1913–90 and filled the 1950 gap in this series by assuming the same proportionate movement 1950–51 as he shows in his industry of origin estimate. GDP movement from 1990 onwards from ADB. Benchmark 1990 GDP level from Summers and Heston, *Penn World Tables,* version 5.6.

Thailand: Population 1820–1913 from Maddison (1995a), 1950 onwards from US Bureau of the Census. GDP movement 1870–1951 from sources cited in Maddison (1995a), 1951–96 from *National Income of Thailand 1951–1996,* National Economic and Social Development Board, Bangkok, updated from ADB. Benchmark 1990 GDP level from ICP5 (see Table A3–g).

25 East Asian Countries

The quality of the estimates for these countries is distinctly inferior to those for the preceding group of 16 countries.

Afghanistan: 1820–1913 population from McEvedy and Jones (1978), 1950 onwards from US Bureau of the Census. 1950–90 GDP movement from OECD Development Centre database, updated from IMF, World Economic Outlook, May 1999, p. 147. No ICP or PWT estimate of 1990 real product level was available; it was assumed that 1990 per capita GDP was 600 dollars.

Cambodia: 1820–1913 population movement from McEvedy and Jones (1978), 1950 onwards from US Bureau of the Census. 1950–90 GDP movement and level from Maddison (1995a), p. 219 and underlying database, updated from ADB.

Laos: 1820–1913 population movement assumed to be proportionately the same as in Vietnam, 1950 onwards from US Bureau of the Census. The output movement shown in Maddison (1995a) for 1950–90 and for 1990–98 from ADB was based on material product rather than GDP and hence overstated growth. I have adjusted the measure to a GDP basis using the same downward adjustment coefficient as for China. 1990 benchmark GDP level from ICP7, see Table A3–h.

Mongolia: Population 1820–1913 from McEvedy and Jones (1978), 1950 onwards from US Bureau of the Census. 1980–98 GDP movement from ADB. There are no estimates of GDP movement for 1950–80. 1950–80 per capita trend movement was assumed to be the same as in China. 1990 per capita GDP level in international dollars derived from OECD, *A PPP Comparison for the NIS,* Paris, February 2000, p. B–24.

North Korea: For years before 1950, North Korea is included in the estimates for Korea as a whole. Population for 1950 onwards from US Bureau of the Census. No estimates of North Korean GDP or material product have been published for years before 1992, so any estimate is likely to be hazardous. We know that in 1940 North Korean GDP per capita was nearly 50 per cent higher than in the South (see source notes for South Korea), so it seems reasonable to suppose that 1950 North Korean per capita GDP was at least as high as in the South. N. Eberstadt, "Material progress in Korea since Partition", in R.H. Myers, ed., *The Wealth of Nations in the Twentieth Century,* Hoover Institution, 1996 is one of the best informed assessments available. He suggests that North Korea was more productive, and more rapidly developing than the South, for "many years after partition" although the military share was undoubtedly larger in the North. I have assumed that per capita GDP was the same in the North as in the South from 1950 to 1973, with no progress to 1991. Thereafter, North Korea stopped receiving Soviet aid, and its per capita income has fallen a great deal. GDP volume movement from 1991 was as taken from M.C. Cho and H. Zang, *The Present and Future Prospects of the North Korean Economy,* Discussion Paper D99–3, Institute of Economic Research, Hitotsubashi University, June 1999, p. 5 (taking the Bank of Korea estimates for the 1991–2 and 1996–7 GDP movement, and the estimates which the North Korean authorities reported to the IMF for 1992–6). I assumed no change in per capita GDP from 1997 to 1998.

Vietnam: 1913 population from Banens (2000). His estimate involved a substantial upward revision for the colonial period, using reconstitution techniques based on birth and death rates. 1820–1913 proportionate movement from McEvedy and Jones (1978). Population for 1950 onwards from US Bureau of the Census.

Estimates of 1950–60 material product, using the former Soviet MPS system, were reported by the statistical authorities in Hanoi to the OECD Development Centre. I have used these estimates from the Centre's data files. New GDP estimates for 1960–98 on an SNA basis were kindly provided by Viet Vu of the UN Statistics Division. 1990 benchmark GDP level derived from ICP 7, see Table A–3h.

Jean–Pascal Bassino (Centre for International Economics and Finance, Aix–en–Provence) is conducting a major study of Vietnamese economic history for the Asian Historical Statistics Project of Hitotsubashi University using the French colonial archives. His provisional findings for 1820–1950 imply the following GDP levels, taking 1950 as 100: 1913 84.3; 1870 31.9; 1820 20.7.

19 Small East Asian Countries:1950–98 population from US Bureau of the Census. 1820–1950 population movement for 15 Pacific islands from McEvedy and Jones (1978), pp. 330–6; Macao 1900–50 from p. 173. 1820–1950 population for Bhutan, Maldives and Brunei assumed to move parallel to India.

GDP movement in Bhutan, Brunei, Macau and Maldives for 1950–90 from Maddison (1995a) database. Update to 1998 from IMF, except for Macau which was assumed to move as in Hong Kong. GDP movement in 15 Pacific islands 1950–90 from Maddison (1995a) database updated from IMF for Fiji, Papua New Guinea, Solomon Islands, Tonga, Vanuatu, Western Samoa, Kiribati, and Micronesia; from ADB for Marshall Islands. GDP movement in French Polynesia, Guam, Pacific Islands, New Caledonia, American Samoa, Wallis and Futuna assumed to move parallel to that in the nine Pacific islands for which estimates were available.

Table A–k. **Population and GDP in 19 Small East Asian Countries, 1950–98**

	Population (000 at mid–year)				GDP (million 1990 international dollars)			
	1950	1973	1990	1998	1950	1973	1990	1998
Bhutan	734	1 111	1 585	1 908	369	645	1 407	2 110
Brunei	45	145	254	315	224	1 156	1 663	1 932
Macao	205	259	352	429	127	735	3 078	4 331
Maldives	79	126	218	290	43	107	497	826
Total 4 Countries	1 063	1 641	2 409	2 942	763	2 641	6 645	9 199
Fiji	287	556	738	803	851	2 348	3 440	4 498
Papua New Guinea	1 412	2 477	3 823	4 600	1 356	4 847	5 865	8 625
13 Other Pacific Islands	649	1 210	1 782	2 148	875	2 296	3 496	4 340
15 Pacific Islands Total	2 348	4 243	6 343	7 551	3 082	9 491	12 711	17 463
19 Small Countries	3 411	5 884	8 752	10 493	3 845	11 952	19 356	26 662

http://dx.doi.org/10.1787/486663055853

1990 benchmark GDP levels in international dollars are from Penn World Tables for Bhutan, Fiji, Papua New Guinea, Solomon Islands, Tonga, Vanuatu and Western Samoa. For ten other countries, proxy estimates were used from Maddison (1995a) pp. 219–220. Macao per capita GDP was taken to be half of that in Hong Kong. In Brunei income levels are dominated by oil production, which was 30.7 tons per capita in 1990, about 6 per cent above that in Kuwait. It was therefore assumed that per capita income was around $6 550 (about 6 per cent higher than in Kuwait).

15 West Asian Countries

1820–1913 population from McEvedy and Jones (1978); 1950 onwards from US Bureau of the Census. The 1820–1913 figures shown for Israel in fact refer to Palestine (including what is now Israel, the West Bank and Gaza).

Volume movement of GDP 1950–90 for Bahrain, Iraq, Jordan, Kuwait, Lebanon, Oman, Qatar, Saudi Arabia, Syria, United Arab Emirates and Yemen from OECD Development Centre database (as in Maddison, 1995a), thereafter from IMF, *World Economic Outlook,* October 1999. For all these countries, except Lebanon and Syria, the benchmark 1990 level of GDP in 1990 international (i.e. Geary–Khamis) dollars was derived from Penn World Tables version 5.6. For Syria the benchmark 1990 GDP level was derived from ICP3 (see Table A3–g). For Lebanon it is conjectural (see Maddison 1995a, p. 214).

Iran: 1950–74 GDP volume movement from OECD Development Centre database, 1974–90 from *World Tables 1995,* 1990 onwards from IMF. Benchmark 1990 GDP level from ICP3 (see Table A3–g).

Turkey: 1950–60 GDP volume movement from Maddison (1995a). 1960–90 from *OECD National Accounts 1960–97,* Vol. 1, 1999, thereafter from *National Accounts of OECD Countries 1988–1998,* vol. 1, 2000. The new figures involve a significant revision of those in Maddison (1995a). The Turkish authorities have revised their estimates, raising the 1990 GDP level substantially and reducing the GDP growth rate from 1968 onwards. 1990 benchmark GDP from ICP7 (see Table A3–g).

Israel: 1950–73 GDP volume movement supplied by the Israeli Central Bureau of Statistics, 1973–90 from World Bank, *World Tables 1995,* 1990 onwards from IMF. Benchmark 1990 GDP derived from ICP 4 (see Table A3–g). For 1922–47 development of Palestine, see entry for the West Bank and Gaza below.

West Bank and Gaza: These areas belonged to the old Palestinian political entity until 1948, when it was split into three parts. Israel got about 75 per cent of the territory, Jordan took over what was then a larger version of the West Bank (including Jerusalem) and Egypt took over the administration of the Gaza strip. In 1967 Israel occupied the West Bank and Gaza, and has been in the process of ceding control of parts of the West Bank to new Palestinian authority since the Oslo Peace accords.

The prepartition characteristics of Palestine are analysed in J. Metzer, *The Divided Economy of Mandatory Palestine,* Cambridge University Press, 1998, who provides annual estimates of population and GDP for the Arab and Jewish sectors for 1922–47 (pp. 29, 217 and 242). These estimates can be extended to 1950, using the 1950 population estimates for the Jewish and non–Jewish population of Israel from D. Patinkin, *The Israel Economy: the First Decade,* Falk Project, Jerusalem, 1960, and estimates of 1947–50 GDP supplied by the Bank of Israel (based mainly on R. Szereszewski, *Essays on the Structure of the Jewish Economy in Palestine and Israel,* Falk Project, Jerusalem, 1968).

From the above sources, it would appear that net domestic product and population moved as in Table A–l:

Table A–I. **Arab and Jewish Population and GDP in Palestine and Israel, 1922–50**

	Net Domestic Product (000 Palestinian pounds at 1936 prices)			Population at mid–year (000)		
	Total	*Arab*	*Jewish*	*Total*	*Arab*	*Jewish*
1922	8 360	6 628	1 732	754.6	674.5	80.1
1947	70 877	32 345	38 532	1 942.8	1 333.8	609.0
1950	93 099	3 971	89 128	1 266.8	163.8	1 103.0

N.B.   1922–47 figures refer to the area of mandatory Palestine, 1950 to Israel. The "Arab" population of Israel includes Christians and Druzes.

http://dx.doi.org/10.1787/486663055853

From Metzer's estimates it appears that Arab per capita income in Palestine rose from 9.83 pounds in 1922 to 24.25 in 1947. In the Jewish economy of Palestine per capita income rose from 24.6 pounds in 1922 to 63.27 in 1947. For 1950, the Bank of Israel GDP estimates cited above are not broken down into the Jewish and non–Jewish groups; but I assumed that non–Jewish real per capita income was the same in 1950 as in 1947. Applying the above 1950 proportionate shares to 1950 Israeli GDP in 1990 international dollars, it would seem that Arab GDP per capita in 1950 was about 950 international dollars.

The Palestine Bureau of Statistics in Ramallah appears to have estimated GDP only in current prices for 1994 onwards. I made a proxy estimate of the trend in real product by linking the 1950 per capita level as derived above, and the 1993 level as estimated by ESCWA (Economic and Social Commission for Western Asia of the United Nations) in the study cited in Table A3–i. These two spot estimates ($950 per capita in 1950 and $4 708 in 1993) are both in 1990 international dollars. I used a logarithmic trend to interpolate between these two years, and to extrapolate from 1993 to 1998, multiplying the per capita estimates by population as estimated by the US Bureau of the Census.

Proxy Procedure to Fill Gaps in the Dataset for 16 Asian Countries

For 1913, there are two gaps in the GDP dataset. I assumed that the 1913–50 movement in per capita GDP in Hong Kong was parallel to that in Japan; in Nepal parallel to India (see Table A–m). For 1870, there were eight holes in the dataset. I assumed that the 1870–1913 per capita GDP movement in Hong Kong and Singapore was proportionately the same as for Japan. In the other six countries (Burma, Korea, Malaysia, Nepal, Philippines and Taiwan), it was assumed to move parallel to the average 1870–1913 per capita movement for Indonesia, Sri Lanka and Thailand see Table A–m). For 1820, there were ten holes in the dataset. Average per capita GDP movement 1820–1870 for these ten countries was assumed to be parallel to that in Japan.

Proxy Procedure to Fill Gaps in the Dataset for 25 East Asian and 16 West Asian Countries

For these countries there were no GDP estimates for any of the years 1820, 1870 and 1913. It was assumed that their average per capita GDP level in 1870 and 1913 was the same as the average for the 16 East Asian countries, and that their 1820 level was the same as in 1870.

Table A–m. **Proxy Entries to Fill Holes in GDP and GDP Per Capita Dataset for 1870 and 1913**

	GDP		GDP per capita	
	1870	1913	1870	1913
Burma	2 156		508	
Hong Kong	106	778	862	1 597
Malaysia	534		667	
Nepal	1 879	3 039	400	539
Philippines	4 005		791	
Singapore	58		691	
South Korea	9 512		663	
Taiwan	1 299		554	
Total Above	19 549	3 817	617	623
25 East Asia	11 050	21 583	552	679
16 West Asia	16 782	26 537	552	679
Total Proxies	47 381	51 937	570	675

http://dx.doi.org/10.1787/486663055853

Proportionate Importance of the Proxy Estimates

For 1913, the proxy estimates represented 7.8 per cent of the Asian GDP total, for 1870, 11.2 per cent and for 1820, 9.5 per cent. Proxy estimates are contestable, as different analysts may have different ideas about how to fill the gaps. However, the proxy proportion is relatively modest, so the all–Asia results are not too sensitive to variations in procedure. The main task of further research is to fill the gaps by direct estimation, which seems likely to be feasible in a number of cases (see note above on Vietnam).

Table A3–a. **Population in 56 Asian Countries**
(000 at mid–year)

	1820	*1870*	*1913*	*1950*	*1973*	*1990*	*1998*
Bangladesh				45 646	72 471	109 897	125 105
Burma	3 506	4 245	12 326	19 488	29 227	41 068	47 305
China	381 000	358 000	437 140	546 815	881 940	1 135 185	1 242 700
Hong Kong	20	123	487	2 237	4 213	5 704	6 690
India[a]	209 000	253 000	303 700	359 000	580 000	839 000	975 000
Indonesia	17 927	28 922	49 934	79 043	124 271	179 248	204 390
Japan	31 000	34 437	51 672	83 563	108 660	123 540	126 486
Malaysia	287	800	3 084	6 434	11 712	17 507	20 933
Nepal	3 881	4 698	5 639	8 990	12 685	19 333	23 698
Pakistan				39 448	71 121	113 914	135 135
Philippines	2 176	5 063	9 384	21 131	42 094	65 037	77 726
Singapore	30	84	323	1 022	2 193	3 039	3 490
South Korea[b]	13 820	14 347	16 070	20 846	34 073	42 869	46 430
Sri Lanka	1 305	2 786	4 817	7 533	13 246	17 193	18 934
Taiwan	2 000	2 345	3 469	7 882	15 427	20 230	21 780
Thailand	4 665	5 775	8 689	20 042	40 302	55 052	60 037
16 East Asia	**670 617**	**714 625**	**906 734**	**1 269 120**	**2 043 635**	**2 787 816**	**3 135 839**
Afghanistan	3 280	4 207	5 730	8 150	13 421	14 767	24 792
Cambodia	2 090	2 340	3 070	4 163	7 202	8 717	11 340
Laos	470	755	1 387	1 886	3 027	4 191	5 261
Mongolia	619	668	725	779	1 360	2 216	2 579
North Korea				9 471	15 161	20 019	21 234
Vietnam	6 314	10 146	18 638	25 348	45 737	66 315	76 236
19 Small Countries	1 798	1 903	2 237	3 411	5 884	8 752	10 493
25 East Asia	**14 571**	**20 019**	**31 787**	**53 208**	**91 792**	**124 977**	**151 935**
41 East Asia	**685 188**	**734 644**	**938 521**	**1 322 328**	**2 135 427**	**2 912 793**	**3 287 774**
Bahrain			104	115	239	502	616
Iran	6 560	8 415	10 994	16 357	31 491	55 717	64 411
Iraq	1 093	1 580	2 613	5 163	10 402	18 135	21 722
Israel	332	429	700	1 286	3 197	4 512	5 644
Jordan	217	266	348	561	1 674	3 277	4 453
Kuwait				145	894	2 131	1 913
Lebanon	332	476	649	1 364	2 824	3 130	3 506
Oman	317	367	421	489	857	1 773	2 364
Qatar				25	142	482	697
Saudi Arabia	2 123	2 464	2 800	3 860	6 667	15 871	20 786
Syria	1 337	1 582	1 994	3 495	6 931	12 620	16 673
Turkey	10 074	11 793	15 000	21 122	38 503	56 125	64 568
UAE				72	391	1 952	2 303
Yemen	2 953	2 840	3 284	4 461	7 077	12 023	16 388
West Bank + Gaza				1 016	1 098	1 715	2 611
15 West Asia	**25 178**	**30 412**	**39 083**	**59 531**	**112 387**	**189 965**	**228 655**
56 Asia	**710 366**	**765 056**	**977 604**	**1 381 859**	**2 247 814**	**3 102 758**	**3 516 429**
Total excluding Japan	**679 366**	**730 619**	**925 932**	**1 298 296**	**2 139 154**	**2 979 218**	**3 389 943**
Total excluding Japan, China, India	**89 366**	**119 619**	**185 092**	**392 481**	**677 214**	**1 005 033**	**1 172 243**

a) 1820–1913 includes Bangladesh and Pakistan. b) 1820–1913 includes North and South Korea.

http://dx.doi.org/10.1787/486663055853

Table A3–b. **GDP Levels in 56 Asian Countries**
(million 1990 international $)

	1820	*1870*	*1913*	*1950*	*1973*	*1990*	*1998*
Bangladesh				24 628	35 997	70 320	101 666
Burma			8 445	7 711	18 352	30 834	48 427
China	228 600	189 740	241 344	239 903	740 048	2 109 400	3 873 352
Hong Kong				4 962	29 931	99 770	135 089
India[a]	111 417	134 882	204 241	222 222	494 832	1 098 100	1 702 712
Indonesia	10 970	18 929	45 152	66 358	186 900	450 901	627 499
Japan	20 739	25 393	71 653	160 966	1 242 932	2 321 153	2 581 576
Malaysia			2 773	10 032	29 982	89 823	148 621
Nepal				4 462	7 894	15 609	22 435
Pakistan				25 366	67 828	182 014	261 497
Philippines			10 000	22 616	82 464	143 025	176 246
Singapore			413	2 268	13 108	43 330	79 025
South Korea[b]			14 343	16 045	96 794	373 150	564 211
Sri Lanka		1 782	4 094	7 241	19 759	42 089	63 408
Taiwan			2 591	7 378	63 519	200 477	326 958
Thailand		4 081	7 251	16 375	75 511	255 732	372 509
16 East Asia	**389 305**	**394 356**	**616 117**	**838 533**	**3 205 851**	**7 525 727**	**11 085 231**
Afghanistan				5 255	9 181	8 861	12 744
Cambodia				2 155	5 858	8 235	11 998
Laos				1 156	2 331	3 912	5 806
Mongolia				339	1 170	2 954	2 821
North Korea				7 293	43 072	56 874	25 130
Vietnam	3 453	5 321	14 062	16 681	38 238	68 959	127 851
19 Small Countries				3 845	11 952	19 356	26 662
25 East Asia	**8 043**	**11 050**	**21 583**	**36 724**	**111 802**	**169 151**	**213 012**
41 East Asia	**397 348**	**405 406**	**637 700**	**875 257**	**3 317 653**	**7 694 878**	**11 298 243**
Bahrain				242	1 046	2 054	2 846
Iran				28 128	171 466	199 819	274 695
Iraq				7 041	39 042	44 583	24 564
Israel				3 623	30 839	58 511	85 520
Jordan				933	3 999	12 371	18 313
Kuwait				4 181	23 847	13 111	21 565
Lebanon				3 313	8 915	6 099	12 077
Oman				304	2 809	11 487	17 179
Qatar				763	6 228	3 276	5 091
Saudi Arabia				8 610	73 601	144 438	170 972
Syria				8 418	27 846	70 894	96 112
Turkey				38 408	144 483	305 395	423 018
UAE				1 130	9 739	25 496	31 913
Yemen				4 353	12 431	28 212	37 656
West Bank + Gaza				965	2 455	7 222	14 807
15 West Asia	**13 894**	**16 782**	**26 537**	**110 412**	**558 746**	**932 968**	**1 236 328**
56 Asia	**411 242**	**422 188**	**664 237**	**985 669**	**3 876 399**	**8 627 846**	**12 534 571**
Total excluding Japan	**390 503**	**396 795**	**592 584**	**824 703**	**2 633 467**	**6 306 693**	**9 952 995**
Total excluding Japan, China, India	**50 486**	**72 173**	**146 999**	**362 578**	**1 398 587**	**3 099 193**	**4 376 931**

a) 1820–1913 includes Bangladesh and Pakistan. b) 1820–1913 includes North and South Korea.

http://dx.doi.org/10.1787/486663055853

ISBN 92-64-02261-9 – © OECD 2006

Table A3–c. GDP Per Capita in 56 Asian Countries
(1990 international $)

	1820	*1870*	*1913*	*1950*	*1973*	*1990*	*1998*
Bangladesh				540	497	640	813
Burma			685	396	628	751	1 024
China	600	530	552	439	839	1 858	3 117
Hong Kong				2 218	7 104	17 491	20 193
India[a]	533	533	673	619	853	1 309	1 746
Indonesia	612	654	904	840	1 504	2 516	3 070
Japan	669	737	1 387	1 926	11 439	18 789	20 410
Malaysia			899	1 559	2 560	5 131	7 100
Nepal				496	622	807	947
Pakistan				643	954	1 598	1 935
Philippines			1 066	1 070	1 959	2 199	2 268
Singapore			1 279	2 219	5 977	14 258	22 643
South Korea[b]			893	770	2 841	8 704	12 152
Sri Lanka		640	850	961	1 492	2 448	3 349
Taiwan			747	936	4 117	9 910	15 012
Thailand		707	835	817	1 874	4 645	6 205
16 East Asia	**581**	**552**	**679**	**661**	**1 569**	**2 700**	**3 535**
Afghanistan				645	684	600	514
Cambodia				518	813	945	1 058
Laos				613	770	933	1 104
Mongolia				435	860	1 333	1 094
North Korea				770	2 841	2 841	1 183
Vietnam	546	524	754	658	836	1 040	1 677
19 Small Countries				1 127	2 031	2 212	2 541
25 East Asia	**552**	**552**	**679**	**690**	**1 218**	**1 353**	**1 402**
41 East Asia	**580**	**552**	**679**	**662**	**1 554**	**2 642**	**3 436**
Bahrain				2 104	4 377	4 092	4 620
Iran				1 720	5 445	3 586	4 265
Iraq				1 364	3 753	2 458	1 131
Israel				2 817	9 646	12 968	15 152
Jordan				1 663	2 389	3 775	4 113
Kuwait				28 834	26 674	6 153	11 273
Lebanon				2 429	3 157	1 949	3 445
Oman				622	3 278	6 479	7 267
Qatar				30 520	43 859	6 797	7 304
Saudi Arabia				2 231	11 040	9 101	8 225
Syria				2 409	4 018	5 618	5 765
Turkey				1 818	3 753	5 441	6 552
UAE				15 694	24 908	13 061	13 857
Yemen				976	1 757	2 347	2 298
West Bank + Gaza				950	2 236	4 211	5 671
15 West Asia	**552**	**552**	**679**	**1 855**	**4 972**	**4 911**	**5 407**
56 Asia	**579**	**552**	**679**	**713**	**1 725**	**2 781**	**3 565**
Total excluding Japan	**575**	**543**	**640**	**635**	**1 231**	**2 117**	**2 936**
Total excluding Japan, China, India	**565**	**603**	**794**	**924**	**2 065**	**3 084**	**3 734**

a) 1820–1913 includes Bangladesh and Pakistan. b) 1820–1913 includes North and South Korea.

http://dx.doi.org/10.1787/486663055853

Table A3–d. **GDP Per Capita Growth Rates in 56 Asian Countries, 1820–1998**

	1820–70	*1870–1913*	*1913–50*	*1950–73*	*1973–98*
Bangladesh				−0.36	1.99
Burma			−1.47	2.03	1.97
China	−0.25	0.10	−0.62	2.86	5.39
Hong Kong				5.19	4.27
India[a]	0.00	0.54	−0.22	1.40	2.91
Indonesia	0.13	0.75	−0.20	2.57	2.90
Japan	0.19	1.48	0.89	8.05	2.34
Malaysia			1.50	2.18	4.16
Nepal				0.99	1.69
Pakistan				1.73	2.87
Philippines			0.01	2.66	0.59
Singapore			1.50	4.40	5.47
South Korea[b]			−0.40	5.84	5.99
Sri Lanka			0.33	1.93	3.29
Taiwan			0.61	6.65	5.31
Thailand		0.39	−0.06	3.67	4.91
16 East Asia	**−0.10**	**0.49**	**−0.08**	**3.83**	**3.30**
Afghanistan				0.26	−1.14
Cambodia				1.98	1.06
Laos				1.00	1.45
Mongolia				3.01	0.97
North Korea				5.84	−3.44
Vietnam	−0.08	0.85	−0.37	1.05	2.82
19 Small Countries				2.59	0.90
25 East Asia	**0.00**	**0.48**	**0.04**	**2.50**	**0.56**
41 East Asia	**−0.10**	**0.49**	**−0.07**	**3.78**	**3.23**
Bahrain				3.23	0.22
Iran				5.14	−0.97
Iraq				4.50	−4.69
Israel				5.50	1.82
Jordan				1.59	2.20
Kuwait				−0.34	−3.39
Lebanon				1.15	0.35
Oman				7.50	3.24
Qatar				1.59	−6.92
Saudi Arabia				7.20	−1.17
Syria				2.25	1.45
Turkey				3.20	2.25
UAE				2.03	−2.32
Yemen				2.59	1.08
West Bank + Gaza				3.79	3.79
15 West Asia	**0.00**	**0.48**	**2.75**	**4.38**	**0.34**
56 Asia	**−0.10**	**0.48**	**0.13**	**3.91**	**2.95**
Total excluding Japan	**−0.11**	**0.38**	**−0.02**	**2.92**	**3.54**
Total excluding Japan, China, India	**0.13**	**0.64**	**0.41**	**3.56**	**2.40**

a) 1820–1913 includes Bangladesh and Pakistan. b) 1820–1913 includes North and South Korea.

http://dx.doi.org/10.1787/486663055853

Table A3–e. **GDP Growth Rates in 56 Asian Countries, 1820–1998**

	1820–70	*1870–1913*	*1913–50*	*1950–73*	*1973–98*
Bangladesh				1.66	4.24
Burma			−0.25	3.84	3.96
China	−0.37	0.56	−0.02	5.02	6.84
Hong Kong				8.13	6.21
India[a]	0.38	0.97	0.23	3.54	5.07
Indonesia	1.10	2.04	1.05	4.61	4.96
Japan	0.41	2.44	2.21	9.29	2.97
Malaysia			3.54	4.88	6.61
Nepal				2.51	4.27
Pakistan				4.37	5.55
Philippines			2.23	5.79	3.08
Singapore			4.71	7.93	7.45
South Korea[b]			0.30	8.13	7.31
Sri Lanka			1.55	4.46	4.77
Taiwan		1.95	2.87	9.81	6.77
Thailand		1.35	2.23	6.87	6.59
16 East Asia	**0.03**	**1.04**	**0.84**	**6.00**	**5.09**
Afghanistan				2.46	1.32
Cambodia				4.44	2.91
Laos				3.10	3.72
Mongolia				5.53	3.58
North Korea				8.03	−2.13
Vietnam	0.86	2.29	0.46	3.67	4.95
19 Small Countries				5.05	3.26
25 East Asia	**0.64**	**1.57**	**1.45**	**4.96**	**2.61**
41 East Asia	**0.04**	**1.06**	**0.86**	**5.96**	**5.02**
Bahrain				6.57	4.08
Iran				8.18	1.90
Iraq				7.73	−1.84
Israel				9.76	4.16
Jordan				6.53	6.28
Kuwait				7.86	−0.40
Lebanon				4.40	1.22
Oman				10.15	7.51
Qatar				9.56	−0.80
Saudi Arabia				9.78	3.43
Syria				5.34	5.08
Turkey				5.93	4.39
UAE				9.82	4.86
Yemen				4.67	4.53
West Bank + Gaza				4.14	7.45
15 West Asia	**0.38**	**1.07**	**3.93**	**7.30**	**3.23**
56 Asia	**0.05**	**1.06**	**1.07**	**6.13**	**4.81**
Total excluding Japan	**0.03**	**0.94**	**0.90**	**5.18**	**5.46**
Total excluding Japan, China, India	**0.72**	**1.67**	**2.47**	**6.05**	**4.67**

a) 1820–1913 includes Bangladesh and Pakistan. b) 1820–1913 includes North and South Korea.

http://dx.doi.org/10.1787/486663055853

Table A3–f. Population Growth Rates in 56 Asian Countries, 1820–1998

	1820–70	1870–1913	1913–50	1950–73	1973–98
Bangladesh				2.03	2.21
Burma	0.38	2.51	1.25	1.78	1.94
China	−0.12	0.47	0.61	2.10	1.38
Hong Kong	3.70	3.25	4.21	2.79	1.87
India[a]	0.38	0.43	0.45	2.11	2.10
Indonesia	0.96	1.28	1.25	1.99	2.01
Japan	0.21	0.95	1.31	1.15	0.61
Malaysia	2.07	3.19	2.01	2.64	2.35
Nepal	0.38	0.43	1.27	1.51	2.53
Pakistan				2.60	2.60
Philippines	1.70	1.45	2.22	3.04	2.48
Singapore	2.08	3.18	3.16	3.38	1.88
South Korea[b]	0.07	0.26	0.71	2.16	1.25
Sri Lanka	1.53	1.28	1.22	2.48	1.44
Taiwan	0.32	0.91	2.24	2.96	1.39
Thailand	0.43	0.95	2.28	3.08	1.61
16 East Asia	**0.13**	**0.56**	**0.91**	**2.09**	**1.73**
Afghanistan	0.50	0.72	0.96	2.19	2.49
Cambodia	0.23	0.63	0.83	2.41	1.83
Laos	0.95	1.42	0.83	2.08	2.24
Mongolia	0.15	0.19	0.19	2.45	2.59
North Korea				2.07	1.36
Vietnam	0.95	1.42	0.83	2.60	2.06
19 Small Countries	0.11	0.38	1.15	2.40	2.34
25 East Asia	**0.64**	**1.08**	**1.40**	**2.40**	**2.04**
41 East Asia	**0.14**	**0.57**	**0.93**	**2.11**	**1.74**
Bahrain			0.27	3.23	3.86
Iran	0.50	0.62	1.08	2.89	2.90
Iraq	0.74	1.18	1.86	3.09	2.99
Israel	0.51	1.15	1.66	4.04	2.30
Jordan	0.41	0.63	1.30	4.87	3.99
Kuwait				8.23	3.09
Lebanon	0.72	0.72	2.03	3.21	0.87
Oman	0.29	0.32	0.41	2.47	4.14
Qatar				7.84	6.57
Saudi Arabia	0.30	0.30	0.87	2.40	4.65
Syria	0.34	0.54	1.53	3.02	3.57
Turkey	0.32	0.56	0.93	2.64	2.09
UAE				7.63	7.35
Yemen	−0.08	0.34	0.83	2.03	3.42
West Bank + Gaza				0.34	3.53
15 West Asia	**0.38**	**0.59**	**1.14**	**2.80**	**2.88**
56 Asia	**0.15**	**0.57**	**0.94**	**2.14**	**1.81**
Total excluding Japan	**0.15**	**0.55**	**0.92**	**2.19**	**1.86**
Total excluding Japan, China, India	**0.58**	**1.02**	**2.05**	**2.40**	**2.22**

a) 1820–1913 includes Bangladesh and Pakistan. b) 1820–1913 includes North and South Korea.

http://dx.doi.org/10.1787/486663055853

Table A3–g. **Derivation of 1990 Benchmark Levels of GDP in 1990 International Dollars for 15 East Asian Countries**

	GDP in million national currency units in reference year	PPP Converter for reference year (units of national currency per dollar)	GDP in reference year in million Geary–Khamis dollars	1990 GDP in Geary–Khamis dollars of reference year	1990 GDP in million 1990 Geary–Khamis dollars
	ICP 3 (Reference Year 1975)				
Iran	3 377 740	39.7	85 073	86 878	199 819
Syria	20 600	1.48	13 919	23 631	70 894
	ICP 4 (Reference Year 1980)				
India	1 360 100	3.37	403 591	695 515	1 098 100
Indonesia	48 914 000	280.0	174 693	285 598	450 901
Israel	107 651	4.14	26 003	37 061	58 511
Philippines	243 750	3.18	76 651	90 591	143 025
South Korea	38 148 400	384.0	99 345	236 350	373 150
	ICP 5 (Reference Year 1985)				
Bangladesh	406 930	6.075	66 984	81 779	98 113
Hong Kong	271 655	4.680	58 046	83 160	99 770
Pakistan	472 160	3.761	125 541	166 380	199 611
Sri Lanka	157 763	5.288	29 834	35 082	42 089
Thailand	1 056 496	8.094	130 528	213 158	255 732
	ICP 6 (Reference Year 1990)				
China	1 956 038	0.9273			2 109 400
Japan	430 040 000	185.27			2 321 153
	ICP 7 (Reference Year 1993)				
Turkey	1 981 867	5 139.3	385 630	333 678	305 395

Source: Column 1 shows GDP in the reference year in national currency units; in most cases the figures are from World Bank, *World Tables* (1995), Japan, Turkey and South Korea from OECD, *National Accounts, 1960–97*, Vol.1 (1999), and Thailand from Asian Development Bank, *Key Indicators* (1999). In most cases these involve minor revisions of the figures used by ICP. Col.2 purchasing power parity (PPP converters) for 1975 from Kravis, Heston and Summers, *World Product and Income* (1982), pp. 176–9; 1980 from UN, *World Comparisons of Purchasing Power and Real Product for 1980* (1987), p. viii; 1985 from UN, *World Comparisons of Real Gross Domestic Product and Purchasing Power, 1985*, (1994), p. 5; 1990 for Japan from OECD, *Purchasing Power Parities and Real Expenditures: GK Results, 1990*, Vol.2 (1993), p. 32 (adjusted to a US PPP = 1.00). Turkey 1993 from *Purchasing Power Parities and Real Expenditures: GK Results, 1993*, vol.2 (1996), p. 35 (adjusted to a US PPP = 1.00). All these PPP converters are multilateral and use the Geary–Khamis method of estimation. The results for China were derived from a 1987 bilateral China/United States comparison, adjusted to a Geary–Khamis basis as described in Maddison, *Chinese Economic Performance in the Long Run* (1998), pp. 153–4, with upward adjustment of the official Chinese GDP estimates in yuan. Column 3 is derived from columns 1 and 2. Column 4 was derived by adjusting column 3 for the volume movement in GDP between the reference year and 1990. Column 5 is column 4 adjusted by the movement in the US GDP deflator from the reference year to 1990.

http://dx.doi.org/10.1787/486663055853

Table A3–h. **Derivation of 1990 Benchmark Levels of GDP in 1990 International Dollars for Five East Asian Countries**

	GDP in million national currency units in reference year	Implicit Geary–Khamis PPP Converter for reference year (units of national currency per dollar)	GDP in reference year in million Geary–Khamis dollars	1990 GDP in million 1993 Geary–Khamis dollars	1990 GDP in million 1990 Geary–Khamis dollars
		ICP 3 (Reference Year 1993)			
Hong Kong	897 463	6.9486	129 158	109 010	99 770
Laos	950 973	191.0865	4 977	4 274	3 912
Malaysia	165 206	1.32718	124 479	98 142	89 823
Nepal	171 386	8.7553	19 575	17 055	15 609
Singapore	92 905	1.5287	60 774	47 343	43 330
Vietnam	136 571 000	1538.281	88 749	75 345	68 959

Source: Column 1 from ADB, *Key Indicators of Developing Asian and Pacific Countries,* 1999. In most cases these involve minor revisions of the figures cited by ESCAP, except for Singapore, where the figure is 13 per cent lower. ESCAP used an adjusted version of the Geary–Khamis procedure. The estimates for Malaysia and Laos were made by the World Bank and used reduced information techniques (see ESCAP *Comparisons of Real Gross Product and Purchasing Power Parities 1993).* ESCAP took Hong Kong as the numeraire country, and the Hong Kong figures were reported without a PPP adjustment. In column 2 above I derived the implicit 1993 Hong Kong PPP in terms of Hong Kong dollars per US dollar by updating the 1990 result shown in Table A3–g. For other countries ESCAP reported PPP in terms of units of national currency per Hong Kong dollar. In column 2 these PPPs were multiplied by the 1993 Hong Kong/US dollar PPP, to link these regional results to the global ICP exercises in which the United States is the numeraire country. Column 3 is derived from columns 1 and 2. Column 4 was derived by adjusting column 3 for the change in the volume movement of GDP between 1990 and 1993. Column 5 is column 4 adjusted by the movement in the US GDP deflator between 1990 and 1993.

Table A3–i. **Derivation of 1990 Benchmark Levels of GDP in 1990 International Dollars for Three West Asian Countries**

	GDP in million national currency units in reference year	Geary–Khamis PPP Converter for reference year (units of national currency per dollar)	GDP in reference year in million Geary–Khamis dollars	1990 GDP in million 1993 Geary–Khamis dollars	1990 GDP in million 1990 Geary–Khamis dollars
		ICP 3 (Reference Year 1993)			
Bahrain	1 754.2	0.6402	2 740	2 244	2 054
Palestine	8 844.63	0.8698	10 169	7 890	7 222
Qatar	26 183.0	6.5951	3 970	3 579	3 276

Source: First three columns from Geary–Khamis results in *Purchasing Power Parities, Volume and Price Level Comparisons for the Middle East, 1993,* Economic and Social Commission for Western Asia and World Bank, p. 59. This study presented figures for 8 West Asian countries and Egypt for 1993. It used a short–cut, "reduced information" approach, using both the Geary–Khamis and the EKS approach. It should be regarded as a first approximation to a full ICP exercise. The results for some of the countries such as Lebanon and Yemen seemed implausible, so I used the results for only three of the countries. Fourth column derived by adjusting column 3 for the change in the volume of GDP between 1990 and 1993. Column 5 adjusts the column 4 entry for the movement in the US GDP deflator between 1990 and 1993.

http://dx.doi.org/10.1787/486663055853

A4

Population, GDP and GDP Per Capita in 57 African Countries

Population 1950 onwards from the International Programs Centre, US Bureau of the Census, which provides comprehensive coverage of the African countries on an annual basis back to 1950. Its estimates are updated and revised regularly. Use of this source involved some significant modifications of the figures used in Maddison (1995a), which were a mixture of OECD Development Centre and World Bank sources. 1913 population for the four sample countries from Maddison (1995a). 1820–1913 total African population derived from McEvedy and Jones (1978), p. 206.

Estimates of benchmark 1990 GDP levels in international (Geary–Khamis) dollars were available for 50 African countries from the Penn World Tables of Robert Summers and Alan Heston. In Maddison (1995a), I used the PWT 5.5 estimates. Here I use the 5.6 version. Table A4–g provides a confrontation of the PWT results and those of the three ICP rounds which cover 24 countries. There are seven countries for which no ICP or PWT benchmark was available. For Equatorial Guinea, Mayotte, St. Helena, S. Tome Principe and Western Sahara, 1990 per capita GDP was assumed to be equal to the average for the 50 countries covered by the PWT. For Libya it was assumed to be the same as in Algeria, and for Eritrea the same as Ethiopia.

1990–98 GDP movement for all African countries from IMF, World Economic Outlook, October 1999. GDP movement 1913–90 for Egypt, Ghana, Morocco and South Africa from the sources cited below; 1950–90 GDP movement for other countries (except Botswana, Nigeria and the seven proxy estimates) from the database of the OECD Development Centre.

Egypt: 1913–50 GDP from Hansen and Marzouk (1965), p. 3, 1950–73 from Ikram (1980) p. 398–9; 1973–90 from World Bank, World Tables, 1995.

Ghana: GDP 1913–50 from Szereszewski (1965) pp. 74, 92 and 149; 1950–5 from Maddison (1970); 1955–90 from the Government Statistical Service, Republic of Ghana.

Morocco: 1913–50 GDP derived from Amin (1966), 1950–90 GDP from World Bank, World Tables (1983 and 1995 editions).

South Africa: 1913–20 current price GDP divided by cost of living index from Bureau of Census and Statistics, Union Statistics for Fifty Years, Jubilee Issue 1910–1960, Pretoria, 1960; 1920–50 from L.J. Fourie, "Contribution of Factors of Production and Productivity to South African Economic Growth", IARIW, processed, 1971. 1946–70 GDP at 1975 prices from Development Bank of South Africa, 1970–90 from World Bank, World Tables.

Botswana: GDP movement in 1950–90 from World Bank, World Tables.

Nigeria: 1950–90 from Bevan, Collier and Gunning (1999).

Estimates for the 15 "non–sample" countries are segregated as they are extremely shaky.

1913–50 per capita GDP for Africa assumed to move parallel to the average for the four countries for which estimates were available. Before 1913 no indicators were available. As a proxy it was assumed that per capita GDP for Africa as a whole moved at the same pace as in "other Asia" (see Table B–21), for 1820–1913.

Table A4–a. **Population of 57 African Countries**
(000 at mid–year)

	1820	1870	1913	1950	1973	1990	1998
Egypt			12 144	21 198	35 480	56 106	66 050
Ghana			2 043	5 297	9 583	15 190	18 497
Morocco			4 500	9 343	16 998	24 685	29 114
South Africa			6 153	13 596	24 549	37 191	42 835
4 Sample Countries			**24 840**	**49 434**	**86 610**	**133 172**	**156 496**
Algeria				8 893	15 198	25 352	30 481
Angola				4 118	6 028	8 430	10 865
Benin				1 673	2 836	4 676	6 101
Botswana				430	643	1 304	1 448
Cameroon				4 888	7 179	11 894	15 029
Cape Verde				146	277	349	400
Central African Rep.				1 260	1 945	2 798	3 376
Chad				2 608	3 995	5 889	7 360
Comoros				148	257	429	546
Congo				768	1 279	2 206	2 658
Côte d'Ivoire				2 860	6 352	11 904	15 446
Djibouti				60	189	370	441
Gabon				416	557	1 078	1 208
Gambia				305	546	964	1 292
Kenya				6 121	12 594	23 674	28 337
Liberia				824	1 528	2 265	2 772
Madagascar				4 620	7 250	11 525	14 463
Mali				3 688	5 909	8 231	10 109
Mauritania				1 006	1 356	1 979	2 511
Mauritius				481	861	1 074	1 168
Mozambique				6 250	10 088	14 056	18 641
Namibia				464	831	1 409	1 622
Niger				2 482	4 559	7 644	9 672
Nigeria				31 797	53 121	86 530	110 532
Reunion				244	469	600	705
Rwanda				2 439	4 110	7 161	7 956
Senegal				2 654	4 727	7 408	9 723
Seychelles				33	58	73	79
Sierra Leone				2 087	2 925	4 283	5 080
Somalia				2 438	3 932	6 675	6 842
Sudan				8 051	15 113	26 628	33 551
Swaziland				277	493	840	966
Tanzania				8 909	15 321	24 886	30 609
Togo				1 172	2 133	3 680	4 906
Tunisia				3 517	5 426	8 207	9 380
Uganda				5 522	10 386	17 227	22 167
Zambia				2 553	4 625	7 957	9 461
Zimbabwe				2 853	6 041	9 958	11 044
38 Other Countries				**129 055**	**221 137**	**361 613**	**448 947**
15 Non–sample Countries				**49 853**	**79 898**	**125 980**	**154 511**
Total 57 Countries	**74 208**	**90 466**	**124 697**	**228 342**	**387 645**	**620 765**	**759 954**
Burkina Faso				4 376	5 947	9 024	11 266
Burundi				2 363	3 529	5 285	5 537
Ethiopia and Eritrea				21 577	34 028	50 960	62 232
Guinea				2 586	3 786	5 936	7 477
Guinea Bissau				573	633	998	1 206
Lesotho				726	1 142	1 744	2 090
Malawi				2 817	4 865	9 139	9 840
Zaire				13 569	23 186	37 978	49 001
6 Other Countries				1 266	2 782	4 916	5 862
15 Non–sample Countries				49 853	79 898	125 980	154 511

http://dx.doi.org/10.1787/486663055853

ISBN 92-64-02261-9 – © OECD 2006

Table A4–b. **GDP Levels in 57 African Countries**
(million 1990 international $)

	1820	1870	1913	1950	1973	1990	1998
Egypt			8 891	15 224	36 249	112 873	140 546
Ghana			1 509	5 943	13 484	16 372	23 014
Morocco			3 630	13 598	28 800	64 082	78 397
South Africa			9 857	34 465	102 498	147 509	165 239
4 Sample Countries			**23 887**	**69 230**	**181 031**	**340 836**	**407 196**
Algeria				12 136	35 814	73 934	81 948
Angola				4 331	10 784	7 207	7 029
Benin				1 813	3 011	5 347	7 668
Botswana				150	722	4 178	6 083
Cameroon				3 279	7 201	14 393	15 157
Cape Verde				66	147	430	544
Central African Rep.				972	1 627	1 982	2 203
Chad				1 240	1 726	2 573	3 463
Comoros				83	229	294	285
Congo				990	2 727	5 394	5 951
Côte d'Ivoire				2 977	12 064	16 330	21 201
Djibouti				90	412	530	467
Gabon				1 292	4 086	4 500	5 901
Gambia				165	533	833	1 098
Kenya				3 982	12 107	26 093	30 451
Liberia				869	2 212	2 245	2 580
Madagascar				4 394	8 292	9 210	9 976
Mali				1 685	3 449	6 040	7 917
Mauritania				467	1 309	1 825	2 494
Mauritius				1 198	3 169	7 652	11 508
Mozambique				7 084	18 894	14 105	22 125
Namibia				1 002	2 895	4 619	6 158
Niger				2 018	3 377	4 289	5 149
Nigeria				23 933	76 585	107 459	136 162
Reunion				485	1 771	2 694	3 174
Rwanda				1 334	2 826	6 125	5 605
Senegal				3 341	6 217	10 032	12 659
Seychelles				63	187	366	471
Sierra Leone				1 370	3 180	4 335	2 837
Somalia				2 576	4 625	7 231	6 044
Sudan				6 609	11 783	19 793	29 535
Swaziland				200	1 114	2 154	2 699
Tanzania				3 362	9 007	13 852	16 933
Togo				673	2 245	2 805	3 159
Tunisia				3 920	12 051	27 387	39 306
Uganda				3 793	8 704	10 206	16 082
Zambia				1 687	4 930	6 432	6 374
Zimbabwe				2 000	8 594	13 766	15 990
38 Other Countries				**107 629**	**290 606**	**448 640**	**554 386**
15 Non–sample Countries				**17 710**	**57 548**	**70 352**	**77 826**
Total 57 Countries	**31 010**	**40 172**	**72 948**	**194 569**	**529 185**	**859 828**	**1 039 408**
Burkina Faso				1 686	3 287	5 482	7 613
Burundi				772	1 781	3 520	3 005
Ethiopia and Eritrea				5 394	13 640	18 964	24 833
Guinea				784	1 861	3 304	4 573
Guinea Bissau				166	558	794	736
Lesotho				232	790	1 828	2 451
Malawi				913	2 756	5 146	6 949
Zaire				6 750	16 915	17 394	10 790
6 Other Countries				1 013	15 960	13 920	16 876
15 Non–sample Countries				17 710	57 548	70 352	77 826

http://dx.doi.org/10.1787/486663055853

223

Table A4–c. GDP Per Capita in 57 African Countries
(1990 international $)

	1820	1870	1913	1950	1973	1990	1998
Egypt			732	718	1 022	2 012	2 128
Ghana			739	1 122	1 407	1 078	1 244
Morocco			807	1 455	1 694	2 596	2 693
South Africa			1 602	2 535	4 175	3 966	3 858
4 Sample Countries			**962**	**1 400**	**2 090**	**2 559**	**2 602**
Algeria				1 365	2 356	2 916	2 688
Angola				1 052	1 789	855	647
Benin				1 084	1 062	1 143	1 257
Botswana				349	1 123	3 204	4 201
Cameroon				671	1 003	1 210	1 009
Cape Verde				452	531	1 232	1 360
Central African Rep.				771	837	708	653
Chad				475	432	437	471
Comoros				561	891	685	522
Congo				1 289	2 132	2 445	2 239
Côte d'Ivoire				1 041	1 899	1 372	1 373
Djibouti				1 500	2 180	1 432	1 059
Gabon				3 106	7 336	4 174	4 885
Gambia				541	976	864	850
Kenya				651	961	1 102	1 075
Liberia				1 055	1 448	991	931
Madagascar				951	1 144	799	690
Mali				457	584	734	783
Mauritania				464	965	922	993
Mauritius				2 491	3 681	7 125	9 853
Mozambique				1 133	1 873	1 003	1 187
Namibia				2 159	3 484	3 278	3 797
Niger				813	741	561	532
Nigeria				753	1 442	1 242	1 232
Reunion				1 988	3 776	4 490	4 502
Rwanda				547	688	855	704
Senegal				1 259	1 315	1 354	1 302
Seychelles				1 909	3 224	5 014	5 962
Sierra Leone				656	1 087	1 012	558
Somalia				1 057	1 176	1 083	883
Sudan				821	780	743	880
Swaziland				722	2 260	2 564	2 794
Tanzania				377	588	557	553
Togo				574	1 053	762	644
Tunisia				1 115	2 221	3 337	4 190
Uganda				687	838	592	725
Zambia				661	1 066	808	674
Zimbabwe				701	1 423	1 382	1 448
38 Other Countries				**834**	**1 314**	**1 241**	**1 235**
15 Non–sample Countries				**355**	**720**	**558**	**504**
Total 57 Countries	**418**	**444**	**585**	**852**	**1 365**	**1 385**	**1 368**
Burkina Faso				385	553	607	676
Burundi				327	505	666	543
Ethiopia and Eritrea				250	401	372	399
Guinea				303	492	557	612
Guinea Bissau				290	882	796	610
Lesotho				320	692	1 048	1 173
Malawi				324	566	563	706
Zaire				497	730	458	220
6 Other Countries				800	5 737	2 832	2 879
15 Non–sample Countries				355	720	558	504

http://dx.doi.org/10.1787/486663055853

ISBN 92-64-02261-9 – © OECD 2006

Table A4–d. **GDP Per Capita Growth Rates in 57 African Countries**

	1820–70	*1870–1913*	*1913–50*	*1950–73*	*1973–98*
Egypt			−0.05	1.54	2.98
Ghana			1.14	0.99	−0.49
Morocco			1.61	0.66	1.87
South Africa			1.25	2.19	−0.32
4 Sample Countries			**1.02**	**1.76**	**0.88**
Algeria				2.40	0.53
Angola				2.34	−3.99
Benin				−0.09	0.68
Botswana				5.21	5.42
Cameroon				1.76	0.02
Cape Verde				0.70	3.84
Central African Rep.				0.35	−0.99
Chad				−0.42	0.34
Comoros				2.03	−2.12
Congo				2.21	0.20
Côte d'Ivoire				2.65	−1.29
Djibouti				1.64	−2.85
Gabon				3.81	−1.61
Gambia				2.60	−0.55
Kenya				1.71	0.45
Liberia				1.39	−1.75
Madagascar				0.81	−2.00
Mali				1.07	1.18
Mauritania				3.23	0.11
Mauritius				1.71	4.02
Mozambique				2.21	−1.81
Namibia				2.10	0.34
Niger				−0.40	−1.31
Nigeria				2.87	−0.63
Reunion				2.83	0.71
Rwanda				1.00	0.10
Senegal				0.19	−0.04
Seychelles				2.30	2.49
Sierra Leone				2.22	−2.63
Somalia				0.47	−1.14
Sudan				−0.22	0.49
Swaziland				5.09	0.85
Tanzania				1.95	−0.24
Togo				2.67	−1.95
Tunisia				3.04	2.57
Uganda				0.87	−0.58
Zambia				2.10	−1.82
Zimbabwe				3.12	0.07
38 Other Countries				**2.00**	**−0.25**
15 Non–sample Countries				**3.12**	**−1.42**
Total 57 Countries	**0.12**	**0.64**	**1.02**	**2.07**	**0.01**
Burkina Faso				1.58	0.81
Burundi				1.91	0.29
Ethiopia and Eritrea				2.07	−0.02
Guinea				2.12	0.88
Guinea Bissau				4.96	−1.46
Lesotho				3.41	2.13
Malawi				2.46	0.89
Zaire				1.68	−4.68
6 Other Countries				8.94	−2.72
15 Non–sample Countries				3.12	−1.42

http://dx.doi.org/10.1787/486663055853

Table A4–e. **GDP Growth Rates in 57 African Countries**

	1820–70	*1870–1913*	*1913–50*	*1950–73*	*1973–98*
Egypt			1.46	3.84	5.57
Ghana			3.77	3.63	2.16
Morocco			3.63	3.32	4.09
South Africa			3.44	4.85	1.93
4 Sample Countries			**2.92**	**4.27**	**3.30**
Algeria				4.82	3.37
Angola				4.05	−1.70
Benin				2.23	3.81
Botswana				7.07	8.90
Cameroon				3.48	3.02
Cape Verde				3.54	5.37
Central African Rep.				2.26	1.22
Chad				1.45	2.82
Comoros				4.51	0.88
Congo				4.50	3.17
Côte d'Ivoire				6.27	2.28
Djibouti				6.84	0.50
Gabon				5.13	1.48
Gambia				5.23	2.93
Kenya				4.95	3.76
Liberia				4.15	0.62
Madagascar				2.80	0.74
Mali				3.16	3.38
Mauritania				4.58	2.61
Mauritius				4.32	5.29
Mozambique				4.36	0.63
Namibia				4.72	3.07
Niger				2.26	1.70
Nigeria				5.19	2.33
Reunion				5.79	2.36
Rwanda				3.32	2.78
Senegal				2.74	2.89
Seychelles				4.84	3.76
Sierra Leone				3.73	−0.46
Somalia				2.58	1.08
Sudan				2.55	3.74
Swaziland				7.75	3.60
Tanzania				4.38	2.56
Togo				5.38	1.38
Tunisia				5.00	4.84
Uganda				3.68	2.49
Zambia				4.77	1.03
Zimbabwe				6.54	2.51
38 Other Countries				**4.41**	**2.62**
15 Non–sample Countries				**5.26**	**1.21**
Total 57 Countries	**0.52**	**1.40**	**2.69**	**4.45**	**2.74**
Burkina Faso				2.95	3.42
Burundi				3.70	2.11
Ethiopia and Eritrea				4.12	2.43
Guinea				3.83	3.66
Guinea Bissau				5.41	1.11
Lesotho				5.47	4.63
Malawi				4.92	3.77
Zaire				4.08	−1.78
6 Other Countries				12.74	0.22
15 Non–sample Countries				5.26	1.21

http://dx.doi.org/10.1787/486663055853

Table A4–f. **Population Growth Rates in 57 African Countries**

	1820–70	1870–1913	1913–50	1950–73	1973–98
Egypt			1.52	2.26	2.52
Ghana			2.61	2.61	2.67
Morocco			1.99	2.64	2.18
South Africa			2.17	2.60	2.25
4 Sample Countries			**1.88**	**2.47**	**2.39**
Algeria				2.36	2.82
Angola				1.67	2.38
Benin				2.32	3.11
Botswana				1.76	3.30
Cameroon				1.69	3.00
Cape Verde				2.82	1.48
Central African Rep.				1.91	2.23
Chad				1.87	2.47
Comoros				2.43	3.06
Congo				2.24	2.97
Côte d'Ivoire				3.53	3.62
Djibouti				5.12	3.45
Gabon				1.28	3.15
Gambia				2.56	3.51
Kenya				3.19	3.30
Liberia				2.72	2.41
Madagascar				1.98	2.80
Mali				2.07	2.17
Mauritania				1.31	2.50
Mauritius				2.56	1.23
Mozambique				2.10	2.49
Namibia				2.57	2.71
Niger				2.68	3.05
Nigeria				2.26	2.97
Reunion				2.88	1.64
Rwanda				2.29	2.68
Senegal				2.54	2.93
Seychelles				2.48	1.24
Sierra Leone				1.48	2.23
Somalia				2.10	2.24
Sudan				2.78	3.24
Swaziland				2.54	2.73
Tanzania				2.39	2.81
Togo				2.64	3.39
Tunisia				1.90	2.21
Uganda				2.78	3.08
Zambia				2.62	2.90
Zimbabwe				3.32	2.44
38 Other Countries				**2.37**	**2.87**
15 Non–sample Countries				**2.07**	**2.67**
Total 57 Countries	**0.40**	**0.75**	**1.65**	**2.33**	**2.73**
Burkina Faso				1.34	2.59
Burundi				1.76	1.82
Ethiopia and Eritrea				2.00	2.44
Guinea				1.67	2.76
Guinea Bissau				0.43	2.61
Lesotho				1.99	2.45
Malawi				2.40	2.86
Zaire				2.36	3.04
6 Other Countries				3.48	3.03
15 Non–sample Countries				2.07	2.67

http://dx.doi.org/10.1787/486663055853

Table A4–g. **Alternative Estimates of African 1990 GDP Level by ICP and PWT**
(million international, Geary–Khamis dollars)

	PWT 5.5	PWT 5.6	ICP 4	ICP 5	ICP 7
Benin	5 248	5 347	n.a.	6 629	1 227
Botswana	5 479	4 178	5 488	5 662	2 591
Cameroon	17 115	14 393	16 781	41 534	7 123
Congo	5 972	5 394	n.a.	5 358	1 096
Côte d'Ivoire	14 568	16 330	16 655	18 528	5 562
Egypt	105 684	112 873	n.a.	194 267	66 855
Ethiopia	17 891	18 964	16 498	18 622	n.a.
Gabon	3 639	4 500	n.a.	n.a.	2 424
Guinea	3 087	3 304	n.a.	n.a.	2 506
Kenya	26 028	26 093	25 698	31 855	7 358
Madagascar	9 093	9 210	8 001	8 531	3 541
Malawi	4 840	5 146	5 131	6 173	1 582
Mali	5 059	6 040	4 561	5 314	1 485
Mauritius	7 211	7 652	n.a.	7 671	1 796
Morocco	60 193	64 082	56 183	83 696	20 338
Nigeria	96 521	107 459	126 035	139 453	24 349
Rwanda	5 360	6 125	n.a.	5 040	n.a.
Senegal	9 351	10 032	8 627	12 139	3 361
Sierra Leone	4 041	4 325	n.a.	3 021	774
Swaziland	1 580	2 154	n.a.	2 181	611
Tanzania	14 676	13 852	13 388	13 199	2 470
Tunisia	26 421	27 387	28 990	35 312	9 409
Zambia	6 935	6 432	8 358	10 684	2 741
Zimbabwe	14 913	13 766	15 256	20 391	5 559

Source: Col. 1 from Penn World Tables, version 5.5, diskette annex to R.S. Summers and A. Heston, "The Penn World Table (Mark 5): An Expanded Set of International Comparisons, 1950–1988", *Quarterly Journal of Economics*, May 1991. Col. 2 from their diskette of version 5.6a of January 1995. In some cases the PWT estimate referred to a year or two earlier than 1990, and I updated using the volume movement of GDP, and the change in the US GDP deflator between that year and 1990. I used the PWT version 5.5 for 50 countries earlier (see Maddison, 1995a, p. 192 and 221), and here have used version 5.6a. This raised the GDP aggregate for the 50 countries from 812 817 million international (Geary–Khamis) dollars in Maddison (1995a) to 845 908 million here. In addition, there were proxy estimates for six countries amounting to $13 883 million int.dollars in both exercises (see Maddison, 1995a, pp. 214 and 221). The PWT estimates are much more comprehensive than those of the ICP, which covered 15 countries for 1980 (ICP 4), 22 countries in ICP 5 for 1985 and ICP 7 for 1993. There was no ICP 6 round for 1990 for Africa. The ICP results were adjusted to a 1990 basis in the same fashion as those in Tables A3–g and A3–h. The 24 countries shown here include all of those which participated in one or other of the ICP exercises. ICP 4 results are from UN/Eurostat, *World Comparisons of Purchasing Power Parity and Real Product for 1980*, New York, 1987, p. viii; ICP 5 from UN/Eurostat, *World Comparisons of Real GDP and Purchasing Power 1985*, New York, 1994, p. 5; ICP 7 Geary–Khamis results from Eurostat, *Comparisons of Price Levels and Economic Aggregates 1993: The Results of 22 African Countries*, Luxembourg 1996, pp. 43, 145–6. The ICP 7 results in the last column are not comparable with those for earlier years. They are intra–African relatives linked to the US dollar via a standardised exchange rate rather than a purchasing power parity with the United States as the *numeraire* country. As a result they show real product levels which are in the aggregate aout one third of those in the ICP 5 exercise. The ratio of the ICP 7 to ICP 5 results varies from .46 for Botswana to .17 for Cameroon. The ICP 5 result for Cameroon is, in fact, rather odd. However, for the biggest countries, the ratio varies from .17 for Nigeria to .34 for Egypt. A major problem with the ICP exercise is that there is no attempt to reconcile discrepancies between the results of different rounds, whereas this is a fundamental feature of the Summers and Heston approach in the Penn World Tables.

http://dx.doi.org/10.1787/486663055853

Appendix B

Growth of World Population, GDP and GDP Per Capita before 1820

Maddison (1995a) contained a rough aggregate estimate of world population, GDP and per capita GDP back to 1500 to provide perspective for the detailed analysis of developments after 1820. The main purpose of the brief look backwards was to emphasise the dramatic acceleration of growth in the succeeding capitalist epoch. Maddison (1998a) provided a confrontation of Chinese and Western economic performance over a longer period of two millennia. This demonstrated important differences in the pace and pattern of change in major parts of the world economy, which have roots deep into the past.

The present exercise provides a more detailed and disaggregated scrutiny of the protocapitalist experience from 1500 to 1820, with a rough sketch of the contours of development over the preceding millennium and a half.

The quantitative analysis in this appendix works backward from the 1820 estimates in Appendix A, using the same techniques of analysis — assembling evidence on changes in population, retaining the 1990 international dollar as the temporal and spatial anchor in the estimation of movements in GDP and per capita GDP, filling holes in the evidence with proxy estimates in order to derive world totals. This appendix is divided into two parts. The first deals with population. The second with GDP growth.

POPULATION

The evidence here on the more distant past is weaker than that in Appendix A, and there are more gaps in the database. Nevertheless, the exercise in quantification is not a product of fantasy. The strongest and most comprehensive evidence is that for population, and the population component is of greater proportionate importance in analysis of centuries when per capita income growth was exiguous.

Demographic material is important in providing clues to per capita income development. One striking example is the urbanisation ratio. Thanks to the work of de Vries for Europe and of Rozman for Asia, one can measure the proportion of population living in towns with more than 10 000 inhabitants. In the year 1000, this ratio was zero in Europe (there were only 4 towns with more than 10 000 inhabitants) and in China it was 3 per cent. By 1800 the West European urban ratio was 10.6 per cent, the Chinese 3.8 per cent and the Japanese 12.3 per cent. When countries are able to expand their urban ratios, it indicates that there was a growing surplus beyond subsistence in agriculture, and that the non–agricultural component of economic activity was increasing. These changes were used to infer differences in per capita progress between China and Europe in Maddison (1998a), and such inference is a feature of the present study. The Chinese bureaucracy kept population registers which go back more than 2 000 years. These bureaucratic records were designed to assess taxable capacity, and include information on cultivated area and crop production, which was used by Perkins (1969) to assess long run movements in Chinese GDP per capita. Bagnall and Frier (1994) have made brilliant use of fragments of ancient censuses to estimate occupational structure, household size, marriage patterns, fertility and life expectation in Roman Egypt of the third century.

Serious work on historical demography started in the seventeenth century with John Graunt (1662). He derived vital statistics, survival tables, and the population of London by processing and analysing christenings and burials recorded in the London bills of mortality from 1603 onwards. Halley (1693) published the first rigorous mathematical analysis of life tables and Gregory King (1696) derived estimates of the population of England and Wales by exploiting information from hearth and poll taxes, a new tax on births, marriages and burials and his own minicensuses for a few towns.

Historical demography gained new vigour in the twentieth century in several important centres: a) the Office of Population Research in Princeton University (established in 1936); b) INED (Institut National des Études Demographiques) founded in the 1950s to exploit family reconstitution techniques developed by Louis Henry; c) the Cambridge Group for the History of Population and Family Structure (established in the 1970s) has carried out a massive research project to reconstitute English population size and structure on an annual basis back to 1541 (Wrigley, et al., 1997); d) research on Japanese population history has blossomed under the leadership of Akira Hayami and Osamu Saito; e) there has been a flood of publications on Latin American demography from the University of California by members of the Berkeley school. For the second half of the twentieth century we have the comprehensive international surveys of the United Nations, and the US Bureau of the Census.

As a result there are now a large number of monographic studies on European, American and Asian countries, and a long series of efforts to construct aggregative estimates of world population. Riccioli (1672) and Gregory King (1696) inaugurated this tradition. Early estimates are usefully surveyed by Willcox (1931) who listed 66 publications between 1650 and 1850. Modern scholarship is represented by Colin Clark (1967), Durand (1974), McEvedy and Jones (1978) and Biraben (1979).

The following detailed estimates for 1500 onwards rely heavily on monographic country studies for the major countries. To fill holes in my dataset I draw on McEvedy and Jones (1978). For the preceding millennium and a half, I used their work extensively.

There are several reasons for preferring McEvedy and Jones rather than Clark, Durand and Biraben. The McEvedy and Jones estimates are the most detailed and best documented. When reconstructing the past, they define countries in terms of 1975 boundaries, which are in most cases identical with the 1990 boundaries I adopted as a general rule (with exceptions for Germany, India, Korea and the United Kingdom). They also show the impact of frontier changes. There are significant differences of judgement amongst the four standard sources on long term population momentum, particularly for Latin America for 1500 and earlier, and for Africa. In both these cases my judgement was closer to that of McEvedy and Jones, than to that of Clark, Durand or Biraben.

Table B–1 summarises my aggregate findings compared with those of McEvedy and Jones, Clark, Durand and Biraben.

Western Europe

Denmark, Finland, Germany, Netherlands, Norway, Sweden and Switzerland 1500–1700 from Maddison (1991) pp. 226–7; Belgium and Italy from de Vries (1984), p. 36. Austria from McEvedy and Jones (1978). France 1500–1700 (refers to present territory) from Bardet and Dupaquier (1997), pp. 446 and 449; 1700–1820 from Henry and Blayo (1975), pp. 97–9. UK estimate is explained in Table B–13 below. Population for the years 0 and 1000 from McEvedy and Jones (1978). Population of 13 small West European countries assumed to move parallel to the total for the 12 countries above.

Portugal 1500–1700 and Spain 1500 from de Vries (1984), p. 36. Spain 1600 and 1700 from *Espana: Anuario Estadistico 1977*, INE, Madrid, p. 49; 0 and 1000 are from McEvedy and Jones. Greece 0–1700 from McEvedy and Jones.

Table B–1. **Alternative Estimates of the Regional Components of World Population, 0–1700 A.D.**
(000)

Year	0	1000	1500	1700
Europe (including area of former USSR)				
Clark	44 500	44 200	73 800	111 800
Durand	42 500	45 500	79 000	n.a.
Biraben	43 000	43 000	84 000	125 000
McEvedy and Jones	32 800	38 800	85 500	126 150
Maddison	33 350	39 013	87 718	126 810
Americas				
Clark	3 000	13 000	41 000	13 000
Durand	12 000	37 500	46 500	n.a.
Biraben	12 000	18 000	42 000	12 000
McEvedy and Jones	4 500	9 000	14 000	13 000
Maddison	6 320	12 860	19 750	13 250
Asia (including Australasia)				
Clark	185 000	173 000	227 000	416 000
Durand	207 000	189 500	304 000	n.a.
Biraben	171 000	152 000	245 000	436 000
McEvedy and Jones	114 200	183 400	277 330	411 250
Maddison	174 650	183 400	284 350	402 350
Africa				
Clark	23 000	50 000	85 000	100 000
Durand	35 000	37 500	54 000	n.a.
Biraben	26 000	38 000	87 000	107 000
McEvedy and Jones	16 500	33 000	46 000	61 000
Maddison	16 500	33 000	46 000	61 000
World				
Clark	225 500	280 200	427 800	640 800
Durand	296 500	310 000	483 500	n.a.
Biraben	252 000	253 000	461 000	680 000
McEvedy and Jones	168 700	264 500	423 600	610 000
Maddison	230 820	268 273	437 818	603 410

Source: Clark (1967), Durand (1974), McEvedy and Jones (1978) and Biraben (1979). The estimates of Durand are high/low ranges. I have taken the mid point of his figures. I included the whole of the former USSR in Europe and the whole of Turkey in Asia, and adjusted the estimates of the other authors to conform to this definition.

http://dx.doi.org/10.1787/675115301353

Eastern Europe

Population 0 — 1700 of what is now Albania, Bulgaria, Czech Republic, Greece, Hungary, Poland, Romania, Slovakia and the five republics of the former Yugoslavia from McEvedy and Jones (1978).

Table B–2. **Population of Western and Eastern Europe and Western Offshoots, 0–1820 A.D.**
(000)

Year	0	1000	1500	1600	1700	1820
Austria	500	700	2 000	2 500	2 500	3 369
Belgium	300	400	1 400	1 600	2 000	3 434
Denmark	180	360	600	650	700	1 155
Finland	20	40	300	400	400	1 169
France	5 000	6 500	15 000	18 500	21 471	31 246
Germany	3 000	3 500	12 000	16 000	15 000	24 905
Italy	7 000	5 000	10 500	13 100	13 300	20 176
Netherlands	200	300	950	1 500	1 900	2 355
Norway	100	200	300	400	500	970
Sweden	200	400	550	760	1 260	2 585
Switzerland	300	300	650	1 000	1 200	1 829
United Kingdom	800	2 000	3 942	6 170	8 565	21 226
12 Countries	17 600[a]	19 700[b]	48 192	62 580	68 796	114 419
Portugal	500	600	1 000	1 100	2 000	3 297
Spain	4 500	4 000	6 800	8 240	8 770	12 203
Greece	2 000	1 000	1 000	1 500	1 500	2 312
13 Small Countries	100	113	276	358	394	657
Total Western Europe	**24 700**	**25 413**	**57 268**	**73 778**	**81 460**	**132 888**
Albania	200	200	200	200	300	437
Bulgaria	500	800	800	1 250	1 250	2 187
Czechoslovakia	1 000	1 250	3 000	4 500	4 500	7 190
Hungary	300	500	1 250	1 250	1 500	4 571
Poland	450	1 200	4 000	5 000	6 000	10 426
Romania	800	800	2 000	2 000	2 500	6 389
Yugoslavia	1 500	1 750	2 250	2 750	2 750	5 215
Total Eastern Europe	**4 750**	**6 500**	**13 500**	**16 950**	**18 800**	**36 415**
United States	640	1 300	2 000	1 500	1 000	9 981
Canada	80	160	250	250	200	816
Australia & New Zealand	450	500	550	550	550	433
Total Western Offshoots	**1 170**	**1 960**	**2 800**	**2 300**	**1 750**	**11 230**

Table B–3. **European and Asian Population of Russia, 0–1870 A.D.**
(000)

Year	0	1000	1500	1600	1700	1820	1870
European Russia	2 000	4 000	12 000	15 000	20 000	44 161	71 726
Siberia	100	100	200	200	300	1 443	3 272
Caucasus	300	500	1 250	1 500	1 750	2 429	4 587
Turkestan	1 500	2 500	3 500	4 000	4 500	6 732	9 087
Total	**3 900**	**7 100**	**16 950**	**20 700**	**26 550**	**54 765**	**88 672**

Source: McEvedy and Jones (1978).

http://dx.doi.org/10.1787/675115301353

Former USSR

Table B–3 refers to population in the geographic area that constituted the USSR before it was dissolved in 1991. 0–1870 from McEvedy and Jones (1978), pp. 78–82, 157–63, broken down for European Russia (excluding Finland and the Polish provinces), Siberia, the Caucasus (present republics of Armenia, Azerbaijan and Georgia), and Turkestan (present republics of Kazakhstan, Kyrgyzstan, Tajikistan, Turkmenistan and Uzbekistan).

Western Offshoots

There is a detailed bibliography and survey of the literature on North America in Daniels (1992). Thornton (1987) analyses the process of indigenous depopulation, and cites Ubelaker's (1976) estimates for the Smithsonian Institution. I took a rounded version of the latter as the basis for my estimate of 2 million in 1500 for the United States, and quarter of a million for Canada. Thornton gives no estimates for 1600 and 1700. My assessment for these two years is based on the assumption that the depopulation ratio was smaller than in Mexico (where population density was much greater). Movement of population for 0–1500 assumed to be proportionately the same as the total for Latin America.

For Australia, the conventional official estimate of the aboriginal population at the time of initial contact with Europeans was 250–300 thousand, but Butlin's (1983) detailed modelling of the likely impact of disease, displacement and deliberate extermination in New South Wales and Victoria suggested a considerably higher figure. I assumed a pre–contact population in Australia and New Zealand combined of 550 000 — smaller than Butlin's estimate but bigger than the old official estimates. For 0–1500 I assumed slower growth than in the Americas.

Latin America

The size of the indigenous population at the time of the Spanish conquest is a matter of considerable controversy. Firm evidence is weak, but there are two very distinct schools of thought. It is clear that population declined substantially after the conquest. The native population had been isolated over millennia from foreign microbes, and suffered from major epidemics of smallpox, measles and other deadly diseases against which they had no immunities.

Mexico

In an assessment based on a careful survey of literary evidence of the conquistadores and documents in Spanish archives, Angel Rosenblat (1945) estimated the pre–conquest population of present day Mexico to have been about 4.5 million. He assumed a rather modest rate of depopulation after the conquest — a drop less than 15 per cent in the sixteenth century. The Berkeley school (Cook and Simpson, 1948) had very much higher estimates of the pre–conquest population — their figure for Central Mexico alone (about a quarter of the territory of present day Mexico) was 11 million. This estimate was based on various flimsy suppositions, e.g. multiplying the number of Franciscan monks by baptismal coefficients or inferring population from the size of Aztec armies as estimated by those who fought them. The Borah and Cook (1963) estimate for Central Mexico was even higher — 25 million on the basis of ambiguous pictographs describing the incidence of Aztec fiscal levies. They assumed a 95 per cent depopulation ratio for the indigenous population between 1519 and 1605, and backcast Spanish estimates for 1605 by a multiplier of 25. They give no detailed specification of the different causes of mortality as Butlin (1983) did for Australia. They did not discuss alternative approaches to measurement as Cook (1981) does for Peru, and they never made an adequate response to Rosenblat's (1967) criticism of their work.

There are two reasons for scepticism about the extremely high mortality estimates of the Berkeley school: a) they assume very much higher mortality than European experience in the wake of the Black Death (a one third loss); b) it is implausible that Central Mexican population did not recover its alleged 1519 level until 1970 in spite of the additions the Spanish conquest made to production potential. Before the conquest there were no wheeled vehicles, no ploughs and no metal tools. The basic diet was close to vegetarianism with no cattle, sheep, pigs or hens. The absence of horses, donkeys, oxen and wheeled vehicles meant that land transport possibilities were confined to human porterage. Europe recovered from the Black Death mortality within a century with virtually no change in technology. It seems inconceivable that Mexican recovery took 450 years.

My own judgement is that Berkeley School's estimates for Mexico are far too high. However, I think Rosenblat understates the pre–conquest level and the subsequent rate of depopulation. Zambardino (1980), in a critical review of the Berkeley School, suggests a plausible range of 5–10 million. I took the midpoint of the Zambardino estimate for Mexico (see the discussion in Maddison, 1995b), and assumed a depopulation ratio of two thirds between 1500 and 1600.

Rosenblat (1945) describes the structure of the Mexican population in 1825, at the end of Spanish rule when the total population was 6.8 million. At the top of the scale was a thin layer of 70 000 peninsulares (peninsular Spaniards). The second group consisted of 1.2 million criollos (whites of Spanish extraction). The third group consisted of 1.9 million *mestizos* or *castas*. Most of them originated from unions between whites and Indians, some were Indians who had abandoned their rural lifestyle, wore Spanish–type clothes and lived in urban areas. At the bottom of the social scale were rural Indians (3.7 million) living mostly in nucleated pueblos, engaged in subsistence agriculture, with some hunter–gatherer groups in the North. This group wore traditional dress, maintained their own languages and customs except religion. There was a small group (about 10 000) of negro slaves in the South of the country. This information on social structure is of considerable use in constructing income accounts (see below).

Brazil

I adopted the Rosenblat (1945) estimate for 1500 which was used by McEvedy and Jones. It is close to the Kroeber (1939) estimate based on hypotheses about the nature of land use and technology by a population who were mainly hunter–gatherers (with some slash and burn agriculture in coastal regions). Hemming (1978) estimates a pre–contact population of 2.4 million (a figure he describes as "pure guess–work") derived by blowing up present day figures for 28 regions by assumed depopulation ratios. Denevan (1976) estimates 4.8 million for North and Central Brazil (including Amazonia) but this was based on agricultural potential and inferences from evidence on Peru. Hemming exaggerates the likely depopulation ratio for a country with a thinly settled hunter–gatherer population, and Denevan's reliance on estimates of agricultural potential is not relevant for an Indian population who were predominantly hunter–gatherers.

In the first century of settlement it became clear that it was difficult to use Indians as serf or slave labour. They were not docile, had high mortality when exposed to Western diseases, could run away and hide very easily. So the Portuguese imported large numbers of African slaves for manual labour. The ultimate fate of Brazilian Indians was like that of North American Indians. They were pushed beyond the bounds of colonial society. The main difference was greater miscegenation with the white invaders and black slaves.

Table B–4. **Ethnic Composition of the Brazilian Population, 1500–1870**
(000)

Year	1500	1600	1700	1820	1870
Indigenous	1 000	700	950	500	400
Black and Mixed		70	200	2 500	5 700[a]
European		30	100	1 500	3 700
Total	**1 000**	**800**	**1 250**	**4 500**	**9 800**

a) including 1.5 million slaves.
Sources: Rosenblat (1945), Simonsen (1962), Merrick and Graham (1979), Marcilio (1984).

Table B–5. **Alternative Estimates of Latin American Population, 0–1820 A.D.**
(000)

Year	0	1000	1500	1600	1700	1820
Maddison estimates						
Mexico		4 500	7 500	2 500	4 500	6 587
Brazil		700	1 000	800	1 250	4 507
Peru		3 000	4 000	1 300	1 300	1 317
Other		3 200	5 000	4 000	5 000	8 809
Total	5 600	11 400	17 500	8 600	12 050	21 220
McEvedy and Jones (1978)						
Mexico	1 500	3 000	5 000	3 500	4 000	6 309[a]
Brazil	400	700	1 000	1 000	1 250	3 827[a]
Peru	750	1 500	2 000	1 500	1 500	1 683[a]
Other	1 550	3 300	5 200	4 500	5 400	10 450[a]
Total	4 200	8 500	13 200	10 500	12 150	22 269[a]
Rosenblat (1945)						
Mexico			4 500	3 645[b]	n.a.	6 800[c]
Brazil			1 000	886[b]	n.a.	4 000[c]
Peru			2 000	1 591[b]	n.a.	1 400[c]
Other			4 885	4 532[b]	n.a.	10 863[c]
Total			12 385	10 654[b]	n.a.	23 063[c]
Clark (1967)						
Total	2 900	12 600	40 000	14 000	12 000	
Biraben (1979)						
Total	10 000	16 000	39 000	10 000	10 000	23 980[a]

a) interpolation of 1800 and 1850 estimates; b) interpolation of 1570 and 1650 estimates; c) 1825.

Sources: My estimates for 1500–1820 (see text above). 0–1500 growth rates from McEvedy and Jones.

http://dx.doi.org/10.1787/675115301353

Peru

I adopted Cook's (1981, Chapter 7) "minimal" estimate of 4 million. Although he calls it "minimal" he cites lower figures derived by other methods he considers respectable. Cook's approach is like that of the Berkeley school, but he shows alternative estimates derived from *a)* the "ecological" approach, which assesses population potential (carrying capacity) in terms of resources and the technology available; *b)* inferences from the extent of archaelogical remains; *c)* retropolation of assumed depopulation ratios from 1571 when the first reasonably documented Spanish population estimates became available. Cook opts for a pre–conquest figure of 9 million (p. 114) which is near the top of the wide range he shows. I assumed the same depopulation ratio of two thirds between 1500 and 1600, as I did for Mexico.

Other Latin American Countries

I adopted the pre–conquest estimates of McEvedy and Jones (1978) which they derive to a large degree from Rosenblat (1945). I assume a higher depopulation ratio for the sixteenth century than McEvedy and Jones, but less than that for Mexico and Peru (see Table B–5).

Total Latin American Population

Table B–5 compares my estimates, those of McEvedy and Jones and Rosenblat. Mine are higher for 1500 and show bigger depopulation in the sixteenth century, but the differences are modest compared with the Berkeley school. Borah (1976) suggested a population of 100 million upwards for the Americas as a whole in 1500. Colin Clark (1967) and Biraben (1979) were impressed by Borah but obviously felt he exaggerated and adopted compromise estimates (without entering into country detail).

China

Chinese population estimates (see Table B–8) are based on bureaucratic records which go much further back than those in any other country. The type of adjustments which are necessary for intertemporal compatibility are discussed in detail in Bielenstein (1987) and Ho (1959). I have used Ho (1970) p.49 for the population in 2A.D. For 960 onwards see Maddison, 1998a, Appendix D, pp. 167–9. Recently (in volume 8 of the *Cambridge History of China)*, Martin Heidra offered a totally different picture of Chinese population with very rapid growth during the Ming dynasty. However, he provides no detail or bibliographic evidence for his revisionism, and shows no decline in the mid seventeenth century wars between the Ming and their Ch'ing successors. His analysis ends in 1650, and his high hypothesis leaves virtually no room for any growth in the Ch'ing period (see Heidra in Twitchett and Mote, 1998, pp. 436–40). It is therefore difficult to give much credence to his views.

Table B–6. **Alternative Estimates of India's Population, 0–1820 A.D.**
(million)

Year	0	1000	1500	1600	1700	1820
Clark (1967)	70	70	79	100	200	190
McEvedy & Jones (1978)	34	77	100	130	160	200
Biraben (1979)	46	40	95	145	175	194
Durand (1974)	75	75	112.5	n.a.	180[a]	n.a.
Maddison	55	75	110	135	165	209

a) 1750.

http://dx.doi.org/10.1787/675115301353

ISBN 92-64-02261-9 – © OECD 2006

India

India does not have statistical records of the same sort as Western Europe, China or Japan, and there is consequently a wide range of views. A good deal of discussion has hinged on the year 1600, for which Moreland estimated 100 million, Davis (1951) 125 million, Habib (1982) around 145 million (a range of 140–150). Virtually all of these estimates are based on an assessment of the productive capacity of the cultivated area (see Raychaudhuri and Habib, 1982), so there is an interdependence between what one assumes about demographic and economic performance. I took an average of the Davis and Habib estimate for 1600. For the year 0, I used the estimates of Durand.

Japan

Reasonably firm evidence is available from 1721 onwards from national population surveys at six–yearly intervals. These were taken for the shogun's own domains and those of approximately 250 *daimyo* in the rest of Japan. The registers excluded samurai households, the imperial nobility, outcastes and beggars (*eta* and *hinin*). They understated the female population and (to a degree which varied between different domains) young children as well. Nevertheless they can be adjusted to provide reasonable estimates for 1721 onwards when the aggregate level was about 30 million. Before the six–yearly surveys were instituted, information was available from annual registers of religious affiliation which were instituted after the Portuguese were expelled from Japan and Christianity was made illegal. Hayami (1986a) shows such retrospective *daimyo* returns for 17 areas for periods varying from 30 to 100 years before the 1730s. Together they covered about 17 per cent of the Japanese population in the 1730s. They show an arithmetic average growth rate of 0.35 per cent a year, and a weighted average of 0.52 per cent. When these rates are backcast they suggest a 1600 population between 16 and 19.7 million, which is close to the Yoshida (1911) estimate of 18.5 million. Yoshida based his estimate on the 1598 cadastral survey which showed 18.5 million *koku* of grain output. He assumed this would support a population of 18.5 million with a consumption of 1 koku (150 kg.) per head.

Table B–7. **Alternative Estimates of Japanese Population, 0–1820 A.D.**
(000)

Year	0	1000	1500	1600	1700	1820
Maddison	3 000	7 500	15 400	18 500	27 000	31 000
Hayami			10 000	12 000	30 000	31 000

Source: For the first century I took the midpoint of the range cited by Farris (1985) p. 3 for the Yayoi period, and for the year 1000 interpolated between the estimate cited by Farris (p. 175) for the mid 7th and by Taeuber (1958), p. 20, for the mid 13th century. For 1500–1600 I assume the same growth rate as Hayami (0.18 per cent a year).

http://dx.doi.org/10.1787/675115301353

Yoshida's reasoning was crude but seems more plausible than Hayami's (1986a) range of 10 to 14 million for 1600. Hayami implies a very rapid growth in the seventeenth century with an abrupt change to more or less complete stagnation in the eighteenth century.

Korea

Korea had a system of household population registers (*hojok*) for purposes of taxation and manpower mobilisation from 1392 to 1910, from which bureaucratic records survive. These registers had very scanty coverage of the child population, there was substantial regional variance, with much better coverage in Seoul, the capital. Kwon (1993) adjusted these records with the help of other historical documents, and information on family structure from the first modern census of 1925. Kwon and Shin (1977) provide annual estimates for 1392 to 1910. I used their estimates of population movement for 1500, 1600, 1700 and 1910 and linked them to estimates of the 1910 level from Mizoguchi and Umemura (1988) as described in Appendix A. The revised estimates are about twice as high as those used in McEvedy and Jones (1978) which were based on the unadjusted results of the population registers as reported in Lee (1936), pp. 40–1. For 0–1500 I assumed the same proportionate movement as in Japan.

Table B–8. **Population of Asia, 0–1820 A.D.**
(million)

Year	0	1000	1500	1600	1700	1820
China	59.6	59.0	103.0	160.0	138.0	381.0
India	75.0	75.0	110.0	135.0	165.0	209.0
Japan	3.0	7.5	15.4	18.5	27.0	31.0
Korea	1.6	3.9	8.0	10.0	12.2	13.8
Indonesia	2.8	5.2	10.7	11.7	13.1	17.9
Indochina	1.1	2.2	4.5	5.0	5.9	8.9
Other East Asia	5.9	9.8	14.4	16.9	19.8	23.6
Iran	4.0	4.5	4.0	5.0	5.0	6.6
Turkey	6.1	7.3	6.3	7.9	8.4	10.1
Other West Asia	15.1	8.5	7.5	8.5	7.4	8.5
Total Asia	**174.2**	**182.9**	**283.8**	**378.5**	**401.8**	**710.4**

Source: China, India, Japan and Korea as described in text. All 1820 figures are from Appendix A. Indonesia 1700 from Maddison (1989*b*), 0–1700 proportionate movement from McEvedy and Jones. Indochina (area of Cambodia, Laos and Vietnam), 0–1820 proportionate movement from McEvedy and Jones. Other East Asia, Iran, Turkey and Other West Asia 0–1700 from McEvedy and Jones. The geographic coverage of Asia is the same here as in Appendix A. The Asian population in the former USSR is excluded. Turkey, Polynesia and Melanesia are included.

http://dx.doi.org/10.1787/675115301353

Africa

Except for Egypt there is virtually no documentation on African population. The available estimates are speculative. The first were by Riccioli, an Italian Jesuit, in 1672. He suggested a population of 100 million in his day without explaining the derivation. Gregory King (1696) estimated 70 million, starting with the land area of the continent and a rough assessment of agricultural productivity to estimate what population could be sustained with the available natural resources, levels of technique and organisation.

The leading American demographer Walter Willcox (1931) thought Riccioli's estimate was plausible and assumed no change in seventeenth and eighteenth centuries. Colin Clark (1967) did the same. Carr–Saunders (1964) accepted Riccioli's estimate for the mid–seventeenth century and allowed for some decline thereafter because of the slave trade. Biraben (1979) also allowed for some decline due to the slave trade.

Durand (1974) and McEvedy and Jones (1978) took a very different view. Working backwards from their estimated population level in 1900, they assumed a more dynamic growth process. They took a position on the interaction between population pressure and production which is nearer to that of Boserup (1965 and 1981), than to the Malthusian constraints which the other school had in mind. The hypothesis of McEvedy and Jones seems the more plausible, and I adopted their estimates for 0–1913.

Table B–9a. **Alternative Estimates of African Population, 0–1950 A.D.**
(million)

Year	Willcox (1931)	Carr–Saunders (1964)	Clark (1967)	Biraben (1979)	Durand (1974)	McEvedy & Jones (1978)	Maddison (1999)
0			23	26	35	16.5	16.5
1000			50	39	37.5	33	33
1500			85	87	54	46	46
1600			95	113	55	55	55
1650	100	100	100				
1700			100	107		61	61
1800	100	90	100	102		70	
1820		(92)				(74.2)	74.2
1870		(104.3)				(90.5)	90.5
1900	141	120	122	138	159	110	110.0
1913						(124.7)	124.7
1950		207		219		205	228.3

Sources: Willcox (1931), p.78; Carr–Saunders (1964), p.42; Clark (1967), pp.64, 104 and 108; Biraben (1979), p. 16; Durand (1974), p. 11 (midpoint of his range); McEvedy and Jones (1978), p. 206. Figures in brackets are interpolations.

Table B–9b. **Regional Distribution of African Population 0–1820 A.D**
(000)

Year	0	1000	1500	1600	1700	1820
Egypt	4 000	5 000	4 000	5 000	4 500	4 195
Other North Africa	4 200	5 500	4 300	6 000	4 800	6 790
Other Africa	8 300	22 500	37 700	44 000	51 700	63 223
Total Africa	16 500	33 000	46 000	55 000	61 000	74 208
North African Share %	49.7	31.8	18.0	20.0	13.6	14.8

Source: McEvedy and Jones (1978). Figure for 1820 is an interpolation of their estimates for 1800 and 1850.

http://dx.doi.org/10.1787/675115301353

McEvedy and Jones (1978) is the only source which provides a detailed analysis of the population of Africa. The most striking aspect of their estimates is the dynamism of the expansion south of the Sahara, and the very large decline in the North African share from about half of the African total in the first century to about one seventh in 1820 (see Table B–9b). For about four millennia Egypt was virtually the only area to practise agriculture, and the rest of the continent was sparsely inhabited by hunter–gatherer populations. In the last millennium B.C., Phoenicians and Greeks settled in North Africa west of Egypt, established cities and brought in sophisticated agricultural techniques. By the first century the whole of the prosperous Mediterranean littoral was under Roman control. Its economy and population declined after the Roman collapse, revived with the seventh century Arab takeover, reaching a new peak around the year 1000 A.D.

The dynamic expansion south of the Sahara was due to the spread of agriculturalists into East and Southern Africa, pushing out hunter—gatherer populations. The introduction of manioc and maize from the Americas in the sixteenth century reinforced the possibilities of agricultural expansion. The introduction of agriculture made it possible to accommodate a substantial increase in population, but per capita income probably did not change much.

The slave trade had a substantial effect on African population growth (see Tables 1–7 and 2–5 and the analysis in Chapter 2). Between 1600 and 1870 more than 9 million slaves were shipped to the Americas. The peak was in the eighteenth century when arrivals in the Americas were over 6 million, and African losses were bigger owing to mortality on the passage. Without this trade, African population growth in the eighteenth century might well have been three times as fast.

Table B–10. World Population, 20 Countries and Regional Totals, 0–1998 A.D.

(000)

Year	0	1000	1500	1600	1700	1820	1870	1913	1950	1973	1998
Austria	500	700	2 000	2 500	2 500	3 369	4 520	6 767	6 935	7 586	8 078
Belgium	300	400	1 400	1 600	2 000	3 434	5 096	7 666	8 640	9 738	10 197
Denmark	180	360	600	650	700	1 155	1 888	2 983	4 269	5 022	5 303
Finland	20	40	300	400	400	1 169	1 754	3 027	4 009	4 666	5 153
France	5 000	6 500	15 000	18 500	21 471	31 246	38 440	41 463	41 836	52 118	58 805
Germany	3 000	3 500	12 000	16 000	15 000	24 905	39 231	65 058	68 371	78 956	82 029
Italy	7 000	5 000	10 500	13 100	13 300	20 176	27 888	37 248	47 105	54 751	57 592
Netherlands	200	300	950	1 500	1 900	2 355	3 615	6 164	10 114	13 438	15 700
Norway	100	200	300	400	500	970	1 735	2 447	3 265	3 961	4 432
Sweden	200	400	550	760	1 260	2 585	4 164	5 621	7 015	8 137	8 851
Switzerland	300	300	650	1 000	1 200	1 829	2 664	3 864	4 694	6 441	7 130
United Kingdom	800	2 000	3 942	6 170	8 565	21 226	31 393	45 649	50 363	56 223	59 237
12 Countries Total	*17 600*	*19 700*	*48 192*	*62 580*	*68 796*	*114 419*	*162 388*	*227 957*	*256 616*	*301 037*	*322 507*
Portugal	500	600	1 000	1 100	2 000	3 297	4 353	6 004	8 512	8 634	9 968
Spain	4 500	4 000	6 800	8 240	8 770	12 203	16 201	20 263	27 868	34 810	39 371
Other	2 100	1 113	1 276	1 858	1 894	2 969	4 590	6 783	12 064	13 909	16 553
Total Western Europe	24 700	25 413	57 268	73 778	81 460	132 888	187 532	261 007	305 060	358 390	388 399
Eastern Europe	4 750	6 500	13 500	16 950	18 800	36 415	52 182	79 604	87 289	110 490	121 006
Former USSR	3 900	7 100	16 950	20 700	26 550	54 765	88 672	156 192	180 050	249 748	290 866
United States	680	1 300	2 000	1 500	1 000	9 981	40 241	97 606	152 271	211 909	270 561
Other Western Offshoots	490	660	800	800	750	1 249	5 892	13 795	23 823	39 036	52 859
Total Western Offshoots	1 170	1 960	2 800	2 300	1 750	11 230	46 133	111 401	176 094	250 945	323 420
Mexico	2 200	4 500	7 500	2 500	4 500	6 587	9 219	14 970	28 485	57 643	98 553
Other Latin America	3 400	6 900	10 000	6 100	7 550	14 633	30 754	65 545	137 352	250 807	409 070
Total Latin America	5 600	11 400	17 500	8 600	12 050	21 220	39 973	80 515	165 837	308 450	507 623
Japan	3 000	7 500	15 400	18 500	27 000	31 000	34 437	51 672	83 563	108 660	126 469
China	59 600	59 000	103 000	160 000	138 000	381 000	358 000	437 140	546 815	881 940	1 242 700
India	75 000	75 000	110 000	135 000	165 000	209 000	253 000	303 700	359 000	580 000	975 000
Other Asia	36 600	41 400	55 400	65 000	71 800	89 366	119 619	185 092	392 481	677 214	1 172 243
Total Asia (excluding Japan)	171 200	175 400	268 400	360 000	374 800	679 366	730 619	925 932	1 298 296	2 139 154	3 389 943
Africa	16 500	33 000	46 000	55 000	61 000	74 208	90 466	124 697	228 342	387 645	759 954
World	230 820	268 273	437 818	555 828	603 410	1 041 092	1 270 014	1 791 020	2 524 531	3 913 482	5 907 680

http://dx.doi.org/10.1787/675115301353

Table B-11. Rates of Growth of World Population, 20 Countries and Regional Totals, 0–1998 A.D.
(annual average compound growth rates)

Year	0–1000	1000–1500	1500–1820	1820–70	1870–1913	1913–50	1950–73	1973–98
Austria	0.03	0.21	0.16	0.59	0.94	0.07	0.39	0.25
Belgium	0.03	0.25	0.28	0.79	0.95	0.32	0.52	0.18
Denmark	0.07	0.10	0.20	0.99	1.07	0.97	0.71	0.22
Finland	0.07	0.40	0.43	0.81	1.28	0.76	0.66	0.40
France	0.03	0.17	0.23	0.42	0.18	0.02	0.96	0.48
Germany	0.02	0.25	0.23	0.91	1.18	0.13	0.63	0.15
Italy	−0.03	0.15	0.20	0.65	0.68	0.64	0.66	0.20
Netherlands	0.04	0.23	0.28	0.86	1.25	1.35	1.24	0.62
Norway	0.07	0.08	0.37	1.17	0.80	0.78	0.84	0.45
Sweden	0.07	0.06	0.48	0.96	0.70	0.60	0.65	0.34
Switzerland	0.00	0.15	0.32	0.75	0.87	0.53	1.39	0.41
United Kingdom	0.09	0.14	0.53	0.79	0.87	0.27	0.48	0.21
12 Countries Total	*0.01*	*0.18*	*0.27*	*0.70*	*0.79*	*0.32*	*0.70*	*0.28*
Portugal	0.02	0.10	0.37	0.56	0.75	0.95	0.06	0.58
Spain	−0.01	0.11	0.18	0.57	0.52	0.87	0.97	0.49
Other	−0.06	0.03	0.26	0.88	0.91	1.57	0.62	0.70
Total Western Europe	**0.00**	**0.16**	**0.26**	**0.69**	**0.77**	**0.42**	**0.70**	**0.32**
Eastern Europe	**0.03**	**0.15**	**0.31**	**0.72**	**0.99**	**0.25**	**1.03**	**0.36**
Former USSR	**0.06**	**0.17**	**0.37**	**0.97**	**1.33**	**0.38**	**1.43**	**0.61**
United States	0.06	0.09	0.50	2.83	2.08	1.21	1.45	0.98
Other Western Offshoots	0.03	0.04	0.14	3.15	2.00	1.49	2.17	1.22
Total Western Offshoots	**0.05**	**0.07**	**0.43**	**2.87**	**2.07**	**1.25**	**1.55**	**1.02**
Mexico	0.07	0.10	−0.04	0.67	1.13	1.75	3.11	2.17
Other Latin America	0.07	0.07	0.12	1.50	1.78	2.02	2.65	1.98
Total Latin America	**0.07**	**0.09**	**0.06**	**1.27**	**1.64**	**1.97**	**2.73**	2.01
Japan	**0.09**	**0.14**	**0.22**	**0.21**	**0.95**	**1.31**	**1.15**	**0.61**
China	0.00	0.11	0.41	−0.12	0.47	0.61	2.10	1.38
India	0.00	0.08	0.20	0.38	0.43	0.45	2.11	2.10
Other Asia	0.01	0.06	0.15	0.58	1.02	2.05	2.40	2.22
Total Asia (excluding Japan)	**0.00**	**0.09**	**0.29**	**0.15**	**0.55**	**0.92**	**2.19**	**1.86**
Africa	**0.07**	**0.07**	**0.15**	**0.40**	**0.75**	**1.65**	**2.33**	**2.73**
World	**0.02**	**0.10**	**0.27**	**0.40**	**0.80**	**0.93**	**1.92**	**1.66**

http://dx.doi.org/10.1787/675115301353

Table B–12. Shares of World Population, 20 Countries and Regional Totals, 0–1998 A.D.
(per cent of world total)

Year	0	1000	1500	1600	1700	1820	1870	1913	1950	1973	1998
Austria	0.2	0.3	0.5	0.4	0.4	0.3	0.4	0.4	0.3	0.2	0.1
Belgium	0.1	0.1	0.3	0.3	0.3	0.3	0.4	0.4	0.3	0.2	0.2
Denmark	0.1	0.1	0.1	0.1	0.1	0.1	0.1	0.2	0.2	0.1	0.1
Finland	0.0	0.0	0.1	0.1	0.1	0.1	0.1	0.2	0.2	0.1	0.1
France	2.2	2.4	3.4	3.3	3.6	3.0	3.0	2.3	1.7	1.3	1.0
Germany	1.3	1.3	2.7	2.9	2.5	2.4	3.1	3.6	2.7	2.0	1.4
Italy	3.0	1.9	2.4	2.4	2.2	1.9	2.2	2.1	1.9	1.4	1.0
Netherlands	0.1	0.1	0.2	0.3	0.3	0.2	0.3	0.3	0.4	0.3	0.3
Norway	0.0	0.1	0.1	0.1	0.1	0.1	0.1	0.1	0.1	0.1	0.1
Sweden	0.1	0.1	0.1	0.1	0.2	0.2	0.3	0.3	0.3	0.2	0.1
Switzerland	0.1	0.1	0.1	0.2	0.2	0.2	0.2	0.2	0.2	0.2	0.1
United Kingdom	0.3	0.7	0.9	1.1	1.4	2.0	2.5	2.5	2.0	1.4	1.0
12 Countries Total	*7.6*	*7.3*	*11.0*	*11.3*	*11.4*	*11.0*	*12.8*	*12.7*	*10.2*	*7.7*	*5.5*
Portugal	0.2	0.2	0.2	0.2	0.3	0.3	0.3	0.3	0.3	0.2	0.2
Spain	1.9	1.5	1.6	1.5	1.5	1.2	1.3	1.1	1.1	0.9	0.7
Other	0.9	0.4	0.3	0.3	0.3	0.3	0.4	0.4	0.5	0.4	0.3
Total Western Europe	**10.7**	**9.5**	**13.1**	**13.3**	**13.5**	**12.8**	**14.8**	**14.6**	**12.1**	**9.2**	**6.6**
Eastern Europe	**2.1**	**2.4**	**3.1**	**3.0**	**3.1**	**3.5**	**4.1**	**4.4**	**3.5**	**2.8**	**2.0**
Former USSR	**1.7**	**2.6**	**3.9**	**3.7**	**4.4**	**5.3**	**7.0**	**8.7**	**7.1**	**6.4**	**4.9**
United States	0.3	0.5	0.5	0.3	0.2	1.0	3.2	5.4	6.0	5.4	4.6
Other Western Offshoots	0.2	0.2	0.2	0.1	0.1	0.1	0.5	0.8	0.9	1.0	0.9
Total Western Offshoots	**0.5**	**0.7**	**0.6**	**0.4**	**0.3**	**1.1**	**3.6**	**6.2**	**7.0**	**6.4**	**5.5**
Mexico	1.0	1.7	1.7	0.4	0.7	0.6	0.7	0.8	1.1	1.5	1.7
Other Latin America	1.5	2.6	2.3	1.1	1.3	1.4	2.4	3.7	5.4	6.4	6.9
Total Latin America	**2.4**	**4.2**	**4.0**	**1.5**	**2.0**	**2.0**	**3.1**	**4.5**	**6.6**	**7.9**	**8.6**
Japan	**1.3**	**2.8**	**3.5**	**3.3**	**4.5**	**3.0**	**2.7**	**2.9**	**3.3**	**2.8**	**2.1**
China	25.8	22.0	23.5	28.8	22.9	36.6	28.2	24.4	21.7	22.5	21.0
India	32.5	28.0	25.1	24.3	27.3	20.1	19.9	17.0	14.2	14.8	16.5
Other Asia	15.9	15.4	12.7	11.7	11.9	8.6	9.4	10.3	15.5	17.3	19.8
Total Asia (excluding Japan)	**74.2**	**65.4**	**61.3**	**64.8**	**62.1**	**65.3**	**57.5**	**51.7**	**51.4**	**54.7**	**57.4**
Africa	**7.1**	**12.3**	**10.5**	**9.9**	**10.1**	**7.1**	**7.1**	**7.0**	**9.0**	**9.9**	**12.9**
World	**100.0**	**100.0**	**100.0**	**100.0**	**100.0**	**100.0**	**100.0**	**100.0**	**100.0**	**100.0**	**100.0**

http://dx.doi.org/10.1787/675115301353

GDP AND GDP PER CAPITA, 1500–1820

Maddison (1995a) pp. 19–20 contained a very crude estimate of the movement of world economic growth from 1500 to 1820, as a supplement to the much more detailed analysis for 1820 onwards. In that study I used three simple hypotheses about the growth of real GDP per capita. For Western Europe it was assumed to rise by 0.2 per cent a year, following the hypothesis of Kuznets (1973), 0.1 per cent a year in the rest of Europe and Latin America, and with zero change in Asia and Africa. Maddison (1998a), pp. 25 and 40 compared the contours of development in China and Europe from the first century of our era to 1995. The evidence for China was examined in considerable detail, but the estimates for Europe contained a large element of conjecture.

This appendix involves a much more detailed scrutiny of the evidence for 1500–1820. It strongly suggests that average per capita West European growth rate was slower (at 0.15 per cent a year) from 1500 to 1820 than the 0.2 per cent which Kuznets hypothesised. Growth was faster in Latin America and in the Western offshoots than was assumed in Maddison (1995a). The hypothesis of a stagnant level of per capita income in Asia is generally confirmed, but Japan is a significant exception.

The last section of this appendix includes rough and tentative estimates of GDP levels by major regions for the first century of our era and for the year 1000. Estimates of world GDP and per capita GDP are set out in Tables B–18 to B–22.

Western Europe

Belgium

Blomme and Van der Wee (1994) provide estimates (for Flanders and Brabant) of GDP by industry of origin for 1510–1812. They give estimates for seven points within the period, which I used to derive approximate estimates for 1500,1600 and 1700.

France

François Perroux, with encouragement and support from Simon Kuznets, set up a group to measure French growth in the 1950s (Marczewski and Toutain were its most productive members). Marczewski (1961) made some preliminary estimates of growth for the eighteenth century which greatly exaggerated industrial performance. These have now been superseded. J.C. Toutain kindly provided me with the revised estimates which I have used here for 1700–1820.

Over the past few decades French economic history has been dominated by members of the *Annales* school who have been rather disdainful of the Kuznetsian approach. From our point of view, there are three main drawbacks to their work: *a)* disinterest in macroquantification; *b)* concentration on regional or supranational characterisations rather than national performance; *c)* Malthusian bias.

Le Roy Ladurie strongly emphasized the long–term stability of the French economy from 1300 to 1700, both in demographic and per capita terms. He first put forward the thesis of stagnant income in a regional study of the peasants of Languedoc (1966) . He argued that there was a tension between the dynamism of population and the rigidity of the agricultural production potential which led to recurrent and prolonged population setbacks. In 1977 he maintained the same conclusions in a survey drawing on a new generation of regional studies.

ISBN 92-64-02261-9 – © OECD 2006

Braudel's pessimism at one time went further than that of Le Roy Ladurie. In a 1967 article with Spooner, he concluded, after summarising the work of Phelps Brown and other real wage analysts and regional studies of the *Annales* school that: "From the late fifteenth century until well into the beginning of the eighteenth century, the standard of living in Europe progressively declined." Later he changed his mind (Braudel, 1985, Vol.III, p. 314): "Visualizing overall quantities throws into relief clear continuities in European history. The first of these is the regular rise in GNP come hell or high water — if Frank Spooner is correct, France's GNP had been rising since the reign of Louis XII and probably even longer." [Louis XII reigned from 1498 to 1515].

My own view is that Braudel's revised judgement is more acceptable than his earlier position, or that of Le Roy Ladurie. However, the graph which Braudel reproduced from Spooner (1972) did not show real GNP, but the movement in value from 1500 to 1800 of a fixed quantity of wheat, multiplied by population, and by a smoothed index of wheat prices in Paris. The quantitative evidence for assessing aggregate French performance from 1500 to 1700 is therefore still quite weak. Judging from the comparative growth of the urban population ratio (Table B–14), it seems clear that French economic growth was slower than that of England. I have assumed that French per capita growth 1500–1700 was about the same as in Belgium.

Italy

Malanima (1995, p. 600) suggests declining per capita income in Italy for 1570–1700, and stability from 1700 to 1820. These conclusions are based on a variety of indicators of industrial and commercial activity in cities, levels of food consumption and real wages, rather than an articulate estimate of GDP movement. The nature of the approach is explained in his short essay, "Italian Economic Performance: Output and Income 1600–1800" in Maddison and van der Wee (1994). Malanima's assumption of a decline up to 1700 fits with the qualitative indicators and assessment of Cipolla (1976, pp. 236–244), who suggests decline from the late fifteenth to seventeenth century. However, there is some dissent on this in Sella's (1979) assessment of seventeenth century development in Spanish Lombardy (centred in Milan) and Rapp's (1976) judgement on the seventeenth century situation in Venice. Both Sella and Rapp assumed some relative decline compared with more dynamic economies in Northern Europe, but not an absolute decline. I assumed that Italian per capita income was stagnant from 1500 to 1820. Italian population growth was slower than that in the rest of Europe and the urban ratio showed little change from 1500 to 1820.

The Netherlands

Estimates of GDP growth for 1580–1820 are from Maddison (1991a) pp. 205 and 277. They are linked at 1820 to new estimates for 1820–1913 by Smits, Horlings and van Zanden (2000). For 1580–1700, GDP movement was inferred from evidence (on explosive urbanisation, the transformation of the rural economy, and the size of household assets as revealed by probate inventories) provided in de Vries (1974). Van Zanden (1987) presented a wide variety of evidence to document his estimates of agricultural and fishery production, industry, transport and services for 1650–1805. The Dutch estimates show rapid growth to 1700, and a significant fall per capita from 1700 to 1820. De Vries and van der Woude (1997), p. 707 give a graphical representation based on alternative assumptions about the decline of Dutch per capita income from its peak to the nadir at the end of the Napoleonic wars. Their profile is not markedly different from the measure I adopted. I interpolated the 1580–1700 per capita growth rate of 0.43 to derive the estimates for 1600, and assumed that the 1500 level was below that of Belgium.

United Kingdom

1700–1820 GDP growth from Maddison (1991a), p. 220, modified for England and Wales to incorporate the results of Crafts and Harley (1992) rather than Crafts 1983). I assumed that Scottish per capita GDP was three–quarters of the level in England and Wales in 1801 and that its movement 1700–1801 was parallel to the Crafts–Harley estimate for England and Wales. For Ireland 1700–1801 per capita income was assumed to rise half as fast as in England and Wales.

For 1500–1700 there are several indicators which suggest that the United Kingdom was more dynamic than most other European countries. Population rose by 0.39 per cent a year compared with 0.15 per cent in the rest of Western Europe. The urban population ratio (population in cities 10 000 and over as a percentage of total population) rose from 3.1 to 13.3 per cent in England and Wales — about twice as fast as in France or the Netherlands. It seems clear that the ratio of foreign trade to GDP increased from 1500 to 1820. There are no satisfactory aggregate measures of crop output back to 1500 (see Overton, 1996), but the evidence on yields per acre in Clark (1991), on labour productivity in Allen (1991), and occupational structure (Wrigley, 1988) help to explain the growing urban ratio, as per capita crop availability was maintained with a decreasing share of the labour force. The faster growth in animal husbandry than crops (Wrigley, 1988) suggests an improvement in diets. Recent research on the growing variety of consumption items, improvements in housing and increased stocks of furniture and household linen revealed by probate inventories for successive generations also demonstrates a long process of improvement in living standards — see chapters by de Vries, Wills, and Shammas in Brewer and Porter (1993).

For these reasons, it seemed reasonable to assume that the Crafts–Harley rate of growth of per capita income for 1700–1801 was also valid for 1500–1700. For Ireland I assumed per capita growth was half as fast. For the United Kingdom as a whole this implies a per capita growth rate of 0.28 per cent a year for 1500–1700.

Snooks (1993) estimated the growth of total and per capita income in England 1086–1688 by linking the nominal income assessments in the Domesday Book survey of rural England south of the river Tees with Gregory King's estimates for 1688 as adjusted by Lindert and Williamson (1982). He deflated nominal income growth with the price index for household consumables of Phelps Brown and Hopkins (1981), pp. 28–30, supplemented by an index of wheat prices from Thorold Rogers. His estimates imply a growth rate of per capita real income averaging 0.35 per cent a year from 1492 to 1688 (p. 24). At this rate per capita income would have doubled from 1500 to 1700. This is faster growth than I have suggested.

The estimates of per capita GDP in Table B–13 show a very different movement from the frequently quoted real wage index for building workers in Southern England of Phelps Brown and Hopkins (1981). From 1500 to 1800 they suggested that real wages fell by 60 per cent, whereas I show per capita real GDP increasing 2.4 fold.

The tradition in real wage measurement is quite simplistic compared with that in demography or national accounts. Phelps Brown and Hopkins use daily wage rates for craftsmen and labourers hired for building work by Oxford and Cambridge colleges, Eton school and some other employers in Southern England. For the most part they had 15 or more wage quotations a year for craftsmen, and about 3 a year for building labourers. For the period 1500–1800, in which we are most interested, there were 82 years for which they show no wage estimate because of wide variance in the quotes they had or absence of data. They have no data for weekly or annual earnings, or days worked. There is no discussion in Phelps Brown and Hopkins of the representativity of their wage index for building workers. Lindert and Williamson (1982, p. 393), show that 5.3 per cent of families (73 000) derived their livelihood from the building trades in 1688. Even if the Phelps Brown coverage of this group is assumed to be adequate, and even if it is reasonable to assume that building workers were paid mainly in cash and not in kind, this is certainly not true of the bulk of the working population.

People employed in agriculture were 56 per cent of the total in 1700, and most of them were producing and directly consuming cereals, meat, butter and cheese which figure so largely in the price index. Many others such as servants, artisans, the clergy, the armed forces were either not wage earners or received an appreciable part of their remuneration in kind. A large part of the working population were thus sheltered from the impact of price rises.

Table B–13. **Regional Components of British GDP, Population and GDP Per Capita, 1500–1920**

	United Kingdom	*England, Wales & Scotland*	*Ireland*	*Scotland*	*England & Wales*
GDP (million 1990 Geary–Khamis dollars)					
1500	2 815	2 394	421	298	2 096
1600	6 007	5 392	615	566	4 826
1700	10 709	9 332	1 377	1 136	8 196
1801	25 426	21 060	4 366	2 445	18 615
1820	36 232	30 001	6 231		
1870	100 179	90 560	9 619		
1913	224 618	212 727	11 891		
1920	212 938	201 860	11 078		
Population (000)					
1500	3 942	3 142	800	500	2 642
1600	6 170	5 170	1 000	700	4 470
1700	8 565	6 640	1 925	1 036	5 604
1801	16 103	10 902	5 201	1 625	9 277
1820	21 226	14 142	7 084	2 071	12 071
1870	31 393	25 974	5 419	3 337	22 637
1913	45 649	41 303	4 346	4 728	36 575
1920	46 821	42 460	4 361	4 864	37 596
Per Capita GDP (1990 Geary–Khamis dollars)					
1500	714	762	526	596	793
1600	974	1 043	615	809	1 080
1700	1 250	1 405	715	1 096	1 463
1801	1 579	1 931	839	1 505	2 006
1820	1 707	2 121	880		
1870	3 191	3 487	1 775		
1913	4 921	5 150	2 736		
1920	4 568	4 754	2 540		

Source: GDP as explained in the text. Population in England (excluding Monmouth) interpolated from quinquennial estimates in Wrigley *et al.* (1997), pp. 614–5 for 1541–1871. 1500 to 1541 growth at the rate suggested by Wrigley and Schofield (1981), p. 737 for 1471–1541. Monmouth and Wales 1700–1820 population movement from Deane and Cole (1964), p. 103, 1500–1600 assumed to move parallel to England. Ireland 1500 and 1600 derived from O Grada in Bardet and Dupaquier (1997) vol. 1, p. 386, 1700–1821 movement from Dickson, O Grada and Daultrey (1982), p. 156. Scotland 1500–1600 from McEvedy and Jones (1978), pp. 45–7, 1700 from Deane and Cole (1964), p. 6, 1820 from Mitchell (1962), pp. 8–10. 1820–1920 population and GDP movement from Maddison (1995a).

http://dx.doi.org/10.1787/675115301353

Jan de Vries (1993) is very critical of the real wage approach compared with alternative quantitative methods of measuring well–being. He questions the representativity of construction worker experience in a society with wide income differences. He emphasises the large number of important items left out of the Phelps Brown index and its use of fixed weights for such a long period, but his strongest doubts arise from the conflict between its sombre conclusions with evidence of a different kind which he found in probate inventories "All the studies I have examined for colonial New England and the Chesapeake, England and the Netherlands consistently reveal two features. With very few exceptions, each generation of decedents from the mid–seventeenth to the late eighteenth century left behind more and better possessions."

Aggregate Performance in the West European Core

The aggregate per capita growth rate for the five countries (Belgium, France, Italy, Netherlands and the United Kingdom) where I have given estimates for 1500–1820 is 0.14 per cent per annum, but they are a rather mixed bunch. The growth rate in the United Kingdom was 0.27, the Netherlands 0.28, France 0.16, Belgium 0.13 and zero in Italy. In fact the United Kingdom and the Netherlands are special cases of fast growth. Italian stagnation was also atypical (as is clear from the stability in its urban ratio), and there were special forces retarding Belgian growth. Belgian growth was adversely affected by the break with the Netherlands. Belgium was one of the most prosperous areas of Europe in 1500, as a centre of international trade and banking and substantial textile production. After the Netherlands became independent, the port of Antwerp was blockaded for two centuries, there was substantial migration of capital and skills to Holland. In order to get an approximate picture for Western Europe as a whole, I made proxy estimates for Austria, Denmark, Finland, Norway, Sweden and Switzerland, assuming that per capita real GDP increased at 0.17 per cent a year for 1500–1820. For Germany, a per capita growth rate of 0.14 per cent was assumed, as there was a decline in Germany's role in banking and Hanseatic trade, as well as the impact of the 30 years war. When the proxy estimates are aggregated with the estimates for the 5 countries for which we have better evidence, we find average per capita growth for the 12 West European core countries of 0.15 per cent a year. This is significantly slower than Kuznets' 0.2 per cent hypothesis which I used in Maddison (1995a). I assume here that average per capita growth in "other" Western Europe (Greece and 13 small countries) was the same as the average for the 12 core countries.

Table B–14. **Urbanisation Ratios in Europe and Asia, 1500–1890**
(population in cities 10 000 and over as percentage of total population)

Year	1500	1600	1700	1800	1890
Belgium	21.1	18.8	23.9	18.9	34.5
France	4.2	5.9	9.2	8.8	25.9
Germany	3.2	4.1	4.8	5.5	28.2
Italy	14.9	16.8	14.7	18.3	21.2
Netherlands	15.8	24.3	33.6	28.8	33.4
Scandinavia	0.9	1.4	4.0	4.6	13.2
Switzerland	1.5	2.5	3.3	3.7	16.0
England & Wales	3.1	5.8	13.3	20.3	61.9
Scotland	1.6	3.0	5.3	17.3	50.3
Ireland	0.0	0.0	3.4	7.0	17.6
Western Europe	6.1	7.8	9.9	10.6	31.3
Portugal	3.0	14.1	11.5	8.7	12.7
Spain	6.1	11.4	9.0	11.1	26.8
China	3.8	4.0[a]	n.a.	3.8	4.4
Japan	2.9	4.4	n.a.	12.3	16.0

a) 1650.

Source: European countries from de Vries (1984), pp. 30, 36, 39 and 46 except Italy which is from Malanima (1988*b*); China and Japan from Rozman (1973) adjusted to refer to the ratio in cities 10 000 and over, see Maddison (1998a) pp. 33–36.

http://dx.doi.org/10.1787/675115301353

Spain and Portugal

Yun's (1994) rough per capita GDP estimates for Castile (about three–quarters of Spain) suggest a per capita growth rate of about 0.22 per cent for 1580–1630, with a decline thereafter, and a level in 1800 slightly below the 1630 peak. He makes spot estimates of output levels in current prices for 6 benchmark years within the period 1580 to 1800 and deflates with a price index for food products. His firmest evidence relates to agricultural output and food consumption, but his indicators for secondary and tertiary activity are weak. He concludes that his "trajectory seems congruent with what we know about the evolution of the Castilian economy: expansion until the end of the sixteenth century; agrarian recession, decomposition of the urban network and industrial and commercial crisis during the seventeenth, with a subsequent fall of the GDP revealed in our numbers; and growth on the basis of the poorly developed urban structures and the greater dynamism of the outlying areas in the eighteenth century". I assumed a growth rate of Spanish GDP per capita of 0.25 per cent a year for 1500–1600, no advance in the seventeenth century and some mild progress from 1700 to 1820. I adopted a similar profile for Portugal.

Eastern Europe and USSR

For these two areas direct evidence was lacking. As a proxy I assumed slower per capita GDP growth than in Western Europe at 0.1 per cent per annum for 1500–1820 (as I did in Maddison, 1995a).

Western Offshoots

For the United States, Gallman (1972) p. 22 estimated per capita growth in net national product of 0.42 per cent a year between 1710 and 1840 (taking the mid–point of the range he suggests for 1710). Adjusting for the faster growth of per capita income in 1820–40 (see Maddison, 1995a, p. 137), Gallman's estimate implies a per capita growth of about .29 per cent a year for the non–indigenous population, from a level of $909 in 1700 to $1 286 in 1820. Gallman's estimate included only the white and black population. In 1820, the indigenous population was only 3 per cent of the total. In 1700, it was three–quarters of the total (see Table B–15). Assuming the indigenous population had a per capita income of $400 in both 1700 and 1820, the average level for the whole population was $527 in 1700 and $1 257 in 1820. For 1500 and 1600, the population consisted entirely of hunter–gatherer Indians, and an average income of $400 a head was assumed.

Mancall and Weiss (1999) have recently estimated US per capita income for 1700 and 1800, with separate assessments for whites, slaves and Indians. Their "multicultural" estimate (p. 35) shows a per capita growth rate of only 0.28 per cent a year for 1700–1800, compared with my 0.73 per cent a year for 1700–1820. I consider their growth rate to be much too slow, given the huge change in the ethnic composition of the population in the period. They show no figures for population or total GDP, so it is not possible to replicate their "multicultural" measure. They make no reference to the Gallman estimate I used.

For the other Western Offshoots, Canada, Australia and New Zealand, the great bulk of the 1500–1700 population were indigenous hunter–gatherers, and I assumed a per capita GDP of $400 for 1500, 1600, and 1700.

Table B–15. **Ethnic Composition of the US Population, 1700–1820**
(000)

	Indigenous	White	Black	Total
1700	750	223	27	1 000
1820	325	7 884	1 772	9 981

Source: US Bureau of the Census, *Historical Statistics of the United States: Colonial Times to 1970*, 1975, pp. 14 and 18 for 1820, p. 1168 for 1700 white and black populations. Indian population figures from Rosenblat (1945) for 1820; 1700 as explained above.

Table B–16. **Ethnic Composition of Latin American Population in 1820**
(000)

	Indigenous	White	Black	Mixed	Total
Mexico	3 500	1 200	10	1 880	6 590
Brazil	500	1 500	2 200	300	4 500
Caribbean Islands	0	420	1 700	350	2 470
Other Latin America	3 160	1 300	200	3 000	7 660
Total Latin America	7 160	4 420	4 110	5 530	21 220

Source: Table B–4 for Brazil, otherwise from Rosenblat (1945).

http://dx.doi.org/10.1787/675115301353

Mexico

My per capita income estimate for 1820 is $759 (see Appendix A). At that time the indigenous population was about 53 per cent of the total (see Table B–16). There was a thin layer of "peninsular" Spaniards (about 1 per cent of the population) who ran the army, administration, the church, trading monopolies and part of the professions. They had a baroque life style with sumptuous residences and retinues of servants. About a sixth of the population were *criollos*, i.e. whites of Spanish origin, who had been born in Mexico. They were hacienda owners, merchants, part of the clergy, army and professions. The third social group, over a quarter of the population, were *mestizos* originating from unions between whites and Indians. They were generally workers, farm hands, servants and some were rancheros. I assume a per capita income of $425 for the native population. The aggregate estimate for 1820 implies an average per capita income of $1 140 for the non–native population. 1500–1700 per capita income level of the two segments of the population was assumed to be the same as in 1820, but the average was lower for the two segments combined, because the non–native population was only a quarter of the total in 1700, 4 per cent in 1600, and negligible in 1500.

Other Latin America

In 1500, other parts of Latin America were poorer than Mexico. Except in Peru, most of the inhabitants were hunter gatherers rather than agriculturalists. They also had a lower per capita income than Mexico at the end of the colonial period in 1820. Thus their per capita income grew more slowly than in Mexico from 1500 to 1820. I assumed that the growth differential between Mexico and the rest of Latin America was stable between 1500 and 1820.

ISBN 92-64-02261-9 – © OECD 2006

China

Maddison (1998a) contains an extensive analysis of the course of population, total output, and per capita product over the past 2000 years. There is a greater mass of survey material on Chinese population for the past two millennia than for any other country, thanks to the bureaucratic system and its efforts to monitor economic activity for tax purposes.

In assessing the growth of agricultural output, Perkins (1969) is a masterpiece of scholarly endeavour, covering the period 1368–1968, on which I relied heavily. Perkins' analysis is basically Boserupian. He feels that China responded successfully to population pressure, and managed to sustain more or less stable per capita consumption over the period he covers. This was achieved by increases in cultivated area, in per capita labour input, and land productivity. It involved heavy inputs of traditional fertilisers, irrigation, development of crop varieties and seeds which permitted multiple cropping, diffusion of best–practice techniques by officially sponsored distribution of agricultural handbooks (available at an early stage due to the precocious development of paper and printing). Crops from the Americas were introduced after the mid–sixteenth century. Maize, peanuts, potatoes and sweet potatoes added significantly to China's output potential because of their heavy yields and the possibility of growing them on inferior land. Tobacco and sugar cane were widely diffused in the Ming period. The pattern of Chinese food consumption was heavily concentrated on proteins and calories supplied by crop production which makes more economic use of land than pastoral activities. Chinese consumption of meat was very much lower than in Europe and concentrated on poultry and pigs which were scavengers rather than grazing animals. Milk and milk products were almost totally absent. Chinese also made very little use of wool. Ordinary clothing came largely from vegetable fibres (hemp, ramie, and then cotton). Quilted clothing supplied the warmth that wool might have provided. The richer part of the population used silk. Silk cocoons were raised on mulberry bushes often grown on hillsides which were not suitable for other crops.

Chinese rural households had many labour–intensive activities outside farming. They raised fish in small ponds, used grass and other biomass for fuel. Important "industrial" activities were centred in rural households. Textile spinning and weaving, making garments and leather goods were largely household activities. The same was true of oil and grain milling; drying and preparation of tea leaves; tobacco products; soybean sauce; candles and tung oil; wine and liqueurs; straw, rattan and bamboo products. Manufacture of bricks and tiles, carts and small boats, and construction of rural housing were also significant village activities. Chinese farmers were engaged in a web of commercial activity carried out in rural market areas to which virtually all villages had access. All these non–farm activities appear to have intensified in the Sung dynasty (960–1280). Thereafter some proportionate increase seems plausible because of the growing importance over the long term of cash crops like cotton, sugar, tobacco and tea. In the nineteenth century well over a quarter of GDP came from traditional handicrafts, transport, trade, construction and housing and most of these were carried out in rural areas. It seems likely that their proportionate importance was just as large in 1500 as it was in 1820.

On the basis of Rozman's (1973) rough estimates, it would seem that there were no dramatic changes in the proportion of the urban population (persons living in towns with a population of 10 000 or more) in China between the Tang dynasty and the beginning of the nineteenth century. This is in striking contrast to the situation in Western Europe, and is a significant piece of corroborative evidence of the comparative performance of China and Europe.

Another type of evidence which is very useful is the detailed documentation and chronology of Chinese technology in Needham's *magnum opus* on Chinese science and civilisation. Although it is weak in analysing the economic impact of invention, it is an invaluable help in assessing comparative development in agriculture, metallurgy, textile production, printing, shipbuilding, navigation etc. and in its assessment of Chinese capacity to develop the fundamentals of science.

The big advance in Chinese land productivity, and the more modest advance in living standards came before the period we are examining here. The big shift from wheat and millet farming in North China, to much more intensive wet rice farming south of the Yangtse came in the Sung dynasty (tenth to thirteenth century). The evidence strongly suggests that per capita GDP stagnated for nearly six centuries thereafter although China was able to accommodate a large rise in population through extensive growth.

India

Maddison (1971) contained an analysis of the social structure and institutions of the Moghul Empire and of British India. For the Moghul period, I relied heavily on the economic survey of Abul Fazl, Akbar's vizier, carried out at the end of the sixteenth century (see translation by Jarrett and Sarkar, 1949). I had no firm conclusions on the growth rate from 1500 to 1820, but there was little evidence to suggest that it was a dynamic economy. There is no reason to think that the British takeover had a positive effect on economic growth before the 1850s.

The Cambridge Economic History of India, Vol.1 (Raychaudhuri and Habib, 1982) does not address the growth question very directly, and deals with India by major area, without trying to generalise for the country as a whole. Habib suggests that farm output per head of population may have been higher in 1595 than in 1870, or 1900, and bases this inference on the availability of more cultivatable land per head at the earlier period and apparently greater relative availability of bullocks and buffaloes as draft animals. On the other hand he also stresses the introduction of new crops in the seventeenth and eighteenth centuries. He is more upbeat about manufacturing: "The expansion of the domestic and foreign markets, and the rising public expenditure on urban developments, public monuments and the army suggest an upward trend in output and possibly labour productivity." (p. 305)

Shireen Moosvi (1987, p. 400) assumes that rural per capita consumption was about the same in 1601 as in 1901, but that urban income was bigger at the earlier date. She therefore assumes an aggregate per capita consumption level 5 per cent higher at the first date. Moreland (1920, p. 274) using the same sort of evidence as Habib and Moosvi, but with less intensive scrutiny, concluded that India was almost certainly not richer at the death of Akbar than in 1910–14, "and probably that she was a little poorer".

My own judgement is that Indian per capita income fell from 1700 to the 1850s due to the collapse of the Moghul Empire and the costs of adjusting to the British regime of governance (see analysis in Chapter 2).

Japan

There are no previous estimates of the long term macroeconomic performance of Japan before the Meiji Restoration of 1868. However, one can get some idea of what happened by comparing Japanese and Chinese experience.

In the seventh century, Japan tried to model its economy, society, religion, literature and institutions on those of China. Admiration for things Chinese continued until the eighteenth century, even though Japan was not integrated into the Chinese international order (with two brief exceptions) as a tributary state. However, Japan never created a meritocratic bureaucracy but let the effective governance of the country fall into the hands of a hereditary and substantially decentralized military elite. The institutional history of Japan from the tenth to the fifteenth century therefore had a closer resemblance to that of feudal Europe than to that of China.

Japan copied the institutions of Tang China in the seventh century, creating a national capital at Nara, on the model of China's Chang–an. It also adopted Chinese style Buddhism, and allowed its religious orders to acquire very substantial properties and economic influence. It adopted Chinese ideograms, the kanji script, Chinese literary style, Chinese clothing fashions, the Chinese calendar, methods of measuring age and hours. There was already a substantial similarity in the cropping mix and food consumption, with a prevalence of rice agriculture, and much smaller consumption of meat and meat products than in Europe. There was greater land scarcity in Japan and China than in Europe or India, so the agriculture of both countries was very labour–intensive.

Although Japanese emperors continued to be nominal heads of state, governance fell into the hands of a hereditary aristocracy. From 1195 to 1868, the effective head of state was a military overlord known as the *shogun*.

From the seventh to the ninth century, the central government controlled land allocation in imitation of Tang China, but ownership gradually devolved on a rural military elite. The *shoen* was a complex and fragmented feudal system. Many layers of proprietors claimed a share of the surplus from a servile peasantry.

Technological progress and its diffusion were facilitated in China by its bureaucracy to a degree which was not possible in Japan, which had no educated secular elite. Knowledge of printing was available almost as early as in China, but there was little printed matter except for Buddhist tallies and talismans. The Chinese, by comparison, used printed handbooks of best–practice farming to disseminate the methods of multicropping, irrigation and use of quick ripening seeds which the Sung dynasty imported from Vietnam. The degree of urbanisation was smaller in Japan than in China. The division of Japan into particularistic and competing feudal jurisdictions meant that farming and irrigation tended to develop defensively on hillsides. The manorial system also inhibited agricultural specialisation and development of cash crops.

Whilst the Chinese had switched from hemp to cotton clothing in the fourteenth century, the change did not come in Japan until the seventeenth. Until the seventeenth century, Japanese production of silk was small, and consumption depended on imports from China. Shipping and mining technology remained inferior to that in China until the seventeenth century. Rural by–employments were slower to develop than in China.

The old regime collapsed in Japan after a century of civil war (*sengoku*) which started in 1467. The capital city, Kyoto, was destroyed early in these conflicts, with the population reduced from 400 000 to 40 000 by 1500. A new type of regime emerged from the wreckage, with a new type of military elite.

Tokugawa Ieyasu established his shogunal dynasty in 1603, after serving two successive military dictators, Nobunaga (1573–82) and Hideyoshi (1582–98) who had developed some of the techniques of governance which Ieyasu adopted (notably the demilitarisation of rural areas, the *kokudaka* system of fiscal levies based initially on a cadastral survey, the reduction in ecclesiastical properties, and the practice of keeping *daimyo* wives and children as hostages).

The Tokugawa shogun controlled a quarter of the land area directly. The imperial household and aristocracy in Kyoto had only 0.5 per cent of the fiscal revenue, the Shinto and Buddhist temple authorities shared 1.5 per cent. A third was assigned to smaller *daimyo* who were under tight control. The rest was allocated to bigger more autonomous (*tozama*) *daimyo* in rather distant areas who were already feudal lords before the establishment of the Tokugawa regime. These were potential rivals of the shogunate and eventually rebelled in the 1860s. But the shogun in fact held unchallenged hegemonial power after 1615 when he killed Hideyoshi's family and destroyed his castle in Osaka. The Tokugawa shoguns neutered potential *daimyo* opposition by keeping their families hostage, and their incomes precarious (between 1601 and 1705, "some 200 *daimyo* had been destroyed; 172 had been newly created; 200 had received increases in holdings; and 280 had their domains transferred" — Hall, 1991 (pp. 150–1). The shogun's magistrates directly administered the biggest cities (Edo, Kyoto, Osaka and some others), operated as the emperor's delegate, controlled foreign relations and the revenue from gold and silver mines.

The Tokugawa shogunate was not ideal for economic growth or resource allocation but it exercised a more favourable influence than the Kamakura (1192–1338) and Ashikaga (1338–1573) shogunates which preceded it. It initiated a successful process of catch–up and forging ahead. Between 1600 and 1868 Japanese per capita income probably rose by about 40 per cent, moving from a level below China, to a significantly higher position, in spite of the heavy burden of supporting a large and functionally redundant elite.

The Tokugawa established a system of checks and balances between the leading members of the military elite (*daimyo*) who had survived the civil war. It ensured internal peace on a lasting basis. Rural areas were completely demilitarised by Hideyoshi's 1588 sword hunt and the Tokugawa government's gradual suppression of the production and use of Western type firearms which the Portuguese had introduced in 1543.

The *daimyo* and their military vassals (the *samurai*) were compelled to live in a single castle town in each domain, and abandon their previous managerial role in agriculture. As compensation they received stipends in kind (rice), which was supplied by the peasantry in their domain. *Daimyo* had no fixed property rights in land and could not buy or sell it. The shogun could move *daimyo* from one part of the country to another, confiscate, truncate or augment their rice stipends in view of their behaviour (or intentions as determined by shogunal surveillance and espionage). *Daimyo* were also required to spend part of the year in the new capital Edo (present day Tokyo), and to keep their families there permanently as hostages for good behaviour. *Daimyo* were not required to remit revenue on a regular basis to the shogunal authority, though they had to meet the very heavy costs of their compulsory (*sankin kotai*) residence in Edo and respond to ad hoc demands for funds for constructing Edo and rebuilding it after earthquake damage.

This system of goverment was very expensive compared with that of China. The shogunal, *daimyo* and samurai households were about 6.5 per cent of the Japanese population, compared with 2 per cent for the bureaucracy, military and gentry in China. Fiscal levies accounted for 20–25 per cent of Japanese GDP compared with about 5 per cent in China, though the Chinese gentry had rental incomes and the Chinese bureaucracy had a substantial income from non–fiscal exactions. The Tokugawa did, however, achieve some savings by a very substantial reduction in Buddhist income and properties. They also made an ideological shift away from religion towards neo–confucianism. In both respects they were replicating changes which occurred in China in the ninth century.

The economic consequences of these political changes were important for all parts of the economy.

Growth of Farm Output in the Tokugawa Period

The farm population were no longer servile households subjected to arbitrary claims to support feudal notables and military. Rice levies were large but more or less fixed and fell proportionately over time as agriculture expanded. The ending of local warfare meant that it was safer to develop agricultural land in open plains. There was greater scope for land reclamation and increases in area under cultivation. This was particularly true in the previously underdeveloped Kanto plain surrounding the new capital Edo.

Printed handbooks of best practice agriculture started to appear on Chinese lines. *Nogyo Zensho* (Encyclopaedia of Farming, 1697) was the earliest commercial publication, and by the early eighteenth century there were hundreds of such books (see Robertson, 1984). Quick ripening seeds and double cropping were introduced. There was increased use of commercial fertiliser (soybean meal, seaweed etc.), and improvement in tools for threshing. There was a major expansion of commercial crops — cotton, tobacco, oil seeds, sugar (in South Kyushu and the Ryuku islands), and a very substantial increase in silkworm cultivation. Large scale land reclamation was initiated in the 1720s — partly financed by merchants.

Some idea of the progress of agricultural production in Tokugawa Japan can be derived from the *kokudaka* cadastral surveys initiated by Hideyoshi between 1582 and 1590. They assessed the productive capacity of land in terms of *koku* of rice equivalent (i.e. enough to provide subsistence for one person for a year). The *koku* as a volumetric measure equivalent to 5.1 US bushels or to 150 kilograms in terms of weight. This *kokudaka* assessment was the basis on which the shogun allocated income to *daimyo*. The smallest *daimyo* were allocated 10 000 *koku*, the biggest got much larger allocations (over a million *koku* in the Kaga domain at Kanazawa on the Japan Sea coast, 770 000 for the Satsuma domain in Southern Kyushu). In 1598, the total was estimated to be 18.5 million. The official estimate increased over time, as the cultivated area increased, but there were substantial and varying degrees of mismeasurement of the aggregate. Craig (1961, p. 11) gives examples of the difference between nominal and actual productive capacity for the late Tokugawa period; the actual yield for the 9 domains he specifies was one third higher than the official assessment. Nakamura (1968) made an estimate of cereal production for 1600 to 1872 which was adjusted to eliminate these variations in coverage of the official statistics. Table B–17 shows that cereal output per capita increased by 18 per cent from 1600 to 1820, and probably by a quarter over the Tokugawa period as a whole. In 1874, rice and other cereals were 72 per cent of the value of gross farm output, other traditional products 10.7 per cent, and relatively new crops (cotton, sugar, tobacco, oil seeds, silk cocoons and potatoes) 17.2 per cent. Most of the latter were absent in 1600 and most of these escaped taxation, so their production grew faster than cereals. If one assumes that these other items were about 5 per cent of output in 1600, this would imply a growth of total farm output per capita of about a quarter from 1600 to 1820, and over 40 per cent for the Tokugawa period as a whole. For the period before 1600 there is no real quantitative evidence, but it seems likely that there was little growth in agricultural output per head in the sixteenth century which was so severely plagued by civil war.

Table B–17. **Japanese Cereal Production and Per Capita Availability, 1600–1874**

| | Cereal Production | | Population | Per Capita Availability |
	(000 koku)	(000 metric tons)	(000)	(kg)
1600	19 731	2 960	18 500	160
1700	30 630	4 565	27 000	169
1820	39 017	5 853	31 000	189
1872	46 812	7 022	34 859	201
1874	49 189	7 378	35 235	209

Source: First column for 1600–1872 from Hayami and Miyamoto (1988), p. 44; with 1820 derived by interpolation of their figures for 1800 and 1850. Their estimates were derived from Satoru Nakamura (1968), pp. 169–171. 1874 cereal production from Ohkawa, Shinohara and Umemura (1966), volume 9, *Agriculture and Forestry*, p. 166, with an upward adjustment of rice output by 1 927 *koku* — see Yamada and Hayami (1979), p. 233. In 1874, adjusted cereal output represented 72 per cent of the value of gross agricultural output at 1874–6 prices, other traditional crops 10.8 per cent, and other crops 17.2 per cent (see vol. 9, p. 148). The latter group consisted of industrial crops, potatoes and sericulture, most of which were unimportant in 1600. It seems highly likely therefore that per capita farm output rose more rapidly than cereal output. Col. 2, *koku* (150 kg.) converted into metric tons. Col. 3 is my estimate of population from Table B–7. Col. 4 equals col. 2 divided by col. 3. The standard production measure in Tokugawa Japan was in terms of husked rice, whereas in China the standard unit was unhusked rice. Perkins (1969) assumed a per capita availability of 250 kg. of unhusked rice for China in the period shown here. Using Perkins' (1969, p. 305) coefficient, this meant a per capita availability of 167 kg. of husked rice — higher than Japan in 1600, but lower from 1700 onwards. In 1872, Japan had net imports of rice which raised per capita availability to 219 kg, and in 1874 to 231 kg.

http://dx.doi.org/10.1787/675115301353

Performance in the Non–Farm Sector

Most analysts of the Tokugawa period (Smith, 1969; Hanley and Yamamura, 1977; Yasuba, 1987) stress the growing importance of industrial and commercial by–employments in rural areas.

Smith (1969) produced the classic analysis of rural non–farm activity, drawing on a 1843 survey of 15 districts of the Choshu domain. Komonoseki county had a population of 6501 families in a region at the extreme south of Honshu, with a big coastline projecting into the inland sea between Kyushu and Shikoku — an area particularly advantageous for trade with other parts of Japan. 82 per cent of the population were farmers, but 55 per cent of net income originated outside agriculture. The arithmetic average of Smith's district ratios suggests that industry produced nearly 28 per cent of family income. I am skeptical of the representativity of the Kaminoseki sample. If it were typical of all rural areas, and urban areas had a proportionately greater commitment to non–agriculture, one could expect over 30 per cent of late Tokugawa GDP to have been derived from industry.

Nishikawa (1987) presents a much more sophisticated and comprehensive account of the Choshu economy in the 1840s. Using the same survey material he constructed a set of aggregate input–output accounts. His analysis covers 107 000 households (520 000 population) including both rural and urban areas, i.e. a sample 16 times bigger than Smith's. His approach is in the national accounting tradition with careful consistency checks, merging of different data sources to estimate the labour force, gross output and value added by economic sector. On a value added basis, manufacturing (including handicrafts) accounts for 18.8 per cent of his aggregate. However, he points out that the survey data were seriously deficient for output. His aggregate therefore excludes *daimyo–samurai* military and civil government services, the activity of monks, nuns, priests and servants, urban services "concentrated in `entertainment' such as inns, restaurants, teahouses, brothels, streetwalking, hair–dressing, massage and so forth". There is no imputation for residential accommodation. The construction sector is also omitted. If we augment Nishikawa's aggregate by a quarter to include the omitted items and bring it to a GDP basis, the structure of value added in Choshu in the 1840s would have been 53 per cent for agriculture, forestry and fisheries, 15 per cent for manufacturing, 32 per cent for the rest (including services and construction). Other very interesting features of the Nishikawa accounts are estimates of Choshu's transactions with other parts of Japan and demonstration of the physiocratic bias in the Tokugawa fiscal regime. 97 per cent of tax revenue consisted of levies on agriculture, 3 per cent was derived from levies on non agriculture. Apart from his structural analysis, Nishikawa also ventures an estimate of the rate of growth of per capita Choshu income between the 1760s and the 1840s of 0.4 per cent a year. However, this is based entirely on land survey estimates for fiscal purposes.

In 1500, less than 3 per cent of Japanese lived in towns of 10 000 population and over. By 1800 more than 12 per cent lived in such cities. Edo which had been a village became a city of a million inhabitants. There were more than two hundred castle towns, half of whose population were *samurai*. Kanazawa and Nagoya were the biggest with a population over 100 000. The old capital, Kyoto, had half a million (being the seat of the Emperor and his court and the centre of a prosperous agricultural area). Osaka became a large commercial metropolis, similar in size to Kyoto. This four–fold increase in the urban proportion contrasted with a stable and much lower ratio in China. Japan had a smaller proportion of small towns than China, because concentration of samurai in one single castle town per domain was accompanied by compulsory destruction of scattered smaller fortified settlements. There was also a decline in the size of Osaka in the eighteenth century as commercial activity increased in smaller towns and rural areas.

The urban centres created a market for the surrounding agricultural areas. They also created a demand for servants, entertainment and theatres. Merchants ceased to be mere quartermasters for the military, and acted as commodity brokers, bankers and money–lenders. They were active in promoting significant expansion of coastal trade and shipping in the inland sea (see Crawcour, 1963). Thus there was clearly a substantial increase in many types of service activity per head of population in Tokugawa Japan. However, the biggest service industry was that of the *samurai* and *daimyo* who supplied an exaggeratedly large amount of military and civil governance. The evidence suggests that they remained a stable proportion of the population throughout the Tokugawa epoch. Yamamura's (1974) study suggests there was not much change in their household real incomes, and Smith's work on the falling incidence of fiscal levies in agriculture helps to reinforce this latter conclusion.

There was a very substantial increase in levels of education in Tokugawa Japan, and an emphasis on secular neo–confucian values rather than Buddhism. This improved the level of popular culture and knowledge of technology. There was a huge increase in book production and circulation of woodblock prints. Between the eighth century and the beginning of the seventeenth fewer than 100 illustrated books appeared in Japan but by the eighteenth there were large editions of books with polychrome illustrations and 40 per cent literacy of the male population.

In 1639, the Jesuits and the Portuguese traders were expelled from Japan, Christianity was suppressed and contact with Europeans was restricted to the small Dutch trading settlement in the South of Japan, near Nagasaki. This was done because the Portuguese were intrusive and thought to be a political threat. The Togugawa were aware of the Spanish takeover in the Philippines and wanted to avoid this in Japan. The Dutch were only interested in commerce, but in the course of their long stay in Japan, their East India Company appointed three very distinguished doctors in Deshima (Engelbert Kaempfer, 1690–2, an adventurous German savant and scientist; C.P. Thunberg, 1775–6, a distinguished Swedish botanist; and Franz Philipp von Siebold, 1823–9 and 1859–62, a German physician and naturalist). These scholars wrote books which were important sources of Western knowledge about Japan, but they also had a significant impact in transmitting European science and technology to Japan.

The Japanese had depended on Chinese books for knowledge of the West (Chinese translations of works by Matteo Ricci and other Jesuits in Peking), but in 1720 the shogun, Yoshimune, lifted the ban on European books. An important turning point occurred in 1771 when two Japanese doctors observed the dissection of a corpse and compared the body parts (lungs, kidneys and intestines) with those described in a Chinese book and a Dutch anatomy text. The Dutch text corresponded to what they found, and the Chinese text was inaccurate (see Keene, 1969). As a result translations of Dutch learning (rangaku) became an important cultural influence. Although they were limited in quantity, they helped destroy Japanese respect for "things Chinese", and accentuate curiosity about "things Western".

Japanese exposure to Western knowledge was more limited than Chinese, but its impact went much deeper. The old tradition was easier to reject in Japan as it was foreign. However, contacts with foreigners and foreign ideas were often frowned upon by the authorities. Von Siebold was expelled from Japan in 1829, and a Japanese friend was executed for giving him copies of Ino Tadataka's magnificent survey maps for the Kuriles and Kamchatka. Nevertheless, the Dutch window into the Western world was important and influential in preparing the ground intellectually for the Meiji Restoration of 1868. Dutch learning (painfully acquired) was the major vehicle of enlightenment for Japan's greatest Westerniser, Yukichi Fukuzawa (1832–1901), whose books sold millions of copies, and who founded Keio University on Western lines.

Although the Tokugawa regime had a positive impact on Japanese growth, it had certain drawbacks.

It involved the maintenance of a large elite whose effective military potential was very feeble in meeting the challenges which came in the nineteenth century, and whose life style involved extremely lavish expenditure. The Meiji regime was able to capture substantial resources for economic development and military modernisation by dismantling these Tokugawa arrangements.

The system of hereditary privilege and big status differentials with virtually no meritocratic element, meant a large waste of potential talent. The frustrations involved are clearly illustrated in Fukuzawa's autobiography. The Tokugawa system was inefficient in its reliance on a clumsy collection of fiscal revenue in kind and overdetailed surveillance of economic activity. It also imposed restrictions on the diffusion of technology. One example of this was the ban on wheeled vehicles on Japanese roads and the virtual absence of bridges. These restrictions were imposed for security reasons, but made journeys very costly and time consuming. There were also restrictions on the size of boats which inhibited coastal shipping, foreign trade, and naval preparedness. There were restrictions on property rights (buying and selling of land), arbitrary levies by the shogun, cancellation of *daimyo* debts, or defaults by samurai which inhibited private enterprise.

All of these, plus increasing pressures on Japan from Russia, England and the United States, eventually led to the breakdown of the Tokugawa system.

Aggregate Japanese Performance

There has been a good deal of research on the economic history of the Tokugawa period, but hitherto no aggregative quantification of performance except at a regional level. Most of the postwar revisionist historians (Akira Hayami, Yasuba, Nishikawa, Hall, Smith, Hanley and Yamamura) agree (in contrast to earlier Marxists) that there was substantial economic advance.

Levels of income were probably depressed in 1500 as a result of civil war but there may have been a modest increase in Japanese per capita income in the sixteenth century. For 1600–1820, there are indicators of substantial increase in performance in several sectors of the economy. For farming as a whole (including new crops — cotton, sugar, tobacco, oil seeds, silk cocoons and potatoes), gross output per head of population rose by about a quarter (see Table B–17 and accompanying text), and value added by somewhat less. In the early Tokugawa period, agriculture probably represented well over half of GDP.

There is substantial evidence of an expansion in the importance of rural household activity, and the large increase in the size of the urban population led to an increase in commercial activity and urban services. There were substantial improvements in education, and a large increase in book production. It seems likely that all these activities rose faster than agriculture.

An offset to these elements of dynamism was the high cost of the Tokugawa system of governance. The elite of samurai, *daimyo* and the shogunate absorbed nearly a quarter of GDP. Their official function was to provide administrative and military services. But the way this fossilised elite functioned was extremely wasteful and put inreasing strain on the economy. The apparatus of government was a system of checks and balances — an armed truce whose original rationale had been to end the civil wars which lasted from the mid–fifteenth to the mid–sixteenth century.

My overall assessment (see Table B–21) is that from 1500 to 1820 Japanese GDP per capita rose by a third. This was enough to raise its level above that of China and most of the rest of Asia.

Other Asia

Other Asia is a miscellaneous conglomerate of countries with about 12.5 per cent of Asia's population and about 12 per cent of GDP in 1820. For most of them, there is not much hard evidence for assessing their GDP performance from 1500 to 1820.

Indonesia is the largest of these countries. The estimates in Tables 2–21c and 2–22 show that most of the modest rise in per capita income from 1700 to 1820 accrued to European and Chinese trading interests. Boomgaard (1993) pp. 208–210 came to a similar conclusion for 1500–1835. He found that the "Dutch and Chinese introduced new technologies, organisational skills and capital, which strengthened the non–agricultural sectors, and led to the introduction of some cash crops (coffee and sugar). However, they also pushed the Javanese out of the more rewarding economic activities and increased the burden of taxation and corvee levies".

Korea was the second biggest of the "other Asia" countries. Until the 1870s, it was a hermit kingdom with only exiguous contact with the outside world except China. Its social organisation and technology were very close to the Chinese model, and there is reason to suppose that its economic performance was similar to that of China, i.e. stagnant per capita income at a level above the Asian norm. The major disturbances to Korean development because of the Mongol and Japanese invasions happened before 1500.

The Indochinese states were also Chinese tributaries. They were more open to foreign trade than Korea, but there do not seem to be grounds for supposing that per capita income changed much in the period under consideration.

In 1500, the Ottoman Empire had control over a large part of Western Asia and the Balkans. In 1517 it took control of Syria and Egypt and suzerainty of Arabia. The Empire had widespread trading interests in Asia. By the eighteenth century, it had entered a long period of decline, and its trading interests in Asia had been taken over by Europeans. Although estimates of per capita income are not available, there is enough evidence (see Inalcik (1994) and Faroqui *et al.*, 1994) to suggest that it was lower in 1820 than in 1500. In Iran; the second biggest country in West Asia, it also seems very unlikely that per capita income in 1820 was as high as in the heyday of the Safavid dynasty in the sixteenth and seventeenth centuries.

Africa

I assumed that African per capita income did not change from 1500 to 1700.

GDP AND GDP PER CAPITA FROM FIRST CENTURY TO 1000 A.D.

Before 1500, the element of conjecture in the estimates is very large indeed. The derivation of per capita GDP levels for China and Europe are explained in Maddison (1998a), and the conjectures for other areas are explained below. In all cases GDP is derived by multiplying the per capita levels by the independently estimated levels of population.

Maddison (1998a) contained estimates of Chinese economic performance from the first century onwards. The evidence suggested that per capita GDP in the first century (in the Han dynasty) was above subsistence levels — about $450 in our numeraire (1990 international dollars), but did not change significantly until the end of the 10th century.

During the Sung dynasty (960 — 1280) Chinese per capita income increased significantly, by about a third, and population growth accelerated. The main reason for this advance was a major transformation in agriculture. Until the Sung dynasty, large parts of South China had been relatively underdeveloped. Primitive slash and burn agriculture and moving cultivation had been practiced, but the climate and accessibility of water gave great potential for intensive rice cultivation. The Sung rulers developed this potential by introducing quick ripening strains of rice imported from Indochina. They exploited new opportunities to diffuse knowledge of agricultural technology by printing handbooks of best practice in farming. As a result there was a major switch in the centre of gravity, with a substantial rise in the proportion of people in rice growing south of the Yangtse, and a sharp drop in the proportionate importance of the dry farming area (millet and wheat) of North China. Increased density of settlement in the South gave a boost to internal trade, a rise in the proportion of farm output which was marketed, productivity gains from increased specialisation of agricultural production in response to higher living standards. The introduction of paper money facilitated the growth of commerce, and raised the proportion of state income in cash from negligible proportions to more than half.

For most of the rest of Asia, it seemed reasonable here to assume that the level of per capita income was similar to that in China and showed no great change from the first century to the year 1000. The $450 level of per capita income assumed here is sufficiently above subsistence to maintain the governing elite in some degree of luxury and to sustain a relatively elaborate system of governance. Japan was a rather special case. In the first century, it was a subsistence economy in course of transition to agriculture from hunting and gathering, and from wooden to metal tools. By the year 1000, it had made some progress but lagged well behind China.

In Maddison (1998a), pp. 25, 37–38, it was assumed that European per capita income levels in the first century were similar to those in China. Goldsmith (1984) provided a comprehensive assessment of economic performance for the Roman Empire as a whole, and also provided a temporal link, suggesting that Roman levels were about two fifths of Gregory King's estimate of English income for 1688.

The West Asian and North African parts of the Roman Empire were at least as prosperous and urbanised as the European component, which warrants the assumption of similar levels of income there.

Between the first century and the year 1000, there was a collapse in living standards in Western Europe. Urbanisation ratios provide the strongest evidence that the year 1000 was a nadir. The urban ratio of Roman Europe was around 5 per cent in the first century. This compares with zero in the year 1000, when there were only 4 towns with more than 10 000 population (see Maddison, 1998a, p. 35). The urban collapse and other signs of decline warrant the assumption of a relapse more or less to subsistence levels ($400 per capita) in the year 1000.

For the Americas, Australasia, Africa south of the Sahara, Eastern Europe and the area of the former USSR, I have assumed that more or less subsistence levels of income ($400 per capita) prevailed from the first century to the end of the first millennium.

ISBN 92-64-02261-9 – © OECD 2006

Table B-18. **World GDP, 20 Countries and Regional Totals, 0–1998 A.D.**
(million 1990 international $)

Year	0	1000	1500	1600	1700	1820	1870	1913	1950	1973	1998
Austria			1 414	2 093	2 483	4 104	8 419	23 451	25 702	85 227	152 712
Belgium			1 225	1 561	2 288	4 529	13 746	32 347	47 190	118 516	198 249
Denmark			443	569	727	1 471	3 782	11 670	29 654	70 032	117 319
Finland			136	215	255	913	1 999	6 389	17 051	51 724	94 421
France			10 912	15 559	21 180	38 434	72 100	144 489	220 492	683 965	1 150 080
Germany			8 112	12 432	13 410	26 349	71 429	237 332	265 354	944 755	1 460 069
Italy			11 550	14 410	14 630	22 535	41 814	95 487	164 957	582 713	1 022 776
Netherlands			716	2 052	4 009	4 288	9 952	24 955	60 642	175 791	317 517
Norway			192	304	450	1 071	2 485	6 119	17 838	44 544	104 860
Sweden			382	626	1 231	3 098	6 927	17 403	47 269	109 794	165 385
Switzerland			482	880	1 253	2 342	5 867	16 483	42 545	117 251	152 345
United Kingdom			2 815	6 007	10 709	36 232	100 179	224 618	347 850	675 941	1 108 568
12 Countries Total			*38 379*	*56 708*	*72 625*	*145 366*	*338 699*	*840 743*	*1 286 544*	*3 660 253*	*6 044 301*
Portugal			632	850	1 708	3 175	4 338	7 467	17 615	63 397	128 877
Spain			4 744	7 416	7 893	12 975	22 295	45 686	66 792	304 220	560 138
Other			590	981	1 169	2 206	4 891	12 478	30 600	105 910	227 300
Total Western Europe	**11 115**	**10 165**	**44 345**	**65 955**	**83 395**	**163 722**	**370 223**	**906 374**	**1 401 551**	**4 133 780**	**6 960 616**
Eastern Europe	**1 900**	**2 600**	**6 237**	**8 743**	**10 647**	**23 149**	**45 448**	**121 559**	**185 023**	**550 757**	**660 861**
Former USSR	**1 560**	**2 840**	**8 475**	**11 447**	**16 222**	**37 710**	**83 646**	**232 351**	**510 243**	**1 513 070**	**1 132 434**
United States			800	600	527	12 548	98 374	517 383	1 455 916	3 536 622	7 394 598
Other Western Offshoots			320	320	300	941	13 781	68 249	179 574	521 667	1 061 537
Total Western Offshoots	**468**	**784**	**1 120**	**920**	**827**	**13 489**	**112 155**	**585 632**	**1 635 490**	**4 058 289**	**8 456 135**
Mexico			3 188	1 134	2 558	5 000	6 214	25 921	67 368	279 302	655 910
Other Latin America			4 100	2 623	3 813	9 120	21 683	95 760	356 188	1 118 398	2 285 700
Total Latin America	**2 240**	**4 560**	**7 288**	**3 757**	**6 371**	**14 120**	**27 897**	**121 681**	**423 556**	**1 397 700**	**2 941 610**
Japan	**1 200**	**3 188**	**7 700**	**9 620**	**15 390**	**20 739**	**25 393**	**71 653**	**160 966**	**1 242 932**	**2 581 576**
China	26 820	26 550	61 800	96 000	82 800	228 600	189 740	241 344	239 903	740 048	3 873 352
India	33 750	33 750	60 500	74 250	90 750	111 417	134 882	204 241	222 222	494 832	1 702 712
Other Asia	16 470	18 630	31 301	36 725	40 567	50 486	72 173	146 999	362 578	1 398 587	4 376 931
Total Asia (excluding Japan)	**77 040**	**78 930**	**153 601**	**206 975**	**214 117**	**390 503**	**396 795**	**592 584**	**824 703**	**2 633 467**	**9 952 995**
Africa	**7 013**	**13 723**	**18 400**	**22 000**	**24 400**	**31 010**	**40 172**	**72 948**	**194 569**	**529 185**	**1 039 408**
World	**102 536**	**116 790**	**247 116**	**329 417**	**371 369**	**694 442**	**1 101 369**	**2 704 782**	**5 336 101**	**16 059 180**	**33 725 635**

http://dx.doi.org/10.1787/675115301353

Table B–19. **Rates of Growth of World GDP, 20 Countries and Regional Totals, 0–1998 A.D.**
(annual average compound growth rates)

Year	0–1000	1000–1500	1500–1820	1820–70	1870–1913	1913–50	1950–73	1973–98
Austria			0.33	1.45	2.41	0.25	5.35	2.36
Belgium			0.41	2.25	2.01	1.03	4.08	2.08
Denmark			0.38	1.91	2.66	2.55	3.81	2.09
Finland			0.60	1.58	2.74	2.69	4.94	2.44
France			0.39	1.27	1.63	1.15	5.05	2.10
Germany			0.37	2.01	2.83	0.30	5.68	1.76
Italy			0.21	1.24	1.94	1.49	5.64	2.28
Netherlands			0.56	1.70	2.16	2.43	4.74	2.39
Norway			0.54	1.70	2.12	2.93	4.06	3.48
Sweden			0.66	1.62	2.17	2.74	3.73	1.65
Switzerland			0.50	1.85	2.43	2.60	4.51	1.05
United Kingdom			0.80	2.05	1.90	1.19	2.93	2.00
12 Countries Total			*0.42*	*1.71*	*2.14*	*1.16*	*4.65*	*2.03*
Portugal			0.51	0.63	1.27	2.35	5.73	2.88
Spain			0.31	1.09	1.68	1.03	6.81	2.47
Other			0.41	1.61	2.20	2.45	5.55	3.10
Total Western Europe	**−0.01**	**0.30**	**0.41**	**1.65**	**2.10**	**1.19**	**4.81**	**2.11**
Eastern Europe	**0.03**	**0.18**	**0.41**	**1.36**	**2.31**	**1.14**	**4.86**	**0.73**
Former USSR	**0.06**	**0.22**	**0.47**	**1.61**	**2.40**	**2.15**	**4.84**	**−1.15**
United States			0.86	4.20	3.94	2.84	3.93	2.99
Other Western Offshoots			0.34	5.51	3.79	2.65	4.75	2.88
Total Western Offshoots	**0.05**	**0.07**	**0.78**	**4.33**	**3.92**	**2.81**	**4.03**	**2.98**
Mexico			0.14	0.44	3.38	2.62	6.38	3.47
Other Latin America			0.25	1.75	3.51	3.61	5.10	2.90
Total Latin America	**0.07**	**0.09**	**0.21**	**1.37**	**3.48**	**3.43**	**5.33**	**3.02**
Japan	**0.10**	**0.18**	**0.31**	**0.41**	**2.44**	**2.21**	**9.29**	**2.97**
China	0.00	0.17	0.41	−0.37	0.56	−0.02	5.02	6.84
India	0.00	0.12	0.19	0.38	0.97	0.23	3.54	5.07
Other Asia	0.01	0.10	0.15	0.72	1.67	2.47	6.05	4.67
Total Asia (excluding Japan)	**0.00**	**0.13**	**0.29**	**0.03**	**0.94**	**0.90**	**5.18**	**5.46**
Africa	**0.07**	**0.06**	**0.16**	**0.52**	**1.40**	**2.69**	**4.45**	**2.74**
World	**0.01**	**0.15**	**0.32**	**0.93**	**2.11**	**1.85**	**4.91**	**3.01**

http://dx.doi.org/10.1787/675115301353

ISBN 92-64-02261-9 – © OECD 2006

Table B–20. **Shares of World GDP, 20 Countries and Regional Totals, 0–1998 A.D.**
(per cent of world total)

Year	0	1000	1500	1600	1700	1820	1870	1913	1950	1973	1998
Austria			0.6	0.6	0.7	0.6	0.8	0.9	0.5	0.5	0.5
Belgium			0.5	0.5	0.6	0.7	1.2	1.2	0.9	0.7	0.6
Denmark			0.2	0.2	0.2	0.2	0.3	0.4	0.6	0.4	0.3
Finland			0.1	0.1	0.1	0.1	0.2	0.2	0.3	0.3	0.3
France			4.4	4.7	5.7	5.5	6.5	5.3	4.1	4.3	3.4
Germany			3.3	3.8	3.6	3.8	6.5	8.8	5.0	5.9	4.3
Italy			4.7	4.4	3.9	3.2	3.8	3.5	3.1	3.6	3.0
Netherlands			0.3	0.6	1.1	0.6	0.9	0.9	1.1	1.1	0.9
Norway			0.1	0.1	0.1	0.2	0.2	0.2	0.3	0.3	0.3
Sweden			0.2	0.2	0.3	0.4	0.6	0.6	0.9	0.7	0.5
Switzerland			0.2	0.3	0.3	0.3	0.5	0.6	0.8	0.7	0.5
United Kingdom			1.1	1.8	2.9	5.2	9.1	8.3	6.5	4.2	3.3
12 Countries Total			*15.5*	*17.2*	*19.5*	*20.9*	*30.7*	*31.1*	*24.1*	*22.8*	*17.9*
Portugal			0.3	0.3	0.5	0.5	0.4	0.3	0.3	0.4	0.4
Spain			1.9	2.1	2.2	1.9	2.0	1.7	1.3	1.9	1.7
Other			0.2	0.3	0.3	0.3	0.4	0.5	0.6	0.7	0.7
Total Western Europe	10.8	8.7	17.9	19.9	22.5	23.6	33.6	33.5	26.3	25.7	20.6
Eastern Europe	1.9	2.2	2.5	2.7	2.9	3.3	4.1	4.5	3.5	3.4	2.0
Former USSR	1.5	2.4	3.4	3.5	4.4	5.4	7.6	8.6	9.6	9.4	3.4
United States			0.3	0.2	0.1	1.8	8.9	19.1	27.3	22.0	21.9
Other Western Offshoots			0.1	0.1	0.1	0.1	1.3	2.5	3.4	3.2	3.1
Total Western Offshoots	0.5	0.7	0.5	0.3	0.2	1.9	10.2	21.7	30.6	25.3	25.1
Mexico			1.3	0.3	0.7	0.7	0.6	1.0	1.3	1.7	1.9
Other Latin America			1.7	0.8	1.0	1.3	2.0	3.5	6.7	7.0	6.8
Total Latin America	2.2	3.9	2.9	1.1	1.7	2.0	2.5	4.5	7.9	8.7	8.7
Japan	1.2	2.7	3.1	2.9	4.1	3.0	2.3	2.6	3.0	7.7	7.7
China	26.2	22.7	25.0	29.2	22.3	32.9	17.2	8.9	4.5	4.6	11.5
India	32.9	28.9	24.5	22.6	24.4	16.0	12.2	7.6	4.2	3.1	5.0
Other Asia	16.1	16.0	12.7	11.2	10.9	7.3	6.6	5.4	6.8	8.7	13.0
Total Asia (excluding Japan)	75.1	67.6	62.1	62.9	57.6	56.2	36.0	21.9	15.5	16.4	29.5
Africa	6.8	11.8	7.4	6.7	6.6	4.5	3.6	2.7	3.6	3.3	3.1
World	100.0	100.0	100.0	100.0	100.0	100.0	100.0	100.0	100.0	100.0	100.0

http://dx.doi.org/10.1787/675115301353

Table B–21. World GDP per Capita, 20 Countries and Regional Averages, 0–1998 A.D.
(1990 international $)

Year	0	1000	1500	1600	1700	1820	1870	1913	1950	1973	1998
Austria			707	837	993	1 218	1 863	3 465	3 706	11 235	18 905
Belgium			875	976	1 144	1 319	2 697	4 220	5 462	12 170	19 442
Denmark			738	875	1 039	1 274	2 003	3 912	6 946	13 945	22 123
Finland			453	538	638	781	1 140	2 111	4 253	11 085	18 324
France			727	841	986	1 230	1 876	3 485	5 270	13 123	19 558
Germany			676	777	894	1 058	1 821	3 648	3 881	11 966	17 799
Italy			1 100	1 100	1 100	1 117	1 499	2 564	3 502	10 643	17 759
Netherlands			754	1 368	2 110	1 821	2 753	4 049	5 996	13 082	20 224
Norway			640	760	900	1 104	1 432	2 501	5 463	11 246	23 660
Sweden			695	824	977	1 198	1 664	3 096	6 738	13 493	18 685
Switzerland			742	880	1 044	1 280	2 202	4 266	9 064	18 204	21 367
United Kingdom			714	974	1 250	1 707	3 191	4 921	6 907	12 022	18 714
12 Countries Total			*796*	*906*	*1 056*	*1 270*	*2 086*	*3 688*	*5 013*	*12 159*	*18 742*
Portugal			632	773	854	963	997	1 244	2 069	7 343	12 929
Spain			698	900	900	1 063	1 376	2 255	2 397	8 739	14 227
Other			462	528	617	743	1 066	1 840	2 536	7 614	13 732
Total Western Europe	450	400	774	894	1 024	1 232	1 974	3 473	4 594	11 534	17 921
Eastern Europe	400	400	462	516	566	636	871	1 527	2 120	4 985	5 461
Former USSR	400	400	500	553	611	689	943	1 488	2 834	6 058	3 893
United States			400	400	527	1 257	2 445	5 301	9 561	16 689	27 331
Other Western Offshoots			400	400	400	753	2 339	4 947	7 538	13 364	20 082
Total Western Offshoots	400	400	400	400	473	1 201	2 431	5 257	9 288	16 172	26 146
Mexico			425	454	568	759	674	1 732	2 365	4 845	6 655
Other Latin America			410	430	505	623	705	1 461	2 593	4 459	5 588
Total Latin America	400	400	416	437	529	665	698	1 511	2 554	4 531	5 795
Japan	400	425	500	520	570	669	737	1 387	1 926	11 439	20 413
China	450	450	600	600	600	600	530	552	439	839	3 117
India	450	450	550	550	550	533	533	673	619	853	1 746
Other Asia	450	450	565	565	565	565	603	794	924	2 065	3 734
Total Asia (excluding Japan)	450	450	572	575	571	575	543	640	635	1 231	2 936
Africa	425	416	400	400	400	418	444	585	852	1 365	1 368
World	444	435	565	593	615	667	867	1 510	2 114	4 104	5 709

http://dx.doi.org/10.1787/675115301353

Table B–22. **Rates of Growth of World GDP per Capita, 20 Countries and Regional Totals, 0–1998 A.D.**
(annual average compound growth rates)

Year	0–1000	1000–1500	1500–1820	1820–70	1870–1913	1913–50	1950–73	1973–98
Austria			0.17	0.85	1.45	0.18	4.94	2.10
Belgium			0.13	1.44	1.05	0.70	3.55	1.89
Denmark			0.17	0.91	1.57	1.56	3.08	1.86
Finland			0.17	0.76	1.44	1.91	4.25	2.03
France			0.16	0.85	1.45	1.12	4.05	1.61
Germany			0.14	1.09	1.63	0.17	5.02	1.60
Italy			0.00	0.59	1.26	0.85	4.95	2.07
Netherlands			0.28	0.83	0.90	1.07	3.45	1.76
Norway			0.17	0.52	1.30	2.13	3.19	3.02
Sweden			0.17	0.66	1.46	2.12	3.07	1.31
Switzerland			0.17	1.09	1.55	2.06	3.08	0.64
United Kingdom			0.27	1.26	1.01	0.92	2.44	1.79
12 Countries Total			*0.15*	*1.00*	*1.33*	*0.83*	*3.93*	*1.75*
Portugal			0.13	0.07	0.52	1.39	5.66	2.29
Spain			0.13	0.52	1.15	0.17	5.79	1.97
Other			0.15	0.72	1.28	0.87	4.90	2.39
Total Western Europe	**−0.01**	**0.13**	**0.15**	**0.95**	**1.32**	**0.76**	**4.08**	**1.78**
Eastern Europe	**0.00**	**0.03**	**0.10**	**0.63**	**1.31**	**0.89**	**3.79**	**0.37**
Former USSR	**0.00**	**0.04**	**0.10**	**0.63**	**1.06**	**1.76**	**3.36**	**−1.75**
United States			0.36	1.34	1.82	1.61	2.45	1.99
Other Western Offshoots			0.20	2.29	1.76	1.14	2.52	1.64
Total Western Offshoots	**0.00**	**0.00**	**0.34**	**1.42**	**1.81**	**1.55**	**2.44**	**1.94**
Mexico			0.18	−0.24	2.22	0.85	3.17	1.28
Other Latin America			0.13	0.25	1.71	1.56	2.38	0.91
Total Latin America	**0.00**	**0.01**	**0.15**	**0.10**	**1.81**	**1.43**	**2.52**	**0.99**
Japan	**0.01**	**0.03**	**0.09**	**0.19**	**1.48**	**0.89**	**8.05**	**2.34**
China		0.06	0.00	−0.25	0.10	−0.62	2.86	5.39
India		0.04	−0.01	0.00	0.54	−0.22	1.40	2.91
Other Asia		0.05	0.00	0.13	0.64	0.41	3.56	2.40
Total Asia (excluding Japan)	**0.00**	**0.05**	**0.00**	**−0.11**	**0.38**	**−0.02**	**2.92**	**3.54**
Africa	**0.00**	**−0.01**	**0.01**	**0.12**	**0.64**	**1.02**	**2.07**	**0.01**
World	**0.00**	**0.05**	**0.05**	**0.53**	**1.30**	**0.91**	**2.93**	**1.33**

http://dx.doi.org/10.1787/675115301353

Appendix C

Annual Estimates of Population, GDP and GDP Per Capita for 124 Countries, 7 Regions and the World, 1950–98

This appendix contains annual estimates of population; and levels of GDP and GDP per capita in 1990 international dollars for 1950–98. Annual estimates are given for 124 individual countries, as well as regional, subregional, and world totals. The sources are given in Appendix A.

Annual estimates for population and GDP movement in earlier years can be found in Maddison (1995a) for 46 countries. They have not been included here for lack of space. See Maddison (1995a), Appendix A (pp. 104–107) for annual estimates of population for 12 West European Countries, Western Offshoots and Japan for 1870–1949; pp. 108–109 for five South European Countries, 1900–49; pp. 110–111 for seven East European Countries 1920–89; pp. 112–113 for seven Latin American Countries 1900–49; pp. 114–115 for ten Asian Countries 1900–49. Annual real GDP indices for the same countries and same years are shown (as far as they are available) on pages 148–159 in Appendix B. These GDP indices are generally compatible with the present estimates for 1950 onwards and can be used to backcast the 1950 levels shown here in Tables C–1b, C–2b and C–3b. Revised annual estimates for 1900–50 for India are shown in Table A–h, and for Japan 1870–1950 in Table A–j of the present work.

Table C1–a. Population of European Countries, Annual Estimates, 1950–98
(000 at mid–year)

Year	Austria	Belgium	Denmark	Finland	France	Germany	Italy	Netherlands
1950	6 935	8 640	4 269	4 009	41 836	68 371	47 105	10 114
1951	6 936	8 679	4 304	4 047	42 156	68 863	47 418	10 264
1952	6 928	8 731	4 334	4 091	42 460	69 193	47 666	10 382
1953	6 933	8 778	4 369	4 139	42 752	69 621	47 957	10 494
1954	6 940	8 820	4 406	4 187	43 057	69 937	48 299	10 616
1955	6 947	8 869	4 439	4 235	43 428	70 310	48 633	10 751
1956	6 952	8 924	4 466	4 282	43 843	70 743	48 921	10 888
1957	6 966	8 989	4 488	4 324	44 311	71 134	49 182	11 026
1958	6 987	9 053	4 515	4 360	44 789	71 554	49 476	11 187
1959	7 014	9 104	4 587	4 395	45 240	72 024	49 832	11 348
1960	7 048	9 118	4 581	4 430	45 684	72 674	50 200	11 483
1961	7 087	9 166	4 612	4 461	46 163	73 310	50 536	11 637
1962	7 130	9 218	4 647	4 491	46 998	73 939	50 879	11 801
1963	7 175	9 283	4 684	4 523	47 816	74 544	51 252	11 964
1964	7 224	9 367	4 720	4 549	48 310	74 963	51 675	12 125
1965	7 271	9 488	4 757	4 564	48 758	75 647	52 112	12 293
1966	7 322	9 508	4 797	4 581	49 164	76 214	52 519	12 455
1967	7 377	9 557	4 839	4 606	49 548	76 368	52 901	12 597
1968	7 415	9 590	4 867	4 626	49 915	76 584	53 236	12 726
1969	7 441	9 613	4 893	4 624	50 315	77 143	53 538	12 873
1970	7 467	9 638	4 929	4 606	50 772	77 709	53 822	13 032
1971	7 501	9 673	4 963	4 612	51 251	78 345	54 073	13 194
1972	7 544	9 709	4 992	4 640	51 701	78 715	54 381	13 330
1973	7 586	9 738	5 022	4 666	52 118	78 956	54 751	13 438
1974	7 599	9 768	5 045	4 691	52 460	78 979	55 111	13 543
1975	7 579	9 795	5 060	4 712	52 699	78 679	55 441	13 660
1976	7 566	9 811	5 073	4 726	52 909	78 317	55 718	13 773
1977	7 568	9 822	5 088	4 739	53 145	78 165	55 955	13 856
1978	7 562	9 830	5 104	4 753	53 376	78 082	56 155	13 939
1979	7 549	9 837	5 117	4 765	53 606	78 104	56 318	14 034
1980	7 549	9 847	5 123	4 780	53 880	78 303	56 434	14 148
1981	7 569	9 854	5 122	4 800	54 182	78 418	56 510	14 247
1982	7 576	9 862	5 118	4 827	54 492	78 335	56 579	14 312
1983	7 567	9 867	5 114	4 856	54 772	78 122	56 626	14 368
1984	7 571	9 871	5 112	4 882	55 026	77 846	56 652	14 423
1985	7 578	9 879	5 114	4 902	55 284	77 668	56 674	14 488
1986	7 588	9 888	5 121	4 918	55 547	77 690	56 675	14 567
1987	7 598	9 901	5 127	4 932	55 824	77 718	56 674	14 664
1988	7 615	9 908	5 130	4 946	56 118	78 115	56 629	14 760
1989	7 659	9 941	5 131	4 964	56 423	78 677	56 672	14 846
1990	7 729	9 971	5 138	4 986	56 735	79 364	56 719	14 947
1991	7 813	10 008	5 150	5 014	57 055	79 984	56 751	15 068
1992	7 914	10 051	5 166	5 042	57 374	80 595	56 859	15 182
1993	7 991	10 088	5 185	5 066	57 654	81 180	57 049	15 290
1994	8 030	10 119	5 201	5 089	57 900	81 422	57 204	15 381
1995	8 047	10 137	5 222	5 108	58 138	81 661	57 301	15 460
1996	8 059	10 157	5 256	5 125	58 372	81 896	57 397	15 523
1997	8 072	10 182	5 280	5 140	58 604	82 053	57 512	15 605
1998	8 078	10 197	5 303	5 153	58 805	82 029	57 592	15 700

http://dx.doi.org/10.1787/667827525313

Table C1–a. **Population of European Countries, Annual Estimates, 1950–98**
(000 at mid–year)

Year	Norway	Sweden	Switzerland	United Kingdom	Average 12 WEC*	Ireland	Greece
1950	3 265	7 015	4 694	50 363	256 616	2 969	7 566
1951	3 296	7 071	4 749	50 574	258 357	2 961	7 659
1952	3 328	7 125	4 815	50 737	259 790	2 953	7 733
1953	3 362	7 171	4 877	50 880	261 333	2 949	7 817
1954	3 395	7 213	4 929	51 066	262 865	2 941	7 893
1955	3 429	7 262	4 980	51 221	264 504	2 921	7 966
1956	3 462	7 315	5 045	51 430	266 271	2 898	8 031
1957	3 494	7 367	5 126	51 657	268 064	2 885	8 096
1958	3 525	7 415	5 199	51 870	269 930	2 853	8 173
1959	3 556	7 454	5 259	52 157	271 970	2 846	8 258
1960	3 585	7 480	5 362	52 373	274 018	2 834	8 327
1961	3 615	7 520	5 512	52 807	276 426	2 819	8 398
1962	3 639	7 562	5 666	53 292	279 262	2 830	8 448
1963	3 667	7 604	5 789	53 625	281 926	2 850	8 480
1964	3 694	7 662	5 887	53 991	284 167	2 864	8 510
1965	3 723	7 734	5 943	54 350	286 640	2 876	8 551
1966	3 753	7 807	5 996	54 643	288 759	2 884	8 614
1967	3 785	7 869	6 063	54 959	290 469	2 900	8 716
1968	3 819	7 912	6 132	55 214	292 036	2 913	8 741
1969	3 851	7 968	6 212	55 461	293 932	2 926	8 773
1970	3 879	8 043	6 267	55 632	295 796	2 950	8 793
1971	3 903	8 098	6 343	55 928	297 884	2 978	8 831
1972	3 933	8 122	6 401	56 097	299 565	3 024	8 889
1973	3 961	8 137	6 441	56 223	301 037	3 073	8 929
1974	3 985	8 160	6 460	56 236	302 037	3 124	8 962
1975	4 007	8 192	6 404	56 226	302 454	3 177	9 046
1976	4 026	8 222	6 333	56 216	302 690	3 228	9 167
1977	4 043	8 251	6 316	56 190	303 138	3 272	9 309
1978	4 060	8 275	6 333	56 178	303 647	3 314	9 430
1979	4 073	8 294	6 351	56 240	304 288	3 368	9 548
1980	4 086	8 311	6 385	56 330	305 176	3 401	9 643
1981	4 100	8 320	6 429	56 352	305 903	3 443	9 729
1982	4 115	8 325	6 467	56 318	306 326	3 480	9 790
1983	4 128	8 329	6 482	56 377	306 608	3 505	9 847
1984	4 140	8 337	6 505	56 506	306 871	3 529	9 896
1985	4 153	8 350	6 534	56 685	307 309	3 541	9 934
1986	4 167	8 370	6 573	56 852	307 956	3 542	9 967
1987	4 187	8 398	6 619	57 009	308 651	3 543	10 001
1988	4 209	8 436	6 671	57 158	309 695	3 531	10 037
1989	4 227	8 493	6 723	57 358	311 114	3 510	10 090
1990	4 241	8 566	6 796	57 561	312 753	3 506	10 161
1991	4 262	8 617	6 873	57 808	314 403	3 526	10 247
1992	4 286	8 668	6 943	58 006	316 086	3 549	10 322
1993	4 312	8 719	6 989	58 191	317 714	3 563	10 379
1994	4 337	8 781	7 037	58 395	318 896	3 583	10 426
1995	4 358	8 827	7 081	58 606	319 946	3 601	10 454
1996	4 381	8 841	7 105	58 801	320 913	3 626	10 476
1997	4 405	8 846	7 113	59 009	321 821	3 661	10 499
1998	4 432	8 851	7 130	59 237	322 507	3 705	10 511

*   WEC = Western European Countries.

http://dx.doi.org/10.1787/667827525313

Table C1–a. **Population of European Countries, Annual Estimates, 1950–98**
(000 at mid–year)

Year	Portugal	Spain	Total 16 WEC	Total 13 small WEC	Total 29 WEC	Total Eastern Europe	Total former USSR	Total EE and former USSR
1950	8 512	27 868	303 531	1 529	305 060	87 288	180 050	267 338
1951	8 547	28 086	305 610	1 544	307 154	88 374	183 200	271 574
1952	8 563	28 332	307 371	1 559	308 930	89 487	186 400	275 887
1953	8 587	28 571	309 257	1 574	310 831	90 770	189 500	280 270
1954	8 607	28 812	311 118	1 591	312 709	92 045	192 700	284 745
1955	8 657	29 056	313 104	1 600	314 704	93 439	196 150	289 589
1956	8 698	29 355	315 253	1 613	316 866	94 721	199 650	294 371
1957	8 737	29 657	317 439	1 636	319 075	95 801	203 150	298 951
1958	8 789	29 962	319 707	1 661	321 368	96 919	206 700	303 619
1959	8 837	30 271	322 182	1 682	323 864	98 003	210 450	308 453
1960	8 891	30 583	324 653	1 701	326 354	99 056	214 350	313 406
1961	8 944	30 904	327 491	1 717	329 208	100 112	218 150	318 262
1962	9 002	31 158	330 700	1 729	332 429	101 010	221 750	322 760
1963	9 040	31 430	333 726	1 747	335 473	101 914	225 100	327 014
1964	9 053	31 741	336 335	1 759	338 094	102 783	228 150	330 933
1965	8 996	32 085	339 148	1 773	340 921	103 610	230 900	334 510
1966	8 871	32 453	341 581	1 787	343 368	104 412	233 500	337 912
1967	8 798	32 850	343 733	1 803	345 536	105 195	236 000	341 195
1968	8 743	33 240	345 673	1 819	347 492	106 264	238 350	344 614
1969	8 696	33 566	347 893	1 837	349 730	107 101	240 600	347 701
1970	8 663	33 876	350 078	1 853	351 931	107 927	242 757	350 684
1971	8 644	34 190	352 527	1 869	354 396	108 782	245 083	353 865
1972	8 631	34 498	354 607	1 883	356 490	109 628	247 459	357 087
1973	8 634	34 810	356 483	1 907	358 390	110 490	249 747	360 237
1974	8 755	35 147	358 025	1 929	359 954	111 461	252 131	363 592
1975	9 094	35 515	359 286	1 915	361 201	112 468	254 469	366 937
1976	9 356	35 937	360 378	1 914	362 292	113 457	256 760	370 217
1977	9 456	36 367	361 542	1 922	363 464	114 442	259 029	373 471
1978	9 559	36 778	362 728	1 939	364 667	115 300	261 253	376 553
1979	9 662	37 108	363 974	1 957	365 931	116 157	263 425	379 582
1980	9 767	37 510	365 497	1 990	367 487	116 921	265 542	382 463
1981	9 851	37 741	366 667	2 009	368 676	117 661	267 722	385 383
1982	9 912	37 944	367 452	2 020	369 472	118 323	270 042	388 365
1983	9 955	38 123	368 038	2 035	370 073	118 926	272 540	391 466
1984	9 989	38 279	368 564	2 049	370 613	119 503	275 066	394 569
1985	10 011	38 420	369 215	2 067	371 282	120 062	277 537	397 599
1986	10 011	38 537	370 013	2 060	372 073	120 574	280 236	400 810
1987	9 994	38 632	370 821	2 082	372 903	121 051	283 100	404 151
1988	9 968	38 717	371 948	2 105	374 053	121 253	285 463	406 716
1989	9 937	38 792	373 443	2 126	375 569	121 650	287 845	409 495
1990	9 899	38 851	375 170	2 154	377 324	121 866	289 350	411 216
1991	9 871	39 920	377 967	2 183	380 150	122 049	291 060	413 109
1992	9 867	39 008	378 832	2 211	381 043	122 070	292 422	414 492
1993	9 880	39 086	380 622	2 240	382 862	121 632	292 417	414 049
1994	9 902	39 150	381 957	2 264	384 221	121 323	292 407	413 730
1995	9 917	39 210	383 128	2 284	385 412	121 126	292 196	413 322
1996	9 927	39 270	384 212	2 302	386 514	120 980	291 660	412 640
1997	9 946	39 323	385 250	2 320	387 570	120 977	291 027	412 004
1998	9 968	39 371	386 062	2 337	388 399	121 006	290 866	411 872

http://dx.doi.org/10.1787/667827525313

Table C1–a. **Population of Western Offshoots, Annual Estimates, 1950–98**
(000 at mid–year)

Year	Australia	New Zealand	Canada	United States	Total 4 Western Offshoots
1950	8 177	1 909	13 737	152 271	176 094
1951	8 418	1 948	14 047	154 878	179 291
1952	8 634	1 996	14 491	157 553	182 674
1953	8 821	2 049	14 882	160 184	185 936
1954	8 996	2 095	15 321	163 026	189 438
1955	9 201	2 139	15 730	165 931	193 001
1956	9 421	2 183	16 123	168 903	196 630
1957	9 640	2 233	16 677	171 984	200 534
1958	9 842	2 286	17 120	174 882	204 130
1959	10 056	2 335	17 522	177 830	207 743
1960	10 275	2 377	17 870	180 671	211 193
1961	10 508	2 427	18 238	183 691	214 864
1962	10 700	2 485	18 583	186 538	218 306
1963	10 907	2 537	18 931	189 242	221 617
1964	11 122	2 589	19 290	191 889	224 890
1965	11 341	2 635	19 644	194 303	227 923
1966	11 599	2 683	20 015	196 560	230 857
1967	11 799	2 728	20 378	198 712	233 617
1968	12 009	2 754	20 701	200 706	236 170
1969	12 263	2 780	21 001	202 677	238 721
1970	12 507	2 820	21 297	205 052	241 676
1971	13 067	2 864	22 026	207 661	245 618
1972	13 304	2 913	22 285	209 896	248 398
1973	13 505	2 971	22 560	211 909	250 945
1974	13 723	3 032	22 865	213 854	253 474
1975	13 893	3 087	23 209	215 973	256 162
1976	14 033	3 116	23 518	218 035	258 702
1977	14 192	3 128	23 796	220 239	261 355
1978	14 359	3 129	24 036	222 585	264 109
1979	14 516	3 138	24 277	225 055	266 986
1980	14 695	3 144	24 593	227 726	270 158
1981	14 923	3 157	24 900	229 966	272 946
1982	15 184	3 183	25 202	232 188	275 757
1983	15 393	3 226	25 456	234 307	278 382
1984	15 579	3 258	25 702	236 348	280 887
1985	15 788	3 272	25 942	238 466	283 468
1986	16 018	3 277	26 204	240 651	286 150
1987	16 264	3 304	26 550	242 804	288 922
1988	16 538	3 318	26 798	245 021	291 675
1989	16 833	3 337	27 286	247 342	294 798
1990	17 085	3 380	27 701	249 984	298 150
1991	17 284	3 488	28 031	252 639	301 442
1992	17 489	3 524	28 377	255 374	304 764
1993	17 657	3 567	28 703	258 083	308 010
1994	17 838	3 617	29 036	260 599	311 090
1995	18 072	3 673	29 354	263 044	314 143
1996	18 311	3 729	29 672	265 463	317 175
1997	18 524	3 771	30 008	268 008	320 311
1998	18 751	3 811	30 297	270 561	323 420

http://dx.doi.org/10.1787/667827525313

Table C1–b. Levels of GDP in European Countries, Annual Estimates, 1950–98
(million 1990 international Geary–Khamis dollars)

	Austria	Belgium	Denmark	Finland	France	Germany	Italy	Netherlands
1950	25 702	47 190	29 654	17 051	220 492	265 354	164 957	60 642
1951	27 460	49 874	29 852	18 501	234 074	289 679	177 272	61 914
1952	27 484	49 486	30 144	19 121	240 287	314 794	190 541	63 162
1953	28 680	51 071	31 859	19 255	247 223	341 150	204 288	68 652
1954	31 611	53 173	32 478	20 941	259 215	366 584	214 884	73 319
1955	35 105	55 696	32 828	22 008	274 098	406 922	227 389	78 759
1956	37 520	57 313	33 225	22 673	287 969	436 086	237 699	81 654
1957	39 818	58 381	35 746	23 739	305 308	461 071	251 732	83 950
1958	41 272	58 316	36 551	23 867	312 966	481 599	265 192	83 701
1959	42 445	60 160	39 270	25 285	321 924	516 821	281 707	87 793
1960	45 939	63 394	40 367	27 598	344 609	558 482	296 981	95 180
1961	48 378	66 478	42 926	29 701	363 754	581 487	321 992	95 455
1962	49 550	69 904	45 295	30 627	387 937	606 292	347 098	101 993
1963	51 567	72 988	45 579	31 636	408 090	623 382	371 822	105 686
1964	54 662	78 128	49 843	33 235	435 296	661 273	386 333	114 446
1965	56 234	80 870	52 117	35 002	456 456	694 798	395 020	120 435
1966	59 399	83 440	53 539	35 843	479 631	715 393	415 639	123 754
1967	61 205	86 695	55 339	36 600	501 799	717 610	445 232	130 267
1968	63 925	90 293	57 613	37 442	523 967	755 463	482 462	138 627
1969	67 945	96 302	61 283	41 048	560 280	805 410	510 051	147 552
1970	72 785	102 265	62 524	44 114	592 389	843 103	521 506	155 955
1971	76 506	106 103	64 191	45 036	621 055	867 917	531 385	162 539
1972	81 256	111 679	67 578	48 473	648 668	903 739	546 933	167 919
1973	85 227	118 516	70 032	51 724	683 965	944 755	582 713	175 791
1974	88 588	123 494	69 379	53 291	704 012	952 571	610 040	182 763
1975	88 267	121 855	68 921	53 905	699 106	947 383	596 946	182 596
1976	92 307	128 743	73 382	53 676	729 326	993 132	635 737	191 194
1977	96 624	129 549	74 573	53 808	756 545	1 021 710	654 108	196 392
1978	96 273	133 231	75 674	54 934	777 544	1 050 404	678 494	201 024
1979	101 525	136 350	78 356	58 756	802 491	1 092 615	716 984	205 501
1980	103 874	142 458	78 010	61 890	813 763	1 105 099	742 299	207 979
1981	103 771	140 680	77 316	63 043	822 116	1 109 276	745 816	206 925
1982	105 750	142 665	79 650	65 090	842 787	1 099 799	749 233	204 517
1983	108 716	142 648	81 656	66 849	852 644	1 119 394	758 360	208 014
1984	109 077	146 180	85 241	68 866	865 172	1 150 951	777 841	214 854
1985	111 525	147 650	88 897	71 184	877 305	1 176 131	799 697	221 470
1986	114 135	149 854	92 135	72 873	898 129	1 202 151	822 404	227 570
1987	116 053	153 392	92 406	75 861	920 822	1 220 284	847 870	230 788
1988	119 730	160 632	93 482	79 581	961 287	1 260 983	880 671	236 824
1989	124 791	166 396	93 728	84 092	1 000 286	1 302 212	906 053	247 906
1990	130 476	171 442	94 863	84 103	1 026 491	1 264 438	925 654	258 094
1991	134 944	174 880	96 184	78 841	1 036 379	1 328 057	938 522	263 950
1992	136 754	177 695	97 413	76 222	1 051 689	1 357 825	945 660	269 298
1993	137 455	175 072	98 232	75 347	1 041 232	1 343 060	937 303	271 347
1994	140 949	180 312	103 884	78 327	1 061 556	1 374 575	957 993	280 094
1995	143 849	185 047	107 713	81 311	1 079 157	1 398 310	986 004	286 416
1996	146 699	186 661	110 778	84 571	1 091 060	1 408 868	994 537	295 118
1997	148 443	192 652	114 250	89 892	1 112 956	1 429 308	1 009 277	306 297
1998	152 712	198 249	117 319	94 421	1 150 080	1 460 069	1 022 776	317 517

http://dx.doi.org/10.1787/667827525313

Table C1–b. **Levels of GDP in European Countries, Annual Estimates, 1950–1998**
(million 1990 international Geary–Khamis dollars)

	Norway	Sweden	Switzerland	United Kingdom	Total 12 WEC	Ireland	Greece
1950	17 838	47 269	42 545	347 850	1 286 544	10 231	14 489
1951	18 665	49 148	45 990	358 234	1 360 663	10 488	15 765
1952	19 332	49 845	46 369	357 585	1 408 150	10 753	15 878
1953	20 225	51 237	48 001	371 646	1 483 287	11 043	18 053
1954	21 229	53 395	50 705	386 789	1 564 323	11 142	18 615
1955	21 639	54 944	54 117	400 850	1 664 355	11 432	20 022
1956	22 771	57 032	57 710	405 825	1 737 477	11 283	21 731
1957	23 432	59 591	60 002	412 315	1 815 085	11 266	23 147
1958	23 218	59 887	58 732	411 450	1 856 751	11 034	24 218
1959	24 411	61 714	62 425	428 107	1 952 062	11 481	25 107
1960	25 813	64 986	66 793	452 768	2 082 910	12 127	26 195
1961	27 377	68 710	72 200	467 694	2 186 152	12 706	28 492
1962	28 159	71 599	75 661	472 454	2 286 569	13 120	29 562
1963	29 254	75 411	79 370	490 625	2 385 410	13 741	32 567
1964	30 662	80 562	83 541	516 584	2 524 565	14 279	35 243
1965	32 305	83 643	86 195	529 996	2 623 071	14 528	38 553
1966	33 556	85 383	88 305	540 163	2 714 045	14 652	40 907
1967	35 690	88 272	91 008	552 277	2 801 994	15 521	43 152
1968	36 498	91 475	94 272	574 775	2 946 812	16 804	46 027
1969	38 140	96 056	99 584	585 207	3 108 858	17 815	50 585
1970	38 902	102 275	105 935	599 016	3 240 769	18 289	54 609
1971	40 683	103 241	110 253	611 705	3 340 614	18 923	58 496
1972	42 785	105 604	113 781	633 352	3 471 767	20 151	65 775
1973	44 544	109 794	117 251	675 941	3 660 253	21 103	68 355
1974	46 858	113 306	118 957	666 755	3 730 014	22 002	65 868
1975	48 811	116 198	110 294	665 984	3 700 266	23 246	69 853
1976	52 135	117 428	108 745	680 933	3 856 738	23 571	74 296
1977	54 002	115 553	111 392	695 699	3 959 955	25 506	76 843
1978	56 453	117 577	111 847	720 501	4 073 956	27 340	81 989
1979	58 894	122 092	114 634	740 370	4 228 568	28 180	85 015
1980	61 811	124 130	119 909	728 224	4 289 446	29 047	86 505
1981	62 406	124 113	121 802	718 733	4 295 997	30 013	86 553
1982	62 514	125 358	120 051	729 861	4 327 275	30 698	86 895
1983	64 729	127 555	120 659	755 779	4 407 003	30 624	87 244
1984	68 530	132 717	124 311	774 665	4 518 405	31 957	89 645
1985	72 105	135 277	128 561	802 000	4 631 802	32 943	92 442
1986	74 687	138 381	130 653	837 280	4 760 252	32 802	93 941
1987	76 203	142 733	131 614	877 143	4 885 169	34 331	93 507
1988	76 117	145 946	135 709	920 841	5 071 803	36 123	97 670
1989	76 818	149 415	141 599	940 908	5 234 204	38 223	101 425
1990	78 333	151 451	146 900	944 610	5 276 855	41 459	101 452
1991	80 774	149 760	145 724	930 493	5 358 508	42 231	104 581
1992	83 413	147 631	145 540	930 975	5 420 115	43 625	105 327
1993	85 694	144 353	144 839	952 554	5 406 488	44 775	103 604
1994	90 400	150 296	145 610	994 384	5 558 380	47 355	105 723
1995	93 879	155 843	146 345	1 022 172	5 686 046	51 855	107 929
1996	98 475	157 523	146 811	1 048 308	5 769 409	55 865	110 474
1997	102 687	160 643	149 273	1 085 122	5 900 800	61 844	114 253
1998	104 860	165 385	152 345	1 108 568	6 044 301	67 368	118 433

http://dx.doi.org/10.1787/667827525313

Table C1–b. **Levels of GDP in European Countries, Annual Estimates, 1950–98**
(million 1990 International Geary–Khamis dollars)

	Portugal	Spain	Total 16 WEC	Total 13 small WEC	Total 29 WEC	Total Eastern Europe	Total former USSR	Total EE and former USSR
1950	17 615	66 792	1 395 671	5 880	1 401 551	185 023	510 243	695 266
1951	18 404	73 874	1 479 194	5 746	1 484 940	195 667	512 566	708 233
1952	18 428	79 676	1 532 885	6 180	1 539 065	198 287	545 792	744 079
1953	19 714	80 589	1 612 686	6 436	1 619 122	209 197	569 260	778 457
1954	20 660	85 204	1 699 944	6 647	1 706 591	218 949	596 910	815 859
1955	21 512	89 635	1 806 956	7 001	1 813 957	233 875	648 027	881 902
1956	22 451	96 077	1 889 019	7 427	1 896 446	239 574	710 065	949 639
1957	23 445	100 188	1 973 131	7 752	1 980 883	257 645	724 470	982 115
1958	23 753	104 666	2 020 422	7 966	2 028 388	272 649	778 840	1 051 489
1959	25 039	102 701	2 116 390	8 279	2 124 669	286 878	770 244	1 057 122
1960	26 711	105 123	2 253 066	8 487	2 261 553	304 633	843 434	1 148 067
1961	28 170	117 549	2 373 069	8 876	2 381 945	322 781	891 763	1 214 544
1962	30 040	128 514	2 487 805	9 269	2 497 074	328 253	915 928	1 244 181
1963	31 823	139 752	2 603 293	9 756	2 613 049	344 112	895 016	1 239 128
1964	33 921	148 387	2 756 395	10 165	2 766 560	364 518	1 010 727	1 375 245
1965	36 446	162 823	2 875 421	10 877	2 886 298	380 016	1 068 117	1 448 133
1966	37 929	179 727	2 987 260	11 398	2 998 658	404 452	1 119 932	1 524 384
1967	40 792	191 468	3 092 927	11 862	3 104 789	420 645	1 169 422	1 590 067
1968	44 421	208 144	3 262 208	12 261	3 274 469	436 444	1 237 966	1 674 410
1969	45 364	231 535	3 454 157	13 144	3 467 301	449 862	1 255 392	1 705 254
1970	49 498	246 976	3 610 141	13 713	3 623 854	465 695	1 351 818	1 817 513
1971	52 781	259 814	3 730 628	14 651	3 745 279	499 790	1 387 832	1 887 622
1972	57 011	281 560	3 896 264	15 548	3 911 812	524 971	1 395 732	1 920 703
1973	63 397	304 220	4 117 328	16 452	4 133 780	550 756	1 513 070	2 063 826
1974	64 122	321 313	4 203 319	16 510	4 219 829	583 528	1 556 984	2 140 512
1975	61 334	323 056	4 177 755	16 005	4 193 760	604 251	1 561 399	2 165 650
1976	65 566	333 729	4 353 900	17 038	4 370 938	619 961	1 634 589	2 254 550
1977	69 239	343 202	4 474 745	18 095	4 492 840	641 681	1 673 159	2 314 840
1978	71 189	348 223	4 602 697	19 058	4 621 755	662 328	1 715 215	2 377 543
1979	75 203	348 367	4 765 333	20 007	4 785 340	672 299	1 707 083	2 379 382
1980	78 655	356 062	4 839 715	20 768	4 860 483	675 819	1 709 174	2 384 993
1981	79 928	355 615	4 848 106	21 257	4 869 363	667 932	1 724 741	2 392 673
1982	81 634	361 106	4 887 608	21 886	4 909 494	674 202	1 767 262	2 441 464
1983	81 492	368 180	4 974 543	22 385	4 996 928	684 326	1 823 723	2 508 049
1984	79 961	374 444	5 094 412	23 512	5 117 924	705 274	1 847 190	2 552 464
1985	82 206	380 795	5 220 188	24 313	5 244 501	706 201	1 863 687	2 569 888
1986	85 610	392 978	5 365 583	25 556	5 391 139	725 733	1 940 363	2 666 096
1987	91 073	415 150	5 519 230	26 754	5 545 984	721 188	1 965 457	2 686 645
1988	97 894	436 576	5 740 066	28 385	5 768 451	727 564	2 007 280	2 734 844
1989	102 922	457 262	5 934 036	30 000	5 964 036	718 039	2 037 253	2 755 292
1990	107 427	474 366	6 001 559	31 205	6 032 764	662 604	1 987 995	2 650 599
1991	110 047	485 126	6 100 493	32 342	6 132 835	590 231	1 863 524	2 453 755
1992	112 134	488 459	6 169 660	33 161	6 202 821	559 157	1 592 085	2 151 242
1993	110 593	482 776	6 148 236	34 633	6 182 869	550 466	1 435 008	1 985 474
1994	113 328	493 643	6 318 429	35 838	6 354 267	572 173	1 235 701	1 807 874
1995	116 640	507 054	6 469 524	36 899	6 506 423	605 352	1 169 446	1 774 798
1996	120 357	518 920	6 575 025	38 136	6 613 161	628 154	1 137 039	1 765 193
1997	124 529	538 824	6 740 250	39 918	6 780 168	646 234	1 156 028	1 802 262
1998	128 877	560 138	6 919 117	41 499	6 960 616	660 861	1 132 434	1 793 295

http://dx.doi.org/10.1787/667827525313

ISBN 92-64-02261-9 – © OECD 2006

Table C1–b. **Levels of GDP in Western Offshoots, Annual Estimates, 1950–98**
(million 1990 international Geary–Khamis dollars)

	Australia	New Zealand	Canada	United States	Total 4 Western Offshoots
1950	61 274	16 136	102 164	1 455 916	1 635 490
1951	63 892	14 904	107 960	1 566 784	1 753 540
1952	64 470	15 552	115 816	1 625 245	1 821 083
1953	66 481	16 084	121 228	1 699 970	1 903 763
1954	70 614	18 298	120 390	1 688 804	1 898 106
1955	74 471	18 639	131 633	1 808 126	2 032 869
1956	77 034	19 605	142 282	1 843 455	2 082 376
1957	78 577	20 165	146 402	1 878 063	2 123 207
1958	82 351	20 957	149 021	1 859 088	2 111 417
1959	87 421	22 449	155 062	1 997 061	2 261 993
1960	91 085	22 449	159 880	2 046 727	2 320 141
1961	91 713	23 704	164 598	2 094 396	2 374 411
1962	97 444	24 215	176 130	2 220 732	2 518 521
1963	103 413	25 749	185 041	2 316 765	2 630 968
1964	110 488	27 004	197 098	2 450 915	2 785 505
1965	116 131	28 724	210 203	2 607 294	2 962 352
1966	119 363	30 536	223 832	2 778 086	3 151 817
1967	127 422	29 142	230 647	2 847 549	3 234 760
1968	134 913	29 095	242 703	2 983 081	3 389 792
1969	143 118	32 099	255 497	3 076 517	3 507 231
1970	152 220	31 644	262 098	3 081 900	3 527 862
1971	158 992	33 285	276 694	3 178 106	3 647 077
1972	163 453	34 711	291 314	3 346 554	3 836 032
1973	172 314	37 177	312 176	3 536 622	4 058 289
1974	176 586	39 390	324 928	3 526 724	4 067 628
1975	181 367	38 937	332 269	3 516 825	4 069 398
1976	188 678	39 887	350 467	3 701 163	4 280 195
1977	190 653	37 944	362 245	3 868 829	4 459 671
1978	196 184	38 097	376 894	4 089 548	4 700 723
1979	206 515	38 874	392 561	4 228 647	4 866 597
1980	210 642	39 141	397 814	4 230 558	4 878 155
1981	218 780	41 041	410 164	4 336 141	5 006 126
1982	218 512	41 809	397 671	4 254 870	4 912 862
1983	218 539	42 955	409 246	4 433 129	5 103 869
1984	233 618	45 072	432 711	4 755 958	5 467 359
1985	245 444	45 420	456 107	4 940 383	5 687 354
1986	250 539	46 372	468 055	5 110 480	5 875 446
1987	262 925	46 564	487 138	5 290 129	6 086 756
1988	274 737	46 435	510 815	5 512 845	6 344 832
1989	286 820	46 850	523 177	5 703 521	6 560 368
1990	291 180	46 729	524 475	5 803 200	6 665 584
1991	288 661	45 908	514 459	5 790 784	6 639 812
1992	296 225	46 304	519 148	5 983 457	6 845 134
1993	307 489	48 654	531 096	6 124 987	7 012 226
1994	322 819	51 554	556 209	6 371 321	7 301 903
1995	336 990	53 599	571 447	6 544 370	7 506 406
1996	350 394	55 331	581 118	6 784 105	7 770 948
1997	363 903	56 455	604 180	7 089 655	8 114 193
1998	382 335	56 322	622 880	7 394 598	8 456 135

http://dx.doi.org/10.1787/667827525313

Table C1–c. Levels of Per Capita GDP in European Countries, Annual Estimates, 1950–98

(1990 international Geary–Khamis dollars)

	Austria	Belgium	Denmark	Finland	France	Germany	Italy	Netherlands
1950	3 706	5 462	6 946	4 253	5 270	3 881	3 502	5 996
1951	3 959	5 747	6 936	4 572	5 553	4 207	3 738	6 032
1952	3 967	5 668	6 955	4 674	5 659	4 550	3 997	6 084
1953	4 137	5 818	7 292	4 652	5 783	4 900	4 260	6 542
1954	4 555	6 029	7 371	5 001	6 020	5 242	4 449	6 906
1955	5 053	6 280	7 395	5 197	6 312	5 788	4 676	7 326
1956	5 397	6 422	7 440	5 295	6 568	6 164	4 859	7 499
1957	5 716	6 495	7 965	5 490	6 890	6 482	5 118	7 614
1958	5 907	6 442	8 095	5 474	6 988	6 731	5 360	7 482
1959	6 051	6 608	8 561	5 753	7 116	7 176	5 653	7 736
1960	6 518	6 953	8 812	6 230	7 543	7 685	5 916	8 289
1961	6 826	7 253	9 307	6 658	7 880	7 932	6 372	8 203
1962	6 950	7 583	9 747	6 820	8 254	8 200	6 822	8 643
1963	7 187	7 863	9 731	6 994	8 535	8 363	7 255	8 834
1964	7 567	8 341	10 560	7 306	9 010	8 821	7 476	9 439
1965	7 734	8 523	10 956	7 669	9 362	9 185	7 580	9 797
1966	8 112	8 776	11 161	7 824	9 756	9 387	7 914	9 936
1967	8 297	9 071	11 436	7 946	10 128	9 397	8 416	10 341
1968	8 621	9 415	11 837	8 094	10 497	9 865	9 063	10 893
1969	9 131	10 018	12 525	8 877	11 135	10 440	9 527	11 462
1970	9 748	10 611	12 685	9 578	11 668	10 849	9 689	11 967
1971	10 199	10 969	12 934	9 765	12 118	11 078	9 827	12 319
1972	10 771	11 503	13 537	10 447	12 547	11 481	10 057	12 597
1973	11 235	12 170	13 945	11 085	13 123	11 966	10 643	13 082
1974	11 658	12 643	13 752	11 360	13 420	12 061	11 069	13 495
1975	11 646	12 441	13 621	11 440	13 266	12 041	10 767	13 367
1976	12 200	13 122	14 465	11 358	13 785	12 681	11 410	13 882
1977	12 767	13 190	14 657	11 354	14 235	13 071	11 690	14 174
1978	12 731	13 554	14 826	11 558	14 567	13 453	12 083	14 422
1979	13 449	13 861	15 313	12 331	14 970	13 989	12 731	14 643
1980	13 760	14 467	15 227	12 948	15 103	14 113	13 153	14 700
1981	13 710	14 276	15 095	13 134	15 173	14 146	13 198	14 524
1982	13 959	14 466	15 563	13 485	15 466	14 040	13 242	14 290
1983	14 367	14 457	15 967	13 766	15 567	14 329	13 392	14 478
1984	14 407	14 809	16 675	14 106	15 723	14 785	13 730	14 897
1985	14 717	14 946	17 383	14 521	15 869	15 143	14 110	15 286
1986	15 042	15 155	17 992	14 818	16 169	15 474	14 511	15 622
1987	15 274	15 493	18 023	15 381	16 495	15 701	14 960	15 738
1988	15 723	16 212	18 223	16 090	17 130	16 143	15 552	16 045
1989	16 293	16 738	18 267	16 940	17 728	16 551	15 988	16 699
1990	16 881	17 194	18 463	16 868	18 093	15 932	16 320	17 267
1991	17 272	17 474	18 677	15 724	18 165	16 604	16 538	17 517
1992	17 280	17 679	18 857	15 117	18 330	16 848	16 632	17 738
1993	17 201	17 354	18 945	14 873	18 060	16 544	16 430	17 747
1994	17 553	17 819	19 974	15 391	18 334	16 882	16 747	18 210
1995	17 876	18 255	20 627	15 918	18 562	17 123	17 207	18 526
1996	18 203	18 378	21 076	16 502	18 691	17 203	17 327	19 012
1997	18 390	18 921	21 638	17 489	18 991	17 419	17 549	19 628
1998	18 905	19 442	22 123	18 324	19 558	17 799	17 759	20 224

http://dx.doi.org/10.1787/667827525313

ISBN 92-64-02261-9 – © OECD 2006

Table C1–c. **Levels of Per Capita GDP in European Countries, Annual Estimates, 1950–98**
(1990 international Geary–Khamis dollars)

	Norway	Sweden	Switzerland	United Kingdom	Total 12 WEC	Ireland	Greece
1950	5 463	6 738	9 064	6 907	5 013	3 446	1 915
1951	5 663	6 951	9 684	7 083	5 267	3 542	2 058
1952	5 809	6 996	9 630	7 048	5 420	3 641	2 053
1953	6 016	7 145	9 842	7 304	5 676	3 745	2 309
1954	6 253	7 403	10 287	7 574	5 951	3 789	2 358
1955	6 311	7 566	10 867	7 826	6 292	3 914	2 513
1956	6 577	7 797	11 439	7 891	6 525	3 893	2 706
1957	6 706	8 089	11 705	7 982	6 771	3 905	2 859
1958	6 587	8 076	11 297	7 932	6 879	3 868	2 963
1959	6 865	8 279	11 870	8 208	7 177	4 034	3 040
1960	7 200	8 688	12 457	8 645	7 601	4 279	3 146
1961	7 573	9 137	13 099	8 857	7 909	4 507	3 393
1962	7 738	9 468	13 354	8 865	8 188	4 636	3 499
1963	7 978	9 917	13 710	9 149	8 461	4 821	3 840
1964	8 300	10 514	14 191	9 568	8 884	4 986	4 141
1965	8 677	10 815	14 504	9 752	9 151	5 051	4 509
1966	8 941	10 937	14 727	9 885	9 399	5 080	4 749
1967	9 429	11 218	15 010	10 049	9 646	5 352	4 951
1968	9 557	11 562	15 374	10 410	10 091	5 769	5 266
1969	9 904	12 055	16 031	10 552	10 577	6 089	5 766
1970	10 029	12 716	16 904	10 767	10 956	6 200	6 211
1971	10 424	12 749	17 382	10 937	11 214	6 354	6 624
1972	10 878	13 002	17 776	11 290	11 589	6 664	7 400
1973	11 246	13 493	18 204	12 022	12 159	6 867	7 655
1974	11 759	13 886	18 414	11 856	12 350	7 043	7 350
1975	12 181	14 184	17 223	11 845	12 234	7 317	7 722
1976	12 950	14 282	17 171	12 113	12 742	7 302	8 105
1977	13 357	14 005	17 636	12 381	13 063	7 795	8 255
1978	13 905	14 209	17 661	12 825	13 417	8 250	8 694
1979	14 460	14 721	18 050	13 164	13 897	8 367	8 904
1980	15 128	14 936	18 780	12 928	14 056	8 541	8 971
1981	15 221	14 917	18 946	12 754	14 044	8 717	8 896
1982	15 192	15 058	18 564	12 960	14 126	8 821	8 876
1983	15 680	15 315	18 614	13 406	14 373	8 737	8 860
1984	16 553	15 919	19 110	13 709	14 724	9 056	9 059
1985	17 362	16 201	19 676	14 148	15 072	9 303	9 306
1986	17 923	16 533	19 877	14 727	15 458	9 261	9 425
1987	18 200	16 996	19 884	15 386	15 827	9 690	9 350
1988	18 084	17 300	20 343	16 110	16 377	10 230	9 731
1989	18 173	17 593	21 062	16 404	16 824	10 890	10 052
1990	18 470	17 680	21 616	16 411	16 872	11 825	9 984
1991	18 952	17 380	21 202	16 096	17 043	11 977	10 206
1992	19 462	17 032	20 962	16 050	17 148	12 292	10 204
1993	19 873	16 556	20 724	16 369	17 017	12 567	9 982
1994	20 844	17 116	20 692	17 029	17 430	13 217	10 140
1995	21 542	17 655	20 667	17 441	17 772	14 400	10 324
1996	22 478	17 817	20 663	17 828	17 978	15 407	10 545
1997	23 311	18 160	20 986	18 389	18 336	16 893	10 882
1998	23 660	18 685	21 367	18 714	18 742	18 183	11 268

http://dx.doi.org/10.1787/667827525313

Table C1-c. Levels of Per Capita GDP in European Countries, Annual Estimates, 1950–98
(million 1990 international Geary–Khamis dollars)

	Portugal	Spain	Total 16 WEC	Total 13 small WEC	Total 29 WEC	Total Eastern Europe	Total former USSR	Average EE and former USSR
1950	2 069	2 397	4 598	3 846	4 594	2 120	2 834	2 601
1951	2 153	2 630	4 840	3 722	4 835	2 214	2 798	2 608
1952	2 152	2 812	4 987	3 964	4 982	2 216	2 928	2 697
1953	2 296	2 821	5 215	4 089	5 209	2 305	3 004	2 778
1954	2 400	2 957	5 464	4 178	5 457	2 379	3 098	2 865
1955	2 485	3 085	5 771	4 376	5 764	2 503	3 304	3 045
1956	2 581	3 273	5 992	4 604	5 985	2 529	3 557	3 226
1957	2 683	3 378	6 216	4 738	6 208	2 689	3 566	3 285
1958	2 703	3 493	6 320	4 796	6 312	2 813	3 768	3 463
1959	2 833	3 393	6 569	4 922	6 560	2 927	3 660	3 427
1960	3 004	3 437	6 940	4 989	6 930	3 075	3 935	3 663
1961	3 150	3 804	7 246	5 169	7 235	3 224	4 088	3 816
1962	3 337	4 125	7 523	5 361	7 512	3 250	4 130	3 855
1963	3 520	4 446	7 801	5 584	7 789	3 376	3 976	3 789
1964	3 747	4 675	8 195	5 779	8 183	3 546	4 430	4 156
1965	4 051	5 075	8 478	6 135	8 466	3 668	4 626	4 329
1966	4 276	5 538	8 745	6 378	8 733	3 874	4 796	4 511
1967	4 637	5 829	8 998	6 579	8 985	3 999	4 955	4 660
1968	5 081	6 262	9 437	6 741	9 423	4 107	5 194	4 859
1969	5 217	6 898	9 929	7 155	9 914	4 200	5 218	4 904
1970	5 714	7 291	10 312	7 400	10 297	4 315	5 569	5 183
1971	6 106	7 599	10 583	7 839	10 568	4 594	5 663	5 334
1972	6 605	8 162	10 988	8 257	10 973	4 789	5 640	5 379
1973	7 343	8 739	11 550	8 627	11 534	4 985	6 058	5 729
1974	7 324	9 142	11 740	8 559	11 723	5 235	6 175	5 887
1975	6 744	9 096	11 628	8 358	11 611	5 373	6 136	5 902
1976	7 008	9 287	12 081	8 902	12 065	5 464	6 366	6 090
1977	7 322	9 437	12 377	9 415	12 361	5 607	6 459	6 198
1978	7 447	9 468	12 689	9 829	12 674	5 744	6 565	6 314
1979	7 783	9 388	13 093	10 223	13 077	5 788	6 480	6 268
1980	8 053	9 492	13 241	10 436	13 226	5 780	6 437	6 236
1981	8 114	9 423	13 222	10 581	13 208	5 677	6 442	6 209
1982	8 236	9 517	13 301	10 835	13 288	5 698	6 544	6 287
1983	8 186	9 658	13 516	11 000	13 503	5 754	6 692	6 407
1984	8 005	9 782	13 822	11 475	13 809	5 902	6 715	6 469
1985	8 212	9 911	14 139	11 762	14 125	5 882	6 715	6 464
1986	8 552	10 197	14 501	12 406	14 489	6 019	6 924	6 652
1987	9 113	10 746	14 884	12 850	14 872	5 958	6 943	6 648
1988	9 821	11 276	15 432	13 485	15 421	6 000	7 032	6 724
1989	10 357	11 788	15 890	14 111	15 880	5 902	7 078	6 729
1990	10 852	12 210	15 997	14 487	15 988	5 437	6 871	6 446
1991	11 149	12 152	16 140	14 815	16 133	4 836	6 403	5 940
1992	11 365	12 522	16 286	14 998	16 279	4 581	5 444	5 190
1993	11 194	12 352	16 153	15 461	16 149	4 526	4 907	4 795
1994	11 445	12 609	16 542	15 830	16 538	4 716	4 226	4 370
1995	11 762	12 932	16 886	16 155	16 882	4 998	4 002	4 294
1996	12 124	13 214	17 113	16 566	17 110	5 192	3 899	4 278
1997	12 521	13 703	17 496	17 206	17 494	5 342	3 972	4 374
1998	12 929	14 227	17 922	17 757	17 921	5 461	3 893	4 354

http://dx.doi.org/10.1787/667827525313

ISBN 92-64-02261-9 – © OECD 2006

Table C1–c. **Levels of Per Capita GDP in Western Offshoots, Annual Estimates, 1950–98**
(1990 international Geary–Khamis dollars)

	Australia	New Zealand	Canada	United States	Average 4 Western Offshoots
1950	7 493	8 453	7 437	9 561	9 288
1951	7 590	7 651	7 686	10 116	9 780
1952	7 467	7 792	7 992	10 316	9 969
1953	7 537	7 850	8 146	10 613	10 239
1954	7 849	8 734	7 858	10 359	10 020
1955	8 094	8 714	8 368	10 897	10 533
1956	8 177	8 981	8 825	10 914	10 590
1957	8 151	9 030	8 779	10 920	10 588
1958	8 367	9 168	8 704	10 631	10 343
1959	8 693	9 614	8 850	11 230	10 888
1960	8 865	9 444	8 947	11 328	10 986
1961	8 728	9 767	9 025	11 402	11 051
1962	9 107	9 744	9 478	11 905	11 537
1963	9 481	10 149	9 774	12 242	11 872
1964	9 934	10 430	10 218	12 773	12 386
1965	10 240	10 901	10 701	13 419	12 997
1966	10 291	11 381	11 183	14 134	13 653
1967	10 799	10 683	11 318	14 330	13 846
1968	11 234	10 565	11 724	14 863	14 353
1969	11 671	11 546	12 166	15 179	14 692
1970	12 171	11 221	12 307	15 030	14 597
1971	12 167	11 622	12 562	15 304	14 849
1972	12 286	11 916	13 072	15 944	15 443
1973	12 759	12 513	13 838	16 689	16 172
1974	12 868	12 991	14 211	16 491	16 048
1975	13 055	12 613	14 316	16 284	15 886
1976	13 445	12 801	14 902	16 975	16 545
1977	13 434	12 130	15 223	17 567	17 064
1978	13 663	12 175	15 680	18 373	17 798
1979	14 227	12 388	16 170	18 789	18 228
1980	14 334	12 449	16 176	18 577	18 057
1981	14 661	13 000	16 472	18 856	18 341
1982	14 391	13 135	15 779	18 325	17 816
1983	14 197	13 315	16 077	18 920	18 334
1984	14 996	13 834	16 836	20 123	19 465
1985	15 546	13 881	17 582	20 717	20 063
1986	15 641	14 151	17 862	21 236	20 533
1987	16 166	14 093	18 348	21 788	21 067
1988	16 612	13 995	19 062	22 499	21 753
1989	17 039	14 040	19 174	23 059	22 254
1990	17 043	13 825	18 933	23 214	22 356
1991	16 701	13 162	18 353	22 921	22 027
1992	16 938	13 140	18 295	23 430	22 460
1993	17 415	13 640	18 503	23 733	22 766
1994	18 097	14 253	19 156	24 449	23 472
1995	18 647	14 593	19 467	24 879	23 895
1996	19 136	14 838	19 585	25 556	24 501
1997	19 645	14 971	20 134	26 453	25 332
1998	20 390	14 779	20 559	27 331	26 146

http://dx.doi.org/10.1787/667827525313

279

Table C2–a. Population of 8 Latin American Countries, Annual Estimates, 1950–98
(000 at mid–year)

	Argentina	Brazil	Chile	Colombia	Mexico	Peru	Uruguay	Venezuela	Total
1950	17 150	53 443	6 091	11 592	28 485	7 633	2 194	5 009	131 597
1951	17 517	54 996	6 252	11 965	29 296	7 826	2 223	5 217	135 292
1952	17 877	56 603	6 378	12 351	30 144	8 026	2 253	5 440	139 070
1953	18 231	58 266	6 493	12 750	31 031	8 232	2 284	5 674	142 961
1954	18 581	59 989	6 612	13 162	31 959	8 447	2 317	5 919	146 985
1955	18 928	61 774	6 743	13 588	32 930	8 672	2 353	6 170	151 158
1956	19 272	63 632	6 889	14 029	33 946	8 905	2 389	6 431	155 493
1957	19 611	65 551	7 048	14 486	35 016	9 146	2 425	6 703	159 985
1958	19 947	67 533	7 220	14 958	36 142	9 397	2 460	6 982	164 639
1959	20 281	69 580	7 400	15 447	37 328	9 658	2 495	7 268	169 457
1960	20 616	71 695	7 585	15 953	38 579	9 931	2 531	7 556	174 446
1961	20 951	73 833	7 773	16 476	39 836	10 218	2 564	7 848	179 498
1962	21 284	76 039	7 961	17 010	41 121	10 517	2 598	8 143	184 674
1963	21 616	78 317	8 147	17 546	42 434	10 826	2 632	8 444	189 963
1964	21 949	80 667	8 330	18 090	43 775	11 144	2 664	8 752	195 370
1965	22 283	83 093	8 510	18 646	45 142	11 467	2 693	9 068	200 903
1966	22 612	85 557	8 686	19 202	46 538	11 796	2 721	9 387	206 499
1967	22 934	88 050	8 859	19 764	47 996	12 132	2 749	9 710	212 193
1968	23 261	90 569	9 030	20 322	49 519	12 476	2 777	10 041	217 994
1969	23 600	93 114	9 199	20 869	51 111	12 829	2 802	10 389	223 913
1970	23 962	95 684	9 369	21 430	52 775	13 193	2 824	10 758	229 994
1971	24 352	98 244	9 540	21 993	54 434	13 568	2 826	11 152	236 110
1972	24 757	100 837	9 718	22 543	56 040	13 955	2 830	11 516	242 193
1973	25 174	103 463	9 897	23 069	57 643	14 350	2 834	11 893	248 323
1974	25 598	106 122	10 077	23 593	59 240	14 753	2 838	12 281	254 502
1975	26 021	108 813	10 252	24 114	60 828	15 161	2 842	12 675	260 706
1976	26 457	111 533	10 432	24 620	62 404	15 573	2 857	13 082	266 960
1977	26 895	114 299	10 600	25 094	63 981	15 990	2 874	13 504	273 237
1978	27 338	117 129	10 760	25 543	65 554	16 414	2 889	13 931	279 558
1979	27 785	120 020	10 923	26 031	67 123	16 849	2 905	14 355	285 990
1980	28 237	122 936	11 094	26 583	68 686	17 295	2 920	14 768	292 519
1981	28 701	125 907	11 282	27 159	70 324	17 755	2 936	15 166	299 230
1982	29 151	128 938	11 487	27 764	71 923	18 234	2 954	15 621	306 072
1983	29 584	131 864	11 687	28 388	73 463	18 706	2 973	16 084	312 750
1984	29 993	134 596	11 879	29 026	74 992	19 171	2 990	16 545	319 192
1985	30 407	137 272	12 067	29 675	76 544	19 624	3 008	16 998	325 595
1986	30 853	140 080	12 260	30 339	78 132	20 073	3 027	17 450	332 214
1987	31 303	142 903	12 463	31 011	79 754	20 531	3 045	17 910	338 922
1988	31 749	145 744	12 678	31 681	81 408	21 000	3 064	18 379	345 702
1989	32 194	148 526	12 901	32 341	83 073	21 487	3 084	18 851	352 457
1990	32 634	151 040	13 128	32 985	84 748	21 989	3 106	19 325	358 955
1991	33 083	153 471	13 353	33 629	86 437	22 501	3 128	19 801	365 402
1992	33 531	155 918	13 573	34 296	88 143	23 015	3 149	20 266	371 891
1993	33 963	158 344	13 788	34 979	89 863	23 531	3 172	20 706	378 346
1994	34 412	160 744	14 000	35 679	91 592	24 047	3 194	21 139	384 807
1995	34 877	163 113	14 205	36 397	93 325	24 563	3 216	21 564	391 261
1996	35 335	165 427	14 403	37 124	95 063	25 079	3 239	21 983	397 653
1997	35 798	167 661	14 597	37 852	96 807	25 595	3 262	22 396	403 969
1998	36 265	169 807	14 788	38 581	98 553	26 111	3 285	22 803	410 192

http://dx.doi.org/10.1787/667827525313

ISBN 92-64-02261-9 – © OECD 2006

Table C2–a. **Population of 15 Latin American Countries, Annual Estimates, 1950–98**
(000 at mid–year)

	Bolivia	Costa Rica	Cuba	Dominican Republic	Ecuador	El Salvador	Guatemala	Haiti
1950	2 766	867	5 785	2 312	3 310	1 940	2 969	3 097
1951	2 824	895	5 892	2 375	3 403	1 989	3 056	3 148
1952	2 883	926	6 008	2 444	3 498	2 042	3 146	3 201
1953	2 945	959	6 129	2 518	3 596	2 097	3 239	3 257
1954	3 009	994	6 254	2 598	3 699	2 156	3 335	3 316
1955	3 074	1 032	6 381	2 685	3 806	2 218	3 434	3 376
1956	3 142	1 072	6 513	2 778	3 918	2 283	3 535	3 441
1957	3 212	1 112	6 641	2 873	4 034	2 351	3 640	3 508
1958	3 284	1 154	6 763	2 968	4 155	2 422	3 749	3 577
1959	3 358	1 200	6 901	3 064	4 281	2 497	3 861	3 648
1960	3 434	1 248	7 027	3 159	4 413	2 574	3 975	3 723
1961	3 513	1 297	7 134	3 225	4 551	2 656	4 090	3 800
1962	3 594	1 345	7 254	3 359	4 696	2 738	4 208	3 880
1963	3 678	1 393	7 415	3 470	4 846	2 825	4 329	3 964
1964	3 764	1 440	7 612	3 588	5 001	2 912	4 454	4 050
1965	3 853	1 488	7 810	3 714	5 162	3 005	4 581	4 137
1966	3 945	1 538	7 985	3 848	5 330	3 114	4 712	4 227
1967	4 041	1 589	8 139	3 981	5 503	3 217	4 847	4 318
1968	4 139	1 638	8 284	4 114	5 682	3 330	4 987	4 412
1969	4 241	1 687	8 421	4 244	5 865	3 450	5 133	4 507
1970	4 346	1 736	8 543	4 373	6 051	3 583	5 287	4 605
1971	4 455	1 786	8 670	4 508	6 240	3 688	5 452	4 653
1972	4 566	1 835	8 831	4 644	6 432	3 767	5 623	4 701
1973	4 680	1 886	9 001	4 781	6 629	3 853	5 801	4 748
1974	4 796	1 938	9 153	4 915	6 829	3 944	5 986	4 795
1975	4 914	1 993	9 290	5 052	7 038	4 042	6 178	4 839
1976	5 025	2 051	9 421	5 192	7 243	4 143	6 375	4 882
1977	5 128	2 112	9 538	5 333	7 455	4 249	6 580	4 925
1978	5 232	2 198	9 634	5 472	7 671	4 361	6 792	4 970
1979	5 335	2 266	9 710	5 613	7 893	4 470	7 009	5 017
1980	5 439	2 307	9 653	5 697	8 123	4 527	7 232	5 056
1981	5 545	2 366	9 712	5 826	8 361	4 475	7 486	5 091
1982	5 653	2 435	9 789	5 957	8 606	4 434	7 710	5 149
1983	5 763	2 506	9 886	6 087	8 831	4 478	7 898	5 248
1984	5 876	2 568	9 982	6 214	9 051	4 543	8 118	5 354
1985	5 992	2 640	10 079	6 343	9 269	4 617	8 351	5 468
1986	6 111	2 716	10 162	6 472	9 484	4 702	8 593	5 588
1987	6 233	2 793	10 240	6 603	9 696	4 791	8 844	5 708
1988	6 359	2 870	10 334	6 734	9 904	4 877	9 103	5 825
1989	6 487	2 947	10 439	6 867	10 110	4 959	9 366	5 939
1990	6 620	3 022	10 545	6 997	10 308	5 041	9 631	6 048
1991	6 756	3 098	10 643	7 127	10 577	5 125	9 901	6 133
1992	6 895	3 172	10 724	7 253	10 852	5 211	10 179	6 215
1993	7 048	3 246	10 789	7 372	11 121	5 301	10 465	6 310
1994	7 202	3 319	10 846	7 489	11 381	5 391	10 759	6 399
1995	7 358	3 391	10 900	7 612	11 629	5 481	11 061	6 488
1996	7 514	3 463	10 952	7 740	11 869	5 571	11 370	6 583
1997	7 670	3 534	11 003	7 869	12 105	5 662	11 686	6 680
1998	7 826	3 605	11 051	7 999	12 337	5 752	12 008	6 781

http://dx.doi.org/10.1787/667827525313

Table C2–a. **Population of 15 Latin American Countries, Annual Estimates, 1950–98**
(000 at mid–year)

	Honduras	Jamaica	Nicaragua	Panama	Paraguay	Puerto Rico	Trinidad & Tobago	Total
1950	1 431	1 385	1 098	893	1 476	2 218	632	32 178
1951	1 474	1 406	1 131	916	1 515	2 235	649	32 908
1952	1 517	1 426	1 166	940	1 556	2 227	663	33 643
1953	1 562	1 446	1 202	962	1 597	2 204	678	34 393
1954	1 611	1 468	1 239	985	1 640	2 214	698	35 214
1955	1 662	1 489	1 277	1 011	1 683	2 250	721	36 099
1956	1 715	1 510	1 317	1 037	1 727	2 249	743	36 980
1957	1 770	1 535	1 359	1 064	1 771	2 260	765	37 894
1958	1 829	1 566	1 402	1 085	1 816	2 299	789	38 857
1959	1 889	1 599	1 446	1 115	1 862	2 322	817	39 859
1960	1 952	1 632	1 493	1 148	1 910	2 358	841	40 886
1961	2 017	1 648	1 541	1 181	1 959	2 403	861	41 877
1962	2 082	1 665	1 591	1 216	2 010	2 448	887	42 974
1963	2 151	1 698	1 642	1 251	2 062	2 497	904	44 126
1964	2 224	1 739	1 695	1 288	2 115	2 552	924	45 359
1965	2 299	1 777	1 750	1 326	2 170	2 597	939	46 610
1966	2 375	1 820	1 807	1 365	2 228	2 627	953	47 875
1967	2 453	1 861	1 865	1 405	2 288	2 649	960	49 118
1968	2 534	1 893	1 926	1 447	2 349	2 674	963	50 372
1969	2 618	1 920	1 988	1 489	2 412	2 722	963	51 660
1970	2 683	1 944	2 053	1 531	2 477	2 722	955	52 888
1971	2 767	1 967	2 120	1 573	2 545	2 766	962	54 150
1972	2 864	1 998	2 180	1 616	2 614	2 847	975	55 493
1973	2 964	2 036	2 241	1 659	2 692	2 863	985	56 819
1974	3 066	2 071	2 311	1 706	2 773	2 887	995	58 167
1975	3 151	2 105	2 383	1 748	2 850	2 935	1 007	59 525
1976	3 237	2 133	2 458	1 790	2 919	3 026	1 021	60 920
1977	3 326	2 157	2 537	1 840	2 984	3 081	1 039	62 286
1978	3 425	2 179	2 587	1 873	3 051	3 118	1 056	63 619
1979	3 520	2 207	2 663	1 915	3 119	3 168	1 073	64 979
1980	3 625	2 229	2 776	1 956	3 193	3 210	1 091	66 113
1981	3 744	2 258	2 869	1 996	3 276	3 239	1 102	67 346
1982	3 847	2 298	2 945	2 036	3 366	3 279	1 116	68 619
1983	3 946	2 323	3 012	2 077	3 463	3 316	1 133	69 967
1984	4 053	2 348	3 083	2 120	3 564	3 350	1 150	71 375
1985	4 164	2 372	3 152	2 164	3 668	3 382	1 166	72 828
1986	4 277	2 396	3 224	2 208	3 776	3 413	1 180	74 302
1987	4 390	2 415	3 302	2 252	3 887	3 444	1 191	75 788
1988	4 473	2 430	3 387	2 297	4 000	3 475	1 198	77 266
1989	4 604	2 446	3 480	2 342	4 117	3 506	1 200	78 809
1990	4 740	2 466	3 591	2 388	4 236	3 537	1 198	80 368
1991	4 880	2 488	3 708	2 434	4 359	3 571	1 194	81 993
1992	5 021	2 509	3 820	2 480	4 484	3 604	1 186	83 605
1993	5 163	2 529	3 935	2 524	4 612	3 644	1 177	85 236
1994	5 304	2 551	4 057	2 567	4 743	3 687	1 166	86 863
1995	5 445	2 574	4 185	2 609	4 876	3 731	1 155	88 495
1996	5 585	2 595	4 317	2 651	5 012	3 783	1 143	90 148
1997	5 725	2 616	4 450	2 693	5 150	3 828	1 130	91 800
1998	5 862	2 635	4 583	2 736	5 291	3 860	1 117	93 441

http://dx.doi.org/10.1787/667827525313

ISBN 92-64-02261-9 – © OECD 2006

Table C2–a. **Total Population of 44 Latin American Countries, Annual Estimates, 1950–98**
(000 at mid–year)

	Total 8 core countries	*Total 15 countries*	*Total 21 small Caribbean countries*	*Total 44 countries*
1950	131 597	32 178	2 062	165 837
1951	135 292	32 908	2 111	170 311
1952	139 070	33 643	2 161	174 875
1953	142 961	34 393	2 211	179 565
1954	146 985	35 214	2 267	184 466
1955	151 158	36 099	2 323	189 580
1956	155 493	36 980	2 378	194 851
1957	159 985	37 894	2 435	200 315
1958	164 639	38 857	2 494	205 990
1959	169 457	39 859	2 555	211 871
1960	174 446	40 886	2 614	217 946
1961	179 498	41 877	2 662	224 038
1962	184 674	42 974	2 711	230 359
1963	189 963	44 126	2 781	236 870
1964	195 370	45 359	2 841	243 570
1965	200 903	46 610	2 900	250 412
1966	206 499	47 875	2 959	257 334
1967	212 193	49 118	3 014	264 325
1968	217 994	50 372	3 071	271 436
1969	223 913	51 660	3 121	278 694
1970	229 994	52 888	3 164	286 046
1971	236 110	54 150	3 214	293 473
1972	242 193	55 493	3 263	300 949
1973	248 323	56 819	3 308	308 451
1974	254 502	58 167	3 340	316 009
1975	260 706	59 525	3 347	323 578
1976	266 960	60 920	3 350	331 230
1977	273 237	62 286	3 364	338 887
1978	279 558	63 619	3 383	346 560
1979	285 990	64 979	3 397	354 366
1980	292 519	66 113	3 410	362 041
1981	299 230	67 346	3 434	370 010
1982	306 072	68 619	3 464	378 155
1983	312 750	69 967	3 494	386 211
1984	319 192	71 375	3 527	394 093
1985	325 595	72 828	3 561	401 985
1986	332 214	74 302	3 593	410 109
1987	338 922	75 788	3 622	418 332
1988	345 702	77 266	3 653	426 621
1989	352 457	78 809	3 684	434 950
1990	358 955	80 368	3 726	443 049
1991	365 402	81 993	3 758	451 153
1992	371 891	83 605	3 790	459 285
1993	378 346	85 236	3 824	467 406
1994	384 807	86 863	3 856	475 526
1995	391 261	88 495	3 889	483 645
1996	397 653	90 148	3 922	491 723
1997	403 969	91 800	3 955	499 724
1998	410 192	93 441	3 990	507 623

http://dx.doi.org/10.1787/667827525313

Table C2–b. **Levels of GDP in 8 Latin American Countries, Annual Estimates, 1950–98**
(million 1990 international Geary–Khamis dollars)

	Argentina	Brazil	Chile	Colombia	Mexico	Peru	Uruguay	Venezuela	Total
1950	85 524	89 342	23 274	24 955	67 368	17 270	10 224	37 377	355 334
1951	88 866	93 608	24 274	25 726	72 578	18 669	11 015	39 979	374 715
1952	84 333	99 181	25 663	27 350	75 481	19 848	11 167	43 472	386 495
1953	88 866	103 957	27 006	29 026	75 688	20 901	11 736	45 147	402 327
1954	92 528	110 836	27 117	31 042	83 258	22 246	12 488	49 820	429 335
1955	99 125	118 960	27 080	32 242	90 307	23 317	12 593	53 991	457 615
1956	101 856	120 674	27 238	33 539	96 502	24 316	12 807	58 677	475 609
1957	107 087	130 717	30 090	34 766	103 812	25 936	12 932	67 414	512 754
1958	113 655	142 577	30 915	35 639	109 333	25 805	13 292	68 540	539 756
1959	106 303	154 538	30 748	38 207	112 599	26 737	12 125	72 658	553 915
1960	114 614	167 397	32 767	39 831	121 723	30 017	12 554	72 889	591 792
1961	122 809	179 951	34 341	41 847	126 365	32 226	12 912	70 643	621 094
1962	120 833	190 932	35 971	44 120	132 039	34 922	12 624	73 762	645 203
1963	117 927	192 912	38 240	45 571	141 839	36 217	12 686	77 134	662 526
1964	130 074	199 423	39 092	48 389	157 312	38 580	12 940	83 688	709 498
1965	141 960	203 444	39 407	50 136	167 116	40 501	13 088	89 240	744 892
1966	142 919	216 181	43 797	52 806	177 427	43 921	13 536	90 842	781 429
1967	146 755	224 877	45 223	55 028	188 258	45 581	12 975	96 334	815 031
1968	153 002	244 921	46 844	58 398	201 669	45 734	13 181	102 916	866 665
1969	166 080	266 292	48 585	62 116	213 924	47 448	13 984	106 612	925 041
1970	174 972	292 480	49 586	66 308	227 970	50 229	14 638	114 807	990 990
1971	183 458	322 159	54 022	70 250	237 480	52 331	14 498	116 494	1 050 692
1972	189 183	356 880	53 373	75 637	257 636	53 838	13 992	117 982	1 118 521
1973	200 720	401 643	50 401	80 728	279 302	56 713	14 098	126 364	1 209 969
1974	213 739	433 322	50 891	85 370	296 370	61 969	14 541	129 038	1 285 240
1975	211 850	455 918	44 316	87 347	312 998	64 075	15 406	132 728	1 324 638
1976	211 327	498 823	45 881	91 488	326 267	65 334	16 026	142 978	1 398 124
1977	224 084	522 154	50 401	95 283	337 499	65 600	16 205	151 927	1 463 153
1978	214 233	548 342	54 540	103 366	365 340	65 784	17 058	155 528	1 524 191
1979	229 547	587 289	59 060	108 906	398 788	69 609	18 110	156 752	1 628 061
1980	232 802	639 093	63 654	113 375	431 983	72 723	19 205	149 735	1 722 570
1981	219 434	611 007	67 192	115 789	469 972	76 035	19 575	149 253	1 728 257
1982	212 518	614 538	57 634	116 938	466 649	76 147	17 724	146 150	1 708 298
1983	220 016	593 575	57 245	118 806	446 602	66 567	16 688	140 665	1 660 164
1984	224 491	625 438	60 875	123 037	462 678	69 650	16 505	142 664	1 725 338
1985	209 641	675 090	62 366	127 076	475 505	71 247	16 746	144 843	1 782 514
1986	224 985	729 252	65 895	134 844	457 655	77 857	18 231	152 244	1 860 963
1987	230 797	753 685	69 674	142 086	466 148	84 237	19 676	157 698	1 924 001
1988	226 438	751 910	74 814	147 896	471 953	77 285	19 676	166 879	1 936 851
1989	212 373	776 547	82 269	152 686	491 767	68 399	19 930	152 577	1 956 548
1990	212 518	743 765	84 038	159 042	516 692	64 979	20 105	160 648	1 961 787
1991	233 770	751 203	90 173	161 587	538 508	66 603	20 687	177 516	2 040 047
1992	254 575	748 949	100 092	167 889	558 049	66 004	22 218	189 942	2 107 718
1993	269 341	782 652	106 698	175 444	568 934	69 766	22 907	189 182	2 184 924
1994	291 696	831 176	112 139	186 496	594 054	79 254	24 166	182 183	2 301 164
1995	282 653	866 086	122 344	196 567	557 419	86 070	23 683	192 931	2 327 753
1996	295 090	891 202	130 786	200 695	586 144	88 050	24 867	192 160	2 408 994
1997	318 698	925 068	139 941	203 706	625 759	95 622	26 112	204 843	2 539 749
1998	334 314	926 918	144 279	205 132	655 910	95 718	27 313	204 433	2 594 017

http://dx.doi.org/10.1787/667827525313

ISBN 92-64-02261-9 – © OECD 2006

Table C2–b. **Levels of GDP in 15 Latin American Countries, Annual Estimates, 1950–98**
(million 1990 international Geary–Khamis dollars)

	Bolivia	Costa Rica	Cuba	Dominican Republic	Ecuador	El Salvador	Guatemala	Haiti
1950	5 309	1 702	19 613	2 416	6 278	2 888	6 190	3 254
1951	5 683	1 747	19 829	2 701	6 346	2 945	6 277	3 302
1952	5 855	1 958	20 045	2 921	7 129	3 166	6 408	3 489
1953	5 301	2 256	20 281	2 884	7 279	3 392	6 643	3 378
1954	5 412	2 275	20 495	3 049	7 867	3 431	6 767	3 654
1955	5 698	2 538	20 731	3 237	8 074	3 608	6 934	3 507
1956	5 360	2 466	20 966	3 562	8 373	3 891	7 565	3 814
1957	5 183	2 676	21 202	3 787	8 751	4 098	7 992	3 587
1958	5 306	3 007	21 438	3 989	9 007	4 187	8 365	3 871
1959	5 289	3 118	21 672	4 012	9 490	4 375	8 778	3 688
1960	5 516	3 389	21 908	4 209	10 106	4 553	8 992	3 926
1961	5 631	3 530	22 222	4 114	10 360	4 713	9 378	3 767
1962	5 945	3 746	22 556	4 815	10 911	5 276	9 709	4 128
1963	6 327	4 067	22 888	5 129	11 189	5 504	10 635	3 860
1964	6 632	4 265	23 241	5 472	11 977	6 017	11 128	3 772
1965	6 958	4 651	23 595	4 791	13 131	6 340	11 613	3 813
1966	7 461	5 013	23 928	5 434	13 475	6 794	12 255	3 790
1967	7 928	5 320	24 301	5 617	14 188	7 164	12 757	3 713
1968	8 604	5 730	24 653	5 628	14 973	7 396	13 877	3 860
1969	8 989	6 111	25 026	6 244	15 792	7 653	14 532	3 986
1970	9 459	6 515	25 399	6 906	16 899	7 881	15 364	4 174
1971	9 820	6 945	24 046	7 637	17 872	8 245	16 221	4 445
1972	10 321	7 556	23 281	8 581	18 972	8 712	17 412	4 603
1973	11 030	8 145	29 165	9 617	21 337	9 084	18 593	4 810
1974	11 598	8 583	25 870	10 171	22 585	9 675	19 779	5 114
1975	12 364	8 755	24 811	10 659	23 772	10 193	20 164	4 995
1976	13 118	9 231	25 125	11 377	26 075	10 572	21 654	5 422
1977	13 670	10 055	25 458	11 930	27 731	11 189	23 344	5 448
1978	14 128	10 677	25 792	12 207	29 664	11 935	24 511	5 710
1979	14 125	11 207	25 811	12 733	31 274	11 744	25 667	6 127
1980	13 995	11 290	25 850	13 511	32 706	10 748	26 632	6 591
1981	14 124	11 035	26 851	14 069	34 041	9 869	26 804	6 410
1982	13 508	10 266	28 204	14 324	34 421	9 324	25 858	6 191
1983	12 905	10 551	29 754	14 959	33 702	9 386	25 193	6 238
1984	13 034	11 379	31 969	14 999	35 081	9 595	25 321	6 256
1985	12 943	11 475	33 284	14 620	36 570	9 819	25 167	6 269
1986	12 530	12 107	32 538	15 057	37 648	9 926	25 199	6 261
1987	12 858	12 683	30 930	16 189	35 288	10 193	26 094	6 214
1988	13 348	13 114	32 029	16 300	39 060	10 384	27 110	6 263
1989	13 735	13 867	32 048	18 377	39 123	10 491	28 179	6 329
1990	14 446	14 370	31 087	17 503	40 267	10 805	29 050	6 323
1991	15 226	14 686	27 481	17 643	42 280	11 108	30 125	6 329
1992	15 485	15 729	24 238	18 772	43 549	11 918	31 601	5 456
1993	16 135	16 641	21 039	19 148	44 507	12 681	32 865	5 336
1994	16 910	17 357	21 039	19 971	46 465	13 442	34 212	4 893
1995	17 705	17 739	21 417	20 870	47 859	14 275	35 923	5 138
1996	17 670	17 650	22 981	22 289	48 960	14 532	37 001	5 281
1997	18 394	18 268	23 555	23 871	50 869	15 143	38 592	5 361
1998	19 241	19 272	23 909	25 304	51 378	15 627	40 522	5 532

http://dx.doi.org/10.1787/667827525313

Table C2–b. Levels of GDP in 15 Latin American Countries, Annual Estimates, 1950–98
(million 1990 international Geary–Khamis dollars)

	Honduras	Jamaica	Nicaragua	Panama	Paraguay	Puerto Rico	Trinidad & Tobago	Total
1950	1 880	1 837	1 774	1 710	2 338	4 755	2 322	64 266
1951	1 982	1 985	1 894	1 695	2 383	4 929	2 526	66 224
1952	2 058	2 145	2 215	1 787	2 343	5 214	2 612	69 345
1953	2 220	2 446	2 268	1 895	2 410	5 445	2 682	70 780
1954	2 094	2 727	2 480	1 963	2 452	5 669	2 730	73 065
1955	2 149	3 008	2 646	2 077	2 564	5 961	3 111	75 843
1956	2 322	3 307	2 645	2 185	2 672	6 388	3 756	79 272
1957	2 429	3 789	2 868	2 414	2 795	6 708	4 088	82 367
1958	2 506	3 849	2 877	2 432	2 952	6 901	4 423	85 110
1959	2 569	4 064	2 920	2 589	2 944	7 521	4 692	87 721
1960	2 728	4 330	2 960	2 744	2 970	8 066	5 258	91 655
1961	2 798	4 453	3 182	3 040	3 111	8 835	5 488	94 622
1962	2 959	4 533	3 529	3 295	3 330	9 500	5 781	100 013
1963	3 069	4 681	3 912	3 606	3 421	10 488	6 076	104 852
1964	3 229	5 050	4 370	3 761	3 569	11 232	6 283	109 998
1965	3 509	5 456	4 786	4 091	3 773	12 254	6 603	115 364
1966	3 713	5 695	4 944	4 395	3 815	13 119	6 891	120 722
1967	3 922	5 915	5 288	4 762	4 058	13 944	7 035	125 912
1968	4 154	6 218	5 360	5 109	4 202	14 606	7 400	131 770
1969	4 187	6 681	5 716	5 507	4 365	15 899	7 604	138 292
1970	4 296	7 481	5 771	5 839	4 636	17 280	7 873	145 773
1971	4 462	7 481	6 055	6 312	4 839	18 375	7 954	150 709
1972	4 635	7 706	6 248	6 645	5 088	19 732	8 414	157 906
1973	4 866	8 411	6 566	7 052	5 487	20 908	8 553	173 624
1974	4 826	8 095	7 505	7 221	5 945	20 919	9 011	176 897
1975	4 949	8 093	7 493	7 338	6 328	20 388	9 181	179 483
1976	5 467	7 603	7 880	7 458	6 758	21 464	10 059	189 263
1977	6 047	7 443	8 556	7 546	7 478	22 867	10 698	199 460
1978	6 662	7 496	7 884	8 285	8 297	24 379	11 947	209 574
1979	6 976	7 363	5 785	8 651	9 215	25 868	12 500	215 046
1980	7 014	6 957	6 043	9 961	10 549	26 263	13 501	221 611
1981	7 196	7 142	6 367	10 367	11 458	26 544	14 096	226 373
1982	7 078	7 237	6 312	10 939	11 058	25 734	13 271	223 725
1983	7 030	7 405	6 609	11 013	10 724	25 855	12 231	223 555
1984	7 312	7 343	6 474	10 963	11 061	27 747	12 967	231 501
1985	7 640	7 003	6 204	11 480	11 501	28 319	12 436	234 730
1986	7 710	7 119	6 077	11 857	11 486	30 630	12 028	238 173
1987	8 167	7 668	6 035	12 150	11 988	32 136	11 473	240 066
1988	8 571	7 889	5 367	10 256	12 764	34 228	11 027	247 710
1989	8 894	8 428	5 296	10 215	13 509	35 919	10 937	255 347
1990	8 898	8 890	5 297	10 688	13 923	37 277	11 110	259 934
1991	9 138	8 917	5 281	11 650	14 271	38 136	11 499	263 770
1992	9 668	9 140	5 323	12 605	14 514	39 877	11 372	269 247
1993	10 355	9 304	5 302	13 273	15 094	41 729	11 236	274 645
1994	10 158	9 481	5 514	13 685	15 547	43 475	11 708	283 857
1995	10 534	9 642	5 762	13 945	16 247	45 453	12 188	294 697
1996	10 934	9 594	6 050	14 321	16 425	46 706	12 675	303 069
1997	11 481	9 373	6 383	15 009	16 820	48 882	13 208	315 209
1998	11 929	9 308	6 651	15 609	16 719	51 159	13 683	325 843

http://dx.doi.org/10.1787/667827525313

Table C2–b. **Total GDP in 44 Latin American Countries, Annual Estimates, 1950–98**
(million 1990 international Geary–Khamis dollars)

	Total 8 core countries	Total 15 countries	Total 21 small Caribbean countries	Total 44 countries
1950	355 334	64 266	3 956	423 556
1951	374 715	66 224	4 180	445 119
1952	386 495	69 345	4 418	460 258
1953	402 327	70 780	4 670	477 777
1954	429 335	73 065	4 935	507 335
1955	457 615	75 843	5 215	538 673
1956	475 609	79 272	5 512	560 393
1957	512 754	82 367	5 825	600 946
1958	539 756	85 110	6 156	631 022
1959	553 915	87 721	6 506	648 142
1960	591 792	91 655	6 876	690 323
1961	621 094	94 622	7 266	722 982
1962	645 203	100 013	7 679	752 895
1963	662 526	104 852	8 116	775 494
1964	709 498	109 998	8 577	828 073
1965	744 892	115 364	9 064	869 320
1966	781 429	120 722	9 579	911 730
1967	815 031	125 912	10 124	951 067
1968	866 665	131 770	10 699	1 009 134
1969	925 041	138 292	11 307	1 074 640
1970	990 990	145 773	11 950	1 148 713
1971	1 050 692	150 709	12 629	1 214 030
1972	1 118 521	157 906	13 347	1 289 774
1973	1 209 969	173 624	14 105	1 397 698
1974	1 285 240	176 897	14 295	1 476 432
1975	1 324 638	179 483	14 487	1 518 608
1976	1 398 124	189 263	14 682	1 602 069
1977	1 463 153	199 460	14 880	1 677 493
1978	1 524 191	209 574	15 081	1 748 846
1979	1 628 061	215 046	15 284	1 858 391
1980	1 722 570	221 611	15 489	1 959 670
1981	1 728 257	226 373	15 698	1 970 328
1982	1 708 298	223 725	15 909	1 947 932
1983	1 660 164	223 555	16 124	1 899 843
1984	1 725 338	231 501	16 341	1 973 180
1985	1 782 514	234 730	16 561	2 033 805
1986	1 860 963	238 173	16 784	2 115 920
1987	1 924 001	240 066	17 010	2 181 077
1988	1 936 851	247 710	17 239	2 201 800
1989	1 956 548	255 347	17 471	2 229 366
1990	1 961 787	259 934	17 706	2 239 427
1991	2 040 047	263 770	18 167	2 321 984
1992	2 107 718	269 247	18 640	2 395 605
1993	2 184 924	274 645	19 126	2 478 695
1994	2 301 164	283 857	19 624	2 604 645
1995	2 327 753	294 697	20 135	2 642 585
1996	2 408 994	303 069	20 659	2 732 722
1997	2 539 749	315 209	21 197	2 876 155
1998	2 594 017	325 843	21 749	2 941 609

http://dx.doi.org/10.1787/667827525313

Table C2–c. **Levels of Per Capita GDP in 8 Latin American Countries, Annual Estimates, 1950–98**
(1990 international Geary–Khamis dollars)

	Argentina	Brazil	Chile	Colombia	Mexico	Peru	Uruguay	Venezuela	Average
1950	4 987	1 672	3 821	2 153	2 365	2 263	4 659	7 462	2 700
1951	5 073	1 702	3 883	2 150	2 477	2 385	4 955	7 663	2 770
1952	4 717	1 752	4 024	2 214	2 504	2 473	4 957	7 992	2 779
1953	4 874	1 784	4 159	2 277	2 439	2 539	5 139	7 956	2 814
1954	4 980	1 848	4 101	2 358	2 605	2 634	5 391	8 417	2 921
1955	5 237	1 926	4 016	2 373	2 742	2 689	5 352	8 750	3 027
1956	5 285	1 896	3 954	2 391	2 843	2 731	5 360	9 124	3 059
1957	5 461	1 994	4 269	2 400	2 965	2 836	5 333	10 058	3 205
1958	5 698	2 111	4 282	2 383	3 025	2 746	5 402	9 816	3 278
1959	5 241	2 221	4 155	2 473	3 016	2 768	4 860	9 997	3 269
1960	5 559	2 335	4 320	2 497	3 155	3 023	4 960	9 646	3 392
1961	5 862	2 437	4 418	2 540	3 172	3 154	5 036	9 002	3 460
1962	5 677	2 511	4 518	2 594	3 211	3 321	4 858	9 058	3 494
1963	5 455	2 463	4 694	2 597	3 343	3 345	4 820	9 134	3 488
1964	5 926	2 472	4 693	2 675	3 594	3 462	4 858	9 562	3 632
1965	6 371	2 448	4 631	2 689	3 702	3 532	4 860	9 841	3 708
1966	6 321	2 527	5 042	2 750	3 813	3 723	4 974	9 677	3 784
1967	6 399	2 554	5 105	2 784	3 922	3 757	4 721	9 922	3 841
1968	6 578	2 704	5 188	2 874	4 073	3 666	4 747	10 249	3 976
1969	7 037	2 860	5 281	2 976	4 185	3 698	4 991	10 262	4 131
1970	7 302	3 057	5 293	3 094	4 320	3 807	5 184	10 672	4 309
1971	7 533	3 279	5 663	3 194	4 363	3 857	5 130	10 446	4 450
1972	7 642	3 539	5 492	3 355	4 597	3 858	4 945	10 245	4 618
1973	7 973	3 882	5 093	3 499	4 845	3 952	4 974	10 625	4 873
1974	8 350	4 083	5 050	3 618	5 003	4 200	5 123	10 507	5 050
1975	8 142	4 190	4 323	3 622	5 146	4 226	5 421	10 472	5 081
1976	7 988	4 472	4 398	3 716	5 228	4 195	5 608	10 929	5 237
1977	8 332	4 568	4 755	3 797	5 275	4 103	5 639	11 251	5 355
1978	7 837	4 682	5 069	4 047	5 573	4 008	5 903	11 164	5 452
1979	8 262	4 893	5 407	4 184	5 941	4 131	6 234	10 920	5 693
1980	8 245	5 199	5 738	4 265	6 289	4 205	6 577	10 139	5 889
1981	7 646	4 853	5 956	4 263	6 683	4 283	6 668	9 841	5 776
1982	7 290	4 766	5 017	4 212	6 488	4 176	6 000	9 356	5 581
1983	7 437	4 501	4 898	4 185	6 079	3 559	5 614	8 745	5 308
1984	7 485	4 647	5 125	4 239	6 170	3 633	5 520	8 623	5 405
1985	6 894	4 918	5 168	4 282	6 212	3 631	5 567	8 521	5 475
1986	7 292	5 206	5 375	4 445	5 857	3 879	6 023	8 725	5 602
1987	7 373	5 274	5 590	4 582	5 845	4 103	6 461	8 805	5 677
1988	7 132	5 159	5 901	4 668	5 797	3 680	6 422	9 080	5 603
1989	6 597	5 228	6 377	4 721	5 920	3 183	6 462	8 094	5 551
1990	6 512	4 924	6 402	4 822	6 097	2 955	6 474	8 313	5 465
1991	7 066	4 895	6 753	4 805	6 230	2 960	6 614	8 965	5 583
1992	7 592	4 803	7 374	4 895	6 331	2 868	7 055	9 373	5 668
1993	7 930	4 943	7 738	5 016	6 331	2 965	7 223	9 137	5 775
1994	8 477	5 171	8 010	5 227	6 486	3 296	7 566	8 618	5 980
1995	8 104	5 310	8 612	5 401	5 973	3 504	7 363	8 947	5 949
1996	8 351	5 387	9 080	5 406	6 166	3 511	7 677	8 741	6 058
1997	8 903	5 518	9 587	5 382	6 464	3 736	8 006	9 146	6 287
1998	9 219	5 459	9 757	5 317	6 655	3 666	8 315	8 965	6 324

http://dx.doi.org/10.1787/667827525313

Table C2–c. **Levels of Per Capita GDP in 15 Latin American Countries, Annual Estimates, 1950–98**
(1990 international Geary–Khamis dollars)

	Bolivia	Costa Rica	Cuba	Dominican Republic	Ecuador	El Salvador	Guatemala	Haiti
1950	1 919	1 963	3 390	1 045	1 897	1 489	2 085	1 051
1951	2 013	1 951	3 366	1 137	1 865	1 481	2 054	1 049
1952	2 031	2 114	3 336	1 195	2 038	1 551	2 037	1 090
1953	1 800	2 353	3 309	1 145	2 024	1 617	2 051	1 037
1954	1 799	2 289	3 277	1 174	2 127	1 591	2 029	1 102
1955	1 853	2 460	3 249	1 206	2 121	1 627	2 019	1 039
1956	1 706	2 301	3 219	1 282	2 137	1 704	2 140	1 108
1957	1 614	2 406	3 193	1 318	2 169	1 743	2 195	1 023
1958	1 616	2 605	3 170	1 344	2 168	1 729	2 231	1 082
1959	1 575	2 598	3 140	1 310	2 217	1 752	2 274	1 011
1960	1 606	2 715	3 118	1 332	2 290	1 769	2 262	1 055
1961	1 603	2 723	3 115	1 276	2 276	1 774	2 293	991
1962	1 654	2 785	3 109	1 433	2 324	1 927	2 307	1 064
1963	1 720	2 919	3 087	1 478	2 309	1 948	2 457	974
1964	1 762	2 961	3 053	1 525	2 395	2 066	2 499	931
1965	1 806	3 127	3 021	1 290	2 544	2 110	2 535	922
1966	1 891	3 258	2 997	1 412	2 528	2 182	2 601	897
1967	1 962	3 349	2 986	1 411	2 578	2 227	2 632	860
1968	2 079	3 497	2 976	1 368	2 635	2 221	2 782	875
1969	2 120	3 622	2 972	1 471	2 693	2 218	2 831	884
1970	2 176	3 754	2 973	1 579	2 793	2 199	2 906	906
1971	2 204	3 889	2 774	1 694	2 864	2 236	2 975	955
1972	2 260	4 118	2 636	1 848	2 950	2 313	3 097	979
1973	2 357	4 319	3 240	2 012	3 219	2 358	3 205	1 013
1974	2 418	4 428	2 826	2 069	3 307	2 453	3 304	1 066
1975	2 516	4 392	2 671	2 110	3 378	2 522	3 264	1 032
1976	2 610	4 500	2 667	2 191	3 600	2 551	3 397	1 111
1977	2 666	4 760	2 669	2 237	3 720	2 633	3 547	1 106
1978	2 700	4 859	2 677	2 231	3 867	2 737	3 609	1 149
1979	2 647	4 945	2 658	2 269	3 962	2 627	3 662	1 221
1980	2 573	4 894	2 678	2 372	4 026	2 374	3 683	1 304
1981	2 547	4 664	2 765	2 415	4 071	2 205	3 580	1 259
1982	2 390	4 217	2 881	2 405	4 000	2 103	3 354	1 202
1983	2 239	4 210	3 010	2 458	3 816	2 096	3 190	1 189
1984	2 218	4 432	3 203	2 414	3 876	2 112	3 119	1 168
1985	2 160	4 346	3 302	2 305	3 945	2 127	3 014	1 146
1986	2 050	4 457	3 202	2 326	3 970	2 111	2 933	1 120
1987	2 063	4 541	3 021	2 452	3 640	2 128	2 950	1 089
1988	2 099	4 569	3 099	2 420	3 944	2 129	2 978	1 075
1989	2 117	4 706	3 070	2 676	3 870	2 115	3 009	1 066
1990	2 182	4 754	2 948	2 501	3 906	2 143	3 016	1 045
1991	2 254	4 741	2 582	2 476	3 997	2 168	3 043	1 032
1992	2 246	4 958	2 260	2 588	4 013	2 287	3 105	878
1993	2 289	5 127	1 950	2 597	4 002	2 392	3 141	846
1994	2 348	5 230	1 940	2 667	4 083	2 493	3 180	765
1995	2 406	5 231	1 965	2 742	4 116	2 604	3 248	792
1996	2 352	5 097	2 098	2 880	4 125	2 608	3 254	802
1997	2 398	5 169	2 141	3 034	4 202	2 675	3 302	803
1998	2 458	5 346	2 164	3 163	4 165	2 717	3 375	816

http://dx.doi.org/10.1787/667827525313

Table C2–c. **Levels of Per Capita GDP in 15 Latin American Countries,
Annual Estimates, 1950–98**
(1990 international Geary–Khamis dollars)

	Honduras	Jamaica	Nicaragua	Panama	Paraguay	Puerto Rico	Trinidad & Tobago	Average
1950	1 313	1 327	1 616	1 916	1 584	2 144	3 674	1 997
1951	1 344	1 412	1 674	1 851	1 573	2 205	3 894	2 012
1952	1 356	1 504	1 900	1 901	1 506	2 341	3 941	2 061
1953	1 421	1 691	1 888	1 969	1 509	2 471	3 954	2 058
1954	1 300	1 858	2 002	1 993	1 495	2 561	3 914	2 075
1955	1 293	2 020	2 072	2 055	1 523	2 649	4 316	2 101
1956	1 354	2 190	2 008	2 108	1 547	2 840	5 059	2 144
1957	1 372	2 468	2 111	2 270	1 578	2 968	5 344	2 174
1958	1 370	2 458	2 052	2 241	1 625	3 002	5 609	2 190
1959	1 360	2 541	2 019	2 322	1 581	3 239	5 743	2 201
1960	1 398	2 654	1 983	2 391	1 555	3 421	6 251	2 242
1961	1 387	2 702	2 065	2 574	1 588	3 677	6 371	2 260
1962	1 421	2 722	2 219	2 710	1 657	3 881	6 514	2 327
1963	1 427	2 757	2 382	2 882	1 659	4 201	6 718	2 376
1964	1 452	2 904	2 578	2 920	1 687	4 401	6 801	2 425
1965	1 526	3 070	2 734	3 085	1 739	4 719	7 030	2 475
1966	1 563	3 129	2 736	3 219	1 712	4 993	7 234	2 522
1967	1 599	3 178	2 835	3 388	1 774	5 264	7 327	2 563
1968	1 639	3 284	2 783	3 531	1 789	5 463	7 684	2 616
1969	1 599	3 480	2 875	3 699	1 810	5 840	7 897	2 677
1970	1 601	3 849	2 812	3 814	1 872	6 349	8 244	2 756
1971	1 613	3 803	2 856	4 012	1 902	6 642	8 272	2 783
1972	1 618	3 858	2 867	4 111	1 946	6 930	8 628	2 846
1973	1 642	4 130	2 929	4 250	2 038	7 302	8 685	3 056
1974	1 574	3 908	3 248	4 232	2 144	7 247	9 053	3 041
1975	1 571	3 845	3 144	4 198	2 220	6 946	9 118	3 015
1976	1 689	3 564	3 205	4 167	2 315	7 093	9 847	3 107
1977	1 818	3 451	3 373	4 102	2 506	7 422	10 296	3 202
1978	1 945	3 439	3 047	4 424	2 719	7 819	11 319	3 294
1979	1 982	3 336	2 172	4 518	2 954	8 164	11 649	3 309
1980	1 935	3 121	2 177	5 091	3 304	8 183	12 380	3 352
1981	1 922	3 162	2 219	5 194	3 498	8 195	12 794	3 361
1982	1 840	3 150	2 144	5 372	3 285	7 848	11 888	3 260
1983	1 781	3 188	2 194	5 301	3 097	7 797	10 794	3 195
1984	1 804	3 128	2 100	5 172	3 104	8 283	11 273	3 243
1985	1 835	2 952	1 968	5 306	3 135	8 373	10 664	3 223
1986	1 803	2 972	1 885	5 370	3 042	8 974	10 192	3 205
1987	1 861	3 176	1 828	5 394	3 085	9 330	9 631	3 168
1988	1 916	3 247	1 585	4 465	3 191	9 850	9 202	3 206
1989	1 932	3 445	1 522	4 361	3 282	10 246	9 112	3 240
1990	1 877	3 605	1 475	4 476	3 287	10 539	9 271	3 234
1991	1 873	3 584	1 424	4 786	3 274	10 678	9 630	3 217
1992	1 925	3 643	1 394	5 083	3 237	11 065	9 586	3 220
1993	2 006	3 679	1 347	5 259	3 273	11 453	9 550	3 222
1994	1 915	3 716	1 359	5 332	3 278	11 791	10 038	3 268
1995	1 935	3 746	1 377	5 345	3 332	12 183	10 550	3 330
1996	1 958	3 697	1 401	5 402	3 277	12 347	11 087	3 362
1997	2 006	3 584	1 434	5 572	3 266	12 769	11 685	3 434
1998	2 035	3 533	1 451	5 705	3 160	13 253	12 254	3 487

http://dx.doi.org/10.1787/667827525313

Table C2–c. Average Levels of Per Capita GDP in 44 Latin American Countries, Annual Estimates, 1950–98

(1990 international Geary–Khamis dollars)

	Total 8 core countries	Total 15 countries	Total 21 small Caribbean countries	Total 44 countries
1950	2 700	1 997	1 919	2 554
1951	2 770	2 012	1 980	2 614
1952	2 779	2 061	2 044	2 632
1953	2 814	2 058	2 112	2 661
1954	2 921	2 075	2 177	2 750
1955	3 027	2 101	2 245	2 841
1956	3 059	2 144	2 318	2 876
1957	3 205	2 174	2 392	3 000
1958	3 278	2 190	2 468	3 063
1959	3 269	2 201	2 546	3 059
1960	3 392	2 242	2 630	3 167
1961	3 460	2 260	2 730	3 227
1962	3 494	2 327	2 833	3 268
1963	3 488	2 376	2 918	3 274
1964	3 632	2 425	3 019	3 400
1965	3 708	2 475	3 126	3 472
1966	3 784	2 522	3 237	3 543
1967	3 841	2 563	3 359	3 598
1968	3 976	2 616	3 484	3 718
1969	4 131	2 677	3 623	3 856
1970	4 309	2 756	3 777	4 016
1971	4 450	2 783	3 929	4 137
1972	4 618	2 846	4 090	4 286
1973	4 873	3 056	4 264	4 531
1974	5 050	3 041	4 280	4 672
1975	5 081	3 015	4 328	4 693
1976	5 237	3 107	4 383	4 837
1977	5 355	3 202	4 423	4 950
1978	5 452	3 294	4 458	5 046
1979	5 693	3 309	4 499	5 244
1980	5 889	3 352	4 542	5 413
1981	5 776	3 361	4 571	5 325
1982	5 581	3 260	4 593	5 151
1983	5 308	3 195	4 615	4 919
1984	5 405	3 243	4 633	5 007
1985	5 475	3 223	4 651	5 059
1986	5 602	3 205	4 671	5 159
1987	5 677	3 168	4 696	5 214
1988	5 603	3 206	4 719	5 161
1989	5 551	3 240	4 742	5 126
1990	5 465	3 234	4 752	5 055
1991	5 583	3 217	4 834	5 147
1992	5 668	3 220	4 918	5 216
1993	5 775	3 222	5 002	5 303
1994	5 980	3 268	5 089	5 477
1995	5 949	3 330	5 177	5 464
1996	6 058	3 362	5 267	5 557
1997	6 287	3 434	5 360	5 755
1998	6 324	3 487	5 451	5 795

http://dx.doi.org/10.1787/667827525313

Table C3–a. Population of 16 East Asian Countries, Annual Estimates 1950–99
(000 at mid–year)

	China	India	Indonesia	Japan	Philippines	South Korea	Thailand	Taiwan
1950	546 815	359 000	79 043	83 563	21 131	20 846	20 042	7 882
1951	557 480	365 000	80 525	84 974	21 777	20 876	20 653	8 255
1952	568 910	372 000	82 052	86 293	22 443	20 948	21 289	8 541
1953	581 390	379 000	83 611	87 463	23 129	21 060	21 964	8 822
1954	595 310	386 000	85 196	88 752	23 836	21 259	22 685	9 134
1955	608 655	393 000	86 807	89 790	24 565	21 552	23 451	9 480
1956	621 465	401 000	88 456	90 727	25 316	22 031	24 244	9 823
1957	637 408	409 000	90 124	91 513	26 090	22 612	25 042	10 133
1958	653 235	418 000	91 821	92 349	26 888	23 254	25 845	10 460
1959	666 005	426 000	93 565	93 237	27 710	23 981	26 667	10 806
1960	667 070	434 000	95 254	94 053	28 557	24 784	27 513	11 155
1961	660 330	444 000	97 085	94 890	29 443	25 614	28 376	11 510
1962	665 770	454 000	99 028	95 797	30 361	26 420	29 263	11 857
1963	682 335	464 000	101 009	96 765	31 313	27 211	30 174	12 210
1964	698 355	474 000	103 031	97 793	32 299	27 984	31 107	12 570
1965	715 185	485 000	105 093	98 883	33 317	28 705	32 062	12 928
1966	735 400	495 000	107 197	99 790	34 359	29 436	33 036	13 283
1967	754 550	506 000	109 343	100 850	35 416	30 131	34 024	13 617
1968	774 510	518 000	111 532	102 050	36 489	30 838	35 028	13 945
1969	796 025	529 000	113 765	103 231	37 577	31 544	36 050	14 264
1970	818 315	541 000	116 044	104 334	38 680	32 241	37 091	14 565
1971	841 105	554 000	118 368	105 677	39 801	32 883	38 202	14 865
1972	862 030	567 000	121 282	107 179	40 939	33 505	39 276	15 142
1973	881 940	580 000	124 271	108 660	42 094	34 073	40 302	15 427
1974	900 350	593 000	127 338	110 160	43 265	34 692	41 306	15 709
1975	916 395	607 000	130 485	111 520	44 447	35 281	42 272	16 001
1976	930 685	620 000	133 713	112 770	45 692	35 860	43 221	16 329
1977	943 455	634 000	137 026	113 880	46 976	36 436	44 148	16 661
1978	956 165	648 000	140 425	114 920	48 306	37 019	45 057	16 974
1979	969 005	664 000	143 912	115 880	49 680	37 534	46 004	17 308
1980	981 235	679 000	147 490	116 800	51 092	38 124	47 026	17 642
1981	993 861	692 000	150 657	117 650	52 423	38 723	47 924	17 970
1982	1 000 281	708 000	153 894	118 450	53 753	39 326	48 802	18 297
1983	1 023 288	723 000	157 204	119 260	55 079	39 910	49 655	18 596
1984	1 036 825	739 000	160 588	120 020	56 416	40 406	50 481	18 873
1985	1 051 040	755 000	164 047	120 750	57 784	40 806	51 275	19 136
1986	1 066 790	771 000	166 976	121 490	59 185	41 214	52 048	19 357
1987	1 084 035	788 000	169 959	122 090	60 602	41 622	52 813	19 564
1988	1 101 630	805 000	172 999	122 610	62 044	42 031	53 571	19 788
1989	1 118 650	822 000	176 094	123 120	63 529	42 449	54 317	20 006
1990	1 135 185	839 000	179 248	123 540	65 037	42 869	55 052	20 230
1991	1 150 780	856 000	182 223	123 920	66 558	43 246	55 702	20 460
1992	1 164 970	872 000	185 259	124 320	68 100	43 657	56 348	20 660
1993	1 178 440	891 000	188 359	124 670	69 664	44 099	56 988	20 850
1994	1 191 835	908 000	191 524	124 960	71 251	44 556	57 620	21 040
1995	1 204 855	927 000	194 755	125 570	72 860	45 018	58 241	21 220
1996	1 217 550	943 000	198 025	125 864	74 481	45 482	58 851	21 390
1997	1 230 075	959 000	201 350	126 166	76 104	45 991	59 451	21 580
1998	1 242 700	975 000	204 390	126 486	77 726	46 430	60 037	21 780
1999	1 252 704	991 691	207 429	126 737	79 376	46 898	60 609	21 984

http://dx.doi.org/10.1787/667827525313

Table C3–a. **Population of 16 East Asian Countries, Annual Estimates 1950–99**
(000 at mid–year)

	Bangladesh	Burma	Hong Kong	Malaysia	Nepal	Pakistan	Singapore	Sri Lanka	Total
1950	45 646	19 488	2 237	6 434	8 990	39 448	1 022	7 533	1 269 120
1951	46 152	19 788	2 015	6 582	9 086	40 382	1 068	7 752	1 292 365
1952	46 887	20 093	2 126	6 742	9 183	41 347	1 127	7 982	1 317 963
1953	47 660	20 403	2 242	6 929	9 280	42 342	1 192	8 221	1 344 708
1954	48 603	20 721	2 365	7 118	9 379	43 372	1 248	8 457	1 373 435
1955	49 602	21 049	2 490	7 312	9 479	44 434	1 306	8 679	1 401 651
1956	50 478	21 385	2 615	7 520	9 580	45 536	1 372	8 898	1 430 446
1957	51 365	21 732	2 736	7 739	9 682	46 680	1 446	9 129	1 462 431
1958	52 399	22 088	2 854	7 966	9 789	47 869	1 519	9 362	1 495 698
1959	53 485	22 456	2 967	8 196	9 906	49 104	1 587	9 610	1 525 282
1960	54 622	22 836	3 075	8 428	10 035	50 387	1 646	9 879	1 543 294
1961	55 741	23 229	3 168	8 663	10 176	51 719	1 702	10 152	1 555 798
1962	56 839	23 634	3 305	8 906	10 332	53 101	1 750	10 422	1 580 785
1963	58 226	24 053	3 421	9 148	10 500	54 524	1 795	10 687	1 617 371
1964	59 403	24 486	3 505	9 397	10 677	55 988	1 842	10 942	1 653 379
1965	60 332	24 933	3 598	9 648	10 862	57 495	1 887	11 202	1 691 130
1966	61 548	25 394	3 630	9 900	11 057	59 046	1 934	11 470	1 731 480
1967	62 822	25 870	3 723	10 155	11 262	60 642	1 978	11 737	1 772 120
1968	64 133	26 362	3 803	10 409	11 473	62 282	2 012	12 010	1 814 876
1969	65 483	26 867	3 864	10 662	11 692	63 970	2 043	12 275	1 858 312
1970	67 403	27 386	3 959	10 910	11 919	65 706	2 075	12 532	1 904 160
1971	69 227	27 919	4 045	11 171	12 155	67 491	2 113	12 776	1 951 798
1972	70 759	28 466	4 116	11 441	12 413	69 326	2 152	13 017	1 998 043
1973	72 471	29 227	4 213	11 712	12 685	71 121	2 193	13 246	2 043 635
1974	74 679	29 828	4 320	11 986	12 973	72 912	2 230	13 450	2 088 198
1975	76 253	30 445	4 396	12 267	12 278	74 712	2 263	13 660	2 129 675
1976	77 928	31 080	4 518	12 554	13 599	76 456	2 293	13 887	2 170 585
1977	80 428	31 735	4 584	12 845	13 933	78 153	2 325	14 117	2 210 702
1978	82 936	32 404	4 668	13 139	14 280	80 051	2 354	14 371	2 251 069
1979	85 492	33 081	4 930	13 444	14 641	82 374	2 384	14 649	2 294 318
1980	88 077	33 766	5 063	13 764	15 016	85 219	2 414	14 900	2 336 628
1981	90 666	34 460	5 183	14 097	15 403	88 417	2 470	15 152	2 377 056
1982	93 074	35 162	5 265	14 442	15 796	91 257	2 528	15 410	2 413 737
1983	95 384	35 873	5 345	14 794	16 200	93 720	2 586	15 618	2 465 512
1984	97 612	36 592	5 398	15 158	16 613	96 284	2 644	15 810	2 508 720
1985	99 753	37 319	5 456	15 546	17 037	99 053	2 703	16 021	2 552 726
1986	101 769	38 055	5 525	15 943	17 472	101 953	2 763	16 256	2 597 796
1987	103 764	38 800	5 585	16 334	17 918	104 887	2 824	16 495	2 645 292
1988	105 771	39 551	5 628	16 732	18 376	107 846	2 893	16 735	2 693 205
1989	107 807	40 308	5 661	17 121	18 848	110 848	2 966	16 971	2 740 695
1990	109 897	41 068	5 704	17 507	19 333	113 914	3 039	17 193	2 787 816
1991	111 936	41 834	5 750	17 911	19 831	116 909	3 096	17 391	2 833 547
1992	113 711	42 607	5 800	18 324	20 345	118 852	3 152	17 587	2 875 692
1993	115 453	43 385	5 900	18 753	20 874	120 853	3 209	17 823	2 920 320
1994	117 283	44 169	6 040	19 184	21 414	123 668	3 268	18 066	2 963 878
1995	119 188	44 955	6 160	19 615	21 966	126 404	3 326	18 290	3 009 423
1996	121 140	45 741	6 310	20 052	22 530	129 276	3 383	18 508	3 051 583
1997	123 112	46 525	6 500	20 491	23 107	132 185	3 441	18 721	3 093 799
1998	125 105	47 305	6 690	20 933	23 698	135 135	3 490	18 934	3 135 839
1999	127 118	48 081	6 830	21 376	24 303	138 123	3 532	19 154	3 175 945

http://dx.doi.org/10.1787/667827525313

Table C3–a. Population of 25 East Asian Countries, Annual Estimates, 1950–98
(000 at mid–year)

	Afghanistan	Cambodia	Laos	Mongolia	North Korea	Vietnam	19 small countries	Total
1950	8 150	4 163	1 886	779	9 471	25 348	3 411	53 208
1951	8 284	4 266	1 921	789	9 162	25 794	3 493	53 709
1952	8 425	4 371	1 957	801	8 865	26 247	3 577	54 243
1953	8 573	4 478	1 995	814	8 580	26 724	3 662	54 826
1954	8 728	4 589	2 035	828	8 572	27 210	3 750	55 712
1955	8 891	4 702	2 077	844	8 839	27 738	3 840	56 931
1956	9 062	4 827	2 121	862	9 116	28 327	3 932	58 247
1957	9 241	4 956	2 166	882	9 411	28 999	4 027	59 682
1958	9 429	5 088	2 213	904	9 727	29 775	4 123	61 259
1959	9 625	5 224	2 261	929	10 054	30 683	4 222	62 998
1960	9 829	5 364	2 309	955	10 392	31 656	4 323	64 828
1961	10 043	5 511	2 359	982	10 651	32 701	4 427	66 674
1962	10 267	5 761	2 409	1 010	10 917	33 796	4 533	68 693
1963	10 501	5 919	2 460	1 031	11 210	34 933	4 642	70 696
1964	10 744	6 079	2 512	1 061	11 528	36 099	4 754	72 777
1965	10 998	6 242	2 565	1 090	11 869	37 258	4 868	74 890
1966	11 262	6 408	2 619	1 119	12 232	38 379	4 984	77 003
1967	11 538	6 578	2 674	1 150	12 617	39 464	5 104	79 125
1968	11 825	6 752	2 730	1 181	13 024	40 512	5 226	81 250
1969	12 123	6 931	2 787	1 214	13 455	41 542	5 352	83 404
1970	12 431	6 996	2 845	1 248	13 912	42 577	5 480	85 489
1971	12 749	7 018	2 904	1 283	14 365	43 614	5 612	87 545
1972	13 079	7 112	2 964	1 321	14 781	44 655	5 746	89 658
1973	13 421	7 202	3 027	1 360	15 161	45 737	5 884	91 792
1974	13 772	7 287	3 092	1 403	15 501	46 902	6 023	93 980
1975	14 132	7 179	3 161	1 446	15 801	48 075	6 165	95 959
1976	14 501	6 906	3 176	1 487	16 069	49 273	6 311	97 723
1977	14 880	6 669	3 208	1 528	16 325	50 534	6 460	99 604
1978	15 269	6 460	3 248	1 572	16 580	51 663	6 613	101 405
1979	15 556	6 393	3 268	1 617	16 840	52 668	6 769	103 111
1980	14 985	6 499	3 293	1 662	17 114	53 661	6 929	104 143
1981	14 087	6 681	3 337	1 709	17 384	54 792	7 093	105 083
1982	13 645	6 903	3 411	1 756	17 648	55 972	7 260	106 595
1983	13 709	7 143	3 495	1 805	17 918	57 205	7 432	108 707
1984	13 826	7 286	3 577	1 856	18 196	58 466	6 708	109 915
1985	13 898	7 399	3 657	1 908	18 481	59 730	7 787	112 860
1986	13 937	7 621	3 753	1 961	18 772	61 006	7 971	115 021
1987	14 074	7 883	3 853	2 015	19 068	62 320	8 160	117 373
1988	14 332	8 153	3 960	2 071	19 371	63 630	8 353	119 870
1989	14 646	8 431	4 073	2 159	19 688	64 906	8 550	122 453
1990	14 767	8 717	4 191	2 216	20 019	66 315	8 752	124 977
1991	14 964	9 012	4 314	2 271	20 361	67 684	8 953	127 559
1992	16 624	9 403	4 440	2 320	20 711	69 021	9 159	131 678
1993	18 888	9 858	4 569	2 366	21 064	70 344	9 369	136 458
1994	20 382	10 210	4 702	2 410	21 361	71 617	9 584	140 266
1995	21 571	10 491	4 837	2 454	21 551	72 815	9 804	143 523
1996	22 664	10 773	4 976	2 497	21 512	73 977	10 030	146 429
1997	23 738	11 055	5 117	2 538	21 334	75 124	10 260	149 166
1998	24 792	11 340	5 261	2 579	21 234	76 236	10 493	151 935

http://dx.doi.org/10.1787/667827525313

Table C3–a. **Population of 15 West Asian Countries, Annual Estimates, 1950–98**
(000 at mid–year)

	Bahrain	Iran	Iraq	Israel	Jordan	Kuwait	Lebanon	Oman	Qatar
1950	115	16 375	5 163	1 286	561	145	1 364	489	25
1951	118	16 809	5 300	1 490	584	152	1 401	498	27
1952	120	17 272	5 442	1 621	608	160	1 440	508	29
1953	123	17 742	5 589	1 667	633	168	1 479	517	31
1954	127	18 226	5 743	1 712	659	177	1 519	528	33
1955	130	18 729	5 903	1 772	687	187	1 561	539	35
1956	134	19 249	6 073	1 850	716	197	1 604	550	37
1957	139	19 729	6 249	1 944	747	213	1 647	562	39
1958	144	20 326	6 433	2 025	779	235	1 692	573	41
1959	150	20 958	6 625	2 082	813	262	1 739	586	43
1960	157	21 577	6 822	2 141	849	292	1 786	599	45
1961	164	22 214	7 026	2 217	887	325	1 836	614	49
1962	172	22 874	7 240	2 311	934	358	1 887	628	53
1963	179	23 554	7 468	2 407	975	394	1 940	645	58
1964	186	24 264	7 711	2 498	1 017	433	1 996	662	64
1965	191	25 000	7 971	2 578	1 061	476	2 058	679	70
1966	197	25 764	8 240	2 641	1 107	523	2 122	697	77
1967	202	26 538	8 519	2 694	1 255	575	2 187	715	85
1968	208	27 321	8 808	2 747	1 383	632	2 254	735	94
1969	214	28 119	9 106	2 817	1 454	690	2 320	756	103
1970	220	28 933	9 414	2 903	1 503	748	2 383	779	113
1971	225	29 763	9 732	2 997	1 556	793	2 529	803	122
1972	231	30 614	10 062	3 096	1 614	842	2 680	829	132
1973	239	31 491	10 402	3 197	1 674	894	2 824	857	142
1974	248	32 412	10 754	3 286	1 738	948	2 986	884	153
1975	259	33 379	11 118	3 354	1 803	1 007	3 095	913	165
1976	274	34 381	11 494	3 424	1 870	1 072	3 115	956	177
1977	297	35 430	11 883	3 496	1 938	1 140	3 110	1 005	189
1978	323	36 519	12 317	3 570	2 007	1 214	3 102	1 059	202
1979	336	37 772	12 768	3 653	2 077	1 292	3 090	1 116	216
1980	348	39 274	13 233	3 737	2 168	1 370	3 075	1 175	231
1981	363	40 906	13 703	3 801	2 262	1 432	3 068	1 238	242
1982	378	42 555	14 173	3 858	2 357	1 497	3 072	1 301	252
1983	393	44 200	14 652	3 927	2 451	1 566	3 073	1 363	284
1984	408	45 868	15 161	4 005	2 546	1 637	3 072	1 424	315
1985	424	47 533	15 694	4 075	2 646	1 720	3 068	1 482	345
1986	440	49 274	16 247	4 137	2 748	1 799	3 066	1 538	375
1987	455	50 873	16 543	4 203	2 851	1 880	3 068	1 594	402
1988	470	52 435	17 038	4 272	2 956	1 962	3 075	1 652	430
1989	486	53 979	17 568	4 344	3 069	2 045	3 088	1 712	457
1990	502	55 717	18 135	4 512	3 277	2 131	3 130	1 773	482
1991	517	57 492	17 491	4 756	3 562	955	3 179	1 843	505
1992	531	58 905	17 905	4 937	3 762	1 398	3 210	1 915	531
1993	546	59 684	18 480	5 062	3 889	1 467	3 247	1 989	558
1994	561	60 424	19 083	5 185	3 999	1 574	3 291	2 059	587
1995	576	61 528	19 713	5 306	4 099	1 673	3 340	2 131	615
1996	590	62 584	20 367	5 422	4 210	1 754	3 394	2 206	643
1997	603	63 531	21 037	5 535	4 322	1 834	3 450	2 283	670
1998	616	64 411	21 722	5 644	4 435	1 913	3 506	2 364	697
1999	629	65 180	22 427	5 750	4 561	1 991	3 563	2 447	724
2000	642	65 865	23 151	5 852	4 701	2 068	3 620	2 533	750

http://dx.doi.org/10.1787/667827525313

Table C3–a. **Population of 15 West Asian Countries, Annual Estimates, 1950–98**
(000 at mid–year)

	Saudi Arabia	*Syria*	*Turkey*	*UAE*	*Yemen*	*West Bank and Gaza*	*Total*
1950	3 860	3 495	21 122	72	4 461	1 016	59 549
1951	3 932	3 577	21 669	73	4 546	1 023	61 199
1952	4 006	3 662	22 236	75	4 635	1 031	62 845
1953	4 082	3 750	22 831	77	4 726	1 040	64 455
1954	4 160	3 842	23 464	80	4 820	1 049	66 139
1955	4 243	3 938	24 145	83	4 916	1 054	67 922
1956	4 329	4 041	24 877	86	5 024	1 061	69 828
1957	4 420	4 150	25 671	89	5 134	1 071	71 804
1958	4 514	4 268	26 506	93	5 247	1 078	73 954
1959	4 614	4 395	27 356	98	5 363	1 101	76 185
1960	4 718	4 533	28 217	103	5 483	1 113	78 435
1961	4 828	4 681	29 030	109	5 597	1 110	80 687
1962	4 943	4 835	29 789	116	5 715	1 133	82 988
1963	5 065	4 993	30 509	124	5 834	1 157	85 302
1964	5 129	5 157	31 227	133	5 956	1 182	87 615
1965	5 327	5 326	31 951	144	6 079	1 211	90 122
1966	5 469	5 500	32 678	157	6 186	1 236	92 594
1967	5 618	5 681	33 411	172	6 294	1 143	95 089
1968	5 775	5 867	34 165	191	6 405	1 001	97 586
1969	5 939	6 059	34 952	218	6 516	1 002	100 265
1970	6 109	6 258	35 758	249	6 628	1 022	103 020
1971	6 287	6 479	36 580	288	6 771	1 045	105 970
1972	6 473	6 701	37 493	336	6 916	1 070	109 089
1973	6 667	6 931	38 503	391	7 077	1 098	112 387
1974	6 868	7 169	39 513	453	7 241	1 134	115 787
1975	7 199	7 416	40 530	523	7 409	1 161	119 331
1976	7 608	7 670	41 485	598	7 629	1 183	122 936
1977	8 108	7 933	42 404	684	7 847	1 209	126 673
1978	8 680	8 203	43 317	779	8 068	1 237	130 597
1979	9 307	8 484	44 223	884	8 295	1 263	134 776
1980	9 949	8 774	45 121	1 000	8 527	1 286	139 268
1981	10 565	9 073	46 222	1 100	8 768	1 308	144 051
1982	11 179	9 412	47 329	1 204	9 018	1 336	148 921
1983	11 822	9 762	48 440	1 316	9 278	1 376	153 903
1984	12 502	10 126	49 554	1 438	9 551	1 416	159 023
1985	13 208	10 502	50 669	1 570	9 842	1 457	164 235
1986	13 859	10 892	51 780	1 714	10 149	1 501	169 519
1987	14 465	11 294	52 884	1 779	10 476	1 549	174 316
1988	15 064	11 711	53 976	1 840	10 823	1 603	179 307
1989	15 646	12 141	55 054	1 898	11 192	1 653	184 332
1990	15 871	12 620	56 125	1 952	12 023	1 715	189 965
1991	16 110	13 115	57 198	2 003	12 889	1 797	193 412
1992	16 739	13 589	58 267	2 051	13 379	1 886	199 005
1993	17 386	14 075	59 330	2 097	13 892	1 977	203 679
1994	18 049	14 575	60 387	2 140	14 395	2 085	208 394
1995	18 730	15 087	61 439	2 181	14 862	2 215	213 495
1996	19 409	15 609	62 486	2 222	15 349	2 352	218 597
1997	20 088	16 138	63 530	2 262	15 857	2 484	223 624
1998	20 786	16 673	64 568	2 303	16 388	2 611	228 637
1999	21 505	17 214	65 599	2 344	16 942	2 724	233 600
2000	22 246	17 759	66 620	2 386	17 521	2 825	238 539

http://dx.doi.org/10.1787/667827525313

ISBN 92-64-02261-9 – © OECD 2006

Table C3–a. Population in 56 Asian Countries, Annual Estimates, 1950–98
(000 at mid–year)

	16 East Asian countries	25 East Asian countries	15 West Asian countries	56 Asian countries
1950	1 269 120	53 208	59 549	1 381 877
1951	1 292 365	53 709	61 199	1 407 273
1952	1 317 963	54 243	62 845	1 435 051
1953	1 344 708	54 826	64 455	1 463 989
1954	1 373 435	55 712	66 139	1 495 286
1955	1 401 651	56 931	67 922	1 526 504
1956	1 430 446	58 247	69 828	1 558 521
1957	1 462 431	59 682	71 804	1 593 917
1958	1 495 698	61 259	73 954	1 630 911
1959	1 525 282	62 998	76 185	1 664 465
1960	1 543 294	64 828	78 435	1 686 557
1961	1 555 798	66 674	80 687	1 703 159
1962	1 580 785	68 693	82 988	1 732 466
1963	1 617 371	70 696	85 302	1 773 369
1964	1 653 379	72 777	87 615	1 813 771
1965	1 691 130	74 890	90 122	1 856 142
1966	1 731 480	77 003	92 594	1 901 077
1967	1 772 120	79 125	95 089	1 946 334
1968	1 814 876	81 250	97 586	1 993 712
1969	1 858 312	83 404	100 265	2 041 981
1970	1 904 160	85 489	103 020	2 092 669
1971	1 951 798	87 545	105 970	2 145 313
1972	1 998 043	89 658	109 089	2 196 790
1973	2 043 635	91 792	112 387	2 247 814
1974	2 088 198	93 980	115 787	2 297 965
1975	2 129 675	95 959	119 331	2 344 965
1976	2 170 585	97 723	122 936	2 391 244
1977	2 210 702	99 604	126 673	2 436 979
1978	2 251 069	101 405	130 597	2 483 071
1979	2 294 318	103 111	134 776	2 532 205
1980	2 336 628	104 143	139 268	2 580 039
1981	2 377 056	105 083	144 051	2 626 190
1982	2 413 737	106 595	148 921	2 669 253
1983	2 465 512	108 707	153 903	2 728 122
1984	2 508 720	109 915	159 023	2 777 658
1985	2 552 726	112 860	164 235	2 829 821
1986	2 597 796	115 021	169 519	2 882 336
1987	2 645 292	117 373	174 316	2 936 981
1988	2 693 205	119 870	179 307	2 992 382
1989	2 740 695	122 453	184 332	3 047 480
1990	2 787 816	124 977	189 965	3 102 758
1991	2 833 547	127 559	193 412	3 154 518
1992	2 875 692	131 678	199 005	3 206 375
1993	2 920 320	136 458	203 679	3 260 457
1994	2 963 878	140 266	208 394	3 312 538
1995	3 009 423	143 523	213 495	3 366 441
1996	3 051 583	146 429	218 597	3 416 609
1997	3 093 799	149 166	223 624	3 466 589
1998	3 135 839	151 935	228 637	3 516 411

http://dx.doi.org/10.1787/667827525313

Table C3–b. Levels of GDP in 16 East Asian Countries, Annual Estimates, 1950–99
(million 1990 international Geary–Khamis dollars)

	China	India	Indonesia	Japan	Philippines	South Korea	Thailand	Taiwan
1950	239 903	222 222	66 358	160 966	22 616	16 045	16 375	7 378
1951	267 228	227 362	71 304	181 025	25 054	14 810	17 532	8 179
1952	305 742	234 148	74 679	202 005	26 609	15 772	18 503	9 093
1953	321 919	248 963	78 394	216 889	28 988	20 345	20 542	10 092
1954	332 326	259 262	83 283	229 151	31 168	21 539	20 381	10 927
1955	350 115	265 527	85 571	248 855	33 331	22 708	22 162	11 853
1956	384 842	280 978	86 700	267 567	35 670	22 815	22 540	12 481
1957	406 222	277 924	92 631	287 130	37 599	24 575	22 792	13 360
1958	452 654	299 137	89 293	303 857	38 900	25 863	23 616	14 510
1959	464 006	305 499	93 129	331 570	41 548	26 865	26 457	15 871
1960	448 727	326 910	97 082	375 090	42 114	27 398	29 665	16 725
1961	368 021	336 744	103 446	420 246	44 480	28 782	31 210	17 931
1962	368 032	344 204	103 332	457 742	46 603	29 654	33 636	19 453
1963	403 732	361 442	99 371	496 514	49 893	32 268	36 360	22 150
1964	452 558	389 262	103 043	554 449	51 613	35 054	38 841	24 971
1965	505 099	373 814	104 070	586 744	54 331	37 166	41 933	26 688
1966	553 676	377 207	104 089	649 189	56 736	41 641	46 654	29 378
1967	536 987	408 349	101 739	721 132	59 756	44 670	50 552	32 688
1968	525 204	418 907	111 662	813 984	62 712	50 371	54 695	35 447
1969	574 669	446 872	125 408	915 556	65 632	58 007	58 980	38 651
1970	640 949	469 584	138 612	1 013 602	68 102	62 988	62 842	43 509
1971	671 780	474 338	146 200	1 061 230	71 799	82 932	65 886	49 591
1972	691 449	472 766	162 748	1 150 516	75 710	85 811	68 666	57 358
1973	740 048	494 832	186 900	1 242 932	82 464	96 794	75 511	63 519
1974	752 734	500 146	196 374	1 227 706	85 398	104 605	78 894	62 384
1975	800 876	544 683	196 374	1 265 661	90 150	111 548	82 799	63 818
1976	793 092	551 402	213 675	1 315 966	98 090	124 664	90 391	75 108
1977	844 157	593 834	230 338	1 373 741	103 585	137 531	99 304	84 267
1978	935 884	625 695	240 853	1 446 165	108 942	150 442	109 112	94 833
1979	1 007 734	594 510	253 961	1 525 477	115 086	161 172	114 828	101 759
1980	1 046 781	637 202	275 805	1 568 457	121 012	156 846	120 116	104 753
1981	1 096 587	675 882	294 768	1 618 185	125 154	166 581	127 211	113 222
1982	1 192 494	697 705	283 922	1 667 653	129 648	179 220	134 020	119 254
1983	1 294 304	753 942	295 296	1 706 380	132 115	199 828	141 504	132 294
1984	1 447 661	783 042	315 677	1 773 223	122 440	217 167	149 644	148 650
1985	1 599 201	814 344	323 451	1 851 315	113 493	231 386	156 598	156 878
1986	1 703 671	848 990	342 452	1 904 918	117 371	258 122	165 264	177 721
1987	1 849 563	886 154	359 323	1 984 142	122 432	287 854	180 996	190 493
1988	2 000 236	978 822	379 917	2 107 060	130 699	320 301	205 047	192 229
1989	2 044 100	1 043 912	414 090	2 208 858	138 809	340 751	230 043	195 311
1990	2 109 400	1 098 100	450 901	2 321 153	143 025	373 150	255 732	200 477
1991	2 232 306	1 104 114	473 680	2 409 304	142 191	407 582	277 618	215 622
1992	2 444 569	1 161 769	524 482	2 433 927	142 668	429 744	300 059	230 203
1993	2 683 336	1 233 796	560 544	2 441 512	145 704	453 344	325 215	244 747
1994	2 950 104	1 330 036	601 301	2 457 252	152 094	490 745	354 283	260 744
1995	3 196 343	1 425 798	648 332	2 493 399	159 199	534 517	385 584	276 463
1996	3 433 255	1 532 733	696 426	2 619 315	168 506	570 598	406 864	292 128
1997	3 657 242	1 609 371	727 953	2 656 686	177 199	599 190	405 097	311 894
1998	3 873 352	1 702 712	627 499	2 581 576	176 246	564 211	372 509	326 958
1999	4 082 513	1 803 172	628 753	2 589 320	181 886	624 582	387 782	345 595

http://dx.doi.org/10.1787/667827525313

ISBN 92-64-02261-9 – © OECD 2006

Table C3–b. **Levels of GDP in 16 East Asian Countries, Annual Estimates, 1950–99**
(million 1990 international Geary–Khamis dollars)

	Bangladesh	Burma	Hong Kong	Malaysia	Nepal	Pakistan	Singapore	Sri Lanka	Total
1950	24 628	7 711	4 962	10 032	4 462	25 366	2 268	7 241	838 533
1951	24 974	8 834	4 626	9 478	4 591	24 534	2 406	7 850	899 787
1952	25 706	9 028	5 054	9 930	4 748	24 625	2 569	8 140	976 351
1953	26 072	9 265	5 515	9 977	5 038	26 983	2 758	8 058	1 039 798
1954	26 581	8 690	6 021	10 607	5 145	27 603	2 896	8 295	1 083 875
1955	25 177	9 822	6 564	10 677	5 248	28 238	3 078	8 808	1 137 734
1956	27 821	10 472	7 136	11 320	5 484	29 069	3 200	8 323	1 216 418
1957	27 231	11 089	7 729	11 257	5 484	30 339	3 352	8 862	1 267 576
1958	26 702	10 785	8 345	11 256	5 792	30 762	3 485	9 280	1 354 237
1959	28 126	12 457	8 981	12 026	5 957	31 095	3 470	9 553	1 416 610
1960	29 733	12 871	9 637	12 899	6 091	32 621	3 803	10 081	1 481 447
1961	31 421	13 183	10 276	13 794	6 238	34 602	4 123	10 257	1 474 754
1962	31 258	14 332	12 072	14 578	6 385	37 111	4 411	10 500	1 533 303
1963	34 573	14 737	13 968	15 271	6 537	39 439	4 848	11 168	1 642 271
1964	34 939	14 999	15 165	16 235	6 689	42 417	4 680	11 860	1 796 775
1965	36 647	15 379	17 360	17 405	6 849	44 307	5 033	12 148	1 884 973
1966	37 115	14 737	17 659	18 278	7 331	47 919	5 593	12 772	2 019 974
1967	36 302	15 151	17 959	18 587	7 216	49 718	6 255	13 546	2 120 607
1968	39 678	16 148	18 557	20 217	7 265	53 195	7 123	14 136	2 249 301
1969	40 227	16 815	20 652	21 382	7 590	56 642	8 098	15 292	2 470 473
1970	42 403	17 575	22 548	22 684	7 787	62 522	9 209	17 711	2 702 627
1971	40 552	18 149	24 144	24 359	7 693	62 824	10 362	17 700	2 829 539
1972	35 732	18 284	26 639	26 195	7 934	63 323	11 752	19 087	2 973 970
1973	35 997	18 352	29 931	29 982	7 894	67 828	13 108	19 759	3 205 851
1974	40 817	19 323	30 629	32 222	8 393	70 141	13 994	20 541	3 244 301
1975	40 308	20 125	30 729	32 489	8 518	73 043	14 549	21 504	3 397 174
1976	42 098	21 350	35 718	36 536	8 893	76 898	15 588	22 458	3 521 927
1977	42 525	22 625	39 908	39 513	9 161	79 951	16 797	23 316	3 740 553
1978	45 657	24 086	43 300	42 970	9 563	86 406	18 245	24 943	4 007 096
1979	47 846	25 222	48 289	46 469	9 790	89 580	19 932	26 539	4 188 194
1980	48 239	27 381	53 177	50 333	9 563	98 907	21 865	28 079	4 368 516
1981	49 877	28 930	58 066	53 901	9 563	106 753	23 960	29 707	4 578 347
1982	50 487	30 499	59 662	57 102	10 749	114 852	25 601	31 222	4 784 090
1983	52 961	31 827	63 055	60 588	10 433	122 649	27 695	32 771	5 057 642
1984	55 833	33 397	69 340	65 290	11 441	127 518	30 006	34 103	5 384 432
1985	57 519	34 349	69 639	64 617	12 146	138 632	29 451	35 793	5 688 812
1986	60 011	33 986	77 122	65 434	12 664	147 421	29 975	37 307	5 982 429
1987	62 521	32 624	87 099	68 898	13 164	155 994	32 817	37 752	6 351 826
1988	64 329	28 921	94 083	74 982	14 199	166 031	36 491	38 770	6 832 117
1989	65 948	29 989	96 478	81 996	14 525	174 001	39 857	39 594	7 158 262
1990	70 320	30 834	99 770	89 823	15 609	182 014	43 330	42 089	7 525 727
1991	72 629	30 633	104 858	97 545	16 603	192 138	45 832	44 118	7 866 773
1992	76 245	33 593	111 343	105 151	17 285	206 957	49 399	46 050	8 313 444
1993	79 722	35 622	118 227	113 927	17 950	211 653	55 622	49 235	8 770 156
1994	82 774	38 285	124 613	124 525	19 425	221 260	61 843	52 016	9 321 300
1995	87 355	40 946	129 402	136 182	20 099	232 849	67 066	54 892	9 888 426
1996	91 705	43 584	135 288	147 899	21 170	244 954	72 108	56 955	10 533 488
1997	96 616	45 600	142 372	159 294	22 025	248 142	77 868	60 541	10 997 090
1998	101 666	48 427	135 089	148 621	22 435	261 497	79 025	63 408	11 085 231
1999	106 139	50 606	139 006	156 647	23 175	269 603	83 292	66 071	11 538 142

http://dx.doi.org/10.1787/667827525313

Table C3–b. Levels of GDP in 25 East Asian Countries, Annual Estimates, 1950–98
(million 1990 international Geary–Khamis dollars)

	Afghanistan	Cambodia	Laos	Mongolia	North Korea	Vietnam	19 small countries	Total
1950	5 255	2 155	1 156	339	7 293	16 681	3 845	36 724
1951	5 408	2 228	1 192	353	6 496	17 445	3 987	37 109
1952	5 591	2 368	1 229	370	6 675	18 209	4 225	38 667
1953	5 933	2 392	1 267	387	8 288	19 034	4 316	41 617
1954	6 059	2 670	1 306	406	8 683	19 920	4 471	43 515
1955	6 180	2 614	1 347	426	9 316	20 806	4 636	45 325
1956	6 458	2 963	1 388	448	9 444	21 631	4 820	47 152
1957	6 458	3 163	1 431	473	10 230	22 486	5 012	49 253
1958	6 821	3 322	1 476	499	10 816	23 372	5 200	51 506
1959	7 016	3 646	1 521	528	11 260	24 289	5 403	53 663
1960	7 268	3 863	1 568	559	11 483	25 297	5 640	55 678
1961	7 331	3 827	1 617	592	11 972	26 554	5 938	57 831
1962	7 457	4 139	1 667	627	12 249	29 917	6 130	62 186
1963	7 594	4 451	1 718	660	13 295	30 821	6 496	65 035
1964	7 741	4 331	1 772	699	14 445	32 322	6 794	68 104
1965	7 914	4 538	1 826	740	15 370	32 666	7 172	70 226
1966	7 993	4 744	1 883	782	17 308	32 975	7 561	73 246
1967	8 214	4 988	1 941	828	18 711	28 829	7 854	71 365
1968	8 508	5 214	2 001	876	21 268	28 329	8 347	74 543
1969	8 645	5 292	2 063	927	24 743	30 702	8 750	81 122
1970	8 819	4 785	2 127	982	27 184	31 295	9 581	84 773
1971	8 398	4 546	2 193	1 041	36 229	32 889	10 376	95 672
1972	8 240	4 301	2 261	1 103	37 854	35 815	10 939	100 513
1973	9 181	5 858	2 331	1 170	43 072	38 238	11 952	111 802
1974	9 680	5 007	2 403	1 243	44 038	36 744	12 594	111 709
1975	10 184	4 342	2 477	1 319	44 891	34 130	12 765	110 108
1976	10 694	4 650	2 554	1 396	45 652	39 879	13 181	118 006
1977	9 959	5 016	2 633	1 479	46 379	41 343	13 403	120 212
1978	10 752	5 484	2 714	1 567	47 104	41 622	14 102	123 345
1979	10 715	5 593	2 798	1 661	47 842	41 873	15 175	125 657
1980	10 427	5 705	2 885	1 758	48 621	40 671	14 880	124 947
1981	10 547	5 774	2 974	1 905	49 388	42 103	14 965	127 656
1982	10 726	6 218	3 066	2 064	50 138	45 526	15 226	132 964
1983	11 157	6 660	3 161	2 184	50 905	48 042	15 662	137 771
1984	11 336	7 106	3 258	2 314	51 695	52 355	15 899	143 963
1985	11 299	7 554	3 359	2 446	52 505	55 481	16 565	149 209
1986	12 161	7 998	3 463	2 675	53 331	57 056	17 368	154 052
1987	10 064	7 839	3 570	2 768	54 172	59 127	17 984	155 524
1988	9 228	8 035	3 681	2 909	55 033	62 685	18 633	160 204
1989	9 284	8 233	3 795	3 031	55 934	65 615	19 306	165 198
1990	8 861	8 235	3 912	2 954	56 874	68 959	19 356	169 151
1991	8 932	8 860	4 031	2 681	57 846	72 963	20 212	175 525
1992	9 021	9 482	4 245	2 426	53 391	79 312	21 107	178 984
1993	8 741	9 870	4 674	2 354	53 552	85 718	22 041	186 950
1994	8 479	10 258	4 964	2 408	39 468	93 292	23 016	181 885
1995	10 700	10 940	5 230	2 560	32 758	102 192	24 034	188 414
1996	11 342	11 543	5 355	2 620	27 091	111 736	25 098	194 785
1997	12 023	11 846	5 636	2 726	25 249	120 845	26 208	204 533
1998	12 744	11 998	5 806	2 821	25 130	127 851	26 662	213 012

http://dx.doi.org/10.1787/667827525313

ISBN 92-64-02261-9 – © OECD 2006

Table C3–b. **Levels of GDP in 15 West Asian Countries, Annual Estimates, 1950–98**
(million 1990 international Geary–Khamis dollars)

	Bahrain	Iran	Iraq	Israel	Jordan	Kuwait	Lebanon	Oman	Qatar
1950	242	28 128	7 041	3 623	933	4 181	3 313	304	763
1951	257	28 128	7 661	4 707	990	4 532	2 972	324	827
1952	273	28 128	8 470	4 910	1 049	4 804	3 157	344	876
1953	290	28 156	11 899	4 852	1 112	5 280	3 634	366	963
1954	309	28 156	14 145	5 776	1 178	5 882	4 171	389	1 073
1955	328	28 156	13 568	6 558	1 116	6 020	4 506	413	1 099
1956	349	30 659	14 511	7 142	1 532	6 464	4 399	439	1 180
1957	371	34 939	14 370	7 761	1 571	6 693	4 476	467	1 223
1958	394	39 013	16 039	8 319	1 729	7 024	3 840	496	1 282
1959	419	42 360	16 715	9 370	1 858	7 747	4 164	528	1 415
1960	445	46 467	18 658	9 986	1 977	8 420	4 274	560	1 496
1961	474	50 405	20 806	11 077	2 381	8 495	4 555	567	1 497
1962	504	51 389	21 841	12 171	2 446	9 474	4 731	681	1 555
1963	536	57 043	21 447	13 461	2 582	9 984	4 771	711	1 657
1964	571	61 178	24 024	14 780	3 032	10 962	5 059	712	1 712
1965	607	68 688	26 206	16 171	3 379	11 205	5 569	715	1 837
1966	646	75 579	27 593	16 349	3 474	12 584	5 950	752	2 493
1967	688	84 102	26 953	16 758	3 839	12 885	5 668	1 250	3 014
1968	732	96 759	31 740	19 320	3 696	14 089	6 381	2 274	3 474
1969	779	109 304	32 818	21 755	4 031	14 474	6 520	2 858	3 706
1970	832	120 865	32 691	23 520	3 600	22 944	6 950	2 957	3 756
1971	898	135 829	34 712	26 107	3 682	24 537	7 590	2 983	4 665
1972	969	157 909	33 430	29 342	3 800	25 503	8 514	3 262	5 263
1973	1 046	171 466	39 042	30 839	3 999	23 847	8 915	2 809	6 228
1974	1 136	186 655	41 133	32 941	4 355	20 799	10 465	3 132	5 661
1975	1 015	195 684	47 977	34 038	4 657	18 287	10 724	3 897	5 823
1976	1 180	229 241	57 735	34 480	5 789	19 466	10 989	4 397	6 263
1977	1 322	226 315	59 320	34 480	6 166	18 722	11 260	4 410	5 586
1978	1 424	199 481	70 127	36 144	7 462	20 072	11 539	4 326	6 114
1979	1 419	182 267	86 258	38 416	8 142	22 827	10 873	4 511	6 364
1980	1 525	156 643	84 392	41 053	9 689	18 178	10 879	4 784	6 816
1981	1 568	151 918	69 078	43 173	10 147	14 737	10 366	5 599	5 834
1982	1 669	175 826	68 501	43 948	10 897	13 006	9 680	6 245	4 731
1983	1 785	199 031	62 544	45 496	11 115	14 039	9 584	7 288	4 246
1984	1 860	202 379	62 699	45 905	12 071	14 775	9 786	8 507	4 143
1985	1 854	207 245	61 714	47 489	12 493	14 148	10 028	9 697	3 699
1986	1 897	187 780	61 073	49 760	13 626	15 352	9 581	9 906	3 130
1987	1 935	184 939	62 812	53 344	13 997	14 733	6 705	10 699	3 192
1988	2 003	174 532	49 540	54 417	13 853	15 247	6 099	11 018	3 240
1989	2 053	181 227	45 160	54 895	12 387	16 389	6 106	11 481	3 275
1990	2 054	199 819	44 583	58 511	12 371	13 111	6 099	11 487	3 276
1991	2 148	220 999	16 540	61 848	12 656	7 735	8 429	12 176	3 263
1992	2 316	234 472	21 370	66 051	14 807	13 723	8 808	13 211	3 566
1993	2 508	239 395	21 370	68 298	15 666	18 416	9 425	14 017	3 552
1994	2 568	241 560	21 370	73 012	16 856	19 963	10 179	14 550	3 634
1995	2 622	248 565	19 938	77 977	17 514	20 163	10 840	15 248	3 594
1996	2 704	262 234	19 938	81 639	17 689	20 586	11 274	15 690	3 953
1997	2 788	270 110	21 932	83 846	17 919	21 101	11 725	16 694	4 566
1998	2 846	274 695	24 564	85 520	18 313	21 565	12 077	17 179	5 091

http://dx.doi.org/10.1787/667827525313

Table C3–b. **Levels of GDP in 15 West Asian Countries, Annual Estimates, 1950–98**
(million 1990 international Geary–Khamis dollars)

	Saudi Arabia	Syria	Turkey	UAE	Yemen	West Bank and Gaza	Total
1950	8 610	8 418	38 408	1 130	4 353	965	110 412
1951	9 334	8 098	43 329	1 225	4 468	1 009	117 858
1952	9 893	10 202	48 521	1 298	4 584	1 055	127 566
1953	10 875	11 566	53 931	1 427	4 708	1 104	140 163
1954	12 115	13 266	52 393	1 590	4 831	1 157	146 430
1955	12 399	11 970	56 626	1 628	4 959	1 206	150 552
1956	13 312	14 175	58 454	1 749	5 091	1 260	160 716
1957	13 785	15 051	63 103	1 812	5 228	1 321	172 171
1958	14 465	12 972	65 998	1 902	5 367	1 380	180 219
1959	15 955	13 460	69 019	2 097	5 510	1 462	192 079
1960	17 548	13 704	71 064	2 312	5 660	1 534	204 105
1961	19 632	14 832	72 258	2 526	5 810	1 588	216 903
1962	21 974	18 351	76 672	2 809	5 970	1 683	232 248
1963	23 885	18 342	83 890	3 097	6 148	1 783	249 337
1964	25 986	18 755	87 346	3 414	6 307	1 891	265 728
1965	29 137	18 704	89 643	3 762	6 486	2 010	284 120
1966	33 374	17 265	100 137	4 147	6 674	2 130	309 146
1967	36 310	18 696	104 674	4 570	6 868	2 045	328 321
1968	39 547	19 394	111 674	5 037	7 052	1 859	363 029
1969	42 578	23 031	117 624	5 554	7 260	1 931	394 223
1970	46 573	22 155	123 378	6 123	8 731	2 044	427 119
1971	53 289	24 352	130 247	7 147	10 253	2 169	468 459
1972	61 469	30 447	139 919	8 343	11 070	2 306	521 546
1973	73 601	27 846	144 483	9 739	12 431	2 455	558 745
1974	84 700	34 563	152 566	12 894	13 152	2 632	606 784
1975	84 924	41 306	163 510	13 307	14 152	2 797	642 097
1976	92 251	45 834	180 618	15 308	16 363	2 958	722 873
1977	106 191	45 254	186 768	17 978	18 167	3 137	745 076
1978	112 511	49 202	189 577	17 557	19 711	3 332	748 578
1979	120 028	50 986	188 394	21 926	20 805	3 531	766 747
1980	132 160	57 097	183 786	27 717	20 918	3 732	759 370
1981	142 630	62 527	192 709	28 492	22 191	3 940	764 909
1982	144 989	63 857	199 575	26 145	22 563	4 176	795 808
1983	129 404	64 766	209 492	24 833	23 856	4 465	811 944
1984	129 258	62 131	223 552	25 893	24 778	4 769	832 507
1985	120 605	65 928	233 034	25 287	24 578	5 094	842 891
1986	113 260	62 670	249 383	19 919	25 115	5 446	827 898
1987	118 495	63 865	273 031	20 631	26 135	5 834	860 347
1988	122 284	72 342	278 823	20 580	27 249	6 265	857 493
1989	126 701	65 860	279 524	22 766	28 203	6 706	862 733
1990	144 438	70 894	305 395	25 496	28 212	7 222	932 968
1991	156 571	75 927	308 227	25 547	28 297	7 853	948 217
1992	160 955	81 318	326 672	26 237	29 683	8 555	1 011 745
1993	159 989	89 938	352 945	26 001	30 544	9 308	1 061 372
1994	160 789	90 388	333 688	26 573	30 391	10 189	1 055 709
1995	161 593	90 840	357 688	28 194	33 005	11 234	1 099 014
1996	163 855	92 111	382 743	31 041	34 853	12 381	1 152 693
1997	168 279	94 598	411 555	31 786	36 666	13 573	1 207 138
1998	170 972	96 112	423 018	31 913	37 656	14 807	1 236 327

http://dx.doi.org/10.1787/667827525313

ISBN 92-64-02261-9 – © OECD 2006

Table C3–b. **Levels of GDP in 56 Asian Countries, Annual Estimates, 1950–98**
(million 1990 international Geary–Khamis dollars)

	16 East Asian countries	25 East Asian countries	15 West Asian countries	56 Asian countries
1950	838 533	36 724	110 412	985 669
1951	899 787	37 109	117 858	1 054 754
1952	976 351	38 667	127 566	1 142 584
1953	1 039 798	41 617	140 163	1 221 578
1954	1 083 875	43 515	146 430	1 273 820
1955	1 137 734	45 325	150 552	1 333 611
1956	1 216 418	47 152	160 716	1 424 286
1957	1 267 576	49 253	172 171	1 489 000
1958	1 354 237	51 506	180 219	1 585 962
1959	1 416 610	53 663	192 079	1 662 352
1960	1 481 447	55 678	204 105	1 741 230
1961	1 474 754	57 831	216 903	1 749 488
1962	1 533 303	62 186	232 248	1 827 737
1963	1 642 271	65 035	249 337	1 956 643
1964	1 796 775	68 104	265 728	2 130 607
1965	1 884 973	70 226	284 120	2 239 319
1966	2 019 974	73 246	309 146	2 402 366
1967	2 120 607	71 365	328 321	2 520 293
1968	2 249 301	74 543	363 029	2 686 873
1969	2 470 473	81 122	394 223	2 945 818
1970	2 702 627	84 773	427 119	3 214 519
1971	2 829 539	95 672	468 459	3 393 670
1972	2 973 970	100 513	521 546	3 596 029
1973	3 205 851	111 802	558 745	3 876 398
1974	3 244 301	111 709	606 784	3 962 794
1975	3 397 174	110 108	642 097	4 149 379
1976	3 521 927	118 006	722 873	4 362 806
1977	3 740 553	120 212	745 076	4 605 841
1978	4 007 096	123 345	748 578	4 879 019
1979	4 188 194	125 657	766 747	5 080 598
1980	4 368 516	124 947	759 370	5 252 833
1981	4 578 347	127 656	764 909	5 470 912
1982	4 784 090	132 964	795 808	5 712 862
1983	5 057 642	137 771	811 944	6 007 357
1984	5 384 432	143 963	832 507	6 360 902
1985	5 688 812	149 209	842 891	6 680 912
1986	5 982 429	154 052	827 898	6 964 379
1987	6 351 826	155 524	860 347	7 367 697
1988	6 832 117	160 204	857 493	7 849 814
1989	7 158 262	165 198	862 733	8 186 193
1990	7 525 727	169 151	932 968	8 627 846
1991	7 866 773	175 525	948 217	8 990 515
1992	8 313 444	178 984	1 011 745	9 504 173
1993	8 770 156	186 950	1 061 372	10 018 478
1994	9 321 300	181 885	1 055 709	10 558 894
1995	9 888 426	188 414	1 099 014	11 175 854
1996	10 533 488	194 785	1 152 693	11 880 966
1997	10 997 090	204 533	1 207 138	12 408 761
1998	11 085 231	213 012	1 236 327	12 534 570

http://dx.doi.org/10.1787/667827525313

Table C3–c. **Levels of Per Capita GDP in 16 East Asian Countries, 1950–99**
(1990 international Geary–Khamis dollars)

	China	India	Indonesia	Japan	Philippines	South Korea	Thailand	Taiwan
1950	439	619	840	1 926	1 070	770	817	936
1951	479	623	885	2 130	1 150	709	849	991
1952	537	629	910	2 341	1 186	753	869	1 065
1953	554	657	938	2 480	1 253	966	935	1 144
1954	558	672	978	2 582	1 308	1 013	898	1 196
1955	575	676	986	2 772	1 357	1 054	945	1 250
1956	619	701	980	2 949	1 409	1 036	930	1 271
1957	637	680	1 028	3 138	1 441	1 087	910	1 318
1958	693	716	972	3 290	1 447	1 112	914	1 387
1959	697	717	995	3 556	1 499	1 120	992	1 469
1960	673	753	1 019	3 988	1 475	1 105	1 078	1 499
1961	557	758	1 066	4 429	1 511	1 124	1 100	1 558
1962	553	758	1 043	4 778	1 535	1 122	1 149	1 641
1963	592	779	984	5 131	1 593	1 186	1 205	1 814
1964	648	821	1 000	5 670	1 598	1 253	1 249	1 987
1965	706	771	990	5 934	1 631	1 295	1 308	2 064
1966	753	762	971	6 506	1 651	1 415	1 412	2 212
1967	712	807	930	7 151	1 687	1 483	1 486	2 401
1968	678	809	1 001	7 976	1 719	1 633	1 561	2 542
1969	722	845	1 102	8 869	1 747	1 839	1 636	2 710
1970	783	868	1 194	9 715	1 761	1 954	1 694	2 987
1971	799	856	1 235	10 042	1 804	2 522	1 725	3 336
1972	802	834	1 342	10 735	1 849	2 561	1 748	3 788
1973	839	853	1 504	11 439	1 959	2 841	1 874	4 117
1974	836	843	1 542	11 145	1 974	3 015	1 910	3 971
1975	874	897	1 505	11 349	2 028	3 162	1 959	3 988
1976	852	889	1 598	11 669	2 147	3 476	2 091	4 600
1977	895	937	1 681	12 063	2 205	3 775	2 249	5 058
1978	979	966	1 715	12 584	2 255	4 064	2 422	5 587
1979	1 040	895	1 765	13 164	2 317	4 294	2 496	5 879
1980	1 067	938	1 870	13 429	2 369	4 114	2 554	5 938
1981	1 103	977	1 957	13 754	2 387	4 302	2 654	6 301
1982	1 192	985	1 845	14 079	2 412	4 557	2 746	6 518
1983	1 265	1 043	1 878	14 308	2 399	5 007	2 850	7 114
1984	1 396	1 060	1 966	14 774	2 170	5 375	2 964	7 876
1985	1 522	1 079	1 972	15 332	1 964	5 670	3 054	8 198
1986	1 597	1 101	2 051	15 680	1 983	6 263	3 175	9 181
1987	1 706	1 125	2 114	16 251	2 020	6 916	3 427	9 737
1988	1 816	1 216	2 196	17 185	2 107	7 621	3 828	9 714
1989	1 827	1 270	2 352	17 941	2 185	8 027	4 235	9 763
1990	1 858	1 309	2 516	18 789	2 199	8 704	4 645	9 910
1991	1 940	1 290	2 599	19 442	2 136	9 425	4 984	10 539
1992	2 098	1 332	2 831	19 578	2 095	9 844	5 325	11 142
1993	2 277	1 385	2 976	19 584	2 092	10 280	5 707	11 738
1994	2 475	1 465	3 140	19 664	2 135	11 014	6 149	12 393
1995	2 653	1 538	3 329	19 857	2 185	11 873	6 620	13 028
1996	2 820	1 625	3 517	20 811	2 262	12 546	6 913	13 657
1997	2 973	1 678	3 615	21 057	2 328	13 028	6 814	14 453
1998	3 117	1 746	3 070	20 410	2 268	12 152	6 205	15 012
1999	3 259	1 818	3 031	20 431	2 291	13 317	6 398	15 720

http://dx.doi.org/10.1787/667827525313

Table C3–c. **Levels of Per Capita GDP in 16 East Asian countries, 1950–99**
(1990 international Geary–Khamis dollars)

	Bangladesh	Burma	Hong Kong	Malaysia	Nepal	Pakistan	Singapore	Sri Lanka	Average	Average ex. Japan
1950	540	396	2 218	1 559	496	643	2 219	961	661	572
1951	541	446	2 296	1 440	505	608	2 253	1 013	696	595
1952	548	449	2 377	1 473	517	596	2 280	1 020	741	629
1953	547	454	2 460	1 440	543	637	2 314	980	773	655
1954	547	419	2 546	1 490	549	636	2 321	981	789	665
1955	508	467	2 636	1 460	554	636	2 357	1 015	812	678
1956	551	490	2 729	1 505	572	638	2 332	935	850	708
1957	530	510	2 825	1 455	566	650	2 318	971	867	715
1958	510	488	2 924	1 413	592	643	2 294	991	905	748
1959	526	555	3 027	1 467	601	633	2 187	994	929	758
1960	544	564	3 134	1 530	607	647	2 310	1 020	960	763
1961	564	568	3 244	1 592	613	669	2 422	1 010	948	722
1962	550	606	3 653	1 637	618	699	2 521	1 007	970	724
1963	594	613	4 083	1 669	623	723	2 701	1 045	1 015	753
1964	588	613	4 327	1 728	626	758	2 541	1 084	1 087	799
1965	607	617	4 825	1 804	631	771	2 667	1 084	1 115	815
1966	603	580	4 865	1 846	663	812	2 892	1 114	1 167	840
1967	578	586	4 824	1 830	641	820	3 162	1 154	1 197	837
1968	619	613	4 880	1 942	633	854	3 540	1 177	1 239	838
1969	614	626	5 345	2 005	649	885	3 964	1 246	1 329	886
1970	629	642	5 695	2 079	653	952	4 438	1 413	1 419	938
1971	586	650	5 969	2 181	633	931	4 904	1 385	1 450	958
1972	505	642	6 472	2 290	639	913	5 461	1 466	1 488	964
1973	497	628	7 104	2 560	622	954	5 977	1 492	1 569	1 014
1974	547	648	7 090	2 688	647	962	6 275	1 527	1 554	1 019
1975	529	661	6 990	2 648	694	978	6 429	1 574	1 595	1 056
1976	540	687	7 906	2 910	654	1 006	6 798	1 617	1 623	1 072
1977	529	713	8 706	3 076	658	1 023	7 225	1 652	1 692	1 129
1978	551	743	9 276	3 270	670	1 079	7 751	1 736	1 780	1 199
1979	560	762	9 795	3 456	669	1 087	8 361	1 812	1 825	1 222
1980	548	811	10 503	3 657	637	1 161	9 058	1 884	1 870	1 261
1981	550	840	11 203	3 824	621	1 207	9 700	1 961	1 926	1 310
1982	542	867	11 332	3 954	680	1 259	10 127	2 026	1 982	1 358
1983	555	887	11 797	4 095	644	1 309	10 710	2 098	2 051	1 428
1984	572	913	12 845	4 307	689	1 324	11 349	2 157	2 146	1 512
1985	577	920	12 764	4 157	713	1 400	10 896	2 234	2 229	1 578
1986	590	893	13 959	4 104	725	1 446	10 849	2 295	2 303	1 647
1987	603	841	15 595	4 218	735	1 487	11 621	2 289	2 401	1 731
1988	608	731	16 717	4 481	773	1 540	12 614	2 317	2 537	1 838
1989	612	744	17 043	4 789	771	1 570	13 438	2 333	2 612	1 891
1990	640	751	17 491	5 131	807	1 598	14 258	2 448	2 700	1 953
1991	649	732	18 236	5 446	837	1 643	14 804	2 537	2 776	2 014
1992	671	788	19 197	5 738	850	1 741	15 672	2 618	2 891	2 137
1993	691	821	20 038	6 075	860	1 751	17 333	2 762	3 003	2 264
1994	706	867	20 631	6 491	907	1 789	18 924	2 879	3 145	2 418
1995	733	911	21 007	6 943	915	1 842	20 164	3 001	3 286	2 564
1996	757	953	21 440	7 376	940	1 895	21 315	3 077	3 452	2 705
1997	785	980	21 903	7 774	953	1 877	22 629	3 234	3 555	2 810
1998	813	1 024	20 193	7 100	947	1 935	22 643	3 349	3 535	2 826
1999	835	1 050	20 352	7 328	954	1 952	23 582	3 451	3 633	2 935

http://dx.doi.org/10.1787/667827525313

Table C3–c. **Levels of Per Capita GDP in 25 East Asian Countries, Annual Estimates, 1950–98**
(1990 international Geary–Khamis dollars)

	Afghanistan	Cambodia	Laos	Mongolia	North Korea	Vietnam	19 small countries	Total
1950	645	518	613	435	770	658	1 127	690
1951	653	522	621	447	709	676	1 141	691
1952	664	542	628	462	753	694	1 181	713
1953	692	534	635	475	966	712	1 179	759
1954	694	582	642	490	1 013	732	1 192	781
1955	695	556	649	505	1 054	750	1 207	796
1956	713	614	654	520	1 036	764	1 226	810
1957	699	638	661	536	1 087	775	1 245	825
1958	723	653	667	552	1 112	785	1 261	841
1959	729	698	673	568	1 120	792	1 280	852
1960	739	720	679	585	1 105	799	1 305	859
1961	730	694	685	603	1 124	812	1 341	867
1962	726	718	692	621	1 122	885	1 352	905
1963	723	752	698	640	1 186	882	1 399	920
1964	720	712	705	659	1 253	895	1 429	936
1965	720	727	712	679	1 295	877	1 473	938
1966	710	740	719	699	1 415	859	1 517	951
1967	712	758	726	720	1 483	731	1 539	902
1968	719	772	733	742	1 633	699	1 597	917
1969	713	764	740	764	1 839	739	1 635	973
1970	709	684	748	787	1 954	735	1 748	992
1971	659	648	755	811	2 522	754	1 849	1 093
1972	630	605	763	835	2 561	802	1 904	1 121
1973	684	813	770	860	2 841	836	2 031	1 218
1974	703	687	777	886	2 841	783	2 091	1 189
1975	721	605	784	912	2 841	710	2 071	1 147
1976	737	673	804	939	2 841	809	2 089	1 208
1977	669	752	821	968	2 841	818	2 075	1 207
1978	704	849	836	997	2 841	806	2 132	1 216
1979	689	875	856	1 027	2 841	795	2 242	1 219
1980	696	878	876	1 058	2 841	758	2 147	1 200
1981	749	864	891	1 115	2 841	768	2 110	1 215
1982	786	901	899	1 175	2 841	813	2 097	1 247
1983	814	932	904	1 210	2 841	840	2 107	1 267
1984	820	975	911	1 247	2 841	895	2 370	1 310
1985	813	1 021	919	1 282	2 841	929	2 127	1 322
1986	873	1 049	923	1 364	2 841	935	2 179	1 339
1987	715	994	927	1 374	2 841	949	2 204	1 325
1988	644	986	930	1 405	2 841	985	2 231	1 336
1989	634	977	932	1 404	2 841	1 011	2 258	1 349
1990	600	945	933	1 333	2 841	1 040	2 212	1 353
1991	597	983	934	1 181	2 841	1 078	2 258	1 376
1992	543	1 008	956	1 046	2 578	1 149	2 305	1 359
1993	463	1 001	1 023	995	2 542	1 219	2 353	1 370
1994	416	1 005	1 056	999	1 848	1 303	2 402	1 297
1995	496	1 043	1 081	1 043	1 520	1 403	2 451	1 313
1996	500	1 071	1 076	1 049	1 259	1 510	2 502	1 330
1997	506	1 072	1 101	1 074	1 184	1 609	2 554	1 371
1998	514	1 058	1 104	1 094	1 183	1 677	2 541	1 402

http://dx.doi.org/10.1787/667827525313

ISBN 92-64-02261-9 – © OECD 2006

Table C3–c. **Levels of Per Capita GDP in 15 West Asian Countries, 1950–98**
(1990 international Geary–Khamis dollars)

	Bahrain	Iran	Iraq	Israel	Jordan	Kuwait	Lebanon	Oman	Qatar
1950	2 102	1 718	1 364	2 818	1 664	28 833	2 429	623	30 510
1951	2 177	1 673	1 445	3 159	1 696	29 816	2 121	650	30 623
1952	2 276	1 629	1 556	3 029	1 726	30 023	2 192	677	30 221
1953	2 360	1 587	2 129	2 910	1 756	31 431	2 457	707	31 076
1954	2 430	1 545	2 463	3 374	1 788	33 234	2 746	736	32 521
1955	2 523	1 503	2 298	3 701	1 625	32 194	2 886	766	31 403
1956	2 603	1 593	2 389	3 860	2 139	32 810	2 743	799	31 891
1957	2 667	1 771	2 300	3 992	2 103	31 425	2 717	831	31 351
1958	2 736	1 919	2 493	4 108	2 219	29 888	2 269	866	31 273
1959	2 792	2 021	2 523	4 501	2 286	29 569	2 395	900	32 905
1960	2 837	2 154	2 735	4 664	2 329	28 836	2 393	935	33 239
1961	2 888	2 269	2 961	4 996	2 685	26 140	2 481	923	30 557
1962	2 928	2 247	3 017	5 267	2 618	26 463	2 507	1 084	29 344
1963	2 996	2 422	2 872	5 592	2 648	25 339	2 459	1 103	28 577
1964	3 068	2 521	3 115	5 917	2 981	25 317	2 534	1 075	26 756
1965	3 180	2 748	3 288	6 273	3 185	23 539	2 706	1 053	26 239
1966	3 278	2 934	3 349	6 190	3 138	24 062	2 804	1 079	32 372
1967	3 405	3 169	3 164	6 221	3 059	22 409	2 592	1 749	35 463
1968	3 517	3 542	3 604	7 033	2 673	22 293	2 831	3 094	36 953
1969	3 639	3 887	3 604	7 723	2 772	20 977	2 810	3 781	35 982
1970	3 780	4 177	3 473	8 102	2 395	30 674	2 917	3 796	33 237
1971	3 989	4 564	3 567	8 711	2 366	30 942	3 001	3 714	38 237
1972	4 194	5 158	3 322	9 478	2 354	30 288	3 177	3 935	39 871
1973	4 375	5 445	3 753	9 646	2 389	26 675	3 157	3 278	43 858
1974	4 580	5 759	3 825	10 025	2 505	21 940	3 505	3 543	37 001
1975	3 919	5 862	4 315	10 149	2 583	18 160	3 465	4 268	35 290
1976	4 308	6 668	5 023	10 070	3 096	18 158	3 528	4 599	35 384
1977	4 450	6 388	4 992	9 863	3 182	16 422	3 621	4 388	29 553
1978	4 409	5 462	5 694	10 124	3 718	16 534	3 720	4 085	30 268
1979	4 223	4 825	6 756	10 516	3 920	17 668	3 519	4 042	29 465
1980	4 383	3 988	6 377	10 986	4 469	13 269	3 538	4 071	29 506
1981	4 318	3 714	5 041	11 358	4 486	10 291	3 379	4 523	24 108
1982	4 414	4 132	4 833	11 392	4 623	8 688	3 151	4 800	18 772
1983	4 542	4 503	4 269	11 585	4 535	8 965	3 119	5 347	14 951
1984	4 560	4 412	4 136	11 462	4 741	9 026	3 186	5 974	13 153
1985	4 374	4 360	3 932	11 654	4 722	8 225	3 269	6 543	10 720
1986	4 312	3 811	3 759	12 028	4 959	8 534	3 125	6 441	8 345
1987	4 253	3 635	3 797	12 692	4 910	7 837	2 186	6 712	7 941
1988	4 263	3 329	2 908	12 738	4 687	7 771	1 983	6 670	7 535
1989	4 225	3 357	2 571	12 637	4 036	8 014	1 977	6 706	7 167
1990	4 092	3 586	2 458	12 968	3 775	6 153	1 949	6 479	6 797
1991	4 156	3 844	946	13 004	3 553	8 100	2 651	6 607	6 461
1992	4 362	3 981	1 194	13 379	3 936	9 816	2 744	6 899	6 716
1993	4 594	4 011	1 156	13 492	4 028	12 553	2 903	7 047	6 366
1994	4 578	3 998	1 120	14 081	4 215	12 683	3 093	7 066	6 190
1995	4 553	4 040	1 011	14 696	4 273	12 052	3 246	7 155	5 844
1996	4 583	4 190	979	15 057	4 202	11 737	3 322	7 113	6 148
1997	4 623	4 252	1 043	15 148	4 146	11 505	3 399	7 313	6 815
1998	4 620	4 265	1 131	15 152	4 129	11 273	3 445	7 267	7 304

http://dx.doi.org/10.1787/667827525313

Table C3–c. **Levels of Per Capita GDP in 15 West Asian Countries, 1950–98**
(1990 international Geary–Khamis dollars)

	Saudi Arabia	Syria	Turkey	UAE	Yemen	West Bank and Gaza	Average
1950	2 231	2 409	1 818	15 692	976	950	1 854
1951	2 374	2 264	2 000	16 777	983	986	1 926
1952	2 470	2 786	2 182	17 309	989	1 023	2 030
1953	2 664	3 084	2 362	18 532	996	1 062	2 175
1954	2 912	3 453	2 233	19 871	1 002	1 103	2 214
1955	2 922	3 040	2 345	19 616	1 009	1 144	2 217
1956	3 075	3 508	2 350	20 337	1 013	1 188	2 302
1957	3 119	3 627	2 458	20 363	1 018	1 233	2 398
1958	3 205	3 039	2 490	20 446	1 023	1 280	2 437
1959	3 458	3 063	2 523	21 398	1 027	1 328	2 521
1960	3 719	3 023	2 518	22 443	1 032	1 378	2 602
1961	4 066	3 169	2 489	23 177	1 038	1 431	2 688
1962	4 445	3 795	2 574	24 214	1 045	1 485	2 799
1963	4 716	3 674	2 750	24 975	1 054	1 541	2 923
1964	5 066	3 637	2 797	25 672	1 059	1 600	3 033
1965	5 470	3 512	2 806	26 128	1 067	1 660	3 153
1966	6 102	3 139	3 064	26 411	1 079	1 723	3 339
1967	6 463	3 291	3 133	26 571	1 091	1 789	3 453
1968	6 848	3 306	3 269	26 371	1 101	1 857	3 720
1969	7 169	3 801	3 365	25 478	1 114	1 927	3 932
1970	7 624	3 540	3 450	24 589	1 317	2 000	4 146
1971	8 476	3 759	3 561	24 817	1 514	2 076	4 421
1972	9 496	4 544	3 732	24 830	1 601	2 155	4 781
1973	11 040	4 018	3 753	24 909	1 756	2 236	4 972
1974	12 333	4 821	3 861	28 463	1 816	2 321	5 241
1975	11 797	5 570	4 034	25 444	1 910	2 409	5 381
1976	12 126	5 976	4 354	25 599	2 145	2 500	5 880
1977	13 097	5 704	4 404	26 284	2 315	2 595	5 882
1978	12 962	5 998	4 377	22 537	2 443	2 694	5 732
1979	12 897	6 010	4 260	24 803	2 508	2 796	5 689
1980	13 284	6 508	4 073	27 717	2 453	2 902	5 453
1981	13 500	6 892	4 169	25 902	2 531	3 012	5 310
1982	12 970	6 785	4 217	21 715	2 502	3 126	5 344
1983	10 946	6 634	4 325	18 870	2 571	3 245	5 276
1984	10 339	6 136	4 511	18 006	2 594	3 368	5 235
1985	9 131	6 278	4 599	16 106	2 497	3 496	5 132
1986	8 172	5 754	4 816	11 621	2 475	3 628	4 884
1987	8 192	5 655	5 163	11 597	2 495	3 766	4 936
1988	8 118	6 177	5 166	11 185	2 518	3 908	4 782
1989	8 098	5 425	5 077	11 995	2 520	4 057	4 680
1990	9 101	5 618	5 441	13 061	2 347	4 211	4 911
1991	9 719	5 789	5 389	12 754	2 195	4 370	4 903
1992	9 616	5 984	5 606	12 792	2 219	4 536	5 084
1993	9 202	6 390	5 949	12 399	2 199	4 708	5 211
1994	8 908	6 202	5 526	12 417	2 111	4 887	5 066
1995	8 627	6 021	5 822	12 927	2 221	5 027	5 148
1996	8 442	5 901	6 125	13 970	2 271	5 264	5 273
1997	8 377	5 862	6 478	14 052	2 312	5 464	5 398
1998	8 225	5 765	6 552	13 857	2 298	5 671	5 407

http://dx.doi.org/10.1787/667827525313

Table C3–c. **Average Levels of Per Capita GDP in 56 Asian Countries, Annual Estimates, 1950–98**
(1990 international Geary–Khamis dollars)

	16 East Asian countries	25 East Asian countries	15 West Asian countries	56 Asian countries
1950	661	690	1 854	713
1951	696	691	1 926	750
1952	741	713	2 030	796
1953	773	759	2 175	834
1954	789	781	2 214	852
1955	812	796	2 217	874
1956	850	810	2 302	914
1957	867	825	2 398	934
1958	905	841	2 437	972
1959	929	852	2 521	999
1960	960	859	2 602	1 032
1961	948	867	2 688	1 027
1962	970	905	2 799	1 055
1963	1 015	920	2 923	1 103
1964	1 087	936	3 033	1 175
1965	1 115	938	3 153	1 206
1966	1 167	951	3 339	1 264
1967	1 197	902	3 453	1 295
1968	1 239	917	3 720	1 348
1969	1 329	973	3 932	1 443
1970	1 419	992	4 146	1 536
1971	1 450	1 093	4 421	1 582
1972	1 488	1 121	4 781	1 637
1973	1 569	1 218	4 972	1 725
1974	1 554	1 189	5 241	1 724
1975	1 595	1 147	5 381	1 769
1976	1 623	1 208	5 880	1 824
1977	1 692	1 207	5 882	1 890
1978	1 780	1 216	5 732	1 965
1979	1 825	1 219	5 689	2 006
1980	1 870	1 200	5 453	2 036
1981	1 926	1 215	5 310	2 083
1982	1 982	1 247	5 344	2 140
1983	2 051	1 267	5 276	2 202
1984	2 146	1 310	5 235	2 290
1985	2 229	1 322	5 132	2 361
1986	2 303	1 339	4 884	2 416
1987	2 401	1 325	4 936	2 509
1988	2 537	1 336	4 782	2 623
1989	2 612	1 349	4 680	2 686
1990	2 700	1 353	4 911	2 781
1991	2 776	1 376	4 903	2 850
1992	2 891	1 359	5 084	2 964
1993	3 003	1 370	5 211	3 073
1994	3 145	1 297	5 066	3 188
1995	3 286	1 313	5 148	3 320
1996	3 452	1 330	5 273	3 477
1997	3 555	1 371	5 398	3 580
1998	3 535	1 402	5 407	3 565

http://dx.doi.org/10.1787/667827525313

Table C4–a. **Population in 57 African Countries, Annual Estimates, 1950–98**
(000 at mid–year)

	Algeria	Angola	Benin	Botswana	Cameroon	Cape Verde	Central African Republic	Chad
1950	8 893	4 118	1 673	430	4 888	146	1 260	2 608
1951	9 073	4 173	1 705	436	4 947	151	1 275	2 644
1952	9 280	4 232	1 738	442	5 009	155	1 292	2 682
1953	9 532	4 294	1 773	448	5 074	160	1 309	2 722
1954	9 611	4 358	1 809	455	5 141	164	1 328	2 763
1955	9 842	4 423	1 846	461	5 211	169	1 348	2 805
1956	10 057	4 491	1 885	468	5 284	174	1 370	2 849
1957	10 271	4 561	1 925	475	5 360	180	1 392	2 895
1958	10 485	4 636	1 967	482	5 439	185	1 416	2 942
1959	10 696	4 715	2 010	489	5 522	191	1 441	2 991
1960	10 909	4 797	2 055	497	5 609	197	1 467	3 042
1961	11 122	4 752	2 102	505	5 699	203	1 495	3 095
1962	11 001	4 826	2 152	513	5 794	210	1 523	3 150
1963	11 273	4 920	2 203	521	5 892	217	1 553	3 208
1964	11 613	5 026	2 256	530	5 996	224	1 585	3 271
1965	11 963	5 135	2 311	538	6 104	232	1 628	3 342
1966	12 339	5 201	2 368	546	6 217	239	1 683	3 416
1967	12 760	5 247	2 427	554	6 336	247	1 729	3 492
1968	13 146	5 350	2 489	562	6 460	254	1 756	3 570
1969	13 528	5 472	2 553	572	6 590	262	1 785	3 650
1970	13 932	5 606	2 620	584	6 727	269	1 827	3 733
1971	14 335	5 753	2 689	600	6 870	273	1 869	3 818
1972	14 761	5 896	2 761	620	7 021	275	1 910	3 905
1973	15 198	6 028	2 836	643	7 179	277	1 945	3 995
1974	15 653	5 988	2 914	672	7 346	279	1 983	4 087
1975	16 140	5 892	2 996	705	7 522	280	2 031	4 181
1976	16 635	5 955	3 080	742	7 723	283	2 071	4 278
1977	17 153	6 184	3 168	783	7 966	286	2 111	4 378
1978	17 703	6 311	3 260	824	8 214	289	2 153	4 480
1979	18 266	6 493	3 355	864	8 461	292	2 197	4 518
1980	18 862	6 794	3 444	903	8 761	296	2 244	4 507
1981	19 484	6 951	3 540	937	9 044	300	2 291	4 606
1982	20 132	7 114	3 642	972	9 280	305	2 338	4 826
1983	20 803	7 260	3 750	1 009	9 563	309	2 385	5 014
1984	21 488	7 400	3 864	1 047	9 870	314	2 451	5 054
1985	22 182	7 572	3 984	1 087	10 199	320	2 516	5 089
1986	22 844	7 750	4 109	1 129	10 544	325	2 556	5 223
1987	23 485	7 913	4 241	1 171	10 890	331	2 600	5 396
1988	24 102	8 090	4 379	1 215	11 236	337	2 653	5 559
1989	24 725	8 249	4 524	1 259	11 562	343	2 727	5 720
1990	25 352	8 430	4 676	1 304	11 894	349	2 798	5 889
1991	25 983	8 671	4 834	1 323	12 261	356	2 870	6 046
1992	26 618	8 960	4 998	1 342	12 636	362	2 946	6 218
1993	27 257	9 232	5 167	1 360	13 017	369	3 032	6 402
1994	27 898	9 494	5 342	1 379	13 405	375	3 117	6 590
1995	28 539	9 877	5 523	1 397	13 800	381	3 183	6 784
1996	29 183	10 250	5 710	1 415	14 202	388	3 243	6 977
1997	29 830	10 549	5 902	1 432	14 611	394	3 308	7 166
1998	30 481	10 865	6 101	1 448	15 029	400	3 376	7 360

http://dx.doi.org/10.1787/667827525313

Table C4–a. **Population in 57 African Countries, Annual Estimates, 1950–98**
(000 at mid–year)

	Comoros	Congo	Côte d'Ivoire	Djibouti	Egypt	Gabon	Gambia	Ghana
1950	148	768	2 860	60	21 198	416	305	5 297
1951	151	781	2 918	62	21 704	418	313	5 437
1952	154	794	2 977	63	22 223	421	321	5 581
1953	157	809	3 037	65	22 755	423	329	5 731
1954	160	824	3 099	66	23 299	426	337	5 887
1955	164	840	3 164	68	23 856	429	346	6 049
1956	167	856	3 231	70	24 426	432	354	6 217
1957	171	874	3 300	72	25 010	435	363	6 391
1958	175	892	3 374	74	25 608	438	372	6 573
1959	179	911	3 463	76	26 220	442	381	6 761
1960	183	931	3 576	78	26 847	446	391	6 958
1961	187	952	3 700	84	27 523	450	401	7 154
1962	192	974	3 832	90	28 173	456	411	7 355
1963	196	996	3 985	96	28 821	461	421	7 564
1964	201	1 020	4 148	103	29 533	468	432	7 782
1965	206	1 044	4 327	111	30 265	474	443	8 010
1966	212	1 070	4 527	119	30 986	482	454	8 245
1967	217	1 097	4 745	128	31 681	489	465	8 490
1968	223	1 124	4 984	137	32 338	497	477	8 744
1969	230	1 153	5 235	147	32 966	504	489	9 009
1970	236	1 183	5 504	158	33 574	514	502	8 789
1971	243	1 214	5 786	169	34 184	525	515	9 040
1972	250	1 246	6 072	179	34 807	536	529	9 306
1973	257	1 279	6 352	189	35 480	557	546	9 583
1974	265	1 314	6 622	198	36 216	591	563	9 823
1975	273	1 358	6 889	208	36 952	640	581	10 023
1976	281	1 406	7 151	217	37 737	676	599	10 229
1977	305	1 456	7 419	229	38 754	709	618	10 427
1978	314	1 509	7 692	248	39 940	760	637	10 604
1979	324	1 563	7 973	263	41 123	786	656	10 753
1980	334	1 620	8 261	279	42 441	808	676	10 880
1981	341	1 680	8 558	294	43 941	854	696	11 027
1982	349	1 742	8 866	306	45 361	904	717	11 236
1983	357	1 807	9 185	316	46 703	947	739	11 982
1984	366	1 883	9 517	289	48 088	984	767	12 653
1985	375	1 936	9 864	297	49 514	1 015	796	13 050
1986	385	1 989	10 221	305	50 974	1 037	827	13 597
1987	395	2 043	10 585	312	52 252	1 050	859	13 985
1988	406	2 097	10 956	329	53 487	1 059	893	14 379
1989	417	2 151	11 362	353	54 704	1 068	928	14 778
1990	429	2 206	11 904	370	56 106	1 078	964	15 190
1991	441	2 261	12 430	381	57 512	1 090	1 001	15 614
1992	454	2 315	12 796	391	58 723	1 106	1 040	16 039
1993	468	2 371	13 223	402	59 929	1 123	1 080	16 461
1994	482	2 427	13 731	413	61 150	1 139	1 121	16 878
1995	497	2 484	14 204	421	62 374	1 156	1 163	17 291
1996	513	2 542	14 653	428	63 599	1 173	1 205	17 698
1997	529	2 600	15 075	434	64 824	1 190	1 248	18 101
1998	546	2 658	15 446	441	66 050	1 208	1 292	18 497

http://dx.doi.org/10.1787/667827525313

Table C4–a. Population in 57 African Countries, Annual Estimates, 1950–98
(000 at mid–year)

	Kenya	Liberia	Madagascar	Mali	Mauritania	Mauritius	Morocco	Mozambique
1950	6 121	824	4 620	3 688	1 006	481	9 343	6 250
1951	6 289	843	4 690	3 761	1 014	499	9 634	6 346
1952	6 464	863	4 763	3 835	1 023	517	9 939	6 446
1953	6 646	884	4 839	3 911	1 032	536	10 206	6 552
1954	6 836	906	4 919	3 988	1 042	554	10 487	6 664
1955	7 034	928	5 003	4 067	1 053	572	10 782	6 782
1956	7 240	952	5 090	4 148	1 065	592	11 089	6 906
1957	7 455	976	5 182	4 230	1 077	610	11 406	7 038
1958	7 679	1 001	5 277	4 314	1 090	628	11 735	7 177
1959	7 913	1 028	5 378	4 399	1 103	645	12 074	7 321
1960	8 157	1 055	5 482	4 486	1 117	663	12 423	7 472
1961	8 412	1 083	5 590	4 576	1 132	681	12 736	7 628
1962	8 679	1 113	5 703	4 668	1 147	701	13 057	7 789
1963	8 957	1 144	5 821	4 763	1 162	715	13 385	7 957
1964	9 248	1 175	5 944	4 862	1 178	736	13 722	8 127
1965	9 549	1 209	6 070	4 963	1 195	756	14 066	8 301
1966	9 864	1 243	6 200	5 068	1 212	774	14 415	8 486
1967	10 192	1 279	6 335	5 177	1 231	789	14 770	8 681
1968	10 532	1 317	6 473	5 289	1 249	804	15 137	8 884
1969	10 888	1 356	6 616	5 405	1 269	816	15 517	9 093
1970	11 272	1 397	6 766	5 525	1 289	830	15 909	9 304
1971	11 685	1 439	6 920	5 649	1 311	841	16 313	9 539
1972	12 126	1 483	7 082	5 777	1 333	851	16 661	9 810
1973	12 594	1 528	7 250	5 909	1 356	861	16 998	10 088
1974	13 090	1 575	7 424	6 046	1 380	873	17 335	10 370
1975	13 615	1 625	7 604	6 188	1 404	885	17 687	10 433
1976	14 171	1 675	7 805	6 334	1 430	898	18 043	10 770
1977	14 762	1 728	8 007	6 422	1 457	913	18 397	11 128
1978	15 386	1 783	8 217	6 517	1 485	929	18 758	11 466
1979	16 045	1 840	8 443	6 620	1 516	947	19 126	11 828
1980	16 685	1 900	8 678	6 731	1 550	964	19 487	12 103
1981	17 341	1 961	8 922	6 849	1 585	979	19 846	12 450
1982	18 015	2 025	9 174	6 975	1 622	992	20 199	12 794
1983	18 707	2 092	9 436	7 110	1 661	1 002	20 740	13 137
1984	19 419	2 161	9 706	7 255	1 702	1 012	21 296	13 487
1985	20 149	2 233	9 987	7 408	1 745	1 022	21 857	13 839
1986	20 890	2 308	10 277	7 569	1 791	1 032	22 422	14 122
1987	21 620	2 386	10 577	7 738	1 838	1 043	22 987	14 066
1988	22 330	2 467	10 885	7 884	1 888	1 052	23 555	13 882
1989	23 016	2 551	11 201	8 051	1 932	1 063	24 122	13 906
1990	23 674	2 265	11 525	8 231	1 979	1 074	24 685	14 056
1991	24 493	2 005	11 858	8 417	2 035	1 085	25 242	14 293
1992	25 410	2 145	12 201	8 574	2 113	1 096	25 797	14 522
1993	26 071	2 271	12 555	8 732	2 198	1 107	26 352	15 047
1994	26 496	2 304	12 917	8 930	2 272	1 118	26 907	16 159
1995	26 864	2 282	13 289	9 182	2 334	1 128	27 461	17 150
1996	27 316	2 397	13 671	9 485	2 389	1 140	28 013	17 694
1997	27 839	2 602	14 062	9 789	2 449	1 154	28 565	18 165
1998	28 337	2 772	14 463	10 109	2 511	1 168	29 114	18 641

http://dx.doi.org/10.1787/667827525313

Table C4–a. **Population in 57 African Countries, Annual Estimates, 1950–98**
(000 at mid–year)

	Namibia	Niger	Nigeria	Reunion	Rwanda	Senegal	Seychelles	Sierra Leone
1950	464	2 482	31 797	244	2 439	2 654	33	2 087
1951	475	2 538	32 449	251	2 486	2 703	33	2 115
1952	486	2 597	33 119	258	2 535	2 756	33	2 143
1953	497	2 659	33 809	266	2 587	2 810	34	2 172
1954	509	2 723	34 518	274	2 641	2 867	35	2 202
1955	522	2 790	35 248	286	2 698	2 927	36	2 233
1956	535	2 859	36 000	296	2 759	2 989	38	2 264
1957	548	2 931	36 774	309	2 822	3 055	38	2 296
1958	562	3 007	37 569	318	2 889	3 123	39	2 328
1959	576	3 085	38 388	327	2 959	3 195	40	2 362
1960	591	3 168	39 230	338	3 032	3 270	42	2 396
1961	606	3 253	40 096	348	3 046	3 348	43	2 432
1962	621	3 343	40 989	359	3 051	3 430	44	2 468
1963	637	3 437	41 908	371	3 129	3 516	45	2 505
1964	654	3 533	42 854	384	3 184	3 636	47	2 543
1965	671	3 633	43 829	393	3 265	3 744	48	2 582
1966	689	3 735	44 838	403	3 358	3 857	49	2 622
1967	707	3 842	45 887	414	3 451	3 966	50	2 662
1968	725	3 951	46 977	425	3 548	4 074	51	2 704
1969	745	4 064	48 110	436	3 657	4 193	53	2 746
1970	765	4 182	49 309	445	3 769	4 318	54	2 789
1971	786	4 303	50 540	453	3 880	4 450	56	2 834
1972	808	4 429	51 796	462	3 992	4 589	57	2 879
1973	831	4 559	53 121	469	4 110	4 727	58	2 925
1974	854	4 695	54 600	475	4 226	4 872	59	2 974
1975	879	4 836	56 224	481	4 357	4 989	61	3 027
1976	905	4 984	57 901	487	4 502	5 101	62	3 084
1977	923	5 139	59 657	492	4 657	5 232	63	3 142
1978	935	5 294	61 533	497	4 819	5 366	64	3 203
1979	955	5 459	63 548	502	4 991	5 501	65	3 267
1980	975	5 629	65 699	507	5 170	5 640	66	3 333
1981	988	5 806	67 905	512	5 362	5 783	68	3 403
1982	1 011	5 988	70 094	518	5 583	5 931	68	3 476
1983	1 045	6 189	71 202	523	5 802	6 083	69	3 553
1984	1 080	6 389	72 597	533	5 984	6 240	70	3 634
1985	1 116	6 589	74 697	542	6 157	6 402	71	3 719
1986	1 154	6 802	76 558	552	6 335	6 569	71	3 809
1987	1 196	7 016	78 892	563	6 539	6 742	72	3 904
1988	1 256	7 237	81 330	575	6 759	6 920	72	4 003
1989	1 339	7 436	83 874	588	6 968	7 159	73	4 109
1990	1 409	7 644	86 530	600	7 161	7 408	73	4 283
1991	1 438	7 863	89 263	613	7 359	7 667	74	4 407
1992	1 464	8 093	92 057	626	7 547	7 935	75	4 348
1993	1 491	8 333	94 934	640	7 721	8 211	76	4 318
1994	1 518	8 583	97 900	653	6 682	8 497	76	4 434
1995	1 544	8 844	100 959	666	5 980	8 790	77	4 589
1996	1 570	9 113	104 095	679	6 273	9 093	78	4 734
1997	1 596	9 389	107 286	692	7 718	9 404	78	4 892
1998	1 622	9 672	110 532	705	7 956	9 723	79	5 080

http://dx.doi.org/10.1787/667827525313

Table C4–a. **Population in 57 African Countries, Annual Estimates, 1950–98**
(000 at mid–year)

	Somalia	South Africa	Sudan	Swaziland	Tanzania	Togo	Tunisia	Uganda
1950	2 438	13 596	8 051	277	8 909	1 172	3 517	5 522
1951	2 482	13 926	8 275	284	9 061	1 195	3 583	5 671
1952	2 527	14 265	8 505	290	9 222	1 219	3 648	5 825
1953	2 574	14 624	8 741	297	9 392	1 244	3 713	5 983
1954	2 623	14 992	8 984	304	9 572	1 271	3 779	6 148
1955	2 673	15 369	9 233	311	9 762	1 298	3 846	6 317
1956	2 726	15 755	9 490	319	9 963	1 327	3 903	6 493
1957	2 780	16 152	9 753	327	10 175	1 357	3 951	6 676
1958	2 837	16 558	10 024	335	10 398	1 389	4 007	6 864
1959	2 895	16 975	10 303	343	10 632	1 422	4 075	7 059
1960	2 956	17 417	10 589	352	10 876	1 456	4 149	7 262
1961	3 017	17 870	10 882	361	11 135	1 491	4 216	7 472
1962	3 080	18 357	11 183	370	11 409	1 528	4 287	7 689
1963	3 145	18 857	11 493	380	11 693	1 566	4 374	7 914
1964	3 213	19 371	11 801	389	11 990	1 606	4 468	8 147
1965	3 283	19 898	12 086	399	12 301	1 648	4 566	8 389
1966	3 354	20 440	12 377	410	12 620	1 691	4 676	8 640
1967	3 429	20 997	12 716	421	12 952	1 736	4 787	8 900
1968	3 506	21 569	13 059	432	13 296	1 782	4 894	9 170
1969	3 585	22 157	13 403	443	13 657	1 830	4 996	9 450
1970	3 667	22 740	13 788	455	14 038	1 964	5 099	9 728
1971	3 752	23 338	14 182	467	14 430	2 019	5 198	9 984
1972	3 840	23 936	14 597	480	14 843	2 075	5 304	10 191
1973	3 932	24 549	15 113	493	15 321	2 133	5 426	10 386
1974	4 027	25 179	15 571	507	15 792	2 192	5 556	10 621
1975	4 128	25 815	16 056	521	16 250	2 254	5 704	10 891
1976	4 238	26 468	16 570	536	16 704	2 317	5 859	11 171
1977	4 354	27 130	17 105	551	17 195	2 382	6 005	11 459
1978	4 678	27 809	17 712	566	17 633	2 450	6 136	11 757
1979	5 309	28 506	18 387	585	18 155	2 521	6 280	12 034
1980	5 791	29 252	19 064	607	18 690	2 596	6 443	12 298
1981	5 825	30 018	19 702	625	19 240	2 686	6 606	12 597
1982	5 829	30 829	20 367	641	19 802	2 775	6 734	12 941
1983	6 003	31 664	21 751	661	20 385	2 870	6 860	13 323
1984	6 207	32 523	22 544	682	20 987	2 970	7 185	13 765
1985	6 446	33 406	23 459	705	21 603	3 075	7 362	14 232
1986	6 700	34 156	24 181	728	22 240	3 185	7 545	14 747
1987	6 922	34 894	24 738	762	22 913	3 301	7 725	15 350
1988	6 900	35 640	25 250	792	23 582	3 422	7 895	15 991
1989	6 748	36 406	25 844	813	24 227	3 548	8 053	16 627
1990	6 675	37 191	26 628	840	24 886	3 680	8 207	17 227
1991	6 427	37 962	27 441	867	25 567	3 818	8 364	17 833
1992	6 057	38 746	28 218	894	26 261	3 959	8 522	18 465
1993	6 044	39 481	28 946	916	27 093	4 105	8 680	19 150
1994	6 174	40 165	29 710	912	28 032	4 255	8 831	19 846
1995	6 256	40 864	30 556	909	28 825	4 410	8 972	20 401
1996	6 420	41 551	31 548	928	29 341	4 571	9 108	20 929
1997	6 590	42 209	32 594	947	29 899	4 736	9 245	21 544
1998	6 842	42 835	33 551	966	30 609	4 906	9 380	22 167

http://dx.doi.org/10.1787/667827525313

Table C4–a. **Population in 57 African Countries, Annual Estimates, 1950–98**
(000 at mid–year)

	Zambia	Zimbabwe	Total 42 countries	Total other 15 countries	Total 57 countries
1950	2 553	2 853	178 488	49 852	228 341
1951	2 611	2 951	182 351	50 688	233 039
1952	2 672	3 081	186 396	51 549	237 944
1953	2 734	3 191	190 552	52 435	242 986
1954	2 800	3 307	194 671	53 353	248 024
1955	2 869	3 409	199 069	54 305	253 374
1956	2 941	3 530	203 599	55 295	258 894
1957	3 016	3 646	208 253	56 324	264 577
1958	3 094	3 764	213 064	57 393	270 456
1959	3 173	3 887	218 047	58 500	276 547
1960	3 254	4 011	223 226	59 649	282 876
1961	3 337	4 140	228 354	60 847	289 201
1962	3 421	4 278	233 414	62 239	295 653
1963	3 508	4 412	239 124	63 658	302 782
1964	3 599	4 537	245 137	64 969	310 107
1965	3 694	4 685	251 355	66 351	317 706
1966	3 794	4 836	257 755	67 845	325 600
1967	3 900	4 995	264 369	69 474	333 843
1968	4 009	5 172	271 142	71 171	342 313
1969	4 123	5 353	278 105	72 886	350 991
1970	4 247	5 515	284 921	74 580	359 501
1971	4 368	5 684	292 306	76 320	368 625
1972	4 493	5 861	299 828	78 018	377 846
1973	4 625	6 041	307 751	79 900	387 651
1974	4 761	6 222	315 794	81 900	397 693
1975	4 895	6 403	323 884	84 066	407 950
1976	5 032	6 570	332 681	86 343	419 024
1977	5 176	6 728	342 148	88 376	430 525
1978	5 324	6 866	352 124	90 312	442 436
1979	5 478	6 999	362 794	92 466	455 260
1980	5 638	7 298	373 902	94 355	468 257
1981	5 832	7 574	385 008	96 373	481 381
1982	6 059	7 798	396 330	99 053	495 383
1983	6 311	8 053	408 360	101 796	510 156
1984	6 555	8 320	420 338	104 766	525 104
1985	6 793	8 597	433 006	107 334	540 340
1986	7 054	8 881	445 493	110 258	555 751
1987	7 314	9 189	457 793	113 875	571 668
1988	7 543	9 493	469 784	117 903	587 687
1989	7 754	9 745	482 024	122 038	604 062
1990	7 957	9 958	494 785	125 980	620 765
1991	8 158	10 157	507 781	129 957	637 738
1992	8 361	10 365	520 795	133 548	654 343
1993	8 561	10 556	534 482	137 169	671 651
1994	8 762	10 612	547 686	140 488	688 174
1995	8 915	10 646	560 972	144 585	705 557
1996	9 068	10 778	575 156	147 594	722 750
1997	9 265	10 915	590 817	150 790	741 607
1998	9 461	11 044	605 442	154 512	759 955

http://dx.doi.org/10.1787/667827525313

Table C4–b. Levels of GDP in 57 African Countries, Annual Estimates, 1950–98

(million 1990 international Geary–Khamis dollars)

	Algeria	Angola	Benin	Botswana	Cameroon	Cape Verde	Central African Republic	Chad
1950	12 136	4 331	1 813	150	3 279	66	972	1 240
1951	12 221	4 491	1 813	155	3 401	69	1 008	1 286
1952	12 767	4 660	1 813	159	3 525	71	1 045	1 333
1953	13 046	4 833	1 762	164	3 653	75	1 083	1 381
1954	13 811	4 703	1 813	169	3 788	76	1 123	1 432
1955	14 224	5 080	1 813	174	3 929	78	1 165	1 485
1956	15 619	4 985	1 813	179	4 073	82	1 207	1 540
1957	17 391	5 461	1 813	184	4 224	81	1 252	1 597
1958	18 022	5 751	1 880	189	4 381	83	1 299	1 657
1959	21 323	5 777	1 950	195	4 542	93	1 346	1 717
1960	22 780	6 011	2 010	200	4 666	100	1 358	1 730
1961	20 013	6 635	2 075	207	4 722	107	1 409	1 753
1962	15 765	6 444	2 005	213	4 867	113	1 373	1 846
1963	19 928	6 791	2 097	220	5 047	120	1 369	1 819
1964	20 971	7 587	2 240	228	5 227	127	1 391	1 773
1965	22 367	8 194	2 356	235	5 332	133	1 409	1 783
1966	21 287	8 635	2 443	258	5 581	140	1 420	1 752
1967	23 277	9 064	2 467	284	5 736	147	1 487	1 764
1968	25 996	8 947	2 561	313	6 109	153	1 494	1 756
1969	28 484	9 255	2 637	344	6 411	160	1 565	1 876
1970	31 336	9 909	2 692	378	6 605	166	1 638	1 912
1971	28 666	9 943	2 704	448	6 801	155	1 590	1 948
1972	34 685	10 091	2 942	592	7 096	148	1 557	1 815
1973	35 814	10 784	3 011	722	7 201	147	1 627	1 726
1974	37 999	10 242	2 784	873	7 523	143	1 580	1 963
1975	40 705	6 314	2 904	862	7 910	147	1 609	2 301
1976	43 387	5 669	3 029	1 024	8 061	147	1 679	2 267
1977	47 319	5 799	3 199	1 061	8 520	148	1 816	2 098
1978	53 387	6 037	3 301	1 264	8 985	164	1 848	2 088
1979	58 193	6 184	3 565	1 391	9 474	182	1 745	1 640
1980	59 273	6 483	3 901	1 589	10 441	249	1 730	1 541
1981	60 766	6 353	4 122	1 736	12 222	271	1 757	1 557
1982	64 662	6 050	4 566	1 865	13 147	279	1 790	1 640
1983	68 012	5 851	4 366	2 159	14 068	306	1 681	1 897
1984	71 774	5 881	4 713	2 400	15 170	317	1 803	1 937
1985	75 512	5 911	5 068	2 577	16 528	345	1 826	2 361
1986	74 747	5 379	5 182	2 773	17 722	355	1 859	2 264
1987	74 225	5 985	5 104	3 017	16 839	380	1 812	2 208
1988	72 672	6 843	5 258	3 492	16 072	392	1 845	2 551
1989	75 123	6 959	5 144	3 944	14 632	413	1 913	2 698
1990	73 934	7 202	5 347	4 178	14 393	430	1 982	2 537
1991	73 047	7 252	5 598	4 379	13 846	283	1 970	2 801
1992	74 216	7 180	5 822	4 510	13 417	231	1 844	2 868
1993	72 583	5 241	6 026	4 600	12 987	434	1 850	2 816
1994	71 784	5 315	6 291	4 757	12 663	490	1 940	2 977
1995	74 584	5 915	6 581	4 980	13 081	500	2 057	3 004
1996	77 418	6 607	6 942	5 324	13 735	513	1 989	3 115
1997	78 270	7 043	7 338	5 739	14 435	525	2 102	3 243
1998	81 948	7 029	7 668	6 083	15 157	544	2 203	3 463

http://dx.doi.org/10.1787/667827525313

ISBN 92-64-02261-9 – © OECD 2006   316

Table C4–b. **Levels of GDP in 57 African Countries, Annual Estimates, 1950–98**
(million 1990 international Geary–Khamis dollars)

	Comoros	Congo	Côte d'Ivoire	Djibouti	Egypt	Gabon	Gambia	Ghana
1950	83	990	2 977	90	15 224	1 292	165	5 943
1951	88	1 027	3 087	95	15 498	1 340	174	6 163
1952	90	1 064	3 201	98	15 788	1 389	180	6 050
1953	94	1 103	3 317	102	16 062	1 440	187	6 888
1954	99	1 144	3 439	108	16 351	1 493	197	7 755
1955	102	1 186	3 567	111	16 655	1 548	203	7 256
1956	106	1 230	3 698	115	17 447	1 605	211	7 684
1957	110	1 275	3 835	120	18 269	1 665	219	7 933
1958	113	1 323	3 978	123	19 137	1 727	225	7 803
1959	120	1 372	4 123	130	20 050	1 791	238	8 932
1960	130	1 419	4 493	139	21 010	1 866	254	9 591
1961	132	1 465	4 912	150	22 395	2 090	296	9 930
1962	144	1 513	5 130	158	23 887	2 153	292	10 412
1963	174	1 563	5 972	171	25 485	2 229	294	10 774
1964	188	1 616	7 041	182	27 191	2 268	314	11 006
1965	188	1 670	6 886	194	28 987	2 306	348	11 154
1966	208	1 757	7 431	209	29 155	2 409	406	11 166
1967	217	1 850	7 538	224	28 789	2 508	421	11 368
1968	218	1 948	8 714	239	29 246	2 572	427	11 529
1969	221	2 050	9 098	256	31 255	2 780	473	11 939
1970	238	2 158	10 087	327	33 235	3 020	426	12 515
1971	280	2 333	10 593	361	34 620	3 330	475	13 514
1972	258	2 523	11 179	385	35 275	3 708	509	13 109
1973	229	2 727	12 064	412	36 249	4 086	533	13 484
1974	279	2 947	12 412	412	37 634	5 699	638	14 411
1975	219	3 185	12 400	430	41 441	6 090	598	12 616
1976	194	3 199	13 886	468	47 850	8 487	668	12 171
1977	190	2 934	14 541	410	54 092	6 732	701	12 450
1978	197	2 883	15 982	427	58 248	4 883	665	13 508
1979	202	3 323	16 282	444	62 846	4 814	773	13 163
1980	215	3 891	17 539	464	69 636	4 837	697	12 747
1981	226	4 697	18 152	491	72 407	4 780	691	12 765
1982	235	5 072	18 188	513	80 141	4 685	779	11 879
1983	244	5 327	17 479	519	86 307	4 756	685	11 339
1984	252	5 667	16 902	521	91 574	4 946	665	12 319
1985	259	5 412	17 732	521	97 618	4 846	609	12 943
1986	266	5 044	18 262	521	100 191	4 603	641	13 621
1987	277	5 079	17 970	521	102 718	4 005	676	14 274
1988	289	5 089	17 646	521	107 027	4 086	747	15 077
1989	290	5 277	17 542	526	110 239	4 261	799	15 843
1990	294	5 394	16 330	530	112 873	4 500	833	16 372
1991	278	5 523	16 330	533	109 261	4 775	851	17 240
1992	302	5 667	16 297	532	112 867	4 617	889	17 912
1993	311	5 610	16 265	511	114 673	4 728	943	18 808
1994	294	5 302	16 590	496	117 998	4 888	979	19 522
1995	283	5 514	17 768	478	120 948	5 231	942	20 401
1996	282	5 861	18 976	460	126 995	5 497	992	21 115
1997	282	5 750	20 115	464	133 345	5 789	999	22 002
1998	285	5 951	21 201	467	140 546	5 901	1 098	23 014

http://dx.doi.org/10.1787/667827525313

Table C4–b. **Levels of GDP in 57 African Countries, Annual Estimates, 1950–98**
(million 1990 international Geary–Khamis dollars)

	Kenya	Liberia	Madagascar	Mali	Mauritania	Mauritius	Morocco	Mozambique
1950	3 982	869	4 394	1 685	467	1 198	13 598	7 084
1951	4 851	919	4 557	1 747	484	1 267	14 046	7 332
1952	4 313	947	4 724	1 811	502	1 306	14 509	7 594
1953	4 205	984	4 895	1 879	520	1 356	14 987	7 857
1954	4 695	1 039	5 075	1 946	539	1 433	15 481	8 041
1955	5 050	1 073	5 264	2 018	559	1 479	15 991	8 537
1956	5 329	1 113	5 457	2 093	580	1 535	16 093	8 579
1957	5 504	1 155	5 660	2 170	601	1 594	16 195	8 770
1958	5 563	1 188	5 870	2 249	623	1 638	16 299	9 188
1959	5 699	1 257	6 086	2 333	647	1 733	16 402	9 684
1960	5 918	1 297	6 169	2 399	698	1 842	16 507	9 918
1961	5 775	1 328	6 297	2 414	817	2 261	17 085	10 202
1962	6 085	1 345	6 442	2 428	799	2 278	17 684	10 903
1963	6 392	1 377	6 380	2 591	750	2 595	18 303	10 513
1964	7 013	1 447	6 635	2 714	974	2 417	18 944	10 967
1965	7 093	1 472	6 604	2 753	1 109	2 495	19 608	11 215
1966	8 005	1 751	6 741	2 869	1 115	2 406	20 700	11 576
1967	8 419	1 740	7 114	2 964	1 154	2 510	21 853	12 369
1968	9 028	1 823	7 597	3 075	1 256	2 338	23 071	13 758
1969	9 590	1 955	7 883	3 060	1 237	2 453	24 356	15 394
1970	10 291	2 083	8 296	3 248	1 365	2 443	25 713	16 216
1971	10 944	2 186	8 621	3 361	1 378	2 563	27 154	17 321
1972	11 509	2 269	8 511	3 535	1 396	2 817	27 807	17 881
1973	12 107	2 212	8 292	3 449	1 309	3 169	28 800	18 894
1974	12 704	2 375	8 459	3 365	1 443	3 511	30 351	17 463
1975	12 652	2 017	8 564	3 831	1 351	3 514	32 385	14 643
1976	13 162	2 096	8 300	4 352	1 459	4 086	35 950	13 942
1977	14 369	2 079	8 498	4 648	1 440	4 353	37 711	14 055
1978	15 663	2 161	8 274	4 524	1 434	4 520	38 808	14 162
1979	16 252	2 257	9 087	5 612	1 500	4 679	40 584	14 367
1980	17 160	2 149	9 157	4 953	1 560	4 208	44 278	14 771
1981	17 555	2 197	8 366	4 787	1 619	4 455	43 054	15 040
1982	18 614	2 134	8 213	4 512	1 586	4 701	47 203	14 629
1983	18 729	2 119	8 278	4 711	1 663	4 719	46 930	13 581
1984	19 056	2 100	7 975	4 918	1 543	4 940	48 894	13 212
1985	19 876	2 071	8 155	5 029	1 587	5 285	51 955	12 022
1986	21 302	2 131	8 213	5 348	1 676	5 817	56 023	12 199
1987	22 569	2 189	8 393	5 449	1 727	6 408	54 762	12 639
1988	23 927	2 189	8 525	5 440	1 792	6 844	60 367	13 361
1989	25 018	2 216	8 867	5 995	1 852	7 145	61 748	13 900
1990	26 093	2 245	9 210	6 040	1 825	7 652	64 082	14 105
1991	26 458	2 281	8 630	5 986	1 872	8 142	68 504	14 796
1992	26 247	2 321	8 733	6 488	1 904	8 533	65 764	13 598
1993	26 352	2 374	8 917	6 333	2 009	9 104	65 106	14 781
1994	27 037	2 426	8 917	6 472	2 101	9 496	71 877	15 889
1995	28 226	2 492	9 068	6 886	2 196	9 828	67 133	16 572
1996	29 384	2 541	9 259	7 162	2 299	10 329	75 256	17 749
1997	30 001	2 555	9 601	7 642	2 410	10 897	73 751	19 755
1998	30 451	2 580	9 976	7 917	2 494	11 508	78 397	22 125

http://dx.doi.org/10.1787/667827525313

Table C4–b. **Levels of GDP in 57 African Countries, Annual Estimates, 1950–98**
(million 1990 international Geary–Khamis dollars)

	Namibia	Niger	Nigeria	Reunion	Rwanda	Senegal	Seychelles	Sierra Leone
1950	1 002	2 018	23 933	485	1 334	3 341	63	1 370
1951	1 033	2 093	25 728	512	1 410	3 464	67	1 448
1952	1 065	2 170	27 571	528	1 454	3 591	69	1 493
1953	1 106	2 248	28 217	549	1 510	3 721	71	1 550
1954	1 168	2 331	30 299	580	1 596	3 858	75	1 638
1955	1 206	2 418	31 089	598	1 646	4 002	78	1 696
1956	1 251	2 507	30 371	621	1 709	4 149	81	1 760
1957	1 299	2 600	31 615	645	1 773	4 303	84	1 826
1958	1 335	2 697	31 256	663	1 824	4 463	86	1 878
1959	1 412	2 797	32 621	701	1 929	4 627	91	1 986
1960	1 545	2 977	34 081	756	1 989	4 724	99	2 050
1961	1 562	3 100	35 229	796	1 904	4 937	94	2 087
1962	1 783	3 427	37 240	859	2 120	5 101	101	2 182
1963	1 961	3 766	40 734	925	1 912	5 298	111	2 219
1964	2 279	3 776	42 481	1 004	1 673	5 452	116	2 245
1965	2 433	4 061	45 353	1 101	1 790	5 656	116	2 405
1966	2 526	4 010	43 893	1 170	1 916	5 816	119	2 559
1967	2 424	4 029	37 072	1 256	2 051	5 746	119	2 542
1968	2 444	4 061	36 665	1 347	2 193	6 107	129	2 791
1969	2 529	3 940	46 502	1 477	2 435	5 709	129	3 045
1970	2 540	4 061	60 814	1 540	2 702	6 197	139	3 149
1971	2 627	4 291	67 970	1 575	2 734	6 187	162	3 120
1972	2 783	4 069	70 530	1 757	2 742	6 588	172	3 086
1973	2 895	3 377	76 585	1 771	2 826	6 217	187	3 180
1974	3 021	3 671	85 465	1 876	2 959	6 478	190	3 309
1975	3 052	3 570	82 904	1 838	3 510	6 965	197	3 408
1976	3 221	3 595	91 927	1 636	3 450	7 587	217	3 305
1977	3 424	3 873	95 277	1 603	3 629	7 383	234	3 353
1978	3 651	4 394	89 653	1 730	3 985	7 092	250	3 363
1979	3 806	4 709	95 852	1 815	4 360	7 590	292	3 554
1980	3 986	4 937	97 646	1 869	4 892	7 339	284	3 721
1981	4 110	4 995	89 820	1 913	5 210	7 283	265	3 951
1982	4 164	4 935	89 007	2 057	5 646	8 388	260	4 019
1983	4 057	4 844	83 000	2 157	5 984	8 602	255	3 961
1984	4 006	4 025	79 290	2 181	5 730	8 205	265	4 014
1985	4 023	4 095	86 302	2 205	5 982	8 515	290	3 904
1986	4 147	4 283	87 930	2 230	6 309	8 926	297	3 767
1987	4 268	4 130	87 284	2 248	6 261	9 290	311	3 965
1988	4 368	4 362	95 947	2 383	6 046	9 765	325	4 072
1989	4 738	4 368	102 146	2 454	6 168	9 598	343	4 164
1990	4 619	4 289	107 459	2 694	6 125	10 032	366	4 335
1991	4 882	4 396	113 907	2 863	5 862	9 992	376	3 988
1992	5 346	4 110	116 868	2 863	6 248	10 212	402	3 605
1993	5 239	4 168	119 439	2 863	5 730	9 987	428	3 609
1994	5 590	4 335	118 723	2 863	2 951	10 277	425	3 735
1995	5 780	4 447	121 809	2 863	3 919	10 842	422	3 362
1996	5 948	4 599	129 605	3 012	4 538	11 406	442	3 530
1997	6 055	4 750	133 623	3 136	5 119	11 976	461	2 817
1998	6 158	5 149	136 162	3 174	5 605	12 659	471	2 837

http://dx.doi.org/10.1787/667827525313

Table C4–b. **Levels of GDP in 57 African Countries, Annual Estimates, 1950–98**
(million 1990 international Geary–Khamis dollars)

	Somalia	South Africa	Sudan	Swaziland	Tanzania	Togo	Tunisia	Uganda
1950	2 576	34 465	6 609	200	3 362	673	3 920	3 793
1951	2 724	36 085	6 926	211	3 786	698	3 963	3 641
1952	2 810	37 360	7 270	218	3 863	723	4 450	3 868
1953	2 915	39 117	7 613	226	3 725	749	4 618	4 039
1954	3 083	41 427	7 983	239	4 028	777	4 720	3 982
1955	3 183	43 494	8 373	247	4 125	806	4 477	4 244
1956	3 301	45 907	9 259	256	4 176	836	4 775	4 479
1957	3 425	47 665	9 133	266	4 277	867	4 579	4 673
1958	3 520	48 664	9 510	273	4 314	899	5 175	4 703
1959	3 726	50 835	10 640	289	4 525	932	4 959	4 942
1960	3 775	52 972	10 838	329	4 710	1 016	5 571	5 177
1961	3 956	55 247	10 838	371	4 657	1 085	6 053	5 124
1962	4 130	58 349	11 592	449	5 080	1 125	5 912	5 332
1963	4 290	62 622	11 261	475	5 400	1 181	6 806	5 943
1964	3 826	66 827	11 142	545	5 695	1 351	7 100	6 394
1965	3 572	70 825	11 896	630	5 901	1 535	7 547	6 535
1966	4 079	73 892	11 717	657	6 657	1 676	7 735	6 941
1967	4 313	78 959	11 354	719	6 926	1 769	7 684	7 312
1968	4 388	82 371	12 048	686	7 282	1 859	8 491	7 498
1969	3 840	87 437	12 781	715	7 417	2 060	8 793	8 325
1970	4 174	91 986	12 246	926	7 847	2 112	9 315	8 450
1971	4 282	96 501	13 092	942	8 177	2 262	10 302	8 700
1972	4 717	98 362	12 814	1 057	8 725	2 340	12 129	8 757
1973	4 625	102 498	11 783	1 114	9 007	2 245	12 051	8 704
1974	3 682	108 254	12 966	1 238	9 216	2 340	13 019	8 719
1975	4 960	110 253	14 612	1 282	9 693	2 326	13 952	8 541
1976	4 944	112 941	17 302	1 324	10 386	2 315	15 054	8 606
1977	6 185	112 734	19 932	1 364	10 678	2 441	15 567	8 738
1978	6 500	116 077	19 621	1 399	10 987	2 689	16 571	8 260
1979	6 270	120 627	17 586	1 424	11 122	2 851	17 657	7 350
1980	6 005	128 416	17 758	1 466	11 216	2 721	18 966	7 100
1981	6 482	135 171	18 128	1 566	11 092	2 551	20 013	7 373
1982	6 716	134 619	20 421	1 656	11 236	2 453	19 915	7 980
1983	6 098	132 172	20 844	1 664	11 186	2 320	20 848	8 571
1984	6 306	138 893	19 800	1 698	11 465	2 389	22 040	7 843
1985	6 816	137 239	18 557	1 804	11 438	2 502	23 279	7 999
1986	7 056	137 307	19 291	1 872	11 811	2 580	22 918	8 025
1987	7 409	140 099	19 720	2 031	12 413	2 616	24 451	8 533
1988	7 359	145 855	19 952	1 984	12 937	2 733	24 478	9 148
1989	7 349	148 888	21 518	2 111	13 371	2 834	25 384	9 815
1990	7 231	147 509	19 793	2 154	13 852	2 805	27 387	10 206
1991	6 505	146 034	21 179	2 208	14 143	2 785	28 455	10 308
1992	5 536	142 967	22 280	2 237	14 228	2 674	30 675	10 628
1993	5 536	144 683	22 904	2 310	14 398	2 235	31 349	11 520
1994	5 701	149 313	24 118	2 391	14 629	2 611	32 384	12 131
1995	5 867	153 941	25 179	2 463	15 155	2 789	33 161	13 405
1996	6 048	160 407	26 362	2 552	15 837	3 059	35 482	14 490
1997	6 044	164 417	28 128	2 646	16 392	3 191	37 399	15 244
1998	6 044	165 239	29 535	2 699	16 933	3 159	39 306	16 082

http://dx.doi.org/10.1787/667827525313

Table C4–b. **Levels of GDP in 57 African countries, Annual Estimates, 1950–98**
(million 1990 international Geary–Khamis dollars)

	Zambia	Zimbabwe	Total 42 countries	Total other 15 countries	Total 57 countries
1950	1 687	2 000	176 858	17 709	194 568
1951	1 795	2 130	184 831	18 968	203 798
1952	1 910	2 232	191 583	20 059	211 642
1953	2 032	2 424	198 303	21 072	219 375
1954	2 161	2 554	208 248	21 873	230 121
1955	2 111	2 756	215 096	22 965	238 060
1956	2 362	3 148	223 320	24 392	247 712
1957	2 465	3 368	231 939	24 971	256 911
1958	2 401	3 412	237 382	25 267	262 649
1959	2 902	3 596	251 054	26 221	277 275
1960	3 123	3 762	261 999	27 609	289 608
1961	3 130	3 956	268 595	27 166	295 761
1962	3 096	4 016	276 171	30 854	307 024
1963	3 164	3 976	295 000	33 783	328 783
1964	3 586	4 326	310 279	36 203	346 482
1965	4 239	4 608	326 095	39 309	365 404
1966	4 007	4 678	333 469	42 439	375 908
1967	4 318	5 068	338 924	44 622	383 546
1968	4 379	5 168	354 074	49 389	403 463
1969	4 355	5 812	382 032	53 292	435 325
1970	4 562	7 072	416 129	55 239	471 369
1971	4 561	7 692	436 466	56 113	492 579
1972	4 979	8 342	455 548	55 180	510 728
1973	4 930	8 594	471 638	57 549	529 186
1974	5 332	8 810	497 754	56 400	554 154
1975	5 124	8 890	503 766	56 651	560 418
1976	5 426	8 816	537 581	59 988	597 569
1977	5 163	8 108	558 850	62 738	621 588
1978	5 195	8 338	573 167	63 348	636 515
1979	5 037	8 338	598 798	67 113	665 911
1980	5 190	9 288	626 270	68 617	694 886
1981	5 509	10 454	635 952	65 439	701 392
1982	5 354	10 726	656 633	65 340	721 973
1983	5 249	10 896	658 433	66 285	724 718
1984	5 231	10 688	673 549	65 872	739 421
1985	5 317	11 430	697 747	64 757	762 503
1986	5 354	11 732	711 972	66 283	778 255
1987	5 497	11 588	721 343	68 259	789 602
1988	5 841	12 672	752 279	69 913	822 192
1989	5 900	13 498	776 990	70 750	847 740
1990	6 432	13 766	789 435	70 352	859 787
1991	6 432	14 523	799 473	68 642	868 115
1992	6 323	13 216	803 175	66 447	869 622
1993	6 753	13 388	809 901	67 746	877 647
1994	6 172	14 298	829 146	68 002	897 149
1995	5 906	14 212	850 191	70 894	921 084
1996	6 284	15 250	898 652	75 305	973 958
1997	6 504	15 738	927 690	77 901	1 005 591
1998	6 374	15 990	961 581	77 825	1 039 407

http://dx.doi.org/10.1787/667827525313

Table C4–c. Levels of Per Capita GDP in 57 African Countries, Annual Estimates, 1950–98
(1990 international Geary–Khamis dollars)

	Algeria	Angola	Benin	Botswana	Cameroon	Cape Verde	Central African Republic	Chad
1950	1 365	1 052	1 084	349	671	450	772	476
1951	1 347	1 076	1 063	355	687	455	790	486
1952	1 376	1 101	1 043	359	704	461	809	497
1953	1 369	1 126	994	366	720	467	827	507
1954	1 437	1 079	1 002	372	737	460	845	518
1955	1 445	1 148	982	377	754	463	864	529
1956	1 553	1 110	962	383	771	469	881	540
1957	1 693	1 197	941	388	788	453	899	552
1958	1 719	1 241	956	392	805	449	917	563
1959	1 994	1 225	970	399	822	486	934	574
1960	2 088	1 253	978	403	832	508	925	569
1961	1 799	1 396	987	410	829	525	943	566
1962	1 433	1 335	932	415	840	539	901	586
1963	1 768	1 380	952	422	857	553	881	567
1964	1 806	1 510	993	430	872	564	878	542
1965	1 870	1 596	1 020	437	874	575	866	533
1966	1 725	1 660	1 032	473	898	585	844	513
1967	1 824	1 727	1 016	513	905	594	860	505
1968	1 977	1 672	1 029	557	946	602	851	492
1969	2 105	1 691	1 033	601	973	611	877	514
1970	2 249	1 768	1 027	647	982	619	896	512
1971	2 000	1 728	1 006	747	990	566	851	510
1972	2 350	1 712	1 065	956	1 011	536	815	465
1973	2 357	1 789	1 061	1 122	1 003	529	837	432
1974	2 428	1 710	955	1 299	1 024	512	797	480
1975	2 522	1 072	969	1 222	1 052	525	792	550
1976	2 608	952	983	1 380	1 044	520	811	530
1977	2 759	938	1 010	1 355	1 070	518	860	479
1978	3 016	957	1 013	1 534	1 094	567	858	466
1979	3 186	952	1 063	1 609	1 120	622	794	363
1980	3 143	954	1 132	1 760	1 192	841	771	342
1981	3 119	914	1 164	1 853	1 351	904	767	338
1982	3 212	850	1 254	1 919	1 417	916	765	340
1983	3 269	806	1 164	2 140	1 471	988	705	378
1984	3 340	795	1 220	2 291	1 537	1 009	736	383
1985	3 404	781	1 272	2 370	1 620	1 079	726	464
1986	3 272	694	1 261	2 457	1 681	1 091	727	433
1987	3 161	756	1 204	2 576	1 546	1 148	697	409
1988	3 015	846	1 201	2 875	1 430	1 163	695	459
1989	3 038	844	1 137	3 133	1 266	1 205	701	472
1990	2 916	854	1 144	3 204	1 210	1 231	708	431
1991	2 811	836	1 158	3 310	1 129	796	686	463
1992	2 788	801	1 165	3 362	1 062	638	626	461
1993	2 663	568	1 166	3 382	998	1 179	610	440
1994	2 573	560	1 178	3 450	945	1 305	622	452
1995	2 613	599	1 192	3 565	948	1 312	646	443
1996	2 653	645	1 216	3 763	967	1 324	613	446
1997	2 624	668	1 243	4 008	988	1 332	635	452
1998	2 689	647	1 257	4 200	1 008	1 360	653	471

http://dx.doi.org/10.1787/667827525313

ISBN 92-64-02261-9 – © OECD 2006

Table C4–c. **Levels of Per Capita GDP in 57 African Countries, Annual Estimates, 1950–98**
(1990 international Geary–Khamis dollars)

	Comoros	Congo	Côte d'Ivoire	Djibouti	Egypt	Gabon	Gambia	Ghana
1950	560	1 289	1 041	1 500	718	3 108	540	1 122
1951	581	1 315	1 058	1 546	714	3 204	557	1 134
1952	587	1 340	1 075	1 554	710	3 302	560	1 084
1953	598	1 364	1 092	1 575	706	3 401	567	1 202
1954	619	1 388	1 110	1 622	702	3 504	584	1 317
1955	625	1 412	1 127	1 632	698	3 611	588	1 200
1956	635	1 436	1 144	1 651	714	3 718	596	1 236
1957	645	1 459	1 162	1 668	730	3 827	604	1 241
1958	649	1 482	1 179	1 665	747	3 939	606	1 187
1959	671	1 506	1 191	1 711	765	4 052	625	1 321
1960	712	1 523	1 256	1 771	783	4 184	650	1 378
1961	703	1 539	1 328	1 783	814	4 639	738	1 388
1962	749	1 553	1 339	1 759	848	4 725	711	1 416
1963	887	1 569	1 499	1 774	884	4 832	698	1 424
1964	932	1 584	1 697	1 758	921	4 851	727	1 414
1965	913	1 599	1 592	1 754	958	4 860	787	1 393
1966	984	1 642	1 642	1 761	941	5 003	896	1 354
1967	999	1 688	1 589	1 758	909	5 130	904	1 339
1968	973	1 732	1 749	1 746	904	5 176	894	1 318
1969	963	1 779	1 738	1 742	948	5 518	965	1 325
1970	1 009	1 825	1 833	2 069	990	5 874	848	1 424
1971	1 154	1 922	1 831	2 142	1 013	6 347	922	1 495
1972	1 032	2 025	1 841	2 150	1 013	6 922	963	1 409
1973	889	2 132	1 899	2 185	1 022	7 337	976	1 407
1974	1 055	2 243	1 874	2 080	1 039	9 635	1 133	1 467
1975	804	2 345	1 800	2 065	1 121	9 521	1 030	1 259
1976	692	2 275	1 942	2 154	1 268	12 549	1 114	1 190
1977	624	2 014	1 960	1 794	1 396	9 497	1 134	1 194
1978	627	1 911	2 078	1 724	1 458	6 426	1 044	1 274
1979	624	2 126	2 042	1 687	1 528	6 124	1 178	1 224
1980	643	2 402	2 123	1 661	1 641	5 990	1 030	1 172
1981	664	2 796	2 121	1 674	1 648	5 596	992	1 158
1982	675	2 912	2 052	1 676	1 767	5 185	1 086	1 057
1983	683	2 948	1 903	1 643	1 848	5 022	926	946
1984	688	3 009	1 776	1 802	1 904	5 025	867	974
1985	691	2 795	1 798	1 756	1 972	4 773	764	992
1986	691	2 535	1 787	1 712	1 966	4 438	775	1 002
1987	701	2 486	1 698	1 669	1 966	3 816	786	1 021
1988	712	2 427	1 611	1 587	2 001	3 860	837	1 048
1989	694	2 453	1 544	1 490	2 015	3 989	862	1 072
1990	685	2 445	1 372	1 432	2 012	4 176	864	1 078
1991	630	2 443	1 314	1 400	1 900	4 379	850	1 104
1992	664	2 448	1 274	1 360	1 922	4 173	855	1 117
1993	664	2 366	1 230	1 272	1 913	4 212	873	1 143
1994	610	2 184	1 208	1 202	1 930	4 292	873	1 157
1995	569	2 219	1 251	1 135	1 939	4 526	810	1 180
1996	549	2 306	1 295	1 077	1 997	4 687	823	1 193
1997	533	2 212	1 334	1 068	2 057	4 864	801	1 216
1998	522	2 239	1 373	1 061	2 128	4 886	850	1 244

http://dx.doi.org/10.1787/667827525313

Table C4–c. Levels of Per Capita GDP in 57 African Countries, Annual Estimates, 1950–98

(1990 international Geary–Khamis dollars)

	Kenya	Liberia	Madagascar	Mali	Mauritania	Mauritius	Morocco	Mozambique
1950	651	1 055	951	457	464	2 490	1 455	1 133
1951	771	1 090	972	465	477	2 540	1 458	1 155
1952	667	1 097	992	472	490	2 528	1 460	1 178
1953	633	1 113	1 012	480	504	2 530	1 468	1 199
1954	687	1 147	1 032	488	517	2 587	1 476	1 207
1955	718	1 156	1 052	496	531	2 587	1 483	1 259
1956	736	1 170	1 072	504	545	2 594	1 451	1 242
1957	738	1 183	1 092	513	558	2 613	1 420	1 246
1958	725	1 187	1 112	521	572	2 610	1 389	1 280
1959	720	1 223	1 132	530	586	2 685	1 358	1 323
1960	726	1 230	1 125	535	625	2 777	1 329	1 327
1961	686	1 226	1 126	528	722	3 319	1 341	1 337
1962	701	1 209	1 129	520	697	3 249	1 354	1 400
1963	714	1 204	1 096	544	645	3 629	1 367	1 321
1964	758	1 231	1 116	558	827	3 283	1 381	1 349
1965	743	1 218	1 088	555	928	3 302	1 394	1 351
1966	812	1 408	1 087	566	920	3 108	1 436	1 364
1967	826	1 360	1 123	572	938	3 180	1 480	1 425
1968	857	1 384	1 174	581	1 006	2 907	1 524	1 549
1969	881	1 442	1 192	566	975	3 006	1 570	1 693
1970	913	1 492	1 226	588	1 059	2 945	1 616	1 743
1971	937	1 519	1 246	595	1 051	3 047	1 665	1 816
1972	949	1 530	1 202	612	1 047	3 309	1 669	1 823
1973	961	1 447	1 144	584	966	3 680	1 694	1 873
1974	971	1 508	1 139	556	1 046	4 020	1 751	1 684
1975	929	1 242	1 126	619	962	3 969	1 831	1 404
1976	929	1 251	1 063	687	1 020	4 551	1 992	1 295
1977	973	1 203	1 061	724	988	4 768	2 050	1 263
1978	1 018	1 212	1 007	694	965	4 863	2 069	1 235
1979	1 013	1 226	1 076	848	989	4 943	2 122	1 215
1980	1 029	1 131	1 055	736	1 006	4 367	2 272	1 220
1981	1 012	1 120	938	699	1 021	4 550	2 169	1 208
1982	1 033	1 054	895	647	978	4 738	2 337	1 143
1983	1 001	1 013	877	663	1 001	4 708	2 263	1 034
1984	981	972	822	678	906	4 882	2 296	980
1985	986	927	817	679	909	5 173	2 377	869
1986	1 020	923	799	707	936	5 635	2 499	864
1987	1 044	917	793	704	940	6 146	2 382	899
1988	1 071	887	783	690	949	6 504	2 563	962
1989	1 087	869	792	745	958	6 725	2 560	1 000
1990	1 102	991	799	734	922	7 128	2 596	1 003
1991	1 080	1 137	728	711	920	7 505	2 714	1 035
1992	1 033	1 082	716	757	901	7 784	2 549	936
1993	1 011	1 046	710	725	914	8 221	2 471	982
1994	1 020	1 053	690	725	925	8 493	2 671	983
1995	1 051	1 092	682	750	941	8 711	2 445	966
1996	1 076	1 060	677	755	963	9 059	2 686	1 003
1997	1 078	982	683	781	984	9 441	2 582	1 087
1998	1 075	931	690	783	993	9 850	2 693	1 187

http://dx.doi.org/10.1787/667827525313

Table C4–c. **Levels of Per Capita GDP in 57 African Countries, Annual Estimates, 1950–98**
(1990 international Geary–Khamis dollars)

	Namibia	Niger	Nigeria	Reunion	Rwanda	Senegal	Seychelles	Sierra Leone
1950	2 160	813	753	1 989	547	1 259	1 912	656
1951	2 176	825	793	2 044	567	1 281	2 019	685
1952	2 191	835	832	2 051	574	1 303	2 050	697
1953	2 223	846	835	2 067	584	1 324	2 084	714
1954	2 292	856	878	2 113	604	1 346	2 174	744
1955	2 310	867	882	2 091	610	1 367	2 164	760
1956	2 339	877	844	2 098	620	1 388	2 143	777
1957	2 370	887	860	2 089	628	1 409	2 186	795
1958	2 376	897	832	2 085	631	1 429	2 200	807
1959	2 451	907	850	2 142	652	1 448	2 254	841
1960	2 616	940	869	2 239	656	1 445	2 367	856
1961	2 579	953	879	2 288	625	1 475	2 176	858
1962	2 869	1 025	909	2 394	695	1 487	2 306	884
1963	3 076	1 096	972	2 495	611	1 507	2 458	886
1964	3 486	1 069	991	2 617	525	1 499	2 488	883
1965	3 626	1 118	1 035	2 803	548	1 511	2 435	932
1966	3 668	1 074	979	2 901	570	1 508	2 434	976
1967	3 430	1 049	808	3 033	594	1 449	2 381	955
1968	3 369	1 028	780	3 169	618	1 499	2 522	1 032
1969	3 396	969	967	3 391	666	1 362	2 455	1 109
1970	3 321	971	1 233	3 463	717	1 435	2 570	1 129
1971	3 342	997	1 345	3 473	705	1 390	2 910	1 101
1972	3 443	919	1 362	3 807	687	1 436	3 013	1 072
1973	3 486	741	1 442	3 774	688	1 315	3 224	1 087
1974	3 539	782	1 565	3 946	700	1 329	3 203	1 113
1975	3 473	738	1 475	3 821	806	1 396	3 251	1 126
1976	3 559	721	1 588	3 361	766	1 487	3 507	1 072
1977	3 712	754	1 597	3 258	779	1 411	3 691	1 067
1978	3 906	830	1 457	3 480	827	1 322	3 885	1 050
1979	3 986	863	1 508	3 615	874	1 380	4 460	1 088
1980	4 089	877	1 486	3 686	946	1 301	4 274	1 117
1981	4 159	860	1 323	3 738	972	1 259	3 914	1 161
1982	4 120	824	1 270	3 972	1 011	1 414	3 794	1 156
1983	3 884	783	1 166	4 124	1 031	1 414	3 695	1 115
1984	3 710	630	1 092	4 094	957	1 315	3 799	1 105
1985	3 606	622	1 155	4 068	972	1 330	4 116	1 050
1986	3 593	630	1 149	4 039	996	1 359	4 163	989
1987	3 569	589	1 106	3 990	958	1 378	4 335	1 016
1988	3 478	603	1 180	4 141	894	1 411	4 483	1 017
1989	3 539	587	1 218	4 176	885	1 341	4 706	1 013
1990	3 278	561	1 242	4 488	855	1 354	4 984	1 012
1991	3 396	559	1 276	4 668	797	1 303	5 065	905
1992	3 651	508	1 270	4 570	828	1 287	5 360	829
1993	3 514	500	1 258	4 476	742	1 216	5 656	836
1994	3 684	505	1 213	4 385	442	1 210	5 562	842
1995	3 744	503	1 207	4 298	655	1 233	5 484	733
1996	3 788	505	1 245	4 435	723	1 254	5 697	746
1997	3 793	506	1 245	4 530	663	1 274	5 900	576
1998	3 796	532	1 232	4 502	704	1 302	5 994	558

http://dx.doi.org/10.1787/667827525313

Table C4–c. **Levels of Per Capita GDP in 57 African Countries, Annual Estimates, 1950–98**
(1990 international Geary–Khamis dollars)

	Somalia	South Africa	Sudan	Swaziland	Tanzania	Togo	Tunisia	Uganda
1950	1 057	2 535	821	721	377	574	1 115	687
1951	1 098	2 591	837	745	418	584	1 106	642
1952	1 112	2 619	855	751	419	593	1 220	664
1953	1 132	2 675	871	762	397	602	1 244	675
1954	1 175	2 763	889	787	421	611	1 249	648
1955	1 191	2 830	907	793	423	621	1 164	672
1956	1 211	2 914	976	803	419	630	1 223	690
1957	1 232	2 951	936	814	420	639	1 159	700
1958	1 241	2 939	949	817	415	647	1 291	685
1959	1 287	2 995	1 033	843	426	656	1 217	700
1960	1 277	3 041	1 024	935	433	698	1 343	713
1961	1 311	3 092	996	1 028	418	728	1 436	686
1962	1 341	3 179	1 037	1 214	445	736	1 379	694
1963	1 364	3 321	980	1 252	462	754	1 556	751
1964	1 191	3 450	944	1 399	475	841	1 589	785
1965	1 088	3 559	984	1 577	480	932	1 653	779
1966	1 216	3 615	947	1 602	527	991	1 654	803
1967	1 258	3 760	893	1 709	535	1 019	1 605	822
1968	1 252	3 819	923	1 588	548	1 043	1 735	818
1969	1 071	3 946	954	1 612	543	1 126	1 760	881
1970	1 138	4 045	888	2 036	559	1 075	1 827	869
1971	1 141	4 135	923	2 015	567	1 121	1 982	871
1972	1 228	4 109	878	2 201	588	1 128	2 287	859
1973	1 176	4 175	780	2 258	588	1 053	2 221	838
1974	914	4 299	833	2 443	584	1 067	2 343	821
1975	1 202	4 271	910	2 462	597	1 032	2 446	784
1976	1 167	4 267	1 044	2 472	622	999	2 569	770
1977	1 421	4 155	1 165	2 477	621	1 025	2 592	763
1978	1 390	4 174	1 108	2 470	623	1 098	2 700	703
1979	1 181	4 232	956	2 434	613	1 131	2 811	611
1980	1 037	4 390	931	2 416	600	1 048	2 944	577
1981	1 113	4 503	920	2 507	576	950	3 030	585
1982	1 152	4 367	1 003	2 581	567	884	2 957	617
1983	1 016	4 174	958	2 518	549	808	3 039	643
1984	1 016	4 271	878	2 491	546	805	3 068	570
1985	1 057	4 108	791	2 560	529	814	3 162	562
1986	1 053	4 020	798	2 572	531	810	3 038	544
1987	1 070	4 015	797	2 666	542	793	3 165	556
1988	1 067	4 092	790	2 506	549	799	3 101	572
1989	1 089	4 090	833	2 597	552	799	3 152	590
1990	1 083	3 966	743	2 565	557	762	3 337	592
1991	1 012	3 847	772	2 546	553	730	3 402	578
1992	914	3 690	790	2 501	542	675	3 599	576
1993	916	3 665	791	2 521	531	545	3 612	602
1994	923	3 717	812	2 621	522	614	3 667	611
1995	938	3 767	824	2 709	526	632	3 696	657
1996	942	3 860	836	2 749	540	669	3 896	692
1997	917	3 895	863	2 793	548	674	4 045	708
1998	883	3 858	880	2 793	553	644	4 190	726

http://dx.doi.org/10.1787/667827525313

Table C4–c. **Levels of Per Capita GDP in 57 African Countries, Annual Estimates, 1950–98**
(1990 international Geary–Khamis dollars)

	Zambia	Zimbabwe	Total 42 countries	Total other 15 countries	Total 57 countries
1950	661	701	991	355	852
1951	688	722	1 014	374	875
1952	715	724	1 028	389	889
1953	743	760	1 041	402	903
1954	772	772	1 070	410	928
1955	736	808	1 081	423	940
1956	803	892	1 097	441	957
1957	817	924	1 114	443	971
1958	776	906	1 114	440	971
1959	915	925	1 151	448	1 003
1960	960	938	1 174	463	1 024
1961	938	956	1 176	446	1 023
1962	905	939	1 183	496	1 038
1963	902	901	1 234	531	1 086
1964	996	953	1 266	557	1 117
1965	1 147	984	1 297	592	1 150
1966	1 056	967	1 294	626	1 155
1967	1 107	1 015	1 282	642	1 149
1968	1 092	999	1 306	694	1 179
1969	1 056	1 086	1 374	731	1 240
1970	1 074	1 282	1 461	741	1 311
1971	1 044	1 353	1 493	735	1 336
1972	1 108	1 423	1 519	707	1 352
1973	1 066	1 423	1 533	720	1 365
1974	1 120	1 416	1 576	689	1 393
1975	1 047	1 388	1 555	674	1 374
1976	1 078	1 342	1 616	695	1 426
1977	998	1 205	1 633	710	1 444
1978	976	1 214	1 628	701	1 439
1979	919	1 191	1 651	726	1 463
1980	920	1 273	1 675	727	1 484
1981	945	1 380	1 652	679	1 457
1982	884	1 375	1 657	660	1 457
1983	832	1 353	1 612	651	1 421
1984	798	1 285	1 602	629	1 408
1985	783	1 330	1 611	603	1 411
1986	759	1 321	1 598	601	1 400
1987	752	1 261	1 576	599	1 381
1988	774	1 335	1 601	593	1 399
1989	761	1 385	1 612	580	1 403
1990	808	1 382	1 596	558	1 385
1991	788	1 430	1 574	528	1 361
1992	756	1 275	1 542	498	1 329
1993	789	1 268	1 515	494	1 307
1994	704	1 347	1 514	484	1 304
1995	663	1 335	1 516	490	1 305
1996	693	1 415	1 562	510	1 348
1997	702	1 442	1 570	517	1 356
1998	674	1 448	1 588	504	1 368

http://dx.doi.org/10.1787/667827525313

Table C5–a. World Population by Regions, Annual Estimates, 1950–98
(000 at mid–year)

	Western Europe	Western Offshoots	Eastern Europe	Former USSR	Latin America	Asia	Africa	World
1950	305 060	176 094	87 288	180 050	165 837	1 381 877	228 341	2 524 547
1951	307 154	179 291	88 374	183 200	170 311	1 407 273	233 039	2 568 643
1952	308 930	182 674	89 487	186 400	174 875	1 435 051	237 944	2 615 361
1953	310 831	185 936	90 770	189 500	179 565	1 463 989	242 986	2 663 577
1954	312 709	189 438	92 045	192 700	184 466	1 495 286	248 024	2 714 668
1955	314 704	193 001	93 439	196 150	189 580	1 526 504	253 374	2 766 752
1956	316 866	196 630	94 721	199 650	194 851	1 558 521	258 894	2 820 132
1957	319 075	200 534	95 801	203 150	200 315	1 593 917	264 577	2 877 369
1958	321 368	204 130	96 919	206 700	205 990	1 630 911	270 456	2 936 474
1959	323 864	207 743	98 003	210 450	211 871	1 664 465	276 547	2 992 943
1960	326 354	211 193	99 056	214 350	217 946	1 686 557	282 876	3 038 332
1961	329 208	214 864	100 112	218 150	224 038	1 703 159	289 201	3 078 732
1962	332 429	218 306	101 010	221 750	230 359	1 732 466	295 653	3 131 974
1963	335 473	221 617	101 914	225 100	236 870	1 773 369	302 782	3 197 125
1964	338 094	224 890	102 783	228 150	243 570	1 813 771	310 107	3 261 365
1965	340 921	227 923	103 610	230 900	250 412	1 856 142	317 706	3 327 615
1966	343 368	230 857	104 412	233 500	257 334	1 901 077	325 600	3 396 148
1967	345 536	233 617	105 195	236 000	264 325	1 946 334	333 843	3 464 850
1968	347 492	236 170	106 264	238 350	271 436	1 993 712	342 313	3 535 737
1969	349 730	238 721	107 101	240 600	278 694	2 041 981	350 991	3 607 818
1970	351 931	241 676	107 927	242 757	286 046	2 092 669	359 501	3 682 507
1971	354 396	245 618	108 782	245 083	293 473	2 145 313	368 625	3 761 291
1972	356 490	248 398	109 628	247 459	300 949	2 196 790	377 846	3 837 560
1973	358 390	250 945	110 490	249 747	308 451	2 247 814	387 651	3 913 488
1974	359 954	253 474	111 461	252 131	316 009	2 297 965	397 693	3 988 687
1975	361 201	256 162	112 468	254 469	323 578	2 344 965	407 950	4 060 793
1976	362 292	258 702	113 457	256 760	331 230	2 391 244	419 024	4 132 709
1977	363 464	261 355	114 442	259 029	338 887	2 436 979	430 525	4 204 680
1978	364 667	264 109	115 300	261 253	346 560	2 483 071	442 436	4 277 395
1979	365 931	266 986	116 157	263 425	354 366	2 532 205	455 260	4 354 330
1980	367 487	270 158	116 921	265 542	362 041	2 580 039	468 257	4 430 445
1981	368 676	272 946	117 661	267 722	370 010	2 626 190	481 381	4 504 586
1982	369 472	275 757	118 323	270 042	378 155	2 669 253	495 383	4 576 385
1983	370 073	278 382	118 926	272 540	386 211	2 728 122	510 156	4 664 410
1984	370 613	280 887	119 503	275 066	394 093	2 777 658	525 104	4 742 924
1985	371 282	283 468	120 062	277 537	401 985	2 829 821	540 340	4 824 495
1986	372 073	286 150	120 574	280 236	410 109	2 882 336	555 751	4 907 229
1987	372 903	288 922	121 051	283 100	418 332	2 936 981	571 668	4 992 957
1988	374 053	291 675	121 253	285 463	426 621	2 992 382	587 687	5 079 134
1989	375 569	294 798	121 650	287 845	434 950	3 047 480	604 062	5 166 354
1990	377 324	298 150	121 866	289 350	443 049	3 102 758	620 765	5 253 262
1991	380 150	301 442	122 049	291 060	451 153	3 154 518	637 738	5 338 109
1992	381 043	304 764	122 070	292 422	459 285	3 206 375	654 343	5 420 302
1993	382 862	308 010	121 632	292 417	467 406	3 260 457	671 651	5 504 436
1994	384 221	311 090	121 323	292 407	475 526	3 312 538	688 174	5 585 279
1995	385 412	314 143	121 126	292 196	483 645	3 366 441	705 557	5 668 520
1996	386 514	317 175	120 980	291 660	491 723	3 416 609	722 750	5 747 411
1997	387 570	320 311	120 977	291 027	499 724	3 466 589	741 607	5 827 805
1998	388 399	323 420	121 006	290 866	507 623	3 516 411	759 955	5 907 680

http://dx.doi.org/10.1787/667827525313

ISBN 92-64-02261-9 – © OECD 2006

Table C5–b. World GDP by Regions, Annual Estimates, 1950–98
(million 1990 International Geary–Khamis dollars)

	Western Europe	Western Offshoots	Eastern Europe	Former USSR	Latin America	Asia	Africa	World
1950	1 401 551	1 635 490	185 023	510 243	423 556	985 669	194 567	5 336 099
1951	1 484 940	1 753 540	195 667	512 566	445 119	1 054 754	203 798	5 650 385
1952	1 539 065	1 821 083	198 287	545 792	460 258	1 142 584	211 641	5 918 710
1953	1 619 122	1 903 763	209 197	569 260	477 777	1 221 578	219 375	6 220 072
1954	1 706 591	1 898 106	218 949	596 910	507 335	1 273 820	230 122	6 431 833
1955	1 813 957	2 032 869	233 875	648 027	538 673	1 333 611	238 060	6 839 072
1956	1 896 446	2 082 376	239 574	710 065	560 393	1 424 286	247 712	7 160 852
1957	1 980 883	2 123 207	257 645	724 470	600 946	1 489 000	256 911	7 433 062
1958	2 028 388	2 111 417	272 649	778 840	631 022	1 585 962	262 649	7 670 927
1959	2 124 669	2 261 993	286 878	770 244	648 142	1 662 352	277 275	8 031 553
1960	2 261 553	2 320 141	304 633	843 434	690 323	1 741 230	289 608	8 450 922
1961	2 381 945	2 374 411	322 781	891 763	722 982	1 749 488	295 761	8 739 132
1962	2 497 074	2 518 521	328 253	915 928	752 895	1 827 737	307 025	9 147 433
1963	2 613 049	2 630 968	344 112	895 016	775 494	1 956 643	328 783	9 544 065
1964	2 766 560	2 785 505	364 518	1 010 727	828 073	2 130 607	346 483	10 232 473
1965	2 886 298	2 962 352	380 016	1 068 117	869 320	2 239 319	365 404	10 770 826
1966	2 998 658	3 151 817	404 452	1 119 932	911 730	2 402 366	375 909	11 364 864
1967	3 104 789	3 234 760	420 645	1 169 422	951 067	2 520 293	383 547	11 784 523
1968	3 274 469	3 389 792	436 444	1 237 966	1 009 134	2 686 873	403 463	12 438 141
1969	3 467 301	3 507 231	449 862	1 255 392	1 074 640	2 945 818	435 325	13 135 568
1970	3 623 854	3 527 862	465 695	1 351 818	1 148 713	3 214 519	471 368	13 803 829
1971	3 745 279	3 647 077	499 790	1 387 832	1 214 030	3 393 670	492 579	14 380 257
1972	3 911 812	3 836 032	524 971	1 395 732	1 289 774	3 596 029	510 728	15 065 078
1973	4 133 780	4 058 289	550 756	1 513 070	1 397 698	3 876 398	529 186	16 059 177
1974	4 219 829	4 067 628	583 528	1 556 984	1 476 432	3 962 794	554 155	16 421 350
1975	4 193 760	4 069 398	604 251	1 561 399	1 518 608	4 149 379	560 418	16 657 212
1976	4 370 938	4 280 195	619 961	1 634 589	1 602 069	4 362 806	597 568	17 468 126
1977	4 492 840	4 459 671	641 681	1 673 159	1 677 493	4 605 841	621 588	18 172 272
1978	4 621 755	4 700 723	662 328	1 715 215	1 748 846	4 879 019	636 515	18 964 401
1979	4 785 340	4 866 597	672 299	1 707 083	1 858 391	5 080 598	665 912	19 636 220
1980	4 860 483	4 878 155	675 819	1 709 174	1 959 670	5 252 833	694 887	20 031 021
1981	4 869 363	5 006 126	667 932	1 724 741	1 970 328	5 470 912	701 392	20 410 793
1982	4 909 494	4 912 862	674 202	1 767 262	1 947 932	5 712 862	721 973	20 646 587
1983	4 996 928	5 103 869	684 326	1 823 723	1 899 843	6 007 357	724 718	21 240 764
1984	5 117 924	5 467 359	705 274	1 847 190	1 973 180	6 360 902	739 421	22 211 250
1985	5 244 501	5 687 354	706 201	1 863 687	2 033 805	6 680 912	762 503	22 978 964
1986	5 391 139	5 875 446	725 733	1 940 363	2 115 920	6 964 379	778 255	23 791 235
1987	5 545 984	6 086 756	721 188	1 965 457	2 181 077	7 367 697	789 602	24 657 761
1988	5 768 451	6 344 832	727 564	2 007 280	2 201 800	7 849 814	822 192	25 721 933
1989	5 964 036	6 560 368	718 039	2 037 253	2 229 366	8 186 193	847 741	26 542 996
1990	6 032 764	6 665 584	662 604	1 987 995	2 239 427	8 627 846	859 787	27 076 007
1991	6 132 835	6 639 812	590 231	1 863 524	2 321 984	8 990 515	868 115	27 407 016
1992	6 202 821	6 845 134	559 157	1 592 085	2 395 605	9 504 173	869 621	27 968 596
1993	6 182 869	7 012 226	550 466	1 435 008	2 478 695	10 018 478	877 647	28 555 388
1994	6 354 267	7 301 903	572 173	1 235 701	2 604 645	10 558 894	897 148	29 524 731
1995	6 506 423	7 506 406	605 352	1 169 446	2 642 585	11 175 854	921 085	30 527 151
1996	6 613 161	7 770 948	628 154	1 137 039	2 732 722	11 880 966	973 958	31 736 947
1997	6 780 168	8 114 193	646 234	1 156 028	2 876 155	12 408 761	1 005 591	32 987 130
1998	6 960 616	8 456 135	660 861	1 132 434	2 941 609	12 534 570	1 039 407	33 725 631

http://dx.doi.org/10.1787/667827525313

Table C5–c. World Per Capita GDP by Regions, Annual Estimates, 1950-98
(million 1990 international Geary–Khamis dollars)

	Western Europe	Western Offshoots	Eastern Europe	Former USSR	Latin America	Asia	Africa	World
1950	4 594	9 288	2 120	2 834	2 554	713	852	2 114
1951	4 835	9 780	2 214	2 798	2 614	750	875	2 200
1952	4 982	9 969	2 216	2 928	2 632	796	889	2 263
1953	5 209	10 239	2 305	3 004	2 661	834	903	2 335
1954	5 457	10 020	2 379	3 098	2 750	852	928	2 369
1955	5 764	10 533	2 503	3 304	2 841	874	940	2 472
1956	5 985	10 590	2 529	3 557	2 876	914	957	2 539
1957	6 208	10 588	2 689	3 566	3 000	934	971	2 583
1958	6 312	10 343	2 813	3 768	3 063	972	971	2 612
1959	6 560	10 888	2 927	3 660	3 059	999	1 003	2 683
1960	6 930	10 986	3 075	3 935	3 167	1 032	1 024	2 781
1961	7 235	11 051	3 224	4 088	3 227	1 027	1 023	2 839
1962	7 512	11 537	3 250	4 130	3 268	1 055	1 038	2 921
1963	7 789	11 872	3 376	3 976	3 274	1 103	1 086	2 985
1964	8 183	12 386	3 546	4 430	3 400	1 175	1 117	3 137
1965	8 466	12 997	3 668	4 626	3 472	1 206	1 150	3 237
1966	8 733	13 653	3 874	4 796	3 543	1 264	1 155	3 346
1967	8 985	13 846	3 999	4 955	3 598	1 295	1 149	3 401
1968	9 423	14 353	4 107	5 194	3 718	1 348	1 179	3 518
1969	9 914	14 692	4 200	5 218	3 856	1 443	1 240	3 641
1970	10 297	14 597	4 315	5 569	4 016	1 536	1 311	3 748
1971	10 568	14 849	4 594	5 663	4 137	1 582	1 336	3 823
1972	10 973	15 443	4 789	5 640	4 286	1 637	1 352	3 926
1973	11 534	16 172	4 985	6 058	4 531	1 725	1 365	4 104
1974	11 723	16 048	5 235	6 175	4 672	1 724	1 393	4 117
1975	11 611	15 886	5 373	6 136	4 693	1 769	1 374	4 102
1976	12 065	16 545	5 464	6 366	4 837	1 824	1 426	4 227
1977	12 361	17 064	5 607	6 459	4 950	1 890	1 444	4 322
1978	12 674	17 798	5 744	6 565	5 046	1 965	1 439	4 434
1979	13 077	18 228	5 788	6 480	5 244	2 006	1 463	4 510
1980	13 226	18 057	5 780	6 437	5 413	2 036	1 484	4 521
1981	13 208	18 341	5 677	6 442	5 325	2 083	1 457	4 531
1982	13 288	17 816	5 698	6 544	5 151	2 140	1 457	4 512
1983	13 503	18 334	5 754	6 692	4 919	2 202	1 421	4 554
1984	13 809	19 465	5 902	6 715	5 007	2 290	1 408	4 683
1985	14 125	20 063	5 882	6 715	5 059	2 361	1 411	4 763
1986	14 489	20 533	6 019	6 924	5 159	2 416	1 400	4 848
1987	14 872	21 067	5 958	6 943	5 214	2 509	1 381	4 939
1988	15 421	21 753	6 000	7 032	5 161	2 623	1 399	5 064
1989	15 880	22 254	5 902	7 078	5 126	2 686	1 403	5 138
1990	15 988	22 356	5 437	6 871	5 055	2 781	1 385	5 154
1991	16 133	22 027	4 836	6 403	5 147	2 850	1 361	5 134
1992	16 279	22 460	4 581	5 444	5 216	2 964	1 329	5 160
1993	16 149	22 766	4 526	4 907	5 303	3 073	1 307	5 188
1994	16 538	23 472	4 716	4 226	5 477	3 188	1 304	5 286
1995	16 882	23 895	4 998	4 002	5 464	3 320	1 305	5 385
1996	17 110	24 501	5 192	3 899	5 557	3 477	1 348	5 522
1997	17 494	25 332	5 342	3 972	5 755	3 580	1 356	5 660
1998	17 921	26 146	5 461	3 893	5 795	3 565	1 368	5 709

http://dx.doi.org/10.1787/667827525313

Table C–6a. **Year to Year Percentage Change in World Population, by Regions, 1950–98**

	Western Europe	Western Offshoots	Eastern Europe	Former USSR	Latin America	Asia	Africa	World
1950								
1951	0.7	1.8	1.2	1.7	2.7	1.8	2.1	1.7
1952	0.6	1.9	1.3	1.7	2.7	2.0	2.1	1.8
1953	0.6	1.8	1.4	1.7	2.7	2.0	2.1	1.8
1954	0.6	1.9	1.4	1.7	2.7	2.1	2.1	1.9
1955	0.6	1.9	1.5	1.8	2.8	2.1	2.2	1.9
1956	0.7	1.9	1.4	1.8	2.8	2.1	2.2	1.9
1957	0.7	2.0	1.1	1.8	2.8	2.3	2.2	2.0
1958	0.7	1.8	1.2	1.7	2.8	2.3	2.2	2.1
1959	0.8	1.8	1.1	1.8	2.9	2.1	2.3	1.9
1960	0.8	1.7	1.1	1.9	2.9	1.3	2.3	1.5
1961	0.9	1.7	1.1	1.8	2.8	1.0	2.2	1.3
1962	1.0	1.6	0.9	1.7	2.8	1.7	2.2	1.7
1963	0.9	1.5	0.9	1.5	2.8	2.4	2.4	2.1
1964	0.8	1.5	0.9	1.4	2.8	2.3	2.4	2.0
1965	0.8	1.3	0.8	1.2	2.8	2.3	2.5	2.0
1966	0.7	1.3	0.8	1.1	2.8	2.4	2.5	2.1
1967	0.6	1.2	0.7	1.1	2.7	2.4	2.5	2.0
1968	0.6	1.1	1.0	1.0	2.7	2.4	2.5	2.0
1969	0.6	1.1	0.8	0.9	2.7	2.4	2.5	2.0
1970	0.6	1.2	0.8	0.9	2.6	2.5	2.4	2.1
1971	0.7	1.6	0.8	1.0	2.6	2.5	2.5	2.1
1972	0.6	1.1	0.8	1.0	2.5	2.4	2.5	2.0
1973	0.5	1.0	0.8	0.9	2.5	2.3	2.6	2.0
1974	0.4	1.0	0.9	1.0	2.5	2.2	2.6	1.9
1975	0.3	1.1	0.9	0.9	2.4	2.0	2.6	1.8
1976	0.3	1.0	0.9	0.9	2.4	2.0	2.7	1.8
1977	0.3	1.0	0.9	0.9	2.3	1.9	2.7	1.7
1978	0.3	1.1	0.7	0.9	2.3	1.9	2.8	1.7
1979	0.3	1.1	0.7	0.8	2.3	2.0	2.9	1.8
1980	0.4	1.2	0.7	0.8	2.2	1.9	2.9	1.7
1981	0.3	1.0	0.6	0.8	2.2	1.8	2.8	1.7
1982	0.2	1.0	0.6	0.9	2.2	1.6	2.9	1.6
1983	0.2	1.0	0.5	0.9	2.1	2.2	3.0	1.9
1984	0.1	0.9	0.5	0.9	2.0	1.8	2.9	1.7
1985	0.2	0.9	0.5	0.9	2.0	1.9	2.9	1.7
1986	0.2	0.9	0.4	1.0	2.0	1.9	2.9	1.7
1987	0.2	1.0	0.4	1.0	2.0	1.9	2.9	1.7
1988	0.3	1.0	0.2	0.8	2.0	1.9	2.8	1.7
1989	0.4	1.1	0.3	0.8	2.0	1.8	2.8	1.7
1990	0.5	1.1	0.2	0.5	1.9	1.8	2.8	1.7
1991	0.7	1.1	0.2	0.6	1.8	1.7	2.7	1.6
1992	0.2	1.1	0.0	0.5	1.8	1.6	2.6	1.5
1993	0.5	1.1	−0.4	0.0	1.8	1.7	2.6	1.6
1994	0.4	1.0	−0.3	0.0	1.7	1.6	2.5	1.5
1995	0.3	1.0	−0.2	−0.1	1.7	1.6	2.5	1.5
1996	0.3	1.0	−0.1	−0.2	1.7	1.5	2.4	1.4
1997	0.3	1.0	0.0	−0.2	1.6	1.5	2.6	1.4
1998	0.2	1.0	0.0	−0.1	1.6	1.4	2.5	1.4

http://dx.doi.org/10.1787/667827525313

Table C6–b. **Year to Year Percentage Change in World GDP Volume, by Regions, 1950–98**

	Western Europe	Western Offshoots	Eastern Europe	Former USSR	Latin America	Asia	Africa	World
1950								
1951	5.9	7.2	5.8	0.5	5.1	7.0	4.7	5.9
1952	3.6	3.9	1.3	6.5	3.4	8.3	3.8	4.7
1953	5.2	4.5	5.5	4.3	3.8	6.9	3.7	5.1
1954	5.4	−0.3	4.7	4.9	6.2	4.3	4.9	3.4
1955	6.3	7.1	6.8	8.6	6.2	4.7	3.4	6.3
1956	4.5	2.4	2.4	9.6	4.0	6.8	4.1	4.7
1957	4.5	2.0	7.5	2.0	7.2	4.5	3.7	3.8
1958	2.4	−0.6	5.8	7.5	5.0	6.5	2.2	3.2
1959	4.7	7.1	5.2	−1.1	2.7	4.8	5.6	4.7
1960	6.4	2.6	6.2	9.5	6.5	4.7	4.4	5.2
1961	5.3	2.3	6.0	5.7	4.7	0.5	2.1	3.4
1962	4.8	6.1	1.7	2.7	4.1	4.5	3.8	4.7
1963	4.6	4.5	4.8	−2.3	3.0	7.1	7.1	4.3
1964	5.9	5.9	5.9	12.9	6.8	8.9	5.4	7.2
1965	4.1	6.3	4.3	5.7	5.0	5.1	5.5	5.2
1966	4.1	6.4	6.4	4.9	4.9	7.3	2.9	5.6
1967	3.5	2.6	4.0	4.4	4.3	4.9	2.0	3.7
1968	5.5	4.8	3.8	5.9	6.1	6.6	5.2	5.5
1969	5.9	3.5	3.1	1.4	6.5	9.6	7.9	5.6
1970	4.5	0.6	3.5	7.7	6.9	9.1	8.3	5.1
1971	3.4	3.4	7.3	2.7	5.7	5.6	4.5	4.2
1972	4.4	5.2	5.0	0.6	6.2	6.0	3.7	4.8
1973	5.7	5.8	4.9	8.4	8.4	7.8	3.6	6.6
1974	2.1	0.2	6.0	2.9	5.6	2.2	4.7	2.3
1975	−0.6	0.0	3.6	0.3	2.9	4.7	1.1	1.4
1976	4.2	5.2	2.6	4.7	5.5	5.1	6.6	4.9
1977	2.8	4.2	3.5	2.4	4.7	5.6	4.0	4.0
1978	2.9	5.4	3.2	2.5	4.3	5.9	2.4	4.4
1979	3.5	3.5	1.5	−0.5	6.3	4.1	4.6	3.5
1980	1.6	0.2	0.5	0.1	5.4	3.4	4.4	2.0
1981	0.2	2.6	−1.2	0.9	0.5	4.2	0.9	1.9
1982	0.8	−1.9	0.9	2.5	−1.1	4.4	2.9	1.2
1983	1.8	3.9	1.5	3.2	−2.5	5.2	0.4	2.9
1984	2.4	7.1	3.1	1.3	3.9	5.9	2.0	4.6
1985	2.5	4.0	0.1	0.9	3.1	5.0	3.1	3.5
1986	2.8	3.3	2.8	4.1	4.0	4.2	2.1	3.5
1987	2.9	3.6	−0.6	1.3	3.1	5.8	1.5	3.6
1988	4.0	4.2	0.9	2.1	1.0	6.5	4.1	4.3
1989	3.4	3.4	−1.3	1.5	1.3	4.3	3.1	3.2
1990	1.2	1.6	−7.7	−2.4	0.5	5.4	1.4	2.0
1991	1.7	−0.4	−10.9	−6.3	3.7	4.2	1.0	1.2
1992	1.1	3.1	−5.3	−14.6	3.2	5.7	0.2	2.0
1993	−0.3	2.4	−1.6	−9.9	3.5	5.4	0.9	2.1
1994	2.8	4.1	3.9	−13.9	5.1	5.4	2.2	3.4
1995	2.4	2.8	5.8	−5.4	1.5	5.8	2.7	3.4
1996	1.6	3.5	3.8	−2.8	3.4	6.3	5.7	4.0
1997	2.5	4.4	2.9	1.7	5.2	4.4	3.2	3.9
1998	2.7	4.2	2.3	−2.0	2.3	1.0	3.4	2.2

http://dx.doi.org/10.1787/667827525313

Table C6–c. **Year to Year Percentage Change in World Per Capita GDP, by Regions, 1950–98**

	Western Europe	Western Offshoots	Eastern Europe	Former USSR	Latin America	Asia	Africa	World
1950								
1951	5.2	5.3	4.5	−1.3	2.3	5.1	2.6	4.1
1952	3.0	1.9	0.1	4.7	0.7	6.2	1.7	2.9
1953	4.6	2.7	4.0	2.6	1.1	4.8	1.5	3.2
1954	4.8	−2.1	3.2	3.1	3.4	2.1	2.8	1.5
1955	5.6	5.1	5.2	6.7	3.3	2.6	1.3	4.3
1956	3.8	0.5	1.1	7.7	1.2	4.6	1.8	2.7
1957	3.7	0.0	6.3	0.3	4.3	2.2	1.5	1.7
1958	1.7	−2.3	4.6	5.7	2.1	4.1	0.0	1.1
1959	3.9	5.3	4.1	−2.9	−0.1	2.7	3.2	2.7
1960	5.6	0.9	5.1	7.5	3.5	3.4	2.1	3.6
1961	4.4	0.6	4.8	3.9	1.9	−0.5	−0.1	2.1
1962	3.8	4.4	0.8	1.0	1.3	2.7	1.5	2.9
1963	3.7	2.9	3.9	−3.7	0.2	4.6	4.6	2.2
1964	5.1	4.3	5.0	11.4	3.8	6.5	2.9	5.1
1965	3.3	4.9	3.4	4.4	2.1	2.7	2.9	3.1
1966	3.4	5.0	5.6	3.7	2.1	4.7	0.4	3.4
1967	2.9	1.4	3.2	3.3	1.6	2.5	−0.5	1.6
1968	4.9	3.7	2.7	4.8	3.3	4.1	2.6	3.4
1969	5.2	2.4	2.3	0.5	3.7	7.0	5.2	3.5
1970	3.9	−0.6	2.7	6.7	4.1	6.5	5.7	3.0
1971	2.6	1.7	6.5	1.7	3.0	3.0	1.9	2.0
1972	3.8	4.0	4.2	−0.4	3.6	3.5	1.2	2.7
1973	5.1	4.7	4.1	7.4	5.7	5.3	1.0	4.5
1974	1.6	−0.8	5.0	1.9	3.1	0.0	2.1	0.3
1975	−1.0	−1.0	2.6	−0.6	0.5	2.6	−1.4	−0.4
1976	3.9	4.1	1.7	3.8	3.1	3.1	3.8	3.0
1977	2.5	3.1	2.6	1.5	2.3	3.6	1.2	2.3
1978	2.5	4.3	2.4	1.6	1.9	4.0	−0.4	2.6
1979	3.2	2.4	0.8	−1.3	3.9	2.1	1.7	1.7
1980	1.1	−0.9	−0.1	−0.7	3.2	1.5	1.5	0.3
1981	−0.1	1.6	−1.8	0.1	−1.6	2.3	−1.8	0.2
1982	0.6	−2.9	0.4	1.6	−3.3	2.7	0.0	−0.4
1983	1.6	2.9	1.0	2.2	−4.5	2.9	−2.5	0.9
1984	2.3	6.2	2.6	0.4	1.8	4.0	−0.9	2.8
1985	2.3	3.1	−0.3	0.0	1.0	3.1	0.2	1.7
1986	2.6	2.3	2.3	3.1	2.0	2.3	−0.8	1.8
1987	2.6	2.6	−1.0	0.3	1.1	3.8	−1.4	1.9
1988	3.7	3.3	0.7	1.3	−1.0	4.6	1.3	2.5
1989	3.0	2.3	−1.6	0.7	−0.7	2.4	0.3	1.4
1990	0.7	0.5	−7.9	−2.9	−1.4	3.5	−1.3	0.3
1991	0.9	−1.5	−11.1	−6.8	1.8	2.5	−1.7	−0.4
1992	0.9	2.0	−5.3	−15.0	1.3	4.0	−2.4	0.5
1993	−0.8	1.4	−1.2	−9.9	1.7	3.7	−1.7	0.5
1994	2.4	3.1	4.2	−13.9	3.3	3.7	−0.2	1.9
1995	2.1	1.8	6.0	−5.3	−0.2	4.1	0.1	1.9
1996	1.4	2.5	3.9	−2.6	1.7	4.7	3.2	2.5
1997	2.2	3.4	2.9	1.9	3.6	2.9	0.6	2.5
1998	2.4	3.2	2.2	−2.0	0.7	−0.4	0.9	0.9

http://dx.doi.org/10.1787/667827525313

Appendix D

Growth and Levels of Performance in 27 Formerly Communist Countries

Table D–1a. **GDP in East European Countries, 1990–99**
(million 1990 international dollars)

	Albania	Bulgaria	Czech Republic	Slovakia	Hungary	Poland	Romania	Former Yugoslavia	Total
1990	8 125	49 779	91 706	40 854	66 990	194 920	80 277	129 953	662 604
1991	5 850	45 617	81 057	34 904	59 019	181 245	69 902	112 637	590 231
1992	5 426	42 277	80 640	32 641	57 212	185 958	63 779	91 224	559 157
1993	5 949	41 674	80 690	31 468	56 884	192 982	64 800	76 019	550 466
1994	6 446	42 441	82 481	32 977	58 561	202 934	67 351	78 982	572 173
1995	7 303	43 646	87 381	35 281	59 430	217 060	72 113	83 138	605 352
1996	7 963	39 210	90 725	37 586	60 227	230 188	75 005	87 250	628 154
1997	7 403	36 472	91 016	40 058	62 981	245 841	69 817	92 646	646 234
1998	7 999	37 786	88 897	41 818	66 089	258 220	64 715	95 337	660 861
1999	8 639	38 731	88 719	42 623	69 063	258 549	62 191		

Source: 1990–98 from OECD, *National Accounts of OECD Countries, 1988–1998*, Paris, 2000, and Statistics Division of Economic Commission for Europe, Geneva. 1999 Czech Republic, Hungary and Poland from OECD *Economic Outlook*, June 2000; 1999 Slovakia from OECD *Main Economic Indicators*, April 2000, p. 242; 1999 Bulgaria and Romania from IMF, *World Economic Outlook*, April 2000.

Table D–1b. **Population in East European Countries,1990–99**
(000)

	Albania	Bulgaria	Czech Republic	Slovakia	Hungary	Poland	Romania	Former Yugoslavia
1990	3 273	8 966	10 310	5 263	10 352	38 109	22 775	22 819
1991	3 259	8 914	10 309	5 283	10 352	38 242	22 728	22 961
1992	3 189	8 869	10 319	5 307	10 343	38 359	22 692	22 993
1993	3 154	8 495	10 329	5 329	10 326	38 456	22 660	22 883
1994	3 178	8 448	10 333	5 352	10 307	38 537	22 627	22 541
1995	3 219	8 399	10 327	5 368	10 285	38 590	22 582	22 357
1996	3 263	8 345	10 313	5 379	10 259	38 611	22 524	22 287
1997	3 300	8 291	10 298	5 388	10 232	38 615	22 463	22 390
1998	3 331	8 240	10 286	5 393	10 208	38 607	22 396	22 545
1999	3 365	8 195	10 281	5 396	10 186	38 609	22 234	22 679

Source: International Programs Center, US Bureau of the Census.

Table D–1c. **GDP Per Capita in East European Countries, 1990–99**
(1990 international $)

	Albania	Bulgaria	Czech Republic	Slovakia	Hungary	Poland	Romania	Former Yugoslavia
1990	2 482	5 552	8 895	7 762	6 471	5 115	3 525	5 695
1991	1 795	5 117	7 863	6 607	5 701	4 739	3 076	4 906
1992	1 701	4 767	7 815	6 151	5 531	4 848	2 811	3 967
1993	1 886	4 906	7 812	5 905	5 509	5 018	2 860	3 322
1994	2 028	5 024	7 982	6 162	5 682	5 266	2 977	3 504
1995	2 269	5 197	8 461	6 572	5 778	5 625	3 193	3 719
1996	2 440	4 699	8 797	6 988	5 871	5 962	3 330	3 915
1997	2 243	4 399	8 838	7 435	6 155	6 366	3 108	4 138
1998	2 401	4 586	8 643	7 754	6 474	6 688	2 890	4 229
1999	2 567	4 726	8 629	7 899	6 780	6 697	2 797	

Source: Derived from Tables D–1a and D–1b.

http://dx.doi.org/10.1787/331258434653

Table D–2a. GDP in Successor Republics of Former Yugoslavia, 1990–98
(million 1990 international dollars)

	Bosnia	Croatia	Macedonia	Slovenia	Serbia–Montenegro
1990	16 530	33 139	7 394	21 624	51 266
1991	14 610	26 147	6 875	19 695	45 310
1992	10 535	23 080	6 323	18 612	32 674
1993	7 287	21 225	5 755	19 153	22 599
1994	7 484	22 473	5 648	20 165	23 212
1995	7 933	24 007	5 583	21 012	24 603
1996	8 400	25 434	5 624	21 742	26 050
1997	9 028	27 182	5 706	22 730	28 000
1998	9 261	27 858	5 871	23 625	28 722

Source: Statistics Division of Economic Commission for Europe, Geneva, and national sources (see Table A–f in Appendix A).

Table D–2b. Population in Successor Republics of Former Yugoslavia,1990–99
(000)

	Bosnia	Croatia	Macedonia	Slovenia	Serbia–Montenegro
1990	4 360	4 754	2 031	1 969	9 705
1991	4 371	4 796	2 039	1 966	9 790
1992	4 327	4 714	2 056	1 959	9 937
1993	4 084	4 687	2 071	1 960	10 080
1994	3 686	4 723	1 946	1 965	10 220
1995	3 282	4 701	1 967	1 970	10 437
1996	3 111	4 661	1 982	1 974	10 558
1997	3 223	4 665	1 996	1 973	10 534
1998	3 366	4 672	2 009	1 972	10 526
1999	3 482	4 677	2 023	1 971	10 526

Source: International Programs Center, US Bureau of the Census.

Table D–2c. GDP Per Capita in Successor Republics of Former Yugoslavia,1990–98
(000)

	Bosnia	Croatia	Macedonia	Slovenia	Serbia–Montenegro
1990	3 791	6 971	3 641	10 982	5 282
1991	3 342	5 452	3 372	10 018	4 628
1992	2 435	4 896	3 075	9 501	3 288
1993	1 784	4 528	2 779	9 772	2 242
1994	2 030	4 758	2 902	10 262	2 271
1995	2 417	5 107	2 838	10 666	2 357
1996	2 700	5 457	2 838	11 014	2 467
1997	2 801	5 827	2 859	11 521	2 658
1998	2 751	5 963	2 922	11 980	2 729

Source: Derived from D–2a and D–2b.

http://dx.doi.org/10.1787/331258434653

ISBN 92-64-02261-9 – © OECD 2006

Table D–3a. GDP in Successor States of Former USSR, 1990–98
(million 1990 international dollars)

	Belarus	Estonia	Latvia	Lithuania	Moldova	Ukraine	6 Country Total	Russian Federation
				Europe				Europe/Asia
1990	73 389	16 980	26 413	32 010	27 112	311 112	487 016	1 151 040
1991	72 491	15 280	23 666	30 189	22 362	284 003	447 991	1 094 081
1992	65 534	13 118	15 427	23 768	15 889	255 602	389 288	935 072
1993	60 596	12 010	13 117	19 928	15 695	219 457	340 803	853 194
1994	52 966	11 770	13 117	17 975	10 834	169 111	275 773	745 209
1995	47 430	12 268	13 091	18 570	10 639	148 456	250 454	714 357
1996	48 776	12 749	13 527	19 431	9 806	133 610	237 899	690 624
1997	54 315	14 098	14 709	20 855	9 972	129 423	243 372	696 609
1998	58 799	14 671	15 222	21 914	9 112	127 151	246 869	664 495

West Asia

	Armenia	Azerbaijan	Georgia	3 Country Total
1990	20 483	33 397	41 325	99 205
1991	18 077	33 159	32 612	83 848
1992	10 534	25 673	17 961	54 168
1993	9 602	19 736	12 704	42 042
1994	10 122	15 842	11 390	37 354
1995	10 816	13 989	11 682	36 487
1996	11 444	14 141	12 996	38 581
1997	11 835	14 979	14 455	41 269
1998	12 679	16 365	14 894	43 938

Central Asia

	Kazakhstan	Kyrgyzstan	Tajikistan	Turkmenistan	Uzbekistan	5 Country Total
1990	122 295	15 787	15 884	13 300	87 468	254 734
1991	108 830	14 537	14 537	12 673	87 027	237 604
1992	103 024	12 533	9 844	10 778	77 328	213 507
1993	93 636	10 590	8 243	10 935	75 565	198 969
1994	81 777	8 466	6 484	9 041	71 597	177 365
1995	75 106	7 999	5 675	8 388	70 980	168 148
1996	75 477	8 571	4 724	8 949	72 214	169 935
1997	76 716	9 415	4 803	7 931	75 913	174 778
1998	74 857	9 595	5 073	8 335	79 272	177 132

Source: Derived from indices in the statistical database of the Statistics Division, Economic Commission for Europe, Geneva.

http://dx.doi.org/10.1787/331258434653

Table D–3b. **Population in Successor States of Former USSR, 1990–98**
(000)

	Belarus	Estonia	Latvia	Lithuania	Moldova	Ukraine	6 Country Total	Russian Federation
	Europe							*Europe/Asia*
1990	10 260	1 582	2 684	3 726	4 365	51 891	74 508	148 290
1991	10 271	1 566	2 662	3 742	4 363	52 001	74 605	148 624
1992	10 313	1 544	2 632	3 742	4 334	52 150	74 715	148 689
1993	10 357	1 517	2 586	3 730	3 618	52 179	73 987	148 520
1994	10 356	1 449	2 548	3 721	3 618	51 921	73 613	148 336
1995	10 329	1 484	2 516	3 715	3 611	51 531	73 186	148 141
1996	10 298	1 469	2 491	3 710	3 599	51 114	72 681	147 739
1997	10 268	1 458	2 469	3 706	3 587	50 697	72 185	147 304
1998	10 239	1 450	2 449	3 703	3 649	50 295	71 785	146 909

West Asia

	Armenia	Azerbaijan	Georgia	3 Country Total
1990	3 335	7 134	5 460	15 929
1991	3 612	7 242	5 464	16 318
1992	3 686	7 332	5 455	16 473
1993	3 732	7 399	5 440	16 571
1994	3 748	7 459	5 425	16 632
1995	3 760	7 511	5 417	16 688
1996	3 774	7 555	5 419	16 748
1997	3 786	7 603	5 431	16 820
1998	3 795	7 666	5 442	16 903

Central Asia

	Kazakhstan	Kyrgyzstan	Tajikistan	Turkmenistan	Uzbekistan	5 Country Total
1990	16 742	4 395	5 303	3 668	20 515	50 623
1991	16 878	4 453	5 465	3 762	20 958	51 516
1992	16 975	4 493	5 571	4 032	21 445	52 516
1993	16 964	4 482	5 638	4 308	21 948	53 340
1994	16 775	4 473	5 745	4 406	22 378	53 777
1995	16 540	4 514	5 835	4 508	22 784	54 181
1996	16 166	4 576	5 927	4 597	23 225	54 491
1997	15 751	4 367	6 018	4 657	23 656	54 449
1998	15 567	4 699	6 115	4 838	24 050	55 269

Source: As for Table D–3a.

http://dx.doi.org/10.1787/331258434653

ISBN 92-64-02261-9 – © OECD 2006   340

Table D–3c. GDP Per Capita in Successor States of Former USSR, 1990–98
(1990 international dollars)

			Europe					Europe/Asia
	Belarus	Estonia	Latvia	Lithuania	Moldova	Ukraine	6 Country Total	Russian Federation
1990	7 153	10 733	9 841	8 591	6 211	5 995	6 536	7 762
1991	7 058	9 757	8 890	8 068	5 125	5 461	6 005	7 361
1992	6 355	8 496	5 861	6 352	3 666	4 901	5 210	6 289
1993	5 851	7 917	5 072	5 343	4 338	4 206	4 606	5 745
1994	5 115	8 123	5 148	4 831	2 994	3 257	3 746	5 024
1995	4 592	8 267	5 203	4 999	2 946	2 881	3 422	4 822
1996	4 736	8 679	5 430	5 237	2 725	2 614	3 273	4 675
1997	5 290	9 669	5 957	5 627	2 780	2 553	3 372	4 729
1998	5 743	10 118	6 216	5 918	2 497	2 528	3 439	4 523

West Asia

	Armenia	Azerbaijan	Georgia	3 Country Total
1990	6 142	4 681	7 569	6 228
1991	5 005	4 579	5 969	5 138
1992	2 858	3 502	3 293	3 288
1993	2 573	2 667	2 335	2 537
1994	2 701	2 124	2 100	2 246
1995	2 877	1 862	2 157	2 186
1996	3 032	1 872	2 398	2 304
1997	3 126	1 970	2 662	2 454
1998	3 341	2 135	2 737	2 599

Central Asia

	Kazakhstan	Kyrgyzstan	Tajikistan	Turkmenistan	Uzbekistan	5 Country Total
1990	7 305	3 592	2 995	3 626	4 264	5 032
1991	6 448	3 265	2 660	3 369	4 152	4 612
1992	6 069	2 789	1 767	2 673	3 606	4 066
1993	5 520	2 363	1 462	2 538	3 443	3 730
1994	4 875	1 893	1 129	2 052	3 199	3 298
1995	4 541	1 772	973	1 861	3 115	3 103
1996	4 669	1 873	797	1 947	3 109	3 119
1997	4 871	2 156	798	1 703	3 209	3 210
1998	4 809	2 042	830	1 723	3 296	3 205

Source: Derived from Tables D–3a and D–3b.

http://dx.doi.org/10.1787/331258434653

Table D–4. Confrontation of OECD and Maddison Estimates of 1990 Real GDP Levels in 15 Successor States of the Former Soviet Union

	1996 GDP in million 1996 EKS dollars	*GDP Volume Ratio 1990–96*	*1990 GDP Level in 1996 EKS dollars*	*1990 GDP Level in 1990 EKS dollars*	*Maddison Estimates of 1990 GDP Level in 1990 Geary–Khamis dollars*
Armenia	7 423	1.7898	13 286	11 467	20 483
Azerbaijan	14 501	2.31265	33 536	28 944	33 397
Belarus	53 198	1.5046	80 042	69 083	73 389
Estonia	9 761	1.33187	13 000	11 220	16 980
Georgia	15 844	3.1798	50 381	43 483	41 325
Kazakhstan	71 548	1.620295	115 929	100 056	122 295
Kyrgyzstan	9 547	1.8419	17 585	15 177	15 787
Latvia	12 584	1.9526	24 572	21 208	26 413
Lithuania	21 320	1.647368	35 122	30 313	32 010
Moldova	7 558	2.764838	20 897	18 036	27 112
Russian Federation	996 051	1.66667	1 660 085	1 432 790	1 151 040
Tajikistan	5 455	3.362405	18 342	15 831	15 884
Turkmenistan	13 510	1.4862	20 079	17 330	13 300
Ukraine	169 933	2.3285	395 690	341 513	311 112
Uzbekistan	46 350	1.211234	56 141	48 454	87 468
Total	1 454 583		2 554 687	2 204 905	1 987 995

Source: First column from *A PPP Comparison for the NIS, 1994, 1995 and 1996*, OECD, Paris, February 2000, Annex B, Table B–1. Column 2 is the ratio of 1990 GDP to that of 1996 (derived from Table D–3 above). Third column is column 1 multiplied by column 2. Fourth column is column 3 multiplied by US GDP deflator 1990–96 (0.863082). Last column shows my estimates (from Table A1–b of Appendix A). My figures are based on the ECE estimates for the former USSR (as shown in Table A1–h of Appendix A). The breakdown by republic for 1990 is from Bolotin (1992). Bolotin also used the ICP approach. I prefer my estimates because they are consistent with those I used for East European countries, because the Geary–Khamis approach is distinctly superior to the EKS approach, and because the quality of the data was probably better in the 1990 comparison than in 1996.

http://dx.doi.org/10.1787/331258434653

ISBN 92-64-02261-9 – © OECD 2006

Appendix E

Employment, Working Hours and Labour Productivity

Table E–1. Total Employment in Europe, Japan, and Western Offshoots, 1870–1998
(000 at mid–year)

	1870	1913	1950	1973	1990	1998
Austria	2 077	3 122	3 215	3 160	3 412	3 723
Belgium	2 141	3 376	3 341	3 748	3 815	3 766
Denmark	820	1 277	1 978	2 426	2 672	2 693
Finland	785	1 323	1 959	2 194	2 487	2 245
France	17 800	19 373	19 663	21 434	22 632	22 693
Germany	16 184	30 333	28 745	35 487	36 808	36 094
Italy	13 770	17 644	18 875	22 708	25 624	24 343
Netherlands	1 382	2 330	4 120	5 150	6 356	7 465
Norway	706	984	1 428	1 676	2 030	2 241
Sweden	1 923	2 602	3 422	3 879	4 465	3 979
Switzerland	1 285	1 904	2 237	3 277	3 563	3 850
United Kingdom	13 157	19 884	22 400	25 076	26 942	27 121
Total 12 West Europe	**72 030**	**104 152**	**111 383**	**130 215**	**140 806**	**140 213**
Ireland			1 220	1 067	1 126	1 503
Spain		7 613	11 662	13 031	12 890	13 378
Australia	630	1 943	3 459	5 838	7 938	8 652
Canada	1 266	3 014	5 030	8 843	13 244	14 386
United States	14 720	38 821	61 651	86 838	120 960	132 953
Czechoslovakia		5 854	5 972	7 092	7 679	7 374
a) Czech Republic					5 201	5 207
b) Slovakia					2 478	2 167
Hungary		3 285	4 379	5 008	4 808	3 698
Poland			12 718	17 319	16 840	15 477
Romania		6 877	9 710	10 015	10 865	10 845
USSR		64 664	85 246	128 278	132 546	
Russian Federation					75 325	64 500
East Germany			7 581	8 327	8 820	6 055
Japan	18 684	25 751	35 683	52 590	62 490	65 141

Source: 1870–1973 from Maddison (1995a), updated from OECD, *Labour Force Statistics 1978–1998,* Paris 1999 for West European countries, Japan and Western Offshoots. In the case of Germany, the 1870–1913 figures refer to the 1913 boundaries (excluding Alsace–Lorraine) and for 1950–98 to 1991 boundaries; for 1950–98, the figures for East Germany (given in the table) were added to those for the Federal Republic. For 1870, and 1913 employment in the territory of the Federal Republic, as given in Maddison (1995a) was adjusted upwards by the ratio of population within the 1913 frontiers including Alsace–Lorraine to population in the territory of the Federal Republic (see Table A–d in Appendix A). For the United Kingdom, the 1870 and 1913 figures include Southern Ireland; the employment estimates in Maddison (1995a) for 1870 and 1913 were adjusted upwards by the population ratio. For the other countries in this group the figures refer throughout to employment within present frontiers.

For Eastern Europe; 1870–1973 from Maddison (1995a). East Germany 1950 and 1973 derived from Merkel and Wahl (1991) p. 73; 1990 and 1998 from Van Ark (1999). The latter source was also used for Hungary, Poland, Romania, Russian Federation and Slovakia for 1990. Czech Republic 1990 and 1998; Hungary and Poland 1998 from OECD, *Labour Force Statistics 1978–1998,* OECD, Paris; Romania, Russian Federation and Slovakia 1998 from OECD, *Main Economic Indicators,* April 2000. USSR 1990 from Maddison (1995b).

http://dx.doi.org/10.1787/233517061144

Table E–2. **Total Employment in Latin America and Asia, 1950–98**
(000 at mid–year)

	1950	*1973*	*1990*	*1998*
Argentina	6 821	9 402	11 932	13 060
Brazil	17 657	33 164	56 108	63 966
Chile	2 256	2 894	4 429	5 541
Colombia	3 844	6 616	10 747	12 673
Mexico	8 766	15 180	24 905	31 519
Peru	2 799	4 471	7 446	9 444
Venezuela	1 571	3 338	5 859	7 716
China	184 984	362 530	567 400	626 630
Hong Kong			2 710	3 140
India	161 386	239 645	324 885	377 548
Indonesia	30 863	46 655	75 851	87 672
Malaysia			6 686	8 563
Pakistan	14 009	50 144	31 290	35 430
Philippines	8 525	14 195	22 532	28 262
Singapore			1 486	1 870
South Korea	6 377	11 140	18 085	19 926
Sri Lanka			4 951	6 085
Taiwan	2 872	5 327	8 283	9 289
Thailand	10 119	18 576	30 844	32 138

Source: Latin American estimates supplied by Andre Hofman. Asia 1950–73 from Maddison (1995a), p. 247, 1990 and 1998 generally from Asian Development Bank, *Key Indicators for Developing Asian and Pacific Countries,* China 1999 and 1998 from SSB, *China Statistical Yearbook 1999,* Beijing. Korea 1990 and 1998 from OECD, *Labour Force Statistics* 1978–1998, Paris, 1999.

http://dx.doi.org/10.1787/233517061144

ISBN 92-64-02261-9 – © OECD 2006

Table E–3. **Annual Hours Worked Per Person Employed, 1870–1998**

	1870	*1913*	*1950*	*1973*	*1990*	*1998*
Austria	2 935	2 580	1 976	1 778	1 590	1 515
Belgium	2 964	2 605	2 283	1 872	1 638	1 568
Denmark	2 945	2 553	2 283	1 742	1 638	1 664
Finland	2 945	2 588	2 035	1 707	1 668	1 637
France	2 945	2 588	1 926	1 771	1 539	1 503
Germany	2 841	2 584	2 316	1 804	1 566	1 523
Italy	2 886	2 536	1 997	1 612	1 500	1 506
Netherlands	2 964	2 605	2 208	1 751	1 347	1 389
Norway	2 945	2 588	2 101	1 721	1 460	1 428
Sweden	2 945	2 588	1 951	1 571	1 508	1 582
Switzerland	2 984	2 624	2 144	1 930	1 644	1 595
United Kingdom	2 984	2 624	1 958	1 688	1 637	1 489
Ireland			2 250	2 010	1 700	1 657
Spain			2 200	2 150	1 941	1 908
Australia	2 945	2 588	1 838	1 708	1 645	1 641
Canada	2 964	2 605	1 967	1 788	1 683	1 663
United States	2 964	2 605	1 867	1 717	1 594	1 610
Argentina			2 034	1 996	1 850	1 903
Brazil			2 042	2 096	1 879	1 841
Chile			2 212	1 955	1 984	1 974
Colombia			2 323	2 141	1 969	1 956
Mexico			2 154	2 061	2 060	2 073
Peru			2 189	2 039	1 930	1 926
Venezuela			2 179	1 965	1 889	1 931
Japan	2 945	2 588	2 166	2 042	1 951	1 758

Source: 1870-1973 from Maddison (1995a), p. 248, 1990 for OECD countries from Maddison (1996), p. 41 and worksheets from Maddison (1991a). Movement in hours 1992-98 linked to 1992 level shown in Maddison (1995a) p. 248, except for the United States which is derived from estimates of the US Bureau of Labor Statistics of average weekly hours of production workers in the private sector, multiplied by average weeks worked per year. Latin American estimates supplied by Andre Hofman (updating those in Hofman, 2000).

http://dx.doi.org/10.1787/233517061144

Table E–4. **Total Hours Worked, 1870–1998**
(million hours)

	1870	*1913*	*1950*	*1973*	*1990*	*1998*
Austria	6 096	8 055	6 353	5 618	5 425	5 640
Belgium	6 346	8 794	7 628	7 016	6 249	5 905
Denmark	2 415	3 260	4 516	4 226	4 377	4 481
Finland	2 312	3 424	3 987	3 745	4 148	3 675
France	52 421	50 137	37 871	37 960	34 831	34 108
Germany	45 979	78 380	66 573	64 019	57 641	54 971
Italy	39 740	44 745	37 693	36 605	38 436	36 661
Netherlands	4 096	6 070	9 097	9 018	8 562	10 369
Norway	2 079	2 547	3 000	2 884	2 964	3 200
Sweden	5 663	6 734	6 676	6 094	6 733	6 295
Switzerland	3 834	4 996	4 796	6 325	5 858	6 141
United Kingdom	39 260	52 176	43 859	42 328	44 104	40 383
Total 12 West Europe	**210 242**	**269 318**	**232 049**	**225 838**	**219 327**	**211 829**
Ireland			2 745	2 145	1 914	2 490
Spain			25 656	28 017	25 019	25 525
Australia	1 855	5 028	6 358	9 971	13 058	14 198
Canada	3 752	7 851	9 894	15 811	22 290	23 924
United States	43 630	101 129	115 102	149 101	192 810	214 054
Argentina			13 874	18 766	22 074	24 853
Brazil			36 056	69 512	105 427	117 761
Chile			4 990	5 658	8 787	10 938
Colombia			8 930	14 165	21 161	24 788
Mexico			18 882	31 286	51 304	65 339
Peru			6 127	9 116	14 371	18 189
Venezuela			3 423	6 559	11 068	14 900
Japan	55 024	66 644	77 289	107 389	121 918	114 518

http://dx.doi.org/10.1787/233517061144

ISBN 92-64-02261-9 – © OECD 2006

Table E–5. **GDP Per Person Employed in Europe, Japan and Western Offshoots, 1870–1998**
(1990 international $)

	1870	1913	1950	1973	1990	1998
Austria	4 053	7 512	7 994	26 971	38 240	41 019
Belgium	6 420	9 581	14 125	31 621	44 939	52 642
Denmark	4 612	9 139	14 992	28 867	35 503	43 564
Finland	2 546	4 829	8 704	23 575	33 817	42 058
France	4 051	7 458	11 214	31 910	45 356	50 680
Germany	4 414	7 824	9 231	26 623	34 352	40 452
Italy	3 037	5 412	8 739	25 661	36 124	42 015
Netherlands	7 201	10 710	14 719	34 134	40 606	42 534
Norway	3 520	6 218	12 492	26 578	38 588	46 792
Sweden	3 602	6 688	13 813	28 305	33 920	41 564
Switzerland	4 566	8 657	19 019	35 780	41 229	39 570
United Kingdom	7 614	11 296	15 529	26 956	35 061	40 875
Weighted Average						
12 West Europe	**4 702**	**8 072**	**11 551**	**28 109**	**37 476**	**43 108**
Ireland				19 778	36 820	44 822
Spain		6 001	5 727	23 346	36 801	41 870
Australia	10 241	14 180	17 714	29 516	36 682	44 190
Canada	5 061	11 585	20 311	35 302	39 601	43 298
United States	6 683	13 327	23 615	40 727	47 976	55 618
Czechoslovakia		4 741	7 262	14 445	17 263	17 726
a) Czech Republic					17 632	17 073
b) Slovakia					16 487	19 298
Hungary		5 007	5 288	11 649	13 933	17 872
Poland			4 776	10 276	11 575	16 684
Romania			1 985	7 230	7 389	5 967
USSR		3 593	5 986	11 795	14 999	
Russian Federation					15 281	10 302
East Germany			6 782	15 608	9 317	20 319
Japan	1 359	2 783	4 511	23 634	37 144	39 631

http://dx.doi.org/10.1787/233517061144

Table E–6. **GDP Per Person Employed in Latin America and Asia, 1950–98**
(1990 international $)

	1950	1973	1990	1998
Argentina	12 538	21 349	17 811	25 598
Brazil	5 060	12 111	13 256	14 491
Chile	10 316	17 416	18 974	26 038
Colombia	6 492	12 202	14 799	16 187
Mexico	7 685	18 399	20 747	20 810
Peru	6 170	12 685	8 727	10 135
Venezuela	23 792	37 856	27 419	26 495
China	1 297	2 041	3 718	6 181
Hong Kong			36 815	43 022
India	1 377	2 065	3 380	4 510
Indonesia			5 945	7 157
Malaysia			13 434	17 356
Pakistan			5 817	7 381
Philippines	2 653	5 809	6 348	6 236
Singapore			29 159	42 259
South Korea	2 516	8 689	20 633	28 315
Sri Lanka			8 501	10 420
Taiwan	2 569	11 924	24 203	35 198
Thailand	1 618	4 065	8 291	11 591

http://dx.doi.org/10.1787/233517061144

Table E–7. **Labour Productivity (GDP Per Hour Worked), 1870–1998**
(1990 international $ per hour)

	1870	1913	1950	1973	1990	1998
Austria	1.38	2.91	4.05	15.17	24.05	27.07
Belgium	2.17	3.68	6.19	16.89	27.44	33.57
Denmark	1.57	3.58	6.57	16.57	21.67	26.18
Finland	0.86	1.87	4.28	13.81	20.27	25.69
France	1.38	2.88	5.82	18.02	29.47	33.72
Germany	1.55	3.03	3.99	14.76	21.94	26.56
Italy	1.05	2.13	4.38	15.92	24.08	27.90
Netherlands	2.43	4.11	6.67	19.49	30.15	30.62
Norway	1.20	2.40	5.95	15.44	26.43	32.77
Sweden	1.22	2.58	7.08	18.02	22.49	26.27
Switzerland	1.53	3.30	8.87	18.54	25.08	24.81
United Kingdom	2.55	4.31	7.93	15.97	21.42	27.45
Weighted Average						
12 West Europe	**1.61**	**3.12**	**5.54**	**16.21**	**24.06**	**28.53**
Ireland			3.73	9.84	21.66	27.05
Spain			2.60	10.86	18.96	21.94
Australia	3.48	5.48	9.64	17.28	22.30	26.93
Canada	1.71	4.45	10.33	19.74	23.53	26.04
United States	2.25	5.12	12.65	23.72	30.10	34.55
Argentina			6.16	10.70	9.63	13.45
Brazil			2.48	5.78	7.05	7.87
Chile			4.66	8.91	9.56	13.19
Colombia			2.79	5.70	7.52	8.28
Mexico			3.57	8.93	10.07	10.04
Peru			2.82	6.22	4.52	5.26
Venezuela			10.92	19.27	14.52	13.72
Japan	0.46	1.08	2.08	11.57	19.04	22.54

http://dx.doi.org/10.1787/233517061144

Table E–8. **Rate of Growth of GDP Per Hour Worked, 1870–1998**
(annual average compound growth rates)

	1870–1913	1913–50	1950–73	1973–98	1973–90	1990–98
Austria	1.75	0.89	5.91	2.34	2.75	1.49
Belgium	1.24	1.42	4.46	2.79	2.89	2.56
Denmark	1.94	1.65	4.11	1.85	1.59	2.39
Finland	1.80	2.27	5.23	2.51	2.28	3.00
France	1.74	1.92	5.03	2.54	2.94	1.70
Germany	1.56	0.75	5.86	2.38	2.36	2.42
Italy	1.66	1.96	5.77	2.27	2.47	1.86
Netherlands	1.23	1.31	4.78	1.82	2.60	0.20
Norway	1.64	2.48	4.24	3.05	3.21	2.72
Sweden	1.75	2.76	4.14	1.52	1.31	1.96
Switzerland	1.80	2.71	3.26	1.17	1.79	−0.14
United Kingdom	1.22	1.67	3.09	2.19	1.74	3.15
Weighted Average 12 West Europe	**1.55**	**1.56**	**4.77**	**2.29**	**2.35**	**2.16**
Ireland			4.31	4.13	4.75	2.82
Spain			6.41	2.85	3.33	1.84
Australia	1.06	1.54	2.57	1.79	1.51	2.39
Canada	2.25	2.30	2.86	1.11	1.04	1.27
United States	1.92	2.48	2.77	1.52	1.41	1.74
Argentina			2.42	0.92	−0.62	4.27
Brazil			3.75	1.24	1.18	1.38
Chile			2.85	1.58	0.42	4.10
Colombia			3.15	1.50	1.64	1.21
Mexico			4.07	0.47	0.71	−0.04
Peru			3.50	−0.67	−1.86	1.91
Venezuela			2.50	−1.35	−1.65	−0.70
Japan	1.99	1.80	7.74	2.70	2.97	2.13

http://dx.doi.org/10.1787/233517061144

ISBN 92-64-02261-9 – © OECD 2006

Table E–9. **Levels of GDP Per Hour Worked, 1870–1998**
(United States = 100)

	1870	*1913*	*1950*	*1973*	*1990*	*1998*
Austria	61	57	32	64	80	78
Belgium	96	72	49	71	91	97
Denmark	69	70	52	70	72	76
Finland	38	36	34	58	67	74
France	61	56	46	76	98	98
Germany	69	59	32	62	73	77
Italy	47	42	35	67	80	81
Netherlands	108	80	53	82	100	89
Norway	53	47	47	65	88	95
Sweden	54	51	56	76	75	76
Switzerland	68	64	70	78	83	72
United Kingdom	113	84	63	67	71	79
Weighted Average						
12 West Europe	**71**	**61**	**44**	**68**	**80**	**83**
Ireland					72	78
Spain					63	64
Australia	154	107	76	73	74	78
Canada	76	87	82	83	78	75
Argentina			49	45	32	39
Brazil			20	24	23	23
Chile			37	38	32	38
Colombia			22	24	25	24
Mexico			28	38	33	29
Peru			22	26	15	15
Venezuela			86	81	48	40
Japan	20	21	16	49	63	65

http://dx.doi.org/10.1787/233517061144

Table E–10. **Annual Hours Worked Per Head of Population, 1870–1998**
(hours)

	1870	1913	1950	1973	1990	1998
Austria	1 349	1 190	916	741	702	698
Belgium	1 245	1 147	883	721	627	579
Denmark	1 279	1 093	1 058	842	852	845
Finland	1 318	1 131	994	803	832	713
France	1 364	1 209	905	728	614	580
Germany	1 172	1 205	974	811	726	670
Italy	1 425	1 201	800	669	678	637
Netherlands	1 133	985	899	671	573	660
Norway	1 198	1 041	919	728	699	722
Sweden	1 360	1 198	952	749	786	711
Switzerland	1 439	1 293	1 022	982	862	861
United Kingdom	1 251	1 143	871	753	766	682
Weighted Average 12 West Europe	1 295	1 181	904	750	701	657
Ireland			925	698	546	672
Spain			921	805	644	648
Australia	1 048	1 043	778	738	764	757
Canada	992	1 000	720	701	805	790
United States	1 084	1 036	756	704	771	791
Argentina			809	745	676	685
Brazil			675	672	698	694
Chile			819	572	669	740
Colombia			770	614	642	643
Mexico			663	543	605	663
Peru			803	635	654	697
Venezuela			683	552	573	653
Japan	1 598	1 290	925	988	987	905

http://dx.doi.org/10.1787/233517061144

Table E–11. **Employment in Europe, Japan and Western Offshoots, as Per Cent of Population, 1870–1998**
(percentage)

	1870	1913	1950	1973	1990	1998
Austria	46.0	46.1	46.4	41.7	44.1	46.1
Belgium	42.0	44.0	38.7	38.5	38.3	36.9
Denmark	43.4	42.8	46.3	48.3	52.0	50.8
Finland	44.8	43.7	48.9	47.0	49.9	43.6
France	46.3	46.7	47.0	41.1	39.9	38.6
Germany	41.3	46.6	42.0	44.9	46.4	44.0
Italy	49.4	47.4	40.1	41.5	45.2	42.3
Netherlands	38.2	37.8	40.7	38.3	42.5	47.5
Norway	40.7	40.2	43.7	42.3	47.9	50.6
Sweden	46.2	46.3	48.8	47.7	52.1	45.0
Switzerland	48.2	49.3	47.7	50.9	52.4	54.0
United Kingdom	41.9	43.6	44.5	44.6	46.8	45.8
Weighted Average						
12 West Europe	**44.4**	**45.7**	**43.4**	**43.3**	**45.0**	**43.5**
Ireland			41.1	34.7	32.1	40.6
Spain		37.6	41.8	37.4	33.2	34.0
Australia	35.6	40.3	42.3	43.2	46.5	46.1
Canada	33.5	38.4	36.6	39.2	47.8	47.5
United States	36.6	39.8	40.5	41.0	48.4	49.1
Czechoslovakia		44.2	48.2	48.7	49.3	47.0
a) Czech Republic					50.4	50.6
b) Slovakia					47.1	40.2
Hungary		41.9	46.9	48.0	46.4	36.2
Poland		0.0	51.2	52.0	44.2	40.1
Romania		54.9	59.5	48.1	47.7	48.4
USSR		41.4	47.3	51.4	45.8	
Russian Federation					50.8	43.9
Japan	54.3	49.8	42.7	48.4	50.6	51.5

http://dx.doi.org/10.1787/233517061144

Table E–12. **Employment in Latin America and Asia, as Per Cent of Population, 1950–1998**
(percentage)

	1950	*1973*	*1990*	*1998*
Argentina	39.8	37.3	36.6	36.0
Brazil	33.0	32.1	37.1	37.7
Chile	37.0	29.2	33.7	37.5
Colombia	33.2	28.7	32.6	32.8
Mexico	30.8	26.3	29.4	32.0
Peru	36.7	31.2	33.9	36.2
Venezuela	31.4	28.1	30.3	33.8
China	33.8	41.1	50.0	50.4
Hong Kong			47.5	46.9
India	45.0	41.3	38.7	38.7
Indonesia	39.0	37.5	42.3	42.9
Malaysia			38.2	40.9
Pakistan	35.5	70.5	27.5	26.2
Philippines	40.3	33.7	34.6	36.4
Singapore			48.9	53.6
South Korea	30.6	32.7	42.2	42.9
Sri Lanka			28.8	32.1
Taiwan	36.4	34.5	40.9	42.6
Thailand	50.5	46.1	56.0	53.5

http://dx.doi.org/10.1787/233517061144

Appendix F

Value and Volume of Exports, 1870–1998

Table F–1. **Value of Merchandise Exports at Current Prices (56 Countries), 1870–1998**
(million dollars at current exchange rate)

	1870	1913	1929	1950	1973	1990	1998
Austria	160	561	308	326	5 283	41 138	62 746
Belgium	133	717	884	1 652	22 450	118 328	177 662
Denmark	42[a]	171	433	665	6 248	35 135	46 915
Finland	9	78	162	390	3 837	26 572	42 963
France	541	1 328	1 965	3 082	36 675	210 169	305 492
Germany	424	2 454	3 212	1 993	67 563	409 958	543 292
Italy	208	485	783	1 206	22 226	170 383	242 147
Netherlands	158[b]	413	800	1 413	27 348	131 787	182 753
Norway	22	105	199	390	4 726	34 045	39 649
Sweden	41	219	486	I 103	12 201	57 542	84 739
Switzerland	132[b]	226	404	894	9 538	63 793	75 439
United Kingdom	971	2 555	3 550	6 325	29 640	185 326	271 850
Total	2 841	9 352	13 186	19 439	247 735	1 484 176	2 075 627
Australia	98	382	592	1 668	9 559	39 760	55 896
Canada	58	421	1 141	3 020	26 437	127 634	214 335
New Zealand	12	112	259	514	2 596	9 394	12 071
United States	403	2 380	5 157	10 282	71404	393 592	682 497
Total	571	3 295	7 149	15 484	109 996	570 380	964 799
Greece	7	23	91	90	I 456	8 106	9 559
Ireland	–	–	225	203	2129	23 747	64 333
Portugal	22	38	48	186	1 842	16 419	24 218
Spain	76	183	407	389	5 200	55 528	109 231
Total	105	244	771	868	10 627	103 800	207 341
Bulgaria	5[b]	94	46	116	3 301	6 836	4292
Czechoslovakia	–	–	606	779	6 035	11 882	37 083
Hungary	–	–	182	329	3 354	9 597	22 955
Poland	–	–	316	634	6 374	13 627	27 191
Romania	32[b]	130	173	300	3 691	5 775	8 300
USSR	216	783	482	1 801	21458	104 177	119 798
Yugoslavia	6[b]	18	139	154	2 853	14 312	I7 324
Total	259	1 025	1 944	4 113	47 066	166 206	236 943

http://dx.doi.org/10.1787/853080005227

Table F–1. **Value of Merchandise Exports at Current Prices (56 Countries), 1870–1998**
(million dollars at current exchange rates)

	1870	*1913*	*1929*	*1950*	*1973*	*1990*	*1998*
Argentina	29	515	908	1 178	3 266	12 353	25 227
Brazil	76	317	462	1 359	6 199	31 414	51 120
Chile	27	149	283	281	1 231	8 373	14 895
Colombia	18	34	124	394	1 177	6 766	10 852
Mexico	28[a]	150	285	532	2 261	27 131	117 500
Peru	25[a]	43	117	193	1 112	3 231	5 736
Venezuela	15[a]	28	149	929	4 680	17 783	15 682
Total	218	1 236	2 328	4 866	19 926	107 051	241 012
Bangladesh	–	–	–	303	358	1 671	3 831
Burma	–	–	–	139	140	325	1 067
China	102	299	660	550	5 876	62 091	183 589
India	255	786	1 177	1 145	2 917	17 970	33 656
Indonesia	31	270	582	800	3 211	25 675	48 847
Japan	15	315	969	825	37 017	287 648	388 117
Pakistan	–	–	–	330	955	5 589	8 501
Philippines	29	48	163	331	1 885	8 068	27 783
South Korea	0	15	159	23	3 225	65 016	132 313
Taiwan	–	26	125	73	4 483	67 142	110 454
Thailand	7	43	94	304	1 564	23 071	54 455
Turkey	49[b]	94	139	159	1 317	12 959	25 938
Total	488	1 896	4 068	4 982	62 948	577 225	1 018 549
Côte d'Ivoire	–	–	–	79	857	3 072	4 504
Egypt	66[a]	156	253	504	1 121	4 957	3 130
Ethiopia	n.a.	n.a.	n.a.	37	239	298	560
Ghana	2	26	60	217	628	863	1 788
Kenya	n.a.	n.a.	34	57	516	1 031	2 007
Morocco	n.a.	n.a.	48	190	910	4 265	12 480
Nigeria	4	36	86	253	3 462	12 961	37 029
South Africa	14	342	454	1 158	6 114	22 834	25 396
Tanzania	n.a.	n.a.	18	68	61	331	675
Zaire	n.a.	n.a.	40	261	1 013	999	592
Total	n.a.	n.a.	n.a.	2 824	14 921	51 611	73 333

a) 1874; b) 1872; c) 1991.

Source: Maddison (1962 and 1989); League of Nations, *Review of World Trade 1938*, Geneva, 1939; UN. *Yearbook of International Trade Statistics*, New York, various issues; IMF, *International Financial Statistics*, Washington, D.C., various issues.

http://dx.doi.org/10.1787/853080005227

Table F–2. Value of Merchandise Exports at Constant Prices (35 Countries), 1820–1998
(million 1990 dollars)

	1820	1870	1913	1929	1950	1973	1998
Austria	47	467	2 024	1 746	1 348	13 899	69 519
Belgium	92	1 237	7 318	7 845	8 182	61 764	175 503
Denmark		314	1 494	2 705	3 579	16 568	49 121
Finland		310	1 597	2 578	3 186	15 641	48 697
France	487	3 512	11 292	16 600	16 848	104 161	329 597
Germany		6 761	38 200	35 068	13 179	194 171	567 372
Italy	339	1 788	4 621	5 670	5 846	72 749	267 378
Netherlands		1 727[a]	4 329	7 411	7 411	71 522	194 430
Norway		223	854	1 427	2 301	11 687	58 141
Sweden		713	2 670	4 167	7 366	34 431	103 341
Switzerland	147	1 107	5 735	5 776	6 493	38 972	78 863
United Kingdom	1 125	12 237	39 348	31 990	39 348	94 670	277 243
Total	n.a.	30 396	119 482	122 983	115 087	730 235	2 219 205
Australia		455	3 392	3 636	5 383	18 869	69 324
Canada		724	4 044	7 812	12 576	60 214	243 015
United States	251	2 495	19 196	30 368	43 114	174 548	745 330
Total	n.a.	3 674	26 632	41 816	61 073	253 631	1 057 669
Spain	137	850	3 697	3 394	2 018	15 295	131 621
USSR		n.a.	6 666	3 420	6 472	58 015	119 978
Argentina		222	1 963	3 096	2 079	4 181	23 439
Brazil		854	1 888	2 592	3 489	9 998	49 874
Chile		166	702	1 352	1 166	2 030	18 228
Colombia		114	267	811	1 112	2 629	11 117
Mexico		242	2 363	3 714	1 999	5 238	70 261
Peru		202	409	1 142	1 172	4 323	6 205
Venezuela		n.a.	1 374	2 593	9 722	23 779	29 411
Total		2 126	8 966	15 300	20 739	52 178	208 535
Bangladesh		-	-	-	284	445	4 146
Burma		-	-	-	269	235	1 075
China		1 398	4 197	6 262	6 339	11 679	190 177
India		3 466	9 480	8 209	5 489	9 679	40 972
Indonesia		172	989	2 609	2 254	9 605	56 232
Japan		51	1 684	4 343	3 538	95 105	346 007
Pakistan		-	-	-	720	1 626	9 868
Philippines		55	180	678	697	2 608	22 712
South Korea		0	171	1 292	112	7 894	204 542
Taiwan		-	70	261	180	5 761	100 639
Thailand		88	495	640	1 148	3 081	48 752
Total		5 230	17 266	24 294	21 030	147 733	1 025 122

a) 1872

Source: Volume movement in Western Europe, Western Offshoots and Japan from A. Maddison, *Dynamic Forces in Capitalist Development*, OUP, 1991, Appendix F, updated from OECD, *Economic Outlook*, December 1999. Spain 1826-1980 from A. Carreras, ed., *Estadisticas Historicas de España: Siglos XIX-XX*, Fundacion Banco Exterior, Madrid, 1989, pp. 346-7. USSR, Latin America and Asia from sources cited in A. Maddison, *The World Economy in the Twentieth Century*, OECD Development Centre, 1989, p. 140, updated with volume movements derivable from IMF, *International Financial Statistics*, various issues. Brazil 1870-1913 from R.W. Goldsmith, *Brasil 1850-1984: Desenvolvimento Financeiro Sob um Secolo de Inflacâo*, Harper and Row, Sao Paulo, 1986, pp. 54-5 and 110-111: Peru 1870-1950 from S.J. Hunt, "Price and Quantum Estimates of Peruvian Exports, 1830-1962", Discussion Paper 33, Research Program in Economic Development, Princeton University, January 1973, (1929 weights for 1900-50, 1900 weights for 1870-1900): Venezuela 1913-29 from A. Baptista, *Bases Cuantitativas de la Economia Venezolana 1830-1989*, C. Corporativas, Caracas, 1991, and 1929-92 from ECLAC sources. 1990-8 movements from ADB, OECD, ECLAC, IMF.

http://dx.doi.org/10.1787/853080005227

Table F–3. **Value of World Exports by Region at Constant Prices, 1870–1998**
(million 1990 dollars)

	1870	1913	1950	1973	1990	1998
Western Europe	32 428	127 839	121 535	773 726	1 597 933	2 490 596
Western Offshoots	3 783	27 425	62 892	254 128	570 380	1 071 432
Eastern Europe & former USSR	2 100	8 726	14 780	127 285	166 252	237 148
Latin America	2 709	10 910	25 235	66 155	139 611	286 043
Asia	7 000	22 900	41 800	372 170	883 309	1 577 571
Africa	2 325	14 625	29 379	97 184	99 277	154 290
World	50 345	212 425	295 621	1 690 648	3 456 762	5 817 080

Source: 1950–98 from IMF *International Financial Statistics,* various issues, supplemented by UN *Yearbook of International Trade Statistics,* various issues. 1870–1950 export volume movement for Western Europe as a whole assumed to move parallel to the 13 country total shown in Table F–2; for Western Offshoots parallel to the three country total in Table F–2; Latin America parallel to the seven country total in Table F–2 (adjusted to include Venezuela for 1870). Asian total assumed to move parallel to sum of the Asian countries shown in Table F–2, with adjustment to include West Asian oil exports. Eastern Europe and former USSR and Africa 1870–1913 are guesstimates based on partial value figures of Table F–1 and unit value estimates for areas with similar commodity structures.

Table F–4. **Rate of Growth in Volume of Merchandise Exports, 11 Countries and World, 1870–1998**
(annual average compound growth rates)

	1870–1913	1913–50	1950–73	1973–98
France	2.8	1.1	8.2	4.7
Germany	4.1	−2.8	12.4	4.4
Netherlands	2.3	1.5	10.4	4.1
United Kingdom	2.8	0.0	3.9	4.4
Spain	3.5	−1.6	9.2	9.0
United States	4.9	2.2	6.3	6.0
Mexico	5.4	−0.5	4.3	10.9
Brazil	1.9	1.7	4.7	6.6
China	2.6	1.1	2.7	11.8
India	2.4	−1.5	2.5	5.9
Japan	8.5	2.0	15.4	5.3
World	3.4	0.9	7.9	5.1

Source: Derived from Tables F–2 and F–3.

http://dx.doi.org/10.1787/853080005227

Table F–5. **Merchandise Exports as Per Cent of GDP in 1990 Prices, 11 Countries and World, 1870–1998**

	1870	*1913*	*1929*	*1950*	*1973*	*1998*
France	4.9	7.8	8.6	7.6	15.2	28.7
Germany	9.5	16.1	12.8	6.2	23.8	38.9
Netherlands	17.4	17.3	17.2	12.2	40.7	61.2
United Kingdom	12.2	17.5	13.3	11.3	14.0	25.0
Spain	3.8	8.1	5.0	3.0	5.0	23.5
United States	2.5	3.7	3.6	3.0	4.9	10.1
Mexico	3.9	9.1	12.5	3.0	1.9	10.7
Brazil	12.2	9.8	6.9	3.9	2.5	5.4
China	0.7	1.7	1.8	2.6	1.5	4.9
India	2.6	4.6	3.7	2.9	2.0	2.4
Japan	0.2	2.4	3.5	2.2	7.7	13.4
World	4.6	7.9	9.0	5.5	10.5	17.2

Source: Tables F–2, F–3, and B–18. See Maddison (1997), Table 13 for a comparison of ratios at current and constant prices. As export prices have risen less over the long run than GDP deflators, the ratios for earlier years are higher in current than in 1990 prices, e.g. the UK ratio in current prices for 1870 was 17.3; for 1913, 20.9; for 1950, 14.4 and for 1973, 16.3.

http://dx.doi.org/10.1787/853080005227

Bibliography

ABEL, W. (1978), *Agrarkrisen und Agrarkonjunktur*, Parey, Hamburg and Berlin.

ABRAMOVITZ, M. (1989), *Thinking About Growth*, Cambridge University Press, Cambridge.

ABULAFIA, D. (1987), "Asia, Africa and the Trade of Medieval Europe", in POSTAN *et al.*, (eds.), vol. II, pp. 402–73.

ABU–LUGHOD, J.L. (1989), *Before European Hegemony: The World System AD 1250–1350*, Oxford University Press, Oxford.

ABU–LUGHOD, J.L. (1971), *Cairo, 1001 Years of the City Victorious*, Princeton University Press, New Jersey.

ADB (Asian Development Bank) (1999), *Key Indicators of Developing Asian and Pacific Countries*, Oxford University Press, Oxford.

ALDEN, D. (1973), *The Colonial Roots of Modern Brazil,* University of California Press, Berkeley.

ALLEN, R.C. (1991), "The Two English Agricultural Revolutions, 1450–1850", in CAMPBELL AND OVERTON.

AMIN, S. (1966), *L'économie du Maghreb*, Editions de Minuit, Paris.

ARASARATNAM, S. (1990), "Recent Trends in the Historiography of the Indian Ocean, 1500 to 1800", *Journal of World History,* Fall, pp. 225–48.

ARK, B. VAN (1999), "Economic Growth and Labour Productivity in Europe: Half a Century of East–West Comparisons", Research Memorandum GD–41, Groningen Growth and Development Centre.

ARK, B. VAN (2000), "Measuring Productivity in the 'New Economy': Towards a European Perspective", *De Economist*, 148,1, pp. 87–105.

ARK, B. VAN AND N. CRAFTS (1996), *Quantitative Aspects of Post–War European Economic Growth,* Cambridge University Press, Cambridge.

ARK, B. VAN , S. KUIPERS AND G. KUPER (2000), *Productivity, Technology and Economic Growth*, Kluwer, Dordrecht.

ASHTOR, E. (1976), *A Social and Economic History of the Near East in the Middle Ages,* University of California Press, Berkeley.

ASHTOR, E. (1980), "The Volume of Medieval Spice Trade", *Journal of European Economic History,* vol. 9, No. 3, Winter, pp. 753–763.

AUBIN, F. (ed.) (1970), *Études Song in Memoriam Etienne Balazs,* Mouton, Paris.

BAGNALL, R.S. AND B.W. FRIER (1994), *The Demography of Roman Egypt*, Cambridge University Press, Cambridge.

BAIROCH, P. (1967), *Diagnostic de l'évolution économique du tiers–monde 1900–1966*, Gauthiers–Villars, Paris.

BAIROCH, P. AND ASSOCIATES (1968), *The Working Population and Its Structure*, Université Libre de Bruxelles, Brussels.

BAIROCH, P. AND M. LEVY–LEBOYER (1981), *Disparities in Economic Development since the Industrial Revolution*, Macmillan, London.

BALCEROWICZ, L. (1995), *Socialism, Capitalism, Transformation*, Central European University Press, Budapest, London and New York.

BANENS, M. (2000), "Vietnam: a Reconstitution of its 20th Century Population History", in BASSINO, GIACOMETTI AND ODAKA (2000).

BARAN, P.A. (1957), *The Political Economy of Growth*, Prometheus Paper Back, New York.

BARCLAY, G.W. *et al.* (1976), "A Reassessment of The Demography of Traditional Rural China", *Population Index*, Winter, pp. 606–35.

BARDET, J–P. AND J. DUPAQUIER (1997), *Histoire des populations de l'Europe*, Fayard, Paris, 2 vols.

BASSINO, J–P., J–D. GIACOMETTI AND K. ODAKA (2000), *Quantitative Economic History of Vietnam, 1900–1990*, Institute of Economic Research, Hitotsubashi University.

BATISTA, D, C. MARTINS, M. PINHEIRO AND J. REIS (1997), "New Estimates of Portugal's GDP, 1910–1958", Bank of Portugal, Lisbon.

BAUGH, A.C. AND T. CABLE (1993), *A History of the English Language,* Macmillan, London.

BAUMOL, W.J. (1986), "Productivity Growth, Convergence and Welfare: What the Long Run Data Show", *American Economic Review*, December.

BELOCH, J. (1886), *Die Bevölkerung der griechisch–römischen Welt*, Duncker and Humblot, Leipzig.

BELOCH, K.J. (1961), *Bevölkerungsgeschichte Italiens,* de Gruyter, Berlin.

BERGSON, A. (1953), *Soviet National Income and Product in 1937*, Columbia University Press, New York.

BERTOLA, L., L. CALICCHIO, M. CAMOU AND L. RIVERO (1998), *El PIB de Uruguay*, Universidad de la Republica, Montevideo.

BETHELL, L. (ed.) (1984–1991), *Cambridge History of Latin America*, 8 vols., Cambridge University Press, Cambridge.

BEVAN, D., P. COLLIER AND J. GUNNING (1999), *The Political Economy of Poverty, Equity and Growth: Indonesia and Nigeria*, Oxford University Press, Oxford.

BHANOJI RAO, V.V. (1976), *National Accounts of West Malaysia, 1947–1971*, Heinemann, Singapore.

BHATTACHARYA, D. (1987), "A Note on the Population of India, 1000–1800 AD" in *Le Peuplement du Monde avant 1800*, Société de Démographie Historique, Paris.

BIDEAU, A., B. DESJARDINS AND H. PEREZ–BRIGNOLI (1997), *Infant and Child Mortality in the Past*, Clarendon Press, Oxford.

BIELENSTEIN, H. (1987), "Chinese Historical Demography AD 2 – 1982", *Bulletin of the Museum of Far Eastern Antiquities*, Stockholm, No. 59.

BIRABEN, J.N. (1972), "Certain Demographic Characteristics of the Plague Epidemic in France, 1720–1722" in GLASS AND REVELLE.

BIRABEN, J.N. (1979), "Essai sur l'évolution du nombre des hommes", *Population*, Jan–Feb., pp. 13–25.

BLACKBURN, R. (1997), *The Making of New World Slavery,* Allen and Unwin, London.

BLAYO, Y. (1975), "La population de la France de 1740 à 1860" and "La mortalité en France de 1740 à 1829", *Population*, November, pp. 71–122 and 124–142, respectively.

BLOMME, J. AND H. VAN DER WEE (1994), "The Belgian Economy in a Long–Term Historical Perspective: Economic Development in Flanders and Brabant, 1500–1812", in MADDISON AND VAN DER WEE.

BLOOM, D.E. AND J.D. SACHS (1998), "Geography, Demography and Economic Growth in Africa", *Brookings Papers on Economic Activity, 2*, pp. 207–296.

BOLOTIN, B.M. (1992), "The Former Soviet Union as Reflected in National Accounts Statistics", in HIRSCH.

BOOMGAARD, P. (1993), "Economic Growth in Indonesia, 500–1990", in SZIRMAI, VAN ARK AND PILAT.

BOOTH, A. AND A. REID (1994), "Population, Trade and Economic Growth in South–East Asia in the Long Term: An Exploratory Analysis 1400–1990", in MADDISON AND VAN DER WEE.

BORAH, W.C. (1976), "The Historical Demography of Aboriginal and Colonial America: An Attempt at Perspective", in DENEVAN, pp. 13–34.

BORAH, W. AND S.F. COOK (1963), *The Aboriginal Population of Central Mexico on the Eve of the Spanish Conquest*, University of California, Berkeley.

BOSERUP, E. (1965), *The Conditions of Agricultural Growth*, Allen and Unwin, London.

BOSERUP, E. (1981), *Population and Technology*, Blackwell, Oxford.

BOWLEY, A.L. (1942), *Studies in the National Income*, Cambridge University Press, Cambridge.

BOWMAN, A.K. AND E. ROGAN (1999), *Agriculture in Egypt from Pharaonic to Modern Times*, Oxford University Press, Oxford.

BOXER, C.R. (1974), *Four Centuries of Portuguese Expansion, 1414–1825: A Succinct Survey,* Witwatersrand University Press, Johannesburg.

BRAUDEL, F. (1985), *Civilisation and Capitalism, 15th–18th Century*, 3 vols., Fontana, London.

BRAUDEL, F. AND F. SPOONER (1967), "Prices in Europe from 1450 to 1750", in RICH AND WILSON.

BRAUDEL, F. AND E. LAROUSSE (eds.) (1977), *Histoire économique et sociale de la France*, Vol. 2, P.U.F., Paris.

BRAY, F. (1984), *Agriculture*, Vol. VI:2 in NEEDHAM (1954–2000).

BRAY, F. (1986), *The Rice Economies: Technology and Development in Asian Societies*, Blackwell, Oxford.

BREWER, J. (1989), *The Sinews of Power: War, Money and the English State, 1688–1783*, Unwin Hyman, London.

BREWER, J. AND R. PORTER (eds.) (1993), *Consumption and the World of Goods*, Routledge, London.

BRUIJN, J.R. AND F.S. GAASTRA (eds.) (1993), *Ships, Sailors and Spices, East India Companies and their Shipping in the 16th, 17th and 18th Centuries,* NEHA, Amsterdam.

BULBECK, D., A. REID, L.C. TAN AND Y. WU (1998), *Southeast Asian Exports since the Fourteenth Century,* KITLV Press, Leiden.

BUTLIN, N.G. (1983), *Our Original Aggression*, Allen and Unwin, Sydney.

BUTLIN, N.G. (1993), *Economics and the Dreamtime,* Cambridge University Press, Melbourne.

CAMPBELL, B.M.S. AND M. OVERTON (eds.), (1991), *Land, Labour and Livestock: Historical Studies in European Agricultural Productivity*, Manchester University Press.

CARR–SAUNDERS, A.M. (1964), *World Population,* Cass, London.

CASELLI, G. (1991), "Health Transition and Cause Specific Mortality", in SCHOFIELD, REHER AND BIDEAU.

CHANDLER, A.D., JR. (1990), *Scale and Scope: The Dynamics of Industrial Capitalism*, Harvard.

CHANG, CHUNG–LI (1962), *The Income of the Chinese Gentry*, Greenwood, Westport.

CHAO, K. (1986), *Man and Land in Chinese History*, Stanford.

CHAUDHURI, K.N. (1978), *The Trading World of Asia and the English East India Company, 1660–1760*, Cambridge University Press, Cambridge.

CHAUDHURI, K.N. (1982), "Foreign Trade", in RAYCHAUDHURI AND HABIB.

CHAUDHURY, S. (1999), *From Prosperity to Decline: Eighteenth Centry Bengal,* Manohar, New Delhi.

CHAUDHURY, S. AND M. MORINEAU (1999), *Merchants, Companies and Trade: Europe and Asia in the Early Modern Era,* Cambridge University Press, Cambridge.

CHESNAIS, J.–C. (1987), *La revanche du tiers–monde*, Laffont, Paris.

CHOU, K.R. (1966), *The Hong Kong Economy*, Academic Publications, Hong Kong.

CIPOLLA, C.M. (1969), *Literacy and Development in the West*, Penguin Books, London.

CIPOLLA, C.M. (1970), *European Culture and Overseas Expansion*, Pelican, London.

CIPOLLA, C.M. (ed.) (1972–76), *The Fontana Economic History of Europe,* 6 vols., Collins/Fontana Books, London.

CIPOLLA, C.M. (1976), *Before the Industrial Revolution: European Society and Economy, 1000–1700*, Norton, New York.

CLARK, C. (1940), *The Conditions of Economic Progress*, Macmillan, London.

CLARK, C. (1967), *Population Growth and Land Use,* Macmillan, London.

CLARK, G. (1991), "Yields per Acre in English Agriculture, 1250–1860: Evidence from Labour Inputs", *Economic History Review*, August, pp. 445–60.

CLARK, G.N. (1968), *Science and Social Welfare in the Age of Newton*, Clarendon Press, Oxford.

COALE, A.J. AND P. DEMENY (1983), *Regional Model Life Tables and Stable Populations*, Academic Press, New York.

COATSWORTH, J.H. (1978), "Obstacles to Economic Growth in Nineteenth Century Mexico", *American Historical Review*, February, pp. 80–100.

COATSWORTH, J.H. (1989), "The Decline of the Mexican Economy, 1800–1860" in LIEHR.

COLLIER, P. AND J.W. GUNNING (1999), "Explaining African Performance", *Journal of Economic Literature*, March, pp. 64–111.

COOK, D.N. (1981), *Demographic Collapse: Indian Peru, 1520–1620*, Cambridge University Press, Cambridge.

COOK, S.F. AND L.B. SIMPSON (1948), *The Population of Central Mexico in the Sixteenth Century*, University of California, Berkeley.

COOPER, J.P. (1967), "The Social Distribution of Land and Men in England, 1436–1700", *Economic History Review* 20, pp. 419–440.

CRAFTS, N.F.R. (1983), "British Economic Growth, 1700–1831: A Review of the Evidence", *Economic History Review*, May, pp. 177–199.

CRAFTS, N.F.R. AND C.K. HARLEY (1992), "Output Growth and the British Industrial Revolution: A Restatement of the Crafts–Harley View", *Economic History Review*, November, pp. 703–730.

CRAIG, A.M. (1961), *Choshu in the Meiji Restoration*, Harvard University Press, Cambridge, Ma.

CRAWCOUR, E.S. (1963), "Changes in Japanese Commerce in the Tokugawa Period", *Journal of Asian Studies*, pp. 387–400.

CROSBY, A.W. (1972), *The Columbian Exchange: Biological and Cultural Consequences of 1492*, Greenwood Press, Westport, Connecticut.

CROSBY, A.W. (1986), *Ecological Imperialism: The Biological Expansion of Europe, 900–1900,* Cambridge University Press, Cambridge.

CROUZET, F. (1964), "Wars, Blockade, and Economic Change in Europe, 1792–1815", *Journal of Economic History,* December, pp. 567–88.

CROUZET, F. (1985), *De la supériorité de l'Angleterre sur La France*, Perrin, Paris.

CURTIN, P.D. (1969), *The Atlantic Slave Trade: A Census,* University of Wisconsin Press, Madison.

CURTIN, P.D. (1984), *Cross–cultural Trade in World History,* Cambridge University Press, Cambridge.

DANIELS, J.D. (1992), "The Indian Population of North America in 1492", *William and Mary Quarterly*, pp. 298–320.

DAS GUPTA, A. AND M.N. PEARSON (1987), *India and the Indian Ocean, 1500–1800,* New Delhi.

DAVID, P.A. (1967), "The Growth of Real Product in the United States Before 1840: New Evidence, Controlled Conjectures", *Journal of Economic History*, June.

DAVID, P.A. (1991), "Computer and Dynamo: The Modern Productivity Paradox in a Not Distant Mirror", in *Technology and Productivity: The Challenge for Economic Policy*, OECD, Paris, pp. 315–48.

Davies, R.T. (1964), *The Golden Century of Spain*, Macmillan, London.

Davis, K. (1951), *The Population of India and Pakistan*, Princeton.

Davis, L. and Associates (eds.) (1972), *American Economic Growth: An Economist's History of the United States*, Harper and Row, New York.

Davis, R. (1962), *The Rise of the English Shipbuilding Industry*, Macmillan, London.

Day, C. (1921), *A History of Commerce*, Longmans Green, New York.

Deane, P. (1955), "The Implications of Early National Income Estimates for the Measurement of Long–Term Economic Growth in the United Kingdom", *Economic Development and Cultural Change*, pp. 3–38.

Deane, P. (1955–6), "Contemporary Estimates of National Income in the First Half of the Nineteenth Century", *Economic History Review*, VIII, 3, pp. 339–354.

Deane, P. (1956–7), "Contemporary Estimates of National Income in the Second Half of the Nineteenth Century", *Economic History Review*, IX, 3, pp. 451–61.

Deane P. (1957), "The Industrial Revolution and Economic Growth: The Evidence of Early British National Income Estimates", *Economic Development and Cultural Change*, pp. 159–74.

Deane, P. and W.A. Cole (1964), *British Economic Growth 1688–1958*, Cambridge University Press, Cambridge.

Deane, P. (1968), "New Estimates of Gross National Product for the United Kingdom, 1830–1914", *Review of Income and Wealth*, June, pp. 95–112.

Denevan, W.M. (ed.) (1976), *The Native Population of the Americas in 1492*, University of Wisconsin.

Denison, E.F. and W.C. Haraldson (1945), "The Gross National Product of Germany 1936–1944", Special Paper 1, (mimeographed appendix to Galbraith, *et al*.

Dickson, D., C. O'Grada and S. Daultrey (1982), "Hearth Tax, Household Size and Irish Population Change 1672–1981", *Proceedings of the Royal Irish Academy*, Vol. 82 C, No. 6, Dublin.

Dickson, P.M.G. (1967), *The Financial Revolution in England,* Macmillan, London.

Domar, E.D. (1989), *Capitalism, Socialism and Serfdom*, Cambridge University Press, Cambridge.

Dore, R.P. (1965), *Education in Tokugawa Japan*, University of California Press, Berkeley.

Dublin, L.I., A.J. Lotka and M. Spiegelman (1963), *Length of Life,* Ronald Press, New York.

Dupaquier, J. (1997), "La connaissance démographique", in Bardet and Dupaquier, Vol. 1, pp. 218–38.

Durand, J.D. (1974), *Historical Estimates of World Population: An Evaluation*, University of Pennsylvania, Philadelphia.

Dyson, T. (ed.) (1989), *India's Historical Demography*, Curzon, Riverdale.

EBRD (European Bank for Reconstruction and Development), (1999), *Transition Report 1999*, London.

ECE (Economic Commission for Europe), (1994), *International Comparison of Gross Domestic Product in Europe 1990*, Geneva.

ECLAC, (Economic Commission for Latin America and the Caribbean) (1978), *Series Historicas del Crecimiento de America Latina*, Santiago, Chile.

ECLAC (1996), *Preliminary Overview of the Economy of Latin America and the Caribbean*, Santiago, Chile.

Eisner, G. (1961), *Jamaica, 1830–1930: a Study in Economic Growth*, Manchester University Press.

Eltis, D. (1995), "The Total Product of Barbados 1667–1701", *Journal of Economic History,* vol. 55:2, pp. 321–38

Engerman, S.L. and R.E. Gallman (1986), *Long Term Factors in American Economic Growth,* NBER, University of Chicago Press, Chicago.

ENGERMAN, S.L. AND R.E. GALLMAN (1996), *The Cambridge History of the United States,* Vol. 1, Cambridge University Press, Cambridge.

ESCAP (Economic and Social Commission for Asia and the Pacific), (1999), *Escap Comparisons of Real Gross Domestic Product and Purchasing Power Parities, 1993,* Bangkok.

EUROSTAT (Statistical Office of the European Communities), (1989), *Comparison of Price Levels and Economic Aggregates 1985: The Results for 22 African Countries,* Luxemburg.

FAGERBERG, J. (1994), "Technology and International Differences in Growth Rates", *Journal of Economic Literature,* September.

FAIRBANK, J.K. (ed.) (1968), *The Chinese World Order,* Harvard University Press, Cambridge, Ma.

FAIRBANK, J.K. (ed.) (1983), *The Cambridge History of China,* Vol. 12, Cambridge University Press, Cambridge.

FAROQHI, S., B. McGOWAN, D. QUATAERT, AND S. PAMUK (1994), *An Economic and Social History of the Ottoman Empire, 1600–1914,* Vol. 2, Cambridge University Press, Cambridge.

FARRIS, W.W. (1985), *Population, Disease and Land in Early Japan, 645–900,* Harvard.

FEINSTEIN, C.H. (1998), "Pessimism Perpetuated: Real Wages and the Standard of Living in Britain during and after the Industrial Revolution", *Journal of Economic History,* September, pp. 625–58.

FERNANDES, F. (1969), *The Negro in Brazilian Society,* Columbia University Press, New York.

FEUERWERKER, A. (1983), "The Foreign Presence in China", IN FAIRBANK.

FIRESTONE, O.J. (1958), *Canada's Economic Development, 1867–1953,* Bowes and Bowes, London.

FOGEL, R.W. (1964), *Railroads and American Economic Growth,* Johns Hopkins, Baltimore.

FOGEL, R.W. (1986), "Nutrition and the Decline in Mortality since 1700: Some Preliminary Findings", in ENGERMAN AND GALLMAN.

FOGEL, R.W. AND S.L. ENGERMAN (1974), *Time on the Cross: The Economics of American Negro Slavery,* Little Brown, London.

FOY, C., Y.–H. KIM AND H. REISEN (2000), *Sustainable Recovery in Asia: Mobilising Resources for Development,* OECD Development Centre, Paris (Preface by Braga de Macedo and Chino).

FRANK, A.G. (1998), *Reorient: Global Economy in the Asian Age,* University of California Press, Berkeley.

FREYRE, G. (1959), *New World in the Tropics,* Knopf, New York.

GALBRAITH, J.K., *et al.* (1945), *The Effects of Strategic Bombing on the German War Economy,* US Strategic Bombing Survey, Washington, D.C.

GALENSON, D.W. (1996), "The Settlement and Growth of the Colonies, Population, Labour and Economic Development", in ENGERMAN AND GALLMAN.

GALLMAN, R.E. (1972), "The Pace and Pattern of American Economic Growth", in DAVIS AND ASSOCIATES.

GALLOWAY, P.R. (1994), "A Reconstitution of the Population of North Italy from 1650 to 1881 using Annual Inverse Projection with Comparisons to England, France and Sweden", *Journal of Population,* 10, pp. 222–74.

GERSCHENKRON, A. (1965), *Economic Backwardness in Historical Perspective,* Praeger, New York.

GILBERT, M. AND I.B. KRAVIS (1954), *An International Comparison of National Products and Purchasing Power of Currencies,* OEEC, Paris.

GILLE, H. (1949), "The Demographic History of the Northern European Countries in the Eighteenth Century", *Population Studies,* III:1, June, pp. 3–65.

GLAMANN, K. (1981), *Dutch Asiatic Trade, 1620–1740,* Nijhoff, the Hague.

GLASS, D.V. (1965), "Two Papers on Gregory King", in GLASS AND EVERSLEY (1965), pp. 159–221.

GLASS, D.V. (1966), *London Inhabitants Within the Walls 1695,* London Record Society, London.

GLASS, D.V. AND D.E.C. EVERSLEY (eds.) (1965), *Population in History: Essays in Historical Demography*, Arnold, London.

GLASS, D.V. AND E. GREBENIK (1966), "World Population, 1800–1950", in H.J. HABAKKUK AND M. POSTAN, *Cambridge Economic History of Europe*, Vol. VI:1, Cambridge University Press, Cambridge.

GLASS, D.V. AND R. REVELLE (1972), *Population and Social Change*, Arnold, London.

GOITEIN, S.D. (1967), *A Mediterranean Society*, vol. 1, *Economic Foundations*, University of California Press, Berkeley.

GOLDSMITH, R.W. (1984), "An Estimate of the Size and Structure of the National Product of the Roman Empire", *Review of Income and Wealth*, September.

GOODMAN, D. AND C.A. RUSSELL (1991), *The Rise of Scientific Europe, 1500–1800*, Hodder and Stoughton, London.

GORDON, R.J. (2000), "Interpreting the 'One Big Wave in US Long–Term Productivity Growth", in VAN ARK, KUIPERS AND KUPER.

GOUBERT, P. (1965), "Recent Theories and Research in French Population Between 1500 and 1700", in GLASS AND EVERSLEY.

GRAUNT, J. (1676), *Natural and Political Observations upon the Bills of Mortality,* fifth edition, reprinted in HULL (1899).

HABAKKUK, H.J. AND M. POSTAN (eds.) (1966), *The Cambridge Economic History of Europe,* vol. VI, Cambridge University Press, Cambridge.

HABIB, I. (1982), "Technology and Economy of Moghul India", *Indian Economic and Social History Review,* XVII(1), pp. 1–34.

HABIB, I. (1995), *Essays in Indian History,* Tulika, New Delhi.

HALL, J.W. (ed.) (1991), *Early Modern Japan*, Vol. 4 of *The Cambridge History of Japan*, Cambridge University Press, Cambridge.

HALL, J.W., N. NAGAHARA, AND K. YAMAMURA (1981), *Japan Before Tokugawa*, Princeton.

HALLEY, E. (1693), "An Estimate of the Degrees of Mortality of Mankind, drawn from curious tables of the births and funerals at the city of Breslaw; with an attempt to ascertain the price of annuities upon lives", *Philosophical Transactions of the Royal Society,* Vol. XVII, No. 198, pp. 596–610.

HANLEY, S.B. AND K. YAMAMURA (1977), *Economic and Demographic Change in Preindustrial Japan*, Princeton.

HANLEY, S.B. (1997), *Everyday Things in Premodern Japan*, University of California Press, Berkeley.

HANSEN, B. AND G.A. MARZOUK (1965), *Development and Economic Policy in the UAR (Egypt)*, North Holland, Amsterdam.

HARLEY, C.K. (1988), "Ocean Freight Rates and Productivity, 1740–1913: The Primacy of Mechanical Invention Reaffirmed", *Journal of Economic History,* December, pp. 851–76.

HAWKE, G.R. (1985), *The Making of New Zealand,* Cambridge University Press, Melbourne.

HAYAMI, A. (1973), *Kinsei Noson no Rekishi Jinkogakuteki Kenkyu* (A Study of Historical Demography of Pre–Modern Rural Japan), Toyo Keizai Shimposha, Tokyo.

HAYAMI, A. (1986a), "Population Trends in Tokugawa Japan, 1600–1868", paper presented at the 46th session of the International Statistical Institute Congress.

HAYAMI, A. (ed.) (1986b), *Preconditions to Industrialization in Japan*, International Economic History Conference, Berne.

HAYAMI, A. AND M. MIYAMOTO (eds.) (1988), *Keizai Shakai no seritsu: 17–18 seiki, Nihon keizai–shi*, Vol. 1, Iwanami Shoten, Tokyo.

HAYAMI, Y., V.W. RUTTAN AND H.M. SOUTHWORTH (eds.) (1979), *Agricultural Growth in Japan, Taiwan, Korea and the Philippines*, Asian Productivity Center, Honolulu.

Hᴀʏᴀᴍɪ, Y. ᴀɴᴅ V.W. Rᴜᴛᴛᴀɴ (1985), *Agricultural Development*, second edition, Johns Hopkins, Baltimore.

Hᴇᴍᴍɪɴɢ, J. (1978), *Red Gold: The Conquest of the Brazilian Indians*, Macmillan.

Hᴇɴʀʏ L. ᴀɴᴅ D. Bʟᴀɴᴄʜᴇᴛ (1983), "La population de l'Angleterre de 1514 à 1871", *Population*, 4–5, pp. 781–826.

Hᴇɴʀʏ L. ᴀɴᴅ Y. Bʟᴀʏᴏ (1975), "La population de la France de 1740 à 1860", *Population*, November.

Hɪɢᴍᴀɴ, B.W. (1996), "Economic and Social Development in the British West Indies", in Eɴɢᴇʀᴍᴀɴ ᴀɴᴅ Gᴀʟʟᴍᴀɴ.

Hɪʀsᴄʜ, S. (ed.) (1992), *Memo 3: In Search of Answers in the Post–Soviet Era*, Bureau of National Affairs, Washington, D.C.

Hʟᴀɪɴɢ, A. (1964), "Trends of Economic Growth and Income Distribution in Burma 1870–1940", *Journal of the Burma Research Society*.

Hᴏ, P.T. (1959), *Studies on the Population of China, 1368–1953*, Harvard University Press, Cambridge, Ma.

Hᴏ, P.T. (1970), "An Estimate of the Total Population of Sung–Chin China", in Aᴜʙɪɴ.

Hᴏꜰꜰᴍᴀɴɴ, W.G. (1965), *Das Wachstum der deutschen Wirtschaft seit der Mitte des 19. Jahrhunderts*, Springer, Berlin.

Hᴏꜰᴍᴀɴ, A.A. (2000), *The Economic Development of Latin America in the Twentieth Century*, Elgar, Cheltenham.

Hᴏᴅɢᴇs, R. ᴀɴᴅ D. Wʜɪᴛᴇʜᴏᴜsᴇ (1998), *Mohammed, Charlemagne and the Origins of Europe*, Duckworth, London.

Hᴏʟᴍᴇs, G.S. (1977), "Gregory King and the Social Structure of Pre–Industrial England", *Transactions of the Royal Historical Society*, 5th series, Vol. 27, pp. 41–68.

Hᴏᴏʟᴇʏ, R.W. (1968), "Long Term Growth of the Philippine Economy, 1902–1961", *Philippine Economic Journal*.

Hᴏɴᴅᴀ, G. (1997), "Differential Structure, Differential Health: Industrialisation in Japan, 1868–1940", in Sᴛᴇᴄᴋᴇʟ ᴀɴᴅ Fʟᴏᴜᴅ.

Hᴏɴᴊᴏ, E. (1935), *The Social and Economic History of Japan*, Kyoto.

Hᴏᴘᴋɪɴs, K. (1980), "Taxes and Trade in the Roman Empire (200 B.C.–400 A.D.)", *Journal of Roman Studies*, Vol. LXX, pp. 101–25.

Hᴏʀɪᴏᴋᴀ, C.Y. (1990), "Why is Japan's Household Saving Rate So High? A Literature Survey", *Journal of Japanese and International Economies*, 4.

Hᴏᴜʀᴀɴɪ, G.F. (1951), *Arab Seafaring in the Indian Ocean in Ancient and Early Medieval Times*, Princeton.

Hsᴜᴇʜ, Tɪᴇɴ–ᴛᴜɴɢ ᴀɴᴅ Lɪ, Qɪᴀɴɢ (1999), *China's National Income, 1952–1995*, Westview Press, Boulder, Colorado.

Hᴜʟʟ, C.H. (ed.) (1899), *The Economic Writings of Sir William Petty*, 2 vols, Cambridge University Press, Cambridge.

IBGE (1960), *O Brasil em Numeros*, Rio de Janeiro.

Iᴋʀᴀᴍ, K. (1980), *Egypt: Economic Management in a Period of Transition*, Johns Hopkins, Baltimore.

IMF (International Monetary Fund) (1999), *World Economic Outlook*, Washington, D.C.

Iɴᴀʟᴄɪᴋ, H. (1994), *An Economic and Social History of the Ottoman Empire, 1300–1600*, Vol. 1, Cambridge University Press, Cambridge.

Isʜɪɪ, R. (1937), *Population Pressure and Economic Life in Japan*, King, London.

Isʀᴀᴇʟ, J.I. (1989), *Dutch Primacy in World Trade, 1585–1740*, Clarendon Press, Oxford.

Isʀᴀᴇʟ, J. (1995), *The Dutch Republic*, Clarendon Press, Oxford.

Jᴀɴɴᴇᴛᴛᴀ, A.B. (1986), *Epidemics and Mortality in Early Modern Japan*, Princeton.

Jᴀɴɴᴇᴛᴛᴀ, A.B. ᴀɴᴅ S.H. Pʀᴇsᴛᴏɴ (1991), "Two Centuries of Mortality Change in Central Japan: The Evidence from a Temple Death Register", *Population Studies*, 45, pp. 417–36.

JARRETT, H.S. AND S–N. SARKAR (1949), *Ain–I–Akbari of Abul Fazl–I–Allami*, Royal Asiatic Society of Bengal, Calcutta.

JONES, E.L. (1981), *The European Miracle,* Cambridge University Press, Cambridge.

JONES, V. (1978), *Sail the Indian Sea,* Gordon and Cremonesi, London.

JORGENSON, D.W. AND K.J. STIROH (2000), "Raising the Speed Limit: US Economic Growth in the Information Age", *Brookings Papers on Economic Activity I*, pp. 125–236.

KALLAND, A. AND J. PEDERSON (1984), "Famine and Population in Fukuoka Domain during the Tokugawa Period", *Journal of Japanese Studies*, 10, pp. 31–72.

KEENE, D. (1969), *The Japanese Discovery of Europe, 1720–1820,* Stanford.

KENDRICK, J.W. (1961), *Productivity Trends in the United States*, Princeton.

KENNEDY, P. (1987), *The Rise and Fall of the Great Powers,* Random House, New York.

KEYNES, J.M. (1919), *The Economic Consequences of the Peace,* Macmillan, LONDON.

KIM, K.S. AND M. ROEMER (1979), *Growth and Structural Transformation: The Republic of Korea,* Harvard University Press, Cambridge, Mass.

KING, G. (1696), *Natural and Political Observations and Conclusions upon the State and Condition of England,* in BARNETT (ed.), Johns Hopkins (1936).

KIRSTEN, E., E.W. BUCHHOLZ AND W. KÖLLMANN (1956), *Raum und Bevölkerung in der Weltgeschichte,* Ploetz–Verlag, Würzburg.

KLEIN, H.S. (1999), *The Atlantic Slave Trade,* Cambridge University Press, Cambridge.

KNODEL, J.E. (1988), *Demographic Behavior in the Past*, Cambridge University Press, Cambridge.

KORNAI, J. (1992), *The Socialist System: The Political Economy of Communism,* Clarendon Press, Oxford.

KRAVIS, I.B., A. HESTON AND R. SUMMERS (1982), *World Product and Income, International Comparisons of Real Gross Product*, Johns Hopkins, Baltimore.

KROEBER, A.L. (1939), *Cultural and National Areas of Native North America*, Berkeley.

KUHN, D. (1988), *Textile Technology: Spinning and Reeling*, Vol. 5, Part IX of Needham, Cambridge University Press, Cambridge.

KUMAR, D. AND M. DESAI (1983), *Cambridge Economic History of India*, Vol. 2, Cambridge.

KUZNETS, S. (1966), *Modern Economic Growth*, Yale.

KUZNETS, S. (1971), *Economic Growth of Nations*, Harvard.

KUZNETS, S. (1973), *Population, Capital and Growth: Selected Essays*, Norton, New York.

KUZNETS, S. (1979), *Growth, Population and Income Distribution*, Norton, New York.

KWON, T.H. (1993), "Reconstructing Population Phenomena in Chosun Korea",International Workshop on Historical Demography, Reitaku University, Chiba, Japan.

KWON, T.H. AND Y–H. SHIN (1977), "On Population Estimates of the Yi Dynasty, 1392–1910", *Tong–A Munhwa*, 14 (in Korean).

LAL, D. (1988), *The Hindu Equilibrium: Cultural Stability and Economic Stagnation,* Oxford University Press, Oxford.

LANDERS, J. (1993), *Death and the Metropolis: Studies in the Demographic History of London, 1670–1830,* Cambridge University Press, Cambridge.

LANDES, D.S. (1966), "Technological Change and Development in Western Europe, 1750–1914", IN HABAKKUK AND POSTAN.

LANDES, D.S. (1969), *The Unbound Prometheus,* Cambridge University Press, Cambridge.

LANDES, D.S. (1998), *The Wealth and Poverty of Nations,* Little Brown, London.

LANE, F.C. (1966), *Venice and History: Collected Papers,* Johns Hopkins Press, Baltimore.

LANE, F.C. (1973), *Venice: A Maritime Republic,* Johns Hopkins Press, Baltimore.

LANE, F.C. AND R.C. MUELLER (1985), *Money and Banking in Medieval and Renaissance Venice,* vol. 1, Johns Hopkins Press, Baltimore.

LASLETT, P. (1969), "John Locke, the Great Recoinage, and the Origins of the Board of Trade" in YOLTON.

LASLETT, P. (ed.) (1973), *The Earliest Classics: John Graunt and Gregory King,* Gregg International, London.

LEBERGOTT, S. (1984), *The Americans: An Economic Record,* Norton, New York.

LEBOUTTE, R. (ed.) (1996), *Proto–industrialization,* Droz, Geneva.

LEE, H.K. (1936), *Land Utilization and Rural Economy in Korea,* Oxford University Press.

LEE, J.Z AND C. CAMPBELL (1997), *Fate and Fortune in Rural China,* Cambridge University Press, Cambridge.

LEE, J.Z. AND F. WANG (forthcoming*), Malthusian Mythology and Chinese Reality: The Population History of One Quarter of Humanity: 1700–2000.*

LEFF, N.H. (1982), *Underdevelopment and Development in Brazil,* 2 vols., Allen and Unwin, London.

LENIHAN, P. (1997), "War and Population, 1649–52", *Irish Economic and Social History, XXIV,* pp. 1–21.

LE ROY LADURIE, E. (1966), *Les paysans de Languedoc,* Mouton, Paris.

LE ROY LADURIE, E. (1977), "Les masses profondes: la paysannerie", in BRAUDEL AND LAROUSSE.

LE ROY LADURIE, E. (1978), *Le territoire de l'historien,* 2 vols., Gallimard, Paris.

LEVATHES, L. (1994), *When China Ruled the Seas,* Simon and Schuster, New York.

LIEHR, R. (1989), *La formacion de las economias latinoamericanos en la epoca de Simon Bolivar,* Colloquium Verlag, Berlin.

LIM, C.H. (1967), *Economic Development of Modern Malaya,* Oxford University Press, Kuala Lumpur.

LINDERT, P.H. (1980), "English Occupations, 1670–1811", *Journal of Economic History, XL,* 4, pp. 685–713.

LINDERT, P.H. AND J.G. WILLIAMSON (1982), "Revising England's Social Tables, 1688–1812", *Explorations in Economic History,* 19, 1982, pp. 385–408.

LIVI BACCI, M. AND D.S. REHER (1993), "Other Paths to the Past: from Vital Series to Population Patterns", in REHER AND SCHOFIELD.

LORIMER, F. (1946), *The Population of the Soviet Union: History and Prospects,* League of Nations, Geneva.

LOVEJOY, P.E. (1982), "The Volume of the African Slave Trade: A Synthesis", *Journal of African History,* pp. 473–75.

LUNDBERG, E. (1968), *Instability and Economic Growth,* Yale University Press, New Haven.

MACEDO, J. BRAGA DE (1995), "Convertibility and Stability 1834–1994: Portuguese Currency Experience Revisited", in *Ensaios de Homenagem a Francisco Pereira de Moura,* UTL, Lisbon.

MACFARLANE, A. (1997), *The Savage Wars of Peace,* Blackwell, Oxford.

MADDISON, A. (1962), "Growth and Fluctuation in the World Economy, 1870–1960", *Banca Nazionale del Lavoro Quarterly Review,* June.

MADDISON, A. (1969), *Economic Growth in Japan and the USSR,* Allen and Unwin, London.

MADDISON, A. (1970), *Economic Progress and Policy in Developing Countries,* Allen and Unwin, London.

MADDISON, A. (1971), *Class Structure and Economic Growth: India and Pakistan Since the Moghuls,* Allen and Unwin, London.

MADDISON, A. (1972), "Explaining Economic Growth", *Banca Nazionale del Lavoro Quarterly Review,* 102, September.

MADDISON, A. (1976), "Economic Policy and Performance in Europe, 1913–70", in CIPOLLA.

MADDISON, A. (1980), "Monitoring the Labour Market", *Review of Income and Wealth*, June.

MADDISON, A. (1982), *Phases of Capitalist Development*, Oxford University Press, Oxford.

MADDISON, A. (1983), "A Comparison of Levels of GDP Per Capita in Developed and Developing Countries, 1700–1980", *Journal of Economic History*, March, pp. 27–41.

MADDISON, A. (1985), *Two Crises: Latin America and Asia, 1929–38 and 1973–83,* OECD Development Centre, Paris.

MADDISON, A. (1987a), "Growth and Slowdown in Advanced Capitalist Economies: Techniques of Quantitative Assessment", *Journal of Economic Literature*, June.

MADDISON, A. (1987b), "Recent Revisions to British and Dutch Growth, 1700–1870 and their Implications for Comparative Levels of Performance", in MADDISON AND VAN DER MEULEN (1987).

MADDISON, A. (1989a), *The World Economy in the Twentieth Century*, OECD Development Centre, Paris.

MADDISON, A. (1989b), "Dutch Income in and from Indonesia 1700–1938", *Modern Asian Studies*, pp. 645–70.

MADDISON, A. (1990a), "The Colonial Burden: A Comparative Perspective", in SCOTT AND LAL.

MADDISON, A. (1990b), "Measuring European Growth: the Core and the Periphery", in E. AERTS AND N. VALERIO, *Growth and Stagnation in the Mediterranean World*, Tenth International Economic History Conference, Leuven.

MADDISON, A. (1991a), *Dynamic Forces in Capitalist Development*, Oxford University Press, Oxford.

MADDISON, A. (1991b), *A Long Run Perspective on Saving*, Research Memorandum 443, Institute of Economic Research, University of Groningen (a shorter version appeared in the *Scandinavian Journal of Economics*, June 1992, pp. 181–96).

MADDISON, A. (1995a), *Monitoring the World Economy 1820–1992*, OECD Development Centre, Paris.

MADDISON, A. (1995b) *Explaining the Economic Performance of Nations: Essays in Time and Space*, Elgar, Aldershot.

MADDISON, A. (1995c), "The Historical Roots of Modern Mexico: 1500–1940", in MADDISON (1995b).

MADDISON, A. (1996), "Macroeconomic Accounts for European Countries", in VAN ARK AND CRAFTS.

MADDISON, A. (1997), "The Nature and Functioning of European Capitalism: A Historical and Comparative Perspective", *Banca Nazionale del Lavoro Quarterly Review*, December.

MADDISON, A. (1998a), *Chinese Economic Performance in the Long Run*, OECD Development Centre, Paris.

MADDISON, A. (1998b), "Measuring the Performance of A Communist Command Economy: An Assessment of the CIA Estimates for the USSR", *Review of Income and Wealth*, September.

MADDISON, A. (1999a), "Poor until 1820", *Wall Street Journal*, January 11th, p.8.

MADDISON, A. (1999b), "Book Review", of Hanley (1997), *Journal of Japanese and International Economies*, 13, pp. 150–151.

MADDISON, A. AND B. VAN ARK (1994), "The International Comparison of Real Product and Productivity", paper presented at IARIW meetings, St. Andrews, New Brunswick, Canada.

MADDISON, A. AND ASSOCIATES (1992), *The Political Economy of Economic Growth: Brazil and Mexico*, Oxford University Press, New York.

MADDISON, A. AND G. PRINCE (eds.) (1989), *Economic Growth in Indonesia, 1820–1940,* Foris, Dordrecht.

MADDISON, A. AND H. VAN DER MEULEN (eds.) (1987), *Economic Growth in Northwestern Europe: The Last 400 Years*, Research Memorandum 214, Institute of Economic Research, University of Groningen.

MADDISON, A. AND H. VAN DER WEE (eds.) (1994), *Economic Growth and Structural Change: Comparative Approaches over the Long Run*, Proceedings of the Eleventh International Economic History Congress, Milan, September.

MADDISON, A., D.S. PRASADA RAO AND W. SHEPHERD (eds.) (2001), *The Asian Economies in the Twentieth Century*, Elgar, Aldershot.

MALANIMA, P. (1995), *Economia Preindustriale*, Mondadori, Milan.

MALANIMA, P. (1998*a*), *La Fina del Primato*, Mondadori, Milan.

MALANIMA, P. (1998*b*), "Italian Cities 1300–1800: A Quantitative Approach", *Revista de Storia Economica*, August, pp. 91–126.

MANCALL, P.C. AND T. WEISS (1999), "Was Economic Growth Likely in British North America?", *Journal of Economic History*, March, pp. 17–40.

MARCILIO, M.L. (1984), "The Population of Colonial Brazil", in BETHELL (1984), Vol. 2.

MARCZEWSKI, J. (1961), "Some Aspects of the Economic Growth of France, 1660–1958", *Economic Development and Cultural Change*, April.

MARI BHAT, P.N. (1989), "Mortality and Fertility in India, 1881–1961: A Reassessment", in DYSON.

MATHIAS, P. (1957), "The Social Structure in the Eighteenth Century: A Calculation by Joseph Massie", *Economic History Review*, pp. 30–45.

McEVEDY, C. (1967), *The Penguin Atlas of Ancient History*, Penguin Books, London.

McEVEDY, C. (1997), *The New Penguin Atlas of Medieval History*, Penguin Books, London.

McEVEDY, C. AND R. JONES (1978), *Atlas of World Population History*, Penguin, Middlesex.

McNEILL, W.H. (1964), *Europe's Steppe Frontier*, University of Chicago Press, Chicago.

McNEILL, W.H. (1974), *Venice: The Fringe of Europe*, University of Chicago Press, Chicago.

McNEILL, W.H. (1977), *Plagues and Peoples*, Anchor Books, Doubleday, New York.

MEIER, G.M. AND D. SEERS (eds.) (1984), *Pioneers in Development*, Oxford University Press, Oxford.

MERKEL, W. AND S. WAHL (1991), *Das geplünderte Deutschland*, IWG, Bonn.

MERRICK, T.W. AND D.H. GRAHAM (1979), *Population and Development in Brazil 1800 to the Present*, Johns Hopkins University Press, Baltimore and London.

METZER, J. (1998), *The Divided Economy of Mandatory Palestine*, Cambridge University Press, Cambridge.

MITCHELL, B.R. (1975), *European Historical Statistics, 1750–1970*, Macmillan, London.

MITCHELL, B.R. AND P. DEANE (1962), *Abstract of British Historical Statistics*, Cambridge University Press, Cambridge.

MITCHELL, B.R. AND H.G. JONES (1971), *Second Abstract of British Historical Statistics*, Cambridge University Press, Cambridge.

MIZOGUCHI, T. (1999), *Long Term Economic Statistics of Taiwan: 1905–1990*, Institute of Economic Research, Hitotsubashi University, Tokyo.

MIZOGUCHI, T. AND M. UMEMURA (1988), *Basic Economic Statistics of Japanese Colonies, 1895–1938*, Toyo Keizai Shinposha, Tokyo.

MOOSVI, S. (1987), *The Economy of the Moghul Empire c.1595: A Statistical Study*, Oxford University Press, Delhi.

MORELAND, W.H. (1920), *India at the Death of Akbar: An Economic Study*, Atmar Ram, Delhi (1962 reprint).

MORINEAU, M. (1985), *Incroyables gazettes et fabuleux métaux*, Cambridge University Press, Cambridge.

MORISON, S.E. (1971), *The European Discovery of America: The Northern Voyages*, A.D. 500–1600, Oxford Univeristy Press, Oxford.

MORISON, S.E. (1974), *The European Discovery of America: The Southern Voyages*, A.D. 1492–1616, Oxford University Press, Oxford.

MOTE, F.W. AND D. TWITCHETT (eds.) (1988), *The Cambridge History of China, The Ming Dynasty, 1368–1644*, Part 1, Cambridge University Press, Cambridge.

MOWERY, D.C. AND N. ROSENBERG (1989), *Technology and the Pursuit of Economic Growth*, Cambridge University Press, Cambridge.

MULHALL, M.G. (1896), *Industries and Wealth of Nations*, Longmans, London.

MULHALL, M.G. (1899), *The Dictionary of Statistics*, Routledge, London, 4th edition.

MYERS, R.H. (ed.) (1996), *The Wealth of Nations in the Twentieth Century*, Hoover Institution, Stanford.

NAKAMURA, J.I. (1966), *Agricultural Production and the Economic Development of Japan, 1873–1922*, Princeton.

NAKAMURA, S. (1968), *Meiji Ishin no Kiso Kozo*.

NAOROJI, D. (1901), *Poverty and Un–British Rule in India,* London, Government of India Reprint, Delhi, 1962.

NDULU, B. AND S.A. O'CONNELL (1999), "Governance and Growth in Sub–Saharan Africa", *Journal of Economic Perspectives,* Summer, pp. 41–66.

NEEDHAM, J. AND ASSOCIATES (1954–2000), *Science and Civilisation in China*, 50 major sections, many co–authors, many volumes, Cambridge University Press, Cambridge.

NEF, J.U. (1987), "Mining and Metallurgy in Medieval Civilisation", in POSTAN *et al.* (eds.), vol. II, pp. 693–762.

NISHIKAWA, S. (1987), "The Economy of Choshu on the Eve of Industrialisation", *Economic Studies Quarterly*, December.

NORTH, D.C. (1966), *Growth and Welfare in the American Past,* Prentice Hall, New Jersey.

NORTH D.C. (1968), "Sources of Productivity Change in Ocean Shipping, 1600–1850", *Journal of Political Economy,* September–October, pp. 953–70.

NORTH D.C. (1990), *Institutions, Institutional Change and Economic Performance*, Cambridge University Press, Cambridge.

Ó GRÁDA, C. (1988), *Ireland Before and After the Famine,* Manchester University Press, Manchester.

OECD (1979), *Demographic Trends 1950–1990*, Paris.

OHKAWA, K. (1957), *The Growth Rate of the Japanese Economy since 1878*, Kinokuniya, Tokyo.

OHKAWA, K., M. SHINOHARA, AND M. UMEMURA (eds.) (1966–1988), *Estimates of Long–Term Economic Statistics of Japan since 1868*, 14 volumes, Toyo Keizai Shinposha, Tokyo.

OHKAWA, K. AND M. SHINOHARA (eds.) (1979), *Patterns of Japanese Economic Development: A Quantitative Appraisal*, Yale.

OHLIN, G. (1955), *The Positive and Preventive Check: A Study of the Rate of Growth of Pre–Industrial Populations,* Harvard Ph.D thesis, reprinted by Arno Press, New York, 1981.

OKAMOTO, Y. (1972), *The Namban Art of Japan*, Heibonsha, Tokyo.

OLINER. S.D. AND D.E. SICHEL (2000), "The Resurgence of Growth in the Late 1990s: Is Information Technology the Story?", Federal Reserve Board, Washington, D.C., February.

OLIVER, R. AND J.D. FAGE (1995), *A Short History of Africa*, Penguin Books, London.

O'ROURKE, K.H. AND J.G. WILLIAMSON (1999), *Globalization and History,* MIT Press, Cambridge, Ma.

OVERTON, M. (1996), *Agricultural Revolution in England: The Transformation of the Agrarian Economy, 1500–1850*, Cambridge University Press, Cambridge.

PAIGE, D. AND G. BOMBACH (1959), *A Comparison of National Output and Productivity of the UK and the United States*, OECD, Paris.

PANNIKAR, K.M. (1953), *Asian and Western Dominance,* Allen and Unwin, London.

PARKER, G. (1979), *Spain and the Netherlands, 1599–1659,* Fontana/Collins, London.

Parry, J.H. (1967), "Transport and Trade Routes", in Rich and Wilson.

Parry, J.H. (1974), *The Discovery of the Sea,* Weidenfeld and Nicolson, London.

Patinkin, D. (1960), *The Israeli Economy: The First Decade*, Falk Project, Jerusalem.

Pebrer, P. (1833), *Taxation, Revenue, Expenditure, Power, Statistics of the Whole British Empire,* Baldwin and Cradock, London.

Perkins, D.W. (1969), *Agricultural Development in China, 1368–1968*, Aldine, Chicago.

Perrin, N. (1979), *Giving up the Gun: Japan's Reversion to the Sword, 1543–1879,* Godine, Boston.

Petty, W. (1690), *Political Arithmetick,* in Hull (1899), Vol. 1.

Petty, W. (1997), *The Collected Works of Sir William Petty*, 8 volumes, Routledge/Thoemes Press, London (includes Hull's (1899) collection of Petty's economic writings; E.G. Fitzmaurice's (1895) biography of Petty; Lansdowne's (1927 and 1928) collection of Petty papers and the Southwell–Petty correspondence; Larcom's (1851) edition of Petty's Irish Land Survey, and critical appraisals by T.W. Hutchinson and others).

Phelps Brown, H. and S.V. Hopkins (1981), *A Perspective on Wages and Prices*, Methuen, London.

Pirenne, H. (1939), *Mohammed and Charlemagne,* Allen and Unwin, London.

Polak, J.J. (1943), *The National Income of the Netherlands Indies, 1921–1939,* New York.

Pomeranz, K. (2000), *The Great Divergence*, Princeton University Press, Princeton.

Postan, M.M., *et al.* (eds.) (1963–87), *The Cambridge Economic History of Europe,* vol. I (1966), vol. II (1987) and vol. III (1963), Cambridge University Press, Cambridge.

Potter, J. (1965), "The Growth of Population in America, 1700–1860", in Glass and Everseley.

Prakash, O. (1998), *European Commercial Enterprise in Pre–colonial India,* Cambridge University Press, Cambridge.

Preston, S.H and E. van der Walle (1978), "Urban French Mortality in the Nineteenth Century", *Population Studies,* 32, 2, pp. 275–297.

Procacci, G. (1978), *History of the Italian People*, Penguin Books, London.

Purcell, V. (1965), *The Chinese in Southeast Asia,* Oxford University Press, Kuala Lumpur.

Qaisar, A.J. (1982), *The Indian Response to European Techgnology and Culture, A.D. 1498–1707,* Oxford University Press, Bombay.

Ranis, G. and T.P. Schultz (eds.) (1988), *The State of Development Economics*, Blackwell, Oxford.

Rapp, R.T. (1976), *Industry and Economic Decline in Seventeenth Century Venice*, Harvard University Press, Cambridge, Ma.

Raychaudhuri, T. and I. Habib (1982) (eds.) *The Cambridge Economic History of India*, Cambridge University Press, Cambridge.

Reher, D.S. and R. Schofield (eds.) (1993), *Old and New Methods in Historical Demography*, Clarendon Press, Oxford.

Reid, A. (1988), *Southeast Asia in the Age of Commerce, 1450–1680, Vol. 1, The Lands Below the Winds*, Yale, New Haven.

Reid, A. (1993), *Southeast Asia in the Age of Commerce, 1450–1680, Vol. 2, Expansion and Crisis*, Yale, New Haven.

Reisen, H. and M. Soto (2000), "The Need for Foreign Savings in Post–Crisis Asia" (see Foy, Kim and Reisen) in Braga de Macedo and Chino (Preface by).

Ruoen, R. (1997), *China's Economic Performance in An International Perspective*, OECD Development Centre, Paris.

Riccioli, G.B. (1672), *Geographiae et Hydrographiae Reformatae, Libri Duodecim, Venice.*

RICH, E.E. AND C.H. WILSON (1967), *The Cambridge History of Europe,* Vol. IV, Cambridge University Press, Cambridge.

RICHARDS, E.G. (1998), *Mapping Time,* Oxford University Press, Oxford.

RICHARDS, J.F. (1983), *Precious Metals in the Later Medieval and Early Modern Worlds,* Carolina Academic Press, Durham, North Carolina.

ROBERTSON, J. (1984), "Japanese Farm Manuals: A Literature of Discovery", *Peasant Studies,* 11, Spring, pp. 169–194.

ROMANELLI, G. (ed.) (1997), *Venice: Art and Architecture,* Könemann, Cologne.

ROMER, P.M. (1986), "Increasing Returns and Long Run Growth", *Journal of Political Economy,* 94, No. 5.

ROSENBLAT, A. (1945), *La Poblacion Indigena de America Desde 1492 Hasta la Actualidad,* ICE, Buenos Aires.

ROSENBLAT, A. (1967), *La Poblacion de America en 1492,* Colegio de Mexico, Mexico D.F.

ROSTOW, W.W. (1960), *The Stages of Economic Growth,* Cambridge University Press, Cambridge.

ROSTOW, W.W. (ed.) (1963), *The Economics of Take–Off into Sustained Growth,* Macmillan, London.

ROSTOW, W.W. (1990), *Theorists of Economic Growth from David Hume to the Present,* Oxford University Press, Oxford.

ROTHERMUND, D. (1999), "The Changing Pattern of British Trade in Indian Textiles, 1701–57", in CHAUDHURY AND MORINEAU.

ROSENZWEIG, F. (1963), "La economia Novo–Hispaña al comenzar del siglo XIX", *Revista de Sciencias Politicas y Sociales,* UNAM, July–September.

ROZMAN, G. (1973), *Urban Networks in Ch'ing China and Tokugawa Japan,* Princeton University Press, Princeton.

RUSSELL, J.C. (1948), *British Medieval Population,* University of New Mexico, Albuquerque.

RUSSELL, J.C. (1958), *Late Ancient and Medieval Population,* American Philosophical Society, Philadelphia.

RUSSELL, P. (2000), *Prince Henry "The Navigator": A Life,* Yale University Press, New Haven.

SAITO, O. (1979), "Who Worked When: Life Time Profiles of Labour Force Participation in Cardington and Corfe Castle in the Late Eighteenth and Mid–Nineteenth Centuries", *Local Population Studies,* pp. 14–29.

SAITO, O. (1996), "Gender, Workload and Agricultural Progress: Japan's Historical Experience in Perspective", in LEBOUTTE.

SAITO, O. (1997), "Infant Mortality in Pre–Transition Japan: Levels and Trends", in BIDEAU, DESJARDINS AND PEREZ BRIGNOLI.

SALTER, W.E.G. (1960), *Productivity and Technical Change,* Cambridge University Press, Cambridge.

SANCHEZ–ALBORNOZ, N. (1984), "The Population of Colonial Spanish America", in BETHELL, vol. 2.

SANCHEZ–ALBORNOZ, N. (1986), "The Population of Latin America, 1850–1930", in BETHELL, vol. 4.

SARKAR, N.K. (1957), *The Demography of Ceylon,* Ceylon Government Press, Colombo.

SCHMOOKLER, J. (1966), *Invention and Economic Growth,* Harvard University Press, Cambridge, Ma.

SCHOFIELD, R., D. REHER AND A. BIDEAU (1991), *The Decline of Mortality in Europe,* Clarendon Press, Oxford.

SCHULTZ, T.W. (1961), "Investment in Human Capital", *American Economic Review,* March.

SCHUMPETER, J.A. (1939), *Business Cycles,* McGraw Hill, New York.

SCHWARTZ, S.B., (1985), *Sugar Plantations in the Formation of Brazilian Society: Bahià, 1550–1835,* Cambridge University Press, Cambridge.

SCOTT, M. AND D. LAL (eds.) (1990), *Public Policy and Economic Development: Essays in Honour of Ian Little,* Clarendon Press, Oxford.

SELLA, D. (1979), *Crisis and Continuity: The Economy of Spanish Lombardy in the Seventeenth Century*, Harvard University Press, Cambridge, Ma.

SHAMMAS, C. (1993), "Changes in English and Anglo–American Consumption from 1550 to 1800", in BREWER AND PORTER.

SHEA, D.E. (1976), "A Defence of Small Population Estimates for the Central Andes in 1520", in DENEVAN (1976), pp. 157–80.

SIMONSEN, R.C. (1962), *Historia Economica do Brasil (1500–1820)*, Editora Nacional, São Paulo.

SIVASUBRAMONIAN, S. (2000), *The National Income of India in the Twentieth Century*, Oxford University Press, New Delhi.

SIVASUBRAMONIAN, S. (2001), "Twentieth Century Economic Performance of India", in MADDISON, PRASADA RAO AND SHEPHERD.

SLICHER VAN BATH, B.H. (1963), *The Agrarian History of Western Europe, AD 500–1850*, Arnold, London.

SMITH, A. (1776), *An Inquiry into the Nature and Causes of the Wealth of Nations*, University of Chicago Reprint, 1976.

SMITH, T.C. (1959), *The Agrarian Origins of Modern Japan*, Stanford.

SMITH, T.C. (1969), "Farm Family By-Employments in Preindustrial Japan", *Journal of Economic History*, December.

SMITH, T.C. (1977), *Nakahara: Family Farming and Population in a Japanese Village, 1717–1830*, Stanford University Press, Stanford, California.

SMITH, T.C. (1988), *Native Sources of Japanese Industrialization, 1750–1920*, University of California, Berkeley.

SMITS, J.P., E. HORLINGS AND J.L. VAN ZANDEN (2000), *The Measurement of Gross National Product and Its Components, 1800–1913*, Groningen Growth and Development Centre Monograph Series, No. 5.

SNODGRASS, D.R. (1966), *Ceylon: An Export Economy in Transition*, Irwin, Illinois.

SNOOKS, G.D. (1993), *Economics Without Time*, Macmillan, London.

SNOOKS, G.D. (1996), *The Dynamic Society: Exploring the Sources of Global Change*, Routledge, London.

SNOOKS, G.D. (1997), *The Ephemeral Civilisation*, Routledge, London.

SOLOW, R.M. (1956), "A Contribution to the Theory of Economic Growth", *Quarterly Journal of Economics*, February.

SOLOW, R.M. (1960), "Investment and Technical Progress", in ARROW, KARLIN AND SUPPES (eds.) *Mathematical Methods in the Social Sciences*, Stanford University Press.

SOLOW, R.M. (1962), "Technical Progress, Capital Formation and Eonomic Growth", *American Economic Review*, May.

SPOONER, F.C. (1972), *The International Economy and Monetary Movements in France, 1493–1725*, Harvard University Press, Cambridge, Ma.

SPULBER, N. (1966), *The State and Economic Development in Eastern Europe*, Random House, New York.

STECKEL, R.H. AND R. FLOUD (1997), *Health and Welfare during Industrialisation*, University of Chicago Press, Chicago.

STEENSGAARD, N. (1972), *Carracks, Caravans and Companies*, Copenhagen.

STONE, R. (1997), *Some British Empiricists in the Social Sciences 1650–1900*, Cambridge University Press, Cambridge.

STUDENSKI, P. (1958), *The Income of Nations: Theory, Measurement and Analysis: Past and Present*, New York University Press, Washington Square.

SUBRAHMANYAM, S. (1997), *The Career and Legend of Vasco de Gama*, Cambridge University Press, Cambridge.

SUH, S.C. (1978), *Growth and Structural Changes in the Korean Economy, 1910–40*, Harvard University Press, Cambridge, Ma.

SUMMERS, R. AND A. HESTON (1991), "The Penn World Table (Mark 5): An Expanded Set of International Comparisons 1950–1988", *Quarterly Journal of Economics*, May, supplemented by January 1995 diskette of P.W.T. Mark 5.6.

SZERESZEWSKI, R. (1965), *Structural Changes in the Economy of Ghana*, Weidenfeld and Nicolson, London.

SZERESZEWSKI, R. (1968), *Essays on the Structure of the Jewish Economy in Palestine and Israel*, Falk Project, Jerusalem.

SZIRMAI, A., B. VAN ARK AND D. PILAT (eds.) (1993), *Explaining Economic Growth: Essays in Honour of Angus Maddison*, North Holland, Amsterdam.

TAEUBER, I.B. (1958), *The Population of Japan*, Princeton University Press, New Jersey.

TAWNEY, A.J. AND R.H. (1934), "An Occupational Census of the Seventeenth Century", *Economic History Review*, October.

TAYLOR, G.R. (1964), "American Economic Growth Before 1840: An Exploratory Essay", *Journal of Economic History*, December, pp. 427–444.

TEMPLE, W. (1693), *Observations upon the United Provinces of the Netherlands,* Tonson, London.

TERRISE, M. (1975), "Aux origines de la méthode de reconstitution des familles: les Suédois d'Estonie", *Population*, numéro spécial.

THIRSK, J. (1978), *Economic Policies and Projects: The Development of a Consumer Society in Early Modern England*, Oxford University Press, Oxford.

THOMAS, R.P. (1965), "A Quantitative Approach to the Study of the Effects of British Imperial Policy upon Colonial Welfare: Some Preliminary Findings", *Journal of Economic History,* December.

THOMAS, R.P. (1968), "The Sugar Colonies of the Old Empire: Profit and Loss to Great Britain", *Economic History Review*.

THORNTON, R. (1987), *American Indian Holocaust and Survival: A Population History since 1492*, University of Oklahoma, Norman.

TIBBETTS, G.R. (1981), *Arab Navigation in the Indian Ocean before the Coming of the Portuguese,* Royal Asiatic Society of Great Britain and Ireland

TRACY, J.D. (ed.) (1990), *The Rise of Merchant Empires: Long Distance Trade in the Early Modern Period, 1350–1750,* Cambridge University Press.

TWITCHETT, D. AND F.W. MOTE (eds.) (1998), *The Cambridge History of China*, Vol. 8, *The Ming Dynasty,* Part 2, *1368–1644*, Cambridge University Press, Cambridge.

UBELAKER, D.H. (1976), "Prehistoric New World Population Size: Historical Review and Current Appraisal of North American Estimates", *American Journal of Physical Anthropology*, pp. 661–6.

UNGER, R.W. (1980), *The Ship in the Medieval Economy, 600–1600,* Croom Helm, London.

UNGER, R.W. (1992), "The Tonnage of Europe's Merchant Fleets, 1300–1800", *The American Neptune (52),* pp. 247–61.

UN POPULATION DIVISON (1973), *The Determinants and Consequences of Population Trends,* New York.

UN POPULATION DIVISON (1999), *World Population Prospects: The 1998 Revision*, New York.

URLANIS, B.TS. (1941), *Rost Naselennie v Evrope*, Ogiz, Moscow.

VALLIN, J. (1991), "Mortality in Europe from 1720 to 1914", in SCHOFIELD, REHER AND BIDEAU.

VAMPLEW, W. (ed.) (1987), *Australians: Historical Statistics,* Cambridge University Press, Cambridge.

VAN DER ENG, P. (1998), "Exploring Exploitation: The Netherlands and Colonial Indonesia, 1870–1940", *Revista de Historia Economica* XVI, 1, pp. 291–320.

VAUBAN, S. (1707), *La disme royale* (1992 edition, with introduction by E. Le Roy Ladurie, Imprimerie nationale, Paris).

VERLINDEN, C. (1963), "Markets and Fairs", in POSTAN *et al.* (eds.) Vol. III, pp. 126–136.

VERLINDEN, C. (1972), "From the Mediterranean to the Atlantic", *Journal of European Economic History,* pp. 625-46.

VISARIA, L. AND P. VISARIA (1983), "Population: 1757–1947", IN KUMAR AND DESAI.

VOGEL, W. (1915), "Zur Grösse der europaischen Handelsflotten im 15., 16. und 17. Jahrhundert", in D. Schäfer (ed.) *Forschungen und Versuche zur Geschichte des Mitelalters und der Neuzeit,* Fischer, Jena.

VON GLAHN, R. (1996), *Fountain of Fortune: Money and Monetary Policy in China, 1000–1700,* University of California Press, California.

VRIES, J. DE (1974), *The Dutch Rural Economy in the Golden Age, 1500–1700,* Yale.

VRIES, J. DE (1976), *Economy of Europe in an Age of Crisis, 1600–1750,* Cambridge University Press, Cambridge.

VRIES, J. DE (1984), *European Urbanization 1500–1800,* Methuen, London.

VRIES, J. DE (1985), "The Population and Economy of the Preindustrial Netherlands", *Journal of Interdisciplinary History,* XV:4, pp. 661–82.

VRIES, J. DE (1993), "Between Purchasing Power and the World of Goods: Understanding the Household Economy in Early Modern Europe", in BREWER AND PORTER.

VRIES, J. DE AND A. VAN DER WOUDE (1997), *The First Modern Economy: Success, Failure and Perseverance of the Dutch Economy, 1500–1815,* Cambridge University Press, Cambridge.

WAKE, C.H.H. (1979), "The Changing Pattern of Europe's Pepper and Spice Imports, ca 1400–1700", *Journal of European Economic History,* vol. 8(2), pp. 361–403.

WAKE, C.H.H. (1986), "The Volume of European Spice Imports at the Beginning and End of the Fifteenth Century", *Journal of European Economic History, vol* 15(3), pp. 621–35.

WALL, R. (1983), "The Household: Demographic and Economic Change in England, 1650–1970", in WALL *et al.*

WALL, R., J. ROBIN AND P. LASLETT (1983), *Family Forms in Historic Europe,* Cambridge University Press, Cambridge.

WALTER, J. AND R. SCHOFIELD (1989), *Famine, Disease and the Social Order in Early Modern Society,* Cambridge University Press, Cambridge.

WARMINGTON, E.H. (1928), *The Commerce Between the Roman Empire and India,* Cambridge University Press, Cambridge.

WESTERGAARD, H. (1932), *Contributions to the History of Statistics,* King, London (Kelley reprint, 1969).

WHITE, L. (1962), *Medieval Tehnology and Social Change,* Clarendon Press, Oxford.

WHITWORTH, C. (ed.) (1771), *The Political and Commercial Works of Charles Davenant,* 5 vols., Horsefield, London.

WILLCOX, W.F. (1931), "Increase in the Population of the Earth and of the Continents since 1650", in W.F. WILLCOX (ed.) *International Migrations,* Vol. II, National Bureau of Economic Research, New York, pp. 33–82.

WILLIAMS, E. (1970), *From Columbus to Castro: The History of the Caribbean 1492–1969,* Deutsch, London.

WILLIAMSON, J.G. (1995), "The Evolution of Global Markets Since 1830: Background Evidence and Hypotheses", *Explorations in Economic History,* 32, pp. 141–196.

WILSON, C. AND G. PARKER (eds.) (1977), *An Introduction to the Sources of European Economic History, 1500–1800,* Weidenfeld and Nicolson, London.

WOLF, J. (1912), *Die Volkswirtschaft der Gegenwart und Zukunft,* Deichert, Leipzig, 19l2.

WORLD BANK (2000), *Global Development Finance,* Washington, D.C.

WRIGLEY, E.A. (1967), "A Simple Model of London's Importance in Changing English Society and Economy 1650–1750", *Past and Present,* July, pp. 44–70.

WRIGLEY, E.A. (1988), *Continuity, Chance and Change*, Cambridge.

WRIGLEY, E.A. AND R.S. SCHOFIELD (1981), *The Population History of England 1541–1871*, Arnold, London.

WRIGLEY, E.A., R.S. DAVIES, J.E. OEPPEN AND R.S. SCHOFIELD (1997), *English Population History from Family Reconstitution 1580–1837*, Cambridge University Press, Cambridge.

WYCKOFF, A.W. (1995), "The Impact of Computer Prices on International Comparisons of Labour Productivity", *Economies of Innovation and New Technology,* vol. 3, pp. *277–93.*

XU, XIANCHUN (1999), "Evaluation and Adjustments of China's Official GDP by the World Bank and Prof. Maddison", *Journal of Econometric Study of Northeast Asia*, Vol. 1, No. 2.

YAMADA, S. AND Y. HAYAMI (1979), "Agricultural Growth in Japan, 1880–1970", in HAYAMI, RUTTAN AND SOUTHWORTH, pp. 33–48 and 230–64.

YAMAMURA, K. (1974), *A Study of Samurai Income and Entrepreneurship*, Harvard.

YAMAMURA, K. (1981), "Returns on Unification Economic Growth in Japan, 1550–1650", in HALL *et al.*

YAMAMURA, K. AND T. KAMIRI (1983), "Silver Mines and Sung Coins — A Monetary History of Medieval and Modern Japan in International Perspective", IN RICHARDS.

YASUBA, Y. (1987), "The Tokugawa Legacy: A Survey", *Economic Studies Quarterly,* December, pp. 290–308.

YOLTON, J.W. (ed.) (1969), *John Locke: Problems and Perspectives.*

YOSHIDA, T. (1911), *Ishinshi Hachi Ko*, Fuzanbo, Tokyo.

YUN, B. (1994), "Proposals to Quantify Long–Run Performance in the Kingdom of Castile, 1550–1800", in MADDISON AND VAN DER WEE.

ZAMBARDINO, R.A. (1980), "Mexico's Population in the Sixteenth Century: Demographic Anomaly or Mathematical Illusion?", *Journal of Interdisciplinary History*, pp. 1–27.

ZANDEN, J.L. VAN (1987), "De economie van Holland in de periode 1650–1805: groei of achteruitgang? Een overzicht van bronnen, problemen en resultaten", *Bijdrage en Mededelingen Geschiedenis der Nederlanden.*

THE WORLD ECONOMY

Volume 2: Historical Statistics

Foreword

This book is intended as a quantitative reference work and guide to current and past research in macroeconomic history. It is a companion volume to *The World Economy: A Millennial Perspective*, published by OECD in 2001. The major purpose of that study was to provide an analytic survey of developments in the world economy over two millennia, and to explore the reasons for the great divergence in the momentum of advance in different regions. The analysis was underpinned by a comprehensive quantification of levels and movement in population, output, and per capita income. The statistical appendices provided annual estimates for 1950–1998, and for 8 benchmark years back to the first century. Annual estimates for 1870–1950 appeared in my earlier book *Monitoring the World Economy 1820–1992*.

The present work revises and updates the population estimates for 1950–2003, GDP and per capita GDP estimates for 1820–2001. It shows annual figures back to 1820 wherever possible and provides fuller source notes and explanations of proxy procedures for filling data gaps. For the period before 1820, there are fewer revisions, but detail is given for more countries and there is closer scrutiny of the contours of development in Latin America and Africa. Estimates of benchmark levels of output in 1990 international dollars are unchanged except for seven African countries.

The possibilities for extended annual coverage of population, GDP and per capita GDP were greatest for Europe and Western Offshoots. There were about 4 200 annual entries for individual countries in the 2001 volume and 15 200 here. For Latin America, Asia and Africa combined, there were about 15 300 entries in the earlier volume and 22 600 here.

The prologue provides a brief survey of the development of historical national accounts and demography from the 17th century to the present. It is based on some of the material I presented in the Kuznets lectures at Yale University in 1998. Sections HS–1 to HS–6 explain the sources and procedures used to derive the basic estimates for countries in the major regions. Section HS–7 summarises the procedures and problems involved in deriving the world totals for 1950–2003. HS–8 does the same for the estimates from the first century to 1950. Research on quantitative economic history has made great strides in the past quarter century, and the efforts of individual scholars have been reinforced by the creation of international networks as explained in HS–8. As a result we have a clearer notion of the range of growth experience, processes of catch–up, convergence and divergence, and underlying causal forces. Research has concentrated on the past two centuries of accelerated growth. Much less has been done on earlier centuries. As a consequence, there are conflicting views on relative levels of income in Europe and Asia around 1800. In my view, it is possible to resolve some of these differences by extending quantitative research further into the past. There were two reasons for indifference to or neglect of distant horizons. One is that quantitative evidence is scarcer the further back one goes in time, and earlier centuries were regarded as impenetrable to quantitative analysis. Another is that economic growth was much slower before the nineteenth century and therefore seemed irrelevant or uninteresting. There was a belief that the roots of modern growth lay in a sudden take–off (an industrial revolution) in the late eighteenth century, that agriculture originated eight thousand years ago and that there was a Malthusian torpor for most of the intervening interval. I disagree with this interpretation for reasons explained in HS–8.

Acknowledgements

I am indebted to Derek Blades for his encouragement and detailed comments on the tables and all of the text. Bart van Ark, Roger Brown, Ian Castles, Colm Foy, David Henderson and Eddy Szirmai gave me helpful comments on parts of it. Elizabeth Maddison helped advance my computer education. I am very grateful to Gerard Ypma for help in organising the basic statistical data in HS–1 to HS–7; and to Ly Na Tang Dollon for help with the tables in HS–8. Sheila Lionet put the manuscript into a form fit for publication. Alan Heston, David Roberts and Michael Ward answered many queries about PWT, OECD, and World Bank derivation of purchasing power parity converters. Steve Broadberry and Dirk Pilat were helpful in providing historical crosschecks on my measure of comparative GDP levels. Cathy Ward provided source material underlying IMF estimates of world GDP. Henk Jan Brinkman and Ian Kinniburgh provided access to UN material on world population and GDP. Nanno Mulder and Thomas Chalaux provided help in measurement of world population. Pierre van der Eng permitted me to use his estimates of Indonesian, Malaysian and Sri Lankan GDP. I received useful comments and research material from Maks Banens and Jean–Pascal Bassino on Vietnam, Luis Bertola on Uruguay, Claes Brundenius on Cuba, John Coatsworth, Stanley Engerman and Andre Hofman on Latin America, Thomas David on Switzerland, David Good and Max–Stephan Schulze on the successor states of the Austro–Hungarian Empire, Bryan Haig on Australia, Richard Hooley on the Philippines, Andrew Kamarck and J.R. McNeill on Africa, Debin Ma, Harry Wu and Xu Xianchun on China, Katya Maddison on the Middle East, Michelangelo van Meerten on Belgium, Patrick O'Brien on Egypt, Cormac O Grada and Mary O'Mahony on Ireland, Sevket Pamuk on Turkey and the successor states of the Ottoman Empire, Leandro Prados on Spain, Siva Sivasubramonian on India, Jean–Claude Toutain on France. Alan Bowman, Carol Kidwell and William McNeill gave me useful comments on chronology. Michèle Alkilic–Girard and Myriam Andrieux helped in locating bibliographic material. Since I did not always follow advice received, I do not suggest that those who gave it would endorse my judgement.

Table of Contents

List of Tables in Prologue and Source Notes

List of Basic Tables

HS–1

HS–2

HS–3A

HS–6

HS–7

HS–8

Preface

This is the eighth study by Angus Maddison published by the Development Centre since 1965. It is a companion volume to *The World Economy: A Millennial Perspective*, which appeared in 2001. This earlier work had an excellent reception from historians, economists and a broader public and has been a best–seller.

This book updates and supplements his earlier panoramic survey of the dynamics of growth, patterns of inequality and their deep–rooted causes. It provides fuller source notes and much more detailed estimates of population, GDP and per capita income. His rigorous handling of the data, systematic comparison and assessment of the reliability of sources and his suggestions about how gaps in the data should be filled are exemplary.

There is a closer scrutiny of the contours of African development over the past two millennia; and of Latin American experience since Columbus. It provides a critical review of the literature on macroeconomic measurement from its seventeenth century origins to the present, and is intended as a research guide for future comparisons of economic performance in space and time.

A comparative quantitative approach to the world's regions over a very long period is useful for policy formulation for several reasons. For developing countries, it augments the statistical information on which to base policy decisions in face of uncertainty. For OECD countries, it is a reminder of the key role of long–term processes such as demographic change, technological change and the operation of market forces in determining economic outcomes. It also provides an insightful account of the forces of convergence or divergence across economies and regions and is a valuable contribution to the complex debate about the benefits and costs of globalisation.

Louka T. Katseli
Director
OECD Development Centre

August 2003

ISBN 92-64-02261-9 – © OECD 2006

Prologue: The Pioneers of Macromeasurement

National accounts are an indispensable tool for assessing the growth potential and performance of contemporary economies. They are fundamental in international comparison of development levels. They have become an important tool of analysis for quantitative economic historians. They are sometimes considered too "modern" to be applicable to the distant past. In fact, national accounting, international income comparisons, and historical demography originated in the seventeenth century, when "the art of reasoning by figures on things relating to government" was called Political Arithmetick.

The 17th Century Pioneers

The pioneer was **William Petty** (1623–87), a major figure in the scientific revolution of the seventeenth century. He was research assistant to the philosopher Thomas Hobbes in Paris in the 1640s, Professor of Anatomy in Oxford and organiser of the cadastral survey of Ireland after the Cromwellian conquest in the 1650s, one of the founders of the Royal Society in the 1660s, inventor, cartographer, economist, entrepreneur and founder of a wealthy dynasty. *Verbum Sapienti* (1665) presented his estimates of population, income, expenditure, stock of land, other physical assets and human capital in an integrated set of accounts for England and Wales. They were intended to provide a quantitative framework for effective implementation of fiscal policy and mobilisation of resources in time of war (the second Anglo–Dutch war of 1664–7).

Political Arithmetick (1676) was a comparative study of the economic performance of the Netherlands and France, using key indicators to demonstrate Dutch superiority. The French population was ten times the Dutch, but the Dutch merchant fleet was nine times as big, its foreign trade four times as big, its interest rate half the French level, its foreign assets large, those of France negligible. The Dutch economy was highly specialised, importing a large part of its food, hiring mercenaries to fight its wars, concentrating its labour force in high productivity sectors. High density of urban settlement, good ports and internal waterways reduced transport and infrastructure costs, cheapened government services and reduced the need for inventories. Property rights were clear and transfers facilitated by maintenance of registers. An efficient legal system and sound banking favoured economic enterprise. Taxes were high but levied on expenditure rather than income. This encouraged savings, frugality and hard work. The Dutch were a model of economic efficiency with obvious lessons for English policy, whereas popular notions of French power were greatly exaggerated.

Both these works were circulated in manuscript in Petty's lifetime, and published posthumously, in 1690 and 1691. Their publication sparked renewed interest in political arithmetic.

The second major contribution came from **Gregory King** (1648–1712), in reaction to Charles Davenant's (1694), *Essay upon Ways and Means of Supplying the War* (war of the League of Augsburg, 1688–97). **Davenant** (1656–1714) had literary talent as a clear expositor of economic issues (his father was poet laureate, and he was reputed by some to be the grandson of William Shakespeare). As former commissioner of excise when tax collection was taken out of the hands of tax farmers, he was able to present a first consolidated and transparent picture of the government's actual and potential revenues and expenditure. King was impressed by the possibilities of using fiscal information for macroeconomic analysis. He established a close relationship with Davenant who quoted his work in detail and called him "that wonderful genius and master in the art of computing". Publications on sensitive matters of public policy required an official license, and exposed the author to sanctions of official disapproval. King preferred to avoid this risk, circulated copies of his manuscript accounts for comment to Davenant, **Robert Harley** (1661–1724) and others, but did not publish them. Unlike Davenant who was a well connected member of parliament, King was a cautious public servant in course of moving from the antiquated world of heraldry to more lucrative employment as Commissioner of Public Accounts. Harley was later Chancellor of the Exchequer and effectively Prime Minister under Queen Anne.

King's work in this field was intense from 1695 to 1700. His *Natural and Political Observations and Conclusions on the State and Condition of England* (1696) presented his results in highly concentrated form, but his 300 page Notebook (published in facsimile form by Laslett, 1973) provides an understanding of his meticulous procedures and the sophistication of his analysis. King's *Observations* was first published in complete form by George Chalmers in 1802 as an annex to his book on the *Comparative Strength of Great Britain*. This sparked the interest of **Patrick Colquhoun** (1745–1820) who exploited new sources of information (the first two censuses and the first income tax accounts) to replicate King's income account, and provide a more comprehensive production account showing value added for 1812. However, King's *Notebook* did not surface until 1917, and was first explored by David Glass in 1965. It is a treasure trove which deserves to be mined more thoroughly by quantitative historians.

The modern standardised system of national accounts provides a coherent macroeconomic framework covering the whole economy, which can be crosschecked in three ways. From the income side, it is the total of wages, rents and profits. It is also the sum of final expenditures by consumers, investors and government. From the production side, it is the sum of value added in different sectors–agriculture, industry and services, net of duplication. The framework can be expanded to include measures of labour input and capital stock, labour and total factor productivity.

King had four dimensions to his accounts which anticipated this modern system of interrelated balances:

a) the best–known is his depiction of the 1688 social hierarchy, showing 26 types of household, their number, average size, income and expenditure, savings or dependency on social transfers, and type of economic activity. In constructing it, King drew on 30 years experience in the Herald's office, making visitations to various parts of England to examine credentials of succession to aristocratic titles, the status and social standing of people who accounted for about two–thirds of national income. As a commissioner for the graduated poll tax on births, deaths, and marriage which came into force in 1695, he had access to a great deal of new information on the structure of incomes. The hearth tax was a further guide to the number of households and their average size;

b) his second account showed government spending and consumer expenditure by type of product, based on information derived from land and excise taxes for food, drink and tobacco, and a special survey he made for clothing and textiles. In *Observations* this account is very summary, but it is clear from the *Notebook* that his aggregate was the fruit of detailed estimation, and contains enough information to provide an approximation to the modern notion of gross domestic product (see Table 1 where I augment his aggregate which had narrower boundaries than is now standard);

c) his production account was incomplete. It showed value added in farming (crops and livestock) and forestry. His *Notebook* provides detailed quantification of many other items–textiles, value added in the paper industry, a breakdown of material inputs and labour costs in construction and shipbuilding. It shows expenditure on furniture, ceramics, pottery, glass, tools and transport equipment which can be converted into production estimates, with adjustment to deduct material inputs, transport and distributive margins;

d) a fourth dimension was his consolidated wealth and income account for 1688, showing property and labour income, the capitalised value of physical assets and of human capital. This resembled Petty's account for 1665, though the techniques of capitalisation were different.

King had a fifth account which compared levels of per capita consumption, public expenditure and revenue in England, France and Holland in 1688 and in 1695 in order to demonstrate differences in capacity to mobilise resources for war. It also contained a forecast of English national income to 1698. The estimates for France and the Netherlands were in most respects very rough, and he did not discuss the problem of measuring changes in the volume of output over time or adjusting for differences in the purchasing power of currency in making international comparisons.

Table 1. Gross Domestic Expenditure in England and Wales in 1688
(£000 at market prices)

Food	**13 900**	**Education and Health**	**1 150**
Bread, Biscuits and Pastry	4 300	Schooling	250
Beef, Mutton and Pork	3 300	Paper, Books and Ink	500
Fish, Poultry and Eggs	1 700	Medical	400[a]
Dairy Products	2 300		
Fruits and Vegetables	1 200	**Personal and Professional Services**	**3 100**
Salt, Spices, Oil, and Sweetmeats	1 100	Domestic Servants	1 600[a]
		Recreation	500
Beverages and Tobacco	**7 350**	Legal, Financial, Hair-dressing,	
Beer and Ale	5 800	Inns and Taverns	1 000[a]
Wine and Brandy	1 300		
Tobacco, Pipes and Snuff	250[a]	**Passenger Transport**	**430**
		Passenger Transport by Road	280[a]
Clothing	**10 393**	Passenger Transport by Water	150[a]
Male Outerwear	2 390		
Shirts, Cravats, and Ruffles	1 300	**Government, Religion and Defence**	**4 844**
Male Underwear	100	Military Pay	1 530[a]
Male Accessories	85	Ecclesiastical Remuneration	514[a]
Female Outerwear	904	Civil Government Pay	1 800[a]
Female Underwear	1 400	Commodities	1 000[a]
Nightgowns and Aprons	500		
Female Accessories	335	**Gross Capital Formation**	**3 675**
Hats, Caps and Wigs	568	Structures	975[a]
Gloves, Mittens and Muffs	410	Transport Equipment	700[a]
Handkerchiefs	200	Other Equipment	2 000
Stockings and Socks	1 011		
Footwear	1 190	**Gross Domestic Expenditure**	**54 042**
		Gregory King's Total	41 643[b]
Household Operation	**9 200**	Additional Items	12 399[a]
Rent and Imputed Rent	2 200[a]		
Fire, Candles and Soap	2 000		
Beds and Bedding	1 500		
Sheets and Table Linen	1 500		
Brass and Pewterware	1 000		
Wood and Glassware	1 000		

a) Indicates items I added from *Notebook*.
b) Total of items shown in *Observations*.
Source: Gregory King's *Notebook* in Laslett (1973) and *Observations* in Barnett (1936).

http://dx.doi.org/10.1787/456125276116

Table 2. **Structure of British Gross Domestic Expenditure, 1688 and 1996**
(per cent of total)

	1688 *England and Wales*	*1996* *United Kingdom*
Food	25.7	6.5
Beverages and Tobacco	13.6	5.9
Clothing and Footwear	19.2	3.7
Light, Fuel and Power	3.7	2.2
Furniture, Furnishings and Household Equipment	9.3	4.0
Personal Services	3.0	1.2
Sub-total	**74.5**	**23.5**
Rent and Imputed Rent	4.1	10.0
Education	1.4	5.4
Health	0.7	6.7
Recreation and Entertainment	0.9	5.7
Transport and Communication	0.8	10.6
Other	1.9	11.5
Sub-total	**9.8**	**49.9**
Total Private Consumption (Total Items 1-12)	84.2	73.4
Government Consumption (except education and health)	9.0	10.9
Gross Capital Formation	6.8	15.8
Total Gross Domestic Expenditure	**100.0**	**100.0**
Level of Per Capita GDP (in 1990 international dollars)	1 411	17 891

Source: 1688 from Table 1; 1996 from OECD, *National Accounts 1984-1996*, Vol.2, Paris 1998.

http://dx.doi.org/10.1787/456125276116

Box 1. **Political arithmeticians were also pioneers of demography**

The first serious demographer was **John Graunt** (1620–74), a close friend of Petty. Graunt's *Observations on the Bills of Mortality* published in 1662 involved a meticulous assemblage and adjustment of a very large weekly and annual database on burials and christenings in London for 1603 onwards. For 20 years he had data on causes of death, broken down by 81 categories. He had access to returns of a partial census for 1631 which provided a benchmark for his growth estimates.

Graunt distinguished the regular pattern of chronic ailments from epidemics. Plague was endemic but recurred at irregular intervals. The worst year was 1603, when it caused 82 per cent of deaths. He had no direct information on age at death, but constructed a rough proxy by grouping illnesses which affected infants and children, and those associated with old age. He constructed a crude survival table which showed 36 per cent mortality for those aged 0–6, with only 3 per cent surviving beyond age 66. This was the ancestor of life tables, and attracted wide interest in England, France and Holland where life annuities and tontines (a lottery on life expectation invented by Lorenzo Tonti in 1652) were part of the public debt. **Edmond Halley** (1656–1742) improved on Graunt's crude analysis of life expectation and articulated the fundamental mathematical principles of life insurance in (1693) "Degrees of Mortality of Mankind; with an Attempt to ascertain the Price of Annuities", *Philosophical Transactions of the Royal Society*.

In confronting data on London burials and christenings, Graunt found that burials were bigger. By comparison of the average discrepancy between births and deaths, he concluded that there was net immigration from small towns and rural areas of about 6 000 persons a year. As a crosscheck, he analysed annual data for Romsey, a town near Southampton. Over 90 years there was a net increase of 1 059 persons, of which 300 remained in Romsey, 400 emigrated to the Americas and 300–400 emigrated to London. In the third edition, in 1665, Graunt extended the analysis of country towns to Tiverton in Devon and Cranbrook in Kent, which confirmed the Romsey/London differentials.

As births were rising substantially over time, it was clear that the population was growing, and the growth of the housing stock corroborated this. Using inferences about age structure and likely fertility in conjunction with his other material, he suggested that London had grown two and a half fold in the previous 56 years.

Graunt concluded that the population of England and Wales was 14 times as big as that of London. His multiplier was derived from several indicators, i.e. London's share of the tax burden; cartographic analysis of the area of different parts of the country, likely density of settlement, the average size of parishes.

Prior to Graunt, nobody had thought of using the mortality bills to reconstruct the demography of London. His meticulous inspection of data, adjustments for coverage, the caution and modesty with which he explained his carefully structured inferences and techniques of analysis are the foundation of modern historical demography, and he clearly belonged to the pantheon of seventeenth century science.

Gregory King made a significant improvement on Graunt's estimate of the population of England and Wales. He had much more information for areas outside London. He had the hearth tax returns on the number of houses (1 million rural and 300 000 urban). From Davenant (1694) he had evidence from the chimney tax on house occupancy. He organised mini–censuses for Lichfield, Harfield and Buckfastleigh as a crosscheck on household size. His estimate of family size was smaller than Graunt's. He found an average household of 4.23 persons, but this included domestic servants, apprentices and unmarried farm labourers who lived in. Deducting these the average family size was 3.8 persons.

King's estimate of the population of England and Wales in 1695 was 5.5 million, significantly lower than Graunt's 6.4 million, but virtually identical with the estimate of Wrigley *et al.* (1997) in their detailed reconstitution of English demographic history 1580–1837 using the sophisticated techniques and massive computing power of modern demography.

King also made an estimate of world population in 1695, based on a calculation of the surface area of the globe, the proportion of land in the total and the likely density of settlement on different types of land. His world total in the *Notebook* was 626 million, much closer to my 604 million for 1700 than Petty's estimate of 320 million in his day or Riccioli's (1672) estimate of 1 billion.

Between 1695 and 1707, there was interest in national income estimation in France. In 1695 **Pierre de Boisguilbert** (1646–1714), lieutenant–general (chief judge and president of the appeals court) in Rouen (capital of the province of Normandy), published anonymously *La France ruinée sous la règne de Louis XIV,* a very pessimistic assessment of the economic condition of France, the need to make its fiscal structure more effective and equitable and to be less dirigiste in economic policy. In 1697 another version appeared, still anonymous but with a less provocative title *Le détail de la France.* Boisguilbert was impressed by the hunger crises and population decline which hit France in the early 1690s. He asserted that the national income had fallen by a third since 1660, but in fact provided no detail. Boisguilbert's books attracted little notice but stimulated the interest of **Sebastien le Prestre de Vauban** (1633–1707), a military engineer, who designed and supervised the construction of fortifications on the Northern and Eastern frontiers, successfully besieged many enemy cities, and constructed ports and forts on the Atlantic coast. Marshal Vauban had experience in galvanising regional and local authorities and mobilising resources for construction projects in many parts of France over a period of decades, so it is not surprising that he developed aspirations as a social engineer at the end of his career. There is a striking difference in tone between the work of Boisguilbert and Vauban and the English school of political arithmetic. The French writers were both convinced that the economy of their country was in a parlous state and the English were much more upbeat about England.

In 1707 Vauban published *La dîme royale,* a detailed proposal to transform the tax structure, which included a detailed assessment of potential revenue under a new tax regime. He was encouraged in this endeavour by the success of a proposal he made to the king in January 1695 for a temporary wartime capitation tax. This was adopted in 1695 and terminated in 1697 when the war ended. It was similar to the English poll tax of 1695–1705. Its incidence was graduated by descending order in the social hierarchy for 22 classes of taxpayer from the Dauphin down; social position being a proxy for income assessment. It was reintroduced in 1701 as a regional supplement to the *taille* without the key feature of graduation by ability to pay (see Collins, 2001, pp. 133–4 and 165–7).

The French revenue system Boiguilbert and Vauban wanted to transform was highly inefficient and inequitable. The main direct tax, the *taille,* involved large exemptions for the nobility and office holders. Some of these were for individuals (*personnelle*), others exempted specified properties (*réelle*). Tax rates varied regionally, between the *pays d'élection* and the *pays d'état* (Brittany, Burgundy, Languedoc and Provence, where tax rates were largely determined by the regional authorities). There were internal transit duties (*traites*) on merchandise crossing regional frontiers, inhibiting the development of a national market. Collection of direct and indirect taxes was done mainly by tax farmers and *traitants,* who made advance payments to the authorities and kept what they could collect. At the bottom level, in the 36 000 parishes, tax liability was fixed collectively. A large proportion of public officials obtained their posts by purchase, or inherited them from relatives. Most of them paid an annual fee (*paulette*) to guarantee inheritability of their office. In fact their salaries (*gages*) were equivalent to interest on the money they paid for their post. As a result the bureaucracy was swollen by officials who were only partially employed. The major indirect tax (*gabelle*), was on salt; the rate of tax varied between regions, virtually zero in producing regions like Brittany, and high in Burgundy, where wine taxes were low. As a consequence, there was large–scale smuggling and expenditure on revenue police. In all these respects, England had a more efficient, transparent and equitable fiscal system. In 1694 it acquired a central bank and established effective foundations for a market in long–term government debt. In France the first attempt a national budget was Necker's *Compte Rendu au Roi* in 1781, and the Banque de France was not created until 1800.

Vauban proposed to abolish all the existing taxes on property, income and internal transit, and replace them with a single tax on income without exemptions or regional variation. He proposed to simplify the rate structure of the salt tax to reduce smuggling. He suggested new indirect taxes on luxuries and on liquor consumed in bars (*cabarets*).

In order to assess potential revenue from his new system he made estimates of national income, population and area. For area, he used a rough average of five different cartographic sources for 38 regions of France. His estimated total was the equivalent of 60 million hectares. This was an exaggeration. The present area is 55 million and at that time (before Lorraine and Savoie were incorporated) was about 50 million (see Le Roy Ladurie, 1992, p. 280). In fact, King's estimate of the area of France (51 million hectares) was much more exact. For population Vauban used estimates from 28 provincial officials for years between 1694–1700. His total was 19.1 million, which tallies fairly well with modern estimates for the area he covered (see Bardet and Dupaquier, 1997, p. 449). King's estimate for France (14 million) was much too low.

Vauban's estimates of national income were rough and hybrid. His measure for agriculture referred to gross output, with no deduction for feed, seed and upkeep of buildings and equipment. He did not distinguish between different categories of agricultural income, and did not cover non–agricultural activity in rural areas. He specified 10 types of non–agricultural income from property and labour. The sophistication of the analysis was greatly inferior to that of Gregory King, and he was dealing with a country where fiscal and other evidence for a coherent national analysis was much more exiguous than in England.

Vauban estimated agricultural output on the basis of a sample study of Normandy. For this he had help from an anonymous friend (possibly Boisguilbert). He assumed that 80 per cent of the land yielded income from crops, livestock, vineyards and forestry, with a third of cropland in fallow. He estimated the physical crop yield for wheat and its value per square league (20 square km.). He assumed this value yield per league was also valid for pastoral activities, vineyards and forestry. From this he estimated a tax yield about 24 per cent higher than the ecclesiastical tithe for Normandy. Nevertheless, he took the latter as representative and blew up it up by the ratio of the land area of France to that of Normandy. After a further conservative reduction of about 10 per cent, he concluded that the tax yield at the national level would be 60 million livres, assuming a 5 per cent levy (*vingtième*) on gross output. If we multiply his 5 per cent tax yield by 20, gross agricultural output for France would have been 1 200 million livres; his first estimate implied 1667 million livres. However, if we deduct inputs into agriculture, adjust for his overstatement of the area of France and the fact that Normandy was more densely populated than the country as a whole, it seems likely that he was overstating national income from agriculture substantially.

Vauban's estimate of non–rural income was 352 million livres. Rent and imputed rent (net of repair and maintenance) from 320 000 urban houses he estimated to be 32 million. Interest on government debt 20 million, mixed income from commerce, banking, fishing, shipping, and grain milling 58 million, pensions and emoluments of government officials 40 million, legal income 10 million. He assumed there were 1.5 million servants with emoluments of 30 million. 2 million non–agricultural labourers and artisans were assumed to earn 162 million–he derived this from their average daily wage, and assumed a working year of 185 days (deducting 52 Sundays, 38 days for public holidays, 50 for intemperate weather, 20 days attending fairs and markets, and 25 for illness). Except for the last three groups, he gave no indication of the number of people involved in rural and non–rural activity. He proposed the introduction of a Chinese–style household registration system to remedy this defect, and appended a form showing the type of detail by age, sex and occupation which should be garnered annually by local worthies. Vauban must have realised that his assessment of non–rural income was inadequate, as he started his analysis by asserting that it was bigger than rural income. However, he could have crosschecked his estimates more closely for consistency. His estimate of the number of non–rural houses (320 000) is manifestly too low for a non–rural labour force of more than 3.5 million and their families.

Vauban insisted that the costs of collection would be greatly reduced with his system and that the transition from the existing order would be painless. He felt that one could dispense with the sevices of tax farmers and traitants whom he classified as bloodsuckers (*Sang-suës d'État*). He felt that there could be a smooth tansition to collection of agricultural levies in kind to be stored in government warehouses. He did not explain how the government would dispose of these commodities. He was also insouciant about the protests of the elite who would lose their tax–exempt status. In chapter VIII he identified all the groups who might oppose his proposition and suggested that with 200 000 armed men at his disposal the king could easily quell any opposition. Politically his proposition was both naïve and provocative. In February 1707, a month before Vauban's death, the book was officially condemned and the remaining copies were destroyed.

The 18th Century Onwards

From the beginning of the eighteenth century to the 1940s, there were about thirty attempts to measure national income in Britain. There were significant differences in their coverage and methodology. Most concentrated on the income dimension without crosschecks from the expenditure or production side. Most were spot estimates for a given point of time and it was difficult to link them to measure economic growth, as there was only a limited and belated effort to develop appropriate price deflators (see Colin Clark, 1937). Nevertheless, these estimates are still very useful to quantitative economic historians. Thanks to detailed scrutiny by Phyllis Deane (1955–7) they provided a starting point and inspiration for pioneering studies of British economic growth by Deane and Cole (1964), Feinstein (1972), Matthews, Feinstein and Odling–Smee (1982) and Crafts (1985). The retrospective estimates of this new generation of quantitative historians are generally based on the modern international standardised system of national accounts.

Studenski (1958) cites nine attempts to measure French national income later in the 18th century. Some of these were an improvement on Vauban, notably Lavoisier's *De la richesse territoriale du royaume de France* (1791), and Arthur Young's (1794, chapter 15) detailed estimates of French agricultural output for 1787–9. Young found that land productivity in Normandy was much higher than in the rest of France, which strengthens the impression that Vauban overstated agricultural output.

Between 1800 and the first world war, the statistical basis for macroeconomic measurement improved a good deal in Europe, North America and the Antipodes. Population censuses provided a much better basis for demographic analysis. Statistical offices collected data on trade, transport, fiscal and monetary matters, employment, wages and prices. There was an increasing array of information on commodity output in agriculture, mining and manufacturing. Index number techniques were developed which would have made it possible to measure temporal change and inter–spatial variance of complex aggregates.

Although there was a proliferation of national income estimates, there was little improvement in their quality or comparability. They provided little help for serious analysis of economic growth, and there were significant differences in their coverage and methodology.

Michael Mulhall (1836–1900) made a serious contribution to international comparison of levels of performance.

Mulhall was Irish, educated in Rome, and spent his early working life as a journalist in Argentina. He published four major books between 1880 and 1896, drawing on census, trade, and commercial information to demonstrate developments in the world economy. His *Industry and Wealth of Nations* (1896) was devoted entirely to providing consistent comparisons of national output and wealth. He gave detailed sources and a mass of carefully structured statistical material in comparative form for 22 countries representing about 60 per cent of world product in 1894–5. He referred to other national income estimates where available, but used his own standard rules of thumb to assess value added for all countries. He also provided standard guidelines for his measures of national wealth. His methods were simple and described transparently. To determine total value added, he divided each national economy into 9 sectors, estimated gross output in each sector, and to avoid double counting, deducted inputs as specified below.

His coverage of Europe and Western offshoots was pretty comprehensive, but for the rest of the world was confined to Argentina and South Africa. He provided current price estimates of the level in income in eight countries at dates ranging from 1812 to 1895. His cross–country comparison for 1894 was at current prices (in £ sterling) using exchange rates.

Mulhall had a powerful influence on Timothy Coghlan, the government statistician for New South Wales who made the first official estimates of national income for the *Seven Colonies of Australasia* which were published regularly from 1886–1905.

Table 3. Mulhall's 1896 Guidelines for Estimating Value Added by Sector of Economic Activity

Economic Sector	*Value Added*
Agriculture	60 per cent of gross product
Manufacturing	50 per cent of gross product
Minerals, forestry and fisheries	100 per cent of gross product
Commerce	10 per cent of aggregate domestic sales
Transport	10.5 per cent of aggregate domestic sales
House-rent	6 per cent of the value of the housing stock
Domestic servants	two-thirds of house rent
Public service	50 per cent of tax revenue
Professional services	10 per cent of the sum of 8 items above

http://dx.doi.org/10.1787/456125276116

Colin Clark (1905–89) took a major step towards world accounts in his *Conditions of Economic Progress* in 1940. He assembled income estimates for 30 countries (pp. 40–1). He adjusted them to mitigate national idiosyncrasies of measurement and made rough proxies for another 20 countries (based on indicators of real wages) to make a rough estimate of world income for 1925–34 (p. 56). He constructed a crude PPP measure to make the individual country estimates additive in terms of his "international unit" (US dollars with average purchasing power of 1925–34). Unlike Mulhall, who made his own multicountry estimates on a standardised basis, Clark was in large degree a compiler of other people's estimates, seeking maximalist coverage. To measure economic growth, he made time series comparisons in real terms for 15 countries for disparate years between 1850 and the 1930s (pp. 146–148), but in many cases these were weak because he was willing to make crude links between different and not always comparable "spot" estimates, and to make use of some dubious deflators.

All of Clark's 1940 estimates have now been superseded, but his work is still of substantial historical interest, because he made an exhaustive survey of the work of virtually all the economists and statisticians who had published in his field in the nineteenth and twentieth centuries and had extensive correspondance with the statisticians of his day who were engaged in such work. He never hesitated to adjust these estimates to conform to his own ideas about the appropriate coverage of the accounts or methods of treatment of particular items. He also used the estimates analytically. Systematic comparative confrontation is a particularly good way of testing the plausibility and consistency of estimates and may well induce careful scrutiny of "outlier countries". In 1940, however, there was no agreement on the coverage and methodology of national accounts, and the comparability of the different estimates was therefore restricted.

The Modern Era

The first official estimates for the United States were made by **Simon Kuznets** (1901–85) in 1934, at a time when the economy was in deep depression. The accounts were felt to be an important tool for improving public policy. In the United Kingdom, the outbreak of war in 1939 led to a replication of the Davenant–King partnership of the 1690s. In February 1940, Maynard Keynes published *How to Pay for the War: A Radical Plan for the Chancellor of the Exchequer*. The structure of his argument was butressed by national accounts developed by Colin Clark (they were already closely associated in 1931–7, when Keynes was analysing the causes and cure for unemployment). Keynes persuaded the chancellor to include a first official set of accounts in his 1941 budget. The accounts were an important tool in Whitehall strategy for winning the war. The integrated statistical perspective led to much more effective resource mobilisatiton than in Germany (see Kaldor, 1946).

In 1944 there were consultations between British, Canadian and US statisticians with a view to standardisation of their concepts and procedures (see Denison, 1947). In the postwar years, comparable accounts were felt to be a political necessity to facilitate assessment of needs for Marshall Aid and burden–sharing in NATO.

The standardised system was designed in large part by **Richard Stone** (1913–1991), who together with James Meade made the first official estimates of national income for the United Kingdom in 1941. He also produced guidelines for OEEC and OECD on *Quantity and Price Indexes* (1956), *Input–Output and National Accounts* (1961) and *Demographic Accounting and Model Building* (1971). His magnum opus was his posthumously published (1997) *Some British Empiricists in the Social Sciences, 1650-1900*. Stone and Milton Gilbert (chief of US national income accounts until 1951 and Director of the OEEC Economics and Statistics Department until 1960) were very active in the 1950s in seeing that the 1952 standardised system was implemented in OEEC countries. Shortly after, the OEEC system was merged with that of the UN which was applied by official statisticians in most countries in the postwar years, except in communist countries whose accounts excluded many service activities, and involved some duplication. **Milton Gilbert** (1909–79) and **Irving Kravis** (1916–92) pioneered the first official measures of the purchasing power parity of currencies, published by OEEC in 1954. Kravis greatly expanded the scope of the PPP measures by starting the International Comparison Project (ICP) in 1968, and in 1978, together with his colleagues Robert Summers and Alan Heston inaugurated the Penn World Tables (PWT) to fill gaps in ICP coverage.

Thanks to these pioneering efforts, there are now official estimates of GDP growth for years since 1950 for 179 countries, and purchasing power parity measures which permit comparison of levels of performance. They have become a major instrument of economic policy in virtually all countries.

HS–1: Western Europe, 1500–2001

Population 1500-1700 and GDP growth rates 1500-1820 (except for France) from Appendix B of Maddison (2001), *The World Economy: A Millennial Perspective*; 1820 onwards as described below.

POPULATION: Sources for the annual estimates, 1820–1950, are described in the country notes below. 1950 onwards from International Programs Center, US Bureau of the Census, October 2002.

GDP: Annual estimates, 1820–1950, as described below. In most cases, the country source notes are abbreviated versions of those in Maddison (1995), *Monitoring the World Economy, 1820–1992*, pp. 126–139, but there are revised estimates for France, the Netherlands, Portugal, Switzerland and Spain. I also comment on new estimates for Austria and Greece which I have not adopted. 1950 onwards from Appendix C of Maddison (2001), *The World Economy: A Millennial Perspective*, updated as follows: GDP volume movement 1995–2001 from OECD, *National Accounts of OECD Countries, 1989–2000*, vol. 1, and OECD, *Quarterly National Accounts Statistics*, 2/2002; Maddison (2001), pp.171–4 and 189–90 explain the derivation of the benchmark 1990 GDP levels. Except for Germany and the United Kingdom, the estimates are adjusted to eliminate the impact of frontier change.

Austria: GDP by industry of origin in 1913 prices for 1830, 1840, 1850, 1860 and annual estimates 1870–1913, from A. Kausel, "Österreichs Volkseinkommen 1830 bis 1913" in *Geschichte und Ergebnisse der zentralen amtlichen Statistik in Österreich 1829–1979, Beitrage zur österreichischen Statistik*, Heft 550, Vienna, 1979, pp. 692–3. 1820–30 per capita movement assumed to be the same as that for 1830–40 (see Kausel, p. 701). 1913–50 gross national product in 1937 prices by expenditure and industry of origin, from A. Kausel, N. Nemeth, and H. Seidel, "Österreichs Volkseinkommen, 1913–63", *Monatsberichte des Österreichischen Institutes für Wirtschaftsforschung*, 14th Sonderheft, Vienna, August 1965, p. 38 and 42; 1937–45 from F. Butschek, *Die Österreichische Wirtschaft 1938 bis 1945*, Fischer, Stuttgart, 1979, p. 65. 1950 onwards from OECD sources. Kausel's estimates are corrected for territorial change, and refer to population and product within the present boundaries of Austria. Kausel (1979) also presented 1830–1913 estimates for Cisleithenia (the Austrian half of the Austro–Hungarian Empire). Other Cisleithenia included Bohemia, Moravia, Galicia, Bukowina, the Trieste region, and Dalmatia (subsequently parts of Czechoslavakia, Poland and Yugoslavia). Kausel was head of the national accounts division and subsequently Vice President of the Austrian Central Statistical Office. His 1979 article was part of a large–scale exercise in quantitative economic history to celebrate the 150th anniversary of the Statistical Office. The anniversary volume contained many other papers, including a comprehensive demographic analysis of the different components of the Austro–Hungarian Empire("Die Bevölkerung Österrreich–Ungarns", by H. Helczmanovszki).

David Good and Tongshu Ma (1999), "The Economic Growth of Central and Eastern Europe in Comparative Perspective, 1870–1989", *European Review of Economic History*, vol. 3, Part 2, pp. 105 and 107 reject the Kausel (1979) estimates as "back–of–the envelope" calculations. They suggest a "more plausible" alternative with "firmer foundations". In fact, it is derived from regression and three proxy measures: letters posted per capita, crude birth rate, and share of non–agricultural employment in the labour force. Their estimate refers to 1870–1910 and shows slower growth than Kausel. In an earlier estimate, using five proxies and a different estimating procedure, Good (1994) appeared satisfied to have found growth "almost identical to that of Kausel". The Good and Ma characterisation of Kausel's direct estimate is inaccurate and there is no justification for dropping it in favour of their proxy for Austria. However, their other proxies are useful as they cover countries and periods for which direct estimates are not available (see HS–2 below).

Max–Stephan Schulze, "Patterns of Growth and Stagnation in the Late Nineteenth Century Habsburg Economy", *European Review of Economic History*, December 2000, pp. 311–40 provides well–documented annual GDP and per capita GDP estimates for 1870–1913 for Cisleithenia and Transleithenia (the Hungarian half of the Habsburg Empire). He made no estimate for present–day Austria, but used Good and Ma results. He shows slower growth for present–day Austria than for Cisleithenia, whereas Kausel showed the opposite. Kausel's 1913 per capita GDP was more than 60 per cent higher than he found for Cisleithenia. The Schulze differential is 29 per cent. Table 1–1 shows my estimates for 1830, 1870 and 1913 derived from Kausel; the bottom panel shows those of Schulze.

Table 1-1. **Population and GDP in Modern and Habsburg Austria, 1830-1913**

	Modern Austria	Other Cisleithenia	Total Cisleithenia
	Population (000s)		
1830	3 538	12 292	15 830
1870	4 520	16 028	20 248
1913	6 767	22 572	29 339
	GDP (million 1990 international Geary-Khamis $)		
1830	4 937	11 150	16 087
1870	8 429	16 574	25 003
1913	23 451	39 187	62 638
	GDP per capita (1990 international Geary-Khamis $)		
1830	1 395	907	1 016
1870	1 865	1 034	1 235
1913	3 465	1 736	2 135
	Schulze GDP per capita estimates		
1870	1 856	n.a.	1 421
1913	2 871	n.a.	2 222

http://dx.doi.org/10.1787/456125276116

Belgium: 1820–46 movement in agricultural output from Martine Goossens, *De Economische Ontwikkeling van de Belgische Landbouw in Regional Perspectief, 1812–1846*, Leuven 1989. 1831–46 industrial output estimates supplied by Jean Gadisseur (1820–31 assumed to increase at same pace as in 1831–42). Service output 1820–46 assumed to move with population. 1846–1913 GDP derived from movements in agricultural and industrial output from J. Gadisseur, "Contribution à l'étude de la production agricole en Belgique de 1846 à 1913", *Revue belge d'histoire contemporaine*, vol. IV, 1–2, 1973. Service output is from the same source and was assumed to move with service employment (derived for census years from P. Bairoch, *La Population active et sa structure*, Brussels, 1968, pp. 87–8). 1913 weights and 1913–50 GDP from C. Carbonnelle, "Recherches sur l'évolution de la production en Belgique de 1900 à 1957", *Cahiers Économiques de Bruxelles*, no. 3, April 1959, p. 358. Carbonnelle gives GDP figures for only a few benchmark years but gives a commodity production series for many more years. Interpolations were made for the service sector to arrive at a figure for GDP for all the years for which Carbonnelle shows total commodity production. GDP movement 1914–19 and 1939–47 are interpolations between the 1913 and 1920 estimates and those for 1938 and 1948 respectively, assuming the same pattern of movement as in France. Population 1820–1950 from *Annuaire statistique de la Belgique et du Congo Belge*, 1955. Figures adjusted to exclude the impact of the cession by Germany of Eupen and Malmedy in 1925, which added 0.81 per cent to population and was assumed to have added the same proportion to output.

Denmark: 1820–1947 GDP at 1929 factor cost by industry of origin from S.A. Hansen, *Økonomisk vaekst i Danmark*, vol. II, Institute of Economic History, Copenhagen, 1974, pp. 229–32. 1947–60 GDP at 1955 factor cost from Søren Larsen, "Reviderede tidsserier for produktionsvaerdi og bruttofaktorindkomst for perioden 1947–65", CBS, Copenhagen, 1992. 1820–1950 population from Hansen (1974). Estimates are adjusted to eliminate the impact of the acquisition of North Schleswig in 1921, which added 5.3 per cent to population, and 4.5 per cent to GDP.

Finland: 1860–1960 GDP by industry of origin at market prices from R. Hjerppe, *The Finnish Economy 1860–1985: Growth and Structural Change*, Bank of Finland, Helsinki, l989, pp. 198–200. 1820–60 per capita GDP assumed to increase by 22.5 per cent, as indicated in S. Heikkinen, R. Hjerppe, Y. Kaukiainen, E. Markkanen and I. Nummela, "Förändringar i levnadsstandarden i Finland, 1750–1913" in G. Karlson, ed., *Levestandarden i Norden 1750–1914*, Reykjavik, l987, p. 74. Population 1820–1950 from O. Turpeinen, *Ikaryhmittainen kuolleisuus Suomessa vv. 1751–1970*, (Mortality by Age-group in Finland, 1751-1970), Helsinki, 1973. The 1940 and 1944 treaties which ceded territory to the USSR had no impact on population as all inhabitants were moved to Finland.

France: GDP estimates for 1820–70 in Maddison (1995) have been revised. I used J–C. Toutain's volume movement for agriculture and services, but not for industry where he showed much faster growth than other scholars (see Toutain, *Le produit intérieur de la France de 1789 à 1982*, Presses Universitaires de Grenoble, 1987). Instead I used the industrial index of M. Levy–Leboyer and F. Bourguignon (1984) *L'économie Francaise au XIXe siècle*, using Toutain's sector weights for 1870. Toutain has revised his 1820–70 estimates significantly (see J.–C. Toutain, "Le produit intérieur brut de la France, 1789–1990", ISMEA, *Histoire et Sociétés, histoire économique et quantitative*, 1, no. 11, 1997, pp. 5–136 Presses Universitaires de Grenoble), showing faster growth for services. I now use his new estimates for agriculture and services, together with the Levy–Leboyer/Bouguignon estimate for industry. Sources for 1870 onwards are unchanged–see Maddison (1995), pp.127–130.

Growth rates of per capita GDP for 1500-1600 and 1700-1820 are unchanged, but modified for 1600-1700. For the second half of the seventeenth century I assume stagnant per capita income because of hunger crises and the depressing impact of more or less continuous warfare as noted by Boisguilbert and Vauban.

Population and GDP estimates refer to the present territory of France, excluding the impact of the loss of Alsace–Lorraine 1871–1918 and acquisition of territory in 1861 (Savoie, Haute Savoie, Nice and surrounding parts of the Alpes Maritimes), which represented 600 000 of the 37 390 000 population of 1861. Population 1820–1860 from L. Henry and Y. Blayo, "La population de la France de 1740 à 1860", *Population*, November 1975, pp. 97–9; 1861–1950 from *Annuaire statistique de la France*, 1966, pp. 66–72.

Germany: The present estimates refer to GDP and population within 1870 frontiers until 1918, 1936 frontiers for 1919–45, and present frontiers from 1946 onwards. Maddison 1995 provided estimates for 1820–1992 adjusted to exclude the impact of territorial change for the area of the Federal republic within its 1989 boundaries. As frontier changes have been very complicated it is difficult to make adjusted estimates at this stage for the whole period for reunified Germany.

a)   In 1871 Germany took Alsace–Lorraine from France. This increased its population and GDP by 4 per cent;

b)   between 1918 and 1922 Germany lost Alsace–Lorraine, Memel, Danzig, Eupen and Malmedy, Saarland, North Schleswig and Eastern Upper Silesia. These territories had a population of 7 330 000 in 1918 out of a total of 66 811 000 within the 1918 Reich frontiers, i.e. the old Reich was 12.3 per cent bigger in terms of population. However, as 1913 per capita income in the truncated area was 2.4 per cent higher than in the former Reich, the total income loss due to these changes was 9.7 per cent (for the population changes see A. Maddison, *Dynamic Forces in Capitalist Development*, 1991, pp. 232–5; for the per capita income difference see F. Grünig, "Die Anfänge der volkswirtschaftlichen Gesamtrechnung in Deutschland", *Beitrage zur empirischen Konjunkturforschung*, Berlin, 1950, p. 76);

c) in 1935, Germany regained the Saarland which added 1.79 per cent to population and income;

d) in 1938, Germany incorporated Austria and took the Sudetenland from Czechoslovakia. Later it took Alsace–Lorraine and parts of Poland and Yugoslavia. In 1941 these areas added 22.4 per cent to the GDP generated with the 1937 frontiers;

e) after the second world war, Germany within its 1936 frontiers was effectively split between the Federal Republic, the DDR (East Germany) and the territory East of the Oder–Neisse which went to Poland, and to the USSR (Koenigsberg became Kaliningrad);

f) in 1991, East German territory became part of the Federal Republic.

A detailed account of German border changes and their impact on GDP can be found in Maddison (1977), "Phases of Capitalist Development", *Banca Nazionale del Lavoro Quarterly Review*, no. 121, pp. 134 and Maddison (1995), p. 130–33. For the impact of territorial change on population see Maddison (1991), *Dynamic Forces in Capitalist Development*, pp.226–237. Maddison (2001), p. 178 provides a summary presentation of the impact of frontier change on population and GDP.

Sources for GDP 1820–2001 were as follows: 1820, 1830 and 1850 derived from Tilly's estimates for Prussia–see R.H. Tilly, "Capital Formation in Germany in the Nineteenth Century", in P. Mathias and M.M. Postan (eds.), *Cambridge Economic History of Europe*, vol. VII, I, 1978, pp. 395, 420, and 441. Prussian per capita output in agriculture and industry were multiplied by population in Germany as a whole. Output in services was assumed to move with population. GDP aggregate estimated with 1850 weights for the three sectors from W.G. Hoffmann, F. Grumbach and H. Hesse, *Das Wachstum der deutschen Wirtschaft seit der Mitte des 19. Jahrhunderts*, Springer, Berlin, 1965, p. 454.

1850–1938 annual GDP volume movement and link to 1950 derived from Hoffmann, Grumbach and Hesse, *op. cit.*, pp. 454–5. As Hoffmann *et al.* omit 1914–24, the pattern of movement in these years in industry and agriculture was derived from the output estimates of J. Dessirier, "Indices comparés de la production industrielle et production agricole en divers pays de 1870 à 1928", *Bulletin de la statistique générale de la France, Études spéciales*, October–December 1928. Service output was interpolated between the 1913 and 1925 estimates of Hoffmann *et al.* for this sector.

1938–44 GNP in 1939 prices (from the expenditure side) for the 1938 territory (including Austria and Sudetenland) from W.C. Haraldson and E.F. Denison, "The Gross National Product of Germany 1936–1944", *Special Paper 1* (mimeographed) in J.K. Galbraith (ed.), *The Effects of Strategic Bombing on the German War Economy*, US Strategic Bombing Survey, 1945. 1946 (linked to 1936) from *Wirtschaftsproblemen der Besatzungszonen*, D.I.W. Duncker and Humblot, Berlin, 1948, p. 135; 1945 onwards, the derivation of GDP for West Germany (Federal Republic) and East Germany (DDR) is explained in Maddison (1995), pp. 131-2 and Maddison (2001), p. 178. Table 1-2 shows the impact of frontier changes 1870-1991.

Table 1-2. **The Impact of Frontier Changes on German GDP, 1870-1991**

	West Germany (1990 frontiers)	East Germany (1990 frontiers)	Germany within 1991 boundaries	Germany within 1936 boundaries	Germany within 1913 frontiers (ex. Alsace–Lorraine)
	GDP in million 1990 international dollars				
1820	16 390				26 819
1870	44 094				72 149
1913	145 045			225 008	237 332
1936	192 910	74 652	267 562	299 753	
1950	213 942	51 412	265 354		
1973	814 786	129 969	944 755		
1990	1 182 261	82 177	1 264 438		
1991	1 242 096	85 961	1 328 057		

http://dx.doi.org/10.1787/456125276116

ISBN 92-64-02261-9 – © OECD 2006

Greece: 1913–29 real product in international units from C. Clark, *Conditions of Economic Progress*, 3rd edition, Macmillan, London, 1957, pp. 148–9; 1929–38 GNP at factor cost from *Ekonomikos Tachydromos*, 22 May 1954; 1938–50 from OEEC, *Europe and the World Economy*, Paris 1960, p.116. 1950 onwards from OECD, *National Accounts*, various issues. 1820–1913 per capita GDP assumed to move with the aggregate for Eastern Europe. 1820–1900 population derived, with interpolation, from B.R. Mitchell *European Historical Statistics 1750–1970*, Macmillan, London, 1975, p. 21, 1900–40 from I. Svennilson, *Growth and Stagnation in the European Economy*, ECE, Geneva, 1954, pp. 236–7, 1941–9 from UN, *Demographic Yearbook 1951*, New York, 1952 pp. 124–5. Figures are adjusted to offset territorial change. Greece gained independence from Turkey in the 1820s, and gradually extended its area to include the Ionian Islands in 1864, Thessaly in 1881, Crete (*de facto*) in 1898, Epirus, Macedonia, Thrace and the Aegean Islands in 1913, Rhodes and the rest of the Dodecanese in 1947.

George Kostelenos, *Money and Output in Modern Greece*, Centre of Planning and Economic Research, Athens, 1995 provides annual estimates of output in current prices for primary, secondary and tertiary activity for 1858–1938. He does not estimate the volume of sector output, but constructs an aggregate deflator to derive a GDP estimate at 1914 prices (pp. 457–9). He measures growth of the money supply for the same period and uses the apparent velocity of circulation as a crosscheck on his GDP estimates (leading him to modify the results for 1858–9). Although Kostelenos throws more light on the available evidence than was previously available, there are three problems with his direct measure: *a)* his GDP deflator is very crude; with prices of only 11 items (6 for the whole period). All are agricultural or mining products, and the weights are gross output of the same items (in 1860, 1875, 1899, and 1914). The acceptibility of the GDP measure would be enhanced by construction of sectoral volume indices. I am not clear whether this is feasible, but it is certainly desirable. *b)* the second problem is territorial change. Kostelenos refers to Greece within the boundaries of the years he covers. His population figures show the impact of change very clearly. There were four major breaks: population jumped by 21 per cent in 1864, by 18 per cent in 1881, 77 per cent in 1913, and 15 per cent in 1920, but he does not discuss the problems this created in finding appropriate data on output, adjusting for differences in level between old and new territories, etc. His estimates suggest that these problems were difficult to resolve. For 1910–12 he shows a rise in per capita income of 63 per cent, a drop of a quarter in 1913, and a rise of a quarter in 1914. There is a similar problem for 1883–87 where his per capita GDP rises by nearly 90 per cent. It is not clear whether it is possible to accommodate these problems successfully, and one cannot criticise Kostelenos for attempting to overcome such an inherently difficult challenge. The third problem is that Kostelenos shows a very stagnant economy in the nineteenth century, with per capita income 6 per cent lower in 1910 than in 1860. If his estimates were linked to mine at 1938, per capita GDP in 1858 would be 1550 international 1990 dollars–a level similar to that in Germany and Sweden and about 70 per cent higher than the average for Eastern Europe. This seeems highly improbable. Recently, Kostelenos has revised his estimates, and his new results (in cooperation with Petmezas and others), show much faster and smoother growth, and are carried back to 1833. The main reason for faster growth is the use of a new deflator — a "rolling index" with a moving base, merging segments with weights of 1860, 1886 and 1914 respectively. The results are more plausible, but are still tentative. They will be more fully explained in a forthcoming publication of the National Bank of Greece. See Kostelenos (2001), "Economic Growth and Inequality in Greece in the 19th and 20th Century: A Tentative Approach", available on the Groningen website: www.eco.rug.nl/ggdc.

Ireland: For Ireland before 1920, see note below for the United Kingdom. 1920 per capita GDP level taken to be 54 per cent of that in the UK (excluding Southern Ireland) as estimated by C.H. Feinstein, *National Income, Expenditure and Output of the United Kingdom 1855–1965*, Cambridge University Press, 1972, Table 6. 1926–50 from K.A. Kennedy, *Productivity and Industrial Growth: The Irish Experience*, Oxford University Press, 1971, p. 3. Population, 1921–49, from UN, *Demographic Yearbook 1960*, New York.

Italy: 1820 and annual 1861–1970 GDP movement from A. Maddison, "A Revised Estimate of Italian Economic Growth 1861–1989", *Banca Nazionale del Lavoro Quarterly Review*, June 1991. The official ISTAT estimates I used for 1970 onwards have a more complete coverage of the underground economy than is the case in other countries (20.2 per cent of total GDP). In other countries, underground activities which escape the net of official national accounts statisticians are typically about 3 per cent of GDP (see D. Blades, "The Hidden Economy and the National Accounts", OECD, *Occasional Studies*, June 1982, p. 39). I therefore made a 3 per cent downward adjustment to the benchmark level of GDP to enhance international comparability. This has no effect on GDP volume movement, but reduces the level for all years.

1820 population derived from K.J. Beloch, *Bevölkerungsgeschichte Italiens*, de Gruyter, Berlin, 1961, pp. 351–4; annual change in resident population, 1861–1950 from *Sommario di statistiche storiche dell Italia, 1861–1975*, Istat, Rome, 1976, adjusted to midyear. Annual estimates for 1821–61 derived by logarithmic interpolation; average annual growth was 0.644 per cent. Galloway's estimates for Northern Italy show an annual growth rate of 0.703 per cent for the period I interpolated (see P.R. Galloway, "A Reconstruction of the Population of Northern Italy from 1650 to 1881 using Annual Inverse Projection", *European Journal of Population*, 10, 1994, pp. 223–274). Population and GDP are adjusted to eliminate the impact of territorial change. In 1866, after the war with Austria, the Venetian territories became part of Italy, and after 1870 the Papal states were added. In 1919 South Tirol, the old Austrian Kustenland provinces and the port of Zara were acquired. Fiume was added in 1922. In 1945, Zara, Fiume and part of Venezia–Giulia were ceded to Yugoslavia. Until the settlement of 1954 Trieste was in dispute and under international occupation; thereafter the city and a strip of coast went to Italy and the hinterland to Yugoslavia. In 1947, Tenda and Briga were added to France. The impact of these changes can be seen in Maddison (1995), p. 231.

Netherlands: annual estimates of population and GDP, 1820–1913 from J.–P. Smits, E. Horlings and J.L.van Zanden, *Dutch GDP and Its Components, 1800–1913*, Groningen, 2000, which Edwin Horlings kindly adjusted to a midyear basis. GDP, 1913–60, from C.A. van Bochove and T.A. Huitker, "Main National Accounting Series, 1900–1986", *CBS Occasional Paper*, No. 17, The Hague, 1987. 1960 onwards from OECD, *National Accounts*. Population 1913–50 from *Zeventig jaren statistiek in tijdreeksen*, CBS, The Hague, 1970, p. 14, adjusted to a midyear basis.

Norway: 1865–1950 GDP by category of expenditure at constant market prices from *National Accounts 1865–1960*, Central Bureau of Statistics, Oslo, 1965, pp. 348–59, with gross fixed investment adjusted downwards by a third to eliminate repairs and maintenance. For the 1939–44 gap in these estimates, I used the movement in national income (excluding shipping and whaling operations carried out from Allied bases 1940–4) from O. Aukrust and P.J. Bjerve, *Hva krigen kostet Norge*, Dreyers, Oslo, 1945, p. 45. 1945 assumed to be midway between 1944 and 1946. For 1820–65 I assume per capita GDP movement was the same as in Sweden.

There are interesting estimates of GDP back to 1835 in F. Hodne and O. H. Grytten, "Gross Domestic Product of Norway 1835-1915", *Occasional Papers in Economic History*, Umeå University, 1994. They adjust and link three nineteenth century spot estimates for 1835, 1845 and 1850 with the official estimate for 1865. They show faster growth than I have assumed (their per capita estimate for 1850 is about one fifth lower than mine). A more definitive estimate for 1820-65 will probably emerge when the Nordic Group complete their review of estimates for Scandinavia. Annual mid–year population estimates 1770–1950 from *Historical Statistics, 1968*, CBS, Oslo, 1969, pp.44–47.

Portugal: Annual GDP movement 1851–1910 derived from C. Bardini, A. Carreras and Pedro Lains, "The National Accounts for Italy, Spain and Portugal", *Scandinavian Economic History Review*, 1, 1995, p.135. They estimate agricultural and industrial output and use the combined movement in these two sectors to measure aggregate physical output, which they use as a proxy for GDP movement. I used their estimates for agriculture and industry, and derived a crude measure of GDP, using sector weights for 1910 and assuming that half of output in the rest of the economy (trade, transport and services) moved parallel to population and half parallel to aggregate physical ouput. GDP 1910–58 and 1910 sector weights from D. Batista, C. Martins, M. Pinheiro, and J. Reis, "New Estimates for Portugal's GDP, 1910–1958", Bank of Portugal and European University Institute, October, 1997. There are annual estimates of GDP movement 1834–1946 in A.B. Nunes, E. Mata, and N. Valerio, "Portuguese Economic Growth, 1833–1985", *Journal of European Economic History*, Fall, 1989, They were derived by regression, using three proxy indicators (exports, fiscal receipts and public expenditure) and their relationship to GDP movement for 1947–85. For 1834–51 they show a bumpy trajectory, without much indication of growth. This was a period of political and economic instability, following the upheavals of the Napoleonic wars and loss of the Brazilian Empire. I used their estimate of the 1850–51 movement and assumed that the per capita GDP level in 1820 was the same as in 1850.

Population: 1820 and annual movement 1833–64 from Nunes, Mata and Valerio (1989), p. 292, interpolation for 1821–32. 1865–1949 from Nuno Valerio, *Portuguese Historical Statistics,* INE, Lisbon, 2001, vol. 1, pp.52–3. Population estimates are adjusted to a midyear basis.

Spain: 1820-50 GDP volume movement derived from Prados (1982) as explained in Maddison (1995), p.138; 1850–1990 from Leandro Prados, *El Progreso Economico de Espana, 1850–2000*, Universidad Carlos III, Madrid, 2002. Population 1820 and 1850 from A. Carreras, ed. *Estadisticas Historicas de Espana: Siglos XIX–XX*, Fundacion Banco Exterior, Madrid, 1989, pp. 68–72; 1821–49 interpolated, 1850–1949 from Prados (2002).

Sweden: 1820–1950 population and provisional estimates of GDP 1820-1960 by industry of origin were kindly supplied by Olle Krantz. His procedures are explained in Olle Krantz, "New Estimates of Swedish Historical GDP Since the Beginning of the Nineteenth Century", *Review of Income and Wealth,* June l988. He has revised these estimates and will present a final version fairly soon.

Switzerland: 1820–51 per capita GDP movement assumed equal to average for France and Germany. 1851–1913 annual estimates of real GDP, average of two alternatively deflated series from H. Ritzmann–Blickenstorfer, *Historical Statistics of Switzerland,* Chronos, Zürich, 1996, pp. 859–79. Real product in international units, 1913, and annual estimates 1924–50 from C. Clark, *Conditions of Economic Progress* (3rd ed.), Macmillan, London, 1957, pp. 188–9. Annual percentage GDP movement, 1913–24, derived from economic activity estimates of F. Andrist, R.G. Anderson, and M.M. Williams, "Real Output in Switzerland: New Estimates for 1914–47", *Federal Reserve Bank of St. Louis Review*, May/June 2000, adjusted to fit 1913–24 movement shown by Clark (1957). 1950 onwards from OECD sources. Population, 1830, 1840 and 1850 from A. Kausel, *150 Jahre Wirtschaftswachstum*, Staatsdruckerei, Vienna, 1985, p.12. 1820–30 assumed to grow at same pace as 1830–40. Annual movement 1851–70 from Ritzmann, *op. cit.*; 1871–1949 from *Annuaire statistique de la Suisse 1952*, Federal Statistical Office, Bern 1953, pp. 42–3.

United Kingdom: 1801–31 GDP movement from N.F.R. Crafts and C.K. Harley, "Output Growth and the British Industrial Revolution: A Restatement of the Crafts–Harley View", *Economic History Review*, November 1992, p. 715 for England, Wales and Scotland, adjusted to a UK basis assuming Irish output per head of population in 1831 to have been half of that in Great Britain (hypothesis of P. Deane, "New Estimates of Gross National Product for the United Kingdom 1830–1914", *Review of Income and Wealth*, June 1968) and to have grown at half the pace from 1801. 1830–1855 annual movement in real gross national product from P. Deane (1968), p. 106. 1855–1960 annual movement of GDP at factor cost (average of real expenditure, output and income estimates) from C.H. Feinstein, *National Income Expenditure and Output of the United Kingdom 1855–1965*, Cambridge, 1972, pp. T18–20.

Population 1815–71 for England, excluding Monmouth, from E.A. Wrigley, R.S. Davies, J.E. Oeppen and R. S. Schofield (1997), *English Population History from Family Reconstitution 1580–1837,* Cambridge, p. 614 derived by interpolation of their quinnquennial estimates. Monmouth and Wales 1811–71 interpolation of the decennial census results shown in B.R. Mitchell, *Abstract of British Historical*

Table 1-3. **Economic Growth in Ireland/Irish Republic and the United Kingdom, 1820-2001**

	United Kingdom	Ireland	E + W + S	Northern Ireland
		Population (000)		
1820	21 239	7 101	14 138	
1840	26 745	8 348	18 396	
1870	31 400	5 419	25 981	
1913	45 649	4 346	41 303	
1920	46 821	4 361	42 460	
1920	43 718	**3 103**	42 460	1 258
1950	50 363	**2 969**	48 986	1 377
1973	56 223	**3 072**		1 530
2001	59 905	**3 839**		1 689
		GDP (million 1990 Geary-Khamis international $)		
1820	36 232	6 231	30 001	
1840	53 234	8 638	44 596	
1870	100 179	9 619	90 560	
1913	224 618	11 891	212 727	
1920	212 938	11 078	201 860	
1920	205 056	**7 882**	201 860	3 196
1950	347 850	**10 231**		
1973	675 941	**21 103**		
2001	1 202 074	**89 113**		
		Per Capita GDP (1990 Geary-Khamis international $		
1820	1 707	880	2 121	
1840	1 990	1 035	2 424	
1870	3 191	1 775	3 487	
1913	4 921	2 736	5 150	
1920	4 568	2 540	4 754	2 540
1920	4 690	**2 540**		
1950	6 907	**3 446**		
1973	12 022	**6 867**		
2001	20 066	**23 201**		

Note: E + W + S means England, Wales and Scotland.
Source: Maddison (2001), p. 247. Figures in **bold** refer to Irish Republic.

http://dx.doi.org/10.1787/456125276116

Statistics, 1962, p. 20. Scotland, 1815–71 from Mitchell, pp. 8–9. Ireland 1791–1821 from D. Dickson, C. O Grada and S. Daultry, "Hearth Tax, Household Size and Irish Population Change 1672–1821", *Proceedings of the Royal Irish Academy*, vol. 82, C, no. 6, Dublin, 1982, p. 156. Ireland 1821–41 from J. Lee, "On the Accuracy of the Pre–Famine Irish Censuses", in J.M. Goldstrom and I.A. Clarkson (1981), *Irish Population, Economy and Society*, Oxford, p. 54; 1842–1920 from Mitchell, *op. cit.*, pp. 8–9, with 2.44 per cent upward adjustment of his 1842–7 figures to link with those of Lee. 1871–1949 UK population from Feinstein (1972), pp. T120–1.

The population and GDP estimates for 1920 and earlier years include the whole of Ireland.

Table 1–3 gives a geographic breakdown for benchmark years 1820–2001. Until the 1990s, Irish per capita income levels were well below those in Great Britain, but have now surged ahead.

Table 1-4. **Population and GDP: 13 Small West European Countries, 1950-2001**

	1950	*1973*	*1990*	*2001*
		Population (000 at mid-year)		
Iceland	143	212	255	278
Luxembourg	296	350	382	443
Cyprus	494	634	681	763
Malta	312	322	359	395
9 Other	285	389	482	516
13 Country Total	1 529	1 907	2 159	2 595
		GDP (million 1990 international dollars)		
Iceland	762	2 435	4 596	6 131
Luxembourg	2 481	5 237	8 819	16 452
Cyprus	930	3 207	6 651	9 823
Malta	278	855	2 987	4 790
9 Other	1 429	4 718	8 152	10 357
13 Country Total	5 880	16 452	31 205	47 553
		Per capita GDP (1990 international dollars)		
Iceland	5 336	11 472	18 024	22 054
Luxembourg	8 382	14 963	23 086	37 138
Cyprus	1 883	5 058	9 767	12 874
Malta	894	2 655	8 320	12 127
9 Other	5 013	12 129	16 913	20 077
13 Country Average	3 846	8 627	14 453	19 855

http://dx.doi.org/10.1787/456125276116

13 Small Countries: Estimates of GDP movement for Iceland and Luxembourg 1950–2001 from OECD National Accounts, various issues; Cyprus and Malta 1950–90 from Maddison (1995) updated from IMF. Per capita GDP in 9 smaller countries (Andorra, Channel Islands, Faeroe Islands, Gibraltar, Greenland, Isle of Man, Liechtenstein, Monaco and San Marino) assumed to be the same as the average for 12 West European countries. Pre–1950 population and GDP per capita levels for the 13–country group assumed to move parallel to the total/average for 12 West European countries.

Table 1a. **Population of 12 West European Countries, 1500-1868**
(000 at mid-year)

	Austria	*Belgium*	*Denmark*	*Finland*	*France*	*Germany*	*Italy*
1500	2 000	1 400	600	300	15 000	12 000	10 500
1600	2 500	1 600	650	400	18 500	16 000	13 100
1700	2 500	2 000	700	400	21 471	15 000	13 300
1820	3 369	3 434	1 155	1 169	31 250	24 905	20 176
1821	3 386	3 464	1 167	1 186	31 460	25 260	20 306
1822	3 402	3 495	1 179	1 202	31 685	25 620	20 437
1823	3 419	3 526	1 196	1 219	31 905	25 969	20 568
1824	3 436	3 557	1 213	1 235	32 127	26 307	20 701
1825	3 452	3 589	1 228	1 252	32 350	26 650	20 834
1826	3 469	3 620	1 243	1 268	32 538	26 964	20 968
1827	3 486	3 652	1 255	1 310	32 727	27 249	21 103
1828	3 504	3 685	1 265	1 326	32 917	27 540	21 239
1829	3 521	3 717	1 270	1 343	33 108	27 807	21 376
1830	3 538	3 750	1 273	1 364	33 300	28 045	21 513
1831	3 555	3 782	1 275	1 374	33 439	28 283	21 652
1832	3 573	3 814	1 276	1 378	33 598	28 535	21 791
1833	3 590	3 846	1 284	1 383	33 718	28 801	21 932
1834	3 608	3 879	1 295	1 387	33 859	29 071	22 073
1835	3 626	3 912	1 306	1 391	34 000	29 390	22 215
1836	3 614	3 945	1 315	1 399	34 178	29 702	22 358
1837	3 662	3 978	1 325	1 409	34 357	30 013	22 502
1838	3 680	4 012	1 335	1 420	34 537	30 365	22 647
1839	3 698	4 046	1 347	1 430	34 718	30 746	22 793
1840	3 716	4 080	1 357	1 441	34 900	31 126	22 939
1841	3 739	4 115	1 371	1 456	35 059	31 475	23 087
1842	3 762	4 151	1 385	1 476	35 218	31 787	23 236
1843	3 785	4 187	1 392	1 495	35 378	32 086	23 385
1844	3 808	4 223	1 414	1 516	35 539	32 394	23 536
1845	3 831	4 259	1 430	1 536	35 700	32 743	23 687
1846	3 855	4 296	1 444	1 555	35 829	33 059	23 840
1847	3 878	4 333	1 456	1 573	35 959	33 231	23 993
1848	3 902	4 371	1 470	1 591	36 089	33 289	24 148
1849	3 926	4 408	1 484	1 610	36 219	33 452	24 303
1850	3 950	4 449	1 499	1 628	36 350	33 746	24 460
1851	3 978	4 477	1 517	1 642	36 479	34 055	24 617
1852	4 006	4 506	1 536	1 652	36 609	34 290	24 776
1853	4 035	4 534	1 552	1 663	36 739	34 422	24 935
1854	4 063	4 563	1 569	1 673	36 869	34 531	25 096
1855	4 092	4 592	1 590	1 683	37 000	34 586	25 257
1856	4 120	4 621	1 612	1 692	37 060	34 715	25 420
1857	4 150	4 651	1 634	1 703	37 120	34 979	25 584
1858	4 178	4 680	1 653	1 715	37 180	35 278	25 748
1859	4 206	4 710	1 674	1 726	37 240	35 633	25 914
1860	4 235	4 740	1 696	1 738	37 300	36 049	26 081
1861	4 263	4 774	1 717	1 754	37 390	36 435	26 249
1862	4 292	4 809	1 739	1 774	37 520	36 788	26 418
1863	4 321	4 844	1 761	1 794	37 710	37 184	26 610
1864	4 350	4 879	1 777	1 813	37 860	37 602	26 814
1865	4 380	4 915	1 799	1 833	38 020	37 955	27 023
1866	4 409	4 950	1 814	1 840	38 080	38 193	27 256
1867	4 439	4 986	1 833	1 831	38 230	38 440	27 411
1868	4 469	5 023	1 852	1 776	38 330	38 637	27 501

http://dx.doi.org/10.1787/456125276116

Table 1a. Population of 12 West European Countries, 1500-1868
(000 at mid-year)

	Netherlands	Norway	Sweden	Switzerland	United Kingdom	12 WEC
1500	950	300	550	650	3 942	**48 192**
1600	1 500	400	760	1 000	6 170	**62 580**
1700	1 900	500	1 260	1 200	8 565	**68 796**
1820	2 333	970	2 585	1 986	21 239	**114 571**
1821	2 365	984	2 611	1 998	21 551	**115 738**
1822	2 400	998	2 646	2 008	21 832	**116 904**
1823	2 435	1 013	2 689	2 020	22 117	**118 076**
1824	2 474	1 028	2 727	2 031	22 407	**119 243**
1825	2 514	1 044	2 771	2 042	22 698	**120 424**
1826	2 543	1 062	2 805	2 054	22 996	**121 530**
1827	2 561	1 079	2 828	2 065	23 275	**122 590**
1828	2 585	1 093	2 847	2 077	23 560	**123 638**
1829	2 610	1 108	2 863	2 088	23 847	**124 658**
1830	2 633	1 124	2 888	2 100	24 139	**125 667**
1831	2 653	1 137	2 901	2 112	24 433	**126 596**
1832	2 665	1 150	2 923	2 123	24 684	**127 510**
1833	2 683	1 163	2 959	2 135	24 937	**128 431**
1834	2 707	1 174	2 983	2 147	25 194	**129 377**
1835	2 732	1 188	3 025	2 159	25 452	**130 396**
1836	2 762	1 202	3 059	2 171	25 715	**131 420**
1837	2 791	1 214	3 076	2 183	25 968	**132 478**
1838	2 821	1 224	3 090	2 195	26 223	**133 549**
1839	2 853	1 233	3 106	2 208	26 483	**134 661**
1840	2 886	1 241	3 139	2 220	26 745	**135 790**
1841	2 921	1 254	3 173	2 235	27 004	**136 889**
1842	2 952	1 271	3 207	2 251	27 277	**137 973**
1843	2 981	1 286	3 237	2 266	27 511	**138 989**
1844	3 014	1 302	3 275	2 282	27 785	**140 088**
1845	3 047	1 319	3 317	2 298	28 040	**141 207**
1846	3 069	1 337	3 343	2 314	28 272	**142 213**
1847	3 071	1 351	3 362	2 330	28 118	**142 655**
1848	3 069	1 363	3 397	2 346	27 683	**142 718**
1849	3 076	1 377	3 441	2 363	27 429	**143 088**
1850	3 098	1 392	3 483	2 379	27 181	**143 615**
1851	3 133	1 409	3 517	2 399	26 945	**144 168**
1852	3 167	1 425	3 540	2 406	27 076	**144 989**
1853	3 194	1 440	3 563	2 412	27 248	**145 737**
1854	3 218	1 457	3 608	2 427	27 446	**146 520**
1855	3 235	1 479	3 641	2 442	27 697	**147 294**
1856	3 253	1 501	3 673	2 457	27 978	**148 102**
1857	3 277	1 521	3 688	2 471	28 186	**148 964**
1858	3 294	1 543	3 734	2 484	28 422	**149 909**
1859	3 304	1 570	3 788	2 497	28 660	**150 922**
1860	3 318	1 596	3 860	2 510	28 888	**152 011**
1861	3 340	1 614	3 917	2 524	29 128	**153 105**
1862	3 366	1 627	3 966	2 538	29 401	**154 238**
1863	3 397	1 646	4 023	2 552	29 630	**155 472**
1864	3 431	1 668	4 070	2 566	29 842	**156 672**
1865	3 460	1 690	4 114	2 579	30 089	**157 857**
1866	3 484	1 707	4 161	2 593	30 315	**158 802**
1867	3 510	1 716	4 196	2 607	30 572	**159 771**
1868	3 543	1 724	4 173	2 623	30 845	**160 496**

http://dx.doi.org/10.1787/456125276116

Table 1a. **Population of 12 West European Countries, 1869-1918**
(000 at mid-year)

	Austria	Belgium	Denmark	Finland	France	Germany	Italy
1869	4 499	5 029	1 871	1 734	38 890	38 914	27 681
1870	4 520	5 096	1 888	1 754	38 440	39 231	27 888
1871	4 562	5 137	1 903	1 786	37 731	39 456	28 063
1872	4 604	5 178	1 918	1 819	37 679	39 691	28 233
1873	4 646	5 219	1 935	1 847	37 887	40 017	28 387
1874	4 688	5 261	1 954	1 873	38 044	40 450	28 505
1875	4 730	5 303	1 973	1 899	38 221	40 897	28 630
1876	4 772	5 345	1 994	1 928	38 398	41 491	28 837
1877	4 815	5 394	2 019	1 957	38 576	42 034	29 067
1878	4 857	5 442	2 043	1 983	38 763	42 546	29 252
1879	4 899	5 492	2 064	2 014	38 909	43 052	29 425
1880	4 941	5 541	2 081	2 047	39 045	43 500	29 534
1881	4 985	5 606	2 101	2 072	39 191	43 827	29 672
1882	5 030	5 673	2 120	2 098	39 337	44 112	29 898
1883	5 075	5 740	2 137	2 130	39 472	44 404	30 113
1884	5 121	5 807	2 160	2 164	39 629	44 777	30 366
1885	5 166	5 876	2 186	2 195	39 733	45 084	30 644
1886	5 212	5 919	2 213	2 224	39 858	45 505	30 857
1887	5 257	5 962	2 237	2 259	39 889	46 001	31 049
1888	5 303	6 007	2 257	2 296	39 920	46 538	31 243
1889	5 348	6 051	2 276	2 331	40 004	47 083	31 468
1890	5 394	6 096	2 294	2 364	40 014	47 607	31 702
1891	5 446	6 164	2 311	2 394	39 983	48 129	31 892
1892	5 504	6 231	2 327	2 451	39 993	48 633	32 091
1893	5 563	6 300	2 344	2 430	40 014	49 123	32 303
1894	5 622	6 370	2 367	2 511	40 056	49 703	32 513
1895	5 680	6 439	2 397	2 483	40 098	50 363	32 689
1896	5 739	6 494	2 428	2 515	40 192	51 111	32 863
1897	5 798	6 548	2 462	2 549	40 348	51 921	33 078
1898	5 856	6 604	2 497	2 589	40 473	52 753	33 285
1899	5 915	6 662	2 530	2 624	40 546	53 592	33 487
1900	5 973	6 719	2 561	2 646	40 598	54 388	33 672
1901	6 035	6 801	2 594	2 667	40 640	55 214	33 877
1902	6 099	6 903	2 623	2 686	40 713	56 104	34 166
1903	6 164	6 997	2 653	2 706	40 786	56 963	34 436
1904	6 228	7 086	2 681	2 735	40 859	57 806	34 715
1905	6 292	7 175	2 710	2 762	40 890	58 644	35 011
1906	6 357	7 258	2 741	2 788	40 942	59 481	35 297
1907	6 421	7 338	2 775	2 821	40 942	60 341	35 594
1908	6 485	7 411	2 809	2 861	41 046	61 187	35 899
1909	6 550	7 478	2 845	2 899	41 109	62 038	36 213
1910	6 614	7 498	2 882	2 929	41 224	62 884	36 572
1911	6 669	7 517	2 917	2 962	41 307	63 852	36 917
1912	6 724	7 590	2 951	2 998	41 359	64 457	37 150
1913	6 767	7 666	2 983	3 027	41 463	65 058	37 248
1914	6 806	7 723	3 018	3 053	41 476	66 096	37 526
1915	6 843	7 759	3 055	3 083	40 481	66 230	37 982
1916	6 825	7 762	3 092	3 105	39 884	66 076	38 142
1917	6 785	7 729	3 130	3 124	39 288	65 763	37 981
1918	6 727	7 660	3 165	3 125	38 542	65 237	37 520

http://dx.doi.org/10.1787/456125276116

Table 1a. Population of 12 West European Countries, 1869-1918
(000 at mid-year)

	Netherlands	Norway	Sweden	Switzerland	United Kingdom	12 WEC
1869	3 575	1 729	4 159	2 639	31 127	**161 847**
1870	3 610	1 735	4 169	2 655	31 400	**162 386**
1871	3 636	1 745	4 186	2 680	31 685	**162 570**
1872	3 662	1 755	4 227	2 697	31 874	**163 337**
1873	3 670	1 767	4 274	2 715	32 177	**164 541**
1874	3 745	1 783	4 320	2 733	32 501	**165 857**
1875	3 788	1 803	4 362	2 750	32 839	**167 195**
1876	3 832	1 829	4 407	2 768	33 200	**168 801**
1877	3 883	1 852	4 457	2 786	33 576	**170 416**
1878	3 834	1 877	4 508	2 803	33 932	**171 840**
1879	3 986	1 902	4 555	2 821	34 304	**173 423**
1880	4 043	1 919	4 572	2 839	34 623	**174 685**
1881	4 079	1 923	4 569	2 853	34 935	**175 813**
1882	4 130	1 920	4 576	2 863	35 206	**176 963**
1883	4 180	1 919	4 591	2 874	35 450	**178 085**
1884	4 226	1 929	4 624	2 885	35 724	**179 412**
1885	4 276	1 944	4 664	2 896	36 015	**180 679**
1886	4 326	1 958	4 700	2 907	36 313	**181 992**
1887	4 378	1 970	4 726	2 918	36 598	**183 244**
1888	4 432	1 977	4 742	2 929	36 881	**184 525**
1889	4 485	1 984	4 761	2 940	37 178	**185 909**
1890	4 535	1 997	4 780	2 951	37 485	**187 219**
1891	4 585	2 013	4 794	2 965	37 802	**188 478**
1892	4 632	2 026	4 805	3 002	38 134	**189 829**
1893	4 684	2 038	4 816	3 040	38 490	**191 145**
1894	4 743	2 057	4 849	3 077	38 859	**192 727**
1895	4 803	2 083	4 896	3 114	39 221	**194 266**
1896	4 866	2 112	4 941	3 151	39 599	**196 011**
1897	4 935	2 142	4 986	3 188	39 987	**197 942**
1898	5 003	2 174	5 036	3 226	40 381	**199 877**
1899	5 070	2 204	5 080	3 263	40 773	**201 746**
1900	5 142	2 230	5 117	3 300	41 155	**203 501**
1901	5 221	2 255	5 156	3 341	41 538	**205 339**
1902	5 305	2 275	5 187	3 384	41 893	**207 338**
1903	5 389	2 288	5 210	3 428	42 246	**209 266**
1904	5 470	2 297	5 241	3 472	42 611	**211 201**
1905	5 551	2 309	5 278	3 461	42 981	**213 064**
1906	5 632	2 319	5 316	3 560	43 361	**215 052**
1907	5 710	2 329	5 357	3 604	43 737	**216 969**
1908	5 786	2 346	5 404	3 647	44 124	**219 005**
1909	5 862	2 367	5 453	3 691	44 520	**221 025**
1910	5 922	2 384	5 449	3 735	44 916	**223 009**
1911	5 984	2 401	5 542	3 776	45 268	**225 112**
1912	6 068	2 423	5 583	3 819	45 426	**226 548**
1913	6 164	2 447	5 621	3 864	45 649	**227 957**
1914	6 277	2 472	5 659	3 897	46 049	**230 052**
1915	6 395	2 498	5 696	3 883	46 340	**230 245**
1916	6 516	2 522	5 735	3 883	46 514	**230 056**
1917	6 654	2 551	5 779	3 888	46 614	**229 286**
1918	6 752	2 578	5 807	3 880	46 575	**227 568**

http://dx.doi.org/10.1787/456125276116

Table 1a. **Population of 12 West European Countries, 1919-1969**
(000 at mid-year)

	Austria	Belgium	Denmark	Finland	France	Germany	Italy
1919	6 420	7 628	3 202	3 117	38 700	60 547	37 250
1920	6 455	7 552	3 242	3 133	39 000	60 894	37 398
1921	6 504	7 504	3 285	3 170	39 240	61 573	37 691
1922	6 528	7 571	3 322	3 210	39 420	61 900	38 086
1923	6 543	7 635	3 356	3 243	39 880	62 307	38 460
1924	6 562	7 707	3 389	3 272	40 310	62 697	38 810
1925	6 582	7 779	3 425	3 304	40 610	63 166	39 165
1926	6 603	7 844	3 452	3 339	40 870	63 630	39 502
1927	6 623	7 904	3 475	3 368	40 940	64 023	39 848
1928	6 643	7 968	3 497	3 396	41 050	64 393	40 186
1929	6 664	8 032	3 518	3 424	41 230	64 739	40 469
1930	6 684	8 076	3 542	3 449	41 610	65 084	40 791
1931	6 705	8 126	3 569	3 476	41 860	65 423	41 132
1932	6 725	8 186	3 603	3 503	41 860	65 716	41 431
1933	6 746	8 231	3 633	3 526	41 890	66 027	41 753
1934	6 760	8 262	3 666	3 549	41 950	66 409	42 093
1935	6 761	8 288	3 695	3 576	41 940	66 871	42 429
1936	6 758	8 315	3 722	3 601	41 910	67 349	42 750
1937	6 755	8 346	3 749	3 626	41 930	67 831	43 068
1938	6 753	8 374	3 777	3 656	41 960	68 558	43 419
1939	6 653	8 392	3 805	3 686	41 900	69 286	43 865
1940	6 705	8 346	3 832	3 698	41 000	69 835	44 341
1941	6 745	8 276	3 863	3 702	39 600	70 244	44 734
1942	6 783	8 247	3 903	3 708	39 400	70 834	45 004
1943	6 808	8 242	3 949	3 721	39 000	70 411	45 177
1944	6 834	8 291	3 998	3 735	38 900	69 865	45 290
1945	6 799	8 339	4 045	3 758	39 700	67 000	45 442
1946	7 000	8 367	4 101	3 806	40 290	64 678	45 725
1947	6 971	8 450	4 146	3 859	40 680	66 094	46 040
1948	6 956	8 557	4 190	3 912	41 110	67 295	46 381
1949	6 943	8 614	4 230	3 963	41 480	67 991	46 733
1950	6 935	8 639	4 271	4 009	41 829	68 375	47 105
1951	6 935	8 678	4 304	4 047	42 156	68 876	47 418
1952	6 928	8 730	4 334	4 091	42 460	69 146	47 666
1953	6 932	8 778	4 369	4 139	42 752	69 550	47 957
1954	6 940	8 819	4 406	4 187	43 057	69 868	48 299
1955	6 947	8 868	4 439	4 235	43 428	70 196	48 633
1956	6 952	8 924	4 466	4 282	43 843	70 603	48 921
1957	6 966	8 989	4 488	4 324	44 311	71 019	49 182
1958	6 987	9 053	4 515	4 360	44 789	71 488	49 476
1959	7 014	9 104	4 547	4 395	45 240	72 014	49 832
1960	7 047	9 119	4 581	4 430	45 670	72 481	50 198
1961	7 086	9 166	4 610	4 461	46 189	73 123	50 523
1962	7 130	9 218	4 647	4 491	47 124	73 739	50 843
1963	7 176	9 283	4 684	4 523	47 808	74 340	51 198
1964	7 224	9 367	4 720	4 549	48 340	74 954	51 600
1965	7 271	9 448	4 758	4 564	48 763	75 639	51 987
1966	7 322	9 508	4 798	4 581	49 194	76 206	52 332
1967	7 377	9 557	4 839	4 606	49 569	76 368	52 667
1968	7 415	9 590	4 867	4 626	49 934	76 584	52 987
1969	7 441	9 613	4 891	4 624	50 353	77 144	53 317

http://dx.doi.org/10.1787/456125276116

Table 1a. **Population of 12 West European Countries, 1919-1969**
(000 at mid-year)

	Netherlands	Norway	Sweden	Switzerland	United Kingdom	12 WEC
1919	6 805	2 603	5 830	3 869	46 534	222 505
1920	6 848	2 635	5 876	3 877	46 821	223 731
1921	6 921	2 668	5 929	3 876	44 072	222 433
1922	7 032	2 695	5 971	3 874	44 372	223 981
1923	7 150	2 713	5 997	3 883	44 596	225 763
1924	7 264	2 729	6 021	3 896	44 915	227 572
1925	7 366	2 747	6 045	3 910	45 059	229 158
1926	7 471	2 763	6 064	3 932	45 232	230 702
1927	7 576	2 775	6 081	3 956	45 389	231 958
1928	7 679	2 785	6 097	3 988	45 578	233 260
1929	7 782	2 795	6 113	4 022	45 672	234 460
1930	7 884	2 807	6 131	4 051	45 866	235 975
1931	7 999	2 824	6 152	4 080	46 074	237 420
1932	8 123	2 842	6 176	4 102	46 335	238 602
1933	8 237	2 858	6 201	4 122	46 520	239 744
1934	8 341	2 874	6 222	4 140	46 666	240 932
1935	8 434	2 889	6 242	4 155	46 868	242 148
1936	8 516	2 904	6 259	4 168	47 081	243 333
1937	8 599	2 919	6 276	4 180	47 289	244 568
1938	8 685	2 936	6 298	4 192	47 494	246 102
1939	8 782	2 954	6 326	4 206	47 991	247 846
1940	8 879	2 973	6 356	4 226	48 226	248 417
1941	8 966	2 990	6 389	4 254	48 216	247 979
1942	9 042	3 009	6 432	4 286	48 400	249 048
1943	9 103	3 032	6 491	4 323	48 789	249 046
1944	9 175	3 060	6 560	4 364	49 016	249 088
1945	9 262	3 091	6 636	4 412	49 182	247 666
1946	9 424	3 127	6 719	4 467	49 217	246 921
1947	9 630	3 165	6 803	4 524	49 519	249 881
1948	9 800	3 201	6 884	4 582	50 014	252 882
1949	9 956	3 234	6 956	4 640	50 312	255 052
1950	10 114	3 265	7 014	4 694	50 127	256 376
1951	10 264	3 296	7 073	4 749	50 290	258 086
1952	10 382	3 328	7 125	4 815	50 430	259 434
1953	10 493	3 361	7 171	4 878	50 593	260 975
1954	10 615	3 394	7 213	4 929	50 765	262 493
1955	10 751	3 427	7 262	4 980	50 946	264 112
1956	10 889	3 460	7 315	5 045	51 184	265 884
1957	11 026	3 492	7 364	5 126	51 430	267 717
1958	11 187	3 523	7 409	5 199	51 652	269 638
1959	11 348	3 553	7 446	5 259	51 956	271 707
1960	11 486	3 581	7 480	5 362	52 372	273 807
1961	11 639	3 610	7 520	5 512	52 807	276 246
1962	11 806	3 639	7 562	5 666	53 292	279 157
1963	11 966	3 667	7 604	5 789	53 625	281 663
1964	12 127	3 694	7 661	5 887	53 991	284 115
1965	12 292	3 723	7 734	5 943	54 350	286 472
1966	12 455	3 754	7 808	5 996	54 643	288 595
1967	12 597	3 786	7 868	6 063	54 959	290 255
1968	12 725	3 819	7 912	6 132	55 214	291 806
1969	12 873	3 851	7 968	6 212	55 461	293 747

http://dx.doi.org/10.1787/456125276116

Table 1a. **Population of 12 West European Countries, 1970-2003**
(000 at mid-year)

	Austria	*Belgium*	*Denmark*	*Finland*	*France*	*Germany*	*Italy*
1970	7 467	9 638	4 929	4 606	50 787	77 783	53 661
1971	7 500	9 673	4 963	4 612	51 285	78 355	54 006
1972	7 544	9 709	4 992	4 640	51 732	78 717	54 366
1973	7 586	9 738	5 022	4 666	52 157	78 950	54 797
1974	7 599	9 768	5 045	4 691	52 503	78 966	55 226
1975	7 579	9 795	5 060	4 711	52 758	78 682	55 572
1976	7 566	9 811	5 073	4 726	52 954	78 299	55 839
1977	7 568	9 822	5 088	4 739	53 165	78 161	56 059
1978	7 562	9 830	5 104	4 753	53 381	78 066	56 240
1979	7 549	9 837	5 117	4 765	53 606	78 081	56 368
1980	7 549	9 847	5 123	4 780	53 870	78 298	56 451
1981	7 565	9 852	5 122	4 800	54 147	78 402	56 502
1982	7 574	9 856	5 118	4 827	54 434	78 335	56 536
1983	7 552	9 856	5 114	4 856	54 650	78 122	56 630
1984	7 553	9 855	5 112	4 882	54 947	77 855	56 697
1985	7 558	9 858	5 114	4 902	55 171	77 685	56 731
1986	7 566	9 862	5 121	4 917	55 387	77 713	56 734
1987	7 576	9 870	5 127	4 932	55 630	77 718	56 730
1988	7 596	9 884	5 130	4 947	55 873	78 031	56 734
1989	7 624	9 938	5 133	4 962	56 417	78 645	56 738
1990	7 718	9 969	5 141	4 986	56 735	79 380	56 743
1991	7 813	10 004	5 154	5 014	57 055	79 984	56 747
1992	7 910	10 045	5 171	5 041	57 374	80 598	56 841
1993	7 983	10 084	5 188	5 065	57 658	81 132	57 027
1994	8 022	10 116	5 206	5 087	57 907	81 414	57 179
1995	8 042	10 137	5 233	5 106	58 150	81 654	57 275
1996	8 056	10 157	5 262	5 122	58 388	81 891	57 367
1997	8 072	10 181	5 284	5 136	58 623	82 011	57 479
1998	8 092	10 203	5 302	5 148	58 866	82 024	57 550
1999	8 111	10 223	5 320	5 158	59 116	82 075	57 604
2000	8 131	10 242	5 336	5 167	59 382	82 188	57 719
2001	8 151	10 259	5 353	5 176	59 658	82 281	57 845
2002	8 170	10 275	5 369	5 184	59 925	82 351	57 927
2003	8 188	10 289	5 384	5 191	60 181	82 398	57 998

http://dx.doi.org/10.1787/456125276116

ISBN 92-64-02261-9 – © OECD 2006   418

Table 1a. **Population of 12 West European Countries, 1970-2003**
(000 at mid-year)

	Netherlands	Norway	Sweden	Switzerland	United Kingdom	12 WEC
1970	13 032	3 877	8 043	6 267	55 632	**295 723**
1971	13 194	3 903	8 098	6 343	55 907	**297 839**
1972	13 330	3 933	8 122	6 401	56 079	**299 565**
1973	13 438	3 961	8 137	6 441	56 210	**301 103**
1974	13 541	3 985	8 161	6 460	56 224	**302 169**
1975	13 653	4 007	8 193	6 404	56 215	**302 629**
1976	13 770	4 026	8 222	6 333	56 206	**302 824**
1977	13 853	4 043	8 252	6 316	56 179	**303 246**
1978	13 937	4 059	8 276	6 333	56 167	**303 706**
1979	14 030	4 073	8 294	6 351	56 228	**304 298**
1980	14 144	4 086	8 310	6 385	56 314	**305 157**
1981	14 246	4 100	8 320	6 425	56 383	**305 864**
1982	14 310	4 115	8 325	6 468	56 340	**306 238**
1983	14 362	4 128	8 329	6 501	56 383	**306 483**
1984	14 420	4 140	8 343	6 530	56 462	**306 795**
1985	14 491	4 152	8 356	6 565	56 620	**307 204**
1986	14 572	4 167	8 376	6 604	56 796	**307 815**
1987	14 665	4 186	8 405	6 651	56 982	**308 472**
1988	14 761	4 209	8 445	6 705	57 160	**309 474**
1989	14 849	4 226	8 493	6 765	57 324	**311 113**
1990	14 952	4 242	8 559	6 838	57 493	**312 757**
1991	15 066	4 262	8 617	6 923	57 666	**314 306**
1992	15 174	4 286	8 676	7 001	57 866	**315 984**
1993	15 275	4 312	8 722	7 064	58 027	**317 539**
1994	15 382	4 337	8 769	7 120	58 213	**318 750**
1995	15 459	4 359	8 825	7 166	58 426	**319 831**
1996	15 533	4 381	8 859	7 198	58 619	**320 832**
1997	15 613	4 406	8 865	7 213	58 808	**321 691**
1998	15 705	4 433	8 868	7 225	59 036	**322 451**
1999	15 800	4 458	8 871	7 242	59 293	**323 271**
2000	15 892	4 481	8 873	7 262	59 522	**324 197**
2001	15 981	4 503	8 875	7 283	59 723	**325 088**
2002	16 068	4 525	8 877	7 302	59 912	**325 884**
2003	16 151	4 546	8 878	7 319	60 095	**326 618**

http://dx.doi.org/10.1787/456125276116

Table 1a. **Population of 4 West European Countries and Total WEC, 1500-1868**
(000 at mid-year)

	Ireland [a]	Greece	Portugal	Spain	13 small WEC	29 WEC
1500	800	1 000	1 000	6 800	276	**57 268**
1600	1 000	1 500	1 100	8 240	358	**73 778**
1700	1 925	1 500	2 000	8 770	394	**81 460**
1820	7 101	2 312	3 297	12 203	657	**133 040**
1821	7 200	2 333	3 316	12 284	665	**134 336**
1822	7 267	2 355	3 335	12 366	672	**135 632**
1823	7 335	2 376	3 354	12 449	678	**136 933**
1824	7 403	2 398	3 373	12 532	685	**138 231**
1825	7 472	2 420	3 393	12 615	692	**139 544**
1826	7 542	2 443	3 412	12 699	698	**140 782**
1827	7 612	2 465	3 432	12 784	704	**141 975**
1828	7 683	2 488	3 452	12 869	710	**143 157**
1829	7 755	2 511	3 472	12 955	716	**144 312**
1830	7 827	2 534	3 491	13 041	722	**145 455**
1831	7 900	2 557	3 512	12 128	727	**145 520**
1832	7 949	2 581	3 532	13 216	733	**147 572**
1833	7 998	2 605	3 552	13 304	738	**148 630**
1834	8 047	2 629	3 475	13 392	743	**149 616**
1835	8 096	2 653	3 595	13 482	749	**150 875**
1836	8 146	2 677	3 617	13 571	755	**152 040**
1837	8 196	2 702	3 639	13 662	761	**153 242**
1838	8 247	2 727	3 661	13 753	767	**154 457**
1839	8 298	2 752	3 683	13 845	774	**155 715**
1840	8 349	2 777	3 704	13 937	780	**156 988**
1841	8 400	2 803	3 715	14 030	787	**158 224**
1842	8 422	2 829	3 726	14 123	793	**159 444**
1843	8 441	2 855	3 738	14 217	799	**160 598**
1844	8 479	2 881	3 749	14 312	805	**161 835**
1845	8 497	2 908	3 760	14 407	811	**163 093**
1846	8 490	2 934	3 771	14 503	817	**164 238**
1847	8 205	2 961	3 783	14 600	820	**164 819**
1848	7 640	2 989	3 794	14 697	820	**165 018**
1849	7 256	3 016	3 804	14 795	822	**165 525**
1850	6 878	3 044	3 816	14 894	825	**166 194**
1851	6 514	3 072	3 827	14 974	828	**166 869**
1852	6 337	3 100	3 839	15 055	833	**167 816**
1853	6 199	3 129	3 850	15 136	837	**168 689**
1854	6 083	3 158	3 858	15 217	842	**169 595**
1855	6 015	3 187	3 867	15 299	846	**170 493**
1856	5 973	3 216	3 875	15 381	851	**171 425**
1857	5 919	3 246	3 889	15 455	856	**172 410**
1858	5 891	3 273	3 925	15 526	861	**173 494**
1859	5 862	3 306	3 963	15 584	867	**174 642**
1860	5 821	3 336	4 000	15 642	873	**175 862**
1861	5 788	3 367	4 074	15 699	880	**177 125**
1862	5 776	3 398	4 113	15 754	886	**178 389**
1863	5 718	3 430	4 131	15 809	893	**179 735**
1864	5 641	3 461	4 176	15 864	900	**181 073**
1865	5 595	3 493	4 201	15 920	907	**182 378**
1866	5 523	3 525	4 226	15 976	912	**183 441**
1867	5 487	3 558	4 251	16 032	918	**184 530**
1868	5 466	3 591	4 276	16 088	922	**185 373**

http://dx.doi.org/10.1787/456125276116

Table 1a. **Population of 4 West European Countries and Total WEC, 1869-1918**
(000 at mid-year)

	Ireland	*Greece*	*Portugal*	*Spain*	*13 small WEC*	*29 WEC*
1869	5 449	3 621	4 302	16 144	930	**186 844**
1870	5 419	3 657	4 327	16 201	933	**187 504**
1871	5 398	3 694	4 353	16 258	941	**187 816**
1872	5 373	3 732	4 379	16 315	949	**188 712**
1873	5 328	3 770	4 405	16 372	958	**190 046**
1874	5 299	3 809	4 431	16 429	966	**191 492**
1875	5 279	3 848	4 458	16 487	975	**192 963**
1876	5 278	3 887	4 484	16 545	983	**194 700**
1877	5 286	3 927	4 511	16 603	992	**196 449**
1878	5 282	3 967	4 538	16 677	1 000	**198 022**
1879	5 266	4 008	4 571	16 768	1 009	**199 779**
1880	5 203	4 049	4 610	16 859	1 018	**201 221**
1881	5 146	4 090	4 651	16 951	1 027	**202 532**
1882	5 101	4 132	4 691	17 043	1 036	**203 865**
1883	5 024	4 174	4 732	17 136	1 045	**205 172**
1884	4 975	4 217	4 773	17 230	1 054	**206 686**
1885	4 939	4 260	4 815	17 323	1 064	**208 141**
1886	4 906	4 303	4 857	17 418	1 073	**209 643**
1887	4 857	4 347	4 899	17 513	1 082	**211 085**
1888	4 801	4 392	4 942	17 600	1 092	**212 551**
1889	4 757	4 437	4 985	17 678	1 101	**214 110**
1890	4 718	4 482	5 028	17 757	1 111	**215 597**
1891	4 680	4 528	5 068	17 836	1 121	**217 031**
1892	4 634	4 574	5 104	17 916	1 131	**218 554**
1893	4 607	4 621	5 141	17 996	1 140	**220 043**
1894	4 589	4 668	5 178	18 076	1 150	**221 799**
1895	4 560	4 716	5 215	18 157	1 161	**223 515**
1896	4 542	4 764	5 252	18 238	1 171	**225 436**
1897	4 530	4 813	5 290	18 320	1 181	**227 546**
1898	4 518	4 862	5 327	18 402	1 191	**229 659**
1899	4 502	4 912	5 366	18 484	1 202	**231 710**
1900	4 469	4 962	5 404	18 566	1 212	**233 645**
1901	4 447	4 997	5 447	18 659	1 223	**235 665**
1902	4 435	5 032	5 494	18 788	1 234	**237 886**
1903	4 418	5 067	5 541	18 919	1 244	**240 037**
1904	4 408	5 102	5 589	19 050	1 255	**242 197**
1905	4 399	5 138	5 637	19 133	1 266	**244 238**
1906	4 398	5 174	5 686	19 316	1 277	**246 505**
1907	4 388	5 210	5 735	19 450	1 289	**248 653**
1908	4 385	5 246	5 784	19 585	1 300	**250 920**
1909	4 387	5 283	5 834	19 721	1 311	**253 174**
1910	4 385	5 320	5 884	19 858	1 323	**255 394**
1911	4 381	5 355	5 935	19 994	1 334	**257 730**
1912	4 368	5 390	5 964	20 128	1 346	**259 376**
1913	4 346	5 425	5 972	20 263	1 358	**260 975**
1914	4 334	5 463	5 980	20 398	1 362	**263 255**
1915	4 278	5 502	5 988	20 535	1 367	**263 637**
1916	4 273	5 541	5 996	20 673	1 371	**263 637**
1917	4 273	5 580	6 005	20 811	1 376	**263 058**
1918	4 280	5 620	6 013	20 950	1 380	**261 531**

a. Figures are shown here for Ireland 1500-1920 for information. They are not included in the total because the UK figures already include the whole of Ireland for 1500-1920, thereafter only the Northern Ireland province.

http://dx.doi.org/10.1787/456125276116

Table 1a. **Population of 4 West European Countries and Total WEC, 1919-1969**
(000 at mid-year)

	Ireland [b]	Greece	Portugal	Spain	13 small WEC	29 WEC
1919	4 352	5 660	6 021	21 091	1 384	**256 661**
1920	4 361	5 700	6 029	21 232	1 389	**258 081**
1921	3 096	5 837	6 071	21 411	1 393	**260 241**
1922	3 002	5 890	6 146	21 628	1 398	**262 045**
1923	3 014	6 010	6 223	21 847	1 402	**264 259**
1924	3 005	6 000	6 300	22 069	1 407	**266 353**
1925	2 985	5 958	6 378	22 292	1 411	**268 182**
1926	2 971	6 042	6 457	22 518	1 416	**270 106**
1927	2 957	6 127	6 538	22 747	1 420	**271 747**
1928	2 944	6 205	6 619	22 977	1 425	**273 430**
1929	2 937	6 275	6 701	23 210	1 429	**275 012**
1930	2 927	6 351	6 784	23 445	1 434	**276 916**
1931	2 933	6 440	6 869	23 675	1 439	**278 776**
1932	2 949	6 516	6 954	23 897	1 443	**280 361**
1933	2 962	6 591	7 040	24 122	1 448	**281 907**
1934	2 971	6 688	7 127	24 349	1 453	**283 520**
1935	2 971	6 793	7 216	24 579	1 457	**285 164**
1936	2 967	6 886	7 305	23 810	1 462	**285 763**
1937	2 948	6 973	7 396	25 043	1 467	**288 395**
1938	2 937	7 061	7 488	25 279	1 471	**290 338**
1939	2 934	7 156	7 581	25 517	1 476	**292 510**
1940	2 958	7 280	7 675	25 757	1 481	**293 568**
1941	2 993	7 362	7 757	25 979	1 485	**293 555**
1942	2 963	7 339	7 826	26 182	1 490	**294 848**
1943	2 946	7 297	7 896	26 387	1 495	**295 067**
1944	2 944	7 284	7 967	26 594	1 500	**295 377**
1945	2 952	7 322	8 038	26 802	1 505	**294 285**
1946	2 957	7 418	8 110	27 012	1 510	**293 928**
1947	2 974	7 529	8 183	27 223	1 514	**297 304**
1948	2 985	7 749	8 256	27 437	1 519	**300 828**
1949	2 981	7 856	8 329	27 651	1 524	**303 393**
1950	2 963	7 566	8 443	28 063	1 529	**304 940**
1951	2 959	7 646	8 490	28 298	1 544	**307 024**
1952	2 952	7 733	8 526	28 550	1 559	**308 754**
1953	2 947	7 817	8 579	28 804	1 574	**310 696**
1954	2 937	7 893	8 632	29 060	1 591	**312 607**
1955	2 916	7 966	8 693	29 319	1 600	**314 605**
1956	2 895	8 031	8 756	29 579	1 613	**316 758**
1957	2 878	8 096	8 818	29 842	1 636	**318 987**
1958	2 852	8 173	8 889	30 106	1 661	**321 318**
1959	2 843	8 258	8 962	30 373	1 682	**323 824**
1960	2 832	8 327	9 037	30 641	1 701	**326 346**
1961	2 818	8 398	9 031	30 904	1 717	**329 115**
1962	2 830	8 448	9 020	31 158	1 729	**332 342**
1963	2 850	8 480	9 082	31 430	1 747	**335 251**
1964	2 864	8 510	9 123	31 741	1 759	**338 111**
1965	2 876	8 550	9 129	32 085	1 773	**340 884**
1966	2 884	8 614	9 109	32 452	1 787	**343 440**
1967	2 900	8 716	9 103	32 850	1 803	**345 628**
1968	2 913	8 741	9 115	33 239	1 819	**347 633**
1969	2 926	8 773	9 097	33 566	1 837	**349 946**

http://dx.doi.org/10.1787/456125276116

Table 1a. **Population of 4 West European Countries and Total WEC, 1970-2003**
(000 at mid-year)

	Ireland [b]	Greece	Portugal	Spain	13 small WEC	29 WEC
1970	2 950	8 793	9 044	33 876	1 853	**352 240**
1971	2 978	8 831	8 990	34 195	1 869	**354 702**
1972	3 024	8 889	8 970	34 513	1 883	**356 845**
1973	3 073	8 929	8 976	34 837	1 907	**358 825**
1974	3 124	8 962	9 098	35 184	1 929	**360 466**
1975	3 177	9 047	9 411	35 564	1 915	**361 743**
1976	3 228	9 167	9 622	35 997	1 914	**362 752**
1977	3 272	9 308	9 663	36 439	1 922	**363 850**
1978	3 314	9 430	9 699	36 861	1 939	**364 949**
1979	3 368	9 548	9 725	37 200	1 957	**366 096**
1980	3 401	9 643	9 778	37 488	1 990	**367 457**
1981	3 443	9 729	9 850	37 751	2 009	**368 647**
1982	3 480	9 790	9 860	37 983	2 020	**369 371**
1983	3 504	9 847	9 872	38 184	2 030	**369 920**
1984	3 529	9 896	9 885	38 363	2 040	**370 509**
1985	3 540	9 936	9 897	38 535	2 050	**371 162**
1986	3 541	9 967	9 907	38 708	2 064	**372 001**
1987	3 540	9 993	9 915	38 881	2 086	**372 887**
1988	3 530	10 004	9 921	39 054	2 110	**374 092**
1989	3 513	10 056	9 923	39 215	2 131	**375 950**
1990	3 508	10 158	9 923	39 351	2 159	**377 856**
1991	3 531	10 283	9 919	39 461	2 188	**379 688**
1992	3 557	10 357	9 915	39 549	2 218	**381 580**
1993	3 577	10 415	9 931	39 628	2 245	**383 334**
1994	3 594	10 462	9 955	39 691	2 268	**384 719**
1995	3 611	10 489	9 969	39 750	2 285	**385 936**
1996	3 633	10 511	9 980	39 804	2 303	**387 063**
1997	3 669	10 533	9 995	39 855	2 322	**388 065**
1998	3 711	10 556	10 012	39 906	2 340	**388 977**
1999	3 754	10 579	10 030	39 953	2 359	**389 945**
2000	3 797	10 602	10 048	40 016	2 377	**391 036**
2001	3 841	10 624	10 066	40 087	2 395	**392 101**
2002	3 883	10 645	10 084	40 153	2 412	**393 061**
2003	3 924	10 666	10 102	40 217	2 429	**393 957**

b.   From 1921 the figures refer to the Irish Republic.

http://dx.doi.org/10.1787/456125276116

Table 1b. GDP Levels in 12 West European Countries, 1500-1868
(million 1990 international Geary-Khamis dollars)

	Austria	Belgium	Denmark	Finland	France	Germany	Italy
1500	1 414	1 225	443	136	10 912	8 256	11 550
1600	2 093	1 561	569	215	15 559	12 656	14 410
1700	2 483	2 288	727	255	19 539	13 650	14 630
1820	4 104	4 529	1 471	913	35 468	26 819	22 535
1821			1 541		38 524		
1822			1 564		37 267		
1823			1 564		38 706		
1824			1 611		40 025		
1825			1 623		38 526		
1826			1 646		39 783		
1827			1 693		39 179		
1828			1 716		39 158		
1829			1 681		40 415		
1830	4 948	5 078	1 693		39 655	37 250	
1831			1 681		40 378		
1832			1 728		44 090		
1833			1 716		43 416		
1834			1 809		43 663		
1835			1 798		45 312		
1836			1 798		44 803		
1837			1 844		45 669		
1838			1 856		47 899		
1839			1 879		46 367		
1840	5 628		1 938		49 828		
1841			1 938		51 045		
1842			1 949		49 933		
1843			2 054		52 595		
1844			2 159		54 497		
1845			2 218		52 833		
1846		7 277	2 265		52 965		
1847		7 633	2 253		58 806		
1848		7 665	2 370		55 198		
1849		7 892	2 510		56 933		
1850	6 519	8 216	2 649	1 483	58 039	48 178	33 019
1851		8 442	2 521		57 188	47 941	
1852		8 668	2 615		60 931	48 890	
1853		8 894	2 626		57 969	48 653	
1854		9 444	2 638		60 763	49 840	
1855		9 509	2 930		59 842	49 128	
1856		10 026	2 766		62 469	53 162	
1857		10 285	2 813		66 038	55 773	
1858		10 350	2 790		70 645	55 536	
1859		10 350	2 977		66 046	55 773	
1860	7 528	10 867	2 953	1 667	70 577	59 096	
1861		11 029	3 000	1 680	66 154	57 672	37 995
1862		11 320	3 093	1 590	71 812	60 520	39 141
1863		11 644	3 292	1 718	74 416	65 029	38 377
1864		12 032	3 257	1 756	75 256	66 928	39 523
1865		12 032	3 373	1 744	73 157	67 165	40 503
1866		12 388	3 373	1 763	73 651	67 640	42 482
1867		12 452	3 373	1 622	69 308	67 877	38 950
1868		12 905	3 432	1 782	75 958	71 912	40 668

http://dx.doi.org/10.1787/456125276116

ISBN 92-64-02261-9 – © OECD 2006   424

Table 1b. **GDP Levels in 12 West European countries, 1500-1868**
(million 1990 international Geary-Khamis dollars)

	Netherlands	Norway	Sweden	Switzerland	United Kingdom	12 WEC
1500	723	192	382	411	2 815	**38 459**
1600	2 072	304	626	750	6 007	**56 822**
1700	4 047	450	1 231	1 068	10 709	**71 077**
1820	4 288	1 071	3 098	2 165	36 232	**142 693**
1821	4 458		3 255			
1822	4 498		3 220			
1823	4 702		3 342			
1824	4 871		3 463			
1825	4 871		3 498			
1826	4 902		3 185			
1827	5 125		3 307			
1828	5 373		3 603			
1829	5 492		3 463			
1830	5 300		3 394		42 228	
1831	5 298		3 255		44 249	
1832	5 638		3 463		43 800	
1833	5 742		3 638		44 249	
1834	5 750		3 638		46 046	
1835	5 823		3 725		48 517	
1836	5 980		3 777		50 314	
1837	6 205		3 638		49 640	
1838	6 380		3 429		52 336	
1839	6 485		3 777		54 806	
1840	6 588		3 864		53 234	
1841	6 734		3 742		52 111	
1842	6 756		3 742		50 988	
1843	6 680		3 899		51 886	
1844	6 723		4 247		55 031	
1845	6 807		4 020		57 951	
1846	6 837		3 933		61 770	
1847	6 869		4 177		62 219	
1848	6 938		4 438		62 893	
1849	7 119		4 595		64 016	
1850	7 345	1 653	4 490	3 541	63 342	**238 474**
1851	7 551		4 334	3 633	66 037	
1852	7 642		4 351	3 863	67 160	
1853	7 578		4 334	3 729	69 631	
1854	7 790		4 769	3 314	71 428	
1855	7 941		5 013	3 873	71 203	
1856	8 036		4 856	3 869	76 370	
1857	8 179		4 995	4 200	77 717	
1858	8 039		5 395	5 298	77 942	
1859	7 810		5 656	5 035	79 964	
1860	7 887		5 743	4 379	81 760	
1861	8 007		5 413	4 691	84 007	
1862	8 123		5 709	5 049	84 680	
1863	8 427		5 918	5 047	85 354	
1864	8 760		6 283	4 778	87 600	
1865	9 015	2 301	6 057	5 183	90 296	
1866	9 255	2 344	6 109	5 135	91 644	
1867	9 335	2 405	6 005	4 514	90 745	
1868	9 286	2 393	6 161	5 333	93 665	

http://dx.doi.org/10.1787/456125276116

Table 1b. GDP Levels in 12 West European Countries, 1869-1918
(million 1990 international Geary-Khamis dollars)

	Austria	Belgium	Denmark	Finland	France	Germany	Italy
1869		13 390	3 630	1 910	78 029	72 386	41 146
1870	8 419	13 716	3 782	1 999	72 100	72 149	41 814
1871	9 029	13 780	3 793	2 013	71 667	71 674	42 272
1872	9 099	14 621	4 003	2 083	78 313	76 658	41 647
1873	8 888	14 718	3 979	2 204	72 822	79 981	43 274
1874	9 287	15 203	4 096	2 255	82 070	85 914	43 130
1875	9 333	15 171	4 166	2 300	84 815	86 389	44 365
1876	9 545	15 365	4 248	2 428	77 880	85 914	43 431
1877	9 873	15 559	4 131	2 370	82 070	85 440	43 409
1878	10 201	16 012	4 295	2 326	81 058	89 474	44 051
1879	10 131	16 174	4 435	2 351	76 001	87 338	44 561
1880	10 272	16 982	4 540	2 364	82 792	86 626	46 690
1881	10 694	17 209	4 586	2 300	85 971	88 762	43 541
1882	10 764	17 791	4 750	2 524	90 017	90 186	47 354
1883	11 210	18 050	4 913	2 619	90 306	95 170	47 218
1884	11 514	18 211	4 936	2 639	89 294	97 543	47 556
1885	11 444	18 438	4 971	2 703	87 705	99 917	48 542
1886	11 819	18 664	5 170	2 837	89 150	100 629	50 695
1887	12 640	19 376	5 357	2 881	89 728	104 663	52 090
1888	12 617	19 505	5 392	2 990	90 595	108 935	51 920
1889	12 499	20 443	5 462	3 092	92 906	112 021	49 686
1890	13 179	20 896	5 788	3 265	95 074	115 581	52 863
1891	13 648	20 929	5 905	3 233	97 241	115 343	52 648
1892	13 953	21 446	6 045	3 137	99 697	120 090	49 688
1893	14 047	21 770	6 162	3 258	101 431	126 023	51 967
1894	14 868	22 093	6 290	3 514	105 188	129 109	51 235
1895	15 267	22 611	6 640	3 706	103 021	135 279	52 027
1896	15 501	23 063	6 885	3 948	107 933	140 026	53 456
1897	15 829	23 484	7 049	4 140	106 488	144 061	51 091
1898	16 721	23 872	7 165	4 319	111 690	150 231	55 646
1899	17 072	24 357	7 469	4 217	118 048	155 690	56 944
1900	17 213	25 069	7 726	4 415	116 747	162 335	60 114
1901	17 283	25 295	8 052	4 364	114 869	158 538	64 016
1902	17 963	25 813	8 239	4 274	112 990	162 335	62 231
1903	18 128	26 395	8 729	4 562	115 447	171 354	65 196
1904	18 409	27 074	8 916	4 734	116 314	178 236	65 805
1905	19 441	27 851	9 068	4 811	118 336	182 034	69 477
1906	20 191	28 433	9 324	5 003	120 504	187 492	72 087
1907	21 434	28 854	9 674	5 175	125 705	195 799	80 214
1908	21 528	29 145	9 978	5 233	124 983	199 122	82 149
1909	21 458	29 695	10 363	5 463	130 185	203 156	88 494
1910	21 763	30 471	10 678	5 584	122 238	210 513	85 285
1911	22 443	31 183	11 250	5 744	134 230	217 633	90 839
1912	23 568	31 926	11 250	6 063	145 356	227 127	91 574
1913	23 451	32 347	11 670	6 389	144 489	237 332	95 487
1914	19 572	30 300	12 405	6 108	134 230	202 207	95 413
1915	18 154	29 935	11 542	5 801	131 485	192 002	106 730
1916	17 933	31 672	12 032	5 878	138 131	193 900	119 746
1917	17 548	27 199	11 320	4 939	117 036	194 138	125 383
1918	17 186	21 917	10 946	4 281	92 328	194 612	127 249

http://dx.doi.org/10.1787/456125276116

ISBN 92-64-02261-9 – © OECD 2006

Table 1b. GDP Levels in 12 West European Countries, 1869-1918
(million 1990 international Geary-Khamis dollars)

	Netherlands	Norway	Sweden	Switzerland	United Kingdom	12 WEC
1869	9 552	2 491	6 474	5 836	94 339	
1870	9 952	2 485	6 927	5 581	100 180	339 103
1871	9 942	2 521	7 048	5 964	105 570	345 273
1872	10 146	2 680	7 379	5 684	105 795	358 108
1873	10 472	2 735	8 058	5 844	108 266	361 242
1874	10 213	2 827	8 371	6 550	110 063	379 979
1875	10 908	2 913	8 005	7 275	112 758	388 398
1876	11 074	2 998	8 527	7 109	113 881	382 400
1877	11 364	3 011	8 249	6 416	115 004	386 896
1878	11 468	2 919	8 197	6 535	115 454	391 988
1879	11 074	2 955	8 058	6 517	115 004	384 599
1880	12 313	3 047	8 440	6 955	120 395	401 416
1881	12 540	3 072	8 458	7 078	124 663	408 873
1882	12 875	3 060	8 806	6 870	128 257	423 253
1883	13 816	3 047	8 893	6 887	129 155	431 284
1884	14 065	3 108	9 137	7 666	129 380	435 051
1885	14 378	3 145	9 102	8 268	128 706	437 319
1886	14 594	3 164	9 067	8 593	130 728	445 109
1887	15 178	3 200	9 102	8 554	135 894	458 663
1888	15 707	3 341	9 345	8 757	141 959	471 062
1889	15 707	3 457	9 833	8 766	149 596	483 468
1890	15 070	3 549	9 972	9 389	150 269	494 895
1891	14 783	3 580	10 094	8 856	150 269	496 530
1892	15 006	3 659	10 303	9 627	146 676	499 328
1893	15 157	3 757	10 320	10 014	146 676	510 582
1894	15 524	3 769	10 529	9 783	156 559	528 460
1895	16 015	3 806	11 051	10 861	161 500	541 783
1896	15 405	3 922	11 695	11 142	168 239	561 217
1897	16 959	4 118	12 112	11 716	170 485	567 533
1898	17 310	4 130	12 374	11 927	178 796	594 181
1899	17 566	4 247	12 652	12 513	186 208	616 982
1900	17 604	4 320	13 104	12 649	184 861	626 156
1901	17 958	4 436	12 965	12 511	184 861	625 148
1902	18 796	4 528	12 948	12 801	189 578	632 497
1903	19 197	4 510	13 905	12 554	187 556	647 532
1904	19 334	4 504	14 044	13 223	188 679	659 273
1905	19 953	4 559	14 201	13 543	194 295	677 567
1906	20 661	4 724	15 123	14 972	200 808	699 323
1907	20 679	4 901	15 454	15 110	204 627	727 627
1908	20 694	5 060	15 419	14 873	196 316	724 500
1909	21 457	5 195	15 315	15 648	200 808	747 235
1910	22 438	5 379	16 237	16 177	207 098	753 860
1911	23 263	5 544	16 637	16 530	213 162	788 458
1912	23 998	5 795	17 107	16 701	216 307	816 772
1913	24 955	6 119	17 403	16 483	224 618	840 743
1914	24 281	6 254	17 246	16 496	226 864	791 376
1915	25 105	6 523	17 246	16 658	245 058	806 239
1916	25 779	6 731	17 020	16 606	250 449	835 878
1917	24 131	6 119	14 932	14 790	252 695	810 230
1918	22 634	5 893	14 706	14 737	254 268	780 758

http://dx.doi.org/10.1787/456125276116

Table 1b. **GDP Levels in 12 West European Countries, 1919-1969**
(million 1990 international Geary-Khamis dollars)

	Austria	*Belgium*	*Denmark*	*Finland*	*France*	*Germany*	*Italy*
1919	14 503	25 854	12 359	5 169	108 800	156 591	105 980
1920	15 571	29 921	12 942	5 782	125 850	170 235	96 757
1921	17 236	30 439	12 569	5 974	120 648	189 511	95 287
1922	18 784	33 414	13 841	6 606	142 322	206 188	100 210
1923	18 597	34 611	15 299	7 092	149 691	171 318	106 266
1924	20 754	35 743	15 346	7 277	168 474	200 557	107 312
1925	22 161	36 293	14 996	7 692	169 197	223 082	114 397
1926	22 536	37 523	15 871	7 986	173 676	229 363	115 595
1927	23 216	38 913	16 186	8 612	170 064	252 321	113 094
1928	24 295	40 951	16 735	9 194	181 912	263 367	121 182
1929	24 647	40 595	17 855	9 302	194 193	262 284	125 180
1930	23 967	40 207	18 917	9 194	188 558	258 602	119 014
1931	22 044	39 496	19 127	8 970	177 288	238 893	118 323
1932	19 769	37 717	18 625	8 932	165 729	220 916	122 140
1933	19 113	38 525	19 220	9 526	177 577	234 778	121 317
1934	19 277	38 202	19 804	10 606	175 843	256 220	121 826
1935	19 652	40 563	20 247	11 059	171 364	275 496	133 559
1936	20 238	40 854	20 749	11 807	177 866	299 753	133 792
1937	21 317	41 404	21 251	12 478	188 125	317 783	142 954
1938	24 037	40 466	21 765	13 123	187 402	342 351	143 981
1939	27 250	43 216	22 803	12 561	200 840	374 577	154 470
1940	26 547	38 072	19 606	11 909	165 729	377 284	155 424
1941	28 446	36 067	17 668	12 299	131 052	401 174	153 517
1942	27 016	32 962	18 065	12 337	117 470	406 582	151 610
1943	27 672	32 198	20 061	13 756	111 546	414 696	137 307
1944	28 376	34 094	22 161	13 762	94 207	425 041	111 562
1945	11 726	36 132	20 493	12 963	102 154	302 457	87 342
1946	13 695	38 267	23 690	14 017	155 326	143 381	114 422
1947	15 102	40 563	25 020	14 343	168 330	161 011	134 446
1948	19 230	42 989	25 697	15 481	180 611	190 695	142 074
1949	22 865	44 736	27 471	16 420	205 174	223 178	152 563
1950	25 702	47 190	29 654	17 051	220 492	265 354	164 957
1951	27 460	49 874	29 852	18 501	234 074	289 679	177 272
1952	27 484	49 486	30 144	19 121	240 287	314 794	190 541
1953	28 680	51 071	31 859	19 255	247 223	341 150	204 288
1954	31 611	53 173	32 478	20 941	259 215	366 584	214 884
1955	35 105	55 696	32 828	22 008	274 098	406 922	227 389
1956	37 520	57 313	33 225	22 673	287 969	436 086	237 699
1957	39 818	58 381	35 746	23 739	305 308	461 071	251 732
1958	41 272	58 316	36 551	23 867	312 966	481 599	265 192
1959	42 445	60 160	39 270	25 285	321 924	516 821	281 707
1960	45 939	63 394	40 367	27 598	344 609	558 482	296 981
1961	48 378	66 478	42 926	29 701	363 754	581 487	321 992
1962	49 550	69 904	45 295	30 627	387 937	606 292	347 098
1963	51 567	72 988	45 579	31 636	408 090	623 382	371 822
1964	54 662	78 128	49 843	33 235	435 296	661 273	386 333
1965	56 234	80 870	52 117	35 002	456 456	695 798	395 020
1966	59 399	83 440	53 539	35 843	479 631	715 393	415 639
1967	61 205	86 695	55 339	36 600	501 799	717 610	445 232
1968	63 925	90 293	57 613	37 442	523 967	755 463	482 462
1969	67 945	96 302	61 283	41 048	560 280	805 410	510 051

http://dx.doi.org/10.1787/456125276116

ISBN 92-64-02261-9 – © OECD 2006

Table 1b. **GDP Levels in 12 West European Countries, 1919-1969**
(million 1990 international Geary-Khamis dollars)

	Netherlands	Norway	Sweden	Switzerland	United Kingdom	12 WEC
1919	28 049	6 890	15 558	15 707	226 640	722 099
1920	28 898	7 324	16 463	16 726	212 938	739 408
1921	30 670	6 719	15 854	16 311	195 642	736 859
1922	32 342	7 502	17 351	17 890	205 750	802 200
1923	33 140	7 667	18 273	18 925	212 264	793 144
1924	35 561	7 630	18 847	19 631	221 024	858 158
1925	37 058	8 102	19 544	21 065	231 806	905 392
1926	40 028	8 279	20 640	22 120	223 270	916 887
1927	41 700	8 597	21 284	23 307	241 240	958 535
1928	43 921	8 879	22 293	24 609	244 160	1 001 498
1929	44 270	9 705	23 651	25 466	251 348	1 028 497
1930	44 170	10 421	24 138	25 301	249 551	1 012 040
1931	41 475	9 613	23 268	24 246	236 747	959 491
1932	40 901	10 255	22 641	23 422	238 544	929 593
1933	40 826	10 500	23 076	24 593	245 507	964 560
1934	40 078	10 837	24 834	24 642	261 680	1 003 848
1935	41 575	11 302	26 418	24 543	271 788	1 047 566
1936	44 195	11 993	27 949	24 626	284 142	1 097 965
1937	46 716	12 422	29 272	25 796	294 025	1 153 541
1938	45 593	12 734	29 759	26 785	297 619	1 185 615
1939	48 687	13 339	31 813	26 752	300 539	1 256 847
1940	42 898	12 152	30 873	27 032	330 638	1 238 163
1941	40 627	12 446	31 395	26 851	360 737	1 252 277
1942	37 133	11 963	33 309	26 175	369 721	1 244 342
1943	36 235	11 724	34 789	25 944	377 807	1 243 734
1944	24 306	11 112	35 972	26 571	362 983	1 190 146
1945	24 880	12 452	36 947	34 202	347 035	1 028 782
1946	41 999	13 786	41 001	36 543	331 985	968 114
1947	48 613	15 365	42 011	40 944	327 044	1 032 793
1948	53 804	16 589	43 316	41 768	337 376	1 109 630
1949	58 546	16 913	44 900	40 631	349 955	1 203 351
1950	60 642	17 838	47 269	42 545	347 850	1 286 544
1951	61 914	18 665	49 148	45 990	358 234	1 360 663
1952	63 162	19 332	49 845	46 369	357 585	1 408 150
1953	68 652	20 225	51 237	48 001	371 646	1 483 287
1954	73 319	21 229	53 395	50 705	386 789	1 564 323
1955	78 759	21 639	54 944	54 117	400 850	1 664 355
1956	81 654	22 771	57 032	57 710	405 825	1 737 477
1957	83 950	23 432	59 591	60 002	412 315	1 815 085
1958	83 701	23 218	59 887	58 732	411 450	1 856 751
1959	87 793	24 411	61 714	62 425	428 107	1 952 062
1960	95 180	25 813	64 986	66 793	452 768	2 082 910
1961	95 455	27 377	68 710	72 200	467 694	2 186 152
1962	101 993	28 159	71 599	75 661	472 454	2 286 569
1963	105 686	29 254	75 411	79 370	490 625	2 385 410
1964	114 446	30 662	80 562	83 541	516 584	2 524 565
1965	120 435	32 305	83 643	86 195	529 996	2 624 071
1966	123 754	33 556	85 383	88 305	540 163	2 714 045
1967	130 267	35 690	88 272	91 008	552 277	2 801 994
1968	138 627	36 498	91 475	94 272	574 775	2 946 812
1969	147 552	38 140	96 056	99 584	585 207	3 108 858

http://dx.doi.org/10.1787/456125276116

Table 1b. GDP Levels in 12 West European Countries, 1970-2001
(million 1990 international Geary-Khamis dollars)

	Austria	Belgium	Denmark	Finland	France	Germany	Italy
1970	72 785	102 265	62 524	44 114	592 389	843 103	521 506
1971	76 506	106 103	64 191	45 036	621 055	867 917	531 385
1972	81 256	111 679	67 578	48 473	648 668	903 739	546 933
1973	85 227	118 516	70 032	51 724	683 965	944 755	582 713
1974	88 588	123 494	69 379	53 291	704 012	952 571	610 040
1975	88 267	121 855	68 921	53 905	699 106	947 383	596 946
1976	92 307	128 743	73 382	53 676	729 326	993 132	635 737
1977	96 624	129 549	74 573	53 808	756 545	1 021 710	654 108
1978	96 273	133 231	75 674	54 934	777 544	1 050 404	678 494
1979	101 525	136 350	78 356	58 756	802 491	1 092 615	716 984
1980	103 874	142 458	78 010	61 890	813 763	1 105 099	742 299
1981	103 771	140 680	77 316	63 043	822 116	1 109 276	745 816
1982	105 750	142 665	79 650	65 090	842 787	1 099 799	749 233
1983	108 716	142 648	81 656	66 849	852 644	1 119 394	758 360
1984	109 077	146 180	85 241	68 866	865 172	1 150 951	777 841
1985	111 525	147 650	88 897	71 184	877 305	1 176 131	799 697
1986	114 135	149 854	92 135	72 873	898 129	1 202 151	822 404
1987	116 053	153 392	92 406	75 861	920 822	1 220 284	847 870
1988	119 730	160 632	93 482	79 581	961 287	1 260 983	880 671
1989	124 791	166 396	93 728	84 092	1 000 286	1 302 212	906 053
1990	130 476	171 442	94 863	84 103	1 026 491	1 264 438	925 654
1991	134 944	174 880	96 184	78 841	1 036 379	1 328 057	938 522
1992	136 754	177 695	97 413	76 222	1 051 689	1 357 825	945 660
1993	137 455	175 072	98 232	75 347	1 041 232	1 343 060	937 303
1994	140 949	180 312	103 884	78 327	1 061 556	1 374 575	957 993
1995	143 849	185 047	107 713	81 311	1 079 157	1 398 310	986 004
1996	146 726	187 268	110 406	84 563	1 091 028	1 409 496	996 850
1997	149 028	193 929	113 745	89 930	1 111 532	1 429 073	1 016 570
1998	154 350	198 370	116 545	94 727	1 150 381	1 457 039	1 035 304
1999	158 665	204 292	119 238	98 549	1 188 152	1 483 607	1 052 066
2000	163 412	212 434	122 793	104 566	1 235 635	1 528 353	1 081 646
2001	164 851	214 655	123 978	105 298	1 258 297	1 536 743	1 101 366

http://dx.doi.org/10.1787/456125276116

ISBN 92-64-02261-9 – © OECD 2006

Table 1b. **GDP Levels in 12 West European Countries, 1970-2001**
(million 1990 international Geary-Khamis dollars)

	Netherlands	Norway	Sweden	Switzerland	United Kingdom	12 WEC
1970	155 955	38 902	102 275	105 935	599 016	3 240 769
1971	162 539	40 683	103 241	110 253	611 705	3 340 614
1972	167 919	42 785	105 604	113 781	633 352	3 471 767
1973	175 791	44 544	109 794	117 251	675 941	3 660 253
1974	182 763	46 858	113 306	118 957	666 755	3 730 014
1975	182 596	48 811	116 198	110 294	665 984	3 700 266
1976	191 194	52 135	117 428	108 745	680 933	3 856 738
1977	196 392	54 002	115 553	111 392	695 699	3 959 955
1978	201 024	56 453	117 577	111 847	720 501	4 073 956
1979	205 501	58 894	122 092	114 634	740 370	4 228 568
1980	207 979	61 811	124 130	119 909	728 224	4 289 446
1981	206 925	62 406	124 113	121 802	718 733	4 295 997
1982	204 517	62 514	125 358	120 051	729 861	4 327 275
1983	208 014	64 729	127 555	120 659	755 779	4 407 003
1984	214 854	68 530	132 717	124 311	774 665	4 518 405
1985	221 470	72 105	135 277	128 561	802 000	4 631 802
1986	227 570	74 687	138 381	130 653	837 280	4 760 252
1987	230 788	76 203	142 733	131 614	877 143	4 885 169
1988	236 824	76 117	145 946	135 709	920 841	5 071 803
1989	247 906	76 818	149 415	141 599	940 908	5 234 204
1990	258 094	78 333	151 451	146 900	944 610	5 276 855
1991	263 950	80 774	149 760	145 724	930 493	5 358 508
1992	269 298	83 413	147 631	145 540	930 975	5 420 115
1993	271 347	85 694	144 353	144 839	952 554	5 406 488
1994	280 094	90 400	150 296	145 610	994 384	5 558 380
1995	286 416	93 879	155 843	146 345	1 022 172	5 686 046
1996	295 008	98 479	157 557	146 784	1 048 748	5 772 913
1997	306 465	103 079	160 830	149 272	1 085 547	5 909 000
1998	319 640	105 614	166 596	152 784	1 117 234	6 068 584
1999	331 670	106 740	174 077	155 272	1 143 810	6 216 138
2000	343 126	109 181	180 310	159 955	1 179 586	6 420 997
2001	347 136	110 683	182 492	162 150	1 202 074	6 509 723

http://dx.doi.org/10.1787/456125276116

Table 1b. **GDP Levels in 4 West European Countries and Total WEC, 1500-1868**
(million 1990 international Geary-Khamis dollars)

	Ireland [a]	Greece	Portugal	Spain	13 small WEC	29 WEC
1500	421	433	606	4 495	169	**44 162**
1600	615	725	814	7 029	250	**65 640**
1700	1 377	795	1 638	7 481	311	**81 302**
1820	6 231	1 482	3 043	12 299	628	**160 145**
1821						
1822						
1823						
1824						
1825						
1826						
1827						
1828						
1829						
1830						
1831						
1832						
1833						
1834						
1835						
1836						
1837						
1838						
1839						
1840						
1841						
1842						
1843						
1844						
1845						
1846						
1847						
1848						
1849						
1850		2 484	3 524	16 066	1 050	**261 598**
1851			3 793	16 311		
1852				17 053		
1853				17 192		
1854				17 506		
1855			3 552	18 391		
1856				17 892		
1857				17 489		
1858				17 902		
1859				18 700		
1860				19 336		
1861			3 597	19 595		
1862				19 729		
1863				20 190		
1864				20 206		
1865			3 745	19 586		
1866			3 887	20 612		
1867			4 000	20 566		
1868			4 042	18 490		

http://dx.doi.org/10.1787/456125276116

ISBN 92-64-02261-9 – © OECD 2006

Table 1b. GDP Levels in 4 West European Countries and Total WEC, 1869-1918
(million 1990 international Geary-Khamis dollars)

	Ireland [a]	Greece	Portugal	Spain	13 small WEC	29 WEC
1869			4 148	19 073		
1870	9 619	3 218	4 219	19 556	1 495	**367 591**
1871			4 061	21 104		
1872			4 179	24 034		
1873			4 353	26 156		
1874			4 282	23 968		
1875			4 277	24 670		
1876			4 177	25 136		
1877			4 372	27 701		
1878			4 375	26 982		
1879			4 384	25 492		
1880			4 367	27 750		
1881			4 513	28 462		
1882			4 655	28 831		
1883			4 770	29 480		
1884			4 934	29 561		
1885			5 064	28 774		
1886			5 343	28 157		
1887			5 457	27 765		
1888			5 523	28 890		
1889			5 425	28 823		
1890		5 280	5 671	28 839	2 253	**536 938**
1891			5 572	29 495		
1892			5 548	31 707		
1893			5 660	30 597		
1894			5 587	30 939		
1895			5 827	30 668		
1896			5 908	28 224		
1897			6 251	29 659		
1898			6 469	31 945		
1899			6 701	32 457		
1900		6 704	7 037	33 164	2 862	**675 923**
1901			6 914	35 471		
1902			6 954	34 440		
1903			7 054	34 600		
1904			7 148	34 485		
1905			6 950	34 005		
1906			6 997	35 760		
1907			7 165	36 885		
1908			7 052	38 331		
1909			7 048	38 998		
1910			7 225	37 633		
1911			7 369	40 332		
1912			7 494	40 028		
1913	11 891	8 635	7 467	41 653	3 843	**902 341**
1914			7 520	41 075	3 594	
1915			7 352	41 746	3 673	
1916			7 397	43 687	3 822	
1917			7 281	43 150	3 732	
1918			6 913	42 844	3 634	

a.   Figures are shown here for Ireland 1500-1920 for information. They are not included in the total because the UK figures already
     include the whole of Ireland for 1500-1920, thereafter only the Northern Ireland province.

http://dx.doi.org/10.1787/456125276116

Table 1b. GDP Levels in 4 West European Countries and Total WEC, 1919-1969
(million 1990 international Geary-Khamis dollars)

	Ireland [b]	Greece	Portugal	Spain	13 small WEC	29 WEC
1919			7 064	43 112	3 446	
1920			7 411	46 226	3 523	
1921	7 841	11 196	7 831	47 370	3 346	814 443
1922	7 800	11 565	8 788	49 390	3 843	883 586
1923	7 760	11 947	9 169	50 028	3 780	875 828
1924	7 720	12 341	8 828	51 443	4 072	942 562
1925	7 680	12 748	9 223	54 627	4 278	993 948
1926	7 640	13 169	9 163	54 424	4 317	1 005 600
1927	7 845	13 603	10 772	59 140	4 503	1 054 398
1928	8 058	13 864	9 732	59 371	4 694	1 097 217
1929	8 294	14 696	10 789	63 570	4 810	1 130 656
1930	8 480	14 342	10 656	61 435	4 719	1 111 672
1931	8 716	13 746	11 204	59 871	4 462	1 057 490
1932	8 508	14 912	11 422	61 163	4 615	1 030 213
1933	8 294	15 784	12 194	59 966	4 470	1 065 268
1934	8 562	16 173	12 714	62 231	4 647	1 108 175
1935	8 812	16 846	12 041	63 482	4 837	1 153 584
1936	9 056	16 907	11 124	49 343	5 061	1 189 456
1937	8 716	19 307	12 997	45 272	5 311	1 245 144
1938	8 965	18 901	13 084	45 255	5 438	1 277 258
1939	8 955	18 875	13 259	48 856	5 743	1 352 535
1940	9 028	16 183	12 396	53 585	5 663	1 335 018
1941	9 135	13 796	13 551	52 726	5 753	1 347 238
1942	9 043	11 588	13 369	55 670	5 713	1 339 725
1943	8 991	9 683	14 263	57 724	5 729	1 340 124
1944	8 985	8 129	15 079	60 407	5 499	1 288 245
1945	8 912	6 865	14 497	56 326	4 798	1 120 180
1946	9 025	10 284	15 635	58 854	4 544	1 066 456
1947	9 196	13 272	16 943	59 823	4 801	1 136 828
1948	9 643	13 936	16 894	59 970	5 114	1 215 187
1949	10 148	14 679	17 129	59 583	5 517	1 310 407
1950	10 231	14 489	17 615	61 429	5 880	1 396 188
1951	10 488	15 765	18 404	67 533	5 746	1 478 599
1952	10 753	15 878	18 428	73 044	6 180	1 532 433
1953	11 043	18 053	19 714	72 806	6 436	1 611 339
1954	11 142	18 615	20 660	78 335	6 647	1 699 722
1955	11 432	20 022	21 512	81 457	7 001	1 805 779
1956	11 283	21 731	22 451	88 083	7 427	1 888 452
1957	11 266	23 147	23 445	90 901	7 752	1 971 596
1958	11 034	24 218	23 753	94 829	7 966	2 018 551
1959	11 481	25 107	25 039	92 651	8 279	2 114 619
1960	12 127	26 195	26 711	94 119	8 487	2 250 549
1961	12 706	28 492	28 170	106 187	8 876	2 370 583
1962	13 120	29 562	30 040	118 386	9 269	2 486 946
1963	13 741	32 567	31 823	130 477	9 756	2 603 774
1964	14 279	35 243	33 921	143 308	10 165	2 761 481
1965	14 528	38 553	36 446	152 794	10 877	2 877 269
1966	14 652	40 907	37 929	164 199	11 398	2 983 130
1967	15 521	43 152	40 792	175 227	11 862	3 088 548
1968	16 804	46 027	44 421	185 747	12 261	3 252 072
1969	17 815	50 585	45 364	202 472	13 144	3 438 238

b.   From 1921 the figures refer to the Irish Republic.

http://dx.doi.org/10.1787/456125276116

ISBN 92-64-02261-9 – © OECD 2006

Table 1b. **GDP Levels in 4 West European Countries and Total WEC, 1970-2001**
(1990 international Geary-Khamis dollars)

	Ireland	*Greece*	*Portugal*	*Spain*	*13 small WEC*	*29 WEC*
1970	18 289	54 609	49 498	214 070	13 713	**3 590 948**
1971	18 923	58 496	52 781	226 319	14 651	**3 711 784**
1972	20 151	65 775	57 011	245 019	15 548	**3 875 271**
1973	21 103	68 355	63 397	266 896	16 452	**4 096 456**
1974	22 002	65 868	64 122	286 732	16 510	**4 185 248**
1975	23 246	69 853	61 334	296 824	16 005	**4 167 528**
1976	23 571	74 296	65 566	309 546	17 038	**4 346 755**
1977	25 506	76 843	69 239	321 868	18 095	**4 471 506**
1978	27 340	81 989	71 189	332 597	19 058	**4 606 129**
1979	28 180	85 015	75 203	337 333	20 007	**4 774 306**
1980	29 047	86 505	78 655	344 987	20 768	**4 849 408**
1981	30 013	86 553	79 928	346 768	21 257	**4 860 516**
1982	30 698	86 895	81 634	352 979	21 886	**4 901 367**
1983	30 624	87 244	81 492	361 902	22 385	**4 990 650**
1984	31 957	89 645	79 961	367 170	23 512	**5 110 650**
1985	32 943	92 442	82 206	374 627	24 313	**5 238 333**
1986	32 802	93 941	85 610	386 998	25 556	**5 385 159**
1987	34 331	93 507	91 073	409 027	26 754	**5 539 861**
1988	36 123	97 670	97 894	431 389	28 385	**5 763 264**
1989	38 223	101 425	102 922	454 166	30 000	**5 960 940**
1990	41 459	101 452	107 427	474 366	31 205	**6 032 764**
1991	42 259	104 597	110 047	485 126	32 342	**6 132 879**
1992	43 672	105 329	112 134	488 459	33 161	**6 202 870**
1993	44 848	103 644	110 593	482 776	34 633	**6 182 982**
1994	47 429	105 717	113 328	493 643	35 838	**6 354 335**
1995	52 163	107 937	116 640	507 054	36 899	**6 506 739**
1996	56 207	110 482	120 722	519 223	38 136	**6 617 683**
1997	62 295	114 500	125 505	540 520	39 918	**6 791 738**
1998	67 658	118 351	131 220	563 844	41 769	**6 991 426**
1999	74 999	122 405	135 886	587 169	43 639	**7 180 236**
2000	83 596	127 681	140 901	611 000	46 112	**7 430 287**
2001	89 113	132 916	143 234	627 733	47 553	**7 550 272**

http://dx.doi.org/10.1787/456125276116

Table 1c. Per Capita GDP in 12 West European Countries, 1500-1868
(1990 international Geary-Khamis dollars)

	Austria	Belgium	Denmark	Finland	France	Germany	Italy
1500	707	875	738	453	727	688	1 100
1600	837	976	875	538	841	791	1 100
1700	993	1 144	1 039	638	910	910	1 100
1820	1 218	1 319	1 274	781	1 135	1 077	1 117
1821			1 320		1 225		
1822			1 327		1 176		
1823			1 308		1 213		
1824			1 328		1 246		
1825			1 322		1 191		
1826			1 324		1 223		
1827			1 349		1 197		
1828			1 357		1 190		
1829			1 324		1 221		
1830	1 399	1 354	1 330		1 191	1 328	
1831			1 318		1 208		
1832			1 354		1 312		
1833			1 336		1 288		
1834			1 397		1 290		
1835			1 377		1 333		
1836			1 367		1 311		
1837			1 392		1 329		
1838			1 390		1 387		
1839			1 395		1 336		
1840	1 515		1 428		1 428		
1841			1 414		1 456		
1842			1 407		1 418		
1843			1 476		1 487		
1844			1 527		1 533		
1845			1 551		1 480		
1846		1 694	1 569		1 478		
1847		1 762	1 547		1 635		
1848		1 754	1 612		1 529		
1849		1 790	1 691		1 572		
1850	1 650	1 847	1 767	911	1 597	1 428	1 350
1851		1 886	1 662		1 568	1 408	
1852		1 924	1 702		1 664	1 426	
1853		1 962	1 692		1 578	1 413	
1854		2 070	1 681		1 648	1 443	
1855		2 071	1 843		1 617	1 420	
1856		2 170	1 716		1 686	1 531	
1857		2 211	1 722		1 779	1 594	
1858		2 212	1 688		1 900	1 574	
1859		2 197	1 778		1 774	1 565	
1860	1 778	2 293	1 741	959	1 892	1 639	
1861		2 310	1 747	958	1 769	1 583	1 447
1862		2 354	1 779	896	1 914	1 645	1 482
1863		2 404	1 869	958	1 973	1 749	1 442
1864		2 466	1 833	969	1 988	1 780	1 474
1865		2 448	1 875	951	1 924	1 770	1 499
1866		2 503	1 859	958	1 934	1 771	1 559
1867		2 497	1 840	886	1 813	1 766	1 421
1868		2 569	1 853	1 003	1 982	1 861	1 479

http://dx.doi.org/10.1787/456125276116

Table 1c. **Per Capita GDP in 12 West European Countries, 1500-1868**
(1990 international Geary-Khamis dollars)

	Netherlands	Norway	Sweden	Switzerland	United Kingdom	12 WEC
1500	761	640	695	632	714	**798**
1600	1 381	760	824	750	974	**908**
1700	2 130	900	977	890	1 250	**1 033**
1820	1 838	1 104	1 198	1 090	1 706	**1 245**
1821	1 885		1 247			
1822	1 874		1 217			
1823	1 931		1 243			
1824	1 969		1 270			
1825	1 938		1 262			
1826	1 928		1 135			
1827	2 001		1 169			
1828	2 079		1 266			
1829	2 104		1 210			
1830	2 013		1 175		1 749	
1831	1 997		1 122		1 811	
1832	2 116		1 185		1 774	
1833	2 140		1 229		1 774	
1834	2 124		1 220		1 828	
1835	2 131		1 231		1 906	
1836	2 165		1 235		1 957	
1837	2 223		1 183		1 912	
1838	2 262		1 110		1 996	
1839	2 273		1 216		2 069	
1840	2 283		1 231		1 990	
1841	2 305		1 179		1 930	
1842	2 289		1 167		1 869	
1843	2 241		1 205		1 886	
1844	2 231		1 297		1 981	
1845	2 234		1 212		2 067	
1846	2 228		1 176		2 185	
1847	2 237		1 242		2 213	
1848	2 261		1 306		2 272	
1849	2 314		1 335		2 334	
1850	2 371	1 188	1 289	1 488	2 330	**1 661**
1851	2 410		1 232	1 514	2 451	
1852	2 413		1 229	1 606	2 480	
1853	2 373		1 216	1 546	2 555	
1854	2 421		1 322	1 365	2 602	
1855	2 455		1 377	1 586	2 571	
1856	2 470		1 322	1 575	2 730	
1857	2 496		1 354	1 700	2 757	
1858	2 440		1 445	2 133	2 742	
1859	2 364		1 493	2 016	2 790	
1860	2 377		1 488	1 745	2 830	
1861	2 397		1 382	1 859	2 884	
1862	2 413		1 439	1 989	2 880	
1863	2 481		1 471	1 978	2 881	
1864	2 553		1 544	1 862	2 935	
1865	2 605	1 362	1 472	2 010	3 001	
1866	2 656	1 373	1 468	1 980	3 023	
1867	2 660	1 402	1 431	1 731	2 968	
1868	2 621	1 388	1 476	2 033	3 037	

http://dx.doi.org/10.1787/456125276116

Table 1c. **Per Capita GDP in 12 West European Countries, 1869-1918**
(1990 international Geary-Khamis dollars)

	Austria	Belgium	Denmark	Finland	France	Germany	Italy
1869		2 663	1 940	1 101	2 006	1 860	1 486
1870	1 863	2 692	2 003	1 140	1 876	1 839	1 499
1871	1 979	2 682	1 993	1 127	1 899	1 817	1 506
1872	1 976	2 824	2 087	1 145	2 078	1 931	1 475
1873	1 913	2 820	2 057	1 193	1 922	1 999	1 524
1874	1 981	2 890	2 096	1 204	2 157	2 124	1 513
1875	1 973	2 861	2 112	1 211	2 219	2 112	1 550
1876	2 000	2 875	2 130	1 259	2 028	2 071	1 506
1877	2 050	2 884	2 046	1 211	2 127	2 033	1 493
1878	2 100	2 942	2 102	1 173	2 091	2 103	1 506
1879	2 068	2 945	2 149	1 167	1 953	2 029	1 514
1880	2 079	3 065	2 181	1 155	2 120	1 991	1 581
1881	2 145	3 070	2 183	1 110	2 194	2 025	1 467
1882	2 140	3 136	2 240	1 203	2 288	2 044	1 584
1883	2 209	3 145	2 299	1 230	2 288	2 143	1 568
1884	2 248	3 136	2 285	1 219	2 253	2 178	1 566
1885	2 215	3 138	2 274	1 231	2 207	2 216	1 584
1886	2 268	3 153	2 336	1 276	2 237	2 211	1 643
1887	2 404	3 250	2 395	1 276	2 249	2 275	1 678
1888	2 379	3 247	2 389	1 302	2 269	2 341	1 662
1889	2 337	3 379	2 400	1 327	2 322	2 379	1 579
1890	2 443	3 428	2 523	1 381	2 376	2 428	1 667
1891	2 506	3 395	2 555	1 350	2 432	2 397	1 651
1892	2 535	3 442	2 598	1 280	2 493	2 469	1 548
1893	2 525	3 455	2 629	1 341	2 535	2 565	1 609
1894	2 645	3 468	2 657	1 399	2 626	2 598	1 576
1895	2 688	3 512	2 770	1 492	2 569	2 686	1 592
1896	2 701	3 551	2 836	1 570	2 685	2 740	1 627
1897	2 730	3 586	2 863	1 624	2 639	2 775	1 545
1898	2 855	3 615	2 870	1 668	2 760	2 848	1 672
1899	2 886	3 656	2 952	1 607	2 911	2 905	1 700
1900	2 882	3 731	3 017	1 668	2 876	2 985	1 785
1901	2 864	3 719	3 104	1 636	2 826	2 871	1 890
1902	2 945	3 739	3 141	1 591	2 775	2 893	1 821
1903	2 941	3 772	3 290	1 686	2 831	3 008	1 893
1904	2 956	3 821	3 326	1 731	2 847	3 083	1 896
1905	3 090	3 882	3 346	1 742	2 894	3 104	1 984
1906	3 176	3 917	3 402	1 794	2 943	3 152	2 042
1907	3 338	3 932	3 486	1 834	3 070	3 245	2 254
1908	3 320	3 933	3 552	1 829	3 045	3 254	2 288
1909	3 276	3 971	3 643	1 884	3 167	3 275	2 444
1910	3 290	4 064	3 705	1 906	2 965	3 348	2 332
1911	3 365	4 148	3 857	1 939	3 250	3 408	2 461
1912	3 505	4 206	3 812	2 022	3 514	3 524	2 465
1913	3 465	4 220	3 912	2 111	3 485	3 648	2 564
1914	2 876	3 923	4 110	2 001	3 236	3 059	2 543
1915	2 653	3 858	3 778	1 882	3 248	2 899	2 810
1916	2 628	4 080	3 891	1 893	3 463	2 935	3 139
1917	2 586	3 519	3 617	1 581	2 979	2 952	3 301
1918	2 555	2 861	3 459	1 370	2 396	2 983	3 392

http://dx.doi.org/10.1787/456125276116

Table 1b. **Per Capita GDP in 12 West European Countries, 1869-1918**
(1990 international Geary-Khamis dollars)

	Netherlands	Norway	Sweden	Switzerland	United Kingdom	12 WEC
1869	2 672	1 441	1 557	2 211	3 031	
1870	2 757	1 432	1 662	2 102	3 190	2 088
1871	2 734	1 445	1 684	2 225	3 332	2 124
1872	2 771	1 527	1 746	2 108	3 319	2 192
1873	2 853	1 548	1 885	2 152	3 365	2 195
1874	2 727	1 586	1 938	2 397	3 386	2 291
1875	2 880	1 615	1 835	2 645	3 434	2 323
1876	2 890	1 639	1 935	2 568	3 430	2 265
1877	2 927	1 626	1 851	2 303	3 425	2 270
1878	2 991	1 555	1 818	2 331	3 403	2 281
1879	2 778	1 554	1 769	2 310	3 353	2 218
1880	3 046	1 588	1 846	2 450	3 477	2 298
1881	3 074	1 597	1 851	2 481	3 568	2 326
1882	3 117	1 593	1 924	2 400	3 643	2 392
1883	3 305	1 588	1 937	2 396	3 643	2 422
1884	3 328	1 611	1 976	2 657	3 622	2 425
1885	3 362	1 618	1 951	2 855	3 574	2 420
1886	3 374	1 616	1 929	2 956	3 600	2 446
1887	3 467	1 624	1 926	2 931	3 713	2 503
1888	3 544	1 690	1 971	2 990	3 849	2 553
1889	3 502	1 743	2 065	2 982	4 024	2 601
1890	3 323	1 777	2 086	3 182	4 009	2 643
1891	3 224	1 778	2 105	2 987	3 975	2 634
1892	3 240	1 806	2 144	3 207	3 846	2 630
1893	3 236	1 844	2 143	3 294	3 811	2 671
1894	3 273	1 832	2 171	3 179	4 029	2 742
1895	3 334	1 827	2 257	3 488	4 118	2 789
1896	3 166	1 857	2 367	3 536	4 249	2 863
1897	3 436	1 923	2 429	3 675	4 264	2 867
1898	3 460	1 900	2 457	3 697	4 428	2 973
1899	3 465	1 927	2 491	3 835	4 567	3 058
1900	3 424	1 937	2 561	3 833	4 492	3 077
1901	3 440	1 967	2 515	3 745	4 450	3 044
1902	3 543	1 990	2 496	3 783	4 525	3 051
1903	3 562	1 971	2 669	3 662	4 440	3 094
1904	3 535	1 961	2 680	3 808	4 428	3 122
1905	3 594	1 974	2 691	3 913	4 520	3 180
1906	3 669	2 037	2 845	4 206	4 631	3 252
1907	3 622	2 104	2 885	4 193	4 679	3 354
1908	3 577	2 157	2 853	4 078	4 449	3 308
1909	3 660	2 195	2 808	4 240	4 511	3 381
1910	3 789	2 256	2 980	4 331	4 611	3 380
1911	3 888	2 309	3 002	4 378	4 709	3 503
1912	3 955	2 392	3 064	4 373	4 762	3 605
1913	4 049	2 501	3 096	4 266	4 921	3 688
1914	3 868	2 530	3 048	4 233	4 927	3 440
1915	3 926	2 611	3 028	4 290	5 288	3 502
1916	3 956	2 669	2 968	4 277	5 384	3 633
1917	3 627	2 399	2 584	3 804	5 421	3 534
1918	3 352	2 286	2 532	3 798	5 459	3 431

http://dx.doi.org/10.1787/456125276116

Table 1c. Per Capita GDP in 12 West European Countries, 1919-1969

(1990 international Geary-Khamis dollars)

	Austria	Belgium	Denmark	Finland	France	Germany	Italy
1919	2 259	3 389	3 860	1 658	2 811	2 586	2 845
1920	2 412	3 962	3 992	1 846	3 227	2 796	2 587
1921	2 650	4 056	3 826	1 884	3 075	3 078	2 528
1922	2 877	4 413	4 166	2 058	3 610	3 331	2 631
1923	2 842	4 533	4 559	2 187	3 754	2 750	2 763
1924	3 163	4 638	4 528	2 224	4 179	3 199	2 765
1925	3 367	4 666	4 378	2 328	4 166	3 532	2 921
1926	3 413	4 784	4 598	2 392	4 249	3 605	2 926
1927	3 505	4 923	4 658	2 557	4 154	3 941	2 838
1928	3 657	5 139	4 785	2 707	4 431	4 090	3 016
1929	3 699	5 054	5 075	2 717	4 710	4 051	3 093
1930	3 586	4 979	5 341	2 666	4 532	3 973	2 918
1931	3 288	4 860	5 359	2 581	4 235	3 652	2 877
1932	2 940	4 607	5 169	2 550	3 959	3 362	2 948
1933	2 833	4 681	5 291	2 702	4 239	3 556	2 906
1934	2 852	4 624	5 402	2 988	4 192	3 858	2 894
1935	2 907	4 894	5 480	3 093	4 086	4 120	3 148
1936	2 995	4 913	5 575	3 279	4 244	4 451	3 130
1937	3 156	4 961	5 668	3 441	4 487	4 685	3 319
1938	3 559	4 832	5 762	3 589	4 466	4 994	3 316
1939	4 096	5 150	5 993	3 408	4 793	5 406	3 521
1940	3 959	4 562	5 116	3 220	4 042	5 403	3 505
1941	4 217	4 358	4 574	3 322	3 309	5 711	3 432
1942	3 983	3 997	4 629	3 327	2 981	5 740	3 369
1943	4 065	3 907	5 080	3 697	2 860	5 890	3 039
1944	4 152	4 112	5 543	3 685	2 422	6 084	2 463
1945	1 725	4 333	5 066	3 450	2 573	4 514	1 922
1946	1 956	4 574	5 777	3 683	3 855	2 217	2 502
1947	2 166	4 800	6 035	3 717	4 138	2 436	2 920
1948	2 764	5 024	6 133	3 957	4 393	2 834	3 063
1949	3 293	5 193	6 494	4 143	4 946	3 282	3 265
1950	3 706	5 462	6 943	4 253	5 271	3 881	3 502
1951	3 959	5 747	6 936	4 571	5 553	4 206	3 738
1952	3 967	5 668	6 955	4 674	5 659	4 553	3 997
1953	4 137	5 818	7 292	4 652	5 783	4 905	4 260
1954	4 555	6 029	7 371	5 002	6 020	5 247	4 449
1955	5 053	6 280	7 395	5 197	6 312	5 797	4 676
1956	5 397	6 422	7 439	5 295	6 568	6 177	4 859
1957	5 716	6 495	7 965	5 490	6 890	6 492	5 118
1958	5 907	6 442	8 095	5 474	6 988	6 737	5 360
1959	6 051	6 608	8 637	5 754	7 116	7 177	5 653
1960	6 519	6 952	8 812	6 230	7 546	7 705	5 916
1961	6 827	7 253	9 312	6 658	7 875	7 952	6 373
1962	6 950	7 583	9 747	6 819	8 232	8 222	6 827
1963	7 186	7 862	9 732	6 994	8 536	8 386	7 262
1964	7 567	8 341	10 560	7 307	9 005	8 822	7 487
1965	7 734	8 559	10 953	7 670	9 361	9 199	7 598
1966	8 112	8 776	11 160	7 824	9 750	9 388	7 942
1967	8 297	9 072	11 437	7 947	10 123	9 397	8 454
1968	8 621	9 416	11 837	8 093	10 493	9 864	9 105
1969	9 131	10 018	12 531	8 878	11 127	10 440	9 566

http://dx.doi.org/10.1787/456125276116

ISBN 92-64-02261-9 – © OECD 2006

Table 1c. Per Capita GDP in 12 West European Countries, 1919-1969
(1990 international Geary-Khamis dollars)

	Netherlands	Norway	Sweden	Switzerland	United Kingdom	12 WEC
1919	4 122	2 647	2 669	4 060	4 870	**3 245**
1920	4 220	2 780	2 802	4 314	4 548	**3 305**
1921	4 431	2 518	2 674	4 208	4 439	**3 313**
1922	4 599	2 784	2 906	4 618	4 637	**3 582**
1923	4 635	2 826	3 047	4 874	4 760	**3 513**
1924	4 895	2 796	3 130	5 039	4 921	**3 771**
1925	5 031	2 949	3 233	5 388	5 144	**3 951**
1926	5 358	2 996	3 404	5 626	4 936	**3 974**
1927	5 504	3 098	3 500	5 892	5 315	**4 132**
1928	5 720	3 188	3 656	6 171	5 357	**4 293**
1929	5 689	3 472	3 869	6 332	5 503	**4 387**
1930	5 603	3 712	3 937	6 246	5 441	**4 289**
1931	5 185	3 404	3 782	5 943	5 138	**4 041**
1932	5 035	3 609	3 666	5 710	5 148	**3 896**
1933	4 956	3 674	3 721	5 966	5 277	**4 023**
1934	4 805	3 771	3 991	5 952	5 608	**4 167**
1935	4 929	3 912	4 232	5 907	5 799	**4 326**
1936	5 190	4 130	4 465	5 908	6 035	**4 512**
1937	5 433	4 255	4 664	6 171	6 218	**4 717**
1938	5 250	4 337	4 725	6 390	6 266	**4 818**
1939	5 544	4 516	5 029	6 360	6 262	**5 071**
1940	4 831	4 088	4 857	6 397	6 856	**4 984**
1941	4 531	4 163	4 914	6 312	7 482	**5 050**
1942	4 107	3 976	5 179	6 107	7 639	**4 996**
1943	3 981	3 867	5 360	6 001	7 744	**4 994**
1944	2 649	3 631	5 484	6 089	7 405	**4 778**
1945	2 686	4 029	5 568	7 752	7 056	**4 154**
1946	4 457	4 409	6 102	8 181	6 745	**3 921**
1947	5 048	4 855	6 175	9 050	6 604	**4 133**
1948	5 490	5 182	6 292	9 116	6 746	**4 388**
1949	5 880	5 230	6 455	8 757	6 956	**4 718**
1950	5 996	5 463	6 739	9 064	6 939	**5 018**
1951	6 032	5 663	6 949	9 684	7 123	**5 272**
1952	6 084	5 809	6 996	9 630	7 091	**5 428**
1953	6 543	6 018	7 145	9 840	7 346	**5 684**
1954	6 907	6 254	7 402	10 287	7 619	**5 959**
1955	7 326	6 314	7 566	10 867	7 868	**6 302**
1956	7 499	6 581	7 797	11 439	7 929	**6 535**
1957	7 614	6 710	8 092	11 705	8 017	**6 780**
1958	7 482	6 590	8 083	11 297	7 966	**6 886**
1959	7 737	6 871	8 288	11 870	8 240	**7 184**
1960	8 287	7 208	8 688	12 457	8 645	**7 607**
1961	8 202	7 584	9 137	13 099	8 857	**7 914**
1962	8 639	7 738	9 469	13 354	8 865	**8 191**
1963	8 832	7 979	9 917	13 710	9 149	**8 469**
1964	9 437	8 300	10 515	14 191	9 568	**8 886**
1965	9 798	8 677	10 815	14 504	9 752	**9 160**
1966	9 936	8 940	10 936	14 727	9 885	**9 404**
1967	10 341	9 427	11 219	15 010	10 049	**9 654**
1968	10 894	9 557	11 561	15 374	10 410	**10 099**
1969	11 462	9 904	12 055	16 031	10 552	**10 583**

http://dx.doi.org/10.1787/456125276116

Table 1c. **Per Capita GDP in 12 West European Countries, 1970-2001**
(1990 international Geary-Khamis dollars)

	Austria	*Belgium*	*Denmark*	*Finland*	*France*	*Germany*	*Italy*
1970	9 747	10 611	12 686	9 577	11 664	10 839	9 719
1971	10 200	10 970	12 934	9 765	12 110	11 077	9 839
1972	10 771	11 503	13 538	10 448	12 539	11 481	10 060
1973	11 235	12 170	13 945	11 085	13 114	11 966	10 634
1974	11 658	12 643	13 751	11 361	13 409	12 063	11 046
1975	11 646	12 441	13 621	11 441	13 251	12 041	10 742
1976	12 201	13 122	14 466	11 358	13 773	12 684	11 385
1977	12 767	13 190	14 655	11 355	14 230	13 072	11 668
1978	12 731	13 554	14 826	11 559	14 566	13 455	12 064
1979	13 448	13 861	15 313	12 332	14 970	13 993	12 720
1980	13 759	14 467	15 227	12 949	15 106	14 114	13 149
1981	13 718	14 279	15 096	13 134	15 183	14 149	13 200
1982	13 962	14 474	15 563	13 485	15 483	14 040	13 252
1983	14 396	14 474	15 966	13 767	15 602	14 329	13 391
1984	14 442	14 833	16 676	14 107	15 746	14 783	13 719
1985	14 757	14 977	17 384	14 522	15 901	15 140	14 096
1986	15 086	15 195	17 993	14 819	16 215	15 469	14 496
1987	15 319	15 541	18 023	15 382	16 553	15 701	14 946
1988	15 762	16 252	18 224	16 088	17 205	16 160	15 523
1989	16 369	16 744	18 261	16 946	17 730	16 558	15 969
1990	16 905	17 197	18 452	16 866	18 093	15 929	16 313
1991	17 272	17 480	18 661	15 725	18 164	16 604	16 539
1992	17 290	17 690	18 837	15 120	18 330	16 847	16 637
1993	17 218	17 361	18 933	14 876	18 059	16 554	16 436
1994	17 570	17 825	19 956	15 398	18 332	16 884	16 754
1995	17 887	18 255	20 585	15 925	18 558	17 125	17 215
1996	18 213	18 438	20 981	16 511	18 686	17 212	17 377
1997	18 462	19 048	21 528	17 511	18 961	17 425	17 686
1998	19 075	19 443	21 981	18 401	19 542	17 764	17 990
1999	19 561	19 984	22 415	19 105	20 099	18 076	18 264
2000	20 097	20 742	23 010	20 235	20 808	18 596	18 740
2001	20 225	20 924	23 161	20 344	21 092	18 677	19 040

http://dx.doi.org/10.1787/456125276116

ISBN 92-64-02261-9 – © OECD 2006

Table 1c. **Per Capita GDP in 12 West European Countries, 1970-2001**
(1990 international Geary-Khamis dollars)

	Netherlands	Norway	Sweden	Switzerland	United Kingdom	12 WEC
1970	11 967	10 033	12 716	16 904	10 767	**10 959**
1971	12 319	10 423	12 748	17 381	10 941	**11 216**
1972	12 597	10 878	13 002	17 774	11 294	**11 589**
1973	13 081	11 247	13 494	18 204	12 025	**12 156**
1974	13 497	11 758	13 885	18 414	11 859	**12 344**
1975	13 374	12 180	14 183	17 224	11 847	**12 227**
1976	13 885	12 949	14 282	17 170	12 115	**12 736**
1977	14 177	13 356	14 004	17 635	12 384	**13 059**
1978	14 424	13 909	14 207	17 662	12 828	**13 414**
1979	14 647	14 461	14 721	18 050	13 167	**13 896**
1980	14 705	15 129	14 937	18 779	12 931	**14 057**
1981	14 525	15 222	14 917	18 956	12 747	**14 045**
1982	14 291	15 193	15 058	18 560	12 955	**14 130**
1983	14 483	15 679	15 315	18 559	13 404	**14 379**
1984	14 900	16 553	15 908	19 036	13 720	**14 728**
1985	15 283	17 365	16 189	19 584	14 165	**15 077**
1986	15 617	17 925	16 521	19 784	14 742	**15 465**
1987	15 737	18 204	16 982	19 788	15 393	**15 837**
1988	16 044	18 086	17 283	20 239	16 110	**16 388**
1989	16 695	18 177	17 593	20 931	16 414	**16 824**
1990	17 262	18 466	17 695	21 482	16 430	**16 872**
1991	17 519	18 953	17 379	21 051	16 136	**17 049**
1992	17 747	19 460	17 017	20 788	16 088	**17 153**
1993	17 764	19 874	16 550	20 504	16 416	**17 026**
1994	18 209	20 846	17 139	20 452	17 082	**17 438**
1995	18 527	21 536	17 658	20 421	17 495	**17 778**
1996	18 992	22 477	17 785	20 393	17 891	**17 994**
1997	19 629	23 397	18 143	20 696	18 459	**18 369**
1998	20 353	23 826	18 787	21 145	18 925	**18 820**
1999	20 992	23 942	19 624	21 440	19 291	**19 229**
2000	21 591	24 364	20 321	22 025	19 817	**19 806**
2001	21 721	24 577	20 562	22 263	20 127	**20 024**

http://dx.doi.org/10.1787/456125276116

Table 1c. **Per Capita GDP in 4 West European Countries and Average WEC, 1500-1868**
(1990 international Geary-Khamis dollars)

	Ireland[a]	Greece	Portugal	Spain	13 small WEC	29 WEC
1500	526	433	606	661	612	**771**
1600	615	483	740	853	698	**890**
1700	715	530	819	853	789	**998**
1820	877	641	923	1 008	956	**1 204**
1821						
1822						
1823						
1824						
1825						
1826						
1827						
1828						
1829						
1830						
1831						
1832						
1833						
1834						
1835						
1836						
1837						
1838						
1839						
1840						
1841						
1842						
1843						
1844						
1845						
1846						
1847						
1848						
1849						
1850		816	923	1 079	1 273	**1 574**
1851			991	1 089		
1852				1 133		
1853				1 136		
1854				1 150		
1855			919	1 202		
1856				1 163		
1857				1 132		
1858				1 153		
1859				1 200		
1860				1 236		
1861			883	1 248		
1862				1 252		
1863				1 277		
1864				1 274		
1865			891	1 230		
1866			920	1 290		
1867			941	1 283		
1868			945	1 149		

http://dx.doi.org/10.1787/456125276116

ISBN 92-64-02261-9 – © OECD 2006   444

Table 1c. **Per Capita GDP in 4 West European Countries and Average WEC, 1869-1918**
(1990 international Geary-Khamis dollars)

	Ireland[a]	Greece	Portugal	Spain	13 small WEC	29 WEC
1869			964	1 181		
1870	1 775	880	975	1 207	1 602	**1 960**
1871			933	1 298		
1872			954	1 473		
1873			988	1 598		
1874			966	1 459		
1875			959	1 496		
1876			932	1 519		
1877			969	1 668		
1878			964	1 618		
1879			959	1 520		
1880			947	1 646		
1881			970	1 679		
1882			992	1 692		
1883			1 008	1 720		
1884			1 034	1 716		
1885			1 052	1 661		
1886			1 100	1 617		
1887			1 114	1 585		
1888			1 118	1 641		
1889			1 088	1 630		
1890		1 178	1 128	1 624	2 028	**2 490**
1891			1 099	1 654		
1892			1 087	1 770		
1893			1 101	1 700		
1894			1 079	1 712		
1895			1 117	1 689		
1896			1 125	1 548		
1897			1 182	1 619		
1898			1 214	1 736		
1899			1 249	1 756		
1900		1 351	1 302	1 786	2 361	**2 893**
1901			1 269	1 901		
1902			1 266	1 833		
1903			1 273	1 829		
1904			1 279	1 810		
1905			1 233	1 777		
1906			1 231	1 851		
1907			1 249	1 896		
1908			1 219	1 957		
1909			1 208	1 977		
1910			1 228	1 895		
1911			1 242	2 017		
1912			1 257	1 989		
1913	2 736	1 592	1 250	2 056	2 830	**3 458**
1914			1 258	2 014	2 639	
1915			1 228	2 033	2 687	
1916			1 234	2 113	2 788	
1917			1 212	2 073	2 712	
1918			1 150	2 045	2 633	

a. Figures are shown here for Ireland 1500-1920 for information. They are not included in the total because the UK figures already include the whole of Ireland for 1500-1920, thereafter only the Northern Ireland province.

http://dx.doi.org/10.1787/456125276116

Table 1c. **Per Capita GDP in 4 West European Countries and Average WEC, 1919-1969**
(1990 international Geary-Khamis dollars)

	Ireland [b]	Greece	Portugal	Spain	13 small WEC	29 WEC
1919			1 173	2 044	2 490	
1920			1 229	2 177	2 536	
1921	2 533	1 918	1 290	2 212	2 402	3 130
1922	2 598	1 963	1 430	2 284	2 749	3 372
1923	2 575	1 988	1 473	2 290	2 696	3 314
1924	2 569	2 057	1 401	2 331	2 894	3 539
1925	2 573	2 140	1 446	2 451	3 032	3 706
1926	2 572	2 180	1 419	2 417	3 049	3 723
1927	2 653	2 220	1 648	2 600	3 171	3 880
1928	2 737	2 234	1 470	2 584	3 294	4 013
1929	2 824	2 342	1 610	2 739	3 366	4 111
1930	2 897	2 258	1 571	2 620	3 291	4 014
1931	2 972	2 134	1 631	2 529	3 101	3 793
1932	2 885	2 289	1 643	2 559	3 198	3 675
1933	2 800	2 395	1 732	2 486	3 087	3 779
1934	2 882	2 418	1 784	2 556	3 198	3 909
1935	2 966	2 480	1 669	2 583	3 320	4 045
1936	3 052	2 455	1 523	2 072	3 462	4 162
1937	2 957	2 769	1 757	1 808	3 620	4 317
1938	3 052	2 677	1 747	1 790	3 697	4 399
1939	3 052	2 638	1 749	1 915	3 891	4 624
1940	3 052	2 223	1 615	2 080	3 824	4 548
1941	3 052	1 874	1 747	2 030	3 874	4 589
1942	3 052	1 579	1 708	2 126	3 834	4 544
1943	3 052	1 327	1 806	2 188	3 832	4 542
1944	3 052	1 116	1 893	2 271	3 666	4 361
1945	3 019	938	1 804	2 102	3 188	3 806
1946	3 052	1 386	1 928	2 179	3 009	3 628
1947	3 092	1 763	2 071	2 198	3 171	3 824
1948	3 230	1 798	2 046	2 186	3 367	4 039
1949	3 404	1 869	2 057	2 155	3 620	4 319
1950	3 453	1 915	2 086	2 189	3 846	4 579
1951	3 544	2 062	2 168	2 386	3 722	4 816
1952	3 642	2 053	2 161	2 558	3 964	4 963
1953	3 747	2 309	2 298	2 528	4 090	5 186
1954	3 794	2 358	2 393	2 696	4 178	5 437
1955	3 920	2 514	2 475	2 778	4 375	5 740
1956	3 897	2 706	2 564	2 978	4 604	5 962
1957	3 914	2 859	2 659	3 046	4 737	6 181
1958	3 870	2 963	2 672	3 150	4 796	6 282
1959	4 038	3 040	2 794	3 050	4 923	6 530
1960	4 282	3 146	2 956	3 072	4 988	6 896
1961	4 508	3 393	3 119	3 436	5 169	7 203
1962	4 636	3 499	3 330	3 800	5 361	7 483
1963	4 821	3 841	3 504	4 151	5 585	7 767
1964	4 986	4 141	3 718	4 515	5 779	8 167
1965	5 051	4 509	3 992	4 762	6 135	8 441
1966	5 080	4 749	4 164	5 060	6 379	8 686
1967	5 352	4 951	4 481	5 334	6 579	8 936
1968	5 770	5 266	4 873	5 588	6 739	9 355
1969	6 089	5 766	4 987	6 032	7 154	9 825

b.   From 1921 the figures refer to the Irish Republic.

http://dx.doi.org/10.1787/456125276116

Table 1c. **Per Capita GDP in 4 West European Countries and Average WEC, 1970-2001**
(1990 international Geary-Khamis dollars)

	Ireland	Greece	Portugal	Spain	13 small WEC	29 WEC
1970	6 199	6 211	5 473	6 319	7 399	**10 195**
1971	6 354	6 624	5 871	6 618	7 841	**10 465**
1972	6 663	7 400	6 355	7 099	8 256	**10 860**
1973	6 867	7 655	7 063	7 661	8 627	**11 416**
1974	7 042	7 350	7 048	8 149	8 560	**11 611**
1975	7 316	7 722	6 517	8 346	8 357	**11 521**
1976	7 302	8 105	6 814	8 599	8 900	**11 983**
1977	7 795	8 255	7 166	8 833	9 415	**12 289**
1978	8 250	8 695	7 340	9 023	9 830	**12 621**
1979	8 366	8 904	7 733	9 068	10 221	**13 041**
1980	8 541	8 971	8 044	9 203	10 436	**13 197**
1981	8 716	8 896	8 114	9 186	10 582	**13 185**
1982	8 821	8 876	8 280	9 293	10 834	**13 270**
1983	8 740	8 860	8 255	9 478	11 026	**13 491**
1984	9 056	9 058	8 089	9 571	11 525	**13 794**
1985	9 306	9 304	8 306	9 722	11 858	**14 113**
1986	9 265	9 425	8 641	9 998	12 381	**14 476**
1987	9 698	9 357	9 185	10 520	12 824	**14 857**
1988	10 234	9 763	9 868	11 046	13 453	**15 406**
1989	10 880	10 086	10 372	11 582	14 080	**15 856**
1990	11 818	9 988	10 826	12 055	14 452	**15 966**
1991	11 969	10 172	11 095	12 294	14 784	**16 152**
1992	12 277	10 170	11 310	12 351	14 952	**16 256**
1993	12 538	9 952	11 136	12 183	15 424	**16 129**
1994	13 198	10 105	11 385	12 437	15 805	**16 517**
1995	14 445	10 290	11 700	12 756	16 145	**16 860**
1996	15 472	10 511	12 097	13 045	16 557	**17 097**
1997	16 978	10 870	12 557	13 562	17 192	**17 502**
1998	18 233	11 212	13 106	14 129	17 847	**17 974**
1999	19 981	11 571	13 548	14 696	18 501	**18 413**
2000	22 015	12 044	14 022	15 269	19 401	**19 002**
2001	23 201	12 511	14 229	15 659	19 859	**19 256**

http://dx.doi.org/10.1787/456125276116

HS–2: WESTERN OFFSHOOTS: 1500–2001
(Australia, Canada, New Zealand, and the United States)

These four countries have experienced much more rapid growth since 1820 than Western Europe or the rest of the world. Between 1820 and 2001 their combined population increased 35–fold, compared with less than 3–fold in Western Europe. Their GDP increased 679–fold compared with 47–fold in Western Europe. Average per capita GDP (in terms of 1990 international dollars) rose from $1 202 to $26 943; Western Europe's from $1 204 to $19 256.

The disparity was due partly to huge differences in natural resource endowment. In 1820, land per head of population in France, Germany and the United Kingdom averaged 1.5 hectares compared to 240 hectares in the Western Offshoots. Their growth was facilitated by large–scale immigration, foreign investment and distance from foreign wars. They inherited institutional arrangements and traditions which gave them political stability, a fair degree of social mobility, relatively high levels of education, secure property rights, and a willingness to use market forces, which were more favourable to growth than was the case of the Iberian offshoots in Latin America.

Table 2-1. **Population and GDP of Australia, 1700-1870**

	Population (000)			GDP (million 1990 international $)			Per capita GDP (international $)		
	European	Aboriginal	Total	European	Aboriginal	Total	European	Aboriginal	Average
1700	0	450	450	0	180	180		400	400
1820	34	300	334	53	120	173	1 559	400	518
1830	70	260	330	176	104	280	2 514	400	848
1840	190	230	420	485	92	577	2 553	400	1 374
1850	405	200	605	1 115	80	1 195	2 951	400	1 975
1860	1 146	180	1 326	3 766	72	3 838	3 349	400	2 894
1870	1 620	155	1 775	5 748	62	5 810	3 548	400	3 273

Table 2-2. **Population and GDP of the United States, 1700-1870**

	Population (000)			GDP (million 1990 international $)			Per capita GDP (international $)		
	European and African	Indigenous	Total	European and African	Indigenous	Total	European and African	Indigenous	Average
1700	250	750	1 000	227	300	527	909	400	527
1820	9 656	325	9 981	12 418	130	12 548	1 286	400	1 257
1830	12 951	289	13 240	18 103	116	18 219	1 398	400	1 376
1840	17 187	257	17 444	27 591	103	27 694	1 605	400	1 588
1850	23 352	228	23 580	42 492	91	42 583	1 820	400	1 806
1860	31 636	203	31 839	69 265	81	69 346	2 189	400	2 178
1870	40 061	180	40 241	98 302	72	98 374	2 454	400	2 445

http://dx.doi.org/10.1787/456125276116

In the past, most measures of their performance have concentrated on the economies created by European settlement, and disregarded the fact that they displaced and destroyed indigenous economies whose output and populations contracted. I have attempted to provide a crude measure of this disruptive impact up to 1870, estimating what Noel Butlin called a "multicultural" estimate of GDP. For the indigenous economies the population figures are rough and the per capita GDP estimates are stylised. For the settler economies the estimates are at least as good as those for Western Europe.

Australia: Australia has a distinguished record of national income measurement. It was the first country with official estimates.. They were started in 1886 by Timothy Coghlan (1857–1926), government statistician for New South Wales who published estimates of the *Wealth and Progress of New South Wales* as well as a *Statistical Abstract for the Seven Colonies of Australasia* covering New Zealand and the six colonies which became the constituent states of Australia. Publication was discontinued in 1905 when he accepted a diplomatic post as agent general for New South Wales in London, and official national accounts did not reappear until 1946. Bryan Haig is the custodian of the Coghlan archive, and has written an as yet unpublished memoir on Coghlan's work "The First Official National Accounting Estimates" (see also Heinz Arndt, "A Pioneer of National Income Estimates", *Economic Journal*, December, 1949).

In 1938, Colin Clark (1905–89) and John Crawford (1910-84) published estimates of income and product for the 1920s and 30s, annual estimates of real income for 1914–39, and rough estimates of productivity for some years back to 1886 (see their *National Income of Australia*, Angus and Robertson, Sydney, 1938). Clark used this material in the first edition of *Conditions of Economic Progress*, 1940, pp. 84–5, improved on it in the 1951 edition, pp. 140–1, and modified his estimates showing faster growth of real product for 1914–38 in the 1957 edition, pp. 90–7 (see Table 2–4).

Noel Butlin (1921–91) published a continuous stream of studies on the quantitative economic history of Australia from 1946 onwards (see Graeme Snooks, "Life and Work of Noel George Butlin", *Australian Economic History Review*, September 1991). He was an admirer of Kuznets and much of his work is in the Kuznetsian tradition with meticulous indication of sources and transparent explanation of methodology. His first major book (1962) provided annual estimates of GDP, GNP, net domestic and net national product from 1861 to1938/9. It showed nominal and real value added by industry of origin at factor cost and market prices, together with very detailed estimates of capital formation and the balance of payments on current and capital account. It contained more than 200 pages describing his sources and estimating procedures, and 274 tables.

As Butlin's work covered the whole span of Australian history, I relied heavily on his estimates in Maddison (1995 and 2001). 1820 to 1828 GDP movement was derived from N.G. Butlin, "Our 200 Years", *Queensland Calendar*, 1988. 1828–60 annual GDP volume movement by eight industries of origin at 1848–50 prices from N.G. Butlin, "Contours of the Australian Economy 1788–1860", *Australian Economic History Review*, Sept. 1986, pp. 96–147. Annual GDP movement 1861–1938/9, by 13 industries of origin in 1910/11 prices from N.G. Butlin, *Australian Domestic Product, Investment and Foreign Borrowing 1861–1938/39*, Cambridge, 1962, pp. 460–l; amended as indicated in N.G. Butlin, *Investment in Australian Economic Development l861–1900*, Cambridge, 1964, p. 453, with revised deflator for 1911–1938/9 shown in M.W. Butlin, *A Preliminary Annual Database 1900/01 to 1973/74*, Discussion Paper 7701, Reserve Bank of Australia, May 1977, p.41. 1938/9–1950 real expenditure aggregates in 1966/7 prices from M.W. Butlin, p. 85. 1860–1 link derived by using the GDP deflator in W. Vamplew (ed.), *Australians: Historical Statistics*, Fairfax, Broadway, 1987, p. 219. 1950 onwards from OECD sources. Where necessary, GDP figures were adjusted to a calendar year basis. Population 1788–1949 from Butlin (1988), adjusted to a calendar year basis from 1870. Butlin's estimate of the pre–contact population is much higher than is conventional (1.1 million instead of 300 000). His analysis of the destructive impact of white settlement makes it difficult to accept the conventional estimate, but his depopulation coefficient seems exaggerated. As a compromise, I assumed a pre–contact population of 450 000, 1820–70 from L.R. Smith, *The Aboriginal Population of Australia*, ANU, Canberra, 1980, p. 210.

Recently, Bryan Haig rejected Butlin's estimates *en bloc* (see his "New Estimates of Australian GDP: 1861–1948/49", *Australian Economic History Review*, March 2001, pp. 1–34). He argues that Butlin's approach (deflation of nominal estimates of value added by price indices) is "unworkable" because of the weakness of existing price indices, and the inherent difficulty of improving them; Butlin "relied on existing series of wholesale prices, wage rates and retail price indices", and "no useful research has been undertaken by academics on Australian price indices since Butlin produced his estimates". Butlin did not take his price indices from the shelf, but constructed ten special deflators for sectors of GDP, and eight for components of capital investment. Butlin's deflators are imperfect but improvable. Australian academics have not abandoned the field (see Ian McLean and S.J. Woodland "Consumer Prices in Australia, 1850–1914" *Working Paper 92–4*, Economics Dept, University of Adelaide, 1992), and Australia seems better endowed with historical price statistics than many other countries (see Shergold's chapter in Vamplew,1987).

Haig's second fundamental objection is that Butlin's results are "unreasonable" as they show contours of development which conflict with traditional views and generated a new interpretation of Australian economic history. I see no harm in this. It is up to those who disagree with Butlin to prove him wrong.

Table 2-3. **Alternative Measures of Australian Sector Growth and Structure, 1861-1938/9**

| | Confrontation of Butlin (1962) and Haig (2001) Estimates | | | | | | | |
| | Annual Growth % 1861-1911 | | 1891 level: million 1891 pounds | | Annual Growth % 1911/12-1938/9 | | 1938/9 level: million 1938/9 pounds | |
	Butlin	Haig	Butlin	Haig	Butlin	Haig	Butlin	Haig
Pastoral	4.81	4.30	29.5	28.7	1.39	0.96	74.5	63.2
Agriculture	3.39	3.81	10.5	15.3	1.13	2.38	41.7	41.2
Dairy	3.69	3.96	9.7	6.8	3.54	2.64	49.3	40.8
Mining	1.83	1.98	11.3	12.0	-2.21	-0.60	27.9	27.1
Manufacturing	6.13	3.72	21.3	29.5	2.01	2.43	157.0	198.0
Construction	3.01	2.37	28.4	15.1	0.34	2.27	56.2	65.0
Water Transport	4.56	n.a.	3.6	n.a.	-0.41	n.a.	7.9	n.a.
Public Undertakings	5.88	n.a.	6.8	n.a.	1.06	n.a.	45.5	n.a.
Public services	1.99	n.a.	8.5	n.a.	2.62	n.a.	40.7	n.a.
Finance	1.55	n.a.	6.7	n.a.	2.73	n.a.	21.1	n.a.
Distribution	4.33	n.a.	23.9	n.a.	2.40	n.a.	159.8	n.a.
Other services	3.16	n.a.	22.5	n.a.	0.89	n.a.	91.0	n.a.
Total Services	**3.63**	**3.33**	**72.0**	**52.0**	**1.77**	**2.35**	**366.0**	**291.0**
Imputed Rent	3.34	3.27	21.9	18.3	2.20	2.19	72.0	60.0
Unallocated	4.91	n.a.	1.8	0.0	2.93	n.a.	-4.1	0.0
GDP	**3.67**	**3.34**	**202.8**	**177.8**	**1.58**	**2.09**	**840.5**	**797.0**
GDP New South Wales	n.a.	4.00	n.a.	57.3				
GDP Victoria	n.a.	2.06	n.a.	53.3				

Source: Columns 1 and 5 from Butlin, pp. 160-1. Butlin shows fiscal years (beginning July 1st) from 1901/2 onwards, Haig from 1911/2 onwards. 1911 calendar year for Butlin derived by averaging his estimates for 1910/11 and 1911/12. Columns 2 and 6 from Haig, pp. 28-34. Columns 3 and 7 from Butlin, pp. 10-11. Columns 4 and 8 from Haig, pp. 28-34.

http://dx.doi.org/10.1787/456125276116

Table 2-4. Alternative Estimates of Australian Real GDP, calendar years 1861-1900

(million 1990 international Geary-Khamis dollars)

	Haig	Butlin		Haig	Butlin	Clark
1861	4 453	4 188	1901	17 764	16 201	
1862	4 625	4 133	1902	16 905	16 366	
1863	4 750	4 271	1903	18 436	17 661	
1864	4 867	4 739	1904	17 733	18 846	
1865	5 132	4 711	1905	19 038	19 066	
1866	5 539	5 014	1906	19 741	20 361	
1867	5 515	5 621	1907	19 936	21 187	
1868	5 929	5 896	1908	20 694	21 904	
1869	6 101	5 951	1909	21 608	23 695	
1870	5 898	6 392	1910	22 662	25 348	
1871	6 210	6 144	1911	22 967	25 541	
1872	6 484	6 805	1912	23 764	26 147	
1873	6 656	7 522	1913	24 861	27 552	
1874	7 187	7 770	1914	24 797	25 430	21 294
1875	7 398	8 624	1915	24 341	23 943	20 782
1876	7 593	8 596	1916	24 172	25 623	19 902
1877	7 796	8 954	1917	23 716	26 202	17 519
1878	7 976	9 809	1918	23 155	26 340	16 138
1879	8 249	9 946	1919	24 488	26 092	17 819
1880	8 421	10 470	1920	25 534	28 075	19 969
1881	8 929	11 241	1921	26 818	30 831	22 263
1882	9 702	10 608	1922	28 225	31 051	25 058
1883	10 694	12 178	1923	29 579	31 685	27 275
1884	11 132	12 233	1924	31 524	34 109	29 324
1885	11 296	13 032	1925	33 002	35 239	30 872
1886	11 702	13 197	1926	33 792	34 798	32 587
1887	12 265	14 603	1927	34 305	34 716	34 068
1888	12 546	14 685	1928	34 368	34 164	34 759
1889	13 702	15 953	1929	33 662	33 834	34 848
1890	13 772	15 402	1930	30 458	32 181	33 411
1891	13 890	16 586	1931	28 416	32 720	31 406
1892	13 640	14 547	1932	30 025	31 878	31 640
1893	13 663	13 748	1933	32 110	33 696	31 199
1894	13 819	14 217	1934	33 810	34 991	34 603
1895	14 015	13 418	1935	35 798	36 424	35 427
1896	14 288	14 437	1936	37 414	38 160	36 195
1897	15 147	13 638	1937	39 306	40 336	37 509
1898	15 749	15 760	1938	40 639	40 639	40 639
1899	16 592	15 760				
1900	17 186	16 697				

Source: Haig, pp. 28-30. He gives calendar year estimates for 1861-1911, fiscal years (beginning July 1st) for 1911/12 onwards. I adjusted the latter to a calendar year basis. For 1910/11, he presents no figures for the primary sector or GDP. To make the link between his two temporal segments, I used the 1910/11-1911/12 primary movement shown by Butlin. Clark (1957), pp. 90-1, real product adjusted to calendar year basis.

http://dx.doi.org/10.1787/456125276116

A more legitimate objection is that Butlin probably exaggerated the long boom from 1861 to 1891 by understating manufacturing employment and output at the beginning of the period. This is a point which Haig should have tackled more rigorously, showing his own employment estimates for Australian manufacturing and comparing them with those of Butlin (see Butlin and Dowie, "Estimates of Australian Work Force and Employment, 1861–1961", *Australian Economic History Review*, September, 1969). Instead he presents a comparison for the state of Victoria.

Haig's alternative to the Butlin approach is to use quantitative measures of output for seven sectors of GDP. This is a desirable crosscheck, but for 1861–1911 Haig does not have quantitative measures for 70 per cent of GDP, and uses employment (available in direct form only for NSW and Victoria) as a proxy. He amalgamates his sector estimates using 1891 output weights which Coghlan published in 1893. Although he makes a few comparisons between his results and those of Butlin they are limited and casual. A further problem is that Haig describes his estimating procedure parsimoniously in five pages whereas Butlin provided 200. Table 2–4 facilitates systematic confrontation of their sector growth rates and structure (Butlin's value added and Coghlan's gross output). Haig relies heavily on measures for New South Wales and Victoria to fill gaps in information for Australia as a whole, whereas Butlin covers a wider and perhaps more representative range of states. For 1861–1911, Haig's estimates imply per capita growth of 1.6 per cent a year in NSW, 0.42 in Victoria, and 0.57 per cent in Australia.

For 1911–12 to 1938–39, Haig's estimates are of better quality. He has quantity indicators for manufacturing from his "Manufacturing Output and Productivity, 1910 to 1948/9", *Australian Economic History Review*, September, 1975. For the rest of the economy he was able to adjust his employment indicators for productivity change. The weights from his "1938/9 National Income Estimates", *Australian Economic History Review*, 1967, p. 176, are also more satisfactory. I have now adopted Haig's estimates for 1911–38, but would like to see more detail of his evidence before adopting his estimates for 1861–1911.

All the above refers to the white settler economy. In the 1980s Butlin made a major innovation in proposing a "multicultural" estimate. In 1983 he published a masterpiece of demographic modelling (*Our Original Aggression*, Allen & Unwin, Sydney and London) analysing the impact of white settlement on the Aboriginal population and its economy, with detailed specification of the different vectors of mortality. This was similar in intent to studies by Borah and others on the impact of European conquest on the Americas, but Butlin was much more rigorous. His analysis of Aboriginal history was enlarged in *Economics and the Dreamtime: A Hypothetical History,* Cambridge University Press, 1993. A further posthumous work *Forming A Colonial Economy: Australia 1810–1850*, Cambridge University Press, appeared in 1994.

Canada: GDP and population of French–Canadian settlers in 1700 derived from Morris Altman, "Economic Growth in Canada, 1695–1739: Estimates and Analysis", *William and Mary Quarterly*, October 1988. 1820–50 per capita product of non–indigenous population assumed to grow at the same rate as in the United States. GDP for 1851, 1860 and 1870 from O.J. Firestone, "Canada's Changing Economy in the Second Half of the 19th Century", NBER, New York, 1957. 1870–1926 GDP from M.C. Urquhart and Associates, ed., *Gross National Product, Canada 1870–1926: The Derivation of the Estimates*, McGill Queen's University Press, Montreal, 1993, pp. 11–12 and 24–5. 1926–60 from Statistics Canada, *National Income and Expenditure Accounts*, vol. 1, *The Annual Estimates 1926–1974*, Ottawa, 1975, p. 323. 1960 onwards from OECD sources. 1820–1948 GDP raised by 1.32 per cent and population by 2.6 to include Newfoundland, acquired in 1949. Indigenous population before 1820 from same sources as for the United States. Population 1820–50 supplied by Marvin McInnis; 1850–1950 from M.C. Urquhart and K.A.H. Buckley, *Historical Statistics of Canada*, Cambridge, 1965, p. 14.

Table 2-5. **Population and GDP of Canada and New Zealand, 1700-1870**

	Population (000)			GDP (million 1990 international $)			Per capita GDP (international $)		
	European	Indigenous	Total	European	Indigenous	Total	European	Indigenous	Average
				Canada					
1700	15	185	200	12	74	86	800	400	430
1820	741	75	816	708	30	738	955	400	904
1830	1 101	68	1 169	1 142	27	1 169	1 038	400	1 000
1840	1 636	61	1 697	1 948	24	1 972	1 191	400	1 162
1850	2 430	55	2 485	3 282	22	3 304	1 351	400	1 330
1860	3 319	50	3 369	4 867	20	4 887	1 466	400	1 451
1870	3 736	45	3 781	6 389	18	6 407	1 710	400	1 695
				New Zealand					
1700	0	100	100	0	40	40		400	400
1820	0	100	100	0	40	40		400	400
1830	0	100	100	0	40	40		400	400
1840	0	70	70	0	28	28		400	400
1850	25	65	90	77	26	103	3 080	400	1 144
1860	76	56	132	270	22	292	3 553	400	2 212
1870	243	48	291	883	19	902	3 633	400	3 100

http://dx.doi.org/10.1787/456125276116

New Zealand: GNP, 1870–1939, in 1910/11 prices from K. Rankin, "New Zealand's Gross National Product: 1859–1939, *Review of Income and Wealth*, March 1992, pp. 60–1. These are proxy estimates based on regression involving assumptions about velocity of circulation, nominal money supply, a variety of price indices (wholesale, export, import, farm and non–farm) and population. 1939–50 from C. Clark, *The Conditions of Economic Progress*, third edition, Macmillan, London, 1957, pp. 171–2 (which Clark derived by deflating official estimates in current prices). 1950 onwards from OECD sources. GDP estimates are for calendar years to 1939 and fiscal years starting April 1st thereafter. For 1820–70 I assumed per capita income of Maoris to have been 400 international 1990 dollars. Per capita GDP of white settlers was assumed to have grown 0.8 per cent a year from 1850 to 1870 (the rate shown by Rankin for 1859–70). Maori population 1820–1919 and non–Maoris 1820–60 from G.R. Hawke, *The Making of New Zealand*, Cambridge University Press, 1985, pp. 10–11 and 20; 1861–1919 non–Maoris from Rankin (1992), pp. 58–9. 1920–49 population from UN, *Demographic Yearbook*, 1960, pp. 148–50.

United States: GDP Estimates

1700–1820: Robert Gallman, "The Pace and Pattern of American Economic Growth", in L. Davis and Associates (eds.), *American Economic Growth: An Economist's History of the United States*, Harper and Row, New York, 1972, estimated per capita growth in net national product of 0.42 per cent a year between 1710 and 1840 (taking the mid–point of the range he suggested for 1710). His figures refer to the neo–European economy of the white and black population. Adjusting for the faster growth of their per capita income in 1820–40 (see below), Gallman's estimate implies a per capita growth of about 0.29 per cent a year from 1700 to 1820 (from a level of $909 to $1 286). Assuming an unchanged per capita income of $400 a year in the indigenous hunter–gatherer economy, the average level for the whole population would have risen from $527 in 1700 to $1 257 in 1820.

P.C. Mancall and Weiss, "Was Econonomic Growth Likely in British North America?", *Journal of Economic History*, March 1999, made a "multicultural" estimate which shows much slower growth for the eighteenth century. I consider their growth rate to be much too slow, given the huge change in the relative size of the neo–European and indigenous populations. They show no figures for total population or GDP, so it is not possible to replicate their multicultural measure. They make no reference to the Gallman estimate I used.

1820–2001

Modern GDP estimation relies heavily on the massive contribution of Simon Kuznets. He took over the NBER research in this field around 1930, and also prepared the first official estimates, *National Income 1929–32*, which were transmitted to the Finance Committee of the US Senate by the Dept. of Commerce in January 1934. This showed the flows of different categories of income broken down by industry together with corresponding employment estimates prepared by Robert Nathan. A cost of living index was provided as a tentative deflator, together with very fully documented appendices with sources. This approach was further elaborated in S. Kuznets, *National Income and Its Composition 1919–38*, NBER, New York, 1941, which contained estimates (at current and 1929 prices) of the industrial distribution of different categories of income (wage, property, and entrepreneurial).

Kuznets also derived estimates by category of expenditure for 1919 onwards by the "commodity flow" method, i.e. he used census and other information on production, and determined what part represented the final flow to consumers and capital formation. These flows from producers were given distributive mark–ups to reflect final sales values. Rougher estimates were made for services. This work was sponsored by the Committee on Credit and Banking which was interested in commodity flows as a counterpart to its interest in flows of financial resources. The details of this approach are described in S. Kuznets, *Commodity Flow and Capital Formation*, NBER, New York, 1938. The expenditure estimates were extended back to 1869 in S. Kuznets, L. Epstein and E. Jenks, *National Product Since 1869*, NBER, New York, 1946 (but these referred to overlapping decades and were not annual). This extension back to 1869 relied very heavily on W.H. Shaw, *Value of Commodity Output Since 1869*, NBER, New York, 1947, who used the same procedure for making commodity flow estimates of values as Kuznets (1938) did. Shaw also supplied price deflators. Estimates in the same form can also be found (in an analytical context) in S. Kuznets, *Income and Wealth of the United States: Trends and Structure*, Income and Wealth Series II, Bowes and Bowes, Cambridge, 1952. This study contains an annex on the estimates for 1800 to 1870 by Martin and King. Kuznets had a poor opinion of these, and although he did not produce alternative estimates, he gave a clear indication of the direction in which they were biased, and some clues for constructing estimates with limited information.

The final version of Kuznets' massive work appeared in his *Capital in the American Economy*, NBER, Princeton, 1961. Here he published annual estimates of GNP by type of expenditure in current and in 1929 dollars (pp. 555–8) back to 1889. As the underlying census information was inadequate before 1889, he showed only 5–year moving averages back to 1871 (pp. 559–64). He had three variants of GNP with different assumptions about which products were intermediate.

The US Department of Commerce did not adopt the Kuznets' definitions of the scope of GNP. He explained his disagreement with their procedures in S. Kuznets, "Discussion of the New Department of Commerce Income Series", *Review of Economics and Statistics*, August 1948. The official side was not convinced by his arguments, see M. Gilbert, G. Jaszi, E.F. Denison and C.F. Schwartz, "Objectives of National Income Measurement: A Reply to Professor Kuznets" in the same publication.

The Kuznets estimates were published in transparent form with the full scholarly apparatus characteristic of the NBER. It was therefore possible for John Kendrick (who in any case had access to the worksheets) to convert the Kuznets annual estimates of GNP (variant III) back to 1889 (with some minor adjustment) by type of expenditure to a Dept. of Commerce basis, see J.W. Kendrick, *Productivity Trends in the United States*, NBER, Princeton, 1961, pp. 298–9. Like Kuznets, Kendrick used fixed 1929 weights for his volume estimates, but he also gave a chain weighted alternative, which for 1889–1929 shows a growth rate of 3.82 per cent a year compared with 3.68 for his fixed weight index for the private domestic economy (p. 327). For 1869–1889 Kendrick presented only decade averages, as it seemed probable that they exaggerated growth. Kendrick (1961) augmented the NBER sectoral production studies (by Barger, Fabricant and others) to show annual movements in output or value added on an annual basis back to 1869 in many cases. However, he did not construct an estimate of GDP by industry of origin. His aggregate (pp. 302–3) covers 9 production sectors in combination with total private GDP by type of expenditure. The bulk of private service activity was derived as a residual. Even then his estimates were presented only for 10 benchmark years. Thus we have the paradox that the United States is one of the few countries where the construction of historical accounts by industry of origin has been neglected, though the statistical basis for such estimates is better than elsewhere.

1820–40: For this period the evidence is still rather weak, and one must still rely on the kind of reasoning which Kuznets (1952) first applied, and which can be found in P.A. David, "The Growth of Real Product in the United States before 1840: New Evidence, Controlled Conjectures", *Journal of Economic History*, June 1967, and more recently in T. Weiss, "US Labor Force Estimates and Economic Growth, 1800–1860", in R.E. Gallman and J.J. Wallis, eds., *American Economic Growth and Standards of Living Before the Civil War*, University of Chicago Press, 1992, p. 27. I used a variant of the Kuznets–David inferential approach. I calculated agricultural productivity 1820–40, taking agricultural value added (output of crops and livestock products plus change in livestock inventories, minus intermediate products consumed) from M.W. Towne and W.D. Rasmussen, "Farm Gross Product and Gross Investment in the Nineteenth Century", in Parker, ed. (1960), p. 25, and agricultural employment from Weiss (1992), p. 51. Agricultural productivity (thus measured) grew by .62 per cent a year from 1820–40. Like Kuznets and David, I assumed that productivity growth in the rest of the economy was faster (1 per cent a year). Although service productivity growth is likely to have been modest, the assumption of faster growth in non–agriculture seems warranted as K.L. Sokoloff found manufacturing productivity to have grown by 2.2 per cent a year, see his "Productivity Growth in Manufacturing During Early Industrialisation: Evidence from the American Northeast, 1820–1860", in S.L. Engerman and R.E. Gallmann, *Long Term Factors in American Economic Growth*, Chicago, 1986, p. 695.

1840–69: derived from Robert Gallman who revised and extended the Kuznets estimates backwards (variant I) using the same commodity flow approach and techniques of presentation. He first estimated value added (in 1879 prices) for agriculture, mining, manufacturing and construction for benchmark years, see R.E. Gallman, "Commodity Output, 1839–1899", in W.N. Parker, *Trends in the American Economy in the Nineteenth Century*, NBER, Princeton, 1960, p. 43. He used these results, census, and other information to construct his estimates of GNP by type of expenditure (four–way breakdown of consumption and three–way breakdown of capital formation) in 1860 prices, see R.E. Gallman, "Gross National Product in the United States 1834–1909", in D.S. Brady, ed., *Output, Employment and Productivity in the United States after 1800*, NBER, New York, 1966, p. 26. Unfortunately he provided figures only for five benchmark years, 1839, 1844, 1849, 1854, and 1859 and for overlapping decades from 1834–43 to 1899–1908, and did not publish the full detail of his procedures.

1869–90: from N.S. Balke and R.J. Gordon, "The Estimation of Prewar Gross National Product: Methodology and New Evidence", *Journal of Political Economy*, February 1989, p. 84. They revamped the Gallman–Kendrick–Kuznets commodity flow estimates, using additional information on construction, transport and communications, to provide annual estimates of nominal GNP, real GNP and a GNP deflator. For 1869–90, their average annual estimate for real GNP growth was 4.16 per cent a year, which is lower than the unpublished Kendrick figure of 5.44 per cent, or the 5.55 per cent of Kuznets. As both Kuznets and Kendrick thought their 1869 level (as described above) was too low, the Balke–Gordon estimate seems acceptable.

1890–1929: GDP volume movement with 1929 weights from J.W. Kendrick (1961), pp. 298–9.

1929–50: GDP movement at 1987 prices as shown by the Bureau of Economic Analysis (BEA) in *National Income and Product Accounts of the United States*, vol. 1, US Dept. of Commerce, Washington, D.C., February 1993.

1950–2001: 1950–59 from "GDP and other Major NIPA Series, 1929–97", *Survey of Current Business*, August 1998; 1959–90 GDP movement and 1990 level in 1990 prices from E.P. Seskin, "Improved Estimates of the National Income and Product Accounts for 1958–98: Results of the Comprehensive Revision", *Survey of Current Business*, December 1999; 1990–8 from S.K.S. Lum, B.C. Moyer and R.E. Yuscavage, "Improved Estimates of Gross Product by Industry for 1947–98", *Survey of Current Business*, June 2000, p. 46; 1998–2001 from E.P. Seskin and S.M. McCulla, "Annual Revision of the National Income and Product Accounts", *Survey of Current Business*, August 2002, p. 11. Figures for years before 1960 are adjusted to include Alaska and Hawaii, which added 0.294 per cent to 1960 GDP (see *Survey of Current Business*, December 1980, p. 17).

Population: Indigenous population before 1820 from R. Thornton, *American Indian Holocaust and Survival: A Population History Since 1492*, University of Oklahoma, 1987 and D.H. Ubelaker, "Prehistoric New World Population Size: Historical Review and Current Appraisal of North American Estimates, *American Journal of Physical Anthropology*, 1976, pp. 661–6, as indicated in Maddison (2001), pp. 232–3. White and black population, 1630–1949 from *Historical Statistics of the United States, Colonial Times to 1970*, US Department of Commerce, 1975, pp. 8 and 1168. The figures refer to the present territory of the United States. 1820–1949 increased by 0.39 per cent to include Alaska and Hawaii, incorporated in l950. 1950–2001 from International Programs Center, US Bureau of the Census. In 1820, the territory of the United States was half of what it is today. The increase was due to the acquisition of Texas, California and other Western lands from Mexico between 1845 and 1853. The settlement of the border with Canada brought in the territory which is now Idaho, Oregon and Washington in 1846. These territories were sparsely settled and consisted very largely of the indigenous population which was not separately specified in US censuses before 1860. Before 1890 the censuses excluded those living in Indian territory or reservations. I added 325 000 for the indigenous population in 1820 and 180 000 for 1850, (see Maddison, 1995, p. 97).

Three Recent Modifications in US Official Measures of GDP

Annual Chain Indices for GDP: The official figures I use for 1950 onwards are based on a chain index as described in J.S. Landefeld and R.P. Parker, "BEA's Chain Indexes, Time Series and Measures of Long Term Growth", *Survey of Current Business*, May 1997. This is an index where the weights change every year. The annual GDP volume change is measured by a Fisher index which is the geometric mean of two indices, one of which (a Laspeyres index) uses the prices of year t-1 as weights, and the other (a Paasche index) uses prices of year t. Annual changes calculated this way are multiplied together to form a time series. This procedure is a sharp break with the tradition of the Department of Commerce which for six decades used a fixed weight for the whole period it covered (though the chosen year was changed quinquennially). Before making the switch, BEA experimented with alternative weighting systems. A.H. Young, "Alternative Measures of Changes in Real Output and Prices, Quarterly Estimates for 1959–92", *Survey of Current Business*, March 1993 presented three alternative indices for 1959–92. The old fixed weight index showed a real GDP growth rate of 2.88 a year, the annual Fisher chain index 3.12 per cent and a Fisher index with weights changed every 5 years 3.16 a year. In Maddison (1995) I used the third measure because it was closer to the procedure used in other OECD countries at that time. BEA did not present these three options for earlier years as it announced. Instead it made a sudden switch to chain indexation back to 1929. The new measure shows a GDP growth of 3.5 per cent a year for 1929–50, the traditional measure 2.6 per cent. This is a much bigger difference between fixed and chain weights than Young found for 1959–92 or Kendrick for 1889–1929. Acceptance of the new measure for this period would involve a major reinterpretation of American economic history. It implies a GDP level in 1929 16 per cent lower than the old index and would lower the level for earlier years. If used as a link, it would imply a US level of labour productivity in 1913 below that in the United Kingdom. The new BEA index also changes the picture of the war and immediate postwar recovery. It seems hazardous to use it for 1929–50 without further investigation of the reasons why the new method had such a big impact. One must also remember that no other country uses a chain index technique for such a long period in the past.

Hedonic Indices for the New Economy: A major reason why BEA switched to chain indexation was its adoption of "hedonic" price indices for computers and peripherals in 1985 and extended use of this type of measure back to 1959. By the year 2000, the components of GDP deflated by this technique represented 18 per cent of the total (see J.S. Landefeld and B.T. Grimm, "A Note on the Impact of Hedonics and Computers on Real GDP", *Survey of Current Business*, December 2000). This technique imputes quality improvements by specifying computing power in terms of several characteristics, e.g. speed, memory etc. and estimating price change by regression. The manufacturers of computers were understandably helpful in suppying detail of these improved characteristics and the application of hedonic techniques to the measuerement of computer prices was in fact pioneered by IBM. The hedonic measure implied that prices dropped 32 per cent a year from 1994 onwards. If this rate had prevailed for the 1990s, it would mean that a consumer who spent $1 000 on a computer in 1990 and again in 2000, would be getting sixteen times as much for his money in the latter year. Hedonic weights (advocated since 1961 by Zvi Griliches) are perfectly respectable, but one can be a bit sceptical about the assumption that quality change was so large and monotonically positive. The hedonic techniques used by BEA imply a direct connection between computing power (speed, memory etc.) and computer output without considering the quality of the software that converts power to output. In addition, hedonic techniques assume competitive markets where prices accurately reflect consumer utility, but recent anti–trust cases suggest that this assumption may be unrealistic. One would like to see a more rigorous and detailed examination of alternatives and a smaller dose of euphoric reassurance that the results are robust. However, adoption of annual chain weights helped moderate the accelerative impact of hedonic indices on GDP growth.

Treatment of Computer Software as Investment: A third innovation which raised the level of GDP modestly and raised the growth rate, was the decision to treat computer software as investment rather than as an intermediate product. This practice was introduced in 1999 and applied retrospectively to 1959. The average service life for such investment is assumed (rather generously) to be 3–5 years (see BEA, "Recognition of Software as Investment in the US National Accounts", *OECD Meeting of National Accounts Experts*, September 1999). The change was recommended in the 1993 revision of the *System of National Accounts* of EU, IMF, OECD and World Bank, and has been adopted by other OECD countries. Given the fact that hedonic indexation already makes generous allowance for quality change in computers which derive in large part from improved software, there is an element of double–counting in the new procedure. It is also a little odd to treat this rapidly depreciating advance in knowledge as investment, whilst ignoring the more durable impact of scientific academies. However, the hallowed status of computer technology seems to be firmly esconced in most statistical offices.

Table 2a. **Population of Western Offshoots, 1500-1899**
(000 at mid-year)

	Australia	New Zealand	Canada	United States	4 Western Offshoots
1500	450	100	250	2 000	**2 800**
1600	450	100	250	1 500	**2 300**
1700	450	100	200	1 000	**1 750**
1820	334	100	816	9 981	**11 231**
1830	330	100	1 169	13 240	**14 839**
1840	420	70	1 697	17 444	**19 631**
1850	605	90	2 485	23 580	**26 760**
1860	1 326	132	3 369	31 839	**36 666**
1870	1 775	291	3 781	40 241	**46 088**
1871	1 675	306	3 801	41 098	**46 880**
1872	1 722	320	3 870	42 136	**48 048**
1873	1 769	335	3 943	43 174	**49 221**
1874	1 822	367	4 012	44 212	**50 413**
1875	1 874	406	4 071	45 245	**51 596**
1876	1 929	434	4 128	46 287	**52 778**
1877	1 995	450	4 184	47 325	**53 954**
1878	2 062	467	4 244	48 362	**55 135**
1879	2 127	494	4 312	49 400	**56 333**
1880	2 197	520	4 384	50 458	**57 559**
1881	2 269	539	4 451	51 743	**59 002**
1882	2 348	555	4 503	53 027	**60 433**
1883	2 447	574	4 560	54 311	**61 892**
1884	2 556	598	4 617	55 595	**63 366**
1885	2 650	614	4 666	56 879	**64 809**
1886	2 741	626	4 711	58 164	**66 242**
1887	2 835	640	4 760	59 448	**67 683**
1888	2 932	649	4 813	60 732	**69 126**
1889	3 022	656	4 865	62 016	**70 559**
1890	3 107	665	4 918	63 302	**71 992**
1891	3 196	674	4 972	64 612	**73 454**
1892	3 274	686	5 022	65 922	**74 904**
1893	3 334	705	5 072	67 231	**76 342**
1894	3 395	722	5 121	68 541	**77 779**
1895	3 460	735	5 169	69 851	**79 215**
1896	3 523	748	5 218	71 161	**80 650**
1897	3 586	764	5 269	72 471	**82 090**
1898	3 642	779	5 325	73 781	**83 527**
1899	3 691	794	5 383	75 091	**84 959**

http://dx.doi.org/10.1787/456125276116

Table 2a. **Population of Western Offshoots, 1900-1955**
(000 at mid-year)

	Australia	*New Zealand*	*Canada*	*United States*	*4 Western Offshoots*
1900	3 741	807	5 457	76 391	**86 396**
1901	3 795	824	5 536	77 888	**88 043**
1902	3 850	844	5 650	79 469	**89 813**
1903	3 896	867	5 813	80 946	**91 522**
1904	3 946	893	5 994	82 485	**93 318**
1905	4 004	919	6 166	84 147	**95 236**
1906	4 062	946	6 282	85 770	**97 060**
1907	4 127	969	6 596	87 339	**99 031**
1908	4 197	996	6 813	89 055	**101 061**
1909	4 278	1 024	6 993	90 845	**103 140**
1910	4 375	1 045	7 188	92 767	**105 375**
1911	4 500	1 067	7 410	94 234	**107 211**
1912	4 661	1 092	7 602	95 703	**109 058**
1913	4 821	1 122	7 852	97 606	**111 401**
1914	4 933	1 143	8 093	99 505	**113 674**
1915	4 971	1 152	8 191	100 941	**115 255**
1916	4 955	1 155	8 214	102 364	**116 688**
1917	4 950	1 152	8 277	103 817	**118 196**
1918	5 032	1 156	8 374	104 958	**119 520**
1919	5 193	1 195	8 548	105 473	**120 409**
1920	5 358	1 241	8 798	106 881	**122 278**
1921	5 461	1 275	9 028	108 964	**124 728**
1922	5 574	1 304	9 159	110 484	**126 521**
1923	5 697	1 326	9 256	112 387	**128 666**
1924	5 819	1 350	9 394	114 558	**131 121**
1925	5 943	1 382	9 549	116 284	**133 158**
1926	6 064	1 412	9 713	117 857	**135 046**
1927	6 188	1 437	9 905	119 502	**137 032**
1928	6 304	1 454	10 107	120 971	**138 836**
1929	6 396	1 471	10 305	122 245	**140 417**
1930	6 469	1 493	10 488	123 668	**142 118**
1931	6 527	1 514	10 657	124 633	**143 331**
1932	6 579	1 527	10 794	125 436	**144 336**
1933	6 631	1 540	10 919	126 180	**145 270**
1934	6 682	1 552	11 030	126 978	**146 242**
1935	6 732	1 562	11 136	127 859	**147 289**
1936	6 783	1 573	11 243	128 681	**148 280**
1937	6 841	1 587	11 341	129 464	**149 233**
1938	6 904	1 604	11 452	130 476	**150 436**
1939	6 971	1 627	11 570	131 539	**151 707**
1940	7 042	1 636	11 688	132 637	**153 003**
1941	7 111	1 629	11 818	133 922	**154 480**
1942	7 173	1 639	11 969	135 386	**156 167**
1943	7 236	1 633	12 115	137 272	**158 256**
1944	7 309	1 654	12 268	138 937	**160 168**
1945	7 389	1 688	12 404	140 474	**161 955**
1946	7 474	1 759	12 634	141 940	**163 807**
1947	7 578	1 797	12 901	144 688	**166 964**
1948	7 715	1 833	13 180	147 203	**169 931**
1949	7 919	1 871	13 469	149 770	**173 029**
1950	8 267	1 908	14 011	152 271	**176 458**
1951	8 511	1 947	14 331	154 878	**179 667**
1952	8 691	1 995	14 786	157 553	**183 025**
1953	8 858	2 047	15 183	160 184	**186 273**
1954	9 064	2 093	15 636	163 026	**189 819**
1955	9 277	2 136	16 050	165 931	**193 395**

http://dx.doi.org/10.1787/456125276116

ISBN 92-64-02261-9 – © OECD 2006

Table 2a. **Population of Western Offshoots, 1956-2003**
(000 at mid-year)

	Australia	New Zealand	Canada	United States	4 Western Offshoots
1956	9 501	2 178	16 445	168 903	**197 027**
1957	9 713	2 229	17 010	171 984	**200 936**
1958	9 915	2 282	17 462	174 882	**204 541**
1959	10 132	2 331	17 872	177 830	**208 165**
1960	10 361	2 372	18 267	180 671	**211 671**
1961	10 599	2 432	18 635	183 691	**215 357**
1962	10 795	2 489	18 986	186 538	**218 807**
1963	11 001	2 541	19 343	189 242	**222 128**
1964	11 218	2 592	19 711	191 889	**225 410**
1965	11 439	2 640	20 071	194 303	**228 454**
1966	11 655	2 688	20 448	196 560	**231 351**
1967	11 872	2 728	20 820	198 712	**234 132**
1968	12 102	2 759	21 143	200 706	**236 710**
1969	12 379	2 789	21 448	202 677	**239 293**
1970	12 660	2 828	21 750	205 052	**242 290**
1971	12 937	2 875	22 026	207 661	**245 500**
1972	13 177	2 929	22 285	209 896	**248 287**
1973	13 380	2 992	22 560	211 909	**250 841**
1974	13 599	3 058	22 875	213 854	**253 386**
1975	13 771	3 118	23 209	215 973	**256 071**
1976	13 916	3 154	23 518	218 035	**258 622**
1977	14 074	3 165	23 796	220 239	**261 274**
1978	14 249	3 166	24 036	222 585	**264 036**
1979	14 422	3 165	24 277	225 055	**266 918**
1980	14 616	3 170	24 593	227 726	**270 106**
1981	14 923	3 185	24 900	229 966	**272 975**
1982	15 184	3 211	25 202	232 188	**275 785**
1983	15 394	3 246	25 456	234 307	**278 403**
1984	15 579	3 279	25 702	236 348	**280 908**
1985	15 788	3 298	25 942	238 466	**283 494**
1986	16 018	3 308	26 204	240 651	**286 181**
1987	16 257	3 317	26 550	242 804	**288 928**
1988	16 520	3 331	26 895	245 021	**291 768**
1989	16 780	3 342	27 379	247 342	**294 843**
1990	17 022	3 360	27 791	250 132	**298 304**
1991	17 258	3 397	28 118	253 493	**302 265**
1992	17 482	3 438	28 524	256 894	**306 337**
1993	17 689	3 475	28 921	260 255	**310 340**
1994	17 893	3 517	29 262	263 436	**314 108**
1995	18 116	3 566	29 619	266 557	**317 858**
1996	18 348	3 621	29 983	269 667	**321 620**
1997	18 565	3 676	30 306	272 912	**325 459**
1998	18 769	3 726	30 629	276 115	**329 239**
1999	18 968	3 774	30 957	279 295	**332 994**
2000	19 165	3 820	31 278	282 339	**336 601**
2001	19 358	3 864	31 593	285 024	**339 838**
2002	19 547	3 908	31 902	287 676	**343 033**
2003	19 732	3 951	32 207	290 343	**346 233**

http://dx.doi.org/10.1787/456125276116

Table 2b. **GDP Levels in Western Offshoots, 1500-1899**
(million 1990 international Geary-Khamis dollars)

	Australia	*New Zealand*	*Canada*	*United States*	*4 Western Offshoots*
1500	180	40	100	800	**1 120**
1600	180	40	100	600	**920**
1700	180	40	86	527	**833**
1820	173	40	738	12 548	**13 499**
1830	280	40	1 169	18 219	**19 708**
1840	577	28	1 972	27 694	**30 271**
1850	1 195	103	3 304	42 583	**47 185**
1860	3 838	292	4 887	69 346	**78 363**
1870	5 810	902	6 407	98 374	**111 493**
1871	5 525	965	6 669	102 289	**115 448**
1872	6 119	1 127	6 599	106 360	**120 205**
1873	6 764	1 283	7 263	110 593	**125 903**
1874	6 987	1 411	7 437	114 994	**130 829**
1875	7 755	1 497	7 263	119 571	**136 086**
1876	7 730	1 572	6 774	124 330	**140 406**
1877	8 052	1 792	7 228	129 278	**146 350**
1878	8 820	1 994	6 948	134 423	**152 186**
1879	8 944	1 763	7 612	139 772	**158 091**
1880	9 415	1 948	7 961	145 335	**164 659**
1881	10 108	2 029	9 078	151 119	**172 334**
1882	9 539	2 023	9 497	157 133	**178 193**
1883	10 951	2 006	9 532	163 387	**185 876**
1884	11 000	2 214	10 300	169 889	**193 403**
1885	11 719	2 203	9 672	176 651	**200 244**
1886	11 867	2 255	9 776	183 681	**207 579**
1887	13 131	2 307	10 091	190 991	**216 519**
1888	13 205	2 307	10 824	198 592	**224 928**
1889	14 345	2 428	10 894	206 496	**234 163**
1890	13 850	2 497	11 697	214 714	**242 758**
1891	14 914	2 515	11 976	224 027	**253 432**
1892	13 081	2 607	11 906	245 757	**273 352**
1893	12 362	2 671	11 837	233 857	**260 726**
1894	12 784	2 584	12 395	227 131	**254 894**
1895	12 066	2 677	12 256	254 552	**281 551**
1896	12 982	2 983	11 941	249 379	**277 285**
1897	12 264	3 018	13 233	273 178	**301 693**
1898	14 172	3 104	13 757	278 869	**309 903**
1899	14 172	3 208	15 049	304 221	**336 650**

http://dx.doi.org/10.1787/456125276116

Table 2b. **GDP Levels in Western Offshoots, 1900-1955**
(million 1990 international Geary-Khamis dollars)

	Australia	New Zealand	Canada	United States	4 Western Offshoots
1900	15 014	3 469	15 887	312 499	**346 869**
1901	14 568	3 480	17 144	347 681	**382 873**
1902	14 717	3 746	18 820	351 303	**388 586**
1903	15 881	4 099	19 378	368 377	**407 735**
1904	16 947	4 081	19 658	363 720	**404 406**
1905	17 145	4 457	21 962	390 624	**434 188**
1906	18 309	4 879	24 162	435 636	**482 987**
1907	19 052	5 174	25 559	442 362	**492 147**
1908	19 697	4 816	24 336	406 146	**454 995**
1909	21 307	4 885	26 920	455 814	**508 927**
1910	22 793	5 556	29 225	460 471	**518 044**
1911	22 967	5 862	31 215	475 475	**535 519**
1912	23 764	5 689	33 275	497 722	**560 450**
1913	24 861	5 781	34 916	517 383	**582 941**
1914	24 797	5 931	32 577	477 545	**540 849**
1915	24 341	5 960	34 672	490 996	**555 969**
1916	24 172	5 914	38 163	558 774	**627 023**
1917	23 716	5 769	39 734	544 804	**614 024**
1918	23 155	5 677	37 186	593 956	**659 973**
1919	24 488	6 313	34 357	599 130	**664 288**
1920	25 534	7 001	33 973	593 438	**659 946**
1921	26 818	6 538	30 307	579 986	**643 650**
1922	28 225	6 313	34 741	612 064	**681 343**
1923	29 579	6 822	36 801	692 776	**765 978**
1924	31 524	6 943	37 360	713 989	**789 816**
1925	33 002	7 313	41 445	730 545	**812 305**
1926	33 792	6 926	43 680	778 144	**862 542**
1927	34 305	6 729	48 010	785 905	**874 948**
1928	34 368	7 475	52 269	794 700	**888 812**
1929	33 662	7 741	52 199	843 334	**936 936**
1930	30 458	7 405	50 454	768 314	**856 631**
1931	28 416	6 775	42 667	709 332	**787 191**
1932	30 025	6 608	39 630	615 686	**691 948**
1933	32 110	7 047	36 801	602 751	**678 710**
1934	33 810	7 400	40 712	649 316	**731 237**
1935	35 798	7 747	43 994	698 984	**786 523**
1936	37 414	9 186	46 368	798 322	**891 290**
1937	39 306	9 683	50 733	832 469	**932 191**
1938	40 639	10 365	52 060	799 357	**902 421**
1939	40 749	10 510	55 167	862 995	**969 421**
1940	43 422	10 308	62 744	929 737	**1 046 211**
1941	48 271	9 984	71 508	1 098 921	**1 228 684**
1942	53 837	11 082	84 182	1 318 809	**1 467 911**
1943	55 738	11 313	87 988	1 581 122	**1 736 162**
1944	53 809	11 360	91 305	1 713 572	**1 870 047**
1945	51 109	11 695	88 477	1 644 761	**1 796 042**
1946	49 291	12 597	87 569	1 305 357	**1 454 814**
1947	50 503	14 100	91 445	1 285 697	**1 441 744**
1948	53 754	12 701	93 121	1 334 331	**1 493 907**
1949	57 308	14 071	95 146	1 339 505	**1 506 030**
1950	61 274	16 136	102 164	1 455 916	**1 635 490**
1951	63 892	14 904	107 960	1 566 784	**1 753 540**
1952	64 470	15 552	115 816	1 625 245	**1 821 083**
1953	66 481	16 084	121 228	1 699 970	**1 903 763**
1954	70 614	18 298	120 390	1 688 804	**1 898 106**
1955	74 471	18 639	131 633	1 808 126	**2 032 869**

http://dx.doi.org/10.1787/456125276116

Table 2b. **GDP Levels in Western Offshoots, 1956-2001**
(million 1990 international Geary-Khamis dollars)

	Australia	*New Zealand*	*Canada*	*United States*	*4 Western Offshoots*
1956	77 034	19 605	142 282	1 843 455	**2 082 376**
1957	78 577	20 165	146 402	1 878 063	**2 123 207**
1958	82 351	20 957	149 021	1 859 088	**2 111 417**
1959	87 421	22 449	155 062	1 997 061	**2 261 993**
1960	91 085	22 449	159 880	2 046 727	**2 320 141**
1961	91 713	23 704	164 598	2 094 396	**2 374 411**
1962	97 444	24 215	176 130	2 220 732	**2 518 521**
1963	103 413	25 749	185 041	2 316 765	**2 630 968**
1964	110 488	27 004	197 098	2 450 915	**2 785 505**
1965	116 131	28 724	210 203	2 607 294	**2 962 352**
1966	119 363	30 536	223 832	2 778 086	**3 151 817**
1967	127 422	29 142	230 647	2 847 549	**3 234 760**
1968	134 913	29 095	242 703	2 983 081	**3 389 792**
1969	143 118	32 099	255 497	3 076 517	**3 507 231**
1970	152 220	31 644	262 098	3 081 900	**3 527 862**
1971	158 992	33 285	276 694	3 178 106	**3 647 077**
1972	163 453	34 711	291 314	3 346 554	**3 836 032**
1973	172 314	37 177	312 176	3 536 622	**4 058 289**
1974	176 586	39 390	324 928	3 526 724	**4 067 628**
1975	181 367	38 937	332 269	3 516 825	**4 069 398**
1976	188 678	39 887	350 467	3 701 163	**4 280 195**
1977	190 653	37 944	362 245	3 868 829	**4 459 671**
1978	196 184	38 097	376 894	4 089 548	**4 700 723**
1979	206 515	38 874	392 561	4 228 647	**4 866 597**
1980	210 642	39 141	397 814	4 230 558	**4 878 155**
1981	218 780	41 041	410 164	4 336 141	**5 006 126**
1982	218 512	41 809	397 671	4 254 870	**4 912 862**
1983	218 539	42 955	409 246	4 433 129	**5 103 869**
1984	233 618	45 072	432 711	4 755 958	**5 467 359**
1985	245 444	45 420	456 107	4 940 383	**5 687 354**
1986	250 539	46 372	468 055	5 110 480	**5 875 446**
1987	262 925	46 564	487 138	5 290 129	**6 086 756**
1988	274 737	46 435	510 815	5 512 845	**6 344 832**
1989	286 820	46 850	523 177	5 703 521	**6 560 368**
1990	291 180	46 729	524 475	5 803 200	**6 665 584**
1991	288 661	45 908	514 459	5 775 948	**6 624 976**
1992	296 225	46 304	519 148	5 952 089	**6 813 766**
1993	307 489	48 654	531 096	6 110 061	**6 997 300**
1994	322 819	51 554	556 209	6 356 710	**7 287 292**
1995	336 990	53 599	571 447	6 526 361	**7 488 397**
1996	350 470	55 368	580 590	6 759 427	**7 745 855**
1997	362 601	57 083	605 162	7 046 304	**8 071 150**
1998	382 147	56 761	630 306	7 349 878	**8 419 092**
1999	399 670	59 173	664 021	7 651 223	**8 774 087**
2000	412 813	61 156	694 308	7 941 969	**9 110 246**
2001	423 596	62 282	704 594	7 965 795	**9 156 267**

http://dx.doi.org/10.1787/456125276116

Table 2c. **Per Capita GDP in Western Offshoots, 1500-1899**
(1990 international Geary-Khamis dollars)

	Australia	New Zealand	Canada	United States	4 Western Offshoots
1500	400	400	400	400	**400**
1600	400	400	400	400	**400**
1700	400	400	430	527	**476**
1820	518	400	904	1 257	**1 202**
1830	848	400	1 000	1 376	**1 328**
1840	1 374	400	1 162	1 588	**1 542**
1850	1 975	1 144	1 330	1 806	**1 763**
1860	2 894	2 212	1 451	2 178	**2 137**
1870	3 273	3 100	1 695	2 445	**2 419**
1871	3 299	3 155	1 755	2 489	**2 463**
1872	3 553	3 523	1 705	2 524	**2 502**
1873	3 824	3 831	1 842	2 562	**2 558**
1874	3 835	3 843	1 854	2 601	**2 595**
1875	4 138	3 688	1 784	2 643	**2 638**
1876	4 007	3 623	1 641	2 686	**2 660**
1877	4 036	3 982	1 727	2 732	**2 712**
1878	4 277	4 271	1 637	2 780	**2 760**
1879	4 205	3 569	1 765	2 829	**2 806**
1880	4 285	3 747	1 816	2 880	**2 861**
1881	4 455	3 765	2 040	2 921	**2 921**
1882	4 063	3 646	2 109	2 963	**2 949**
1883	4 475	3 495	2 090	3 008	**3 003**
1884	4 304	3 703	2 231	3 056	**3 052**
1885	4 422	3 587	2 073	3 106	**3 090**
1886	4 329	3 602	2 075	3 158	**3 134**
1887	4 632	3 604	2 120	3 213	**3 199**
1888	4 504	3 554	2 249	3 270	**3 254**
1889	4 747	3 701	2 239	3 330	**3 319**
1890	4 458	3 755	2 378	3 392	**3 372**
1891	4 666	3 731	2 409	3 467	**3 450**
1892	3 995	3 801	2 371	3 728	**3 649**
1893	3 708	3 788	2 334	3 478	**3 415**
1894	3 766	3 579	2 420	3 314	**3 277**
1895	3 487	3 642	2 371	3 644	**3 554**
1896	3 685	3 988	2 288	3 504	**3 438**
1897	3 420	3 950	2 512	3 769	**3 675**
1898	3 891	3 985	2 583	3 780	**3 710**
1899	3 840	4 041	2 796	4 051	**3 963**

http://dx.doi.org/10.1787/456125276116

Table 2c. **Per Capita GDP in Western Offshoots, 1900-1955**
(1990 international Geary-Khamis dollars)

	Australia	New Zealand	Canada	United States	4 Western Offshoots
1900	4 013	4 298	2 911	4 091	**4 015**
1901	3 839	4 223	3 097	4 464	**4 349**
1902	3 823	4 438	3 331	4 421	**4 327**
1903	4 076	4 727	3 334	4 551	**4 455**
1904	4 295	4 570	3 280	4 410	**4 334**
1905	4 282	4 850	3 562	4 642	**4 559**
1906	4 507	5 158	3 846	5 079	**4 976**
1907	4 616	5 340	3 875	5 065	**4 970**
1908	4 693	4 835	3 572	4 561	**4 502**
1909	4 981	4 770	3 850	5 017	**4 934**
1910	5 210	5 316	4 066	4 964	**4 916**
1911	5 104	5 494	4 213	5 046	**4 995**
1912	5 098	5 209	4 377	5 201	**5 139**
1913	5 157	5 152	4 447	5 301	**5 233**
1914	5 027	5 189	4 025	4 799	**4 758**
1915	4 897	5 174	4 233	4 864	**4 824**
1916	4 878	5 120	4 646	5 459	**5 373**
1917	4 791	5 008	4 801	5 248	**5 195**
1918	4 602	4 911	4 441	5 659	**5 522**
1919	4 716	5 283	4 019	5 680	**5 517**
1920	4 766	5 641	3 861	5 552	**5 397**
1921	4 911	5 128	3 357	5 323	**5 160**
1922	5 064	4 841	3 793	5 540	**5 385**
1923	5 192	5 144	3 976	6 164	**5 953**
1924	5 417	5 143	3 977	6 233	**6 024**
1925	5 553	5 292	4 340	6 282	**6 100**
1926	5 573	4 905	4 497	6 602	**6 387**
1927	5 544	4 683	4 847	6 576	**6 385**
1928	5 452	5 141	5 172	6 569	**6 402**
1929	5 263	5 262	5 065	6 899	**6 673**
1930	4 708	4 960	4 811	6 213	**6 028**
1931	4 354	4 475	4 004	5 691	**5 492**
1932	4 564	4 327	3 671	4 908	**4 794**
1933	4 842	4 576	3 370	4 777	**4 672**
1934	5 060	4 768	3 691	5 114	**5 000**
1935	5 318	4 959	3 951	5 467	**5 340**
1936	5 516	5 840	4 124	6 204	**6 011**
1937	5 746	6 102	4 473	6 430	**6 247**
1938	5 886	6 462	4 546	6 126	**5 999**
1939	5 846	6 460	4 768	6 561	**6 390**
1940	6 166	6 300	5 368	7 010	**6 838**
1941	6 788	6 129	6 051	8 206	**7 954**
1942	7 505	6 762	7 033	9 741	**9 400**
1943	7 703	6 928	7 263	11 518	**10 971**
1944	7 362	6 868	7 443	12 333	**11 676**
1945	6 917	6 928	7 133	11 709	**11 090**
1946	6 595	7 161	6 931	9 197	**8 881**
1947	6 664	7 846	7 088	8 886	**8 635**
1948	6 967	6 929	7 065	9 065	**8 791**
1949	7 237	7 521	7 064	8 944	**8 704**
1950	7 412	8 456	7 291	9 561	**9 268**
1951	7 507	7 653	7 533	10 116	**9 760**
1952	7 418	7 796	7 833	10 316	**9 950**
1953	7 505	7 856	7 984	10 613	**10 220**
1954	7 791	8 743	7 699	10 359	**10 000**
1955	8 027	8 725	8 201	10 897	**10 512**

http://dx.doi.org/10.1787/456125276116

ISBN 92-64-02261-9 – © OECD 2006

Table 2c. **Per Capita GDP in Western Offshoots, 1956-2001**
(1990 international Geary-Khamis dollars)

	Australia	New Zealand	Canada	United States	4 Western Offshoots
1956	8 108	9 000	8 652	10 914	**10 569**
1957	8 090	9 045	8 607	10 920	**10 567**
1958	8 305	9 185	8 534	10 631	**10 323**
1959	8 628	9 630	8 676	11 230	**10 866**
1960	8 791	9 465	8 753	11 328	**10 961**
1961	8 653	9 745	8 833	11 402	**11 025**
1962	9 027	9 731	9 277	11 905	**11 510**
1963	9 400	10 132	9 566	12 242	**11 844**
1964	9 849	10 418	9 999	12 773	**12 357**
1965	10 152	10 879	10 473	13 419	**12 967**
1966	10 241	11 362	10 946	14 134	**13 624**
1967	10 733	10 682	11 078	14 330	**13 816**
1968	11 148	10 545	11 479	14 863	**14 320**
1969	11 561	11 511	11 912	15 179	**14 657**
1970	12 024	11 189	12 050	15 030	**14 560**
1971	12 290	11 576	12 562	15 304	**14 856**
1972	12 404	11 850	13 072	15 944	**15 450**
1973	12 878	12 424	13 838	16 689	**16 179**
1974	12 985	12 879	14 205	16 491	**16 053**
1975	13 170	12 489	14 316	16 284	**15 892**
1976	13 559	12 648	14 902	16 975	**16 550**
1977	13 546	11 989	15 223	17 567	**17 069**
1978	13 769	12 034	15 680	18 373	**17 803**
1979	14 320	12 284	16 170	18 789	**18 233**
1980	14 412	12 347	16 176	18 577	**18 060**
1981	14 660	12 884	16 472	18 856	**18 339**
1982	14 391	13 022	15 779	18 325	**17 814**
1983	14 197	13 234	16 076	18 920	**18 333**
1984	14 995	13 746	16 836	20 123	**19 463**
1985	15 546	13 772	17 582	20 717	**20 062**
1986	15 641	14 017	17 862	21 236	**20 531**
1987	16 173	14 037	18 348	21 788	**21 067**
1988	16 630	13 939	18 993	22 499	**21 746**
1989	17 093	14 020	19 108	23 059	**22 250**
1990	17 106	13 909	18 872	23 201	**22 345**
1991	16 727	13 514	18 297	22 785	**21 918**
1992	16 945	13 470	18 201	23 169	**22 243**
1993	17 383	14 001	18 364	23 477	**22 547**
1994	18 042	14 657	19 008	24 130	**23 200**
1995	18 602	15 031	19 293	24 484	**23 559**
1996	19 101	15 290	19 364	25 066	**24 084**
1997	19 531	15 528	19 968	25 819	**24 799**
1998	20 361	15 233	20 579	26 619	**25 571**
1999	21 070	15 679	21 450	27 395	**26 349**
2000	21 540	16 010	22 198	28 129	**27 065**
2001	21 883	16 118	22 302	27 948	**26 943**

http://dx.doi.org/10.1787/456125276116

HS–3: A. EASTERN EUROPE AND FORMER USSR

Until 1990, there were 8 countries in this group, 5 still have the same frontiers, but 22 successor states have emerged, 2 from Czechoslovakia, 5 from Yugoslavia, and 15 from USSR. The tables show GDP, population and per capita GDP for the 8 countries, 1820–2001 within their 1989 frontiers and 1990–2001 for the 22 successor states within their new boundaries.

The former DDR (German Democratic Republic) lasted from 1946 to 1990, when it was absorbed into the Federal Republic. As the estimates for Germany in HS–1 include the area of the former DDR, it is not shown here (see Maddison, 1995, p.132 for East German population and GDP, 1936–1993).

Estimates for 1820–2001

POPULATION: 1950 onwards all countries of Eastern Europe and the former USSR from the International Programs Center of the US Bureau of the Census, October 2002 revision. For 1820–1949, I have made some revisions and filled gaps from Colin McEvedy and Richard Jones (1978), *Atlas of World Population History,* Penguin, London. They provide estimates adjusted throughout to 1978 frontiers. Sources for 1820–1949 are indicated in the country notes below.

GDP LEVELS: sources are indicated in the country notes below. For 1820–1913, there are significant gaps in the GDP estimates for Eastern European countries, which makes it difficult to get meaningful group totals and averages. I have therefore used the proxy estimates of Good and Ma (1999) to fill most of these gaps as indicated below. In all cases the GDP estimates for the communist period have been adjusted to correspond to the norms of the UN standardised system of national accounts. The problems in doing this and the relevant sources are discussed in Maddison (1995), pp. 139–43 and in Maddison "Measuring the Performance of a Communist Command Economy: An Assessment of CIA Estimates for the USSR", *Review of Income and Wealth*, September, 1998.

Albania: 1950 and 1990 GDP levels from Maddison, 1995, p. 217. 1870–1950 per capita GDP was assumed to move in the same proportion as the average for the other 6 East European countries.

Bulgaria: 1926–39 from A. Chakalov, *The National Income and Outlay of Bulgaria: 1924–1945* (in Bulgarian), Knipegraph, Sofia, 1946; 1939–65 from T.P. Alton, "Economic Structure and Growth in Eastern Europe", in *Economic Developments in Countries of Eastern Europe*, Joint Economic Committee, US Congress, 1970, p. 46. 1965–75 from T.P. Alton, "East European GNPs: Origins of Product, Final Uses, Rates of Growth and International Comparisons", in *East European Economies: Slow Growth in the 1980s*, vol. I, *Economic Performance and Policy*, Joint Economic Committee, US Congress, October 1985, pp. 109–10. 1975–90 real GNP by industry of origin from T.P. Alton and Associates, "Economic Growth in Eastern Europe", *Occasional Papers* 120 and 124, Research Project on National Income in East Central Europe, New York, 1992 and 1993. GDP movement 1990–2001 from Statistics Division, Economic Commission for Europe, Geneva. Population 1820–50 from McEvedy and Jones (1978); 1870–1940 from I. Svennilson, *Growth and Stagnation in the European Economy*, ECE, Geneva, 1954, p. 237 (adjusted to postwar frontiers); 1941–9 from UN, *Demographic Yearbook*, New York, 1960.

Czechoslovakia: 1820–1913 growth rate of per capita GDP assumed to fall midway between those for Austria proper and for rest of Cisleithania in A. Kausel, "Österreichs Volkseinkommen 1830 bis 1913", in "Geschichte und Ergebnisse der zentralen amtlichen Statistik in Österreich 1829–1979", *Beiträge zum Österreichischen Statistik*, 550, Vienna, 1979. 1913–37 GDP from F.L. Pryor, Z.P. Pryor, M. Stadnik, and G.J. Staller "Czechoslovakia: Aggregate Production in the Inter–war Period", *Review of Income and Wealth*, March 1971, p.36. 1937–65 from G. Lazarcik, "Czechoslovak Gross National Product by Sector of Origin and Final Use, 1937, and 1948–65", *Occasional Paper* 26, Research Project on National Income in East Central Europe, New York, 1969. 1965–90 as for Bulgaria. 1990–2001 for Czech republic from OECD sources; Slovakia from Statistics Division, Economic Commission for Europe. Population 1820–50 from McEvedy and Jones (1978), 1870–1910 supplied by David Good, 1913–49 as for Bulgaria.

Hungary: 1870–1900 GDP from Max–Stephan Schulze, "Patterns of Growth and Stagnation in the Late Nineteenth Century Habsburg Economy", *European Review of Economic History*, no. 4, 2000, pp. 311–340. Schulze's estimates refer to imperial Hungary, but the movement he shows is the best available proxy for development within present frontiers. 1900–38 net national product within present frontiers from A. Eckstein, "National Income and Capital Formation in Hungary, 1900–50", in S. Kuznets, ed., *Income and Wealth*, series V, Bowes and Bowes, London, 1955, p. 175; 1938–65 real GNP by industry of origin from L. Czirjak, "Hungarian GNP by Sectors of Origin of Product and End Uses, 1938 and 1946–67", *Occasional Paper* 43, Research Project on East Central Europe, New York, 1973. 1965–91 as for Bulgaria. Thereafter from OECD sources. Population 1820–70 assumed to grow at the same pace as in imperial Hungary as shown in Kausel (1985), p. 12. 1870–1949 as for Bulgaria.

Friedich von Fellner estimated the breakdown of population, income, and wealth between present–day Hungary and other successor states of imperial Hungary for 1910. Present–day Hungary had 36.7 per cent of the population (7 605 thousand out of a total 20 745) and 39.7 per cent of the national income. 21.4 per cent of income went to an area which became part of Romania, 20.2 to Yugoslavia, 16.9 to Czechoslovakia and 1.8 per cent to present–day Austria. See "Die Verteilung des Volksvermögens und Volkseinkommens der Länder der ungarischen Heiligen Krone zwischen dem heutigen Ungarn und der Successions–Staaten", *Metron*, July 1923, pp. 302–3. Per capita income was about 8 per cent higher in present–day Hungary than in the rest.

Poland: 1929–38 from K. Laski, *Akumulacja i spozycie w procesie uprzemyslowienia Polski Ludowej*, Ksiazka i Wiedza, Warsaw, 1956, pp. 86–90 as cited by N. Spulber, *The State and Economic Development in Eastern Europe*, Random House, New York, 1966, p. 59; 1937–65 from T.P. Alton (1970), p. 46, 1965–90 as for Bulgaria. 1990 onwards from OECD sources. Population 1820–70 from McEvedy and Jones (1978), thereafter as for Bulgaria.

Romania: 1926–38 from "Venitul National", in *Enciclopedia Romaniei*, Bucharest, 1940, vol. 4, pp. 941–966 as cited by N. Spulber, p. 54, *op. cit.*; 1938–50 from D. Grindea, *Venitul National in Republica Socialista Romania*, Stiintifica, Bucharest, 1967, p. 113; 1950–65 from Alton (1970), *op. cit.*, p. 46; 1965–75 from T.P. Alton (1985), *op. cit.*, pp. 109–10; 1975–90 as for Bulgaria. 1990–2001 from Statistics Division, Economic Commission for Europe, Geneva. Population 1820–1900 from McEvedy and Jones (1978), thereafter as for Bulgaria.

Yugoslavia: Movement of net domestic product adjusted to enhance international comparability 1909–12, 1920–39, and 1947–50 from I. Vinski, "National Product and Fixed Assets in the Territory of Yugoslavia 1900–59", in P. Deane, ed., *Income and Wealth*, Series IX, Bowes and Bowes, London, 1961, p. 221 1950–68 from T.P. Alton, *op. cit.* (1970). 1968–75 from World Bank, *World Tables*, various issues. 1975–90 from "Economic Growth in Eastern Europe 1975–91" in T.P. Alton and Associates, *Occasional Paper*, 120, Research Project on National Income in East Central Europe, New York, 1992. 1990–2001 GDP for Bosnia–Herczegovina, Croatia, Macedonia, Slovenia, and Serbia–Montenegro from Statistics Division, Economic Commission for Europe. Population 1820–1949 as for Bulgaria.

USSR: 1820–70 per capita GDP movement assumed to parallel the average for Eastern Europe. 1870–1913 volume movement of GDP components from R.W. Goldsmith, "The Economic Growth of Tsarist Russia 1860–1913", *Economic Development and Cultural Change*, April 1961, pp. 450, and 462–3. I used his estimates of crop and livestock output, his industrial index and estimate for handicraft activity. I assumed forestry and fishing to move parallel to agriculture; construction, transport and communication parallel to industry. I used 1913 weights for the components from M.E. Falkus, "Russia's National Income 1913: A Revaluation", *Economica*, February 1968, pp. 62 and 67. For 1913–28, I used the same technique of estimation and weights, taking net agricultural product from S.G. Wheatcroft in R.W. Davies, ed., *From Tsarism to the New Economic Policy*, Macmillan, London, 1990, p. 279, and industrial output from G.W. Nutter, *Growth of Industrial Production in the Soviet Union*, Princeton, 1962, p. 150. 1928–40 and 1945–50 gross national product at 1937 prices by industry of origin from R. Moorsteen and R.P. Powell, *The Soviet Capital Stock 1928–1962*, Irwin, Illinois, 1966, p. 361 with the 1939–40 increase reduced to offset the population increase due to territorial acquisitions at that time. 1950–90 from CIA, "Sector of Origin GNP for the Soviet Union, Factor Cost Prices", March 29, 1991, processed. This was an update of *Measures of Soviet Gross National Product in 1982 Prices*, Joint Economic Committee, US Congress, November 1990. 1990 breakdown of GDP level for the 15 successor republics derived from B.M. Bolotin, "The Former Soviet Union as Reflected in National Accounts Statistics", in S. Hirsch, ed., *Memo 3:In Search of Answers in the Post–Soviet Era*, Bureau of National Affairs, Washington DC, 1992. 1973–93 GDP level for the fifteen successor states from Maddison (2001), pp. 182, 184 and 339. Annual movement 1994–2002 from IMF, *World Economic Outlook*, September, 2002.

Population 1820–1900 from McEvedy and Jones, pp. 79 and 159–163; 1913–40 from F. Lorimer, *The Population of the Soviet Union: History and Prospects*, League of Nations, Geneva, 1946. 1946–9 movement from G.W. Nutter, *The Growth of Industrial Production in the Soviet Union*, NBER, Princeton, 1962, p. 519.

For the Tsarist period to 1928 there are alternative estimates by P.R. Gregory, *Russian National Income 1885–1913*, Cambridge University Press, 1982, pp. 56–7. He measures expenditure components (private consumption, government current spending, and investment) in current prices and deflates by price indices. The two methods concord well. The industry of origin approach yields a GDP index of 43.2 for 1890, 66.3 for 1900 and 100.0 for 1913. Gregory's two net national product alternatives average 42.9, 66.2 and 100.0 for these years.

Proxy Estimates to Fill Gaps in GDP Estimates for Eastern Europe, 1820–1913

David Good and Tongshu Ma, "The Economic Growth of Central and Eastern Europe, 1870–1989", *European Review of Economic History*, August 1999 provide proxy estimates of the level and movement of GDP per capita for the years 1870, 1890 and 1910 for Austria and 6 East European countries. For the 1920s onwards they used Maddison (1995) estimates, and my *numeraire* (1990 international Geary–Khamis dollars). These estimates are shown as relatives to the United States. Virtually identical results are given in Good and Ma (1998), "New Estimates of Income levels in Central and Eastern Europe, 1870–1910", in F. Baltzarek, F. Butschek and G. Tichy (eds.), (1998), *Von der Theorie zur Wirtschaftspolitik–ein österreichische Weg*, Lucius, Stuttgart, where they are shown as levels rather than relatives. In 1998, they showed figures for 1880 and 1900, but not the link with years after the first world war.

Their proxy estimates are derived by regression using three indicators (letters posted per capita, crude birth rate and the share of non–agricultural employment in the labour force). The relationship of GDP per capita to this cocktail of indicators is tested for 12 countries deemed to have reasonably good national income data. Although I reject the proxies as a substitute for direct estimates, they seem plausible enough to fill gaps in the database until direct estimates become available. Table 3–1 shows their proxies. Table 3–2 shows my estimates and my use of their proxies (in italics). I extrapolated the proxies to 1913, using 1900–1910 growth rates. Per capita proxies were multiplied by population to derive GDP.

It should be noted that the Good and Ma proxies refer mostly to territory within the Austro–Hungarian empire where comparison was facilitated by the existence of a currency and customs union. Their estimates are likely to be less representative for Poland, where only 15 per cent of the population lived within the borders of the Habsburg empire.

Table 3-1. **Good and Ma Proxy Measures of Per Capita GDP**

(1990 international Geary-Khamis dollars)

	1870	*1890*	*1910*	*1920*	*1929*
Austria	*1 892*	*2 289*	*3 017*	2 429	3 722
Bulgaria		*1 131*	*1 456*	589	1 181
Czechoslovakia	*1 509*	*1 912*	*2 495*	1 935	3 046
Hungary	*1 179*	*1 572*	*2 192*	1 707	2 473
Poland	*946*	*1 284*	*1 690*	678	2 120
Romania	*931*	*1 246*	*1 660*	828	1 153
Yugoslavia	*864*	*1 216*	*1 525*	1 056	1 368
United States	2 457	3 396	4 970	5 559	6 907

Source: Good and Ma (1999), p.111. They show their proxies as relatives to the US level in the given year. I have unscrambled them, using the Maddison (1995) estimates for the US shown above. Proxies are in italics.

Table 3-2. **Maddison Estimates of Per Capita GDP and Proxies Derived from Good and Ma**

(1990 international Geary-Khamis dollars)

	1870	*1890*	*1910*	*1920*	*1929*
Austria	1 863	2 443	3 290	2 412	3 699
Bulgaria		*1 131*	*1 456*		1 180
Czechoslovakia	1 164	1 505	1 991	1 933	3 042
Hungary	1 092	1 473	2 000	1 709	2 476
Poland	*946*	*1 284*	*1 690*		2 117
Romania	*931*	*1 246*	*1 660*		1 152
Yugoslavia	*599*	*843*	1 057	1 031	1 364

Source: For Bulgaria, Poland and Romania, I used the Good-Ma proxies without adjustment as they are benchmarked on my estimates for 1929. For Yugoslavia I made the link at 1910 and adjusted the Good-Ma proxies for the difference in level in 1910. Proxies are in italics.

http://dx.doi.org/10.1787/456125276116

Estimates for 1500–1820

Population 1500–1820 from McEvedy and Jones (1978), except for Hungary 1820, as noted above. Direct estimates of GDP movement for 1500–1820 are not available. As a proxy, I assumed slower per capita growth than in Western Europe at 0.1 per cent per annum for 1500–1820 (as I did in Maddison, 1995).

Table 3-3. **Eastern Europe and Russia (Former USSR area): Population and GDP, 1500-1820**

	Population (000)			
	1500	*1600*	*1700*	*1820*
Albania	200	200	300	437
Bulgaria	800	1 250	1 250	2 187
Czechoslovakia	3 000	4 500	4 500	7 657
Hungary	1 250	1 250	1 500	4 146
Poland	4 000	5 000	6 000	10 426
Romania	2 000	2 000	2 500	6 389
Yugoslavia	2 250	2 750	2 750	5 215
Total	13 500	16 950	18 800	36 457
Russia	16 950	20 700	26 550	54 765

	GDP (million 1990 international $)			
Total E. Europe	6 696	9 289	11 393	24 906
Russia	8 458	11 426	16 196	37 678

	Per Capita GDP (1990 international $)			
Average E. Europe	496	548	606	683
Russia	499	552	610	688

Source: see text.

http://dx.doi.org/10.1787/456125276116

Table 3a. Population of Former Eastern Europe and USSR, 1820-1949
(000 at mid-year)

	Albania	Bulgaria	Czecho-slovakia	Hungary	Poland	Romania	Yugoslavia	Total 7 EE	USSR
1820	437	2 187	7 657	4 146	10 426	6 389	5 215	36 457	54 765
1850	500	2 500	9 250	5 161	13 000	8 000	6 000	44 411	73 750
1870	603	2 586	10 155	5 917	16 865	9 179	8 252	53 557	88 672
1890	726	3 445	11 253	6 622	22 854	10 373	9 690	64 963	110 664
1900	800	4 000	12 142	7 127	24 750	11 000	11 174	70 993	124 500
1910	874	4 520	12 984	7 644	26 644	11 866	13 052	77 584	
1913	898	4 720	13 245	7 840	26 710	12 527	13 590	79 530	156 192
1920	932	5 072	12 979	7 950	23 968	12 340	12 422	75 663	154 607
1921	937	5 148	13 008	8 029	24 330	12 479	12 607	76 538	152 836
1922	942	5 255	13 159	8 103	24 935	12 666	12 796	77 856	152 403
1923	947	5 365	13 293	8 173	25 569	12 843	12 987	79 177	153 055
1924	952	5 476	13 413	8 232	25 992	13 020	13 180	80 265	155 581
1925	956	5 590	13 537	8 299	26 425	13 209	13 378	81 394	158 983
1926	962	5 705	13 644	8 383	26 815	13 399	13 578	82 486	162 621
1927	967	5 798	13 728	8 454	27 148	13 574	13 780	83 449	166 117
1928	972	5 873	13 807	8 520	27 509	13 760	13 986	84 427	169 269
1929	977	5 950	13 884	8 583	27 856	13 952	14 194	85 396	172 017
1930	982	6 027	13 964	8 649	28 204	14 141	14 407	86 374	174 212
1931	988	6 106	14 052	8 723	28 615	14 355	14 618	87 457	175 987
1932	993	6 186	14 138	8 785	29 022	14 554	14 819	88 497	176 807
1933	998	6 267	14 216	8 848	29 421	14 730	15 022	89 502	177 401
1934	1 003	6 349	14 282	8 919	29 771	14 924	15 228	90 476	178 453
1935	1 009	6 415	14 339	8 985	30 129	15 069	15 439	91 385	179 636
1936	1 014	6 469	14 387	9 046	30 471	15 256	15 651	92 294	181 502
1937	1 030	6 514	14 429	9 107	30 791	15 434	15 860	93 165	184 626
1938	1 040	6 564	14 603	9 167	31 062	15 601	16 084	94 121	188 498
1939	1 070	6 614	14 683	9 227	31 365	15 751	16 305	95 015	192 379
1940	1 088	6 666	14 713	9 287	30 021	15 907			195 970
1941	1 100	6 715	14 671	9 344		15 774			
1942	1 117	6 771	14 577	9 396		15 839			
1943	1 119	6 828	14 538	9 442		15 840			
1944	1 122	6 885	14 593	9 497		15 946			
1945	1 138	6 942	14 152	9 024		15 929			
1946	1 154	7 000	12 916	9 042	23 959	15 971			173 900
1947	1 175	7 064	12 164	9 079	23 734	15 849	15 596	84 661	174 000
1948	1 192	7 130	12 339	9 158	23 980	15 893	15 817	85 509	175 100
1949	1 209	7 195	12 339	9 250	24 410	16 084	16 040	86 527	177 500

http://dx.doi.org/10.1787/456125276116

Table 3a. **Population of Former Eastern Europe and USSR, 1950-2003**
(000 at mid-year)

	Albania	Bulgaria	Czecho-slovakia	Hungary	Poland	Romania	Yugoslavia	Total 7 EE	USSR
1950	1 227	7 251	12 389	9 338	24 824	16 311	16 298	87 637	179 571
1951	1 254	7 258	12 532	9 423	25 262	16 464	16 519	88 713	182 677
1952	1 283	7 275	12 683	9 504	25 731	16 630	16 708	89 814	185 856
1953	1 315	7 346	12 820	9 595	26 221	16 847	16 937	91 081	188 961
1954	1 353	7 423	12 952	9 706	26 715	17 040	17 151	92 341	192 171
1955	1 392	7 499	13 093	9 825	27 221	17 325	17 364	93 719	195 613
1956	1 434	7 576	13 229	9 911	27 744	17 583	17 508	94 985	199 103
1957	1 477	7 651	13 358	9 839	28 235	17 829	17 659	96 049	202 604
1958	1 521	7 728	13 474	9 882	28 693	18 056	17 796	97 149	206 201
1959	1 571	7 798	13 565	9 937	29 152	18 226	17 968	98 217	209 928
1960	1 623	7 867	13 654	9 984	29 590	18 403	18 133	99 254	213 780
1961	1 677	7 943	13 779	10 029	29 979	18 567	18 318	100 292	217 618
1962	1 728	8 013	13 858	10 063	30 330	18 681	18 500	101 172	221 227
1963	1 780	8 078	13 948	10 091	30 662	18 813	18 685	102 057	224 585
1964	1 832	8 144	14 052	10 124	30 976	18 927	18 852	102 908	227 698
1965	1 884	8 201	14 147	10 153	31 262	19 027	19 038	103 713	230 513
1966	1 933	8 258	14 224	10 185	31 532	19 141	19 221	104 494	233 139
1967	1 984	8 310	14 277	10 223	31 785	19 285	19 390	105 256	235 630
1968	2 039	8 370	14 323	10 264	32 035	19 721	19 552	106 302	237 983
1969	2 100	8 434	14 284	10 303	32 281	20 010	19 705	107 117	240 253
1970	2 157	8 490	14 319	10 337	32 526	20 253	19 840	107 921	242 478
1971	2 209	8 536	14 381	10 365	32 778	20 470	20 015	108 753	244 887
1972	2 264	8 576	14 456	10 394	33 040	20 663	20 197	109 589	247 343
1973	2 296	8 621	14 549	10 426	33 331	20 828	20 367	110 418	249 712
1974	2 348	8 679	14 658	10 471	33 643	21 029	20 550	111 377	252 111
1975	2 401	8 721	14 772	10 532	33 969	21 245	20 732	112 372	254 519
1976	2 455	8 755	14 884	10 589	34 299	21 446	20 930	113 357	256 883
1977	2 509	8 797	14 990	10 637	34 621	21 659	21 126	114 339	259 225
1978	2 563	8 803	15 089	10 673	34 929	21 832	21 309	115 199	261 525
1979	2 618	8 812	15 182	10 698	35 257	22 001	21 490	116 058	263 751
1980	2 671	8 844	15 255	10 711	35 578	22 130	21 615	116 804	265 973
1981	2 724	8 869	15 312	10 712	35 902	22 257	21 707	117 483	268 217
1982	2 780	8 892	15 352	10 706	36 227	22 357	21 860	118 173	270 533
1983	2 837	8 910	15 388	10 689	36 571	22 407	21 968	118 772	273 010
1984	2 896	8 928	15 423	10 668	36 904	22 454	22 012	119 285	275 574
1985	2 957	8 944	15 455	10 649	37 226	22 521	22 115	119 866	278 108
1986	3 015	8 959	15 481	10 631	37 504	22 600	22 213	120 402	280 646
1987	3 075	8 972	15 511	10 613	37 741	22 686	22 283	120 881	283 124
1988	3 137	8 982	15 537	10 443	37 867	22 769	22 358	121 092	285 482
1989	3 196	8 990	15 559	10 398	37 970	22 852	22 429	121 394	287 011
1990	3 258	8 894	15 572	10 372	38 119	22 866	22 488	121 569	289 045
1991	3 238	8 772	15 587	10 365	38 253	22 826	22 806	121 847	290 754
1992	3 175	8 659	15 619	10 349	38 371	22 797	22 912	121 880	292 079
1993	3 172	8 441	15 650	10 329	38 469	22 769	22 775	121 605	292 686
1994	3 198	8 360	15 676	10 313	38 551	22 739	22 543	121 379	292 755
1995	3 237	8 272	15 687	10 296	38 603	22 693	22 347	121 135	292 597
1996	3 280	8 181	15 686	10 274	38 633	22 628	22 303	120 983	292 188
1997	3 318	8 085	15 685	10 245	38 656	22 562	22 391	120 942	291 750
1998	3 367	7 985	15 684	10 211	38 664	22 509	22 506	120 924	291 373
1999	3 443	7 889	15 682	10 174	38 658	22 459	22 600	120 904	291 012
2000	3 490	7 797	15 680	10 139	38 646	22 411	22 750	120 913	290 654
2001	3 510	7 707	15 679	10 106	38 634	22 364	22 911	120 912	290 349
2002	3 545	7 621	15 679	10 075	38 625	22 318	23 001	120 864	290 154
2003	3 582	7 538	15 679	10 045	38 623	22 272	23 066	120 805	290 062

http://dx.doi.org/10.1787/456125276116

Table 3b. GDP Levels in Former Eastern Europe and USSR, 1820-1949[a]
(million 1990 international Geary-Khamis dollars)

	Albania	Bulgaria	Czecho-slovakia	Hungary	Poland	Romania	Yugoslavia	Total 7 EE	USSR
1820			6 501					24 906	37 678
1850			9 981					38 593	
1870	*269*	*2 172*	11 820	6 459	*15 954*	*8 546*	*4 943*	50 163	83 646
1890	*434*	*3 896*	16 936	9 751	*29 345*	*12 925*	*8 169*	81 456	
1900	*548*	*4 892*	20 994	11 990	*38 016*	*15 565*	*10 079*	102 084	154 049
1910	*682*	*6 581*	25 851	15 291	*45 028*	*19 698*	13 795	126 926	
1913	*728*	*7 240*	27 755	16 447	*46 449*	*21 810*	14 364	134 793	232 351
1920			25 091	13 585			12 810		
1921			27 117				13 129		
1922			26 395				13 522		
1923			28 588				14 234		
1924		4 976	31 558	15 740			15 264		
1925		5 156	35 277	18 914			16 025		
1926		6 671	35 138	18 125		16 850	17 154		
1927		7 274	37 775	18 914		16 850	16 884		
1928		7 160	41 106	20 576		16 850	18 381		231 886
1929	905	7 023	42 240	21 250	58 980	16 079	19 363	165 840	238 392
1930		7 741	40 856	20 789	56 247	17 235	18 995		252 333
1931		8 876	39 468	19 786	52 177	17 640	18 430		257 213
1932		8 933	37 886	19 260	48 107	16 657	16 712		254 424
1933		9 084	36 276	21 003	46 771	17 447	17 228		264 880
1934		8 308	34 889	21 135	47 439	17 640	17 866		290 903
1935		7 928	34 556	22 204	48 107	18 026	17 596		334 818
1936		9 659	37 387	23 684	49 504	18 218	19 878		361 306
1937		10 204	41 578	23 158	58 980	17 447	20 197		398 017
1938		10 470		24 342	67 788	19 375	21 817		405 220
1939		10 599		26 184			23 019		430 314
1940		10 319		24 391					420 091
1941		10 520		24 539					333 656
1942		10 018		25 773					333 656
1943		10 334							333 656
1944		9 551							333 656
1945		7 447							333 656
1946				15 559					332 727
1947				16 102			20 516		369 903
1948			38 108	20 148		12 975	24 492		420 555
1949			40 218	21 776			26 921		465 631

a)   proxies are shown in bold italics.

http://dx.doi.org/10.1787/456125276116

ISBN 92-64-02261-9 – © OECD 2006

Table 3b. GDP Levels in Former Eastern Europe and USSR, 1950-2002
(million 1990 international Geary-Khamis dollars)

	Albania	Bulgaria	Czecho-slovakia	Hungary	Poland	Romania	Yugoslavia	Total 7 EE	USSR
1950	1 229	11 971	43 368	23 158	60 742	19 279	25 277	185 023	510 243
1951	1 310	14 434	44 159	25 395	63 414	20 674	26 284	195 670	512 566
1952	1 342	13 773	45 630	26 250	64 872	22 169	24 200	198 236	545 792
1953	1 431	15 317	45 436	26 727	68 638	23 773	27 823	209 145	569 260
1954	1 516	15 030	47 295	27 664	72 526	25 493	29 362	218 886	596 910
1955	1 644	16 107	51 348	30 164	76 049	27 337	31 208	233 857	648 027
1956	1 711	16 121	54 373	28 799	79 450	28 544	30 495	239 494	710 065
1957	1 874	17 831	57 704	31 184	83 641	29 805	35 573	257 611	724 470
1958	2 018	19 382	62 117	33 273	87 711	31 121	37 014	272 635	778 840
1959	2 170	20 926	64 837	34 622	90 262	32 496	41 574	286 886	770 244
1960	2 355	22 908	69 749	36 431	95 121	33 931	44 190	304 685	843 434
1961	2 453	24 401	72 525	38 273	102 714	36 225	46 190	322 781	891 763
1962	2 612	26 405	73 496	39 868	101 317	37 497	47 057	328 253	915 928
1963	2 782	27 611	72 109	42 056	107 391	40 196	51 967	344 112	895 016
1964	2 962	29 787	75 495	44 424	112 190	42 741	56 919	364 518	1 010 727
1965	3 156	31 575	78 270	44 770	118 386	45 402	58 458	380 016	1 068 117
1966	3 360	34 067	81 657	47 319	125 857	50 588	61 605	404 452	1 119 932
1967	3 579	35 898	85 154	50 033	130 412	52 901	62 668	420 645	1 169 422
1968	3 810	36 559	89 123	50 641	138 309	54 019	63 983	436 444	1 237 966
1969	4 058	38 340	90 760	52 155	136 912	56 506	71 131	449 862	1 255 392
1970	4 321	40 523	92 592	51 974	144 018	57 779	74 489	465 695	1 351 818
1971	4 602	41 844	95 756	54 293	154 284	65 934	83 078	499 790	1 387 832
1972	4 901	43 826	99 142	55 460	165 521	70 175	85 945	524 971	1 395 732
1973	5 218	45 557	102 445	58 339	177 973	72 411	88 813	550 756	1 513 070
1974	5 357	46 986	106 165	59 852	188 421	76 479	100 269	583 528	1 556 984
1975	5 497	50 849	109 301	61 135	197 289	79 911	100 269	604 251	1 561 399
1976	5 643	52 371	111 050	61 316	202 209	83 998	103 375	619 961	1 634 589
1977	5 793	51 869	116 073	65 164	205 975	85 906	110 901	641 681	1 673 159
1978	5 945	52 989	117 489	66 743	213 446	88 702	117 014	662 328	1 715 215
1979	6 101	55 028	118 488	66 875	209 498	91 266	125 043	672 299	1 707 083
1980	6 270	53 449	121 763	67 549	204 213	91 517	131 058	675 819	1 709 174
1981	6 428	54 870	121 153	68 026	193 341	90 957	133 156	667 932	1 724 741
1982	6 596	56 644	123 512	70 477	191 579	91 035	134 359	674 202	1 767 262
1983	6 771	55 574	125 371	69 753	201 055	90 225	135 576	684 326	1 823 723
1984	6 951	57 412	128 313	71 579	208 526	93 811	138 682	705 274	1 847 190
1985	7 133	55 682	129 313	69 819	210 713	93 657	139 885	706 201	1 863 687
1986	7 321	57 154	131 700	71 217	217 394	95 257	145 690	725 733	1 940 363
1987	7 514	57 262	132 366	72 319	214 479	93 252	143 997	721 188	1 965 457
1988	7 713	56 903	135 308	73 421	219 217	93 020	141 983	727 564	2 007 280
1989	7 917	55 883	136 418	71 776	215 815	90 051	140 179	718 039	2 037 253
1990	8 125	49 779	132 560	66 990	194 920	80 277	129 953	662 604	1 987 995
1991	5 850	45 598	115 937	59 019	181 245	69 921	112 710	590 280	1 863 524
1992	5 429	42 689	113 318	57 211	185 804	63 768	91 392	559 611	1 592 084
1993	5 950	41 635	112 191	56 881	192 749	64 725	76 268	550 399	1 435 008
1994	6 444	42 384	115 603	58 557	202 815	67 249	79 190	572 242	1 231 738
1995	7 301	43 613	122 621	59 430	217 060	72 024	83 343	605 392	1 163 401
1996	7 965	39 514	128 423	60 226	230 147	74 833	87 483	628 591	1 125 992
1997	7 408	37 301	129 782	62 980	244 450	70 268	92 850	645 039	1 149 255
1998	8 000	38 793	130 452	66 039	257 765	66 895	95 527	663 471	1 124 868
1999	8 584	39 868	131 431	68 794	268 213	66 092	92 675	675 657	1 171 952
2000	9 252	41 829	135 313	72 366	278 826	67 282	96 878	701 746	1 264 526
2001	9 855	43 502	139 777	75 127	289 421	70 848	100 262	728 792	1 343 230
2002									1 405 639

http://dx.doi.org/10.1787/456125276116

477

Table 3c. Per Capita GDP in Former Eastern Europe and USSR, 1820-1949[a]
(1990 international Geary-Khamis dollars)

	Albania	Bulgaria	Czecho-slovakia	Hungary	Poland	Romania	Yugoslavia	Average 7 EE	USSR
1820			849					683	688
1850			1 079					869	
1870	*446*	*840*	1 164	1 092	*946*	*931*	*599*	937	943
1890	*598*	*1 131*	1 505	1 473	*1 284*	*1 246*	*843*	1 254	
1900	*685*	*1 223*	1 729	1 682	*1 536*	*1 415*	902	1 438	1 237
1910	*780*	*1 456*	1 991	2 000	*1 690*	*1 660*	1 057	1 636	
1913	*811*	*1 534*	2 096	2 098	*1 739*	*1 741*	1 057	1 695	1 488
1920			1 933	1 709			1 031		
1921			2 085				1 041		
1922			2 006				1 057		
1923			2 151				1 096		
1924		909	2 353	1 912			1 158		
1925		922	2 606	2 279			1 198		
1926		1 169	2 575	2 162		1 258	1 263		
1927		1 255	2 752	2 237		1 241	1 225		
1928		1 219	2 977	2 415		1 225	1 314		1 370
1929	*926*	1 180	3 042	2 476	2 117	1 152	1 364	1 942	1 386
1930		1 284	2 926	2 404	1 994	1 219	1 318		1 448
1931		1 454	2 809	2 268	1 823	1 229	1 261		1 462
1932		1 444	2 680	2 192	1 658	1 144	1 128		1 439
1933		1 450	2 552	2 374	1 590	1 184	1 147		1 493
1934		1 309	2 443	2 370	1 593	1 182	1 173		1 630
1935		1 236	2 410	2 471	1 597	1 196	1 140		1 864
1936		1 493	2 599	2 618	1 625	1 194	1 270		1 991
1937		1 567	2 882	2 543	1 915	1 130	1 273		2 156
1938		1 595		2 655	2 182	1 242	1 356		2 150
1939		1 603		2 838			1 412		2 237
1940		1 548		2 626					2 144
1941		1 567		2 626					
1942		1 479		2 743					
1943		1 513							
1944		1 387							
1945		1 073							
1946				1 721					1 913
1947				1 774			1 315		2 126
1948			3 088	2 200		816	1 548		2 402
1949			3 259	2 354			1 678		2 623

a) proxies are shown in bold italics.

http://dx.doi.org/10.1787/456125276116

Table 3c. **Per Capita GDP in Former Eastern Europe and USSR, 1950-2002**
(1990 international Geary-Khamis dollars)

	Albania	Bulgaria	Czecho-slovakia	Hungary	Poland	Romania	Yugoslavia	Average 7 EE	USSR
1950	1 001	1 651	3 501	2 480	2 447	1 182	1 551	2 111	2 841
1951	1 045	1 989	3 524	2 695	2 510	1 256	1 591	2 206	2 806
1952	1 046	1 893	3 598	2 762	2 521	1 333	1 448	2 207	2 937
1953	1 089	2 085	3 544	2 786	2 618	1 411	1 643	2 296	3 013
1954	1 120	2 025	3 652	2 850	2 715	1 496	1 712	2 370	3 106
1955	1 181	2 148	3 922	3 070	2 794	1 578	1 797	2 495	3 313
1956	1 193	2 128	4 110	2 906	2 864	1 623	1 742	2 521	3 566
1957	1 269	2 330	4 320	3 169	2 962	1 672	2 014	2 682	3 576
1958	1 326	2 508	4 610	3 367	3 057	1 724	2 080	2 806	3 777
1959	1 381	2 684	4 780	3 484	3 096	1 783	2 314	2 921	3 669
1960	1 451	2 912	5 108	3 649	3 215	1 844	2 437	3 070	3 945
1961	1 463	3 072	5 263	3 816	3 426	1 951	2 522	3 218	4 098
1962	1 511	3 295	5 304	3 962	3 341	2 007	2 544	3 244	4 140
1963	1 563	3 418	5 170	4 168	3 502	2 137	2 781	3 372	3 985
1964	1 616	3 657	5 372	4 388	3 622	2 258	3 019	3 542	4 439
1965	1 675	3 850	5 533	4 410	3 787	2 386	3 071	3 664	4 634
1966	1 738	4 125	5 741	4 646	3 991	2 643	3 205	3 871	4 804
1967	1 804	4 320	5 964	4 894	4 103	2 743	3 232	3 996	4 963
1968	1 869	4 368	6 223	4 934	4 317	2 739	3 272	4 106	5 202
1969	1 932	4 546	6 354	5 062	4 241	2 824	3 610	4 200	5 225
1970	2 004	4 773	6 466	5 028	4 428	2 853	3 755	4 315	5 575
1971	2 084	4 902	6 658	5 238	4 707	3 221	4 151	4 596	5 667
1972	2 165	5 110	6 858	5 336	5 010	3 396	4 255	4 790	5 643
1973	2 273	5 284	7 041	5 596	5 340	3 477	4 361	4 988	6 059
1974	2 282	5 414	7 243	5 716	5 601	3 637	4 879	5 239	6 176
1975	2 289	5 831	7 399	5 805	5 808	3 761	4 836	5 377	6 135
1976	2 299	5 982	7 461	5 791	5 895	3 917	4 939	5 469	6 363
1977	2 309	5 896	7 744	6 126	5 949	3 966	5 250	5 612	6 454
1978	2 319	6 019	7 786	6 253	6 111	4 063	5 491	5 749	6 559
1979	2 331	6 245	7 804	6 251	5 942	4 148	5 819	5 793	6 472
1980	2 347	6 044	7 982	6 306	5 740	4 135	6 063	5 786	6 426
1981	2 360	6 186	7 912	6 351	5 385	4 087	6 134	5 685	6 430
1982	2 373	6 370	8 045	6 583	5 288	4 072	6 146	5 705	6 533
1983	2 387	6 237	8 147	6 525	5 498	4 027	6 172	5 762	6 680
1984	2 400	6 430	8 319	6 710	5 650	4 178	6 300	5 913	6 703
1985	2 413	6 226	8 367	6 557	5 660	4 159	6 325	5 892	6 701
1986	2 428	6 380	8 507	6 699	5 797	4 215	6 559	6 028	6 914
1987	2 443	6 382	8 534	6 814	5 683	4 110	6 462	5 966	6 942
1988	2 459	6 335	8 709	7 031	5 789	4 085	6 351	6 008	7 031
1989	2 477	6 216	8 768	6 903	5 684	3 941	6 250	5 915	7 098
1990	2 494	5 597	8 513	6 459	5 113	3 511	5 779	5 450	6 878
1991	1 806	5 198	7 438	5 694	4 738	3 063	4 942	4 844	6 409
1992	1 710	4 930	7 255	5 528	4 842	2 797	3 989	4 591	5 451
1993	1 876	4 933	7 169	5 507	5 010	2 843	3 349	4 526	4 903
1994	2 015	5 070	7 374	5 678	5 261	2 957	3 513	4 714	4 207
1995	2 256	5 272	7 817	5 772	5 623	3 174	3 729	4 998	3 976
1996	2 428	4 830	8 187	5 862	5 957	3 307	3 923	5 196	3 854
1997	2 233	4 614	8 274	6 148	6 324	3 114	4 147	5 333	3 939
1998	2 376	4 858	8 318	6 467	6 667	2 972	4 245	5 487	3 861
1999	2 493	5 054	8 381	6 762	6 938	2 943	4 101	5 588	4 027
2000	2 651	5 365	8 630	7 138	7 215	3 002	4 258	5 804	4 351
2001	2 807	5 644	8 915	7 434	7 491	3 168	4 376	6 027	4 626
2002									4 844

http://dx.doi.org/10.1787/456125276116

HS–3: B. 7 Successor States of Former Czechoslovakia and Yugoslavia

Table 3a. **Population of Successor Republics of Yugoslavia and Czechoslovakia, 1950-2003**
(000 at mid-year)

	Bosnia	Croatia	Macedonia	Slovenia	Serbia/ Montenegro	Former Yugoslavia	Czech Republic	Slovakia	Former Czecho-slovakia
1950	2 662	3 837	1 225	1 468	7 106	16 298	8 925	3 463	12 389
1951	2 721	3 860	1 256	1 483	7 199	16 519	9 023	3 509	12 532
1952	2 791	3 882	1 272	1 490	7 274	16 708	9 125	3 558	12 683
1953	2 863	3 906	1 299	1 498	7 370	16 937	9 221	3 599	12 820
1954	2 916	3 930	1 325	1 509	7 471	17 151	9 291	3 661	12 952
1955	2 974	3 956	1 340	1 517	7 577	17 364	9 366	3 727	13 093
1956	3 025	3 973	1 340	1 525	7 644	17 508	9 442	3 787	13 229
1957	3 076	3 991	1 345	1 533	7 714	17 659	9 514	3 844	13 358
1958	3 126	4 004	1 345	1 540	7 780	17 796	9 575	3 900	13 474
1959	3 185	4 021	1 354	1 549	7 860	17 968	9 619	3 946	13 565
1960	3 240	4 036	1 366	1 558	7 932	18 133	9 660	3 994	13 654
1961	3 299	4 055	1 382	1 572	8 010	18 318	9 587	4 192	13 779
1962	3 349	4 077	1 401	1 583	8 091	18 500	9 620	4 237	13 858
1963	3 399	4 099	1 422	1 595	8 170	18 685	9 666	4 282	13 948
1964	3 445	4 114	1 445	1 606	8 243	18 852	9 726	4 326	14 052
1965	3 493	4 133	1 470	1 620	8 322	19 038	9 777	4 370	14 147
1966	3 541	4 156	1 490	1 632	8 403	19 221	9 815	4 409	14 224
1967	3 585	4 174	1 512	1 647	8 472	19 390	9 835	4 442	14 277
1968	3 627	4 190	1 533	1 658	8 545	19 552	9 851	4 472	14 323
1969	3 669	4 201	1 554	1 667	8 615	19 705	9 807	4 478	14 284
1970	3 703	4 205	1 574	1 676	8 681	19 840	9 795	4 524	14 319
1971	3 761	4 216	1 596	1 686	8 756	20 015	9 825	4 557	14 381
1972	3 819	4 225	1 618	1 695	8 841	20 197	9 862	4 593	14 456
1973	3 872	4 235	1 639	1 703	8 918	20 367	9 912	4 637	14 549
1974	3 925	4 246	1 662	1 713	9 004	20 550	9 976	4 682	14 658
1975	3 980	4 255	1 684	1 722	9 091	20 732	10 042	4 730	14 772
1976	4 033	4 286	1 706	1 734	9 169	20 930	10 105	4 779	14 884
1977	4 086	4 319	1 728	1 747	9 246	21 126	10 162	4 828	14 990
1978	4 135	4 349	1 747	1 759	9 318	21 309	10 213	4 876	15 089
1979	4 181	4 380	1 768	1 773	9 388	21 490	10 260	4 923	15 182
1980	4 092	4 383	1 792	1 833	9 515	21 615	10 289	4 966	15 255
1981	4 136	4 391	1 808	1 839	9 533	21 707	10 298	5 014	15 312
1982	4 173	4 413	1 827	1 851	9 595	21 860	10 304	5 048	15 352
1983	4 207	4 431	1 838	1 858	9 633	21 968	10 307	5 081	15 388
1984	4 241	4 442	1 848	1 866	9 615	22 012	10 309	5 114	15 423
1985	4 275	4 458	1 859	1 873	9 650	22 115	10 310	5 145	15 455
1986	4 308	4 472	1 868	1 880	9 685	22 213	10 309	5 172	15 481
1987	4 339	4 484	1 878	1 883	9 698	22 283	10 312	5 199	15 511
1988	4 370	4 494	1 884	1 889	9 722	22 358	10 314	5 223	15 537
1989	4 398	4 501	1 891	1 892	9 746	22 429	10 314	5 245	15 559
1990	4 424	4 508	1 893	1 896	9 766	22 488	10 310	5 263	15 572
1991	4 449	4 541	1 903	1 894	10 018	22 806	10 305	5 282	15 587
1992	4 427	4 432	1 929	1 892	10 232	22 912	10 316	5 303	15 619
1993	4 152	4 421	1 962	1 896	10 345	22 775	10 327	5 324	15 650
1994	3 704	4 488	1 983	1 903	10 464	22 543	10 331	5 345	15 676
1995	3 356	4 455	1 986	1 909	10 641	22 347	10 325	5 362	15 687
1996	3 247	4 373	1 993	1 914	10 775	22 303	10 313	5 373	15 686
1997	3 335	4 320	2 002	1 918	10 817	22 391	10 301	5 384	15 685
1998	3 502	4 265	2 015	1 921	10 803	22 506	10 291	5 393	15 684
1999	3 690	4 254	2 032	1 924	10 698	22 600	10 281	5 401	15 682
2000	3 836	4 282	2 041	1 928	10 663	22 750	10 272	5 408	15 680
2001	3 922	4 334	2 046	1 930	10 678	22 911	10 264	5 415	15 679
2002	3 964	4 391	2 055	1 933	10 658	23 001	10 257	5 422	15 679
2003	3 989	4 422	2 063	1 936	10 656	23 066	10 249	5 430	15 679

http://dx.doi.org/10.1787/456125276116

Table 3b. GDP Levels in Successor Republics of Yugoslavia and Czechoslovakia, 1990-2001
(million 1990 international Geary-Khamis dollars)

	Bosnia	Croatia	Macedonia	Slovenia	Serbia/ Montenegro	Former Yugoslavia	Czech Republic	Slovakia	Former Czecho- slovakia
1990	16 530	33 139	7 394	21 624	51 266	129 953	91 706	40 854	132 560
1991	14 610	26 147	6 935	19 699	45 319	112 710	81 068	34 869	115 937
1992	10 535	23 088	6 478	18 616	32 675	91 392	80 662	32 656	113 318
1993	7 287	21 241	5 992	19 137	22 611	76 268	80 743	31 448	112 191
1994	7 484	22 494	5 884	20 152	23 176	79 190	82 520	33 083	115 603
1995	7 933	24 023	5 819	20 978	24 590	83 343	87 388	35 233	122 621
1996	8 400	25 441	5 889	21 712	26 041	87 483	91 146	37 277	128 423
1997	9 028	27 171	5 972	22 711	27 968	92 850	90 417	39 365	129 782
1998	9 261	27 850	6 175	23 574	28 667	95 527	89 512	40 940	130 452
1999	10 243	27 599	6 440	24 800	23 593	92 675	89 960	41 471	131 431
2000	10 704	28 400	6 730	25 941	25 103	96 878	92 929	42 384	135 313
2001	10 950	29 479	6 454	26 719	26 660	100 262	95 995	43 782	139 777

Table 3c. Per Capita GDP in Successor Republics of Yugoslavia and Czechoslovakia, 1990-2001
(1990 international Geary-Khamis dollars)

	Bosnia	Croatia	Macedonia	Slovenia	Serbia/ Montenegro	Former Yugoslavia	Czech Republic	Slovakia	Former Czecho- slovakia
1990	3 737	7 351	3 905	11 404	5 249	5 779	8 895	7 763	8 513
1991	3 284	5 758	3 644	10 402	4 524	4 942	7 867	6 602	7 438
1992	2 380	5 209	3 358	9 842	3 194	3 989	7 819	6 158	7 255
1993	1 755	4 805	3 055	10 094	2 186	3 349	7 819	5 907	7 169
1994	2 021	5 012	2 967	10 590	2 215	3 513	7 988	6 189	7 374
1995	2 364	5 392	2 930	10 987	2 311	3 729	8 464	6 571	7 817
1996	2 587	5 818	2 954	11 341	2 417	3 923	8 838	6 938	8 187
1997	2 707	6 290	2 983	11 842	2 586	4 147	8 777	7 312	8 274
1998	2 644	6 530	3 065	12 272	2 654	4 245	8 698	7 592	8 318
1999	2 776	6 487	3 169	12 886	2 205	4 101	8 750	7 679	8 381
2000	2 791	6 632	3 297	13 458	2 354	4 258	9 047	7 837	8 630
2001	2 792	6 802	3 154	13 843	2 497	4 376	9 352	8 085	8 915

http://dx.doi.org/10.1787/456125276116

HS–3: C. 15 Successor States of Former USSR

Table 3a. Population of Successor Republics of USSR, 1950-2003
(000 at mid-year)

	Armenia	Azerbaijan	Belarus	Estonia	Georgia	Kazakhstan	Kyrgyzstan	Latvia
1950	1 355	2 885	7 722	1 096	3 516	6 693	1 739	1 936
1951	1 379	2 983	7 742	1 112	3 579	6 936	1 767	1 951
1952	1 417	3 091	7 698	1 130	3 628	7 123	1 787	1 964
1953	1 456	3 159	7 667	1 140	3 687	7 261	1 817	1 976
1954	1 506	3 223	7 699	1 148	3 760	7 517	1 858	1 991
1955	1 565	3 314	7 781	1 154	3 827	7 977	1 901	2 002
1956	1 617	3 417	7 857	1 163	3 887	8 414	1 939	2 026
1957	1 672	3 526	7 913	1 174	3 937	8 710	1 976	2 056
1958	1 733	3 631	7 983	1 185	3 995	9 063	2 027	2 072
1959	1 796	3 741	8 075	1 197	4 071	9 500	2 096	2 089
1960	1 869	3 882	8 168	1 211	4 147	9 982	2 171	2 115
1961	1 944	4 034	8 263	1 224	4 211	10 467	2 255	2 146
1962	2 007	4 157	8 365	1 239	4 279	10 946	2 333	2 173
1963	2 066	4 283	8 439	1 255	4 344	11 312	2 413	2 199
1964	2 135	4 430	8 502	1 272	4 407	11 602	2 495	2 227
1965	2 206	4 567	8 591	1 288	4 465	11 902	2 573	2 254
1966	2 274	4 702	8 694	1 300	4 518	12 180	2 655	2 279
1967	2 338	4 827	8 787	1 312	4 565	12 452	2 737	2 301
1968	2 402	4 945	8 865	1 324	4 607	12 692	2 818	2 322
1969	2 463	5 059	8 946	1 343	4 650	12 900	2 896	2 342
1970	2 520	5 169	9 027	1 363	4 694	13 106	2 964	2 361
1971	2 582	5 284	9 101	1 381	4 742	13 325	3 029	2 382
1972	2 647	5 394	9 169	1 397	4 786	13 542	3 095	2 401
1973	2 713	5 498	9 236	1 411	4 826	13 754	3 161	2 421
1974	2 777	5 599	9 304	1 422	4 865	13 972	3 232	2 442
1975	2 834	5 696	9 360	1 432	4 898	14 157	3 301	2 462
1976	2 893	5 790	9 406	1 442	4 930	14 304	3 367	2 477
1977	2 955	5 887	9 457	1 453	4 963	14 455	3 432	2 491
1978	3 014	5 986	9 520	1 464	4 991	14 624	3 496	2 505
1979	3 067	6 082	9 582	1 472	5 019	14 804	3 559	2 514
1980	3 115	6 173	9 644	1 482	5 048	14 994	3 623	2 525
1981	3 165	6 271	9 713	1 493	5 078	15 192	3 690	2 538
1982	3 217	6 369	9 779	1 504	5 109	15 389	3 763	2 554
1983	3 267	6 470	9 845	1 515	5 141	15 582	3 842	2 572
1984	3 319	6 579	9 914	1 526	5 174	15 775	3 924	2 591
1985	3 369	6 682	9 982	1 538	5 208	15 966	4 006	2 610
1986	3 417	6 776	10 044	1 550	5 237	16 154	4 089	2 631
1987	3 463	6 874	10 097	1 562	5 260	16 349	4 176	2 654
1988	3 509	6 976	10 150	1 569	5 343	16 478	4 244	2 670
1989	3 319	7 102	10 184	1 571	5 424	16 568	4 304	2 674
1990	3 366	7 200	10 215	1 573	5 457	16 708	4 390	2 672
1991	3 413	7 308	10 245	1 568	5 478	16 855	4 468	2 663
1992	3 448	7 414	10 306	1 546	5 466	16 985	4 532	2 631
1993	3 458	7 497	10 361	1 517	5 422	17 016	4 552	2 586
1994	3 440	7 573	10 388	1 499	5 359	16 990	4 544	2 552
1995	3 414	7 630	10 404	1 484	5 287	16 943	4 535	2 523
1996	3 394	7 668	10 409	1 470	5 216	16 882	4 537	2 496
1997	3 378	7 695	10 404	1 458	5 154	16 824	4 552	2 470
1998	3 365	7 714	10 394	1 449	5 100	16 779	4 581	2 447
1999	3 354	7 729	10 382	1 440	5 055	16 749	4 626	2 426
2000	3 344	7 748	10 367	1 431	5 020	16 733	4 685	2 405
2001	3 336	7 771	10 350	1 423	4 989	16 731	4 753	2 385
2002	3 330	7 798	10 335	1 416	4 961	16 742	4 822	2 367
2003	3 326	7 831	10 322	1 409	4 934	16 764	4 893	2 349

http://dx.doi.org/10.1787/456125276116

Table 3a. **Population of Successor Republics of USSR, 1950-2003**
(000 at mid-year)

	Lithuania	Moldova	Russian Federation	Tajikistan	Turkmenistan	Ukraine	Uzbekistan	Former USSR
1950	2 553	2 336	101 937	1 530	1 204	36 775	6 293	179 571
1951	2 562	2 422	103 507	1 585	1 226	37 436	6 490	182 677
1952	2 584	2 467	105 385	1 641	1 253	38 006	6 681	185 856
1953	2 594	2 506	107 303	1 684	1 283	38 541	6 886	188 961
1954	2 597	2 566	109 209	1 730	1 313	38 994	7 061	192 171
1955	2 614	2 622	111 125	1 781	1 348	39 368	7 232	195 613
1956	2 641	2 682	112 859	1 837	1 382	39 940	7 441	199 103
1957	2 652	2 759	114 555	1 899	1 426	40 656	7 694	202 604
1958	2 672	2 838	116 259	1 954	1 478	41 359	7 952	206 201
1959	2 718	2 919	117 957	2 009	1 530	42 006	8 223	209 928
1960	2 765	2 999	119 632	2 081	1 585	42 644	8 531	213 780
1961	2 810	3 069	121 324	2 163	1 644	43 196	8 868	217 618
1962	2 850	3 136	122 878	2 253	1 705	43 697	9 210	221 227
1963	2 886	3 205	124 277	2 340	1 765	44 256	9 547	224 585
1964	2 923	3 271	125 522	2 424	1 825	44 786	9 878	227 698
1965	2 959	3 334	126 541	2 511	1 882	45 235	10 206	230 513
1966	2 997	3 394	127 415	2 593	1 936	45 674	10 530	233 139
1967	3 034	3 452	128 184	2 672	1 994	46 111	10 864	235 630
1968	3 069	3 506	128 876	2 759	2 054	46 510	11 232	237 983
1969	3 102	3 549	129 573	2 850	2 116	46 871	11 591	240 253
1970	3 138	3 595	130 245	2 939	2 181	47 236	11 940	242 478
1971	3 178	3 649	130 977	3 039	2 247	47 637	12 334	244 887
1972	3 213	3 703	131 769	3 145	2 313	48 027	12 742	247 343
1973	3 246	3 753	132 556	3 243	2 380	48 367	13 148	249 712
1974	3 276	3 801	133 379	3 345	2 451	48 677	13 569	252 111
1975	3 305	3 847	134 293	3 449	2 524	48 973	13 988	254 519
1976	3 334	3 886	135 269	3 554	2 594	49 234	14 404	256 883
1977	3 361	3 920	136 264	3 659	2 664	49 454	14 809	259 225
1978	3 387	3 947	137 246	3 761	2 734	49 643	15 207	261 525
1979	3 411	3 970	138 164	3 863	2 804	49 835	15 605	263 751
1980	3 436	3 996	139 045	3 969	2 875	50 047	16 000	265 973
1981	3 464	4 026	139 913	4 079	2 947	50 236	16 413	268 217
1982	3 494	4 055	140 841	4 194	3 018	50 397	16 850	270 533
1983	3 526	4 083	141 888	4 316	3 091	50 573	17 298	273 010
1984	3 559	4 113	142 955	4 446	3 165	50 769	17 764	275 574
1985	3 592	4 148	143 978	4 587	3 240	50 944	18 258	278 108
1986	3 625	4 183	145 013	4 738	3 324	51 095	18 769	280 646
1987	3 660	4 217	146 013	4 891	3 411	51 218	19 280	283 124
1988	3 681	4 290	146 926	5 036	3 492	51 423	19 694	285 482
1989	3 689	4 359	147 419	5 183	3 574	51 528	20 112	287 011
1990	3 702	4 398	148 082	5 332	3 668	51 658	20 624	289 045
1991	3 709	4 428	148 460	5 481	3 761	51 782	21 137	290 754
1992	3 707	4 448	148 587	5 601	3 848	51 946	21 614	292 079
1993	3 694	4 460	148 479	5 682	3 934	51 978	22 049	292 686
1994	3 682	4 463	148 300	5 771	4 019	51 712	22 462	292 755
1995	3 673	4 460	148 115	5 864	4 102	51 316	22 847	292 597
1996	3 662	4 451	147 757	5 964	4 184	50 879	23 220	292 188
1997	3 652	4 442	147 364	6 071	4 267	50 423	23 597	291 750
1998	3 642	4 436	146 964	6 186	4 350	49 989	23 977	291 373
1999	3 631	4 432	146 516	6 309	4 434	49 566	24 363	291 012
2000	3 621	4 431	146 001	6 441	4 518	49 153	24 756	290 654
2001	3 611	4 432	145 470	6 579	4 603	48 760	25 155	290 349
2002	3 601	4 435	144 979	6 720	4 689	48 396	25 563	290 154
2003	3 593	4 440	144 526	6 864	4 776	48 055	25 982	290 062

http://dx.doi.org/10.1787/456125276116

Table 3b. **GDP Levels in Successor Republics of USSR, 1973-2002**
(million 1990 international Geary-Khamis dollars)

	Armenia	Azerbaijan	Belarus	Estonia	Georgia	Kazakhstan	Kyrgyzstan	Latvia
1973	16 691	24 378	48 333	12 214	28 627	104 875	11 781	18 998
1990	20 483	33 397	73 389	16 980	41 325	122 295	15 787	26 413
1991	18 077	33 159	72 491	15 280	32 612	108 830	14 537	23 666
1992	10 534	25 673	65 534	13 118	17 961	103 024	12 533	15 426
1993	9 602	19 736	60 596	12 010	12 704	93 636	10 590	13 117
1994	10 121	15 848	55 142	11 770	11 383	81 838	8 493	13 196
1995	10 819	13 978	49 408	12 276	11 679	75 045	8 035	13 090
1996	11 457	14 160	45 079	12 755	12 905	75 421	8 597	13 522
1997	12 294	14 981	56 581	14 005	14 196	76 246	9 448	14 685
1998	13 191	16 479	61 277	14 649	14 607	74 797	9 646	15 258
1999	13 626	17 698	63 361	14 561	15 045	76 817	10 003	15 425
2000	14 443	19 663	67 036	15 595	15 331	84 345	10 544	16 295
2001	15 830	21 433	69 784	16 375	16 021	95 478	11 102	17 534
2002	17 025	23 126	72 227	17 111	16 582	103 117	11 591	18 411

Table 3c. **Per Capita GDP in Successor Republics of USSR, 1973-2002**
(1990 international Geary-Khamis dollars)

	Armenia	Azerbaijan	Belarus	Estonia	Georgia	Kazakhstan	Kyrgyzstan	Latvia
1973	6 152	4 434	5 233	8 657	5 932	7 625	3 727	7 846
1990	6 086	4 639	7 184	10 794	7 573	7 319	3 596	9 886
1991	5 297	4 537	7 076	9 744	5 954	6 457	3 253	8 888
1992	3 055	3 463	6 359	8 488	3 286	6 066	2 766	5 863
1993	2 776	2 632	5 849	7 916	2 343	5 503	2 326	5 071
1994	2 942	2 093	5 308	7 850	2 124	4 817	1 869	5 171
1995	3 169	1 832	4 749	8 274	2 209	4 429	1 772	5 189
1996	3 376	1 847	4 331	8 680	2 474	4 468	1 895	5 418
1997	3 640	1 947	5 438	9 605	2 755	4 532	2 076	5 944
1998	3 920	2 136	5 895	10 112	2 864	4 458	2 105	6 236
1999	4 062	2 290	6 103	10 112	2 976	4 586	2 162	6 359
2000	4 319	2 538	6 466	10 894	3 054	5 041	2 250	6 776
2001	4 745	2 758	6 742	11 505	3 211	5 707	2 336	7 351
2002	5 112	2 965	6 988	12 087	3 343	6 159	2 404	7 780

http://dx.doi.org/10.1787/456125276116

Table 3b. GDP Levels in Successor Republics of USSR, 1973-2002
(million 1990 international Geary-Khamis dollars)

	Lithuania	Moldova	Russian Federation	Tajikistan	Turkmenistan	Ukraine	Uzbekistan	Former USSR
1973	24 643	20 134	872 466	13 279	11 483	238 156	67 012	1 513 070
1990	32 010	27 112	1 151 040	15 884	13 300	311 112	87 468	1 987 995
1991	30 189	22 362	1 094 081	14 537	12 673	284 003	87 027	1 863 524
1992	23 768	15 889	935 072	9 844	10 778	255 602	77 328	1 592 084
1993	19 928	15 695	853 194	8 243	10 935	219 457	75 565	1 435 008
1994	17 975	10 845	738 013	6 479	9 043	169 201	72 391	1 231 738
1995	18 568	10 693	707 016	5 669	8 392	148 559	70 174	1 163 401
1996	19 181	10 063	682 978	5 420	7 863	133 703	72 888	1 125 992
1997	20 581	10 224	689 125	5 512	6 975	129 692	74 710	1 149 255
1998	21 631	9 559	655 357	5 804	7 463	127 228	77 922	1 124 868
1999	22 474	9 234	690 747	6 019	8 695	126 974	81 273	1 171 952
2000	23 328	9 428	752 914	6 518	10 260	134 465	84 361	1 264 526
2001	24 705	10 003	790 560	7 183	12 363	146 701	88 158	1 343 230
2002	25 791	10 483	825 345	7 686	12 863	153 743	90 538	1 405 639

Table 3c. Per Capita GDP in Successor Republics of USSR, 1973-2002
(1990 international Geary-Khamis dollars)

	Lithuania	Moldova	Russian Federation	Tajikistan	Turkmenistan	Ukraine	Uzbekistan	Former USSR
1973	7 593	5 365	6 582	4 095	4 826	4 924	5 097	6 059
1990	8 646	6 165	7 773	2 979	3 626	6 023	4 241	6 878
1991	8 139	5 051	7 370	2 652	3 370	5 485	4 117	6 409
1992	6 412	3 572	6 293	1 758	2 801	4 921	3 578	5 451
1993	5 395	3 519	5 746	1 451	2 780	4 222	3 427	4 903
1994	4 881	2 430	4 976	1 123	2 250	3 272	3 223	4 207
1995	5 055	2 398	4 773	967	2 046	2 895	3 071	3 976
1996	5 237	2 261	4 622	909	1 879	2 628	3 139	3 854
1997	5 636	2 302	4 676	908	1 635	2 572	3 166	3 939
1998	5 940	2 155	4 459	938	1 716	2 545	3 250	3 861
1999	6 189	2 083	4 714	954	1 961	2 562	3 336	4 027
2000	6 443	2 128	5 157	1 012	2 271	2 736	3 408	4 351
2001	6 842	2 257	5 435	1 092	2 686	3 009	3 505	4 626
2002	7 162	2 364	5 693	1 144	2 743	3 177	3 542	4 844

http://dx.doi.org/10.1787/456125276116

HS–4: Latin America

1500–1820s: Impact of Conquest and Colonisation on Output and Population

At the end of the fifteenth century, at the time of Spanish conquest, the Americas were thinly settled. The population was a third of that in Western Europe and the land area eleven times as large. The technological level was greatly inferior. There were no wheeled vehicles or draught animals, no metal tools, weapons or ploughs. There were no cattle, sheep, pigs or hens. The most densely populated areas (Mexico and Peru) had significant urban centres and a sophisticated vegetarian agriculture. Elsewhere, most of the inhabitants were hunter–gatherers.

American populations had no resistance to European (smallpox, measles, influenza and typhus) and African diseases (yellow fever and malaria). By the middle of the sixteenth century two thirds of them were wiped out. Mortality was twice that of Europe during the Black Death of the fourteenth century.

The two advanced civilisations (Aztec in Mexico and Inca in Peru) were destroyed. Their populations were reduced to anomie and serfdom. Hunter–gatherer populations elsewhere were marginalised or exterminated. The economy of these relatively empty lands was completely revamped. The Latin part of the continent was repopulated by shipment of 7.5 million African slaves and arrival of 1.5 million European settlers. By 1820, 22 per cent of the population were white, 24 per cent black or mulatto, 37 per cent indigenous and 16 per cent mestizo. European settlers had higher fertility, longer life expectation, and very much higher average incomes than African slaves and the indigenous population.

Although the initial impact of conquest was massively destructive, the long–term economic potential was greatly enhanced. Capacity to support a bigger population was augmented by the introduction of new crops and animals. The new items were wheat, rice, sugar cane, vines, cabbages, lettuce, olives, bananas, yams and coffee. The new animals for food were cattle, pigs, chickens, sheep and goats. The introduction of transport and traction animals — horses, oxen, asses and mules — along with wheeled vehicles and ploughs (which replaced digging sticks) were a major contribution to productive capacity. There was a reciprocal transfer of New World crops to Europe, Asia and Africa–maize, potatoes, sweet potatoes, manioc, chilis, tomatoes, groundnuts, haricot, lima and string beans, pineapples, cocoa and tobacco–which enhanced the rest of the world's production capacity and ability to sustain population growth.

The experience of the Americas from 1500 to 1820 was very different from other continents. The demographic catastrophe of the sixteenth century and the collapse of the indigenous economy had no parallel elsewhere. Population and output recovered somewhat in the seventeenth century, but in 1700 were still well below 1500 levels. Growth accelerated in the eighteenth century. By 1820, GDP was twice as big as in 1500, and average per capita income above the world average. The economy, technology and economic institutions had been transformed. Most of the continent was in process of attaining political independence. From 1820 to 2001, demographic expansion was the most dynamic aspect of Latin American development. Population rose 24–fold, compared to 3–fold in the former metropoles (Spain and Portugal). Per capita performance was less impressive. GDP per head rose 8–fold, compared with 15–fold in the old metropoles and 22–fold in North America.

Table 4-1. **The Economies of the Americas, Five Regions, 1500-2001**
(population in 000; per capita GDP in 1990 int. $; GDP in million 1990 int. $)

	1500	1600	1700	1820	2001
			Mexico		
Population	7 500	2 500	4 500	6 587	101 879
Per Capita GDP	425	454	568	759	7 089
GDP	3 188	1 134	2 558	5 000	722 198
		15 Other Spanish America (ex. Caribbean)			
Population	8 500	5 100	5 800	7 691	212 919
Per Capita GDP	412	432	498	683	5 663
GDP	3 500	2 201	2 889	5 255	1 205 630
		30 Caribbean Countries			
Population	500	200	500	2 920	38 650
Per Capita GDP	400	430	650	636	4 373
GDP	200	86	325	1 857	169 032
			Brazil		
Population	1 000	800	1 250	4 507	177 753
Per Capita GDP	400	428	459	646	5 570
GDP	400	342	574	2 912	990 076
		United States and Canada			
Population	2 250	1 750	1 200	10 797	316 617
Per Capita GDP	400	400	511	1 231	27 384
GDP	900	700	613	13 286	8 670 389
			Latin America		
Population	17 500	8 600	12 050	21 705	531 201
Per Capita GDP	416	438	527	692	5 811
GDP	7 288	3 763	6 346	15 024	3 086 936

http://dx.doi.org/10.1787/456125276116

ISBN 92-64-02261-9 – © OECD 2006

Table 4-2. **Ethnic Composition of the Americas in 1820**
(000)

	Indigenous	Mestizo	Black and Mulatto	White	Total
Mexico	3 570	1 777	10	1 230	6 587
Brazil	500		2 500	1 507	4 507
Caribbean			2 366	554	2 920
Other	4 000	1 800	400	1 491	7 691
Total Latin America	8 070	3 577	5 276	4 776	21 705
United States	325		1 772	7 884	9 981
Canada	75			741	816
Total Americas	8 470	3 577	7 048	13 407	32 502

Source: Maddison (2001), p. 250 amended (see text for Caribbean).

Table 4-3. **Net Non-Slave Migration to the Americas, 1500-1998**
(000)

	1500-1820	1820-1998
Brazil	500	4 500
Spanish America	475	6 500
Caribbean	450	2 000
Canada	30	6 395
United States	718	53 150
Total Americas	2 173	72 545

Table 4-4. **Arrivals of African Slaves in the Americas, 1500-1870**
(000)

	1500-1810	1811-1870	1500-1870
Brazil	2 501	1 145	3 647
Spanish America	947	606	1 552
Non-Spanish Caribbean	3 698	96	3 793
United States	348	51	399
Total Americas	7 494	1 898	9 391

Source: P.D. Curtin (1969), *The Atlantic Slave Trade*, University of Wisconsin, Madison, p. 268.

http://dx.doi.org/10.1787/456125276116

The striking differences between the growth trajectories of Latin and North America were due in significant degree to differences in the type of colonialism and their enduring impact on institutions and social structure.

Spain concentrated its colonial activity in Mexico and Peru, which were the most densely populated at the time of conquest. The Aztec and Inca elites and their priesthood were exterminated. Old gods, calendars, records, relics, property rights and indigenous institutions disappeared. Churches and convents were built on the ruins of Aztec and Inca temples. The main agents of social control were the religious orders. Land was allocated to a privileged elite of Spaniards, giving them control of a traumatised Indian population, which was compelled to supply labour to mines and agriculture. There were rigid social distinctions between the ruling elite and the indigenous population which had no legal rights, access to education or land. The main aim of this tribute imperialism was to transfer a fiscal surplus (in precious metals) to finance government aspirations in Europe. Spain was well prepared to exercise this type of hegemony. It had several centuries of experience in reconquest of territory from the Moors. It had the military know–how and organisation for conquest, and a church experienced in evangelising, converting and indoctrinating a conquered population. Islam and Judaism were proscribed in Spain, just as the Aztec and Inca religions were extirpated in Mexico and Peru. The church was firmly under national control; the king being free to appoint bishops under a sixteenth century treaty with the Papacy. Centuries of militant struggle had concentrated power and legitimacy on the monarchy as the ultimate arbiter, against which rebellion even in very distant colonies was seldom imagined before the last quarter of the eighteenth century.

By 1825, the American empire had collapsed and more than 14 million people were no longer Spanish. In 1790, it had covered 16 million square km. Cuba and Puerto Rico were all that was left– with an area of 12 thousand square km, and a population less than 700 000. In South America, nine new nations had emerged with a total area of 8.8 million square km. Mexico had an area of 4.4 million square km. Five countries in Central America had formed a temporary union. Independence was achieved by armed struggle, and the process of state–formation was not smooth. The new states inherited the deep inequalities of the colonial period. In Mexico there were five decades of political anarchy after independence, half the land area was lost to the United States, and per capita income was a good deal lower in 1870 than in 1820. This was not untypical of what happened elsewhere.

Portugal had much more pragmatic objectives in Brazil, developing an export agriculture based on sugar plantations, with much looser imperial control. As indigenous labour was scarce, its labour force was composed largely of African slaves. Between 1500 and 1870, 3.6 million were shipped to Brazil. At the end of the colonial period, half the population were slaves. They were worked to death after a few years of service, and fed on a crude diet of beans and jerked beef. A privileged fraction of the white population enjoyed high incomes but the rest of the population (indigenous, free blacks, mulattos, and large numbers of whites) were poor. Land–ownership was concentrated on slave owners. A very unequal distribution of property buttressed a highly unequal distribution of income. Independence came very smoothly by Latin American standards. In 1808, the Portuguese Queen and the Regent fled to Rio to escape the French invasion of the motherland. They brought 10 000 of the mainland establishment with them. After the Napoleonic wars, Brazil became independent with an Emperor who was the son of the Portuguese monarch. Brazil abolished slavery and became a republic in 1889.

The Netherlands, the United Kingdom and France copied the Portuguese model in Caribbean islands they seized from Spain in the seventeenth century. These colonies were highly specialised in sugar production, importing most of their food. By 1820, they had imported 3.7 million African slaves. Output rose tenfold between the 1660s and the 1780. A large part of the profits were siphoned off to absentee owners who preferred the healthier climate of the metropoles. The loss of privileged export markets in North America after 1776, interruptions to trade during the Napoleonic wars, and the successful slave revolt in Haiti persuaded the planting lobby that their days were numbered and that it was in their interest to settle for compensation. The prohibition of the slave trade and subsequent abolition of slavery raised costs and weakened the competitive position of most Caribbean producers (in spite of the introduction of 700 000 indentured Asian workers between 1838 and 1913). In 1787 the Caribbean accounted for 90 per cent of world sugar exports; in 1913 about a sixth. Except for Cuba and Puerto Rico, the Caribbean became an economic backwater. Real GDP per head fell by a quarter in Jamaica between 1832 and 1870, exports fell from 41 to 15 per cent of GDP. In 1930, the per capita GDP level was about the same as in 1832. For the British and French islands, this experience was probably fairly typical.

Sources for 1500–1820

Population: The size of the indigenous population at the time of the Spanish conquest was a matter of considerable controversy, and there were two extreme schools of thought. Borah and Cook (1963) estimated 25 million for central Mexico on the basis of ambiguous pictographs describing the incidence of Aztec fiscal levies. They assumed a 95 per cent depopulation ratio for the indigenous population for 1519–1605, and backcast Spanish estimates for 1605 by a multiplier of 25. Rosenblat (1945) made a careful survey of literary evidence, and estimated the pre–conquest population to have been 4.5 million with a drop of less than 15 per cent in the sixteenth century. There are two reasons for scepticism about the Borah estimates for Mexico and Latin America as a whole: *a)* they assume very much higher disease mortality than European experience with the Black Death; *b)* they assume that population did not recover its alleged pre–conquest levels until the twentieth century. On the other hand, Rosenblat's depopulation ratio is clearly too low. There is a discussion of the subsequent literature and rationale for the estimates I adopted in Maddison (2001), pp. 232–236.

GDP: I made a multicultural estimate, with a stylised per capita GDP for the indigenous population ($400 international 1990 dollars for the hunter–gatherers and $425 for Mexico and Peru, which had developed agriculture and urbanisation). For the non–indigenous population, I assumed the 1820 level of per capita GDP was valid for the whole period 1500–1820. The income level for each group was assumed to be stable, but the average for the two combined was lower in earlier years when the non–indigenous proportion was smaller — see Maddison (2001), p. 250. For the Caribbean, the estimates for 1600–1820 were based largely on evidence about sugar production, inferences on per capita GDP levels at the end of the period from G. Eisner (1961), *Jamaica, 1830–1930: A Study in Economic Growth*, Manchester University Press, and the work of David Eltis and others on earlier development, see Eltis, "The Total Product of Barbados, 1664–1701", *Journal of Economic History*, (June 1995) and, "The Slave Economies of the Caribbean, Performance, Evolution and Significance", in F.W. Knight (1997), *General History of the Caribbean*, vol. III, UNESCO, London.

Sources for 1820–2001
Core Countries (Argentina, Brazil, Chile, Colombia, Mexico, Peru, Uruguay and Venezuela)

Population: 1820–1949 generally as in Maddison (1995), p. 99. Uruguay from Luis Bertola and Associates, *PBI de Uruguay 1870–1936*, Montevideo, 1998, and supplementary information supplied by Luis Bertola. Venezuela from Asdrubal Baptista, *Bases de la Economia Venezolana 1830–1989*, CCD, Caracas, 1991. 1950 onwards, all countries from US Bureau of the Census (http://www.census.gov./ipc), October 2002.

GDP: movement 1820–1949 generally from Maddison (1995), p.143; 1901–12 Colombia and Peru interpolated with average per capita movement in Brazil and Chile. 1911–12 and 1914–20 movement in Mexico from A.A. Hofman, *The Economic Development of Latin America in the Twentieth Century*, Elgar, Cheltenham, 2000, pp. 163–4. Uruguay 1820 1949 from Bertola, *op. cit.* For Brazil and Mexico, 1820–1949, see Maddison 2001, p. 191. Updating 1998–2001 from IMF, *World Economic Outlook*. 1990 benchmark GDP levels in 1990 international dollars from Maddison (2001), p. 199.

15 Other Countries

Population: Gaps in Maddison (2001) were filled as follows: 1820 from *Cambridge History of Latin America,* vol. III, pp. 238–9, 245 and 258 for Haiti and Dominican republic; p.478 for Costa Rica, El Salvador, Guatemala, Honduras and Nicaragua; p. 508 for Ecuador; p.564 for Bolivia; pp. 668 and 673 for Paraguay. Cuba and Puerto Rico from Shepherd and Beckles, eds, (2000) *Caribbean Slavery in the Atlantic World,* Wiener, Princeton, pp. 274 and 285 respectively. Jamaica, Trinidad and Tobago from Higman (1984), *Slave Populations of the British Caribbean,* 1807–1834, Johns Hopkins University Press, Baltimore, p. 417. 1850 generally from Sanchez–Albornoz in *Cambridge History of Latin America,* vol. IV, 1986, p. 122; Jamaica from Eisner (1961), p. 153; Trinidad and Tobago from Mitchell (1983), p. 50. 1870 and 1913 generally from Maddison (2001). Annual figures for 1871–1912 for thirteen countries are interpolations of estimates for benchmark years in Sanchez Albornoz (1986). Jamaica from Eisner (1961), p. 134; 1870–1950 movement in Trinidad and Tobago assumed to be proportionately the same as in Jamaica.

Annual estimates 1920–49 from Bulmer–Thomas (1987) *The Political Economy of Central America since 1920,* C.U.P, p. 310 for Costa Rica, El Salvador, Guatemala, Honduras and Nicaragua; other countries generally from UN, *Demographic Yearbook 1960,* p. 132–8 (with some interpolation for Haiti); Cuba 1900–28 derived from C. Brundenius (1984), *Revolutionary Cuba: The Challenge of Economic Growth with Equity,* Westview Press, Boulder and London p. 140, 1929–49 from CEPAL (ECLAC), Statistics Division, (1962) *Cuadros del producto interno bruto a precios del mercado en dollares de 1950,* Santiago (mimeo). 1950–2001 as for the 8 core countries.

GDP: I added estimates for Jamaica 1820–1930 from Eisner (1961), p. 119, linked to 1938–50 from Findlay and Wellisz (1999) *The Political Economy of Poverty, Equity and Growth: Five Small Open Economies,* OUP, New York, p. 149. Jamaica is the only Caribbean economy for which GDP estimates are available for this period. Eisner's estimates imply a 24 per cent fall in per capita GDP between 1820 and 1870 as Jamaica's sugar economy decayed. I assumed that the 1820–70 per capita GDP movement in this group paralleled that in Jamaica. For the benchmark years 1870, 1913 and 1950, average per capita GDP movement in these economies was assumed parallel to the average for the 8 core countries. Annual GDP movement, 1920–50, for Costa Rica, El Salvador, Guatemala, Honduras and Nicaragua from Bulmer–Thomas (1987), p. 308, Bolivia (1945–9), Ecuador (1939), Haiti (1945–9), Panama (1945–9), and Paraguay (1939–49) from ECLAC (1978), *Series Historicas del Crecimiento de America Latina,* Santiago, pp. 14–15. 1950–98 from Maddison (2001) Appendix C, updated to 2001 from IMF *World Economic Outlook,* 2/2002. Derivation of 1990 benchmark levels from Maddison (2001), p. 199.

Estimates for Cuba are revised. 1929–59 from ECLAC (1962), *Cuadros del producto interno bruto.* At that time Cuban national accounts were compiled according to UN standardised (SNA) procedures. After the revolution, Cuba adopted the Soviet material product system (MPS), which exaggerated growth. 1959–65 from OECD Development Centre, *Latest Information on National Accounts of Developing Countries,* various issues. 1965–82 from J.F. Perez Lopez (1987), *Measuring Cuban Economic Performance,* University of Texas Press, Austin, p. 111 who recalculated Cuban GDP according to SNA concepts. The Cuban Statistical Office published estimates of GDP by industry of origin for 1975–2000 (see Oficina Nacional de Estadisticas, *Cuba: Indicadores Seleccionados, 1950–2000,* Havana, 2001, pp. 15–16. Where these estimates overlap with those of Perez Lopez (for 1975–82) they show a growth rate twice as fast. I used these official estimates for 1982–90, but scaled down the year–to–year growth by a coefficient of the differential between them and those of Perez Lopez for the overlap years. 1990–1998 from ECLAC, *Economic Survey of Latin America and the Caribbean: Current Conditions and Outlook* (2001); 1998–2001 ECLAC, *Preliminary Overview of the Economies of Latin America and the Caribbean,* Santiago (2002). These ECLAC figures are based on official Cuban sources which now seem more acceptable as the estimating procedure has been revised to conform with the UN standardised system (see *Anuario Estadistico de Cuba 2001,* Oficina Nacional de Estadisticas, Havana, 2002).

24 Small Caribbean Countries

Estimates for this group are substantially revised for 1820–1913.

Population: 1820–70 from S.L. Engerman and B.W. Higman (1997), "The demographic situation of the Caribbean slave societies in the eighteenth and nineteenth centuries", in F.W. Knight (ed.), *General History of the Caribbean,* vol. III, UNESCO, London pp. 50–7 and Higman (1984); 1913 from League of Nations, (1928), *International Statistical Yearbook 1927,* Geneva, pp. 16–17; 1920–49 from UN, *Demographic Yearbook 1960,* pp. 132–6. 1950 onwards from US Bureau of the Census estimates, October 2002.

GDP: 1820 average per capita GDP level assumed equal to that of the 15 country group; 1870–1950 per capita GDP movement assumed to parallel that in the 8 core countries. GDP 1950–90 from Maddison (2001), updated and revised as shown in Table 4–5.

Table 4-5. **GDP and Population in 24 Small Caribbean Countries, 1950-2001**

	GDP in million 1990 international $				Population (000)			
	1950	*1973*	*1990*	*2001*	*1950*	*1973*	*1990*	*2001*
Bahamas	756	3 159	3 946	4 700	70	182	257	293
Barbados	448	1 595	2 138	2 419	211	244	263	275
Belize	110	341	735	1083	66	130	191	253
Dominica	82	182	279	352	51	74	73	71
Grenada	71	180	310	459	76	97	92	89
Guyana	462	1 309	1 159	2 080	428	755	742	698
St. Lucia	61	199	449	532	79	109	140	158
St. Vincent	79	175	392	545	66	90	107	116
Suriname	315	1 046	1 094	1 099	208	384	395	432
Total A (9 countries)	2 384	8 186	10 502	13 269	1 255	2 065	2 260	2 385
Antigua & Barbuda	82	328	413	535	46	68	63	67
Bermuda	65	238	310		39	53	58	63
Guadeloupe	359	1 568	1 801		208	329	378	431
Guyana (Fr.)	138	238	516		26	53	116	178
Martinique	293	1 568	1 857		217	332	374	418
Neth. Antilles	393	1 097	980	1 057	110	165	189	212
St. Kitts Nevis	61	215	233	402	44	45	41	39
Total B (7 countries)	1 391	5 252	6 110	8 315	690	1 045	1 219	1 408
Total C (8 countries)	298	926	1 441	1 809	117	197	250	298
24 countries	4 073	14 364	18 053	23 393	2 062	3 308	3 727	4 091

Source: 1950–98 GDP from Maddison (2001), p. 192, updated to 2001 from IMF, *World Economic Outlook,* September, 2002. For countries for which estimates were not available, aggregate GDP movement assumed to be proportionate to that for the group A average. Population from Maddison (2001), updated from 1950 onwards from the International Programs Center, US Bureau of the Census, October 2002. The 8 countries in the third group are Anguilla, Aruba, Cayman Islands, Montserrat, St. Pierre and Miquelon, Turks and Caicos Islands, Virgin Islands, and British Virgin Islands.

http://dx.doi.org/10.1787/456125276116

Table 4a. **Population of 8 Latin American Countries, 1820-1913**
(000s at mid-year)

	Argentina	Brazil	Chile	Colombia	Mexico	Peru	Uruguay	Venezuela	Total
1820	534	4 507	885	1 206	6 587	1 317	55	718	15 809
1850	1 100	7 234	1 443	2 065	7 662	2 001	132	1 324	22 961
1870	1 796	9 797	1 943	2 392	9 219	2 606	343	1 653	29 749
1871		9 980			9 331		354	1 675	
1872		10 167			9 444		364	1 699	
1873		10 358			9 558		376	1 725	
1874		10 552			9 674		387	1 753	
1875		10 749			9 791		399	1 784	
1876		10 951			9 910		411	1 816	
1877		11 156			10 030		424	1 849	
1878		11 365			10 151		437	1 883	
1879		11 578			10 274		450	1 917	
1880		11 794			10 399		464	1 952	
1881		12 015			10 524		482	1 986	
1882		12 240			10 652		502	2 019	
1883		12 470			10 781		522	2 052	
1884		12 703			10 912		543	2 083	
1885		12 941			11 044		564	2 113	
1886		13 183			11 178		587	2 129	
1887		13 430			11 313		610	2 147	
1888		13 682			11 450		635	2 173	
1889		13 938			11 589		660	2 198	
1890	3 376	14 199	2 651	3 369	11 729	3 346	686	2 224	41 580
1891		14 539			11 904		706	2 255	
1892		14 886			12 083		727	2 285	
1893		15 242			12 263		748	2 314	
1894		15 607			12 447		770	2 346	
1895		15 980			12 663		792	2 375	
1896		16 362			12 822		815	2 408	
1897		16 753			13 014		839	2 442	
1898		17 154			13 209		864	2 475	
1899		17 564			13 406		889	2 509	
1900	4 693	17 984	2 974	3 998	13 607	3 791	915	2 542	50 504
1901	4 873	18 392	3 011	4 079	13 755	3 831	930	2 576	51 447
1902	5 060	18 782	3 048	4 162	13 904	3 871	945	2 609	52 381
1903	5 254	19 180	3 086	4 247	14 055	3 911	961	2 643	53 337
1904	5 455	19 587	3 124	4 334	14 208	3 952	977	2 690	54 327
1905	5 664	20 003	3 163	4 422	14 363	3 993	993	2 706	55 307
1906	5 881	20 427	3 202	4 512	14 519	4 035	1 009	2 720	56 305
1907	6 107	20 860	3 242	4 604	14 676	4 077	1 026	2 741	57 333
1908	6 341	21 303	3 282	4 697	14 836	4 119	1 043	2 761	58 382
1909	6 584	21 754	3 323	4 793	14 997	4 162	1 062	2 780	59 455
1910	6 836	22 216	3 364	4 890	15 000	4 206	1 081	2 805	60 398
1911	7 098	22 687	3 406	4 990	14 990	4 250	1 112	2 834	61 367
1912	7 370	23 168	3 448	5 091	14 980	4 294	1 144	2 856	62 351
1913	7 653	23 660	3 491	5 195	14 970	4 339	1 177	2 874	63 359

http://dx.doi.org/10.1787/456125276116

Table 4a. **Population of 8 Latin American Countries, 1914-1949**
(000s at mid-year)

	Argentina	Brazil	Chile	Colombia	Mexico	Peru	Uruguay	Venezuela	Total
1914	7 885	24 161	3 537	5 330	14 960	4 384	1 223	2 899	64 379
1915	8 072	24 674	3 584	5 468	14 950	4 430	1 246	2 918	65 342
1916	8 226	25 197	3 631	5 609	14 940	4 477	1 269	2 929	66 278
1917	8 374	25 732	3 679	5 754	14 930	4 523	1 292	2 944	67 228
1918	8 518	26 277	3 728	5 903	14 920	4 571	1 316	2 958	68 191
1919	8 672	26 835	3 777	6 056	14 910	4 619	1 341	2 973	69 183
1920	8 861	27 404	3 827	6 213	14 900	4 667	1 371	2 992	70 235
1921	9 092	27 969	3 877	6 374	14 895	4 730	1 402	3 008	71 347
1922	9 368	28 542	3 928	6 539	15 129	4 793	1 433	3 025	72 757
1923	9 707	29 126	3 980	6 709	15 367	4 859	1 465	3 049	74 262
1924	10 054	29 723	4 033	6 882	15 609	4 927	1 498	3 077	75 803
1925	10 358	30 332	4 086	7 061	15 854	4 996	1 534	3 114	77 335
1926	10 652	30 953	4 140	7 243	16 103	5 067	1 571	3 152	78 881
1927	10 965	31 587	4 195	7 431	16 356	5 141	1 608	3 185	80 468
1928	11 282	32 234	4 250	7 624	16 613	5 216	1 646	3 221	82 086
1929	11 592	32 894	4 306	7 821	16 875	5 294	1 685	3 259	83 726
1930	11 896	33 568	4 370	7 914	17 175	5 374	1 713	3 300	85 310
1931	12 167	34 256	4 434	8 009	17 480	5 456	1 741	3 336	86 879
1932	12 402	34 957	4 500	8 104	17 790	5 540	1 770	3 368	88 431
1933	12 623	35 673	4 567	8 201	18 115	5 626	1 799	3 401	90 005
1934	12 834	36 404	4 634	8 299	18 445	5 715	1 829	3 431	91 591
1935	13 044	37 150	4 703	8 398	18 781	5 806	1 859	3 465	93 206
1936	13 260	37 911	4 773	8 498	19 040	5 899	1 889	3 510	94 780
1937	13 490	38 687	4 843	8 599	19 370	5 995	1 921	3 565	96 470
1938	13 724	39 480	4 915	8 702	19 705	6 093	1 952	3 623	98 194
1939	13 984	40 289	5 003	8 935	20 047	6 194	1 944	3 699	100 095
1940	14 169	41 114	5 093	9 174	20 393	6 298	1 965	3 784	101 990
1941	14 402	42 069	5 184	9 419	20 955	6 415	1 987	3 858	104 289
1942	14 638	43 069	5 277	9 671	21 532	6 537	2 010	3 934	106 668
1943	14 877	44 093	5 371	9 930	22 125	6 661	2 032	4 020	109 109
1944	15 130	45 141	5 467	10 196	22 734	6 787	2 055	4 114	111 624
1945	15 390	46 215	5 565	10 469	23 724	6 919	2 081	4 223	114 586
1946	15 654	47 313	5 665	10 749	24 413	7 053	2 107	4 347	117 301
1947	15 942	48 438	5 767	11 036	25 122	7 192	2 134	4 486	120 117
1948	16 307	49 590	5 870	11 332	25 852	7 335	2 160	4 656	123 102
1949	16 737	50 769	5 975	11 635	26 603	7 480	2 188	4 843	126 230

http://dx.doi.org/10.1787/456125276116

Table 4a. Population of 8 Latin American Countries, 1950-2003
(000s at mid-year)

	Argentina	Brazil	Chile	Colombia	Mexico	Peru	Uruguay	Venezuela	Total
1950	17 150	53 443	6 091	11 592	28 485	7 633	2 194	5 009	131 597
1951	17 517	54 996	6 252	11 965	29 296	7 826	2 223	5 217	135 292
1952	17 877	56 603	6 378	12 351	30 144	8 026	2 253	5 440	139 070
1953	18 231	58 266	6 493	12 750	31 031	8 232	2 284	5 674	142 961
1954	18 581	59 989	6 612	13 162	31 959	8 447	2 317	5 919	146 985
1955	18 928	61 774	6 743	13 588	32 930	8 672	2 353	6 170	151 158
1956	19 272	63 632	6 889	14 029	33 946	8 905	2 389	6 431	155 493
1957	19 611	65 551	7 048	14 486	35 016	9 146	2 425	6 703	159 985
1958	19 947	67 533	7 220	14 958	36 142	9 397	2 460	6 982	164 639
1959	20 281	69 580	7 400	15 447	37 328	9 658	2 495	7 268	169 457
1960	20 616	71 695	7 585	15 953	38 579	9 931	2 531	7 556	174 446
1961	20 951	73 833	7 773	16 476	39 836	10 218	2 564	7 848	179 498
1962	21 284	76 039	7 961	17 010	41 121	10 517	2 598	8 143	184 674
1963	21 616	78 317	8 147	17 546	42 434	10 826	2 632	8 444	189 963
1964	21 949	80 667	8 330	18 090	43 775	11 144	2 664	8 752	195 370
1965	22 283	83 093	8 510	18 646	45 142	11 467	2 693	9 068	200 903
1966	22 612	85 557	8 686	19 202	46 538	11 796	2 721	9 387	206 499
1967	22 934	88 050	8 859	19 764	47 996	12 132	2 749	9 710	212 193
1968	23 261	90 569	9 030	20 322	49 519	12 476	2 777	10 041	217 994
1969	23 600	93 114	9 199	20 869	51 111	12 829	2 802	10 389	223 913
1970	23 962	95 684	9 369	21 430	52 775	13 193	2 824	10 758	229 994
1971	24 364	98 245	9 540	21 993	54 434	13 568	2 826	11 152	236 122
1972	24 780	100 840	9 718	22 543	56 040	13 955	2 830	11 516	242 220
1973	25 210	103 469	9 897	23 069	57 643	14 350	2 834	11 893	248 365
1974	25 646	106 131	10 077	23 593	59 240	14 753	2 838	12 281	254 559
1975	26 082	108 824	10 252	24 114	60 828	15 161	2 842	12 675	260 777
1976	26 531	111 545	10 432	24 620	62 404	15 573	2 857	13 082	267 046
1977	26 984	114 314	10 600	25 094	63 981	15 990	2 874	13 504	273 340
1978	27 440	117 147	10 760	25 543	65 554	16 414	2 889	13 931	279 678
1979	27 902	120 040	10 923	26 031	67 123	16 849	2 905	14 355	286 128
1980	28 370	122 958	11 094	26 583	68 686	17 295	2 920	14 768	292 673
1981	28 863	125 930	11 282	27 159	70 321	17 755	2 936	15 166	299 412
1982	29 341	128 963	11 487	27 765	71 910	18 234	2 954	15 621	306 275
1983	29 802	131 892	11 687	28 389	73 435	18 706	2 973	16 084	312 968
1984	30 236	134 626	11 879	29 028	74 945	19 171	2 990	16 545	319 420
1985	30 675	137 303	12 067	29 678	76 475	19 624	3 008	16 998	325 828
1986	31 146	140 112	12 260	30 327	78 035	20 073	3 027	17 450	332 430
1987	31 621	142 938	12 463	30 964	79 623	20 531	3 045	17 910	339 095
1988	32 091	145 782	12 678	31 589	81 231	21 000	3 064	18 379	345 813
1989	32 559	148 567	12 901	32 217	82 840	21 487	3 084	18 851	352 505
1990	33 022	151 084	13 128	32 859	84 446	21 989	3 106	19 325	358 959
1991	33 492	153 512	13 353	33 519	86 055	22 501	3 128	19 801	365 358
1992	33 959	155 976	13 573	34 203	87 667	23 015	3 149	20 266	371 808
1993	34 412	158 471	13 788	34 897	89 280	23 531	3 171	20 704	378 255
1994	34 864	160 994	14 000	35 589	90 888	24 047	3 193	21 135	384 711
1995	35 311	163 543	14 205	36 281	92 488	24 556	3 215	21 556	391 155
1996	35 754	166 074	14 404	36 971	94 080	25 058	3 237	21 969	397 547
1997	36 203	168 547	14 599	37 658	95 667	25 556	3 260	22 374	403 865
1998	36 644	170 956	14 789	38 340	97 245	26 049	3 284	22 773	410 079
1999	37 074	173 294	14 974	39 016	98 807	26 535	3 309	23 162	416 170
2000	37 498	175 553	15 154	39 686	100 350	27 013	3 334	23 543	422 131
2001	37 917	177 753	15 328	40 349	101 879	27 484	3 360	23 917	427 987
2002	38 331	179 914	15 499	41 008	103 400	27 950	3 387	24 288	433 777
2003	38 741	182 033	15 665	41 662	104 908	28 410	3 413	24 655	439 487

http://dx.doi.org/10.1787/456125276116

Table 4a. Population of 15 Latin American Countries, 1820-1949
(000s at mid-year)

	Bolivia	Costa Rica	Cuba	Dominican Republic	Ecuador	El Salvador	Guatemala	Haiti
1820	1 100	63	605	89	500	248	595	723
1850	1 374	101	1 186	146	816	366	850	938
1870	1 495	137	1 331	242	1 013	492	1 080	1 150
1900	1 696	297	1 658	515	1 400	766	1 300	1 560
1901	1 710	310	1 716	530	1 420	782	1 313	1 583
1902	1 723	320	1 775	546	1 441	799	1 327	1 607
1903	1 737	320	1 837	562	1 462	816	1 341	1 631
1904	1 751	330	1 879	578	1 483	834	1 355	1 655
1905	1 765	340	1 927	595	1 505	851	1 369	1 680
1906	1 779	340	1 979	613	1 527	869	1 383	1 705
1907	1 793	350	2 034	631	1 549	888	1 397	1 730
1908	1 808	350	2 092	649	1 571	907	1 412	1 756
1909	1 822	360	2 154	668	1 594	926	1 426	1 782
1910	1 837	363	2 219	688	1 617	946	1 441	1 809
1911	1 851	366	2 287	708	1 641	966	1 456	1 836
1912	1 866	369	2 358	729	1 665	987	1 470	1 863
1913	1 881	372	2 431	750	1 689	1 008	1 486	1 891
1914	1 915	390	2 507	767	1 703	1 030	1 501	1 923
1915	1 951	390	2 585	785	1 717	1 052	1 517	1 955
1916	1 986	400	2 664	803	1 731	1 074	1 533	1 988
1917	2 023	400	2 746	821	1 746	1 098	1 549	2 021
1918	2 060	410	2 828	840	1 760	1 121	1 565	2 055
1919	2 098	420	2 912	859	1 774	1 145	1 581	2 089
1920	2 136	420	2 997	879	1 790	1 170	1 597	2 124
1921	2 161	430	3 083	912	1 805	1 190	1 614	2 152
1922	2 186	430	3 170	946	1 820	1 220	1 631	2 181
1923	2 212	440	3 257	981	1 835	1 240	1 648	2 209
1924	2 237	450	3 345	1 017	1 850	1 270	1 665	2 239
1925	2 263	460	3 432	1 054	1 865	1 300	1 682	2 268
1926	2 289	470	3 519	1 092	1 881	1 330	1 699	2 298
1927	2 316	470	3 606	1 131	1 896	1 350	1 717	2 328
1928	2 343	480	3 693	1 172	1 912	1 390	1 735	2 359
1929	2 370	490	3 742	1 213	1 928	1 410	1 753	2 390
1930	2 397	500	3 837	1 256	1 944	1 440	1 771	2 422
1931	2 425	510	3 910	1 300	1 995	1 460	1 810	2 453
1932	2 453	520	3 984	1 345	2 050	1 470	1 860	2 485
1933	2 482	530	4 060	1 391	2 095	1 490	1 910	2 517
1934	2 511	540	4 137	1 438	2 140	1 510	1 940	2 549
1935	2 540	550	4 221	1 484	2 196	1 530	1 980	2 582
1936	2 569	560	4 289	1 520	2 249	1 550	2 020	2 615
1937	2 599	580	4 357	1 558	2 298	1 570	2 070	2 648
1938	2 629	590	4 428	1 596	2 355	1 590	2 110	2 682
1939	2 659	610	4 497	1 634	2 412	1 610	2 150	2 716
1940	2 690	620	4 566	1 674	2 466	1 630	2 200	2 751
1941	2 721	630	4 635	1 715	2 541	1 650	2 250	2 786
1942	2 753	650	4 704	1 757	2 575	1 680	2 300	2 820
1943	2 785	660	4 779	1 800	2 641	1 690	2 340	2 856
1944	2 817	680	4 849	1 844	2 712	1 720	2 390	2 892
1945	2 850	700	4 932	1 889	2 781	1 740	2 440	2 928
1946	2 883	710	5 039	1 935	2 853	1 760	2 500	2 961
1947	2 916	730	5 152	1 982	2 936	1 780	2 570	2 994
1948	2 950	750	5 268	2 031	3 017	1 810	2 640	3 028
1949	2 984	770	5 386	2 080	3 104	1 840	2 720	3 062

http://dx.doi.org/10.1787/456125276116

Table 4a. **Population of 15 Latin American Countries, 1820-1949**
(000s at mid-year)

	Honduras	Jamaica	Nicaragua	Panama	Paraguay	Puerto Rico	Trinidad and Tobago	Total
1820	135	401	186	–	143	248	60	5 096
1850	350	399	300	135	350	495	80	7 886
1870	404	499	337	176	384	645	124	9 509
1900	500	720	478	263	440	959	268	12 820
1901	511	728	485	269	450	974	274	13 055
1902	522	737	492	275	461	990	279	13 294
1903	533	745	499	281	472	1 006	285	13 527
1904	545	754	507	287	483	1 022	291	13 754
1905	556	763	514	293	494	1 039	298	13 989
1906	568	772	522	299	505	1 056	304	14 221
1907	581	781	529	306	517	1 073	310	14 469
1908	593	790	537	312	529	1 090	317	14 713
1909	606	799	545	319	542	1 108	324	14 975
1910	619	808	553	326	554	1 126	331	15 237
1911	632	818	561	333	567	1 144	338	15 504
1912	646	827	570	341	580	1 162	345	15 778
1913	660	837	578	348	594	1 181	352	16 058
1914	668	840	580	365	608	1 199	357	16 353
1915	677	842	595	383	622	1 217	362	16 650
1916	685	845	604	402	637	1 235	367	16 954
1917	694	847	613	422	652	1 254	373	17 259
1918	702	850	622	442	667	1 273	378	17 573
1919	711	852	631	464	683	1 292	383	17 894
1920	720	855	640	487	699	1 312	389	18 215
1921	740	860	640	489	715	1 336	367	18 494
1922	770	879	650	491	732	1 359	371	18 836
1923	800	891	650	493	749	1 383	376	19 164
1924	820	900	660	495	767	1 407	379	19 501
1925	850	910	660	497	785	1 431	382	19 839
1926	880	930	670	499	803	1 455	385	20 200
1927	890	946	670	502	822	1 478	388	20 510
1928	910	966	670	504	841	1 502	392	20 869
1929	930	985	680	506	860	1 526	398	21 181
1930	950	1 009	680	515	880	1 552	405	21 558
1931	970	1 039	690	527	901	1 584	412	21 986
1932	990	1 061	690	543	922	1 615	417	22 405
1933	1 010	1 082	700	559	944	1 647	422	22 839
1934	1 020	1 098	710	576	966	1 679	428	23 242
1935	1 040	1 113	730	592	988	1 710	435	23 691
1936	1 060	1 130	750	608	1 012	1 743	442	24 117
1937	1 080	1 142	770	623	1 036	1 777	450	24 558
1938	1 100	1 163	780	640	1 061	1 810	458	24 992
1939	1 120	1 191	810	656	1 086	1 844	466	25 461
1940	1 150	1 212	830	697	1 111	1 880	476	25 953
1941	1 170	1 230	840	720	1 137	1 935	492	26 452
1942	1 200	1 254	860	773	1 164	1 987	510	26 987
1943	1 210	1 249	880	795	1 191	2 033	525	27 434
1944	1 240	1 259	900	784	1 219	2 062	536	27 904
1945	1 260	1 266	920	791	1 247	2 099	547	28 390
1946	1 290	1 298	950	788	1 275	2 141	561	28 944
1947	1 320	1 327	980	804	1 305	2 162	583	29 541
1948	1 350	1 350	1 000	822	1 335	2 187	600	30 138
1949	1 390	1 374	1 030	838	1 366	2 197	616	30 757

http://dx.doi.org/10.1787/456125276116

Table 4a. **Population of 15 Latin American Countries, Annual Estimates, 1950-2003**
(000s at mid-year)

	Bolivia	Costa Rica	Cuba	Dominican Republic	Ecuador	El Salvador	Guatemala	Haiti
1950	2 766	867	5 785	2 353	3 370	1 940	2 969	3 097
1951	2 824	895	5 892	2 419	3 458	1 990	3 056	3 148
1952	2 883	926	6 008	2 491	3 549	2 043	3 146	3 201
1953	2 945	959	6 129	2 569	3 643	2 099	3 239	3 257
1954	3 009	994	6 254	2 651	3 740	2 159	3 335	3 316
1955	3 074	1 032	6 381	2 737	3 842	2 221	3 434	3 376
1956	3 142	1 072	6 513	2 828	3 949	2 287	3 536	3 441
1957	3 212	1 112	6 641	2 923	4 058	2 356	3 641	3 508
1958	3 284	1 154	6 763	3 023	4 172	2 428	3 749	3 577
1959	3 358	1 200	6 901	3 126	4 291	2 503	3 861	3 648
1960	3 434	1 248	7 027	3 231	4 416	2 582	3 976	3 723
1961	3 513	1 297	7 134	3 341	4 546	2 665	4 091	3 800
1962	3 594	1 345	7 254	3 453	4 682	2 748	4 209	3 880
1963	3 678	1 393	7 415	3 569	4 822	2 836	4 330	3 964
1964	3 764	1 440	7 612	3 687	4 968	2 924	4 454	4 050
1965	3 853	1 488	7 810	3 806	5 118	3 018	4 582	4 137
1966	3 945	1 538	7 985	3 926	5 273	3 128	4 713	4 227
1967	4 041	1 589	8 139	4 049	5 432	3 233	4 849	4 318
1968	4 139	1 638	8 284	4 173	5 597	3 347	4 989	4 412
1969	4 241	1 687	8 421	4 298	5 766	3 469	5 135	4 507
1970	4 346	1 736	8 543	4 423	5 939	3 604	5 289	4 605
1971	4 455	1 786	8 670	4 547	6 117	3 710	5 454	4 653
1972	4 566	1 835	8 831	4 671	6 299	3 791	5 625	4 701
1973	4 680	1 886	9 001	4 796	6 485	3 878	5 803	4 748
1974	4 796	1 937	9 153	4 922	6 676	3 972	5 988	4 795
1975	4 914	1 992	9 290	5 048	6 872	4 071	6 180	4 839
1976	4 956	2 049	9 421	5 176	7 073	4 175	6 378	4 882
1977	5 080	2 108	9 538	5 303	7 279	4 283	6 583	4 925
1978	5 205	2 192	9 634	5 431	7 489	4 396	6 795	4 970
1979	5 327	2 260	9 710	5 562	7 704	4 508	7 012	5 017
1980	5 441	2 299	9 653	5 697	7 920	4 566	7 235	5 056
1981	5 545	2 357	9 712	5 832	8 141	4 515	7 489	5 091
1982	5 642	2 424	9 789	5 968	8 366	4 475	7 714	5 149
1983	5 737	2 494	9 886	6 105	8 593	4 521	7 904	5 248
1984	5 834	2 568	9 982	6 241	8 826	4 588	8 124	5 355
1985	5 935	2 644	10 079	6 378	9 062	4 664	8 358	5 469
1986	6 041	2 723	10 162	6 516	9 301	4 751	8 601	5 588
1987	6 156	2 800	10 240	6 655	9 545	4 842	8 856	5 710
1988	6 283	2 875	10 334	6 796	9 794	4 930	9 118	5 833
1989	6 423	2 951	10 439	6 937	10 048	5 016	9 384	5 955
1990	6 574	3 027	10 545	7 076	10 317	5 100	9 654	6 075
1991	6 731	3 101	10 643	7 213	10 566	5 186	9 931	6 174
1992	6 893	3 173	10 724	7 347	10 819	5 275	10 216	6 272
1993	7 055	3 244	10 789	7 472	11 077	5 370	10 510	6 388
1994	7 217	3 315	10 846	7 595	11 337	5 467	10 814	6 500
1995	7 377	3 384	10 900	7 722	11 599	5 568	11 127	6 614
1996	7 536	3 452	10 952	7 851	11 862	5 674	11 449	6 727
1997	7 693	3 518	11 003	7 979	12 126	5 783	11 781	6 837
1998	7 849	3 583	11 051	8 105	12 391	5 895	12 121	6 952
1999	8 002	3 647	11 098	8 230	12 656	6 008	12 467	7 066
2000	8 153	3 711	11 142	8 354	12 920	6 123	12 820	7 177
2001	8 300	3 773	11 184	8 475	13 184	6 238	13 179	7 288
2002	8 445	3 835	11 224	8 596	13 447	6 354	13 542	7 405
2003	8 586	3 896	11 263	8 716	13 710	6 470	13 909	7 528

http://dx.doi.org/10.1787/456125276116

ISBN 92-64-02261-9 – © OECD 2006

Table 4a. **Population of 15 Latin American Countries, 1950-2003**
(000s at mid-year)

	Honduras	Jamaica	Nicaragua	Panama	Paraguay	Puerto Rico	Trinidad and Tobago	Total
1950	1 431	1 385	1 098	893	1 476	2 218	632	32 279
1951	1 474	1 406	1 131	916	1 515	2 235	649	33 008
1952	1 517	1 426	1 166	940	1 556	2 227	663	33 743
1953	1 562	1 446	1 202	962	1 597	2 204	678	34 492
1954	1 611	1 468	1 239	985	1 640	2 214	698	35 311
1955	1 662	1 489	1 277	1 011	1 683	2 250	721	36 192
1956	1 715	1 510	1 317	1 037	1 727	2 249	743	37 064
1957	1 770	1 535	1 359	1 064	1 771	2 260	765	37 974
1958	1 829	1 566	1 402	1 085	1 816	2 299	789	38 935
1959	1 889	1 599	1 446	1 115	1 862	2 322	817	39 939
1960	1 952	1 632	1 493	1 148	1 910	2 358	841	40 969
1961	2 017	1 648	1 541	1 181	1 959	2 403	861	41 997
1962	2 082	1 665	1 591	1 216	2 010	2 448	887	43 064
1963	2 151	1 698	1 642	1 251	2 062	2 497	904	44 213
1964	2 224	1 739	1 695	1 288	2 115	2 552	924	45 437
1965	2 299	1 777	1 750	1 326	2 170	2 597	939	46 671
1966	2 375	1 820	1 807	1 365	2 228	2 627	953	47 912
1967	2 453	1 861	1 865	1 405	2 288	2 649	960	49 132
1968	2 534	1 893	1 926	1 447	2 349	2 674	963	50 365
1969	2 618	1 920	1 988	1 489	2 412	2 722	963	51 636
1970	2 683	1 944	2 053	1 531	2 477	2 722	955	52 849
1971	2 767	1 967	2 120	1 573	2 545	2 766	962	54 091
1972	2 864	1 998	2 183	1 616	2 614	2 847	975	55 416
1973	2 964	2 036	2 247	1 659	2 692	2 863	985	56 725
1974	3 066	2 071	2 320	1 706	2 773	2 887	995	58 057
1975	3 152	2 105	2 394	1 748	2 850	2 935	1 007	59 399
1976	3 240	2 133	2 473	1 790	2 919	3 026	1 021	60 711
1977	3 331	2 157	2 554	1 840	2 984	3 081	1 039	62 085
1978	3 431	2 179	2 608	1 873	3 051	3 118	1 056	63 430
1979	3 528	2 207	2 688	1 915	3 119	3 168	1 073	64 799
1980	3 635	2 229	2 804	1 956	3 193	3 210	1 091	65 986
1981	3 756	2 258	2 900	1 996	3 276	3 239	1 102	67 210
1982	3 861	2 298	2 978	2 036	3 366	3 279	1 116	68 463
1983	3 963	2 323	3 047	2 077	3 463	3 316	1 133	69 811
1984	4 072	2 347	3 119	2 120	3 564	3 350	1 150	71 239
1985	4 186	2 371	3 188	2 164	3 668	3 382	1 166	72 713
1986	4 301	2 394	3 258	2 208	3 776	3 413	1 180	74 216
1987	4 417	2 413	3 334	2 252	3 887	3 444	1 191	75 743
1988	4 505	2 428	3 415	2 297	4 000	3 475	1 198	77 282
1989	4 634	2 444	3 502	2 342	4 117	3 506	1 200	78 898
1990	4 757	2 463	3 643	2 388	4 236	3 537	1 198	80 591
1991	4 878	2 485	3 817	2 434	4 359	3 562	1 193	82 272
1992	5 009	2 505	3 947	2 480	4 484	3 585	1 184	83 915
1993	5 148	2 525	4 055	2 524	4 612	3 615	1 175	85 560
1994	5 293	2 547	4 164	2 568	4 744	3 649	1 167	87 222
1995	5 443	2 569	4 274	2 615	4 878	3 683	1 160	88 912
1996	5 594	2 589	4 384	2 663	5 015	3 725	1 151	90 623
1997	5 747	2 608	4 493	2 705	5 154	3 759	1 141	92 328
1998	5 902	2 624	4 600	2 745	5 296	3 781	1 136	94 032
1999	6 044	2 639	4 706	2 792	5 440	3 800	1 131	95 727
2000	6 201	2 653	4 813	2 836	5 586	3 816	1 125	97 428
2001	6 358	2 666	4 918	2 879	5 734	3 840	1 118	99 135
2002	6 514	2 680	5 024	2 920	5 884	3 863	1 112	100 846
2003	6 670	2 696	5 129	2 961	6 037	3 886	1 104	102 561

http://dx.doi.org/10.1787/456125276116

Table 4a. **Population of 47 Latin American Countries, 1820-1949**
(000s at mid-year)

	Total 8 core countries	Total 15 countries	Total 24 small Caribbean countries	Total 47 countries
1820	15 809	5 096	800	21 705
1850	22 961	7 886	946	31 793
1870	29 749	9 509	1 141	40 399
1890	41 580	10 859	1 383	53 822
1900	50 504	12 820	1 440	64 764
1901	51 447	13 055	1 446	65 948
1902	52 381	13 294	1 452	67 127
1903	53 337	13 527	1 458	68 322
1904	54 327	13 754	1 464	69 545
1905	55 307	13 989	1 470	70 766
1906	56 305	14 221	1 475	72 001
1907	57 333	14 469	1 481	73 283
1908	58 382	14 713	1 488	74 583
1909	59 455	14 975	1 494	75 924
1910	60 398	15 237	1 500	77 135
1911	61 367	15 504	1 506	78 377
1912	62 351	15 778	1 512	79 641
1913	63 359	16 058	1 518	80 935
1914	64 379	16 353	1 531	82 263
1915	65 342	16 650	1 543	83 535
1916	66 278	16 954	1 556	84 788
1917	67 228	17 259	1 569	86 056
1918	68 191	17 573	1 582	87 346
1919	69 183	17 894	1 596	88 673
1920	70 235	18 215	1 609	90 059
1921	71 347	18 494	1 622	91 463
1922	72 757	18 836	1 635	93 228
1923	74 262	19 164	1 649	95 075
1924	75 803	19 501	1 663	96 967
1925	77 335	19 839	1 677	98 851
1926	78 881	20 200	1 690	100 771
1927	80 468	20 510	1 705	102 683
1928	82 086	20 869	1 719	104 674
1929	83 726	21 181	1 733	106 640
1930	85 310	21 558	1 747	108 615
1931	86 879	21 986	1 762	110 627
1932	88 431	22 405	1 777	112 613
1933	90 005	22 839	1 791	114 635
1934	91 591	23 242	1 806	116 639
1935	93 206	23 691	1 821	118 718
1936	94 780	24 117	1 836	120 733
1937	96 470	24 558	1 852	122 880
1938	98 194	24 992	1 867	125 053
1939	100 095	25 461	1 883	127 439
1940	101 990	25 953	1 898	129 841
1941	104 289	26 452	1 914	132 655
1942	106 668	26 987	1 930	135 585
1943	109 109	27 434	1 946	138 489
1944	111 624	27 904	1 962	141 490
1945	114 586	28 390	1 978	144 954
1946	117 301	28 944	1 995	148 240
1947	120 117	29 541	2 011	151 669
1948	123 102	30 138	2 028	155 268
1949	126 230	30 757	2 045	159 032

http://dx.doi.org/10.1787/456125276116

Table 4a. **Population of 47 Latin American Countries, 1950-2003**
(000s at mid-year)

	Total 8 core countries	Total 15 countries	Total 24 small Caribbean countries	Total 47 countries
1950	131 597	32 279	2 062	165 938
1951	135 292	33 008	2 111	170 411
1952	139 070	33 743	2 161	174 975
1953	142 961	34 492	2 211	179 664
1954	146 985	35 311	2 267	184 563
1955	151 158	36 192	2 323	189 673
1956	155 493	37 064	2 378	194 935
1957	159 985	37 974	2 435	200 395
1958	164 639	38 935	2 494	206 069
1959	169 457	39 939	2 555	211 951
1960	174 446	40 969	2 614	218 029
1961	179 498	41 997	2 662	224 157
1962	184 674	43 064	2 711	230 450
1963	189 963	44 213	2 781	236 957
1964	195 370	45 437	2 841	243 648
1965	200 903	46 671	2 900	250 474
1966	206 499	47 912	2 959	257 370
1967	212 193	49 132	3 014	264 339
1968	217 994	50 365	3 071	271 430
1969	223 913	51 636	3 121	278 670
1970	229 994	52 849	3 164	286 007
1971	236 122	54 091	3 215	293 427
1972	242 220	55 416	3 264	300 900
1973	248 365	56 725	3 308	308 399
1974	254 559	58 057	3 341	315 957
1975	260 777	59 399	3 348	323 524
1976	267 046	60 711	3 351	331 109
1977	273 340	62 085	3 366	338 791
1978	279 678	63 430	3 385	346 493
1979	286 128	64 799	3 399	354 326
1980	292 673	65 986	3 410	362 069
1981	299 412	67 210	3 435	370 057
1982	306 275	68 463	3 466	378 204
1983	312 968	69 811	3 499	386 279
1984	319 420	71 239	3 534	394 193
1985	325 828	72 713	3 569	402 110
1986	332 430	74 216	3 602	410 248
1987	339 095	75 743	3 632	418 470
1988	345 813	77 282	3 663	426 758
1989	352 505	78 898	3 694	435 097
1990	358 959	80 591	3 727	443 276
1991	365 358	82 272	3 757	451 387
1992	371 808	83 915	3 790	459 512
1993	378 255	85 560	3 824	467 639
1994	384 711	87 222	3 857	475 790
1995	391 155	88 912	3 890	483 957
1996	397 547	90 623	3 923	492 093
1997	403 865	92 328	3 956	500 150
1998	410 079	94 032	3 983	508 094
1999	416 170	95 727	4 019	515 916
2000	422 129	97 428	4 055	523 612
2001	427 987	99 135	4 091	531 213
2002	433 777	100 846	4 128	538 751
2003	439 487	102 561	4 164	546 212

http://dx.doi.org/10.1787/456125276116

GDP LEVELS IN LATIN AMERICA

Table 4b. **GDP Levels in 8 Latin American Countries, 1820-1913**
(million 1990 international Geary-Khamis dollars)

	Argentina	Brazil	Chile	Colombia	Mexico	Peru	Uruguay	Venezuela	Total
1820		2 912			5 000				11 275
1850		4 959							
1870	2 354	6 985			6 214		748	941	22 273
1871		7 154					771		
1872		7 327					958		
1873		7 504					978		
1874		7 686					896		
1875		7 872					775		
1876		8 062					865		
1877		8 257					900		
1878		8 457					982		
1879		8 662					877		
1880		8 871					966		
1881		9 086					931		
1882		9 306					1 044		
1883		9 531					1 251		
1884		9 761					1 262		
1885		9 998					1 449		
1886		10 240					1 531		
1887		10 487					1 383		
1888		10 741					1 726		
1889		11 001					1 594		
1890	7 265	11 267			11 860		1 473		
1891		11 232					1 617		
1892		10 865					1 668		
1893		9 474					1 823		
1894		9 695					2 046		
1895		12 519			14 337		2 034		
1896		11 616					2 155		
1897		11 712					2 092		
1898		12 300					1 944		
1899		12 347					2 010		
1900	12 932	12 201	5 798	3 891	18 585	3 096	2 030	2 087	60 619
1901	14 036	13 425	5 992	4 169	20 167	3 287	2 077	2 053	65 206
1902	13 746	13 425	6 196	4 245	18 741	3 310	2 431	2 233	64 327
1903	15 722	13 693	6 400	4 374	20 840	3 379	2 513	2 414	69 334
1904	17 407	13 961	6 622	4 503	21 203	3 446	2 579	2 357	72 078
1905	19 703	14 365	6 844	4 656	23 407	3 530	2 318	2 329	77 152
1906	20 691	15 735	7 076	4 977	23 147	3 732	2 556	2 173	80 087
1907	21 127	15 754	7 317	5 069	24 495	3 767	2 829	2 173	82 530
1908	23 190	15 639	7 557	5 148	24 469	3 789	3 101	2 322	85 216
1909	24 353	16 886	7 687	5 421	25 195	3 950	3 140	2 405	89 036
1910	26 125	17 078	8 317	5 682	25 403	4 101	3 390	2 484	92 580
1911	26 590	18 959	8 243	5 993	25 584	4 284	3 288	2 655	95 596
1912	28 770	18 747	9 160	6 292	25 740	4 453	4 013	2 747	99 922
1913	29 060	19 188	9 261	6 420	25 921	4 500	3 896	3 172	101 419

http://dx.doi.org/10.1787/456125276116

Table 4b. **GDP Levels in 8 Latin American Countries, 1914-1949**
(million 1990 international Geary-Khamis dollars)

	Argentina	Brazil	Chile	Colombia	Mexico	Peru	Uruguay	Venezuela	Total
1914	26 038	18 844	8 632	6 199	26 095	4 063	3 246	2 773	95 890
1915	26 183	19 688	8 020	6 173	26 270	4 315	3 078	2 858	96 586
1916	25 428	20 263	9 511	6 854	26 446	5 620	3 183	2 697	100 002
1917	23 364	21 664	10 280	7 434	26 624	5 418	3 511	3 147	101 442
1918	27 665	21 223	10 299	7 391	26 803	5 274	3 721	3 128	105 504
1919	28 683	24 024	8 141	7 588	26 983	6 088	4 204	2 922	108 632
1920	30 775	26 393	9 298	7 797	27 164	6 209	3 666	3 509	114 811
1921	31 559	26 944	8 002	7 999	27 346	4 378	3 857	3 651	113 737
1922	34 059	28 801	8 558	8 206	27 994	4 959	4 411	3 753	120 740
1923	37 837	30 454	10 651	8 420	28 953	6 403	4 644	4 330	131 691
1924	40 772	30 434	11 614	8 637	28 487	6 493	5 089	5 016	136 541
1925	40 597	30 556	11 753	8 860	30 250	5 782	4 890	6 481	139 169
1926	42 544	31 210	11 456	9 707	32 064	6 443	5 338	7 839	146 603
1927	45 567	33 476	10 984	10 581	30 664	7 249	6 106	8 794	153 420
1928	48 414	37 333	13 327	11 357	30 846	7 757	6 429	9 847	165 312
1929	50 623	37 415	14 624	11 768	29 653	8 572	6 483	11 167	170 305
1930	48 531	35 187	13 735	11 666	27 787	7 613	7 368	11 367	163 253
1931	45 160	34 401	10 345	11 595	28 720	6 700	6 094	9 187	152 202
1932	43 678	35 599	10 234	12 243	24 417	6 362	5 657	8 800	146 991
1933	45 712	38 374	12 114	12 930	27 191	8 572	4 948	9 628	159 469
1934	49 344	41 585	13 790	12 661	29 031	10 016	5 891	10 275	172 594
1935	51 524	42 722	14 050	14 080	31 183	10 291	6 238	11 021	181 108
1936	51 873	46 824	14 587	14 824	33 671	10 750	6 534	12 106	191 168
1937	55 650	48 355	15 698	15 055	34 786	10 984	6 651	13 889	201 068
1938	55 883	50 376	15 430	16 038	35 356	10 705	7 176	15 015	205 978
1939	58 004	50 876	15 902	17 020	37 248	11 668	7 177	15 926	213 820
1940	58 963	51 381	16 596	17 386	37 767	11 483	7 193	15 307	216 077
1941	61 986	54 981	16 615	17 681	40 851	12 815	7 317	15 056	227 302
1942	62 712	52 944	17 532	17 713	43 754	11 483	6 709	13 166	226 013
1943	62 218	60 317	18 263	17 790	45 387	10 943	6 768	14 371	236 058
1944	69 280	62 562	18 523	18 991	49 094	12 455	7 613	17 727	256 245
1945	67 042	64 236	20 199	19 883	50 623	13 872	7 832	21 547	265 235
1946	73 029	71 013	21 449	21 681	53 967	14 430	8 603	25 855	290 028
1947	81 136	73 523	20 014	22 535	55 807	14 858	9 203	30 925	308 001
1948	85 641	79 157	22 339	23 235	58 114	15 357	9 515	34 427	327 784
1949	84 478	84 239	22 200	24 519	61 303	16 446	9 854	36 534	339 572

http://dx.doi.org/10.1787/456125276116

Table 4b. GDP Levels in 8 Latin American Countries, 1950-2001
(million 1990 international Geary-Khamis dollars)

	Argentina	Brazil	Chile	Colombia	Mexico	Peru	Uruguay	Venezuela	Total
1950	85 524	89 342	23 274	24 955	67 368	17 270	10 224	37 377	355 334
1951	88 866	93 608	24 274	25 726	72 578	18 669	11 015	39 979	374 715
1952	84 333	99 181	25 663	27 350	75 481	19 848	11 167	43 472	386 495
1953	88 866	103 957	27 006	29 026	75 688	20 901	11 736	45 147	402 327
1954	92 528	110 836	27 117	31 042	83 258	22 246	12 488	49 820	429 335
1955	99 125	118 960	27 080	32 242	90 307	23 317	12 593	53 991	457 615
1956	101 856	120 674	27 238	33 539	96 502	24 316	12 807	58 677	475 609
1957	107 087	130 717	30 090	34 766	103 812	25 936	12 932	67 414	512 754
1958	113 655	142 577	30 915	35 639	109 333	25 805	13 292	68 540	539 756
1959	106 303	154 538	30 748	38 207	112 599	26 737	12 125	72 658	553 915
1960	114 614	167 397	32 767	39 831	121 723	30 017	12 554	72 889	591 792
1961	122 809	179 951	34 341	41 847	126 365	32 226	12 912	70 643	621 094
1962	120 833	190 932	35 971	44 120	132 039	34 922	12 624	73 762	645 203
1963	117 927	192 912	38 240	45 571	141 839	36 217	12 686	77 134	662 526
1964	130 074	199 423	39 092	48 389	157 312	38 580	12 940	83 688	709 498
1965	141 960	203 444	39 407	50 136	167 116	40 501	13 088	89 240	744 892
1966	142 919	216 181	43 797	52 806	177 427	43 921	13 536	90 842	781 429
1967	146 755	224 877	45 223	55 028	188 258	45 581	12 975	96 334	815 031
1968	153 002	244 921	46 844	58 398	201 669	45 734	13 181	102 916	866 665
1969	166 080	266 292	48 585	62 116	213 924	47 448	13 984	106 612	925 041
1970	174 972	292 480	49 586	66 308	227 970	50 229	14 638	114 807	990 990
1971	183 458	322 159	54 022	70 250	237 480	52 331	14 498	116 494	1 050 692
1972	189 183	356 880	53 373	75 637	257 636	53 838	13 992	117 982	1 118 521
1973	200 720	401 643	50 401	80 728	279 302	56 713	14 098	126 364	1 209 969
1974	213 739	433 322	50 891	85 370	296 370	61 969	14 541	129 038	1 285 240
1975	211 850	455 918	44 316	87 347	312 998	64 075	15 406	132 728	1 324 638
1976	211 327	498 823	45 881	91 488	326 267	65 334	16 026	142 978	1 398 124
1977	224 084	522 154	50 401	95 283	337 499	65 600	16 205	151 927	1 463 153
1978	214 233	548 342	54 540	103 366	365 340	65 784	17 058	155 528	1 524 191
1979	229 547	587 289	59 060	108 906	398 788	69 609	18 110	156 752	1 628 061
1980	232 802	639 093	63 654	113 375	431 983	72 723	19 205	149 735	1 722 570
1981	219 434	611 007	67 192	115 789	469 972	76 035	19 575	149 253	1 728 257
1982	212 518	614 538	57 634	116 938	466 649	76 147	17 724	146 150	1 708 298
1983	220 016	593 575	57 245	118 806	446 602	66 567	16 688	140 665	1 660 164
1984	224 491	625 438	60 875	123 037	462 678	69 650	16 505	142 664	1 725 338
1985	209 641	675 090	62 366	127 076	475 505	71 247	16 746	144 843	1 782 514
1986	224 985	729 252	65 895	134 844	457 655	77 857	18 231	152 244	1 860 963
1987	230 797	753 685	69 674	142 086	466 148	84 237	19 676	157 698	1 924 001
1988	226 438	751 910	74 814	147 896	471 953	77 285	19 676	166 879	1 936 851
1989	212 373	776 547	82 269	152 686	491 767	68 399	19 930	152 577	1 956 548
1990	212 518	743 765	84 038	159 042	516 692	64 979	20 105	160 648	1 961 787
1991	233 770	751 203	90 173	161 587	538 508	66 603	20 687	177 516	2 040 047
1992	254 575	748 949	100 092	167 889	558 049	66 004	22 218	189 942	2 107 718
1993	269 341	782 652	106 698	175 444	568 934	69 766	22 907	189 182	2 184 924
1994	291 696	831 176	112 139	186 496	594 054	79 254	24 166	182 183	2 301 164
1995	282 653	866 086	122 344	196 567	557 419	86 070	23 683	192 931	2 327 753
1996	295 090	891 202	130 786	200 695	586 144	88 050	24 867	192 160	2 408 994
1997	318 698	925 068	139 941	203 706	625 759	95 622	26 112	204 843	2 539 749
1998	334 314	926 918	144 279	205 132	655 910	95 718	27 313	204 433	2 594 017
1999	322 947	934 333	142 836	196 722	679 523	96 579	26 548	191 963	2 591 451
2000	320 364	975 444	149 121	202 230	724 371	99 573	26 203	198 105	2 695 411
2001	308 510	990 076	153 296	205 263	722 198	99 773	25 391	203 454	2 707 961

http://dx.doi.org/10.1787/456125276116

Table 4b. GDP Levels in 15 Latin American Countries, 1820-1949
(million 1990 international Geary-Khamis dollars)

	Bolivia	Costa Rica	Cuba	Dominican Republic	Ecuador	El Salvador	Guatemala	Haiti
1820								
1850								
1870								
1913								
1914								
1915								
1916								
1917								
1918								
1919								
1920		682				1 091	2 032	
1921		668				1 094	2 231	
1922		727				1 159	2 106	
1923		672				1 208	2 316	
1924		769				1 292	2 504	
1925		766				1 203	2 456	
1926		847				1 422	2 480	
1927		769				1 250	2 643	
1928		809				1 466	2 702	
1929		775	6 132			1 468	3 016	
1930		813	5 776			1 505	3 145	
1931		803	4 853			1 349	2 933	
1932		739	3 894			1 210	2 567	
1933		880	4 213			1 374	2 593	
1934		776	4 948			1 419	2 933	
1935		840	5 788			1 562	3 390	
1936		896	6 747			1 527	4 657	
1937		1 045	7 753			1 672	4 567	
1938		1 107	6 012			1 554	4 693	
1939		1 139	6 345		3 137	1 667	5 282	
1940		1 093	5 516		3 344	1 811	6 033	
1941		1 224	7 410		3 361	1 772	6 356	
1942		1 097	6 214		3 502	1 925	6 439	
1943		1 095	6 889		3 946	2 087	4 293	
1944		992	7 907		3 998	1 980	4 162	
1945	4 816	1 130	8 759		4 014	1 898	4 226	3 059
1946	4 902	1 249	9 541		4 492	1 928	5 006	3 085
1947	4 987	1 486	10 925		4 991	2 425	5 076	3 137
1948	5 095	1 571	9 706		5 673	3 090	5 248	3 168
1949	5 202	1 635	10 547		5 776	2 806	5 741	3 202

http://dx.doi.org/10.1787/456125276116

Table 4b. GDP Levels in 15 Latin American Countries, 1820-1949
(million 1990 international Geary-Khamis dollars)

	Honduras	Jamaica	Nicaragua	Panama	Paraguay	Puerto Rico	Trinidad and Tobago	Total
1820		281						3 240
1850		217						
1870		267						4 620
1913		509						16 670
1914								
1915								
1916								
1917								
1918								
1919								
1920	917		809					
1921	927		840					
1922	1 008		769					
1923	1 002		823					
1924	936		872					
1925	1 130		963					
1926	1 140		837					
1927	1 252		841					
1928	1 408		1 065					
1929	1 394		1 190					
1930	1 485		962					
1931	1 517		900					
1932	1 359		810					
1933	1 275		1 019					
1934	1 235		925					
1935	1 180		940					
1936	1 201		748					
1937	1 148		811					
1938	1 215	1 131	839					
1939	1 249		1 042		2 057			
1940	1 334		1 139		1 947			
1941	1 331		1 246		1 979			
1942	1 217	1 217	1 200		2 095			
1943	1 219	1 436	1 316		2 139			
1944	1 247		1 303		2 185			
1945	1 536		1 309	1 671	2 108			
1946	1 653	2 141	1 422	1 698	2 314			
1947	1 760	2 007	1 426	1 769	2 012			
1948	1 797		1 550	1 664	2 035			
1949	1 822		1 522	1 702	2 377			

http://dx.doi.org/10.1787/456125276116

ISBN 92-64-02261-9 – © OECD 2006

Table 4b. GDP Levels in 15 Latin American Countries, 1950-2001
(million 1990 international Geary-Khamis dollars)

	Bolivia	Costa Rica	Cuba	Dominican Republic	Ecuador	El Salvador	Guatemala	Haiti
1950	5 309	1 702	11 837	2 416	6 278	2 888	6 190	3 254
1951	5 683	1 747	12 818	2 701	6 346	2 945	6 277	3 302
1952	5 855	1 958	13 257	2 921	7 129	3 166	6 408	3 489
1953	5 301	2 256	11 647	2 884	7 279	3 392	6 643	3 378
1954	5 412	2 275	12 238	3 049	7 867	3 431	6 767	3 654
1955	5 698	2 538	12 794	3 237	8 074	3 608	6 934	3 507
1956	5 360	2 466	13 967	3 562	8 373	3 891	7 565	3 814
1957	5 183	2 676	15 980	3 787	8 751	4 098	7 992	3 587
1958	5 306	3 007	15 980	3 989	9 007	4 187	8 365	3 871
1959	5 289	3 118	14 263	4 012	9 490	4 375	8 778	3 688
1960	5 516	3 389	14 419	4 209	10 106	4 553	8 992	3 926
1961	5 631	3 530	14 625	4 114	10 360	4 713	9 378	3 767
1962	5 945	3 746	14 845	4 815	10 911	5 276	9 709	4 128
1963	6 327	4 067	15 064	5 129	11 189	5 504	10 635	3 860
1964	6 632	4 265	15 296	5 472	11 977	6 017	11 128	3 772
1965	6 958	4 651	15 529	4 791	13 131	6 340	11 613	3 813
1966	7 461	5 013	16 380	5 434	13 475	6 794	12 255	3 790
1967	7 928	5 320	18 294	5 617	14 188	7 164	12 757	3 713
1968	8 604	5 730	17 230	5 628	14 973	7 396	13 877	3 860
1969	8 989	6 111	17 018	6 244	15 792	7 653	14 532	3 986
1970	9 459	6 515	16 380	6 906	16 899	7 881	15 364	4 174
1971	9 820	6 945	17 656	7 637	17 872	8 245	16 221	4 445
1972	10 321	7 556	18 507	8 581	18 972	8 712	17 412	4 603
1973	11 030	8 145	20 209	9 617	21 337	9 084	18 593	4 810
1974	11 598	8 583	21 272	10 171	22 585	9 675	19 779	5 114
1975	12 364	8 755	22 336	10 659	23 772	10 193	20 164	4 995
1976	13 118	9 231	22 974	11 377	26 075	10 572	21 654	5 422
1977	13 670	10 055	24 038	11 930	27 731	11 189	23 344	5 448
1978	14 128	10 677	25 527	12 207	29 664	11 935	24 511	5 710
1979	14 125	11 207	26 165	12 733	31 274	11 744	25 667	6 127
1980	13 995	11 290	25 527	13 511	32 706	10 748	26 632	6 591
1981	14 124	11 035	27 654	14 069	34 041	9 869	26 804	6 410
1982	13 508	10 266	28 292	14 324	34 421	9 324	25 858	6 191
1983	12 905	10 551	29 104	14 959	33 702	9 386	25 193	6 238
1984	13 034	11 379	30 146	14 999	35 081	9 595	25 321	6 256
1985	12 943	11 475	30 694	14 620	36 570	9 819	25 167	6 269
1986	12 530	12 107	30 714	15 057	37 648	9 926	25 199	6 261
1987	12 858	12 683	30 468	16 189	35 288	10 193	26 094	6 214
1988	13 348	13 114	31 022	16 300	39 060	10 384	27 110	6 263
1989	13 735	13 867	31 128	18 377	39 123	10 491	28 179	6 329
1990	14 446	14 370	31 087	17 503	40 267	10 805	29 050	6 323
1991	15 226	14 686	27 481	17 643	42 280	11 108	30 125	6 329
1992	15 485	15 729	23 689	18 772	43 549	11 918	31 601	5 456
1993	16 135	16 641	19 898	19 148	44 507	12 681	32 865	5 336
1994	16 910	17 357	20 296	19 971	46 465	13 442	34 212	4 893
1995	17 705	17 739	20 986	20 870	47 859	14 275	35 923	5 138
1996	18 484	17 899	22 812	22 373	48 816	14 532	37 000	5 349
1997	19 408	18 901	23 565	24 230	50 476	15 157	38 518	5 493
1998	20 417	20 489	23 871	25 998	50 678	15 732	40 482	5 614
1999	20 499	22 415	25 494	28 078	46 978	16 268	42 020	5 765
2000	20 991	22 908	26 896	30 600	40 059	16 626	43 533	5 817
2001	21 243	23 114	27 703	30 943	50 750	16 925	44 317	5 718

http://dx.doi.org/10.1787/456125276116

Table 4b. **GDP Levels in 15 Latin American Countries, 1950-2001**
(million 1990 international Geary-Khamis dollars)

	Honduras	Jamaica	Nicaragua	Panama	Paraguay	Puerto Rico	Trinidad and Tobago	Total
1950	1 880	1 837	1 774	1 710	2 338	4 755	2 322	56 490
1951	1 982	1 985	1 894	1 695	2 383	4 929	2 526	59 213
1952	2 058	2 145	2 215	1 787	2 343	5 214	2 612	62 557
1953	2 220	2 446	2 268	1 895	2 410	5 445	2 682	62 146
1954	2 094	2 727	2 480	1 963	2 452	5 669	2 730	64 808
1955	2 149	3 008	2 646	2 077	2 564	5 961	3 111	67 906
1956	2 322	3 307	2 645	2 185	2 672	6 388	3 756	72 273
1957	2 429	3 789	2 868	2 414	2 795	6 708	4 088	77 145
1958	2 506	3 849	2 877	2 432	2 952	6 901	4 423	79 652
1959	2 569	4 064	2 920	2 589	2 944	7 521	4 692	80 312
1960	2 728	4 330	2 960	2 744	2 970	8 066	5 258	84 166
1961	2 798	4 453	3 182	3 040	3 111	8 835	5 488	87 025
1962	2 959	4 533	3 529	3 295	3 330	9 500	5 781	92 302
1963	3 069	4 681	3 912	3 606	3 421	10 488	6 076	97 028
1964	3 229	5 050	4 370	3 761	3 569	11 232	6 283	102 053
1965	3 509	5 456	4 786	4 091	3 773	12 254	6 603	107 298
1966	3 713	5 695	4 944	4 395	3 815	13 119	6 891	113 174
1967	3 922	5 915	5 288	4 762	4 058	13 944	7 035	119 905
1968	4 154	6 218	5 360	5 109	4 202	14 606	7 400	124 347
1969	4 187	6 681	5 716	5 507	4 365	15 899	7 604	130 284
1970	4 296	7 481	5 771	5 839	4 636	17 280	7 873	136 754
1971	4 462	7 481	6 055	6 312	4 839	18 375	7 954	144 319
1972	4 635	7 706	6 248	6 645	5 088	19 732	8 414	153 132
1973	4 866	8 411	6 566	7 052	5 487	20 908	8 553	164 668
1974	4 826	8 095	7 505	7 221	5 945	20 919	9 011	172 299
1975	4 949	8 093	7 493	7 338	6 328	20 388	9 181	177 008
1976	5 467	7 603	7 880	7 458	6 758	21 464	10 059	187 112
1977	6 047	7 443	8 556	7 546	7 478	22 867	10 698	198 040
1978	6 662	7 496	7 884	8 285	8 297	24 379	11 947	209 309
1979	6 976	7 363	5 785	8 651	9 215	25 868	12 500	215 400
1980	7 014	6 957	6 043	9 961	10 549	26 263	13 501	221 288
1981	7 196	7 142	6 367	10 367	11 458	26 544	14 096	227 176
1982	7 078	7 237	6 312	10 939	11 058	25 734	13 271	223 813
1983	7 030	7 405	6 609	11 013	10 724	25 855	12 231	222 905
1984	7 312	7 343	6 474	10 963	11 061	27 747	12 967	229 678
1985	7 640	7 003	6 204	11 480	11 501	28 319	12 436	232 140
1986	7 710	7 119	6 077	11 857	11 486	30 630	12 028	236 349
1987	8 167	7 668	6 035	12 150	11 988	32 136	11 473	239 604
1988	8 571	7 889	5 367	10 256	12 764	34 228	11 027	246 703
1989	8 894	8 428	5 296	10 215	13 509	35 919	10 937	254 427
1990	8 898	8 890	5 297	10 688	13 923	37 277	11 110	259 934
1991	9 138	8 917	5 281	11 650	14 271	38 136	11 499	263 770
1992	9 668	9 140	5 323	12 605	14 514	39 877	11 372	268 698
1993	10 355	9 304	5 302	13 273	15 094	41 729	11 236	273 504
1994	10 158	9 481	5 514	13 685	15 547	43 475	11 708	283 114
1995	10 534	9 642	5 762	13 945	16 247	45 453	12 188	294 266
1996	10 913	9 497	6 033	14 280	16 458	46 953	12.651	304 050
1997	11 459	9 355	6 340	14 908	16 886	48 549	13 043	316 288
1998	11 791	9 317	6 600	15 504	16 819	50 103	13 669	327 084
1999	11 567	9 308	7 889	16 000	16 903	52 207	14 598	335 989
2000	12 134	9 411	7 500	16 400	16 835	53 826	15 299	338 835
2001	12 449	9 693	7 725	16 450	16 970	55 494	15 988	355 482

http://dx.doi.org/10.1787/456125276116

Table 4b. GDP Levels in 47 Latin American Countries, 1820-1949
(million 1990 international Geary-Khamis dollars)

	Total 8 core countries	Total 15 countries	Total 24 small Caribbean countries	Total 47 countries
1820	11 275	3 240	509	15 024
1850				
1870	22 273	4 620	626	27 519
1900	60 619	9 974	1 217	71 810
1901	65 206			
1902	64 327			
1903	69 334			
1904	72 078			
1905	77 152			
1906	80 087			
1907	82 530			
1908	85 216			
1909	89 036			
1910	92 580			
1911	95 596			
1912	99 922			
1913	101 419	16 670	1 782	119 871
1914	95 890			
1915	96 586			
1916	100 002			
1917	101 442			
1918	105 504			
1919	108 632			
1920	114 811			
1921	113 737			
1922	120 740			
1923	131 691			
1924	136 541			
1925	139 169			
1926	146 603			
1927	153 420			
1928	165 312			
1929	170 305			
1930	163 253			
1931	152 202			
1932	146 991			
1933	159 469			
1934	172 594			
1935	181 108			
1936	191 168			
1937	201 068			
1938	205 978			
1939	213 820			
1940	216 077			
1941	227 302			
1942	226 013			
1943	236 058			
1944	256 245			
1945	265 235			
1946	290 028			
1947	308 001			
1948	327 784			
1949	339 572			

http://dx.doi.org/10.1787/456125276116

Table 4b. **GDP Levels in 47 Latin American Countries, 1950-2001**
(million 1990 international Geary-Khamis dollars)

	Total 8 core countries	Total 15 countries	Total 24 small Caribbean countries	Total 47 countries
1950	355 334	56 490	4 083	415 907
1951	374 715	59 213	4 313	438 241
1952	386 495	62 557	4 556	453 608
1953	402 327	62 146	4 813	469 286
1954	429 335	64 808	5 083	499 226
1955	457 615	67 906	5 370	530 891
1956	475 609	72 273	5 671	553 553
1957	512 754	77 145	5 991	595 890
1958	539 756	79 652	6 328	625 736
1959	553 915	80 312	6 685	640 912
1960	591 792	84 166	7 060	683 018
1961	621 094	87 025	7 458	715 577
1962	645 203	92 302	7 878	745 383
1963	662 526	97 028	8 321	767 875
1964	709 498	102 053	8 790	820 341
1965	744 892	107 298	9 285	861 475
1966	781 429	113 174	9 808	904 411
1967	815 031	119 905	10 359	945 295
1968	866 665	124 347	10 942	1 001 954
1969	925 041	130 284	11 558	1 066 883
1970	990 990	136 754	12 210	1 139 954
1971	1 050 692	144 319	12 897	1 207 908
1972	1 118 521	153 132	13 544	1 285 197
1973	1 209 969	164 668	14 392	1 389 029
1974	1 285 240	172 299	14 585	1 472 124
1975	1 324 638	177 008	14 783	1 516 429
1976	1 398 124	187 112	14 983	1 600 219
1977	1 463 153	198 040	15 187	1 676 380
1978	1 524 191	209 309	15 392	1 748 892
1979	1 628 061	215 400	15 601	1 859 062
1980	1 722 570	221 288	15 812	1 959 670
1981	1 728 257	227 176	16 026	1 971 459
1982	1 708 298	223 813	16 243	1 948 354
1983	1 660 164	222 905	16 462	1 899 531
1984	1 725 338	229 678	16 686	1 971 702
1985	1 782 514	232 140	16 912	2 031 566
1986	1 860 963	236 349	17 142	2 114 454
1987	1 924 001	239 604	17 374	2 180 979
1988	1 936 851	246 703	17 611	2 201 165
1989	1 956 548	254 427	17 851	2 228 826
1990	1 961 787	259 934	18 094	2 239 815
1991	2 040 047	263 770	18 545	2 322 362
1992	2 107 718	268 698	19 007	2 395 423
1993	2 184 924	273 504	19 481	2 477 909
1994	2 301 164	283 114	19 966	2 604 244
1995	2 327 753	294 266	20 464	2 642 483
1996	2 408 994	304 050	20 975	2 734 019
1997	2 539 749	316 288	21 497	2 877 534
1998	2 594 017	327 084	22 033	2 943 134
1999	2 591 451	335 989	22 634	2 950 074
2000	2 695 411	338 835	22 846	3 057 092
2001	2 707 961	355 482	23 563	3 087 006

http://dx.doi.org/10.1787/456125276116

ISBN 92-64-02261-9 – © OECD 2006

Per Capita GDP in Latin America

Table 4c. Per Capita GDP in 8 Latin American Countries, 1820-1913
(1990 international Geary-Khamis dollars)

	Argentina	Brazil	Chile	Colombia	Mexico	Peru	Uruguay	Venezuela	Average
1820		646			759				713
1850		686							
1870	1 311	713			674		2 181	569	749
1871		717					2 178		
1872		721					2 632		
1873		724					2 601		
1874		728					2 315		
1875		732					1 942		
1876		736					2 105		
1877		740					2 123		
1878		744					2 247		
1879		748					1 949		
1880		752					2 082		
1881		756					1 932		
1882		760					2 080		
1883		764					2 397		
1884		768					2 324		
1885		773					2 569		
1886		777					2 608		
1887		781					2 267		
1888		785					2 718		
1889		789					2 415		
1890	2 152	794			1 011		2 147		
1891		773					2 290		
1892		730					2 294		
1893		622					2 437		
1894		621					2 657		
1895		783			1 132		2 568		
1896		710					2 644		
1897		699					2 493		
1898		717					2 250		
1899		703					2 261		
1900	2 756	678	1 949	973	1 366	817	2 219	821	1 200
1901	2 880	730	1 990	1 022	1 466	858	2 233	797	1 267
1902	2 717	715	2 033	1 020	1 348	855	2 572	856	1 228
1903	2 992	714	2 074	1 030	1 483	864	2 615	913	1 300
1904	3 191	713	2 120	1 039	1 492	872	2 640	876	1 327
1905	3 479	718	2 164	1 053	1 630	884	2 334	861	1 395
1906	3 518	770	2 210	1 103	1 594	925	2 533	799	1 422
1907	3 459	755	2 257	1 101	1 669	924	2 757	793	1 439
1908	3 657	734	2 303	1 096	1 649	920	2 973	841	1 460
1909	3 699	776	2 313	1 131	1 680	949	2 957	865	1 498
1910	3 822	769	2 472	1 162	1 694	975	3 136	886	1 533
1911	3 746	836	2 420	1 201	1 707	1 008	2 957	937	1 558
1912	3 904	809	2 656	1 236	1 718	1 037	3 508	962	1 603
1913	3 797	811	2 653	1 236	1 732	1 037	3 310	1 104	1 601

http://dx.doi.org/10.1787/456125276116

ISBN 92-64-02261-9 – © OECD 2006

Table 4c. **Per Capita GDP in 8 Latin American Countries, 1914-1949**
(1990 international Geary-Khamis dollars)

	Argentina	Brazil	Chile	Colombia	Mexico	Peru	Uruguay	Venezuela	Average
1914	3 302	780	2 440	1 163	1 744	927	2 654	956	1 489
1915	3 244	798	2 238	1 129	1 757	974	2 470	980	1 478
1916	3 091	804	2 620	1 222	1 770	1 255	2 508	921	1 509
1917	2 790	842	2 794	1 292	1 783	1 198	2 717	1 069	1 509
1918	3 248	808	2 763	1 252	1 796	1 154	2 828	1 057	1 547
1919	3 307	895	2 155	1 253	1 810	1 318	3 135	983	1 570
1920	3 473	963	2 430	1 255	1 823	1 331	2 674	1 173	1 635
1921	3 471	859	2 064	1 255	1 836	926	2 751	1 214	1 594
1922	3 636	1 009	2 179	1 255	1 850	1 035	3 078	1 241	1 659
1923	3 898	1 046	2 676	1 255	1 884	1 318	3 170	1 420	1 773
1924	4 055	1 024	2 880	1 255	1 825	1 318	3 397	1 630	1 801
1925	3 919	1 007	2 876	1 255	1 908	1 157	3 188	2 081	1 800
1926	3 994	1 008	2 767	1 340	1 991	1 272	3 398	2 487	1 859
1927	4 156	1 060	2 618	1 424	1 875	1 410	3 797	2 761	1 907
1928	4 291	1 158	3 136	1 490	1 857	1 487	3 906	3 057	2 014
1929	4 367	1 137	3 396	1 505	1 757	1 619	3 847	3 426	2 034
1930	4 080	1 048	3 143	1 474	1 618	1 417	4 301	3 444	1 914
1931	3 712	1 004	2 333	1 448	1 643	1 228	3 500	2 754	1 752
1932	3 522	1 018	2 274	1 511	1 373	1 148	3 196	2 613	1 662
1933	3 621	1 076	2 652	1 577	1 501	1 524	2 750	2 831	1 772
1934	3 845	1 142	2 976	1 526	1 574	1 753	3 221	2 995	1 884
1935	3 950	1 150	2 987	1 677	1 660	1 772	3 356	3 181	1 943
1936	3 912	1 235	3 056	1 744	1 768	1 822	3 459	3 449	2 017
1937	4 125	1 250	3 241	1 751	1 796	1 832	3 462	3 896	2 084
1938	4 072	1 276	3 139	1 843	1 794	1 757	3 676	4 144	2 098
1939	4 148	1 263	3 178	1 905	1 858	1 884	3 692	4 305	2 136
1940	4 161	1 250	3 259	1 895	1 852	1 823	3 661	4 045	2 119
1941	4 304	1 307	3 205	1 877	1 949	1 998	3 682	3 903	2 180
1942	4 284	1 229	3 322	1 832	2 032	1 757	3 338	3 347	2 119
1943	4 182	1 368	3 400	1 792	2 051	1 643	3 331	3 575	2 164
1944	4 579	1 386	3 388	1 863	2 159	1 835	3 705	4 309	2 296
1945	4 356	1 390	3 630	1 899	2 134	2 005	3 764	5 102	2 315
1946	4 665	1 501	3 786	2 017	2 211	2 046	4 083	5 948	2 473
1947	5 089	1 518	3 470	2 042	2 221	2 066	4 313	6 894	2 564
1948	5 252	1 596	3 806	2 050	2 248	2 094	4 405	7 394	2 663
1949	5 047	1 659	3 715	2 107	2 304	2 199	4 504	7 544	2 690

http://dx.doi.org/10.1787/456125276116

Table 4c. **Per Capita GDP in 8 Latin American Countries, 1950-2001**
(1990 international Geary-Khamis dollars)

	Argentina	*Brazil*	*Chile*	*Colombia*	*Mexico*	*Peru*	*Uruguay*	*Venezuela*	*Average*
1950	4 987	1 672	3 821	2 153	2 365	2 263	4 659	7 462	2 700
1951	5 073	1 702	3 883	2 150	2 477	2 385	4 955	7 663	2 770
1952	4 717	1 752	4 024	2 214	2 504	2 473	4 957	7 992	2 779
1953	4 874	1 784	4 159	2 277	2 439	2 539	5 139	7 956	2 814
1954	4 980	1 848	4 101	2 358	2 605	2 634	5 391	8 417	2 921
1955	5 237	1 926	4 016	2 373	2 742	2 689	5 352	8 750	3 027
1956	5 285	1 896	3 954	2 391	2 843	2 731	5 360	9 124	3 059
1957	5 461	1 994	4 269	2 400	2 965	2 836	5 333	10 058	3 205
1958	5 698	2 111	4 282	2 383	3 025	2 746	5 402	9 816	3 278
1959	5 241	2 221	4 155	2 473	3 016	2 768	4 860	9 997	3 269
1960	5 559	2 335	4 320	2 497	3 155	3 023	4 960	9 646	3 392
1961	5 862	2 437	4 418	2 540	3 172	3 154	5 036	9 002	3 460
1962	5 677	2 511	4 518	2 594	3 211	3 321	4 858	9 058	3 494
1963	5 455	2 463	4 694	2 597	3 343	3 345	4 820	9 134	3 488
1964	5 926	2 472	4 693	2 675	3 594	3 462	4 858	9 562	3 632
1965	6 371	2 448	4 631	2 689	3 702	3 532	4 860	9 841	3 708
1966	6 321	2 527	5 042	2 750	3 813	3 723	4 974	9 677	3 784
1967	6 399	2 554	5 105	2 784	3 922	3 757	4 721	9 922	3 841
1968	6 578	2 704	5 188	2 874	4 073	3 666	4 747	10 249	3 976
1969	7 037	2 860	5 281	2 976	4 185	3 698	4 991	10 262	4 131
1970	7 302	3 057	5 293	3 094	4 320	3 807	5 184	10 672	4 309
1971	7 530	3 279	5 663	3 194	4 363	3 857	5 130	10 446	4 450
1972	7 635	3 539	5 492	3 355	4 597	3 858	4 945	10 245	4 618
1973	7 962	3 882	5 093	3 499	4 845	3 952	4 974	10 625	4 872
1974	8 334	4 083	5 050	3 618	5 003	4 200	5 123	10 507	5 049
1975	8 122	4 190	4 323	3 622	5 146	4 226	5 421	10 472	5 080
1976	7 965	4 472	4 398	3 716	5 228	4 195	5 608	10 929	5 236
1977	8 304	4 568	4 755	3 797	5 275	4 103	5 639	11 251	5 353
1978	7 807	4 681	5 069	4 047	5 573	4 008	5 903	11 164	5 450
1979	8 227	4 892	5 407	4 184	5 941	4 131	6 234	10 920	5 690
1980	8 206	5 198	5 738	4 265	6 289	4 205	6 577	10 139	5 886
1981	7 603	4 852	5 956	4 263	6 683	4 283	6 668	9 841	5 772
1982	7 243	4 765	5 017	4 212	6 489	4 176	6 000	9 356	5 578
1983	7 383	4 500	4 898	4 185	6 082	3 559	5 614	8 745	5 305
1984	7 425	4 646	5 125	4 239	6 174	3 633	5 520	8 623	5 401
1985	6 834	4 917	5 168	4 282	6 218	3 631	5 567	8 521	5 471
1986	7 224	5 205	5 375	4 446	5 865	3 879	6 023	8 725	5 598
1987	7 299	5 273	5 590	4 589	5 854	4 103	6 461	8 805	5 674
1988	7 056	5 158	5 901	4 682	5 810	3 680	6 422	9 080	5 601
1989	6 523	5 227	6 377	4 739	5 936	3 183	6 462	8 094	5 550
1990	6 436	4 923	6 402	4 840	6 119	2 955	6 474	8 313	5 465
1991	6 980	4 893	6 753	4 821	6 258	2 960	6 614	8 965	5 584
1992	7 497	4 802	7 374	4 909	6 366	2 868	7 055	9 373	5 669
1993	7 827	4 939	7 738	5 028	6 372	2 965	7 224	9 137	5 776
1994	8 367	5 163	8 010	5 240	6 536	3 296	7 567	8 620	5 982
1995	8 005	5 296	8 612	5 418	6 027	3 505	7 365	8 950	5 951
1996	8 253	5 366	9 080	5 428	6 230	3 514	7 681	8 747	6 060
1997	8 803	5 488	9 586	5 409	6 541	3 742	8 009	9 155	6 289
1998	9 123	5 422	9 756	5 350	6 745	3 675	8 317	8 977	6 326
1999	8 711	5 392	9 539	5 042	6 877	3 640	8 024	8 288	6 227
2000	8 544	5 556	9 841	5 096	7 218	3 686	7 859	8 415	6 385
2001	8 137	5 570	10 001	5 087	7 089	3 630	7 557	8 507	6 327

http://dx.doi.org/10.1787/456125276116

ISBN 92-64-02261-9 – © OECD 2006

Table 4b. **Per Capita GDP in 15 Latin American Countries, 1820-1949**
(1990 international Geary-Khamis dollars)

	Bolivia	Costa Rica	Cuba	Dominican Republic	Ecuador	El Salvador	Guatemala	Haiti
1820								
1850								
1870								
1913								
1914								
1915								
1916								
1917								
1918								
1919								
1920		1 624				932	1 272	
1921		1 553				919	1 382	
1922		1 691				950	1 291	
1923		1 527				974	1 405	
1924		1 709				1 017	1 504	
1925		1 665				925	1 460	
1926		1 802				1 069	1 460	
1927		1 636				926	1 539	
1928		1 685				1 055	1 557	
1929		1 582	1 639			1 041	1 720	
1930		1 626	1 505			1 045	1 776	
1931		1 575	1 241			924	1 620	
1932		1 421	977			823	1 380	
1933		1 660	1 038			922	1 358	
1934		1 437	1 982			940	1 512	
1935		1 527	1 371			1 021	1 712	
1936		1 600	1 573			985	2 305	
1937		1 802	1 779			1 065	2 206	
1938		1 876	1 358			977	2 224	
1939		1 867	1 411		1 301	1 035	2 457	
1940		1 763	1 208		1 356	1 111	2 742	
1941		1 943	1 599		1 323	1 074	2 825	
1942		1 688	1 321		1 360	1 146	2 800	
1943		1 659	1 442		1 494	1 235	1 835	
1944		1 459	1 631		1 474	1 151	1 741	
1945	1 690	1 614	1 776		1 443	1 091	1 732	1 045
1946	1 700	1 759	1 893		1 574	1 095	2 002	1 042
1947	1 710	2 036	2 121		1 700	1 362	1 975	1 048
1948	1 727	2 095	1 842		1 880	1 707	1 988	1 046
1949	1 743	2 123	1 958		1 861	1 525	2 111	1 046

http://dx.doi.org/10.1787/456125276116

Table 4b. Per Capita GDP in 15 Latin American Countries, 1820-1949
(1990 international Geary-Khamis dollars)

	Honduras	Jamaica	Nicaragua	Panama	Paraguay	Puerto Rico	Trinidad and Tobago	Total
1820		700						636
1850		522						
1870		535						486
1913		620						1 038
1914								
1915								
1916								
1917								
1918								
1919								
1920	1 274		1 264					
1921	1 253		1 313					
1922	1 309		1 183					
1923	1 253		1 266					
1924	1 141		1 321					
1925	1 329		1 459					
1926	1 295		1 249					
1927	1 407		1 255					
1928	1 547		1 590					
1929	1 499		1 750					
1930	1 563		1 415					
1931	1 564		1 304					
1932	1 373		1 174					
1933	1 262		1 456					
1934	1 211		1 303					
1935	1 135		1 288					
1936	1 133		997					
1937	1 063		1 053					
1938	1 105	972	1 076					
1939	1 115		1 286		1 894			
1940	1 160		1 372		1 752			
1941	1 138		1 483		1 741			
1942	1 014	970	1 395		1 800			
1943	1 007	1 150	1 495		1 796			
1944	1 006		1 448		1 792			
1945	1 219		1 423	2 113	1 690			
1946	1 281	1 649	1 497	2 155	1 815			
1947	1 333	1 512	1 455	2 200	1 542			
1948	1 331		1 550	2 024	1 524			
1949	1 311		1 478	2 031	1 740			

http://dx.doi.org/10.1787/456125276116

ISBN 92-64-02261-9 – © OECD 2006

Table 4b. **Per Capita GDP in 15 Latin American Countries, 1950-2001**
(1990 international Geary-Khamis dollars)

	Bolivia	Costa Rica	Cuba	Dominican Republic	Ecuador	El Salvador	Guatemala	Haiti
1950	1 919	1 963	2 046	1 027	1 863	1 489	2 085	1 051
1951	2 013	1 951	2 176	1 117	1 835	1 480	2 054	1 049
1952	2 031	2 114	2 207	1 172	2 009	1 550	2 037	1 090
1953	1 800	2 353	1 900	1 123	1 998	1 616	2 051	1 037
1954	1 799	2 289	1 957	1 150	2 103	1 589	2 029	1 102
1955	1 853	2 460	2 005	1 183	2 101	1 624	2 019	1 039
1956	1 706	2 301	2 145	1 260	2 121	1 701	2 140	1 108
1957	1 614	2 406	2 406	1 296	2 156	1 740	2 195	1 023
1958	1 616	2 605	2 363	1 320	2 159	1 725	2 231	1 082
1959	1 575	2 598	2 067	1 284	2 211	1 748	2 273	1 011
1960	1 606	2 715	2 052	1 302	2 289	1 764	2 262	1 055
1961	1 603	2 723	2 050	1 232	2 279	1 769	2 292	991
1962	1 654	2 785	2 046	1 394	2 331	1 920	2 307	1 064
1963	1 720	2 919	2 032	1 437	2 320	1 941	2 456	974
1964	1 762	2 961	2 009	1 484	2 411	2 058	2 498	931
1965	1 806	3 127	1 988	1 259	2 566	2 101	2 534	922
1966	1 891	3 258	2 051	1 384	2 556	2 172	2 600	897
1967	1 962	3 349	2 248	1 387	2 612	2 216	2 631	860
1968	2 079	3 497	2 080	1 349	2 675	2 210	2 782	875
1969	2 120	3 622	2 021	1 453	2 739	2 206	2 830	884
1970	2 176	3 754	1 917	1 561	2 845	2 187	2 905	906
1971	2 204	3 889	2 037	1 680	2 922	2 222	2 974	955
1972	2 260	4 118	2 096	1 837	3 012	2 298	3 096	979
1973	2 357	4 319	2 245	2 005	3 290	2 342	3 204	1 013
1974	2 418	4 430	2 324	2 067	3 383	2 436	3 303	1 066
1975	2 516	4 396	2 404	2 111	3 459	2 504	3 263	1 032
1976	2 647	4 506	2 439	2 198	3 687	2 532	3 395	1 111
1977	2 691	4 769	2 520	2 250	3 810	2 613	3 546	1 106
1978	2 715	4 870	2 650	2 248	3 961	2 715	3 607	1 149
1979	2 652	4 959	2 695	2 289	4 060	2 605	3 661	1 221
1980	2 572	4 911	2 644	2 372	4 129	2 354	3 681	1 304
1981	2 547	4 681	2 847	2 413	4 181	2 186	3 579	1 259
1982	2 394	4 235	2 890	2 400	4 114	2 084	3 352	1 202
1983	2 249	4 230	2 944	2 450	3 922	2 076	3 187	1 189
1984	2 234	4 432	3 020	2 403	3 975	2 091	3 117	1 168
1985	2 181	4 340	3 045	2 292	4 036	2 105	3 011	1 146
1986	2 074	4 446	3 022	2 311	4 048	2 089	2 930	1 120
1987	2 089	4 530	2 975	2 432	3 697	2 105	2 947	1 088
1988	2 124	4 561	3 002	2 399	3 988	2 106	2 973	1 074
1989	2 138	4 698	2 982	2 649	3 894	2 092	3 003	1 063
1990	2 197	4 747	2 948	2 474	3 903	2 119	3 009	1 041
1991	2 262	4 736	2 582	2 446	4 002	2 142	3 034	1 025
1992	2 246	4 957	2 209	2 555	4 025	2 259	3 093	870
1993	2 287	5 129	1 844	2 563	4 018	2 362	3 127	835
1994	2 343	5 237	1 871	2 629	4 099	2 459	3 164	753
1995	2 400	5 242	1 925	2 703	4 126	2 564	3 229	777
1996	2 453	5 186	2 083	2 850	4 115	2 561	3 232	795
1997	2 523	5 372	2 142	3 037	4 163	2 621	3 269	803
1998	2 601	5 718	2 160	3 208	4 090	2 669	3 340	808
1999	2 562	6 146	2 297	3 412	3 712	2 708	3 370	816
2000	2 575	6 174	2 414	3 663	3 101	2 716	3 396	810
2001	2 559	6 126	2 477	3 651	3 849	2 713	3 363	785

http://dx.doi.org/10.1787/456125276116

Table 4b. Per Capita GDP in 15 Latin American Countries,1950-2001
(1990 international Geary-Khamis dollars)

	Honduras	Jamaica	Nicaragua	Panama	Paraguay	Puerto Rico	Trinidad and Tobago	Total
1950	1 313	1 327	1 616	1 916	1 584	2 144	3 674	1 750
1951	1 344	1 412	1 674	1 851	1 573	2 205	3 894	1 794
1952	1 356	1 504	1 900	1 901	1 506	2 341	3 941	1 854
1953	1 421	1 691	1 888	1 969	1 509	2 471	3 954	1 802
1954	1 300	1 858	2 002	1 993	1 495	2 561	3 914	1 835
1955	1 293	2 020	2 072	2 055	1 523	2 649	4 316	1 876
1956	1 354	2 190	2 008	2 108	1 547	2 840	5 059	1 950
1957	1 372	2 468	2 111	2 270	1 578	2 968	5 344	2 032
1958	1 370	2 458	2 052	2 241	1 625	3 002	5 609	2 046
1959	1 360	2 541	2 019	2 322	1 581	3 239	5 743	2 011
1960	1 398	2 654	1 983	2 391	1 555	3 421	6 251	2 054
1961	1 387	2 702	2 065	2 574	1 588	3 677	6 371	2 072
1962	1 421	2 722	2 219	2 710	1 657	3 881	6 514	2 143
1963	1 427	2 757	2 382	2 882	1 659	4 201	6 718	2 195
1964	1 452	2 904	2 578	2 920	1 687	4 401	6 801	2 246
1965	1 526	3 070	2 734	3 085	1 739	4 719	7 030	2 299
1966	1 563	3 129	2 736	3 219	1 712	4 993	7 234	2 362
1967	1 599	3 178	2 835	3 388	1 774	5 264	7 327	2 440
1968	1 639	3 284	2 783	3 531	1 789	5 463	7 684	2 469
1969	1 599	3 480	2 875	3 699	1 810	5 840	7 897	2 523
1970	1 601	3 849	2 812	3 814	1 872	6 349	8 244	2 588
1971	1 613	3 803	2 856	4 012	1 902	6 642	8 272	2 668
1972	1 618	3 858	2 862	4 111	1 946	6 930	8 628	2 763
1973	1 642	4 130	2 921	4 250	2 038	7 302	8 685	2 903
1974	1 574	3 908	3 236	4 232	2 144	7 247	9 053	2 968
1975	1 570	3 845	3 129	4 198	2 220	6 946	9 118	2 980
1976	1 687	3 564	3 187	4 167	2 315	7 093	9 847	3 082
1977	1 815	3 451	3 350	4 102	2 506	7 422	10 296	3 190
1978	1 942	3 439	3 023	4 424	2 719	7 819	11 319	3 300
1979	1 977	3 336	2 152	4 518	2 954	8 164	11 649	3 324
1980	1 930	3 121	2 155	5 091	3 304	8 183	12 380	3 354
1981	1 916	3 162	2 195	5 194	3 498	8 195	12 794	3 380
1982	1 833	3 150	2 119	5 372	3 285	7 848	11 888	3 269
1983	1 774	3 188	2 169	5 301	3 097	7 797	10 794	3 193
1984	1 795	3 128	2 076	5 172	3 104	8 283	11 273	3 224
1985	1 825	2 953	1 946	5 306	3 135	8 373	10 664	3 193
1986	1 793	2 973	1 865	5 370	3 042	8 974	10 192	3 185
1987	1 849	3 178	1 810	5 394	3 085	9 330	9 631	3 163
1988	1 903	3 249	1 571	4 465	3 191	9 850	9 202	3 192
1989	1 919	3 449	1 512	4 361	3 282	10 246	9 112	3 225
1990	1 871	3 609	1 454	4 476	3 287	10 539	9 271	3 225
1991	1 873	3 588	1 384	4 786	3 274	10 706	9 641	3 206
1992	1 930	3 648	1 348	5 083	3 237	11 123	9 603	3 202
1993	2 011	3 684	1 308	5 259	3 273	11 542	9 560	3 197
1994	1 919	3 722	1 324	5 329	3 277	11 913	10 032	3 246
1995	1 935	3 753	1 348	5 333	3 331	12 341	10 503	3 310
1996	1 951	3 668	1 376	5 363	3 282	12 606	10 989	3 355
1997	1 994	3 588	1 411	5 512	3 276	12 914	11 426	3 426
1998	1 998	3 550	1 435	5 647	3 176	13 251	12 036	3 478
1999	1 914	3 526	1 676	5 731	3 107	13 738	12 908	3 510
2000	1 957	3 548	1 558	5 782	3 014	14 106	13 598	3 478
2001	1 958	3 636	1 571	5 715	2 959	14 452	14 295	3 586

http://dx.doi.org/10.1787/456125276116

Table 4c. **Per Capita GDP in 47 Latin American Countries, 1820-1949**
(1990 international Geary-Khamis dollars)

	Average 8 core countries	Average 15 countries	Average 24 small Caribbean countries	Average 47 countries
1820	713	636	636	692
1850				
1870	749	486	549	681
1900	1 200	778	880	1 110
1901	1 267			
1902	1 228			
1903	1 300			
1904	1 327			
1905	1 395			
1906	1 422			
1907	1 439			
1908	1 460			
1909	1 498			
1910	1 533			
1911	1 558			
1912	1 603			
1913	1 601	1 038	1 174	1 481
1914	1 489			
1915	1 478			
1916	1 509			
1917	1 509			
1918	1 547			
1919	1 570			
1920	1 635			
1921	1 594			
1922	1 659			
1923	1 773			
1924	1 801			
1925	1 800			
1926	1 859			
1927	1 907			
1928	2 014			
1929	2 034			
1930	1 914			
1931	1 752			
1932	1 662			
1933	1 772			
1934	1 884			
1935	1 943			
1936	2 017			
1937	2 084			
1938	2 098			
1939	2 136			
1940	2 119			
1941	2 180			
1942	2 119			
1943	2 164			
1944	2 296			
1945	2 315			
1946	2 473			
1947	2 564			
1948	2 663			
1949	2 690			

http://dx.doi.org/10.1787/456125276116

Table 4c. **Per Capita GDP in 47 Latin American Countries, 1950-2001**
(1990 international Geary-Khamis dollars)

	Average 8 core countries	Average 15 countries	Average 24 small Caribbean countries	Average 47 countries
1950	2 700	1 750	1 980	2 506
1951	2 770	1 794	2 043	2 572
1952	2 779	1 854	2 109	2 592
1953	2 814	1 802	2 177	2 612
1954	2 921	1 835	2 242	2 705
1955	3 027	1 876	2 311	2 799
1956	3 059	1 950	2 385	2 840
1957	3 205	2 032	2 460	2 974
1958	3 278	2 046	2 537	3 037
1959	3 269	2 011	2 616	3 024
1960	3 392	2 054	2 701	3 133
1961	3 460	2 072	2 801	3 192
1962	3 494	2 143	2 905	3 234
1963	3 488	2 195	2 992	3 241
1964	3 632	2 246	3 094	3 367
1965	3 708	2 299	3 201	3 439
1966	3 784	2 362	3 315	3 514
1967	3 841	2 440	3 437	3 576
1968	3 976	2 469	3 563	3 691
1969	4 131	2 523	3 703	3 828
1970	4 309	2 588	3 859	3 986
1971	4 450	2 668	4 012	4 117
1972	4 618	2 763	4 150	4 271
1973	4 872	2 903	4 350	4 504
1974	5 049	2 968	4 366	4 659
1975	5 080	2 980	4 415	4 687
1976	5 236	3 082	4 471	4 833
1977	5 353	3 190	4 512	4 948
1978	5 450	3 300	4 547	5 047
1979	5 690	3 324	4 589	5 247
1980	5 886	3 354	4 636	5 412
1981	5 772	3 380	4 665	5 327
1982	5 578	3 269	4 686	5 152
1983	5 305	3 193	4 704	4 918
1984	5 401	3 224	4 721	5 002
1985	5 471	3 193	4 738	5 052
1986	5 598	3 185	4 759	5 154
1987	5 674	3 163	4 784	5 212
1988	5 601	3 192	4 808	5 158
1989	5 550	3 225	4 833	5 123
1990	5 465	3 225	4 855	5 053
1991	5 584	3 206	4 937	5 145
1992	5 669	3 202	5 016	5 213
1993	5 776	3 197	5 095	5 299
1994	5 982	3 246	5 177	5 474
1995	5 951	3 310	5 261	5 460
1996	6 060	3 355	5 347	5 556
1997	6 289	3 426	5 434	5 753
1998	6 326	3 478	5 532	5 793
1999	6 223	3 510	5 632	5 718
2000	6 378	3 478	5 634	5 838
2001	6 314	3 586	5 759	5 811

http://dx.doi.org/10.1787/456125276116

ISBN 92-64-02261-9 – © OECD 2006   528

HS–5: Asia

Estimates for Asia are shown in three groups. The first consists of 16 East Asian countries which produced 88 per cent of Asian GDP and had 89 per cent of Asian population in 2001. For these countries the GDP estimates are well documented and of reasonable quality for 1950 onwards and scholars have been active in developing historical accounts for earlier years. There have been major problems for China where official estimates of GDP exaggerate growth and understate its level. Maddison (1998), *Chinese Economic Performance in the Long Run*, OECD, Paris, provides a detailed examination of these problems and makes adjustments to provide a close approximation to Western SNA accounting practice. Chinese official statisticians adopted SNA norms several years ago. Misstatement is not deliberate, but is a transitional problem in moving away from a detailed reporting practice inherited from the long period in which the norms of the Soviet material product system (MPS) prevailed.

The second group consists of 26 East Asian countries, which produced 1.6 per cent of Asian GDP and had 4.3 per cent of Asian population in 2001.

The third group consists of 15 West Asian countries, which produced about 10 per cent of Asian GDP and had 6.5 per cent of Asian population in 2001. The biggest countries in this group, in terms of GDP are Turkey, Iran, and Saudi Arabia.

Eight independent Asian countries emerged from the collapse of the former Soviet Union in 1991, and a third of the GDP of the Russian Federation is generated in Asia. It is not possible to construct satisfactory GDP estimates for this area before 1973, because the problem of disaggregating the former USSR is compounded by the difficulty of converting from an MPS to an SNA basis. Estimates for 1973–2001 are shown in HS–3. Inclusion of the 8 new states would have added 1.9 per cent to our Asian GDP for 2001.

16 East Asian Countries

Population: 1820–1949 as in Maddison (2001) and Maddison (1995), except as specified below. 1950 onwards revised and updated from International Programs Center, US Bureau of the Census (October 2002), except for China, India and Indonesia where estimates were derived from sources specified below.

GDP: 1820–1993 movement from Maddison (2001) revised and updated to 2001 from IMF, *World Economic Outlook,* April 2002, except as specified below. Benchmark 1990 levels in international Geary–Khamis dollars were derived as shown in Maddison (2001), pp. 174, 219–20.

China: Population and GDP 1820–1998 from Maddison (1998), pp. 155–9, 167–170. 1933 GDP level from Maddison (1998), p. 158, and annual volume movement 1929–38 from Maddison (1995), p. 158. Updating to 2001 from *China Statistical Yearbook,* Beijing, (2001) with adjustment of growth rate to conform to SNA measurement procedure as indicated in Maddison (2001), p. 202, and described in detail in Maddison (1998). Unfortunately the IMF and many journalists continue to cite the official growth rates or levels without caveat or correction. One also finds frequent references to Japan being the world's second biggest economy. My estimates show a GDP growth rate for China about threequarters the official estimate and a GDP level about 70 per cent higher than in Japan (when converted by purchasing power parity rather than exchange rates). See Xu Xianchun, Ye Yanfei and Derek Blades (2000), *National Accounts for China: Sources and Methods,* OECD, Paris and Maddison (1998).

India: 1900–1990 real GDP and population from Siva Sivasubramonian, *The National Income of India in the Twentieth Century,* Oxford University Press, Delhi, 2000, updated from his posthumous work, *The Sources of Economic Growth in India,* 1950 to 1999, OUP, Delhi, forthcoming. GDP movement 1820–1900 from Maddison 2001, pp. 202–3, annual movement 1884–99 from Alan Heston, in Kumar and Desai, eds., *Cambridge Economic History of India,* vol. 2, 1983, pp. 397–8. The present estimates refer to undivided India until 1946, and to the Indian Union since 1947. The GDP and population estimates are centred on October 1st (the middle of the fiscal year). The following table shows the population breakdown for India, Bangladesh and Pakistan for 1820–1946. Population figures for 1932–46 were misplaced in Maddison (2001), p. 203 and have been corrected. Per capita GDP in 1946 in undivided India was 622 in 1990 Geary–Khamis dollars, 624 in the Indian Union, 566 in Bangladesh, and 672 in Pakistan.

Table 5-1. **Population of Undivided India, Bangladesh and Pakistan, 1820-1946**

(000s)

	Undivided India	Indian Union	Bangladesh	Pakistan
1820	209 000	175 349	20 000	13 651
1870	253 000	212 189	24 721	16 090
1913	303 700	251 906	31 786	20 008
1929	333 100	275 861	34 427	22 812
1941	391 700	321 565	41 966	28 169
1946	415 200	340 857	41 660	32 683

Source: Maddison (1995), pp. 109, 114-5, and 232. Population of Bangladesh and Pakistan for benchmark year 1941 from M.W.M Yeatts, *Census of India 1941, vol. 1, Part I. Tables, Delhi, 1943,* pp. 62-3. Bangladesh assumed to move (with intercensal interpolation) as in prepartition Bengal (plus native states and agencies); Pakistan as in the prepartition total for Punjab (province, states, etc.), Sind and North West Frontier Province. Rough estimates 1946 for areas of Bangladesh and Pakistan when they were "wings" of undivided Pakistan from *20 Years of Pakistan in Statistics1947-1967, Karachi,* 1968. Figures are for 1st October, the midpoint of the fiscal year.

http://dx.doi.org/10.1787/456125276116

Indonesia: Population and GDP 1820–70 from Maddison (1989) "Dutch Income in and from Indonesia, 1700–1938", *Modern Asian Studies,* pp. 645–70; 1870–1993 supplied by Pierre van der Eng (see Maddison, 2001, p. 204). Estimates include East Timor.

Japan: GDP 1820–1990 from Maddison (2001), pp. 204–7, revised and updated 1990–2001 from OECD, *Quarterly National Accounts,* vol. 2002/2.

Malaysia: The estimates refer to modern Malaysia (old federated and unfederated Malay states, Sabah and Sarawak) excluding Brunei and Singapore. Population 1820–1913 supplied by Don Hoerr, 1913–49 by Pierre van der Eng. Annual GDP estimates 1911–90 supplied by Pierre van der Eng. They are an extension of the estimates by industry of origin for West Malaysia of V.V. Bhanoji Rao, *National Accounts of West Malaysia, 1947–1971,* Heinemann, Kuala Lumpur, 1976, adjusted to include Sabah and Sarawak. New estimates for West Malaysia, by type of expenditure, are under preparation by a research team at the Asia–Europe Institute, University of Malaya. The preliminary results for 1900–1939 were presented by HRH Raja Nazrin at the International Economic History Congress in Buenos Aires, July 2002.

Philippines: GDP movement 1902–50 from unpublished estimates of Richard Hooley. They are a substantially revised version of R.W. Hooley, "Long term Growth of the Philippine Economy 1902–1961", *The Philippine Economic Journal* (1968). GDP movement 1950–90 from the National Statistical Coordination Board, Manila, updated from Asian Development Bank (ADB) *Key Indicators,* see Maddison (2001), p. 205.

South Korea: Population movement, 1820–1910, for the whole of Korea from T.H. Kwon and Y.–H. Shin, "On Population Estimates of the Yi Dynasty, 1392–1910", *Tong–a Munhwa,* 14, 1977, p. 328 linked to 1910–44 level estimates of S.–C. Suh, *Growth and Structural Change in the Korean Economy,* 1910–1940, Harvard, 1978, p. 41. Suh, p. 132 gives a breakdown of population in the North and South for 1925–44; in 1925, South Korea had 68.375 per cent of total population. I assumed this ratio applied for 1820–1924. 1944–49 from *UN Demographic Yearbook 1960,* p. 142. GDP movement 1911–53 from Maddison (1995), pp. 146, 158–9, 1953–70 from *National Income in Korea 1975,* Bank of Korea, pp. 142–3, 1970–90 from OECD *National Accounts 1960–97,* vol.1, Paris, 1999. 1990–2001 from OECD *Quarterly National Accounts,* vol. 2002/2.

Table 5-2. **Population of Korea, North and South, 1820-1950**
(000s)

	Korea	South	North
1820	13 740	9 395	4 345
1870	14 264	9 753	4 511
1910	14 766	10 096	4 670
1913	15 486	10 589	4 897
1925	19 020	13 005	6 014
1930	20 438	13 900	6 537
1935	22 280	15 020	7 187
1940	23 547	15 627	7 920
1944	25 133	16 574	8 558
1950	30 317	20 846	9 471

Source: 1910-44 total from Suh (1978), p. 41,linked to 1820-1910 population movement from Kwon and Shin (1977), p. 328. The latter estimates are an upward adjustment of the old household registers. Suh used the population censuses which began in 1925, as the basis of his estimates. For the overlap year, 1910, Kwon and Shin show a higher level than Suh. I assume that their upward adjustment was too big, but this should not affect their 1820-1910 growth rate.

http://dx.doi.org/10.1787/456125276116

Sri Lanka: New annual estimates of population, 1820–1949, and GDP, 1820–1990, were supplied by Pierre van der Eng. His GDP estimates are by industry of origin for 11 major sectors, with considerable commodity detail for agriculture. He draws to some extent on the statistical appendix in D.R. Snodgrass, *Ceylon: An Export Economy in Transition,* Irwin, Illinois, 1966, and on N.K. Sarkar, *The Demography of Ceylon,* Colombo, 1957, but there is substantial new research, significant revision, and a much more complete annual coverage.

Thailand: GDP movement 1870–1951 from Maddison (2001), pp. 208 and 298, with slight revision.

Taiwan: GDP movement 1912–90 from expenditure estimates of Toshiyuki Mizoguchi, *Long Term Economic Statistics of Taiwan 1905–1990,* Institute of Economic Research, Hitotsubashi University, 1999, pp. 22–4.; the 1939–45 gap in these estimates was filled by Hsing's figures as cited by S.P.S. Ho, *Economic Development of Taiwan,1860–1970,* Yale, 1978, pp. 298–9; 1945–9 interpolated assuming equal percentage growth each year. GDP movement from 1990 onwards from ADB, *Key Indicators.*

Bangladesh, Burma, Hong Kong, Nepal, Pakistan, and Singapore: as indicated in Maddison (2001).

Conjectures to Fill Gaps in the Estimates: There are no gaps for population for benchmark years 1820, 1870 and 1913, but several countries for which GDP estimates are not available. As the objective is to provide a picture for the world as a whole, it was necessary to fill gaps in the dataset by conjectures (see Table 5–3).

Table 5-3. **16 East Asian Countries: GDP Conjectures and Estimates, 1820-1913**

	GDP (million international $)			GDP Per Capita (1990 int. $)			Population (000)		
	1820	1870	1913	1820	1870	1913	1820	1870	1913
Burma	1 767	2 139		504	504		3 506	4 245	
HongKong	12	84	623	615	682	1 279	20	123	487
Malaysia	173	530		603	663		287	800	
Nepal	1 541	1 865	3 039	397	397	539	3 881	4 698	5 639
Philippines	1 532	3 929		704	776		2 176	5 063	
Singapore	18	57		615	682		30	84	
South Korea	5 637	5 891		600	604		9 395	9 753	
Taiwan	998	1 290		499	550		2 000	2 345	
Thailand	3 014			646			4 665		
Total Conjectures	14 693	15 785	3 661	567	582	598	25 960	27 111	6 126
East Asia Sample	**372 323**	**375 428**	**608 413**	**581**	**550**	**680**	**640 140**	**682 920**	**895 121**
16 East Asia Total	**387 016**	**391 213**	**612 074**	**581**	**551**	**679**	**666 100**	**710 031**	**901 247**

http://dx.doi.org/10.1787/456125276116

For 1913, there were two gaps. I assumed the 1913–50 per capita GDP movement in Hong Kong was parallel to that in Singapore; in Nepal parallel to India.

For 1870, there were eight gaps. For Hong Kong and Singapore I assumed 1870–1913 per capita GDP movement was proportionately the same as in Japan. For the other six countries (Burma, South Korea, Malaysia, Nepal, Philippines and Taiwan), per capita GDP was assumed to move parallel to the average 1870–1913 for Indonesia, Sri Lanka and Thailand.

For 1820, there were nine gaps. Per capita GDP in Korea was taken to be the same as in China. Per capita GDP in Burma and Nepal was assumed to have been stagnant between 1820 and 1870 as it was in India. Average per capita GDP movement for the other six countries was assumed to be parallel to that in Japan.

For 1820, the proxy estimates represented 3.8 per cent of the total GDP of the 16 countries, 4 per cent in 1870, and 0.6 per cent in 1913. In the basic tables the proxy entries are shown in italics.

Other East Asian Countries

GDP for 1950 onwards from Maddison (2001) updated from IMF, *World Economic Outlook,* 1/2002 wherever possible. Revisions and updating for 6 of the small countries (Bhutan, Brunei, Fiji, Macao, Maldives and Papua New Guinea) are shown in Table 5–4, with consolidated figures for the other 14 (American Samoa, French Polynesia, Guam, Kiribati, Marshall Islands, Micronesia, New Caledonia, Northern Mariana Islands, Palau, Solomon Islands, Tonga, Vanuatu, Wallis and Futuna, and Western Samoa). Population from US Bureau of the Census (October 2002).

Table 5-4. **Population and GDP in 20 Small East Asian Countries, 1950–2001**

	Population (000 at mid–year)				GDP (million 1990 international dollars)			
	1950	1973	1990	2001	1950	1973	1990	2001
Bhutan	734	1 111	1 598	2 049	369	645	1 407	2 511
Brunei	45	145	258	344	224	1 156	1 663	2 030
Macao	205	259	352	454	127	735	3 078	4 935
Maldives	79	126	216	311	43	107	497	993
Total 4 Countries	1 063	1 641	2 424	3 158	763	2 641	6 645	10 469
Fiji	287	556	738	844	851	2 348	3 440	4 961
Papua New Guinea	1 412	2 477	3 825	5 049	1 356	4 847	5 865	8 893
14 Other Pacific Islands	649	1 210	1 782	2 014	875	2 296	3 496	4 729
16 Pacific Islands Total	2 279	4 104	6 164	7 924	3 082	9 491	12 711	18 582
20 Small Countries	3 342	5 748	8 588	11 082	3 845	11 952	19 356	29 051

Table 5-5. **26 East Asian Countries: Conjectures and Estimates for GDP, 1820-1913**

	Population (000)			GDP (million international $)			Per Capita GDP (1990 int. $)		
	1820	1870	1913	1820	1870	1913	1820	1870	1913
Afghanistan	3 280	4 207	5 730						
Cambodia	2 090	2 340	3 070						
Laos	470	755	1 387						
Mongolia	619	668	725						
20 Small Countries	1 798	1 903	2 237						
Total	8 257	9 873	13 149	4 591	5 282	9 796	556	535	745
North Korea	4 345	4 511	4 670	2 607	2 725	3 829	600	604	820
Vietnam	6 551	10 528	19 339	3 453	5 321	14 062	527	505	727
North Korea + Vietnam	10 896	15 039	24 009	6 060	8 046	17 891	556	535	745
Grand Total	19 153	24 912	37 158	10 651	13 328	27 687	556	535	745

http://dx.doi.org/10.1787/456125276116

For 1820–1913, provisional estimates of Vietnamese GDP volume movement were supplied by Jean–Pascal Bassino; North Korea was assumed to have the same per capita GDP as South Korea. For other countries no GDP estimates were available. I assumed the average per capita GDP, 1820–1913, for the whole group was the same as the average for North Korea and Vietnam (see Table 5–5). Population levels from McEvedy and Jones (1978), except for Vietnam, where I used Maks Banens' provisional estimate for 1913, with 1820–1913 population movement from McEvedy and Jones. See Table 5–5.

West Asian Countries

GDP for 1950 onwards from Maddison (2001) updated for 1993–2002 for 11 countries from ESCWA, *National Accounts Bulletin*, No. 21, Beirut, (November, 2002), Iran and Israel from IMF, *World Economic Outlook*, 2/2002, Turkey 1991–2000 from OECD *National Accounts, 1989–2000,* thereafter from IMF. No estimates were available for the West Bank and Gaza where the assumed volume increase 1998/9 was the same as 1997–8, with no change between 1999–2000, and 20 per cent falls in 2001 and 2002. Population 1950 onwards from US Bureau of the Census (October 2002).

Before the First World War, most of this area was part the Ottoman Empire. It accounted for 28 million of the 1913 population. The other 11 million lived in Iran. The 1820, 1870 and 1913 population figures shown in Table 5–6 are from Colin McEvedy and Richard Jones, *Atlas of World Population History,* Penguin (1978), pp. 133–154.

Sevket Pamuk has recently made tentative estimates of per capita GDP for several countries which permit estimates for the region much better than those in Maddison (2001), pp. 210–215. See Pamuk, "Economic Growth in Southeastern Europe and the Middle East since 1820", European Historical Economics Society Conference, Oxford, September 2001. They were derived from a variety of evidence in Ottoman archives and other research material on the region. He linked them to the Maddison (2001) estimates for later years and used the same numeraire, i.e. 1990 international Geary–Khamis dollars.

Table 5–6 contains estimates for three groups of countries in the region. For the countries in Arabia no GDP estimates are available before the second world war. They have now been transformed by the discovery and development of oil resources, but production did not start until the inter–war period. However, in the nineteenth century there was significant income from trade in the Persian Gulf, Southern Arabia and the Red Sea coast. Oman controlled large trading territories on the East African littoral. Yemen was a major exporter of coffee. For this group, I assumed a modest increase in per capita income from $550 to $600 between 1820 and 1913, as world trade expanded.

Table 5-6. **West Asian Population, GDP and Per Capita GDP, 1820-1913**

	Population (000)			GDP (million international $)			Per Capita GDP (1990 int. $)		
	1820	*1870*	*1913*	*1820*	*1870*	*1913*	*1820*	*1870*	*1913*
Gulf Coast (a)	200	200	254						
Oman	318	367	444						
Saudi Arabia	2 091	2 338	2 676						
Yemen	2 593	2 840	3 284						
Total Arabia (a)	5 202	5 745	6 658	*2 861*	*3 303*	*3 995*	*550*	*575*	*600*
Iraq	1 093	1 580	2 613	643	1 136	2 613	588	719	1 000
Jordan	217	266	348	128	191	348	588	719	1 000
Palestine-Israel	332	429	700	204	322	875	613	750	1 250
Syria	1 337	1 582	1 994	880	1 335	2 692	658	844	1 350
Lebanon	332	476	649	218	402	876	658	844	1 350
Total 5 countries	3 311	4 333	6 304	2 073	3 386	7 404	626	781	1 174
Iran	6 560	8 415	10 994	*3 857*	*6 050*	*10 994*	*588*	*719*	*1 000*
Turkey	10 074	11 793	15 000	6 478	9 729	18 195	643	825	1 213
Grand Total	25 147	30 286	38 956	15 269	22 468	40 588	607	742	1 042

a)   Includes Bahrain, Kuwait, Qatar and UAE.
Source: Population from McEvedy and Jones (1978) pp. 133-154. Turkish GDP as shown below, otherwise derived from Sevket Pamuk (2001).

http://dx.doi.org/10.1787/456125276116

The second group consists of five more prosperous countries (Iraq, Jordan, Palestine, Syria and Lebanon) with an ancient history as sophisticated traders with East Asia, Africa and Europe. Pamuk provides per capita estimates for Syria, which I assumed valid for Lebanon as well. His estimate for Jordan was taken to be valid for Iraq and Iran. I used his estimate for Palestine.

For Turkey see Table 5–7. The GDP benchmark for 1990 is from Maddison (2001), p. 219. GDP volume movement for 1948 onwards from OECD *National Accounts,* various issues, 1923–48 from T. Bulutay, Y.S. Tezel and N. Yilderim, *Turkiye Milli Geliri* 1923–48, Ankara, 1974, with 1913 per capita GDP assumed to be the same as in 1929. I linked the 1913 level to the per capita volume movement for 1820–1913 shown in Pamuk (2001). His major source was V. Eldem, *Osmanli Imparatorlugunun Iktisadi sartlari Hakkinda Bir Tetkik* (A Study of Economic Conditions in the Ottoman Empire), Is Bank, Istanbul, (1970). Population is from McEvedy and Jones (1978).

Table 5-7. **Turkish Population, GDP and Per Capita GDP, 1820-1950**

	Population (000s)	GDP (million 1990 int. $)	Per Capita GDP (1990 int. $)
1820	10 074	6 478	643
1870	11 793	9 729	825
1913	15 000	18 195	1 213
1923	13 877	9 882	712
1924	13 968	11 819	846
1925	14 059	13 159	936
1926	14 151	15 275	1 079
1927	14 250	13 886	974
1928	14 476	15 388	1 063
1929	14 705	17 842	1 213
1930	14 928	18 649	1 249
1931	15 174	19 763	1 302
1932	15 414	18 568	1 205
1933	15 658	21 007	1 342
1934	15 906	21 491	1 351
1935	16 158	21 927	1 357
1936	16 434	26 093	1 588
1937	16 725	26 965	1 612
1938	17 016	29 338	1 724
1939	17 517	31 776	1 814
1940	17 821	29 855	1 675
1941	18 011	27 158	1 508
1942	18 203	28 337	1 557
1943	18 396	25 721	1 398
1944	18 592	24 623	1 324
1945	18 790	21 297	1 133
1946	19 235	27 514	1 430
1947	19 690	29 064	1 476
1948	20 156	33 003	1 637
1949	20 634	31 340	1 519
1950	21 122	34 279	1 623

http://dx.doi.org/10.1787/456125276116

Summary Totals for Asia, 1820–1913

Table 5–8 shows the regional components and the totals for the 57 Asian countries, 1820–1913. Estimates for 1700 and earlier years in Maddison (2001) are unchanged (see tables in HS–8).

Table 5-8. **Total Asian Population, GDP and Per Capita GDP, 1820-1913**

	Population (000s)			GDP (million 1990 int. $)			Per Capita GDP (1990 int. $)		
	1820	1870	1913	1820	1870	1913	1820	1870	1913
16 East Asia	666 100	710 031	901 247	387 016	391 213	612 074	581	551	679
26 East Asia	19 153	24 912	37 158	10 651	13 328	27 687	556	535	745
15 West Asia	25 147	30 286	38 956	15 269	22 468	40 588	607	742	1 042
57 Asia	710 400	765 229	977 361	412 936	427 009	680 349	581	558	696

http://dx.doi.org/10.1787/456125276116

POPULATION, GDP LEVELS AND PER CAPITA GDP IN ASIA

Table 5a. **Population of 16 East Asian Countries, 1820-1913**
(000 at mid-year)

	China	India	Indonesia	Japan	Philippines	South Korea	Thailand	Taiwan
1820	381 000	209 000	17 927	31 000	2 176	9 395	4 665	2 000
1850	412 000	235 800	22 977	32 000	3 612	9 545	5 230	2 200
1870	358 000	253 000	28 922	34 437	5 063	9 753	5 775	2 345
1871	358 988	253 417	29 463	34 648				
1872	359 978	253 834	30 060	34 859				
1873	360 971	254 253	30 555	35 070				
1874	361 967	254 672	30 962	35 235				
1875	362 966	255 091	31 197	35 436				
1876	363 967	255 512	31 394	35 713				
1877	364 971	255 933	31 740	36 018				
1878	365 978	256 354	32 035	36 315				
1879	366 988	256 777	32 293	36 557				
1880	368 000	257 200	32 876	36 807				
1881	369 183	259 359	33 213	37 112				
1882	370 369	261 536	33 394	37 414				
1883	371 560	263 732	33 816	37 766				
1884	372 754	265 946	34 162	38 138				
1885	373 952	268 179	34 790	38 427				
1886	375 154	270 430	35 402	38 622				
1887	376 359	272 700	35 898	38 866				
1888	377 569	274 990	36 345	39 251				
1889	378 783	277 298	36 662	39 688				
1890	380 000	279 626	37 579	40 077	6 476	9 848	6 670	2 500
1891	381 979	280 110	37 792	40 380				
1892	383 969	280 594	38 288	40 684				
1893	385 969	281 079	38 263	41 001				
1894	387 979	281 565	38 782	41 350				
1895	390 000	282 052	39 476	41 775				
1896	391 980	282 540	39 936	42 196				
1897	393 970	283 029	40 620	42 643				
1898	395 970	283 518	41 316	43 145				
1899	397 980	284 009	42 025	43 626				
1900	400 000	284 500	42 746	44 103	7 324	9 896	7 320	2 864
1901	402 243	286 200	43 275	44 662	7 465		7 413	2 903
1902	404 498	288 000	43 810	45 255	7 609		7 507	2 942
1903	406 766	289 700	44 352	45 841	7 755		7 602	2 982
1904	409 047	291 500	44 901	46 378	7 904		7 699	3 022
1905	411 340	293 300	45 457	46 829	8 056		7 797	3 085
1906	413 646	295 100	45 993	47 227	8 211		7 896	3 140
1907	415 965	296 900	46 535	47 691	8 369		7 996	3 172
1908	418 297	298 700	47 085	48 260	8 530		8 098	3 200
1909	420 642	300 500	47 642	48 869	8 694		8 201	3 232
1910	423 000	302 100	48 206	49 518	8 861	10 096	8 305	3 275
1911	427 662	303 100	48 778	50 215	9 032	10 258	8 431	3 334
1912	432 375	303 400	49 358	50 941	9 206	10 422	8 559	3 402
1913	437 140	303 700	49 934	51 672	9 384	10 589	8 689	3 469

http://dx.doi.org/10.1787/456125276116

ISBN 92-64-02261-9 – © OECD 2006

Table 5a. **Population of 16 East Asian Countries, 1820-1913**
(000 at mid-year)

	Bangladesh	Burma	Hong Kong	Malaysia	Nepal	Pakistan	Singapore	Sri Lanka	16 country Total
1820		3 506	20	287	3 881		30	1 213	666 100
1850		3 932	33	530	4 352		56	2 217	734 484
1870		4 245	123	800	4 698		84	2 786	710 031
1871								2 820	
1872								2 842	
1873								2 863	
1874								2 885	
1875								2 908	
1876								2 930	
1877								2 952	
1878								2 975	
1879								2 998	
1880								3 021	
1881								3 044	
1882								3 073	
1883								3 107	
1884								3 144	
1885								3 170	
1886								3 194	
1887								3 221	
1888								3 261	
1889								3 311	
1890		7 489	214	1 585	5 192		157	3 343	780 756
1891								3 404	
1892								3 470	
1893								3 524	
1894								3 584	
1895								3 626	
1896								3 693	
1897								3 752	
1898								3 820	
1899								3 874	
1900		10 174	306	2 232	5 283		215	3 912	804 251
1901		10 490		2 288				4 031	
1902		10 642		2 345				4 071	
1903		10 796		2 404				4 156	
1904		10 953		2 467				4 233	
1905		11 112		2 532				4 383	
1906		11 273		2 601				4 458	
1907		11 437		2 672				4 467	
1908		11 603		2 745				4 520	
1909		11 771		2 821				4 585	
1910		11 942		2 893				4 668	
1911		12 115		2 967				4 757	
1912		12 220		3 025				4 784	
1913		12 326	487	3 084	5 639		323	4 811	901 247

http://dx.doi.org/10.1787/456125276116

Table 5a. **Population of 16 East Asian Countries, 1914-1949**
(000 at mid-year)

	China	India	Indonesia	Japan	Philippines	South Korea	Thailand	Taiwan
1914	441 958	304 000	50 517	52 396	9 565	10 764	8 822	3 528
1915	446 829	304 200	51 108	53 124	9 749	10 911	8 957	3 562
1916	451 753	304 500	51 705	53 815	9 937	11 086	9 094	3 583
1917	456 732	304 800	52 083	54 437	10 128	11 263	9 232	3 621
1918	461 766	305 100	52 334	54 886	10 323	11 443	9 418	3 658
1919	466 855	305 300	53 027	55 253	10 522	11 627	9 608	3 692
1920	472 000	305 600	53 723	55 818	10 725	11 804	9 802	3 736
1921	473 673	307 300	54 367	56 490	10 932	12 040	10 000	3 797
1922	475 352	310 400	55 020	57 209	11 143	12 281	10 202	3 870
1923	477 037	313 600	55 683	57 937	11 358	12 526	10 435	3 940
1924	478 728	316 700	56 354	58 686	11 577	12 777	10 673	4 009
1925	480 425	319 900	57 036	59 522	11 800	13 005	10 916	4 095
1926	482 128	323 200	57 727	60 490	12 026	13 179	11 165	4 195
1927	483 837	326 400	58 429	61 430	12 305	13 356	11 419	4 289
1928	485 552	329 700	59 140	62 361	12 543	13 535	11 734	4 388
1929	487 273	333 100	59 863	63 244	12 890	13 716	12 058	4 493
1930	489 000	336 400	60 596	64 203	13 194	13 900	12 392	4 614
1931	492 640	341 000	61 496	65 205	13 507	14 117	12 735	4 742
1932	496 307	345 800	62 400	66 189	13 829	14 338	13 087	4 867
1933	500 000	350 700	63 314	67 182	14 158	14 562	13 399	4 995
1934	502 639	355 600	64 246	68 090	14 497	14 789	13 718	5 128
1935	505 292	360 600	65 192	69 238	14 843	15 020	14 045	5 255
1936	507 959	365 700	66 154	70 171	15 199	15 139	14 379	5 384
1937	510 640	370 900	67 136	71 278	15 563	15 260	14 721	5 530
1938	513 336	376 100	68 131	71 879	15 934	15 381	14 980	5 678
1939	516 046	381 400	69 145	72 364	16 275	15 504	15 244	5 821
1940	518 770	386 800	70 175	72 967	16 585	15 627	15 513	5 987
1941	521 508	391 700	71 316	74 005	16 902	15 859	15 787	6 163
1942	524 261	396 300	72 475	75 029	17 169	16 094	16 060	6 339
1943	527 028	400 900	73 314	76 005	17 552	16 332	16 462	6 507
1944	529 810	405 600	73 565	77 178	17 887	16 574	16 868	6 520
1945	532 607	410 400	73 332	76 224	18 228	17 917	17 284	6 533
1946	535 418	<u>415 200</u>	74 132	77 199	18 775	19 369	17 710	6 546
1947	538 244	346 000	75 146	78 119	19 338	19 886	18 148	6 346
1948	541 085	350 000	76 289	80 155	19 918	20 027	18 569	6 697
1949	543 941	355 000	77 654	81 971	20 516	20 208	19 000	7 280

http://dx.doi.org/10.1787/456125276116

Table 5a. **Population of 16 East Asian Countries, 1914-1949**
(000 at mid-year)

	Bangladesh	Burma	Hong Kong	Malaysia	Nepal	Pakistan	Singapore	Sri Lanka	16 country Total
1914		12 433	507	3 144			331	4 838	
1915		12 541	528	3 207			341	4 905	
1916		12 650	550	3 271			351	4 971	
1917		12 760	573	3 337			360	5 040	
1918		12 871	597	3 404			370	5 109	
1919		12 893	622	3 473			380	5 179	
1920		13 096	648	3 545			391	5 250	
1921		13 212	625	3 618			418	5 304	
1922		13 351	638	3 698			436	5 367	
1923		13 491	668	3 779			458	5 426	
1924		13 633	696	3 863			469	5 452	
1925		13 776	725	3 949			492	5 505	
1926		13 921	710	4 038			511	5 545	
1927		14 067	725	4 128			532	5 591	
1928		14 215	753	4 221			553	5 730	
1929		14 364	785	4 316			575	5 669	
1930		14 515	821	4 413			596	5 707	
1931		14 667	840	4 513			563	5 748	
1932		14 870	901	4 604			580	5 788	
1933		15 075	923	4 697			515	5 825	
1934		15 283	944	4 793			525	5 872	
1935		15 494	966	4 890			572	5 897	
1936		15 708	988	4 993			603	5 943	
1937		15 925	1 282	5 099			651	5 989	
1938		16 145	1 479	5 207			710	6 045	
1939		16 368	1 750	5 317			728	6 095	
1940		16 594	1 786	5 434			751	6 134	
1941		16 824	1 639	5 554			769	6 169	
1942		16 727		5 592				6 191	
1943		16 908		5 630				6 296	
1944		17 090		5 668				6 442	
1945		17 272		5 707				6 650	
1946		17 454	1 550	5 746				6 854	
1947		17 636	1 750	5 786			938	7 037	
1948		17 818	1 800	5 922			961	7 244	
1949		18 000	1 857	6 061			979	7 455	

http://dx.doi.org/10.1787/456125276116

Table 5a. **Population of 16 East Asian Countries, 1950-2003**
(000 at mid-year)

	China	India	Indonesia	Japan	Philippines	South Korea	Thailand	Taiwan
1950	546 815	359 000	79 043	83 805	21 131	20 846	20 042	7 981
1951	557 480	365 000	80 525	85 164	21 775	20 876	20 653	8 251
1952	568 910	372 000	82 052	86 459	22 439	20 948	21 289	8 550
1953	581 390	379 000	83 611	87 655	23 122	21 060	21 964	8 850
1954	595 310	386 000	85 196	88 754	23 827	21 259	22 685	9 160
1955	608 655	393 000	86 807	89 815	24 553	21 552	23 451	9 486
1956	621 465	401 000	88 456	90 766	25 301	22 031	24 244	9 825
1957	637 408	409 000	90 124	91 563	26 072	22 612	25 042	10 164
1958	653 235	418 000	91 821	92 389	26 867	23 254	25 845	10 500
1959	666 005	426 000	93 565	93 297	27 685	23 981	26 667	10 853
1960	667 070	434 000	95 254	94 092	28 529	24 784	27 513	11 209
1961	660 330	444 000	97 085	94 943	29 410	25 614	28 376	11 563
1962	665 770	454 000	99 028	95 832	30 325	26 420	29 263	11 919
1963	682 335	464 000	101 009	96 812	31 273	27 211	30 174	12 277
1964	698 355	474 000	103 031	97 826	32 254	27 984	31 107	12 631
1965	715 185	485 000	105 093	98 883	33 268	28 705	32 062	12 978
1966	735 400	495 000	107 197	99 790	34 304	29 436	33 036	13 321
1967	754 550	506 000	109 343	100 825	35 357	30 131	34 024	13 649
1968	774 510	518 000	111 532	101 961	36 424	30 838	35 028	13 962
1969	796 025	529 000	113 765	103 172	37 507	31 544	36 050	14 282
1970	818 315	541 000	116 044	104 345	38 604	32 241	37 091	14 598
1971	841 105	554 000	118 368	105 697	39 718	32 883	38 202	14 918
1972	862 030	567 000	121 282	107 188	40 850	33 505	39 276	15 226
1973	881 940	580 000	124 271	108 707	41 998	34 073	40 302	15 526
1974	900 350	593 000	127 338	110 162	43 162	34 692	41 306	15 824
1975	916 395	607 000	130 485	111 573	44 337	35 281	42 272	16 122
1976	930 685	620 000	133 713	112 775	45 574	35 860	43 221	16 450
1977	943 455	634 000	137 026	113 872	46 851	36 436	44 148	16 785
1978	956 165	648 000	140 425	114 913	48 172	37 019	45 057	17 112
1979	969 005	664 000	143 912	115 890	49 537	37 534	46 004	17 450
1980	981 235	679 000	147 490	116 807	50 940	38 124	47 026	17 848
1981	993 861	692 000	150 657	117 648	52 195	38 723	47 941	18 177
1982	1 000 281	708 000	153 894	118 455	53 457	39 326	48 837	18 501
1983	1 023 288	723 000	157 204	119 270	54 698	39 910	49 709	18 803
1984	1 036 825	739 000	160 588	120 035	55 964	40 406	50 553	19 083
1985	1 051 040	755 000	164 047	120 754	57 288	40 806	51 367	19 337
1986	1 066 790	771 000	166 976	121 492	58 649	41 214	52 160	19 556
1987	1 084 035	788 000	169 959	122 091	60 018	41 622	52 946	19 758
1988	1 101 630	805 000	172 999	122 613	61 385	42 031	53 725	19 976
1989	1 118 650	822 000	176 094	123 108	62 814	42 449	54 493	20 208
1990	1 135 185	839 000	179 248	123 537	64 318	42 869	55 250	20 279
1991	1 150 780	856 000	182 223	123 946	65 789	43 313	55 982	20 493
1992	1 164 970	872 000	185 259	124 329	67 186	43 795	56 718	20 687
1993	1 178 440	891 000	188 359	124 668	68 611	44 279	57 449	20 883
1994	1 191 835	908 000	191 524	125 014	70 112	44 758	58 173	21 088
1995	1 204 855	927 000	194 755	125 341	71 717	45 236	58 894	21 283
1996	1 217 550	943 000	198 025	125 645	73 386	45 695	59 608	21 449
1997	1 230 075	959 000	201 350	125 956	75 013	46 131	60 311	21 629
1998	1 242 700	975 000	204 390	126 246	76 576	46 535	61 003	21 823
1999	1 252 704	991 691	207 429	126 494	78 134	46 903	61 684	21 993
2000	1 264 093	1 007 702	210 875	126 700	79 740	47 261	62 352	22 151
2001	1 275 392	1 023 590	214 303	126 892	81 370	47 619	63 007	22 304
2002				127 066	82 995	47 963	63 645	22 454
2003				127 214	84 620	48 289	64 265	22 603

http://dx.doi.org/10.1787/456125276116

Table 5a. Population of 16 East Asian Countries, 1950-2003
(000 at mid-year)

	Bangladesh	Burma	Hong Kong	Malaysia	Nepal	Pakistan	Singapore	Sri Lanka	16 country Total
1950	45 646	19 488	2 237	6 434	8 990	39 448	1 022	7 533	1 269 461
1951	46 152	19 788	2 015	6 582	9 086	40 382	1 068	7 752	1 292 551
1952	46 887	20 093	2 126	6 748	9 183	41 347	1 127	7 982	1 318 140
1953	47 660	20 403	2 242	6 929	9 280	42 342	1 192	8 221	1 344 923
1954	48 603	20 721	2 365	7 118	9 379	43 372	1 248	8 457	1 373 454
1955	49 602	21 049	2 490	7 312	9 479	44 434	1 306	8 679	1 401 669
1956	50 478	21 385	2 615	7 520	9 580	45 536	1 372	8 898	1 430 473
1957	51 365	21 732	2 736	7 739	9 682	46 680	1 446	9 129	1 462 494
1958	52 399	22 088	2 854	7 966	9 789	47 869	1 519	9 362	1 495 757
1959	53 485	22 456	2 967	8 196	9 906	49 104	1 587	9 610	1 525 365
1960	54 622	22 836	3 075	8 428	10 035	50 387	1 646	9 879	1 543 360
1961	55 741	23 229	3 168	8 663	10 176	51 719	1 702	10 152	1 555 872
1962	56 839	23 634	3 305	8 906	10 332	53 101	1 750	10 422	1 580 848
1963	58 226	24 053	3 421	9 148	10 500	54 524	1 795	10 687	1 617 447
1964	59 403	24 486	3 505	9 397	10 677	55 988	1 842	10 942	1 653 429
1965	60 332	24 933	3 598	9 648	10 862	57 495	1 887	11 202	1 691 130
1966	61 548	25 394	3 630	9 900	11 057	59 046	1 934	11 470	1 731 464
1967	62 822	25 870	3 723	10 155	11 262	60 642	1 978	11 737	1 772 067
1968	64 133	26 362	3 803	10 409	11 473	62 282	2 012	12 010	1 814 741
1969	65 483	26 867	3 864	10 662	11 692	63 970	2 043	12 275	1 858 201
1970	67 403	27 386	3 959	10 910	11 919	65 706	2 075	12 532	1 904 127
1971	69 227	27 919	4 045	11 171	12 155	67 491	2 113	12 776	1 951 789
1972	70 759	28 466	4 116	11 441	12 413	69 326	2 152	13 017	1 998 048
1973	72 471	29 227	4 213	11 712	12 685	71 121	2 193	13 246	2 043 683
1974	74 679	29 799	4 320	11 986	12 973	72 912	2 230	13 450	2 088 182
1975	76 253	30 357	4 396	12 267	13 278	74 712	2 263	13 660	2 130 651
1976	77 928	30 929	4 518	12 554	13 599	76 456	2 293	13 887	2 170 444
1977	80 428	31 514	4 584	12 845	13 933	78 153	2 325	14 117	2 210 473
1978	82 936	32 024	4 668	13 139	14 280	80 051	2 354	14 371	2 250 684
1979	85 492	32 611	4 930	13 444	14 641	82 374	2 384	14 649	2 293 856
1980	88 077	33 283	5 063	13 764	15 016	85 219	2 414	14 900	2 336 207
1981	90 666	33 884	5 183	14 097	15 403	88 417	2 533	15 152	2 376 537
1982	93 074	34 490	5 265	14 442	15 796	91 257	2 647	15 410	2 413 132
1983	95 384	35 103	5 345	14 793	16 200	93 720	2 681	15 618	2 464 726
1984	97 612	35 699	5 398	15 157	16 613	96 284	2 732	15 810	2 507 760
1985	99 753	36 257	5 456	15 545	17 038	99 053	2 736	16 021	2 551 498
1986	101 769	36 783	5 525	15 941	17 472	101 955	2 733	16 256	2 596 270
1987	103 764	37 277	5 585	16 332	17 917	104 893	2 775	16 495	2 643 467
1988	105 771	37 735	5 628	16 729	18 374	107 863	2 846	16 735	2 691 040
1989	107 807	38 152	5 661	17 118	18 843	110 883	2 931	16 971	2 738 182
1990	109 897	38 526	5 688	17 504	19 325	113 975	3 016	17 193	2 784 811
1991	111 936	38 855	5 752	17 906	19 819	117 001	3 097	17 391	2 830 283
1992	113 705	39 073	5 834	18 320	20 326	118 975	3 179	17 587	2 871 942
1993	115 448	39 336	5 944	18 748	20 846	121 009	3 268	17 826	2 916 114
1994	117 280	39 750	6 083	19 180	21 373	123 858	3 367	18 075	2 959 469
1995	119 186	40 166	6 247	19 611	21 907	126 630	3 481	18 304	3 004 613
1996	121 189	40 539	6 420	20 045	22 450	129 538	3 610	18 510	3 046 659
1997	123 315	40 876	6 607	20 476	23 001	132 485	3 741	18 699	3 088 664
1998	125 573	41 193	6 813	20 912	23 560	135 471	3 871	18 885	3 130 552
1999	127 943	41 491	6 992	21 354	24 127	138 496	4 008	19 065	3 175 945
2000	130 407	41 772	7 116	21 793	24 702	141 554	4 152	19 239	3 211 608
2001	132 975	42 035	7 211	22 229	25 284	144 617	4 300	19 409	3 252 537
2002	135 657	42 282	7 303	22 662	25 874	147 663	4 453	19 577	
2003	138 448	42 511	7 394	23 093	26 470	150 695	4 609	19 742	

http://dx.doi.org/10.1787/456125276116

Table 5a. **Population of 15 West Asian Countries, 1950-2003**
(000 at mid-year)

	Bahrain	Iran	Iraq	Israel	Jordan	Kuwait	Lebanon	Oman	Qatar
1950	115	16 357	5 163	1 286	561	145	1 364	489	25
1951	118	16 809	5 300	1 490	584	152	1 401	498	27
1952	120	17 272	5 442	1 621	608	160	1 440	508	29
1953	123	17 742	5 589	1 667	633	168	1 479	517	31
1954	127	18 226	5 743	1 712	659	177	1 519	528	33
1955	130	18 729	5 903	1 772	687	187	1 561	539	35
1956	134	19 249	6 073	1 850	716	197	1 604	550	37
1957	139	19 792	6 249	1 944	747	213	1 647	562	39
1958	144	20 362	6 433	2 025	779	235	1 692	573	41
1959	150	20 958	6 625	2 082	813	262	1 739	586	43
1960	157	21 577	6 822	2 141	849	292	1 786	599	45
1961	164	22 214	7 026	2 217	887	325	1 836	614	49
1962	172	22 874	7 240	2 311	934	358	1 887	628	53
1963	179	23 554	7 468	2 407	975	394	1 940	645	58
1964	186	24 264	7 711	2 498	1 017	433	1 996	662	64
1965	191	25 000	7 971	2 578	1 061	476	2 058	679	70
1966	197	25 764	8 240	2 641	1 107	523	2 122	697	77
1967	202	26 538	8 519	2 694	1 255	575	2 187	715	85
1968	208	27 321	8 808	2 747	1 383	632	2 254	735	94
1969	214	28 119	9 106	2 817	1 454	690	2 320	756	103
1970	220	28 933	9 414	2 903	1 503	748	2 383	779	113
1971	225	29 763	9 732	2 997	1 556	793	2 529	803	122
1972	231	30 614	10 062	3 096	1 614	842	2 680	829	132
1973	239	31 491	10 402	3 197	1 674	894	2 825	857	142
1974	248	32 412	10 754	3 286	1 738	948	2 988	884	153
1975	259	33 379	11 118	3 354	1 803	1 007	3 098	913	165
1976	274	34 381	11 494	3 424	1 870	1 072	3 119	956	177
1977	297	35 473	11 883	3 496	1 938	1 140	3 116	1 005	189
1978	323	36 634	12 317	3 570	2 007	1 214	3 109	1 059	202
1979	336	37 963	12 768	3 653	2 077	1 292	3 099	1 116	216
1980	348	39 548	13 233	3 737	2 163	1 370	3 086	1 175	231
1981	363	41 270	13 703	3 801	2 254	1 432	3 081	1 238	242
1982	378	43 016	14 173	3 858	2 347	1 497	3 087	1 301	252
1983	393	44 764	14 652	3 927	2 440	1 566	3 090	1 363	284
1984	408	46 542	15 161	4 005	2 533	1 637	3 090	1 424	315
1985	424	48 344	15 694	4 075	2 628	1 733	3 088	1 482	345
1986	440	50 162	16 247	4 137	2 724	1 811	3 087	1 538	375
1987	455	51 983	16 543	4 203	2 820	1 891	3 089	1 594	402
1988	469	53 650	17 038	4 272	2 917	1 973	3 096	1 652	430
1989	485	55 355	17 568	4 344	3 019	2 057	3 107	1 712	457
1990	500	57 551	18 135	4 512	3 262	2 142	3 147	1 773	481
1991	515	59 590	17 472	4 756	3 631	954	3 193	1 843	505
1992	529	60 800	17 862	4 937	3 867	1 418	3 220	1 915	529
1993	544	61 001	18 405	5 062	3 984	1 484	3 252	1 989	557
1994	558	61 133	18 970	5 185	4 082	1 551	3 291	2 059	585
1995	573	61 925	19 557	5 305	4 202	1 621	3 335	2 131	613
1996	586	62 768	20 162	5 420	4 364	1 693	3 382	2 206	641
1997	599	63 655	20 776	5 531	4 526	1 765	3 430	2 284	667
1998	611	64 487	21 398	5 639	4 686	1 836	3 479	2 364	694
1999	623	65 240	22 031	5 743	4 843	1 905	3 529	2 447	719
2000	634	66 006	22 676	5 842	4 999	1 974	3 578	2 533	744
2001	645	66 791	23 332	5 938	5 153	2 042	3 628	2 622	769
2002	656	67 538	24 002	6 030	5 307	2 112	3 678	2 713	793
2003	667	68 279	24 683	6 117	5 460	2 183	3 728	2 807	817

http://dx.doi.org/10.1787/456125276116

Table 5a. **Population of 15 West Asian Countries, 1950-2003**
(000 at mid-year)

	Saudi Arabia	Syria	Turkey	UAE	Yemen	West Bank and Gaza	Total
1950	3 860	3 495	21 122	72	4 777	1 017	59 847
1951	3 932	3 577	21 669	73	4 869	1 022	61 522
1952	4 006	3 662	22 236	75	4 964	1 031	63 172
1953	4 082	3 750	22 831	77	5 061	1 040	64 792
1954	4 160	3 842	23 464	80	5 162	1 049	66 482
1955	4 243	3 938	24 145	83	5 265	1 054	68 271
1956	4 329	4 041	24 877	86	5 380	1 061	70 184
1957	4 420	4 150	25 671	89	5 498	1 070	72 230
1958	4 514	4 268	26 506	93	5 619	1 078	74 361
1959	4 614	4 395	27 356	98	5 744	1 101	76 563
1960	4 718	4 533	28 217	103	5 872	1 113	78 825
1961	4 828	4 681	29 030	109	5 994	1 110	81 083
1962	4 943	4 835	29 789	116	6 120	1 133	83 392
1963	5 065	4 993	30 509	124	6 248	1 156	85 716
1964	5 192	5 157	31 227	133	6 378	1 182	88 101
1965	5 327	5 326	31 951	144	6 510	1 211	90 554
1966	5 469	5 500	32 678	157	6 625	1 236	93 033
1967	5 618	5 681	33 411	172	6 741	1 143	95 535
1968	5 775	5 867	34 165	191	6 859	1 000	98 038
1969	5 939	6 059	34 952	218	6 978	1 006	100 731
1970	6 109	6 258	35 758	249	7 098	1 032	103 500
1971	6 287	6 479	36 580	288	7 251	1 060	106 467
1972	6 473	6 701	37 493	336	7 407	1 090	109 598
1973	6 667	6 931	38 503	391	7 580	1 124	112 918
1974	6 868	7 169	39 513	453	7 755	1 167	116 336
1975	7 199	7 416	40 530	523	7 934	1 201	119 899
1976	7 608	7 670	41 485	598	8 171	1 228	123 525
1977	8 108	7 933	42 404	684	8 404	1 261	127 330
1978	8 680	8 203	43 317	779	8 641	1 296	131 349
1979	9 307	8 484	44 223	884	8 883	1 330	135 631
1980	9 949	8 774	45 121	1 000	9 133	1 360	140 226
1981	10 565	9 073	46 222	1 100	9 390	1 389	145 126
1982	11 179	9 410	47 329	1 204	9 658	1 426	150 116
1983	11 822	9 757	48 440	1 316	9 936	1 475	155 225
1984	12 502	10 114	49 554	1 438	10 229	1 525	160 477
1985	13 208	10 481	50 669	1 570	10 540	1 576	165 856
1986	13 858	10 857	51 780	1 714	10 870	1 630	171 230
1987	14 461	11 243	52 881	1 778	11 219	1 691	176 255
1988	15 055	11 632	53 966	1 839	11 591	1 758	181 339
1989	15 631	12 018	55 031	1 897	11 986	1 821	186 488
1990	15 847	12 436	56 085	1 951	12 416	1 897	192 136
1991	16 075	12 849	57 135	2 002	12 882	1 997	195 399
1992	16 692	13 219	58 179	2 049	13 368	2 105	200 689
1993	17 324	13 579	59 213	2 093	13 886	2 216	204 589
1994	17 970	13 939	60 221	2 136	14 395	2 346	208 421
1995	18 632	14 310	61 189	2 176	14 859	2 502	212 929
1996	19 290	14 691	62 128	2 216	15 327	2 666	217 539
1997	19 946	15 081	63 048	2 254	15 826	2 826	222 216
1998	20 620	15 481	63 946	2 293	16 352	2 932	226 816
1999	21 311	15 889	64 820	2 331	16 905	3 041	231 376
2000	22 024	16 306	65 667	2 369	17 479	3 152	235 983
2001	22 757	16 729	66 494	2 407	18 078	3 269	240 655
2002	23 513	17 156	67 309	2 446	18 701	3 390	245 344
2003	24 294	17 586	68 109	2 485	19 350	3 512	250 077

http://dx.doi.org/10.1787/456125276116

Table 5a. **Population of 26 East Asian Countries, 1950-2003**
(000 at mid-year)

	Afghanistan	Cambodia	Laos	Mongolia	North Korea	Vietnam	20 small countries	26 country Total
1950	8 150	4 163	1 886	779	9 471	25 348	3 342	53 139
1951	8 284	4 266	1 921	789	9 162	25 794	3 401	53 617
1952	8 425	4 371	1 957	801	8 865	26 247	3 461	54 127
1953	8 573	4 478	1 995	814	8 580	26 724	3 530	54 695
1954	8 728	4 589	2 035	828	8 572	27 210	3 599	55 561
1955	8 891	4 702	2 077	844	8 839	27 738	3 675	56 766
1956	9 062	4 827	2 121	862	9 116	28 327	3 755	58 070
1957	9 241	4 956	2 166	882	9 411	28 999	3 833	59 488
1958	9 429	5 088	2 213	904	9 727	29 775	3 922	61 059
1959	9 625	5 224	2 261	929	10 054	30 683	4 013	62 788
1960	9 829	5 364	2 309	955	10 392	31 656	4 106	64 612
1961	10 043	5 511	2 359	982	10 651	32 701	4 205	66 453
1962	10 267	5 761	2 409	1 010	10 917	33 796	4 315	68 476
1963	10 501	5 914	2 460	1 031	11 210	34 932	4 434	70 482
1964	10 744	6 071	2 512	1 061	11 528	36 099	4 547	72 562
1965	10 998	6 232	2 565	1 090	11 869	37 258	4 670	74 683
1966	11 262	6 396	2 619	1 119	12 232	38 378	4 799	76 807
1967	11 538	6 565	2 674	1 150	12 617	39 464	4 923	78 930
1968	11 825	6 738	2 730	1 181	13 024	40 512	5 055	81 065
1969	12 123	6 917	2 787	1 214	13 455	41 542	5 186	83 223
1970	12 431	6 984	2 845	1 248	13 912	42 577	5 332	85 327
1971	12 749	7 011	2 904	1 283	14 365	43 614	5 483	87 410
1972	13 079	7 110	2 964	1 321	14 781	44 655	5 617	89 528
1973	13 421	7 205	3 027	1 360	15 161	45 736	5 748	91 658
1974	13 772	7 294	3 092	1 403	15 501	46 902	5 866	93 831
1975	14 132	7 188	3 161	1 446	15 801	48 075	5 999	95 802
1976	14 501	6 915	3 176	1 487	16 069	49 273	6 131	97 553
1977	14 880	6 679	3 208	1 528	16 325	50 534	6 270	99 425
1978	15 269	6 472	3 248	1 572	16 580	51 663	6 417	101 220
1979	15 556	6 436	3 268	1 617	16 840	52 668	6 571	102 956
1980	14 985	6 586	3 293	1 662	17 114	53 661	6 733	104 034
1981	14 087	6 801	3 337	1 709	17 384	54 792	6 893	105 002
1982	13 645	7 064	3 411	1 756	17 648	55 972	7 060	106 556
1983	13 709	7 347	3 495	1 805	17 918	57 204	7 240	108 718
1984	13 826	7 535	3 577	1 856	18 196	58 466	7 425	110 880
1985	13 898	7 695	3 657	1 908	18 481	59 730	7 608	112 977
1986	13 936	7 965	3 762	1 961	18 772	61 006	7 796	115 199
1987	14 071	8 277	3 869	2 015	19 068	62 320	7 986	117 606
1988	14 326	8 599	3 980	2 071	19 371	63 630	8 177	120 153
1989	14 635	8 930	4 094	2 159	19 688	65 206	8 378	123 090
1990	14 750	9 271	4 210	2 216	20 019	66 637	8 588	125 692
1991	14 939	9 622	4 331	2 268	20 361	68 008	8 798	128 326
1992	16 589	10 068	4 454	2 313	20 711	69 321	9 014	132 470
1993	18 840	10 569	4 581	2 349	21 064	70 633	9 233	137 270
1994	20 319	10 950	4 712	2 383	21 340	71 935	9 453	141 091
1995	21 489	11 240	4 846	2 421	21 562	73 172	9 676	144 406
1996	22 429	11 510	4 971	2 459	21 649	74 341	9 901	147 260
1997	23 234	11 754	5 099	2 495	21 585	75 448	10 131	149 745
1998	24 065	11 982	5 229	2 531	21 455	76 487	10 365	152 113
1999	24 961	12 208	5 362	2 566	21 445	77 497	10 602	154 640
2000	25 889	12 433	5 498	2 601	21 648	78 518	10 841	157 426
2001	26 813	12 660	5 636	2 637	21 940	79 544	11 082	160 312
2002	27 756	12 890	5 778	2 674	22 215	80 577	11 326	163 217
2003	28 717	13 125	5 922	2 712	22 466	81 625	11 571	166 138

http://dx.doi.org/10.1787/456125276116

Table 5a. **Population of 57 Asian Countries, 1820-2001**
(000 at mid-year)

	16 East Asia	26 East Asia	15 West Asia	Total 57 Asia
1820	666 100	19 153	25 147	710 400
1870	710 031	24 912	30 286	765 229
1900	804 251	32 972	36 101	873 324
1913	901 247	37 158	38 956	977 361
1950	1 269 461	53 139	59 847	1 382 447
1951	1 292 551	53 617	61 522	1 407 689
1952	1 318 140	54 127	63 172	1 435 439
1953	1 344 923	54 695	64 792	1 464 409
1954	1 373 454	55 561	66 482	1 495 497
1955	1 401 669	56 766	68 271	1 526 707
1956	1 430 473	58 070	70 184	1 558 727
1957	1 462 494	59 488	72 230	1 594 212
1958	1 495 757	61 059	74 361	1 631 177
1959	1 525 365	62 788	76 563	1 664 717
1960	1 543 360	64 612	78 825	1 686 796
1961	1 555 872	66 453	81 083	1 703 409
1962	1 580 848	68 476	83 392	1 732 716
1963	1 617 447	70 482	85 716	1 773 645
1964	1 653 429	72 562	88 101	1 814 092
1965	1 691 130	74 683	90 554	1 856 366
1966	1 731 464	76 807	93 033	1 901 303
1967	1 772 067	78 930	95 535	1 946 533
1968	1 814 741	81 065	98 038	1 993 844
1969	1 858 201	83 223	100 731	2 042 155
1970	1 904 127	85 327	103 500	2 092 954
1971	1 951 789	87 410	106 467	2 145 665
1972	1 998 048	89 528	109 598	2 197 174
1973	2 043 683	91 658	112 918	2 248 260
1974	2 088 182	93 831	116 336	2 298 349
1975	2 130 651	95 802	119 899	2 346 352
1976	2 170 444	97 553	123 525	2 391 522
1977	2 210 473	99 425	127 330	2 437 228
1978	2 250 684	101 220	131 349	2 483 253
1979	2 293 856	102 956	135 631	2 532 444
1980	2 336 207	104 034	140 226	2 580 468
1981	2 376 537	105 002	145 126	2 626 665
1982	2 413 132	106 556	150 116	2 669 803
1983	2 464 726	108 718	155 225	2 728 669
1984	2 507 760	110 880	160 477	2 779 117
1985	2 551 498	112 977	165 856	2 830 331
1986	2 596 270	115 199	171 230	2 882 699
1987	2 643 467	117 606	176 255	2 937 328
1988	2 691 040	120 153	181 339	2 992 532
1989	2 738 182	123 090	186 488	3 047 760
1990	2 784 811	125 692	192 136	3 102 638
1991	2 830 283	128 326	195 399	3 154 008
1992	2 871 942	132 470	200 689	3 205 102
1993	2 916 114	137 270	204 589	3 257 972
1994	2 959 469	141 091	208 421	3 308 981
1995	3 004 613	144 406	212 929	3 361 948
1996	3 046 659	147 260	217 539	3 411 457
1997	3 088 664	149 745	222 216	3 460 624
1998	3 130 552	152 113	226 816	3 509 481
1999	3 175 945	154 640	231 376	3 561 961
2000	3 211 608	157 426	235 983	3 605 017
2001	3 252 537	160 312	240 655	3 653 504

http://dx.doi.org/10.1787/456125276116

Table 5b. GDP Levels in 16 East Asian Countries, 1820-1913
(million 1990 international Geary-Khamis dollars)

	China	India	Indonesia	Japan	Philippines	South Korea	Thailand	Taiwan
1820	228 600	111 417	10 970	20 739	*1 532*	*5 637*	*3 014*	*998*
1850	247 200							
1870	189 740	134 882	18 929	25 393	*3 929*	*5 891*	4 112	*1 290*
1871			19 021	25 709				
1872			19 158	26 005				
1873			19 660	26 338				
1874			20 162	26 644				
1875			20 481	28 698				
1876			21 028	28 019				
1877			21 302	28 910				
1878			21 028	28 825				
1879			21 439	30 540				
1880			21 758	31 779				
1881			23 218	30 777				
1882			22 443	31 584				
1883			22 214	31 618				
1884		146 409	24 495	31 872				
1885		151 985	24 815	33 052				
1886		148 134	24 678	35 395				
1887		155 899	24 951	36 982				
1888		158 358	25 179	35 310				
1889		155 063	25 316	37 016				
1890	205 304	163 341	24 815	40 556			5 229	
1891		148 317	25 362	38 621				
1892		160 224	26 411	41 200				
1893		164 280	27 187	41 344				
1894		166 799	27 643	46 288				
1895		162 696	28 281	46 933				
1896		150 699	28 099	44 353				
1897		178 236	28 509	45 285				
1898		178 599	28 874	53 883				
1899		164 690	30 608	49 870				
1900	218 074	170 466	31 748	52 020				
1901		173 957	31 352	53 883				
1902		188 504	30 904	51 089	5 320			
1903		191 141	32 637	54 671	6 450			
1904		192 060	33 314	55 101	5 979			
1905		188 587	33 823	54 170	5 979			
1906		193 979	34 869	61 263	6 322			
1907		182 234	35 698	63 198	6 648			
1908		184 844	35 800	63 628	6 834			
1909		210 241	37 659	63 556	6 944			
1910		210 439	40 180	64 559	7 984			
1911		209 354	42 442	68 070	8 539	7 966		
1912		208 946	42 818	70 507	8 969	8 148		2 456
1913	241 344	204 242	45 152	71 653	9 877	8 678	7 304	2 591

http://dx.doi.org/10.1787/456125276116

Table 5b. **GDP Levels in 16 East Asian Countries, 1820-1913**
(million 1990 international Geary-Khamis dollars)

	Bangladesh	Burma	Hong Kong	Malaysia	Nepal	Pakistan	Singapore	Sri Lanka	16 country Total
1820		*1 767*	*12*	*173*	*1 541*		*18*	597	387 016
1850								1 250	
1870		*2 139*	*84*	*530*	*1 865*		*57*	2 372	391 213
1871								2 332	
1872								2 230	
1873								2 257	
1874								2 235	
1875								2 270	
1876								2 311	
1877								2 341	
1878								2 135	
1879								2 307	
1880								2 509	
1881								2 699	
1882								2 874	
1883								2 925	
1884								2 844	
1885								2 670	
1886								2 588	
1887								3 044	
1888								3 004	
1889								2 985	
1890								3 494	
1891								3 529	
1892								3 651	
1893								3 709	
1894								3 739	
1895								3 934	
1896								4 018	
1897								4 221	
1898								4 461	
1899								4 779	
1900								5 048	500 686
1901		7 332						4 804	
1902								4 785	
1903								5 093	
1904								5 144	
1905								5 167	
1906		6 385						5 307	
1907								5 509	
1908								5 520	
1909								5 286	
1910								5 639	
1911		7 348		2 376				5 519	
1912				2 486				5 533	
1913		8 445	*623*	2 776	*3 039*		413	5 938	612 075

http://dx.doi.org/10.1787/456125276116

Table 5b. GDP Levels in 16 East Asian Countries, 1914-1949
(million 1990 international Geary-Khamis dollars)

	China	India	Indonesia	Japan	Philippines	South Korea	Thailand	Taiwan
1914		215 400	45 076	69 503	9 713	9 276		2 634
1915		210 110	45 647	75 952	9 017	10 535		2 725
1916		216 245	46 350	87 703	10 332	10 743		3 449
1917		212 341	46 513	90 641	11 924	11 498		3 826
1918		185 202	47 597	91 573	13 649	12 435		3 384
1919		210 730	51 402	100 959	13 400	12 201		3 624
1920		194 051	50 779	94 654	13 826	11 914		3 581
1921		208 785	51 212	105 043		12 654		3 316
1922		217 594	52 033	104 757		12 496		3 793
1923		210 511	52 858	104 828		12 904		4 046
1924		220 763	55 683	107 766		13 095		4 110
1925		223 375	57 610	112 209	16 361	13 216		4 502
1926		230 410	60 781	113 212	17 170	13 685		4 314
1927		230 426	64 989	114 860	17 732	14 500		4 337
1928		232 745	68 099	124 246	18 483	14 171		5 315
1929	273 991	242 409	70 015	128 116	19 363	13 902	9 568	5 149
1930	277 467	244 097	70 525	118 801	19 478	14 179		5 073
1931	280 292	242 489	65 218	119 804	19 481	13 980		5 055
1932	289 200	245 209	64 461	129 835	21 154	14 570		5 747
1933	289 200	245 433	64 035	142 589	20 628	16 670		5 288
1934	263 996	247 712	64 400	142 876	21 567	16 488		5 677
1935	285 300	245 361	66 674	146 817	18 730	18 648		6 807
1936	303 324	254 896	71 517	157 493	21 373	19 915		6 639
1937	295 937	250 768	78 485	165 017	23 335	22 614		6 986
1938	288 549	251 375	80 044	176 051	24 252	22 440	12 380	7 395
1939		256 924	80 861	203 781	26 130	20 115		8 094
1940		265 455	86 682	209 728	26 326	22 536		8 064
1941		270 531	89 316	212 594		22 848		8 871
1942		269 278		211 448		22 718		9 524
1943		279 898		214 457		23 048		6 492
1944		276 954		205 214		22 050		4 459
1945		272 503		102 607		11 029		4 849
1946		258 164		111 492	12 131	11 984		5 274
1947		213 680		120 377	16 922	12 886		5 736
1948		215 927		138 290	19 772	13 867		6 238
1949		221 631	61 872	147 534	21 022	14 917		6 784

http://dx.doi.org/10.1787/456125276116

ISBN 92-64-02261-9 – © OECD 2006

Table 5b. GDP Levels in 16 East Asian Countries, 1914-1949
(million 1990 international Geary-Khamis dollars)

	Bangladesh	Burma	Hong Kong	Malaysia	Nepal	Pakistan	Singapore	Sri Lanka	16 country Total
1914				2 893				5 853	
1915				3 007				5 574	
1916		10 405		3 258				5 829	
1917				3 449				6 137	
1918				3 300				5 658	
1919				4 020				6 041	
1920				3 936				5 733	
1921		9 392		3 889				5 617	
1922				4 259				5 831	
1923				4 194				5 782	
1924				4 095				6 148	
1925				4 743				6 534	
1926		11 326		5 316				7 022	
1927				5 165				7 053	
1928				5 865				7 202	
1929				7 261				7 571	
1930				7 219				7 220	
1931		13 235		6 988				6 914	
1932				6 431				6 604	
1933				6 762				6 699	
1934				7 380				7 397	
1935				6 672				6 982	
1936		13 167		7 380				6 981	
1937				6 672				7 466	
1938		11 942		7 089				7 407	
1939				8 557				7 230	
1940				6 945				7 673	
1941				6 878				7 875	
1942				9 354				8 189	
1943								8 085	
1944								7 437	
1945								7 420	
1946								7 199	
1947				6 186				7 554	
1948	25 197			7 017		23 477		8 397	
1949	23 266			9 277		23 764		8 939	

http://dx.doi.org/10.1787/456125276116

Table 5b. **GDP Levels in 16 East Asian Countries, 1950-2001**
(million 1990 international Geary-Khamis dollars)

	China	India	Indonesia	Japan	Philippines	South Korea	Thailand	Taiwan
1950	239 903	222 222	66 358	160 966	22 616	16 045	16 375	7 378
1951	267 228	227 362	71 304	181 025	25 054	14 810	17 532	8 179
1952	305 742	234 148	74 679	202 005	26 609	15 772	18 503	9 093
1953	321 919	248 963	78 394	216 889	28 988	20 345	20 542	10 092
1954	332 326	259 262	83 283	229 151	31 168	21 539	20 381	10 927
1955	350 115	265 527	85 571	248 855	33 331	22 708	22 162	11 853
1956	384 842	280 978	86 700	267 567	35 670	22 815	22 540	12 481
1957	406 222	277 924	92 631	287 130	37 599	24 575	22 792	13 360
1958	452 654	299 137	89 293	303 857	38 900	25 863	23 616	14 510
1959	464 006	305 499	93 129	331 570	41 548	26 865	26 457	15 871
1960	448 727	326 910	97 082	375 090	42 114	27 398	29 665	16 725
1961	368 021	336 744	103 446	420 246	44 480	28 782	31 210	17 931
1962	368 032	344 204	103 332	457 742	46 603	29 654	33 636	19 453
1963	403 732	361 442	99 371	496 514	49 893	32 268	36 360	22 150
1964	452 558	389 262	103 043	554 449	51 613	35 054	38 841	24 971
1965	505 099	373 814	104 070	586 744	54 331	37 166	41 933	26 688
1966	553 676	377 207	104 089	649 189	56 736	41 641	46 654	29 378
1967	536 987	408 349	101 739	721 132	59 756	44 670	50 552	32 688
1968	525 204	418 907	111 662	813 984	62 712	50 371	54 695	35 447
1969	574 669	446 872	125 408	915 556	65 632	58 007	58 980	38 651
1970	640 949	469 584	138 612	1 013 602	68 102	62 988	62 842	43 509
1971	671 780	474 338	146 200	1 061 230	71 799	82 932	65 886	49 591
1972	691 449	472 766	162 748	1 150 516	75 710	85 811	68 666	57 358
1973	740 048	494 832	186 900	1 242 932	82 464	96 794	75 511	63 519
1974	752 734	500 146	196 374	1 227 706	85 398	104 605	78 894	62 384
1975	800 876	544 683	196 374	1 265 661	90 150	111 548	82 799	63 818
1976	793 092	551 402	213 675	1 315 966	98 090	124 664	90 391	75 108
1977	844 157	593 834	230 338	1 373 741	103 585	137 531	99 304	84 267
1978	935 884	625 695	240 853	1 446 165	108 942	150 442	109 112	94 833
1979	1 007 734	594 510	253 961	1 525 477	115 086	161 172	114 828	101 759
1980	1 046 781	637 202	275 805	1 568 457	121 012	156 846	120 116	104 753
1981	1 096 587	675 882	294 768	1 618 185	125 154	166 581	127 211	113 222
1982	1 192 494	697 705	283 922	1 667 653	129 648	179 220	134 020	119 254
1983	1 294 304	753 942	295 296	1 706 380	132 115	199 828	141 504	132 294
1984	1 447 661	783 042	315 677	1 773 223	122 440	217 167	149 644	148 650
1985	1 599 201	814 344	323 451	1 851 315	113 493	231 386	156 598	156 878
1986	1 703 671	848 990	342 452	1 904 918	117 371	258 122	165 264	177 721
1987	1 849 563	886 154	359 323	1 984 142	122 432	287 854	180 996	190 493
1988	2 000 236	978 822	379 917	2 107 060	130 699	320 301	205 047	192 229
1989	2 044 100	1 043 912	414 090	2 208 858	138 809	340 751	230 043	195 311
1990	2 109 400	1 098 100	450 901	2 321 153	143 025	373 150	255 732	200 477
1991	2 232 306	1 112 340	473 680	2 393 300	142 191	407 899	277 618	215 622
1992	2 444 569	1 169 301	524 482	2 415 691	142 668	429 817	300 059	230 203
1993	2 683 336	1 238 272	560 544	2 425 642	145 704	453 340	325 215	244 747
1994	2 950 104	1 328 047	602 585	2 450 521	152 115	490 762	354 484	262 124
1995	3 196 343	1 425 623	651 997	2 487 838	159 264	534 599	387 097	278 900
1996	3 433 255	1 537 439	704 156	2 574 912	168 507	570 952	409 936	295 913
1997	3 657 242	1 610 621	735 844	2 619 694	177 264	599 285	404 197	315 739
1998	3 873 352	1 716 369	639 448	2 592 327	176 200	559 190	361 756	330 263
1999	4 082 513	1 825 709	644 564	2 609 742	182 191	620 135	377 673	348 097
2000	4 329 913	1 924 297	675 503	2 669 450	190 207	677 871	395 046	368 635
2001	4 569 790	2 003 193	697 794	2 624 523	196 294	698 721	402 157	361 631

http://dx.doi.org/10.1787/456125276116

Table 5b. **GDP Levels in 16 East Asian Countries, 1950-2001**
(million 1990 international Geary-Khamis dollars)

	Bangladesh	Burma	Hong Kong	Malaysia	Nepal	Pakistan	Singapore	Sri Lanka	16 country Total
1950	24 628	7 711	4 962	10 032	4 462	25 366	2 268	9 438	840 730
1951	24 974	8 834	4 626	9 478	4 591	24 534	2 406	10 025	901 962
1952	25 706	9 028	5 054	9 930	4 748	24 625	2 569	10 485	978 696
1953	26 072	9 265	5 515	9 977	5 038	26 983	2 758	10 688	1 042 428
1954	26 581	8 690	6 021	10 607	5 145	27 603	2 896	10 979	1 086 559
1955	25 177	9 822	6 564	10 677	5 248	28 238	3 078	11 621	1 140 547
1956	27 821	10 472	7 136	11 320	5 484	29 069	3 200	11 698	1 219 793
1957	27 231	11 089	7 729	11 257	5 484	30 339	3 352	11 869	1 270 583
1958	26 702	10 785	8 345	11 256	5 792	30 762	3 485	12 214	1 357 171
1959	28 126	12 457	8 981	12 026	5 957	31 095	3 470	12 385	1 419 442
1960	29 733	12 871	9 637	12 899	6 091	32 621	3 803	12 841	1 484 207
1961	31 421	13 183	10 276	13 794	6 238	34 602	4 123	13 104	1 477 601
1962	31 258	14 332	12 072	14 578	6 385	37 111	4 411	13 575	1 536 378
1963	34 573	14 737	13 968	15 271	6 537	39 439	4 848	13 856	1 644 959
1964	34 939	14 999	15 165	16 235	6 689	42 417	4 680	14 515	1 799 430
1965	36 647	15 379	17 360	17 405	6 849	44 307	5 033	14 971	1 887 796
1966	37 115	14 737	17 659	18 278	7 331	47 919	5 593	14 804	2 022 006
1967	36 302	15 151	17 959	18 587	7 216	49 718	6 255	16 157	2 123 218
1968	39 678	16 148	18 557	20 217	7 265	53 195	7 123	17 362	2 252 527
1969	40 227	16 815	20 652	21 382	7 590	56 642	8 098	18 053	2 473 234
1970	42 403	17 575	22 548	22 684	7 787	62 522	9 209	18 912	2 703 828
1971	40 552	18 149	24 144	24 359	7 693	62 824	10 362	18 752	2 830 591
1972	35 732	18 284	26 629	26 195	7 934	63 323	11 752	19 147	2 974 030
1973	35 997	18 352	29 931	29 982	7 894	67 828	13 108	19 922	3 206 014
1974	40 817	19 323	30 629	32 222	8 393	70 141	13 994	20 570	3 244 330
1975	40 308	20 125	30 729	32 489	8 518	73 043	14 549	21 047	3 396 717
1976	42 098	21 350	35 718	36 536	8 893	76 898	15 588	21 669	3 521 138
1977	42 525	22 625	39 908	39 513	9 161	79 951	16 797	23 082	3 740 319
1978	45 657	24 086	43 300	42 970	9 563	86 406	18 245	24 523	4 006 676
1979	47 846	25 222	48 289	46 469	9 790	89 580	19 932	26 125	4 187 780
1980	48 239	27 381	53 177	50 333	9 563	98 907	21 865	27 550	4 367 987
1981	49 877	28 930	58 066	53 901	9 563	106 753	23 960	29 302	4 577 942
1982	50 487	30 499	59 662	57 102	10 749	114 852	25 601	30 788	4 783 656
1983	52 961	31 827	63 055	60 588	10 433	122 649	27 695	32 366	5 057 237
1984	55 833	33 397	69 340	65 290	11 441	127 518	30 006	33 951	5 384 280
1985	57 519	34 349	69 639	64 617	12 146	138 632	29 451	35 381	5 688 400
1986	60 011	33 986	77 122	65 434	12 664	147 421	29 975	37 163	5 982 285
1987	62 521	32 624	87 099	68 898	13 164	155 994	32 817	37 529	6 351 603
1988	64 329	28 921	94 083	74 982	14 199	166 031	36 491	38 520	6 831 867
1989	65 948	29 989	96 478	81 996	14 525	174 001	39 857	39 543	7 158 211
1990	70 320	30 834	99 770	89 823	15 609	182 014	43 330	42 089	7 525 727
1991	72 629	30 633	104 858	97 545	16 603	192 138	45 832	44 118	7 859 312
1992	76 245	33 593	111 343	105 151	17 285	206 957	49 399	46 050	8 302 813
1993	79 722	35 622	118 227	113 927	17 950	211 653	55 622	49 235	8 758 758
1994	83 309	38 044	124 611	124 408	19 425	220 966	61 963	51 992	9 315 460
1995	87 308	40 783	129 471	136 600	20 099	231 793	66 920	54 852	9 889 487
1996	91 674	43 394	135 297	150 260	21 170	238 515	72 073	56 936	10 504 389
1997	96 532	45 867	142 062	161 229	22 025	242 808	78 271	60 580	10 969 260
1998	102 324	48 527	134 533	149 298	22 435	250 335	78 193	63 427	11 097 977
1999	107 850	53 817	138 569	158 406	23 175	260 599	83 588	66 155	11 582 783
2000	113 890	56 508	152 980	171 553	24 681	271 805	92 198	70 124	12 184 661
2001	119 242	59 220	153 286	172 411	25 989	281 590	90 354	69 142	12 525 337

http://dx.doi.org/10.1787/456125276116

Table 5b. GDP Levels in 15 West Asian Countries, 1950-2002
(million 1990 international Geary-Khamis dollars)

	Bahrain	Iran	Iraq	Israel	Jordan	Kuwait	Lebanon	Oman	Qatar
1950	242	28 128	7 041	3 623	933	4 181	3 313	304	763
1951	257	28 128	7 661	4 707	990	4 532	2 972	324	827
1952	273	28 128	8 470	4 910	1 049	4 804	3 157	344	876
1953	290	28 156	11 899	4 852	1 112	5 280	3 634	366	963
1954	309	28 156	14 145	5 776	1 178	5 882	4 171	389	1 073
1955	328	28 156	13 568	6 558	1 116	6 020	4 506	413	1 099
1956	349	30 659	14 511	7 142	1 532	6 464	4 399	439	1 180
1957	371	34 939	14 370	7 761	1 571	6 693	4 476	467	1 223
1958	394	39 013	16 039	8 319	1 729	7 024	3 840	496	1 282
1959	419	42 360	16 715	9 370	1 858	7 747	4 164	528	1 415
1960	445	46 467	18 658	9 986	1 977	8 420	4 274	560	1 496
1961	474	50 405	20 806	11 077	2 381	8 495	4 555	567	1 497
1962	504	51 389	21 841	12 171	2 446	9 474	4 731	681	1 555
1963	536	57 043	21 447	13 461	2 582	9 984	4 771	711	1 657
1964	571	61 178	24 024	14 780	3 032	10 962	5 059	712	1 712
1965	607	68 688	26 206	16 171	3 379	11 205	5 569	715	1 837
1966	646	75 579	27 593	16 349	3 474	12 584	5 950	752	2 493
1967	688	84 102	26 953	16 758	3 839	12 885	5 668	1 250	3 014
1968	732	96 759	31 740	19 320	3 696	14 089	6 381	2 274	3 474
1969	779	109 304	32 818	21 755	4 031	14 474	6 520	2 858	3 706
1970	832	120 865	32 691	23 520	3 600	22 944	6 950	2 957	3 756
1971	898	135 829	34 712	26 107	3 682	24 537	7 590	2 983	4 665
1972	969	157 909	33 430	29 342	3 800	25 503	8 514	3 262	5 263
1973	1 046	171 466	39 042	30 839	3 999	23 847	8 915	2 809	6 228
1974	1 136	186 655	41 133	32 941	4 355	20 799	10 465	3 132	5 661
1975	1 015	195 684	47 977	34 038	4 657	18 287	10 724	3 897	5 823
1976	1 180	229 241	57 735	34 480	5 789	19 466	10 989	4 397	6 263
1977	1 322	226 315	59 320	34 480	6 166	18 722	11 260	4 410	5 586
1978	1 424	199 481	70 127	36 144	7 462	20 072	11 539	4 326	6 114
1979	1 419	182 267	86 258	38 416	8 142	22 827	10 873	4 511	6 364
1980	1 525	156 643	84 392	41 053	9 689	18 178	10 879	4 784	6 816
1981	1 568	151 918	69 078	43 173	10 147	14 737	10 366	5 599	5 834
1982	1 669	175 826	68 501	43 948	10 897	13 006	9 680	6 245	4 731
1983	1 785	199 031	62 544	45 496	11 115	14 039	9 584	7 288	4 246
1984	1 860	202 379	62 699	45 905	12 071	14 775	9 786	8 507	4 143
1985	1 854	207 245	61 714	47 489	12 493	14 148	10 028	9 697	3 699
1986	1 897	187 780	61 073	49 760	13 626	15 352	9 581	9 906	3 130
1987	1 935	184 939	62 812	53 344	13 997	14 733	6 705	10 699	3 192
1988	2 003	174 532	49 540	54 417	13 853	15 247	6 099	11 018	3 240
1989	2 053	181 227	45 160	54 895	12 387	16 389	6 106	11 481	3 275
1990	2 054	199 819	44 583	58 511	12 371	13 111	6 099	11 487	3 276
1991	2 148	220 999	16 540	61 848	12 656	7 735	8 429	12 176	3 263
1992	2 316	234 472	21 370	66 051	14 807	13 723	8 808	13 211	3 566
1993	2 508	239 395	21 370	68 298	15 666	18 416	9 425	14 017	3 552
1994	2 502	244 901	20 306	74 172	16 445	19 970	10 179	14 556	3 635
1995	2 600	252 983	18 475	79 215	17 495	20 186	10 841	15 259	3 742
1996	2 707	267 403	20 799	82 938	17 861	19 518	11 274	15 700	3 922
1997	2 791	280 773	19 996	85 675	18 409	19 708	11 725	16 671	4 865
1998	2 924	285 827	22 993	88 246	18 950	19 354	12 077	17 121	5 275
1999	3 050	296 117	24 948	87 903	19 530	19 173	12 198	16 954	5 443
2000	3 212	312 995	27 692	94 408	20 288	20 151	12 198	17 462	5 987
2001	3 341	328 019	30 185	93 558	20 896	20 654	12 442	18 161	6 359
2002	3 454	347 044	32 297	92 155	21 732	21 068	12 753	18 796	6 740

http://dx.doi.org/10.1787/456125276116

Table 5b. **GDP Levels in 15 West Asian Countries, 1950-2002**
(million 1990 international Geary-Khamis dollars)

	Saudi Arabia	Syria	Turkey	UAE	Yemen	West Bank and Gaza	Total
1950	8 610	8 418	34 279	1 130	4 353	965	106 283
1951	9 334	8 098	38 667	1 225	4 468	1 009	113 196
1952	9 893	10 202	43 295	1 298	4 584	1 055	122 340
1953	10 875	11 566	48 128	1 427	4 708	1 104	134 360
1954	12 115	13 266	46 757	1 590	4 831	1 157	140 794
1955	12 399	11 970	50 528	1 628	4 959	1 206	144 454
1956	13 312	14 175	52 173	1 749	5 091	1 260	154 435
1957	13 785	15 051	56 321	1 812	5 228	1 321	165 389
1958	14 465	12 972	58 892	1 902	5 367	1 380	173 113
1959	15 955	13 460	61 600	2 097	5 510	1 462	184 660
1960	17 548	13 704	63 417	2 312	5 660	1 534	196 458
1961	19 632	14 832	64 480	2 526	5 810	1 588	209 125
1962	21 974	18 351	68 422	2 809	5 970	1 683	223 998
1963	23 885	18 342	74 866	3 097	6 148	1 783	240 313
1964	25 986	18 755	77 951	3 414	6 307	1 891	256 333
1965	29 137	18 704	80 008	3 762	6 486	2 010	274 485
1966	33 374	17 265	89 366	4 147	6 674	2 130	298 375
1967	36 310	18 696	93 377	4 570	6 868	2 045	317 024
1968	39 547	19 394	99 650	5 037	7 052	1 859	351 005
1969	42 578	23 031	104 929	5 554	7 260	1 931	381 528
1970	46 573	22 155	110 071	6 123	8 731	2 044	413 812
1971	53 289	24 352	120 046	7 147	10 253	2 169	458 258
1972	61 469	30 447	127 931	8 343	11 070	2 306	509 558
1973	73 601	27 846	133 858	9 739	12 431	2 455	548 120
1974	84 700	34 563	144 829	12 894	13 152	2 632	599 047
1975	84 924	41 306	157 855	13 307	14 152	2 797	636 442
1976	92 251	45 834	171 601	15 308	16 363	2 958	713 856
1977	106 191	45 254	179 005	17 978	18 167	3 137	737 313
1978	112 511	49 202	184 113	17 557	19 711	3 332	743 114
1979	120 028	50 986	182 536	21 926	20 805	3 531	760 889
1980	132 160	57 097	181 165	27 717	20 918	3 732	756 749
1981	142 630	62 527	189 014	28 492	22 191	3 940	761 214
1982	144 989	63 857	198 495	26 145	22 563	4 176	794 728
1983	129 404	64 766	205 811	24 833	23 856	4 465	808 263
1984	129 258	62 131	217 637	25 893	24 778	4 769	826 592
1985	120 605	65 928	228 744	25 287	24 578	5 094	838 601
1986	113 260	62 670	244 752	19 919	25 115	5 446	823 267
1987	118 495	63 865	266 108	20 631	26 135	5 834	853 424
1988	122 284	72 342	276 460	20 580	27 249	6 265	855 130
1989	126 701	65 860	279 614	22 766	28 203	6 706	862 823
1990	144 438	70 894	305 395	25 496	28 212	7 222	932 968
1991	156 571	75 927	308 227	25 547	28 297	7 853	948 217
1992	160 955	81 318	326 672	26 237	29 683	8 555	1 011 745
1993	159 989	89 938	352 945	26 001	30 544	9 308	1 061 372
1994	160 811	96 821	333 688	28 228	31 205	10 189	1 067 608
1995	161 564	102 698	357 688	30 459	34 594	11 234	1 119 033
1996	163 815	109 904	382 743	32 356	36 631	12 381	1 179 952
1997	167 106	112 640	411 555	34 517	39 592	13 573	1 239 596
1998	169 987	121 201	424 282	35 916	41 532	14 807	1 280 492
1999	168 674	119 012	404 302	37 296	43 067	*16 153*	1 273 820
2000	176 233	121 988	433 220	39 233	45 229	*16 153*	1 346 449
2001	182 402	126 258	401 162	39 626	46 889	*12 922*	1 342 874
2002	186 961	130 046	416 807	40 577	48 862	*10 338*	1 389 630

http://dx.doi.org/10.1787/456125276116

Table 5b. **GDP Levels in 26 East Asian Countries, 1950-2001**
(million 1990 international Geary-Khamis dollars)

	Afghanistan	Cambodia	Laos	Mongolia	North Korea	Vietnam	20 small countries	26 country Total
1950	5 255	2 155	1 156	339	7 293	16 681	3 845	36 724
1951	5 408	2 228	1 192	353	6 496	17 445	3 987	37 109
1952	5 591	2 368	1 229	370	6 675	18 209	4 225	38 667
1953	5 933	2 392	1 267	387	8 288	19 034	4 316	41 617
1954	6 059	2 670	1 306	406	8 683	19 920	4 471	43 515
1955	6 180	2 614	1 347	426	9 316	20 806	4 636	45 325
1956	6 458	2 963	1 388	448	9 444	21 631	4 820	47 152
1957	6 458	3 163	1 431	473	10 230	22 486	5 012	49 253
1958	6 821	3 322	1 476	499	10 816	23 372	5 200	51 506
1959	7 016	3 646	1 521	528	11 260	24 289	5 403	53 663
1960	7 268	3 863	1 568	559	11 483	25 297	5 640	55 678
1961	7 331	3 827	1 617	592	11 972	26 554	5 938	57 831
1962	7 457	4 139	1 667	627	12 249	29 917	6 130	62 186
1963	7 594	4 451	1 718	660	13 295	30 821	6 496	65 035
1964	7 741	4 331	1 772	699	14 445	32 322	6 794	68 104
1965	7 914	4 538	1 826	740	15 370	32 666	7 172	70 226
1966	7 993	4 744	1 883	782	17 308	32 975	7 561	73 246
1967	8 214	4 988	1 941	828	18 711	28 829	7 854	71 365
1968	8 508	5 214	2 001	876	21 268	28 329	8 347	74 543
1969	8 645	5 292	2 063	927	24 743	30 702	8 750	81 122
1970	8 819	4 785	2 127	982	27 184	31 295	9 581	84 773
1971	8 398	4 546	2 193	1 041	36 229	32 889	10 376	95 672
1972	8 240	4 301	2 261	1 103	37 854	35 815	10 939	100 513
1973	9 181	5 858	2 331	1 170	43 072	38 238	11 952	111 802
1974	9 680	5 007	2 403	1 243	44 038	36 744	12 594	111 709
1975	10 184	4 342	2 477	1 319	44 891	34 130	12 765	110 108
1976	10 694	4 650	2 554	1 396	45 652	39 879	13 181	118 006
1977	9 959	5 016	2 633	1 479	46 379	41 343	13 403	120 212
1978	10 752	5 484	2 714	1 567	47 104	41 622	14 102	123 345
1979	10 715	5 593	2 798	1 661	47 842	41 873	15 175	125 657
1980	10 427	5 705	2 885	1 758	48 621	40 671	14 880	124 947
1981	10 547	5 774	2 974	1 905	49 388	42 103	14 965	127 656
1982	10 726	6 218	3 066	2 064	50 138	45 526	15 226	132 964
1983	11 157	6 660	3 161	2 184	50 905	48 042	15 662	137 771
1984	11 336	7 106	3 258	2 314	51 695	52 355	15 899	143 963
1985	11 299	7 554	3 359	2 446	52 505	55 481	16 565	149 209
1986	12 161	7 998	3 463	2 675	53 331	57 056	17 368	154 052
1987	10 064	7 839	3 570	2 768	54 172	59 127	17 984	155 524
1988	9 228	8 035	3 681	2 909	55 033	62 685	18 633	160 204
1989	9 284	8 233	3 795	3 031	55 934	65 615	19 306	165 198
1990	8 861	8 235	3 912	2 954	56 874	68 959	19 356	169 151
1991	8 932	8 860	4 031	2 681	57 846	72 963	20 212	175 525
1992	9 021	9 482	4 245	2 426	53 391	79 312	21 107	178 984
1993	8 741	9 870	4 674	2 354	53 552	85 718	22 041	186 950
1994	8 479	10 258	4 964	2 408	39 468	93 292	23 016	181 885
1995	10 700	10 940	5 230	2 560	32 758	102 192	24 034	188 414
1996	11 342	11 543	5 355	2 620	27 091	111 736	25 098	194 785
1997	12 023	11 846	5 636	2 726	25 249	120 845	26 208	204 533
1998	12 744	11 998	5 806	2 821	25 130	127 851	26 662	213 012
1999	13 508	12 826	6 096	2 821	25 310	133 221	28 797	222 579
2000	13 508	13 518	6 450	2 821	25 310	140 548	28 820	230 975
2001	12 157	14 235	6 785	2 821	25 310	147 154	29 051	237 513

http://dx.doi.org/10.1787/456125276116

Table 5b. **GDP Levels in 57 Asian Countries, 1820-2001**
(million 1990 international Geary-Khamis dollars)

	16 East Asia	26 East Asia	15 West Asia	Total 57 Asia
1820	387 016	10 651	15 269	412 936
1870	391 213	13 328	22 468	427 009
1900	500 686	22 224	33 935	556 845
1913	612 074	27 687	40 588	680 349
1950	840 730	36 724	106 283	983 737
1951	901 962	37 109	113 196	1 052 267
1952	978 696	38 667	122 340	1 139 703
1953	1 042 428	41 617	134 360	1 218 405
1954	1 086 559	43 515	140 794	1 270 868
1955	1 140 547	45 325	144 454	1 330 326
1956	1 219 793	47 152	154 435	1 421 380
1957	1 270 583	49 253	165 389	1 485 225
1958	1 357 171	51 506	173 113	1 581 790
1959	1 419 442	53 663	184 660	1 657 765
1960	1 484 207	55 678	196 458	1 736 343
1961	1 477 601	57 831	209 125	1 744 557
1962	1 536 378	62 186	223 998	1 822 562
1963	1 644 959	65 035	240 313	1 950 307
1964	1 799 430	68 104	256 333	2 123 867
1965	1 887 796	70 226	274 485	2 232 507
1966	2 022 006	73 246	298 375	2 393 627
1967	2 123 218	71 365	317 024	2 511 607
1968	2 252 527	74 543	351 005	2 678 075
1969	2 473 234	81 122	381 528	2 935 884
1970	2 703 828	84 773	413 812	3 202 413
1971	2 830 591	95 672	458 258	3 384 521
1972	2 974 030	100 513	509 558	3 584 101
1973	3 206 014	111 802	548 120	3 865 936
1974	3 244 330	111 709	599 047	3 955 086
1975	3 396 717	110 108	636 442	4 143 267
1976	3 521 138	118 006	713 856	4 353 000
1977	3 740 319	120 212	737 313	4 597 844
1978	4 006 676	123 345	743 114	4 873 135
1979	4 187 780	125 657	760 889	5 074 326
1980	4 367 987	124 947	756 749	5 249 683
1981	4 577 942	127 656	761 214	5 466 812
1982	4 783 656	132 964	794 728	5 711 348
1983	5 057 237	137 771	808 263	6 003 271
1984	5 384 280	143 963	826 592	6 354 835
1985	5 688 400	149 209	838 601	6 676 210
1986	5 982 285	154 052	823 267	6 959 604
1987	6 351 603	155 524	853 424	7 360 551
1988	6 831 867	160 204	855 130	7 847 201
1989	7 158 211	165 198	862 823	8 186 232
1990	7 525 727	169 151	932 968	8 627 846
1991	7 859 312	175 525	948 217	8 983 054
1992	8 302 813	178 984	1 011 745	9 493 542
1993	8 758 758	186 950	1 061 372	10 007 080
1994	9 315 460	181 885	1 067 608	10 564 953
1995	9 889 487	188 414	1 119 033	11 196 934
1996	10 504 389	194 785	1 179 952	11 879 126
1997	10 969 260	204 533	1 239 596	12 413 389
1998	11 097 977	213 012	1 280 492	12 591 481
1999	11 582 783	222 579	1 273 820	13 079 182
2000	12 184 661	230 975	1 346 449	13 762 085
2001	12 525 337	237 513	1 342 874	14 105 724

http://dx.doi.org/10.1787/456125276116

Table 5c. **Per Capita GDP in 16 East Asian Countries, 1820-1913**
(1990 international Geary-Khamis dollars)

	China	India	Indonesia	Japan	Philippines	South Korea	Thailand	Taiwan
1820	600	533	612	669	*704*	*600*	*646*	*499*
1850	600							
1870	530	533	654	737	*776*	*604*	712	*550*
1871			646	742				
1872			637	746				
1873			643	751				
1874			651	756				
1875			657	810				
1876			670	785				
1877			671	803				
1878			656	794				
1879			664	835				
1880			662	863				
1881			699	829				
1882			672	844				
1883			657	837				
1884		551	717	836				
1885		567	713	860				
1886		548	697	916				
1887		572	695	952				
1888		576	693	900				
1889		559	691	933				
1890	540	584	660	1 012			784	
1891		529	671	956				
1892		571	690	1 013				
1893		584	711	1 008				
1894		592	713	1 119				
1895		577	716	1 123				
1896		533	704	1 051				
1897		630	702	1 062				
1898		630	699	1 249				
1899		580	728	1 143				
1900	545	599	743	1 180				
1901		608	724	1 206				
1902		655	705	1 129	699			
1903		660	736	1 193	832			
1904		659	742	1 188	756			
1905		643	744	1 157	742			
1906		657	758	1 297	770			
1907		614	767	1 325	794			
1908		619	760	1 318	801			
1909		700	790	1 301	799			
1910		697	834	1 304	901			
1911		691	870	1 356	945	777		
1912		689	867	1 384	974	782		722
1913	552	673	904	1 387	1 053	820	841	747

http://dx.doi.org/10.1787/456125276116

ISBN 92-64-02261-9 – © OECD 2006

Table 5c. Per Capita GDP in 16 East Asian Countries, 1820-1913
(1990 international Geary-Khamis dollars)

	Bangladesh	Burma	Hong Kong	Malaysia	Nepal	Pakistan	Singapore	Sri Lanka	16 country average
1820		504	615	603	397		615	492	581
1850								564	
1870		504	683	663	397		682	851	551
1871								827	
1872								785	
1873								788	
1874								775	
1875								781	
1876								789	
1877								793	
1878								718	
1879								770	
1880								831	
1881								887	
1882								935	
1883								941	
1884								905	
1885								842	
1886								810	
1887								945	
1888								921	
1889								902	
1890								1 045	
1891								1 037	
1892								1 052	
1893								1 052	
1894								1 043	
1895								1 085	
1896								1 088	
1897								1 125	
1898								1 168	
1899								1 234	
1900								1 290	623
1901								1 192	
1902								1 175	
1903								1 225	
1904								1 215	
1905								1 179	
1906								1 190	
1907								1 233	
1908								1 221	
1909								1 153	
1910								1 208	
1911					801			1 160	
1912					822			1 157	
1913		685	1 279	900	539		1 279	1 234	679

http://dx.doi.org/10.1787/456125276116

Table 5c. **Per Capita GDP in 16 East Asian Countries, 1914-1949**
(1990 international Geary-Khamis dollars)

	China	India	Indonesia	Japan	Philippines	South Korea	Thailand	Taiwan
1914		709	892	1 327	1 015	862		747
1915		691	893	1 430	925	966		765
1916		710	896	1 630	1 040	969		963
1917		697	893	1 665	1 177	1 021		1 057
1918		607	909	1 668	1 322	1 087		925
1919		690	969	1 827	1 274	1 049		982
1920		635	945	1 696	1 289	1 009		959
1921		679	942	1 860		1 051		873
1922		701	946	1 831		1 018		980
1923		671	949	1 809		1 030		1 027
1924		697	988	1 836		1 025		1 025
1925		698	1 010	1 885	1 387	1 016		1 099
1926		713	1 053	1 872	1 428	1 038		1 028
1927		706	1 112	1 870	1 441	1 086		1 011
1928		706	1 151	1 992	1 474	1 047		1 211
1929	562	728	1 170	2 026	1 502	1 014	793	1 146
1930	567	726	1 164	1 850	1 476	1 020		1 099
1931	569	711	1 061	1 837	1 442	990		1 066
1932	583	709	1 033	1 962	1 530	1 016		1 181
1933	578	700	1 011	2 122	1 457	1 145		1 059
1934	525	697	1 002	2 098	1 488	1 115		1 107
1935	565	680	1 023	2 120	1 262	1 242		1 295
1936	597	697	1 081	2 244	1 406	1 315		1 233
1937	580	676	1 169	2 315	1 499	1 482		1 263
1938	562	668	1 175	2 449	1 522	1 459	826	1 302
1939		674	1 169	2 816	1 606	1 297		1 390
1940		686	1 235	2 874	1 587	1 442		1 347
1941		691	1 252	2 873		1 441		1 439
1942		679		2 818		1 412		1 502
1943		698		2 822		1 411		998
1944		683		2 659		1 330		684
1945		664		1 346		616		742
1946		622		1 444	646	619		806
1947		618		1 541	875	648		904
1948		617		1 725	993	692		931
1949		624	797	1 800	1 025	738		932

http://dx.doi.org/10.1787/456125276116

Table 5c. **Per Capita GDP in 16 East Asian Countries, 1914-1949**
(1990 international Geary-Khamis dollars)

	Bangladesh	Burma	Hong Kong	Malaysia	Nepal	Pakistan	Singapore	Sri Lanka	16 country average
1914				920				1 210	
1915				938				1 136	
1916		823		996				1 173	
1917				1 034				1 218	
1918				969				1 107	
1919				1 158				1 166	
1920				1 110				1 092	
1921		711		1 075				1 059	
1922				1 152				1 086	
1923				1 110				1 066	
1924				1 060				1 128	
1925				1 201				1 187	
1926		814		1 316				1 266	
1927				1 251				1 261	
1928				1 389				1 257	
1929				1 682				1 336	
1930				1 636				1 265	
1931		902		1 548				1 203	
1932				1 397				1 141	
1933				1 440				1 150	
1934				1 540				1 260	
1935				1 364				1 184	
1936		838		1 478				1 175	
1937				1 308				1 247	
1938		740		1 361				1 225	
1939				1 609				1 186	
1940				1 278				1 251	
1941				1 238				1 277	
1942				1 673				1 323	
1943								1 284	
1944								1 154	
1945								1 116	
1946								1 050	
1947				1 069				1 073	
1948				1 185				1 159	
1949				1 531				1 199	

http://dx.doi.org/10.1787/456125276116

Table 5c. **Per Capita GDP in 16 East Asian Countries, 1950-2001**
(1990 international Geary-Khamis dollars)

	China	India	Indonesia	Japan	Philippines	South Korea	Thailand	Taiwan
1950	439	619	840	1 921	1 070	770	817	924
1951	479	623	885	2 126	1 151	709	849	991
1952	537	629	910	2 336	1 186	753	869	1 063
1953	554	657	938	2 474	1 254	966	935	1 140
1954	558	672	978	2 582	1 308	1 013	898	1 193
1955	575	676	986	2 771	1 358	1 054	945	1 250
1956	619	701	980	2 948	1 410	1 036	930	1 270
1957	637	680	1 028	3 136	1 442	1 087	910	1 314
1958	693	716	972	3 289	1 448	1 112	914	1 382
1959	697	717	995	3 554	1 501	1 120	992	1 462
1960	673	753	1 019	3 986	1 476	1 105	1 078	1 492
1961	557	758	1 066	4 426	1 512	1 124	1 100	1 551
1962	553	758	1 043	4 777	1 537	1 122	1 149	1 632
1963	592	779	984	5 129	1 595	1 186	1 205	1 804
1964	648	821	1 000	5 668	1 600	1 253	1 249	1 977
1965	706	771	990	5 934	1 633	1 295	1 308	2 056
1966	753	762	971	6 506	1 654	1 415	1 412	2 205
1967	712	807	930	7 152	1 690	1 483	1 486	2 395
1968	678	809	1 001	7 983	1 722	1 633	1 561	2 539
1969	722	845	1 102	8 874	1 750	1 839	1 636	2 706
1970	783	868	1 194	9 714	1 764	1 954	1 694	2 980
1971	799	856	1 235	10 040	1 808	2 522	1 725	3 324
1972	802	834	1 342	10 734	1 853	2 561	1 748	3 767
1973	839	853	1 504	11 434	1 964	2 841	1 874	4 091
1974	836	843	1 542	11 145	1 979	3 015	1 910	3 942
1975	874	897	1 505	11 344	2 033	3 162	1 959	3 958
1976	852	889	1 598	11 669	2 152	3 476	2 091	4 566
1977	895	937	1 681	12 064	2 211	3 775	2 249	5 020
1978	979	966	1 715	12 585	2 262	4 064	2 422	5 542
1979	1 040	895	1 765	13 163	2 323	4 294	2 496	5 831
1980	1 067	938	1 870	13 428	2 376	4 114	2 554	5 869
1981	1 103	977	1 957	13 754	2 398	4 302	2 653	6 229
1982	1 192	985	1 845	14 078	2 425	4 557	2 744	6 446
1983	1 265	1 043	1 878	14 307	2 415	5 007	2 847	7 036
1984	1 396	1 060	1 966	14 773	2 188	5 375	2 960	7 790
1985	1 522	1 079	1 972	15 331	1 981	5 670	3 049	8 113
1986	1 597	1 101	2 051	15 679	2 001	6 263	3 168	9 088
1987	1 706	1 125	2 114	16 251	2 040	6 916	3 418	9 641
1988	1 816	1 216	2 196	17 185	2 129	7 621	3 817	9 623
1989	1 827	1 270	2 352	17 942	2 210	8 027	4 222	9 665
1990	1 858	1 309	2 516	18 789	2 224	8 704	4 629	9 886
1991	1 940	1 299	2 599	19 309	2 161	9 417	4 959	10 522
1992	2 098	1 341	2 831	19 430	2 123	9 814	5 290	11 128
1993	2 277	1 390	2 976	19 457	2 124	10 238	5 661	11 720
1994	2 475	1 463	3 146	19 602	2 170	10 965	6 094	12 430
1995	2 653	1 538	3 348	19 849	2 221	11 818	6 573	13 104
1996	2 820	1 630	3 556	20 494	2 296	12 495	6 877	13 796
1997	2 973	1 679	3 655	20 798	2 363	12 991	6 702	14 598
1998	3 117	1 760	3 129	20 534	2 301	12 016	5 930	15 134
1999	3 259	1 841	3 107	20 631	2 332	13 222	6 123	15 827
2000	3 425	1 910	3 203	21 069	2 385	14 343	6 336	16 642
2001	3 583	1 957	3 256	20 683	2 412	14 673	6 383	16 214

http://dx.doi.org/10.1787/456125276116

Table 5c. **Per Capita GDP in 16 East Asian Countries, 1950-2001**
(1990 international Geary-Khamis dollars)

	Bangladesh	Burma	Hong Kong	Malaysia	Nepal	Pakistan	Singapore	Sri Lanka	16 country average
1950	540	396	2 218	1 559	496	643	2 219	1 253	662
1951	541	446	2 295	1 440	505	608	2 253	1 293	698
1952	548	449	2 377	1 471	517	596	2 280	1 314	742
1953	547	454	2 460	1 440	543	637	2 314	1 300	775
1954	547	419	2 546	1 490	549	636	2 320	1 298	791
1955	508	467	2 636	1 460	554	635	2 358	1 339	814
1956	551	490	2 729	1 505	572	638	2 333	1 315	853
1957	530	510	2 825	1 455	566	650	2 318	1 300	869
1958	510	488	2 924	1 413	592	643	2 295	1 305	907
1959	526	555	3 027	1 467	601	633	2 186	1 289	931
1960	544	564	3 134	1 530	607	647	2 310	1 300	962
1961	564	568	3 244	1 592	613	669	2 422	1 291	950
1962	550	606	3 652	1 637	618	699	2 520	1 303	972
1963	594	613	4 083	1 669	623	723	2 701	1 297	1 017
1964	588	613	4 327	1 728	626	758	2 541	1 326	1 088
1965	607	617	4 825	1 804	631	771	2 667	1 336	1 116
1966	603	580	4 865	1 846	663	812	2 891	1 291	1 168
1967	578	586	4 824	1 830	641	820	3 163	1 377	1 198
1968	619	613	4 880	1 942	633	854	3 540	1 446	1 241
1969	614	626	5 345	2 005	649	885	3 965	1 471	1 331
1970	629	642	5 695	2 079	653	952	4 439	1 509	1 420
1971	586	650	5 968	2 180	633	931	4 904	1 468	1 450
1972	505	642	6 473	2 289	639	913	5 460	1 471	1 488
1973	497	628	7 105	2 560	622	954	5 977	1 504	1 569
1974	547	648	7 091	2 688	647	962	6 276	1 529	1 554
1975	529	663	6 991	2 648	642	978	6 430	1 541	1 594
1976	540	690	7 906	2 910	654	1 006	6 797	1 560	1 622
1977	529	718	8 707	3 076	657	1 023	7 224	1 635	1 692
1978	551	752	9 277	3 271	670	1 079	7 752	1 706	1 780
1979	560	773	9 796	3 457	669	1 087	8 362	1 783	1 826
1980	548	823	10 503	3 657	637	1 161	9 058	1 849	1 870
1981	550	854	11 202	3 824	621	1 207	9 460	1 934	1 926
1982	542	884	11 333	3 954	680	1 259	9 674	1 998	1 982
1983	555	907	11 797	4 096	644	1 309	10 330	2 072	2 052
1984	572	936	12 846	4 307	689	1 324	10 982	2 147	2 147
1985	577	947	12 763	4 157	713	1 400	10 764	2 208	2 229
1986	590	924	13 960	4 105	725	1 446	10 966	2 286	2 304
1987	603	875	15 597	4 219	735	1 487	11 827	2 275	2 403
1988	608	766	16 716	4 482	773	1 539	12 821	2 302	2 539
1989	612	786	17 043	4 790	771	1 569	13 599	2 330	2 614
1990	640	800	17 541	5 132	808	1 597	14 365	2 448	2 702
1991	649	788	18 230	5 447	838	1 642	14 801	2 537	2 777
1992	671	860	19 084	5 740	850	1 740	15 537	2 618	2 891
1993	691	906	19 889	6 077	861	1 749	17 018	2 762	3 004
1994	710	957	20 486	6 486	909	1 784	18 404	2 876	3 148
1995	733	1 015	20 726	6 965	917	1 830	19 225	2 997	3 291
1996	756	1 070	21 075	7 496	943	1 841	19 963	3 076	3 448
1997	783	1 122	21 503	7 874	958	1 833	20 921	3 240	3 551
1998	815	1 178	19 748	7 139	952	1 848	20 198	3 359	3 545
1999	843	1 297	19 819	7 418	961	1 882	20 854	3 470	3 647
2000	873	1 353	21 499	7 872	999	1 920	22 207	3 645	3 794
2001	897	1 409	21 259	7 756	1 028	1 947	21 011	3 562	3 851

http://dx.doi.org/10.1787/456125276116

Table 5c. **Per Capita GDP in 15 West Asian Countries, 1950-2002**
(1990 international Geary-Khamis dollars)

	Bahrain	Iran	Iraq	Israel	Jordan	Kuwait	Lebanon	Oman	Qatar
1950	2 104	1 720	1 364	2 817	1 663	28 878	2 429	623	30 387
1951	2 185	1 673	1 445	3 159	1 695	29 777	2 121	650	30 550
1952	2 267	1 629	1 557	3 029	1 726	30 023	2 193	677	30 161
1953	2 351	1 587	2 129	2 910	1 757	31 361	2 457	707	31 002
1954	2 436	1 545	2 463	3 374	1 787	33 200	2 745	736	32 418
1955	2 518	1 503	2 298	3 701	1 625	32 257	2 886	766	31 277
1956	2 599	1 593	2 389	3 860	2 139	32 876	2 744	799	31 933
1957	2 674	1 765	2 300	3 992	2 104	31 447	2 717	831	31 547
1958	2 739	1 916	2 493	4 109	2 220	29 907	2 269	866	31 620
1959	2 796	2 021	2 523	4 501	2 287	29 568	2 395	900	33 161
1960	2 843	2 154	2 735	4 663	2 330	28 813	2 393	935	33 104
1961	2 882	2 269	2 961	4 996	2 685	26 112	2 482	923	30 737
1962	2 931	2 247	3 017	5 267	2 620	26 443	2 507	1 084	29 362
1963	2 994	2 422	2 872	5 593	2 649	25 331	2 459	1 103	28 505
1964	3 073	2 521	3 115	5 916	2 981	25 303	2 534	1 075	26 799
1965	3 173	2 748	3 288	6 272	3 183	23 533	2 706	1 053	26 132
1966	3 283	2 934	3 349	6 190	3 137	24 050	2 804	1 080	32 239
1967	3 402	3 169	3 164	6 222	3 059	22 409	2 592	1 749	35 393
1968	3 520	3 542	3 604	7 033	2 674	22 300	2 831	3 094	36 982
1969	3 646	3 887	3 604	7 723	2 773	20 963	2 810	3 782	35 884
1970	3 788	4 177	3 473	8 101	2 395	30 695	2 917	3 799	33 160
1971	3 983	4 564	3 567	8 711	2 366	30 930	3 001	3 716	38 182
1972	4 198	5 158	3 323	9 478	2 355	30 291	3 177	3 934	39 933
1973	4 376	5 445	3 753	9 645	2 388	26 689	3 155	3 279	43 806
1974	4 574	5 759	3 825	10 025	2 506	21 934	3 503	3 541	36 914
1975	3 922	5 862	4 315	10 148	2 583	18 162	3 461	4 267	35 198
1976	4 313	6 668	5 023	10 071	3 096	18 166	3 524	4 597	35 424
1977	4 444	6 380	4 992	9 863	3 182	16 417	3 614	4 390	29 562
1978	4 415	5 445	5 693	10 125	3 718	16 539	3 711	4 086	30 278
1979	4 222	4 801	6 756	10 515	3 919	17 675	3 508	4 044	29 491
1980	4 388	3 961	6 377	10 984	4 480	13 271	3 526	4 072	29 552
1981	4 313	3 681	5 041	11 357	4 502	10 290	3 364	4 523	24 061
1982	4 414	4 087	4 833	11 390	4 643	8 685	3 136	4 800	18 750
1983	4 542	4 446	4 269	11 586	4 556	8 966	3 102	5 346	14 955
1984	4 557	4 348	4 136	11 461	4 767	9 024	3 167	5 976	13 163
1985	4 374	4 287	3 932	11 654	4 754	8 165	3 247	6 545	10 718
1986	4 316	3 743	3 759	12 028	5 002	8 475	3 104	6 442	8 345
1987	4 257	3 558	3 797	12 691	4 963	7 789	2 170	6 712	7 938
1988	4 267	3 253	2 908	12 739	4 750	7 727	1 970	6 670	7 540
1989	4 235	3 274	2 571	12 637	4 103	7 968	1 965	6 708	7 173
1990	4 104	3 472	2 458	12 968	3 792	6 121	1 938	6 479	6 804
1991	4 170	3 709	947	13 003	3 486	8 108	2 640	6 606	6 467
1992	4 374	3 856	1 196	13 380	3 829	9 677	2 735	6 898	6 737
1993	4 611	3 924	1 161	13 492	3 932	12 412	2 898	7 048	6 377
1994	4 481	4 006	1 070	14 305	4 029	12 872	3 093	7 071	6 210
1995	4 540	4 085	945	14 932	4 164	12 454	3 251	7 161	6 103
1996	4 619	4 260	1 032	15 302	4 093	11 529	3 333	7 117	6 123
1997	4 663	4 411	962	15 489	4 067	11 164	3 418	7 300	7 290
1998	4 787	4 432	1 075	15 649	4 044	10 542	3 471	7 242	7 605
1999	4 899	4 539	1 132	15 307	4 033	10 063	3 457	6 928	7 567
2000	5 065	4 742	1 221	16 159	4 059	10 210	3 409	6 893	8 042
2001	5 177	4 911	1 294	15 756	4 055	10 115	3 430	6 926	8 268
2002	5 262	5 138	1 346	15 284	4 095	9 977	3 468	6 927	8 496

http://dx.doi.org/10.1787/456125276116

Table 5c. **Per Capita GDP in 15 West Asian Countries, 1950-2002**
(1990 international Geary-Khamis dollars)

	Saudi Arabia	Syria	Turkey	UAE	Yemen	West Bank and Gaza	15 country Average
1950	2 231	2 409	1 623	15 798	911	949	1 776
1951	2 374	2 264	1 784	16 709	918	987	1 840
1952	2 470	2 786	1 947	17 246	924	1 024	1 937
1953	2 664	3 084	2 108	18 418	930	1 061	2 074
1954	2 912	3 453	1 993	19 884	936	1 103	2 118
1955	2 922	3 039	2 093	19 683	942	1 144	2 116
1956	3 075	3 508	2 097	20 377	946	1 187	2 200
1957	3 119	3 627	2 194	20 282	951	1 234	2 290
1958	3 204	3 039	2 222	20 372	955	1 280	2 328
1959	3 458	3 062	2 252	21 426	959	1 328	2 412
1960	3 719	3 023	2 247	22 433	964	1 378	2 492
1961	4 066	3 168	2 221	23 180	969	1 431	2 579
1962	4 445	3 796	2 297	24 250	975	1 485	2 686
1963	4 715	3 673	2 454	25 025	984	1 542	2 804
1964	5 005	3 637	2 496	25 676	989	1 600	2 910
1965	5 469	3 512	2 504	26 164	996	1 660	3 031
1966	6 102	3 139	2 735	26 483	1 007	1 724	3 207
1967	6 463	3 291	2 795	26 610	1 019	1 790	3 318
1968	6 848	3 306	2 917	26 374	1 028	1 858	3 580
1969	7 170	3 801	3 002	25 495	1 040	1 919	3 788
1970	7 624	3 540	3 078	24 552	1 230	1 980	3 998
1971	8 475	3 759	3 282	24 806	1 414	2 046	4 304
1972	9 497	4 544	3 412	24 806	1 495	2 116	4 649
1973	11 040	4 017	3 477	24 887	1 640	2 184	4 854
1974	12 333	4 821	3 665	28 449	1 696	2 256	5 149
1975	11 797	5 570	3 895	25 465	1 784	2 329	5 308
1976	12 126	5 976	4 136	25 598	2 003	2 408	5 779
1977	13 097	5 705	4 221	26 296	2 162	2 488	5 791
1978	12 963	5 998	4 250	22 545	2 281	2 571	5 658
1979	12 897	6 010	4 128	24 802	2 342	2 656	5 610
1980	13 284	6 508	4 015	27 709	2 290	2 744	5 397
1981	13 500	6 891	4 089	25 894	2 363	2 837	5 245
1982	12 969	6 786	4 194	21 721	2 336	2 929	5 294
1983	10 946	6 638	4 249	18 870	2 401	3 028	5 207
1984	10 339	6 143	4 392	18 007	2 422	3 128	5 151
1985	9 131	6 290	4 514	16 104	2 332	3 231	5 056
1986	8 173	5 772	4 727	11 624	2 311	3 340	4 808
1987	8 194	5 681	5 032	11 601	2 329	3 450	4 842
1988	8 122	6 219	5 123	11 189	2 351	3 564	4 716
1989	8 106	5 480	5 081	12 003	2 353	3 683	4 627
1990	9 115	5 701	5 445	13 070	2 272	3 806	4 856
1991	9 740	5 909	5 395	12 764	2 197	3 932	4 853
1992	9 643	6 152	5 615	12 806	2 220	4 065	5 041
1993	9 235	6 623	5 961	12 420	2 200	4 200	5 188
1994	8 949	6 946	5 541	13 216	2 168	4 344	5 122
1995	8 671	7 177	5 846	13 995	2 328	4 490	5 255
1996	8 492	7 481	6 161	14 604	2 390	4 644	5 424
1997	8 378	7 469	6 528	15 312	2 502	4 803	5 578
1998	8 244	7 829	6 635	15 666	2 540	5 050	5 646
1999	7 915	7 490	6 237	16 001	2 548	5 312	5 505
2000	8 002	7 481	6 597	16 560	2 588	5 124	5 706
2001	8 015	7 547	6 033	16 460	2 594	3 953	5 580
2002	7 951	7 580	6 192	16 589	2 613	3 050	5 664

http://dx.doi.org/10.1787/456125276116

Table 5c. Per Capita in 26 East Asian Countries, 1820-2001
(1990 "International"Geary-Khamis dollars)

	Afghanistan	Cambodia	Laos	Mongolia	North Korea	Vietnam	20 small countries	26 country Total
1950	645	518	613	435	770	658	1 151	691
1951	653	522	621	447	709	676	1 172	692
1952	664	542	628	462	753	694	1 221	714
1953	692	534	635	476	966	712	1 223	761
1954	694	582	642	490	1 013	732	1 242	783
1955	695	556	649	505	1 054	750	1 261	798
1956	713	614	655	520	1 036	764	1 284	812
1957	699	638	661	536	1 087	775	1 308	828
1958	723	653	667	552	1 112	785	1 326	844
1959	729	698	673	569	1 120	792	1 346	855
1960	739	720	679	586	1 105	799	1 374	862
1961	730	694	686	603	1 124	812	1 412	870
1962	726	719	692	621	1 122	885	1 421	908
1963	723	753	698	640	1 186	882	1 465	923
1964	720	713	705	659	1 253	895	1 494	939
1965	720	728	712	679	1 295	877	1 536	940
1966	710	742	719	699	1 415	859	1 576	954
1967	712	760	726	720	1 483	731	1 595	904
1968	719	774	733	742	1 633	699	1 651	920
1969	713	765	740	764	1 839	739	1 687	975
1970	709	685	748	787	1 954	735	1 797	994
1971	659	648	755	811	2 522	754	1 892	1 095
1972	630	605	763	835	2 561	802	1 947	1 123
1973	684	813	770	860	2 841	836	2 079	1 220
1974	703	686	777	886	2 841	783	2 147	1 191
1975	721	604	784	912	2 841	710	2 128	1 149
1976	737	672	804	939	2 841	809	2 150	1 210
1977	669	751	821	968	2 841	818	2 138	1 209
1978	704	847	836	997	2 841	806	2 198	1 219
1979	689	869	856	1 027	2 841	795	2 309	1 220
1980	696	866	876	1 058	2 841	758	2 210	1 201
1981	749	849	891	1 115	2 841	768	2 171	1 216
1982	786	880	899	1 175	2 841	813	2 157	1 248
1983	814	906	904	1 210	2 841	840	2 163	1 267
1984	820	943	911	1 247	2 841	895	2 141	1 298
1985	813	982	918	1 282	2 841	929	2 177	1 321
1986	873	1 004	921	1 364	2 841	935	2 228	1 337
1987	715	947	923	1 374	2 841	949	2 252	1 322
1988	644	934	925	1 405	2 841	985	2 279	1 333
1989	634	922	927	1 404	2 841	1 006	2 304	1 342
1990	601	888	929	1 333	2 841	1 035	2 254	1 346
1991	598	921	931	1 182	2 841	1 073	2 297	1 368
1992	544	942	953	1 049	2 578	1 144	2 342	1 351
1993	464	934	1 020	1 002	2 542	1 214	2 387	1 362
1994	417	937	1 054	1 010	1 849	1 297	2 435	1 289
1995	498	973	1 079	1 058	1 519	1 397	2 484	1 305
1996	506	1 003	1 077	1 066	1 251	1 503	2 535	1 323
1997	517	1 008	1 105	1 093	1 170	1 602	2 587	1 366
1998	530	1 001	1 110	1 115	1 171	1 672	2 572	1 400
1999	541	1 051	1 137	1 100	1 180	1 719	2 716	1 439
2000	522	1 087	1 173	1 085	1 169	1 790	2 658	1 467
2001	453	1 124	1 204	1 070	1 154	1 850	2 621	1 482

http://dx.doi.org/10.1787/456125276116

Table 5c. **Per Capita GDP in 57 Asian Countries, 1820-2001**
(1990 international Geary-Khamis dollars)

	16 East Asia	*26 East Asia*	*15 West Asia*	*Average 57 Asia*
1820	581	556	607	581
1870	551	535	742	558
1910	623	674	940	638
1913	679	745	1 042	696
1950	662	691	1 854	712
1951	698	692	1 926	748
1952	742	714	2 030	794
1953	775	761	2 175	832
1954	791	783	2 214	850
1955	814	798	2 217	871
1956	853	812	2 302	912
1957	869	828	2 398	932
1958	907	844	2 437	970
1959	931	855	2 521	996
1960	962	862	2 602	1 029
1961	950	870	2 688	1 024
1962	972	908	2 799	1 052
1963	1 017	923	2 923	1 100
1964	1 088	939	3 033	1 171
1965	1 116	940	3 153	1 203
1966	1 168	954	3 339	1 259
1967	1 198	904	3 453	1 290
1968	1 241	920	3 720	1 343
1969	1 331	975	3 932	1 438
1970	1 420	994	4 146	1 530
1971	1 450	1 095	4 421	1 577
1972	1 488	1 123	4 781	1 631
1973	1 569	1 220	4 972	1 720
1974	1 554	1 191	5 241	1 721
1975	1 594	1 149	5 381	1 766
1976	1 622	1 210	5 880	1 820
1977	1 692	1 209	5 882	1 887
1978	1 780	1 219	5 732	1 962
1979	1 826	1 220	5 689	2 004
1980	1 870	1 201	5 453	2 034
1981	1 926	1 216	5 310	2 081
1982	1 982	1 248	5 344	2 139
1983	2 052	1 267	5 276	2 200
1984	2 147	1 298	5 235	2 287
1985	2 229	1 321	5 132	2 359
1986	2 304	1 337	4 884	2 414
1987	2 403	1 322	4 936	2 506
1988	2 539	1 333	4 782	2 622
1989	2 614	1 342	4 680	2 686
1990	2 702	1 346	4 911	2 781
1991	2 777	1 368	4 903	2 848
1992	2 891	1 351	5 084	2 962
1993	3 004	1 362	5 211	3 072
1994	3 148	1 289	5 066	3 193
1995	3 291	1 305	5 148	3 330
1996	3 448	1 323	5 273	3 482
1997	3 551	1 366	5 398	3 587
1998	3 545	1 400	5 407	3 588
1999	3 647	1 439	5 417	3 672
2000	3 794	1 467	5 426	3 817
2001	3 851	1 482	5 435	3 861

http://dx.doi.org/10.1787/456125276116

HS–6: Africa

Contours of African Development

As the long–term economic development of Africa is difficult to quantify with any precision, it is useful to consider the broad contours and salient features I had in mind when making conjectures about the development of per capita income.

There is a marked difference between the historical experience of the lands North of the Sahara and the rest of the continent. For most of the past two millennia, there were higher levels of income and urbanisation, more sophisticated economic and political institutions in the North than in the South. North African history is reasonably well documented because there are substantial written records. Knowledge of the South is based on archaeological or linguistic evidence until the ninth century when written evidence of northern visitors becomes available.

Over the long run, population growth was much more dynamic South of the Sahara. Two thousand years ago, about half lived in the north; by 1820, four–fifths in the south. Between the first century AD and 1820, the population of the North had increased by a third (with many intervening setbacks). In the South it increased nearly eightfold (see Table 6–1). In terms of extensive growth (i.e. capacity to accommodate population increase), the south clearly had the edge. In terms of per capita real income, it seems likely that the average Northern level was lower in 1820 than in the first century. South of the Sahara, it is probable that it increased modestly (see Table 6–2).

The greater demographic dynamism of the south is surprising, because of its substantial losses from the slave trade. There seem to be three reasons for this: a) in Egypt and the Maghreb, plague seems to have been endemic from the sixth to the early nineteenth century. It does not seem to have crossed the Sahara; b) before the eighth century, there was virtually no contact between North and South. Possibilities for trade across the Sahara were revolutionised by the introduction of camels between the fifth and eighth centuries. They could carry about a third of a ton of freight, go without food for several days, and without water for up to 15 days. The growth in trade benefitted both parties. The partial Islamisation of black Africa increased the sophistication and organisational ability of the ruling elites in the Sahel and savannah lands of West Africa south of the Sahara; c) probably the most important was the spread of improved agricultural technology and new crops. Two thousand years ago, much of black Africa was inhabited by hunter–gatherers using stone–age technology. By 1820, they had been pushed aside and were a fraction of the population. The proportion of agriculturalists and pastoralists with iron–age tools and weapons increased dramatically. Land productivity was also helped by the introduction and gradual diffusion of maize, cassava and sweet potatoes from the Americas from 1500 onwards.

Egypt

In the first century AD, all of North Africa was under Roman rule. The Mediterranean was a Roman lake with magnificent ports in Italy and Alexandria and substantial flows of trade between Africa, Europe and the Middle East. Egypt was the most prosperous area, with a relatively large urban population, a sedentary agriculture, a substantially monetised economy, a significant industrial and

Table 6-1. **African Population, 1-2001 AD**
(000)

	1	1000	1500	1600	1700	1820	2001
Egypt	4 000	5 000	4 000	5 000	4 500	4 194	71 902
Morocco	1 000	2 000	1 500	2 250	1 750	2 689	30 645
Algeria	2 000	2 000	1 500	2 250	1 750	2 689	31 736
Tunisia	800	1 000	800	1 000	800	875	9 705
Libya	400	500	500	500	500	538	5 241
Total North Africa	**8 200**	**10 500**	**8 300**	**11 000**	**9 300**	**10 985**	**149 229**
Sahel	1 000	2 000	3 000	3 500	4 000	4 887	32 885
Other West Africa	3 000	7 000	11 000	14 000	18 000	20 777	218 393
Total West Africa	**4 000**	**9 000**	**14 000**	**17 500**	**22 000**	**25 664**	**251 278**
Ethiopia and Eritrea	500	1 000	2 000	2 250	2 500	3 154	68 208
Sudan	2 000	3 000	4 000	4 200	4 400	5 156	36 080
Somalia	200	400	800	800	950	1 000	7 489
Other East Africa	300	3 000	6 000	7 000	8 000	10 389	103 338
Total East Africa	**3 000**	**7 400**	**12 800**	**14 250**	**15 850**	**19 699**	**215 115**
Angola, Zaire, Equatoria	**1 000**	**4 000**	**8 000**	**8 500**	**9 000**	**10 757**	**87 235**
Malawi, Zambia, Zimbabwe	75	500	1 000	1 100	1 200	1 345	33 452
Mozambique	50	300	1 000	1 250	1 500	2 096	17 142
South Africa, Swaziland and Lesotho	100	300	600	700	1 000	1 550	45 562
Namibia and Botswana	75	100	200	200	200	219	3 444
Madagascar	0	200	700	800	1 000	1 683	15 983
Indian Ocean	0	0	10	20	30	238	2 648
Southern Africa	**300**	**1 400**	**3 510**	**4 070**	**4 930**	**7 131**	**118 231**
Total Africa	**16 500**	**32 300**	**46 610**	**55 320**	**61 080**	**74 236**	**821 088**

Source: 1-1820 from McEvedy and Jones (1978), 2001 from US Bureau of Census. **Sahel** includes Chad, Mauritania, Mali, Niger. **Other West Africa** includes Senegal, Gambia, Guinea Bissau, Guinea, Sierra Leone, Liberia, Burkina Faso, Côte d'Ivoire, Ghana, Togo, Benin, Nigeria, Cape Verde, W. Sahara. **Equatoria** includes Cameroon, Central African Rep., Congo, Equatorial Guinea, Gabon, São Tomé & Principe. **Indian Ocean** includes Comoros, Mauritius, Mayotte, Reunion, Seychelles. **Other East Africa** includes Burundi, Djibouti, Kenya, Rwanda, Tanzania, Uganda.

http://dx.doi.org/10.1787/456125276116

commercial sector, and a very long history as an organised state. Its natural waterways lowered the cost of transporting freight and passengers through its most densely populated area. As the prevailing winds blew from the North, one could sail upstream and float downstream. Agricultural productivity was high because of the abundant and reliable flow of Nile water and the annual renewal of topsoil in the form of silt.

Egypt produced a surplus that the Pharoahs and the Ptolemies used to support a brilliant civilisation. From the first to the tenth century, it was siphoned off; first to Rome, then to Constantinople. After the Muslim conquest, it was redirected by the authorities in Damascus then Baghdad. Under the Fatimid, Ayyubid and Mamluk regimes, tribute ceased, but in 1516 Egypt became a provincial backwater under a Turkish viceroy, paying tribute to the Ottoman sultan. Foreign rule generally impeded trade through the Red Sea to the Indian Ocean which had flourished in the first and second centuries, and was restored from the tenth to the fifteenth century. Virtually all trade with Europe disappeared from the fourth until the twelfth century. The entrepot trade, manufactured exports and population of Alexandria withered away.

Table 6-2. **Tentative Conjectures for African Per Capita GDP and GDP, 1-1820 AD**

	1	1000	1500	1600	1700	1820
	(per cent of African Population)					
Egypt	24.2	15.5	8.6	9.0	7.4	5.7
Morocco	6.1	6.2	3.2	4.1	2.9	3.6
Other North Africa	19.4	10.8	6.0	6.8	5.0	5.5
Total North Africa	**49.7**	**32.5**	**17.8**	**19.9**	**15.3**	**14.8**
Sahel and West Africa	24.2	27.9	30.0	31.6	36.0	34.6
Rest of Africa	24.1	39.6	52.2	48.5	48.7	50.6
Total	100.0	100.0	100.0	100.0	100.0	100.0
	(Conjectured per capita GDP in 1990 international $)					
Egypt	500	500	475	475	475	475
Morocco	400	430	430	430	430	430
Other North Africa	430	430	430	430	430	430
Average North Africa	**460**	**463**	**452**	**451**	**452**	**447**
Sahel and West Africa	400	415	415	415	415	415
Rest of Africa	400	400	400	415	415	415
Average Africa	430	425	414	422	421	420
	(Estimated GDP in million 1990 international $)					
Egypt	2 000	2 500	1 900	2 375	2 138	1 992
Morocco	400	860	645	968	753	1 156
Other North Africa	1 376	1 505	1 204	1 613	1 312	1 764
Total North Africa	**3 776**	**4 865**	**3 749**	**4 956**	**4 203**	**4 912**
Sahel and West Africa	1 600	3 735	5 810	7 263	9 130	10 650
Rest of Africa	1 720	5 120	9 724	11 130	12 359	15 599
Total Africa	7 096	13 720	19 283	23 349	25 692	31 161

Source: The stylised conjectures are for per capita income in each of the five regions at different points of time; GDP is derivative (i.e. per capita conjectures are multiplied by population estimates in Table 6-1). The rationale for the conjectures is derived from the analysis of main currents in African history in the following text. In the first century AD, North Africa belonged to the Roman Empire. Egypt was the richest part of the Roman world because of the special character of its agriculture, which had yielded a large surplus for governance and monuments in Pharaonic times, and was generally siphoned off as tribute by Roman and Arab rulers. Libya and most of the Maghreb (except Morocco) had a prosperous and urbanised coastal fringe in Roman times, with Berber tribes between them and the Sahara. There was no contact then with black Africa which I assume had an average income only slightly above subsistence ($400 in my *numeraire*). After the Arab conquest of North Africa in the seventh century, camel transport permitted trade across the Sahara, permitting a rise in per capita income in Morocco, the Sahel and West Africa. I assume that the gradual transition within Black Africa from a hunter-gatherer to an agricultural mode of production permitted greatly increased density of settlement with higher per capita labour inputs, but had little impact on per capita income.

http://dx.doi.org/10.1787/456125276116

By 1820, the Egyptian population was below its level in the eleventh century and the same is likely to have been true for per capita income. In the same period, Western Europe trebled its per capita income and increased its population more than fivefold.

The Maghreb

In West Africa, Roman ships did not venture beyond Cape Bojador (just south of the Canary Islands), because the prevailing winds made it impossible for them to make the return journey. Overland trade between the western provinces of Africa and the lands to the south was negligible. Roman settlement was essentially coastal except in Tunisia where large irrigated estates were worked mainly by tenant farmers. Exports from these provinces were heavily concentrated on grain shipped to Italy from Carthage and olive oil from Tripolitania. Roman economic activity in Morocco was vestigial.

When the Arabs conquered the Maghreb they severed the Mediterranean trading links which had previously existed and explored new opportunities across the desert. They established camel caravan routes from Tunisia and Libya deep into the Sahara to places where it was possible to trade horses for black slaves. Bigger profits could be derived from the gold trade with ancient Ghana (about 800 kilometres north–west of modern Ghana, between the Senegal and Niger rivers, just inside the southern boundary of modern Mauretania), which had a lengthy history as state before the Arabs established contact in the early eighth century. The most direct route was through Morocco, the area which received the greatest stimulus from the new contacts with black Africa. Muslim merchants on these new routes were active in making converts to Islam. Early in the eleventh century, ancient Ghana was the first of the black African states to convert to Islam.

Gold production increased steadily in West Africa from the eighth century onwards. Until the twelfth century most of the output circulated within the Muslim world, but from then onwards there was increasing demand from Europe, mainly from Genoa, Venice, Pisa, Florence and Marseilles. European traders conducted their operations in Muslim ports on the Mediterranean coast. They had only minimal contact with African gold producing areas until the second half of the fifteenth century when Portugal gained access to the West African coast.

From the eighth to the twelfth century, the main market for Muslim traders was Awdaghast in Ghana. The goldfield was at Bambuk, somewhat further south, but its exact whereabouts was kept secret. Most exports were in the form of gold dust which was melted and moulded into ingots. In the fourteenth century, pressure of demand was such that production was started further south at the Akan mines (in present–day Ghana). In the fifteenth and sixteenth centuries the main trading centre for gold was Timbuktu in the empire of Songhay. Mining wealth was the main reason why ancient Ghana, Mali and Songhay were able to emerge as powerful states. Income from gold produced an economic surplus which allowed the rulers to maintain the attributes of power. It made it possible for them to import horses and weapons and maintain cavalry forces.

The main barter transactions between the Maghreb and black Africa were exchange of salt for gold. In the Sahel region, salt was very scarce, but was a necessity for people doing heavy work. Some of the salt came from maritime sources on the Atlantic coast. But it was much easier to transport rock salt. From the eleventh to the sixteenth century, the main source was in the Sahara at Taghaza, where it was mined by slave labour, cut into large blocks, and transported south by camel. Salt was not the only trade item in this north–south trade. There was also a lively exchange between trading centres within the Sahel and West Africa, particularly in kola nuts — the African equivalent of coffee or tobacco. Further east, Kanem was the main centre of the slave trade. At a later stage there was a diversity of gold routes to Morocco, Algeria, Tunisia and Egypt and from Mediterranean ports to European customers. In the eleventh and twelfth centuries, Muslim countries were the only ones to mint gold coins. Marseilles first issued them in 1227, Florence in 1252, and Venice in 1284.

Black Africa

In spite of the advance beyond hunter–gatherer techniques, the agriculture of black Africa contrasted sharply with that of Egypt. There was an abundance of land in relation to population, but soils were poor, and were not regenerated by manure, crop rotation, natural or human provision of irrigation. As a consequence, there was an extensive, shifting cultivation, with land being left fallow for a decade or more after the first crops. Nomadic pastoralists were generally transhumant over wide areas for the same reason — poor soils. The main agricultural implements were digging sticks, iron hoes for tillage, axes and machetes for clearing trees and bush. There were no ploughs (except in Ethiopia) and virtually no use of traction animals in agriculture. There were no wheeled vehicles, no water mills, windmills or other instruments of water management.

There were no individual property rights in land. Tribes, kin–groups or other communities had customary rights to farm or graze in the areas where they lived, but collective property rights and boundaries were vague. Chiefs and rulers did not collect rents, land taxes, or feudal levies. Their main instrument of exploitation was slavery. Slaves were generally acquired by raids on neighbouring groups. Hence there was a substantial beggar–your–neighbour element in inter–group relations.

It is not clear how widespread slavery was before contact with Muslim Africa, but the contact certainly reinforced the institution because it made it possible to derive a substantial income from export of slaves across the Sahara. The traffic was organised by Muslim traders from the North. The flow from north to south was negligible. Slaves usually walked through the desert with a caravan of camels carrying food, water, slave drivers and other passengers.

Transport facilities in black Africa were poor. Camels thrived in the dry heat of the desert but could not function further south. Muslim Africa had ships which could navigate and trade in the Mediterranean, and in Egypt there was substantial and relatively safe travel on the sailing boats of the Nile. In the Sahel and West Africa, there were partially navigable rivers, particularly the Niger, the Senegal and Gambia, but river traffic moved in rather primitive paddle–boats made of hollowed–out tree trunks and the frequency of cataracts meant that merchandise frequently had to be trans–shipped by head porterage. Horses were very expensive and had a short life expectation, because of the climate and the fact that they were highly sensitive to tsetse flies. They were used almost exclusively for military and prestige purposes by the ruling groups and their lightly armed cavalry (horses and riders wore padded armour as a defence against arrows).

A striking feature of black Africa before contact with the Islamic world, was universal illiteracy and absence of written languages (except in Ethiopia). This made it difficult to transmit knowledge across generations and between African societies. Contact with Islam brought obvious advantages. The Arabs who came as traders had a written language, and an evangelising bent. They included sophisticated members of the Muslim intelligentsia (ulama), who were able to promote knowledge of property institutions, law, and techniques of governance as well cutting business deals. Before the Moroccan conquest of Songhay in 1591, Muslim visitors were generally peaceful and posed no threat to African chiefs and rulers. They saw clear advantages in Islamisation which helped them build bigger empires and acquire stronger instruments of coercion. They were able to exchange gold and slaves for horses and weapons (steel sword blades and tips for spears, and, at a later stage, guns and gunpowder). Black African traders also saw the advantages of conversion. As converts (dyulas) they became members of an œcumene with free access to markets well beyond their previous horizons. Thus there was a gradual spread of hybrid Islam in black Africa from the eleventh century onwards. Conversion had its main effect on the ruling groups whose insignia and sanctions of power were a mix of Islam and tradition, whilst most of their subjects continued to be animists.

Analysts of state formation in black Africa make a distinction between complex and acephalous groups (see Goody, 1971). There were a great variety of polities within black Africa. The differentiation grew wider as a result of the varying degree of contact with Islam. Slave traders were generally the most Islamised. Slaves tended to be taken from the acephalous, stateless, and least Islamised groups. There were two reasons for this. The Muslim states tended to have the most powerful armed forces, and they generally avoided enslaving Muslims.

The European Encounter with Africa

Between the eleventh and the fourteenth centuries, European contact with Africa took place in the Mediterranean. European merchants were able to buy Asian spices in Alexandria and African gold on the Tunisian coast until the Ottomans captured Egypt and most of North Africa early in the sixteenth century.

Table 6-3. **World Gold Output by Major Region, 1493-1925**
(million fine ounces)

	1493-1600	1601-1700	1701-1800	1801-50	1851-1900	1901-25
Africa	8.153	6.430	5.466	2.025	23.810	200.210
Americas	8.976	19.043	52.014	22.623	140.047	152.463
Europe	4.758	3.215	3.480	6.034	17.379	8.296
Asia			0.085	6.855	49.150	51.900
Australasia					104.859	62.658
Other	1.080	0.161	0.161	0.498	0.986	
World	22.968	28.849	61.206	38.036	336.231	477.527

Note: There are 32 150 fine ounces in a metric ton.
Source: R.H. Rigway, *Summarised Data of Gold Production*, US Dept of Commerce, 1929, p. 6.

Table 6-4. **Akan (Ghanaian) Gold Production and Exports, 1400-1900**
(million fine ounces)

	1400-1500	1501-1600	1601-1700	1701-1800	1801-1900
Production	1.350	2.700	4.200	3.100	2.650
Exports to Maghreb	0.750	1.450	1.000	0.800	0.250
Exports to Europe	0.550	1.150	3.000	2.000	2.650

Note: There are 32 150 fine ounces in a metric ton.
Source: T.F. Garrard, *Akan Weights and the Gold Trade*, Longman, London, 1980, pp. 163-6.

Table 6-5. **Slave Exports from Black Africa, 650-1900, by Destination**
(000)

	650-1500	1500-1800	1800-1900	650-1900
Americas	81	7 766	3 314	11 159
Trans-Sahara	4 270	1 950	1 200	7 420
Asia	2 200	1 000	934	4 134
Total	**6 551**	**10 716**	**5 448**	**22 713**

Source: P.E. Lovejoy (2000), *Transformations in Slavery*, CUP, pp. 19, 26, 47, 142 and 147. His figures for the Americas are bigger than those of Curtin (see Table 4-4). Curtin's total for 1500-1870 is 9.4 million compared to more than 11 here. Part of the difference is that Curtin shows arrivals whereas Lovejoy does not allow for deaths in transit. The difference is also due to Lovejoy's use of the Du Bois archive in Harvard. So far, this appears to be available only as a CDROM, without the meticulously documented description of the source material which Curtin provided.

http://dx.doi.org/10.1787/456125276116

Portugal attacked Morocco in 1415 with intent to conquer and get access to African gold. It captured Ceuta, and, by 1521, established several bases on its Atlantic coast, but Moroccan forces recaptured these in 1541 and in 1578 annihilated a Portuguese invasion force. However, Portuguese innovations in the design of ships and navigational instruments made it possible to circumnavigate Africa and trade directly with India and other Asian destinations from 1497 onwards.

They created a trading base at Arquim on the Mauretanian coast in 1445, where they exchanged cloth, horses, trinkets and salt for gold. In 1482, a strongly fortified base was created at Elmina, on the coast of present day Ghana, which gave better access to the Ashanti gold mines. They succeeded in diverting a substantial part of West African gold exports from the Maghreb (see Table 6–4), and got smaller amounts in East Africa from Mutapa in Northern Zimbabwe. The Portuguese discovered quickly that the disease environment in sub–Saharan Africa was very hostile to European settlement. It was, in fact, the reverse of the situation in the Americas. Europeans had very high mortality from African diseases, but Africans were not particularly susceptible to European diseases.

Portugal created an island settlement at São Tomé (in the Bight of Guinea), where sugar production was developed with slave labour. Portuguese also acted as intermediaries in the slave trade, buying and selling between African coastal markets. With the discovery of the Americas, it became more profitable and healthier for Europeans to expand sugar production in Brazil than in Africa. Portugal became the major slave–trader across the Atlantic.

Although the Portuguese pioneered the export of African slaves for plantation agriculture in the Americas, they did not invent African slavery. Between 650 and 1500, 6.5 million slaves had been shipped from black Africa across the Sahara; to Arabia, the Persian Gulf, and India (see Table 6–5). However the Atlantic trade led to a massive increase in enslavement.

In the course of the seventeenth century, Portuguese slaving activity in Africa met fierce competition from the Dutch, British and French. The British exported more than 2.5 million slaves; most of them from Sierra Leone and the Guinea coast. The French took 1.2 million from the Senegal–Gambia region and the Dutch about half a million, mainly from the Gold Coast. The Portuguese were driven out of these regions and concentrated on shipments from Angola to Brazil and Spanish America. Their total shipments from 1500 to 1870 were about 4.5 million.

In the majority of cases, African traders controlled the slaves until the moment of sale. They brought them to the coast or the riverbanks where they were sold to European traders. Within Africa, slaves were acquired in several ways. Some were the offspring of slaves. A large proportion were captured in wars or were supplied as tribute by subject or dependent tribes. Criminals of various kinds were a steady source. There was large–scale raiding of poorly armed tribes without strong central authorities, and kidnapping of individual victims.

The flow across the Atlantic rose from an average of 9 000 a year in 1662–80 to a peak of 76 000 in 1760–89. Lovejoy shows the average price per slave in constant (1601) prices for 1663–1775. In 1663–82, the average price was £2.9 and £15.4 in 1733–75. African income from slavery therefore appears to have risen more than 40–fold from the end of the seventeenth to the end of the eighteenth century. At their peak, in the late eighteenth century, H.S. Klein (1999), *The Atlantic Slave Trade*, CUP, p. 125, suggests that it probably represented less than 5 per cent of West African income.

The demographic losses were concentrated on tribes and people who were least able to protect themselves. Population growth in black Africa was certainly reduced by slave exports. Between 1500 and 1820 it grew about 0.16 per cent a year compared with 0.26 in Western Europe and 0.29 in Asia. The disruption caused by slavery reduced income in the areas from which slaves were seized. The trade goods which slave exporters received in exchange raised consumption but had little impact on production potential. In the eighteenth century, they included Indian textiles made specially for the West African market, tobacco and alcohol, jewellery, bar iron, weapons, gunpowder and cowrie shells from the Maldives.

Slavery within black Africa rose substantially after the abolition movement reduced the Atlantic flow and the price of slaves dropped. The momentum of enslavement continued, and a much larger proportion of the captives were absorbed within Africa. Lovejoy (2000), pp. 191–210 estimates that, at the end of the nineteenth century, 30–50 per cent of the population of the western, central and Nilotic Sudan were slaves. In the 1850s half the people in the caliphate of Sokoto in northern Nigeria were slaves. In Zanzibar, the slave population rose from 15 000 in 1818 to 100 000 in the 1860s. There was a large increase of slave employment in peasant and plantation agriculture producing palm oil products, peanuts, cloves and cotton for export. In the Belgian Congo, Southeast and South Africa there was a rapid expansion of mining activity at the end of the century, with a servile labour force, whose *de facto* situation was equivalent to slavery.

An important result of Portuguese contact with black Africa was the introduction of crops from the Americas. The most important for the food supply and capacity to expand population were roots and tubers. Cassava (manioc) was brought from Brazil to the Congo, the Niger delta and the Bight of Benin early in the sixteenth century. It had high yields, was rich in starch, calcium, iron and vitamin C. It was a perennial plant, tolerant of a wide variety of soils, invulnerable to locusts, drought resistant and easy to cultivate. It could be left in reserve, unharvested, for long periods in good condition after ripening. Cassava flour could be made into cakes for long distance travel and was a staple food for slaves in transit across the Atlantic. Maize was an American crop which the Portuguese introduced on the west and east African coasts. By the seventeenth century it was present in Senegal, the Congo basin, South Africa and Zanzibar. Sweet potatoes were another significant addition to Africa's food supply.

Over the centuries these crops were widely diffused. In the mid–1960s, threequarters (43 million tons) of African output of roots and tubers came from cassava and sweet potatoes (see FAO, *Production Yearbook*, 1966). Maize (15 million tons) represented a third of black Africa's cereal output, the traditional millet and sorghum 47 per cent, rice 12 per cent and other cereals 8 per cent. Other significant American plants which were important in the long term were beans, peanuts, tobacco and cocoa. Bananas and plantains were Asian crops widely diffused in East Africa before the Portuguese arrived; coffee, tea, rubber and cloves were later introductions from Asia.

European countries did nothing to transmit technical knowledge to Africa, nor did they attempt to promote education, printing, development of alphabets etc. China had printing in the ninth century, Western Europe from 1453, Mexico in 1539, Peru 1584, and the north American colonies from the beginning of the seventeenth century. The first printing press in Africa was established in Cairo in 1822.

In 1820, there were only 50 thousand people of European descent in Africa (half of them at the Cape), compared to 13.4 million in the Americas. Africa had diseases which caused very high rates of mortality to Europeans, though Africans were not particularly susceptible to European diseases. Africans had much better weapons to defend themselves than the indigenous population of the Americas. The situation changed in the nineteenth century. Due to improvements in European weaponry, transport (steamboats and railways) and medicine (quinine), the number of European origin in Africa rose to 2.5 million in 1913.

We should note some African institutions which hindered development, but were not due to European influence. One of these, on which Ibn Khaldun commented at length, was the fragility of the states which emerged in the Muslim world (a point which applies *a fortiori* to black Africa). He demonstrated the persistence of tribal affiliations and lineages, and the continuence of nomadic traditions destructive of attempts to develop sedentary agriculture and urban civilisation. He stressed the cyclical rise and fall of Muslim regimes and saw no measure of progress from the seventh to the fourteenth century in which he lived.

African societies failed to secure property rights. The power elite were autocratic and predatory, which inhibited accumulation of capital and willingness to take business risks. This was very obvious in the Mamluk regime in Egypt. There were few countervailing forces in African societies. Goitein's (1967–93) detailed scrutiny of the Cairo Geniza archive led him to be very upbeat about the emergence of a commercial business class in Fatimid Egypt, but freedom of enterprise was snuffed out in later dynasties. The most striking example of deficient property rights was slavery itself, which was closely linked with the polgygamous family structure and limitation on the rights of women. These two institutions were probably the major impediment to physical and human capital formation.

Evidence and Conjectures on the Pace of Development, 1820–1950

Six Country Sample: Maddison (2001) contained pre–1950 estimates for Egypt, Ghana, Morocco and South Africa. I have added Algeria and Tunisia, and extended the estimates for Egypt and Ghana. Sources for the sample countries were as follows:

Egypt: Population to 1870 from McEvedy and Jones (1978); 1886–1945 from D.C. Mead (1967), *Growth and Structural Change in the Egyptian Economy,* Irwin, Illinois, pp. 295 and 302. GDP 1945–50 from Mead, p.286; 1913–45 from B. Hansen and G.A. Marzouk (1965) *Development and Economic Policy in the UAR* (Egypt), North Holland, Amsterdam, p. 3 for 1913–39, p. 318 for 1939–45; 1886/7–1912 movement of per capita GDP from B. Hansen (1979), "Income and Consumption in Egypt, 1886/1887 to 1937", *International Journal of Middle Eastern Studies,* no. 10, p. 29. 1929–39 GDP movement from B. Hansen (1991), *The Political Economy of Poverty, Equity and Growth: Egypt and Turkey,* OUP, New York, p. 6. Per capita estimate for 1870 derived by logarithmic interpolation between the 1886/7 estimate and my conjecture for 1820.

The last column of Table 6–6 compares my results with the proxy estimates of Tarik Yousef (2002), "Egypt's Growth Performance under Economic Liberalism: A Reassessment with New GDP Estimates, 1886–1945", *Review of Income and Wealth,* 48/4 December, pp. 561–79. He derives nominal GDP by a regression procedure using the money supply and assumed velocity of its circulation. He deflates it with a price index and divides by population. I show his per capita GDP movement linked to my estimate of the 1945 level. Yousef cites a miscellany of sources (including those I have used) to show that the broad contours of his proxy estimates are congruent with direct estimates for the first half of the twentieth century. However, there is a big discrepancy between his 1886–1913 per capita movement and mine. His 1886/7 level seems implausibly low, given the substantial expansion in agricultural output, exports and infrastructure investment between 1820 and the 1880s (which he acknowledges at the beginning of his article).

Table 6-6. **Egyptian Population, GDP and Per Capita GDP, 1820-2001**

	Population (000)	GDP (million 1990 int. $)	Per capita GDP (1990 int. $)	Yousef Proxy per capita GDP (1990 int. $)
1820	4 194	1 992	475	
1870	7 049	4 573	649	
1886/7	7 572	5 443	719	452
1913	12 144	10 950	902	825
1929	14 602	12 744	873	828
1939	16 588	14 790	892	812
1945	18 460	14 790	801	801
1950	21 198	19 288	910	
2001	71 902	215 109	2 992	

http://dx.doi.org/10.1787/456125276116

Algeria, Morocco and Tunisia: GDP from Samir Amin (1966), *l'Économie du Maghreb,* Editions de Minuit, Paris, pp. 104–5. For Algeria, Amin's estimates cover benchmark years between 1880 and 1955. I linked his GDP volume movement to my estimate of the 1955 level in 1990 international dollars; 1870 per capita GDP derived by logarithmic interpolation between his 1880 estimate and my conjecture for 1820, 1913 by interpolation between his figures for 1910 and 1920. I followed a similar procedure for Tunisia and Morocco, where his measures covered 1910–55 and 1920–55 respectively. Algerian population 1820–1930, Tunisian 1820–1913 and Moroccan 1820–1870 from McEvedy and Jones (1978), p. 223.

Table 6.7. Algerian Population, GDP and Per Capita GDP, 1820-2001

	Population (000)	GDP (million 1990 int. $)	Per Capita GDP (1990 int. $)
1820	2 689	1 157	430
1870	3 776	2 700	715
1880	4 183	3 312	792
1910	5 378	6 040	1 123
1913	5 497	6 395	1 163
1920	5 785	7 307	1 263
1930	6 507	8 963	1 377
1950	8 893	12 136	1 365
1955	9 842	14 224	1 445
2001	31 736	89 286	2 813

http://dx.doi.org/10.1787/456125276116

Ghana: R. Szereszewski (1965), *Structural Changes in the Economy of Ghana,* Weidenfeld and Nicolson, London, pp. 74, 92–3, 126, and 149 presents detailed estimates of GDP and population for 1891–1911, and 1960. Table 6–8 links his GDP movement to the 1960 level in 1990 international dollars. 1913 GDP is an extrapolation of his 1901–11 sector growth rates; the 1870 per capita level an interpolation between 1891 and my conjecture for 1820. Population 1820-1870 derived from McEvedy and Jones (1978), p. 245.

Table 6-8. Ghanaian Population, GDP and Per Capita GDP, 1820-2001

	Population (000)	GDP (million 1990 int. $)	Per Capita GDP (1990 int. $)
1820	1 374	570	415
1870	1 500	693	462
1891	1 650	798	484
1901	1 800	960	533
1911	2 000	1 393	697
1913	2 043	1 595	781
1950	5 297	5 943	1 122
1960	6 958	9 591	1 378
2001	19 843	26 012	1 311

http://dx.doi.org/10.1787/456125276116

Szereszewski distinguished between the traditional and modern sectors. He assumed the traditional sector expanded in line with population from 1891–1911 and rose about half in per capita terms from 1911 to 1960. The new components rose nearly 8 per cent a year in the two decades he scrutinised in detail. Cocoa exports rose from 80 lbs. in 1891 to 89 million in 1911, when 600 thousand acres and 185 thousand man–years were absorbed in its production. To a large degree the cocoa boom was sustained by more intensive use of land and previously underemployed rural labour.

The second dynamic element was gold. It had been exported for centuries, and in the 1870s there was a beginning of modern operations. The discovery of huge reserves in South Africa in 1886 sparked an analogous euphoria and investment boom in Ghana. By 1901, 42 companies were operating, and by 1911, a railway connection had been built from the coast to Kumasi through the gold mining areas. There were also improvements in transport facilities from Accra to its cocoa– growing hinterland, investment in modern port facilities in Secondi and Accra, and development of internal river transport by steam launches. The export ratio rose from 8 to 19 per cent of GDP between 1891 and 1911. The main benefits of growth were felt by the locals. In 1911 there were 2 245 Europeans (about 0.1 per cent of the population). In Algeria at that time there were three–quarters of a million European settlers (about 14 per cent of the total).

South Africa: GDP movement 1912–20 from Bureau of Census and Statistics, *Union Statistics for Fifty Years,* Pretoria, 1960; 1920–50 from L.J. Fourie, "Contribution of Factors of Production and Productivity to South African Economic Growth" IARIW, processed, 1971. 1870 per capita GDP level was derived by interpolation of the direct estimate for 1913 and my conjecture for 1820. Although direct GDP estimates are not available, it seems clear that South Africa was the most dynamic of the sample countries from 1820 to 1913. The chief beneficiaries were white settlers. In 1820 they were 30 000 (2 per cent of the population) displacing relatively weak and thinly settled indigenous herdsmen and hunters (Khoisan) in the Cape settlement which was then mainly a staging post for trade with Asia. By 1870 there were quarter of a million whites who had fanned out East and North into Natal, the Orange Free State and Transvaal, taken the best land and water supplies from Xhosa, Zulu and other indigenous groups and exploited various forms of semi–servile labour. In the next twenty years the discovery of diamonds and gold created a boom in investment and immigration. By 1913, there were 1.3 million whites (22 per cent of the population), with an elaborate system of social segregation to buttress their privileged position. Table 6–9 on the expansion of the rail network per head of population provides a clue to the comparative dynamics of African development.

Table 6-9. **Length of Railway Line in Service, 1870-1913**
(kilometres per million population)

	1870	1913
Algeria	70	632
Egypt	168	359
Ghana	0	165
Morocco	0	84
Tunisia	0	1 105
South Africa	0	2 300
Argentina	408	4 374
Australia	861	6 944
India	38	184
United Kingdom	685	715
United States	2 117	9 989

Source: *International Historical Statistics: Africa and Asia,* Macmillan, London, 1982 and Maddison, 1995, p. 64.

http://dx.doi.org/10.1787/456125276116

The top panel of Table 6–10 shows population in the 6 sample countries 1820–2001, the total for the non–sample countries and for Africa as a whole. The pace of population growth, 1820–1950, was about twice as fast in the sample as in the other countries, 1.19 per cent a year compared with 0.77 per cent. Average per capita income in the sample countries in 1950 was more than twice the level in the rest of Africa, as can be seen from the bottom panel, and in 2001, it was more than three times as high.

Table 6-10. African GDP and Population Movement, 1820-2001[a]

Population (000)

	1820	1870	1913	1950	2001
Algeria	2 689	3 776	5 497	8 893	31 736
Egypt	4 194	7 049	12 144	21 198	71 902
Ghana	1 374	1 500	2 043	5 297	19 843
Morocco	2 689	3 776	5 111	9 343	30 645
Tunisia	875	1 176	1 870	3 517	9 705
South Africa	1 550	2 547	6 153	13 596	42 573
6 country total	13 371	19 824	32 818	61 844	206 404
51 other countries	60 865	70 642	91 879	165 489	614 684
African Total	74 236	90 466	124 697	227 333	821 088

GDP (million 1990 international Geary-Khamis $)

	1820	1870	1913	1950	2001
Algeria	*1 157*	*2 700*	6 395	12 136	89 286
Egypt	*1 992*	*4 573*	10 950	19 288	215 109
Ghana	*570*	*693*	1 595	5 943	26 012
Morocco	*1 156*	*2 126*	3 630	13 598	82 255
Tunisia	*376*	*744*	1 651	3 920	45 714
South Africa	*643*	*2 185*	9 857	34 465	179 162
6 country total	*5 894*	*13 021*	*34 078*	89 350	637 538
51 other countries	*25 267*	*32 213*	*45 408*	113 781	585 038
African Total	*31 161*	*45 234*	79 486	203 131	1 222 577

Per Capita GDP (1990 international Geary-Khamis $)

	1820	1870	1913	1950	2001
Algeria	*430*	*715*	1 163	1 365	2 813
Egypt	*475*	*649*	902	910	2 992
Ghana	*415*	*462*	781	1 122	1 311
Morocco	*430*	*563*	*710*	1 455	2 782
Tunisia	*430*	*633*	883	1 115	4 710
South Africa	*415*	*858*	1 602	2 535	4 208
6 country average	*441*	*657*	1 038	1 445	3 089
51 other countries	*415*	*456*	*494*	688	952
African Average	*420*	*500*	637	894	1 489

a) Conjectures are in italics.

http://dx.doi.org/10.1787/456125276116

Per capita income was assumed to increase at the same pace in the non–sample as the average for the sample countries between 1913 and 1950. Non–sample per capita GDP in 1870 is an interpolation between the conjecture for 1820 and that for 1913.

ISBN 92-64-02261-9 – © OECD 2006

Updates for 1950–2001

Annual estimates for 1950–2001 are an update and revision of those for 1950–1998 in Maddison (2001), pp. 310–327; with detail for another nine countries. Population 1950–2001 is from International Programs Center, US Bureau of the Census, October 2002 (USBC at www.census.gov). GDP volume movement 1950–2001 revised and updated for 1993 onwards from IMF, *World Economic Outlook*, September, 2000.

I amalgamated Eritrea and Ethiopia. Eritrea became part of a federation with Ethiopia in 1952. Ten years later it was annexed as a province. It seceded in 1991, and independence was approved in a 1993 referendum. There was a border war 1998–2000. Eritrean population was 6.5 per cent of the total for the two countries in 1950, 6.2 per cent in 2001.

1990 benchmark GDP levels in million 1990 international Geary–Khamis dollars were derived from Penn World Tables version 5.6 in Maddison (2001). Here (see Table 6–11), I have used the new PWT 6.1 (October 2002) and raised the 1990 GDP level for Burkina Faso (from $5 482 to $6 748 million), Burundi (from $3 520 to $3 879), Egypt (from $112 873 to $143 000), Ethiopia and Eritrea (from $18 964 to $29 593), Lesotho (from $1 828 to $2 033), and Zaire from ($17 304 to $19 922).

Table 6-11. **Alternative Estimates of African 1990 GDP Levels by ICP and PWT**
(million international Geary-Khamis dollars)

	PWT 5.5	*PWT 5.6*	*PWT 6.1*	*ICP 5*
Benin	5 248	5 347	4 333	6 629
Botswana	5 479	4 178	6 382	5 662
Cameroon	17 115	14 393	21 881	41 534
Congo	5 972	5 394	3 578	5 358
Côte d'Ivoire	14 568	16 330	20 009	18 528
Egypt	105 684	112 873	143 000	194 267
Ethiopia	17 891	18 964	26 496	18 622
Gabon	3 639	4 500	7 736	n.a.
Guinea	3 087	3 304	13 351	n.a.
Kenya	26 028	26 093	24 354	31 855
Madagascar	9 093	9 210	8 949	8 531
Malawi	4 840	5 146	4 719	6 173
Mali	5 059	6 040	5 878	5 314
Mauritius	7 211	7 652	8 646	7 671
Morocco	60 193	64 082	72 464	83 696
Nigeria	96 521	107 459	94 572	139 453
Rwanda	5 360	6 125	6 050	5 040
Senegal	9 351	10 032	10 298	12 139
Sierra Leone	4 041	4 325	4 571	3 021
Swaziland	1 580	2 154	n.a.	2 181
Tanzania	14 676	13 852	11 043	13 199
Tunisia	26 421	27 387	35 131	35 312
Zambia	6 935	6 432	7 879	10 684
Zimbabwe	14 913	13 766	24 712	20 391

Source: This table compares three sets of PWT estimates with ICP5 results (which are available for only 22 African countries). Col. 1 from annex to R.S. Summers and A. Heston, "The Penn World Table (Mark 5): An Expanded Set of International Comparisons, 1950–1988", *Quarterly Journal of Economics*, May 1991. Col. 2 from their January 1995 diskette. Col. 3 from Alan Heston, Robert Summers and Bettina Aten, PWT Version 6.1, Center for International Comparisons at the University of Pennsylvania (CICUP), October 2002 (http://pwt.econ.upenn.edu). In some cases PWT 5.6 referred to a year before 1990, and in Maddison (2001) I updated using the volume movement of GDP, and the change in the US GDP deflator between that year and 1990. I also made proxy estimates for Libya, Equatorial Guinea, Mayotte, St. Helena, São Tomé & Principe, and W. Sahara. Although some PWT 6.1 estimates are lower than those of 5.6, the overall result for the 45 countries now available is to raise African GDP by 28 percent. Italics indicate countries where the GDP level has been raised. Other striking cases are a 63 percent rise for South Africa and a 47 percent rise for Algeria. As some of the changes are very large, I prefer to wait until a further PWT round is available before adopting the new African estimates *en bloc*. I have adopted 6.1 estimates for Burkina Faso, Burundi, Egypt, Ethiopia and Eritrea, Lesotho and Zaire, as PWT 5.6 estimates seemed implausibly low. ICP 5 from UN/Eurostat, *World Comparisons of Real GDP and Purchasing Power 1985*, New York, 1994, p. 5. adjusted to a 1990 basis.

http://dx.doi.org/10.1787/456125276116

Table 6a. **Population of 57 African Countries, 1950-2003**
(000 at mid-year)

	Algeria	Angola	Benin	Botswana	Burkina Faso	Burundi	Cameroon	Cape Verde
1950	8 893	4 118	1 673	430	4 376	2 363	4 888	146
1951	9 073	4 173	1 705	436	4 423	2 403	4 947	151
1952	9 280	4 232	1 738	442	4 470	2 445	5 009	155
1953	9 532	4 294	1 773	448	4 518	2 487	5 074	160
1954	9 611	4 358	1 809	455	4 566	2 531	5 141	164
1955	9 842	4 423	1 846	461	4 614	2 575	5 211	169
1956	10 057	4 491	1 885	468	4 664	2 619	5 284	174
1957	10 271	4 561	1 925	475	4 713	2 665	5 360	180
1958	10 485	4 636	1 967	482	4 764	2 712	5 439	185
1959	10 696	4 715	2 010	489	4 814	2 760	5 522	191
1960	10 909	4 797	2 055	497	4 866	2 812	5 609	197
1961	11 122	4 752	2 102	505	4 920	2 890	5 699	203
1962	11 001	4 826	2 152	513	4 978	2 957	5 794	210
1963	11 273	4 920	2 203	521	5 041	3 003	5 892	217
1964	11 613	5 026	2 256	530	5 109	3 083	5 996	224
1965	11 963	5 135	2 311	538	5 182	3 164	6 104	232
1966	12 339	5 201	2 368	546	5 261	3 247	6 217	239
1967	12 760	5 247	2 427	554	5 344	3 323	6 336	247
1968	13 146	5 350	2 489	562	5 434	3 393	6 460	254
1969	13 528	5 472	2 553	572	5 529	3 451	6 590	262
1970	13 932	5 606	2 620	584	5 626	3 513	6 727	269
1971	14 335	5 751	2 689	600	5 726	3 587	6 870	273
1972	14 761	5 891	2 761	620	5 833	3 520	7 021	275
1973	15 198	6 021	2 836	645	5 947	3 529	7 179	277
1974	15 653	5 978	2 914	675	6 069	3 583	7 346	279
1975	16 140	5 879	2 996	709	6 199	3 664	7 522	280
1976	16 635	5 938	3 080	748	6 336	3 736	7 721	283
1977	17 153	6 161	3 168	789	6 478	3 821	7 960	286
1978	17 703	6 279	3 260	832	6 626	3 915	8 207	289
1979	18 266	6 450	3 355	874	6 780	4 013	8 451	292
1980	18 862	6 736	3 444	914	6 942	4 138	8 748	296
1981	19 484	6 877	3 540	950	7 111	4 214	9 024	300
1982	20 132	7 020	3 641	986	7 288	4 344	9 251	305
1983	20 803	7 143	3 748	1 023	7 474	4 531	9 522	309
1984	21 488	7 256	3 861	1 063	7 670	4 668	9 816	314
1985	22 182	7 399	3 980	1 103	7 876	4 809	10 130	319
1986	22 844	7 544	4 104	1 145	8 072	4 952	10 457	325
1987	23 485	7 669	4 234	1 189	8 275	5 110	10 779	331
1988	24 102	7 805	4 371	1 232	8 517	5 284	11 096	337
1989	24 722	7 919	4 513	1 273	8 799	5 459	11 390	343
1990	25 341	8 049	4 662	1 312	9 090	5 285	11 685	349
1991	25 958	8 237	4 817	1 349	9 390	5 393	12 006	356
1992	26 570	8 472	4 976	1 384	9 701	5 478	12 323	362
1993	27 176	8 689	5 140	1 418	10 005	5 590	12 635	368
1994	27 775	8 894	5 309	1 451	10 302	5 761	12 942	373
1995	28 364	9 218	5 484	1 481	10 608	5 392	13 245	379
1996	28 946	9 443	5 664	1 509	10 922	5 366	13 547	384
1997	29 521	9 560	5 848	1 533	11 242	5 405	13 853	388
1998	30 088	9 736	6 037	1 554	11 564	5 487	14 162	393
1999	30 646	9 922	6 230	1 569	11 889	5 603	14 475	397
2000	31 194	10 132	6 428	1 578	12 217	5 714	14 792	401
2001	31 736	10 342	6 630	1 581	12 549	5 838	15 110	405
2002	32 278	10 554	6 835	1 579	12 887	5 965	15 428	409
2003	32 819	10 766	7 041	1 573	13 228	6 096	15 746	412

http://dx.doi.org/10.1787/456125276116

ISBN 92-64-02261-9 – © OECD 2006

Table 6a. **Population of 57 African Countries, 1950-2003**
(000 at mid-year)

	Central African Rep.	Chad	Comoros	Congo	Côte d'Ivoire	Djibouti	Egypt	Eritrea and Ethiopia	Gabon
1950	1 260	2 608	148	768	2 860	60	21 198	21 577	416
1951	1 275	2 644	151	781	2 918	62	21 704	21 939	418
1952	1 292	2 682	154	794	2 977	63	22 223	22 314	421
1953	1 309	2 722	157	809	3 037	65	22 755	22 703	423
1954	1 328	2 763	160	824	3 099	66	23 299	23 107	426
1955	1 348	2 805	164	840	3 164	68	23 856	23 526	429
1956	1 370	2 849	167	856	3 231	70	24 426	23 961	432
1957	1 392	2 895	171	874	3 300	72	25 010	24 412	435
1958	1 416	2 942	175	892	3 374	74	25 608	24 880	438
1959	1 441	2 991	179	911	3 463	76	26 220	25 364	442
1960	1 467	3 042	183	931	3 576	78	26 847	25 864	446
1961	1 495	3 095	187	952	3 700	84	27 523	26 380	450
1962	1 523	3 150	192	974	3 832	90	28 173	26 913	456
1963	1 553	3 208	196	996	3 985	96	28 821	27 464	461
1964	1 585	3 271	201	1 020	4 148	103	29 533	28 034	468
1965	1 628	3 345	206	1 044	4 327	111	30 265	28 621	474
1966	1 683	3 420	212	1 070	4 527	119	30 986	29 228	482
1967	1 729	3 496	217	1 097	4 745	128	31 681	29 839	489
1968	1 756	3 573	223	1 124	4 984	137	32 338	30 480	497
1969	1 785	3 650	230	1 153	5 235	147	32 966	31 154	504
1970	1 827	3 731	236	1 183	5 504	158	33 574	31 826	515
1971	1 869	3 814	243	1 214	5 786	169	34 184	32 519	526
1972	1 910	3 899	250	1 246	6 072	179	34 807	33 257	538
1973	1 945	3 989	257	1 279	6 352	189	35 480	34 028	561
1974	1 983	4 082	265	1 314	6 622	198	36 216	34 838	597
1975	2 031	4 180	273	1 360	6 889	208	36 952	35 673	648
1976	2 071	4 282	281	1 409	7 151	217	37 737	36 588	688
1977	2 111	4 389	305	1 461	7 419	229	38 784	37 443	706
1978	2 153	4 499	314	1 515	7 692	248	40 020	38 084	726
1979	2 197	4 544	324	1 571	7 973	263	41 258	38 568	722
1980	2 244	4 542	334	1 629	8 261	279	42 634	38 967	714
1981	2 291	4 648	341	1 691	8 558	294	44 196	39 555	731
1982	2 338	4 877	349	1 755	8 866	306	45 682	40 463	754
1983	2 385	5 074	357	1 822	9 185	316	47 093	41 565	779
1984	2 451	5 125	366	1 901	9 517	289	48 550	42 815	805
1985	2 516	5 170	375	1 955	9 864	297	50 052	43 448	833
1986	2 556	5 316	385	2 010	10 221	304	51 593	44 434	859
1987	2 600	5 502	395	2 067	10 585	311	52 799	45 816	881
1988	2 654	5 678	406	2 123	10 956	327	54 024	47 439	900
1989	2 728	5 834	417	2 181	11 361	350	55 263	49 174	919
1990	2 803	6 030	429	2 240	11 901	366	56 694	50 902	938
1991	2 882	6 242	441	2 298	12 421	375	58 139	53 199	961
1992	2 964	6 443	454	2 356	12 775	384	59 402	55 240	987
1993	3 053	6 675	468	2 415	13 185	393	60 677	56 537	1 014
1994	3 139	6 912	482	2 474	13 669	403	61 983	57 967	1 041
1995	3 204	7 138	497	2 532	14 115	409	63 322	59 511	1 070
1996	3 262	7 374	512	2 590	14 503	414	64 705	61 042	1 099
1997	3 322	7 619	528	2 647	14 830	418	66 134	62 536	1 129
1998	3 383	7 875	544	2 703	15 119	422	67 602	64 004	1 160
1999	3 442	8 144	561	2 757	15 475	427	69 067	65 502	1 191
2000	3 501	8 419	578	2 809	15 866	431	70 492	66 895	1 223
2001	3 562	8 693	596	2 860	16 234	438	71 902	68 208	1 255
2002	3 623	8 971	614	2 908	16 598	447	73 313	69 560	1 288
2003	3 684	9 253	633	2 954	16 962	457	74 719	70 920	1 322

http://dx.doi.org/10.1787/456125276116

Table 6a. Population of 57 African Countries, 1950-2003
(000 at mid-year)

	Gambia	Ghana	Guinea	Guinea Bissau	Kenya	Lesotho	Liberia	Madagascar
1950	271	5 297	2 586	573	6 121	726	824	4 620
1951	278	5 437	2 625	577	6 289	737	843	4 690
1952	284	5 581	2 664	581	6 464	749	863	4 763
1953	291	5 731	2 705	584	6 646	761	884	4 839
1954	299	5 887	2 745	588	6 836	773	906	4 919
1955	306	6 049	2 787	592	7 034	786	928	5 003
1956	315	6 217	2 831	596	7 240	800	952	5 090
1957	323	6 391	2 877	601	7 455	813	976	5 182
1958	332	6 573	2 925	606	7 679	828	1 001	5 277
1959	342	6 761	2 975	611	7 913	843	1 028	5 378
1960	352	6 958	3 028	617	8 157	859	1 055	5 482
1961	363	7 154	3 083	622	8 412	875	1 083	5 590
1962	374	7 355	3 140	628	8 679	893	1 113	5 703
1963	386	7 564	3 199	634	8 957	912	1 144	5 821
1964	399	7 782	3 259	610	9 248	932	1 175	5 944
1965	412	8 010	3 321	604	9 549	952	1 209	6 070
1966	426	8 245	3 385	598	9 864	974	1 243	6 200
1967	440	8 490	3 451	601	10 192	996	1 279	6 335
1968	454	8 744	3 519	611	10 532	1 019	1 317	6 473
1969	469	9 009	3 589	616	10 888	1 043	1 356	6 616
1970	485	8 789	3 661	620	11 272	1 067	1 397	6 766
1971	501	9 066	3 735	623	11 685	1 092	1 439	6 920
1972	517	9 354	3 811	625	12 126	1 117	1 483	7 082
1973	534	9 650	3 890	633	12 594	1 142	1 528	7 250
1974	552	9 905	3 970	640	13 090	1 169	1 575	7 424
1975	570	10 119	4 053	681	13 615	1 195	1 624	7 604
1976	589	10 333	4 139	733	14 171	1 223	1 675	7 805
1977	608	10 538	4 227	745	14 762	1 252	1 727	8 007
1978	628	10 721	4 318	758	15 386	1 281	1 780	8 217
1979	649	10 878	4 411	771	16 045	1 312	1 835	8 442
1980	671	11 016	4 508	789	16 698	1 344	1 892	8 677
1981	693	11 177	4 607	807	17 369	1 377	1 951	8 920
1982	716	11 401	4 710	826	18 059	1 412	2 011	9 171
1983	739	12 157	4 816	846	18 769	1 447	2 074	9 432
1984	767	12 829	5 046	865	19 499	1 484	2 138	9 702
1985	796	13 228	5 327	886	20 247	1 521	2 205	9 981
1986	827	13 778	5 504	906	21 006	1 559	2 274	10 270
1987	858	14 170	5 650	928	21 761	1 596	2 345	10 569
1988	891	14 569	5 800	950	22 504	1 631	2 418	10 877
1989	926	14 977	5 955	973	23 229	1 664	2 493	11 194
1990	962	15 400	6 280	996	23 934	1 693	2 189	11 522
1991	999	15 837	6 727	1 020	24 670	1 718	1 892	11 860
1992	1 036	16 278	6 988	1 051	25 524	1 740	1 985	12 210
1993	1 075	16 784	7 194	1 084	26 269	1 760	2 063	12 573
1994	1 115	17 272	7 429	1 116	26 852	1 778	2 057	12 950
1995	1 156	17 668	7 682	1 142	27 463	1 794	1 980	13 340
1996	1 197	18 046	7 949	1 165	28 074	1 807	2 025	13 746
1997	1 238	18 419	8 048	1 193	28 681	1 820	2 296	14 165
1998	1 281	18 795	8 176	1 221	29 266	1 830	2 655	14 598
1999	1 324	19 159	8 434	1 250	29 811	1 840	2 974	15 045
2000	1 367	19 509	8 642	1 278	30 310	1 847	3 149	15 506
2001	1 411	19 843	8 717	1 306	30 777	1 853	3 206	15 983
2002	1 456	20 163	8 816	1 333	31 223	1 858	3 262	16 473
2003	1 501	20 468	9 030	1 361	31 639	1 862	3 317	16 980

http://dx.doi.org/10.1787/456125276116

Table 6a. **Population of 57 African Countries, 1950-2003**
(000 at mid-year)

	Malawi	Mali	Mauritania	Mauritius	Morocco	Mozambique	Namibia	Niger	Nigeria
1950	2 817	3 688	1 006	481	9 343	6 250	464	2 482	31 797
1951	2 866	3 761	1 014	499	9 634	6 346	475	2 538	32 449
1952	2 918	3 835	1 023	517	9 939	6 446	486	2 597	33 119
1953	2 972	3 911	1 032	536	10 206	6 552	497	2 659	33 809
1954	3 029	3 988	1 042	554	10 487	6 664	509	2 723	34 632
1955	3 088	4 067	1 053	572	10 782	6 782	522	2 790	35 464
1956	3 152	4 148	1 065	592	11 089	6 906	535	2 859	36 311
1957	3 221	4 230	1 077	610	11 406	7 038	548	2 931	37 178
1958	3 295	4 314	1 090	628	11 735	7 177	562	3 007	38 068
1959	3 370	4 399	1 103	645	12 074	7 321	576	3 085	38 981
1960	3 450	4 486	1 117	663	12 423	7 472	591	3 168	39 920
1961	3 532	4 576	1 132	681	12 736	7 628	606	3 253	40 884
1962	3 629	4 668	1 147	701	13 057	7 789	621	3 343	41 876
1963	3 726	4 763	1 162	715	13 385	7 957	637	3 437	42 897
1964	3 816	4 862	1 178	736	13 722	8 127	654	3 533	43 946
1965	3 914	4 963	1 195	756	14 066	8 301	671	3 633	45 025
1966	4 023	5 068	1 212	774	14 415	8 486	689	3 735	46 143
1967	4 147	5 177	1 231	789	14 770	8 681	707	3 842	47 305
1968	4 264	5 289	1 249	804	15 137	8 884	725	3 951	48 515
1969	4 379	5 405	1 269	816	15 517	9 093	745	4 064	49 776
1970	4 489	5 525	1 289	830	15 909	9 304	765	4 182	51 113
1971	4 606	5 649	1 311	841	16 313	9 539	786	4 303	52 495
1972	4 731	5 777	1 333	851	16 661	9 810	808	4 429	53 914
1973	4 865	5 909	1 356	861	16 998	10 088	831	4 559	55 415
1974	5 031	6 046	1 380	873	17 335	10 370	854	4 695	57 084
1975	5 268	6 188	1 404	885	17 687	10 433	879	4 836	58 916
1976	5 473	6 334	1 430	898	18 043	10 770	905	4 984	60 819
1977	5 637	6 422	1 457	913	18 397	11 128	923	5 139	62 822
1978	5 792	6 517	1 485	929	18 758	11 466	935	5 294	64 953
1979	5 956	6 620	1 516	947	19 126	11 828	955	5 459	67 224
1980	6 129	6 731	1 550	964	19 487	12 103	975	5 629	69 629
1981	6 311	6 849	1 585	979	19 846	12 364	988	5 806	72 092
1982	6 503	6 975	1 622	992	20 199	12 588	1 011	5 988	74 538
1983	6 703	7 110	1 662	1 002	20 740	12 775	1 045	6 189	75 901
1984	6 909	7 255	1 703	1 012	21 296	12 926	1 080	6 389	77 544
1985	7 124	7 408	1 747	1 022	21 857	13 065	1 116	6 589	79 884
1986	7 391	7 569	1 793	1 032	22 422	13 143	1 154	6 802	81 971
1987	7 817	7 738	1 841	1 043	22 987	12 889	1 196	7 016	84 505
1988	8 327	7 884	1 892	1 052	23 555	12 517	1 256	7 237	87 115
1989	8 800	8 050	1 937	1 063	24 122	12 467	1 339	7 428	89 801
1990	9 215	8 228	1 984	1 074	24 686	12 649	1 409	7 630	92 566
1991	9 549	8 412	2 041	1 085	25 244	12 912	1 450	7 844	95 390
1992	9 871	8 565	2 119	1 096	25 798	13 149	1 491	8 069	98 270
1993	9 997	8 719	2 205	1 107	26 351	13 638	1 532	8 307	101 227
1994	9 767	8 911	2 279	1 118	26 901	14 663	1 575	8 557	104 260
1995	9 656	9 157	2 342	1 129	27 447	15 522	1 618	8 819	107 372
1996	9 855	9 452	2 389	1 139	27 990	15 898	1 661	9 085	110 552
1997	10 103	9 746	2 445	1 150	28 530	16 184	1 704	9 345	113 787
1998	10 356	10 054	2 515	1 160	29 066	16 453	1 746	9 611	117 072
1999	10 613	10 360	2 591	1 169	29 597	16 704	1 787	9 888	120 397
2000	10 874	10 665	2 668	1 179	30 122	16 934	1 826	10 174	123 750
2001	11 134	10 980	2 747	1 190	30 645	17 142	1 863	10 465	127 120
2002	11 393	11 300	2 829	1 200	31 168	17 324	1 897	10 760	130 500
2003	11 651	11 626	2 913	1 210	31 689	17 479	1 927	11 059	133 882

http://dx.doi.org/10.1787/456125276116

Table 6a. Population of 57 African Countries, 1950-2003
(000 at mid-year)

	Reunion	Rwanda	Senegal	Seychelles	Sierra Leone	Somalia	South Africa	Sudan	Swaziland
1950	244	2 439	2 654	33	2 087	2 438	13 596	8 051	277
1951	251	2 486	2 703	33	2 115	2 482	13 926	8 275	284
1952	258	2 535	2 756	33	2 143	2 527	14 265	8 505	290
1953	266	2 587	2 810	34	2 172	2 574	14 624	8 741	297
1954	274	2 641	2 867	35	2 202	2 623	14 992	8 984	304
1955	286	2 698	2 927	36	2 233	2 673	15 369	9 233	311
1956	296	2 759	2 989	38	2 264	2 726	15 755	9 490	319
1957	309	2 822	3 055	38	2 296	2 780	16 152	9 753	327
1958	318	2 889	3 123	39	2 328	2 837	16 558	10 024	335
1959	327	2 959	3 195	40	2 362	2 895	16 975	10 303	343
1960	338	3 032	3 270	42	2 396	2 956	17 417	10 589	352
1961	348	3 046	3 348	43	2 432	3 017	17 870	10 882	361
1962	359	3 051	3 430	44	2 468	3 080	18 357	11 183	370
1963	371	3 129	3 516	45	2 505	3 145	18 857	11 493	380
1964	384	3 184	3 636	47	2 543	3 213	19 371	11 801	389
1965	393	3 265	3 744	48	2 582	3 283	19 898	12 086	399
1966	403	3 358	3 857	49	2 622	3 354	20 440	12 377	410
1967	414	3 451	3 966	50	2 662	3 429	20 997	12 716	421
1968	425	3 548	4 074	51	2 704	3 506	21 569	13 059	432
1969	436	3 657	4 193	53	2 746	3 585	22 157	13 403	443
1970	445	3 769	4 318	54	2 789	3 667	22 740	13 788	455
1971	453	3 880	4 450	56	2 834	3 752	23 338	14 182	467
1972	462	3 992	4 589	57	2 879	3 840	23 936	14 597	480
1973	469	4 110	4 727	58	2 925	3 932	24 549	15 113	493
1974	475	4 226	4 872	59	2 974	4 027	25 179	15 571	507
1975	481	4 357	4 989	61	3 027	4 128	25 815	16 056	521
1976	487	4 502	5 101	62	3 083	4 238	26 468	16 570	536
1977	492	4 657	5 232	63	3 141	4 354	27 130	17 105	551
1978	497	4 819	5 365	64	3 201	4 678	27 809	17 712	568
1979	502	4 976	5 501	65	3 263	5 309	28 506	18 387	588
1980	507	5 139	5 640	66	3 327	5 791	29 252	19 064	611
1981	512	5 311	5 783	68	3 394	5 825	30 018	19 702	631
1982	518	5 510	5 930	68	3 465	5 829	30 829	20 367	650
1983	523	5 705	6 082	69	3 538	6 003	31 664	21 751	673
1984	533	5 868	6 239	70	3 615	6 207	32 523	22 543	697
1985	542	6 023	6 400	71	3 696	6 446	33 406	23 454	722
1986	551	6 186	6 568	71	3 781	6 700	34 156	24 171	751
1987	562	6 375	6 740	72	3 870	6 922	34 894	24 726	779
1988	574	6 584	6 918	72	3 963	6 900	35 640	25 240	817
1989	585	6 781	7 137	73	4 061	6 748	36 406	25 838	852
1990	597	6 962	7 362	73	4 226	6 675	37 191	26 627	885
1991	610	7 150	7 592	74	4 340	6 448	37 924	27 446	926
1992	622	7 328	7 821	75	4 270	6 100	38 656	28 228	963
1993	635	7 489	8 050	76	4 229	6 060	39 271	28 964	992
1994	647	6 441	8 284	76	4 332	6 178	39 762	29 771	997
1995	660	5 723	8 525	77	4 507	6 291	40 256	30 567	1 005
1996	672	6 008	8 774	78	4 633	6 461	40 723	31 307	1 031
1997	685	7 199	9 022	78	4 727	6 634	41 194	32 161	1 057
1998	697	7 159	9 273	78	4 895	6 843	41 658	33 108	1 080
1999	709	7 291	9 527	79	5 053	7 044	42 048	34 085	1 101
2000	721	7 405	9 784	79	5 203	7 253	42 351	35 080	1 120
2001	733	7 532	10 046	80	5 388	7 489	42 573	36 080	1 136
2002	744	7 668	10 311	80	5 565	7 753	42 716	37 090	1 150
2003	755	7 810	10 580	80	5 733	8 025	42 769	38 114	1 161

http://dx.doi.org/10.1787/456125276116

Table 6a. **Population of 57 African Countries, 1950-2003**
(000 at mid-year)

	Tanzania	Togo	Tunisia	Uganda	Zaire	Zambia	Zimbabwe	6 Country Total	57 Country Total
1950	7 935	1 172	3 517	5 522	13 569	2 553	2 853	1 266	227 333
1951	8 125	1 195	3 583	5 671	13 819	2 611	2 951	1 299	232 068
1952	8 323	1 219	3 648	5 825	14 075	2 672	3 081	1 334	237 008
1953	8 529	1 244	3 713	5 983	14 335	2 734	3 191	1 370	242 086
1954	8 745	1 271	3 779	6 148	14 605	2 800	3 307	1 409	247 273
1955	8 971	1 298	3 846	6 317	14 886	2 869	3 409	1 451	252 759
1956	9 206	1 327	3 903	6 493	15 178	2 941	3 530	1 496	258 409
1957	9 453	1 357	3 951	6 676	15 481	3 016	3 646	1 543	264 222
1958	9 711	1 389	4 007	6 864	15 796	3 094	3 764	1 592	270 231
1959	9 979	1 422	4 075	7 059	16 123	3 173	3 887	1 645	276 454
1960	10 260	1 456	4 149	7 262	16 462	3 254	4 011	1 701	282 919
1961	10 555	1 491	4 216	7 472	16 798	3 337	4 140	1 760	289 385
1962	10 864	1 528	4 287	7 689	17 300	3 421	4 278	1 819	295 977
1963	11 185	1 566	4 374	7 914	17 819	3 508	4 412	1 882	303 251
1964	11 522	1 606	4 468	8 147	18 203	3 599	4 537	1 951	310 725
1965	11 870	1 648	4 566	8 389	18 604	3 694	4 685	2 022	318 478
1966	12 231	1 691	4 676	8 640	19 068	3 794	4 836	2 103	326 534
1967	12 607	1 736	4 787	8 900	19 640	3 900	4 995	2 179	334 945
1968	12 999	1 782	4 894	9 170	20 242	4 009	5 172	2 266	343 591
1969	13 412	1 830	4 996	9 450	20 822	4 123	5 353	2 368	352 457
1970	13 842	1 964	5 099	9 728	21 395	4 252	5 515	2 458	361 168
1971	14 285	2 019	5 198	9 984	21 969	4 376	5 684	2 546	370 534
1972	14 769	2 075	5 304	10 191	22 559	4 506	5 861	2 659	380 026
1973	15 279	2 133	5 426	10 386	23 186	4 643	6 002	2 783	390 034
1974	15 775	2 192	5 556	10 621	23 810	4 785	6 173	2 903	400 314
1975	16 258	2 254	5 704	10 891	24 467	4 924	6 342	2 992	410 827
1976	16 754	2 317	5 859	11 171	25 175	5 067	6 496	3 078	422 188
1977	17 276	2 382	6 005	11 459	25 776	5 217	6 642	3 148	433 995
1978	17 814	2 450	6 136	11 757	26 462	5 371	6 767	3 239	446 294
1979	18 355	2 521	6 280	12 034	27 418	5 532	6 887	3 413	459 413
1980	18 915	2 596	6 443	12 298	28 129	5 700	7 170	3 600	472 721
1981	19 496	2 686	6 606	12 597	28 821	5 885	7 429	3 772	486 060
1982	20 093	2 777	6 734	12 941	29 780	6 101	7 637	3 944	500 253
1983	20 718	2 875	6 860	13 323	30 536	6 339	7 930	4 110	515 235
1984	21 367	2 979	7 185	13 765	31 280	6 565	8 243	4 276	530 353
1985	22 036	3 088	7 362	14 232	32 260	6 783	8 562	4 347	545 742
1986	22 732	3 202	7 545	14 746	33 302	7 026	8 879	4 391	561 280
1987	23 485	3 321	7 725	15 348	34 409	7 268	9 217	4 509	577 158
1988	24 236	3 446	7 895	15 991	35 564	7 483	9 558	4 644	593 250
1989	24 946	3 574	8 053	16 633	36 742	7 683	9 865	4 779	609 818
1990	25 651	3 705	8 207	17 242	37 969	7 876	10 154	4 915	626 814
1991	26 376	3 837	8 364	17 857	39 270	8 068	10 439	5 051	644 889
1992	27 134	3 972	8 523	18 499	40 530	8 262	10 729	5 188	662 410
1993	28 029	3 960	8 680	19 193	41 844	8 452	10 997	5 324	679 567
1994	29 096	4 001	8 831	19 897	43 256	8 641	11 127	5 459	696 273
1995	30 016	4 229	8 972	20 455	45 706	8 827	11 233	5 554	713 856
1996	30 618	4 435	9 105	20 984	46 623	9 010	11 436	5 614	730 822
1997	31 282	4 612	9 234	21 599	47 451	9 206	11 643	5 715	748 865
1998	32 098	4 759	9 359	22 221	48 831	9 397	11 839	5 858	766 842
1999	32 920	4 897	9 479	22 855	50 288	9 590	12 022	6 006	785 235
2000	33 768	5 033	9 593	23 496	51 810	9 799	12 186	6 158	803 311
2001	34 583	5 167	9 705	24 170	53 455	9 986	12 332	6 313	821 088
2002	35 302	5 299	9 816	24 889	55 042	10 149	12 463	6 471	838 720
2003	35 922	5 429	9 925	25 633	56 625	10 307	12 577	6 633	856 261

http://dx.doi.org/10.1787/456125276116

Table 6a. **Population of 57 African Countries, 1950-2003**
(000 at mid-year)

	Equatorial Guinea	Libya	SãoTomé & Principe	Mayotte + St. Helena + W. Sahara	6 Country Total
1950	211	961	60	34	1 266
1951	214	990	60	36	1 299
1952	217	1 020	60	37	1 334
1953	220	1 052	60	39	1 370
1954	223	1 086	60	40	1 409
1955	226	1 122	60	42	1 451
1956	229	1 161	61	45	1 496
1957	233	1 202	61	47	1 543
1958	237	1 245	62	49	1 592
1959	240	1 290	63	52	1 645
1960	244	1 338	63	55	1 701
1961	248	1 389	64	59	1 760
1962	249	1 442	65	63	1 819
1963	250	1 499	66	67	1 882
1964	252	1 560	67	72	1 951
1965	253	1 624	69	77	2 022
1966	256	1 694	70	83	2 103
1967	260	1 759	71	90	2 179
1968	263	1 834	72	97	2 266
1969	267	1 923	73	105	2 368
1970	270	1 999	74	114	2 458
1971	274	2 077	75	120	2 546
1972	278	2 184	77	121	2 659
1973	271	2 312	78	121	2 783
1974	250	2 451	80	122	2 903
1975	213	2 570	82	128	2 992
1976	191	2 666	84	137	3 078
1977	193	2 722	87	147	3 148
1978	195	2 797	89	158	3 239
1979	221	2 929	92	171	3 413
1980	256	3 065	94	184	3 600
1981	272	3 204	96	199	3 772
1982	285	3 344	99	216	3 944
1983	300	3 485	101	225	4 110
1984	314	3 625	103	233	4 276
1985	325	3 675	106	242	4 347
1986	333	3 700	108	250	4 391
1987	341	3 800	111	258	4 509
1988	350	3 913	114	267	4 644
1989	359	4 027	116	277	4 779
1990	368	4 140	119	288	4 915
1991	378	4 252	123	298	5 051
1992	388	4 365	126	309	5 188
1993	398	4 476	129	321	5 324
1994	408	4 585	133	332	5 459
1995	418	4 654	137	344	5 554
1996	429	4 686	141	357	5 614
1997	440	4 760	146	369	5 715
1998	451	4 875	150	382	5 858
1999	463	4 993	155	395	6 006
2000	474	5 115	160	408	6 158
2001	486	5 241	165	421	6 313
2002	498	5 369	170	434	6 471
2003	510	5 499	176	448	6 633

http://dx.doi.org/10.1787/456125276116

Table 6b. **GDP Levels in 57 African Countries, 1950-2001**
(million 1990 international Geary-Khamis dollars)

	Algeria	Angola	Benin	Botswana	Burkina Faso	Burundi	Cameroon	Cape Verde
1950	12 136	4 331	1 813	150	2 076	851	3 279	66
1951	12 221	4 491	1 813	155	2 155	899	3 401	69
1952	12 767	4 660	1 813	159	2 233	927	3 525	71
1953	13 046	4 833	1 762	164	2 314	965	3 653	75
1954	13 811	4 703	1 813	169	2 399	1 018	3 788	76
1955	14 224	5 080	1 813	174	2 489	1 050	3 929	78
1956	15 619	4 985	1 813	179	2 582	1 090	4 073	82
1957	17 391	5 461	1 813	184	2 676	1 132	4 224	81
1958	18 022	5 751	1 880	189	2 777	1 163	4 381	83
1959	21 323	5 777	1 950	195	2 877	1 230	4 542	93
1960	22 780	6 011	2 010	200	2 962	1 249	4 666	100
1961	20 013	6 635	2 075	207	3 080	1 078	4 722	107
1962	15 765	6 444	2 005	213	3 269	1 176	4 867	113
1963	19 928	6 791	2 097	220	3 228	1 224	5 047	120
1964	20 971	7 587	2 240	228	3 302	1 298	5 227	127
1965	22 367	8 194	2 356	235	3 429	1 347	5 332	133
1966	21 287	8 635	2 443	258	3 446	1 409	5 581	140
1967	23 277	9 064	2 467	284	3 749	1 537	5 736	147
1968	25 996	8 947	2 561	313	3 865	1 520	6 109	153
1969	28 484	9 255	2 637	344	3 942	1 501	6 411	160
1970	31 336	9 909	2 692	378	3 950	1 902	6 605	166
1971	28 666	9 943	2 704	448	4 106	2 052	6 801	155
1972	34 685	10 091	2 942	592	4 272	1 831	7 096	148
1973	35 814	10 784	3 011	722	4 045	1 963	7 201	147
1974	37 999	10 242	2 784	873	3 969	1 947	7 523	143
1975	40 705	6 314	2 904	862	3 798	1 966	7 910	147
1976	43 387	5 669	3 029	1 024	3 761	2 121	8 061	147
1977	47 319	5 799	3 199	1 061	4 027	2 383	8 520	148
1978	53 387	6 037	3 301	1 264	4 496	2 357	8 985	164
1979	58 193	6 184	3 565	1 391	4 542	2 404	9 474	182
1980	59 273	6 483	3 901	1 589	4 616	2 594	10 441	249
1981	60 766	6 353	4 122	1 736	4 820	2 877	12 222	271
1982	64 662	6 050	4 566	1 865	4 926	2 865	13 147	279
1983	68 012	5 851	4 366	2 159	4 870	2 954	14 068	306
1984	71 774	5 881	4 713	2 400	4 948	2 951	15 170	317
1985	75 512	5 911	5 068	2 577	5 596	3 295	16 528	345
1986	74 747	5 379	5 182	2 773	6 474	3 421	17 722	355
1987	74 225	5 985	5 104	3 017	6 364	3 562	16 839	380
1988	72 672	6 843	5 258	3 492	6 893	3 694	16 072	392
1989	75 123	6 959	5 144	3 944	6 814	3 747	14 632	413
1990	73 934	7 202	5 347	4 178	6 748	3 879	14 393	430
1991	73 047	7 252	5 598	4 379	7 423	4 073	13 846	283
1992	74 216	7 180	5 822	4 510	7 608	4 101	13 417	231
1993	72 583	5 241	6 026	4 600	7 548	3 859	12 987	434
1994	71 929	5 310	6 291	4 761	7 654	3 716	12 662	463
1995	74 663	5 861	6 581	4 975	7 999	3 445	13 081	499
1996	77 500	6 518	6 942	5 259	8 598	3 156	13 734	532
1997	78 353	7 033	7 338	5 611	9 010	3 169	14 435	573
1998	82 349	7 511	7 675	5 942	9 588	3 320	15 156	615
1999	84 984	7 759	8 037	6 317	10 191	3 287	15 823	668
2000	87 109	7 991	8 503	6 860	10 416	3 284	16 488	713
2001	89 286	8 247	8 928	7 196	11 007	3 362	17 362	734

http://dx.doi.org/10.1787/456125276116

589

Table 6b. GDP Levels in 57 African Countries, 1950-2001
(million 1990 international Geary-Khamis dollars)

	Central African Rep.	Chad	Comoros	Congo	Côte d'Ivoire	Djibouti	Egypt	Eritrea & Ethiopia	Gabon
1950	972	1 240	83	990	2 977	90	19 288	8 417	1 292
1951	1 008	1 286	88	1 027	3 087	95	19 635	8 652	1 340
1952	1 045	1 333	90	1 064	3 201	98	20 001	8 896	1 389
1953	1 083	1 381	94	1 103	3 317	102	20 349	9 410	1 440
1954	1 123	1 432	99	1 144	3 439	108	20 715	9 410	1 493
1955	1 165	1 485	102	1 186	3 567	111	21 101	9 915	1 548
1956	1 207	1 540	106	1 230	3 698	115	22 104	10 243	1 605
1957	1 252	1 597	110	1 275	3 835	120	23 145	10 167	1 665
1958	1 299	1 657	113	1 323	3 978	123	24 245	10 504	1 727
1959	1 346	1 717	120	1 372	4 123	130	25 402	10 790	1 791
1960	1 358	1 730	130	1 419	4 493	139	26 617	11 346	1 866
1961	1 409	1 753	132	1 465	4 912	150	28 372	11 901	2 090
1962	1 373	1 846	144	1 513	5 130	158	30 263	12 389	2 153
1963	1 369	1 819	174	1 563	5 972	171	32 288	14 031	2 229
1964	1 391	1 773	188	1 616	7 041	182	34 448	14 721	2 268
1965	1 409	1 783	188	1 670	6 886	194	36 724	15 588	2 306
1966	1 420	1 752	208	1 757	7 431	209	36 936	16 194	2 409
1967	1 487	1 764	217	1 850	7 538	224	36 473	16 875	2 508
1968	1 494	1 756	218	1 948	8 714	239	37 052	17 162	2 572
1969	1 565	1 876	221	2 050	9 098	256	39 598	17 801	2 780
1970	1 638	1 912	238	2 158	10 087	327	42 105	18 811	3 020
1971	1 590	1 948	280	2 333	10 593	361	43 861	19 602	3 330
1972	1 557	1 815	258	2 523	11 179	385	44 690	20 604	3 708
1973	1 627	1 726	229	2 727	12 064	412	45 924	21 286	4 086
1974	1 580	1 963	279	2 947	12 412	412	47 680	21 547	5 699
1975	1 609	2 301	219	3 185	12 400	430	52 501	21 580	6 090
1976	1 679	2 267	194	3 199	13 886	468	60 622	22 170	8 487
1977	1 816	2 098	190	2 934	14 541	410	68 530	22 776	6 732
1978	1 848	2 088	197	2 883	15 982	427	73 795	22 523	4 883
1979	1 745	1 640	202	3 323	16 282	444	79 620	23 971	4 814
1980	1 730	1 541	215	3 891	17 539	464	88 223	25 023	4 837
1981	1 757	1 557	226	4 697	18 152	491	91 733	25 536	4 780
1982	1 790	1 640	235	5 072	18 188	513	101 531	25 940	4 685
1983	1 681	1 897	244	5 327	17 479	519	109 343	27 262	4 756
1984	1 803	1 937	252	5 667	16 902	521	116 016	26 698	4 946
1985	1 826	2 361	259	5 412	17 732	521	123 674	24 913	4 846
1986	1 859	2 264	266	5 044	18 262	521	126 933	26 529	4 603
1987	1 812	2 208	277	5 079	17 970	521	130 135	29 021	4 005
1988	1 845	2 551	289	5 089	17 646	521	135 593	29 585	4 086
1989	1 913	2 698	290	5 277	17 542	526	139 663	30 064	4 261
1990	1 982	2 537	294	5 394	16 330	530	143 000	29 593	4 500
1991	1 970	2 801	278	5 523	16 330	533	138 424	28 202	4 775
1992	1 844	2 868	302	5 667	16 297	532	142 992	26 764	4 617
1993	1 850	2 816	311	5 610	16 265	511	145 280	30 350	4 728
1994	1 972	2 971	294	5 301	16 590	506	151 052	30 835	4 903
1995	2 075	2 983	320	5 514	17 768	489	158 065	32 747	5 148
1996	1 919	3 075	316	5 751	19 136	464	165 950	36 219	5 333
1997	2 067	3 204	330	5 716	20 227	461	175 073	37 921	5 637
1998	2 147	3 451	333	5 928	21 198	461	185 115	37 389	5 835
1999	2 225	3 531	340	5 750	21 537	472	196 044	39 633	4 845
2000	2 265	3 566	336	6 221	21 042	475	205 845	41 774	4 753
2001	2 287	3 869	342	6 402	21 063	484	215 109	44 990	4 867

http://dx.doi.org/10.1787/456125276116

Table 6b. **GDP Levels in 57 African Countries, 1950-2001**
(million 1990 international Geary-Khamis dollars)

	Gambia	Ghana	Guinea	Guinea Bissau	Kenya	Lesotho	Liberia	Madagascar
1950	165	5 943	784	166	3 982	258	869	4 394
1951	174	6 163	831	176	4 851	273	919	4 557
1952	180	6 050	857	187	4 313	281	947	4 724
1953	187	6 888	889	200	4 205	292	984	4 895
1954	197	7 755	941	240	4 695	308	1 039	5 075
1955	203	7 256	972	230	5 050	318	1 073	5 264
1956	211	7 684	1 009	262	5 329	331	1 113	5 457
1957	219	7 933	1 045	279	5 504	343	1 155	5 660
1958	225	7 803	1 077	288	5 563	356	1 188	5 870
1959	238	8 932	1 139	292	5 699	366	1 257	6 086
1960	254	9 591	1 187	309	5 918	393	1 297	6 169
1961	296	9 930	1 265	331	5 775	400	1 328	6 297
1962	292	10 412	1 359	353	6 085	462	1 345	6 442
1963	294	10 774	1 286	369	6 392	511	1 377	6 380
1964	314	11 006	1 370	392	7 013	553	1 447	6 635
1965	348	11 154	1 464	414	7 093	565	1 472	6 604
1966	406	11 166	1 496	436	8 005	562	1 751	6 741
1967	421	11 368	1 543	463	8 419	624	1 740	7 114
1968	427	11 529	1 590	485	9 028	622	1 823	7 597
1969	473	11 939	1 637	513	9 590	631	1 955	7 883
1970	426	12 515	1 694	540	10 291	645	2 083	8 296
1971	475	13 514	1 747	519	10 944	585	2 186	8 621
1972	509	13 109	1 783	552	11 509	697	2 269	8 511
1973	533	13 484	1 861	558	12 107	878	2 212	8 292
1974	638	14 411	1 992	584	12 704	931	2 375	8 459
1975	598	12 616	2 076	630	12 652	855	2 017	8 564
1976	668	12 171	2 280	661	13 162	996	2 096	8 300
1977	701	12 450	2 332	614	14 369	1 172	2 079	8 498
1978	665	13 508	2 394	694	15 663	1 351	2 161	8 274
1979	773	13 163	2 400	708	16 252	1 262	2 257	9 087
1980	697	12 747	2 484	595	17 160	1 351	2 149	9 157
1981	691	12 765	2 499	703	17 555	1 365	2 197	8 366
1982	779	11 879	2 546	745	18 614	1 414	2 134	8 213
1983	685	11 339	2 578	685	18 729	1 292	2 119	8 278
1984	665	12 319	2 651	713	19 056	1 402	2 100	7 975
1985	609	12 943	2 713	752	19 876	1 450	2 071	8 155
1986	641	13 621	2 782	747	21 302	1 479	2 131	8 213
1987	676	14 274	2 870	735	22 569	1 555	2 189	8 393
1988	747	15 077	3 043	765	23 927	1 754	2 189	8 525
1989	799	15 843	3 168	769	25 018	1 947	2 216	8 867
1990	833	16 372	3 304	794	26 093	2 033	2 245	9 210
1991	851	17 240	3 383	834	26 458	2 116	2 281	8 630
1992	889	17 912	3 502	844	26 247	2 214	2 321	8 733
1993	943	18 808	3 673	861	26 352	2 296	2 374	8 917
1994	979	19 429	3 820	889	27 064	2 287	2 426	8 917
1995	945	20 206	3 999	928	28 254	2 575	2 492	9 069
1996	1 003	21 135	4 203	970	29 441	2 819	2 541	9 259
1997	1 052	22 023	4 413	1 024	30 059	2 954	2 555	9 602
1998	1 089	23 058	4 625	736	30 540	2 866	2 580	9 976
1999	1 159	24 073	4 838	795	30 937	2 934	2 623	10 445
2000	1 224	24 963	4 939	870	30 906	3 037	2 667	10 946
2001	1 291	26 012	5 117	872	31 277	3 158	2 712	11 680

http://dx.doi.org/10.1787/456125276116

Table 6b. **GDP Levels in 57 African Countries, 1950-2001**
(million 1990 international Geary-Khamis dollars)

	Malawi	Mali	Mauritania	Mauritius	Morocco	Mozambique	Namibia	Niger	Nigeria
1950	913	1 685	467	1 198	13 598	7 084	1 002	2 018	23 933
1951	951	1 747	484	1 267	14 046	7 332	1 033	2 093	25 728
1952	990	1 811	502	1 306	14 509	7 594	1 065	2 170	27 571
1953	1 031	1 879	520	1 356	14 987	7 857	1 106	2 248	28 217
1954	1 074	1 946	539	1 433	15 481	8 041	1 168	2 331	30 299
1955	1 093	2 018	559	1 479	15 991	8 537	1 206	2 418	31 089
1956	1 184	2 093	580	1 535	16 093	8 579	1 251	2 507	30 371
1957	1 233	2 170	601	1 594	16 195	8 770	1 299	2 600	31 615
1958	1 279	2 249	623	1 638	16 299	9 188	1 335	2 697	31 256
1959	1 324	2 333	647	1 733	16 402	9 684	1 412	2 797	32 621
1960	1 360	2 399	698	1 842	16 507	9 918	1 545	2 977	34 081
1961	1 428	2 414	817	2 261	17 085	10 202	1 562	3 100	35 229
1962	1 428	2 428	799	2 278	17 684	10 903	1 783	3 427	37 240
1963	1 403	2 591	750	2 595	18 303	10 513	1 961	3 766	40 734
1964	1 369	2 714	974	2 417	18 944	10 967	2 279	3 776	42 481
1965	1 554	2 753	1 109	2 495	19 608	11 215	2 433	4 061	45 353
1966	1 714	2 869	1 115	2 406	20 700	11 576	2 526	4 010	43 893
1967	1 889	2 964	1 154	2 510	21 853	12 369	2 424	4 029	37 072
1968	1 868	3 075	1 256	2 338	23 071	13 758	2 444	4 061	36 665
1969	1 988	3 060	1 237	2 453	24 356	15 394	2 529	3 940	46 502
1970	2 017	3 248	1 365	2 443	25 713	16 216	2 540	4 061	60 814
1971	2 307	3 361	1 378	2 563	27 154	17 321	2 627	4 291	67 970
1972	2 543	3 535	1 396	2 817	27 807	17 881	2 783	4 069	70 530
1973	2 756	3 449	1 309	3 169	28 800	18 894	2 895	3 377	76 585
1974	2 955	3 365	1 443	3 511	30 351	17 463	3 021	3 671	85 465
1975	3 117	3 831	1 351	3 514	32 385	14 643	3 052	3 570	82 904
1976	3 269	4 352	1 459	4 086	35 950	13 942	3 221	3 595	91 927
1977	3 437	4 648	1 440	4 353	37 711	14 055	3 424	3 873	95 277
1978	3 747	4 524	1 434	4 520	38 808	14 162	3 651	4 394	89 653
1979	3 919	5 612	1 500	4 679	40 584	14 367	3 806	4 709	95 852
1980	3 945	4 953	1 560	4 208	44 278	14 771	3 986	4 937	97 646
1981	3 746	4 787	1 619	4 455	43 054	15 040	4 110	4 995	89 820
1982	3 783	4 512	1 586	4 701	47 203	14 629	4 164	4 935	89 007
1983	3 945	4 711	1 663	4 719	46 930	13 581	4 057	4 844	83 000
1984	4 123	4 918	1 543	4 940	48 894	13 212	4 006	4 025	79 290
1985	4 446	5 029	1 587	5 285	51 955	12 022	4 023	4 095	86 302
1986	4 463	5 348	1 676	5 817	56 023	12 199	4 147	4 283	87 930
1987	4 572	5 449	1 727	6 408	54 762	12 639	4 268	4 130	87 284
1988	4 690	5 440	1 792	6 844	60 367	13 361	4 368	4 362	95 947
1989	4 923	5 995	1 852	7 145	61 748	13 900	4 738	4 368	102 146
1990	5 146	6 040	1 825	7 652	64 082	14 105	4 619	4 289	107 459
1991	5 594	5 986	1 872	8 142	68 504	14 796	4 882	4 396	113 907
1992	5 185	6 488	1 904	8 533	65 764	13 598	5 346	4 110	116 868
1993	5 688	6 333	2 009	9 104	65 106	14 781	5 239	4 168	119 439
1994	5 102	6 498	2 101	9 505	71 877	15 890	5 595	4 335	118 700
1995	5 954	6 952	2 198	9 837	67 133	16 573	5 830	4 447	121 809
1996	6 389	7 251	2 319	10 349	75 323	17 749	6 005	4 599	129 605
1997	6 632	7 737	2 393	10 970	73 566	19 720	6 257	4 727	133 363
1998	6 850	8 116	2 482	11 628	79 339	22 204	6 470	5 219	135 764
1999	7 124	8 660	2 583	12 244	79 259	23 870	6 703	5 188	137 122
2000	7 388	8 981	2 713	12 563	80 052	24 252	6 931	5 115	143 018
2001	7 499	9 115	2 837	13 467	85 255	27 623	7 104	5 504	147 022

http://dx.doi.org/10.1787/456125276116

Table 6b. **GDP Levels in 57 African Countries, 1950-2001**
(million 1990 international Geary-Khamis dollars)

	Reunion	Rwanda	Senegal	Seychelles	Sierra Leone	Somalia	South Africa	Sudan	Swaziland
1950	485	1 334	3 341	63	1 370	2 576	34 465	6 609	200
1951	512	1 410	3 464	67	1 448	2 724	36 085	6 926	211
1952	528	1 454	3 591	69	1 493	2 810	37 360	7 270	218
1953	549	1 510	3 721	71	1 550	2 915	39 117	7 613	226
1954	580	1 596	3 858	75	1 638	3 083	41 427	7 983	239
1955	598	1 646	4 002	78	1 696	3 183	43 494	8 373	247
1956	621	1 709	4 149	81	1 760	3 301	45 907	9 259	256
1957	645	1 773	4 303	84	1 826	3 425	47 665	9 133	266
1958	663	1 824	4 463	86	1 878	3 520	48 664	9 510	273
1959	701	1 929	4 627	91	1 986	3 726	50 835	10 640	289
1960	756	1 989	4 724	99	2 050	3 775	52 972	10 838	329
1961	796	1 904	4 937	94	2 087	3 956	55 247	10 838	371
1962	859	2 120	5 101	101	2 182	4 130	58 349	11 592	449
1963	925	1 912	5 298	111	2 219	4 290	62 622	11 261	475
1964	1 004	1 673	5 452	116	2 245	3 826	66 827	11 142	545
1965	1 101	1 790	5 656	116	2 405	3 572	70 825	11 896	630
1966	1 170	1 916	5 816	119	2 559	4 079	73 892	11 717	657
1967	1 256	2 051	5 746	119	2 542	4 313	78 959	11 354	719
1968	1 347	2 193	6 107	129	2 791	4 388	82 371	12 048	686
1969	1 477	2 435	5 709	129	3 045	3 840	87 437	12 781	715
1970	1 540	2 702	6 197	139	3 149	4 174	91 986	12 246	926
1971	1 575	2 734	6 187	162	3 120	4 282	96 501	13 092	942
1972	1 757	2 742	6 588	172	3 086	4 717	98 362	12 814	1 057
1973	1 771	2 826	6 217	187	3 180	4 625	102 498	11 783	1 114
1974	1 876	2 959	6 478	190	3 309	3 682	108 254	12 966	1 238
1975	1 838	3 510	6 965	197	3 408	4 960	110 253	14 612	1 282
1976	1 636	3 450	7 587	217	3 305	4 944	112 941	17 302	1 324
1977	1 603	3 629	7 383	234	3 353	6 185	112 734	19 932	1 364
1978	1 730	3 985	7 092	250	3 363	6 500	116 077	19 621	1 399
1979	1 815	4 360	7 590	292	3 554	6 270	120 627	17 586	1 424
1980	1 869	4 892	7 339	284	3 721	6 005	128 416	17 758	1 466
1981	1 913	5 210	7 283	265	3 951	6 482	135 171	18 128	1 566
1982	2 057	5 646	8 388	260	4 019	6 716	134 619	20 421	1 656
1983	2 157	5 984	8 602	255	3 961	6 098	132 172	20 844	1 664
1984	2 181	5 730	8 205	265	4 014	6 306	138 893	19 800	1 698
1985	2 205	5 982	8 515	290	3 904	6 816	137 239	18 557	1 804
1986	2 230	6 309	8 926	297	3 767	7 056	137 307	19 291	1 872
1987	2 248	6 261	9 290	311	3 965	7 409	140 099	19 720	2 031
1988	2 383	6 046	9 765	325	4 072	7 359	145 855	19 952	1 984
1989	2 454	6 168	9 598	343	4 164	7 349	148 888	21 518	2 111
1990	2 694	6 125	10 032	366	4 335	7 231	147 509	19 793	2 154
1991	2 863	5 862	9 992	376	3 988	6 505	146 034	21 179	2 208
1992	2 863	6 248	10 212	402	3 605	5 536	142 967	22 280	2 237
1993	2 863	5 730	9 987	428	3 609	5 536	144 683	22 904	2 310
1994	2 863	2 854	10 277	418	3 735	5 701	149 313	23 362	2 389
1995	2 863	3 858	10 811	420	3 362	5 867	153 942	24 063	2 479
1996	3 012	4 348	11 362	462	2 528	6 048	160 561	25 242	2 576
1997	3 136	4 948	11 930	518	2 083	6 044	164 786	27 766	2 674
1998	3 174	5 388	12 611	548	2 066	6 044	166 054	29 432	2 759
1999	3 240	5 798	13 254	532	1 899	6 151	169 541	31 699	2 856
2000	3 308	6 146	14 022	504	1 971	6 260	175 305	34 773	2 919
2001	3 377	6 557	14 808	463	2 078	6 371	179 162	36 616	2 966

http://dx.doi.org/10.1787/456125276116

Table 6b. **GDP Levels in 57 African Countries, 1950-2001**
(million 1990 international Geary-Khamis dollars)

	Tanzania	Togo	Tunisia	Uganda	Zaire	Zambia	Zimbabwe	6 Country Total	57 Country Total
1950	3 362	673	3 920	3 793	7 731	1 687	2 000	1 014	203 131
1951	3 786	698	3 963	3 641	8 635	1 795	2 130	1 113	212 653
1952	3 863	723	4 450	3 868	9 424	1 910	2 232	1 186	220 780
1953	3 725	749	4 618	4 039	9 957	2 032	2 424	1 210	228 858
1954	4 028	777	4 720	3 982	10 560	2 161	2 554	1 218	239 781
1955	4 125	806	4 477	4 244	10 970	2 111	2 756	1 476	248 054
1956	4 176	836	4 775	4 479	11 712	2 362	3 148	1 763	258 153
1957	4 277	867	4 579	4 673	12 083	2 465	3 368	1 838	267 612
1958	4 314	899	5 175	4 703	11 735	2 401	3 412	2 014	273 683
1959	4 525	932	4 959	4 942	12 145	2 902	3 596	2 164	288 734
1960	4 710	1 016	5 571	5 177	12 423	3 123	3 762	2 743	301 578
1961	4 657	1 085	6 053	5 124	11 070	3 130	3 956	3 010	308 136
1962	5 080	1 125	5 912	5 332	13 420	3 096	4 016	3 919	320 322
1963	5 400	1 181	6 806	5 943	14 124	3 164	3 976	5 208	343 186
1964	5 695	1 351	7 100	6 394	13 776	3 586	4 326	7 253	361 570
1965	5 901	1 535	7 547	6 535	13 915	4 239	4 608	9 222	381 330
1966	6 657	1 676	7 735	6 941	14 858	4 007	4 678	10 861	392 226
1967	6 926	1 769	7 684	7 312	14 712	4 318	5 068	12 066	400 067
1968	7 282	1 859	8 491	7 498	15 345	4 379	5 168	15 971	420 309
1969	7 417	2 060	8 793	8 325	16 776	4 355	5 812	17 968	453 131
1970	7 847	2 112	9 315	8 450	16 737	4 562	7 072	18 805	490 102
1971	8 177	2 262	10 302	8 700	17 804	4 561	7 692	17 710	512 138
1972	8 725	2 340	12 129	8 757	17 827	4 979	8 342	15 777	530 848
1973	9 007	2 245	12 051	8 704	19 373	4 930	8 594	15 959	549 993
1974	9 216	2 340	13 019	8 719	20 038	5 332	8 810	13 739	575 500
1975	9 693	2 326	13 952	8 541	19 041	5 124	8 890	14 736	582 627
1976	10 386	2 315	15 054	8 606	17 951	5 426	8 816	18 023	621 584
1977	10 678	2 441	15 567	8 738	18 043	5 163	8 108	19 518	647 589
1978	10 987	2 689	16 571	8 260	17 023	5 195	8 338	20 212	663 511
1979	11 122	2 851	17 657	7 350	17 000	5 037	8 338	22 877	694 654
1980	11 216	2 721	18 966	7 100	17 355	5 190	9 288	23 085	725 905
1981	11 092	2 551	20 013	7 373	17 765	5 509	10 454	18 863	733 452
1982	11 236	2 453	19 915	7 980	17 680	5 354	10 726	18 333	756 255
1983	11 186	2 320	20 848	8 571	17 927	5 249	10 896	18 156	761 138
1984	11 465	2 389	22 040	7 843	18 925	5 231	10 688	16 897	777 297
1985	11 438	2 502	23 279	7 999	19 010	5 317	11 430	15 442	801 420
1986	11 811	2 580	22 918	8 025	19 907	5 354	11 732	14 216	818 732
1987	12 413	2 616	24 451	8 533	20 440	5 497	11 588	13 837	831 716
1988	12 937	2 733	24 478	9 148	20 556	5 841	12 672	13 980	865 804
1989	13 371	2 834	25 384	9 815	20 417	5 900	13 498	14 112	892 376
1990	13 852	2 805	27 387	10 206	19 922	6 432	13 766	13 917	904 898
1991	14 143	2 785	28 455	10 308	18 249	6 432	14 523	13 183	911 693
1992	14 228	2 674	30 675	10 628	16 332	6 323	13 216	12 748	912 598
1993	14 398	2 235	31 349	11 520	14 128	6 753	13 388	12 272	921 183
1994	14 628	2 626	32 352	12 257	13 577	5 855	14 165	12 182	941 178
1995	15 155	2 807	33 129	13 716	13 672	5 708	14 193	12 276	969 734
1996	15 837	3 080	35 481	14 895	13 536	6 080	15 669	12 915	1 024 994
1997	15 685	2 928	37 397	15 655	12 777	6 286	16 092	14 302	1 060 213
1998	16 266	2 867	39 192	16 391	12 572	6 167	16 559	14 321	1 099 966
1999	16 835	2 950	41 582	17 637	12 032	6 302	16 443	15 379	1 136 130
2000	17 694	2 894	43 537	18 518	11 286	6 529	15 604	16 413	1 175 890
2001	18 685	2 971	45 714	19 555	10 789	6 849	14 278	18 257	1 222 577

http://dx.doi.org/10.1787/456125276116

Table 6b. **GDP Levels in 57 African Countries, 1950-2001**
(million 1990 international Geary-Khamis dollars)

	Equatorial Guinea	Libya	SãoTomé & Principe	Mayotte + St. Helena + W. Sahara	6 Country Total
1950	114	824	49	27	1 014
1951	120	915	49	29	1 113
1952	124	982	49	31	1 186
1953	129	998	49	34	1 210
1954	136	994	51	37	1 218
1955	140	1 251	46	39	1 476
1956	146	1 525	49	43	1 763
1957	151	1 592	49	46	1 838
1958	156	1 755	54	49	2 014
1959	165	1 897	49	53	2 164
1960	182	2 448	55	58	2 743
1961	200	2 688	60	62	3 010
1962	221	3 566	65	67	3 919
1963	252	4 814	70	72	5 208
1964	288	6 812	75	78	7 253
1965	325	8 733	80	84	9 222
1966	339	10 345	86	91	10 861
1967	362	11 515	91	98	12 066
1968	375	15 395	96	105	15 971
1969	364	17 389	101	114	17 968
1970	354	18 222	106	123	18 805
1971	325	17 142	111	132	17 710
1972	284	15 241	109	143	15 777
1973	289	15 410	106	154	15 959
1974	282	13 186	108	163	13 739
1975	276	14 172	116	172	14 736
1976	277	17 438	126	182	18 023
1977	281	18 904	140	193	19 518
1978	306	19 553	149	204	20 212
1979	341	22 155	166	215	22 877
1980	378	22 290	189	228	23 085
1981	387	18 098	137	241	18 863
1982	403	17 502	173	255	18 333
1983	418	17 311	158	269	18 156
1984	528	15 939	145	285	16 897
1985	455	14 529	157	301	15 442
1986	474	13 265	159	318	14 216
1987	502	12 842	156	337	13 837
1988	538	12 927	159	356	13 980
1989	560	13 014	162	376	14 112
1990	576	12 780	166	395	13 917
1991	603	12 013	166	401	13 183
1992	668	11 508	167	405	12 748
1993	710	10 979	169	414	12 272
1994	746	10 836	173	427	12 182
1995	852	10 804	176	444	12 276
1996	1 100	11 160	179	476	12 915
1997	1 884	11 741	181	496	14 302
1998	2 298	11 318	185	520	14 321
1999	3 250	11 397	190	542	15 379
2000	3 773	11 879	196	565	16 413
2001	5 490	11 970	204	593	18 257

http://dx.doi.org/10.1787/456125276116

PER CAPITA GDP IN AFRICA

Table 6c. **Per Capita GDP in 57 African Countries, 1950-2001**
(1990 international Geary-Khamis dollars)

	Algeria	Angola	Benin	Botswana	Burkina Faso	Burundi	Cameroon	Cape Verde
1950	1 365	1 052	1 084	349	474	360	671	450
1951	1 347	1 076	1 063	355	487	374	687	455
1952	1 376	1 101	1 043	359	500	379	704	461
1953	1 369	1 126	994	366	512	388	720	467
1954	1 437	1 079	1 002	372	526	402	737	460
1955	1 445	1 148	982	377	539	408	754	463
1956	1 553	1 110	962	383	554	416	771	469
1957	1 693	1 197	941	388	568	425	788	453
1958	1 719	1 241	956	392	583	429	805	449
1959	1 994	1 225	970	399	598	446	822	486
1960	2 088	1 253	978	403	609	444	832	508
1961	1 799	1 396	987	410	626	373	829	525
1962	1 433	1 335	932	415	657	398	840	539
1963	1 768	1 380	952	422	640	408	857	553
1964	1 806	1 510	993	430	646	421	872	564
1965	1 870	1 596	1 020	437	662	426	874	575
1966	1 725	1 660	1 032	473	655	434	898	585
1967	1 824	1 727	1 016	513	701	463	905	594
1968	1 977	1 672	1 029	557	711	448	946	602
1969	2 105	1 691	1 033	601	713	435	973	611
1970	2 249	1 768	1 027	647	702	542	982	619
1971	2 000	1 729	1 006	747	717	572	990	566
1972	2 350	1 713	1 065	954	732	520	1 011	536
1973	2 357	1 791	1 061	1 119	680	556	1 003	529
1974	2 428	1 713	955	1 293	654	543	1 024	512
1975	2 522	1 074	969	1 215	613	537	1 052	525
1976	2 608	955	983	1 370	594	568	1 044	520
1977	2 759	941	1 010	1 344	622	624	1 070	518
1978	3 016	961	1 013	1 519	679	602	1 095	567
1979	3 186	959	1 063	1 591	670	599	1 121	622
1980	3 143	962	1 133	1 738	665	627	1 194	841
1981	3 119	924	1 164	1 827	678	683	1 354	904
1982	3 212	862	1 254	1 891	676	659	1 421	916
1983	3 269	819	1 165	2 110	652	652	1 477	988
1984	3 340	810	1 220	2 259	645	632	1 545	1 009
1985	3 404	799	1 273	2 336	711	685	1 632	1 079
1986	3 272	713	1 263	2 421	802	691	1 695	1 092
1987	3 161	780	1 205	2 538	769	697	1 562	1 148
1988	3 015	877	1 203	2 833	809	699	1 448	1 164
1989	3 039	879	1 140	3 097	774	686	1 285	1 206
1990	2 918	895	1 147	3 183	742	734	1 232	1 231
1991	2 814	880	1 162	3 245	790	755	1 153	797
1992	2 793	848	1 170	3 258	784	749	1 089	639
1993	2 671	603	1 172	3 244	754	690	1 028	1 182
1994	2 590	597	1 185	3 282	743	645	978	1 241
1995	2 632	636	1 200	3 359	754	639	988	1 318
1996	2 677	690	1 226	3 485	787	588	1 014	1 387
1997	2 654	736	1 255	3 659	802	586	1 042	1 475
1998	2 737	771	1 271	3 824	829	605	1 070	1 565
1999	2 773	782	1 290	4 026	857	587	1 093	1 681
2000	2 792	789	1 323	4 348	853	575	1 115	1 777
2001	2 813	797	1 347	4 552	877	576	1 149	1 812

http://dx.doi.org/10.1787/456125276116

ISBN 92-64-02261-9 – © OECD 2006

Table 6c. **Per Capita GDP in 57 African Countries, 1950-2001**
(1990 international Geary-Khamis dollars)

	Central African Rep.	Chad	Comoros	Congo	Côte d'Ivoire	Djibouti	Egypt	Eritrea & Ethiopia	Gabon
1950	772	476	560	1 289	1 041	1 500	910	390	3 108
1951	790	486	581	1 315	1 058	1 546	905	394	3 204
1952	809	497	587	1 340	1 075	1 554	900	399	3 302
1953	827	507	598	1 364	1 092	1 575	894	414	3 401
1954	845	518	619	1 388	1 110	1 622	889	407	3 504
1955	864	529	625	1 412	1 127	1 632	885	421	3 611
1956	881	540	635	1 436	1 144	1 651	905	427	3 718
1957	899	552	645	1 459	1 162	1 668	925	416	3 827
1958	917	563	649	1 482	1 179	1 665	947	422	3 939
1959	934	574	671	1 506	1 191	1 711	969	425	4 052
1960	925	569	712	1 523	1 256	1 771	991	439	4 184
1961	943	566	703	1 539	1 328	1 783	1 031	451	4 639
1962	901	586	749	1 553	1 339	1 759	1 074	460	4 725
1963	881	567	887	1 569	1 499	1 774	1 120	511	4 832
1964	878	542	932	1 584	1 697	1 758	1 166	525	4 851
1965	866	533	913	1 599	1 592	1 754	1 213	545	4 860
1966	844	512	984	1 642	1 642	1 761	1 192	554	5 003
1967	860	505	999	1 688	1 589	1 758	1 151	566	5 130
1968	851	491	973	1 732	1 749	1 746	1 146	563	5 176
1969	877	514	963	1 779	1 738	1 742	1 201	571	5 518
1970	896	513	1 009	1 825	1 833	2 069	1 254	591	5 869
1971	851	511	1 154	1 922	1 831	2 142	1 283	603	6 332
1972	815	465	1 032	2 025	1 841	2 150	1 284	620	6 892
1973	837	433	889	2 132	1 899	2 185	1 294	626	7 286
1974	797	481	1 055	2 242	1 874	2 080	1 317	618	9 541
1975	792	550	804	2 342	1 800	2 065	1 421	605	9 399
1976	811	529	692	2 270	1 942	2 154	1 606	606	12 342
1977	860	478	624	2 008	1 960	1 794	1 767	608	9 531
1978	858	464	627	1 904	2 078	1 724	1 844	591	6 723
1979	794	361	624	2 115	2 042	1 687	1 930	622	6 666
1980	771	339	643	2 388	2 123	1 661	2 069	642	6 779
1981	767	335	664	2 778	2 121	1 674	2 076	646	6 543
1982	765	336	675	2 890	2 052	1 676	2 223	641	6 213
1983	705	374	683	2 923	1 903	1 643	2 322	656	6 107
1984	736	378	688	2 981	1 776	1 802	2 390	624	6 143
1985	726	457	691	2 768	1 798	1 758	2 471	573	5 818
1986	727	426	691	2 509	1 787	1 717	2 460	597	5 357
1987	697	401	701	2 458	1 698	1 677	2 465	633	4 546
1988	695	449	712	2 397	1 611	1 597	2 510	624	4 541
1989	701	462	694	2 420	1 544	1 502	2 527	611	4 636
1990	707	421	685	2 408	1 372	1 448	2 522	581	4 795
1991	683	449	630	2 403	1 315	1 420	2 381	530	4 969
1992	622	445	664	2 405	1 276	1 384	2 407	485	4 678
1993	606	422	664	2 323	1 234	1 299	2 394	537	4 664
1994	628	430	610	2 143	1 214	1 257	2 437	532	4 708
1995	648	418	644	2 177	1 259	1 195	2 496	550	4 811
1996	588	417	617	2 220	1 319	1 122	2 565	593	4 851
1997	622	421	625	2 159	1 364	1 103	2 647	606	4 992
1998	635	438	612	2 193	1 402	1 092	2 738	584	5 031
1999	646	434	606	2 085	1 392	1 107	2 838	605	4 068
2000	647	424	581	2 214	1 326	1 103	2 920	624	3 887
2001	642	445	574	2 239	1 297	1 106	2 992	660	3 877

http://dx.doi.org/10.1787/456125276116

Table 6c. **Per Capita GDP in 57 African Countries, 1950-2001**
(1990 international Geary-Khamis dollars)

	Gambia	Ghana	Guinea	Guinea Bissau	Kenya	Lesotho	Liberia	Madagascar
1950	607	1 122	303	289	651	355	1 055	951
1951	627	1 134	317	306	771	370	1 090	972
1952	632	1 084	322	323	667	375	1 097	992
1953	640	1 202	329	342	633	384	1 113	1 012
1954	660	1 317	343	408	687	399	1 147	1 032
1955	664	1 200	349	389	718	405	1 156	1 052
1956	671	1 236	357	439	736	413	1 170	1 072
1957	678	1 241	363	465	738	422	1 183	1 092
1958	678	1 187	368	476	725	430	1 187	1 112
1959	697	1 321	383	478	720	435	1 223	1 132
1960	722	1 378	392	501	726	458	1 230	1 125
1961	815	1 388	410	532	686	457	1 226	1 126
1962	781	1 416	433	562	701	517	1 209	1 129
1963	762	1 424	402	583	714	560	1 204	1 096
1964	787	1 414	420	642	758	593	1 231	1 116
1965	846	1 393	441	685	743	593	1 218	1 088
1966	955	1 354	442	728	812	577	1 408	1 087
1967	957	1 339	447	771	826	626	1 360	1 123
1968	939	1 318	452	794	857	610	1 384	1 174
1969	1 007	1 325	456	833	881	605	1 442	1 192
1970	879	1 424	463	872	913	604	1 492	1 226
1971	949	1 491	468	833	937	535	1 519	1 246
1972	985	1 401	468	883	949	624	1 530	1 202
1973	997	1 397	478	882	961	769	1 447	1 144
1974	1 157	1 455	502	912	971	797	1 508	1 139
1975	1 050	1 247	512	925	929	715	1 242	1 126
1976	1 134	1 178	551	902	929	814	1 252	1 063
1977	1 152	1 181	552	823	973	936	1 204	1 061
1978	1 058	1 260	555	915	1 018	1 054	1 214	1 007
1979	1 191	1 210	544	918	1 013	962	1 230	1 076
1980	1 039	1 157	551	754	1 028	1 005	1 136	1 055
1981	997	1 142	542	871	1 011	991	1 126	938
1982	1 088	1 042	541	902	1 031	1 001	1 061	895
1983	926	933	535	810	998	893	1 022	878
1984	867	960	525	824	977	944	982	822
1985	765	978	509	849	982	953	939	817
1986	776	989	505	824	1 014	949	937	800
1987	787	1 007	508	793	1 037	974	934	794
1988	838	1 035	525	805	1 063	1 075	905	784
1989	863	1 058	532	790	1 077	1 170	889	792
1990	866	1 063	526	797	1 090	1 201	1 025	799
1991	853	1 089	503	818	1 072	1 232	1 206	728
1992	858	1 100	501	803	1 028	1 272	1 169	715
1993	877	1 121	511	795	1 003	1 304	1 151	709
1994	878	1 125	514	797	1 008	1 286	1 179	689
1995	818	1 144	521	812	1 029	1 435	1 259	680
1996	838	1 171	529	832	1 049	1 560	1 255	674
1997	849	1 196	548	858	1 048	1 623	1 113	678
1998	850	1 227	566	602	1 044	1 566	972	683
1999	876	1 256	574	636	1 038	1 595	882	694
2000	895	1 280	572	681	1 020	1 645	847	706
2001	915	1 311	587	668	1 016	1 705	846	731

http://dx.doi.org/10.1787/456125276116

Table 6c. **Per Capita GDP in 57 African Countries, 1950-2001**
(1990 international Geary-Khamis dollars)

	Malawi	Mali	Mauritania	Mauritius	Morocco	Mozambique	Namibia	Niger	Nigeria
1950	324	457	464	2 490	1 455	1 133	2 160	813	753
1951	332	465	477	2 540	1 458	1 155	2 176	825	793
1952	339	472	490	2 528	1 460	1 178	2 191	835	832
1953	347	480	504	2 530	1 468	1 199	2 223	846	835
1954	355	488	517	2 587	1 476	1 207	2 292	856	875
1955	354	496	531	2 587	1 483	1 259	2 310	867	877
1956	376	504	545	2 594	1 451	1 242	2 339	877	836
1957	383	513	558	2 613	1 420	1 246	2 370	887	850
1958	388	521	572	2 610	1 389	1 280	2 376	897	821
1959	393	530	586	2 685	1 358	1 323	2 451	907	837
1960	394	535	625	2 777	1 329	1 327	2 616	940	854
1961	404	528	722	3 319	1 341	1 337	2 579	953	862
1962	393	520	697	3 249	1 354	1 400	2 869	1 025	889
1963	376	544	645	3 629	1 367	1 321	3 076	1 096	950
1964	359	558	827	3 283	1 381	1 349	3 486	1 069	967
1965	397	555	928	3 302	1 394	1 351	3 626	1 118	1 007
1966	426	566	920	3 108	1 436	1 364	3 668	1 074	951
1967	456	572	938	3 180	1 480	1 425	3 430	1 049	784
1968	438	581	1 006	2 907	1 524	1 549	3 369	1 028	756
1969	454	566	975	3 006	1 570	1 693	3 396	969	934
1970	449	588	1 059	2 945	1 616	1 743	3 321	971	1 190
1971	501	595	1 051	3 047	1 665	1 816	3 342	997	1 295
1972	537	612	1 047	3 309	1 669	1 823	3 443	919	1 308
1973	567	584	966	3 680	1 694	1 873	3 486	741	1 382
1974	587	556	1 046	4 020	1 751	1 684	3 539	782	1 497
1975	592	619	962	3 969	1 831	1 404	3 473	738	1 407
1976	597	687	1 020	4 551	1 992	1 295	3 559	721	1 511
1977	610	724	988	4 768	2 050	1 263	3 712	754	1 517
1978	647	694	965	4 863	2 069	1 235	3 906	830	1 380
1979	658	848	989	4 943	2 122	1 215	3 986	863	1 426
1980	644	736	1 006	4 367	2 272	1 220	4 089	877	1 402
1981	594	699	1 021	4 550	2 169	1 216	4 159	860	1 246
1982	582	647	978	4 738	2 337	1 162	4 120	824	1 194
1983	589	663	1 001	4 708	2 263	1 063	3 884	783	1 094
1984	597	678	906	4 882	2 296	1 022	3 710	630	1 023
1985	624	679	908	5 173	2 377	920	3 606	622	1 080
1986	604	707	935	5 635	2 499	928	3 593	630	1 073
1987	585	704	938	6 146	2 382	981	3 569	589	1 033
1988	563	690	947	6 504	2 563	1 067	3 478	603	1 101
1989	559	745	956	6 725	2 560	1 115	3 539	588	1 137
1990	558	734	920	7 128	2 596	1 115	3 278	562	1 161
1991	586	712	917	7 505	2 714	1 146	3 366	560	1 194
1992	525	758	898	7 784	2 549	1 034	3 586	509	1 189
1993	569	726	911	8 221	2 471	1 084	3 419	502	1 180
1994	522	729	922	8 502	2 672	1 084	3 553	507	1 138
1995	617	759	939	8 716	2 446	1 068	3 604	504	1 134
1996	648	767	971	9 082	2 691	1 116	3 615	506	1 172
1997	656	794	979	9 541	2 579	1 218	3 671	506	1 172
1998	661	807	987	10 027	2 730	1 350	3 705	543	1 160
1999	671	836	997	10 471	2 678	1 429	3 750	525	1 139
2000	679	842	1 017	10 652	2 658	1 432	3 795	503	1 156
2001	674	830	1 033	11 318	2 782	1 611	3 813	526	1 157

http://dx.doi.org/10.1787/456125276116

Table 6c. **Per Capita GDP in 57 African Countries, 1950-2001**
(1990 international Geary-Khamis dollars)

	Reunion	Rwanda	Senegal	Seychelles	Sierra Leone	Somalia	South Africa	Sudan	Swaziland
1950	1 989	547	1 259	1 912	656	1 057	2 535	821	721
1951	2 044	567	1 281	2 019	685	1 098	2 591	837	745
1952	2 051	574	1 303	2 050	697	1 112	2 619	855	751
1953	2 067	584	1 324	2 084	714	1 132	2 675	871	762
1954	2 113	604	1 346	2 174	744	1 175	2 763	889	787
1955	2 091	610	1 367	2 164	760	1 191	2 830	907	793
1956	2 098	620	1 388	2 143	777	1 211	2 914	976	803
1957	2 089	628	1 409	2 186	795	1 232	2 951	936	814
1958	2 085	631	1 429	2 200	807	1 241	2 939	949	817
1959	2 142	652	1 448	2 254	841	1 287	2 995	1 033	843
1960	2 239	656	1 445	2 367	856	1 277	3 041	1 024	935
1961	2 288	625	1 475	2 176	858	1 311	3 092	996	1 028
1962	2 394	695	1 487	2 306	884	1 341	3 179	1 037	1 214
1963	2 495	611	1 507	2 458	886	1 364	3 321	980	1 252
1964	2 617	525	1 499	2 488	883	1 191	3 450	944	1 399
1965	2 803	548	1 511	2 435	932	1 088	3 559	984	1 577
1966	2 901	570	1 508	2 434	976	1 216	3 615	947	1 602
1967	3 033	594	1 449	2 381	955	1 258	3 760	893	1 709
1968	3 169	618	1 499	2 522	1 032	1 252	3 819	923	1 588
1969	3 391	666	1 362	2 455	1 109	1 071	3 946	954	1 612
1970	3 463	717	1 435	2 570	1 129	1 138	4 045	888	2 036
1971	3 473	705	1 390	2 910	1 101	1 141	4 135	923	2 015
1972	3 807	687	1 436	3 013	1 072	1 228	4 109	878	2 201
1973	3 774	688	1 315	3 224	1 087	1 176	4 175	780	2 258
1974	3 946	700	1 329	3 203	1 113	914	4 299	833	2 443
1975	3 821	806	1 396	3 251	1 126	1 202	4 271	910	2 462
1976	3 361	766	1 487	3 507	1 072	1 167	4 267	1 044	2 472
1977	3 258	779	1 411	3 691	1 068	1 421	4 155	1 165	2 474
1978	3 480	827	1 322	3 885	1 051	1 390	4 174	1 108	2 462
1979	3 615	876	1 380	4 460	1 089	1 181	4 232	956	2 421
1980	3 686	952	1 301	4 274	1 119	1 037	4 390	931	2 397
1981	3 738	981	1 259	3 914	1 164	1 113	4 503	920	2 481
1982	3 972	1 025	1 415	3 794	1 160	1 152	4 367	1 003	2 548
1983	4 124	1 049	1 414	3 695	1 120	1 016	4 174	958	2 474
1984	4 094	976	1 315	3 799	1 110	1 016	4 271	878	2 437
1985	4 070	993	1 330	4 116	1 056	1 057	4 108	791	2 497
1986	4 045	1 020	1 359	4 163	996	1 053	4 020	798	2 494
1987	4 000	982	1 378	4 335	1 025	1 070	4 015	798	2 607
1988	4 155	918	1 411	4 483	1 028	1 067	4 092	790	2 428
1989	4 193	910	1 345	4 706	1 025	1 089	4 090	833	2 478
1990	4 510	880	1 363	4 984	1 026	1 083	3 966	743	2 434
1991	4 695	820	1 316	5 065	919	1 009	3 851	772	2 384
1992	4 601	853	1 306	5 360	844	908	3 698	789	2 323
1993	4 510	765	1 241	5 656	853	914	3 684	791	2 329
1994	4 423	443	1 241	5 477	862	923	3 755	785	2 395
1995	4 338	674	1 268	5 458	746	933	3 824	787	2 467
1996	4 479	724	1 295	5 960	546	936	3 943	806	2 498
1997	4 579	687	1 322	6 640	441	911	4 000	863	2 531
1998	4 554	753	1 360	6 983	422	883	3 986	889	2 555
1999	4 569	795	1 391	6 741	376	873	4 032	930	2 593
2000	4 588	830	1 433	6 354	379	863	4 139	991	2 606
2001	4 610	871	1 474	5 808	386	851	4 208	1 015	2 610

http://dx.doi.org/10.1787/456125276116

ISBN 92-64-02261-9 – © OECD 2006

Table 6c. **Per Capita GDP in 57 African Countries, 1950-2001**
(1990 international Geary-Khamis dollars)

	Tanzania	Togo	Tunisia	Uganda	Zaire	Zambia	Zimbabwe	6 Country Total	57 Country Total
1950	424	574	1 115	687	570	661	701	801	894
1951	466	584	1 106	642	625	688	722	857	916
1952	464	593	1 220	664	670	715	724	889	932
1953	437	602	1 244	675	695	743	760	883	945
1954	461	611	1 249	648	723	772	772	864	970
1955	460	621	1 164	672	737	736	808	1 017	981
1956	454	630	1 223	690	772	803	892	1 179	999
1957	452	639	1 159	700	781	817	924	1 191	1 013
1958	444	647	1 291	685	743	776	906	1 265	1 013
1959	453	656	1 217	700	753	915	925	1 315	1 044
1960	459	698	1 343	713	755	960	938	1 613	1 066
1961	441	728	1 436	686	659	938	956	1 710	1 065
1962	468	736	1 379	694	776	905	939	2 154	1 082
1963	483	754	1 556	751	793	902	901	2 767	1 132
1964	494	841	1 589	785	757	996	953	3 717	1 164
1965	497	932	1 653	779	748	1 147	984	4 560	1 197
1966	544	991	1 654	803	779	1 056	967	5 164	1 201
1967	549	1 019	1 605	822	749	1 107	1 015	5 536	1 194
1968	560	1 043	1 735	818	758	1 092	999	7 048	1 223
1969	553	1 126	1 760	881	806	1 056	1 086	7 589	1 286
1970	567	1 075	1 827	869	782	1 073	1 282	7 652	1 357
1971	572	1 121	1 982	871	810	1 042	1 353	6 956	1 382
1972	591	1 128	2 287	859	790	1 105	1 423	5 934	1 397
1973	590	1 053	2 221	838	836	1 062	1 432	5 734	1 410
1974	584	1 067	2 343	821	842	1 114	1 427	4 732	1 438
1975	596	1 032	2 446	784	778	1 041	1 402	4 925	1 418
1976	620	999	2 569	770	713	1 071	1 357	5 855	1 472
1977	618	1 025	2 592	763	700	990	1 221	6 200	1 492
1978	617	1 098	2 700	703	643	967	1 232	6 241	1 487
1979	606	1 131	2 811	611	620	910	1 211	6 703	1 512
1980	593	1 048	2 944	577	617	911	1 295	6 413	1 536
1981	569	950	3 030	585	616	936	1 407	5 001	1 509
1982	559	883	2 957	617	594	878	1 405	4 648	1 512
1983	540	807	3 039	643	587	828	1 374	4 418	1 477
1984	537	802	3 068	570	605	797	1 297	3 952	1 466
1985	519	810	3 162	562	589	784	1 335	3 552	1 468
1986	520	806	3 038	544	598	762	1 321	3 238	1 459
1987	529	788	3 165	556	594	756	1 257	3 068	1 441
1988	534	793	3 101	572	578	781	1 326	3 010	1 459
1989	536	793	3 152	590	556	768	1 368	2 953	1 463
1990	540	757	3 337	592	525	817	1 356	2 831	1 444
1991	536	726	3 402	577	465	797	1 391	2 610	1 414
1992	524	673	3 599	574	403	765	1 232	2 457	1 378
1993	514	565	3 612	600	338	799	1 217	2 305	1 356
1994	503	656	3 663	616	314	678	1 273	2 232	1 352
1995	505	664	3 692	671	299	647	1 263	2 210	1 358
1996	517	695	3 897	710	290	675	1 370	2 301	1 403
1997	501	635	4 050	725	269	683	1 382	2 503	1 416
1998	507	602	4 188	738	257	656	1 399	2 445	1 434
1999	511	602	4 387	772	239	657	1 368	2 561	1 447
2000	524	575	4 538	788	218	666	1 280	2 665	1 464
2001	540	575	4 710	809	202	686	1 158	2 892	1 489

http://dx.doi.org/10.1787/456125276116

Table 6c. **Per Capita GDP in 57 African Countries, 1950-2001**
(1990 international Geary-Khamis dollars)

	Equatorial Guinea	Libya	SãoTomé & Principe	Mayotte + St. Helena + W. Sahara	6 Country Total
1950	540	857	820	790	801
1951	561	925	818	816	857
1952	572	963	817	837	889
1953	587	949	817	879	883
1954	610	915	850	915	864
1955	620	1 115	764	920	1 017
1956	636	1 314	806	965	1 179
1957	648	1 325	799	981	1 191
1958	660	1 410	875	991	1 265
1959	687	1 470	784	1 014	1 315
1960	746	1 830	867	1 047	1 613
1961	806	1 936	933	1 053	1 710
1962	887	2 473	995	1 068	2 154
1963	1 006	3 212	1 055	1 074	2 767
1964	1 145	4 366	1 112	1 086	3 717
1965	1 285	5 378	1 165	1 089	4 560
1966	1 322	6 107	1 233	1 097	5 164
1967	1 393	6 545	1 286	1 094	5 536
1968	1 424	8 395	1 337	1 083	7 048
1969	1 364	9 043	1 389	1 084	7 589
1970	1 309	9 115	1 440	1 076	7 652
1971	1 186	8 252	1 483	1 103	6 956
1972	1 023	6 979	1 423	1 187	5 934
1973	1 065	6 664	1 355	1 268	5 734
1974	1 128	5 379	1 356	1 331	4 732
1975	1 294	5 515	1 421	1 348	4 925
1976	1 452	6 540	1 497	1 330	5 855
1977	1 458	6 945	1 613	1 314	6 200
1978	1 572	6 991	1 667	1 291	6 241
1979	1 541	7 565	1 808	1 257	6 703
1980	1 477	7 272	2 009	1 237	6 413
1981	1 424	5 648	1 421	1 209	5 001
1982	1 412	5 234	1 755	1 181	4 648
1983	1 395	4 968	1 567	1 196	4 418
1984	1 679	4 397	1 405	1 222	3 952
1985	1 402	3 953	1 486	1 246	3 552
1986	1 425	3 586	1 470	1 270	3 238
1987	1 472	3 380	1 408	1 308	3 068
1988	1 538	3 303	1 400	1 332	3 010
1989	1 560	3 232	1 391	1 357	2 953
1990	1 564	3 087	1 390	1 374	2 831
1991	1 596	2 825	1 354	1 344	2 610
1992	1 723	2 637	1 326	1 309	2 457
1993	1 785	2 453	1 306	1 291	2 305
1994	1 828	2 363	1 299	1 284	2 232
1995	2 036	2 321	1 284	1 289	2 210
1996	2 563	2 381	1 267	1 334	2 301
1997	4 281	2 467	1 243	1 343	2 503
1998	5 093	2 322	1 232	1 361	2 445
1999	7 025	2 282	1 226	1 372	2 561
2000	7 956	2 322	1 226	1 385	2 665
2001	11 295	2 284	1 236	1 408	2 892

http://dx.doi.org/10.1787/456125276116

HS–7: The World Economy, 1950–2001

Tables 7a–7c show annual estimates of economic activity in 7 regions and the world for the year 1900, and annually 1950–2001. They aggregate the detailed estimates by country in HS–1 to HS–6 and there are analytical tables showing percentage year–to–year movement in real terms. Three basic ingredients are necessary for these estimates. These are time series on population which we have for 221 countries, time series showing the volume movement in GDP in constant national prices for 179 countries, and purchasing power converters for 99.3 per cent of world GDP in our benchmark year 1990. With these converters we can transform the GDP volume measures into comparable estimates of GDP level across countries for every year between 1950 and 2001. For countries where all three types of measure are available, the estimates of per capita GDP level are derivative. However, to arrive at a comprehensive world total, we need proxy measures of GDP movement for 42 countries, and proxy per capita GDP levels for 48 countries for the year 1990. These proxies collectively represent less than 1 per cent of world output.

a) World Population Movement 1950–2003

There are two comprehensive and detailed estimates of world population which are regularly updated and revised. They both provide annual estimates back to 1950 and projections 50 years into the future. No other source provides such comprehensive detail, length of perspective, or causal analysis of birth and death rates, fertility and migration. Here I have used the latest (October 2002) estimates of the US Bureau of the Census (USBC) for all countries except China, India and Indonesia. In Maddison (2001), I used the USBC 1999 version for 178 countries, OECD sources for 20 countries and Soviet sources for 15 countries. USBC estimates are available at http://www.census.gov/ipc. The United Nations Population Division (UNPD) is the alternative. Its latest estimates, *World Population Prospects: The 2000 Revision*, were prepared in February 2001; the previous version was issued in 1998. The UN shows estimates for quinquennial intervals, but annual country detail is available for purchase on a CD ROM. Table 7a shows my estimates, based mainly on USBC. Table 7* shows UNPD figures with the same regional breakdown. The easiest way to compare the two sources is the ratio of the two alternatives shown in Table 7**. On the world level the differences are minimal, and the regional differences are not very large after 1973. On the country level there are larger differences between the two sources. These are biggest for small countries and the UNPD omits Taiwan. Both sources provide a similar long–term view, showing the fastest demographic momentum in Africa and a general reduction in the pace of growth in the 1990s. Differences are mainly due to use of different sources or conjectures for cases where evidence is poor. It is clear from inspection of the country detail that the USBC takes better account of short–term interruptions due to war, flight of population or natural disasters. Their impact is smoothed by UNPD interpolation between census intervals. One example is the genocide and exodus from Rwanda: USBC shows a 25 per cent fall of population in 1993–5, UNPD 9 per cent. USBC shows a 55 per cent fall in Kuwait in 1991 during the Gulf war, UNPD 2 per cent. USBC shows a 70 per cent fall in Montserrat in 1998 due to volcanic activity, UNPD tapers this decline over several years. In fact, a major objective of the UN is to provide alternative projections of population trends which are of fundamental importance in assessing prospects for its development programmes. USBC is probably more interested in monitoring past and present performance.

b) Movement in Volume of GDP 1950–2001

Table 7–1 shows the coverage of our GDP estimates for five benchmark years since 1820. For 2001 there were direct estimates for 179 countries representing 99.8 per cent of world output with proxies for 42 other countries (mostly very small), for which direct measures were not available (see Tables 1–4, 4–5 and 5–4). Generally speaking the proxies assume per capita GDP movement parallel to the average for other countries in the same region. The total number of countries was bigger in 2001 than 1950, but this was due to the emergence of new states in Eastern Europe and the USSR. The area covered and the degree of reliance on proxies was in fact similar in 1950. Coverage was much more comprehensive than for the nineteenth century.

Table 7-1. Coverage of World GDP Sample and Proportionate Role of Proxy Measures, 1820-2001
(GDP in billion international dollars and number of countries)

	1820		1870		1913		1950		2001	
Sample countries										
Western Europe	135.4	(9)	326.9	(14)	898.5	(15)	1 394.8	(20)	7 540.4	(20)
Western Offshoots	12.7	(2)	110.6	(3)	577.2	(3)	1 635.5	(4)	9 156.3	(4)
Eastern Europe and former USSR	6.5	(1)	101.9	(3)	290.9	(3)	694.0	(7)	2 072.0	(27)
Latin America	8.2	(3)	17.5	(6)	101.9	(9)	315.6	(39)	3 078.8	(35)
Asia	383.5	(10)	392.3	(11)	644.6	(17)	969.0	(39)	14 050.4	(39)
Africa	n.a.		n.a.		30.7	(5)	202.1	(54)	1 204.3	(54)
World	546.2	(25)	985.2	(37)	2 543.8	(52)	5 310.9	(163)	37 056.9	(179)
Total GDP including proxy component										
Western Europe	160.1		367.6		902.3	(28)	1 396.2	(29)	7 550.3	(29)
Western Offshoots	13.5		111.5		582.9	(4)	1 635.5	(4)	9 156.3	(4)
Eastern Europe and former USSR	62.6		133.8		367.1	(8)	695.3	(8)	2 072.0	(27)
Latin America	15.0		27.5		119.9	(47)	415.9	(47)	3 087.0	(47)
Asia	412.9		427.0		680.3	(55)	983.7	(57)	14 105.7	(57)
Africa	31.2		45.6		80.9	(57)	203.1	(57)	1 222.6	(57)
World	695.3		1 113.0		2 733.5	(199)	5 329.7	(202)	37 193.9	(221)
Coverage of Sample, per cent of regional and world total										
Western Europe	84.5		98.7		99.6		99.9		99.9	
Western Offshoots	94.2		99.2		99.0		100.0		100.0	
Eastern Europe and former USSR	10.4		76.2		79.2		99.8		100.0	
Latin America	54.5		63.6		85.0		99.9		99.7	
Asia	92.9		91.8		94.8		98.5		99.6	
Africa	0.0		0.0		37.9		99.5		98.5	
World	78.6		88.5		93.1		99.6		99.8	

http://dx.doi.org/10.1787/456125276116

ISBN 92-64-02261-9 – © OECD 2006

Measures of GDP volume movement for 1950–2001 are mainly derived from official sources, because of the widespread governmental commitment to their publication, and, from 1953, adherence to the methodology of a standardised system of national accounts (SNA), now endorsed by the EU, IMF, OECD, United Nations, and World Bank (see UN, 1993). Communist countries were an exception. They used the Soviet material product approach (MPS), which exaggerated growth and left out most service activities. Fortunately Kremlinologists (guided by the work of Abram Bergson and Thad Alton) were able to adjust estimates for many of these countries to conform more closely to SNA criteria — see the assessment of their work in Maddison (1995) for Eastern Europe; Maddison (1997) for the USSR; and Maddison (1998) on China. The MPS system has now been abandoned, but there are still residual measurement problems of adjustment to the SNA in the successor countries of the USSR, China, Cuba, North Korea and Vietnam. There are also countries, particularly in Africa, where real GDP estimates are still of low quality, because resources for statistics and trained statisticians are very scarce and in many cases, data collection has been interrupted by war.

For OECD countries, a full set of national accounts statistics, with adjustment to secure comparability, has been published regularly since 1954, with annual data for 1938, and for 1947 onwards. For Eastern Europe official estimates are available in publications of the Economic Commission for Europe (ECE), and adjusted figures by the CIA were published regularly for 1950–90 in the proceedings of the Joint Economic Committee of the US Congress. The Economic Commission for Latin America and the Caribbean (ECLAC) has published detailed national accounts annually since 1950 in its *Statistical Yearbook for Latin America*, with updates in its monthly *ECLAC Notes*. East Asian national accounts are published in detail by the Asian Development Bank in its annual *Key Indicators*. West Asian accounts are published by the Economic and Social Commission for Western Asia (ESCWA) in its annual *National Accounts Studies of the ESCWA Region*. Estimates for African countries 1950–90 were derived mainly from the database of the OECD Development Centre whose *Latest Information on National Accounts of Developing Countries* was published annually from 1969 to 1991. For 1990 onwards, annual GDP movements for virtually all African countries are shown in the IMF *Economic Outlook*.

c) Derivation of 1990 Benchmark Purchasing Power Converters in order to Permit Cross–country Comparison of GDP Levels and Construction of Regional and World Aggregates

In order to make cross–country comparison of GDP levels and aggregate estimates of regional or world totals, we need to convert national currencies into a common unit (numeraire). Table 7–2 shows the derivation of the numeraire for measurement of GDP levels in my benchmark year 1990, which is the interspatial–intertemporal anchor for my comprehensive world estimates. The 1990 cross–section level estimates are merged with the time series for real GDP growth to show GDP levels for all other years. There are four options for deriving GDP converters:

i) Exchange Rates: Conversion of nominal estimates by exchange rates is the simplest option, but exchange rates are mainly a reflection of purchasing power over tradeable items. They may also move erratically because of speculative capital movements or surges of inflation. In poor countries where wages are low, non–tradeable services, like haircuts, government services, building construction, are generally cheaper than in high–income countries, so there is a general tendency for exchange rates to understate purchasing power of their currencies. China is an extreme case. Mr Patten, the last British governor of Hong Kong, stated in an article in the *Economist* newspaper of 4 January 1997 that "Britain's GDP today is almost twice the size of China's". This was an exchange rate comparison. PPP conversion shows British GDP to have been less than a third of China's in 1997. There are very strong reasons for preferring PPP converters which are now available for most of the world economy. Correction for the wide disparity in price levels between countries is a logical interspatial corollary to the use of national GDP deflators to correct for intertemporal changes in the price level. However, there was understandable reluctance on the part of some countries to abandonment of exchange rate comparisons. Although the World Bank made a major contribution to finance work on PPPs, it did not use them for its analytical work because they raise the relative income levels of poor countries substantially compared to their standing in an exchange rate ranking. They feared that this would make them ineligible to borrow from IDA (the cheap loan window of the Bank). For this reason the Bank continued to rank countries by income level in its *Atlas,* by using a three–year moving average of exchange rates.

ii) Purchasing Power Parity (PPP) conversion: This concept was first used by Gustav Cassel in 1918, and crudely implemented by Colin Clark in 1940. A substantial part of Clark's price material was derived from a survey made for the Ford Motor Company, together with his own price comparisons for luxury goods and ILO material on rents in different countries. Much more sophisticated measures have been developed by co–operative research of national statistical offices and international agencies in the past few decades. They have become highly sophisticated comparative pricing exercises involving collection of carefully specified price information on a massive scale by national statistical offices for representative items of consumption, investment goods and government services. The latest OECD exercise for 1999 involved collection of prices for 2 740 items. The OEEC first developed these comparisons of real levels of expenditure and the purchasing parity of currencies in the 1950s for 8 of its member countries and rough proxies for the rest. OECD reactivated this work in 1982 in cooperation with Eurostat (see Michael Ward, 1985). In the meantime Irving Kravis, Alan Heston and Robert Summers set up their International Comparisons Project (ICP) in 1968 and published three major studies in 1975, 1978 and 1982. Their work made major contributions to the methodology of international income comparisons and greatly expanded their coverage. Their last volume covered 34 countries. Their work was taken over by the United Nations Statistical Office which made comparisons for 1980 and 1985. Altogether the two UN comparisons covered 82 countries. There were regional comparisons for some Asian, African and Middle Eastern countries by UN agencies in 1993, but UNSO did not attempt to integrate them. ICP estimation has now been taken over by the World Bank and the next exercise is planned for 2004. The main current activity in this field is by OECD–Eurostat; in 2002 they published a 1999 level comparison for 43 countries.

When the ICP approach was originally developed in OEEC, the main emphasis was on binary comparison. The three most straightforward options were: i) a Paasche PPP (with "own" country quantity weights); ii) a Laspeyres PPP (with the quantity weights of the numeraire country — the United States); or iii), as a compromise, the Fisher geometric average of the two measures. The corresponding measures of real expenditure levels were i) Laspeyres level comparisons based on the prices (unit values) of the numeraire country; ii) Paasche level comparisons based on own country prices (unit values); or iii) a Fisher geometric average of the two measures. Binary comparisons, e.g. France/US, and UK/US can be linked with the United States as the "star" country. The derivative France–UK comparison will not necessarily produce the same results as direct binary comparison of France and the United Kingdom. Such star system comparisons are not "transitive". However, in studies I made of comparative performance of advanced capitalist countries (Maddison, 1982 and 1991), I preferred to use the Laspeyres level comparison at US prices, because this was the price structure to which the other countries in this group were converging as their productivity and demand patterns approached US levels.

Comparisons can be made transitive if they are done on a "multilateral" rather than a "binary" basis. The Geary–Khamis approach (named for R.S. Geary and S.H. Khamis) is an ingenious method for multilaterising the results which provides transitivity and other desirable properties. It was used by Kravis, Heston and Summers as a method for aggregating ICP results available at the basic heading level. They used it in conjunction with the commodity product dummy (CPD) method (invented by Robert Summers) for filling holes in the basic dataset. I used PPPs of this type for 70 countries representing

93.7 per cent of world GDP in 1990 (see Table 7–2). The Geary–Khamis approach gives a weight to countries corresponding to the size of their GDP, so that a large economy, like the United States, has a strong influence on the results. Eurostat (the statistical office of EU) uses a multilateral method in which all its member countries have an equal weight. This is the EKS technique (named for its inventors, Eltöto, Kovacs and Szulc). For my purpose an equi–country weighting system which treats Luxemburg and Germany as equal partners in the world economy is inappropriate, so I have a strong preference for the Geary–Khamis approach. Fortunately the OECD–Eurostat joint exercise derives both EKS and Geary–Khamis measures — see Maddison (1995), pp. 164–79 for a detailed confrontation of all the binary and multilateral PPPs published up to that time.

iii) Penn World Tables (PWT): For countries not covered by ICP, Summers and Heston devised short–cut estimates. Their latest Penn World Tables (PWT 6.1, October 2002) provide PPP converters for 168 countries. Their estimates for countries which have never had an ICP exercise are necessarily rougher than for those where these exercises are available. For these they use much more limited price information from cost of living surveys (of diplomats, UN officials, and people working abroad for private business) as a proxy for the ICP specification prices. I used PPPs from PWT for 84 countries, 5.6 per cent of world GDP in 1990 (see Table 7–2).

iv) ICOP (International Comparison of Real Output and Productivity): The fourth option is to compare levels of real output (value added) using census of production material on output quantities and prices. Rostas (1948) pioneered this approach for manufacturing. The first study of this type for the whole economy was a binary comparison of the United Kingdom and the United States by Paige and Bombach (1959) published by OEEC. This approach was not used in subsequent ICP comparisons, but I used it in a comparative study of economic growth in 29 countries (*Economic Progress and Policy in Developing Countries,* 1970, Norton, New York). At that time there were no ICP estimates for non–OECD countries. I made estimates of value added and productivity in agriculture, industry and services and total GDP in US relative prices for the 29 countries for 1965. I merged these benchmark estimates to time series of GDP movement in the 29 countries back to 1950, 1938, 1913 and 1870, wherever possible. The basic approach was very similar to that in this volume, although the measures of GDP levels in the benchmark year and the time series for GDP growth were much cruder than they are now. In Maddison (1983) I compared my production–side estimates with those of Kravis, Heston and Summers (1982). I also used the two sets of estimates as benchmarks for merger with time series on economic growth to see what the implications were for comparative levels of performance back to 1820. I concluded provisionally that the ICP approach probably exaggerated service output in the poorer countries, but that an authoritative view on this topic required more careful study on the production side. I therefore set up the ICOP (International Comparison of Output and Productivity) project at the University of Groningen in 1983. The Groningen Growth and Development Centre has produced nearly 100 research memoranda on productivity as well as Ph. D theses on economic growth and levels of performance by Bart van Ark, Tom Elfring, Pierre van der Eng, Andre Hofman, Sompop Manarungsan, Kees van der Meer, Nanno Mulder, Dirk Pilat, Jaap Sleifer and Marcel Timmer. These theses are in the Kuznetsian tradition with fully transparent and complete statistical appendices showing sources and methods of approach (see Maddison and van Ark, 2000). The ICOP programme puts primary emphasis on analysis of labour, capital and joint factor productivity for major sectors of the economy. It was not intended as a rival to IPC, but provides and alternative and complementary approach to the problem of international comparison of GDP levels. So far, the project has covered one or more sectors of the economy for more than 30 countries which together represent more than half of world GDP (see http://www.eco.rug.nl/ggdc/dseries/icop.shtml#top). Recently the scale of its systemic comparative exercises has increased in country coverage and sector detail, in co–operation with international agencies including Euostat, ILO and OECD. The most recent ICOP work was a study for 19 countries, covering more than 30 sectors. These results are a useful crosscheck on the ICP measures and on the validity of my 1990 benchmarks as an anchor for analysis of levels of performance in the past (see HS–8 below).

Table 7-2. **Nature of PPP Converters Used to Estimate GDP Levels in the Benchmark Year 1990**
(billion 1990 Geary-Khamis dollars and number of countries)

	Europe and Western Offshoots	*Latin America*	*Asia*	*Africa*	*World*
ICP	15 273 (28)	2 131 (18)	8 017 (24)	0 (0)	25 421 (70)
PWT	59 (3)	71 (14)	524 (16)	891 (51)	1 516 (84)
Proxies	16 (10)	38 (15)	87 (17)	14 (6)	155 (48)
Total	15 349 (41)	2 240 (47)	8 628 (57)	905 (57)	27 122 (202)

Source: The PPP converters used here are the same as those in Maddison (2001) except for 7 African countries.

http://dx.doi.org/10.1787/456125276116

Europe and Western Offshoots: 99.5 per cent of regional GDP from ICP 6 for 1990; 22 countries from OECD–Eurostat and 6 countries from ECE (see OECD, 1993; ECE, 1994; Maddison, 1995, p. 172 and Maddison, 2001, pp. 189–90); 0.4 per cent of regional GDP (Bulgaria, Cyprus and Malta) from PWT version 5.6; 0.1 per cent from proxy estimates (Albania, Andorra, Channel Isles, Faeroe Isles, Gibraltar, Greenland, Isle of Man, Liechtenstein, Monaco and San Marino).

Latin America: 95.1 per cent of regional GDP (18 countries) from ICP. As there was no Latin America ICP exercise for 1990 or later; I used ICP 3 for 2 countries and ICP 4 for 16 countries updated to 1990 (see Kravis, Heston and Summers, 1982; UN, 1987; and Maddison, 2001, p. 199). Updating involves adjustment for the GDP volume change in the specified country between the reference year and 1990, and for the movement in the US GDP deflator in the same interval. 3.2 per cent of regional GDP (Bahamas, Barbados, Belize, Dominica, Grenada, Guyana, Haiti, Nicaragua, Puerto Rico, St. Kitts Nevis, St. Lucia, St. Vincent, Suriname, Trinidad and Tobago) from PWT version 5.6; 1.7 per cent from proxy estimates (Anguilla, Antigua and Barbuda, Aruba, Bermuda, Cayman Islands, Cuba, French Guyana, Guadeloupe, Martinique, Montserrat, Netherlands Antilles, St. Pierre and Miquelon, Turks and Caicos, Virgin Islands and British Virgin Islands).

Asia: 92.9 per cent of regional GDP (24 countries) from ICP or equivalent. I used ICP 3 for 2 countries, ICP 4 for 5 countries. ICP 5 for 3 countreis and linked Bangladesh and Pakistan to their 1950 level relative to India. All 12 were updated to 1990. OECD estimates were available for Japan and Mongolia for 1990, and I made an estimate for China for 1990 based on Maddison (1998) and Ren (1997). ICP 7 estimates were available from ESCAP(1999) and ESCWA (1997) for 9 countries for 1993 and backdated to 1990 (see Maddison, 2001, pp. 202, 208, 219–20). Backdating involves the same procedure as updating. 6.1 per cent of regional GDP (Bhutan, Burma, Fiji, Iraq, Jordan, Kuwait, Oman, Papua New Guinea, Saudi Arabia, Solomon Islands, Taiwan, Tonga, UAE, Vanuatu, Western Samoa, and Yemen) from PWT version 5.6; 1 per cent of regional GDP from proxy estimates (Afghanistan, American Samoa, Brunei, Cambodia, French Polynesia, Guam, Kiribati, Lebanon, Macao, Maldives, Marshall Islands, Micronesia, New Caledonia, North Korea, Northern Marianas, Palau, Wallis and Futuna.

Africa: 75.8 per cent of regional GDP from PWT 5.6 and 22.7 per cent from PWT 6.1; proxy estimates for 1.5 per cent of regional GDP (Equatorial Guinea, Libya, Mayotte, St. Helena, São Tomé & Principe and Western Sahara); see source note HS–6 and Table 6–11.

d) Alternative Estimates of Movement of World GDP, 1970 onwards

The IMF now makes annual estimates of the growth of world GDP in real terms, available back to 1970. Their preference is for PPP adjustment, but they publish an alternative with exchange rate weights (see IMF, *Economic Outlook*, September 2002, pp. 189–199, which describes their method). Their PPP estimates (with 1996 weights) are derived from ICP. For countries not covered by ICP, they estimate PPPs using a regression technique in which exchange rates are one of the independent variables.

Table 7–3 compares the year–to–year movement of their world aggregate and mine. The IMF measure with PPP weights shows faster growth for 1970–2001 than I do (3.9 per cent a year instead of 3.3 per cent). One would not expect complete concordance as my PPP weights are different and my coverage more complete, but it seems clear that the IMF exaggerates growth. Its measure excludes non–member countries, and makes no proxy estimates for countries where estimation is difficult. Some of these — Afghanistan, Bosnia, Cuba, North Korea, Serbia — have had negative growth. It is clear from their database that they have not adjusted growth estimates for countries which formerly used the Soviet system of national accounts. For China they show GDP growth averaging 8.5 per cent a year for 1970–2001, whereas my adjusted estimate is 6.5 per cent. For Germany for the same period, they show growth averaging 2.2 per cent a year. I show 2.0 per cent as I include East Germany for the whole post–war period. For 1973–2001 they show Russian growth averaging 0.7 per cent and –0.7 for the Ukraine, whereas I have –0.2 per cent for Russia and –1.5 for Ukraine

The Department of Economic and Social Affairs of the United Nations also publishes annual estimates of world GDP, available back to 1980. Their preference is for an aggregate with exchange rate conversion, but they publish an alternative using PPP converters (see *World Economic Survey 2002*, pp. 4, 278–280 and 285). Their PPP weights are for 1995, and are derived from ICP and PWT. It is not clear from the published description how many countries are included, but their world aggregate is probably more comprehensive than that of the IMF. The UN measure shows slower growth than the IMF, and is closer to mine.

Table 7-3. **Annual Change of World GDP, IMF and Maddison Measures, 1970-2001**
(percentage change)

	IMF with Ex. Rate	IMF with PPP	Maddison PPP		IMF with Ex. Rate	IMF with PPP	Maddison PPP
1970	4.6	5.2	5.1	1986	3.3	3.7	3.5
1971	4.3	4.6	4.2	1987	3.7	4.1	3.6
1972	5.0	5.4	4.7	1988	4.5	4.7	4.3
1973	6.4	6.9	6.6	1989	3.7	3.7	3.2
1974	2.2	2.8	2.3	1990	2.7	2.8	2.0
1975	1.5	1.9	1.5	1991	0.7	1.5	1.1
1976	5.0	5.2	4.9	1992	1.0	2.1	2.0
1977	4.2	4.4	4.1	1993	1.0	2.2	2.2
1978	4.5	4.7	4.4	1994	2.9	3.7	3.4
1979	3.7	3.8	3.6	1995	2.8	3.7	3.4
1980	2.5	2.9	2.0	1996	3.3	4.0	3.9
1981	2.0	2.2	1.9	1997	3.5	4.2	3.9
1982	0.6	1.2	1.2	1998	2.2	2.8	2.5
1983	2.9	3.0	2.9	1999	3.1	3.6	3.3
1984	4.8	4.9	4.5	2000	3.9	4.7	4.4
1985	3.5	3.7	3.5	2001	1.1	2.2	1.9

http://dx.doi.org/10.1787/456125276116

Table 7a. World Population by Region, 1900 and Annual Estimates 1950-2001
(000 at mid-year)

	Western Europe	Western Offshoots	Eastern Europe	Former USSR	Latin America	Asia	Africa	World
1900	233 645	86 396	70 993	124 500	64 764	873 324	110 000	1 563 622
1950	304 940	176 458	87 637	179 571	165 938	1 382 447	227 333	2 524 324
1951	307 024	179 667	88 713	182 677	170 411	1 407 689	232 068	2 568 249
1952	308 754	183 025	89 814	185 856	174 975	1 435 439	237 008	2 614 871
1953	310 696	186 273	91 081	188 961	179 664	1 464 409	242 086	2 663 170
1954	312 607	189 819	92 341	192 171	184 563	1 495 497	247 273	2 714 271
1955	314 605	193 395	93 719	195 613	189 673	1 526 707	252 759	2 766 471
1956	316 758	197 027	94 985	199 103	194 935	1 558 727	258 409	2 819 944
1957	318 987	200 936	96 049	202 604	200 395	1 594 212	264 222	2 877 405
1958	321 318	204 541	97 149	206 201	206 069	1 631 177	270 231	2 936 686
1959	323 824	208 165	98 217	209 928	211 951	1 664 717	276 454	2 993 256
1960	326 346	211 671	99 254	213 780	218 029	1 686 796	282 919	3 038 795
1961	329 115	215 357	100 292	217 618	224 157	1 703 409	289 385	3 079 333
1962	332 342	218 807	101 172	221 227	230 450	1 732 716	295 977	3 132 691
1963	335 251	222 128	102 057	224 585	236 957	1 773 645	303 251	3 197 874
1964	338 111	225 410	102 908	227 698	243 648	1 814 092	310 725	3 262 592
1965	340 884	228 454	103 713	230 513	250 474	1 856 366	318 478	3 328 882
1966	343 440	231 351	104 494	233 139	257 370	1 901 303	326 534	3 397 631
1967	345 628	234 132	105 256	235 630	264 339	1 946 533	334 945	3 466 463
1968	347 633	236 710	106 302	237 983	271 430	1 993 844	343 591	3 537 493
1969	349 946	239 293	107 117	240 253	278 670	2 042 155	352 457	3 609 891
1970	352 240	242 290	107 921	242 478	286 007	2 092 954	361 168	3 685 058
1971	354 702	245 500	108 753	244 887	293 427	2 145 665	370 534	3 763 468
1972	356 845	248 287	109 589	247 343	300 900	2 197 174	380 026	3 840 164
1973	358 825	250 841	110 418	249 712	308 399	2 248 260	390 034	3 916 489
1974	360 466	253 386	111 377	252 111	315 957	2 298 349	400 314	3 991 960
1975	361 743	256 071	112 372	254 519	323 524	2 346 352	410 827	4 065 408
1976	362 752	258 622	113 357	256 883	331 109	2 391 522	422 188	4 136 433
1977	363 850	261 274	114 339	259 225	338 791	2 437 228	433 995	4 208 702
1978	364 949	264 036	115 199	261 525	346 493	2 483 253	446 294	4 281 749
1979	366 096	266 918	116 058	263 751	354 326	2 532 444	459 413	4 359 006
1980	367 457	270 106	116 804	265 973	362 069	2 580 468	472 721	4 435 598
1981	368 647	272 975	117 483	268 217	370 057	2 626 665	486 060	4 510 104
1982	369 371	275 785	118 173	270 533	378 204	2 669 803	500 253	4 582 122
1983	369 920	278 403	118 772	273 010	386 279	2 728 669	515 235	4 670 288
1984	370 509	280 908	119 285	275 574	394 193	2 779 117	530 353	4 749 939
1985	371 162	283 494	119 866	278 108	402 110	2 830 331	545 742	4 830 813
1986	372 001	286 181	120 402	280 646	410 248	2 882 699	561 280	4 913 457
1987	372 887	288 928	120 881	283 124	418 470	2 937 328	577 158	4 998 776
1988	374 092	291 768	121 092	285 482	426 758	2 992 532	593 250	5 084 974
1989	375 950	294 843	121 394	287 011	435 097	3 047 760	609 818	5 171 873
1990	377 856	298 304	121 569	289 045	443 276	3 102 638	626 814	5 259 502
1991	379 688	302 265	121 847	290 754	451 387	3 154 008	644 889	5 344 838
1992	381 580	306 337	121 880	292 079	459 512	3 205 102	662 410	5 428 900
1993	383 334	310 340	121 605	292 686	467 639	3 257 972	679 567	5 513 143
1994	384 719	314 108	121 379	292 755	475 790	3 308 981	696 273	5 594 005
1995	385 936	317 858	121 135	292 597	483 957	3 361 948	713 856	5 677 287
1996	387 063	321 620	120 983	292 188	492 093	3 411 457	730 822	5 756 226
1997	388 065	325 459	120 942	291 750	500 150	3 460 624	748 865	5 835 855
1998	388 977	329 239	120 924	291 373	508 094	3 509 481	766 842	5 914 930
1999	389 945	332 994	120 904	291 012	515 916	3 561 961	785 235	5 997 967
2000	391 036	336 601	120 913	290 654	523 612	3 605 017	803 311	6 071 144
2001	392 101	339 838	120 912	290 349	531 213	3 653 504	821 088	6 149 005

http://dx.doi.org/10.1787/456125276116

ISBN 92-64-02261-9 – © OECD 2006

Table 7b. World GDP by Region, 1900 and Annual Estimates 1950-2001
(million 1990 international Geary-Khamis dollars)

	Western Europe	Western Offshoots	Eastern Europe	Former USSR	Latin America	Asia	Africa	World
1900	675 923	346 869	102 084	154 049	71 810	556 845	66 136	1 973 716
1950	1 396 188	1 635 490	185 023	510 243	415 897	983 737	203 131	5 329 719
1951	1 478 599	1 753 540	195 670	512 566	438 230	1 052 267	212 653	5 643 536
1952	1 532 433	1 821 083	198 236	545 792	453 597	1 139 703	220 780	5 911 635
1953	1 611 339	1 903 763	209 145	569 260	469 274	1 218 405	228 858	6 210 056
1954	1 699 722	1 898 106	218 886	596 910	499 214	1 270 868	239 781	6 423 499
1955	1 805 779	2 032 869	233 857	648 027	530 878	1 330 326	248 054	6 829 803
1956	1 888 452	2 082 376	239 494	710 065	553 540	1 421 380	258 153	7 153 473
1957	1 971 596	2 123 207	257 611	724 470	595 876	1 485 225	267 612	7 425 611
1958	2 018 551	2 111 417	272 635	778 840	625 722	1 581 790	273 683	7 662 653
1959	2 114 619	2 261 993	286 886	770 244	640 897	1 657 765	288 734	8 021 152
1960	2 250 549	2 320 141	304 685	843 434	683 003	1 736 343	301 578	8 439 748
1961	2 370 583	2 374 411	322 781	891 763	715 561	1 744 557	308 136	8 727 808
1962	2 486 946	2 518 521	328 253	915 928	745 366	1 822 562	320 322	9 137 914
1963	2 603 774	2 630 968	344 112	895 016	767 858	1 950 307	343 186	9 535 239
1964	2 761 481	2 785 505	364 518	1 010 727	820 323	2 123 867	361 570	10 228 009
1965	2 877 269	2 962 352	380 016	1 068 117	861 456	2 232 507	381 330	10 763 066
1966	2 983 130	3 151 817	404 452	1 119 932	904 391	2 393 627	392 226	11 349 595
1967	3 088 548	3 234 760	420 645	1 169 422	945 275	2 511 607	400 067	11 770 344
1968	3 252 072	3 389 792	436 444	1 237 966	1 001 933	2 678 075	420 309	12 416 612
1969	3 438 238	3 507 231	449 862	1 255 392	1 066 861	2 935 884	453 131	13 106 621
1970	3 590 948	3 527 862	465 695	1 351 818	1 139 930	3 202 413	490 102	13 768 791
1971	3 711 784	3 647 077	499 790	1 387 832	1 207 883	3 384 521	512 138	14 351 050
1972	3 875 271	3 836 032	524 971	1 395 732	1 285 171	3 584 101	530 848	15 032 152
1973	4 096 456	4 058 289	550 756	1 513 070	1 389 001	3 865 936	549 993	16 023 529
1974	4 185 248	4 067 628	583 528	1 556 984	1 472 097	3 955 086	575 500	16 396 098
1975	4 167 528	4 069 398	604 251	1 561 399	1 516 401	4 143 267	582 627	16 644 898
1976	4 346 755	4 280 195	619 961	1 634 589	1 600 191	4 353 000	621 584	17 456 303
1977	4 471 506	4 459 671	641 681	1 673 159	1 676 351	4 597 844	647 589	18 167 829
1978	4 606 129	4 700 723	662 328	1 715 215	1 748 863	4 873 135	663 511	18 969 933
1979	4 774 306	4 866 597	672 299	1 707 083	1 859 032	5 074 326	694 654	19 648 326
1980	4 849 408	4 878 155	675 819	1 709 174	1 959 640	5 249 683	725 905	20 047 814
1981	4 860 516	5 006 126	667 932	1 724 741	1 971 428	5 466 812	733 452	20 431 038
1982	4 901 367	4 912 862	674 202	1 767 262	1 948 323	5 711 348	756 255	20 671 650
1983	4 990 650	5 103 869	684 326	1 823 723	1 899 500	6 003 271	761 138	21 266 508
1984	5 110 650	5 467 359	705 274	1 847 190	1 971 670	6 354 835	777 297	22 234 307
1985	5 238 333	5 687 354	706 201	1 863 687	2 031 533	6 676 210	801 420	23 004 771
1986	5 385 159	5 875 446	725 733	1 940 363	2 114 420	6 959 604	818 732	23 819 491
1987	5 539 861	6 086 756	721 188	1 965 457	2 180 944	7 360 551	831 716	24 686 508
1988	5 763 264	6 344 832	727 564	2 007 280	2 201 128	7 847 201	865 804	25 757 109
1989	5 960 940	6 560 368	718 039	2 037 253	2 228 787	8 186 232	892 376	26 584 033
1990	6 032 764	6 665 584	662 604	1 987 995	2 239 774	8 627 846	904 898	27 121 506
1991	6 132 879	6 624 976	590 280	1 863 524	2 322 319	8 983 054	911 693	27 428 768
1992	6 202 870	6 813 766	559 611	1 592 084	2 395 378	9 493 542	912 598	27 969 895
1993	6 182 982	6 997 300	550 399	1 435 008	2 477 861	10 007 080	921 183	28 571 861
1994	6 354 335	7 287 292	572 242	1 231 738	2 604 244	10 564 953	941 178	29 555 982
1995	6 506 739	7 488 397	605 392	1 163 401	2 642 430	11 196 934	969 734	30 573 080
1996	6 617 683	7 745 855	628 591	1 125 992	2 733 963	11 879 126	1 024 994	31 756 260
1997	6 791 738	8 071 150	645 039	1 149 255	2 877 476	12 413 389	1 060 213	33 008 319
1998	6 991 426	8 419 092	663 471	1 124 868	2 943 073	12 591 481	1 099 966	33 833 438
1999	7 180 236	8 774 087	675 657	1 171 952	2 950 010	13 079 182	1 136 130	34 967 319
2000	7 430 287	9 110 246	701 746	1 264 526	3 057 026	13 762 085	1 175 890	36 501 872
2001	7 550 272	9 156 267	728 792	1 343 230	3 086 936	14 105 724	1 222 577	37 193 868

http://dx.doi.org/10.1787/456125276116

Table 7c. **World Per Capita GDP by Region, 1900 and Annual Estimates 1950-2001**
(1990 international Geary-Khamis dollars)

	Western Europe	Western Offshoots	Eastern Europe	Former USSR	Latin America	Asia	Africa	World
1900	2 893	4 015	1 438	1 237	1 109	638	601	1 262
1950	4 579	9 268	2 111	2 841	2 506	712	894	2 111
1951	4 816	9 760	2 206	2 806	2 572	748	916	2 197
1952	4 963	9 950	2 207	2 937	2 592	794	932	2 261
1953	5 186	10 220	2 296	3 013	2 612	832	945	2 332
1954	5 437	10 000	2 370	3 106	2 705	850	970	2 367
1955	5 740	10 511	2 495	3 313	2 799	871	981	2 469
1956	5 962	10 569	2 521	3 566	2 840	912	999	2 537
1957	6 181	10 567	2 682	3 576	2 974	932	1 013	2 581
1958	6 282	10 323	2 806	3 777	3 037	970	1 013	2 609
1959	6 530	10 866	2 921	3 669	3 024	996	1 044	2 680
1960	6 896	10 961	3 070	3 945	3 133	1 029	1 066	2 777
1961	7 203	11 025	3 218	4 098	3 192	1 024	1 065	2 834
1962	7 483	11 510	3 245	4 140	3 234	1 052	1 082	2 917
1963	7 767	11 844	3 372	3 985	3 241	1 100	1 132	2 982
1964	8 167	12 358	3 542	4 439	3 367	1 171	1 164	3 135
1965	8 441	12 967	3 664	4 634	3 439	1 203	1 197	3 233
1966	8 686	13 624	3 871	4 804	3 514	1 259	1 201	3 340
1967	8 936	13 816	3 996	4 963	3 576	1 290	1 194	3 395
1968	9 355	14 320	4 106	5 202	3 691	1 343	1 223	3 510
1969	9 825	14 657	4 200	5 225	3 828	1 438	1 286	3 631
1970	10 195	14 560	4 315	5 575	3 986	1 530	1 357	3 736
1971	10 465	14 856	4 596	5 667	4 117	1 577	1 382	3 813
1972	10 860	15 450	4 790	5 643	4 271	1 631	1 397	3 914
1973	11 416	16 179	4 988	6 059	4 504	1 720	1 410	4 091
1974	11 611	16 053	5 239	6 176	4 659	1 721	1 438	4 107
1975	11 521	15 892	5 377	6 135	4 687	1 766	1 418	4 094
1976	11 983	16 550	5 469	6 363	4 833	1 820	1 472	4 220
1977	12 289	17 069	5 612	6 454	4 948	1 887	1 492	4 317
1978	12 621	17 803	5 749	6 559	5 047	1 962	1 487	4 430
1979	13 041	18 233	5 793	6 472	5 247	2 004	1 512	4 508
1980	13 197	18 060	5 786	6 426	5 412	2 034	1 536	4 520
1981	13 185	18 339	5 685	6 430	5 327	2 081	1 509	4 530
1982	13 269	17 814	5 705	6 533	5 152	2 139	1 512	4 511
1983	13 491	18 333	5 762	6 680	4 918	2 200	1 477	4 554
1984	13 794	19 463	5 913	6 703	5 002	2 287	1 466	4 681
1985	14 113	20 062	5 892	6 701	5 052	2 359	1 468	4 762
1986	14 476	20 531	6 028	6 914	5 154	2 414	1 459	4 848
1987	14 857	21 067	5 966	6 942	5 212	2 506	1 441	4 939
1988	15 406	21 746	6 008	7 031	5 158	2 622	1 459	5 065
1989	15 856	22 250	5 915	7 098	5 123	2 686	1 463	5 140
1990	15 966	22 345	5 450	6 878	5 053	2 781	1 444	5 157
1991	16 152	21 918	4 844	6 409	5 145	2 848	1 414	5 132
1992	16 256	22 243	4 591	5 451	5 213	2 962	1 378	5 152
1993	16 129	22 547	4 526	4 903	5 299	3 072	1 356	5 182
1994	16 517	23 200	4 715	4 207	5 474	3 193	1 352	5 284
1995	16 860	23 559	4 998	3 976	5 460	3 330	1 358	5 385
1996	17 097	24 084	5 196	3 854	5 556	3 482	1 403	5 517
1997	17 502	24 799	5 333	3 939	5 753	3 587	1 416	5 656
1998	17 974	25 571	5 487	3 861	5 793	3 588	1 434	5 720
1999	18 413	26 349	5 588	4 027	5 718	3 672	1 447	5 830
2000	19 002	27 065	5 804	4 351	5 838	3 817	1 464	6 012
2001	19 256	26 943	6 027	4 626	5 811	3 861	1 489	6 049

http://dx.doi.org/10.1787/456125276116

ISBN 92-64-02261-9 – © OECD 2006

Table 7a. Year–to–Year Percentage Change in World Population, by Region, 1950-2001

	Western Europe	Western Offshoots	Eastern Europe	Former USSR	Latin America	Asia	Africa	World
1950								
1951	0.7	1.8	1.2	1.7	2.7	1.8	2.1	1.7
1952	0.6	1.9	1.2	1.7	2.7	2.0	2.1	1.8
1953	0.6	1.8	1.4	1.7	2.7	2.0	2.1	1.8
1954	0.6	1.9	1.4	1.7	2.7	2.1	2.1	1.9
1955	0.6	1.9	1.5	1.8	2.8	2.1	2.2	1.9
1956	0.7	1.9	1.4	1.8	2.8	2.1	2.2	1.9
1957	0.7	2.0	1.1	1.8	2.8	2.3	2.2	2.0
1958	0.7	1.8	1.1	1.8	2.8	2.3	2.3	2.1
1959	0.8	1.8	1.1	1.8	2.9	2.1	2.3	1.9
1960	0.8	1.7	1.1	1.8	2.9	1.3	2.3	1.5
1961	0.8	1.7	1.0	1.8	2.8	1.0	2.3	1.3
1962	1.0	1.6	0.9	1.7	2.8	1.7	2.3	1.7
1963	0.9	1.5	0.9	1.5	2.8	2.4	2.5	2.1
1964	0.9	1.5	0.8	1.4	2.8	2.3	2.5	2.0
1965	0.8	1.4	0.8	1.2	2.8	2.3	2.5	2.0
1966	0.7	1.3	0.8	1.1	2.8	2.4	2.5	2.1
1967	0.6	1.2	0.7	1.1	2.7	2.4	2.6	2.0
1968	0.6	1.1	1.0	1.0	2.7	2.4	2.6	2.0
1969	0.7	1.1	0.8	1.0	2.7	2.4	2.6	2.0
1970	0.7	1.3	0.8	0.9	2.6	2.5	2.5	2.1
1971	0.7	1.3	0.8	1.0	2.6	2.5	2.6	2.1
1972	0.6	1.1	0.8	1.0	2.5	2.4	2.6	2.0
1973	0.6	1.0	0.8	1.0	2.5	2.3	2.6	2.0
1974	0.5	1.0	0.9	1.0	2.5	2.2	2.6	1.9
1975	0.4	1.1	0.9	1.0	2.4	2.1	2.6	1.8
1976	0.3	1.0	0.9	0.9	2.3	1.9	2.8	1.7
1977	0.3	1.0	0.9	0.9	2.3	1.9	2.8	1.7
1978	0.3	1.1	0.8	0.9	2.3	1.9	2.8	1.7
1979	0.3	1.1	0.7	0.9	2.3	2.0	2.9	1.8
1980	0.4	1.2	0.6	0.8	2.2	1.9	2.9	1.8
1981	0.3	1.1	0.6	0.8	2.2	1.8	2.8	1.7
1982	0.2	1.0	0.6	0.9	2.2	1.6	2.9	1.6
1983	0.1	0.9	0.5	0.9	2.1	2.2	3.0	1.9
1984	0.2	0.9	0.4	0.9	2.0	1.8	2.9	1.7
1985	0.2	0.9	0.5	0.9	2.0	1.8	2.9	1.7
1986	0.2	0.9	0.4	0.9	2.0	1.9	2.8	1.7
1987	0.2	1.0	0.4	0.9	2.0	1.9	2.8	1.7
1988	0.3	1.0	0.2	0.8	2.0	1.9	2.8	1.7
1989	0.5	1.1	0.2	0.5	2.0	1.8	2.8	1.7
1990	0.5	1.2	0.1	0.7	1.9	1.8	2.8	1.7
1991	0.5	1.3	0.2	0.6	1.8	1.7	2.9	1.6
1992	0.5	1.3	0.0	0.5	1.8	1.6	2.7	1.6
1993	0.5	1.3	-0.2	0.2	1.8	1.6	2.6	1.6
1994	0.4	1.2	-0.2	0.0	1.7	1.6	2.5	1.5
1995	0.3	1.2	-0.2	-0.1	1.7	1.6	2.5	1.5
1996	0.3	1.2	-0.1	-0.1	1.7	1.5	2.4	1.4
1997	0.3	1.2	0.0	-0.1	1.6	1.4	2.5	1.4
1998	0.2	1.2	0.0	-0.1	1.6	1.4	2.4	1.4
1999	0.2	1.1	0.0	-0.1	1.5	1.5	2.4	1.4
2000	0.3	1.1	0.0	-0.1	1.5	1.2	2.3	1.2
2001	0.3	1.0	0.0	-0.1	1.5	1.3	2.2	1.3

http://dx.doi.org/10.1787/456125276116

Table 7b. **Year–to–Year Percentage Change in World GDP Volume, by Region, 1950-2001**

	Western Europe	Western Offshoots	Eastern Europe	Former USSR	Latin America	Asia	Africa	World
1950								
1951	5.9	7.2	5.8	0.5	5.4	7.0	4.7	5.9
1952	3.6	3.9	1.3	6.5	3.5	8.3	3.8	4.8
1953	5.1	4.5	5.5	4.3	3.5	6.9	3.7	5.0
1954	5.5	-0.3	4.7	4.9	6.4	4.3	4.8	3.4
1955	6.2	7.1	6.8	8.6	6.3	4.7	3.5	6.3
1956	4.6	2.4	2.4	9.6	4.3	6.8	4.1	4.7
1957	4.4	2.0	7.6	2.0	7.6	4.5	3.7	3.8
1958	2.4	-0.6	5.8	7.5	5.0	6.5	2.3	3.2
1959	4.8	7.1	5.2	-1.1	2.4	4.8	5.5	4.7
1960	6.4	2.6	6.2	9.5	6.6	4.7	4.4	5.2
1961	5.3	2.3	5.9	5.7	4.8	0.5	2.2	3.4
1962	4.9	6.1	1.7	2.7	4.2	4.5	4.0	4.7
1963	4.7	4.5	4.8	-2.3	3.0	7.0	7.1	4.3
1964	6.1	5.9	5.9	12.9	6.8	8.9	5.4	7.3
1965	4.2	6.3	4.3	5.7	5.0	5.1	5.5	5.2
1966	3.7	6.4	6.4	4.9	5.0	7.2	2.9	5.4
1967	3.5	2.6	4.0	4.4	4.5	4.9	2.0	3.7
1968	5.3	4.8	3.8	5.9	6.0	6.6	5.1	5.5
1969	5.7	3.5	3.1	1.4	6.5	9.6	7.8	5.6
1970	4.4	0.6	3.5	7.7	6.8	9.1	8.2	5.1
1971	3.4	3.4	7.3	2.7	6.0	5.7	4.5	4.2
1972	4.4	5.2	5.0	0.6	6.4	5.9	3.7	4.7
1973	5.7	5.8	4.9	8.4	8.1	7.9	3.6	6.6
1974	2.2	0.2	6.0	2.9	6.0	2.3	4.6	2.3
1975	-0.4	0.0	3.6	0.3	3.0	4.8	1.2	1.5
1976	4.3	5.2	2.6	4.7	5.5	5.1	6.7	4.9
1977	2.9	4.2	3.5	2.4	4.8	5.6	4.2	4.1
1978	3.0	5.4	3.2	2.5	4.3	6.0	2.5	4.4
1979	3.7	3.5	1.5	-0.5	6.3	4.1	4.7	3.6
1980	1.6	0.2	0.5	0.1	5.4	3.5	4.5	2.0
1981	0.2	2.6	-1.2	0.9	0.6	4.1	1.0	1.9
1982	0.8	-1.9	0.9	2.5	-1.2	4.5	3.1	1.2
1983	1.8	3.9	1.5	3.2	-2.5	5.1	0.6	2.9
1984	2.4	7.1	3.1	1.3	3.8	5.9	2.1	4.6
1985	2.5	4.0	0.1	0.9	3.0	5.1	3.1	3.5
1986	2.8	3.3	2.8	4.1	4.1	4.2	2.2	3.5
1987	2.9	3.6	-0.6	1.3	3.1	5.8	1.6	3.6
1988	4.0	4.2	0.9	2.1	0.9	6.6	4.1	4.3
1989	3.4	3.4	-1.3	1.5	1.3	4.3	3.1	3.2
1990	1.2	1.6	-7.7	-2.4	0.5	5.4	1.4	2.0
1991	1.7	-0.6	-10.9	-6.3	3.7	4.1	0.8	1.1
1992	1.1	2.8	-5.2	-14.6	3.1	5.7	0.1	2.0
1993	-0.3	2.7	-1.6	-9.9	3.4	5.4	0.9	2.2
1994	2.8	4.1	4.0	-14.2	5.1	5.6	2.2	3.4
1995	2.4	2.8	5.8	-5.5	1.5	6.0	3.0	3.4
1996	1.7	3.4	3.8	-3.2	3.5	6.1	5.7	3.9
1997	2.6	4.2	2.6	2.1	5.2	4.5	3.4	3.9
1998	2.9	4.3	2.9	-2.1	2.3	1.4	3.7	2.5
1999	2.7	4.2	1.8	4.2	0.2	3.9	3.3	3.4
2000	3.5	3.8	3.9	7.9	3.6	5.2	3.5	4.4
2001	1.6	0.5	3.9	6.2	1.0	2.5	4.0	1.9

http://dx.doi.org/10.1787/456125276116

Table 7b. **Year-to-Year Percentage Change in World Per Capita GDP, by Region, 1950-2001**

	Western Europe	Western Offshoots	Eastern Europe	Former USSR	Latin America	Asia	Africa	World
1950								
1951	5.2	5.3	4.5	-1.3	2.6	5.0	2.6	4.1
1952	3.1	1.9	0.1	4.7	0.8	6.2	1.7	2.9
1953	4.5	2.7	4.0	2.6	0.8	4.8	1.5	3.1
1954	4.8	-2.2	3.2	3.1	3.6	2.1	2.6	1.5
1955	5.6	5.1	5.3	6.7	3.5	2.5	1.2	4.3
1956	3.9	0.5	1.0	7.7	1.5	4.6	1.8	2.8
1957	3.7	0.0	6.4	0.3	4.7	2.2	1.4	1.7
1958	1.6	-2.3	4.6	5.6	2.1	4.1	0.0	1.1
1959	3.9	5.3	4.1	-2.9	-0.4	2.7	3.1	2.7
1960	5.6	0.9	5.1	7.5	3.6	3.4	2.1	3.6
1961	4.4	0.6	4.8	3.9	1.9	-0.5	-0.1	2.1
1962	3.9	4.4	0.8	1.0	1.3	2.7	1.6	2.9
1963	3.8	2.9	3.9	-3.7	0.2	4.5	4.6	2.2
1964	5.2	4.3	5.1	11.4	3.9	6.5	2.8	5.1
1965	3.3	4.9	3.4	4.4	2.2	2.7	2.9	3.1
1966	2.9	5.1	5.6	3.7	2.2	4.7	0.3	3.3
1967	2.9	1.4	3.3	3.3	1.8	2.5	-0.6	1.6
1968	4.7	3.7	2.7	4.8	3.2	4.1	2.4	3.4
1969	5.0	2.3	2.3	0.4	3.7	7.0	5.1	3.4
1970	3.8	-0.7	2.7	6.7	4.1	6.4	5.6	2.9
1971	2.6	2.0	6.5	1.7	3.3	3.1	1.9	2.1
1972	3.8	4.0	4.2	-0.4	3.8	3.4	1.1	2.7
1973	5.1	4.7	4.1	7.4	5.5	5.4	0.9	4.5
1974	1.7	-0.8	5.0	1.9	3.4	0.1	2.0	0.4
1975	-0.8	-1.0	2.6	-0.7	0.6	2.6	-1.4	-0.3
1976	4.0	4.1	1.7	3.7	3.1	3.1	3.8	3.1
1977	2.6	3.1	2.6	1.4	2.4	3.6	1.3	2.3
1978	2.7	4.3	2.4	1.6	2.0	4.0	-0.4	2.6
1979	3.3	2.4	0.8	-1.3	3.9	2.1	1.7	1.7
1980	1.2	-0.9	-0.1	-0.7	3.2	1.5	1.6	0.3
1981	-0.1	1.5	-1.7	0.1	-1.6	2.3	-1.7	0.2
1982	0.6	-2.9	0.3	1.6	-3.3	2.8	0.2	-0.4
1983	1.7	2.9	1.0	2.3	-4.5	2.8	-2.3	0.9
1984	2.2	6.2	2.6	0.3	1.7	3.9	-0.8	2.8
1985	2.3	3.1	-0.4	0.0	1.0	3.2	0.2	1.7
1986	2.6	2.3	2.3	3.2	2.0	2.4	-0.7	1.8
1987	2.6	2.6	-1.0	0.4	1.1	3.8	-1.2	1.9
1988	3.7	3.2	0.7	1.3	-1.0	4.6	1.3	2.6
1989	2.9	2.3	-1.6	1.0	-0.7	2.4	0.3	1.5
1990	0.7	0.4	-7.9	-3.1	-1.4	3.5	-1.3	0.3
1991	1.2	-1.9	-11.1	-6.8	1.8	2.4	-2.1	-0.5
1992	0.6	1.5	-5.2	-15.0	1.3	4.0	-2.5	0.4
1993	-0.8	1.4	-1.4	-10.1	1.6	3.7	-1.6	0.6
1994	2.4	2.9	4.2	-14.2	3.3	3.9	-0.3	1.9
1995	2.1	1.5	6.0	-5.5	-0.2	4.3	0.5	1.9
1996	1.4	2.2	4.0	-3.1	1.8	4.6	3.2	2.4
1997	2.4	3.0	2.7	2.2	3.6	3.0	0.9	2.5
1998	2.7	3.1	2.9	-2.0	0.7	0.0	1.3	1.1
1999	2.4	3.0	1.9	4.3	-1.3	2.3	0.9	1.9
2000	3.2	2.7	3.9	8.0	2.1	4.0	1.2	3.1
2001	1.3	-0.5	3.9	6.3	-0.5	1.1	1.7	0.6

http://dx.doi.org/10.1787/456125276116

Table 7a*. Alternative UNPD World Population Estimates by Region, 1950-2000
(000 at mid-year)

	Western Europe	Western Offshoots	Eastern Europe	Former USSR	Latin America	Asia	Africa	World
1950	305 346	181 677	87 673	180 980	167 030	1 375 431	220 888	2 519 025
1951	306 928	184 495	89 008	183 626	171 440	1 404 108	225 634	2 565 238
1952	308 740	187 617	90 307	186 630	176 038	1 431 671	230 526	2 611 528
1953	310 693	190 973	91 574	189 877	180 796	1 458 753	235 583	2 658 249
1954	312 722	194 501	92 809	193 275	185 695	1 485 891	240 822	2 705 716
1955	314 794	198 147	94 014	196 752	190 728	1 513 524	246 257	2 754 214
1956	316 900	201 863	95 184	200 259	195 895	1 541 990	251 899	2 803 991
1957	319 062	205 608	96 318	203 771	201 209	1 571 534	257 757	2 855 260
1958	321 323	209 350	97 410	207 281	206 690	1 602 308	263 838	2 908 200
1959	323 739	213 060	98 456	210 795	212 363	1 634 396	270 146	2 962 955
1960	326 359	216 716	99 451	214 322	218 248	1 667 851	276 686	3 019 633
1961	329 197	220 297	100 394	217 854	224 354	1 702 748	283 464	3 078 307
1962	332 210	223 784	101 290	221 354	230 665	1 739 223	290 486	3 139 011
1963	335 287	227 156	102 149	224 755	237 144	1 777 493	297 763	3 201 746
1964	338 280	230 396	102 984	227 968	243 734	1 817 804	305 307	3 266 473
1965	341 080	233 495	103 808	230 936	250 396	1 860 282	313 125	3 333 121
1966	343 641	236 437	104 624	233 624	257 114	1 904 964	321 237	3 401 640
1967	345 987	239 229	105 434	236 060	263 896	1 951 655	329 644	3 471 903
1968	348 156	241 914	106 242	238 325	270 756	1 999 935	338 319	3 543 647
1969	350 222	244 550	107 055	240 537	277 718	2 049 230	347 225	3 616 536
1970	352 234	247 183	107 875	242 782	284 800	2 099 059	356 340	3 690 271
1971	354 199	249 835	108 703	245 091	291 995	2 149 357	365 655	3 764 836
1972	356 094	252 499	109 540	247 446	299 295	2 200 035	375 204	3 840 112
1973	357 905	255 153	110 391	249 818	306 704	2 250 556	385 056	3 915 583
1974	359 610	257 758	111 263	252 162	314 230	2 300 282	395 306	3 990 612
1975	361 194	260 291	112 160	254 445	321 875	2 348 797	406 026	4 064 789
1976	362 669	262 743	113 083	256 663	329 641	2 395 837	417 236	4 137 873
1977	364 044	265 141	114 026	258 840	337 514	2 441 605	428 928	4 210 098
1978	365 304	267 539	114 964	261 001	345 458	2 486 754	441 103	4 282 122
1979	366 427	270 009	115 868	263 183	353 425	2 532 225	453 754	4 354 891
1980	367 408	272 605	116 714	265 411	361 380	2 578 728	466 871	4 429 118
1981	368 237	275 349	117 489	267 671	369 308	2 626 370	480 450	4 504 874
1982	368 943	278 229	118 195	269 949	377 210	2 675 010	494 482	4 582 017
1983	369 609	281 207	118 841	272 279	385 096	2 724 796	508 941	4 660 769
1984	370 346	284 231	119 445	274 702	392 981	2 775 840	523 797	4 741 343
1985	371 234	287 262	120 019	277 233	400 878	2 828 160	539 016	4 823 802
1986	372 294	290 286	120 572	279 898	408 783	2 881 900	554 594	4 908 327
1987	373 506	293 319	121 092	282 641	416 690	2 936 899	570 508	4 994 655
1988	374 859	296 382	121 543	285 302	424 597	2 992 473	586 684	5 081 841
1989	376 328	299 510	121 876	287 665	432 504	3 047 698	603 029	5 168 610
1990	377 885	302 725	122 060	289 574	440 408	3 101 898	619 477	5 254 027
1991	379 537	306 028	122 079	290 967	448 310	3 154 793	635 996	5 337 710
1992	381 267	309 403	121 954	291 886	456 206	3 206 517	652 604	5 419 837
1993	382 990	312 834	121 739	292 411	464 094	3 257 320	669 345	5 500 733
1994	384 595	316 298	121 512	292 670	471 971	3 307 635	686 288	5 580 970
1995	386 001	319 774	121 329	292 761	479 836	3 357 778	703 487	5 660 967
1996	387 172	323 261	121 211	292 711	487 684	3 407 796	720 952	5 740 787
1997	388 124	326 752	121 143	292 504	495 515	3 457 557	738 675	5 820 270
1998	388 894	330 214	121 103	292 142	503 325	3 506 994	756 680	5 899 353
1999	389 544	333 606	121 055	291 620	511 109	3 562 826	774 991	5 984 752
2000	390 121	336 903	120 970	290 940	518 865	3 604 492	793 627	6 055 918

http://dx.doi.org/10.1787/456125276116

Table 7a**. **World Population: Confrontation of UNPD and USBC-Maddison Estimates**
(ratio UNPD to USBC-Maddison)

	Western Europe	Western Offshoots	Eastern Europe	Former USSR	Latin America	Asia	Africa	World
1950	1.001	1.030	1.000	1.008	1.007	0.995	0.972	0.998
1951	1.000	1.027	1.003	1.005	1.006	0.997	0.972	0.999
1952	1.000	1.025	1.005	1.004	1.006	0.997	0.973	0.999
1953	1.000	1.025	1.005	1.005	1.006	0.996	0.973	0.998
1954	1.000	1.025	1.005	1.006	1.006	0.994	0.974	0.997
1955	1.001	1.025	1.003	1.006	1.006	0.991	0.974	0.996
1956	1.000	1.025	1.002	1.006	1.005	0.989	0.975	0.994
1957	1.000	1.023	1.003	1.006	1.004	0.986	0.976	0.992
1958	1.000	1.024	1.003	1.005	1.003	0.982	0.976	0.990
1959	1.000	1.024	1.002	1.004	1.002	0.982	0.977	0.990
1960	1.000	1.024	1.002	1.003	1.001	0.989	0.978	0.994
1961	1.000	1.023	1.001	1.001	1.001	1.000	0.980	1.000
1962	1.000	1.023	1.001	1.001	1.001	1.004	0.981	1.002
1963	1.000	1.023	1.001	1.001	1.001	1.002	0.982	1.001
1964	1.000	1.022	1.001	1.001	1.000	1.002	0.983	1.001
1965	1.001	1.022	1.001	1.002	1.000	1.002	0.983	1.001
1966	1.001	1.022	1.001	1.002	0.999	1.002	0.984	1.001
1967	1.001	1.022	1.002	1.002	0.998	1.003	0.984	1.002
1968	1.002	1.022	0.999	1.001	0.998	1.003	0.985	1.002
1969	1.001	1.022	0.999	1.001	0.997	1.003	0.985	1.002
1970	1.000	1.020	1.000	1.001	0.996	1.003	0.987	1.001
1971	0.999	1.018	1.000	1.001	0.995	1.002	0.987	1.000
1972	0.998	1.017	1.000	1.000	0.995	1.001	0.987	1.000
1973	0.997	1.017	1.000	1.000	0.995	1.001	0.987	1.000
1974	0.998	1.017	0.999	1.000	0.995	1.001	0.987	1.000
1975	0.998	1.016	0.998	1.000	0.995	1.001	0.988	1.000
1976	1.000	1.016	0.998	0.999	0.996	1.002	0.988	1.000
1977	1.001	1.015	0.997	0.999	0.996	1.002	0.988	1.000
1978	1.001	1.013	0.998	0.998	0.997	1.001	0.988	1.000
1979	1.001	1.012	0.998	0.998	0.997	1.000	0.988	0.999
1980	1.000	1.009	0.999	0.998	0.998	0.999	0.988	0.999
1981	0.999	1.009	1.000	0.998	0.998	1.000	0.988	0.999
1982	0.999	1.009	1.000	0.998	0.997	1.002	0.988	1.000
1983	0.999	1.010	1.001	0.997	0.997	0.999	0.988	0.998
1984	1.000	1.012	1.001	0.997	0.997	0.999	0.988	0.998
1985	1.000	1.013	1.001	0.997	0.997	0.999	0.988	0.999
1986	1.001	1.014	1.001	0.997	0.996	1.000	0.988	0.999
1987	1.002	1.015	1.002	0.998	0.996	1.000	0.988	0.999
1988	1.002	1.016	1.004	0.999	0.995	1.000	0.989	0.999
1989	1.001	1.016	1.004	1.002	0.994	1.000	0.989	0.999
1990	1.000	1.015	1.004	1.002	0.994	1.000	0.988	0.999
1991	1.000	1.012	1.002	1.001	0.993	1.000	0.986	0.999
1992	0.999	1.010	1.001	0.999	0.993	1.000	0.985	0.998
1993	0.999	1.008	1.001	0.999	0.992	1.000	0.985	0.998
1994	1.000	1.007	1.001	1.000	0.992	1.000	0.986	0.998
1995	1.000	1.006	1.002	1.001	0.991	0.999	0.985	0.997
1996	1.000	1.005	1.002	1.002	0.991	0.999	0.986	0.997
1997	1.000	1.004	1.002	1.003	0.991	0.999	0.986	0.997
1998	1.000	1.003	1.001	1.003	0.991	0.999	0.987	0.997
1999	0.999	1.002	1.001	1.002	0.991	1.000	0.987	0.998
2000	0.998	1.001	1.000	1.001	0.991	1.000	0.988	0.997

http://dx.doi.org/10.1787/456125276116

HS–8: The World Economy, 1–2001 AD

Tables HS–8 show levels of population, GDP and per capita GDP in 20 countries, 7 regions and the world for eight benchmark years in the past two millennia. There are also 5 analytical tables showing rates of growth and shares of world population and GDP. HS–7 explained the derivation of estimates for 1950–2001. Earlier than this, it is useful to distinguish between estimates for 1820–1950 and those for the centuries before 1820 where the documentation is weaker and the element of conjecture bigger.

Population Movement 1820–1950

For West European countries and Western Offshoots, population estimates for this period are based mainly on censuses dating back to the eighteenth century for Scandinavia and Spain and the early nineteenth for most other countries. The sources are described in HS–1 and HS–2. For Western Europe, annual estimates, adjusted to a midyear basis are shown for all countries back to 1820. For Western Offshoots, they are shown separately for the indigenous population and those of European/African origin at decade intervals for 1820–1870, with annual estimates for the total population thereafter.

For Eastern Europe, annual estimates are shown from 1920. Before the first world–war, these countries were divided between the Austro–Hungarian, Ottoman, Russian and German Empires. Derivation of estimates in the territory corresponding to present boundaries is possible, but they are too rough to warrant presentation on an annual basis. Estimates for the territory of the former USSR are also too rough to warrant annual presentation before 1920. Population sources are described in HS–3.

For Latin America annual estimates are shown back to 1900 for 23 countries. The 1820 and 1870 estimates in Maddison (2001) for the smaller countries are revised and augmented from the *Cambridge History of Latin America*, Engerman and Higman (1997) and other sources cited in HS–4.

For Asia annual estimates are shown from 1913 for the 16 core countries, and for benchmark years 1820, 1850 1870 1890 and 1900. For China, India, Indonesia and Japan annual estimates are shown back to 1870. For other countries there are estimates for benchmark years 1820, 1870, 1900 and 1913. In most cases the sources in HS–5 are the same as in Maddison (2001).

For Africa, the statistical basis is weaker than elsewhere. I show no annual estimates before 1950, but give detail for the sample countries for 1820, 1870 and 1913 in Table 6–10 of HS–6.

Population Change 1–1820 AD

For the centuries before 1820 the most comprehensive evidence is for population and it is of greater proportionate importance for analysis as per capita income growth was much slower then and economic growth was largely extensive.

Demographic changes, e.g. increases in life expectancy, changes in average age which affect labour force participation, changes in the structure of the labour force, are important in providing clues to per capita income development. A striking example is the urbanisation ratio. Thanks to the work of de Vries for Europe and of Rozman for Asia, one can, for some countries, measure the proportion of population living in towns with more than 10 000 inhabitants. In the year 1000, this ratio was virtually zero in Europe (there were only 4 towns with more than 10 000 inhabitants) and in China it was 3 per cent. By 1800 the West European urban ratio was 10.6 per cent, the Chinese 3.8 per cent. When countries are able to expand their urban ratios, it indicates a growing surplus beyond subsistence in agriculture, and suggests that the non–agricultural component of economic activity is increasing. These changing differentials in urban ratios were used to buttress other evidence on per capita progress in China and Europe in Maddison (1998). The Chinese bureaucracy kept population registers which go back more than 2 000 years. These records were designed to assess taxable capacity, and include information on cultivated area and crop production, which was used by Perkins (1969) to assess long run movements in Chinese output per capita. Bagnall and Frier (1994) made brilliant use of fragments of ancient censuses to estimate occupational structure, household size, marriage patterns, fertility and life expectation in Roman Egypt of the third century.

Serious work on historical demography started in the seventeenth century with John Graunt (see Prologue). Modernised techniques and similar types of evidence have been used to make retrospective estimates of population for other European countries for periods before census material was available. Investigations of this character have been carried out by a) the Office of Population Research in Princeton University (established in 1936); b) INED (Institut National des Études Démographiques) founded in the 1950s to exploit family reconstitution techniques developed by Louis Henry; c) the Cambridge Group for the History of Population and Family Structure (established in the 1970s) has carried out a massive research project to reconstitute English population size and structure on an annual basis back to 1541 (Wrigley et al., 1997). This kind of analysis has been sharpened by the application of massive computing power.

Research on Japanese population history has blossomed under the leadership of Akira Hayami and Osamu Saito. Ester Boserup's (1965) analysis of the interaction between demographic pressure, agricultural technology and intensity of labour input in Asia has helped discredit simplistic Malthusian interpretations. There has been a flood of publications on Latin American demography and the shipment of slaves from Africa. As a result of these efforts we are better placed to measure long term changes in world population. The most detailed and best documented are those in McEvedy and Jones (1978). This was the source of my estimates for Africa (see also the masterly analysis of African development in McEvedy, 1995).

Appendix B of Maddison 2001 provided source notes and estimates for 20 countries and 7 regions for benchmark years between the first century and 1700. In this study more country detail is shown for Western Europe, Western Offshoots, Latin America back to 1500 and for Africa back to the first century. There are some changes in the regional totals for Africa (see Table 6–1), but none for other regions.

GDP Growth 1820–1950

Before the second worldwar, only 10 countries had official estimates of national income, assembled without international guidelines to provide comparability. None of these are suitable for our purpose, but there are retrospective official estimates of fairly recent vintage which I used for Austria from 1830, Norway from 1865, Netherlands from 1913, Canada from 1926 and the United States from 1929.

There were non–official estimates in pre–war years. Colin Clark (1940) made a comprehensive survey, but all those he cited have now been superseded. In the past 60 years, work on retrospective national accounts has been undertaken by a large number of scholars who have generally linked their series to official post–war estimates. The initial thrust for these exercises in quantitative economic history was given by Simon Kuznets. His very long career included creation of official US accounts in 1934 and 5 monographs of historical accounts for the United States in 1941–61. These set high standards of scholarship with meticulous and transparent description of sources and methods. These characteristics have permitted succeeding generations of scholars to stand on his shoulders. His persuasive power and influence stemmed from professional integrity and depth of scholarship. He was free from partisanship, open to new ideas and willing to comment sympathetically in detail on the work of others. His influence was reinforced by his style of analysis–use of ideas that could be clearly expressed in literary form, and implemented with relatively simple statistical techniques. He encouraged a band of scholars all over the world to consider that such an enterprise was feasible, exciting, important and rewarding. He encouraged comparable studies for Australia, China, France, Germany, Italy, Japan, Sweden and the United Kingdom. To facilitate this research he helped found the International Association for Income and Wealth in 1947, persuaded the US Social Science Research Council to finance comparative research in other countries, and played a major role in the creation of the Yale Growth Center, which produced basic growth studies for Argentina, Egypt, Korea, Sri Lanka, Taiwan, and the USSR. Between 1953 and 1989 he published 8 volumes containing 70 analytical essays comparing the results which emerged from these quantitative studies and assessing their significance for the study of "modern economic growth". The temporal horizon of this new generation of Kuznetsian scholarship was concentrated on developments since the mid–nineteenth century.

Several university centres are now active in this field, sponsoring their own research and strengthening international networks by holding workshops. Kazushi Ohkawa organised a 14–volume study (1966–1988) of Japanese growth at Hitotsubashi University. The University now has an ambitious comparative project on the quantitative economic history of China, Indonesia, Korea, Taiwan and Vietnam. In the Netherlands, the University of Groningen has been active in this field since 1982. Its Growth and Development Centre has played a major role in international studies of productivity levels and in developing an international database on economic growth. It has published research studies on GDP growth in Brazil, Germany, Indonesia, Japan, Korea, Mexico, the Netherlands, Taiwan, Thailand, and a six–country comparison for Latin America. It maintained close links with Jan Luiten van Zanden's team working on Dutch growth in the University of Utrecht and with the University of Leuven's research on long–run growth in Belgium. It is also linked with the COPPAA group (Comparisons of Output, Productivity and Purchasing Power in Asia and Australia), based in Brisbane, which has carried out a number of studies of comparative performance of economies in the Asia–Pacific region, and was associated with the research of Maddison (1998) on China and Sivasubramonian (2000) on India. Scandinavia has a long history in this field. There have been five rounds of research in Sweden since 1937, and Olle Krantz has made annual estimates of GDP growth since 1800. Riitta Hjerppe supervised a 13 volume study for Finland which was completed in 1989. Svend Aage Hansen produced the second major study of Danish growth in 1974, with annual GDP estimates back to 1818. There is now a Nordic Group, which is revising the Scandinavian historical accounts to enhance their comparability. The International Association for Research in Income and Wealth (IARIW) has held conferences and workshops on measurement of comparative GDP growth and levels of performance, problems of methodology and definition since 1949, and has published its quarterly *Review of Income and Wealth* since 1968. Its membership has always included official statisticians, established scholars working on historical accounts, and younger researchers serving their apprenticeship in this field and has played a major role in developing a standardised approach and extending the range of countries for which studies are available. The European Historical Economics Society (EHES) has also been active in promoting research on quantitative economic history since 1997 when it created the *European Review of Economic History*.

The vitality of recent research activity is clear from Table 8–1 which shows amendments to my estimates since publication of Maddison (2001). The proxy estimates I use for Bulgaria, Poland, Romania and Yugoslavia for 1870 to the 1920s were derived from David Good and Tongshu Ma (1999). Their approach is a variant of that developed originally by Wilfred Beckerman (1966) as a shortcut cross–section technique to measure comparative income levels. Nick Crafts (1983) was the first to use it for diachronic analysis (see Maddison, 1990).

Table 8-1. **Amendments to GDP Estimates in Maddison (2001) for 1820-1950**

Western Europe	Western Offshoots	Eastern Europe and former USSR	Latin America	Asia	Africa
Amendments and New Estimates					
France 1820-70	Australia 1820-70, and 1911-38	Hungary 1870-1900	Cuba 1929-50	Jordan 1820-1950	Algeria 1880–1950
Netherlands 1820-1913			Jamaica 1820-1950	Malaysia 1911-50	Egypt 1886-1950
Portugal 1851-1910			Uruguay 1870-1913	Palestine 1820-1950	Ghana 1891-1950
Spain 1850-1950				Philippines 1902-50	Tunisia 1910-50
Switzerland 1851-1913				Sri Lanka 1820-1950	
				South Korea 1913-50	
				Syria 1820-1950	
				Turkey 1820-1950	
				Vietnam 1820-1950	
Amended and New Proxy Estimates					
Greece 1820-1913	New Zealand 1870-1913	Albania 1870-1950	Caribbean 1820-1950	Arabia 1820-1950	Algeria 1820-80
Switzerland 1820-51, and 1914-24		Bulgaria 1870-1924		Iran 1820-1950	Egypt 1820-86
		Poland 1870-1929		Iraq 1820-1950	Ghana 1820-91
		Romania 1870-1926		Lebanon 1820-1950	Morocco 1820-1920
		Yugoslavia 1870-1912		North Korea 1820-1950	Tunisia 1820-1910
					South Africa 1820-1912

http://dx.doi.org/10.1787/456125276116

GDP Growth before 1820

Western Europe: Per capita GDP growth rates prior to 1820 in Maddison (2001) are unchanged for Germany, Greece, the Netherlands, Portugal, Spain, Sweden and 13 small territories, but *levels* for 1500–1700 for these countries are affected by the amendments for 1820. In the case of France, the 1700–1820 growth rate is unchanged, but for the second half of the seventeenth century I assume stagnant per capita income because of hunger crises and the depressing influence of more or less continuous warfare, as noted by Boisguilbert and Vauban.

Western Offshoots: There are changes in the "multicultural" per capita GDP estimates 1700–1820 for Australia, Canada and New Zealand, as specified in detail in Tables 2–1 and 2–5; estimates for earlier centuries are unchanged.

Eastern Europe: Per capita GDP growth rates prior to 1820 are unchanged (0.1 percent a year), but the level for 1500–1700 is higher due to use of the Good–Ma proxies for the nineteenth century. There was no significant change for Russia.

Latin America: More detailed scrutiny of the evidence for the Caribbean sugar colonies led to upward revision of their per capita GDP and population levels in 1700–1820. See Table 4–1 for a more detailed sub–regional specification for 1500–1820 than in Maddison (2001).

Asia: GDP estimates for China, India, Indonesia and Japan in Maddison (2001) are unchanged, but I was able to make a more detailed scrutiny for West Asia thanks to recent work by Sevket Pamuk (see Tables 5–6 and 5–8). This raised the 1820 per capita GDP level for this group and its rate of growth 1700–1820. However the level estimates for 1700 and earlier are unchanged.

Africa: I have made more detailed sub–regional conjectures of long–run per capita GDP movement than in Maddison (2001), and presented a detailed analysis of the forces affecting the contours of demographic development. See source note HS–6, and Tables 6–1 and 6–2.

Crosschecking Measures of Comparative Levels of Performance before 1950

In this study, the bulk of the evidence consists of measures of inter–temporal change in GDP volume in individual countries, moving backwards from 2001. These are merged with measures of comparative GDP levels in the reference year 1990 at 1990 prices. The derivation of the inter–spatial estimates is explained in the source notes to HS–7 and in Table 7–2. A more comprehensive survey of the array of level estimates available for years between 1970 and 1990 can be found in Maddison (1995) pp. 162–179. This indicates the range of variance between the results of the successive ICP and PWT rounds and compares the attributes of alternative aggregation procedures (Paasche, Laspeyres, Fisher, EKS and Geary–Khamis). Heston and Summers (1993) compare the GDP growth rates implicit in ICP cross–section estimates of the relative standing of countries at different points of time with direct measures of inter–temporal GDP growth. They do not suggest that deviations between implicit and direct measures cast serious doubt on the latter. But such deviations are obviously a useful crosscheck.

I am satisfied that the 1990 benchmark estimates I used are the best presently available, with the possible exception of those for Eastern Europe and Africa, where the results of the OECD (2002) and PWT 6.1 exercises were too recent to be fully digested here (see Table 6–11). My 1990 benchmark can be subjected to comprehensive review when the World Bank's ICP exercise for 2004 becomes available.

However, updates of the 1990 benchmarks are less important than crosschecks on their validity as measures of relative performance in the distant past. It is clear that patterns of expenditure have changed radically over the long–term (as illustrated by the comparison of British expenditure patterns in 1688 and 1996 in Table 1), and there have also been big changes in relative prices and output structure. Some of these changes may have had a similar impact across countries, but this certainly needs to be investigated.

The most promising crosschecks on my estimates of relative standing in the past have come from binary comparisons of countries which have a significant weight in the world total. Some of these I have done myself, and there are several others which confirm my findings, e. g. those of Broadberry, Toda and van Zanden cited below.

It would also be useful to have ICOP or ICP type multilateral cross–section studies for different points of time in the past. It would not be possible replicate the detail or systemic rigour of modern ICP exercises (prices for more than 2000 items for 200 categories of expenditure), but real wage analysts have accumulated quite a lot of material on price structures which could be mobilised for this purpose. It would be useful and probably feasible to construct such a measure e. g. for 1900 or 1870, using reduced information, on the same lines as PWT estimates for countries where there has been no ICP exercise.

In the absence of such measures, Leandro Prados has made proxy estimates of PPPs and per capita income relatives for benchmark years since 1820, using econometrics, but no information on relative price structures. The results are too shaky to be a serious challenge to my estimates of relative levels in 1820 (see Table 8–2).

There are some authors (Paul Bairoch, Susan Hanley and Kenneth Pomeranz) whose judgement of the relative standing of major Asian countries and Western Europe is very different from mine. I give my reasons for disagreeing with them below.

Finally, I would like to comment on the real wage literature, some of which contradicts my view of West European development over the past few centuries.

a) Confirmatory Crosschecks

i) Stephen Broadberry (1997a): provides the most important of the binary cross–checks because he scrutinises the relative standing of the two successive lead counties (the United Kingdom and the United States) for benchmark years between 1870 and 1990. He found US productivity in manufacturing ahead of the United Kingdom by the middle of the 19th century, whereas I found that US productivity leadership at the aggregate level (GDP per man hour) began several decades later. At first sight these judgements seemed incompatible. As a test, Broadberry (1997a) made an ICOP type analysis of performance in 9 sectors and aggregate GDP in the two countries for 1870–1990 using 1937 value added weights. His results were compatible with my aggregate comparison with 1990 expenditure weights.

Broadberry, 1997b, compared UK and German performance for the same period with 1935 weights. He arrived at a similar confirmatory result, reconciling my estimate of the relative standing of the two countries in terms of aggregate GDP using 1990 expenditure weights, with his aggregate of value added by sector, using 1935 weights.

ii) Yasushi Toda (1990): presented a binary comparison of Japanese and Russian urban consumption levels in 1913 and Japan/USSR in 1975–6. He had a matched sample of 46 items at Japanese and Russian prices for 1913, and 110 items for 1975–6. He found the Japanese real per capita consumption level below that in Russia in 1913 and significantly higher in 1975–6. He had no explicit measure of growth, but the implicit differential in growth rates was very similar to what I found for per capita GDP for this period.

iii) Jan Luiten van Zanden (2003) expressed his concern that distortions may arise in using 1990 benchmarks back to 1820 because of changes in relative price structures. As a test, he compared Dutch growth to his new estimates of Javanese GDP growth for 1815–1880 and made PPP adjustments to compare *levels* of per capita income in the 1820s. He concludes that "in the 1820s per capita GDP in Java was about one third of Dutch per capita GDP" and that my estimates of relative levels of the two economies in 1820 are "by and large correct". He also makes comparative estimates of real wages, food consumption patterns, life expectation, and comparative physical stature of Dutch and Indonesians. These "direct indicators" show a narrower gap. He suggests that the relationship between real wages and average per capita GDP is highly variable and dependent on many factors such as the length of the working year, distribution of income, relative prices etc.

b) Conflicting Interpretations

i) Leandro Prados (2000) offers proxy estimates of per capita GDP levels relative to the United States for 17 benchmark years between 1820 and 1990. For 1880 he shows estimates for 23 countries but the coverage drops to 6 countries in 1820. He restricts the coverage to OECD countries, Argentina and Russia. He makes no use of inter-temporal measures of change in real GDP to estimate past levels of performance, nor does he measure price structures. Instead he backcasts an econometric relationship between purchasing power parity converters and exchange rates which prevailed in 1950-90.

He has 89 ICP or OEEC direct measures of this relationship to support the 155 estimates he shows for 7 reference years from 1950 to 1990 (see his tables 3 and 9). The gaps are filled by a structural equation, which attributes spreads between PPPs and exchange rates to four variables: *a)* openness of the economies as measured by the ratio of foreign trade (exports and imports) to GDP; *b)* the ratio of net capital inflows to GDP: *c)* the size of the country in terms of its surface area and population; and *d)* a periphery dummy (in cases where per capita income is less than half of the average level). His cross–section relatives are derived from estimates of these four items for the years he covers, and knowledge of the exchange rates prevailing in those years. With this information he infers the Paasche PPP for a given year in the past for each of the countries. He applies these PPPs to convert estimates of nominal GDP in each country from national currencies into US dollars of the year in question. For years before 1950, he has no ICP or PWT (reduced-information) measures of PPPs. He assumes that the PPP/exchange rate relationships for 1950-1990 are a good guide to the situation in 1820-1938.

He provides two pages of source notes, but shows only his results and none of the basic material on PPPs, his four variables and estimates of nominal GDP. Estimates of variables a and b are likely to be pretty shaky for the early years, and nominal estimates of GDP are often not available. This is the case for his benchmark country, the United States where he derived a nominal value by reflating the real GDP estimates for 1820–1860 with a cost of living and a wholesale price index.

Table 8–2 shows the Prados results for the 6 countries where his estimates go back to 1820. It compares his per capita relatives and mine for 1900 and 1820. It shows my estimates in 1990 international dollars, and his implicit absolute levels, derived by multiplying his relatives by my estimate for the United States. In the bottom panel I compare my estimates of per capita growth with his implicit growth rates. There are very big differences between his relatives and mine for 1820, smaller but appreciable differences for 1900. My growth rates for per capita GDP 1820–1900 are very different from his implicit rates. His growth rate for Australia is much slower than mine, but he shows much faster growth for the four European countries, with France and Denmark growing faster than the United States.

Table 8–2. **Comparison of Maddison Per Capita GDP Levels and Prados' Proxies, 1820–1900**

	Maddison per capita GDP in 1990 int. $	*Maddison per capita GDP % of US*	*Prados per capita GDP % of US*	*Implicit Prados per capita GDP in 1990 int. $*	*Maddison nominal per capita GDP % of US*	*Prados nominal per capita GDP % of US*
			1820			
Australia	518	41.2	102.2	1 285	n.a.	136.1
United States	1 257	100.0	100.0	1 257	n.a.	100.0
United Kingdom	1 706	135.7	96.5	1 213	n.a.	122.8
Netherlands	1 838	146.2	80.0	1 006	n.a.	95.9
France	1 135	90.3	71.3	896	n.a.	69.0
Denmark	1 274	101.4	51.3	645	n.a.	54.8
			1900			
Australia	4 013	98.1	97.6	3 993	104.5	99.3
United States	4 091	100.0	100.0	4 091	100.0	100.0
United Kingdom	4 492	109.8	91.7	3 751	91.9	92.3
Netherlands	3 424	83.7	71.5	2 925	45.6	50.2
France	2 876	70.3	76.8	3 142	52.6	66.6
Denmark	3 017	73.7	66.8	2 733	56.0	59.4
			1820–1900 annual average compound growth rate			
Australia	2.59			1.43		
United States	1.49			1.49		
United Kingdom	1.22			1.42		
Netherlands	0.78			1.34		
France	1.17			1.58		
Denmark	1.08			1.82		

Source: Maddison estimates from basic tables, column 5 from Maddison (1991c). Columns 3 and 6 from Prados (2000), Table 9. Col. 4 derived by multiplying my estimate for the United States by Prados' relatives in column 3. The United States is his benchmark country but he does not show his estimate in absolute terms. He shows estimates labelled "Maddison Revised", but I could not see from the description how he derived these and must therefore register a disclaimer. For Australia 1820, he refers to the white population, whereas my estimate includes aborigines (see HS–2 for white population).

http://dx.doi.org/10.1787/456125276116

ii) Paul Bairoch (1930-1999) was a very prolific quantitative historian, who published many comparative studies of GNP levels, urbanisation and labour force participation. A good deal of his analysis concentrated on the forces making for divergence in the growth of advanced capitalist countries and the third world. He argued (see Bairoch, 1967) that the third world was impoverished by the development process and policies of the rich countries. In Bairoch, 1981, pp 8, 12, 14, he showed the "third world" with a slightly higher average per capita GNP than the "developed countries" in 1750, and slightly lower in 1800. He showed China at more or less the same level as Western Europe in 1800, and Latin America ahead of North America. Bairoch's source notes were frequently cryptic and often cited "personal estimates" he did not publish. They were most exiguous for Asia or Latin America and his results for these continents must therefore be taken with a pinch of salt. The most detailed documentation of his estimates can be found in "Europe's Gross National Product: 1800-1975", *Journal of European Economic History*, Fall 1976. I commented on the quality of these estimates in Maddison (1990), p. 104.

Bairoch's last major work, (*Victoires et Déboires,* Gallimard, Paris, 1997, 3 vols., 2 788 pages) is a massive, comprehensive and fascinating survey of world economic history from 1492 to 1995. It is much less quantitative than most of his other work. He has a very small table P.4 on p. 111 of volume 1 comparing the aggregate per capita GNP performance of the "developed countries" (Europe, Western Offshoots and Japan) and the "third world" (Africa, Asia and Latin America) for 6 benchmark years between 1750 and 1995. As in his earlier work, the third world is credited with a higher level than the developed group in 1750, with minimal progress until after 1950, but he shows no country detail for the third world. Table XII.2 in volume 2, pp. 252–3, presents estimates for each of his 24 "developed countries" for 7 benchmark years from 1800 to 1913. The estimates for Europe are similar to those he presented in 1976 and are in 1960 dollars derived mainly from the OEEC (1958) study of purchasing power, augmented by the proxy PPPs in Beckerman (1966).

To me the most surprising and interesting part of his 1997 study is his discussion of the relative performance and interaction of the European and Asian economies between 1500 and 1800 (pp. 527–645). He suggests that Asia was probably somewhat more advanced than Europe around 1500 and that by the eighteenth century this advantage had disappeared. The Muslim advantage over Europe in the Abbasid caliphate peaked in the 10th century; Chinese superiority had been greatest in the 12th century; the peak for Moghul India was in the 16th century, and that of the Ottoman Empire around 1600. Stagnation or decline followed thereafter, whereas Europe made substantial progress from 1500 to 1800 (see pp. 642–5). This analysis is difficult to reconcile with his earlier position, or the estimates in Table P.4, but it is much nearer to my view of the relative performance of these two parts of the world economy between 1500 and 1800.

iii) Susan Hanley is a demographer and social historian who has concentrated mainly on the economic history of Tokugawa Japan. She is a member of the revisionist school which found evidence to warrant a much more positive view of economic performance from 1600 to the 1860s than that of an earlier generation of scholars. However, she is an unconstrained admirer of Japan, and greatly exaggerates its level of performance in the 1860s. In Hanley (1997) she asserted that "Japanese physical well–being in the 1860s was at least as high as in nineteenth century England". Her evidence for England is pretty flimsy. She admits that Japanese ate virtually no meat, but alleges that this was also the case in mid–nineteenth century England. She alleges that English working class diets in the mid–nineteenth century consisted largely of "bread and margarine" (i.e. at a time before margarine was invented). In fact, we can see from Table 1 (in the Prologue) that already in 1695 only 20 per cent of English food and drink expenditure consisted of bread or things made of meal or flour, and 35 per cent consisted of meat, fish, and dairy products.

In assessing the relative position of two countries at a given point in the past, it is always useful to consider their growth trajectories since that point. The historical accounts of both Japan and the United Kingdom are of high quality. Our basic tables show that per capita income has risen 28–fold in Japan since 1870. In Britain it rose 6–fold. If Hanley's judgement on nineteenth century levels were correct, Japan would now have a gigantic lead over the United Kingdom. In fact the two countries had a similar level of per capita GDP in 2001.

Table 8–3. **The China/West European Dichotomy, 1–2001 AD**

	China	*West Europe*
Population (million)		
1	59.6	24.7
1000	59.0	25.4
1300	100.0	58.4
1400	72.0	41.5
1500	103.0	57.3
1820	381.0	133.0
1913	437.1	261.0
1950	546.8	304.9
2001	1 275.4	392.1
Per Capita GDP (1990 int. $)		
1	450	450
1000	450	400
1300	600	593
1400	600	676
1500	600	771
1820	600	1 204
1913	552	3 458
1950	439	4 579
2001	3 583	19 256
GDP (billion 1990 int $)		
1	26.8	11.1
1000	26.6	10.2
1300	60.0	34.6
1400	43.2	28.1
1500	61.8	44.2
1820	228.6	160.1
1913	241.3	902.3
1950	239.9	1 396.2
2001	4 569.8	7 550.3

Source: HS–1, HS–5, and HS–8 basic tables, Maddison (1998 and 2001).

http://dx.doi.org/10.1787/456125276116

iv) Kenneth Pomeranz (2000) presents a fascinating comparative picture of Chinese economic performance in the eighteenth and early nineteenth centuries. The comparison is mainly with Western Europe. There are many penetrating insights into the differences between these two areas. His main argument is that both were subject to Malthusian/ecological constraints, that Chinese performance was in many respects better than that of Europe before 1800. He suggests that Western Europe was "a non–too–unusual economy; it became a fortunate freak only when unexpected and significant discontinuities in the late eighteenth and especially nineteenth centuries enabled it to break through the fundamental constraints of energy and resource availability that had previously limited *everyone's* horizons". Pomeranz relies mainly on illustrative evidence and partial indicators of performance to back his judgement. There are only four tables with no attempt at macro–quantification (except for his comparison of life expectancy). He does not provide a chronological profile of development in Europe or China before and beyond his point of comparison. He has one passing reference to Needham, and little discussion of the forces affecting the divergent development of technology in China and Europe. His conclusions are very different from mine. In Maddison (1998) I concluded that Western Europe drew level with China in the fourteenth century and that its average per capita level was twice the Chinese in 1820 (see Table 8–3).

I find Pomeranz's judgements unconvincing. In 1800, the degree of urbanisation was three times higher in Western Europe than in China, the proportion of the population employed in agriculture was a good deal smaller, though the European diet included a much higher proportion of meat and dairy products. Chinese life expectation was two–thirds of that in Western Europe. Pomeranz stresses Western Europe's benefits from international trade, which augmented its supply of food and raw materials from the "ghost acreage" of distant lands. He treats this benefit as if it were a windfall gain. In fact, China turned its back on international trade in the middle of the fifteenth century, and the Ching dynasty forbade settlement on its own ghost acres in Manchuria.

The Pomeranz position is stated with four degrees of nuance. On p. 49 he says "it seems likely that average incomes in Japan, China and parts of southeast Asia were comparable to (or higher than) those in western Europe even in the late eighteenth century." Elsewhere his position is more cautious, and he claims Asian superiority was characteristic only for "core regions". Thus on p. 17, he says "core regions in China and Japan circa 1750 seem to resemble the most advanced parts of western Europe". For China, his core region is the lower Yangtse (which had about 18 per cent of China's population). Here he is on firmer ground, but I think he still exaggerates Chinese performance. Research on Chinese economic history has increased substantially in quantity and quantity in the past two decades. Li (1998) has shown significant advances in productivity and income in the lower Yangtse area during the Ching dynasty. Ma (2003) shows its per capita land tax revenue was about 145 per cent of that for China as a whole in 1753. My estimate of Chinese and West European income levels in 1750 can be derived by interpolating between the estimates for 1700 and 1820 in Table 8c. If Ma's fiscal estimate is taken as a proxy for lower Yangtse per capita income around 1750, it would have been about 870 dollars compared to 1 080 for western Europe as a whole and more than 1 400 for the United Kingdom.

On p. 44, Pomeranz states that "Europeans were not ahead in overall productivity in 1750". This proposition I find completely implausible, because Chinese multi–cropping of rice, intensive water management and rural industry demanded much higher labour inputs, (particularly in the lower Yangtse region) than was the case in Europe. Ester Boserup has stressed increased labour intensity as the Chinese response to land shortage. Pomeranz's obsession with Malthusian constraints leads him to neglect this Chinese–European differential in labour inputs.

Pomeranz, p. 37 suggests that Chinese longevity was "quite comparable" to European. He cites an estimate of Chinese life expectancy of 32 years at age 1 for both sexes combined in Manchuria in 1792–1867 (from Lee and Campbell, 1997). He compares this with the Wrigley and Schofield (1981) estimate of English life expectancy at birth of 37 years for 1600–1749. Following a critique by Razzell, he suggests that Wrigley and Schofield got it wrong and that their figure should be reduced to "somewhere between 31.6 and 34.0", i.e. an average of 32.8. If this were a legitimate correction, it would mean that longevity in England and China were indeed "quite comparable". However, their estimate for England should be adjusted upwards, not downwards. Life expectation at age 1 in eighteenth century England was about 7 years higher than at birth, because 17 per cent of infants died before their first birthday (I am grateful to Jim Oeppen for this information). The Cambridge group rebutted Razzell's critique in their 1997 study (Wrigley, Davies, Oeppen, and Schofield). In Maddison (2001) I compared life expectation in different parts of the world in 1820. The average for Western Europe was 36 years and 24 for Asia at birth.

There are at least four views on the contours of long–run Chinese development and two on West European.

On China, Joseph Needham's view was that its technology gave it a lead over Western Europe from the second century AD. "Chinese evolution represented a slowly rising curve. Running at a higher and sometimes much higher level than Europe between the second and fifteenth centuries". Because of its meritocratic bureaucracy, its precocity in developing printing and the existence of a common written language, best–practice technology was more easily diffused than in Europe (a point stressed by Justin Yifu Lin, 1995). China lost its leadership position because it had no counterpart to Europe's scientific revolution. Needham gave a graphical comparison of the contours of Chinese and European technological development in *Clerks and Craftsmen in China and the West* (1970), p. 414. It is similar in shape to my graph of Chinese and West European per capita GDP in Maddison, 2001, p. 42, except that Needham makes no allowance for Sung exceptionalism.

Mark Elvin's (1973) interpretation is that China made a major advance in the Sung dynasty (960–1280), and had high–level stagnation until the nineteenth century. I think Elvin is correct in stressing the special character of Sung experience. However, he did not attempt macro–quantification, and his qualitative judgement probably implies a bigger leap in the Sung than I find. I think Elvin overstates stagnation after the Sung. Between 1400 and 1820, Chinese population grew significantly faster than that of Western Europe, and its GDP growth was only slightly less than Europe's. China experienced extensive growth, whereas Europe had a mild degree of intensive growth.

My interpretation is a hybrid of Needham and Elvin. It is summarised in quantitative terms in Table 8–3 and in graphical form in Maddison (2001), p. 42.

The least plausible interpretation is that of Kang Chao (1986, pp. 87, 89, 216–220). He suggests that per capita grain output rose by half from the 1st to the 11th century, followed by a millennium of decline, with per capita output falling back to 1st century levels in 1949, because of Malthusian pressure of population on limited land resources. The sources for his estimates are not adequately documented, and their plausibility is not heightened when he throws in supposedly corroborative estimates of real wages which rise (in sheng of grain per person) from 120 in the first century to 800 in 1086 and fall to 12 in 1818!

My view of the contours of West European development is that there was a decline in per capita income after the fall of the Roman Empire, which has no counterpart in China, and a sustained process of slow per capita growth from the eleventh to the early nineteenth century. Thereafter there was a substantial acceleration of growth. The alternative view is that there were centuries of Malthusian torpor followed by an industrial revolution and a sudden take–off. Pomeranz's interpretation involves acceptance of this second view.

v) The Real Wage Literature and its Relation to National Accounts.

The serious study of real wages began with Thorold Rogers (1823–1890). His major works in this field were *A History of Agriculture and Prices in England* (7 vols. 1866–1902) and *Six Centuries of Work and Wages* (1884). Rogers was an active politician, as well as a prolific price historian and professor of political economy in Oxford. He was a Liberal member of parliament (1880–1886) and an advocate of political reform who argued that the condition of English wage earners could be improved by extending the franchise and encouraging trade union activity. Later generations of real wage analysts have generally followed his lead: *a)* adopting a very long–term perspective; *b)* giving almost exclusive emphasis to labour income; *c)* giving substantial attention to price history, *d)* reaching pessimistic conclusions. However, Rogers differed from some of his disciples in two important respects. He was not a Malthusian, and would certainly not have regarded real wages as a proxy for real GDP. For him low wages were the result of exploitation of the labourer by the ruling elite. He made a clear distinction between wage income and national income, as is clear in his citation of Gregory King's estimates of inequality (Rogers, 1884 pp. 463–465). He summarised his position, saying (p. 355) "society may make notable progress in wealth, and wages remain low, ...relatively speaking, the working man of today is not so well off as he was in the fifteenth century"

It is interesting to compare his work with that of his near–contemporary Michael Mulhall (1836–1900). Mulhall was a pioneer in comparative analysis of national income. His main concern was to measure aggregate value added (see Table 3 in the Prologue), whereas Rogers concentrated on one kind of income. Mulhall's temporal horizon was much shorter than that of Rogers, and he was not a social or political reformer. Mulhall's estimates all referred to nominal income, except for the United Kingdom, where he used wheat prices as a crude deflator. Rogers devoted massive effort to price history.

The Rogers–Mulhall dichotomy is interesting because real wage analysis and historical national accounts have continued to tread separate paths. Historical national accountants have progressed well beyond Mulhall. They have developed techniques for measuring real output and real expenditure, and have deflators for the components of these aggregates, but they almost never attempt separate deflation of the components of nominal income (see Maddison, 1995, pp. 120–123). Until recently real wage analysis had not progressed much beyond Rogers. It continued to ignore non–wage income, and used data for a small fraction of wage earners without indicating what proportion of the labour force were covered. National accountants take a macroeconomic view, have developed a standardised system (which defines coverage within clearly defined boundaries of activity) and there are fairly comprehensive crosschecks on consistency. However, their time horizon was, until recently, much shorter than that of real wage analysts.

In the 1920s–40s there was a coordinated European–US research effort with financial support from the International Committee on Price History. Some of the researchers (Beveridge and Posthumus) concentrated on price history, but there was also a substantial effort to measure long–term trends in real wages. It is clear from the account of Cole and Crandall (1964) that they had no guidelines on coverage and methodology. They measured wage rates rather than earnings, without indicating annual hours worked. There was no attempt to determine the relative size of non–wage income. Within the field of wage–income, sample coverage was usually quite small. The validity of the inter–temporal measures was questionable and there were no cross–country comparisons of wage levels. From 1939 to 1968, Jürgen Kuczynski (1904–95) provided a Marxist counterpart, producing 40 volumes on the deteriorating condition of the proletariat under capitalism. At that time there was some interaction with national accountants. Colin Clark (1940) used real wages as a real income proxy for 20 countries. Arthur Bowley (1869–1957) made a considerable effort to incorporate real wage and real income analysis into national accounts.

A third wave of interest in real wages was sparked in 1952–57, when Henry Phelps Brown (1906–94), Sheila Hopkins and other associates produced scholarly articles developing new annual measures of wages and prices in England from 1264 to 1954. (Phelps Brown and Hopkins, 1981) They synthesised the work of the pre–war group (Elsas, Hamilton and Pribram) on Austria, Germany, and Spain, and made new estimates for France. For England, they had daily wage rates for building workers hired by Oxford and Cambridge colleges, Eton school and some other employers in the south of England. For the most part, they had 15 or more quotations a year for craftsmen and 3 for building workers. Between 1500 and 1800 there were 82 years for which they had no wage estimates. They had no data on weekly or annual earnings or days worked. They did not discuss the representativity of their measure. Even if their coverage of building workers is assumed to be adequate, they represented only 5 per cent of the workforce in 1700. People employed in agriculture were 56 per cent of the total and most of them were producing and directly consuming the items which figure in the price index. Many others, such as servants, artisans, the clergy, and the armed forces received an appreciable part of their remuneration in kind. A large part of the working population were thus sheltered from the impact of price rises. In spite of these shortcomings, their findings attracted interest because of the long period they covered and their meticulous scholarship in providing detailed and transparent discussion of sources and methods. As there was no work in historical national accounts for this period, their results were readily accepted.

The conclusions of Phelps Brown and Hopkins were extremely pessimistic. From 1500 to 1800, they suggested that real wages for building workers in southern England fell by 60 per cent. Their results were enthusiastically received by Braudel and Spooner (Cambridge Economic History of Europe, 1967, p. 429). They concluded that "from the late fifteenth century until well into the beginning of the eighteenth century, the standard of living in Europe progressively declined. Before this time, in the fourteenth and fifteenth centuries ...conditions were better". This judgement was easily accepted in France because members of the Annales school were profoundly Malthusian. Le Roy Ladurie's judgement in 1960 was that Languedoc had suffered recurrent and prolonged population setbacks because limited land resources had set rigid limits to agricultural production. His inaugural lecture at the Collège de

France in 1973 restated this notion of *l'histoire immobile*. Wilhelm Abel (1978), the German historian, suggested that real living standards fell in Germany from the first half of the fourteenth to the first half of the eighteenth century.

The Phelps Brown analysis was also accepted by Wrigley and Schofield (1981) as a complement to their analysis of English demographic experience from 1541 to 1871. They found it convenient because it was "an approximate guide to fluctuations in the standard of living" in their period (pp. 312–313). They adjusted the results to interpolate gaps (pp. 638–41), they made some judicious comments on its deficiencies, but they took the real wage index to be a representative picture of living standards. In their analysis (pp. 402–412) of the relation between population growth and living standards they concluded that Malthus was right "Before 1800 matters fell out much as Malthus insisted they must..the faster population grew, the lower the standard of living and the grimmer the struggle to exist" A "decisive break" occurred during the industrial revolution. They rejected Boserup's view that "population growth in a pre–industrial economy tended to spark off changes in agricultural techniques which would allow productivity per head in agriculture to be maintained, albeit at the cost of longer hours of work, while at the same time encouraging changes elsewhere in the economy that would lead to a rise in output per head overall".

The Phelps Brown results have now been almost universally rejected as a proxy for the movement of real GDP per capita. Braudel reversed his judgement with characteristic insouciance. In Braudel (1985) p. 314, he stated that there were "clear continuities in European history. The first of these is the regular rise in GNP come hell or high water". Wrigley (1988) concluded his penetrating new analysis thus: "The single most remarkable feature of the economic history of England between the later sixteenth and the early nineteenth century was the rise in output per head in agriculture"(p. 39).

Jan de Vries (1993) joined the attack on the real wage approach. He questioned the representativity of construction worker experience, emphasised the large number of items omitted from the Phelps Brown price index, and contrasted its sombre and stagnant conclusions with his own evidence from probate inventories "All the studies I have examined for colonial New England and the Chesapeake, England and the Netherlands consistently reveal two features. With very few exceptions, each generation of decedents from the mid–seventeenth to the late eighteenth century left behind more and better possessions". He concluded that "economic growth began earlier than previously thought, that the transforming power of industry was felt later than previously thought , and that the century of the Industrial Revolution witnessed no sharp acceleration–not in production, not in consumption". In de Vries (1994) he developed the notion of an "industrious revolution" which is similar to Ester Boserup's (1965) analysis in the Asian context. It helps explain how intensified labour inputs overcame what were previously considered Malthusian constraints.

One reason real wage analysis remained primitive was that historical national accountants and their leading figure, Kuznets, showed no interest in it. Kuznets' (1973, pp. 139–140) speculations on the likely growth of European real per capita GDP between 1500 and 1750 contrasted sharply with the conclusions of Phelps Brown and his disciples, but he made no reference to their work. The two major historians of the national accounting tradition, Studenski (1958) and Stone (1997) made no mention of the real wage literature.

There was a fifth wave of real wage analysis in the past decade. This includes 2 articles on Asia; Feinstein, 1998, is the first rigorous and comprehensive measurement of real earnings of manual workers (1770–1870) by a historical national accountant since Bowley (1900); repair work on the second generation estimates by Robert Allen (2001), and new estimates by Jeffrey Williamson (1995) for 17 countries 1830–1988, which incorporate inter–spatial as well as inter–temporal comparisons.

The articles on Asia break new ground and are discussed below.

Özmucur and Pamuk (2002) present estimates of real wages of building workers in Istanbul for 1489–1914. They find a level in 1820 similar to that at the end of the fifteenth century (with some big dips in between) and about 40 per cent higher by 1910–14. They do not suggest that their measure is a satisfactory proxy for per capita income, but as they have no estimates of the latter before the nineteenth century, they conclude from their evidence that the decline of the Ottoman empire in the sixteenth century was reversed, and it adapted successfully to changing circumstances from the seventeenth to the nineteenth century. Their research is well documented, their conclusions are cautious and Pamuk has also made tentative estimates for of GDP in Turkey and other parts of the Ottoman Empire back to 1820. This study throws new light on a region that has played a significant role in world history for centuries.

Parthasarathi (1998), is a cross–country level comparison of weavers' wages in South India and England in the eighteenth century. He also covers spinners and farm labourers where his evidence is much thinner. He converts weekly wages of weavers in both countries into grain units, assuming a lb of Indian rice equivalent to 1500 calories and a lb of British bread 1000 calories. In Britain weekly earnings of weavers bought 40 to 140 lbs of grain and in South India 65 to 160. He claims that labourers in South India were in a better bargaining position than their English counterparts because they operated as village collectives, appealing to even–handed political authorities in case of dispute. In England legislation prohibited combinations of workers. The article is useful in shaking up conventional views, but is certainly contestable. It may be true that individual workers in England had a weak bargaining position, but it seems likely that in Indian village "collectives" lower castes and untouchables were exploited by the brahmin elite. The sources of his Indian wage estimates are not very clear, and his assumption that British workers got their calories from wheaten loaves bought from bakeries is rather odd. They probably got quite a lot of calories from meat and potatoes, cheese and beer which were not available in south India. A good deal of their bread must have been home–baked.

Chronology

In surveying economic development over the last two millennia in Maddison (2001), it seemed logical to start with the year zero, as official celebrations treated the year 2000 as the beginning of a new millennium. In fact, there is no year zero in the Christian era which begins in AD 1, with I BC as the preceding year. In tables HS–8, I have bowed to convention, and substituted year 1 for year zero. This makes no difference to estimates of growth rates for the first millennium.

It is perhaps useful to consider changes in conventions for measuring time over these two millennia. The Julian calendar, with an average year of 365.25 days was inaugurated by the Roman dictator, Julius Caesar in 46 BC, on the advice of the Alexandrian astronomer Sosigenes. It exaggerated the length of the year by a tiny fraction, and was replaced in the Catholic countries of Europe on October 4th 1582, as decreed in a papal bull of Gregory XIII, on advice from the astronomer Clavius and others. The Gregorian year was a little shorter (averaging of 365.2425 days). 10 days (5–14th October) were dropped from that year to link the two systems. The Protestant countries of Europe started to adopt this calendar in 1700. The last European country to switch was the USSR in 1918.

England and its colonies changed over in 1752. Until then their year began with Lady Day, on 25th March. The British parliament endorsed the change in 1751, stipulating that the year would end on 31st December, and the new Gregorian year would start on 1st January. To complete the transition, 3rd to 13th September were omitted from the 1752 calendar (Wednesday 2nd September being followed by Thursday 14th). The previous anachronistic system meant that anything published from 1st January to 24th March was attributed to the preceding year.

There have also been changes in the dating and denomination of eras. The traditional Roman era began with the foundation of Rome (*ab urbe condita*) which was thought to have been in 753 BC. There was an era of the Emperor Augustus, dating from the battle of Actium in 31BC, and an era of the Emperor Diocletian dating from his accession in 284 AD. The Christian era was first proposed by Dionysius Exiguus in AD 532. He had been asked by Pope John the 1st to provide clear guidelines for calculating the date of Easter. He also suggested the creation of a Christian era to replace that of Diocletian (who martyred Christians). Dionysius believed that Christ was born in 1BC, and that the first year of the new era (anno domini) should be the following year which he called AD 1 (see Richards, pp. 106, 217–8 and 351). There was no symbol for zero in the Roman system of numeration, and the concept of zero as a number did not come to Europe until several centuries later. The Christian era does not seem to have been inaugurated by a papal bull, and did not come into general use until the eleventh century. The first author to use the concept systematically for his chronology was Bede in his *Ecclesiastical History of the English People,* completed in 731. He did not use the term *anno domini,* referring instead to a year in the era as *"anno dominicae incarnationis"*(see Colgrave and Mynors, 1969).

In fact, there is a precedent for starting the Christian era in year zero. Gregory King in his *Notebook,* p. 4, made a comprehensive survey and forecast of world population, using the concept of anno mundi, with continuous numbering since the creation which he assumed had occurred 5630 years before 1695. He provided an alternative numbering system for years before and after Christ, with a dividing point in the year 0. He did not use the terms BC and AD, but distinguished years *ante* and *post Christum*.

Table 8a. World Population, 20 Countries and Regional Totals, 1-2001 AD

(000)

	1	1000	1500	1600	1700	1820	1870	1913	1950	1973	2001
Austria	500	700	2 000	2 500	2 500	3 369	4 520	6 767	6 935	7 586	8 151
Belgium	300	400	1 400	1 600	2 000	3 434	5 096	7 666	8 639	9 738	10 259
Denmark	180	360	600	650	700	1 155	1 888	2 983	4 271	5 022	5 353
Finland	20	40	300	400	400	1 169	1 754	3 027	4 009	4 666	5 176
France	5 000	6 500	15 000	18 500	21 471	31 250	38 440	41 463	41 829	52 157	59 658
Germany	3 000	3 500	12 000	16 000	15 000	24 905	39 231	65 058	68 375	78 950	82 281
Italy	7 000	5 000	10 500	13 100	13 300	20 176	27 888	37 248	47 105	54 797	57 845
Netherlands	200	300	950	1 500	1 900	2 333	3 610	6 164	10 114	13 438	15 981
Norway	100	200	300	400	500	970	1 735	2 447	3 265	3 961	4 503
Sweden	200	400	550	760	1 260	2 585	4 169	5 621	7 014	8 137	8 875
Switzerland	300	300	650	1 000	1 200	1 986	2 655	3 864	4 694	6 441	7 283
United Kingdom	800	2 000	3 942	6 170	8 565	21 239	31 400	45 649	50 127	56 210	59 723
12 Country Total	**17 600**	**19 700**	**48 192**	**62 580**	**68 796**	**114 571**	**162 386**	**227 957**	**256 377**	**301 103**	**325 088**
Portugal	500	600	1 000	1 100	2 000	3 297	4 327	5 972	8 443	8 976	10 066
Spain	4 500	4 000	6 800	8 240	8 770	12 203	16 201	20 263	28 063	34 837	40 087
Other	2 100	1 113	1 276	1 858	1 894	2 969	4 590	6 783	12 058	13 909	16 860
Total Western Europe	**24 700**	**25 413**	**57 268**	**73 778**	**81 460**	**133 040**	**187 504**	**260 975**	**304 941**	**358 825**	**392 101**
Eastern Europe	**4 750**	**6 500**	**13 500**	**16 950**	**18 800**	**36 457**	**53 557**	**79 530**	**87 637**	**110 418**	**120 912**
Former USSR	**3 900**	**7 100**	**16 950**	**20 700**	**26 550**	**54 765**	**88 672**	**156 192**	**179 571**	**249 712**	**290 349**
United States	680	1 300	2 000	1 500	1 000	9 981	40 241	97 606	152 271	211 909	285 024
Other Western Offshoots	490	660	800	800	750	1 250	5 847	13 795	24 186	38 932	54 815
Total Western Offshoots	**1 170**	**1 960**	**2 800**	**2 300**	**1 750**	**11 231**	**46 088**	**111 401**	**176 457**	**250 841**	**339 839**
Mexico	2 200	4 500	7 500	2 500	4 500	6 587	9 219	14 970	28 485	57 643	101 879
Other Latin America	3 400	6 900	10 000	6 100	7 550	15 118	31 180	65 965	137 453	250 756	429 334
Total Latin America	**5 600**	**11 400**	**17 500**	**8 600**	**12 050**	**21 705**	**40 399**	**80 935**	**165 938**	**308 399**	**531 213**
Japan	**3 000**	**7 500**	**15 400**	**18 500**	**27 000**	**31 000**	**34 437**	**51 672**	**83 805**	**108 707**	**126 892**
China	59 600	59 000	103 000	160 000	138 000	381 000	358 000	437 140	546 815	881 940	1 275 392
India	75 000	75 000	110 000	135 000	165 000	209 000	253 000	303 700	359 000	580 000	1 023 590
Other Asia	36 600	41 400	55 400	65 000	71 800	89 400	119 792	184 849	392 827	677 613	1 227 630
Total Asia (excluding Japan)	**171 200**	**175 400**	**268 400**	**360 000**	**374 800**	**679 400**	**730 792**	**925 689**	**1 298 642**	**2 139 553**	**3 526 612**
Africa	**16 500**	**32 300**	**46 610**	**55 320**	**61 080**	**74 236**	**90 466**	**124 697**	**227 333**	**390 034**	**821 088**
World	**230 820**	**267 573**	**438 428**	**556 148**	**603 490**	**1 041 834**	**1 271 915**	**1 791 091**	**2 524 324**	**3 916 489**	**6 149 006**

http://dx.doi.org/10.1787/456125276116

ISBN 92-64-02261-9 – © OECD 2006

Table 8a. **Rate of Growth of World Population, 20 Countries and Regional Totals, 1-2001 AD**
(annual average coumpound growth rates)

	1-1000	1000-1500	1500-1820	1820-70	1870-1913	1913-50	1950-73	1973-2001
Austria	0.03	0.21	0.16	0.59	0.94	0.07	0.39	0.26
Belgium	0.03	0.25	0.28	0.79	0.95	0.32	0.52	0.19
Denmark	0.07	0.10	0.20	0.99	1.07	0.97	0.71	0.23
Finland	0.07	0.40	0.43	0.81	1.28	0.76	0.66	0.37
France	0.03	0.17	0.23	0.42	0.18	0.02	0.96	0.48
Germany	0.02	0.25	0.23	0.91	1.18	0.13	0.63	0.15
Italy	-0.03	0.15	0.20	0.65	0.68	0.64	0.66	0.19
Netherlands	0.04	0.23	0.28	0.88	1.25	1.35	1.24	0.62
Norway	0.07	0.08	0.37	1.17	0.80	0.78	0.84	0.46
Sweden	0.07	0.06	0.48	0.96	0.70	0.60	0.65	0.31
Switzerland	0.00	0.15	0.35	0.58	0.88	0.53	1.39	0.44
United Kingdom	0.09	0.14	0.53	0.79	0.87	0.25	0.50	0.22
12 Country average	0.01	**0.18**	**0.27**	**0.70**	**0.79**	**0.32**	**0.70**	**0.27**
Portugal	0.02	0.10	0.37	0.55	0.75	0.94	0.27	0.41
Spain	-0.01	0.11	0.18	0.57	0.52	0.88	0.94	0.50
Other	-0.06	0.03	0.26	0.88	0.91	1.57	0.62	0.69
Total Western Europe	**0.00**	**0.16**	**0.26**	**0.69**	**0.77**	**0.42**	**0.71**	**0.32**
Eastern Europe	**0.03**	**0.15**	**0.31**	**0.77**	**0.92**	**0.26**	**1.01**	**0.32**
Former USSR	**0.06**	**0.17**	**0.37**	**0.97**	**1.33**	**0.38**	**1.44**	**0.54**
United States	0.06	0.09	0.50	2.83	2.08	1.21	1.45	1.06
Other Western Offshoots	0.03	0.04	0.14	3.13	2.02	1.53	2.09	1.23
Total Western Offshoots	**0.05**	**0.07**	**0.44**	**2.86**	**2.07**	**1.25**	**1.54**	**1.09**
Mexico	**0.07**	**0.10**	-0.04	0.67	1.13	1.75	3.11	2.05
Other Latin America	0.07	0.07	0.13	1.46	1.76	2.00	2.65	1.94
Total Latin America	**0.07**	**0.09**	**0.07**	**1.25**	**1.63**	**1.96**	**2.73**	**1.96**
Japan	**0.09**	**0.14**	**0.22**	**0.21**	**0.95**	**1.32**	**1.14**	**0.55**
China	0.00	0.11	0.41	-0.12	0.47	0.61	2.10	1.33
India	0.00	0.08	0.20	0.38	0.43	0.45	2.11	2.05
Other Asia	0.01	0.06	0.15	0.59	1.01	2.06	2.40	2.15
Total Asia (excl. Japan)	**0.00**	**0.09**	**0.29**	**0.15**	**0.55**	**0.92**	**2.19**	**1.80**
Africa	**0.07**	**0.07**	**0.15**	**0.40**	**0.75**	**1.64**	**2.37**	**2.69**
World	**0.01**	**0.10**	**0.27**	**0.40**	**0.80**	**0.93**	**1.93**	**1.62**

http://dx.doi.org/10.1787/456125276116

Table 8a. Share of World Population, 20 Countries and Regional Totals, 1-2001 AD
(per cent of world total)

	1	1000	1500	1600	1700	1820	1870	1913	1950	1973	2001
Austria	0.2	0.3	0.5	0.4	0.4	0.3	0.4	0.4	0.3	0.2	0.1
Belgium	0.1	0.1	0.3	0.3	0.3	0.3	0.4	0.4	0.3	0.2	0.2
Denmark	0.1	0.1	0.1	0.1	0.1	0.1	0.1	0.2	0.2	0.1	0.1
Finland	0.0	0.0	0.1	0.1	0.1	0.1	0.1	0.2	0.2	0.1	0.1
France	2.2	2.4	3.4	3.3	3.6	3.0	3.0	2.3	1.7	1.3	1.0
Germany	1.3	1.3	2.7	2.9	2.5	2.4	3.1	3.6	2.7	2.0	1.3
Italy	3.0	1.9	2.4	2.4	2.2	1.9	2.2	2.1	1.9	1.4	0.9
Netherlands	0.1	0.1	0.2	0.3	0.3	0.2	0.3	0.3	0.4	0.3	0.3
Norway	0.0	0.1	0.1	0.1	0.1	0.1	0.1	0.1	0.1	0.1	0.1
Sweden	0.1	0.1	0.1	0.1	0.2	0.2	0.3	0.3	0.3	0.2	0.1
Switzerland	0.1	0.1	0.1	0.2	0.2	0.2	0.2	0.2	0.2	0.2	0.1
United Kingdom	0.3	0.7	0.9	1.1	1.4	2.0	2.5	2.5	2.0	1.4	1.0
12 Country total	**7.6**	**7.4**	**11.0**	**11.3**	**11.4**	**11.0**	**12.8**	**12.7**	**10.2**	**7.7**	**5.3**
Portugal	0.2	0.2	0.2	0.2	0.3	0.3	0.3	0.3	0.3	0.2	0.2
Spain	1.9	1.5	1.6	1.5	1.5	1.2	1.3	1.1	1.1	0.9	0.7
Other	0.9	0.4	0.3	0.3	0.3	0.3	0.4	0.4	0.5	0.4	0.3
Total Western Europe	**10.7**	**9.5**	**13.1**	**13.3**	**13.5**	**12.8**	**14.7**	**14.6**	**12.1**	**9.2**	**6.4**
Eastern Europe	**2.1**	**2.4**	**3.1**	**3.0**	**3.1**	**3.5**	**4.2**	**4.4**	**3.5**	**2.8**	**2.0**
Former USSR	**1.7**	**2.7**	**3.9**	**3.7**	**4.4**	**5.3**	**7.0**	**8.7**	**7.1**	**6.4**	**4.7**
United States	0.3	0.5	0.5	0.3	0.2	1.0	3.2	5.4	6.0	5.4	4.6
Other Western Offshoots	0.2	0.2	0.2	0.1	0.1	0.1	0.5	0.8	1.0	1.0	0.9
Total Western Offshoots	**0.5**	**0.7**	**0.6**	**0.4**	**0.3**	**1.1**	**3.6**	**6.2**	**7.0**	**6.4**	**5.5**
Mexico			1.7	0.4	0.7	0.6	0.7	0.8	1.1	1.5	1.7
Other Latin America			2.3	1.1	1.3	1.5	2.5	3.7	5.4	6.4	7.0
Total Latin America	**2.4**	**4.3**	**4.0**	**1.5**	**2.0**	**2.1**	**3.2**	**4.5**	**6.6**	**7.9**	**8.6**
Japan	**1.3**	**2.8**	**3.5**	**3.3**	**4.5**	**3.0**	**2.7**	**2.9**	**3.3**	**2.8**	**2.1**
China	25.8	22.1	23.5	28.8	22.9	36.6	28.1	24.4	21.7	22.5	20.7
India	32.5	28.0	25.1	24.3	27.3	20.1	19.9	17.0	14.2	14.8	16.6
Other Asia	15.9	15.5	12.6	11.7	11.9	8.6	9.4	10.3	15.6	17.3	20.0
Total Asia (excl. Japan)	**74.2**	**65.6**	**61.2**	**64.7**	**62.1**	**65.2**	**57.5**	**51.7**	**51.4**	**54.6**	**57.4**
Africa	**7.1**	**12.1**	**10.6**	**9.9**	**10.1**	**7.1**	**7.1**	**7.0**	**9.0**	**10.0**	**13.4**
World	**100.0**	**100.0**	**100.0**	**100.0**	**100.0**	**100.0**	**100.0**	**100.0**	**100.0**	**100.0**	**100.0**

http://dx.doi.org/10.1787/456125276116

Table 8b. **World GDP, 20 Countries and Regional Totals, 1-2001 AD**
(million 1990 international Geary-Khamis dollars)

	1	1000	1500	1600	1700	1820	1870	1913	1950	1973	2001
Austria			1 414	2 093	2 483	4 104	8 419	23 451	25 702	85 227	164 851
Belgium			1 225	1 561	2 288	4 529	13 716	32 347	47 190	118 516	214 655
Denmark			443	569	727	1 471	3 782	11 670	29 654	70 032	123 978
Finland			136	215	255	913	1 999	6 389	17 051	51 724	105 298
France			10 912	15 559	19 539	35 468	72 100	144 489	220 492	683 965	1 258 297
Germany			8 256	12 656	13 650	26 819	72 149	237 332	265 354	944 755	1 536 743
Italy			11 550	14 410	14 630	22 535	41 814	95 487	164 957	582 713	1 101 366
Netherlands			723	2 072	4 047	4 288	9 952	24 955	60 642	175 791	347 136
Norway			192	304	450	1 071	2 485	6 119	17 838	44 544	110 683
Sweden			382	626	1 231	3 098	6 927	17 403	47 269	109 794	182 492
Switzerland			411	750	1 068	2 165	5 581	16 483	42 545	117 251	162 150
United Kingdom			2 815	6 007	10 709	36 232	100 180	224 618	347 850	675 941	1 202 074
12 Country Total			**38 459**	**56 822**	**71 077**	**142 693**	**339 104**	**840 743**	**1 286 544**	**3 660 253**	**6 509 723**
Portugal			606	814	1 638	3 043	4 219	7 467	17 615	63 397	143 234
Spain			4 495	7 029	7 481	12 299	19 556	41 653	61 429	266 896	627 733
Other			602	975	1 106	2 110	4 712	12 478	30 600	105 910	269 582
Total Western Europe	11 115	10 165	**44 162**	**65 640**	**81 302**	**160 145**	**367 591**	**902 341**	**1 396 188**	**4 096 456**	**7 550 272**
Eastern Europe	1 900	2 600	**6 696**	**9 289**	**11 393**	**24 906**	**50 163**	**134 793**	**185 023**	**550 756**	**728 792**
Former USSR	1 560	2 840	**8 458**	**11 426**	**16 196**	**37 678**	**83 646**	**232 351**	**510 243**	**1 513 070**	**1 343 230**
United States			800	600	527	12 548	98 374	517 383	1 455 916	3 536 622	7 965 795
Other Western Offshoots			320	320	306	951	13 129	65 558	179 574	521 667	1 190 472
Total Western Offshoots	468	784	**1 120**	**920**	**833**	**13 499**	**111 493**	**582 941**	**1 635 490**	**4 058 289**	**9 156 267**
Mexico			3 188	1 134	2 558	5 000	6 214	25 921	67 368	279 302	722 198
Other Latin America			4 100	2 629	3 788	10 024	21 305	93 950	348 539	1 109 727	2 364 808
Total Latin America	2 240	4 560	**7 288**	**3 763**	**6 346**	**15 024**	**27 519**	**119 871**	**415 907**	**1 389 029**	**3 087 006**
Japan	1 200	3 188	**7 700**	**9 620**	**15 390**	**20 739**	**25 393**	**71 653**	**160 966**	**1 242 932**	**2 624 523**
China	26 820	26 550	61 800	96 000	82 800	228 600	189 740	241 344	239 903	740 048	4 569 790
India	33 750	33 750	60 500	74 250	90 750	111 417	134 882	204 242	222 222	494 832	2 003 193
Other Asia	16 470	18 630	31 301	36 725	40 567	52 177	76 994	163 109	363 646	1 388 124	4 908 218
Total Asia (excluding Japan)	77 040	78 930	153 601	206 975	214 117	392 194	401 616	608 695	822 771	2 623 004	11 481 201
Africa	7 096	13 720	19 283	23 349	25 692	31 161	45 234	79 486	203 131	549 993	1 222 577
World	102 619	116 787	248 308	330 982	371 269	695 346	1 112 655	2 732 131	5 329 719	16 023 529	37 193 868

http://dx.doi.org/10.1787/456125276116

Table 8b. Rate of Growth of World GDP, 20 Countries and Regional Totals, 1-2001 AD
(annual average compound growth rates)

	1-1000	1000-1500	1500-1820	1820-70	1870-1913	1913-50	1950-73	1973-2001
Austria			0.33	1.45	2.41	0.25	5.35	2.38
Belgium			0.41	2.24	2.02	1.03	4.08	2.14
Denmark			0.38	1.91	2.66	2.55	3.81	2.06
Finland			0.60	1.58	2.74	2.69	4.94	2.57
France			0.37	1.43	1.63	1.15	5.05	2.20
Germany			0.37	2.00	2.81	0.30	5.68	1.75
Italy			0.21	1.24	1.94	1.49	5.64	2.30
Netherlands			0.56	1.70	2.16	2.43	4.74	2.46
Norway			0.54	1.70	2.12	2.93	4.06	3.30
Sweden			0.66	1.62	2.17	2.74	3.73	1.83
Switzerland			0.52	1.91	2.55	2.60	4.51	1.16
United Kingdom			0.80	2.05	1.90	1.19	2.93	2.08
12 Country Average			**0.41**	**1.75**	**2.13**	**1.16**	**4.65**	**2.08**
Portugal			0.51	0.66	1.34	2.35	5.73	2.95
Spain			0.32	0.93	1.77	1.06	6.60	3.10
Other			0.39	1.62	2.29	2.45	5.55	3.39
Total Western Europe	**-0.01**	**0.29**	**0.40**	**1.68**	**2.11**	**1.19**	**4.79**	**2.21**
Eastern Europe	**0.03**	**0.19**	**0.41**	**1.41**	**2.33**	**0.86**	**4.86**	**1.01**
Former USSR	**0.06**	**0.22**	**0.47**	**1.61**	**2.40**	**2.15**	**4.84**	**-0.42**
United States			0.86	4.20	3.94	2.84	3.93	2.94
Other Western Offshoots			0.34	5.39	3.81	2.76	4.75	2.99
Total Western Offshoots	**0.05**	**0.07**	**0.78**	**4.31**	**3.92**	**2.83**	**4.03**	**2.95**
Mexico			0.14	0.44	3.38	2.62	6.38	3.45
Other Latin America			0.28	1.52	3.51	3.61	5.16	2.74
Total Latin America	**0.07**	**0.09**	**0.23**	**1.22**	**3.48**	**3.42**	**5.38**	**2.89**
Japan	**0.10**	**0.18**	**0.31**	**0.41**	**2.44**	**2.21**	**9.29**	**2.71**
China	0.00	0.17	0.41	-0.37	0.56	-0.02	5.02	6.72
India	0.00	0.12	0.19	0.38	0.97	0.23	3.54	5.12
Other Asia	0.01	0.10	0.16	0.78	1.76	2.19	6.00	4.61
Total Asia (excl. Japan)	**0.00**	**0.13**	**0.29**	**0.05**	**0.97**	**0.82**	**5.17**	**5.41**
Africa	**0.07**	**0.07**	**0.15**	**0.75**	**1.32**	**2.57**	**4.43**	**2.89**
World	**0.01**	**0.15**	**0.32**	**0.93**	**2.11**	**1.82**	**4.90**	**3.05**

http://dx.doi.org/10.1787/456125276116

Table 8b. **Share of World GDP, 20 Countries and Regional Totals, 1-2001 AD**
(per cent of world total)

	1	1000	1500	1600	1700	1820	1870	1913	1950	1973	2001
Austria			0.6	0.6	0.7	0.6	0.8	0.9	0.5	0.5	0.4
Belgium			0.5	0.5	0.6	0.7	1.2	1.2	0.9	0.7	0.6
Denmark			0.2	0.2	0.2	0.2	0.3	0.4	0.6	0.4	0.3
Finland			0.1	0.1	0.1	0.1	0.2	0.2	0.3	0.3	0.3
France			4.4	4.7	5.3	5.1	6.5	5.3	4.1	4.3	3.4
Germany			3.3	3.8	3.7	3.9	6.5	8.7	5.0	5.9	4.1
Italy			4.7	4.4	3.9	3.2	3.8	3.5	3.1	3.6	3.0
Netherlands			0.3	0.6	1.1	0.6	0.9	0.9	1.1	1.1	0.9
Norway			0.1	0.1	0.1	0.2	0.2	0.2	0.3	0.3	0.3
Sweden			0.2	0.2	0.3	0.4	0.6	0.6	0.9	0.7	0.5
Switzerland			0.2	0.2	0.3	0.3	0.5	0.6	0.8	0.7	0.4
United Kingdom			1.1	1.8	2.9	5.2	9.0	8.2	6.5	4.2	3.2
12 Country total			**15.5**	**17.2**	**19.1**	**20.5**	**30.5**	**30.8**	**24.1**	**22.8**	**17.5**
Portugal			0.2	0.2	0.4	0.4	0.4	0.3	0.3	0.4	0.4
Spain			1.8	2.1	2.0	1.8	1.8	1.5	1.2	1.7	1.7
Other			0.2	0.3	0.3	0.3	0.4	0.5	0.6	0.7	0.7
Total Western Europe	**10.8**	**8.7**	**17.8**	**19.8**	**21.9**	**23.0**	**33.0**	**33.0**	**26.2**	**25.6**	**20.3**
Eastern Europe	**1.9**	**2.2**	**2.7**	**2.8**	**3.1**	**3.6**	**4.5**	**4.9**	**3.5**	**3.4**	**2.0**
Former USSR	**1.5**	**2.4**	**3.4**	**3.5**	**4.4**	**5.4**	**7.5**	**8.5**	**9.6**	**9.4**	**3.6**
United States			0.3	0.2	0.1	1.8	8.8	18.9	27.3	22.1	21.4
Other Western Offshoots			0.1	0.1	0.1	0.1	1.2	2.4	3.4	3.3	3.2
Total Western Offshoots	**0.5**	**0.7**	**0.5**	**0.3**	**0.2**	**1.9**	**10.0**	**21.3**	**30.7**	**25.3**	**24.6**
Mexico			1.3	0.3	0.7	0.7	0.6	0.9	1.3	1.7	1.9
Other Latin America			1.7	0.8	1.0	1.4	1.9	3.4	6.5	6.9	6.4
Total Latin America	**2.2**	**3.9**	**2.9**	**1.1**	**1.7**	**2.2**	**2.5**	**4.4**	**7.8**	**8.7**	**8.3**
Japan	**1.2**	**2.7**	**3.1**	**2.9**	**4.1**	**3.0**	**2.3**	**2.6**	**3.0**	**7.8**	**7.1**
China	26.1	22.7	24.9	29.0	22.3	32.9	17.1	8.8	4.5	4.6	12.3
India	32.9	28.9	24.4	22.4	24.4	16.0	12.1	7.5	4.2	3.1	5.4
Other Asia	16.0	16.0	12.6	11.1	10.9	7.5	6.9	6.0	6.8	8.7	13.2
Total Asia (excl. Japan)	**75.1**	**67.6**	**61.9**	**62.5**	**57.7**	**56.4**	**36.1**	**22.3**	**15.4**	**16.4**	**30.9**
Africa	**6.9**	**11.7**	**7.8**	**7.1**	**6.9**	**4.5**	**4.1**	**2.9**	**3.8**	**3.4**	**3.3**
World	**100.0**	**100.0**	**100.0**	**100.0**	**100.0**	**100.0**	**100.0**	**100.0**	**100.0**	**100.0**	**100.0**

http://dx.doi.org/10.1787/456125276116

Table 8c. **World Per Capita GDP, 20 Countries and Regional Averages, 1-2001 AD**
(1990 international Geary-Khamis dollars)

	1	1000	1500	1600	1700	1820	1870	1913	1950	1973	2001
Austria			707	837	993	1 218	1 863	3 465	3 706	11 235	20 225
Belgium			875	976	1 144	1 319	2 692	4 220	5 462	12 170	20 924
Denmark			738	875	1 039	1 274	2 003	3 912	6 943	13 945	23 160
Finland			453	538	638	781	1 140	2 111	4 253	11 085	20 344
France			727	841	910	1 135	1 876	3 485	5 271	13 114	21 092
Germany			688	791	910	1 077	1 839	3 648	3 881	11 966	18 677
Italy			1 100	1 100	1 100	1 117	1 499	2 564	3 502	10 634	19 040
Netherlands			761	1 381	2 130	1 838	2 757	4 049	5 996	13 082	21 722
Norway			640	760	900	1 104	1 432	2 501	5 463	11 246	24 580
Sweden			695	824	977	1 198	1 662	3 096	5 463	13 493	20 562
Switzerland			632	750	890	1 090	2 102	4 266	6 739	18 204	22 264
United Kingdom			714	974	1 250	1 706	3 190	4 921	9 064	12 025	20 127
12 Country Average			**798**	**908**	**1 033**	**1 245**	**2 088**	**3 688**	**5 018**	**12 156**	**20 024**
Portugal			606	740	819	923	975	1 250	2 086	7 063	14 229
Spain			661	853	853	1 008	1 207	2 056	2 189	7 661	15 659
Other			472	525	584	711	1 027	1 840	2 538	7 614	15 989
West European average	450	400	**771**	**890**	**998**	**1 204**	**1 960**	**3 458**	**4 579**	**11 416**	**19 256**
Eastern Europe	400	400	496	548	606	683	937	1 695	2 111	4 988	6 027
Former USSR	400	400	499	552	610	688	943	1 488	2 841	6 059	4 626
United States			400	400	527	1 257	2 445	5 301	9 561	16 689	27 948
Other Western Offshoots			400	400	408	761	2 245	4 752	7 425	13 399	21 718
Average Western Offshoots	400	400	400	400	476	1 202	2 419	5 233	9 268	16 179	26 943
Mexico			425	454	568	759	674	1 732	2 365	4 845	7 089
Other Latin America			410	431	502	663	683	1 424	2 536	4 426	5 508
Latin American Average	400	400	416	438	527	692	681	1 481	2 506	4 504	5 811
Japan	400	425	500	520	570	669	737	1 387	1 921	11 434	20 683
China	450	450	600	600	600	600	530	552	439	839	3 583
India	450	450	550	550	550	533	533	673	619	853	1 957
Other Asia	450	450	565	565	565	584	643	882	926	2 049	3 998
Asian average (excl. Japan)	450	450	572	575	571	577	550	658	634	1 226	3 256
Africa	430	425	414	422	421	420	500	637	894	1 410	1 489
World	445	436	566	595	615	667	875	1 525	2 111	4 091	6 049

http://dx.doi.org/10.1787/456125276116

ISBN 92-64-02261-9 – © OECD 2006

Table 8b. **Rate of Growth of World Per Capita GDP, 20 Countries and Regional Averages, 1-2001 AD**
(annual average compound growth rates)

	1-1000	*1000-1500*	*1500-1820*	*1820-70*	*1870-1913*	*1913-50*	*1950-73*	*1973-2001*
Austria			0.17	0.85	1.45	0.18	4.94	2.12
Belgium			0.13	1.44	1.05	0.70	3.54	1.95
Denmark			0.17	0.91	1.57	1.56	3.08	1.83
Finland			0.17	0.76	1.44	1.91	4.25	2.19
France			0.14	1.01	1.45	1.12	4.04	1.71
Germany			0.14	1.08	1.61	0.17	5.02	1.60
Italy			0.00	0.59	1.26	0.85	4.95	2.10
Netherlands			0.28	0.81	0.90	1.07	3.45	1.83
Norway			0.17	0.52	1.30	2.13	3.19	2.83
Sweden			0.17	0.66	1.46	2.12	3.06	1.52
Switzerland			0.17	1.32	1.66	2.06	3.08	0.72
United Kingdom			0.27	1.26	1.01	0.93	2.42	1.86
12 Country Average			**0.14**	**1.04**	**1.33**	**0.84**	**3.92**	**1.80**
Portugal			0.13	0.11	0.58	1.39	5.45	2.53
Spain			0.13	0.36	1.25	0.17	5.60	2.59
Other			0.13	0.74	1.37	0.87	4.89	2.68
Total Western Europe	**-0.01**	**0.13**	**0.14**	**0.98**	**1.33**	**0.76**	**4.05**	**1.88**
Eastern Europe	**0.00**	**0.04**	**0.10**	**0.63**	**1.39**	**0.60**	**3.81**	**0.68**
Former USSR	**0.00**	**0.04**	**0.10**	**0.63**	**1.06**	**1.76**	**3.35**	**-0.96**
United States			0.36	1.34	1.82	1.61	2.45	1.86
Other Western Offshoots			0.20	2.19	1.76	1.21	2.60	1.74
Total Western Offshoots	**0.00**	**0.00**	**0.34**	**1.41**	**1.81**	**1.56**	**2.45**	**1.84**
Mexico			0.18	-0.24	2.22	0.85	3.17	1.37
Other Latin America			0.15	0.06	1.72	1.57	2.45	0.78
Total Latin America	**0.00**	**0.01**	**0.16**	**-0.03**	**1.82**	**1.43**	**2.58**	**0.91**
Japan	**0.01**	**0.03**	**0.09**	**0.19**	**1.48**	**0.88**	**8.06**	**2.14**
China	**0.00**	0.06	0.00	-0.25	0.10	-0.62	2.86	5.32
India	**0.00**	0.04	-0.01	0.00	0.54	-0.22	1.40	3.01
Other Asia	**0.00**	0.05	0.01	0.19	0.74	0.13	3.51	2.42
Total Asia (excl. Japan)	**0.00**	**0.05**	**0.00**	**-0.10**	**0.42**	**-0.10**	**2.91**	**3.55**
Africa	**0.00**	**-0.01**	**0.00**	**0.35**	**0.57**	**0.92**	**2.00**	**0.19**
World	**0.00**	**0.05**	**0.05**	**0.54**	**1.30**	**0.88**	**2.92**	**1.41**

http://dx.doi.org/10.1787/456125276116

Select Bibliography

ALDCROFT, D.H. AND A. SUTCLIFFE (eds.) (1999). *Europe in the International Economy: 1500 to 2000*, Elgar, Cheltenham.

ALLEN, R.C. (2001), "The Great Divergence in European Wages and Prices from the Middle Ages to the First World War", *Explorations in Economic History*, 38, pp. 411–447.

BAIROCH, P. (1967), *Diagnostic de l'évolution économique du tiers–monde, 1900–1966*, Gauthiers–Villars, Paris.

BAIROCH, P. (1976), "Europe's Gross National Product: 1800–1975", *Journal of European Economic History*, Fall, pp. 273–340.

BAIROCH, P. (1977), "Estimations du revenu national dans les sociétés occidentales pré–industrielles et au dix–neuvième siècle: propositions d'approches indirectes", *Revue économique*, March, pp. 177–208.

BAIROCH, P. (1997), *Victoires et Déboires*, 3 vols., Gallimard, Paris.

BAIROCH, P. AND M. LEVY–LEBOYER (1981), *Disparities in Economic Development since the Industrial Revolution*, Macmillan, London.

BAGNALL, R.S. AND B.W. FRIER (1994*)*, *The Demography of Roman Egypt*, Cambridge University Press.

BARDET, J.–P. AND J. DUPAQUIER (1997), *Histoire des populations de l'Europe*, Fayard, Paris, 2 vols.

BECKERMAN, W. (1966), *International Comparisons of Real Incomes*, OECD Development Centre, Paris.

BELOCH, J. (1886), *Die Bevölkerung der Griechisch–Römischen Welt*, Duncker and Humblot, Leipzig.

BERGSON, A. (1953), *Soviet National Income and Product in 1937*, Columbia University Press, New York.

BETHELL, L. (1985–6), *The Cambridge History of Latin America*, vols. III and IV, Cambridge University Press.

BOISGUILBERT, P. DE (1696*)*, *La France ruinée sous la règne de Louis XIV par qui et comment*, Marteau, Cologne (author not shown, publisher fictitious, clandestinely printed in Rouen).

BOISGUILBERT, P. DE (1697), *Le détail de la France* (author and publisher not shown).

BOISGUILBERT, P. DE (1966), see INED.

BOOMGAARD, P. (1993), "Economic Growth in Indonesia, 500–1990", *in* SZIRMAI, VAN ARK AND PILAT.

BOOMGAARD, P., see Creutzberg.

BORAH, W. AND S.F. COOK (1963), *The Aboriginal Population of Central Mexico on the Eve of the Spanish Conquest*, University of California, Berkeley.

BORDO, M.D. AND R. CORTÉS–CONDE (2001), *Transferring Wealth and Power from the Old to the New World*, Cambridge University Press.

BOSERUP, E. (1965), *The Conditions of Agricultural Growth*, Allen and Unwin, London.

BOWLEY, A.L. (1900),*Wages in the United Kingdom in the Nineteenth Century*, Cambridge University Press.

BOWLEY, A.L. (1942), *Studies in the National Income*, Cambridge University Press.

BOWMAN A.K. AND E. ROGAN (eds.) (1999), *Agriculture in Egypt from Pharaonic to Modern Times*, Oxford University Press.

BRAUDEL, F. (1985), *Civilization and Capitalism: 15th–18th Century*, vol. 3, Fontana, London.

BRESNAHAN, T.F. AND R.J. GORDON (1997), *The Economics of New Goods*, NBER and University of Chicago Press.

BREWER, J. (1989), *The Sinews of Power: War, Money and the English State, 1688–1783*, Unwin Hyman, London.

BREWER, J. AND R. PORTER (eds.) (1993*), Consumption and the World of Goods*, Routledge, London.

BROADBERRY, S.N. (1997a),"Forging Ahead, Falling Behind and Catching–up: A Sectoral Analysis of Anglo–American Productivity Differences, 1870–1990", *Research In Economic History*, 17, pp. 1–37.

BROADBERRY, S.N. (1997b), "Anglo–German Productivity Differences 1870–1990: A Sectoral Analysis", *European Review of Economic History*, I, pp. 247–267.

BROADBERRY, S.N. (1998), "How did the United States and Germany Overtake Britain? A Sectoral Analysis of Comparative Productivity Levels, 1870–1990", *Journal of Economic History,* June, pp. 375–407.

BUTLIN, N.G. (1983), *Our Original Aggression*, Allen and Unwin, Sydney.

CHALMERS, G. (1802), *An Estimate of the Comparative Strength of Great Britain*, Stockdale, Piccadilly, London.

CHAO, K. (1986), *Man and Land in Chinese History: An Economic Analysis*, Stanford University Press, Stanford.

CHRISTENSEN, J.P., R. HJERPPE, O. KRANTZ AND C.–A. NILSSON (1995),"Nordic Historical National Accounts since the 1880s", *Scandinavian Economic History Review*, XLIII, no. 1.

CIPOLLA, C.M. (1976), *Before the Industrial Revolution: European Society and Economy, 1000–1700*, Norton, New York.

CLARK, C. (1937), *National Income and Outlay*, Macmillan, London.

CLARK, C. (1940), *The Conditions of Economic Progress*, Macmillan, London.

CLARK, C. (1951), *The Conditions of Economic Progress*, second edition, Macmillan, London.

CLARK, C. (1957), *The Conditions of Economic Progress*, third edition, Macmillan, London.

COLE, A.H. AND R. CRANDALL (1964), "The International Scientific Committee on Price History", *Journal of Economic History*, September, pp. 381–388.

COLGRAVE, B. AND R.A.B. MYNORS (eds.) (1969), *Bede's Ecclesiastical History of the English People*, Clarendon Press, Oxford.

COLLINS, J.B. (1995), *The State in Early Modern France*, Cambridge University Press.

COLQUHOUN, P. (1815), *A Treatise on the Wealth, Power, and Resources of the British Empire in Every Quarter of the World*, Mawman, London.

CRAFTS, N.F.R. (1983), Gross National Product in Europe 1870–1910: Some New Estimates", *Explorations in Economic History* (20), pp. 387–401.

CRAFTS, N.F.R. AND C.K. HARLEY (1992), "Output Growth and the British Industrial Revolution: A Restatement of the Crafts–Harley View", *Economic History Review*, November, pp. 703–730.

CREUTZBERG, P. AND P. BOOMGAARD (eds.) (1975–1996), *Changing Economy in Indonesia: A Selection of Statistical Resource Material from the Early 19th century up to 1940*, 16 volumes, Royal Tropical Institute, Amsterdam.

CROSBY, A.W. (1972), *The Columbian Exchange:Biological and Cultural Consequences of 1492*, Greenwood Press, Westport.

CROUZET, F. AND A. CLESSE (eds.) (2003), *Leading the World Economically*, Dutch University Press, The Netherlands.

DAVENANT, C. (1694), *An Essay on Ways and Means of Supplying the War*, (see Whitworth, 1771).

DAVENANT, C. (1699), *An Essay upon the Probable Methods of Making a People Gainers in the Balance of Trade*, (see Whitworth, 1771)

DEANE, P. (1955), "The Implications of Early National Income Estimates for the Measurement of Long–Term Economic Growth in the United Kingdom", *Economic Development and Cultural Change*, pp. 3–38.

DEANE, P. (1955–6), "Contemporary Estimates of National Income in the First Half of the Nineteenth Century", *Economic History Review*, VIII, 3, pp. 339–354.

DEANE, P. (1956–7), "Contemporary Estimates of National Income in the Second Half of the Nineteenth Century", *Economic History Review*, IX, 3, pp. 451–61.

DEANE, P. (1957), "The Industrial Revolution and Economic Growth: The Evidence of Early British National Income Estimates", *Economic Development and Cultural Change*, pp. 159–74.

DEANE, P. (1968), "New Estimates of Gross National Product for the United Kingdom, 1830–1914", *Review of Income and Wealth*, June, pp. 95–112.

DEANE, P. AND W.A. COLE (1964), *British Economic Growth, 1688–1959*, Cambridge University Press.

DENISON, E.F. (1947), "Report on Tripartite Discussions of National Income Measurement", *in Studies in Income and Wealth*, Vol.10, NBER, New York.

DENISON, E.F. (1967), *Why Growth Rates Differ*, Brookings, Washington, D.C.

ECE (ECONOMIC COMMISSION FOR EUROPE) and UN (1994), *International Comparison of Gross Domestic Product in Europe 1990*, New York and Geneva.

ELTIS, D. (1995), "The Total Product of Barbados, 1664–1701", *Journal of Economic History*, June.

ELTIS, D. (1997), "The Slave Economies of the Caribbean: Structure, Perfomance, Evolution and Significance", *in* KNIGHT, pp. 105–137.

ELVIN, M. (1973), *The Pattern of the Chinese Past*, Methuen, London.

ENG, P. VAN DER (1993), *Agricultural Growth in Indonesia Since 1880*, University of Groningen.

ENGERMAN, S.L. AND R.E. GALLMAN (1996–2000), *The Cambridge History of the United States*, 3 vols., Cambridge University Press.

ENGERMAN, S.L. AND B.W. HIGMAN (1997), "The demographic structure of the Caribbean slave societies in the eighteenth and nineteenth centuries" *in* Knight, pp. 45–104.

ESCAP (ECONOMIC COMMISSION FOR ASIA AND THE PACIFIC) (1999), *ESCAP Comparisons of Real Gross Domestic Product and Purchasing Power Parities, 1993*, Bangkok.

ESCWA (ECONOMIC AND SOCIAL COMMISSION FOR WESTERN ASIA) and WORLD BANK (1997), *Purchasing Power Parities: Volume and Price Level Comparisons for the Middle East, 1993*, Beirut.

EUROSTAT (1996), *Comparisons of Price Levels and Economic Aggregates 1993: The Results of 22 African Countries*, Luxembourg.

FEINSTEIN, C.H. (1972), *National Income, Expenditure and Output of the United Kingdom, 1855–1965*, Cambridge University Press.

FEINSTEIN, C.H. (1988),"The Rise and Fall of the Williamson Curve", Journal of Economic History, September, pp. 699–729.

FEINSTEIN, C.H. (1998), "Pessimism Perpetuated: Real Wages and the Standard of Living in Britain during and after the Industrial Revolution", *Journal of Economic History*, September, pp. 625–58.

FOGEL, J.A. (1964), *Railroads and American Economic Growth*, Johns Hopkins University Press, Baltimore.

FRANK, A.G. (1998), *Reorient: Global Economy in the Asian Age*, University of California Press, Berkeley.

GALBRAITH, J.K. *et al.* (1945), *The Effects of Strategic Bombing on the German War Economy*, US Strategic Bombing Survey, Washington, D.C.

GILBERT, M. AND I.B. KRAVIS (1954), *An International Comparison of National Products and Purchasing Power of Currencies*, OEEC, Paris.

GILBERT, M. AND ASSOCIATES (1958), *Comparative National Products and Price Levels*, OEEC, Paris.

GLASS, D.V. (1965), "Two Papers on Gregory King", *in* Glass and Eversley (1965), pp. 159–221.

GLASS, D.V. AND D.E.C. EVERSLEY (eds.) (1965), *Population in History: Essays in Historical Demography*, Arnold, London.

GOITEIN, S.D.F. (1967–93*), A Mediterranean Society: The Jewish Communities of the Arab World as Portrayed in the Documents of the Cairo Geniza*, 6 vols.,University of California Press, Berkeley and Los Angeles.

GOLDSMITH, R.W. (1984), "An Estimate of the Size and Structure of the National Product of the Roman Empire", *Review of Income and Wealth,* September.

GOODY, J. (1971), *Technology, Tradition and the State in Africa*, Oxford University Press.

GRAUNT, J. (1662), *Natural and Political Observations Made Upon the Bills of Mortality*, reprinted in Laslett.

HABIB, I. (1978–9), "The Technology and Economy of Moghul India", *Indian Economic and Social History Review,* vol. XVII, No. 1, pp. 1–34.

HABIB, I. (1995), *Essays in Indian History*, Tulika, New Delhi.

HAIG, B. (2001), *The First Official National Accounting Estimates*, Canberra (processed).

HANLEY, S. (1997), *Everyday Things in Premodern Japan*, University of California, Berkeley.

HANLEY, S.B. AND K. YAMAMURA (1977), *Economic and Demographic Change in Preindustrial Japan, 1600–1868*, Princeton University Press.

HARALDSON, W.C. AND E.F. DENISON, (1945), "The Gross National Product of Germany 1936–44", Special Paper I (mimeographed), *in* GALBRAITH *et al.*

HAYAMI, A. (1986), "Population Trends in Tokugawa Japan 1600–1970", International Statistical Institute Conference.

HESTON, A. AND R. SUMMERS (1993), "What Can be Learned from Successive ICP Benchmark Estimates?" *in* SZIRMAI, VAN ARK AND PILAT (*op. cit.*).

HESTON, A., R. SUMMERS AND B. ATEN (2002), PWT Version 6.1 (CICUP), http:/pwt.econ.upenn.edu).

HJERPPE, R. (1996), *Finland's Historical National Accounts 1860–1994*, University of Jyväskylä, Jyväskylä.

HO, P.T. (1959), *Studies on the Population of China, 1368–1953*, Columbia University Press, New York.

HOFMAN, A.A. (2000), *The Economic Development of Latin America in the Twentieth Century*, Elgar, Cheltenham.

HOPKINS, K. (1980), "Taxes and Trade in the Roman Empire (200 BC–400 AD)", *Journal of Roman Studies*, vol. LXX, pp. 101–25.

IBN KHALDUN (1958), *The Muqqadimah: An Introduction to History*, 3 vols., translated by Franz Rosenthal, Routledge and Kegan Paul, London.

INED (1966), *Pierre de Boisguilbert ou la naissance de l'économie politique,* vol. I, Biographie, correspondance, bibliographies, vol. II, œuvres manuscrites et imprimées, Paris.

JARRETT, H.S. AND J.–N. SARKAR (1949), *'Ain–I–Akbari of Abul Fazl–I–'Allami*, Royal Asiatic Society of Bengal, Calcutta.

JONES, E.L. (1981), *The European Miracle*, Cambridge University Press.

JONES, E.L. (1988), *Growth Recurring: Economic Change in World History*, Clarendon Press, Oxford.

KALDOR, N. (1946), "The German War Economy", *Review of Economic Studies*, vol. XIII, 1.

KING, G. (1696), *Natural and Political Observations and Conclusions upon the State and Condition of England*, reproduced in G.E. Barnett (1936), *Two Tracts by Gregory King*, Johns Hopkins Press, Baltimore.

KING, G. (1697), *Natural and Political Observations and Conclusions upon the State and Condition of England*, manuscript copy of above, interleaved with detailed comments by Robert Harley and King's replies, Manuscript (MS 1458) in National Library of Australia.

KING, G. (1695–70), *Manuscript Notebook*, reproduced in Laslett (1973).

KNIGHT, F.W. (ed.) (1997), *General History of the Caribbean*, vol III, UNESCO, London.

Kravis, I.B., A. Heston and R. Summers (1978), "Real GDP Per Capita For More Than One Hundred Countries", *Economic Journal,* June.

Kravis, I.B., A. Heston and R. Summers (1982), *World Product and Income, International Comparisons of Real Gross Product*, Johns Hopkins, Baltimore.

Kuznets, S. (1948), "Discussion of the New Department of Commerce Income Series", *Review of Economics and Statistics*, August, with reply by Gilbert, Jaszi, Denison and Schwartz, and comment by Kalecki.

Kuznets, S. (1973), *Population, Capital and Growth: Selected Essays*, Norton, New York.

Lal, D. (1988), *The Hindu Equilibrium*, Oxford University Press.

Lal, D. (1998), *Unintended Consequences*, MIT Press, Cambridge, Mass.

Landes, D.S. (1969), *The Unbound Prometheus*, Cambridge University Press.

Landes, D.S. (1998),*The Wealth and Poverty of Nations*, Little, Brown and Company, London.

Larsen, H. K. (2001), *Convergence? Industrialisation of Denmark, Finland and Sweden 1870–1940*, Finnish Society of Science and Letters, Helsinki.

Laslett, P. (ed.) (1973), *The Earliest Classics: John Graunt and Gregory King*, Gregg International, London.

Lee, B. and A. Maddison (1997), "A Comparison of Output, Purchasing Power and Productivity in Indian and Chinese Manufacturing in the mid–1980s", *COPPAA Paper, No. 5,* Brisbane.

Le Roy Ladurie, E. (1978), "Les comptes fantastiques de Gregory King", *in Le territoire de l'historien*, vol. 1, Gallimard, Paris.

Li, B. (1998), *Agricultural Development in Jiangnan, 1620–1850*, Macmillan, London.

Lin, J.Y. (1995), "The Needham Puzzle: Why the Industrial Revolution did not Originate in China", *Economic Development and Cultural Change*, January.

Lindert, P.H. and J.G. Williamson (1983), "English Workers Living Standards during the Industrial Revolution: A New Look", *Economic History Review*, February, pp. 1–25.

Ma, D. (2003), "Modern Economic Growth in the Lower Yangzi: A Quantitative and Historical Perspective", http://aghistory,ucdavis.edu/ma.pdf.

Maddison, A. (1962), "Growth and Fluctuation in the World Economy, 1870–1960", *Banca Nazionale del Lavoro Quarterly Review,* June.

Maddison, A. (1969), *Economic Growth in Japan and the USSR*, Allen and Unwin, London.

Maddison, A. (1970), *Economic Progress and Policy in Developing Countries*, Allen and Unwin, London.

Maddison, A. (1971), *Class Structure and Economic Growth: India and Pakistan Since the Moghuls*, Allen and Unwin, London.

Maddison, A. (1982), *Phases of Capitalist Development*, Oxford University Press.

Maddison, A. (1983), "A Comparison of Levels of GDP Per Capita in Developed and Developing Countries, 1700–1980", *Journal of Economic History*, March, pp. 27–41.

Maddison, A. (1987a), "Growth and Slowdown in Advanced Capitalist Economies: Techniques of Quantitative Assessment", *Journal of Economic Literature*, June, pp. 649–698.

Maddison, A. (1987b), "Recent Revisions to British and Dutch Growth, 1700–1870 and their Implications for Comparative Levels of Performance", *in* Maddison and van der Meulen (1987).

Maddison, A. (1989a), *The World Economy in the Twentieth Century*, Development Centre Studies, OECD, Paris.

Maddison, A. (1989b), "Dutch Income in and from Indonesia 1700–1938", *Modern Asian Studies*, pp. 645–70.

Maddison, A. (1990), "Measuring European Growth: the Core and the Periphery", *in* E. Aerts and N. Valerio, *Growth and Stagnation in the Mediterranean World,* Tenth International Economic History Conference, Leuven.

MADDISON, A. (1991), *Dynamic Forces in Capitalist Development*, Oxford University Press.

MADDISON, A. (1991b), "A Revised Estimate of Italian Economic Growth, 1861–1989", *Banca Nazionale del Lavoro Quarterly Review*, June, pp. 225–41.

MADDISON, A. (1991c), *A Long Run Perspective on Saving*, Research Memorandum 443, Institute of Economic Research, University of Groningen (shorter version in *Scandinavian Journal of Economics*, June 1992, pp. 181–96).

MADDISON, A. (1995), *Monitoring the World Economy 1820–1992*, Development Centre Studies, OECD, Paris.

MADDISON, A. (1995b) *Explaining the Economic Performance of Nations: Essays in Time and Space*, Elgar, Aldershot.

MADDISON, A. (1995c), "The Historical Roots of Modern Mexico: 1500–1940", in Maddison (1995b).

MADDISON, A. (1998), *Chinese Economic Performance in the Long Run*, Development Centre Studies, OECD, Paris.

MADDISON, A. (1998b), "Measuring the Performance of A Communist Command Economy: An Assessment of the CIA Estimates for the USSR", *Review of Income and Wealth*, September.

MADDISON, A. (1999), Review of Hanley (1997), *Journal of Japanese and International Economies*.

MADDISON, A. (2001), *The World Economy: A Millennial Perspective*, Development Centre Studies, OECD, Paris.

MADDISON, A. (2002), "The Nature of US Economic Leadership: A Historical and Comparative View", *in* O'BRIEN AND CLESSE.

MADDISON, A. (2003), "Growth Accounts, Technological Change, and the Role of Energy in Western Growth" in *Economia e Energia Secc. XIII–XVIII*, Instituto Internazionale di Storia Economica "E. Datini", Prato.

MADDISON, A. (2003), website: http://eco.rug.nl/~Maddison/

MADDISON, A. (2004), *The West and the Rest in the World Economy*, forthcoming.

MADDISON, A. AND ASSOCIATES (1992), *The Political Economy of Economic Growth: Brazil and Mexico*, Oxford University Press, New York.

MADDISON, A. AND B. VAN ARK (1988), *Comparisons of Real Output in Manufacturing*, Policy, Planning and Research Working Papers WPS 5, World Bank, Washington, D.C.

MADDISON, A. AND B. VAN ARK (1989), "International Comparisons of Purchasing Power, Real Output and Labour Productivity: A Case Study of Brazilian, Mexican and US Manufacturing, 1975", *Review of Income and Wealth*, March.

MADDISON, A. AND B. VAN ARK (2000), "The International Comparison of Real Product and Productivity" in MADDISON, PRASADA RAO AND SHEPHERD.

MADDISON, A. AND H. VAN DER MEULEN (eds.) (1987), *Economic Growth in Northwestern Europe: The Last 400 Years*, Research Memorandum 214, Institute of Economic Research, University of Groningen.

MADDISON, A. AND H. VAN DER WEE (eds.) (1994), *Economic Growth and Structural Change: Comparative Approaches over the Long Run*, Proceedings of the Eleventh International Economic History Congress, Milan, September.

MADDISON, A., D.S. PRASADA RAO AND W. SHEPHERD (eds.) (2000), *The Asian Economies in the Twentieth Century*, Elgar, Aldershot.

MADDISON, A. AND G. PRINCE (eds.) (1989), *Economic Growth in Indonesia, 1820–1940*, Foris, Dordrecht.

MANARUNGSAN, S. (1989), *Economic Development of Thailand, 1850–1950*, University of Groningen.

McEVEDY, C. (1995), *Penguin Atlas of African History*, London.

McEVEDY, C. AND R. JONES (1978), *Atlas of World Population History*, Penguin, Middlesex.

McNEILL, W.H. (1963), *The Rise of the West*, University of Chicago Press.

McNEILL, W.H. (1977), *Plagues and Peoples*, Anchor Books, Doubleday, New York.

McNeill, W.H. (1990), "The Rise of the West after Twenty–Five Years", *Journal of World History*, vol. 1, no. 1.

Meade, J. R. and R. Stone (1941), "The Construction of Tables on National Income, Expenditure, Savings and Investment", *Economic Journal*, Jun–Sep, pp. 216–33.

Mitchell, B.R. (1975), *European Historical Statistics 1750–1970*, Macmillan, London.

Mitchell, B.R. (1982), *International Historical Statistics: Africa and Asia*, Macmillan, London.

Mitchell, B.R. (1983), *International Historical Statistics: the Americas and Australasia*, Macmillan, London.

Moosvi, S. (1987), *The Economy of the Moghul Empire c.1595: A Statistical Study*, Oxford University Press, Delhi.

Mulder, N. (2002), *Economic Performance in the Americas*, Elgar, Cheltenham.

Mulhall, M.G. (1880), *The Progress of the World*, Stanford, London.

Mulhall, M.G. (1881), *Balance Sheet of the World for 10 Years 1870–1880*, Stanford, London.

Mulhall, M.G. (1884), *The Dictionary of Statistics*, Routledge, London, 4th edition 1899.

Mulhall, M.G. (1896), *Industries and Wealth of Nations*, Longmans, London.

Needham, J. (1954–97), *Science and Civilisation in China*, Cambridge University Press.

Needham, J. (1970), *Clerks and Craftsmen in China and the West*, Cambridge University Press.

Nordhaus, W.D. (1997),"Do Real–Wage Measures Capture Reality? The Evidence of Lighting Suggests Not", *in* Bresnahan and Gordon.

North, D.C. (1990), *Institutions, Institutional Change and Economic Performance*, Cambridge University Press.

North, D.C. and R.P. Thomas (1973), *The Rise of the Western World*, Cambridge University Press.

O'Brien P.K. and A. Clesse (eds.) (2002), *Two Hegemonies: Britain 1846–1914 and the United States 1941–2001*, Ashgate, Aldershot.

OECD (1993), *Purchasing Power Parities and Real Expenditures 1990: GK Results,* Vol. II, Paris.

OECD (2002), *Purchasing Power Parities and Real Expenditures, 1999 Benchmark Year*, Paris.

OECD (2003), *Measuring Productivity Levels–A Reader*, Paris.

Ohkawa, K., M. Shinohara and M. Umemura (eds.) (1966–1988), *Estimates of Long–Term Economic Statistics of Japan since 1868*, 14 volumes, Toyo Keizai Shinposha, Tokyo.

Özmucur, S. and S. Pamuk (2002), "Real Wages and Standards of Living in the Ottoman Empire, 1489–1914", *Journal of Economic History*, June, pp. 293–321.

Paige, D. and G. Bombach (1959), *A Comparison of National Output and Productivity of the United Kingdom and the United States*, OEEC, Paris.

Parthasarathi, P. (1998), "Rethinking Wages and Competitiveness in the Eighteenth Century: Britain and South India", *Past and Present*, 158, pp. 79–109.

Perkins, D.W. (1969), *Agricultural Development in China, 1368–1968*, Aldine, Chicago.

Petty, W. (1997), *The Collected Works of Sir William Petty*, 8 volumes, Routledge/Thoemes Press, London (includes Hull's (1899) collection of Petty's economic writings; E.G. Fitzmaurice's (1895) biography of Petty; Lansdowne's (1927 and 1928) collection of Petty papers and the Southwell–Petty correspondence; Larcom's (1851) edition of Petty's Irish Land Survey, and critical appraisals by T.W. Hutchinson and others).

Phelps Brown, H. and S.V. Hopkins (1981), *A Perspective on Wages and Prices*, Methuen, London.

Pilat, D. (1994), *The Economics of Rapid Growth: The Experience of Japan and Korea*, Elgar, Aldershot.

Pomeranz, K. (2000), *The Great Divergence: China, Europe and the Making of the Modern World Economy*, Princeton University Press, New Jersey.

PRADOS DE LA ESCOSURA, L. (2000), "International Comparisons of Real Product, 1820–1990: An alternative Dataset", in *Explorations in Economic History*, 37 (1), pp1–41.

RAYCHAUDHURI, T. AND I. HABIB (1982), *The Cambridge Economic History of India, c.1200–1750,* vol. I, Cambridge University Press.

RICHARDS, E.G. (1998), *Mapping Time*, Oxford University Press.

REN, R. (1997), *China's Economic Performance in an International Perspective*, Development Centre Studies, OECD, Paris.

RICCIOLI, G.B. (1672), *Geographiae et Hydrographiae Reformatae, Libri Duodecim,* Venice.

ROSENBLAT, A. (1945), *La Poblacion Indigena de America Desde 1492 Hasta la Actualidad*, ICE, Buenos Aires.

ROSTAS, L. (1948), *Comparative Productivity in British and American Industry*, Cambridge University Press, Cambridge.

ROSTOW, W.W. (1960), *The Stages of Economic Growth*, Cambridge University Press.

SHEPHERD, V. AND H. M. BECKLES (eds.) (2000), *Caribbean Slavery in the Atlantic World*, Wiener, Princeton.

SIVASUBRAMONIAN, S. (2000), *The National Income of India in the Twentieth Century*, Oxford University Press, New Delhi.

SIVASUBRAMONIAN, S. (2003), *The Sources of Economic Growth in India 1950–2000*, Oxford University Press, New Delhi.

SMITS, J.P., E. HORLINGS AND J.L. VAN ZANDEN (2000), *Dutch GNP and Its Components, 1800–1913*, Groningen Growth and Development Centre, Monograph Series, No. 5.

SNOOKS, G.D. (1993), *Economics Without Time*, Macmillan, London.

SNOOKS, G.D. (1996), *The Dynamic Society: Exploring the Sources of Global Change*, Routledge, London.

SNOOKS, G.D. (1997), *The Ephemeral Civilisation*, Routledge, London.

STONE, R. (1956), *Quantity and Price Indexes in National Accounts*, OEEC, Paris.

STONE, R. (1961), *Input–Output and National Accounts,* OEEC, Paris.

STONE, R. (1971), *Demographic Accounting and Model Building*, OECD, Paris.

STONE, R. (1997a), "The Accounts of Society"(1984 Nobel Memorial Lecture), *American Economic Review,* December, pp. 17–29.

STONE, R. (1997b), *Some British Empiricists in the Social Sciences 1650–1900*, Cambridge University Press, Cambridge.

STUDENSKI, P. (1958), *The Income of Nations: Theory, Measurement and Analysis: Past and Present*, New York University Press, Washington Square.

SUMMERS, R., I.B. KRAVIS AND A. HESTON (1980), "International Comparison of Real Product and its Composition: 1950–77", *Review of Income and Wealth*, March, pp. 19–66.

SUMMERS R. AND A. HESTON (1988), "A New Set of International Comparisons of Real Product and Prices: Estimates for 130 Countries, 1950–1985", *Review of Income and Wealth*, March, pp. 1–26.

SZIRMAI, A., B. VAN ARK AND D. PILAT (eds.) (1993), *Explaining Economic Growth: Essays in Honour of Angus Maddison*, North Holland, Amsterdam.

THOROLD ROGERS, J.E. (1866–1902), *A History of Agriculture and Prices in England*, 7 vols. Clarendon Press, Oxford.

THOROLD ROGERS, J.E (1884), *Six Centuries of Work and Wages*, Swan Sonnenschein, London.

TODA, YASUSHI (1990), "Catching–up and Convergence: the Standard of Living and the Consumption Pattern of the Russians and the Japanese in 1913 and 1975–1976", paper presented at session C28, 10th World Congress of the International Economic History Association, Leuven, mimeographed.

UN (1987), *World Comparisons of Purchasing Power and Real Product for 1980*, New York.

UN (1993), *System of National Accounts 1993*, Paris (jointly with EU, IMF, OECD and World Bank), earlier versions in 1953 and 1968.

UN (1994), *World Comparisons of Real Gross Domestic Product and Purchasing Power, 1985*, New York.

UN (2001) *World Population Prospects: The 2000 Revision*, vol 1, *Comprehensive Tables,* Population Division, Dept. of Economic and Social Affairs, New York. Annual estimates on CD ROM Disk 2: Extensive Set.

VAUBAN, S. (1707), *La dîme royale* (1992 edition, with introduction by E. Le Roy Ladurie, Imprimerie nationale, Paris).

VRIES, J. DE (1984), *European Urbanization 1500–1800*, Methuen, London.

VRIES, J. DE (1993), "Between Purchasing Power and the World of Goods: Understanding the Household Economy in Early Modern Europe", *in* BREWER AND PORTER (1993).

VRIES, J. DE (1994),"The Industrial Revolution and the Industrious Revolution", *Journal of Economic History,* June, pp. 249–270.

VRIES, J. DE AND A. VAN DER WOUDE (1997), *The First Modern Economy; Success, Failure and Perseverance of the Dutch Economy, 1500–1815*, Cambridge University Press, Cambridge.

WARD, M. (1985), *Purchasing Power Parities and Real Expenditures in the OECD*, OECD, Paris.

WESTERGAARD, H. (1932), *Contributions to the History of Statistics*, King, London (Kelley reprint, 1969).

WHITWORTH, C. (ed.) (1771), *The Political and Commercial Works of Charles Davenant*, 5 vols., London.

WHITE, E.N. (2001), "France and the Failure to Modernise Macroeconomic Institutions", *in* BORDO AND CORTÉS–CONDE.

WILLIAMS, E. (1944), *Capitalism and Slavery*, Russell and Russell, New York.

WILLIAMS, E. (1970), *From Columbus to Castro: The History of the Caribbean 1492–1969*, Deutsch, London.

WILLIAMSON, J.G. (1985),*Did British Capitalism Breed Inequality?* Allen and Unwin, London.

WILLIAMSON, J.G. (1995), "The Evolution of Global Labor Markets since 1930: Background Evidence and Hypotheses", *Explorations in Economic History*, 32, pp. 141–196.

WRIGLEY, E.A. (1988), *Continuity, Chance and Change*, Cambridge.

WRIGLEY, E.A. AND R.S. SCHOFIELD (1981), *The Population History of England 1541–1871*, Arnold, London.

WRIGLEY, E.A., R.S. DAVIES, J.E. OEPPEN AND R.S. SCHOFIELD (1997), *English Population History from Family Reconstitution 1580–1837*, Cambridge University Press, Cambridge.

YOUNG, A. (1794), *Travels During the Years 1787–9 with a View to Ascertaining the Cultivation, Wealth, Resources and National Prosperity of the Kingdom of France*, Richardson, London, (2nd edition).

VAN ZANDEN, J.L. (1999),"Wages and the Standard of Living in Europe, 1500–1800", *European Review of Economic History*, August, pp. 175–198.

VAN ZANDEN, J.L. AND E. HORLINGS (1999), "The Rise of the European Economy 1500–1800", *in* ALDCROFT AND SUTCLIFFE.

VAN ZANDEN, J.L. (2002), "Taking the Measure of the Early Modern Economy: Historical National Accounts for Holland in 1510/14", *European Review of Economic History*, 6, pp. 131–163.

VAN ZANDEN, J.L. (2003), "Rich and Poor before the Industrial Revolution: A Comparison between Java and the Netherlands at the beginning of the 19th Century", *Explorations in Economic History*, 40, pp. 1–23.

VAN ZANDEN, J.L. (forthcoming), "Economic Growth in Java, 1815–1939: Reconstruction of the Historical National Accounts of a Colonial Economy" (http://iisg.nl/research/jvz–reconstruction.pdf).

U.W.E.L. LEARNING RESOURCES

OECD PUBLICATIONS, 2, rue André-Pascal, 75775 PARIS CEDEX 16
PRINTED IN FRANCE
(41 2006 02 1 P) ISBN 92-64-02261-9 – No. 55257 2006